Marketing

 12th Edition

The McGraw-Hill/Irwin Series in Marketing

Marketing

 12th Edition

Michael J. Etzel
University of Notre Dame

Bruce J. Walker
University of Missouri-Columbia

William J. Stanton
University of Colorado-Boulder

 **McGraw-Hill Irwin**

Boston   Burr Ridge, IL   Dubuque, IA   Madison, WI   New York   San Francisco   St. Louis
Bangkok   Bogotá   Caracas   Lisbon   London   Madrid
Mexico City   Milan   New Delhi   Seoul   Singapore   Sydney   Taipei   Toronto

McGraw-Hill Higher Education

A Division of The **McGraw-Hill** *Companies*

Marketing

Published by McGraw-Hill/Irwin, an imprint of The McGraw-Hill Companies, Inc. 1221 Avenue of the Americas, New York, NY, 10020. Copyright © 2001, 1997, 1994, 1991, 1987, 1984, 1981, 1978, 1975, 1971, 1967, 1964, by The McGraw-Hill Companies, Inc. All rights reserved. No part of this publication may be reproduced or distributed in any form or by any means, or stored in a database or retrieval system, without the prior written consent of The McGraw-Hill Companies, Inc., including, but not limited to, in any network or other electronic storage or transmission, or broadcast for distance learning.

Some ancillaries, including electronic and print components, may not be available to customers outside the United States.

This book is printed on acid-free paper.

domestic   2 3 4 5 6 7 8 9 0 VNH/VNH 0 9 8 7 6 5 4 3 2 1
international   2 3 4 5 6 7 8 9 0 VNH/VNH 0 9 8 7 6 5 4 3 2 1

ISBN 0-07-366031-0

Publisher: *David Kendric Brake*
Developmental editor: *Christine Parker*
Senior marketing manager: *Colleen J. Suljic*
Project manager: *Susanne Riedell*
Production supervisor: *Michael R. McCormick*
Freelance design coordinator: *Pam Verros*
Supplement coordinator: *Rose M. Range*
Media technology producer: *Burke Broholm*
Senior photo research coordinator: *Keri Johnson*
Cover photographs: *©Photodisc*
Compositor: *GTS Graphics, Inc.*
Typeface: *10/12 Sabon*
Printer: *Von Hoffmann Press, Inc.*

Library of Congress Cataloging-in-Publication Data

Etzel, Michael J.
   Marketing / Michael J. Etzel, Bruce J. Walker, William J. Stanton.—12th ed.
      p. cm.—(McGraw-Hill series in marketing)
   Includes bibliographical references and index.
   ISBN 0-07-366031-0 (softcover : alk. paper)
   1. Marketing. I. Walker, Bruce J. II. Stanton, William J. III. Title. IV. Series.

HF5415 .S745 2001
658.8—dc21   00-027784

INTERNATIONAL EDITION ISBN 0-07-118034-6
Copyright © 2001. Exclusive rights by The McGraw-Hill Companies, Inc. for manufacture and export. This book cannot be re-exported from the country to which it is sold by McGraw-Hill. The International Edition is not available in North America.

www.mhhe.com.

About the Authors

Michael J. Etzel received his Ph.D. in marketing from the University of Colorado. Since 1980, he has been a professor of marketing at the University of Notre Dame. He also has been on the faculties at Utah State University and the University of Kentucky. He has held visiting faculty positions at the University of South Carolina and the University of Hawaii. In 1990, he was a Fulbright Fellow at the University of Innsbruck, Austria. His other overseas assignments include directing and teaching in the University of Notre Dame's program in Fremantle, Australia, in 1994, and the University's London MBA program in 1998.

Professor Etzel has taught marketing courses from the introductory through the doctoral level. He is also a frequent presenter in executive training programs. His research, primarily in marketing management and buyer behavior, has appeared in the *Journal of Marketing*, *Journal of Marketing Research*, *Journal of Consumer Research*, and other publications. He is the coauthor of another college-level text, *Retailing Today*.

He has been active in many aspects of the American Marketing Association at the local and national levels. He served as chairman of AMA's board in 1996–1997.

Bruce J. Walker became professor of marketing and dean of the College of Business at the University of Missouri–Columbia in 1990. Professor Walker received his undergraduate degree in economics from Seattle University and his master's and Ph.D. degrees in business from the University of Colorado.

Professor Walker was a member of the marketing faculties at the University of Kentucky and then at Arizona State University. Dr. Walker has taught a variety of courses, including principles of marketing. His research, focusing primarily on franchising, marketing channels, and survey-research methods, has been published in the *Journal of Marketing, California Management Review, Journal of Marketing Research*, and other periodicals. He has also coedited or coauthored conference proceedings and books, including *Retailing Today*.

Dr. Walker has been involved with both the American Marketing Association and the Western Marketing Educators Association. He served as vice president of AMA's Education Division and president of WMEA. Currently, he is a trustee for the International Franchise Association's Education Foundation.

William J. Stanton is professor emeritus of marketing at the University of Colorado–Boulder. He received his Ph.D. in marketing from Northwestern University, where he was elected to Beta Gamma Sigma. He has worked in business and has taught in several management development programs for marketing executives. He has served as a consultant for various business organizations and has engaged in research projects for the federal government. Professor Stanton also has lectured at universities in Europe, Asia, Mexico, and New Zealand.

A coauthor of the leading text in sales management, Professor Stanton has also published several journal articles and monographs. *Marketing* has been translated into Spanish, and separate editions have been adapted (with coauthors) for Canada, Italy, Australia, and South Africa. In a survey of marketing educators, Professor Stanton was voted one of the leaders in marketing thought. And he is listed in *Who's Who in America* and *Who's Who in the World*.

Dedication

Mike Etzel
To the memory of my parents, Al and Audrey

Bruce Walker
To my wife, Pam, and my father, Frank

Bill Stanton
To Kelley and Little Joe

Brief Contents

Contents

Chapter 19
Advertising, Sales Promotion, and Public Relations 538

How Can Intel Go from Being Inside to Staying Ahead? 539

Part Seven
Managing the Marketing Effort 575

Chapter 20
Strategic Marketing Planning 576

Can Starbucks Continue to Brew Plans for Profitable Growth? 577

Chapter 21
Marketing Implementation and Evaluation 600

Has Disney's Go.com Come to a Stop Sign? 601

Preface

Whether you are a student, professor, manager, owner of a small business, fundraiser for a charity, physician, or even a politician, you are either engaged in marketing or should be. This is an exciting time to be involved in marketing. Unprecedented economic prosperity, increasing attention to international markets, continuing growth of services, and commercialization of the Internet are creating many new business opportunities. Coincidentally, the demands in marketing are increasing. Customers are seeking greater value in their purchases, society is raising the standards for ethical behavior, and organizations are expecting more accountability for marketing expenditures. Amid all of these developments, the fundamental purpose of marketing—satisfying customers while meeting organizational objectives—remains unchanged.

The most fundamental challenge—actually, the opportunity—associated with marketing is to do it well, and that requires an understanding of what marketing is and how to conduct it. Our intent in this twelfth edition of *Marketing* is to help students learn important and fundamental concepts, strategies, and techniques that are needed for effective marketing management.

The book is divided into seven parts to reflect the marketing management process:

- **Part 1: The Field of Marketing.** This introductory section contains an overview of what marketing is, the environment in which it occurs, and the global nature of marketing today.

- **Part 2: Identifying and Selecting Markets.** This section begins with an examination of consumer and business markets, and the decision making made by customers in both of these markets. The discussion then moves to the process of market segmentation, targeting, and positioning, followed by demand forecasting. The part concludes with a description of marketing research and market information used to identify and better understand markets.

- **Part 3: Product.** An essential activity of marketing is translating the needs of prospects into products that can be sold. The design, development, and testing of products are a part of the process, along with more visible features like brands and packaging. An important addition to this part is the chapter on services marketing.

- **Part 4: Price.** Factors such as demand, costs, competition, and the various approaches and strategies used by sellers determine the choice of a price and the adjustments made to that choice.

- **Part 5: Distribution.** To appreciate the modern miracle of having products available when and where they are desired, this section looks at both the institutions that conduct the transactions and those that arrange for the movement of goods from point of production to point of final sale.

- **Part 6: Promotion.** Formulating a message and transmitting it effectively are essential ingredients in a marketing effort to inform and persuade potential customers, and knowing the right blend of promotion methods is crucial to a marketing campaign. Under the umbrella of integrated marketing communications, this section gives special attention to advertising, sales promotion, public relations, personal selling, and sales force management.

- **Part 7: Managing the Marketing Effort.** The first two chapters in this section underscore that an effective marketing management process must be planned and then carefully guided through implementation and evaluation. However, in this dynamic environment, many organizations are rethinking their marketing plans in light of the growing impact of technology. Thus the relationship between marketing and technology is described and discussed in the final chapter of the text.

Coverage and Organizational Changes

In preparing this edition of *Marketing,* our goal was to present the fundamental building blocks of marketing while capturing its dynamism. We were guided by a commitment to preserve the straightforward organization, reader-friendly style, and extensive use of examples that characterized earlier editions. At the same time, we made changes that allow the reader to better understand and appreciate today's marketing. The major changes are:

- Global marketing is moved from Chapter 20 to Chapter 3 in recognition of its prominence in today's marketing world. Global examples also are still integrated throughout the text, and there are Global Perspective boxes in all the chapters except Chapter 3.

- Positioning, a logical extension of segmentation and targeting, is now presented in Chapter 6.

- Chapter 6 also contains demand forecasting, logically following the discussion of market identification.

- Chapter 7, "Marketing Research and Market Information," has been relocated so it follows the explanation of markets, consumer and business buying behavior, and segmentation.

- Services marketing is now included in Part 3 which focuses on the product part of the marketing mix.

- Part 6 contains a chapter (Chapter 17) on integrated marketing communications, which replaces a chapter that introduced promotion.

- Part 7 now includes "Strategic Marketing Planning" (Chapter 20) along with "Marketing Implementation and Evaluation" (Chapter 21).

- Chapter 22, "Marketing in the Information Economy" is a new chapter added to Part 7 in place of the previous concluding chapter, "Marketing: Appraisal and Prospects."

- The book now consists of seven parts instead of eight.

Noteworthy Features of the 12th Edition

The changes in coverage and organization have produced a number of features that enhance this edition as a learning tool. Among the most noteworthy are:

- Discussions of the consumer market (Chapter 4) and the business market (Chapter 5) have similar structures. Each includes a description of the respective market as well as an overview of the buying process in that particular market.

- Chapter 6, which covers market segmentation and target marketing, now includes a discussion of positioning, the managerial application of the process.

- Because adequate demand is a necessary condition for effective target marketing, demand forecasting is also addressed in Chapter 6.

- Two important developments in promotion are the growing number of methods available and the increasing level of accountability demanded by organizations for promotion expenditures. In response, organizations are focusing on creating integrated promotional programs. These developments are reflected in the restructured Part 6.

- Because of the positive response, this edition again combines wholesaling and physical distribution in one chapter, and integrates services marketing by for-profit and nonprofit organizations in a single chapter.

- Two appendices are included as complements to the 22 chapters. The first, "Marketing Math," provides additional detail on price elasticity of demand, the basics of operating statements, markups, and return on investment as a measure of performance. We've found these topics to be a useful review for many students and essential concepts for students who have not been exposed to them previously. The second appendix, "Careers and Marketing," draws students' attention to the opportunities that exist in marketing. It begins by outlining a procedure for choosing a career, then describes a variety of marketing jobs and organizations that are heavily dependent on marketing. The last portion guides students through the job search process.

- The coverage is a mix of classic and emerging topics. The following list illustrates the concepts, strategies, and techniques as well as the issues students will explore in this text:

• Generation Y	• Power centers
• Value chain	• Contract logistics
• Venture team	• Major accounts organization
• Disintermediation	• Mass customization
• North American Industrial Classification System	• Electronic commerce (e-commerce)
• Return on marketing investment	• Co-branding
• Strategic alliances	• First-mover advantage
• Ethics in marketing	• Internet
• Competitive intelligence	• Supply chain management
• Decision support systems	• Integrated marketing communications
• Online retailing (e-tailing)	• World Wide Web
• Reverse auctions	• Collaborative planning, forecasting, and replenishment
• Brand equity	
• Product counterfeiting	• Everyday low prices
• Value pricing	• Banner ads
• Slotting fees	• Fulfillment
• Global marketing	• Cannibalization
• Market fragmentation	• Cookies
• Cause marketing	
• Service encounters	

As this list indicates, every chapter has been updated to reflect recent developments in the business environment and in marketing.

Chapter-Related Cases

- Each chapter begins with a contemporary case that introduces some of the concepts, strategies, and techniques covered in the chapter. Virtually all of these cases deal with highly recognizable companies and brands. At the conclusion of the chapter, the case is revisited and additional information is presented. By addressing the questions at the end of each case, students discover how they can apply what they have learned in the chapter to a marketing situation.

- In this edition, many of the cases deal with firms that are technology based or have made electronic commerce a key component of their operations. A sampling of these cases includes:
    - eBay—Internet auctions
    - Iridium—satellite-linked cellular phones (an unsuccessful enterprise)
    - Wingspan.com—totally online retail banking
    - FreeMarkets—reverse auctions for business-to-business products
    - Intel—branding a computer microprocessor
    - PETsMART.com—online retailing of pet supplies and related products

- Other chapter-opening cases involve well-known companies that are dealing with significant marketing challenges and opportunities. These cases include:
    - Apple computers
    - General Motors' EV1 electric car
    - adidas in America

- Volkswagen's new Beetle
- Campbell Soup's Intelligent Quisine frozen meals (a failed product)
- Mindstorms, a new toy, by Lego

- Three-quarters of the chapter-related cases are new to the 12th edition. The carryovers from the 11th edition have been completely updated and revised.

Part-Ending Cases

- Each of the seven parts of the text ends with two cases. Designed to be realistic, each case focuses on a relatively specific aspect of marketing to prevent the beginning student from being overwhelmed by the complexity common to many business issues. Some of the part-ending cases are:
  - Cracker Barrel Old Country Stores
  - Southwest Airlines
  - Buy.com
  - Ford, General Motors, and DaimlerChrysler on the Internet

- An innovation in the 11th edition that received a positive reaction and has therefore been carried over to the 12th edition is the inclusion of several cases that focus on competitive rivalries. This format allows students to examine intensely competitive situations in which marketing strategy often determines ultimate success. These "versus" cases are:
  - Amazon.com versus Barnes & Noble
  - Sega versus Nintendo versus Sony
  - Toys "R" Us versus eToys

- Almost two-thirds of the part-ending cases are brand new, prepared specifically for the 12th edition.

Pedagogical Support

- A number of the chapter-opening cases and the part-ending cases will be updated periodically by the authors on the website for the 12th edition. Students will be provided with the latest developments and sources of additional material that will keep the material fresh and challenging from semester to semester.

- Technology has become so important to marketing that *Marketing in the Information Economy* boxes have been added to almost all chapters. These boxes, which are tied to the subject matter of the chapter, illustrate the pervasive impact technology is having on marketing. Topics covered in these boxes include:
  - The introduction of electronic books
  - Challenges of branding on the Internet
  - The potential of networked homes
  - The Internet's impact on China
  - "Shopping robots" that perform price comparisons on the Internet

- *Global Perspective* boxes are included in the chapters as well. These boxes, along with numerous international examples used throughout the book, emphasize the global nature of marketing in highly interesting ways. Examples of *Global Perspective* boxes include:
  - Pitfalls in foreign markets
  - Databases and privacy in the European Union
  - Online retailing in Japan
  - Discovering new product ideas abroad
  - Brand disputes across borders
  - Roadblocks to global e-commerce

- *You Make the Decision* boxes are interspersed throughout the text. These boxes present synopses of actual situations faced by marketers and ask students how they would respond to them. The boxes move the student from a passive observer of marketing to an active participant who makes decisions about marketing actions. Among the decisions are:

- Should fast-food firms redefine their businesses?
- How can companies appeal to Generations X and Y?
- Is self-scanning in supermarkets a sound concept?
- What are the limits to using focus group data to make decisions?
- Are there limits to product and brand proliferation?

- Every chapter also contains an *Ethical Dilemma* box. These boxes raise the student's awareness of the nature and frequency of ethical challenges in marketing. They are also intended to help a student formulate an ethical perspective. Topics covered in the *Ethical Dilemma* boxes include:

  - Genetically modified foods
  - Paying bribes in foreign markets
  - Overbooking by airlines and "no-shows" by passengers
  - Special promotions conducted in grammar schools
  - Use of "cookies" by Internet marketers
  - "Copycat" packaging

- Each chapter is followed by two types of assignments. The first is a set of *Questions and Problems* that require applying the text material rather than simply reviewing terms or memorizing definitions. The second type of assignment is called *Hands-On Marketing*. These assignments require that students get out of the classroom and interact with customers and/or marketers. In carrying out these assignments, students will gather information first-hand or observe real marketing situations. As a result, they will develop a practical sense of how marketing is actually performed.

Teaching and Learning Supplements

The text is the primary element in a complete package of teaching and learning resources. The supporting items include:

- An *Instructor's Manual* that contains the following resources: lecture material in the form of additional examples and vignettes; suggested answers to the end-of-chapter questions; and commentaries on the chapter-related and part-ending cases and the *Ethical Dilemma* and *You Make the Decision* boxes.

- An electronic version of the *Instructor's Manual* that can be downloaded from the website.

- A *Test Bank* of over 2,500 objective questions. The questions are coded to indicate the type (definition, concept, application) and text location.

- An electronic version of the Test Bank, *Computest*, that allows the instructor to tailor and edit the exam questions to meet specific class needs.

- A comprehensive *color transparency program* with over 100 acetates to enhance classroom lectures

- A *classroom presentation tool*, using Microsoft PowerPoint "slides," which is available to adopters.

- A *video program* that features a wide variety of organizations and complements text coverage.

- A *website* that includes chapter quizzes, Internet exercises, current events, *Business Week* articles with discussion questions, career profiles, "You Make the Call," that invites students to suggest solutions to REAL marketing challenges, a link to McGraw-Hill's PageOut that will help professors create a course-specific web page, and downloadable instructor supplements.

- McGraw-Hill's *PowerWeb* that offers students and faculty the following: Annual Editions Online—course-specific current articles tied to a course curriculum; a real-time newswire; a database of 6,000 journals called Northern Light Research Engine; weekly Web updates specific to the discipline; assessment tools such as quizzing and review forms; and student study materials such as web research, and time management tools.

Acknowledgments

We have benefited from the contributions of our students, past and present colleagues, other professors, and business executives in preparing this and previous editions of *Marketing*. To all these people, although too numerous to identify by name, we owe a debt of gratitude.

Special thanks are extended to Therese Basham, who prepared drafts of a number of the cases. We are also grateful to several of our students—Eric Schupp, Dan Whitley, and Daniela Papi—who assisted with research and other tasks at various times during this revision.

Several individuals have contributed significantly to the supplementary materials accompanying the text. An extensive set of objective test questions was developed by Professors Tom and Betty Pritchett of Kennesaw State College. Professor Bonnie Guy of Appalachian State University prepared the Instructor's Manual with us and completed the PowerPoint presentation materials.

We'd like to recognize those who helped shape the previous edition, including: **Ronald J. Adams,** *University of North Florida;* **Thomas J. Adams,** *Sacramento City College;* **Carol Bienstock,** *Valdosta State University;* **Roy Cabaniss,** *Western Kentucky University;* **Steven Engel,** *University of Colorado–Boulder;* **Mort Ettinger,** *Salem State College;* **Stephen Goodwin,** *Illinois State University;* **Craig A. Hollingshead,** *Marshall University;* **Denise M. Johnson,** *University of Louisville;* **Craig A. Kelley,** *California State University-Sacramento;* **Kenneth Laird,** *Southern Connecticut State University;* **Mary Lou Lockerby,** *College of Du Page;* **Irving Mason,** *Herkimer County Community College;* **Darryl W. Miller,** *Washburn University;* **Mark Mitchell,** *University of South Carolina–Spartanburg;* **Keith B. Murray,** *Bryant College;* **John Phillips,** *University of San Francisco;* **Charles Prohaska,** *Central Connecticut State University;* **Robert G. Roe,** *University of Wyoming;* **Louise Smith,** *Towson State College;* **Michael J. Swenson,** *Brigham Young University;* **Jack L. Taylor,** *Portland State University;* **Robert E. Thompson,** *Indiana State University;* **Timothy L. Wilson,** *Clarion University.*

A number of professors examined the previous edition and reviewed early drafts of the current edition. Their advice and insights contributed to numerous improvements. **Bruce L. Conners,** *Kaskaskia College;* **Larry Crowson,** *Florida Institute of Technology;* **Jennifer Friestad,** *Anoka Ramsey Community College;* **Madeline Johnson,** *University of Houston;* **Justin Peart,** *Florida International University;* **Ed Timmerman,** *University of Tennessee;* **Joyce H. Wood,** *Northern Virginia Community College;* and **Sharon Wagner,** *Missouri Western State College.*

Finally, we would like to take this opportunity to thank the professionals at McGraw-Hill/Irwin, who did so much to make this book an effective and attractive teaching and learning resource. We especially want to thank our development editors, initially Nancy Barbour and later Christine Parker, for their energy, support, and conscientiousness. Susanne Riedell, the project manager, worked diligently to maintain quality as well as keep the revision on schedule. Michael Hruby coordinated the photo program in a capable manner. Pam Verros brought this book to life with her contemporary and appealing design. Gretlyn Cline was an efficient, yet thorough copyeditor, and Carrie Peters did an excellent job compiling the glossary as did Rose Carmellino with the indexes. Without the team effort of the editorial, design, and production departments, this textbook would not have materialized.

Michael J. Etzel
Bruce J. Walker
William J. Stanton

The Field of Marketing

An introduction to the nature and scope of marketing

Marketing is a large part of all of our lives. For example, if you bought a cup of coffee or a soft drink on the way to school today, visited the website of a business, or noticed an ad on television or the radio, you were touched by a marketing effort. These and literally hundreds of other routine activities bring us into contact with some aspect of marketing. In fact, it would be an unusual day if you did not have some direct marketing experience.

Besides being part of our lives, marketing is also essential to the survival of most organizations, highly rewarding to its successful practitioners and frustrating to the less fortunate, and sometimes controversial. There is another point that's true about marketing. It is never dull!

Today you are beginning a journey that will help you understand the role marketing plays in organizations of all types. You'll learn about the many tools marketers have at their disposal and how they use those tools as they plan and implement strategies. And by the time you finish this course, you'll be better prepared to make effective use of marketing in whatever you do.

To get started, Part 1 provides an introduction and overview. Chapter 1 explains what marketing is, how it has developed, the kinds of decisions marketers make, and how marketing affects all of us. In Chapter 2 we examine the environmental forces that shape an organization's marketing program. Chapter 3 explores the implications of marketing on a global scale.

An Overview of Marketing

"For the most part, auctions had become weekend novelties or fund raisers. The Internet may be changing that."

Can eBay Define a New Way?

Have you ever been to a silent auction? The sales area could be a warehouse, a gymnasium, or even a city park. Although many auctions have a theme, such as antique furniture or works of art, almost anything you can imagine is sold in this fashion. Each item up for auction is accompanied by a sheet of paper on which to post bids. A prospective buyer can examine the most recent bid made on an item and replace it with a higher bid or move on. At a predetermined time the bidding is closed and the items are sold to the persons who made the highest bids.

Many people enjoy silent auctions because they inject an element of suspense in the buying process. It's a little like haggling without the face-to-face confrontation. Also at an auction you can see how others value things. And the flurry of activity just before the bidding closes creates plenty of excitement. Of course, there's always the prospect of the good feeling that comes from paying less for an item than you were willing to bid.

But auctions also have some drawbacks. For example, they aren't very efficient. The bidding process can go on for several hours or even days, and if you're not around to frequently check on an item, it can easily go to a higher bidder. There are also problems associated with the physical space to display the items. Finally, just scheduling an auction at a convenient time for the sellers and the prospective bidders can be a challenge. As a result, we rely on retail stores that offer standardized goods at fixed prices for nearly all purchases. For the most part, auctions had become weekend novelties or fund raisers. The Internet may be changing that. Firms like eBay, Amazon.com, and OnSale, Inc., are creating ways of buying and selling at auction that retain the advantages and reduce many of the disadvantages.

There are over 150 websites described as "online auctions." The most common operating format is to invite prospective sellers to submit descriptions of items they'd like to sell. These descriptions are then placed on the auction's website. Shoppers search the site for specific items or just browse from the comfort of their homes or offices at any time of the night or day. The shopper can read the detailed descriptions of specific products and submit bids over the Internet. All listed items have "closing times" and the highest submitted bid at the close buys the item.

OnSale, Inc., which specializes in buying and reselling surplus computer and electronic goods, receives over 10,000 bids a day. Amazon.com, widely known as a book, music, and video seller on the Internet, has broadened its offerings through an online auction. Over 100 small companies specializing in merchandise as varied as collectibles, jewelry, and photography equipment list items on the Amazon site. The additional merchandise gives consumers already familiar with Amazon another reason to visit the site.

eBay, Inc., founded in 1995, is one of the most successful of the online auction companies. It is headquartered in San Jose, California, employs less than 150 people, and has no merchandise. Yet in 1999 eBay had revenues of $225 million. How was that accomplished? Anyone with something to sell can create an electronic classified ad that for a small fee is placed on the eBay website. If the merchandise is purchased, eBay collects 1.25% to 5% of the sale price as a commission. With about 2 million items for sale every day, ranging from works of art to stuffed animals, and over 10 million registered shoppers, this firm has proved to be very popular.

The concept spread quickly with well-known Internet firms such as Yahoo! adding auctions. Variations have also been created. For example, most of the online auctions are open to anyone, but others are restricted. Electronic Travel Auction allows hotels, airlines, and cruise operators to offer their "excess inventory" to travel agents, but excludes the general public from the site. This allows the travel industry to fill capacity that would otherwise be wasted, and travel agents to provide their customers with last-minute bargains.[1]

How are these electronic forms of marketing likely to evolve and what impact will they have on retail stores? See www.ebay.com for more details.

Marketing Online

The Internet is a powerful marketing tool that we have incorporated into our learning package. Please check our website <http://www.mhhe.com/etzel> for all kinds of tools that will make your learning experience more productive and enjoyable. There are Internet addresses throughout the text to help you find the "home pages" of many organizations that are mentioned in the text. Space limitations occasionally require us to break addresses onto two lines; actual Internet addresses are always written on one line.

www.ebay.com

eBay is an excellent example of marketing. Both buyers and sellers have found the service the firm offers attractive—it has met a need. Meeting needs effectively and efficiently is what marketing is all about. To begin to understand the topic, we need to address the question, "What is marketing?" After studying this chapter, you should be able to explain:

chapter goals

- The centrality of exchange to marketing.
- How marketing applies to nonbusiness as well as business situations.
- The way marketing has evolved in the U.S.
- The marketing concept and related issues.
- The heightened concern about ethics in marketing.
- The components of a company's marketing program.
- The many ways in which marketing influences our lives.

Nature and Scope of Marketing

Most often marketing is associated with the efforts of business firms selling their goods and services. However, a careful examination of what's happening in these business situations suggests that a broader notion of marketing is not only appropriate, but also highly useful. Have you considered, for example, that you may also engage in a form of marketing when you vote, donate to charity, and prepare your résumé?

Exchange as the Focus

Marketing can occur any time a person or organization strives to exchange something of value with another person or organization. Thus, the essence of marketing is a transaction or exchange. In this broad sense, marketing consists of activities designed to generate and facilitate exchanges intended to satisfy human or organizational needs or wants.

Exchange is one of three ways we can satisfy our needs. If you want something, you can make it yourself, acquire it by theft or some form of coercion, or you can offer something of value (perhaps your money, your services, or another good) to a person who has that desired good or service and will exchange it for

Cows on Parade was an exhibit of 320 life-size fiberglass cows, decorated in every way imaginable by local artists. The cows were placed throughout the downtown-Chicago area, often in the most unlikely spots. The exhibit was a promotional bonanza, attracting international media attention and drawing thousands of visitors to the city.

what you offer. Only this last alternative is an exchange in the sense that marketing is occurring.

The following conditions must exist for a marketing exchange to take place:

- Two or more people or organizations must be involved, and each must have needs or wants to be satisfied. If you are totally self-sufficient in some area, there is no need for an exchange.
- The parties to the exchange must be involved voluntarily.
- Each party must have something of value to contribute in the exchange, and each must believe that it will benefit from the exchange. In the case of an election, for example, the things of value are the votes of the electorate and the representation of the voters by the candidate.
- The parties must communicate with each other. The communication can take many forms and may even be through a third party, but without awareness and information there can be no exchange.

These exchange conditions introduce a number of terms that deserve some elaboration. First there are the parties involved in the exchange. On one side of the exchange is the marketer. *Marketers* take the initiative by trying to stimulate and facilitate exchanges. They develop marketing plans and programs and implement them in hopes of creating an exchange. A college or university recruiting students, the American Cancer Society soliciting donors, and United Airlines seeking passengers are all marketers.

On the other side of the exchange is the *market*, which consists of people or organizations with needs to satisfy, money to spend, and the willingness to spend it. Marketing programs are directed at markets that either accept or reject the offer. Markets are made up of current and prospective *customers*, defined as any person or group with whom a marketer has an existing or potential exchange relationship.

Note also that an organization's markets encompass more than the customers for its primary product. For example, in addition to students who consume an education and the parents who frequently pay for all or some of it, a state university markets to legislators to secure funds, to citizens living near the university who may be affected by its activities, and to graduates who support university programs. A firm's markets include government regulatory agencies, environmentalists, and stockholders.

We most often think of *something of value* as money. However, barter (trading one product for another) is still fairly common among small businesses and even between countries. Of course, many exchanges in the nonbusiness world, such as donating blood in exchange for a sense of helping others, do not involve cash.

Marketers use many forms of *communication*, ranging from billboards to personal selling, to inform and persuade their desired markets. Because there are so many communication methods available, selecting the most effective combination is an important marketing task.

In describing exchanges, we use the terms *needs* and *wants* interchangeably because marketing is relevant to both. Technically, needs can be viewed in a strict physiological sense (food, clothing, and shelter), with everything else defined as a want. However, from a customer's perspective, the distinction is not as clear. For example, many people would consider a cellular phone or a personal computer a necessity.

Finally, the object of the exchange or what is being marketed is referred to generically as the *product*. It can be a good, service, idea, person, or place. All of these can be marketed, as we shall see.

Definition of Marketing

This book focuses on the activities carried out by organizations to facilitate mutually beneficial exchanges. These organizations may be profit-seeking business firms, or they may have a primary objective other than profit—a university, charity, church, police department, or political party, for example. (Marketing can also be performed by individuals. As you approach graduation, you can use marketing principles to maximize the effectiveness of your job search. We'll have more to say about this in Appendix B, "Careers and Marketing.")

www.aol.com

Both types of organizations face essentially the same marketing challenges and opportunities. eBay, the online auction firm discussed in the chapter-opening case, must attract both sellers and buyers. To expand its buyer pool, eBay is paying America Online (AOL) $75 million over four years so AOL will make it easy for its 16 million subscribers to have access to the eBay site.[2] Similarly, community leaders found they could successfully market Steubenville, Ohio, as a tourist attraction by decorating the city's downtown buildings with large murals depicting historic scenes. Consequently, we need a definition of marketing to guide executives in business and nonbusiness organizations in the management of their marketing efforts, and to direct our examination of the subject.

Therefore, our definition of marketing—based on the concept of exchange and applicable in any organization—is as follows: **Marketing** is a total system of business activities designed to plan, price, promote, and distribute want-satisfying products to target markets in order to achieve organizational objectives. This definition has two significant implications:

- *Focus:* The entire system of business activities should be customer-oriented. Customers' wants must be recognized and satisfied.
- *Duration:* Marketing should start with an idea about a want-satisfying product and should not end until the customers' wants are completely satisfied, which may be some time after the exchange is made.

As you will see in the discussion below, these conditions are not always met.

Evolution of Marketing

The foundations of marketing in America were laid in Colonial times, when the early settlers traded among themselves and with the Native Americans. Some settlers became retailers, wholesalers, and itinerant peddlers. However, large-scale marketing in the U.S. did not begin to take shape until the Industrial Revolution in the latter part of the 1800s. Since then, marketing has evolved through three successive stages of development: product orientation, sales orientation, and market orientation.

Our description links each stage with a period of time. But you should understand that these stages depict the general evolution of marketing and reflect states of mind as much as they do historical periods. Thus, although many firms have progressed to the market-orientation stage, some are still in the first or second stage, as shown in Figure 1.1.

Product-Orientation Stage

Manufacturers in the **product-orientation stage** typically focused on the quality and quantity of output while assuming that customers would seek out and buy reasonably priced, well-made products. Managers with backgrounds in manufacturing and engineering shaped a firm's strategy. In an era when the demand for goods generally exceeded the supply, the primary focus in business was to efficiently produce large quantities of products. Finding the customers was viewed as a relatively minor function.

The term *marketing* was not in use. Instead, producers had sales departments headed by executives whose primary responsibility was to supervise a sales force. The function of the sales department was simply to carry out the transaction, at a price often dictated by the cost of production. The philosophy of the Pillsbury

Figure 1.1

Three stages of market-
ing evolution in the
United States.

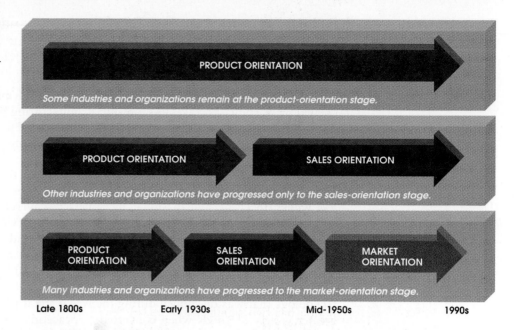

PRODUCT ORIENTATION

Some industries and organizations remain at the product-orientation stage.

PRODUCT ORIENTATION   SALES ORIENTATION

Other industries and organizations have progressed only to the sales-orientation stage.

PRODUCT
ORIENTATION   SALES
ORIENTATION   MARKET
ORIENTATION

Many industries and organizations have progressed to the market-orientation stage.

Late 1800s   Early 1930s   Mid-1950s   1990s

company in the late 1800s is characteristic of this stage: "Blessed with a supply of the finest North American Wheat, plenty of water power, and excellent milling machinery, we produce flour of the highest quality. Our basic function is to mill high-quality flour, and of course (and almost incidentally) we must hire salesmen to sell it, just as we hire accountants to keep our books."[3]

Manufacturers, wholesalers, and retailers operating in this stage emphasized internal operations and focused on efficiency and cost control. There wasn't much need to worry about what customers wanted because it was highly predictable. Most people spent the vast majority of their incomes on necessities. If a firm could make a good quality shoe inexpensively, for example, a market almost certainly existed.

This emphasis on products and operations dominated until the early 1930s. The approach is understandable when you consider that for generations the primary concern of business was how to produce and distribute an adequate quantity of acceptable products to meet the needs of a rapidly growing population.

Sales-Orientation Stage

The world economic crisis of the late 1920s (the Great Depression) changed perceptions. As the developed countries emerged from the depression it became clear that the main economic problem no longer was how to produce efficiently, but rather it was how to sell the resulting output. Just offering a quality product was no assurance of market success. Managers began to realize that to sell their products in an environment where consumers had limited resources and numerous options required substantial postproduction effort. Thus, the sales-orientation stage was characterized by a heavy reliance on promotional activity to sell the products the firm wanted to make. In this stage, advertising consumed a larger share of a firm's resources and sales executives began to gain respect and responsibility from company management.

Along with responsibility came expectations for performance. Unfortunately, these pressures resulted in some managers resorting to overly aggressive selling— the "hard sell"—and unscrupulous advertising tactics. As a result, selling developed an unsavory reputation in the eyes of many. Old habits die hard, and even now some organizations believe that they must use a hard-sell approach to prosper.

In the United States the sales stage was common into the 1950s, when modern marketing began to emerge.

Market-Orientation Stage

At the end of World War II there was strong pent-up demand for consumer goods created by wartime shortages. As a result, manufacturing plants turned out tremendous quantities of goods that were quickly purchased. However, the postwar surge in consumer spending slowed down as supply caught up with demand, and many firms found that they had excess production capacity.

In an attempt to stimulate sales, firms reverted to the aggressive promotional and sales activities of the sales-orientation era. However, this time consumers were less willing to be persuaded. What the sellers discovered was that the war years had also changed the consumer. The thousands of service men and women who spent time overseas came home more sophisticated and worldly. In addition, the war effort brought many women out of the home and into the work force for the first time. Because of their experiences, consumers had become more knowledgeable, less naive, and less easily influenced. In addition, they had more choices. The technology that was developed during the war made it possible to produce a much greater variety of goods when converted to peacetime activity.

Thus the evolution of marketing continued. Many companies recognized that to put idle capacity to work they had to make available what consumers wanted. In the **market-orientation stage**, companies identify what customers want and tailor all the activities of the firm to satisfy those needs as efficiently as possible.

In this third stage, firms are marketing rather than merely selling. Several tasks that were once associated with other business functions became the responsibility of the top marketing executive, called the marketing manager or vice president of marketing. For instance, inventory control, warehousing, and some aspects of product planning are turned over to the head of marketing as a way to serve customers better. To increase effectiveness, input from the marketplace is sought before a product is produced as well as at the end of a production cycle. In addition, marketing is included in long-term as well as short-term company planning.

A market orientation is often reflected in an executive's attitude toward marketing. Philip Knight, chairman and CEO of Nike, makes this point: "For years we thought of ourselves as a production-oriented company, meaning we put all our emphasis on designing and manufacturing the product. But now we understand that the most important thing we do is market the product."[4]

We are *not* saying that marketing is more important than other business functions. They are all essential. Nor are we suggesting that marketing executives should hold the top positions in a company. But it is necessary that everyone in an organization understand the importance of the market, that is, be *market-oriented*.

Many American business firms and not-for-profit organizations are presently in this third stage in the evolution of marketing. Others may recognize the importance of a market orientation, but have difficulty implementing it. Implementation requires accepting the notion that the wants and needs of customers, not the desires of management, direct the organization. Forty-five years ago Peter Drucker, the most influential business writer of the 20th century, observed that companies exist not to make a profit, but to create and satisfy customers. In a recent interview, he commented that the statement is even more true today because the customer has the ultimate power to choose.[5]

A basic implication of a market orientation is the way an organization describes what it does. Table 1.1 shows how some well-known organizations might define their businesses under a product orientation and invites you to try your hand at defining them based on a market orientation.

Note that not every organization needs to be market-oriented to prosper. A monopolist selling a necessity is guaranteed of having customers. Therefore, its man-

Table 1.1	How Should a Business Be Defined?	
(Try your hand at composing a market-oriented answer and then see note 6 for some possibilities.)[6]		
Company	**Product-Oriented Answer**	**Market-Oriented Answer**
Kodak	We make cameras and film.	We help preserve beautiful memories.
Amazon.com	We sell books and recordings.	?
Hewlett-Packard	We make computer printers.	?
Levi Strauss	We make blue jeans.	?
Steelcase	We make office furniture.	?
Caterpillar	We make construction machinery.	?

agement should be much more concerned with low-cost, efficient production than with marketing. Such was the case for public utilities prior to deregulation. Now many electricity and natural gas providers are scrambling to find ways to satisfy customers who have alternative sources of supply. There are also instances in which the potential customers consider the product to be so superior that they will seek it out. For example, the world's best heart surgeons or particularly popular artists find a market for their services regardless of their orientations.

Contrasting Sales and Market Orientations

There is a vast difference between a sales orientation and a market orientation. However, because most firms have both a marketing and a sales staff, and the terms *marketing* and *selling* are often used interchangeably, some people see little difference between them. The most fundamental difference is that a sales orientation is internally focused, while a market orientation is externally focused. Let's see what that means.

When a company makes a product and then tries to persuade prospects to buy it, that's a sales orientation. In effect, the firm attempts to alter consumer demand to fit the firm's supply of the product. But when a firm finds out what the customer wants and develops a marketing mix that includes a product to satisfy that need and also yield a profit, that's a market orientation. Firms with a market orientation adjust their supply to meet the needs of customers.

Some distinctions between a sales orientation and a market orientation in practice are:

	Sales Orientation	**Market Orientation**
Organization's priority	Needs of the seller	Needs of the buyers
Planning horizon	Short term	Long term
Focus	Sales	Customer satisfaction
Performance measure	Market share	Profitable sales

The Marketing Concept

Managers who adopt a market orientation recognize that marketing is vital to the success of their organizations. This realization is reflected in a fundamental approach to doing business that gives the customer the highest priority. Called the **marketing concept**, it emphasizes customer orientation and coordination of marketing activities to achieve the organization's performance objectives.

Is it time for fast-food marketers to redefine their businesses?

After years of remarkable domestic growth, fast-food performance flattened in the 1980s and firms such as McDonald's, Burger King, and Pizza Hut looked for opportunities overseas. They found a ready market for American-style hamburgers and pizza, but by the late 1990s that market was also becoming saturated. In 1995 growth in the supply of fast-food capacity was more than twice the growth in demand. According to an industry analyst, "The 'If you build it, they will come' business model (in fast food) no longer works as it used to."

To increase demand for their existing products, some firms engage in price promotions. One result of price promotions in fast food has been burger price wars with Big Macs and Whoppers selling for 99 cents, undercutting the revenues and the images of both firms.

Another way of increasing demand is to modify the offering to create some variety for regular customers and hopefully also attract new customers. For example, a number of years ago McDonald's introduced a breakfast menu, adding an entirely new day part to its business. However, most fast-food marketers have gone about as far as they can with menu alterations while still maintaining their core businesses.

A third approach to attracting customers is to change the existing internal operation. In 1998 McDonald's introduced a new cooking system that allows sandwiches to be assembled to order rather than standardized. Burger King has opted for a different type of internal change, updating the décor of its outlets and introducing interactive video games to entertain patrons. According to Burger King's CEO, the changes were necessary because "most (fast-food) restaurants look the same, which annoys me as a marketing man."

Another option is to diversify, to branch out into a related but somewhat different business. For example, McDonald's ventured into a chain of children's play areas called Discovery Zone, but that proved unsuccessful. More recently McDonald's bought Donatos Pizza, an established Midwestern firm; Chipotle Mexican Grill, a Denver-based casual-dining chain; and Aroma, a London coffee and sandwich operation. All are quite different from McDonald's traditional outlets. According to Jack Greenberg, McDonald's CEO, they provide opportunities to take advantage of the firm's expertise in the food business.

Despite their efforts, none of the fast-food firms have been able to show substantial growth in recent years. One idea is that they need to step back and develop a more market-oriented definition of the business they are in.

How would you define the fast-food business?

Sources: Richard Gibson, "McDonald's to Branch Out, Its CEO Says," *The Wall Street Journal*, Apr. 12, 1999, p. B2; Andrew Edgecliffe-Johnson, "Burger with Fries and Video to Go," *Financial Times*, Apr. 17 and 18, 1999, p. 7; James P. Miller and Richard Gibson, "Did Somebody Say Pizza? McDonald's to Buy Ohio Chain," *The Wall Street Journal*, May 6, 1999, p. A4.

Nature and Rationale

The marketing concept is based on three beliefs that are illustrated in Figure 1.2:

- All planning and operations should be *customer-oriented*. That is, every department and employee should be focused on contributing to the satisfaction of customers' needs. The inspiration for the "hub and spoke" concept created by FedEx was the customer need for reliable, overnight package delivery. Making it work requires the coordination provided by sophisticated information management, state-of-the-art material handling, and dedicated customer service personnel. What seemed like an impractical idea 30 years ago is now the basis for a $10 billion business that delivers 2.3 million packages a day in over 200 countries.[7]
- All marketing activities in an organization should be *coordinated*. This means that marketing efforts (product planning, pricing, distribution, and promotion) should be designed and combined in a coherent, consistent way, and that one executive should have overall authority and responsibility for the complete set of marketing activities. At Barnes & Noble stores, consumers discover a relaxing environment where they can enjoy a cup of coffee in a store that's big enough to offer a broad selection of books and small enough to provide local

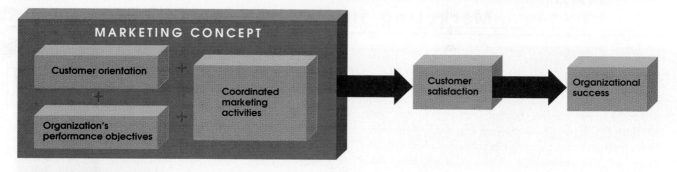

entertainment and children's story hours. The combination of carefully selected inventory, discount pricing, and inviting surroundings produces over $3 billion a year in sales for the firm.[8]

- Customer-oriented, coordinated marketing is essential to achieve the *organization's performance objectives*. The ultimate objective for a business is typically a profitable sales volume. However, the immediate objective might be something less ambitious that will move the organization closer to its ultimate goal. For example, Cinergy, Inc., the electric utility in Cincinnati that now must compete with other power companies in a deregulated environment, wants its customers to know the company that has been faithfully supplying their energy needs for years. By paying $6 million to put its name on Cincinnati's Riverfront Stadium, the firm was able to increase the proportion of area residents who recognize its name from 36% to 95%.[9]

Sometimes the marketing concept is simply stated as a customer orientation, as expressed in these words of the late Sam Walton, founder of Wal-Mart: "There is only one boss: the customer."[10] As important as it is to stress a customer focus, however, it should not replace achievement of objectives as the fundamental rationale for the marketing concept.

Refinements of the Marketing Concept

All ideas are subject to refinement and the marketing concept is no exception. As business learns more about consumers, competitive pressure increases both domestically and globally, and technology alters the way organizations function, priorities are reconsidered and old ideas are examined in new ways. Several of these developments are discussed below.

Quality

Looking for an effective way to compete with highly successful U.S. manufacturers, a number of prominent foreign firms chose to focus on **quality.** Although U.S. firms had not ignored quality, they had a tendency to concentrate on keeping prices down and to think in terms of "acceptable" levels of quality as determined by their engineers and manufacturing people. When the foreign firms added quality as *defined by customers* as a key ingredient of their strategies, it wasn't long before U.S. consumers responded. Soon the benefits of a commitment to quality became evident in the success of firms such as Sony and Honda. Thus, beginning in the 1980s improving quality became a priority for most organizations. And the interest in quality has not diminished. Seven of the ten most respected companies in Europe, including British Telecommunications, rate managing quality as a top priority.[11]

Some suggest that American executives became complacent about quality. However, it is more likely that American businesspeople had come to believe that quality and cost were directly related. That is, as quality is increased, costs must

Is there any place you won't find technology?

We've already described how eBay brings buyers and sellers together via the Internet, creating an electronic auction. No doubt you are aware that many firms have developed websites to communicate with prospects and customers. The Web is also becoming an important sales channel. The success of companies such as Amazon.com selling books and Autobytel.com selling cars has encouraged virtually every significant manufacturer, wholesaler, and retailer to consider how the World Wide Web can be incorporated into their marketing efforts.

But the Web is not the only important technological development impacting marketing. Consider for example:

- Marketers such as American Express, which has on file every AmEx credit card purchase ever made by every one of its cardholders, are using computers to analyze these massive amounts of customer information to improve existing products and develop new offerings.

- Large retailers such as Kroger and Wal-Mart are using electronic cash registers to improve the efficiency and accuracy of checking customers out. However, the registers also allow stores to instantaneously capture information about what is and is not selling so inventories can be most effectively managed.

- Marketing researchers are conducting surveys using e-mail instead of mailed questionnaires, gathering data in days rather than the weeks it used to take.

- Trucking companies such as Roberts Express are installing satellite dishes and computers in their fleets to monitor the location of every truck. The information allows them to predict delays, reroute shipments, and improve on-time deliveries.

- Borders, the bookstore chain, has a computerized database that contains thousands of complete books. When a customer requests a title, store personnel can electronically search the database, download the book, and print and bind a high-quality copy in the store in about 15 minutes. Accessibility to this centralized database will greatly reduce the need to stock obscure and slow-selling titles.

These are just a few examples to illustrate how technology in many forms is having a dramatic effect on marketing. Throughout the book we will describe these and other technological developments in more detail.

How should the use of technology in marketing be integrated with the marketing concept?

Sources: Penelope Ody, "Sharing Data Is Just the Beginning of the Process," *Financial Times*, Sept. 1, 1999, p. VI; Kendra Parker, "Got Questions? All You Have to Do Is Ask," *American Demographics*, November 1999, pp. 36–39; Rodney Ho, "Borders to Try a New Weapon: Printing Books Inside the Stores," *The Wall Street Journal*, June 1, 1999, p. B1+; Chuck Salter, "Roberts Rules the Road," *Fast Company*, September 1998, pp. 114–128.

---

go up. Although that is generally true, the relationship is not as strong as first thought. Through careful study, firms found it is possible to substantially increase quality without unacceptable cost increases by:

- Obtaining and responding to input from customers about how they define quality in a particular product.
- Improving designs to reduce problems in manufacturing, and identifying and correcting problems early in the production process to reduce expensive reworking and waste.
- Encouraging employees to call attention to quality problems, and empowering them to initiate action to improve quality.

Concerns about quality are not limited to manufacturing and service. Every business function has a quality component. Within marketing there are quality aspects to making sales calls, answering customers' questions, preparing advertisements, and every other activity. The breadth of quality issues, along with the realization that achieving and maintaining quality depends on the efforts of employees, led to the development of **total quality management (TQM)** in the 1980s. TQM is a system for implementing organization-wide commitment to quality that involves every employee accepting responsibility for continuous quality improvement. Despite the good intentions that surrounded TQM programs, their focus on introducing change led many proponents to overlook the costs and benefits of the changes. As a result, firms are now evaluating the impact of quality proposals on customer satisfaction, and treating quality improvements as investments. This is known as a return on quality (ROQ) approach.

Relationships

The value of a good relationship is not a new idea. Marketers have long recognized that identifying the needs of customers and satisfying them can be profitable. However, it is only recently that organizations have made a concerted effort at relationship marketing—establishing a connection with a customer such that the organization is viewed as a partner. By examining successful partnerships in business and elsewhere, marketers have discovered that enduring relationships are built on trust and commitment, require a lot of time and effort to create and maintain, and are not appropriate for every exchange situation.[12] Applying these observations to their marketing programs, many firms are dedicating much of their marketing effort to building lasting relationships with selected customers.

Consider, for example, what motorcycle maker Harley-Davidson has done. The firm created a club for bike owners and offers the more than 450,000 members insurance, a travel agency, roadside emergency assistance, magazines, free safety courses, safe riding competitions, and 1,100 local chapters that hold regular meetings.[13] The Internet, with its two-way communication capability, makes it easier for some firms to build relationships with customers by personalizing their interactions. Garden Escape Inc., like many Internet marketers, invites site visitors to submit some information about themselves and their interests. Then, on subsequent visits to the site, the customer is greeted with a personalized message, directed to merchandise tailored to their interests, and provided with an electronic notepad where they can store gardening tips and shopping information.[14] What do these companies hope to get in return? A feeling of goodwill, and a sense that the firm cares about more than making a sale. That is, they are seeking a long-term relationship with their customers that will be mutually beneficial.

More recently, the notion of establishing relationships has been extended beyond customers to all the groups an organization interacts with. These include suppliers, employees, the government, and even competitors. For example, Ford Motor Co. and Daimler-Benz AG (maker of the Mercedes) are working with an engine manufacturer to develop an engine powered by electric fuel cells.

Mass Customization

The modern marketing system was built on identifying a need experienced by a large number of people (a mass market), and using mass production techniques and mass marketing (relying heavily on network television advertising) to satisfy

www.garden.com

Harley-Davidson has created a cultlike following by focusing on customer relationship building. The Harley Owners Group (HOG) holds an annual rally that attracts 10,000 to 12,000 motorcycle enthusiasts.

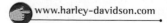
www.harley-davidson.com

that need. By producing and selling large quantities of standardized products, firms were able to keep the unit costs low and offer need-satisfying products at attractive prices. However, the market has changed. Mass marketing is being replaced by **mass customization,** that is, developing, producing, and delivering affordable products with enough variety and uniqueness that nearly every potential customer can have exactly what he or she wants.[15] Deere and Co., maker of John Deere farm machinery, produces 45 different models of seed planters with a total of 1.7 million options in order to meet the varied needs of all types of farmers. What may be more remarkable is that they can all be built on the same assembly line in Moline, Illinois.[16]

The movement toward mass customization is made possible by the tremendous advances in information technology. Firms are now able to learn a lot more about their current and prospective customers, and use that information in designing products, manufacturing, and distribution. They also can advertise to very specific audiences through cable television and the many special interest magazines now on newsstands. The result is a proliferation of products in many product categories. Consider, for example, the variety of dry breakfast cereals available from General Mills and the snack alternatives offered by Frito-Lay.

Marketers are coming to realize, however, that more variety is not always better. In some areas the number of choices creates as much confusion as satisfaction. Consider, for example, the number of different pain relievers available in the drugstore. Retailers are also concerned by the explosion of products because they have to find shelf space for them.

Value Creation

Value is the customer's perception of all the benefits of a product weighed against all the costs of acquiring and consuming the product.[17] The benefits can be functional (the roominess of a minivan for a large family), aesthetic (the attractiveness of the minivan), or psychological (the peace of mind that the van is designed to withstand a collision). Besides the money paid to the seller, the costs might include learning about the product in order to make a choice, negotiating the purchase, arranging financing, waiting for delivery, learning how to use the product, and disposal of the product when it is no longer useful.

Marketers are taking a closer look at what customers value in a product. As we have noted above, the heavy emphasis on mass production and mass marketing were largely driven by the desire to offer products at the lowest possible price. The focus on price overshadowed other benefits sought by customers. With better information about what customers desire and constant improvements in technology that make meeting those desires possible, marketers are engaging in **value creation** that extends beyond just offering the lowest possible prices.

Two points are important to note here. First, value means much more to the buyer than the amount of money charged for a product. Second, the determination of value is distinctive for each individual. To meet customers' different needs, frequently sellers must adapt their products. For example, Capital One, one of the largest issuers of credit cards in the U.S. with nearly 17 million cardholders, offers 6,000 credit cards differing slightly in benefits, payment terms, and requirements.[18]

Return on Marketing Investment

Recall that one element of the marketing concept is the accomplishment of organizational goals. In the past the impact of marketing on organizational goals has been defined rather broadly. Because marketing is only one of many factors that influence how customers behave, it was assumed that a specific cause-and-effect relationship between marketing efforts and sales or profits could not be measured. As a result, marketing expenditures generally have been treated as expenses rather than investments, and managers adopted a short-term approach of trying to minimize these expenses as opposed to investing in marketing for both the short and long term. Today that thinking is changing. Just as they would with any other asset, firms are looking for a measurable return on the marketing investment.

Recognizing that marketing now accounts for at least 50% of all corporate costs, while manufacturing has gone from 50% to less than 30%, managers are demanding greater accountability. In response, organizations are searching for new and creative ways to measure marketing's effects.[19] For example, Kraft has committed nearly one-third of its marketing research staff to identifying the return on its marketing investment.

The Societal Marketing Concept

Not long after the marketing concept became a widely accepted approach to doing business, it came under fire. For more than 40 years critics have persistently charged that marketing ignores social responsibility. That is, although the marketing concept may help an organization achieve its goals, it may at the same time encourage actions that conflict with society's best interests.

From one point of view, these charges are true. A firm may totally satisfy its customers (and in the process achieve a hefty profit), while also adversely affecting society. To illustrate, a pulp and paper mill in the Pacific Northwest might be supplying its newspaper customers with quality newsprint at a reasonable price, but to do so it might be polluting the air and water near the mill.

However, this need not be the case. A firm's social responsibility can be quite compatible with the marketing concept. Compatibility depends on two things: how broadly a firm perceives its marketing goals and what the firm is willing to invest to achieve those goals. A firm that sufficiently extends the *breadth* and *commitment* dimensions of its marketing goals to fulfill its social responsibility is practicing what has become known as the societal marketing concept.

When the marketing concept's breadth is extended, a company recognizes that its market includes not only the buyers of its products but also anyone directly affected by its operations. In our example, the paper mill has several markets to satisfy, including (1) the newspaper publishers, (2) the consumers of the air that contains impurities given off by the mill, and (3) the recreational users of the local river where the mill releases its waste matter.

Extending the commitment dimension of its marketing goals means a firm must recognize that meeting the broader needs of society may require more time, technology, and skill than meeting just the needs of its immediate customers. Although these investments seem costly when they are made, they reflect a long-term view of customer satisfaction and performance objectives, rather than a focus only on today.

For a company to prosper in the long run, it must satisfy its customers' social needs as well as their economic needs. General Motors and Toyota have launched a joint effort to speed development of advanced technology vehicles. The project will involve hundreds of engineers in a long-term research and development program. If their efforts are successful in producing more fuel-efficient, cleaner-operating cars, both firms will benefit—and so will society.[20] Thus the marketing concept and a company's social responsibility are compatible if management strives over the long run to (1) satisfy the wants of its product-buying customers, (2) meet the societal needs of others affected by the firm's activities, and (3) achieve the company's performance objectives.

If the marketing concept and the refinements we've just discussed direct a modern marketer's approach to the marketing task, just what is it that marketers do? In the next section we'll describe the areas of responsibility and decision making that are generally referred to as marketing management.

Toyota is the first automaker to receive a United Nations award for environmental initiatives. Noted in the award is Toyota's Prius, the first mass-produced car to be powered by a hybrid gasoline and electric system that reduces pollution by as much as 90%. Toyota's subsequent cooperative effort with GM is intended to speed up the development of advanced technology vehicles in the 21st century.

www.toyota.com

A Company's Marketing Program

Recall that we said a market consists of people or organizations with needs to satisfy, money to spend, and the willingness to spend it. For example, many people need transportation and are willing to pay for it. However, this large group is made up of many subgroups or segments with different transportation needs. For example, among the people who want to travel long distances by air, there are some who want low prices and efficiency, whereas others are willing to pay for luxury and privacy. These subgroups or market segments are consumers or organizations that share similar wants, buying preferences, or product-use behaviors. If a segment is large and sufficiently distinct, marketers typically respond with a specially designed offering. Thus, we often see the same basic need satisfied in very different ways. For example, Southwest Airlines, with low prices but no meals and no reserved seats, and NetJets Inc., which offers private jets on a time-share basis, are both highly successful air transportation marketers.

Ordinarily it is impractical for a firm to satisfy all or even most of the segments of a market. Instead, a company first identifies the segments and then selects one or more at which to target its efforts. Thus a target market refers to a market segment at which a firm directs a marketing program.

Usually several firms are pursuing a particular target market at the same time, and each attempts to be viewed in a distinct and attractive way by prospective customers. That is, each firm uses strategies and tactics in an effort to establish a unique position in the prospects' minds. For example, Volvo is perceived by consumers as a safe car, IBM PCs as business computers, and Target as a discount general merchandiser. Segmenting markets, selecting targets, and devising positioning strategies are fundamental marketing tasks.

Usually firms do a considerable amount of research to identify markets and define segments. Among the many questions market research seeks to answer, one of the most important is the sales potential of particular market segments. To determine sales potential, a firm must **forecast demand** (that is, sales) in its target markets. The results of demand forecasting will indicate whether the segments are worth pursuing, or whether alternatives need to be identified.

Next, management must design a **marketing mix**—the combination of a product, how it is distributed and promoted, and its price. Together, these four components of strategy must satisfy the needs of the target market(s) and, at the same time, achieve the organization's marketing objectives. Some of the challenges facing marketing managers in developing a marketing mix are:

- *Product.* Strategies are needed for deciding what products to offer, managing existing products over time, and dropping failed products. Strategic decisions must also be made regarding branding, packaging, and other product features such as warranties.

- *Price.* Setting the price for a product is a marketing decision. Other necessary strategies pertain to changing price, pricing related items within a product line, terms of sale, and possible discounts. An especially challenging decision is selecting the price for a new product.

- *Distribution.* Here, strategies relate to the channel(s) by which ownership of products is transferred from producer to customer and, in many cases, the means by which goods are moved from where they are produced to where they are purchased by the final customer. In addition, strategies applicable to any middlemen, such as wholesalers and retailers, must be designed.

- *Promotion.* Strategies are needed to combine individual methods such as advertising, personal selling, and sales promotion into an integrated communications campaign. In addition, promotional strategies must be adjusted as a product moves from the early stages to the later stages of its life.

The four marketing-mix elements are interrelated; decisions in one area affect actions in another. To illustrate, design of a marketing mix is certainly affected by whether a firm chooses to compete on the basis of price *or* on one or more other elements. When a firm relies on price as its primary competitive tool, the other elements must be designed to support aggressive pricing. For example, the promotional campaign likely will be built around a theme of "low, low prices." In nonprice competition, however, product, distribution, and/or promotion strategies come to the forefront. For instance, the product must have features worthy of a higher price, and promotion must create a high-quality image for the product.

Each marketing-mix element contains countless alternatives. For instance, a producer may make and market one product or many, and the products may be related or unrelated to each other. They may be distributed through wholesalers, to retailers without the benefit of wholesalers, or even directly to final customers. Ultimately, from the multitude of alternatives, management must select a combination of elements that will satisfy target markets and achieve organizational and marketing goals.

Like many areas of business, marketers sometimes face seemingly contradictory goals. The desire to satisfy customers, for example, may seem to conflict with a particular revenue or profit objective. When this occurs, ethical predicaments may arise. Thus ethics in marketing deserves our attention.

Ethics and Marketing

Marketers are responsible to a variety of groups. Certainly their customers depend on them to satisfy their needs. Also, their employers expect them to generate sales and profits, suppliers and distributors look to them for their continued business, and society expects them to be responsible citizens. The frequently divergent interests of these groups create a wide variety of ethical challenges for marketers.

What Is Ethical Behavior?

A discussion of the philosophical underpinnings of ethics is beyond the scope of this book.[21] However, it is safe to say that there is considerable disagreement over what is and what is not ethical conduct. For example, ethics vary from society to society. Take bribery; although repugnant in most societies, it is an accepted and even necessary aspect of business behavior in many parts of the world. Thus, for our purposes it is sufficient to say that ethics are the standards of behavior generally accepted by a society. Note that ethics goes beyond laws, which establish the minimum rules a society agrees to follow. Thus, it is possible to behave legally but still be unethical.

To draw attention to how common unethical behavior has become, Transparency International annually compiles a "Corruption Perceptions Index" that ranks 85 countries according to their perceived levels of unethical behavior. Table 1.2 contains the 20 best-performing countries.

The temptation to act in an ethically questionable fashion can be very strong, particularly when the behavior can be rewarding. Take, for example, a development in the drugstore business. For years it has been a common practice for suppliers to grant discounts to retailers for damaged or outdated merchandise. However, some firms appear to be taking advantage of the policy. There have been a number of mergers among retail drugstore chains, giving them enormous power. As suppliers have become more dependent on these chains, they charge that some chains have gotten more liberal in their interpretation of "damaged and outdated," and are taking unauthorized deductions from their invoices.[22] Is this unethical? The suppliers think so, but others say the suppliers have had the upper hand for years. In the past they had been able to dictate terms to the retailers and now "turnabout is fair play."

Instilling an Ethical Orientation

Organizations are not ignoring ethical issues. For example, most firms have a code of ethics for their employees. However, as long as there are conflicting goals and the opportunity for people to make judgments, ethical failures will occur. To relieve some of the pressure on employees faced with ethical challenges and perhaps reduce the frequency and severity of ethical problems, organizations have taken several steps:

- Clearly communicating the organization's ethical standards and expectations through initial training and frequent reminders and updates.

Table 1.2	The Countries with the Least Amount of Corruption		
Country	**Rank**	**Country**	**Rank**
Denmark	1	Australia	11 (tie)
Finland	2	Luxemburg	11 (tie)
Sweden	3	United Kingdom	11 (tie)
New Zealand	4	Ireland	14
Iceland	5	Germany	15
Canada	6	Hong Kong	16
Singapore	7	Austria	17 (tie)
Netherlands	8 (tie)	United States	17 (tie)
Norway	8 (tie)	Israel	19
Switzerland	10	Chile	20

Note: The Corruption Perceptions Index is a "poll of polls." It is the result of compiling numerous surveys on the extent of corruption in countries around the world. For more details see the Transparency International website.

Source: Transparency International website.

www.transparency.de

- Ensuring that employee requirements in terms of goals, quotas, and deadlines are reasonable.
- Creating a senior-level position of "ethics officer" occupied by a person with the skill to provide advice as well as the authority to respond to complaints and inquiries.
- Commending extraordinary ethical behavior and dealing decisively with ethical violations.

The Benefits of Ethical Behavior

One could argue that ethical behavior should in itself be rewarding. However, there are tangible benefits as well. Business is built on relationships with suppliers, customers, employees, and other groups. The strength of those relationships is largely a function of the amount of trust the parties have in each other. Unethical behavior undermines trust and destroys relationships.

However, there is a need for constant vigilance. Johnson & Johnson is probably the most often cited example of an ethical firm. Its corporate code of ethics is one of the oldest, written in 1932. And its handling of the Tylenol crisis in 1982, when eight people died as a result of products that had been tampered with, is considered a near-perfect example of ethical behavior. Yet, even this exemplar of ethics has admitted that employees intentionally destroyed documents sought by the government that dealt with the firm's promotion of Retin-A.[23]

Issues related to ethics are often ambiguous. There are situations in which the behavior of a marketer might be judged inappropriate and unethical by some, and totally acceptable by others. It is important for you to be aware of typical ethical challenges in marketing and to consider how you would respond to them. To help you in that regard, we have included Ethical Dilemma boxes throughout the book. In most, there are no absolutely right or wrong answers. That's why we call them dilemmas. We hope you find them interesting and helpful in refining your own sense of ethics.

An Ethical Dilemma?

The Environmental Protection Agency (EPA) has formulated new pollution-emission regulations for vehicles. The rules, which require auto manufacturers to reduce the nitrogen oxide emissions of cars and trucks, are to be phased in between 2004 and 2009. During the phase-in, a manufacturer will be permitted to sell some vehicles with pollution levels that exceed the requirement as long as the average pollution level across all of the cars and trucks up to 8,500 pounds it sells does not exceed the maximum. The 8,500 pound cutoff includes all cars and trucks except the largest pickups and sport utility vehicles.

Averaging the pollution level across a manufacturer's entire fleet of cars and trucks will permit the highest polluting trucks to be sold without any changes until about 2007. The manufacturers view this as good news because trucks are very popular with consumers and are the most profitable vehicles they make.

No one questions the fact that cars and trucks pollute the air. Nor is there any doubt that emissions can be substantially reduced. According to the senior manager of vehicle emissions planning for DaimlerChrysler, "The industry has stopped saying, 'We can't do it,' because we know that even if we can't do it today, if we apply our engineering resources, we can get it done." The standards are not a surprise given that the auto industry has been a target of the EPA for years.

Is it ethical for automakers to just meet the "letter of the law" in terms of the permissible amount of pollution and the deadlines for implementing changes?

Source: Jeffery Ball and Anna Wilde Mathews, "New EPA Emissions Rules Won't Stem Flow of Trucks," *The Wall Street Journal*, Apr. 19, 1999, p. B4.

Importance of Marketing

It would be difficult to imagine a world without marketing. But it may be equally difficult to appreciate the importance effective marketing plays in most aspects of our lives. We take for granted the media that are largely supported by advertising, the vast assortment of goods distributed through stores close to our homes, and the ease with which we can make purchases. Let's consider for a moment how marketing plays a major role in the global economy, in the American socioeconomic system, in any individual organization, and in your life.

Globally

Until the late 1970s, American firms had a large and secure domestic market. The only significant foreign competition was in selected industries, such as agriculture, or for relatively narrow markets, such as luxury automobiles. But this changed dramatically through the 1980s as more foreign firms developed attractive products, honed their marketing expertise, and then successfully entered the U.S. market. Imported products in some industries, such as office equipment, autos, apparel, watches, semiconductors, and consumer electronics, have been very successful. As a result, in recent years the U.S. has been importing more than it exports, creating large annual trade deficits.

In the not too distant future there will be new challenges. The dramatic changes taking place in the governments and economies of eastern Europe and growing capitalism in China and the former Soviet Union will certainly create new and stronger international competitors.

Trade agreements are also altering the global business picture. The European Union, the North American Free Trade Agreement, and the Asia-Pacific Economic Cooperation are reducing economic barriers and liberalizing trade between their members. However, as trade agreements increase the marketing opportunities for firms within the member countries, they often result in stiffened competition for firms from outside.

In response to these developments, more and more U.S. firms are looking abroad. They are concluding that their profit and growth objectives are most likely to be achieved through a combination of domestic and international marketing,

Invented over 40 years ago, there are over 2,300 container ships that account for a major portion of the nearly $6 trillion in goods transported between countries. Containers are ideal for bulky products that need protection. However, in today's technology-driven world, more of the products shipped are high in value, low in weight, and time sensitive. As a result, intercontinental air freight is growing at 6% a year.

Table 1.3	U.S. International Trade and Major Trading Partners, 1998	
Total Exports = $683 Billion		**Total Imports = $914 Billion**
Primary Destinations:		**Primary Sources:**
Canada		Canada
Mexico		Japan
Japan		Mexico
United Kingdom		China
Germany		Germany

Source: Statistical Abstract of the United States: 1999, 119th ed., U.S. Bureau of the Census, Washington, DC, 1999.

rather than solely from domestic marketing. Table 1.3 gives you some insight into how important foreign trade is for U.S. firms.

Although we don't yet know everything that will result from these developments, one thing is certain. We live in a global economy. Most nations today— regardless of their degree of economic development or their political philosophy— recognize the importance of marketing beyond their own national borders. Indeed, economic growth in the less developed nations of the world depends greatly on their ability to design effective marketing systems to produce global customers for their raw materials and industrial output. We will explore these issues in more detail throughout the book.

Domestically

Aggressive, effective marketing practices have been largely responsible for the high standard of living in the United States. The efficiency of mass marketing—extensive and rapid communication with customers through a wide variety of media and a distribution system that makes products readily available—combined with mass production brought the cost of many products within reach of most consumers. Since about 1920 (except during World War II), the available supply of products in the United States has far surpassed total demand. Making most products has been relatively easy; the real challenge has been marketing them.

Now mass customization means even more products virtually tailored to our individual tastes. As a result, the average American enjoys things that once were considered luxuries and in many countries are still available only to people earning high incomes.

Employment and Costs

We can get an idea of the significance of marketing in the U.S. economy by looking at how many of us are employed in some way in marketing and how much of what we spend covers the cost of marketing. *Between one-fourth and one-third of the U.S. civilian labor force is engaged in marketing activities.* This figure includes employees in retailing, wholesaling, transportation, warehousing, and communications industries, as well as people who work in marketing departments of manufacturers and those who work in marketing in agricultural, mining, and service industries. Furthermore, over the past century, jobs in marketing have increased at a much more rapid rate than jobs in production, reflecting marketing's expanded role in the economy. On the average, *about 50 cents of each dollar we spend as consumers goes to cover marketing costs.* The money pays for designing the products to meet our needs, making products readily available when and where we want them, and informing us about products. These activities add want-satisfying ability, or what is called utility, to products.

A Global Perspective

Where do firms look for markets?

Quick, what do Uzbekistan, Azerbaijan, and Turkmenistan have in common? If you said they are republics that were formerly part of the Soviet Union, you'd be correct. But did you also know that they are part of a Central Asian region with 55 million consumers, rich oil and gas reserves, and a growing consumer market? Those are the features noticed by companies such as Coca-Cola, Mattel, and Philip Morris.

Developing these markets has not been easy. In Uzbekistan consumers saw "Made in Hong Kong" on Mattel's Barbie dolls, and concluded the products were counterfeit because they assume all American products must be made in America. And when consumers noticed the "sell by" dates were much shorter on American food products than on Russian-made products, they concluded the Russian goods were of higher quality.

In recent years Seagram undertook an effort to produce and sell its Tropicana orange juice in China, but was faced with skeptical farmers leery of switching crops and a primitive transportation system that makes it difficult to get products to market in a timely fashion. General Motors committed to marketing Cadillacs in 40 countries outside the U.S. To be taken seriously as a global brand, GM management believed it would have to attract European luxury car buyers, a group that has not been receptive to products made

outside Europe. Unfortunately for GM, Cadillac hasn't proved to be the breakthrough product. And Campbell Soup has tried to sell its canned condensed soups, a product found in virtually every American pantry, in countries as varied as Mexico, Poland, and Australia with only limited success. Although duck gizzard soup was a success for Campbell in Hong Kong, it found that most of the world's consumers prefer soup made from scratch or, more familiar to them, dry soup sold in envelopes.

So why do established firms enter these new (to them) geographic areas and struggle to become established? One reason is that their "home" territories are saturated and provide little opportunity for additional growth. Often these foreign markets appear to offer, at least in the long run, the characteristics that we have used to define a market—people or organizations with needs to satisfy, money to spend, and a willingness to spend it. The challenge for these firms is to put together marketing programs that will create the desired exchanges.

Sources: Hugh Pope, "Plying Ex-Soviet Asia with Pepsi, Barbie, and Barf," *The Wall Street Journal*, May 6, 1998, pp. B1+; Rebecca Blumenstein, "Cadillac Has Designs on Europe's Luxury-Car Buyers," *The Wall Street Journal*, Sept. 9, 1997, p. B1; Kathy Chen, "Tea and Tropicana? Seagram Wants Juice to Be Chinese Staple," *The Wall Street Journal*, Jan. 2, 1998, p. A1; Joseph Weber, "What's Not Cookin' at Campbell's," *Business Week*, Sept. 23, 1996, p. 40.

Creating Utility

A customer purchases a product because it provides satisfaction. The want-satisfying power of a product is called its **utility**, and it comes in many forms. It is through marketing that much of a product's utility is created.

Consider eBay as an example. Pierre Omidyar and Jeff Skoll, two San Jose, California, entrepreneurs, envisioned operating a giant auction where many buyers and sellers could gather and trade goods. But an auction in San Jose was not likely to generate the kind of crowds they desired. Faced with the challenge of how to increase access to their auction, they came upon the Internet. They wondered if the Internet could transport information from sellers about their products and bids from buyers interested in making purchases. Even if the technology could be made to work, potential buyers and sellers had to be made aware of this unique auction format and informed about how to use it. Excited by the possibilities, they created eBay, Inc., and the rest, as we say, is history.

Let's see what kinds of utility have been created in this process:

- *Form utility* is associated primarily with production—the physical or chemical changes that make a product more valuable. When lumber is made into furniture, form utility is created. This is production, not marketing. However, marketing contributes to decisions on the style, size, and color of the furniture.

Similarly, marketing is involved in developing almost all products. In the case of eBay, an attractive, easy-to-use website had to be designed. Visitors to the site had to be able to find goods that interested them quickly and easily. These features contribute to the product's form utility.

- *Place utility* exists when a product is readily accessible to potential customers. An auction on the Internet can increase the number of buyers and sellers, but once products are purchased they still have to be delivered quickly and in good condition. Physically moving a purchased item to a successful bidder is an essential element of its value.

- *Time utility* means having a product available when you want it. In the case of eBay, this may be one of its primary attractions. Prospective buyers can visit the eBay Internet site day or night at their convenience. There's no need to have a store open or staffed.

- *Information utility* is created by informing prospective buyers that a product exists. Unless you know about a product and where you can get it, the product has no value. Advertising that describes the eBay auction concept and provides some information about how to list an item and how to make bids creates information utility. To create awareness of eBay, it had to be advertised. *Image utility* is a special type of information utility. It is the emotional or psychological value that a person attaches to a product or brand because of its reputation or social standing. Image utility is ordinarily associated with prestige or high-status products such as designer clothes, expensive foreign automobiles, or certain residential neighborhoods. However, the image-utility value of a given product may vary considerably depending on different consumers' perceptions. Shopping on the Internet using an online auction is still a novelty for many consumers. For some it may even be a status symbol that they can tell their friends about. Thus, for some consumers using eBay also provides image utility.

- *Possession utility* is created when a customer buys the product—that is, ownership is transferred to the buyer. This is a concern for eBay because there is virtually no policing of the buyers or the sellers. It's possible for sellers to misrepresent goods and for buyers to renege on paying. Clearly this is much less of an issue in face-to-face transactions. For eBay, providing possession utility is taking on growing significance as the number of users of the service increases.

Organizationally

Marketing considerations should be an integral part of all short-range and long-range planning in any company. Here's why:

- The success of any business comes from satisfying the wants of its customers, which is the social and economic basis for the existence of all organizations.

- Although many activities are essential to a company's growth, marketing is the only one that produces revenue directly. (This is sometimes overlooked by the production managers who use these revenues and the financial executives who manage them.)

When managers are internally focused, products are designed by designers, manufactured by manufacturing people, priced by financial managers, and then given to sales managers to sell. This approach generally won't work in today's environment of intense competition and constant change. Just making a good product will not result in sales. Two special applications, services marketing and not-for-profit marketing, are described below.

Service Marketers

The U.S. has gone from primarily a manufacturing economy to the world's first service economy. As opposed to goods, services are activities that are the object of a transaction. Examples are transportation, communications, entertainment,

After several years of poor performance, Disneyland Paris (formerly called EuroDisney) is now one of the most popular attractions in Europe. The theme park draws more than 12 million visitors a year. Studio Disney, a companion facility similar to Disney-MGM Studios Theme Park in Florida, will open nearby in 2003.

 www.disney.com

medical care, financial services, education, and repairs. Services account for over two-thirds of the nation's gross domestic product. Almost three-fourths of the country's nonfarm labor force is employed in service industries, and over one-half of all consumer expenditures are for the purchase of services. Projections indicate that services' share of all these categories (gross domestic product, employment, expenditures) will continue to grow.

Because the production of goods dominated our economy until fairly recently, most marketing knowledge was derived from experience with goods (such as groceries, clothing, machine tools, and automobiles) rather than from services. But progress in services has been rapid, and now some service sector firms such as FedEx, Disney, and Marriott Corp. are generally considered to be among the most market-oriented companies in the world.

Not-for-Profit Marketers

During the 1980s and early 1990s many not-for-profit organizations realized they needed effective marketing programs to make up for shrinking government subsidies, a decrease in charitable contributions, and other unfavorable economic conditions. Colleges with declining enrollments, hospitals with empty beds, and symphony orchestras playing to vacant seats all began to understand that marketing was essential to help them turn their situations around.

Today charities, museums, and even churches—all organizations that formerly rejected any thought of marketing—are embracing it as a means of growth and, for some, survival. This trend is likely to accelerate for two reasons:

- Increasing competition among nonprofit organizations. For example, the competition among colleges and universities for students is intensifying, and the search for donors has become more intense as the number of charities has increased.

- Not-for-profit organizations need to improve their images and gain greater acceptance among donors, government agencies, news media, and of course, consumers, all of which collectively determine an organization's success.

Though many traditional symphonies experience problems, some are successful in part because of their marketing. Ravinia Festival, the summer home of the Chicago Symphony orchestra, generates nearly 10% of its ticket sales to mostly new customers through an Internet marketing effort.

 www.ravinia.com

Personally

Okay, so marketing is important globally, in our economy, and in an individual organization. But what's in it for you? Why should you study marketing? There are a number of reasons:

- Consider how many marketers view you as part of their market. With people like you in mind, firms such as Nike, VISA, Microsoft, and Kellogg's have designed products, set prices, created advertisements, and chosen the best methods of making their products available to you. In response, you watch television with its commercials, buy various articles over the Internet and in stores, and sometimes complain about prices or quality. As we said at the outset of the chapter, marketing occupies a large part of your daily life. If you doubt this, just imagine for a moment what it would be like if there were no marketing institutions—no retail stores to buy from or no advertising to give you information, for example. Clearly it is important to be informed about such a significant part of our society.

- Studying marketing will make you a better-informed consumer. You'll understand more about what underlies a seller's pricing and how brand names are selected, as well as the role of promotion and distribution.

- Last, marketing probably relates—directly or indirectly—to your career aspirations. If you are thinking about a marketing major and employment in a marketing position, you can develop a feel for what marketing managers do. (For an introduction to the many career opportunities in the field, we especially suggest you read Appendix B, "Careers and Marketing.") If you're planning a career in accounting, finance, or some other business field, you can learn how marketing affects managerial decision making in these areas. Finally, if you are thinking about a career in a nonbusiness field such as health care, government, music, or education, you will learn how to use marketing in these organizations.

Summary

The foundation of marketing is exchange, in which one party provides to another party something of value in return for something else of value. In a broad sense, marketing consists of all activities designed to generate or facilitate an exchange intended to satisfy human needs.

Business firms and nonprofit organizations engage in marketing. Products marketed include goods as well as services, ideas, people, and places. Marketing activities are targeted at markets consisting of product purchasers and also individuals and groups that influence the success of an organization.

In a business context, marketing is a total system of business activities designed to plan, price, promote, and distribute want-satisfying products to target markets in order to achieve organizational objectives. The main difference between marketing and selling is that in selling, the emphasis is on the sellers' needs; in marketing, the emphasis is on customers' wants.

Marketing's evolution in the United States has gone through three stages: It began with a product orientation, passed through the sales orientation, and is now in a market orientation. In this third stage a company's efforts are focused on identifying and satisfying customers' needs.

Some successful organizations remain at the first or second stage, not progressing to the market-orientation stage, because they have monopoly power or because their products are in such great demand. Other firms have difficulty accepting a market-driven approach to business or have problems implementing a market orientation.

A business philosophy called the marketing concept was developed to aid companies with supply capabilities that exceed consumer demand. According to the marketing concept, a firm is best able to achieve its performance objectives by adopting a customer orientation, coordinating all of its marketing activities, and fulfilling the organization's goals. Refinements in the market concept include heightened sensitivity to quality, relationship building, mass customization, value creation, and the societal marketing concept. Ethics, the standards of behavior accepted by society, are important concerns of market-oriented organizations.

Marketing management involves segmenting markets, selecting target markets, and establishing a position in the minds of buyers. The primary focus of marketing is the marketing mix—the combination of a product, price, promotion, and distribution process to meet the needs of a targeted segment of a market.

Marketing is practiced today in all modern nations, regardless of their political philosophy. As international competition has heated up, the attention paid to marketing has increased. In the U.S. between one-fourth and one-third of the civilian work force is involved with marketing, and about one-half of consumer spending covers the cost of marketing. This investment in marketing is justified by the form, information, place, time, and possession utilities it creates.

Depending on circumstances, marketing can be vital to an organization's success. In recent years numerous service firms and nonprofit organizations have found marketing to be necessary and worthwhile. Marketing also is useful to individuals. Students particularly find marketing helpful in the search for career opportunities.

More about **eBay**

For a company such as eBay, Internet auctions offer many attractions. For example, most of the work is done by the buyers and sellers. The sellers write the descriptions of the merchandise and submit them to the site for posting. The site operator does not carry any inventory, nor does it worry about what prices to charge for the merchandise. If an item is sold, the seller is notified by eBay, and the buyer and seller work out the arrangements for payment and delivery. All eBay does is maintain the site, provide some minimal customer support, and collect a commission on every transaction.

Observers have been surprised by a number of Internet auction developments. One is their rapid growth. In less than four years after it began, eBay-auctioned items accounted for over 5% of all person-to-person package shipments in the U.S.

Another surprise is the range of merchandise being offered. There seems to be almost no limit, with items from blocks of cheese to dance lessons finding their way to auction.

Then there is the issue of abuse. A 13-year-old recently bid more than $3 million on a variety of items, and had the winning bid on a 1971 Corvette and a wrestling championship belt. The only problem was, he had no money or credit. According to his mother, "To him it was like a game." Finally, there is intentional fraud when buyers and sellers are many miles apart and only communicate electronically. Although the amount of fraud has been relatively small, it has sometimes been rather blatant. For example, the stolen 1961 Kentucky Derby Trophy showed up for sale on eBay.[24]

1. How can Internet auctions more effectively meet the conditions of the marketing concept?

2. What form(s) of utility does eBay provide?

Key Terms and Concepts

The numbers next to the terms refer to the pages on which the terms and concepts are defined. In addition, the Glossary at the end of the book defines key terms and concepts.

Exchange (4)
Marketing (6)
Product-orientation stage (6)
Sales-orientation stage (7)
Market-orientation stage (8)
Marketing concept (9)
Quality (11)
Total quality management
  (TQM) (12)

Relationship marketing (13)
Mass customization (14)
Value (14)
Value creation (14)
Return on marketing
  investment (15)
Societal marketing concept (16)
Market (16)
Market segment (16)

Target market (16)
Position (16)
Forecast demand (17)
Marketing mix (17)
Ethics (18)
Utility (22)

Questions and Problems

1. Explain the concept of an exchange, including the conditions that must exist for an exchange to occur, and give one example each of a business exchange that does not involve money and a non-business exchange.

2. Name some companies that you believe are still in the product or sales stages in the evolution of marketing. Explain why you chose each of them.

3. Describe how each of the following could go beyond an exchange situation to establishing a relationship with customers.
   a. Online fresh-cut flower retailer
   b. CPA firm
   c. Blood bank
   d. Automobile dealership
   e. University
   f. Appliance manufacturer

4. Describe how the actions of a shoe manufacturer engaged in "marketing" might be different from a show manufacturer engaged in "selling."

5. Explain the three elements that constitute the marketing concept.

6. "The marketing concept does not imply that marketing executives will run the firm. The concept requires only that whoever is in top management be market-oriented." Give examples of how a production manager, company treasurer, or personnel manager can be market-oriented.

7. For each of the following organizations, describe the marketing mix.
   a. Luxor hotel and casino in Las Vegas
   b. Airline Pilots Association labor union
   c. Professor teaching a first-year chemistry course
   d. Police department in your city

8. One way to explain the utilities provided by marketing is to consider how we would live if there were no marketing facilities. Describe some of the ways in which your daily activities would be affected if there were no retail stores or advertising.

9. Name two service firms that, in your opinion, do a good marketing job. Then name some that you think do a poor marketing job. Explain your reasoning in each case.

Hands-On Marketing

1. Select an organizational unit at your school (for example, food service, placement office, intramural sports, library), observe the operation, and interview an administrator and some customers to identify (a) what is being exchanged; and (b) whether the unit is product-, sales-, or market-oriented.

2. Visit the sites of two different online book retailers (for example, Amazon.com and Barnes & Noble.com) and request information about this book. Keep track of the length of time it takes to find the book on the site and what information the site provides about the book. Next, note what information a customer is required to provide in order to purchase the book (but don't actually order one unless you need another copy!). How does the search process compare with visiting a bookstore?

2

The Dynamic Marketing Environment

"New products in other areas of the company, especially breakthrough products such as IQ, were critical to Campbell's future financial health."

Can **Intelligent Quisine** Make the Campbell Soup Co. Healthy?

Intelligent Quisine (labeled IQ, which prompted the intentional misspelling of *cuisine*) is a line of nutrient-fortified foods that were developed in the laboratories of the famous Campbell Soup Co. IQ was aimed at adults with health problems, particularly at the growing numbers of senior citizens. The market includes 60 million Americans who are troubled by adult-onset diabetes, high blood pressure, or high levels of harmful cholesterol. Thus it's not surprising that so-called *functional foods* or *nutraceuticals,* which are food products that yield specific health improvements, are of great interest to manufacturers of prepared food products. Predecessors to IQ include ConAgra's Healthy Choice and Heinz's Weight Watchers frozen meals.

The IQ product line consisted of 41 meals and snacks, such as raisin bran, French toast, clam chowder, chicken parmigiana, and even strawberry-topped cheesecake. A week's supply of 21 meals (most of them frozen) cost about $80, including shipping to the customer's home via United Parcel Service.

What sets IQ apart from most other foods was the claim, and supporting scientific evidence, that these entrées and snacks reduce dangerously high levels of blood pressure, heightened cholesterol levels, and blood sugar. This evidence came out of clinical trials at eight universities. For example, one documented benefit for diabetics was a reduction in blood glucose of almost 10%. Further, the products received generally favorable ratings in consumer taste tests.

Given these positive signs, Campbell had very high hopes for IQ. In fact, the company described IQ as its most important breakthrough since developing the technology that led to condensed soup. In January 1997, Campbell started to sell IQ to consumers in Ohio. The firm planned to monitor the results of this test market, which they fully expected to be hugely successful, before launching the product nationally.

Campbell executives forecast at least $200 million in annual sales for IQ nationally. And despite having more than $7 billion in annual sales, the company needed a big hit in the area of new products. Sales of canned soups in the U.S. declined each year during the mid-1990s, losing out to other foods including fancier soups. Further, sales of Campbell's familiar soups dropped more than sales of competing brands—probably because of stiff price competition.

One of the firm's top executives even admitted that another cause of the falling sales of Campbell's canned soups was a lack of exciting new products. Thus new products in other areas of the company, especially breakthrough products such as IQ, were critical to Campbell's future financial health. As a result, the launch of IQ in Ohio was backed by ample funds for advertising and other marketing tools. Campbell even hired two dozen part-timers who promoted the product to doctors, a practice that is used to market drug products.[1]

1. Does Intelligent Quisine coincide with, or run counter to, major demographic, social, and cultural trends in the U.S.?

2. What marketing considerations (e.g., price, advertising) will be particularly important in making Intelligent Quisine successful?

As the Intelligent Quisine situation illustrates, any organization must identify and then respond to numerous environmental forces. Some of these forces are external to the firm; others come from within. Management can't do much about controlling the external forces, but it generally can control the internal ones.

Many of these forces influence what can and should be done in the area of marketing. Ultimately, a firm's ability to adapt to its operating environment determines, in large part, its level of business success. Thus Campbell Soup Co., like any organization, must manage its marketing program within its combined external and internal environment.

After studying this chapter, you should be able to explain:

- The concept of environmental monitoring.
- How external environmental forces such as demographics, economic conditions, and social and cultural trends can affect an organization's marketing.
- How external forces such as markets, as well as suppliers and intermediaries that are specific to a given firm, can influence that firm's marketing.
- How nonmarketing resources within a firm can affect its marketing.

• Environmental Monitoring

Environmental monitoring—also called *environmental scanning*—is the process of (1) gathering information regarding a company's external environment, (2) analyzing it, and (3) forecasting the impact of whatever trends the analysis suggests. Today, much of the environmental discussion is about our physical environment—air quality, water pollution, solid-waste disposal, and natural-resource conservation. However, we use the term *environment* in a much broader sense in this chapter.

An organization operates within an *external* environment that it generally *cannot* control. At the same time, marketing and nonmarketing resources exist *within* the organization that generally *can* be controlled by its executives.

There are two levels of external forces:

- *Macro* influences (so called because they affect all firms), such as demographics, economic conditions, culture, and laws.
- *Micro* influences (so called because they affect a particular firm) consist of suppliers, marketing intermediaries, and customers. Micro influences, although external, are closely related to a specific company.

Successful marketing depends largely on a company's ability to manage its marketing programs within its environment. To do this, a firm's marketing executives must determine what makes up the firm's environment and then monitor it in a systematic, ongoing fashion. They must be alert to environmental trends that could be opportunities or problems for their organization. According to one source, "Successful trend-spotting is necessary for companies big and small . . . ; not only does being able to ride a trend boost profits for existing products, but it also can revive sales for products that are flagging."[2] Among the guidelines for identifying trends is the following: "Look to the margins; trends tend to bubble up from the fringes of society."

How important is environmental monitoring to business success? In a word, *very*. One study of about 100 large companies concluded, "Firms having advanced systems to monitor events in the external environment exhibited higher growth and greater profitability than firms that did not have such systems."[3]

External Macroenvironment

The following external forces have considerable influence on any organization's marketing opportunities and activities (see Figure 2.1). Therefore, they are *macroenvironmental forces:*

- Demographics
- Economic conditions
- Competition

- Social and cultural forces
- Political and legal forces
- Technology

A change in any one of them can cause changes in one or more of the others. Hence, they are interrelated. One thing they all have in common is that they are dynamic forces—that is, they are subject to change *and* at an increasing rate! These forces are largely uncontrollable by management; but they are not *totally* uncontrollable. A company may be able to influence its external environment to some extent. For instance, a firm may influence its political–legal environment by lobbying or by contributing to a legislator's campaign fund. Or, in international marketing, a company can improve its competitive position by a joint venture with a foreign firm that markets a complementary product. Coca-Cola and Swiss-owned Nestlé, the world's largest food manufacturer, joined forces to market ready-to-drink iced Nestea in the U.S. and chocolate, coffee, and tea drinks in Europe.[4]

On the technological frontier, new-product research and development can strengthen a firm's competitive position. For instance, G. D. Searle & Co., a pharmaceuticals firm, is enjoying a blockbuster success with its new drug, Celebrex, which fights pain caused by arthritis. At the same time, Searle's own technology has become an external competitive force that affects other pharmaceutical companies.[5]

Now let's take a look at these six external forces in more detail.

www.searlehealthnet.com
www.celebrex.com

Demographics

Demographics refer to the characteristics of populations, including such factors as size, distribution, and growth. Because people constitute markets, demographics are of special interest to marketing executives. Here we'll just cover a few examples of how demographic factors influence marketing programs; some aspects of demographics related to consumer buying behavior will be considered in Chapter 4.

Figure 2.1

External macroenvironment of a company's marketing program.

Six largely uncontrollable external forces influence an organization's marketing activities.

The U.S. population is aging, to the point that the 50-and-over group is a particularly attractive target market for a variety of businesses and non-business organizations. AARP, a not-for-profit entity, provides a range of services to its members, who must be at least age 50 but do not have to be retired. Over 30 million people belong to AARP, formerly called the American Association of Retired Persons. Key member benefits are travel-related discounts, the *Modern Maturity* magazine, opportunities for service and friendship through local chapters, and even information about "grandparenting."

www.aarp.org

According to projections, there will be over 320 million Americans by the year 2020, an increase of almost 50 million over the present total. Perhaps the most significant demographic trend at this time is the aging of the U.S. population, a shift that is expected to continue for a while. The statistics in Table 2.1 underscore how the age distribution of the population changes over time. Changes in the age distribution are the result of many factors, including the quality of health care and nutrition. Two key factors are the number of women who are of child-bearing age and the birth rate. The number of women of child-bearing age is a function of the births that occurred some years before and thus is highly predictable. However, the birth rate at any one point in time is influenced by a wide variety of social and economic factors that are much less predictable. For example, attitudes toward careers and family size certainly affect the birth rate.

Table 2.1	Projected Changes in the Distribution of the U.S. Population	

Age Group	Percent Change: 2010–2020
Under 5 years old	15.8
5–17 years old	7.4
18–24 years old	13.9
25–34 years old	15.3
35–44 years old	−11.3
45–54 years old	1.9
55–64 years old	74.1
65–74 years old	73.1
Over 74 years old	31.7
Total population	17.5

Source: Adapted from *Statistical Abstract of the United States: 1999,* 119th ed., U.S. Census Bureau, Washington, DC, 1999, p. 17.

There are several noteworthy points in Table 2.1. First, in a 20-year period, there can be quite dramatic shifts in the population. For instance, the number of people in the 55 to 74 age group will increase by nearly 75% from 2000 to 2020, which means growing markets for products such as health care and retirement communities. Second, peaks and valleys in the population distribution move through time. To mention one example, the projected 13% decline in the 35 to 44 age group can be traced back to lower birth rates between 1975 and 1984. Therefore, it is possible to track changes and, to the extent that behavior is related to age, anticipate what impacts they will have.

Another notable demographic trend is the rapid growth of minority markets. Now, minorities represent about 28% of the total U.S. population; by the year 2025, the proportion is expected to increase to 38%. Over the next quarter century, particularly rapid growth is forecasted for Asians (a 97% increase) and persons of Hispanic origin (88%). As a result, early in the 21st century, Hispanics will surpass African Americans as the largest minority group in the U.S. Marketers are interested in these overall projections as well as the fact that there is a large and growing middle class in minority markets.[6]

None of these ethnic groups is homogeneous, however. The Hispanic market, for instance, really consists of separate markets built around subgroups of Cubans, Mexicans, Puerto Ricans, and other Latin Americans. A simple product such as beans illustrates the differences among subgroups. Cubans prefer black beans, Mexicans eat refried beans, and Puerto Ricans go for red beans.[7] Many consumer-product companies realized only recently that they must target their products and advertising at each of the Hispanic subgroups.

Economic Conditions

People alone do not make a market. They must have money to spend and be willing to spend it. Consequently, the economic environment is a significant force that affects the marketing activities of just about any organization. A marketing program is affected especially by such economic factors as the current and anticipated stages of the business cycle, as well as inflation and interest rates.

What are effective appeals to Generations X and Y?

You've probably heard of **baby boomers**, Americans born in the 10 years following World War II. This cohort, or age group, is special because it is so large, has much of the buying power in the American economy, and is now approaching retirement age. Other cohorts are also of great interest to marketers.

In all likelihood, you're a member of either **Generation X**—sometimes termed *baby busters, twentysomethings,* or *boomerangers*—or **Generation Y**—sometimes termed *echo boomers* or *millennium generation.* Whatever the label, both cohorts spend upwards of $200 billion annually. Younger consumers are also attractive because they tend to be trend setters for many products and brands. However, developing effective marketing programs for these cohorts is challenging, because it's difficult to describe either group precisely, much less understand their needs and behavior as consumers.

As distinguished from other cohorts such as *baby boomers,* Generation X refers to about 40 million people born roughly between 1966 and 1976. This group is different than its predecessors in several important respects. For example, they earn less and aren't optimistic about their financial prospects but they believe education is vital to earning a decent living. Another complication for marketers is that Generation X, often perceived as homogeneous, actually contains different segments, ranging from *cynical disclaimers* to *traditional materialists.*

Generation Y represents the successors to Generation X. However, there's little agreement regarding the age span of this younger cohort. At one extreme, Generation Y is said to consist of those born between 1976 and 1994; at the other extreme, it is limited to those born between 1978 and 1982. If the group is defined as young people with birth dates in the 10-year span from 1977 to 1987, it numbers over 50 million consumers. Generation Y is diverse—in fact, more diverse than previous cohorts—in that about one-third are minorities, one-quarter come from single-parent households, and three-quarters have working mothers. Although it's difficult (and often dangerous) to generalize, members of Generation Y tend to be cynical, yet practical.

Like preceding cohorts, Generation Y is brand conscious. However, the brands typically are different than those favored by Generation X, which gave tremendous boosts to Pepsi, Levi, and Nike. Generation Y prefers previously unknown brands such as Delia's (clothing for teenage girls), Hard Candy (nail polish), and Vans (shoes, especially good for skateboarding), along with some better-known brands such as Tommy Hilfiger, Sprite, and Jeep Wrangler.

Companies are trying various approaches to sell goods and services to Generation Y, often using media that allow specific targeting. Many firms have designed websites aimed at this youngest cohort. Others even rely on e-mail and sponsorship of events such as snowboarding tournaments. In 1999, Ford used live TV ads to promote its Focus compact car. In the ads, comedienne Annabelle Gurwitch touted different features of the car as she visited various locales around the country.

What marketing strategies would you suggest to a company that wants to appeal to Generation Y consumers? What strategies should be avoided?

Sources: Alyssa Royse, "Generation X-cited," *St. Louis Post-Dispatch,* Jan. 10, 2000, p. BP11; Kathryn Kranhold, "Ford Woos 'Echo Boomers' with Live TV," *The Wall Street Journal,* Aug. 13, 1999, p. B8; Len Lewis, "Just-in-Time Generation," *Progressive Grocer,* March 1999, p. 3; Ellen Neuborne, "Generation Y," *Business Week,* Feb. 15, 1999, pp. 81–84, 86, 88; Maricris G. Briones, "Ad Biz Faces Technology, Gen Y and Competition," *Marketing News,* Dec. 7, 1998, pp. 2, 10; Faye Rice, "Making Generational Marketing Come of Age," *Fortune,* June 26, 1995, pp. 110–112, 114; Nicholas Zill and John Robinson, "The Generation X Difference," *American Demographics,* April 1995, pp. 24–29, 32–33; and Jennifer Steinhauer, "How Do You Turn On the Twentysomething Market?" *The New York Times,* Apr. 17, 1994, p. F5.

Stage of the Business Cycle

The traditional business cycle goes through four stages: prosperity, recession, depression, and recovery. However, economic strategies adopted by the federal government have averted the depression stage in the U.S. for about 60 years. Consequently, today we think in terms of a three-stage **business cycle**—prosperity, recession, and recovery, which then returns full cycle to prosperity. Marketing executives need to know which stage of the business cycle the economy currently is in, because a company's marketing programs usually must be changed from one stage of the business cycle to another.

Prosperity is a period of economic growth. During this stage, organizations tend to expand their marketing programs as they add new products and enter new markets.

A *recession* is a period of retrenchment for consumers and businesses—we tighten our economic belts. People can become discouraged, scared, and angry. Naturally, these feelings affect their buying behavior. For example, some consumers cut back on eating out and entertainment outside the home. As a result, firms catering to these needs face serious marketing challenges, and some may incur economic losses.

Recovery is the period when the economy is moving from recession to prosperity. The marketers' challenge is to determine how quickly prosperity will return and to what level. As unemployment declines and disposable income increases, companies expand their marketing efforts to improve sales and profits. As you read this, what stage of the business cycle do you think the U.S. economy is in currently?

Inflation

A rise in the prices of goods and services represents **inflation.** When prices rise at a faster rate than personal incomes, consumer buying power declines. Inflation rates affect government policies, consumer psychology, and also marketing programs.

During the late 1970s and early 1980s, the U.S. experienced what for us was a high inflation rate above 10%. But inflation dropped below 5% in the early 1990s and to one-half that rate in the late 1990s. Some countries around the world are plagued by extremely high rates of inflation—increases of 20, 30, or even 50% yearly. However, many countries have inflation under control to the point that Jack Welch, the head of General Electric Co. told shareholders, "Inflation has yielded to deflation as the shaping economic force."[8]

Perhaps surprisingly, periods of declining prices—called *deflation*—or low inflation—sometimes termed *disinflation*—present challenges for marketers. In particular, it is very difficult for firms to raise prices because of consumer resistance. As a result, they need to cut their costs or else profits will evaporate. To do so, companies must take such steps as redesigning products to pare production costs and cutting back on coupons and other promotions that in effect lower prices.[9]

Interest Rates

Interest rates are another external economic factor that influences marketing programs. When interest rates are high, for instance, consumers tend not to make long-term purchases such as housing. Marketers sometimes offer below-market interest rates (a form of price cut) as a promotional device to increase business. Auto manufacturers use this tactic occasionally.

Competition

A company's competitive environment obviously is a major influence on its marketing programs. A firm generally faces three types of competition:

 www.toysrus.com

- *Brand competition* comes from marketers of directly similar products. Toys "R" Us has suffered as a result of growing competition from discounters such as Wal-Mart and Target and online retailers such as eToys.[10] VISA, MasterCard, Discover, and American Express compete internationally in the credit card field. And, yes, even the authors' three schools compete with each other for charitable contributions from business firms and from alumni who hold degrees from two of these schools.

For decades, virtually all American homeowners covered their floors with wall-to-wall carpeting. But home decorating styles change over time. Consequently, there is intense competition among substitute products in the flooring market. Armstrong has sought to capitalize on the changing tastes in flooring by promoting laminate, which consists of thin layers of wood that are bonded together. In this ad, Armstrong stresses durability as the product's advantage compared to other forms of flooring.

 www.armstrong.com

- *Substitute products* satisfy the same need. During winter in Chicago, for example, the Bulls professional basketball team, the Blackhawks hockey team, the Lyric Opera, the Chicago Symphony Orchestra, and stores selling or renting videos all compete for the entertainment dollar. In recent years, a growing number of homeowners have been choosing wood laminate flooring instead of carpeting, causing carpet sales to stagnate.[11]

- In a third, more general type of competition, *every company* is a rival for the customer's limited buying power. So the competition faced by the maker of Prince tennis rackets might be several new pairs of Levi's Docker slacks, a Nissan repair bill, or a cash contribution to some charity.

Skillful marketing executives constantly monitor all aspects of competitors' marketing activities—their products, pricing, distribution systems, and promotional programs. Any enterprise strives to gain a **differential advantage**, which is any feature of an organization or brand that is perceived to be desirable and different from those of the competition. In contrast, this same enterprise has to work hard to avoid a differential *dis*advantage. A differential advantage attracts customers, whereas a differential disadvantage drives them away.

Social and Cultural Forces

The task facing marketing executives is becoming more complex because our sociocultural patterns—life-styles, values, and beliefs—are changing much more quickly than they used to. Here are a few changes in **social and cultural forces** that have significant marketing implications.

Does competition exist all around the globe?

The answer to the preceding question is a resounding *Yes!* Indeed, the destiny of many American firms is affected by international competition. Foreign companies are selling their products in the U.S., and American firms are marketing in foreign countries.

Several developments on the international scene have presented American marketers with profound challenges and attractive opportunities. In many countries, especially in eastern Europe, there has been a radical change from a government-controlled system to a relatively free-market economy. To a large degree, prices have been decontrolled and government subsidies have been removed on many products in Poland, Russia, and Argentina. Furthermore, some major companies and industries, formerly 100% government-owned, have been sold in whole or in part to private interests.

Further, enterprises from the four "Asian tigers" (Hong Kong, Korea, Taiwan, and Singapore) have added to the competitive pressures facing American firms. Previously, the competition facing U.S. firms came primarily from Canadian, Mexican, Japanese, and western European companies. And, with the surge of the Internet, competition is increasingly global.

Another development stems from an old saying, "If you can't lick 'em, join 'em." With that in mind, many U.S. and foreign firms have formed strategic alliances to compete in international markets. Some alliances involve past rivals. For example, Ford and Volkswagen merged in Brazil and Argentina to create "Autolatina."

A firm typically forms a strategic alliance for one or more of three reasons: to gain added resources (ranging from new technology to skilled management); achieve

economies of scale (which might provide more marketing "muscle"); and/or enter a new geographic market. Given the barriers facing foreign firms seeking to enter the Japanese market, a growing number of American companies are forming alliances with Japanese enterprises. Recent examples include Carrier and Toshiba in heating and air-conditioning products, Goodyear and Sumitomo in tires, and Mattel and Bandai in toys. The last alliance illustrates the desired benefits. Bandai will market Mattel's lines, such as Barbie and Hot Wheels, in Japan. In turn, Mattel will sell Bandai's products, including Power Rangers, in Latin America (Bandai is already in the U.S.). The two firms also intend to work cooperatively in developing new products.

Alliances that bring together firms from different countries are not a panacea, however. Problems can result. According to a study by the McKinsey & Co. consulting firm, only one-half of the alliances examined had been economically advantageous for both companies. Further, even those alliances that are beneficial seem to have a limited life, as the average length of such an arrangement is seven years. If not through strategic alliances, U.S. firms will seek other ways of coping with—and beating—foreign competition.

Sources: "Mattel Forms Toy Alliance with Bandai of Japan," *The Wall Street Journal,* July 22, 1999, p. A20; John Griffiths, "Tyre-Makers Sign Up for Strategic Alliances," *Financial Times,* June 14, 1999, p. 30; "Carrier and Toshiba Make Their Global Alliance Official," *Air Conditioning, Heating & Refrigeration News,* Apr. 12, 1999, p. 8; Harvey D. Shapiro, "After NAFTA," *Hemispheres,* March 1995, pp. 74–79; and Richard House, "Cross-Border Alliances: What Works, What Doesn't," *Institutional Investor,* May 1994, pp. 113–115+.

The Greening of America

Many Americans are placing a greater emphasis on the *quality* of life rather than on the *quantity* of goods consumed. The theme is "not more, but better." High on the list of what people consider integral to quality of life is the natural environment. Thus we hear more concerns expressed about air and water pollution, holes in the ozone layer, acid rain, solid waste disposal, and the destruction of rainforests and other natural resources. These concerns have raised the public's level of environmental consciousness, which is what we mean by the "greening of America."

A growing number of businesses have noticed—and are responding to—consumers' environmental consciousness. Specific efforts have focused on using resources efficiently and, in particular, conserving fossil fuels.[12] To cite several examples:

 www.greendisk.com

- GreenDisk Inc. acquires diskettes from unsold boxes of software, erases them, and resells them.

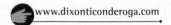

- Dixon Ticonderoga developed a crayon using soybeans rather than paraffin wax, which is a petroleum-based product.
- Many firms, such as Heinz, Anheuser-Busch, and Body Shop, are not only stressing their use of recyclable containers, but also promoting recycling.

The proportion of consumers who buy environmentally friendly products at least occasionally is growing gradually. By the mid-1990s, almost one-half of all consumers exhibited such behavior. Only a few consumers will purchase a product strictly because it is environmentally friendly. According to Roper Starch Worldwide, a market research firm, a common mistake by companies is neglecting to mention the product's benefit to the consumer, not just to the environment.[13] To satisfy "green consumers," a product must also be competitive with alternatives on such factors as price.

Many people who hold favorable attitudes toward environmentally friendly products do not purchase them. Further, and perhaps most perplexing, some products that consumers think are good for the environment—and that companies promote as being environmentally friendly—are more harmful than alternatives. For example, is a paper cup more environmentally friendly than a plastic cup? Actually, "a plastic cup takes half as much energy to make and results in 35 percent fewer pounds of toxic chemicals . . . than a paper cup does."[14]

Environmental consciousness is greater in many other parts of the world—ranging from the European Union to Japan—than it is in the U.S.[15] As a result, a company must be environmentally sensitive in its marketing activities, especially product development, all around the world.

Changing Gender Roles

For many reasons, most notably the increasing number of two-income households, male–female roles related to families, jobs, recreation, and buying behavior are changing dramatically. Now, for example, more men shop for household necessities, notably groceries, whereas more women purchase such products as cars, mutual funds, and business travel. In an interesting reversal, for the first time ever women are buying more athletic shoes than men are.[16] In contrast, a growing number of "house husbands" are staying home and assuming primary responsibility for child care and homemaking while their wives work full-time.

One of the most dramatic shifts in our culture has been the changing role of women. Over one-half of American women, including almost three-quarters of those in the 25–54 age group, work outside the home today. According to a study by the Leo Burnett advertising agency, women need to be segmented not just by age or employment status but also by other variables such as the father's degree of involvement in the family and the mother's interest in self-fulfillment.[17] Marketers obviously need different approaches to reach, and appeal to, stay-at-home mothers versus women who are working full-time and raising children on their own.

Women's attitudes toward careers, shopping, and products continue to evolve. Now, employed women are seeking a better balance between work and family. In turn, they are very interested in products that help them do that, especially by saving time. Thus working women represent a prime market for frozen and prepared food, more efficient appliances and cleaning products, and services such as house cleaning and fast food. Further, they are more likely to reward themselves by going to the beauty salon for a makeover or by buying a new CD player for their cars. Seeing that, Johnson & Johnson has promoted its new Neutrogena makeup line with a "be free to spend more on yourself" theme.[18]

Recognizing women's changing roles and growing economic power, many companies have developed new or altered marketing programs to reach the market of adult females. For example, for some time Nike and its competitors have been designing athletic shoes for the female market.[19] After some delay, American auto manufacturers started to train sales people to treat women as serious prospects

More and more—but far from all—people are paying attention to physical fitness. Women, whether they work or stay at home, have become a particularly attractive target market for various campanies that sell fitness-related products. Some women join health clubs, others buy fitness equipment for in-home use. All females who engage in vigorous exercise are candidates for athletic shoes. Therefore, Reebok and most other shoe manufacturers have a line of products designed especially for women and tailored for specific purposes, such as power walking.

 www.reebok.com

when they venture into dealer showrooms. Still, some industries, such as consumer electronics and personal computers, have been slower to adapt to shifts in male–female buying patterns.[20]

Changing gender roles have affected men as well. Some men are doing more shopping and housework only because it's demanded of them, whereas other men hold more favorable attitudes toward the shift in gender roles. Research shows that "change adapters" are younger, better educated, and more affluent than the "change opposers." Marketers should be aware that these two groups of men buy different items and shop in different ways.[21]

A Premium on Time

Many Americans are working longer hours than their parents did. This has been especially true since the early 1990s, when many large companies downsized, thereby expanding the workload for the remaining employees. Further, a substantial number of people also consider it necessary to be involved in activities such as continuing education, personal fitness, and various kinds of professional or civic endeavors. In recent years, many people have also placed more emphasis on family activities.

Time-short people seek to gain more free time, if possible, and to maximize the benefit of whatever free time they have. From a marketing standpoint, this means many people, especially two-income households with more income but less time, are willing to pay for greater convenience.

Every phase of a company's marketing program is affected by consumers' desire for convenience:

- Product planning should consider the opportunity to provide convenience related to a myriad of factors ranging from ease of preparation (with a food product, for example) to learning time (with a new computer, for example).

- Distribution arrangements should offer convenient locations and store hours. Convenience stores (such as 7-Eleven) and copy centers (such as Kinko's) responded by remaining open 24 hours a day in some cities. More and more shoppers are using the Internet to save time in purchasing a wide variety of consumer and business products. Five product categories, in particular, are receiving a great deal of early attention from Internet entrepreneurs, venture capitalists, and consumers: health and beauty supplies, watches and jewelry, groceries, sporting goods, and pet supplies. As demonstrated by the struggles of online grocers, Internet retailers in these areas are not assured of success.[22]

- Pricing policies should take into account the costs of providing the various kinds of convenience. Online grocers, for example, charge delivery fees that typically range from $2 to $10, with the fee waived on very large orders.[23]

- A company's commitment to saving time for consumers is a possible basis for promotion, perhaps creating a differential advantage for the firm.

Physical Fitness and Health

Most demographic and economic segments of our society seem to reflect an increased interest in physical fitness and health. Participation in fitness activities from aerobics to yoga (we could not think of an activity beginning with a *z*) is on the rise. Fitness centers as well as manufacturers of exercise equipment have benefitted from this trend. However, with an expanding number of competitors, there is no assurance of success for an individual firm.

Paralleling the fitness phenomenon, many Americans are changing their dietary habits. The public is constantly made aware of the relationship between diet, on the one hand, and heart disease and cancer, on the other. Consequently, a large number of consumers have become more interested in diets for weight loss; foods low in salt, additives, and cholesterol; and foods high in vitamins, minerals, and fiber content. (Some habits are hard to shake, however; so some of us still consume bacon double cheeseburgers.)

Companies need to recognize and respond to the public's growing interest in health. Thus, at the retailing level, most supermarkets now stock an assortment of health foods. At the manufacturing level, Campbell Soup Co. developed and introduced Intelligent Quisine, as described in the chapter-opening case. Again, the success of new products that try to address consumer needs is not assured. For example, initial sales of Frito-Lay's new Wow! line of fat-free salty snacks were hurt by reports that some consumers who ate them experienced digestive problems.[24]

Political and Legal Forces

Every company's conduct is influenced more and more by the political and legal processes in our society. The political and legal forces on marketing can be grouped into the following four categories:

- *Monetary and fiscal policies.* Marketing efforts are affected by the level of government spending, the money supply, and tax legislation.

- *Social legislation and regulations.* Legislation affecting the environment—antipollution laws, for example—and regulations set by the Environmental Protection Agency fall into this category.

- *Governmental relationships with industries.* Here we find subsidies in agriculture, shipbuilding, passenger rail transportation, and other industries. Tariffs and import quotas also affect specific industries. Government *deregulation* continues to have an effect on financial institutions and public utilities (such as electric and natural gas suppliers) as well as on the telecommunications and transportation industries.

- *Legislation related specifically to marketing.* Marketing executives do not have to be lawyers, but they should know something about laws affecting marketing—why they were passed, their main provisions, and current ground rules set by the courts and regulatory agencies for administering them.

These laws, which are summarized in Table 2.2, are designed either to regulate competition or to protect consumers. Note that there has been very little new legislation affecting marketing since 1980. However, court decisions and agency rulings based on these laws have been quite frequent. To forestall added legislation, individual companies and perhaps even entire industries

Table 2.2 Summary of Selected Legislation Affecting Marketing

To Regulate Competition

1. **Sherman Antitrust Act (1890).** Prohibits monopolies and combinations in restraint of trade.

2. **Federal Trade Commission (FTC) Act (1914).** Prohibits unfair competition.

3. **Clayton Antitrust Act (1914).** Regulates several activities, notably price discrimination.

4. **State Unfair Trade Practices Acts (1930s).** Prohibit "loss-leader" pricing (selling below cost). Laws still in effect in about half the states.

5. **Robinson-Patman Act (1936).** Amends the Clayton Act by strengthening the prohibition of price discrimination. Regulates price discounts and allowances.

6. **Wheeler-Lea Act (1938).** Amends the FTC Act; broadens and strengthens regulation of unfair or deceptive competition.

7. **Lanham Trademark Act (1946).** Regulates brands and trademarks.

8. **Consumer Goods Pricing Act (1975).** Repeals *federal* laws supporting *state* fair-trade laws. Does away with state laws allowing manufacturers to set retail prices.

9. Various *deregulation* laws pertaining to specific industries:
   a) Natural Gas Policy Act (1978)
   b) Airline Deregulation Act (1978)
   c) Motor Carrier Act (1980)
   d) Staggers Rail Act (1980)
   e) Depository Institutions Act (1981)
   f) Drug Price Competition and Patent Restoration Act (1984)

To Protect Consumers

1. **Pure Food and Drug Act (1906).** Regulates labeling of food and drugs and prohibits manufacture or marketing of adulterated food or drugs. Amended in 1938 by Food, Drug, and Cosmetics Act.

2. **Automobile Information Disclosure Act (1958).** Requires manufacturers to post suggested retail prices on new passenger vehicles.

3. **Kefauver-Harris Drug Amendments (1962).** Requires that drugs be labeled with their generic names, new drugs be pretested, and new drugs get approval of Food and Drug Administration before being marketed.

4. **National Traffic and Motor Vehicle Safety Act (1966).** Provides safety standards for tires and autos.

5. **Fair Packaging and Labeling Act (1966).** Regulates packaging and labeling.

6. **Cigarette Labeling and Advertising Acts (1966, 1969).** Require manufacturers to label cigarettes as being hazardous to health and prohibit TV advertising of cigarettes.

7. **Consumer Credit Protection Act (1968).** The "truth in lending" law that requires full disclosure of interest rates and other financing charges on loans and credit purchases.

8. **Consumer Product Safety Act (1972).** Establishes the Consumer Product Safety Commission with broad powers to limit or even halt the marketing of products ruled unsafe by the commission.

9. **Consumer Product Warranty Act (1975).** Increases consumers' rights and sellers' responsibilities under product warranties.

10. **FTC Improvement Act (1980).** Limits the power of the Federal Trade Commission to set and enforce industry trade regulations. In effect, reverses the trend toward more FTC protection of consumers.

11. **Nutritional Labeling and Education Act (1990).** Requires that detailed nutritional information be stated on labels of most food products.

12. **Children's Television Act (1990).** Limits the number of minutes of advertising that can be shown on programs designed for children.

sometimes respond to government signals and modify troublesome business practices.

Occasionally, a company or even a group of companies is charged with violating a long-standing law. For example, the American Booksellers Association, on behalf of independent bookstores around the U.S., has filed suits alleging that publishers give unfair discounts to giant chains ranging from Barnes & Noble to Sam's Club. The independents claim that such discounts put independent sellers at a competitive disadvantage and violate antitrust law.[25]

Up to this point, our discussion of political and legal forces affecting marketing has dealt essentially with the activities of the *federal* government. However, there are also strong political and legal influences at the *state and local* levels. For instance, many firms' marketing programs are affected by zoning requirements, interest-rate regulations, state and local taxes, prohibitions against unsubstantiated environmental claims, and laws affecting door-to-door selling. All of these have been put in place by numerous states and municipalities.

Technology

Technology has a tremendous impact on our life-styles, our consumption patterns, and our economic well-being. Just think of the effect of technological developments such as the airplane, plastics, television, computers, antibiotics, lasers, and—of course—video games. Except perhaps for the airplane, all these technologies reached their major markets in your lifetime or your parents' lifetime. Think how your life in the future might be affected by cures for the common cold, development of energy sources to replace fossil fuels, low-cost methods for making ocean water drinkable, or even commercial travel to the moon.

Technological breakthroughs can affect markets in three ways:

- By starting entirely new industries, as computers, lasers, and robots have.

- By radically altering, or virtually destroying, existing industries. When it first came out, television crippled the radio and movie industries. And computers all but replaced typewriters, sending Smith Corona Corp. into bankruptcy protection in the mid-1990s.

- By stimulating markets and industries not related to the new technology. New home appliances and microwavable foods give people additional time in which to engage in other activities.

A technological breakthrough, the Independence 3000 IBOT Transporter, should provide more mobility to people who have multiple sclerosis, spinal-cord injuries, or other disabilities that cause them to rely on wheelchairs. By means of gyroscopes and electronic sensors, the high-tech wheelchair—which is expected to cost at least $20,000—can navigate stairs, move through sand and other soft surfaces, and elevate while balancing on two wheels.

 www.indetech.org

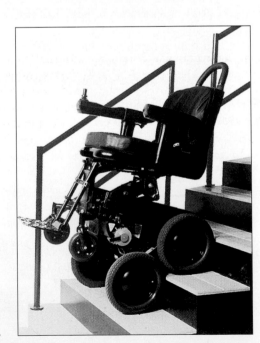

Some grains and vegetables can now be genetically modified so they are more resistant to insects and chemicals that are used to kill weeds. Such products have been criticized by some consumer and environmental groups, including Greenpeace, as having health risks. Responding to this kind of criticism, a frozen-foods retailer in the United Kingdom named Iceland stopped using genetically engineered ingredients in products carrying its brand name. More recently, Gerber banned genetically modified corn and soybeans in its baby food, notably dry cereal. Other businesspeople, however, contend that there are no harmful outcomes from ingredients that are altered in this way. Going a step further, it's been stated that genetically modified seeds would boost agricultural productivity in third-world countries.

Is it ethical for manufacturers to use genetically modified ingredients in food products? If they do so, must they inform consumers that the products contain genetically engineered ingredients?

Sources: "Gerber Drops Grain Suppliers Who Use Genetic Engineering," *St. Louis Post-Dispatch,* July 31, 1999, p. 26OT; Lucette Lagnado, "Gerber Baby Food, Grilled by Greenpeace, Plans Swift Overhaul," *The Wall Street Journal,* July 30, 1999, pp. A1, A6; and John Willman, "Consumer Power Forces Food Industry to Modify Approach," *Financial Times,* June 10, 1999, p 11.

Advances in technology also affect how marketing is carried out. For example, breakthroughs in communications now permit people and organizations to transact business from almost any location at any time of the day. During the past five or so years, the Internet has had a profound effect on millions of Americans as well as on countless enterprises.

We should also note that technology is a mixed blessing in some ways. A new technology may improve our lives in one area while creating environmental and social problems in other areas. Television provides built-in baby-sitters, but it's criticized for reducing family discussions and reading by children. The automobile is a convenient form of personal transportation, but it also creates traffic jams and air pollution. In turn, technology is expected to solve some problems it is criticized for having caused (air pollution, for example).

External Microenvironment

Three additional environmental forces are external to an organization and affect its marketing activities. These are the firm's market, suppliers, and marketing intermediaries. They represent *microenvironmental forces* for a company (see Figure 2.2). Dealing effectively with them is critical to business success. Recognizing that, Compaq Computer Corp. developed a complex computer simulation to help executives monitor the activities and attitudes of its customers, dealers, and suppliers.[26]

www.compaq.com

Figure 2.2

External microenvironment of a company's marketing program.

The arrows reflect the interrelationships—flows of products, payments, information, and influence—between the company and its external environment.

Is it the biggest business advance since the Industrial Revolution?

"It" is the Internet, a network of computers that was created to expedite communications among scientists around the world. The Internet is already having an enormous impact—perhaps an unprecedented impact—on the means by which business is carried out. Between 1990 and 2000, the number of Americans having access to the Internet exploded from about 2.5 million to well over 100 million. Thus, at the beginning of the new century, about one-half of all households in the U.S. were able to use the Internet.

But are any sales being transacted via the Internet? Absolutely yes, with sharp increases annually. Consumers' online spending topped $10 *billion* for 1999. Perhaps surprisingly, business firms' online purchases are much greater, surpassing $100 *billion* for the same year. According to one forecast, business-to-business trade via the Internet will exceed $1 *trillion* by 2003.

In many respects, the Internet provides consumers with maximum convenience. Assuming no malfunctions, the Internet and, more specifically, companies' websites are always open for business. Further, consumers control whether they are exposed to a product and ultimately whether they want to learn more about it or even place an order. There are even online services that do comparison shopping for consumers. Other sites allow consumers to name a price for a particular product, such as an airline flight, after which the vendor accepts or rejects the offer.

With the Internet, a firm can present consumers with a combination of advertising, information, and entertainment related to its product. In a very real sense, the Internet represents a new distribution channel for marketers. Of course, this outlet exists in cyberspace rather than in a mall or other physical location.

The Internet isn't free of problems for companies. According to many observers, for reasons such as the existence of price-comparison services, companies will find it difficult to earn more than small profits on products sold via the Internet. Providing adequate customer service, both before and after transactions, is another significant challenge for online marketers.

All factors considered, how big is the Internet from a business standpoint? Recently, Louis Gerstner, the head of International Business Machines Corp., said that it has become "the ultimate medium for business." A consultant who specializes in electronic commerce stated, "The Internet fundamentally changes the economics of transactions." And a recent business school graduate offered the following explanation for accepting an employment offer from a small electronic commerce firm: "I didn't want to miss the next Industrial Revolution. I didn't want to have any regrets."

Sources: Betsy Morris, "MBAs Get .Com Fever," *Fortune,* Aug. 2, 1999, pp. 60–66; George Anders, "Buying Frenzy," *The Wall Street Journal,* July 12, 1999, pp. R6, R10; David Bank, "A Site-Eat-Site World," *The Wall Street Journal,* July 12, 1999, pp. R8, R10; and Paul M. Eng, "Big Business on the Net? Not Yet," *Business Week,* June 26, 1995, p. 100.

Although all three of these external forces are generally uncontrollable, they can be influenced in some situations. As such, they are different than the *macro*environmental forces discussed previously. A marketing organization, for example, may be able to exert pressure on its suppliers or middlemen. And, through its advertising, a firm should have some influence on its market.

The Market

The market really is what marketing is all about—how to reach it and serve it profitably and in a socially responsible manner. The market should be the focus of all marketing decisions in an organization. But just what is a market? A *market* may be defined as a place where buyers and sellers meet, goods or services are offered for sale, and transfers of ownership occur. A *market* may also be defined as the demand made by a certain group of potential buyers for a good or service. For instance, there is a farm *market* for petroleum products.

These definitions are not sufficiently precise to be useful to us here. For marketing purposes, we define a **market** as people or organizations with needs to satisfy, money to spend, and the willingness to spend money. Thus, in marketing any given good or service, three specific factors need to be considered:

- People or organizations with needs,
- Their purchasing power, and
- Their buying behavior.

When we consider *needs,* we do so from the perspective of the dictionary definition of need as the lack of anything that is required, desired, or useful. We do not limit needs to the physiological requirements of food, clothing, and shelter essential for survival. Recall from Chapter 1 that the words *needs* and *wants* are used interchangeably.

Suppliers

A business cannot sell a product without being able to make or buy it. That's why the people or firms that supply the goods or services required by a producer in order to make what it sells are critical to our marketing success. So too are the firms that provide the merchandise a wholesaler or retailer resells. And that's why we consider a firm's **suppliers** a vital part of its marketing environment.

Marketing executives often are not concerned enough with the supply side of marketing. However, when shortages occur, they recognize the need for cooperative relationships with suppliers. Further, as online sales rise, Internet companies are paying much more attention to sources of supply and also the methods by which orders will be processed and delivered to buyers.

Marketing Intermediaries

Marketing intermediaries are independent business organizations that directly aid in the flow of goods and services between a marketing organization and its markets. There are two types of intermediaries: (1) the firms we call *middlemen*—wholesalers and retailers, and (2) various *facilitating organizations* furnishing such services as transportation, warehousing, and financing that are needed to complete exchanges between buyers and sellers. These intermediaries operate between a company and its markets and between a company and its suppliers. Thus they are part of what we call *channels of distribution.*

In some cases, it may be more efficient for a company to not use marketing intermediaries. A producer can deal *directly* with its suppliers or sell *directly* to its customers and do its own shipping, financing, and so on. But marketing intermediaries are specialists in their respective fields. They often do a better job at a lower cost than the marketing organization can by itself.

Collectively, the company, its suppliers, and its intermediaries (both middlemen and facilitating organizations) comprise a **value chain.** That is, all of these enterprises—each in its own way—perform activities to add value to the product that is eventually bought by an individual or an organization. It's relatively easy to comprehend the value added by a manufacturer when it combines various materials to form a finished product. But it's more difficult to detect the value added by other members of the value chain. For example, consider a financial institution that agrees to provide credit to consumers who buy vehicles from an auto dealership. This facilitating organization has added value to the product, essentially by making it easier for a prospective buyer to make a purchase.

Organization's Internal Environment

An organization's marketing effort is also shaped by *internal* forces that are controllable by management. As shown in Figure 2.3, these internal influences include a firm's production, financial, and personnel activities. If the Colgate-Palmolive Co. is considering adding a new brand of soap, for example, it must determine whether

Figure 2.3

Internal environment
affecting a company's
marketing activities.

A company's internal,
nonmarketing resources
influence and support its
marketing program.

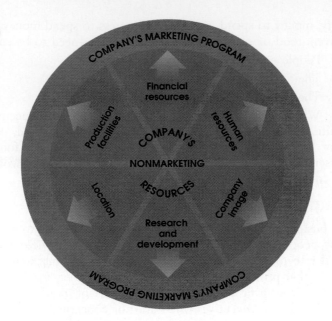

existing production facilities and expertise can be used. If the new product requires
a new plant or machinery, financial capability enters the picture. Although this
example involves a manufacturer, we are viewing *production* in a broad sense, referring to the various activities that create the set of products an organization offers
to its markets. Therefore, all concerns—retailers, wholesalers, service firms, and
not-for-profit organizations—engage in production, in this broad sense.

Other nonmarketing forces are the company's location, its research and development (R&D) strength, and the overall image the firm projects to the public. For
a manufacturer, plant location often determines the geographic limits of the company's market, particularly if transportation costs are high or its products are perishable. For a middleman, location of a store (in the case of a retailer) or a warehouse (in the case of a wholesaler) affects the number of customers drawn to the
firm as well as its operating expenses. Of course, online retailers may not have to
worry about the location of physical stores, but they still need to be concerned
about the location of warehouses. The R&D factor may determine whether a firm
will lead or follow in its industry. An organization's image has an impact on its
ability to attract capital, employees, and customers.

Another thing we must consider in a firm's internal environment is the need to
coordinate its marketing and nonmarketing activities. Sometimes this can be difficult because of conflicts in goals and executive personalities. Production people,
for example, like to see long production runs of standardized items. However, marketing executives may want a variety of models, sizes, and colors to satisfy different market segments. Financial executives typically want tighter credit and
expense limits than the marketing people consider necessary to be competitive.

To wrap up our discussion of the marketing environment, Figure 2.4 shows
how all environmental forces combine to shape an organization's marketing program. Within the framework of these constraints, management should develop a
marketing program to satisfy the needs of its markets.

Summary

Various environmental forces influence an organization's marketing activities. Some
are external to the firm and are largely uncontrollable by the organization. Other
forces are within the firm and are generally controllable by management. Successful
marketing requires that a company develop and implement marketing programs that
take into account its environment. To start with, management should set up a system

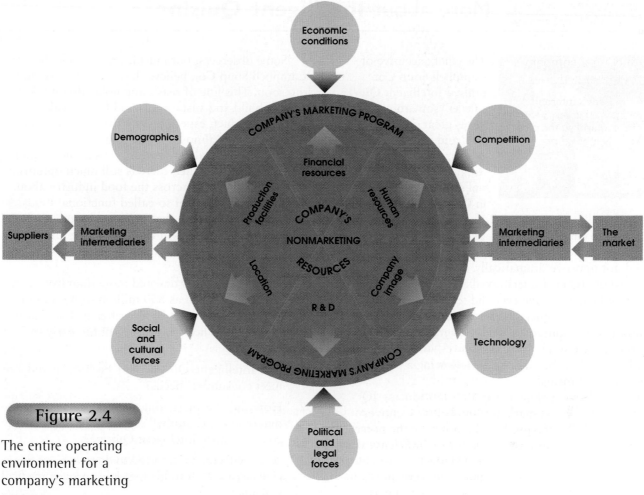

Economic
conditions

COMPANY'S MARKETING PROGRAM

Demographics

Competition

Financial
resources

Production
facilities

Human
resources

COMPANY'S

Suppliers

Marketing
intermediaries

NONMARKETING

Marketing
intermediaries

The
market

RESOURCES

Location

Company
image

Social
and
cultural
forces

R & D

Technology

COMPANY'S MARKETING PROGRAM

Political
and
legal
forces

Figure 2.4

The entire operating
environment for a
company's marketing
program.

A marketing program must
take into account both
internal resources and
external forces.

for environmental monitoring—the process of gathering and evaluating environmental information.

Six broad variables constitute the external environment that generally cannot be controlled by an organization. Demographic factors are one of these macro influences. Another is economic conditions such as the business cycle, inflation, and interest rates. Management also must be aware of the various types of competition and the competitive structure within which its firm operates. Social and cultural forces, such as changes in life-styles, values, and beliefs, must be taken into account as marketing programs are developed. Four noteworthy sociocultural trends are the greening of America, changing gender roles, a greater premium on time, and added emphasis on physical fitness and health. Political and legal forces, ranging from monetary and fiscal policies to legislation, also affect marketing. As with the other external macroenvironmental influences, technology can present both opportunities and challenges for marketers.

Another set of environmental factors—suppliers, marketing intermediaries, and the market itself—is also external to the firm. But these forces can be controlled to some extent by the firm. Although all three of these external forces are generally uncontrollable, they can be influenced in some situations. As such, these *micro*environmental forces are different from *macro*environmental forces such as economic conditions and technology.

At the same time, a set of nonmarketing resources *within* the firm—production facilities, personnel, finances, location, research and development, and company image—affects its marketing effort. These variables generally are controllable by management.

More about **Intelligent Quisine**

The chief executive of Campbell Soup Co. praised Intelligent Quisine as "something that tastes great, is good for you, and is therapeutically as effective as a drug." Nevertheless initial sales of IQ products in Ohio fell far short of Campbell's expectations. To boost sales, calls were placed to customers who had ordered IQ, offering them discounts on repeat purchases. Even then, sales did not improve dramatically.

Many IQ customers raved about the product's health benefits; some even did testimonials used in ads. Other customers, however, complained that the product line contained too little variety or that the products were relatively expensive—or both. Some admitted that they didn't like following a regimented schedule of meals.

A little more than a year after introducing IQ into the Ohio test market, Campbell's executives concluded that the product did not have the potential to be successful (that is, generate sufficient sales and profits on a national scale). Therefore, prodded by a chief executive who wanted the company to focus on its core products, notably soups, IQ was deemed a failure and pulled from the market.

Some observers, both inside and outside the Campbell Soup Co., believe that the firm gave up too soon. This line of reasoning holds that it takes time to build and sustain demand for a breakthrough product, especially one that would benefit from—perhaps almost require—favorable recommendations by medical professionals about its therapeutic benefits. Further, there is still much optimism (or maybe it's hope) across the food industry about the long-term future of so-called functional foods. They believe (or hope) that such meals and snacks with medical benefits will be the next big hit, perhaps even a home run, in the area of prepared food products.

In total, Campbell devoted more than five years and perhaps as much as $50 million to IQ. Executives at Campbell might have written a short obituary for IQ: "Too healthy to die, but too early to survive."[27]

1. Did Intelligent Quisine fail because it did not meet consumers' needs?

2. How did the marketing environment affect the outcome of Campbell's efforts to successfully commercialize Intelligent Quisine?

3. What will companies need to do to achieve financial success with foods that have proven medical benefits?

Key Terms and Concepts

Environmental monitoring (32)
Demographics (33)
Economic environment (35)
Baby boomers (36)
Generation X (36)
Generation Y (36)

Business cycle (36)
Inflation (37)
Interest rates (37)
Differential advantage (38)
Social and cultural forces (38)
Political and legal forces (42)

Technology (44)
Market (46)
Suppliers (47)
Marketing intermediaries (47)
Value chain (47)

Questions and Problems

1. In areas where the number of college-age students is still declining, what marketing measures should a school take to adjust to this trend?

2. For each of the following companies, give some examples of how its marketing program is likely to differ during periods of prosperity as contrasted with periods of recession:
   a. Schwinn bicycles
   b. Living.com (an Internet retailer of furniture)
   c. General Cinema movie theaters
   d. Salvation Army

3. What would be the likely effect of high interest rates on the market for the following goods or services?
   a. Swatch watches
   b. Building materials
   c. Nursery school programs

4. Explain the three types of competition faced by a company. What marketing strategies or programs would you recommend to meet each type?

5. Name three U.S.–manufactured products you think would be highly acceptable to "green consumers" in European markets. Name three products you think would be environmentally unacceptable.

6. Give some examples of how the changing role of women has been reflected in American marketing.

7. What are some marketing implications of the increasing public interest in physical fitness and health?

8. Using examples other than those in this chapter, explain how a firm's marketing can be influenced by the environmental factor of technology.

9. Specify some external macroenvironmental forces affecting the marketing programs of:
   a. Pizza Hut
   b. Your school
   c. Drugstore.com
   d. Clairol (hair care products)

10. Other than technology, which macroenvironmental forces are particularly important to Internet companies?

11. Explain how each of the following resources within a company might influence its marketing program:
    a. Plant or store location
    b. Company image
    c. Financial resources
    d. Personnel capabilities

Hands-On Marketing

1. Identify two controversial social or cultural issues in the community where your school is located, and explain their impact on firms that market in the community.

2. After doing some "Net surfing," identify two product categories (other than those mentioned in the chapter) that you believe can be sold well over the Internet. Then identify two categories that you think will be hard to sell online.

3

Global Markets and Marketing

"By 1985, even though adidas was one of the most recognized brand names in the world, its share of the American athletic shoe market had declined from 70% to 2%."

How Well Does **adidas** Play around the World?

In the 1920s Adolph (Adi) Dassler began designing and making athletic training shoes in his hometown of Herzogenaurach, Germany. Dassler, an athlete himself, grew up working in his family's business, which specialized in making house slippers. In producing his first athletic shoes, Dassler focused on enhancing performance, and included input from athletes, physicians, coaches, and trainers. Although a common practice today, such a strong customer orientation was virtually unheard of at the time.

He initially focused his attention on track and field. His reputation and the popularity of Dassler shoes grew as word spread about athletes breaking records wearing his shoes. Eventually he added soccer and tennis shoes to the product line. By the late 1930s the Dassler brand was well known among European athletes, and the company was making 800 pairs of athletic shoes a day.

In 1948 Adi's brother Rudolph started a competing shoe company, Puma. At about the same time Adi renamed his company, combining his nickname and the first three letters of his last name to form adidas (and using a lowercase "a" for additional uniqueness). Distribution was limited as Dassler was satisfied to focus on designing shoes to meet the unique demands of individual sports. His creativity is reflected by the fact that in his lifetime Dassler acquired over 700 patents related to various shoe features.

Although the company was viewed as the industry's technology leader and was faced with little competition, Dassler was content to let it grow slowly. First there was expansion in Europe; in 1955 adidas licensed a factory in Norway to man-

ufacture athletic shoes. In 1966 the company moved into the U.S., granting distribution rights to an American firm. But then, more intense competition from Nike and Reebok, the loss of Adi Dassler's leadership because of his death, and some internal operating problems caused the firm to spiral downward. By 1985, even though adidas was one of the most recognized brand names in the world, its share of the American athletic shoe market had declined from 70% to 2%. By 1993 the company was losing $100 million a year.

A new president, Robert Louis-Dryfus, came on board in 1993 and instituted a number of changes. First, all remaining production was moved out of Europe to lower-cost countries, including Indonesia, Thailand, and China. Next, staff was reduced and marketing budgets were increased. Then the company was split into two units by sports: the U.S. division handles basketball, baseball, and cross training, whereas the European headquarters focuses on soccer and tennis. In 1997 adidas acquired Sports Development S.C.A., a French sportswear maker. This led to a change in the firm's name to adidas-Salomon AG, an expansion into winter sports gear, and an increased emphasis on clothing. Sportswear now accounts for over half of total revenue, and shoes about 45%. Under Louis-Dryfus's leadership, especially reflected in a wide variety of international initiatives, adidas has gone from the brink of bankruptcy to once again being a major player in the sportswear and athletic shoe business.[1]

How can adidas continue to capitalize on international opportunities? See www.adidas.com for more details.

 www.adidas.org

International marketing has much in common with domestic marketing—but it also has distinctive features that require special attention. A firm interested in marketing its product in a foreign country is faced with many decisions. A basic choice is the level of involvement, which can range from selling products to exporters, as adidas did initially, to setting up an entire business abroad, as the firm has done in the U.S. Then there are marketing-mix decisions, such as what to call the product and how best to inform the market about its existence. These and many more considerations are influenced by cultural, economic, and legal systems that are likely to be quite different from those in the firm's home country. Given this complexity we need to examine international marketing in some detail.

After studying this chapter, you should be able to explain:

chapter goals

- The significance of international marketing to firms and countries.
- What makes foreign markets attractive.
- Challenges in designing marketing strategies for international markets.
- Alternative organizational structures for operating in foreign markets.
- Marketing-mix issues and some concepts unique to international marketing such as countertrade and gray marketing.

The Significance of International Trade

International trade is not a new phenomenon. There is evidence that it was an important part of the lives of many ancient civilizations, including the Etruscans, Egyptians, and the Chinese. The economic reasons for international trade are:

- *Access to products otherwise unavailable.* A large number of goods, including many foodstuffs, spices, and even types of wood, are available only in certain parts of the world. Without foreign trade, consumers in other regions could not experience these products.

- *Comparative advantage.* Some countries possess unique natural or human resources that give them an edge when it comes to producing particular products. This factor, for example, explains South Africa's dominance in diamonds, and the ability of developing Asian and Central American countries with low-wage rates to compete successfully in products assembled by hand. By specializing where it has a comparative advantage and trading for other products, a country maximizes its economic prosperity.

International trade also has political and social implications. In fact, historians give trade much of the credit for the peace and well-being that existed for centuries in the far-flung Roman Empire. In today's world, the interaction fostered by trade reduces social barriers and prejudices and increases tolerance.

To get an idea of how significant international marketing is, consider that the U.S. exports an amount equal to more that 10% of what it produces each year, while France and Germany each export an amount equal to 25% of what they produce per year. In fact, international trade plays a key role in the economy of virtually every country of the world. To illustrate, Germany exports over $400 billion in goods and services annually, Brazil over $50 billion a year, and India over $30 billion. Table 3.1 indicates the relationship between the amount produced and the amount exported by several major countries. As you can see from the table, exports are significant for all of these countries, but they play a larger role in some countries than in others.

Table 3.1	Importance of Exports to Selected Countries
Country	Exports as a Percent of Gross Domestic Product
United States	11%
United Kingdom	28
France	27
Germany	25
Japan	11
Canada	41
Mexico	30
S. Korea	38

Source: International Financial Statistics Yearbook, International Monetary Fund, Washington, DC, 1999, various pages.

What are the prospects for international business? At both the national and individual firm levels, international trade is important to the health of a nation. However, the relationship between how much a country imports and how much it exports has significant implications. To appreciate this, we need to examine the concepts of balance of payments and balance of trade, and we will use the U.S. as an example.

A country's **balance of payments** is an accounting record of all its transactions with all the other nations of the world. The major categories of expenditures and income in a country's balance of payments are military and foreign aid, investments abroad, profits returned on foreign investments, tourism, and its trade balance. These terms are self-explanatory except for a country's **trade balance,** which is the difference between what it exports and what it imports. When exports exceed imports, the balance is positive and the country is said to have a trade *surplus*. When imports exceed exports, the balance is negative and the country has a trade *deficit.*

By definition, a country's balance of payments must balance. That is, the outflow of wealth must equal the inflow. So, for example, if the foreign tourism expenditures of a country's citizens (outflow) exceed the expenditures of tourists visiting the country (inflow), the difference must be made up by one of the other balance-of-payment categories. What happens if there is not enough surplus in the other categories to offset a deficit? Then the country must borrow to make up the difference, and that is where a problem lies. If a country's debt grows, it is faced with pressure to raise taxes and lower government spending.

Historically, the U.S. has had large expenditures in four areas that significantly affect the balance of payments: (1) military forces stationed overseas, (2) foreign aid, (3) oil imports, and (4) American tourist travel abroad. To offset these expenditures and maintain equilibrium in the U.S. balance of payments, American businesses had to generate a substantial trade surplus. That is, exports of goods and services had to greatly exceed imports. Up to about 1970, this was not a problem because the U.S. generally had a positive balance of trade. Then the balance declined to the point where it was not sufficient to offset the expenditures abroad.

Through most of the 1980s, the U.S. was in an unfavorable trade position with large trade deficits. The relationship between imports and exports improved in the late 1980s and early 1990s, with the deficit reaching a low of $31 billion in 1991, but the balance was consistently unfavorable. Since then, the deficit has steadily increased, amounting to $169 billion in 1998.[2] Large trade deficits have a direct negative effect on jobs, investment, and growth.

Unilever's stated purpose is "to meet the everyday needs of people everywhere." When necessary, its food, personal care, and home care products are adapted to local culture and tastes. However, the firm has several well-known global brands including Lipton, Dove, and Close-Up. Liptonice, pictured here in the United Arab Emirates, is one of Unilever's most successful international products.

 www.unilever.com

Several factors affect a country's balance of trade. In the case of the U.S., the most significant are:

- *Consumer preferences.* U.S. consumers have come to know and buy many imported products.
- *Technology.* The "technology gap" between the U.S. and other major industrial countries is narrowing or has disappeared entirely, so the U.S. does not enjoy the same technology advantage it once did.
- *Trade barriers.* Some countries have barriers that severely limit, or entirely prohibit, the importation of products that might compete with their domestic output.
- *Subsidized industries.* Some foreign governments aid their export trade more than the U.S. These subsidies often enable the producers to sell their products in foreign markets at prices lower than the prices of domestic producers.
- *Tax structure.* Some countries derive substantial revenue from indirect taxes, such as a value-added tax, which are often rebated when products are exported. As a result, companies in these countries have an added incentive to seek markets abroad.
- *Relative marketing capabilities.* Firms worldwide have narrowed the gap between their marketing skills and those of the more developed nations.

The foreign trade situation in the U.S. has changed from a bright spot to a problem. Imports probably will remain high because of the factors described above. Consequently, the U.S. must continue to expand its exports by:

- Offsetting higher labor costs with improved productivity.
- Adapting marketing efforts to foreign cultures to improve the attractiveness of products.
- Investing in the future by taking a longer-range view than currently is typical among most U.S. firms.

The Attraction of International Marketing

International trade describes any type of business that firms carry out beyond their domestic borders. More specific to our interests, **international marketing** takes

Coca-Cola is often considered the ultimate global marketer. However, along with its flagship brand, shown here in a Hanoi promotion, Coke markets over 300 diverse ready-to-drink beverage products around the world. Coca-Cola management envisions a time when the company will market 2,000 beverage brands.

 www.cocacola.com

 www.ibm.com

place when an organization actively markets its products in two or more countries. For many U.S. companies, international markets account for a substantial share of their operations. For example, IBM and Boeing regularly get about half their annual sales revenues from outside the U.S. Likewise, many non-U.S. companies, such as Sony, Benetton, Bic, Gucci, Toyota, Lipton, Shell Oil, and adidas, rely heavily on the U.S. market.

A firm moves beyond domestic markets into international trade for several reasons:

- *Potential demand in foreign markets.* There is a strong demand for a wide variety of products all over the world. Within the developing as well as the developed nations of the world, there is a demand for business products such as machine tools, construction equipment, and computers. Starbucks Coffee Company is a good example of a consumer product that has been successfully marketed internationally. After opening 425 outlets in the U.S., Starbucks began to expand internationally in 1995, first in Canada and more recently in Asia and Europe. The firm's combination of good coffee and an atmosphere that encourages relaxation and conversation seems to work almost anywhere.

- *Saturation of domestic markets.* Firms—even those with no previous international experience—look to foreign markets when domestic demand plateaus. As attractive domestic locations become harder to find, a greater proportion of new McDonald's outlets are being located overseas. Even though McDonald's opened its first outlet in 1955, and its first nondomestic outlet in 1967, it now has nearly an equal number at home and abroad (12,600 stores in the U.S., and 12,000 in 117 other countries). Over the next five years, 95% of all new McDonald's outlets will be outside the U.S.[3]

- *Technological advantage.* In a country one particular industry, often encouraged by government and spurred by the efforts of a few firms, develops a technological advantage over the rest of the world. For example, the U.S. dominated the computer industry for many years because of technology developed by companies such as IBM and Hewlett-Packard.

Strategic Planning for International Marketing

Firms that have been very successful in domestic marketing have no assurance whatsoever that their success will be duplicated in foreign markets. Satisfactory

Will the Internet open China to the world?

China's first Internet business was started by Jack Ma Yun in 1995 following a trip to the U.S. where he witnessed firsthand the potential of the technology. A few months later, in the initial demonstration of his new Internet operation, it took three hours for the first page to load. Since that inauspicious beginning, Internet and e-commerce growth rates in China have been among the highest in the world.

There are several barriers to Chinese consumers using the Internet to make purchases. First, few Chinese have credit cards. Second, China is a land of many small shops, so most items can be purchased from a local retailer close to home or work. Third, the package delivery infrastructure is limited and relatively inefficient. Finally, Chinese banks are suspicious of Internet businesses aimed at consumers and have not encouraged their development. For all these reasons, only about 6 million Chinese consumers have Internet access. That has not, however, discouraged entrepreneurs,

often working in joint ventures with Western firms, from seeing the potential.

On the other hand, the Chinese have been especially receptive to businesses using the Internet to buy from or sell to other businesses, especially in international trade. Frequently companies in Europe and North America insist that their trading partners exchange information electronically. Many Chinese businesses, most of which are small or medium-sized, have been unable to afford the necessary systems. However, the Internet changes that since even the smallest firms can afford a PC and a dial-up Internet connection. When the Chinese government encouraged Mr. Ma to create a business Internet server (called ChinaMarket), 4,500 companies joined before the first advertisement appeared.

Sources: "Asia Online," *The Economist,* Apr. 17, 1999, pp. 69–70; Leslie Chang, "Chinese Upstart Surprises with E-commerce Success," *The Wall Street Journal,* Nov. 11, 1999, p. A22.

performance overseas is based on (1) understanding the environment of a foreign market and (2) gauging which domestic management practices and marketing-mix elements should be transferred directly to foreign markets, which ones modified, and which ones not used at all.

A **global strategy** is one in which essentially the same marketing program is employed around the world. Because it is very cost efficient, a global strategy is an ideal situation. FedEx is an example of a company that has globalized its strategy. According to a senior marketing executive, "We're the largest all-cargo carrier in the world, and as a result we've got a pretty good formula for attacking any market whether it's China or Japan or Germany, it really doesn't make any difference."[4]

The firm probably most often associated with a globalized strategy is Coca-Cola, which worldwide sells the equivalent of over a billion 8-ounce servings of its products a day, and uses common promotional themes in many countries. However, Coca-Cola's management recognizes that accommodating customers in particular markets is more important than cost savings. For example, in India, Coca-Cola acquired two popular local brands, Thums Up, a cola, and Limca, a lime-flavored drink. Rather than replace them with its own brands, Coca-Cola continues to market the two drinks and has plans to export them to other Asian countries with large Indian populations.[5]

When large geographic areas have much in common, but are quite distinct from other regions because of factors such as climate, custom, or taste, a firm might develop a **regional strategy.** For example, Unilever markets a fabric softener in five parts of the world using the same advertising message and a teddy bear as a symbol, but with five different brand names. In the U.S. you would know it as Snuggle, but elsewhere in the world you would have to look for Cajoline, Kuschelweich, Mimosin, or Yumos.

In some cases markets differ so much that a firm must develop customized marketing programs for each area it enters. When a firm employs a **local strategy,** there are relatively few marketing-mix dimensions that are transferred from one market to another. Surprisingly, that can be the case even for a commodity. To market its packaged flour in India, Pillsbury had to change the ingredients (for local taste), the package size and packaging material (because of the climate), the advertising (to demonstrate local uses), and the distribution (because small retail stores carry little inventory).[6] Even in countries with quite similar cultures such as the U.S. and the United Kingdom, the flour differs in texture and additives.

To develop a strategic plan, a firm must examine the operating environment that exists in a foreign market. Several of the most important dimensions of the environment are described below.

Analysis of the Environment

Throughout the world, market demand is determined by the number of people, the ability to buy, and buying behavior. Also, human wants and needs have a universal similarity. People need food, clothing, and shelter. They seek a better quality of life in terms of lighter workloads, more leisure time, and social recognition and acceptance. But at about this point, the similarities in foreign and domestic markets seem to end, and the differences in culture, the economic environment, and political and legal forces must be considered.

Social and Cultural Forces

Culture is a set of shared values passed down from generation to generation in a society. These values determine what is socially acceptable behavior. Some of the many cultural elements that can influence a company's marketing program are described below.

Family. The priorities of families and the relationships among family members with regard to purchasing and consumption vary considerably from culture to culture. In some countries a mother would always accompany a teenager shopping for clothes, whereas in other cultures shopping "with Mom" would be avoided at all costs. In China, where one-child families are the norm, parents typically spend one-third to one-half of their disposable incomes on their children. The family situations in each country may require a distinctive type of promotion, and perhaps even different types of products.

Customs and behavior. Customary behavior is often hard to understand. In taking medicine, for example, English and Dutch consumers prefer white pills, the French like purple, and all three dislike red, which is the most popular color in the U.S. Customs also can be difficult to change, as Wal-Mart discovered in Mexico. Although Mexican consumers bought general merchandise in the Wal-Mart stores, they preferred to buy groceries elsewhere. Because many Mexicans don't have cars and most have small refrigerators, they seldom buy food in advance of their needs. In addition, many are accustomed to buying fresh food from specialty shops and outdoor markets, so they find packaged items in the store less appealing.[7] As a result, Wal-Mart had to adapt its merchandise assortment to local preferences. When Ford Motor Co. was developing the Ikon, a passenger car sold in India, the product manager sat in the backseat of a prototype wearing a turban to ensure there was sufficient headroom.[8]

Education. The educational level in a country affects the literacy rate, which in turn influences advertising, branding, and labeling. The brand mark may become the dominant marketing feature if potential customers cannot read and must recognize the article by the picture on the label.

Language differences. Language differences pose many problems in international marketing, from being one of the primary explanations for the high failure rate of cross-border mergers to making it difficult to complete customs forms. Language is often the hurdle that discourages firms from entering foreign markets. In marketing strategy, a literal translation of advertising copy or a brand name may result in ridicule of a product, or even hostility toward it. For example, in Chinese KFC's well-known slogan "Finger lickin' good" translates as "Eat your fingers off."

Economic Environment

In international marketing a firm must closely examine the economic conditions in a particular country. A nation's infrastructure and stage of economic development are key economic factors that affect the attractiveness of a market and suggest what might be an appropriate marketing strategy.

Infrastructure. A country's ability to provide transportation, communications, and energy is its **infrastructure.** Depending on the product and the method of marketing, an international marketer will need certain levels of infrastructure development. For example, an Internet marketer such as Amazon.com selling a low-priced product requires a warehouse and transportation system that will permit widespread distribution. How about communications? Some firms would find it impossible to do business without the availability of newspapers in which to advertise or telephones with which to contact other businesses.

There is a danger in assuming that systems a marketer takes for granted domestically will be available elsewhere. The international marketer must recognize what infrastructure is needed and what is available. For example, in the U.S. there are 50 phones for every 100 people, whereas in the former East Germany there are about 1.5 phones for every 100 people.

Level of economic development. The level of development in a country is a general indication of the types of products that are likely to be in demand. The most common criterion for assessing economic development is gross domestic product (GDP), a measure of the value of all goods and services produced in a country during a year.

Among the world's approximately 190 independent countries, about 115 are categorized as *less developed countries* because they have a GDP of less than $1,700 per capita. These countries lack most or all resources for growth and often rely heavily on foreign aid. They frequently have unstable governments and over-population problems. Countries in this category include Ethiopia, Cambodia, Sudan, Afghanistan, Burma, Haiti, and Bangladesh. These less developed countries are not attractive markets for most consumer goods or for highly technical products. However, they should not be totally ignored. Less developed countries are very eager to acquire technology that will, for example, allow them to increase agricultural output.

In the next level are countries that have an average GDP between $1,700 and $5,500. This group of about 40 nations, including Chile, Thailand, Malaysia, and Mexico, are described as *newly industrialized countries*. They combine an eager work force, low wages, and reasonably stable governments to produce high rates of economic growth. They typically export manufactured goods and import technology and consumer goods. These are highly attractive markets for firms that have a technological advantage.

Finally, there are the *highly industrialized countries*, which have an average per capita GDP over $5,500. About 35 nations fall into this category, including the U.S., Canada, Japan, Taiwan, Germany, France, and England. They have well-developed infrastructures, high levels of education and literacy, stable governments, constantly advancing technology, and well-trained work forces. These countries are heavily involved in exporting a wide variety of goods. Although these are the wealthiest countries, they are also the ones in which a foreign firm is likely to face the stiffest competition.

Note that a classification like this can be useful, but its simplicity may make it misleading. For example, Saudi Arabia, because of its oil revenues and small population, is in the highly industrialized group. However, Saudi Arabia's level of economic development is quite different from countries such as Japan and Switzerland. On the other hand, China, with a per capita GDP of only $750, attracts many foreign firms that see enormous potential in its huge population. Thus, when analyzing a given foreign market, management must also consider other indications of development. Common economic indicators include the (1) distribution of income, (2) rate of growth of buying power, and (3) extent of available financing. Useful noneconomic indicators are (1) infant mortality rate, (2) percent of the population that lives in urban areas, and (3) the number of daily newspapers.

Competition.   Sometimes overlooked by firms considering international opportunities are the strength and resilience of the native competition. The new entrant must have a differential advantage sufficiently strong to overcome the loyalty built up by established brands and the nationalism that may motivate buyers to support local producers.

International marketers can also expect local competitors to design strategies to protect their businesses. On discovering that a foreign competitor is entering the market, local firms often introduce new products, spruce up customer service, and increase promotion and advertising. As an alternative, the local competitor may also retaliate in the foreign competitor's home market as Kodak did by creating a Japanese subsidiary when Fuji boosted its marketing efforts in the U.S.[9]

Political and Legal Forces

International marketers often discover laws quite different from those experienced in domestic markets. To protect small stores, Japan has a law that requires large retailers to shut down for 20 days a year and close daily by 8 p.m. And to protect Greek toy makers that cannot afford television advertising, Greece does not permit toys to be advertised on television. The principal political concerns of international marketers are the stability of governments and their attitudes toward free trade. Obviously, an unstable government adds to the risk of doing business in a country. For example, the frequent coups in several central African countries make them less attractive places to do business than Southeast Asia.

A developing legal issue is the global regulation of electronic commerce. For example, existing laws in Europe require that disputes over cross-border consumer purchases be resolved in the courts of the consumer's country. This has been a cumbersome but workable solution because the majority of foreign consumer purchases have taken place in neighboring or nearby countries. However, one of the most attractive features of the Internet is the ability to shop for goods and services worldwide. Some observers believe that the growth of electronic commerce will be stifled if small website operators outside of Europe are faced with the possibility of lawsuits that must be defended in Europe. Thus, they are pressing for alternative solutions that will safeguard consumers but not unduly constrain the growing popularity of global Internet shopping.[10]

Trade barriers.   The most common legal forces affecting international marketers are barriers created by governments to restrict trade and protect domestic industries. Examples include the following:

- **Tariff**—a tax imposed on a product entering a country. Tariffs are used to protect domestic producers and/or raise revenue. To illustrate, South Korea has a combination of tariffs and taxes that double the price of a car imported from the U.S.[11]
- **Import quota**—a limit on the amount of a particular product that can be brought into a country. Like tariffs, quotas are intended to protect local industry. For example, agreements between the U.S. and Mexico are phasing out quotas on U.S. corn sales to Mexico, and Mexican sales of peanuts, oranges, and sugar to the U.S.
- **Local-content law**—a regulation specifying the proportion of a finished product's components and labor that must be provided by the importing country.

For example, to be sold in Taiwan, Japanese cars must be at least partially assembled there. To comply with a local-content law, a firm may import most of a product's parts, buy some locally, and have the final product assembled locally. These laws are used to provide jobs and protect domestic businesses.

- **Local operating laws**—a constraint on how, when, or where retailing can be conducted. These regulations, many intended to protect small businesses, are having an impact on Internet shopping. For example, in Germany the retail price of a product has to be the same for everyone. As a result, a system like Priceline.com, where consumers propose a price for an airline seat, rental car, or hotel room and the seller decides if it is acceptable, is illegal. In Austria, France, and the Netherlands publishers specify the retail price of books regardless of where or how they are sold. This prevents Internet firms, despite having a cost advantage over bookstores, from offering a lower price to consumers.[12]

- **Standards and certification**—a requirement that a product contain or exclude certain ingredients or that it be tested and certified as meeting certain restrictive standards. European countries, for example, have restricted genetically altered corn and also beef that has been fed growth hormones.

- **Boycott**—a refusal to buy products from a particular company or country. Boycotts, also called embargoes, are used by a government to punish another country for what are perceived to be unfair importation rules.

Trade agreements. Trade agreements reduce trade barriers by giving preferential treatment to firms in the member countries. However, they may also result in member countries establishing barriers to trade with the rest of the world. Thus they have implications for all marketers. By examining several major trade agreements, we can form an impression of the role they play in international marketing:

www.wto.org

- **World Trade Organization (WTO).** This organization was created in 1995, as the governing body of global commerce. It has 135-member countries that account for 90% of world trade. The members participate in periodic negotiations on issues such as tariff reductions, import restrictions, local-content rules, and subsidization of industry by government. The WTO provides a forum for airing trade disputes between countries, but it does not guarantee that solutions to disagreements will be found. Recently it has addressed the issue of safeguarding intellectual property rights.

  The WTO is the successor to the *General Agreement on Tariffs and Trade,* or GATT, founded in 1948. GATT negotiations resulted in the liberalization of trade in 50,000 products and a 40% reduction in tariffs around the world, significant decreases in the subsidies provide for firms engaged in exporting, and the extension of trading rules beyond just goods to include investments.

www.europa.eu.int

- **European Union (EU).** This political and economic alliance evolved from the Treaty of Rome in 1957 that brought together France, Italy, Belgium, West Germany (now the combined East and West Germanys), Luxembourg, and the Netherlands. It was originally called the European Common Market and later the European Community. It is now known as the European Union or EU. Over the years membership has grown to include Denmark, Great Britain, Greece, Spain, Ireland, Portugal, Austria, Sweden, and Finland (see Figure 3.1).

  The EU's overriding objective is to liberalize trade among its members. More specifically, the goal is a single market for its members that would permit the free movement of goods, services, people, and capital. In addition, the members would be governed by the same set of rules for transporting goods, regulating business, and protecting the environment. Fully accomplishing these goals entails adopting a common currency, a single central bank, and a shared foreign policy, among other things.

  A major milestone was accomplished in 1999 when the Euro became the official currency of 11 of the members (Sweden, Denmark, and the United Kingdom declined to participate, and Greece was judged to be economically

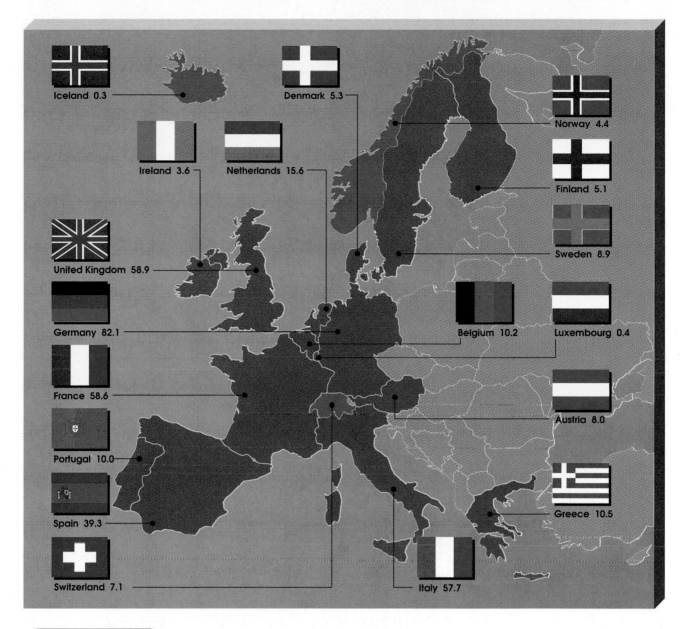

Iceland 0.3

Denmark 5.3

Norway 4.4

Ireland 3.6

Netherlands 15.6

Finland 5.1

Sweden 8.9

United Kingdom 58.9

Germany 82.1

Belgium 10.2

Luxembourg 0.4

France 58.6

Austria 8.0

Portugal 10.0

Spain 39.3

Greece 10.5

Switzerland 7.1

Italy 57.7

Figure 3.1

The European Union Countries (green) and the European Economic Area countries (purple) in 2000 (with population figures in millions).

too weak). Euro notes and coins will not appear until 2002. Given the historic animosities and rivalries that exist among the European countries, it is not surprising that progress has been slow. However, despite delays and setbacks, it is clear that greater liberalization of trade in Europe is inevitable.

The prospect of a market of 370 million consumers with the same regulations for advertising, packaging, and distribution is very attractive. To illustrate, because of national border restrictions and administrative delays, a truck traveling from London to Milan under the old system could be expected to average only about 12 miles per hour. Without the delays, the duration of the trip would be reduced by at least 50%.

Several European countries, notably Switzerland, Norway, and Iceland, object to certain aspects of the EU agreement and have chosen not to join at least for now. The EU will certainly continue to expand. A dozen or more central and eastern European countries are being considered for membership. These countries, which now consume very small amounts of western goods, are seen as primary growth markets.

Canada 30.7

United States 270.3

Mexico 95.8

Colombia 37.7

Venezuela 23.2

Ecuador 12.2

Brazil 161.8

Chile 14.8   Argentina 36.1   Peru 24.8

Uruguay 3.2

Paraguay 5.2

Bolivia 8.0

Figure 3.2

The Americas (with population figures in millions).

www.nafta-sec-alena.org

www.apec.org

- **North American Free Trade Agreement (NAFTA).** The U.S. and Canada forged a pact in 1989 that over a 10-year period phased out tariffs on goods traded between the two countries. The agreement was expanded in 1994 to include Mexico, creating a North American free-trade zone. Several other Western Hemisphere countries are interested in joining and may eventually become members. (See Figure 3.2.)

  Canada is already the U.S.'s largest trading partner, and Mexico is third (behind Japan). As a result, NAFTA is unlikely to produce a dramatic *increase* in trade. More likely there will be *shifts* in trade. That is, most analysts expect to see greater specialization, with some assembly jobs and commodity production moving from the U.S. to Mexico, and more technical production occurring in the U.S. This, in turn, is expected to raise incomes in Mexico and create greater demand for U.S. and Canadian goods.

- **Asia-Pacific Economic Cooperation forum (APEC).** Eighteen Pacific Rim nations participate in this trade pact—Australia, Brunei, Canada, Chile, China, Hong Kong, Indonesia, Japan, Malaysia, Mexico, New Zealand, Papua New Guinea, the Philippines, Singapore, South Korea, Taiwan, Thailand, and the U.S. The objective of the members, which account for 45% of the world's inter-

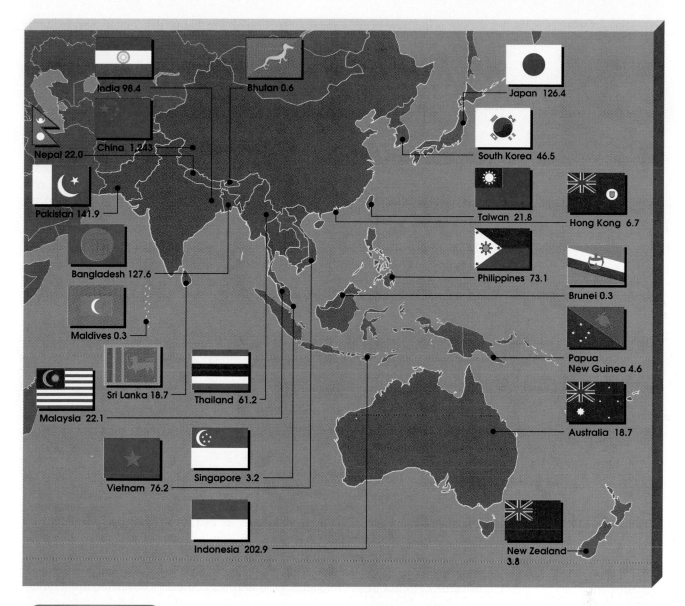

Figure 3.3

South Asia and the Asian side of the Pacific Rim (with population figures in millions).

www.aseansec.org

www.mercosurinvestment.com

national trade, is to create a free-trade zone in the Pacific. South Asia and the Asian side of the Pacific Rim are shown in Figure 3.3. Not surprisingly, given the number of participants in APEC, progress is slow. Their representatives met for the first time in 1992, and the current goal is to have the major trade barriers substantially eliminated by 2020.[13]

- **Association of Southeast Asian Nations (ASEAN).** This pact was established in 1967 as a free-trade zone joining Brunei, Indonesia, Malaysia, the Philippines, Singapore, and Thailand. The ASEAN nations have a combined population of 330 million and a gross domestic product of over $400 billion. The U.S. has exports exceeding $30 billion to ASEAN and imports of nearly $45 billion. Despite some recent setbacks, the rapid growth in these nations has led analysts to predict that soon their imports from the U.S. could triple.[14]

- **Common Market of the South (MERCOSUR).** Consisting of Argentina, Brazil, Paraguay, and Uruguay, and encompassing 190 million people, this pact permits 90% of the trade among these countries to occur tariff-free. The objectives of MERCOSUR are very similar to the EU, the elimination of tariffs among the members and the establishment of common external tariffs. A similar agreement, called the Andean Common Market (ANCOM), has reduced trade barriers among Venezuela, Colombia, Ecuador, Peru, and Bolivia.

Other trade agreements are in existence or are being developed. Seven South Asian nations—India, Pakistan, Bhutan, Bangladesh, the Maldives, Nepal, and Sri Lanka—have formed the South Asian Association for Regional Cooperation (SAARC). With a population of over a billion people, these countries acting in concert have the potential to become a global force. However, traditional rivalries and political problems have thus far hindered the implementation of an effective free-trade arrangement.

What do regional trade agreements mean for the rest of the world? Although they may eventually eliminate *internal* trade barriers among the members, trade agreements create fears that *external* barriers may restrict entry of products from outside the member countries. For example, the EU accounts for 5% of Mexico's imports today, as compared to 20% in 1994, before NAFTA opened Mexico up to U.S. and Canadian exports.[15] Recognizing these concerns, some coalitions are undertaking efforts to build good relations with nonmember countries. For example, Mexico and the EU have reached a free-trade agreement that will be phased in beginning in 2003. And the U.S. and the EU established an accord called the New Transatlantic Agenda that commits them to working toward establishing common product standards, agreement on standards for television programming, and many other trade-related issues.[16]

It is too soon to measure the impact of trade agreements. However, the growth of regional economic trading blocs is a significant development that will create both opportunities and challenges for international marketers.

These accords should not cause us to overlook other areas of the world. An unknown at this time is the potential in eastern Europe, Russia, and the rest of the former Soviet Union. It is impossible to predict how successful these countries will be in moving toward capitalism, or how long it will take. However, the potential of the Commonwealth of Independent States (CIS), headed by Russia, and other countries such as Poland and Hungary, is enormous.

In the 21st century, perhaps the area with the greatest international marketing potential is China, with its *1.2 billion* people. Already we have seen glimpses of these possibilities. Foreign cosmetic sales in China, unheard of a few years ago, are soaring. KFC opened the largest store in its chain on the square across from Chairman Mao's mausoleum. China also has significant potential as an exporter. By 1990, the country was a major exporter of clothing. And China is using American and European investments in a quest to become a significant international exporter of automobiles, semiconductors, and telecommunications equipment.[17]

Organization Structures for International Markets

Having evaluated the opportunities and conditions in a foreign country, management must select an appropriate organizational structure for its marketing effort. There is a range of methods for operating in foreign markets (see Table 3.2), which represents successively greater international involvement.

Exporting

The simplest way to operate in foreign markets is by **exporting,** selling goods either directly to foreign importers or through import-export middlemen. Because it is the easiest way to get into international markets, exporting is popular with small firms. The Internet has created new export opportunities for many companies. Amazon.com, the best known online bookseller, derives 25% of its revenue from foreign customers.[18] However, using the Internet to sell directly to consumers in other countries presents some interesting challenges. There are issues of the lan-

www.amazon.com

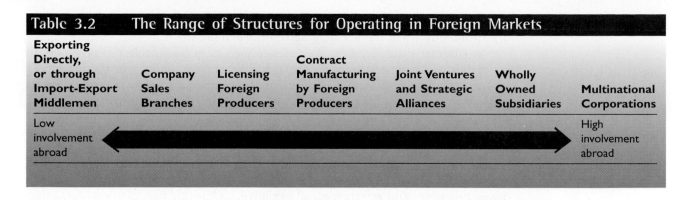

Table 3.2   The Range of Structures for Operating in Foreign Markets

Exporting Directly, or through Import-Export Middlemen	Company Sales Branches	Licensing Foreign Producers	Contract Manufacturing by Foreign Producers	Joint Ventures and Strategic Alliances	Wholly Owned Subsidiaries	Multinational Corporations
Low involvement abroad						High involvement abroad

guage or languages to use on the site, the currency in which to quote prices, selection of the method of payment, and arrangements for reliable delivery of the goods.

In international markets, just as in domestic markets, middlemen may own the goods they deal in or simply bring buyers and sellers together. An **export merchant** is a middleman operating in the manufacturer's country that buys goods and exports them. Very little risk or investment on the part of the manufacturer is involved. Also, minimal time and effort are required on the part of the exporting producer. However, the exporter has little or no control over merchant middlemen.

An **export agent** may be located in either the manufacturer's country or in the destination country. The agent negotiates the sale of the product and may provide additional services such as arranging for international financing, shipping, and insurance on behalf of the manufacturer, but does not own the goods. Greater risk is involved, because the manufacturer retains title to the goods. Because they typically deal with a number of manufacturers, both types of middlemen generally are not aggressive marketers, nor do they generate a large sales volume.

To counteract some of these deficiencies, management can export through its own **company sales branches** located in foreign markets. Operating a sales branch enables a company to (1) promote its products more aggressively, (2) tailor its distribution network to the product, and (3) control its sales effort more completely. Several brewers, including Dutch-based Heineken, Stroh's of the U.S., and Bass in Britain, use company branches to market nonalcoholic beverages in Saudi Arabia.[19] Branch offices are used rather than export agents because the marketing task demands special attention. Alcoholic beverages are illegal in Saudi Arabia, so the marketing effort for products made by beer companies are required to meet numerous regulations. It's unlikely that an export agent would provide the necessary care.

With an international sales branch, management now has the task of managing a sales force. The difficulty is that these sales people are either employees sent from the home country who are unfamiliar with the local market, or foreign nationals who are unfamiliar with the product and the company's marketing practices.

Contracting

Contracting involves a legal relationship that allows a firm to enter a foreign market indirectly, quickly establish a market presence, and experience a limited amount of risk. Three frequently used forms of contracting are licensing, contract manufacturing, and franchising.

Licensing means granting to another producer—for some amount of compensation—the right to use one's production process, patents, trademarks, or other assets. For example, in Japan, the Suntory brewery is licensed by Anheuser-Busch to produce Budweiser beer, whereas in England, Budweiser is brewed under license by the Watney brewery. Producers run the risk of encouraging future competition by licensing. A licensee may learn all it can from the producer and then proceed independently when the licensing agreement expires.

In **contract manufacturing,** a marketer such as Sears Roebuck contracts with a foreign producer to supply products that Sears then markets in the producer's country. For example, rather than import U.S.–made tools and hardware for its department stores in Mexico, Brazil, and Spain, Sears contracts with local manufacturers to supply many of these products.

If you have traveled outside the U.S., most likely you have seen the impact of one form of contracting firsthand. **Franchising** has allowed many U.S. retailers, such as McDonald's, KFC, and Toys "R" Us, to expand overseas rapidly and with minimal risk. Franchising combines a proven operating formula with local knowledge, financing, and entrepreneurial initiative.

Contracting offers companies flexibility with minimal investment. It allows a producer to enter a market that might otherwise be closed to it because of exchange restrictions, import quotas, or prohibitive tariffs.

Direct Investment

Another alternative is **direct foreign investment,** through which a company can build or acquire production or distribution facilities in a foreign country. U.S. firms have about $980 billion in direct investments around the world. In comparison, the foreign direct investment in the U.S. amounts to about $865 billion.[20] Table 3.3 indicates where U.S. firms have made the greatest amounts of foreign investments. Note that these are not sales figures; they are the value of the owned assets such as plants and equipment at a point in time.

The magnitude of foreign investments is a direct reflection of the strength and stability of a country's economy in comparison to the rest of the world. The amount invested in a particular country reflects its political and social receptivity to foreign investment as well as its economic attractiveness.

Direct investment can take the form of a joint venture or a wholly owned foreign subsidiary. A **joint venture** is a partnership arrangement in which the foreign operation is owned in part by a domestic company and in part by a foreign company. PepsiCo entered a joint venture with Empresas Polar to produce soft drinks for western Venezuela. The company, called Sorpresa, combines the bottling, warehousing, and distribution skills of Polar with the marketing, promotion, and advertising expertise of PepsiCo.[21] A joint venture between Ford Motor Co. and

Table 3.3	Direct Foreign Investment in Selected Countries by U.S. Firms
Country	**Direct Investment in 1998 ($ billions)**
United Kingdom	179
Canada	103
Netherlands	79
Germany	43
Bermuda	41
Brazil	38
Japan	38
Switzerland	38
Australia	34
Mexico	26
China	6

Source: Statistical Abstract of the United States: 1999, 119th ed., U.S. Bureau of the Census, Washington, DC, 1999, p. 797.

Recognizing the specialized needs of international business travelers, several major airlines formed an alliance to facilitate ticketing to multiple destinations, rerouting on other alliance-member airlines to avoid delays, access to airport lounges (the feature emphasized in this ad), and other benefits. The Star Alliance network includes flights to 760 destinations in 112 countries. This arrangement greatly extends the ability of each airline to serve its customers without a major investment.

Mahindra & Mahindra Ltd. of India to initially assemble Ford Escorts and eventually manufacture Ford Fiestas in India suggests how volatile these projects can be. Anticipating a receptive market, the plant was designed to produce 20,000 vehicles a year. However, an economic downturn in the Indian economy resulted in sales of only 5,000 vehicles.[22]

When the controlling interest (more than 50%) is owned by foreign nationals, the domestic firm has no real control over the marketing or production activities. However, a joint venture may be the only structure, other than licensing, through which a firm is legally permitted to enter some foreign markets. Joint ventures are frequently undertaken on a country-by-country basis. For example, in less than a year, Royal Crown Cola entered Mexico, Argentina, Syria, Portugal, Australia, and Indonesia on the basis of joint ventures.[23]

Some major corporations have created a hybrid version of a joint venture called a strategic alliance. A **strategic alliance** is a formal, long-term agreement between firms to combine their capabilities and resources to accomplish global objectives without joint ownership. For example, there are several airline alliances. One of the biggest, called Star, includes Air Canada, Lufthansa, United, and six other companies. The alliance permits each member airline to arrange flights for its originating passengers to virtually anywhere in the world.[24]

Joint ventures and alliances in international marketing are particularly attractive when:

- Local laws create barriers to foreign ownership of a business. For example, the national regulations countries impose on airlines led Lufthansa, United Airlines, and other airlines to form alliances for passenger sharing and pooling maintenance facilities.

- Local knowledge is especially important. Retailing in particular requires an understanding of local customs and tastes. Powerful firms like British retailer

Tesco, in an alliance with Samsung when it entered South Korea, and Wal-Mart, working with Cifra in Mexico, recognized that much can be learned from established local firms.

- A firm wants access to a market but does not want to expand its resources or expertise. If the risks of a foreign venture are too great for a firm to assume or gaining the necessary expertise would be too costly or time-consuming, a joint venture may be an option. Turner Broadcasting Services joined with Philips, a Dutch electronics firm, to gain quick access to digital communications hardware.[25]

Wholly owned subsidiaries in foreign markets are foreign-based assembly or manufacturing facilities. They are commonly used by companies that have evolved to an advanced stage of international business. Nissan built Europe's most efficient auto manufacturing plant in England, where it will make a car for the European market using a design provided by Renault.

With a wholly owned foreign subsidiary, a company has maximum control over its marketing program and production operations. To ensure that the product is made and presented according to the same standards around the world, the company makes use of subsidiaries rather than licensees. For example, adidas America, a wholly owned subsidiary of adidas-Salomon AG, produces a broad range of footwear and apparel targeted at U.S. preferences and tastes. The line includes baseball and football cleats, adventure shoes, and women's workout shoes for which there are strong U.S. markets. Because it is a subsidiary, the actions of adidas America come under the scrutiny of the parent organization. Thus, consistent with the corporate philosophy, there is a stronger emphasis on designs for performance enhancement than on fashion. A wholly owned subsidiary requires a substantial investment of money, labor, and managerial attention.

Multinational Corporations

We've now come to the highest level of international involvement—one reached by relatively few companies. It is the truly global enterprise—the **multinational corporation**—in which both the foreign and the domestic operations are integrated and are not separately identified except possibly for legal reasons. A regional sales office in Atlanta is basically the same as one in Paris. Business opportunities abroad are viewed in the same way as those in the home country. That is, domestic opportunities are no longer automatically considered to be more attractive. From a legal point of view, a multinational has a home country. Thus, Nestlé is a Swiss firm and Shell Oil is Dutch. However, from a strategic perspective, a true multinational firm is a worldwide enterprise and does strategic marketing planning on a global basis. The result can create interesting arrangements, such as General Motors manufacturing the Opel Zaifira in Thailand for export to Australia and other Pacific Rim countries.

Even though we have described these operating methods as distinct, it is not uncommon for a firm to use more than one of them at the same time. To illustrate, Honda Motor Company exports cars from Japan, imports minivans to Japan from its subsidiary in Canada, and manufactures cars and trucks for the U.S. market at subsidiaries in the U.S. Likewise, Hershey exports candy to Canada, is involved in a joint venture with the largest candy company in Scandinavia, and has a wholly owned subsidiary in Germany—Gubor, a boxed-chocolate company.

•Designing the Marketing Mix

As in domestic marketing, the manager must design a marketing mix that will effectively meet customers' needs and accomplish the organization's objectives. However, as the following discussion suggests, domestic practices may have to be modified or entirely replaced in international marketing.

Marketing Research

The scarcity of reliable statistical data is often a major impediment in many foreign markets. Typically, the quality of the data is related directly to a country's level of economic development. However, the nature of the data varies widely. For example, most nations (including England, Japan, France, Spain, and Italy) do not even ask their citizens for income figures in their national censuses.

Another problem is a lack of uniformity among countries in how they define basic measures such as unemployment and the cost of living. As a result, comparisons across countries are often unreliable. In some parts of the world, figures on population and production may be only crude estimates. In less developed countries, studies on such things as buying habits or newspaper readership are even less likely. It was only in the 1990s that China was able to report television audience figures, even in the largest urban areas.

Other challenges arise when collecting data directly from customers and prospects. The absence of reliable lists makes it very difficult even to select a representative sample. Telephone surveys, for example, are likely to be invalid if telephone service is not available to virtually the entire population of a country. Even conducting a focus group can be very difficult. The quality of data also depends on the willingness of people to respond accurately when researchers pose questions about attitudes or buying behavior. Gathering useful data is very difficult in societies where opinion polls are relatively uncommon or strangers are viewed with suspicion.

Product Planning

A critical question in product planning concerns the extent to which a company can market the same product in several different countries. *Product extension* describes the situation in which a standard product is sold in two or more countries. For example, Gillette sells the same razor blades worldwide, and Levi Strauss also has been successful in marketing its 501 brand of jeans in many countries.

We can make a few broad generalizations regarding product extensions. The best bet for standardization is in the area of durable business goods. In such industries as aircraft, computers, and tractors, the worldwide market (at least among industrialized nations) is quite uniform. For example, the Boeing Company is selling its two-engine 777 airliner to both Singapore Airlines and United Airlines.

Consumer durable goods such as cameras, watches, pocket calculators, small appliances, and television sets are only slightly more difficult to extend into foreign markets virtually unchanged. The benefits of standardization are reflected in the efforts of automakers to develop "world cars." If Ford is able to design cars that can be sold around the world, it estimates that its $8 billion annual product-development budget can be reduced by *billions*.[26]

The most difficult products to standardize globally are food and drink products, health and beauty aids, and wearing apparel. (Here Gillette blades and Levi's 501 jeans are exceptions.) This difficulty can be traced to national tastes and habits. For example, U.S. consumers eat four times as much dry cereal per capita as the French. This should come as no surprise, because even in large national markets such as the U.S., we often find strong regional differences in food and clothing preferences. Marketers frequently respond with a second product strategy option, *product adaptation,* or modifying a product that sells successfully in one market to suit the unique needs or requirements of other markets. Procter & Gamble modified its Max Factor line of cosmetics with brighter colors for Latin Americans, and its Vidal Sassoon shampoo with more conditioners for the Asian market.[27]

The third alternative product strategy is *invention,* the development of an entirely new product for a foreign market. For example, Maybelline developed a high-humidity face makeup formula for the Asian Pacific market.

Marketers must study carefully the cultural and economic environment of any market—foreign or domestic—before planning products for that particular area.

Well-known brand names, familiar retail stores, and fast-food outlets that look just like the ones at home are now common in foreign locations. Often the products carrying those brands and company names have been adapted or changed dramatically to meet local needs and tastes. For example, Campbell Soup offers duck gizzard soup in Hong Kong in its familiar red and white can. For other products the changes are less visible. Coca-Cola is made from beet sugar in Poland rather than the high-fructose corn syrup used in the U.S. And

Hershey's Kisses in the U.K. contain more milk and less chocolate to create a smoother taste preferred by British consumers. These are pragmatic decisions made on the basis of local tastes and the availability of ingredients.

With the amount of business and pleasure travel today (over 53 million U.S. citizens traveled outside the country last year, and about the same number of foreigners visited the U.S.), does a firm risk damaging its reputation if a product performs or tastes differently from market to market?

In Europe, for example, large refrigerators are popular in the north because consumers prefer to shop once a week. In contrast, southern Europeans enjoy shopping at open-air markets daily and therefore opt for small refrigerators. And in Europe, where washing machines are often in the kitchen, consumers prefer smaller, quieter versions than U.S. households.

Branding and labeling are other considerations in foreign marketing. Most firms would prefer to use the same brand name in domestic and foreign markets, because it provides greater overall familiarity and recognition and can also produce some economies in promotion. However, care must be taken with translating brand names. Clairol introduced a curling iron in Germany called the Mist Stick only to discover that mist is a German slang word for manure.

A concern of many marketers is **trademark infringement.** In many countries copyright laws are nonexistent or poorly enforced. As a result, local firms manufacture products with names and packaging very similar to well-known imported goods in hopes of deceiving consumers. Often these products are of inferior quality, so not only do they steal business from the imported brand, they also damage its reputation.

Global pirating of computer software, music, and videos—virtually anything that can be transmitted electronically—is another serous problem. In the past, firms were provided with at least some protection from pirating by domestic laws and the physical limitations of making and shipping a video tape or CD. With those constraints reduced or eliminated, it's been suggested that the makers of these electronic products will be forced to find new ways to market their products. One approach, already used by some software firms, is to give their products away via the Internet, and generate revenue by selling advertising space on the Internet site.

Marketers must also be alert to shifting tastes. In Europe during the 1970s and 1980s, there was a definite preference for European brands. However, in the mid-1990s, many U.S. brands developed a special appeal. For example, sales increased for Jeeps advertised as "The American Legend," Goodyear tires with images of the Indianapolis 500 race, and Budweiser beer at premium prices. Some of this popularity may be attributable to U.S. films and TV shows shown in Europe.

Pricing

Determining the price for a product is a complex and inexact task, frequently involving trial-and-error decision making. This process is often even more complex in international marketing. An exporter faces variables such as currency conversion, differences in what is included in the price (such as postsale service), and often a lack of control over middlemen's pricing.

Clothing, handbags, jewelry, watches, sports gear, software, CDs, cosmetics, and pharmaceuticals have all been frequently counterfeited in the past. Most recently, less expensive items including toys and trading cards are being illegally copied. As shown in this photo from Thailand, when counterfeit products are discovered they are often publicly destroyed. To deter counterfeiting, some manufacturers place hard-to-duplicate holograms on products or packages.

Cost-plus pricing (setting price by adding an amount to provide a profit to the cost of manufacturing a product) is relatively common in export marketing. Because of additional physical distribution expenses, tariffs, and other export costs, foreign prices usually are considerably higher than domestic prices for the same product. For example, a Jeep Cherokee costs about 50% more in Japan than in the U.S. At the retail level, price bargaining is quite prevalent in many foreign markets—especially in Asia, Africa, and South America—and must be taken into consideration in setting the initial price.

Sometimes companies engage in a practice called **dumping**—selling products in foreign markets at prices below those charged for the same goods in their home markets. The price may be lowered to meet foreign competition or to dispose of slow-moving products. Recently Taiwan accused U.S. manufacturers of dumping computer memory chips in the Taiwanese market, and U.S. steelmakers claim firms in Russia, Brazil, South Africa, and China are dumping products in America.[28] Dumping, which frequently involves selling goods below cost, is viewed as an unfair business practice by most governments, and generally results in threats of tariffs or establishment of quotas.

An issue of growing concern is the **price differential** charged for an identical brand in different, often neighboring, countries. Differentials of 30 to 150% are not uncommon. A French consumer can cross the border into Germany and buy a Volkswagen Jetta for one-third less than it costs in France. European consumers will become much more aware of these differentials with the introduction of the Euro as the common EU currency.[29]

Price differences result from the strength of demand, the complexity of the distribution structures in various countries, and differences in tax systems. With the easy flow of information across borders and increased travel by consumers, price differentials add considerable complexity to the job of middlemen, especially retailers, doing business in several countries. They also encourage arbitrage—the purchase and sale of a product in different markets to benefit from the unequal prices.

Prices may be quoted in the seller's currency or in the currency of the foreign buyer. Here we encounter problems of **foreign exchange** and conversion of currencies. As a general rule, a firm engaged in foreign trade—whether it is exporting or importing—prefers to have the price quoted in its own national currency. If a seller deals in a foreign currency and that currency declines in value between the signing of a contract and the receipt of the foreign currency, the seller incurs a loss. Similarly, a buyer dealing in a foreign currency would lose money if the foreign currency increased in value before payment was made. The risks from fluctuations in foreign exchange are shifted to the other party in the transaction if a firm deals in its national currency.

An alternative to currency-based pricing is **countertrade** or **barter.** Rather than buy goods with cash, some countries arrange to trade domestically made products for imported goods. PepsiCo, for example, has traded soft drinks to Poland for wooden chairs that are used in its U.S. Pizza Hut stores. Two reasons for countertrade are:

- *Lack of hard currency.* Less developed countries may not have enough "hard" currency (the money of countries viewed in world markets as reasonably stable) to buy needed capital goods. So they trade their less-sophisticated products for equipment and technology. A Canadian firm selling steel in Indonesia was compensated in palm oil, coffee, timber, and rattan furniture.
- *Inadequate marketing structure.* Some countries do not have a marketing structure that encourages or permits international trade. Without global distribution systems, adequate promotion, or the ability to provide service, they cannot sell their domestic goods overseas. To overcome this problem, these countries may require foreign firms that import products into the country to accept local goods in total or partial payment. Both China and Romania require that importers accept countertrade.

Agreements between manufacturers and middlemen in the same industry are tolerated to a far greater extent in many foreign countries than in the U.S. They are allowed even when the avowed purpose of the combination is to restrain trade and reduce competition. Recognizing this, Congress passed the Webb-Pomerene Act in 1918. This law allows American firms to join this type of trade combination in a foreign country without being charged with violation of American antitrust laws.

The best known of these international marketing combinations is the cartel. A **cartel** is a group of companies that produce similar products and act collectively to restrain competition in manufacturing and marketing. Cartels exist to varying degrees in steel, aluminum, fertilizers, petroleum products, rayon, and sulfur. Probably the world's best-known cartel is OPEC, the Organization of Petroleum Exporting Countries, which has tried—with varying degrees of success—to control the price of crude oil.

Distribution Systems

The different environments in foreign markets force firms to adjust their distribution systems, because marketing institutions, such as various types of retailers, are responses to the environment. They can also provide an opportunity to experiment with new strategies. For example, in Taiwan, General Motors owns its retail dealers. Freed of the constraint of trying to keep franchised dealers happy (as it must do in the U.S.), GM can install and test a system that allows consumers to configure, order, and buy cars on the Internet.[30]

Middlemen and Channels of Distribution

International middlemen were introduced earlier in this chapter in connection with organizational structures for international marketing. Foreign middlemen representing importers and operating within foreign countries are, in general, less aggressive and perform fewer marketing services than their counterparts selling domestically produced products. The foreign marketing situation, however, usually argues against bypassing these middlemen. Often the demand is too small to warrant establishing a sales office or branch in the foreign country. Also, in many countries, knowledge of the market may be more important than knowledge of the product, even for high-technology products. And sometimes government controls preclude the use of a firm's sales organization abroad. Thus, middlemen in foreign countries ordinarily are a part of the channel structure.

A deceptive practice employed by some middlemen is called export diversion or **gray marketing.** When a distributor buys a product made in one country and agrees to distribute it in a second country, but instead diverts the product to a third country, gray marketing is occurring. The term used to describe the practice comes from the fact that the goods are typically sold in a reputable outlet, typically at a substantial discount, and thus do not appear on the "black market." The discounts stem from the fact that the gray marketer does not bear any of the promotional costs for the product, instead capitalizing on the promotional efforts of the authorized dealers, nor do gray marketer provide the service and warranty protection of an authorized dealer. An investigation of a health scare associated with Coke bottled in Belgium led to the discovery that as much as 20% of all the soft drinks sold in Great Britain are diverted goods.[31] One reason gray marketing occurs is because manufacturers selling their products in several countries often have more difficulty monitoring the activities of middlemen than they do in the domestic market.

Physical Distribution

Various aspects of physical distribution in foreign marketing are quite different from anything found on the domestic scene. Generally, physical distribution expenses account for a much larger share of the final selling price in foreign markets than in domestic markets. Problems caused by climate, pilferage, handling, and inadequate marking must be considered in international shipments. Requirements regarding commercial shipping, insurance, and government documents complicate foreign shipping. As noted earlier, one of the primary benefits of economic alliances like the EU is the efficiency they bring to physical distribution. With the free movement of goods across European borders, distribution time and expense will be drastically reduced.

Bribes, kickbacks, and sometimes even extortion payments are facts of life in international distribution. Bribery is so rooted in many cultures that it is described with special slang words. It's called *mordida* (small bite) in Latin America. The French call it *pot de vin* (jug of wine). In Italy there is *la bustarella* (the little envelope), left on a bureaucrat's desk to cut the red tape. South Koreans use *ttuk kab* (rice cake expenses).

Revelations about the amount of bribery led Congress to pass the Foreign Corrupt Practices Act in 1977. The act prohibits U.S. companies, their subsidiaries, or representatives from making payments to high-ranking foreign government officers and political parties. The law, however, does not exclude small, facilitating payments to lower-level foreign government employees who are not policymakers, because these payments are a way of life in many parts of the world.

What complicates this situation is the fact that bribery is not a sharply defined activity. Sometimes the lines are blurred among a bribe, a gift to show appreciation, a reasonable commission for services rendered, and a finder's fee to open a distribution channel. For example, businesses in South Korea make contributions to government officials to mark major holidays. According to South Korean executives, the payments are not made to obtain favors. Rather, they serve to protect a firm from punitive treatment by government bureaucrats. Realistically, in some foreign markets a seller must pay a fee or commission to an agent to get in touch with prospective buyers. Without paying such fees, there is simply no effective access to those markets.

Advertising

Rather than discuss promotion in its entirety, we limit our discussion to standardizing advertising messages as illustrative of the strategic challenges in international promotion. Recognize, however, that there are issues related to other aspects of advertising, as well as personal selling and sales promotion that international marketers must deal with. For example, Avon's sales in the U.S., entirely dependent on the door-to-door efforts of Avon representatives, are flat. So the firm is opening retail stores and selling its products through health spas. At the same time, Avon's international door-to-door sales are booming from Argentina to Vietnam. However, the firm adapts its techniques to each country's culture.[32]

Because advertisers must capture and hold attention, they make use of a variety of communication devices such as humor, contrast, and surprise. The difficulty in international advertising is that what works in one culture might take on quite a different meaning in another. For example, a major controversy was generated by a Toyota ad in Italy that presented a lighthearted contrast between the Italian government's image as corrupt and the value and reliability of a Toyota Carina.[33]

This, as well as many other advertising failures by international marketers, raises the question of how much advertising can be standardized in international markets. In the past, little thought was given to standardization, and separate programs (copy, appeals, and media) were tailored for each country, or even for regions within a country. For example, as recently as 1988, Parker Pens were advertised around the world using over 30 different themes.

Although complete uniformity is not typical, today there is much support for the idea of commonality in international ad campaigns. Many companies use basically the same appeals, theme, copy, and layout in all or much of their international advertising—particularly in western European countries. Unilever successfully uses the same appeal for Dove bar soap—contains "one-quarter cleansing cream"—in Australia, France, Germany, Italy, and the U.S. Similarly, Toys "R" Us only slightly modifies television ads developed in the U.S. for use in Germany and Japan. Other examples of firms and the brands for which they've adopted global appeals are Gillette for its Sensor razor, and Procter & Gamble with Pert Plus/Wash and Go shampoo, Snuggle fabric softener, and Nescafé coffee. However, in each of these cases the advertiser customizes the way the appeal is presented to fit the local markets. For example, in some cultures it would be inappropriate to depict a woman shampooing her hair in the bathroom.

Standardization of advertising is spurred by the increase in international communications and entertainment. Many TV broadcasts reach audiences all over the world through satellite and cable networks. Many American and European magazines and newspapers circulate across national borders. In addition, vacation and business travel from one country to another is quite common.

A second factor contributing to the standardization of advertising is production costs. Producing quality advertising is very expensive, so the opportunity to achieve savings by repeating the same ideas or executions in various parts of the world is attractive.

Perhaps the issue comes down to this point: The goal of advertising is the same in any country, namely to communicate information and persuasive appeals effectively. For some products, the appeals are sufficiently universal and the markets are sufficiently homogeneous to permit the use of very similar advertising in several countries. It is only the media strategy and the details of a message that must be fine-tuned to each country's cultural, economic, and political environment. However, care must be taken to recognize when differences in national identity and characteristics are sufficient to require specialized advertising in a particular country.

Our discussion has described environmental factors, organizational arrangements, and tactical issues related to the marketing mix elements of product, price, distribution and promotion that are fundamental to designing an international marketing strategy. There are other issues that further distinguish domestic from international or global marketing. A primary purpose of this chapter is to make you aware of the fact that along with the opportunities, marketing beyond one's domestic borders raises new and unique strategic challenges.

Summary

Countries encourage international trade for economic, social, and political reasons. In particular, it provides access to goods that otherwise would be unavailable and, because of comparative advantage, it maximizes a country's economic potential. Firms engage in international marketing because of demand abroad, the saturation of domestic markets, or to take advantage of a technological advantage. Many companies in the U.S. and abroad derive a substantial share of their total sales and profits from their foreign marketing operations.

Although international trade can contribute to the growth of a nation's economy, a country must be concerned about the relationship between exports and imports. For the U.S., trade surpluses are needed to offset deficits in other balance-of-payment categories. In recent years, the U.S. balance of trade has been adversely affected by consumers' preferences for imported products, entry barriers, and other policies of foreign governments, as well as the growing technological and marketing capabilities of other countries.

In terms of organizational structure, the simplest way to operate in a foreign market is to export. This can be done directly to consumers via the Internet or through middlemen specializing in foreign trade. Another method is to export through company sales branches located in foreign countries. More involved approaches include contracting, engaging in a joint venture, or forming a wholly owned subsidiary. The most fully developed organizational structure for international marketing is the multinational corporation.

The macroenvironment faced by an international marketer in various countries will determine whether a global, regional, or local strategy is appropriate. Differences in the social and cultural environment are reflected in family values, customs, education, and language. Critical economic conditions include the infrastructure in a market and a country's stage of economic development. Political and legal forces unique to international marketing are trade barriers and international trade agreements. Organizations such as the World Trade Organization (WTO) as well as trade agreements and economic alliances in Europe (EU), North America (NAFTA), South America (MERCOSUR), Asia (ASEAN), and elsewhere in the world have implications for marketers in both member and nonmember nations.

To develop an international marketing program, a basic issue is how global or standardized the marketing can be. This is made difficult by the fact that market data may be less plentiful in many parts of the world, and conducting marketing research can be very difficult. In some cases each of the marketing-mix elements requires modification or adaptation. Often times operating in a foreign market entails accommodating unique conditions. Chief among these are dumping, foreign exchange, countertrade, price differentials, gray markets, cartels, and bribery.

More about **adidas**

The founder of adidas, Adi Dassler, concentrated on the sports he knew best and the customers closest to his home. In the 1920s he was truly a domestic manufacturer and marketer. However, the realities of competing in the modern athletic shoe world made that strategy impractical. To compete with companies such as Nike and Reebok, major changes were required.

To lower its costs, the firm entered into joint ventures to manufacture products in Asia. In order to gain access to new and less familiar markets in the U.S., adidas first exported its products working with a distributor. Eventually adidas purchased Sports, Inc., creating a wholly owned subsidiary in the U.S. Adidas U.S. concentrates on sports more popular in the U.S., such as baseball and American football. To both capitalize on the adidas name and increase its exposure, the firm has entered into licensing agreements around the globe. For example, Coty Australia has introduced a line of men's toiletries under the adidas name, and a Malaysian firm manufactures adidas sports eyeglasses. Adidas also has entered into joint venture arrangements in Singapore, Hong Kong, Thailand, and other Asian countries to operate Adidas retail sporting goods stores.

What lies ahead for adidas? Long associated with athletic shoes, the firm expanded into other sports including skiing and golf. More recently, it has increased its sportswear business such that clothing sales now exceed footwear volume. At the same time, adidas has expanded the geographic scope of its manufacturing and marketing operations. Although it may not be a truly global enterprise yet, like many firms today it appears to be moving in that direction.[34]

1. In 1999 a dispute between the players and the owners in the National Basketball Association resulted in half the season being cancelled. The absence of games and the subsequent lack of television coverage led to a 25% decline (amounting to $500 million) in basketball shoe sales. All manufacturers, including adidas, were hurt by this environmental development. How can international marketing by adidas reduce the impact of such uncontrollable environmental factors?

2. From the beginning adidas built its reputation on how well its products function. What implications does this have for the way the firm expands internationally?

Key Terms and Concepts

Balance of payments (55)
Trade balance (55)
International marketing (56)
Global strategy (58)
Regional strategy (58)
Local strategy (58)
Infrastructure (60)
Trade barriers (61)
Tariff (61)
Import quota (61)
Local-content law (61)
Local operating laws (62)
Standards and certification (62)
Boycott (62)
World Trade Organization (WTO) (62)

European Union (EU) (62)
North American Free Trade Agreement (NAFTA) (64)
Asia-Pacific Economic Cooperation forum (APEC) (64)
Association of Southeast Asian Nations (ASEAN) (65)
Common Market of the South (MERCOSUR) (65)
Exporting (66)
Export merchant (67)
Export agent (67)
Company sales branch (67)
Contracting (67)
Licensing (67)

Contract manufacturing (68)
Franchising (68)
Direct foreign investment (68)
Joint venture (68)
Strategic alliance (69)
Wholly owned subsidiary (70)
Multinational corporation (70)
Trademark infringement (72)
Dumping (73)
Price differential (73)
Foreign exchange (73)
Countertrade or barter (74)
Cartel (74)
Gray marketing (75)
Bribes (75)

Questions and Problems

1. Find out which U.S. products have the largest volume of exports. (*Hint:* Check *International Financial Statistics* or *International Marketing Data and Statistics*—two publications that are likely in your school's library and on the Internet.) What explains the popularity of these products outside the U.S.?

2. What should a country such as the U.S. do to reduce its trade deficits?

3. A U.S. manufacturer of premium-quality luggage has been exporting its products to Europe. However, the firm has discovered that its luggage is often sold alongside much lower-quality products in discount stores. What approach to international marketing should the firm consider if it wants greater control over how its products are sold at retail?

4. Interview some foreign students on your campus to determine how the grocery buying behavior of people in their countries differ from yours. Consider such factors as when, where, and how people in their countries buy. What roles do various family members play in buying decisions?

5. Many countries have a low literacy rate. In what ways might a company adjust its marketing program to overcome this problem?

6. If an American company uses foreign middlemen, it must usually stand ready to supply them with financial, technical, and promotional help. If this is the case, why is it not customary to bypass these middlemen and deal directly with the ultimate foreign buyers?

7. Examine the ads in a foreign magazine in your college or city library. Particularly note the ads for American products, and compare these with the ads for the same products in American magazines. In what respect do the foreign ads differ from the domestic ads? Are there significant similarities?

8. "Prices of American products are always higher in foreign countries than at home because of the additional risks, expenses of physical distribution, and extra middlemen involved." Discuss.

9. Some U.S. firms have been accused of manufacturing products in "sweatshops" in less developed countries to keep their production costs down. See the Nike website (www.nike.com) for more on this controversy. Should a firm be allowed to pay wages in a foreign market that are below the going wage for the same job in its domestic market?

Hands-On Marketing

1. Report on export marketing activities of companies in the state where your school is located. Consider such topics as the following: What products are exported? How many jobs are created by export marketing? What is the dollar value of exports? How does this figure compare with the value of foreign-made goods imported into the state?

2. Select one product—manufactured or nonmanufactured—for export, and choose the country to which you would like to export it. Examine the macroenvironmental factors described in the chapter and prepare an analysis of the market for this product in the selected country. Be sure to include the sources of information you use.

Cases for Part 1

Always Searching for a Better Recipe for Success

For many years, the McDonald's Corporation enjoyed success built on a few well-known ingredients. The company with the Golden Arches served a fairly simple menu featuring hamburgers, french fries, and soft drinks. The food was relatively inexpensive, consistent in quality, and was served speedily from establishments that all looked alike and were extremely clean.

By the mid-1990s, though, McDonald's was facing a whole menu of problems, including a stagnant product line, a fuzzy marketing strategy, and disenchanted restaurant owners (franchisees). At a time when more Americans were dining out, McDonald's encountered declining sales and market share. In 1998, in fact, the corporation was forced to lay off part of its corporate staff for the first time ever.

Also in 1998, Jack Greenberg was appointed CEO. Since then he has implemented changes that have produced positive results for the chain's domestic restaurants. In addition McDonald's continues to expand its operations internationally and now has restaurants in about 120 countries around the world.

Beefing Up Its Product Line

McDonald's tinkers with its menu continually. However, after introducing Chicken McNuggets, the chain went 15 years without a hugely successful new product. It wasn't for lack of effort, however. Failed products included the Arch Deluxe, the McLean Deluxe, carrot sticks, fried chicken, pasta, and fajitas. In contrast, Burger King (BK) has successfully introduced six new menu items since 1988. Even worse, consumers ranked the taste of McDonald's food 87th out of 91 restaurants in a survey conducted by *Restaurants and Institutions* in 1998.

McDonald's next actions suggested that the leader was no longer being pursued, but rather was the pursuer. The company introduced a burger to compete with BK's flagship product, the Whopper. McDonald's also unveiled a new food-preparation system, "Made for You," which does away with its traditional way of preparing batches of food and keeping them warm in holding bins. "They're going to mass customization the way Burger King has for 40 years," commented Barry Gibbons, BK's former CEO. That may be true, but the new "Made for You" system allows McDonald's to fill special orders much more easily than it could in the past. In addition, many consumers believe it improves the taste of the food without sacrificing the speed of delivery for which McDonald's is famous. It also eliminates waste, thereby reducing costs.

Besides improving the taste of its current menu, McDonald's is aggressively pursuing new options that will appeal to adults. Some parents, the chain realizes, treat their children to Happy Meals, but don't partake in McDonald's fare themselves. Recent introductions, notably a new breakfast bagel sandwich and the McFlurry ice cream dessert, had favorable initial reviews. McDonald's also recognizes that many adults want to reduce fat intake and, in general, eat healthier foods. Thus the giant firm continues to test salads and veggie burgers.

McDonald's Corp. has also made several surprising investments lately. For the first time ever, McDonald's Corp. acquired a stake in another restaurant chain, Chipotle Mexican Grill. Next it purchased Donatos, a small pizza chain based in Columbus, Ohio, and then rescued Boston Market from Chapter 11 bankruptcy proceedings.

Spicing Up Its Distribution Strategy

For many years, McDonald's pursued an aggressive strategy of expansion in the U.S.—some might say too aggressive. After launching under 200 domestic restaurants in 1991 and 1992, McDonald's accelerated its pace, adding more than 1,900 new outlets in the U.S. in 1994 and 1995. This rapid expansion led to a backlash from McDonald's franchisees, who charged that the company was beginning to cannibalize the sales of existing restaurants. Indeed, sales at existing restaurants declined 2.5% in 1995 and 6.4% in 1996. To the increasingly frustrated store owners, this drop was a clear sign that the U.S. market was saturated.

A group of disenchanted franchisees formed Consortium Members Inc. in order to voice their complaints to the corporate offices. They claimed that new McDonald's outlets were being opened to increase overall domestic sales, even though nearby outlets suffered sales decreases. The Consortium may have had an impact. In 1998, only 49 new restaurants were opened and 200 unprofitable restaurants were closed, bringing the total number of domestic sites to about 12,500. In addition, franchisees are speculating (or hoping) that they will have the opportunity to purchase a Donatos, Boston Market, or Chipotle franchise. If so, they will be able to expand their businesses without cannibalizing their current McDonald's restaurants.

According to one franchisee, Greenberg has made a concerted effort to listen more to his owner/operators. "Things are being bubbled up from the stores rather than coming down from the corporation." This seems like smart business when you consider that individual franchisees developed some of McDonald's most popular products, including the Egg McMuffin, Hot Apple Pie, Filet o' Fish, Big Mac, and now the McFlurry. To improve its capability to listen to its franchisees, Greenberg split the company into five geographic divisions and gave each division's management team more decision-making authority. The intent of the reorganization was to eliminate several layers of management and, in turn, to make the corporate offices more responsive and the local operations more autonomous.

Taking a Bite Out of Pricing Problems

During the 1990s, McDonald's has occasionally struggled with pricing decisions. The most notable problem occurred in 1997, when the chain temporarily discounted the price of a Big Mac to 55 cents, symbolizing 1955, the year McDonald's was founded. Consumers were confused by the offer, however, because a soft drink and fries also had to be purchased in order to get the discounted price. Franchisees, concerned that the promotion would be unprofitable for them, were unhappy with management's decision to offer the discounted price. Within two weeks of announcing the discount, sales fell by 6% compared to the previous year's figure. During the same period, Burger King offered its Whopper for 99 cents—with no strings attached. McDonald's discontinued the special price later in the year.

Since then, McDonald's executives have relied on market research and input from franchisees when making pricing decisions. It has also given more autonomy to individual restaurants to offer discounts. This flexibility has allowed franchise owners to respond to tough local competition when necessary.

Putting Some Sizzle Back in Promotions

If you saw a line of people at a McDonald's at some point during the past few years, chances are they weren't there just for the food. More likely, they wanted to get their hands on the Teenie Beanie Babies that were periodically being included in children's Happy Meals. When one of these promotions was announced in April

1997, average sales rose 15%. McDonald's also negotiated an exclusive arrangement to offer toys that tie in to Disney's children-oriented films.

As a result of such appealing promotions, McDonald's remains a perennial favorite with children. Unfortunately, the company is still searching for a menu item that will be a big hit with adults. One misguided effort was the Arch Deluxe hamburger, which flopped when it was promoted with pictures of kids making faces after tasting it.

In the early 1980s, McDonald's moved the bulk of its advertising from DDB Needham to Leo Burnett. The company switched back in 1997 after a nostalgic "My McDonald's" campaign failed to boost sales substantially. Needham introduced a campaign with the tag line, "Did Somebody Say McDonald's?" The company also reallocated a large share of the $600 million promotion budget by making 50% available for local spending instead of the previous 25%. Local ads still use the national slogan, but some observers believe the McDonald's brand is being watered down by the smaller-scale campaigns. Despite these concerns, McDonald's is the most recognized brand in the world, even better known than Coca-Cola.

Gobbling Up Foreign Market Share

The high level of familiarity with McDonald's is not surprising considering its worldwide presence. In 1991, the company had approximately 2,300 restaurants in 47 countries. That number has since grown to more than 12,000 restaurants in almost 120 countries. The international division accounts for about 50% of sales and 60% of total profits. Although McDonald's has been challenged domestically, it is booming in countries like Japan, England, and Germany. McDonald's duplicated its early formula for success in the U.S. by delivering consistent quality, fast service, and a pleasant eating experience.

McDonald's has started to experience growing pains in some foreign markets. In Brazil, after several consecutive years of large increases, sales at outlets open at least a year slowed in 1997. As a result, McDonald's began promoting discount prices to lift sales. Nevertheless, the restaurant chain continues to expand in Brazil.

Because of its aggressive expansion, McDonald's has an 80% share of the fast-food market in some countries. However, profit margins are becoming slimmer, and just eight countries account for 80% of the firm's international earnings. Further, McDonald's is approaching a saturation level in a number of countries. As prime locations become harder to find, the Golden Arches are starting to appear in economically underdeveloped countries.

Brazil is an excellent proving ground for McDonald's international business, because it includes middle- and upper-class segments that are eager to get a taste of America and a large lower-income segment that is unfamiliar with hamburgers and french fries. However, success in Brazil—as in other countries—is not a "sure thing." Brazil's custom of an early-afternoon siesta poses a challenge for McDonald's lunch business. Further, generating breakfast sales is even more difficult because most Brazilians won't consider eating breakfast anywhere but home. Adding to the challenges, Brazil's economy is tumultuous, and many Brazilians are hesitant to spend their hard-earned money on unfamiliar American food.

Many years ago, Ray Kroc, the founder of McDonald's, said, "I don't know what we'll be serving in the year 2000, but we'll be serving more of it than anybody." If Kroc were still alive, he might be surprised that McDonald's menu has not changed that much during the past 45 years. But considering that McDonald's has about 40% of the domestic fast-food market and even more in some countries outside the U.S., his words ring true today.

Questions

1. a. Is McDonald's doing a good job of identifying and satisfying consumer needs?

b. How should McDonald's modify its assortment of products, both domestically and internationally?

2. a. Do you agree with McDonald's decision to continue its global expansion?

b. How should McDonald's marketing strategies be adapted for international expansion?

 www.mcdonalds.com

Sources: Jennifer Ordonez, "McDonald's Appoints Chief Executive of International Division as President," *The Wall Street Journal,* Dec. 3, 1999, p. B10; Andrew Edgecliffe-Johnson, "McDonald's Buys Small Slice of US Pizza Market," *Financial Times,* May 7, 1999, p. 19; David Leonhardt, "Getting off Their McButts," *Business Week,* Feb. 22, 1999, pp. 84, 88; Claire Murphy, "How McDonald's Conquered the UK," *Marketing,* Feb. 18, 1999, pp. 30–31; Louise Kramer, "More-Nimble McDonald's Is Getting Back on Track," *Advertising Age,* Jan. 18, 1999, p. 6; Kevin Helliker and Richard Gibson, "The New Chief Is Ordering Up Changes at McDonald's," *The Wall Street Journal,* Aug. 24, 1998, p. B1; "McDonald's Customizes Food Strategy," *St. Louis Post-Dispatch,* June 7, 1998, p. E8; David Leonhardt, "McDonald's: Can It Regain Its Golden Touch?" *Business Week,* Mar. 9, 1998, pp. 70–74+; Richard Gibson and Matt Moffett, "Why You Won't Find Any Egg McMuffins for Breakfast in Brazil," *The Wall Street Journal,* Oct. 23, 1997, pp. A1, A12; Shelly Branch, "What's Eating McDonald's?" *Fortune,* Oct. 13, 1997, pp. 122–125; Richard Gibson, "Burger Wars Sizzle as McDonald's Clones the Whopper," *The Wall Street Journal,* Sept. 17, 1997, p. B1; Greg Burns, "Fast-Food Fight," *Business Week,* June 2, 1997, pp. 34–36; and Richard Gibson, "Big Price Cut at McDonald's Seems a McFlop," *The Wall Street Journal,* May 9, 1997, pp. B1, B2.

Case 2 • Amazon vs. Barnes and Noble
Booking Sales—and Seeking Profits—on the Internet

As many businesses have learned, the Internet poses an array of new marketing challenges, particularly when trying to sell products online. Nevertheless, it has created a host of opportunities, with numerous—almost countless—upstart entrepreneurs and existing companies seeking success in cyberspace. Two such companies, Amazon.com and Barnes & Noble Inc., are vying for market share in the highly competitive field of online book retailing. Although both companies are generating impressive sales, neither has yet found the formula for online profits. Investors, however, continue to be particularly impressed by Amazon, a company that lives up to its name as the largest current "e-tailer" (the name given to an online retailer).

Amazon.com Makes Its Mark in the Book Industry

When Jeffrey Bezos quit his job on Wall Street and decided to start a new business by selling products over the Internet, he hadn't decided what those products would be. He quickly settled on books and named his company Amazon.com, a reference to the largest river, by volume, in the world. Bezos established the company's headquarters just outside Seattle.

In 1996, its first full year of business, Amazon generated more than $10 million in sales. The company also utilized the advanced technology of the Web to create a differential advantage over other traditional booksellers by offering a variety of unique online services. Open for business 24 hours a day, seven days a week, Amazon shoppers can peruse a database of more than 3 million titles (many times more than the largest superstore) and can search by title, author, or subject.

When making a purchase, customers receive recommendations regarding related or similar titles. Shoppers may provide information to Amazon about their reading preferences and then receive e-mails notifying them of new releases that may be of interest to them. Online visitors are also invited to provide book reviews, one of the main attractions of the site according to many Amazon regulars. By setting up an interactive, easy-to-use website, Amazon has created a "cyber-community" of book lovers to rival even the coziest, well-stocked corner bookshop.

Bezos also decided that Amazon typically would use the Ingram Book Co., a major book wholesaler, to obtain the books ordered by customers. This approach allowed Amazon to carry a very small inventory of best sellers. By having no retail outlets and relatively little warehouse space, Amazon curtailed its overhead costs, allowing it to spend heavily on technology and especially promotion. Bezos said heavy promotion was absolutely essential because it was vital to build market share first and then seek profits later on. Amazon placed ads on a variety of popular websites as well as in traditional media outlets, including the *New York Times Book Review*.

Despite Amazon's features and notoriety, some consumers saw a downside to doing business with the e-tailer. Starting out, Amazon offered most books at 10 to 30% less than a traditional bookstore; however, it added a per-book charge of 95 cents plus a $3 service charge for each order. It took Amazon about a week to deliver a book that was not a best seller, and even longer for more obscure titles. It wasn't long before another giant in the book industry forced Amazon to reevaluate these policies.

Barnes and Noble Takes a Page from Amazon

It was virtually impossible for other booksellers to ignore the success of Amazon.com. In 1997, Barnes & Noble (B&N), the nation's leading bookseller, opened its own online sales site, barnesandnoble.com. The long-time "bricks and mortar" chain certainly noticed that Amazon generated more than $100 million in second-year sales. B&N also saw that following an initial public offering in March 1997, the price of Amazon's stock headed to new heights.

What made Amazon so successful, however, made it fairly simple for B&N to enter online book retailing. B&N already had the necessary bookselling infrastructure in place, not to mention a well-known brand name. Taking many of the best aspects of Amazon's website, B&N designed a user-friendly home page and supplemented it with easy-to-use search engines, online book reviews, and electronic author chats.

When it first began selling online, B&N also beat Amazon on price and delivery. As the largest bookseller in the U.S., B&N receives the lowest wholesale costs from publishers. Thus it started selling all hardcovers at a 30% discount. Amazon felt compelled to match the new lower prices. In addition, because it stocks an enormous inventory of books, B&N was able to shave several days off Amazon's delivery time.

But B&N's expansion into cyberspace raised some concerns for the giant bookseller. For instance, B&N worried that by offering larger discounts online than in its traditional stores, it would irritate its regular bookstore customers and eventually cannibalize its own business.

Barnes and Noble Tests a Novel Concept

The competition between these two booksellers intensified with each passing month. Both Amazon.com and barnesandnoble.com made the list of top 10 online retailers for 1998. However, other start-ups are now clamoring for a piece of the pie as well. And so far, the only companies making a profit are the wholesalers that supply the online booksellers. That explains Barnes & Noble's interest in acquiring the Ingram Book Co., the largest book distributor in the U.S.

Although B&N insisted its purchase of Ingram would improve its ability to serve traditional bookstores as well as its website, industry analysts believe the move was precipitated by B&N's desire to compete with Amazon online. And at the time of B&N's announcement, Amazon was getting 58% of its books from Ingram. If B&N owned Ingram, barnesandnoble.com would be able to ship directly from Ingram to retail customers, delivering most of its orders overnight. Of course, Amazon could do this too—but almost certainly at a higher cost.

Amazon modified its business as well. For instance, it now discounts many titles 40%, and can typically deliver an order within one to three days. However, in order to be more aggressive in its delivery time and to reduce its dependence on Ingram, Amazon significantly enlarged its warehouse space and buys more books directly from publishers, thereby diminishing the importance of Ingram in its marketing channel.

In what might be viewed as an incestuous move, Bertelsmann AG, a German publishing company, purchased a 50% stake in barnesandnoble.com. Bertelsmann is the parent company of the U.S.-based publisher, Random House, which could mean lower wholesale costs for B&N. And every cent counts in the low-margin world of books, especially as online booksellers have yet to turn a profit.

Amazon's Stock Becomes a Bestseller

Facing an alliance of B&N, Bertelsmann, Random House, and Ingram, is Amazon stymied? Not really. For one thing, B&N eventually called off the Ingram deal because of antitrust concerns expressed by federal regulators. Plus, Amazon began discounting bestsellers by an outrageous 50% in order to sustain, perhaps even increase, its online market share. This move particularly irritated B&N's CEO, Leonard Riggio, because Amazon's announcement came only one week prior to barnesandnoble.com's initial public offering (IPO).

Riggio expected B&N to capitalize on Wall Street's love affair with Internet stock offerings. B&N's IPO was disappointing in that the stock price did not rise much over the initial offering price. This scenario resulted in a new term, "getting Amazoned," which means being outsmarted or upstaged by an Internet competitor.

In just one day in December 1998, the market value of Amazon increased 20% as the stock price surged upward. As unfair as it may seem, at that time Amazon's market value was seven times B&N's value, even though B&N had $3 billion in annual sales and a 15% share of the total book market in the U.S. compared to Amazon's $600 million in sales and 3% share. But Wall Street remained enamored with the fact that Amazon.com sold 75% of all books ordered online, compared to just 15% for barnesandnoble.com.

Amazon's New Strategy Speaks Volumes

Apparently, Amazon held off B&N's onslaught in cyberspace. Amazon is winning the battle for online market share. By the year 2000, Amazon had over 8 million registered book customers, about four times the number for barnesandnoble.com.

An analyst for J. P. Morgan said, "Early on, we thought that online sales could be incremental. But now the industry data suggest that online sales are coming at the expense of someone else's market share." Since B&N is the nation's largest retail bookseller, evidently Amazon is luring away many of the giant bookseller's traditional customers. In the last quarter of 1999, barnesandnoble.com's sales surpassed $80 million, three times the level of a year earlier. Despite rising sales, the endeavor remained unprofitable, losing almost $40 million that quarter. Then, for some reason, the online unit changed its name to Barnes & Noble.com. The choice is unusual in that blank spaces are not recognized when they are typed in as part of an Internet domain name.

Not satisfied just with being the largest Internet bookseller, Amazon diversified its offerings to include music, videos, electronics, toys, online auctions, and more. Within days of its entry into the toy business, Amazon became the #1 online retailer of toys. Bezos boldly declared that he wants Amazon to be a place where consumers can find "anything and everything." Besides selling merchandise directly to consumers on its own account, Amazon is entering into alliances with other Internet retailers to broaden the offerings that consumers can acquire at its site. Under this kind of arrangement, a smaller online firm pays Amazon a substantial fee to become a "featured merchant" on the Amazon site. Living.com, for example, is paying Amazon almost $150 million over five years to present its assortment of couches, beds, and related products to Amazon's 16 million customers.

Bezos' sweeping vision may further delay Amazon's becoming profitable; in fact, the firm lost $350 million on sales of about $1 billion in 1999. While closing the book on 1999, Bezos declared that Amazon's original three product lines—books, music, and videos—would generate profits by the end of 2000. Also in December 1999, Bezos was named *Time* magazine's Person of the Year. And just to top it off, Amazon's stock increased 32% in value—compared to the prior month!

"Amazon," which at one time simply referred to the world's largest river, has become a formidable brand name in the world of Internet retailing. The firm intends to use its strong brand to sell a wide assortment of goods and services online. As Amazon extends its breadth, perhaps barnesandnoble.com can gain a differential advantage in online book retailing by stressing its singular focus on books. Already Barnes & Noble.com is testing the concept of same-day deliveries in the borough of Manhattan in New York City. If the test goes well, the company would like to expand this service to take advantage of its national network of warehouses and physical stores. It remains to be seen which retailer is able to sustain an advantage, because the final chapter in this online competition has yet to be written.

www.amazon.com

www.bn.com

Questions

1. How has Amazon integrated the three components of the marketing concept into its organization?

2. a. Describe which factors in the external macroenvironment will significantly affect the future of both Amazon and Barnes & Noble.

   b. How will each individual factor influence the companies' marketing activities?

3. Which of the two firms, Amazon or Barnes & Noble, is in the best position to expand internationally?

Sources: Rebecca Quick, "Barnes & Noble.com's Deficit Widens; Sales Triple with 2002 Profit Forecast," *The Wall Street Journal,* Feb. 9, 2000, p. B12; George Anders, "Amazon Moves into Furniture with Living.com," *The Wall Street Journal,* Feb. 2, 2000, p. B10; Joshua Cooper Ramo, "Jeffrey Preston Bezos: 1999 Person of the Year," *Time,* Dec. 27, 1999, pp. 50+; Joshua Quittner, "An Eye on the Future: Jeff Bezos Merely Wants Amazon.com to Be Earth's Biggest Seller of Everything," *Time,* Dec. 27, 1999, pp. 56+; Rebecca Quick, "Barnesandnoble.com Tests Same-Day Deliveries, *The Wall Street Journal,* Dec. 1, 1999, p. B3; Robert D. Hof, "Amazon.com Throws Open the Doors," *Business Week,* Oct. 11, 1999, p. 44; George Anders, "Amazon Posts $138 Million Loss but Sales Surge," *The Wall Street Journal,* July 22, 1999, p. B6; Nina Munk, "Title Fight," *Fortune,* June 21, 1999, pp. 84–94; "Barnes & Noble Won't Buy Big Book Wholesaler," *St. Louis Post-Dispatch,* June 3, 1999, p. C2; Caroline Daniel, "Low-Tech Book Has Set the Pace for Internet Retailing," *Financial Times,* June 2, 1999, p. X; Yahlin Chang, "Books Caught in the Web," *Newsweek,* Nov. 23, 1998, p. 85; Jodi Mardesich and Marc Gunther, "Is Competition Closing In on Amazon.com?" *Fortune,* Nov. 9, 1998, pp. 229–231; Anthony Bianco, "Virtual Bookstores Start to Get Real," *Business Week,* Oct. 27, 1997, pp. 146, 148; Randall E. Stross, "Why Barnes & Noble May Crush Amazon," *Fortune,* Sept. 29, 1997, pp. 248–250; Michael H. Martin, "The Next Big Thing: A Bookstore?" *Fortune,* Dec. 9, 1996, pp. 168–170; and G. Bruce Knecht, "How Wall Street Whiz Found a Niche Selling Books on the Internet," *The Wall Street Journal,* May 16, 1996, pp. A1, A12.

Identifying and Selecting Markets 2

An examination of the people and organizations who buy, how they buy, and the methods used to learn more about them

Our analysis of marketing began with an emphasis on the customer. And for good reason: virtually all successful organizations place a very high priority on satisfying customers. It stands to reason that the more an organization knows about its potential customers, the greater the likelihood that it will be able to satisfy them. So now we move to an identification and examination of customers—both individuals and organizations.

We will investigate how an organization identifies its intended customers—its target markets. To do this, we begin with a description of consumer markets and consumer decision making in Chapter 4. Chapter 5 covers business markets and organizational buying behavior. In Chapter 6 we introduce the concepts critical to developing marketing strategy in both consumer and business markets—market segmentation, target-marketing strategies, and positioning. Part 2 concludes with Chapter 7 on market and marketing research, with a discussion of how organizations gather and make use of information.

4

Consumer Markets and Buying Behavior

"Why is it so difficult to make a car (or truck) that consumers want to buy? At least part of the answer lies in the difficulty of understanding consumers' needs and desires."

Do the Plans at **Volkswagen** Risk Exterminating the Bug?

Automobile manufacturers have a hard time deciding what consumers want. It seems for every success, like the Ford Taurus or Honda Accord, there are many more flops. Why is it so difficult to make a car (or truck) that consumers want to buy? At least part of the answer lies in the difficulty of understanding consumers' needs and desires.

The car or truck a person drives says a lot about them. A vehicle is expensive and publicly consumed, so it serves an expressive as well as a functional role for consumers. An automobile consultant observed, "Baby boomers buy in a herd. A vehicle gets anointed as the one to buy." The "in" sedans are foreign imports from Japan and Europe. A 34-year-old law professor described her choice of a car by saying "I don't want to be seen getting out of a Ford; a Honda is cooler." Thus, the image of a car brand and who else owns a particular model is as important as its functionality. The problem for the "out" brands is how to change the attitudes of consumers.

Pickup trucks, sport utility vehicles (SUVs), and minivans were extremely successful in the 1990s, accounting for 45% of total vehicle sales to consumers. As a result, auto manufacturers have invested in additional models such as the Cadillac Escalade, Buick Rendezvous, Lincoln Navigator, and bigger versions of existing SUVs such as the Ford Expedition. However, developments in the environment, like global warming, and higher car insurance rates for large vehicles may have an impact on future demand.

Tastes may also be changing. Some carmakers believe consumers have grown bored with trucks as they observe a resurgence in demand for station wagons. Equally important, the demographics of the consumers who buy these vehicles are changing. Because they are purchased primarily as "people haulers," minivans and SUVs lose their attraction as the kids grow up and leave home. The baby boomers, who made these vehicles successful in the 1980s, will soon be empty nesters. Will they opt for the greater comfort and prestige of imported sedans?

Into this scene Volkswagen introduced a reborn Beetle. Today's version has little in common with its inspiration of 40 years ago except a similar look. It is bigger, more powerful, and has air-conditioning and a six-speaker stereo as standard equipment. Volkswagen of America president, Clive Warrilow, observed, "Where the original Beetle provided basic transportation, the new Beetle is an up-market, lifestyle vehicle."

The new VW "Bug" has found buyers among baby boomers, many of whom once owned the original version, as well as young people looking for a nontraditional compact car. As a result, it has breathed new life into the VW line. Annual sales are increasing at 50% a year in the U.S., reaching over 300,000 vehicles. The management of VW is anxious to capitalize on this surge of popularity, and has formulated plans to introduce a minivan, a full-size pickup with carlike amenities, and a luxury sedan. However, not everyone is in agreement. Some executives think that these additions will compete with existing VW models and the company's other auto lines (VW owns Audi). More important, they fear that these models could undermine the quirky, offbeat image the Beetle has cultivated among consumers, making it seem ordinary and result in VW being perceived as just another car company lost in the shuffle.[1]

Volkswagen and other carmakers are faced with trying to predict and influence consumer behavior. To accomplish that, what do they need to know?

 www.volkswagen.com

The total market is divided into two broad segments, consumers and businesses. In this chapter we examine the consumer market, and in Chapter 5 we will discuss the business market. First, we will describe today's consumers, highlighting recent demographic changes that are influencing marketing. As Volkswagen and other auto manufacturers have discovered, these changes can have profound effects on performance. Then we will examine how consumers go about making purchase decisions, a process influenced by information sources, social environment, psychological forces, and situational factors.

After studying this chapter, you should be able to explain:

- The factors that are commonly used by marketers to describe the consumer market.
- Important changes taking place within the consumer market.
- How consumers make purchase decisions.
- The situational factors that influence consumers' decisions.

The Consumer Market

Ultimate consumers buy goods and services for their own personal or household use. In the U.S., there are over 270 million consumers, living in 100 million households. They spend over $5.5 trillion a year on goods and services. The efforts of many marketers are focused on these (or more likely a subset of these) potential customers.

The consumer market is not only large, it is dynamic. Consider that the U.S. is the fastest-growing industrialized nation, and that every hour there are 445 births, 274 deaths, and 95 new immigrants.[2] These statistics convert to a net change of over half a million people a month in the mix of consumers. Thus, the first challenge is to gain an understanding of what this market looks like and how it is changing. To develop an appreciation of this dynamic consumer market, we will examine its geographic distribution, several demographic dimensions, and some representative behaviors.

Geographic Distribution

About 16% of the U.S. population moves to a different home every year. Marketing executives monitor current patterns and projected trends in the regional distribution of the population in order to make decisions that range from where to locate retail stores to the appropriate mix of products to offer. The largest population concentrations are in the eastern half of the country, as they always have been. However, the greatest rate of population growth over the past four decades has occurred in the Southern and Western regions. Figure 4.1 shows the states projected to grow at the fastest rates between 2000 and 2010. By the year 2010, the four most populous states will be California, Texas, New York, and Florida, in that order.

The Rural Population

Rural areas of the U.S. lost population to the cities for decades, but this trend seems to have reversed. In the 1990s nearly four times as many Americans took up residence in rural areas as in the 1980s. Rural areas, although they contain only about one-fourth the total population, are now growing at nearly the same rate as cities. There are several explanations for this development. One is the growth in employment opportunities on the outer edges of large urban areas. People can take advantage of these jobs while still living in the country. Another factor is the growing number of retirees who are leaving the cities for rural areas with smaller communities and slower-paced life-styles.

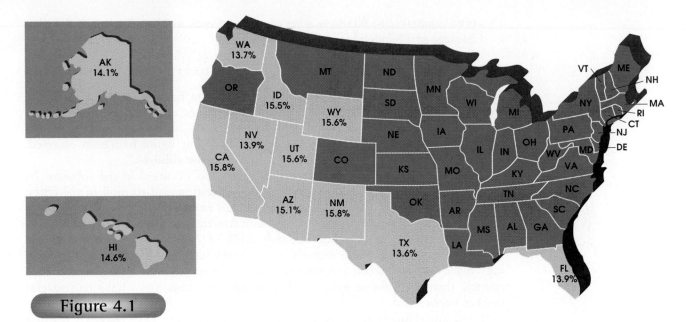

Figure 4.1

The twelve states expected to grow at the fastest rates between 2000 and 2010, with their projected population increases.

Source: *Statistical Abstract of the United States: 1999*, 119th ed., U.S. Bureau of the Census, Washington, DC, 1999, p. 35.

Rather than view the increasing popularity of rural living as a temporary adjustment, some see it as a gradual deconcentration of the U.S. population. With advances in communication technology and the decline in industrial jobs, the need for people to concentrate in small areas is greatly diminished. As a result, the population may be slowly moving toward a country of smaller, more widely dispersed cities and towns.

There is also a change in the mix of the rural population. In the past, young adults migrated from rural to urban areas, and the primary source of replacements was births. Now the replacements of young adults leaving rural areas come largely from older adults moving away from urban areas.[3] Certainly these are developments to watch because changes in the size and mix of the rural population have many implications. For example, retailers such as Kmart and Wal-Mart that depend on masses of customers must consider these shifts as store locations and the assortment of merchandise are selected. On the other hand, catalog retailers and merchants using the Internet to reach customers are likely beneficiaries of this shift.

The Urban Population

About 75% of the U.S. population live in large urban areas. Recognizing the importance of the urban population, the federal government established a three-part classification of metropolitan areas. Observing trends within these classifications provides marketers with a means of identifying growing and declining areas. The three categories are as follows:

- The **Metropolitan Statistical Area (MSA)** is the basic urban unit. An MSA has a city with at least 50,000 residents and a total area population of at least 100,000. The boundaries of an MSA are drawn along county lines and may cross state borders. But the counties must be socially and economically integrated, and virtually all employment must be nonagricultural. There are about 255 MSAs. Of the 25 areas projected to grow the fastest, only two (Orem, Utah, and Tacoma, Washington) are outside the South or Southwest.[4]

- A **Primary Metropolitan Statistical Area (PMSA)** is an MSA that has a population of at least 1 million. About 70 of the largest MSAs are categorized as PMSAs.

- A **Consolidated Metropolitan Statistical Area (CMSA)** is a giant urban center consisting of two or more adjacent PMSAs. The hub of each of the approximately 20 CMSAs is a very large city such as New York, Los Angeles, Chicago, or Philadelphia.

The Suburban Population

As metropolitan areas have grown, their composition has also changed. The central cities are growing very slowly, and in some cases older, established parts of the cities are actually losing population. In 1950, 60% of the people living in metropolitan areas lived in the central city. By 1990 that figure had been reversed, with over 65% of metropolitan residents living in the suburbs.

Most of the real growth in the last 25 years has occurred in the suburbs. As families moved to the suburbs to escape the congestion and turmoil in the cities, the economic, racial, and ethnic compositions of many cities (especially the core areas) changed. For example, 60% of African American households live in the central cities of large metro areas, but only 25% of African American households reside in the suburbs. More recently, the suburbs have expanded outward, creating "inner-ring" suburban communities that are more like the urban centers they encircle than the affluent suburbs. The changes in these areas have had several market implications.

First, suburbanites are more likely than city dwellers to have two cars because of the unavailability of mass transit. They also are inclined to spend more leisure time at home, so they are a big market for home entertainment and recreation.

Second, services providers typically locate close to their markets. That's why retail services firms such as banks, fast-food establishments, florists, and travel agents open branches or start new ventures in the suburbs. In addition, many investment and insurance brokers, realtors, physicians and dentists, and other professional service firms have left the central cities to pursue suburbanites.

The slow but steady migration of retailers to the suburbs created a void in many inner cities, and led to the assumption that inner cities have little market potential. However, that view may be changing. The Initiative for a Competitive Inner City (ICIC) has identified several advantages inner-city locations offer businesses. Of particular interest to retailers are a ready supply of employees and underserved markets. For example, inner-city residents annually spend $85 billion, but more than 25% of that spending is done with retailers outside the inner city.[5]

Another important urban development has been the relocation of sports and entertainment facilities in the downtown area. Cities such as Baltimore and San

In 1992, Camden Yard was erected in downtown Baltimore to serve as the home of the Baltimore Orioles major league baseball team. Total annual attendance for baseball, which seldom exceeded 1 million for a full season before Camden Yard, has not dropped below 3 million since the stadium opened. The consumers attracted by the events in the stadium have reinvigorated the downtown area.

Francisco are contributing to the rejuvenation of the inner city by attracting crowds to sporting events and concerts with facilities like Camden Yard and Three Com Stadium.

Consumer Demographics

Demographics are the vital statistics that describe a population. Marketers make use of a variety of demographic characteristics including age, gender, family life cycle, education, income, and ethnicity. They are important to marketers because they are closely related to the demand for many products.

Changes in demographics signal the rise of new markets and the elimination of others. Some noteworthy demographic developments and their significance for marketers are described below.

Age

As was pointed out in Chapter 2, the U.S. population is getting older. The marketing implications of this aging trend are substantial. Many companies recognize that the 50-and-over group possesses one-half of the discretionary income and more than three-quarters of the total financial assets in the U.S.[6] Thus investment firms such as Merrill Lynch, Paine Webber, and Shearson Lehman are especially targeting this segment of the population in their promotional campaigns. Movie theaters and ski resorts offer discounts to people over 65. Internationally, Best Western, a worldwide association of independently owned and operated motels and hotels, has used "dependable lodging on a retirement budget" as an advertising theme.

Family Life Cycle

Family life-cycle stages, the various forms families can take over time, are major determinants of behavior. A single-parent family (divorced, widowed, or never married) with dependent children faces social and economic problems quite different from those of a two-parent family. Young married couples with no children typically devote large shares of their income to clothing, autos, and recreation. When children start arriving, expenditure patterns shift as many young families buy and furnish a home. Families with teenagers find larger portions of the budget going for food, clothing, and educational needs.

Researchers have identified nine distinct life-cycle stages with different buying behavior:[7]

- *Bachelor stage:* young, single people
- *Young married:* couples with no children
- *Full nest I:* young married couples with children
- *Single parents:* young or middle-aged people with dependent children
- *Divorced and alone:* divorced without dependent children
- *Middle-aged married:* middle-aged married couples without children
- *Full nest II:* middle-aged married couples with dependent children
- *Empty nest:* older married couples with no children living with them
- *Older single:* single people still working or retired

Rapidly growing groups that reflect our changing life-styles are singles, single-parent households, and mingles—unmarried couples of the opposite sex living together. The Census Bureau reports that over 80 million adults are unmarried, nearly twice as many as in 1970. The number of singles households is also increasing at a much faster rate than family households. The impact that single people of either sex have on the market is demonstrated by the availability of such services as apartments for singles, social clubs for singles, and special tours, cruises, and eating places seeking the patronage of singles.

There are projected to be 9 million single-parent households with children under 18 by 2010, an increase of 10% from the number in 2000. Although they typically have less money to spend than traditional households, more purchase decisions and a greater proportion of actual purchases are made by the children in these families. As a result, advertisers that normally focus on adults are increasingly looking for ways to reach children.

Singles in the 25 to 39 age bracket are especially attractive to marketers because they are such a large and affluent group. However, marketing to singles can be tricky. As Campbell Soup found out, even a good product can send the wrong message. When its Soup for One, a single-serving can of soup, didn't do well, a focus group explained why. Participants called it the "lonely soup." They liked the product but hated the name, because it reminded them that they would be eating alone.[8]

The number of mingles increased by more than 45% during the 1990s, reaching a total of 4.1 million couples. They still represent only a small part (4%) of all households. Nevertheless, the social and demographic phenomenon of mingles bears watching.

Education and Income

Education has a significant impact on income. A high school diploma is worth about $600,000 in additional income over a lifetime, and a college degree is worth $1.5 million. For families where both spouses work (that is, over half of all the couples in the U.S.), these earnings figures can be doubled. About 80% of Americans over 25 have completed high school, and 25% have at least a bachelor's degree. Combine these observations with the fact that 15 million Americans are enrolled in institutions of higher learning, an increase of 50% over just 20 years ago, and it suggests that the U.S. population is well educated and prosperous.

However, these figures don't represent the complete picture. In spite of the considerable increase in disposable income in the past 30 years, 37 million people (about 14% of the population) live below the government-defined poverty level. And the situation may get worse. It was recently reported that 90 million Americans over age 16 lack the basic skills necessary to hold a moderately demanding job.[9] Besides impacting earning potential, the skill deficiencies are also likely to affect these consumers' ability to perform such marketing-related tasks as reading package labels, understanding advertising messages, and following product directions.

Knowing what is happening to incomes is important because spending patterns are influenced by how much income people have. Here are some findings from Department of Labor studies of consumer spending:

- For all product categories, people in a given income bracket spend significantly more *total* dollars than those in lower brackets. However, the lower-income households devote a larger *percentage* of their total expenditures to some product categories, such as housing.

- In each successively higher-income group, the amount spent for food declines as a percentage of total expenditures.

- The percentage of total expenditures devoted to the total of housing, utilities, and home operation remains reasonably constant in the middle- and high-income brackets.

- The percentage of total expenditures for transportation, including the purchase of automobiles, tends to grow as incomes increase in low- and middle-income groups. The proportion levels off or drops a bit in higher-income brackets.

- In each successively higher-income group, a smaller percentage of total family expenditures goes for health care, but a higher percentage goes for insurance and pensions.

Consumer product companies link their brands with well-known celebrities to reach specific markets. In addition to pop star Ricky Martin, pictured here, Pepsi has also recently employed the band KISS, baseball players Ken Griffey, Jr., and Sammy Sosa, and race driver Jeff Gordon. Take a look at the Pepsi website and see who the most recent celebrity endorsers are. Why does a firm such as Pepsi use this method of influence?

 www.pepsi.com

Race and Ethnicity

In many cities, the ethnic population is especially large. African Americans, Hispanics, and Asians constitute over 50% of the population in 25 of the nation's largest cities. These cities include Los Angeles, San Antonio, New Orleans, Miami, Atlanta, Baltimore, Washington, DC, Detroit, and Chicago. During the 1990s, ethnic minorities accounted for nearly 70% of total U.S. population growth.[10]

Segmenting markets based on ethnicity presents an interesting challenge. On the one hand, a company must understand an ethnic group's buying behavior and motivation. Studies by the Bureau of Labor Statistics and private research firms show that there are some distinct differences among races. For example, on average, African American and white Americans differ in income, level of education, and the likelihood of living in urban or rural areas. In addition, in some product categories, spending is distinctly different. Compared to whites, African Americans as a group spend a greater portion of their income on meat, poultry, fish, sugar and other sweets, personal care products, laundry and cleaning products, and children's apparel, and less on entertainment, medical services, household furnishings, and alcoholic beverages.[11]

On the other hand, ethnic markets are not homogeneous units any more than any other population segment consisting of 20 or 30 million people. There is nearly as much diversity within every ethnic group as there is similarity. African American and Hispanic markets contain subgroups based on income, occupation, geographic location, and life-cycle stage. Thus, it would be a serious marketing error to be misled by aggregate figures and averages. For example, firms that make products for which skin color is a major choice determinant recognize this diversity. Prescriptives, a subsidiary of Estée Lauder cosmetic company, has a line of makeup foundations for black women with 115 different shades.[12]

Figure 4.2

The consumer buying-decision process and the factors that influence it.

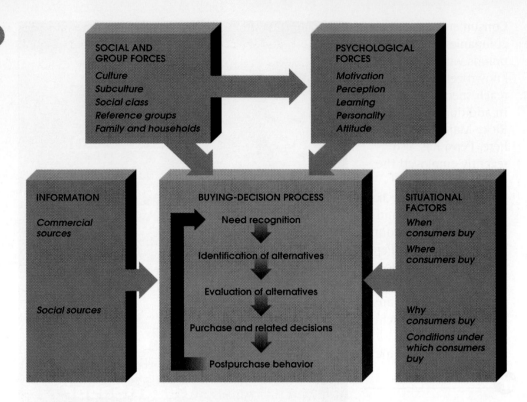

This broad overview of the consumer market is intended to suggest its vibrancy and diversity. It also indicates that there are many ways to describe consumers. A challenge faced by marketers, which we will discuss in detail in Chapter 6, is how to most effectively describe particular markets. But first, let's continue our examination of consumers with a look at their decision making.

Consumer Decision Making

Why is consumer marketing difficult? We've just described one reason: The mix of people in the market is constantly changing. Not only is it difficult to anticipate what marketing program will work, but what worked yesterday may not work today—or tomorrow. Another challenge is understanding how consumers make decisions. This is reflected in the chapter-opening case about Volkswagen. There is a strong market for cars and trucks, but because of past experiences, current beliefs, and changes in their lives, consumers can be quite unpredictable. Thus, Volkswagen and all other marketers must constantly improve their understanding of consumers and adapt their strategies.

Figure 4.2 brings all the dimensions of buying behavior together in a model that provides the structure for our discussion. The model features the buying-decision process and the four primary forces that influence each stage.

The Consumer Buying-Decision Process

To deal with the marketing environment and make purchases, consumers engage in a decision process. One way to look at that process is to view it as problem solving. When faced with a problem that can be resolved through a purchase ("I'm bored. How do I satisfy my need for entertainment?"), the consumer goes through a series of logical stages to arrive at a decision.

As shown in the center of Figure 4.2, the stages of the **consumer buying-decision process** are:

1. *Need recognition.* The consumer is moved to action by a need.

2. *Identification of alternatives.* The consumer identifies alternative products and brands and collects information about them.

3. *Evaluation of alternatives.* The consumer weighs the pros and cons of the alternatives identified.

4. *Decisions.* The consumer decides to buy or not to buy and makes other decisions related to the purchase.

5. *Postpurchase behavior.* The consumer seeks reassurance that the choice made was the correct one.

Although this model is a useful starting point for examining purchase decisions, the process is not always as straightforward as it may appear. Consider these possible variations:

- The consumer can withdraw at any stage prior to the actual purchase if the need diminishes or no satisfactory alternatives are available.
- The stages usually are of different lengths, may overlap, and some may even be skipped.
- The consumer is often involved in several different buying decisions simultaneously, and the outcome of one can affect the others.

A significant factor influencing how consumer decisions are made is the consumer's **level of involvement,** reflected in the amount of effort that is expended in satisfying a need. Some situations are *high* involvement. That is, when a need arises a consumer decides to actively collect and evaluate information about the purchase situation. These purchases entail all five stages of the buying-decision process.

Although it is risky to generalize because consumers are so different, involvement tends to be *greater* under any of the following conditions:

- The consumer lacks information about alternatives for satisfying the need.
- The consumer considers the amount of money involved to be large.
- The product has considerable social importance.
- The product is seen as having a potential for providing significant benefits.

Most buying decisions are for relatively low-priced products that have close, acceptable substitutes and therefore do not meet any of these conditions. These are *low*-involvement situations, in which the consumer either skips or moves very quickly through stages 2 and 3 of the decision process—identification of alternatives and evaluation of alternatives. Typical examples of low-involvement situations are the majority of purchases made in supermarkets, variety stores, and hardware stores.

The notion of involvement raises two important marketing issues: loyalty and impulse purchases. **Loyalty** exists when a consumer, because of past experience, is sufficiently satisfied with a particular brand or retailer that he or she buys that brand or from that retailer when the need arises without considering other alternatives. This is low-involvement purchasing because the decision does not involve gathering and analyzing information. However, the product may be very important to the consumer.

Impulse buying, or purchasing with little or no advance planning, is also a form of low-involvement decision making. A shopper waiting in the checkout line at a grocery store who notices the headline "Plane Missing since 1939 Lands at LaGuardia" on an issue of *Weekly World News* and purchases a copy to satisfy his or her curiosity is engaging in impulse buying. Self-service, open-display retailing has conditioned shoppers to do more impulse buying. Marketing researchers have found that an increasingly large proportion of purchases are unplanned. Consider, for example, how many of your purchases are unplanned (or impulsive). Because of the growth of this type of low-involvement purchasing, greater emphasis must be placed on promotional programs such as in-store videos demonstrating product benefits. Also, displays and packages must be made appealing, because they serve as silent sales people.

In the following discussion we examine the complete five-stage process that characterizes high-involvement buying decisions. However, keep in mind that the stages may have to be adjusted to fit the circumstances of a particular purchase situation. For a wealthy person, the purchase of a country club membership could be a low-involvement experience, whereas for a person with a high need for social acceptance, purchase of toothpaste might be highly involving. Thus involvement must be viewed from the perspective of the consumer, not the product.

Recognition of an Unsatisfied Need

Everyone has unsatisfied needs and wants that create discomfort. Some needs can be satisfied by acquiring and consuming goods and services. Thus the process of deciding what to buy begins when a need that can be satisfied through consumption becomes strong enough to motivate a person. This need recognition may arise internally (for example, when you feel hungry). Or the need may be dormant until it is aroused by an external stimulus, such as an ad or the sight of a product. The decision process can also be triggered by the depletion of an existing product (your pen runs out of ink) or dissatisfaction with a product currently being used.

Becoming aware of a need, however, is not enough to generate a purchase. As consumers we have many needs and wants, but finite amounts of time and money. Thus there is competition among our needs.

Identification of Alternatives

Once a need has been recognized, the consumer must next identify the alternatives capable of satisfying the need. Typically alternative products are identified first, and then alternative brands are identified. Product and brand identification may range from a simple memory scan of previous experiences to an extensive external search.

The search for alternatives is influenced by:

- How much information the consumer already has from past experiences and other sources.
- The consumer's confidence in that information.
- The expected value of additional information or, put another way, what more information is worth in terms of the time and money to get it.

Evaluation of Alternatives

When a satisfactory number of alternatives have been identified, the consumer must evaluate them before making a decision. The evaluation may involve a single criterion, or several criteria, against which the alternatives are compared. For example, you might select a frozen dinner on price alone or on price, taste, and ease of preparation. When multiple criteria are involved, they typically do not carry equal weight. For example, preparation time might be more important than nutrition.

Because experience is often limited or dated and information from sources such as advertising or friends can be biased, evaluations can be factually incorrect. That is, a consumer may believe that the price of brand A is higher than that of brand B, when in fact the opposite is true. Marketers monitor consumers to determine what choice criteria they use, to identify any changes that may be taking place in their criteria or priorities, and to correct any unfavorable misperceptions.

Purchase and Related Decisions

After searching and evaluating, the consumer must decide whether to buy. Thus the first outcome is the decision to purchase or not to purchase the alternative evaluated as most desirable. If the decision is to buy, a series of related decisions must be made regarding features, where and when to make the actual transaction,

Will self-scanning benefit consumers and retailers?

When electronic scanning at retail store checkout counters was introduced, it was hailed as a way to reduce labor costs for the merchants, save time for consumers, and reduce human errors when ringing up prices. However, subsequent studies uncovered that discrepancies between the posted price and the price charged by the scanners occur with disturbing frequency. As a result, consumers have grown skeptical.

Grocery retailers are testing a device that could help alleviate consumers' concerns by increasing their involvement in the checkout procedure and still provide the stores with substantial cost savings. When they enter the store consumers are provided with a handheld scanner that looks like a telephone receiver. The shopper scans each selected item as it is dropped in the shopping cart. Items can also be "unscanned" if the customer changes his or her mind. When the shopping is completed, the scanner prints a bill and the customer pays by swiping a credit card through the scanner.

The benefits of self-scanning are that it makes the checkout procedure quicker and less labor intensive. But there are some potential problems as well. The most obvious is theft. However, when the device was tested in supermarkets in the Netherlands, overall theft from the stores actually declined. Other problems are mistakes by consumers, for example, forgetting to delete an item returned to the shelf, and the added effort required of the customer. Albertson's, a U.S. grocery chain is testing the concept.

Which dimensions of the consumer decision-making process will U.S. retailers have to address to make this concept work?

Sources: Tara Parker-Pope, "New Devices Add Up Bill, Measure Shoppers' Honesty," *The Wall Street Journal*, June 6, 1995, pp. B11+; "Scanners More Accurate, but Consumers Beware," *Columbia Daily Tribune*, Dec. 17, 1998, p. 12B.

---

how to take delivery or possession, the method of payment, and other issues. So the decision to make a purchase is really the beginning of an entirely new series of decisions that may be as time-consuming and difficult as the initial one.

Alert marketers recognize that the outcome of these additional decisions affects satisfaction, so they find ways to help consumers make them as efficiently as possible. For example, car dealers have speeded up loan approval, streamlined the process of tracking down a car that meets the buyer's exact specifications, and, in the case of Saturn, made delivery of the car a "miniceremony" to make the customer feel important.

Selecting a source from which to make a purchase is one of the buying decisions. Sources can be as varied as Internet websites or manufacturers' outlets. The most common source is a retail store, and the reasons a consumer chooses to shop at a certain store are called **patronage buying motives.**

People want to feel comfortable when they shop. They want the assurance of being around people like themselves and in an environment that reflects their values. There are consumers, for example, who would feel uncomfortable shopping in an upscale store such as I. Magnin or Bergdorf-Goodman.

Patronage motives can range from something as simple as convenience when you want a soft drink, to something more complex, such as the atmosphere of a restaurant. Some common patronage motives are:

- Location convenience
- Service speed
- Merchandise accessibility
- Crowding
- Prices

- Merchandise assortment
- Services offered
- Store appearance
- Sales personnel
- Mix of other shoppers

Like the criteria consumers use to choose products and brands, their patronage motives will vary depending on the purchase situation. Successful retailers evaluate their customers carefully and design their stores accordingly. For example, some shoppers might be surprised to learn that such different apparel outlets as Limited, Lerner New York, Lane Bryant, Henri Bendel, Structure, Galyan's, and Express are part of The Limited Corp. A manufacturer, in turn, selects retailers with the patronage characteristics that complement its product and appeal to its market.

Firms selling on the Internet must also identify and appeal to patronage motives. For example, one of the features attributed to Internet shopping is convenience. Thus it's essential that a firm's website be easy to access and navigate. Fancy, animated graphics may be pretty, but they may not be what Internet shoppers are seeking.

Postpurchase Behavior

What a consumer learns from going through the buying process has an influence on how he or she will behave the next time the same need arises. Furthermore, new opinions and beliefs have been formed and old ones have been revised. It's this change in the consumer that is indicated by an arrow in Figure 4.2 from the *postpurchase behavior* stage of the buying-decision process model back to the need-recognition stage.

Something else often occurs following a purchase. Have you ever gone through a careful decision process for a major purchase, selected what you thought was the best alternative, but then had doubts about your choice after the purchase? What you were experiencing is **postpurchase cognitive dissonance**—a state of anxiety brought on by the difficulty of choosing from among alternatives. Unfortunately for marketers, dissonance is quite common, and if the anxiety is not relieved, the consumer may be unhappy with the chosen product even if it performs as expected!

Postpurchase cognitive dissonance occurs when each of the alternatives seriously considered by the consumer has both attractive and unattractive features. For example, in purchasing tires, the set selected may be the most expensive (unattractive), but they provide better traction on wet roads (attractive). The brand not chosen was recommended by a friend (attractive), but came with a very limited warranty (unattractive). After the purchase is made, the unattractive features of the product purchased grow in importance in the consumer's mind, as do the attractive features offered by the rejected alternatives. As a result, we begin to doubt the wisdom of the choice and experience anxiety over the decision. Internet shoppers may be especially prone to dissonance because they are unable to physically examine or test the product. Dissonance typically increases (1) the greater the importance of the purchase decision and (2) the greater the similarity between the item selected and item(s) rejected. Thus buying a house or car is likely to create more dissonance than buying a TV set.

Consumers try to reduce their postpurchase anxieties. They avoid information (such as ads for the rejected products) that is likely to increase the dissonance. And they seek out information that supports their decision, such as reassurance from friends. For Internet shoppers, the use of electronic shopping agents, known as bots, to compare prices and find the best deals may reduce postpurchase dissonance.[13] Also, prior to the purchase, putting more effort into evaluating alternatives can increase a consumer's confidence and reduce dissonance. Sellers can reduce the likelihood of dissonance with guarantees and liberal return policies, high-quality postsale service programs, and reassuring communications after the purchase.

With this background on the buying-decision process, we can examine what influences buying behavior. We'll begin with the sources and types of information used by consumers.

 www.botspot.com

Information and Purchase Decisions

Purchase decisions require information. Until consumers know what products and brands are available, what features and benefits they offer, who sells them at what prices, and where they can be purchased, there won't be a decision process because there won't be any decisions to make.

As shown in Figure 4.2, there are two sources of buying information—the commercial environment and the social environment. The **commercial information environment** consists of all marketing organizations and individuals that attempt to communicate with consumers. It includes manufacturers, retailers, advertisers, and sales people whenever any of them are engaged in efforts to inform or persuade.

Advertising is the most familiar type of commercial information. In the U.S., $200 billion is spent every year on advertising of all types.[14] It's estimated that on average, the typical adult is exposed to about 300 ad messages a day, or almost 10,000 per month.[15] Commercial sources also include retail store clerks, business websites, and telephone solicitors as well as consumers' physical involvement with products, such as trial product use and sampling.

The **social information environment** is comprised of family, friends, and acquaintances who directly or indirectly provide information about products. To appreciate the marketing significance of these social sources, consider how often your conversations with friends or family deal with purchases you are considering or have made.

The most common kind of social information is word-of-mouth communication—two or more people discussing a product. "Chat rooms" on the Internet have become popular places for consumers with similar interests to gather and exchange information. Other social sources include observing others using products and exposure to products in the homes of others. Recognizing the power of word-of-mouth communication, marketers try to stimulate it. For example, Daewoo, the Korean carmaker, and adidas, among other firms, have hired student representatives on college campuses to encourage more informal exposure to their products.

When all the different types of information are considered, it becomes apparent that there is enormous competition for the consumer's attention. Consequently, the consumer's mind has to be marvelously efficient to sort and process this barrage of information. To better understand consumer behavior, we will begin by examining the social and group forces that influence the individual's psychological makeup and also play a role in specific buying decisions.

Social Influences

The ways we think, believe, and act are determined to a great extent by social forces. And our individual buying decisions—including the needs we experience, the alternatives we consider, and the ways in which we evaluate them—are affected by the social forces that surround us. To reflect this dual impact, the arrows in Figure 4.2 extend from the social forces in two directions—to the psychological makeup of the individual and to the buying-decision process. Our description begins with culture, the force with the most *indirect* impact, and moves to the force with the most *direct* impact, the household.

Culture

Culture is a set of symbols and artifacts created by a society and handed down from generation to generation as determinants and regulators of human behavior. The symbols may be intangible (attitudes, beliefs, values, language) or tangible (tools, housing, products, works of art). Although culture does not include instinctive biological acts, the way people perform instinctive acts such as eating is culturally influenced. Thus, everybody gets hungry, but what, when, and how people eat vary among cultures. For example, in the Ukraine, raw pig fat is considered a delicacy.

Cultures do change over time, as old patterns gradually give way to the new. During recent years in the U.S., cultural trends of far-reaching magnitude have occurred. Marketing executives must be alert to these changes so they can adjust their planning to be in step with, or even a little ahead of, the times. Some cul-

How much standardization is enough?

There is a vexing contradiction for marketers moving from a domestic to an international strategy—consumers around the world are both the same and different. For example, there is a high demand for cosmetics nearly everywhere, but the notion of what looks or smells good can be quite different from country to country. Likewise, spectator sports are popular in virtually all countries, but the sports of choice are often quite different. Many firms have found, sometimes after considerable trial and error, what works very well at home may have to be modified substantially to please customers in a new region. Several examples are described below:

- Domino's Pizza found that the "bigger the better" philosophy in the U.S. did not appeal to Germans who prefer smaller, individual pizzas. In Japan the firm had difficulty until it introduced local favorite toppings like squid, and sweet mayonnaise and potatoes. In India pickled vinegar is a popular pizza flavoring.

- McDonald's added wine to its menu in France, beer in Germany and Austria, and Cadbury chocolates to its ice cream desserts in England.

- Pillsbury sells canned sweet corn in the U.S. and advertises it as primarily a hot side dish. The ads have to be changed when the same product is sold elsewhere because the French prefer corn cold in a salad, the British put it on sandwiches, and Koreans sprinkle it on ice cream.

- Frito-Lay's orange and cheesy-tasting Cheetos are cheeseless in China where the more popular flavors of the product are Peking duck and fried egg.

- One of Ben & Jerry's most popular U.S. flavors, chocolate chip cookie dough, was a flop in Britain. The company introduced instead a concoction of vanilla ice cream, strawberries, and chocolate-covered Scottish shortbread.

What's the basis for these consumer differences? Some may be physiological. For example, many Chinese are lactose intolerant so cheese-based Cheetos are difficult to digest. However most are the result of culture, perception, learning, and attitudes. International marketers have found it is usually easier to conform to local behavior than it is to try to change it.

Sources: "Think Globally, Bake Locally," *Fortune,* Oct. 14, 1996, p. 205; Tara Parker-Pope, "Custom-Made," *The Wall Street Journal,* Sept. 26, 1996, pp. R22+.

---

tural trends affecting the buying behavior of U.S. consumers in recent years include the following:[16]

- *Time has become as valuable as money.* Americans feel overcommitted, with more obligations and demands on their time than they can fulfill. This has contributed to the growth in time-saving services (such as home cleaning services and Internet shopping) and labor-saving products (such as prepared entrées in grocery store delis).

- *Two-income families are the norm.* When both adults in a household work outside the home, it affects not only the ability to buy but also the choice of products and the time in which to buy and consume them. It has also created a demand for preschools and day-care centers.

- *Gender roles are losing their identity.* This is reflected in educational opportunities, occupations, clothing styles, sports participation, and language.

- *Youthfulness is admired.* To be thought of as younger than your chronological age (once you're over 21!) is seen by most as a compliment. To remain healthy and free from disease, more Americans have made exercise a regular part of their lives.

Subcultures

In any society as heterogeneous as the U.S., there are bound to be subcultures. **Subcultures** are groups in a culture that exhibit characteristic behavior patterns

Meeting the shared needs of a heterogeneous population often requires marketers to adapt. Citibank, with about 1,900 proprietary ATMs in the United States and 3,000 worldwide, is faced with interesting challenges. In addition to conducting transactions in English, Spanish, Greek, Korean, and Chinese, the bank is developing audio-equipped ATMs that give voice instructions through earphones to vision-impaired users who can't read on-screen information.

sufficient to distinguish them from other groups within the same culture. The behavior patterns that distinguish subcultures are based on factors such as race, nationality, religion, and urban-rural identification. Some of these were discussed earlier in the chapter in the context of demographic market forces.

A subculture takes on importance in marketing if it constitutes a significant part of the population and specific purchasing patterns can be traced to it. For example, increasing attention is being paid in the U.S. to behavioral influences stemming from racial and ethnic subcultures. Early immigrants came to America primarily from Europe. Now the principal sources are Asia and Latin America. West Coast cities have had large Chinese and Japanese populations for over a century. The new wave of Asian immigrants, however, includes people from Korea, Vietnam, and Thailand. The U.S. Census Bureau has observed that over 40 separate languages are spoken by substantial segments of the Los Angeles area population. These new subcultures bring with them different beliefs, customs, and values, not to mention languages, that must be taken into consideration by firms attempting to sell to them.

Social Class

Social class is a ranking within a society determined by the members of the society. Social classes exist in virtually all societies, and people's buying behavior is often strongly influenced by the class to which they belong or to which they aspire.

Without making value judgments about whether one class is superior to or happier than another, sociologists have attempted to describe class structure in a meaningful way. One scheme useful to marketing managers is the five-class model developed by Coleman and Rainwater,[17] classifying people by education, occupation, and type of residential neighborhood.

Notice that income is not one of the classification factors. Social class is not an indication of spending capability; rather, it is an indication of preferences and life-style. For example, a young lawyer might make the same income as a middle-aged steel worker, but they probably have quite different family backgrounds, tastes, and aspirations.

In the summary of the five classes in U.S. society that follows, the population percentages are only approximations and may vary from one geographic area to another.

- The *upper class,* about 2% of the population, includes two groups: (1) socially prominent "old families," often with inherited wealth, and (2) newly rich corporate executives, owners of large businesses, and professionals. They live in exclusive neighborhoods and patronize fancy shops. They buy expensive goods and services, but they do not conspicuously display their wealth.

- The *upper-middle class,* about 12% of the population, is composed of moderately successful business and professional people and owners of medium-sized companies. They are well educated, have a strong desire for success, and push their children to do well. Their purchases are more conspicuous than those of the upper class. They live well, belong to private clubs, and support the arts and various social causes.

- The *lower-middle class,* about 32% of the population, consists of office workers, most sales people, teachers, technicians, and small business owners. As a group they are often referred to as white-collar workers. They strive for respectability and buy what is popular. Their homes are well cared for, and they save money to send their children to college. They are future oriented, strive to move up to the higher social classes, have self-confidence, and are willing to take risks.

- The *upper-lower class,* about 38% of the population, is the blue-collar working class of production workers, semiskilled workers, and service personnel. These people are tied closely to family for economic and emotional support. Male-female roles are quite clearly defined. They live in smaller houses than the lower-middle class, drive larger cars, have more appliances, and watch bigger television sets. They buy American products, and stay close to home on vacations. Their orientation is short term, and they are very concerned about security.

- The *lower-lower class,* about 16% of the population, is composed of unskilled workers, the chronically unemployed, unassimilated immigrants, and people frequently on welfare. They are typically poorly educated, have low incomes, and live in substandard houses and neighborhoods. They tend not to have many opportunities; hence they focus on the present. Often their purchases are not based on economic considerations. The public tends to differentiate within this class between the "working poor" and the "welfare poor."

Marketers recognize that there are substantial differences among classes with respect to buying behavior. Because of this diversity, different social classes are likely to respond differently to a seller's marketing program. Thus, it may be necessary to design marketing programs tailored to specific social classes.

Reference Groups

Each group in a society develops its own standards of behavior that then serve as guides, or frames of reference, for the members. Families and a circle of friends are such groups. Members share values and are expected to conform to the group's behavioral patterns. But a person does not have to be a member of a group to be influenced by it. There are groups we aspire to join (a campus honor society or club) and groups we admire even though membership may be impossible (a professional athletic team). All of these are potential **reference groups**—groups of people who influence a person's attitudes, values, and behavior.

Studies have shown that personal advice in face-to-face groups is much more effective as a behavioral determinant than advertising. That is, in selecting products or changing brands, we are more likely to be influenced by word-of-mouth information from members of our reference groups than by ads or sales people. This is especially true when the information comes from someone we consider knowledgeable about the product and/or whom we trust.

Advertisers are relying on reference-group influence when they use celebrity spokespersons. Professional athletes, musicians, models, and actors can influence people who would like to be associated with them in some way—for example, Lance Armstrong for Nike and Jennifer Love Hewitt for Neutrogena.

On its website, the America Dairy Farmers and Milk Processors shows over 40 of the groups and individuals that have appeared in its "Got Milk?" ads with milk mustaches. This long-running campaign uses the celebrities as both attention getters and as referents for target cutstomers.

 www.whymilk.com

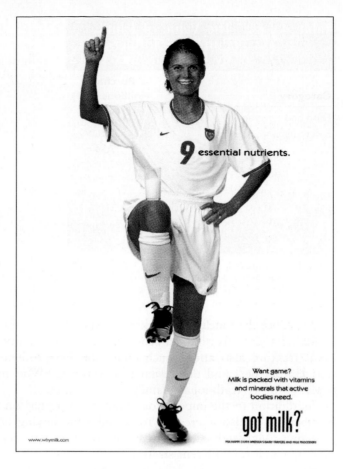

Reference-group influence in marketing is not limited to well-known personalities. Any group whose qualities a person admires can serve as a reference. For example, the physically fit, the socially conscious, and the professionally successful have all served as reference groups in advertising. The result of this process is reflected in advertising appeals using reference groups, such as The Gap's "Everyone in (leather, vests)" series and adidas's "Long Live Sports" campaigns.

Families and Households

A **family** is a group of two or more people related by blood, marriage, or adoption living together in a household. During their lives many people will belong to at least two families—the one into which they are born and the one they form at marriage. The birth family primarily determines core values and attitudes. The marriage family, in contrast, has a more direct influence on specific purchases. For example, family size is important in the purchase of a car.

A household is a broader concept that relates to a dwelling rather than a relationship. A **household** consists of a single person, a family, or any group of unrelated persons who occupy a housing unit. Thus an unmarried homeowner, college students sharing an off-campus apartment, and cohabiting couples are examples of households.

Average household size at the end of the 1990s was 2.64 members, whereas average family size was 3.19 persons. Although household size has remained about the same since 1990, family size has been slowly declining for years. This long-term trend is due in large part to more single-parent families, childless married couples, and unmarried people living together.

Sensitivity to household and family structure is important in designing marketing strategy. When research indicated that singles found mealtime particularly lonely, and often combined a meal with another activity such as reading or work-

Table 4.1	The Value of Family Purchases Influenced by Children Aged 4–12

Category	Purchase (millions of $)
Food and beverages	$110,320
Entertainment	25,260
Clothing	17,540
Automobiles	17,740
Electronics	6,400
Health and Beauty	3,550
Other	5,570
Total	187,740

Source: James U. McNeal, "Tapping the Three Kids' Markets," *American Demographics*, April 1998, pp. 37–41.

ing to reduce the loneliness, marketers responded. Campbell's LeMenu line of individual serving meals is such a product, combining quality and convenience. Household structure also affects such dimensions as product size (How large should refrigerators be?) and the design of advertising (Who might be offended by the depiction of a "traditional" family in a TV ad?).

In addition to the impact household structure has on the purchase behavior of members, it is also interesting to consider the buying behavior of the household as a unit. Marketers should treat this issue as four separate questions, because each may call for different strategies:

- Who influences the buying decision?
- Who makes the buying decision?
- Who makes the actual purchase?
- Who uses the product?

Different household members may assume these various roles, or one individual may play several roles in a particular purchase. Table 4.1 suggests that children aged 4 to 12 influence over $187 billion in family purchases. There have also been changes in who does the shopping. In families, for many years the female household head did most of the day-to-day buying. However, as was described earlier, this behavior has changed as more women have entered the work force, and men and children have assumed greater household responsibility.

Psychological Factors

In discussing the psychological influences on consumer behavior, we will continue to use the model in Figure 4.2. One or more motives within a person activate goal-oriented behavior. One such behavior is perception; that is, the collection and processing of information. Other important psychological activities that play a role in buying decisions are learning, attitude formation, personality, and self-concept.

Motivation—the Starting Point

To understand why consumers behave as they do, we must first ask why a person acts at all. The answer is, "Because he or she experiences a need." All behavior starts with a need. Security, social acceptance, and prestige are examples of needs. A need must be aroused or stimulated before it becomes a motive. Thus, a **motive** is a need sufficiently stimulated to move an individual to seek satisfaction.

We have many dormant needs that do not produce behavior because they are not sufficiently intense. Hunger strong enough to impel us to search for food and fear great enough to motivate a search for security are examples of aroused needs that become motives for behavior.

The broadest classification of motives is based on the source from which a need arises:

- Needs aroused from physiological states of tension (such as the need for sleep).
- Needs aroused from psychological states of tension (such as the needs for affection and self-respect).

A refinement of this concept was formulated by the psychologist Abraham Maslow. He identified a hierarchy of five need levels, arrayed in the order in which people seek to gratify them.[18] **Maslow's need hierarchy** is shown in Figure 4.3. Maslow recognized that a normal person is most likely to be working toward need satisfaction on several levels at the same time, and that rarely are all needs on a given level fully satisfied. However, the hierarchy indicates that the majority of needs on a particular level must be reasonably well satisfied before a person is motivated at the next higher level.

For marketers attempting to design appealing products, persuasive ad messages, inviting retail store layouts, and the like, Maslow's five levels may be too general. Fortunately, there are continuing efforts to better understand and describe motives. For example, a recently proposed model suggests that all behavior is determined by 15 fundamental motives, and individual differences are the result of varying priorites and intensities among these motives.[19] The 15 motives are:

- Curiosity
- Rejection
- Order
- Citizenship
- Family
- Food
- Sex
- Independence
- Pain avoidance
- Social contact
- Honor
- Physical exercise
- Power
- Prestige
- Vengeance

Identifying the motive(s) for a particular action can range from simple to impossible. To illustrate, buying motives may be grouped on three different levels depending on consumers' awareness of them and their willingness to divulge them. At one level, buyers recognize, and are quite willing to talk about, their motives for buying most common, everyday products. At a second level, they are aware of their reasons for buying but will not admit them to others. Some people probably buy luxury cars to impress others. But when questioned about their motives, they may offer other reasons that they think will be more socially appropriate. The most difficult motives to uncover are those at the third level, where even the buyers cannot explain the factors motivating their buying actions. These are called

Figure 4.3

Maslow's hierarchy of needs.

Airlines regularly use a tactic called *overbooking* to cope with the often unpredictable behavior of consumers. That is, an airline will accept reservations for more seats than a plane has on any given flight. Flights are overbooked because in almost every case some number of people make reservations, but do not show up for the flight. So, to protect against unfilled seats and lost revenue, the airlines sell more seats than they have available.

As you probably know, sometimes all the people holding reservations do show up, and there are not enough seats on the plane for everybody. As a result, some people must be "bumped"—that is, switched to a later flight. To entice some travelers to give up their reservations, the airlines often offer cash incentives and/or a totally or partially free ticket on a future flight.

Is the consumer behavior in this case—making a reservation and then failing to show up or cancel it—unethical? What about overbooking—selling something you don't have?

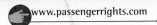

www.passengerrights.com

unconscious or subconscious motives, and we will have more to say about them when we discuss personality.[20]

To further complicate our understanding, a purchase is often the result of multiple motives. Moreover, various motives may conflict with one another. In buying a new suit, a young man may want to (1) feel comfortable, (2) please his girlfriend, and (3) spend as little as possible. Accomplishing all three objectives in one purchase may be truly difficult! Finally, a particular motive may produce different behavior at different times.

Despite the challenges, significant advances have been made in understanding buyer's needs. However, because marketers are unable to precisely describe the needs operating in many purchase situations, more work needs to be done to identify consumption-specific motives and measure their strengths. Some of the methods for gaining insights into motives will be described in Chapter 7 in the discussion of marketing research.

Perception

In many purchase situations, a person gathers information before making a choice. **Perception** is the process of receiving, organizing, and assigning meaning to information or stimuli detected by our five senses. It is in this way that we interpret or understand the world around us. Perception plays a major role in the stage of the buying-decision process where alternatives are identified.

What we perceive—the meaning we give something sensed—depends on the object and our experiences. In an instant the mind is capable of receiving information, comparing it to a huge store of images in memory, and providing an interpretation. Consumers make use of all five senses. Scents, for example, are powerful behavior triggers. Who can resist the aroma of popcorn in a theater or of fresh cookies in a supermarket bakery? As with all perception, memory plays a large part with aromas. Research on common odors found that scents such as vanilla, chocolate, cedar, lavendar, and rosemary create comforting associations for people.[21] Marketers are using this type of information to odorize products and shopping environments to create positive perceptions.

Every day we come in contact with an enormous number of marketing stimuli. However, with the aid of **selective perception** techniques we are able to deal with the commercial environment.

- We pay attention by exception. That is, of all the marketing stimuli our senses are exposed to, only those with the power to capture and hold our attention have the potential of being perceived. Using a somewhat insensitive analogy, an ad executive compared consumers to roaches—"you spray them and spray

Advertisers often go to great lengths to attract and hold attention long enough for a message to be communicated. This highway billboard for a subsidiary of DaimlerChrysler that produces electronic products is certainly eye-catching, even at autobahn speeds, but does the attention-getting device overwhelm the message?

De ongelofelijke zuigkracht van de AEG Vampyr Rosso.

them and they get immune after a while."[22] This phenomenon is called *selective attention*.

- As part of perception, new information is compared with a person's existing store of knowledge, or frame of reference. If an inconsistency is discovered, the new information will likely be distorted to conform to the established beliefs. Despite the fact that the prices for the 100 most frequently purchased packaged goods increased at a lower rate than consumer prices in general over the last four years, most consumers believe grocery prices are unreasonably high. Why? The proliferation of new, heavily advertised premium products, manufacturers' discount coupons, and store specials all contribute to an impression that prices in general are too high.[23] This is *selective distortion*.

- We retain only part of what we have selectively perceived. For example, nearly 80% of Americans cannot remember a typical TV commercial one day after seeing it.[24] This is known as *selective retention*.

There are many communication implications in this selectivity process. For example, to grasp and hold attention, an ad must be involving enough to stimulate the consumer to seek more information. If the ad is too familiar, it will be ignored. On the other hand, if it is too complex, the ad will be judged not worth the time and effort to figure out. Thus, the goal is a mildly ambiguous first impression that heightens the consumer's interest.

Selective distortion tells us that marketers cannot assume that a message, even if it is factually correct, will necessarily be accepted as fact by consumers. In designing a message, the distance between the audience's current belief and the position proposed by the message must be considered. If the distance is large, a moderate claim may be more believable than a dramatic claim, and therefore more effective in moving consumers in the desired direction.

Even messages received undistorted are subject to selective retention. Consequently, ads are repeated many times. The hope is that numerous exposures will etch the message into the recipient's memory. This aim partially explains why a firm with very familiar products, such as Wrigley's, spends over $100 million a year advertising chewing gum.

Learning

Learning involves changes in behavior resulting from observation and experience. It excludes behavior that is attributable to instinct such as breathing or temporary states such as hunger or fatigue. Interpreting and predicting consumer learning enhances our understanding of buying behavior, because learning plays a role at every stage of the buying-decision process.

There is no universally accepted learning theory. However, one with direct application to marketing strategy is stimulus-response.[25] According to **stimulus-response theory,** learning occurs as a person (1) responds to some stimulus by behaving in a particular way and (2) is rewarded for a correct response or penalized for an incorrect one. When the same correct response is repeated in reaction to the same stimulus, a behavior pattern, or learning, is established.

From a marketer's perspective, learning can be desirable or undesirable. As examples of desirable learning, marketers have "taught" consumers to respond to certain cues, such as:

- End-of-aisle displays in supermarkets suggest that the displayed item is on sale.
- Sale signs in store windows suggest that bargains can be found inside.
- Large type in newspaper grocery ads suggests that the item is a particularly good bargain.

On the other hand, by their own admission, U.S. automakers have contributed to some undesirable learning. Thirty years ago three auto manufacturers—General Motors, Ford, and Chrysler (now DaimlerChrysler)—accounted for the bulk of U.S. car sales. Their quality slipped badly in the 1970s, which alienated many baby boomers who were buying their first new cars at that time. According to a Ford researcher describing that period, "We taught them that we build junk (and) the lessons learned in the 1970s will stay with baby boomers the rest of their lives." Despite substantial quality improvements in subsequent years, the Big Three automakers have had a difficult time overcoming this early learning and its generalization to their later products. Today only 44 percent of baby boomers own cars made by these three companies.[26]

Once a behavior pattern has been established it becomes a habit and replaces conscious, willful behavior. In terms of the purchase-decision process, this means that the consumer would skip several of the steps in the buying process, and might go directly from the recognized need to the purchase.

Learning is not a perfect predictor of behavior because a variety of other factors also influence a consumer. For example, a pattern of repeatedly purchasing the same brand may be disrupted by a person's desire for variety or novelty. Or a temporary situation such as being short of money or pressed for time may produce behavior different than a learned response. Thus a learned response does not necessarily occur every time a stimulus appears.

Personality

Personality is defined broadly as an individual's pattern of traits that influence behavioral responses. For example, we speak of people as being self-confident, domineering, introverted, flexible, and/or friendly, and as being influenced (but not controlled) by such personality traits in their responses to situations.

It is generally agreed that personality traits do influence consumers' perceptions and buying behavior. However, there is considerable disagreement as to the nature of this relationship—that is, *how* personality influences behavior. Many studies have been made of personality traits in relation to product and brand preferences in a wide variety of product categories, with mixed results. The findings generally have been too inconclusive to be of much practical value. Although we know, for example, that people's personalities often are reflected in the clothes they wear, the cars they drive (or whether they use a bicycle or motorcycle instead of a car), and the restaurants they eat in, we have not been successful in predicting behavior from particular personality traits. The reason is simple: Many things besides personality enter into the consumer buying-decision process.

The **psychoanalytic theory** of personality, formulated by Sigmund Freud at the turn of the century and later modified by his followers and critics, has had a tremendous impact on the study of human behavior and also marketing. Freud contended that people have subconscious drives that cannot be satisfied in socially acceptable ways. As we learn that we cannot gratify these needs in a direct manner, we develop other, more subtle means of seeking satisfaction. This results in very complex reasons for some behavior.

One significant marketing implication is that a person's real motive(s) for buying a product or shopping at a certain store may be hidden. Sometimes even we ourselves do not understand why we feel or act as we do. Psychoanalytic theory has caused marketers to realize that they must appeal to buyers' dreams, hopes, fantasies, and fears. Yet at the same time they must provide buyers with socially acceptable rationalizations for many purchases. Thus, we see ads emphasizing the practicality of $60,000 cars, the comfort of fur coats, and the permanence of diamond jewelry.

Self-concept is a marketing application of personality theory. Your **self-concept,** or *self-image,* is the way you see yourself. At the same time it is the picture you think others have of you. Psychologists distinguish between the *actual self-concept*—the way you see yourself—and the *ideal self-concept*—the way you want to be seen or would like to see yourself.

Studies of purchases show that people generally prefer brands and products that are compatible with their self-concepts. However, there are mixed reports concerning the degree of influence actual and ideal self-concepts have on brand and product preferences. Some researchers contend that consumption preferences correspond to a person's actual self-concept. Others hold that the ideal self-concept is dominant in consumers' choices.

Perhaps there is no consensus here because in real life we often switch back and forth between our actual and ideal self-concepts. A middle-aged man may buy some comfortable, but not fashionable, clothing to wear at home on a weekend, where he is reflecting his actual self-concept. But he may also buy some expensive, high-fashion clothing, envisioning himself as a young, active, upwardly mobile guy (ideal self-concept).

Attitudes

An **attitude** is a learned predisposition to respond to an object or class of objects in a consistently favorable or unfavorable way.[27] In our buying-decision process model, attitudes play a major role in the evaluation of alternatives. All attitudes have the following characteristics in common:

- Attitudes are *learned.* They are formed as a result of direct experiences with a product or an idea, indirect experiences (such as reading about a product in *Consumer Reports*), and interactions with social groups. For example, the opinions expressed by a friend about diet foods plus the consumer's favorable or unfavorable experience as a result of using diet foods will contribute to an attitude toward diet foods in general.

- Attitudes have an *object.* By definition, we can hold attitudes only toward something. The object can be general (professional sports) or specific (Chicago Cubs); it can be abstract (campus life) or concrete (the computer lab). In attempting to determine consumers' attitudes, the object of the attitude must

How far off is the "networked home?"

Most consumers take a certain amount of technology in the home for granted. A water heater that measures water temperature and shuts on and off to keep a supply of hot water available, a furnace and/or air conditioner controlled by a thermostat that keeps a home comfortable, and a programmable VCR that can record favorite television shows are widespread. Other technology, such as cellular phones, personal computers, and security systems, are less common but not unusual. What's in store for the future, and how soon will it be here? Several companies are hoping to produce answers to these questions.

Two Swedish companies, Electrolux and Ericcson, have launched a joint venture to link household appliances with each other and the outside world using the Internet, personal computers, and mobile phones. They envision a home in which the refrigerator will notify you when its time to restock certain items, or better yet, automatically order the items and have them delivered to the home; where suggested recipes will pop up on your PC screen based on the content of the refrigerator; and where you will be able to operate appliances while away from home using a mobile phone.

On another front, Sony, Honda, Matsushita, and other firms are developing robots that they foresee performing household chores, running errands, and assisting the handicapped. However, the complex technology to operate the robots will take years to develop. As an interim step, Sony is developing robotic toys that allow the firm to experiment with artificial intelligence designs, generate some revenue from sales, and slowly educate the public about the potential of household robots. The first product is AIBO, a $2,000 robotic dog that can chase a ball, bark, sit up, lie down, and wag its tail. You can see this early version of what the future may hold on the Sony website. (www.sony.com)

What consumer behavior issues do the marketers of household technology face?

Sources: Matej Vipotnik, "Smart Fridge Gets Wired," *Financial Times*, Nov. 8, 1999, p. 24; Irene M. Kunii, "This Cute Little Pet Is a Robot," *Business Week*, May 24, 1999, pp. 56–58.

---

be carefully defined. This is because a person might have a favorable attitude toward the general concept (exercise), but a negative attitude toward a specific dimension of the concept (jogging).

- Attitudes have *direction* and *intensity*. Our attitudes are either favorable or unfavorable toward the object. They cannot be neutral. In addition, they have a strength. For example, you may mildly like this text or you may like it very much (we hope!). This factor is important for marketers, because both strongly held favorable and strongly held unfavorable attitudes are difficult to change.

- Finally, attitudes tend to be *stable* and *generalizable*. Once formed, attitudes usually endure, and the longer they are held, the more resistant to change they become. People also have a tendency to generalize attitudes. For instance, a person who likes the produce section in a particular supermarket has a tendency to form a favorable attitude toward the entire store.

A consumer's attitudes do not always predict purchase behavior. A person may hold very favorable attitudes toward a product but not buy it because of some inhibiting factor. Typical inhibitors are not having enough money or discovering that your preferred brand is not available when you want to buy it. Under such circumstances, purchase behavior may even contradict attitudes.

Changing attitudes can be difficult or impossible. When change is accomplished, it normally takes a long time and a lot of money. Consider how long it took to gain widespread acceptance of air bags in cars. They were initially ridiculed but now are frequently demanded by car buyers. When faced with unfavorable attitudes, and recognizing how difficult changing them will be, marketers frequently alter the product to conform to the attitudes.

Situational Influences

Often the situations in which we find ourselves play a large part in determining how we behave. Students, for example, act differently in class than they do when they are in a stadium watching a football game. The same holds true of buying behavior. On spring break you might buy a souvenir that seems very strange when you get home. This is an example of **situational influence**, a temporary force associated with the immediate purchase environment that affects behavior.

Situational influences tend to be less significant when the consumer is very loyal to a brand and when the consumer is highly involved in the purchase. However, they often play a major role in buying decisions. The four categories of situational influences are related to when, where, and how consumers buy as well as the conditions under which they buy.

The Time Dimension

In designing strategy for a product, a marketer should be able to answer at least three time-related questions about consumer buying:

- How is it influenced by the season, week, day, or hour?
- What impact do past and present events have on the purchase decision?
- How much time does the consumer have to make the purchase and consume the product?

The time of day influences the demand for some products. For example, because they associate it with breakfast, Americans drink 10 times as much orange juice as the Japanese. The time dimension of buying has implications for promotion scheduling. Promotional messages must reach consumers when they are in a decision-making frame of mind. It also influences pricing decisions, as when marketers adjust prices in an attempt to even out demand. For instance, supermarkets may offer double coupons on Tuesdays, usually a slow business day. If seasonal buying patterns exist, marketers can tailor their merchandise accordingly. In most parts of the U.S., the demand for bowling products peaks when the weather gets cold. However, in warm-weather areas, the reverse is true. The demand for bowling equipment peaks in the summer, when it is too hot for outdoor recreation. In response, Kmart stores in the Phoenix area stock up on bowling products in the spring, whereas Kmarts in Detroit increase their stock in the fall.[28]

The second question concerns the impact of past or future events. For example, the length of time since you last went out to dinner at a nice restaurant may influence a decision on whether to go to a fancy restaurant tonight. Marketers need to know enough about the recent and planned behavior of consumers to anticipate the effects of these past and future events.

The growth and popularity of fast-food restaurants, quick-service oil-change outlets, and catalog retailers such as L. L. Bean and Lands' End are marketers' responses to the time pressure experienced by consumers. Certainly a factor in the Internet's growing popularity as a place to make purchases is the desire to spend less time shopping. To help consumers conserve time, marketers are making large and small changes. For example, some photoprocessing operations return the developed prints by mail to eliminate the customers' second trip to pick up the pictures. To help customers locate specific products and therefore reduce shopping time, a number of supermarkets have electronic directories attached to their shopping carts.

The Surroundings

Physical surroundings are the features of a situation that are apparent to the senses, such as lighting, smells, weather, and sounds. Think of the importance of atmosphere in a restaurant or the sense of excitement and action created by the sights and sounds in a gambling casino. Music can be an important element in a store's strategy. In an experiment involving supermarket shoppers, the beat of background music apparently influenced behavior. Despite the fact that the shoppers reported paying little or no attention to the music, sales were 38% higher with slower background music than with faster music![29]

The social surroundings are the number, mix, and actions of other people at the purchase site. You probably would not go into a strange restaurant that has an empty parking lot at dinnertime. In a crowded store with other customers waiting, you will probably ask the clerk fewer questions and spend less time comparing products.

Terms of the Purchase

Terms and conditions of sale as well as the transaction-related activities that buyers are willing to perform affect consumer buying. For instance, for many years credit was extended only by retailers selling big-ticket items. However, today consumers can use credit cards at fast-food restaurants and grocery stores. Over 65% of families in the U.S. have credit cards, and the average credit card debt in the U.S. has increased to nearly $5,600 per household. It is anticipated that by the year 2000 there will be 1.5 *billion* credit cards in circulation. Installment credit (including car loans but excluding home mortgages) now exceeds $1.2 *trillion*. Not only do consumers use credit for installment purchases (to buy things today with future income), but many now use credit for convenience. The ability to use American Express, VISA, MasterCard, or Discover Card to make a wide variety of purchases while not carrying cash is an attractive option to many consumers.

Marketers have also experimented with transferring functions or activities to consumers. What were once called "service stations" are now called "gas stations" because you pump your own gas and wash your own windshield. Consumers have shown a willingness to assemble products, sack their own groceries, and buy in case quantities—all in exchange for lower prices.

Consumer Moods and Motives

Sometimes consumers are in a temporary state that influences their buying decisions. When you are feeling ill or late for an appointment, you may be unwilling to wait in line or to take the time or care that a particular purchase deserves. Moods can also influence purchases. Feelings such as anger or excitement can result in purchases that otherwise would not have been made. In the atmosphere accompanying a rock concert, for example, you might pay more for a commemorative T-shirt than you would under normal circumstances. Part of the success of online auctions such as eBay and television shopping networks such as QVC can be attributed to the excitement of competing against other consumers.

Marketers must also monitor long-term situational influences. The optimistic U.S. consumers of the 1990s have been free spending and apparently carefree. According to a 1998 Roper-Starch study, low inflation and a strong economy made U.S. consumers the most confident in the world going into the end of the decade. However, in other parts of the world recessions in the 1990s rocked local economies, creating more conservative buyers. For example, in Japan less than one-fourth of the consumers were as confident about their economic futures as their counterparts in the U.S.[30] Because uncertainty leads to more saving and fewer purchases, exports to Japan during this period were down significantly.

This chapter has dealt with the willingness to buy—part of our definition of marketing. We described the consumer market and examined the consumer's decision-making process. You should now appreciate just how difficult it is for marketers to identify needs and predict consumer buying behavior. In the next chapter we will examine the other category of buyers—the business market.

Summary

The dynamic nature of the consumer market is reflected in its geographic distribution and its demographic characteristics. The U.S. population is shifting toward the West and the South. Further, the mix of people in rural communities is changing as the out-migration of young people continues but an in-migration of older Americans increases.

Demographics are the vital statistics that describe a population. They are useful to marketers because they are related to behavior and they are relatively easy to gather. Demographics frequently used to describe consumers are age, gender, family life cycle, income, ethnicity, and other characteristics such as education, occupation, religion, and nationality.

The buying behavior of ultimate consumers can be examined using a five-part model: the buying-decision process, information, social and group forces, psychological forces, and situational factors.

The buying-decision process is composed of five stages consumers go through in making purchases. The stages are need recognition, identification of alternatives, evaluation of alternatives, purchase and related decisions, and postpurchase behavior. Buying decisions are either high or low involvement. Low-involvement decisions include fewer stages; high-involvement decisions consist of all five stages. Low-involvement situations occur when there is brand and store loyalty and in impulse buying.

Information fuels the buying-decision process. Without it, there would be no decisions. There are two categories of information sources: commercial and social. Commercial sources include advertising, personal selling, selling by phone, and personal involvement with a product. Word of mouth, observation, and experience with a product owned by someone else are social sources.

Social and group forces are composed of culture, subculture, social class, reference groups, family, and households. Culture has the broadest and most general influence on buying behavior, whereas other household occupants have the most immediate impact on an individual. These social and group forces have a direct impact on individual purchase decisions as well as a person's psychological makeup.

Psychological forces that impact buying decisions are motivation, perception, learning, personality, and attitudes. All behavior is motivated by some aroused need. Perception is the way we interpret the world around us and is subject to three types of selectivity: attention, distortion, and retention.

Learning is a change in behavior as a result of experience. Stimulus-response learning involves drives, cues, responses, reinforcement, and punishment. Continued reinforcement leads to habitual buying and brand loyalty.

Personality is the sum of an individual's traits that influence behavioral responses. The Freudian psychoanalytic theory of personality has had a significant impact on marketing. It has caused marketers to realize that the true motives for behavior are often hidden. The self-concept is related to personality. Because purchasing and consumption are very expressive actions, they allow us to communicate to the world our actual and ideal self-concepts.

Attitudes are learned predispositions to respond to an object or class of objects in a consistent fashion. Besides being learned, all attitudes are directed toward an object, have direction and intensity, and tend to be stable and generalizable. Strongly held attitudes are difficult to change.

Situational influences deal with when, where, how, and why consumers buy, and the consumer's personal condition at the time of purchase. Situational influences are often so powerful that they can override all the other forces in the buying-decision process.

More about the **Volkswagen** Beetle

The challenge of figuring out what vehicles consumers want and producing them is not without constraints. Developing a new car can easily cost $1 billion. And every make and model that is produced requires money for advertising and distribution. The manufacturers have also found that once a car is introduced it is not easy to eliminate. There are production facilities, jobs, and dealers to worry about, not to mention the consumers who bought the car and expect to be able to have it serviced and repaired.

The "Holy Grail" that all carmakers seek is a car design that will stretch across several markets. The ideal is a "world car" that will meet the needs of customers in Tokyo, New York, and Paris. Ford attempted it with the compact Mondeo, first introduced in Europe in 1993, and later sold as the Contour in the U.S. Unfortunately, after an investment of $6 billion the car is far from fulfilling the goals set for it. Similarly, Volkswagen hopes to capitalize on the international success of the Beetle in the 1960s with a new version that has modern features and a higher price tag. However, because of the differences in consumers' tastes and driving conditions around the world, a single-model approach may not be possible.

Honda addressed the challenge differently and may have found a solution. By developing a platform or frame (the most expensive part of a new car) that can be easily modified, Honda can adjust the size of a car without redesigning the entire vehicle. That allows it to adapt the Accord to differing demands around the world. As a result, a narrower car can be produced to accommodate the tighter roads in Europe, and a car with more head and leg room can be produced for the U.S. market. What Honda has done is "think globally, and act locally." The company recognized the opportunities provided by markets around the world and at the same time acknowledged that important differences exist in consumers' needs and desires.[31]

1. In which areas of the consumer buying-decision process would you expect to find the greatest difference between U.S. and European automobile buyers? How about between U.S. and Japanese buyers?

2. Given your answers to the first question, do you think it is possible for any product to satisfy the needs of consumers around the world?

Key Terms and Concepts

Questions and Problems

1. Give two examples of goods or services whose market demand would be particularly affected by each of the following population factors:
   a. Regional distribution
   b. Urban-rural-suburban distribution
   c. Marital status
   d. Gender
   e. Age

2. List three population trends noted in this chapter (for instance, the over-65 segment is growing). Speculate on how each of the following types of retail operations might be affected by each of the trends:
   a. Supermarket
   b. Sporting goods store
   c. Online auction
   d. Restaurant

3. When might the purchase of a color television be a low-involvement decision?

4. From a consumer behavior perspective, why is it incorrect to view the European Union or the countries of Asia as single markets?

5. Provide examples of a person and a group that could serve as reference groups in the choice of the following products:
   a. Shampoo
   b. Auto tune-up
   c. Office furniture
   d. Cellular phone service

6. What roles would you expect a husband, a wife, and their young child to play in the purchase of the following items?
   a. Nintendo
   b. Choice of a fast-food outlet for dinner
   c. Personal computer
   d. Lawn-care service

7. Does the psychoanalytic theory of personality have any practical application in the marketing of cars that have a top speed of 120 mph when the speed limit on most U.S. highways is 65 mph or less?

8. Explain how self-concept might come into play in the purchase or use of the following:
   a. Eyeglasses
   b. Man's suit
   c. Online brokerage
   d. College education

9. Interview the manager of a store that sells big-ticket items (furniture, appliances, electronic equipment) about the methods, if any, the store uses to reinforce purchase decisions and to reduce the cognitive dissonance of its customers. What additional methods can you suggest?

10. What situational influences might affect a family's choice of a motel in a strange town while on vacation?

Hands-On Marketing

1. From the most recent "Survey of Buying Power" (from *Sales & Marketing Management* magazine), record the available demographic data for the county in which you live and one other county in your home state. Comment on how any differences you find may be useful to a fast-food franchisee looking for a location for a new outlet.

2. Have a friend describe a high-involvement purchase that he or she recently made. Show how each of the five stages described in the chapter is reflected in the description. Identify the primary social influences that played a part in the decision.

5

Business Markets and Buying Behavior

"The traditional system of business buying has worked for years, but it has left buyers with a nagging question: Am I paying the lowest possible price for the desired product?"

Should **FreeMarkets** Be
Equally Attractive to Buyers and Sellers?

When a manufacturer buys a large quantity of a product, for example a component part for a personal computer, typically several potential suppliers are invited to make offers. The offers are submitted in writing, and the buyer selects the most attractive one. The traditional system of business buying has worked for years, but it has left the buyer with a nagging question: Am I paying the lowest possible price for the desired product? A new method of buying over the Internet, called a reverse auction (because it involves sellers bidding a price down instead of buyers bidding a price up), is providing an answer.

FreeMarkets, Inc., is a firm that offers an Internet business-to-business auction service. It assists buyers of direct materials, commodities, and service products in the identification of potential suppliers, and then conducts electronic, real-time auctions over the Internet in which the suppliers bid for the business.

The auctions are held on FreeMarket's private Internet site, so only invited suppliers are permitted to participate. At a designated time, the buyer and all the prospective suppliers log in to the site. The buyer's computer screen shows all the suppliers and all the offers. The suppliers, however, see only the lowest offer on their individual screens. The suppliers don't know the identities or the number of firms participating in the bidding. The bidding goes on for a specified time, usually two to three hours. When the auction closes, the buyer decides which bid it wants to accept. Typically the result is a price as much as 20 percent below what a buyer would pay under the old, single-bid process. For its service, FreeMarkets charges the buyer a fee.

Procter & Gamble, Caterpillar, and Zenith are among the major firms that have used FreeMarkets' service. United Technologies, an electronics manufacturer, purchased circuit boards for $18 million that had a list price of $24 million, a 35% savings, after three hours of bidding by 10 suppliers on three different continents.

According to its founder, FreeMarkets provides clients with three services. First, it assists in identifying the best prospective suppliers. Consultants at FreeMarkets help the buyer prepare a comprehensive request for quotation (RFQ) which, depending on the product being purchased, may consist of several hundred pages of specifications. Then FreeMarkets narrows down the list of qualified suppliers based on its research and the responses of potential suppliers to the RFQ. Second, FreeMarkets has developed a global electronic market system that allows the prequalified suppliers to participate in a real-time competitive bidding process. By operating on a private Internet network (or extranet), and using its proprietary software, FreeMarkets can provide privacy and security for both the buyers and the sellers. Third, FreeMarkets contend it provides unequaled research on the suppliers' firm and industry to help the buyer evaluate the bids. For example, at the end of a bidding session, FreeMarkets may recommend that a buyer reject the lowest bid and accept instead a supplier with a more reliable delivery record.

Buyers like the speed of the process and, of course, the lower prices. Also, using FreeMarkets allows firms that choose not to invest in creating their own electronic procurement system to enjoy the benefits of Internet bidding. However, there is concern that pitting prospective suppliers against one another in a bidding battle may undermine loyalties that can benefit a company during difficult economic times or when it needs special consideration, such as a rush order.

Some suppliers dislike the system because they think it puts too much emphasis on price, discouraging consideration of other factors that may be equally important. On the other hand, they like the idea that it gives them a chance for business that they might have been closed out of because of a long-standing relationship between a buyer and seller.

Whatever buyers and sellers think about the procedure, it's been a success for FreeMarkets. Begun in 1995 with just 13 employees, the firm has a staff of nearly 300 and arranged for over $1 billion in sales in 1999.[1]

How does the approach developed by FreeMarkets for the business market differ from marketing to consumers?

 www.freemarkets.com

Although most people recognize large, technical equipment such as the robots used in assembling cars or the air-conditioning units used in office buildings as business products, many other products, like paper bags or bottle caps are easily overlooked. In fact, the business market is big, dynamic, and widely diversified. It employs millions of workers in thousands of different jobs, and is actually larger than the consumer market. And, as the chapter-opening case describing FreeMarkets, Inc., suggests, there is plenty of room for innovation in the way business products are bought and sold.

In many ways business markets are similar to the consumer markets we examined in Chapter 4, but there are also important differences. After studying this chapter, you should be able to explain:

chapter goals

- The nature and scope of the business market.
- The seven categories of business buyers.
- The differentiating characteristics of business markets.
- What determines business market demand.
- The buying processes in business markets.

Nature and Scope of the Business Market

The business market consists of all individuals and organizations that buy goods and services for one or more of the following purposes:

- *To make other goods and services.* Dell buys microprocessors to make computers, and Henredon buys wood to make furniture.
- *To resell to other business users or to consumers.* Toys "R" Us buys electronic games to sell to consumers, and ReCellular, Inc., buys used cellular phones to refurbish and sell to cellular service providers.
- *To conduct the organization's operations.* Kroger buys bags to sack groceries, the University of Vermont buys office supplies and computer software for use in the registrar's office, and the Mayo Clinic buys hazardous-materials disposal services to get rid of its medical refuse.

So, any good or service purchased for a reason other than personal or household consumption is part of the **business market,** and each buyer within this market is termed a **business user.** The activity of marketing goods and services to business users, rather than to ultimate consumers, is **business marketing.**

The distinction of whether a good or service is a consumer or business product depends on the reason it is purchased, not on the item itself. For example, a PC purchased from Dell by a small business to keep track of its orders, inventory, and accounts receivable would be a business good. The same PC (with different software), also purchased from Dell but as a family Christmas gift for educational and entertainment use at home, would be a consumer good. This is not simply a semantic distinction because, as you will see, the marketing activities in these two situations are very different.

Because the business market is largely unknown to the average consumer, it is easy to underrate its significance. Actually, it is huge in terms of total sales volume and the number of firms involved. About 50% of all manufactured products are sold to the business market. In addition, about 80% of all farm products and virtually all mineral, forest, and sea products are business goods. These are sold to firms for further processing.[2]

The magnitude and complexity of the business market are also evident from the many transactions required to produce and market a product. Consider, for example, the business marketing transactions and total sales volume involved in getting leather workshoes to their actual users. First, cattle are sold through one or two middlemen before reaching a meatpacker. Then the hides are sold to a tanner, who in turn sells the leather to a shoe manufacturer. The shoe manufacturer may sell finished shoes to a wholesaler, who markets them to retail stores or to employers that supply shoes for their workers. Each sale in the chain is a business marketing transaction.

In addition, the shoe manufacturer buys metal eyelets, laces, thread, glue, steel safety toe plates, heels and soles, and shoe polish. Consider something as simple as the shoelaces. Other industrial firms must first buy the raw cotton. Then they must spin, weave, dye, and cut the cotton so that it becomes shoestring material. All the manufacturers involved have factories and offices with furniture, machinery, furnaces, lights, and maintenance equipment and supplies required to run them—and these also are business goods that have to be produced and marketed. In short, thousands of business products and business marketing activities come into play before almost any product—consumer good or business good—reaches its final destination.

The magnitude and complexity of the business market loom even larger when we consider all the business services involved throughout our workshoe example. Each firm engaged in any stage of the production process probably uses outside accounting and law firms. Several of the producers may use advertising agencies. And all the companies will use services of various financial institutions.

Every retail store and wholesaling establishment is a business user. Every bus company, airline, and railroad is part of this market. So is every hotel, restaurant, bank, insurance company, hospital, theater, and school. In fact, the total sales volume in the business market far surpasses total sales to consumers. This difference is due to the very many business marketing transactions that take place before a product is sold to its ultimate user.

Components of the Business Market

Traditionally, business markets were referred to as industrial markets. This caused many people to think the term referred only to manufacturing firms. But as you can see from what we just explained, the business market is a lot more than that. Certainly manufacturers constitute a major portion of the business market, but there are also six other components—agriculture, reseller, government, services, nonprofit, and international. Although they are often underrated or overlooked because of the heavy attention devoted to manufacturing, each is a significant part of the business market.

The Agriculture Market

The high level of income from the sale of agricultural products—over $202 billion in 1996, the most recent data available—gives farmers, as a group, the purchasing power that makes them a highly attractive business market. Moreover, world population forecasts and food shortages in many countries undoubtedly will keep pressure on farmers to increase their output. Companies hoping to sell to the farm market must analyze it carefully and be aware of significant trends. For example, both the proportion of farmers in the total population and the number of farms have been decreasing and probably will continue to decline. Counterbalancing this has been an increase in large corporate farms. Even the remaining "family farms" are expanding in order to survive. Also, farming is becoming more automated and mechanized. These developments mean that capital investment in farming is increasing. **Agribusiness**—farming, food processing, and other large-scale farming-related businesses—is big business in every sense of the word.

Agribusiness has been high tech for many years. The accompanying photo of a sugarcane harvester is an example. The industry has also joined the Internet age. Three firms with large stakes in agribusiness, Cenex Harvest States, Cargill, and DuPont, have created a website. The site permits farmers to purchase agricultural products including seeds, fertilizers, chemicals, equipment, and other supplies as well as market their crops online while maintaining their ties with local dealers and cooperatives.

 www.rooster.com

Agriculture has become a modern industry. Like other business executives, farmers are looking for ways to increase their productivity, cut their expenses, and manage their cash flows. Technology is an important part of the process. For example, an Illinois firm, Tri-R Innovations, has developed a sensor and remote steering system that guides a tractor between the rows in a field to avoid destroying any crops. And, as farms become fewer and larger, effectively marketing to them requires sophisticated approaches. A joint industry-government project that will soon make possible satellite-generated pictures of individual farm fields is a good illustration. By analyzing the pictures, farmers and agricultural specialists will be able to determine when specific areas need irrigation or spot fertilization. Representatives of fertilizer producers such as International Mineral and Chemical Company can use this information to design unique strategies for individual farms and adapt them as necessary to best serve their customers.[3]

The Reseller Market

Intermediaries in the American marketing system—over 500,000 wholesaling middlemen and 2.7 million retail establishments—constitute the **reseller market.** The basic activity of resellers—unlike any other business market segment—is buying products from supplier organizations and reselling these items in essentially the same form to the resellers' customers. In economic terms, resellers create time, place, information, and possession utilities, rather than form utility.

Resellers are also business users, buying many goods and services for use in operating their businesses—items such as office supplies, warehouses, materials-handling equipment, legal services, electrical services, and janitorial supplies. In these buying activities, resellers essentially do not differ from manufacturers, financial institutions, or any other segment of the business market.

It is their role as buyers for resale that differentiates resellers and attracts special marketing attention from their suppliers. To resell an item, you must please your customer. Usually it is more difficult to determine what will please an outside customer than to find out what will satisfy someone within your own organization. Consider an airline that decides to redesign the uniforms of its flight crews. Management can carefully study the conditions under which the uniforms will be worn and work closely with the people who will be wearing the uniforms to get their views. As a result, the airline should be able to select a design that will be both functional and acceptable. Contrast that with a retailer trying to anticipate what clothing fashions will be popular. The Gap, Express, and Ann Taylor have all had their ups and downs as they try to predict tastes. In both cases clothing is being purchased. However, the opportunity for interaction with the users and the greater interest by those likely to be affected by the purchase make buying for internal use less difficult and less risky than buying for resale.

Especially in a large reseller's organization, buying for resale can be a complex procedure. For a supermarket chain such as Kroger or Vons, buying is frequently done by a buying committee made up of experts on demand, supply, and prices. Department stores may retain resident buyers—independent buying agencies—located in New York or other major market centers to be in constant touch with the latest fashion developments.

Resellers, also called "middlemen" or "intermediaries," are the business marketers most directly affected by electronic commerce. The growth of Internet-based selling is contributing to the replacement of some traditional intermediaries in a process that has become so commonplace it has a name—**disintermediation.** Only resellers that can create utility will continue to prosper.

The Government Market

The fantastically large **government market** includes over 87,000 federal, state, and local units that spend over $2.8 *trillion* a year buying for government institutions, such as schools, offices, hospitals, and military bases. Spending by the federal government alone accounts for almost 25% of our gross domestic product. Spending at the state and local levels accounts for another 20%.

Government procurement processes are different from those in the private sector of the business market. A unique feature of government buying is the competitive bidding system. Much government procurement, by law, must be done on a bid basis. That is, the government agency advertises for bids using a standard format called a request for proposals (RFP) that states specifications for the intended purchase. Then it must accept the lowest bid that meets these specifications.

In other buying situations, the government may negotiate a purchase contract with an individual supplier. This marketing practice might be used, for instance, when the Department of Defense wants someone to develop and build a new weapons system, and there are no comparable products on which to base bidding specifications.

www.cbdnet.access.gpo.gov

A glance at an issue of the *Commerce Business Daily,* a U.S. government publication that lists business opportunities with the government, will give you some idea of the size of this market. The potential is sufficiently attractive that some firms concentrate exclusively on it, and for others it can be a springboard to additional opportunities. AM General Corporation, for example, developed the HUMMER, an all-terrain vehicle, in response to a Department of Defense RFP. The firm eventually expanded its marketing effort for the vehicle to other government agencies such as the Forest Service, and business firms such as mining and oil exploration companies. Now a civilian version of the HUMMER is being marketed by General Motors.

Despite its potential, many companies make no effort to sell to the government because they are intimidated by the red tape. There is no question that dealing

All branches and all levels of government are important markets. The National Aeronautic and Space Administration (NASA), pictured here launching the space shuttle, is one of the more dramatic government agencies that buys goods and services. Annually NASA awards more than $12 billion in contracts to suppliers. Of the total, $1.2 billion goes to small businesses. More information can be found at their website.

 www.nasa.gov

with the government to any significant extent usually requires specialized marketing techniques and information. Some firms, such as ZDS (Zenith Data Systems), have established special departments to deal with government markets. Also, there are information and guidelines available from agencies such as the General Services Administration and the Small Business Administration on the proper procedures for doing business with the government.

The Services Market

Currently, firms that produce services greatly outnumber firms that produce goods. That is, there are more service firms than the total of all manufacturers, mining companies, construction firms, and enterprises engaged in farming, forestry, and fishing. The **business services market** includes all firms that deal in data and information such as marketing research firms and ad agencies. Also part of this market are transportation carriers and public utilities, and the many financial, insurance, legal, and real estate firms. It includes organizations that provide such diverse services as rental housing, recreation and entertainment, temporary help, repairs, health care, personal care, and executive search services.

Brokers, firms that bring buyers and sellers together, are an important part of the service market. With the growth of electronic commerce in recent years, their significance is growing. Business marketers are using Internet-based brokers to inform buyers about the goods they have available, and buyers are publicizing their needs electronically. For example, PurchasePro is an Internet service that brings together hotels and casinos such as Mirage Resorts with vendors of all types. With over 4,000 firms posting their goods and services on its site, Purchase-Pro says a buyer can find everything from "soup to nuts."[4] Firms in industries as

 www.purchasepro.com

An example of nonbusiness marketing is the recruiting effort to attract enlistees into the military. Today's all-volunteer military must compete with college and civilian jobs. In addition to ads that are more contemporary and informative, the armed services are hiring celebrity spokespersons, sponsoring made-for-TV extreme-sports competitions, and visiting schools and shopping malls with technology-filled exhibits. They also are making use of the Internet. In short, they are adopting the practices of corporate marketers.

 www.marines.com

diverse as paper stock and metals are finding that Internet brokers provide more alternative sources of supply while saving them time and money.[5]

Service firms constitute a huge market that buys goods and other services. Hilton Hotels, for example, buy blankets and sheets from textile manufacturers. Hospitals in the U.S. and abroad buy supplies from Baxter Healthcare Corporation. The Chicago Cubs and other major-league teams buy their Louisville Slugger baseball bats from Hillerich and Bradsby. And all these service firms buy legal, accounting, and consulting advice from other service marketers.

The "Nonbusiness" Business Market

In recent years some long-overdue marketing attention has been given to the multi-billion-dollar market comprised of so-called nonbusiness or not-for-profit organizations. The **nonbusiness market** includes such diverse institutions as churches, colleges and universities, museums, hospitals and other health care institutions, political parties, labor unions, and charitable organizations. To prosper, each of these so-called nonbusiness organizations should think of itself as a business enterprise. In the past, however, our society (and the institutions themselves) did not perceive a museum or a charity as a business because its primary objective is something other than making a profit. And many people today still feel uncomfortable thinking of their church, school, or political party as a business. Nevertheless, these organizations do virtually all the things that businesses do—offer a product, collect money, make investments, hire employees—except having profit as one of their goals. Therefore, they require professional management.

Not-for-profit organizations also conduct marketing campaigns—albeit under a different name—in an effort to attract billions of dollars in donations, grants, and contributions. In turn, they spend billions of dollars buying goods and services to run their operations and to provide for their clients.

Can a business marketer afford to have a local outlook?

While international markets may appear attractive to firms faced with intense competitive or regulatory pressures at home, there are many uncertainties and potential pitfalls for the unwary. One problem is the condition of the economy in a foreign market and its impact on imported goods. A firm or an industry can be lulled into complacency by a rosy domestic economy, while the situation beyond its borders where it does business may be far less attractive. Another problem is concentration. A firm or industry can become too dependent on one or two foreign markets, making a downturn in those markets devastating. A few recent examples illustrate these points:

- Problems in the Indonesian economy led to production cuts in its paper industry. This, in turn, had a large impact on several softwood pulp mills in the U.S. that had become heavily dependent on these Asian customers.

- Some Alaskan fishermen and fish processors relied on the Thai market for sales of surimi, a fish paste used in a number of products such as artificial crab. However, problems in the Japanese and South Korean economies caused competitors there to lower their prices to Thailand customers, taking much of the business away from the Alaskans.

- The demand for Australian beef in South Korea dropped by more than 95% in one year.

Foreign economic problems can also create headaches for firms not engaged in exporting. Many construction projects planned in Malaysia, Japan, and other Asian countries were canceled or postponed when the recession struck that region in the late 1990s. As a result, heavy construction equipment, bought in anticipation of those projects, was not needed. The Asian builders, hoping to recoup some of their investment, sold the new equipment back into the U.S. at 50% off the list price. The impact was felt by equipment manufacturers like Caterpillar and Deere, and even more dramatically by their dealers.

Sources: Steve Glain, "From Alaska Fisheries to Australian Outback, Asian Crisis Hits Home," *The Wall Street Journal*, Mar. 3, 1998, pp. A1+; De'Ann Weimer, "The Earth Is Shifting under Heavy Equipment," *Business Week*, Apr. 6, 1998, p. 44.

The International Market

Annual exports of goods and services by U.S. firms amount to approximately $1 trillion, a figure that has increased steadily since the mid-1980s. The biggest recent growth in the **international market** has been in medical products, scientific instruments, environmental protection systems, and consumer goods.

 www.usatrade.gov

Many small organizations are also heavily involved in the export market. These firms benefit from help from the U.S. Commerce Department with trade fairs and "matchmaking" programs, reduced language barriers as English becomes more common in global business, and greater access to markets via the Internet. The market-expanding potential of the Internet for small businesses is unprecedented. For example, Neoforma, a medical supplies distributor in California, uses its website to conduct business with the government of Oman and other international customers it could not reach any other way.[6]

Another dimension of international business is foreign-based subsidiaries. Alhough these sales do not count as exports, they are a significant part of the operations of many firms. McDonald's domestic sales are growing, but its foreign sales are growing nearly four times as fast, and now account for half the firm's total volume. A significant number of U.S. firms receive over half their total revenue from overseas subsidiaries. Included are Exxon, IBM, Philip Morris, Procter & Gamble, and Coca-Cola.

Operating overseas has several benefits for U.S. firms:

- It gains them access to countries participating in trade agreements that restrict imports from nonmembers. For example, a joint operation between Dow Chemical and Sumitomo in Japan to make high-performance plastics gives Dow greater access to the countries of the Pacific Rim than it would otherwise have.

- Manufacturing abroad allows firms to gain a better understanding of local markets and customers. Ford could have tried to export a windshield wiper to Europe that was designed for the U.S. market. Instead, through its German subsidiary, Ford learned that it had to produce a specially designed wiper to accommodate the speeds on German autobahns (where there are no speed limits!).
- Foreign operations contribute to the volume of a firm's exports. About 25% of all exports by U.S. firms are sales to affiliates located overseas.[7]

Characteristics of Business Market Demand

Four demand characteristics differentiate the business market from the consumer market. In business markets demand is derived, demand for a product tends to be inelastic, demand is widely fluctuating, and the market is well informed.

Demand Is Derived

The demand for a business product is derived from the demand for the consumer products in which that business product is used. Thus the demand for steel depends partially on consumer demand for automobiles and refrigerators, but it also depends on the demand for butter, baseball gloves, and CD players. This is because the tools, machines, and other equipment needed to make these items are made of steel. Consequently, as the demand for baseball gloves increases, Wilson Sporting Goods may buy more sewing machines with steel components and more steel filing cabinets for an expanding executive staff.

There are two significant marketing implications in the fact that business market demand is a derived demand. First, to estimate the demand for a product, a business marketer must be very familiar with how it is used. This is fairly easy for a company like Pratt & Whitney, a maker of jet engines. But what about the manufacturer of rubber O-rings (doughnut-shaped rings of all sizes that are used to seal connections)? Considerable research may be necessary to identify uses and users.

Second, the producer of a business product may find it worthwhile to engage in marketing efforts to encourage the sale of its buyers' products. For example, Intel advertises to consumers, urging them when buying PCs to ask specifically for products that contain Intel memory chips. Similarly, the NutraSweet Company ran a consumer advertising campaign designed to build consumer loyalty for products sweetened with NutraSweet. The idea, of course, is that increases in demand for these consumer products will, in turn, trigger increases in derived demand for their ingredients.

Demand Is Inelastic

Another characteristic of the business market is the demand elasticity of business products. **Elasticity of demand** refers to how responsive demand is to a change in the price of a product. (If you would like to review some economics relative to marketing, see Appendix A in Part 4 where demand elasticity and other concepts are explained.)

The demand for many business products is relatively inelastic, which means that the demand for a product responds very little to changes in its price. Two situations contribute to *inelasticity:*

- *If the cost of a part or of material is a small portion of the total cost of a finished product.* For example, Boeing, the maker of passenger jet airplanes, has over 1,200 suppliers. One, Huck International, produces fasteners for aerospace applications. If the price of fasteners should suddenly rise or fall considerably, how much effect would it have on the price of Boeing jets? Despite the fact that the fasteners are critical parts, they are such a small portion of a jet's cost that the price increase would not likely change the price of the plane. As a result, demand for passenger jets would remain the same, so there would be no appreciable change in the demand for fasteners either.

Even the cost of expensive capital equipment such as a robot used in assembling automobiles, when spread over the thousands of units it helps produce, becomes a very small part of the final price of each one. As a result, when the price of the business product changes, there is very little change in the price of the related consumer products. Because there is no appreciable shift in the demand for the consumer goods, then—by virtue of the derived-demand feature—there is no change in the demand for the business product.

- *If the part or material has no substitute.* In the mid-1990s the cost of white bond paper increased over 50% because of a shortage of supply. Because paper is a major component of catalogs and magazines, producers of these products had no alternative but to buy it. The catalog and magazine publishers were unable to pass the increase along to their customers because it would have nearly doubled the price of their publications. As a result, they were severely affected by the price change. The bond paper manufacturers, on the other hand, sold all they could produce at the higher price. However, an interesting longer-run effect was that catalog producers and other firms dependent on paper began looking at the Internet as a communication alternative sooner than they would have if paper prices had remained stable.

From a marketing point of view, three factors can moderate the inelasticity of business demand. The quantity of a product demanded is likely to be affected by a change in price:

- *If the price change occurs in a single firm.* An industry-wide cut in the price of aerospace fasteners used in jets will have little effect on the price of planes and therefore little effect on the demand for Boeing aircraft. Consequently, it will cause minimal shift in the total demand for fasteners. The pricing policy of an individual firm, however, can substantially alter the demand for its products. If one supplier cuts the price of its fasteners significantly, the drop in price may draw business away from competitors. Thus, in the short run, the demand curve faced by a single firm may be quite elastic. However, any advantage will likely be temporary, because competitors will almost certainly retaliate in some way to recapture their lost business.

- *If we adopt a long-run time perspective.* Much of our discussion thus far applies to short-term situations. Over the long run, the demand for a given business product is more elastic. If the price of cloth for women's suits rises, there probably will be no immediate change in the price of the finished garment. However, the increase in the cost of materials could very well be reflected in a rise in suit prices for next year. This rise could then influence the demand for suits, and thus for cloth, a year or more hence.

- *If the cost of a specific business product is a significant portion of the cost of the finished good.* We may generalize to this extent: The greater the cost of a business product as a percentage of the total price of the finished good, the greater the elasticity of demand for this business product.

Demand Is Widely Fluctuating

Although the demand for many business goods does not change much in response to price changes, it does respond to other factors. In fact, market demand for most classes of business goods fluctuates considerably more than the demand for consumer products. The demand for installations—major plant equipment, factories, and so on—is especially subject to change. Substantial fluctuations also exist in the market for accessory equipment—office furniture and machinery, delivery trucks, and similar products. The fluctuating demand for finished goods tends to accentuate the swings in the demand for raw materials and fabricating parts. We can see this very clearly when changes in demand in the construction and auto industries affect suppliers of lumber, steel, and other materials and parts. For example, Navistar, the manufacturer of diesel engines for trucks, has benefited greatly from the increase in demand for vans, pickups, and sport-utility vehicles.[8]

A major reason for these fluctuations is that individual businesses are very concerned about having a shortage of inventory when consumer demand increases or, alternatively, being caught with excess inventory should consumer demand decline. Thus they tend to overreact to signals from the economy, building inventories when they see signs of growth in the economy and working inventories down when the signs suggest a downturn. When the actions of all the individual firms are combined, the effect on their suppliers is widely fluctuating demand. This is known as the *acceleration principle*. One exception to this generalization is found in agricultural products intended for processing. Because people have to eat, there is a reasonably consistent demand for animals intended for meat products, for fruits and vegetables that will be canned or frozen, and for grains and dairy products used in cereals and baked goods.

Fluctuations in the demand for business products can influence all aspects of a marketing program. In product planning, fluctuating demand may stimulate a firm to diversify into other products to ease production and marketing problems. For example, IBM moved from concentrating on large, mainframe computers to software and consulting. Distribution strategies may also be affected. When demand declines, a manufacturer may discover that selling to some resellers is unprofitable, so they are dropped as customers. In its pricing, management may attempt to stem a decline in sales by cutting prices, hoping to attract customers away from competing firms. In a long struggle with imported steel and alternative products such as aluminum and fiberglass, Bethlehem Steel has repeatedly reduced prices.

Buyers Are Well Informed

Typically, business buyers are better informed about what they are buying than ultimate consumers. They know more about the relative merits of alternative sources of supply and competitive products for three reasons. First, there are relatively few alternatives for a business buyer to consider. Consumers generally have many more brands and sellers from which to choose than do business buyers. Consider, for example, how many options you would have in purchasing a TV set. However, in most business situations a buyer has only a few firms that offer the particular combination of product features and service desired. Second, the responsibility of a buyer in an organization is ordinarily limited to a few products. Unlike a consumer who buys many different things, a purchasing agent's job is to be very knowledgeable about a narrowly defined set of products. Third, for most consumer purchases, an error is only a minor inconvenience. However, in business buying the cost of a mistake may be thousands of dollars or even the decision maker's job!

The importance of information in business marketing has two significant implications. For sellers of business products, it means placing greater emphasis on personal selling than do firms that market consumer products. Business sales people must be carefully selected, properly trained, and adequately compensated. They must give effective sales presentations and furnish satisfactory service both before and after each sale is made. Sales executives are devoting increased effort to the assignment of sales people to important customers, called key accounts, to ensure that these reps are compatible with business buyers.

For buyers and sellers, information is valuable, and the Internet has made information even more accessible. As the chapter-opening case demonstrates, FreeMarkets makes it possible for a buyer to consider the bids of many sellers in a short period of time. Thus, it and similar online auction services permit unprecedented comparison shopping. The Internet has also made it efficient for buyers to pool their purchasing power to get better prices. By combining their needs over an intranet and buying on the Internet, various divisions of General Electric have saved 20% on $1 billion in purchases of operating supplies. Finally, the Internet has extended the geographic reach of both buyers and sellers. Firms that previously did business only domestically have discovered entirely new opportunities on the Internet.[9]

Determinants of Business Market Demand

Recall from Chapter 4 that to analyze a consumer market a marketer would study the distribution of population and various demographics such as income, and then try to determine the consumers' buying motives and habits. Essentially the same type of analysis is used by a firm selling to the business market. The only difference, but a very important one, is the attributes selected for analysis. The factors affecting the market for business products include the number of potential business users and their purchasing power, their buying motives, and their buying habits. In the following discussion we'll identify several basic differences between consumer markets and business markets.

Number and Types of Business Users

Number of Buyers

The business market contains relatively few buying units compared to the consumer market. In the U.S. there are about 20 million business users, in contrast to about 270 million consumers divided among more than 100 million households. The business market is even more limited because most companies sell to only a small segment of the total market. For example, a firm that sells to U.S. manufacturers of light bulbs can cover 97% of the manufacturing capacity of the industry by contacting only 39 firms. Similarly, four firms produce 78% of lead pencils, and eight firms make 85% of household vacuum cleaners. Consequently, business marketing executives are able to pinpoint their market carefully by type of industry and geographic location, sometimes down to the level of individually identifying every prospect. A firm that markets hard-rock mining equipment is not interested in the total business market, or even in all 30,000 firms engaged in all forms of mining and quarrying. It needs only focus on the hard-rock mining companies.

For many years marketers have relied on a method for organizing industry information called the **Standard Industrial Classification (SIC) system.** In this system designed by the federal government, all types of businesses in the U.S. are divided into 10 groups, with a range of two-digit code numbers assigned to each group. Then additional numbers are used to subdivide each of the major industries into smaller segments. For example, food manufacturing is designated 20, dairy products within the food industry are classified as 202, and butter, as a subset of dairy products, is 2022. The federal government publishes a considerable amount of market information for each four-digit industry classification, including

Table 5.1 NAICS Industry Sectors and the Classification of the Pager Industry

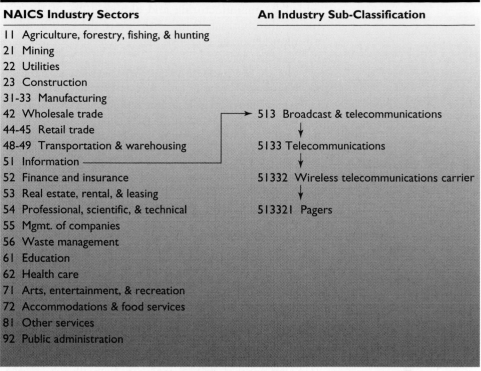

NAICS Industry Sectors	An Industry Sub-Classification
11 Agriculture, forestry, fishing, & hunting	
21 Mining	
22 Utilities	
23 Construction	
31-33 Manufacturing	
42 Wholesale trade	→ 513 Broadcast & telecommunications
44-45 Retail trade	↓
48-49 Transportation & warehousing	5133 Telecommunications
51 Information	↓
52 Finance and insurance	51332 Wireless telecommunications carrier
53 Real estate, rental, & leasing	↓
54 Professional, scientific, & technical	513321 Pagers
55 Mgmt. of companies	
56 Waste management	
61 Education	
62 Health care	
71 Arts, entertainment, & recreation	
72 Accommodations & food services	
81 Other services	
92 Public administration	

Source: North American Industry Classification System—United States, 1997, U.S. Government Printing Office, Washington, DC, 1997.

the number of establishments, employment, and sales volume—all by geographic area. These valuable data are used by marketers to identify potential target industries, geographic markets, and patterns of growth and decline.[10]

www.census.gov/epcd/ www/naics.html

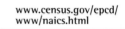

All federal government data reported prior to 1997 rely on the SIC system. Subsequent data use the new **North American Industry Classification System (NAICS)**, jointly adopted by the U.S., Canada, and Mexico. The NAICS is similar to the SIC code, but has 20 (rather than 10) industry sectors, providing a more detailed and contemporary classification scheme. These 20 NAICS groups are subdivided into 96 three-digit subsectors, 313 four-digit industry groups, and 1,170 five and six-digit industries. Table 5.1 lists the NAICS two-digit industry sector codes, and shows the breakdown for one industry, pagers—a segment of the wireless telecommunications industry—within the information sector.[11]

One limitation of data reported using these codes is that a multiproduct company is listed in only its largest four-digit category. Thus, the diversity of a conglomerate such as Sara Lee, which produces bakery goods and hosiery, is hidden. Also, the government's nondisclosure rules prevent revealing information that will identify a given establishment. Consequently, four-digit detail is not available for an industry in a geographic location where this information would easily identify a particular company.

Size of Business Users

Although the business market may be limited in the total number of buyers, it is large in purchasing power. A relatively small percentage of firms account for the greatest share of the value added to products by manufacturing. **Value added** is the dollar value of a firm's output minus the value of the inputs it purchased from other firms. If a manufacturer buys lumber for $40 and converts it into a table that it sells for $100, the value added by the manufacturer is $60.

According to the *Census of Manufactures,*[12] less than 2% of all firms—those with 500 or more employees—accounted for almost 50% of the total dollar value added by manufacturing and almost 40% of the total employment in manufacturing. In contrast, firms with fewer than 100 employees accounted for 90% of all manufacturing establishments, but they produced only 23% of the value added by manufacturing.

The marketing significance of these facts is that buying power in many business markets is highly concentrated in a relatively few firms. That is, a high percentage of industry sales are accounted for by a very small number of firms. That's obvious in some major industries such as automobiles, mainframe computers, and jet aircraft, but it is also true in many smaller industries To illustrate, according to the *Census of Manufactures,* the U.S. has only:

- 65 thread mills
- 31 manufacturers of house slippers
- 26 producers of vegetable oil
- 17 cane sugar refineries

When industries have such a small number of firms, suppliers have the opportunity to deal with them directly. As a result, middlemen often are not as essential in business markets as they are in the consumer market.

Of course, these statements are broad generalizations covering the total business market. They do not take into account the variation in business concentration from one industry to another. In some industries—women's dresses, upholstered furniture, natural and processed cheese, and ready-mix concrete, for example—there are many producers and, therefore, a relatively low level of concentration. Nevertheless, even a so-called low-concentration industry represents far more concentration than anything in the consumer market.

Regional Concentration of Business Users

There is substantial regional concentration in many major industries and among business users as a whole. A firm that sells products used in copper mining will find the bulk of its American market in Utah and Arizona, and a large percentage of American-produced shoes come from the Southeast.

The eight states constituting the Middle Atlantic and East North Central census regions account for almost 40% of the total value added by manufacturing. Just 10 Standard Metropolitan Areas alone account for about 25% of the total U.S. value added by manufacturing.

Vertical and Horizontal Business Markets

For effective marketing planning, a company should know whether the market for its products is vertical or horizontal. A **vertical business market** exists when a firm's product is usable by virtually all the firms in only one or two industries. For example, aircraft landing gear is intended only for the airplane manufacturing market, but every plane maker is a potential customer. A **horizontal business market** is one in which the firm's product is usable by many industries. Business supplies, such as Pennzoil lubricating oils and greases, General Electric small motors, and Weyerhauser paper products, are examples of products with horizontal markets.

A company's marketing program ordinarily is influenced by whether its markets are vertical or horizontal. In a vertical market, a product can be tailor-made to meet the specific needs of one industry. However, the industry must buy enough to support this specialization. In addition, advertising and personal selling can be directed more effectively in vertical markets. In a horizontal market, a product is developed as an all-purpose item, to reach a larger market. Because of the larger potential market, however, the product is likely to face more competition.

Buying Power of Business Users

Another determinant of business market demand is the purchasing power of business customers. This can be measured either by the expenditures of business users or by their sales volume. Unfortunately, such information is not always available or is very difficult to estimate. In such cases purchasing power is estimated indirectly using an **activity indicator of buying power**—that is, some market factor related to sales and expenditures. Sometimes an activity indicator is a combined measure of purchasing power and the number of business users. Government agencies from the local level to the federal level compile a wide range of useful statistics. Go to www.census.gov and click on "The Economic Census" for more details. Following are examples of activity indicators that give some idea of the purchasing power of business users.

Measures of Manufacturing Activity

Firms that sell to manufacturers might use as activity indicators the number of employees, the number of plants, or the dollar value added by manufacturing. One firm that sells work gloves determined the relative attractiveness of various geographic areas from the number of employees in manufacturing establishments within the areas. Another company that sells a product to control stream pollution used two indicators to estimate potential demand: (1) the number of firms processing wood products (paper mills, plywood mills, and so forth) and (2) the manufacturing value added by these firms. These types of data are available in the *Census of Manufactures,* conducted and reported every five years. Yearly updates are available in the *Annual Survey of Manufactures,* a report based on a sample of 55,000 manufacturing firms.

Measures of Mining Activity

The number of mines operating, the volume of their output, and the dollar value of the product as it leaves the mine may all indicate the purchasing power of mining and mining-related firms. These data are published every five years in the *Census of Mineral Industries.* This information is useful to any firm marketing business products related to extracting and processing everything from aluminum to zirconium.

Measures of Agricultural Activity

A company marketing agricultural products or equipment can estimate the buying power of its farm market by studying such indicators as cash farm income, commodity prices, acreage planted, or crop yields. A chemical producer that sells to a fertilizer manufacturer might study the same indices, because the demand for chemicals in this case derives from the demand for fertilizer. These data are in the *Census of Agriculture.*

Measures of Construction Activity

If a business is marketing building materials, such as lumber, brick, gypsum products, or builders' hardware, its market depends on construction activity. This can be gauged by the number and value of building permits issued. Another indicator is the number of construction starts by type of structure (single-family residence, apartment, or commercial). Local data are available from county and city records, whereas *Current Construction Reports,* published monthly by the U.S. Commerce Department, provides regional and national statistics.

These sources illustrate the kinds of information available for predicting buying power of business markets. Many other public and private information sources are useful in forecasting demand. We will have more to say about forecasting in Chapter 6.

Business Buying Behavior

Business buying behavior, like consumer buying behavior, is initiated when an aroused need (a motive) is recognized. This leads to goal-oriented activity designed to satisfy the need. Once again, marketers must try to determine what motivates the buyer, and then understand the buying process and buying patterns of business organizations in their markets. The actual process is very similar to consumer decision-making, except the influences are different. Figure 5.1 summarizes the business buying-decision process and the primary influences.

The Importance of Business Buying

Business buying or purchasing, formerly a relatively minor function in most firms, is now an activity of great interest to top management. Once viewed as an isolated activity that focused primarily on searching out low prices, purchasing has become an important part of overall strategy for at least three reasons:

- *Companies are making less and buying more.* For example, Toyota annually buys $8 billion worth of parts, materials, and services from hundreds of U.S. suppliers for use in its production both in the U.S. and overseas. When outside suppliers become this significant, buying becomes a prime strategic issue.
- *Firms are under intense quality and time pressures.* To reduce costs and improve efficiency, firms no longer tolerate defective parts and supplies. In cooperation with its suppliers, DaimlerChrysler, which relies on outside suppliers for 70% of its production parts and materials, has implemented a widely

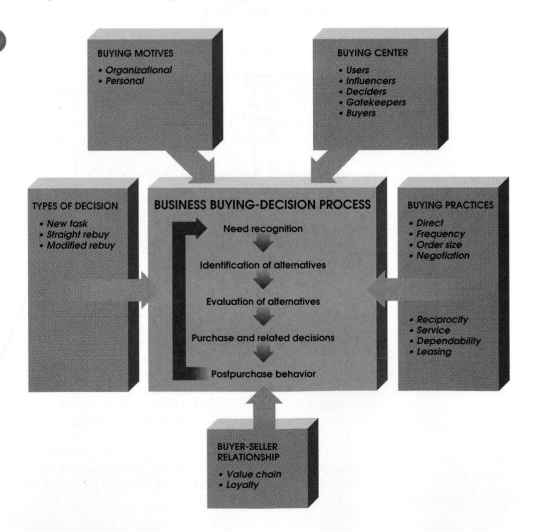

Figure 5.1

The business buying-decision process and the factors that influence it.

copied quality and innovation program called supplier cost reduction effort (SCORE). The program provides incentives to suppliers that can reduce costs or enhance product performance at the same cost. In addition, DaimlerChrysler has implemented a real-time computer system that allows suppliers to check on the performance of their parts and supplies on a daily basis.[13]

- *Firms are concentrating their purchases.* To get what they need, companies are dealing with fewer suppliers but are developing long-term "partnering" relationships with them. This level of involvement extends beyond a purchase to include such things as working together to develop new products and providing financial support.

Buying-Decision Process in Business

The buying-decision process in business markets is a sequence of five stages. It is depicted in the center of Figure 5.1. To illustrate the process, let's assume that Continental Baking Company, responding to increased concerns about nutrition, is considering using a fat substitute in some baked goods:

- *Need recognition.* Continental's marketing executives are sensitive to the concerns of many consumers about fat in their diets. The opportunity to produce high-quality, good-tasting baked goods without fat is very attractive, but finding the right substitute is the challenge.

- *Identification of alternatives.* The managers draw up a list of product-performance specifications for the fat-free baked goods—attractive appearance, good taste, and competitive price—and some requirements for the fat substitute—ease of use, reasonable cost, and available supply. Then the purchasing department identifies the alternative brands and supply sources of fat substitutes that generally meet these specifications. Possibilities include Olean made

The similarities in how business buyers and consumers make decisions are apparent in this ad for business products. Ricoh makes copiers, facsimile machines, scanners, printers, cameras, and related supplies. In the U.S. alone it is a $1.6 billion company. Just like an ad directed to consumers, this ad first gets the reader's attention (using a slightly ambiguous illustration), conveys an appealing message (a history of leadership and innovations), stresses a brand name (Aficio), and asks for action (invites contact with the company).

 www.ricoh.usa.com

by Procter & Gamble, Simplesse produced by Monsanto, Stella made by Staley, and a few others.

- *Evaluation of alternatives.* The production, research, and purchasing people jointly evaluate both the alternative products and sources of supply. Familiar suppliers are invited to make presentation, and knowledgeable sources are contacted for information. They discover that some brands cannot withstand high temperatures, there are differences in how well they simulate the taste and texture of fat, and the approval from the Food and Drug Administration restricts the uses for others. The complete evaluation considers such factors as product performance and price as well as the suppliers' abilities to meet delivery schedules and provide consistent quality.

- *Purchase decision.* Based on the evaluation, the buyer decides on a specific brand and supplier. Next, the purchasing department negotiates the contract. Because large sums are involved, the contract will likely include many details. For example, the contract might go beyond price and delivery schedules to include provision of marketing support for Continental's finished baked goods by the producer of the fat substitute.

- *Postpurchase behavior.* Continental continues to evaluate the performances of the fat substitute and the selected supplier to ensure that both meet expectations. Future dealings with a supplier will depend on this performance evaluation and on how well the supplier handles any problems that may later arise involving its product.

In the following sections we will explore several of the differences between consumer buying behavior and business buying behavior that are reflected in this scenario.

Buying Motives of Business Users

Business buying motives are the needs that direct the purchasing behavior of business users. As shown in Figure 5.1, they fall into two broad categories—organizational and personal. Generally, business purchases are methodical and structured. Thus business buying motives are presumed to be, for the most part, practical and unemotional. Business buyers are assumed to be motivated to achieve organizational goals by securing the optimal combination of price, quality, and service in the products they buy.

An opposing view is that business buyers are human, and their business decisions are certainly influenced by their attitudes, perceptions, and values. In fact, many sales people would maintain that business buyers seem to be motivated more toward personal goals than organizational goals, and the two are often in conflict.

The truth is actually somewhere in between. Business buyers have two goals—to further their company's position (in profits, in acceptance by society) and to protect or improve their position in their firms (self-interest). Sometimes these goals are mutually consistent. For example, the firm's highest priority may be to save money, and the buyer expects to be rewarded for negotiating a low price. Obviously the more consistent the goals are, the better for both the organization and the individual, and the easier it is to make buying decisions.

However, there are often significant areas where the buyer's goals do not coincide with those of the firm, such as when the firm insists on dealing with the lowest-price supplier, but the buyer has developed a good relationship with another supplier and doesn't want to change. In these cases a seller must appeal to the buyer both on a rational "what's good for the firm" basis, and on a self-interest "what's in it for you" basis. Promotional appeals directed to the buyer's self-interest are particularly useful when two or more competing sellers are offering essentially the same products, prices, and postsale services.

Types of Buying Situations

In Chapter 4 we observed that consumer purchases can range from routine to complex buying decisions. In like manner the buying situations in business organizations vary widely in their complexity, number of people involved, and time required. Thus, not every purchase involves all five steps of the buying decision process.

To account for these different situations, Figure 5.1 depicts three classes of business buying situations. The three **buy classes** are new-task buying, straight rebuy, and modified rebuy:

- **New-task buying.** This is the most difficult and complex buying situation because it is a first-time purchase of a major product. Typically more people are involved in new-task buying than in the other two situations because the risk is great. Information needs are high and the evaluation of alternatives is difficult because the decision makers have little experience with the product. Sellers have the challenge of discovering the buyer's needs and communicating the product's ability to provide satisfaction. A hospital's first-time purchase of laser surgical equipment and a company buying robots for a factory (or buying the factory itself) are likely to be new-task buying conditions.

- **Straight rebuy.** This is a routine, low-involvement purchase with minimal information needs and no great consideration of alternatives. The buyer's extensive experience with the seller has been satisfactory, so there is no incentive to search. An example is the repeat purchase of linens and towels by a hospital. These buying decisions are made in the purchasing department, usually from a predetermined list of acceptable suppliers. If a supplier is not on this list, it may have difficulty getting in to make a sales presentation to the buyer.

- **Modified rebuy.** This buying situation is somewhere between the other two in terms of time and people involved, information needed, and alternatives considered. For example, in selecting diagnostic equipment to test blood samples, a hospital would consider a small number of reputable suppliers and evaluate the new features added to the products since its last purchase. Similarly, a school district would review textbooks from a defined group of publishers in selecting a book to replace an outdated edition.

Understanding how the buyer views a buying situation is very important to a seller. The allocation of sales resources, the nature of the presentation made to the buyer, and even the prices offered are influenced by the buyer's need for information.

Multiple Buying Influences—the Buying Center

A **buying center** consists of all the individuals or groups involved in the process of making a decision to purchase. This includes the individuals within and outside an organization that influence the buying decision as well as the person ultimately responsible for the decision. Typically the members of a buying center are not formally identified. That is, there is no list of the buying center members to which a supplier or sales person can refer. One of the biggest challenges in business-to-business marketing is identifying the members of the buying center and their roles for a particular purchase.

Research suggests that the average size of a buying center ranges from three to five persons.[14] In other words, there are *multiple* buying influences, particularly in medium-sized and large firms. Even in small companies where the owner-managers make all major decisions, knowledgeable employees are usually consulted before certain purchases are made. The size and makeup of a buying center will vary depending on the product's cost, the complexity of the decision, and the stage of the buying process. The buying center for a straight rebuy of office supplies

Should a business marketer try to overcome a price disadvantage?

For years consumers carried their groceries home in paper bags. In fact, in 1982, fully 95% of all groceries purchased in the U.S. left the store in paper. However, by 1998 the figure had slipped to 20%, with the difference made up by plastic. The decline in the use of paper has little to do with consumer preferences and everything to do with cost, because plastic bags cost about half of what paper bags cost (2 cents versus 4 cents). With grocery stores operating on profit margins of 1 to 2% of sales, savings in any area are viewed as critical.

How do consumers feel about the bagging situation? According to a national survey, about 60% say they prefer paper for several reasons, citing strength, size, and the opportunity to reuse the bags. Grocers are aware of this preference. According to the director of operations in a 56-store Arizona chain, if his stores began offering paper bags "there would be no going back. Customers would get hooked on them."

S&G Packaging, a paper bag maker, has taken the battle a step further, producing a paper bag with handles. Consumers like it, but it costs even more than standard paper bags. According to a sales executive from a paper bag company, "The person making the buying decision on bags is a buyer who has a gun to his head to reduce costs."

Should S&G try to sell paper bags to supermarkets? If so, what approach should it use with the buying center of a supermarket?

Sources: Calmetta Y. Coleman, "Pushing Paper in a Plastic World," *The Wall Street Journal,* Feb. 24, 1998, pp. B1+; "It's in the Bag," *Progressive Grocer,* May 1996, p. SR14.

will be quite different from the center handling the purchase of a building or a fleet of trucks. Recognizing the existence of buying centers helps sellers appreciate that a successful sales effort seldom can be directed to a single individual.

As shown in Figure 5.1, a buying center includes the people who play any of the following **buying roles:**

- *Users*—the people who actually use the business product, perhaps a secretary, an executive, a production-line worker, or a truck driver.
- *Influencers*—the people who set the specifications and aspects of buying decisions because of their technical expertise, their organizational position, or even their political power in the firm.
- *Deciders*—the people who make the actual buying decision regarding the business product and the supplier. A purchasing agent may be the decider in a straight-rebuy situation. But someone in top management may make the decision regarding whether to buy an expensive computer system.
- *Gatekeepers*—the people who control the flow of purchasing information within the organization as well as between the firm and potential vendors. These people may be purchasing agents, secretaries, receptionists, or technical personnel.
- *Buyers*—the people who interact with the suppliers, arrange the terms of sale, and process the actual purchase orders. Typically this is the purchasing department's role. But again, if the purchase is an expensive, complex new buy, the buyer's role may be filled by someone in top management.

Several people in an organization may play the same role. For example, in the same firm, accountants and product designers use PCs for different purposes. As a result, they may prefer different brands. Or the same person may occupy more than one role. A secretary may be a user, an influencer, and a gatekeeper in the purchase of word processing equipment.

The variety of people contributing to any business buying decision, plus the differences among companies, present real challenges to sales people. As they try to determine "who's on first"—that is, determine who does what in a buying situation—sales reps often call on the wrong people. Even knowing who the decision makers are is not enough, because these people may be very difficult to reach and people move into and out of the buying center as the purchase proceeds through the decision process. This, in part, explains why a sales person typically has only a few major accounts.

Certainly the challenges presented in the business buying-decision process should suggest the importance of coordinating the selling activities of the business marketer with the buying needs of the purchasing organization.

Buyer-Seller Relationships

A purchase can be looked upon as an isolated transaction or as part of a larger relationship that involves more parties than the buyer and seller and more interaction than the specific exchange. Figure 5.1 notes two dimensions of this relationship perspective—the value chain and loyalty.

Rather than focus only on the immediate customer, many marketers approach marketing as a series of links between buyers and sellers. This **value chain** approach considers the roles of suppliers, producers, distributors, and end users to see how each adds value to and benefits from the final product. This perspective leads to a recognition and understanding of the roles played by all the parties involved in successfully bringing a product to market.

Business marketers are also placing greater emphasis on building repeat customers. Research has shown that it is as much as six times less expensive to make a repeat sale than it is to make a sale to a new customer. Repeat sales are often the result of **loyalty**—a willingness of the buyer to purchase from the seller without an extensive evaluation of alternatives. Loyalty requires a high level of trust on the part of the buyer. The time and effort necessary to build such trust

At first glance this may appear to be an ad for Goodyear, and in a sense it is. When you go to www.cabletron.com/ goodyear, you'll see a complete explanation of how Goodyear is implementing operational enhancements including faster product introductions and enhanced internal communications by utilizing Cabletron's networking systems for its computers. So why would Cabletron emphasize Goodyear in an ad for its products? First, because Goodyear is a better known company and is more likely to attract the attention of readers. Second, because the relationship with Goodyear gives Cabletron greater credibility with other prospective customers.

www.cabletron.com/ goodyear

is a major undertaking for both parties. For example, it typically entails sharing information about costs, processes, and plans for the future. The process of moving toward long-term, cost effective, mutually beneficial trust with selected customers is known as **relationship marketing,** and is the goal of many businesses today.[15]

Several traditional business practices tend to discourage relationship building. For example, compensation plans for sales people that reward the volume of sales may result in customers' needs being overlooked. Likewise, the common accounting practice of treating each department in a firm as a cost center may cause managers to focus on cost minimization rather than customer service. And even the procedure of setting individual department performance goals may foster an environment of competition rather than cooperation.

Building and maintaining relationships may require changing the way business is done. For example, Apple Computer, which once relied exclusively on dealers, recognized that many of its larger customers needed specialized service. To satisfy this segment of the market and maintain strong ties to these key customers, the computer firm now has its own sales force calling directly on about 1,000 large accounts. However, many of the orders taken by the sales force are passed along to the dealers for fulfillment to ensure that they are protected as well.

Buying Practices of Business Users

Buying practices in the business market are similar to situational influences in consumer behavior. Several are shown in Figure 5.1. These practices, which are described below, stem from the nature and use of the products and characteristics of the markets.

Direct Purchase

In the consumer market, consumers rarely buy directly from the producer except in the case of services. In the business market, however, direct purchase by the business user from the producer is quite common even for goods. This is true especially when the order is large and the buyer needs much technical assistance. Makers of microprocessors and semiconductors, such as Intel Corp. and Micron Technology, deal directly with personal computer manufacturers because the memory technology is changing so rapidly. From a seller's point of view, direct sale in the business market is reasonable, especially when there are relatively few potential buyers, they are big, or they are geographically concentrated.

Frequency of Purchase

In the business market, firms buy certain products very infrequently. Large installations are purchased only once in many years. Small parts and materials to be used in the manufacture of a product may be ordered on long-term contracts, thus a selling opportunity exists as seldom as once a year. Even standard operating supplies, such as office supplies or cleaning products, may be bought only once a month. Because of this buying pattern, a great burden is placed on the personal selling programs of business sellers. The sales force must call on potential customers often enough to keep them familiar with the company's products and to know when a customer is considering a purchase.

Size of Order

The average business order is considerably larger than its counterpart in the consumer market. This fact, coupled with the infrequency of purchase, spotlights the significance of each sale in the business market. Verson, in its Chicago operation, makes metal presses that are sold to appliance manufacturers and automakers. Its newest product is 49 feet tall and weighs 5 million pounds. Recently Daimler-Chrysler bought three of the presses for $30 million apiece. Given the relatively few number of automakers and the length of time a metal press of this size will be used, each prospective sale is very important to Verson.

Length of Negotiation Period

The period of negotiation in a business sale is usually much longer than in a consumer transaction. Some reasons for extended negotiations follow:
- Several executives participate in the buying decision.
- The sale involves a large amount of money.
- The business product is made to order and considerable discussion is required to establish the specifications.

Reciprocity Arrangements

A highly controversial business buying practice is reciprocity: the policy of "I'll buy from you if you'll buy from me." Traditionally, reciprocity was common among firms marketing homogeneous basic business products (oil, steel, rubber, paper products, and chemicals).

There has been a significant decline, but not elimination, of reciprocity. This decline has occurred for two reasons, one legal and the other economic. Both the Federal Trade Commission and the Antitrust Division of the Department of Justice have forbidden the practice of reciprocity in any *systematic* manner, particularly in large companies. A firm can buy from a customer, but it must be able to prove that it is not given any special privileges regarding price, quality, or service.

From an economic point of view, reciprocity may not make sense because the price, quality, or service offered by the seller may not be competitive. In addition, when a firm fails to pursue objectives that maximize profits, morale of both the sales force and the purchasing department may suffer.

Reciprocity is an area in which U.S. firms run into problems in doing business overseas. In many parts of the world, it is taken for granted that if I buy your product, you will buy mine.

Service Expectation

The user's desire for excellent service is a strong business buying motive that may determine buying practices. Frequently a firm's only differentiating feature is its service, because the product itself is so standardized that it can be purchased from any number of companies. Consider the choice of suppliers that provide elevators for a major office building or hotel. The installation of the elevators is no more important than keeping them operating safely and efficiently. Consequently, in its marketing efforts, a firm such as Montgomery Elevator emphasizes its maintenance service as much as its products.

Sellers must be ready to furnish services both before and after the sale. For example, suppliers such as Kraft Foods conduct a careful analysis of a supermarket's customers and sales performance and then suggest a product assortment and layout for the store's dairy department. In the case of office copiers, manufacturers train the buyers' office staffs in the use of the equipment and, after the machines have been installed, offer other services, such as repairs by specially trained technicians.

Market-oriented companies recognize the value of extraordinary service. For example, when a timing belt on a piece of equipment failed at a Frito-Lay processing plant, the manager contacted Motion Industries, a nearby industrial supplier, for a replacement part. Normally an emergency delivery would take an hour. However, on this particular day heavy rains had isolated the small town where the plant is located. Motion's owner rented a small plane, had the pilot fly over the Frito-Lay plant, and the needed part was dropped to the waiting maintenance manager on the ground. Motion Industries almost certainly lost money on the sale, but because it helped the plant manager save 25,000 pounds of potatoes, it may have won a customer for life.

Dependability of Supply

Another business buying practice is the user's insistence on an adequate quantity of uniform-quality products. Variations in the *quality* of materials going into finished products can cause considerable trouble for manufacturers. They may be faced with costly disruptions in their production processes if the imperfections exceed quality control limits. The emphasis on total quality has increased the significance of dependability. Because it has been established that firms can operate with virtually zero defects, buyers expect a very high standard of performance.

Adequate *quantities* are as important as good quality. A work stoppage caused by an insufficient supply of materials is just as costly as one caused by inferior quality of materials. However, firms refuse to buy well in advance of their needs, because doing so would tie up their resources in large inventories of supplies. In order for suppliers to provide sufficient quantities of a product just in time for the buyer's intended use, called just-in-time (JIT) delivery, unprecedented amounts of information must be exchanged. For example, Ford permits its automotive suppliers to have access to its detailed production schedule in order that critical parts and components can be delivered exactly when they are needed.

Leasing

Many firms in the business market lease business goods instead of buying them. In the past this practice was limited to large equipment, such as computers (IBM), packaging equipment (American Can Company), and heavy construction equipment. Presently, industrial firms are expanding leasing arrangements to include delivery trucks, automobiles used by sales people, machine tools, and other items that are generally less expensive than major installations.

Leasing has several merits for the lessor—the firm providing the equipment:

- Total net income—the income after charging off repairs and maintenance expenses—is often higher than it would be if the equipment were sold.
- The lessor's market may be expanded to include users who could not afford to buy the product, especially for large equipment.

Where will electronic commerce have the greatest impact?

It's hard to ignore the various types of electronic commerce designed for consumers. Hardly a day goes by that there isn't a major media story about a bizarre item up for auction on eBay.com, the unusual grocery products available online from Peapod.com, or the price wars being waged by Amazon.com against other Internet book sellers. These stories could create the impression that electronic commerce—marketing over the Internet—is primarily a retail phenomenon. However, nothing could be further from the truth.

The major driver behind e-commerce is companies using the Internet to conduct transactions with other companies. This is called business-to-business marketing, or B2B, to distinguish it from business-to-consumers marketing. In 1998, it is estimated that $43 billion in B2B transaction were made over websites, while e-commerce sales to consumers amounted to $8 billion. In 1999, the comparable figures were $109 billion for B2B and $19 billion for business-to-consumers. As an increasing number of firms see the benefits of e-commerce, the spread is expected to widen even more. Forecasts for 2003 have B2B e-commerce at $1.3 *trillion*, with consumer online sales at less than $100 *billion*.

B2B auctions (such as ones created by FreeMarkets in the chapter opening) are made possible by electronic networks on the Internet. They have generated considerable interest because they introduce purchasers to new potential suppliers and sellers to new customers. However, the bulk of B2B e-commerce transactions are routine purchases simply made more efficient by the Internet.

Among the many possible implications attributed to the growth of Internet B2B marketing are:

- Salespeople will not be the primary source of added value in transactions because much of what they do can be accomplished on the Internet at a lower cost. If just 5% of the firms in an industry shift their transactions to e-commerce, it will change the entire structure of the industry because longstanding inefficiencies will be uncovered and eliminated.

- Small manufacturers who do not move to the Internet quickly will be unable to compete because larger firms will become even more cost effective by buying and selling online. Entrepreneurs will identify new ways to bring buyers and sellers together in cyberspace that will replace many of today's middlemen.

Sources: Peter Svensson, "Business Deals Are Pushing Beanie Baby Auctions Aside," *The St. Louis Post-Dispatch*, Nov. 24, 1999, p. C7; Michelle V. Rafter, "Internet E-Commerce Expects Business-to-Business Growth," *The St. Louis Post-Dispatch*, Oct. 27, 1999, p. C8; Michael Casey, "Internet Changes the Face of Supply and Demand," *The Wall Street Journal*, Oct. 18, 1999, p. A43K.

- Leasing offers an effective method of getting users to try a new product. They may be more willing to rent a product than to buy it. If they are not satisfied, their expenditure is limited to a few monthly payments.

From the lessee's—or customer's—point of view, the benefits of leasing follow:

- Leasing allows users to retain their investment capital for other purposes.
- Firms can enter a new business with less capital outlay than would be necessary if they had to buy equipment.
- Leased products are usually repaired and maintained by lessors, eliminating one headache associated with ownership.
- Leasing is particularly attractive to firms that need equipment seasonally or sporadically, as in food canning or construction.

The Impact of Electronic Commerce

The most important feature differentiating business from consumer marketing is the customization of products. Because of the significance of a purchase on the buyer's operation, business products often have to be adapted to the user's specific circumstances. For example, Freightliner, a truck manufacturer, works with customers to design individual trucks to meet the buyer's needs. Thus, hundreds of decisions are required, all the way from the engine type and size to the configuration of the outside mirrors. Verson's metal presses, described earlier, each take 18 months to build to meet the customized needs of the buyer. As a result, in many business marketing situations there must be a close, personal working relationship between many levels and functions of buyers and sellers.

However, there are also many business purchases of standardized products. For example, the sale of commodities such as bulk plastic, diesel fuel, and steel stock require much less buyer-seller interaction. There are also many low-technology, standardized products such as office supplies, maintenance products, and many component parts that are purchased in large quantities. An increasing number of firms are using the World Wide Web to facilitate buying these standardized products. For example, Ford Motor Co. plans to shift all of its 1.5 million annual purchases of non-production related items, to the Internet by 2003.[16]

Electronic commerce, which involves interactions and transactions over the Internet, takes many forms. The reverse auctions conducted by FreeMarkets, the subject of the chapter-opening case, is a version that is growing in popularity. Also, electronic bulletins boards (where sellers can post their offerings and prospective buyers can post their needs) are expanding rapidly. Web-based firms such as Ariba and Commerce One are giving buyers and sellers 24-hour, real time access to each other.[17]

www.ariba.com

www.commerceone.com

Electronic commerce will not change all business marketing. There is still a need for personalized relationships in most situations. However, the impact and growth of business transactions on the Internet is a major development that requires the attention of all business marketers. Therefore, we will describe it in detail in Chapter 22.

At this point you know what marketing is and how it fits into an organization's strategy. You also appreciate the nature of consumer and business markets, and how they function. With this background, we are now ready to examine how firms identify the particular markets they wish to serve.

Summary

The business market consists of organizations that buy goods and services to produce other goods and services, to resell to other business users or consumers, or to conduct the organization's operations. It is an extremely large and complex market spanning a wide variety of business users that buy a broad array of business goods and services. Besides manufacturing, the business market includes agriculture, reseller, government, services, nonprofit, and international components.

Business market demand generally is derived, inelastic, and widely fluctuating. Business buyers usually are well informed about what they are buying. Business market demand is analyzed by evaluating the number and kinds of business users and their buying power.

Business buying, or purchasing, has taken on greater strategic importance. Organizations are buying more and making less, under intense time and quality pressures, and developing long-term partnering relationships with suppliers.

The buying-decision process in business markets may involve as many as five stages: need recognition, identification of alternatives, evaluation of alternatives, purchase decision, and postpurchase behavior. The actual number of stages in a given purchase decision depends on a number of factors including buying motives, the type of decision, the buying center, the buyer-seller relationship, and business buying patterns.

Business buying motives are focused on achieving a firm's objectives, but the business buyer's self-interest must also be considered. The types of business buying situations are new-task buy, straight rebuy, or modified rebuy.

The concept of a buying center reflects the multiple buying influences in business purchasing decisions. In a typical buying center are people playing the roles of users, influencers, deciders, gatekeepers, and buyers.

Developing a buyer-seller relationship stems from recognizing the importance of the customer's value chain and the benefits of developing loyalty. Relationships require commitment and are built on trust and sharing of information.

Buying practices of business users often are quite different from buying practices in the consumer market. In the business market, direct purchases (that is, without middlemen) are more common, purchases are made less frequently, and orders are larger. The negotiation period usually is longer, and reciprocity arrangements are more common. The demand for service is greater, and the dependability of supply is more critical. Finally, leasing (rather than product ownership) is quite common in business marketing.

Electronic commerce is having a major impact on business transactions involving standardized products. Even though it will not replace the need for personalized relationships in many situations, the Internet will affect nearly every aspect of business marketing.

More about **FreeMarkets**

Although consumer Internet auction sites like eBay and Priceline get most of the media attention, business-to-business marketers are actually much heavier users of e-commerce. For example, the predictions by Forrester Research are that by 2003 business buyers will spend $1.3 trillion via the Internet versus consumer spending of $108 billion.

FreeMarkets intends to be part of that growth, and it appears to be headed in the right direction. The firm has conducted successful bidding events for a number of major firms such as General Motors, Unilever, and SmithKline Beecham, as well as for public utilities (in the purchase of coal), and government agencies. (The state of Pennsylvania used the service to buy aluminum for license plates, saving over $250,000.)

The fundamental necessities that make buying successful—information and preparation—have not changed with the introduction of the Internet. What has changed is the *amount* of information that can be gathered and processed, and the *speed* with which it can be updated and transferred. As a result, buyers and sellers who might not have known of the existence of one another in the past can now become business partners. To that end, FreeMarkets set up a branch office in Brussels where 30 languages from Mandarin to Hungarian are spoken.

FreeMarkets has thus far focused on low-technology, commodity products such as coal, metal, and foodstuffs, and services such as trucking. Other reverse auction sites have taken a different approach, specializing in business markets for particular industries. For example, USBid, Inc., creates auctions for electronic products, and Seafax, Inc., brings together buyers and sellers of fish.

Auctions come close to the notion of a market where the buyer has "complete information," something that previously had been only a simplifying assumption in economic models. According to the founder of FreeMarkets, electronic auctions cause all suppliers to improve their businesses by forcing them to become more efficient in order to compete.[18]

1. Which business-to-business purchases are most likely to be affected by reverse auctions?

2. Which buying patterns of business users are most likely to be changed by FreeMarkets and similar business-to-business auction sites?

Key Terms and Concepts

Business market (120)
Business user (120)
Business marketing (120)
Agribusiness (121)
Reseller market (122)
Disintermediation (123)
Government market (123)
Business services market (124)
Nonbusiness market (125)
International market (126)
Elasticity of demand (127)

Standard Industrial Classification
(SIC) system (130)
North American Industry
Classification System (NAICS)
(131)
Value added (131)
Vertical business market (132)
Horizontal business market (132)
Activity indicator of buying
power (133)
Buying motives (136)

Buy classes (137)
New-task buying (137)
Straight rebuy (137)
Modified rebuy (137)
Buying center (137)
Buying roles (138)
Value chain (139)
Loyalty (139)
Relationship marketing (140)
Electronic commerce (144)

Questions and Problems

1. What are some marketing implications in the fact that the demand for business goods:
   a. Fluctuates widely.
   b. Is inelastic.
   c. Is derived.

2. What are the marketing implications for a seller in the facts that business customers are typically geographically concentrated and limited in number?

3. What differences would you expect to find between the marketing strategies of a company that sells to horizontal business markets and those of a company that sells to vertical business markets?

4. An American manufacturer has been selling word processors to a large oil company in Norway for 10 years. In which of the three buy classes would you place this buyer-seller relationship? Is there any aspect of the relationship that is likely to fall into the straight-rebuy category?

5. Explain how the five stages in the buying-decision process might be applied in the following buying situations:
   a. New-task buying of a conveyor belt for a soft-drink bottling plant.
   b. Straight rebuying of maintenance services for that conveyor belt.

6. How would you go about determining who influences the buying decisions of business users?

7. NCR, IBM, Xerox, and other manufacturers of office equipment make a substantial proportion of their sales directly to business users. At the same time, wholesalers of office equipment are thriving. Are these two market situations inconsistent? Explain.

Hands–On Marketing

1. Find an ad for a business good or service that is directed toward the business market and another ad for the same product that is directed toward consumers (such as an ad for leasing fleets of Chevrolets and an ad for Chevrolet aimed at consumers). Discuss the buying motives appealed to in the ads.

2. Interview a purchasing agent about buying a product that would qualify as a modified rebuy. Draw a diagram that shows the purchasing agent's perceptions of (a) the stages of the decision process; (b) who was in the buying center at each stage of the decision process; and (c) what role(s) each person played at each stage of the process. Comment on how this diagram might be useful to a sales person representing the product in question.

6

Market Segmentation, Targeting, and Positioning

"NetJet had the fractional ownership market virtually to itself during the early years. However, success has attracted competition. Now the firm must focus its efforts."

Is the Market for **NetJet** Up in the Air?

Inspired by the U.S. Air Force's special squadron that provides on-demand air transportation for military VIPs, retired Brigadier General O. F. Lassiter founded Executive Jet Airways in 1964. The concept was to provide a service similar to the Air Force's special squadron for civilians who wanted to charter a jet for personal travel. Starting with five Lear jets, the business grew slowly. In 1974 a dozen more Lear jets were added to the fleet, and by 1986 the company had logged over 175,000 passenger flights.

In 1986 the company, now called Executive Jet Aviation (EJA), added a new twist. In addition to offering its charter service, EJA made jet service available under a time-share arrangement called NetJet. A time-share, most often associated with vacation properties, allows a person to buy a share of one property and, as a result, gain access to many others. In the case of NetJet, an individual or company can buy as little as a one-sixteenth share of a plane and have access to the entire fleet 24 hours a day. Thus, the plane a company's executives fly in may not be the one it partially owns.

Here's an example of how a NetJet arrangement works. Say a business buys a one-eighth share in a jet for 12.5% of its $38 million price. That guarantees the business access to 100 hours of flying time per year. Additional fees are $6,000 a month for pilots, maintenance, and insurance, and an hourly charge of $1,120 (and up, depending on the size of the jet) for actual flying time. Because NetJet spreads its fleet of planes across the country, it can have a plane available on four to six hours' notice at any one of 5,000 airports. The NetJet fleet consists of over 200 Cessnas, Raytheons, and large-cabin Gulfstreams for international travel. Another 450 planes are on order.

Private companies make up 55% of NetJet fractional owners. The remainder is made up of individuals (25%), and large private companies (20%). Private owners include radio personality Don Imus and professional golfers Ben Crenshaw and Dale Douglass. With over 1,000 fractional owners, NetJet is forging ahead with plans to expand its operation in Europe, the Middle East, Latin America, and Asia.

NetJet had the fractional ownership market virtually to itself during the early years. However, success has attracted competitors. Now the firm must focus its efforts. Bombardier, the third-largest civil aircraft manufacturer in the world, introduced its fractional ownership program called FlexJet in 1995. FlexJet offers virtually the same availability guarantee as NetJet, and now claims to have 25% of the market. Some more recent entrants to the business such as Flight Options, Travel Air, and Jet One are also eager to grab a piece of the action.[1]

How should NetJet focus its marketing effort now that competition is intensifying?

www.netjets.com

NetJet has been in an enviable position, but the situation is changing. As the time-share jet market grows and the number of competitors increases, it's likely that segments will be identified and different marketing mixes—products, distribution, pricing, and promotion—will be designed for each. In this chapter we will see why markets are segmented and how it is done. We will also consider the alternatives a firm faces in selecting which segments or target markets it wishes to pursue. Then we will introduce the concept of positioning or how a firm makes its offering attractive to a target market. Finally, we'll examine forecasting, the process of estimating the sales potential of a market. After studying this chapter, you should be able to explain:

chapter goals

- The related concepts of market segmentation, target marketing, and positioning.
- The process of market segmentation, including its benefits and conditions for use.
- Bases for segmenting consumer and business markets.
- Three target-market strategies: aggregation, single-segment strategy, and multiple-segment strategy.
- The three steps in developing a positioning strategy.
- The most frequently used methods of forecasting the demand of market segments.

An Overview of Market Segments and Target Markets

In Chapter 2 we defined a market as people or organizations with (1) needs to satisfy, (2) money to spend, and (3) the willingness to spend it. However, within a total market, there is always some diversity among the buyers. Not all consumers who wear pants want to wear jeans. Some vacationers take a cruise for rest and relaxation, others look for adventure and excitement. Among businesses, not all firms that use computers want the same amount of memory or speed, and not every software buyer needs the same amount of expert advice.

What we are seeing here is that within the same general market there are groups of customers—**market segments**—with different wants, buying preferences, or product-use behavior. In some markets these differences are relatively minor, and the benefits sought by consumers can be satisfied with a single marketing mix. In other markets, customers are unwilling to make the compromises necessitated by a single marketing mix. As a result, the segments must be targeted individually and alternative marketing mixes are required to reach them. Whether it is large or small, the specific market segment (people or organizations) for which the seller designs a particular marketing mix is a **target market**. Using the marketing mix, a firm attempts to establish an attractive position for its offering in the minds of the target market.

Before positions can be defined and marketing mixes designed, however, potential target markets must be identified and described. This process is called *market segmentation*.

Market Segmentation

The variation in customers' responses to a marketing mix can be traced to differences in buying habits, in ways in which the good or service is used, or in motives for buying. Customer-oriented marketers take these differences into consideration, but they usually cannot afford to design a different marketing mix for every customer. Consequently, most marketers operate between the extremes of one marketing mix for all and a different one for each customer. To do so involves **market segmentation,** a process of dividing the total market for a good or service into several smaller, internally homogeneous groups. The essence of segmentation is that the members of each group are similar with respect to the factors that influence demand. A major element in a company's success is the ability to segment its market effectively.

Benefits of Market Segmentation

Market segmentation is customer-oriented, and thus it is consistent with the marketing concept. In segmenting, we first identify the wants of customers within a submarket and then decide if it is practical to develop a marketing mix to satisfy those wants.

By tailoring marketing programs to individual market segments, any company can do a better marketing job and make more efficient use of its marketing resources. Focus is especially important for a small firm with limited resources. Such a firm might compete very effectively in one or two small market segments; however, it would likely be overwhelmed by the competition if it aimed for a major segment. For example, Estee Corp. has segmented the food market on the basis of dietary restrictions. By producing items for diabetics—sugarless cookies, candy, salad dressings, jams, and desserts—the firm is able to meet the needs of a specific group. Although giants in the food industry such as Kraft or General Foods do not totally ignore this segment, they do not give it the special attention provided by Estee.

The potential for advertising efficiency illustrates the benefits possible from segmentation. Estee's ads are especially effective because promotional messages—and

 www.estee.com

Examine this adidas ad for running shoes and ads for some other brands (Nike, Puma, New Balance) and then go to their websites and consider the market segments the companies are pursuing. For example, adidas is stressing individuality while New Balance makes use of famous marathoner Frank Shorter, and Puma associates its brand with contemporary musical groups. Could the choice of a particular segment preclude attracting other segments in a market?

www.adidas.com
www.nike.com
www.Puma.com
www.newbalance.com

the media chosen to present them—can be aimed toward a specific segment of the market. With a limited budget, Estee communicates with its target market by placing ads in specialty magazines for physicians and diabetics and doing direct-mail advertising to diabetics.

By developing strong positions in specialized market segments, medium-sized firms can grow rapidly. For example, the Oshkosh Truck Company in Wisconsin has become the world's largest producer of fire and rescue trucks for airports.

Even very large companies with the resources to engage in mass marketing supported by expensive national advertising campaigns are abandoning mass-market strategies. These companies embrace market segmentation as a more effective strategy to reach the fragments that once constituted a mass, or homogeneous, market in the U.S.

The marketing of bar soap illustrates these changing conditions nicely. At the turn of the century, there were two major brands: Lifebuoy, a Lever Bros. product; and Ivory, made by Procter & Gamble. The Lever Bros. line has been extended to include Dove, Caress, Knight's Castile, Shield, Lux, and Lever 2000 as well as Lifebuoy. Today, in addition to Ivory, P&G offers Zest, Coast, Safeguard, Camay, Noxema, and Oil of Olay soaps. And the variation doesn't end with brands. Zest comes in eight versions, including two fragrances, three bar sizes, and a liquid body wash. Other variations are differently shaped bars, colors to match bathroom decor, and liquid hand soap in pump dispensers. These developments reflect a market that has been segmented by skin type (dry versus oily), fragrance preference, the desire for convenience, and the primary benefit sought (such as cleaning dirty hands or body deodorizing). It is clear that all consumers use soap for cleansing, but they also expect other benefits from the soap they use. Hence, many segments exist.

The Process of Market Segmentation

Markets are sometimes segmented intuitively; that is, a marketer relies on experience and judgment to make a decision about the segments that exist in a market and how much potential each offers. Others follow the lead of competitors or earlier market entrants. For example, Gatorade established the fact that the soft drink market includes a sports drink segment motivated by the desire to rapidly replenish body fluids. Following the success of Gatorade, brands such as Powerade from Coca-Cola and All Sport from Pepsi are attempting to appeal to the same segment. Another alternative is to perform a structured analysis, often supported by some marketing research, in order to identify segments and measure their potential. This approach, even if done with a small budget, often produces insights and opportunities that would be overlooked otherwise.

The steps involved in segmenting a market in an organized fashion are:

1. *Identify the current and potential wants that exist within a market.* The marketer carefully examines the market to determine the specific needs being satisfied by current offerings, the needs current offerings fail to adequately satisfy, and the needs that may not yet be recognized. This step may involve interviewing and/or observing consumers or firms to determine their behavior, levels of satisfaction, and frustrations. Within the market for wristwatches there is a shared desire among all customers to know the time, and certainly all watches must accurately tell time. But there are customers who also want a watch to be a fashion accessory, a status symbol, an exercise timer, or an appointment reminder. There might be others who would like a watch to function as a computer, a voice recorder, a pulse monitor, a television receiver, or a telephone. Each of these wants represents a potential market segment within the wristwatch market.

2. *Identify characteristics that distinguish among the segments.* In this step the focus is on what prospects who share a particular want have in common to distinguish them from other segments in the market that have different wants.

Among business firms it could be a physical feature (like size or location). Among consumers it might be an attitude or a behavior pattern. From the results of this step, potential marketing mixes (including product ideas) for the various segments can be designed. These alternatives can then be further analyzed.

3. *Determine the size of the segments and how well they are being satisfied.* The final step is to estimate how much demand (or potential sales) each segment represents and the strength of the competition. These forecasts will determine which segments are worth pursuing. American Express launched an Internet banking service that allows customers to make deposits, purchase certificates of deposit, and pay bills online. Despite the fact that online competition from conventional banks and other credit card companies is fierce, American Express' existing cardholders make up an attractive initial market segment.[2]

A group that shares a want distinguishable from the rest of the market is a market segment. However, to be useful to marketers, results of a segmentation effort must also meet some conditions:

- The bases for segmenting—that is, the characteristics used to describe what segments customers fall into—must be *measurable,* and data describing the characteristics must be *obtainable.* The age of customers is both measurable and obtainable. On the other hand, the "desire for ecologically compatible products" may be a factor useful in segmenting the market for mulching lawn mowers. But this characteristic is not easily measured, nor can the data be easily obtained.

- The market segment should be *accessible* through existing marketing institutions—middlemen, advertising media, the company's sales force—with a minimum of cost and wasted effort. To increase the benefits of segmentation, most national magazines such as *Time* and *Sports Illustrated* and large metropolitan newspapers publish separate geographic editions. This allows an advertiser to run a magazine ad aimed at, say, a Southern segment of the market or a newspaper ad for particular suburbs, without having to pay for exposure in other, nontargeted areas.

- Each segment should be *large enough* to be profitable. Procter & Gamble found a segment of candy consumers that wants a low-calorie product. However, it is too small to justify the investment a line of confections would require.[3] In concept, management could treat each single customer as a separate segment. Actually, this situation, called *micromarketing,* is becoming more common in consumer markets and is quite common in some business markets, as when Boeing markets passenger airplanes to individual airlines, or when Citibank makes a loan to the government of Mexico or Argentina. Micromarketing occurs in selected consumer markets such as custom-designed homes. But in segmenting most consumer markets, a firm must not develop too broad an array of styles, colors, sizes, and prices, because the production and inventory costs would make it unprofitable.

Ultimate Consumers and Business Users—the First Cut

As we shall see, a company can segment its market in many different ways, and the bases for segmentation vary from one market to another. Often the first step is to divide a potential market into two broad categories: ultimate consumers and business users. Black & Decker did this, introducing the DeWalt line of power tools for professionals and the Quantum line for the do-it-yourself segment.

The sole criterion for this first cut at segmenting a market is the customer's reason for buying. Recall from Chapter 4 that ultimate consumers buy goods or

Black & Decker recognizes that differences in the business and consumer market segments for power tools are sufficient to require distinct product lines. DeWalt is professional caliber. Quantum meets the needs of the do-it-yourself frequent tool users. And the Black & Decker brand is intended for the occasional household user. The products have different features, prices, packaging, and even distribution outlets.

services for their own personal or household use and are satisfying strictly non-business wants. They constitute the consumer market. Business users, described in Chapter 5, are business, industrial, or institutional organizations that buy goods or services to use in their organizations, to resell, or to make other products. Black & Decker recognized that professionals who earn their living in the building trades need durable tools that perform precisely. Do-it-yourselfers, on the other hand, use their tools less often, typically take on less complicated projects, and are satisfied with less powerful equipment. These segments were judged to be so different that they required separate marketing mixes.

Segmenting a market into these two groups—consumers and businesses—is extremely significant from a marketing point of view because the two segments buy differently. Consequently, the composition of a seller's marketing mix will depend on whether it is directed toward the consumer market or the business market.

Segmenting Consumer Markets

Dividing a total market into ultimate consumers and business users results in segments that are still too broad and varied for most products. We need to identify some characteristics within each of these segments that will enable us to divide them further into more specific targets.

As shown in Table 6.1, there are a number of ways the consumer market can be segmented. The bases for segmentation include many of the characteristics used to describe the consumer market in Chapter 4, as well as some psychological and behavioral dimensions. To illustrate, we will discuss four bases for segmenting consumer markets:

1. Geographic
2. Demographic
3. Psychographic
4. Behavioral

Geographic Segmentation

Subdividing markets into segments based on location—the regions, counties, cities, and towns where people live and work—is **geographic segmentation**. The reason

Table 6.1 Segmentation Bases for Consumer Markets

Segmentation Basis	Possible Market Segments
Geographic	
Region	New England, Middle Atlantic, and other census regions
City or metro-area size	Population under 25,000; 25,001–100,000; 100,001–500,000; 500,001–1,000,000; etc.
Urban-rural	Urban, suburban, rural
Climate	Hot, cold, sunny, rainy, cloudy
Demographic	
Income	Under $15,000; $15,000–$25,000; $25,001–$35,000; $35,001–$50,000; over $50,000
Age	Under 6, 6–12, 13–19, 20–34, 35–49, 50–64, 65 and over
Gender	Male, female
Family life cycle	Young, single; young, married, no children; etc.
Social class	Upper class, upper-middle, lower-middle, upper-lower, etc.
Education	Grade school only, high school graduate, college graduate
Occupation	Professional, manager. clerical, sales, student, homemaker, unemployed, etc.
Ethnic background	African, Asian, European, Hispanic, Middle Eastern, etc.
Psychographic	
Personality	Ambitious, self-confident, aggressive, introverted, extroverted, sociable, etc.
Life-style	Activities (golf, travel); interests (politics, modern art); opinions (conservation, capitalism)
Values	Values and life-styles 2 (VALS2), list of values (LOV)
Behavioral	
Benefits desired	Examples vary widely depending on product: appliance—cost, quality, operating life; toothpaste—no cavities, plaque control, bright teeth, good taste, low price
Usage rate	Nonuser, light user, heavy user

for this is simply that consumers' wants and product usage often are related to one or more of these subcategories. Geographic characteristics are also measurable and accessible—two of the conditions for effective segmentation. Let's consider how the geographic distribution of population may serve as a basis for segmentation.

Regional Population Distribution

Many firms market their products in a limited number of geographic regions, or they may market nationally but prepare a separate marketing mix for each region. Supermarket chains such as Alpha Beta and Winn-Dixie concentrate their marketing efforts in specific geographic regions. Even supermarket giants such as Kroger and Safeway are unknown in some parts of the country. Campbell Soup Company has altered some of its soup and bean recipes to suit regional tastes, and Friday's restaurants, with 345 units nationwide, allows each outlet to offer up to 30 regional items on its menu.

The regional distribution of population is important to marketers because people *within* a given region generally tend to share similar values, attitudes, and style preferences. However, significant differences often exist *among* regions because of differences in climate, social customs, and other factors. Thus bright, warm colors are preferred in Florida and the Southwest, whereas grays and cooler colors predominate in New England and the Midwest. People in the West are less formal than Easterners, and they spend more time outdoors. Consequently, in the western region there is a relatively large market for patio furniture, sports clothes, and outdoor recreation equipment.

Many organizations segment their markets on the basis of city size or population concentration; that is, they utilize an urban-suburban-rural distribution. Toys "R" Us, the largest chain of toy stores in the U.S., initially located stores only in metropolitan areas with populations exceeding 250,000 to ensure a sufficiently large customer base. In contrast, Wal-Mart's initial strategy was to locate only in towns of less than 35,000 people in order to minimize the amount of competition.

A popular reference source used for geographic segmentation is *Sales & Marketing Management* magazine's annual "Survey of Buying Power." This two-part report provides information on population, income, and spending behavior by state, county, major metropolitan area, television market, and newspaper market. With these data, a marketer can compare spending power and purchasing behavior across geographic areas.

Demographic Segmentation

Demographics are also a common basis for segmenting consumer markets. They are frequently used because they are often strongly related to demand and are relatively easy to measure. Recall that several demographic variables were discussed in Chapter 4 in descriptions of the consumer market. The most popular characteristics, used alone or in combination, for **demographic segmentation** are age, gender, family life-cycle stage, income, and education. For example, Toyota has three models designed specifically for drivers in their twenties and thirties: the Echo, a fuel-efficient compact sedan; the MR-Spyder, a two-seater convertible; and the XYR, a sporty subcompact.[4] Examples of demographic segmentation characteristics are shown in Table 6.1.

It is important to note that there are no rules for the number or breadth of categories used in a segmentation effort. The market and the need being satisfied should dictate the choices. For example, there may be a certain symmetry in an age category that includes all teenagers (and data may be available on "teens"), but the purchase behavior and motivations of 13- and 14-year-olds in a particular market may be quite different from 18- and 19-year-olds.

Social class, a composite measure made up of several demographic dimensions, illustrates this approach to segmenting a market. The most commonly used indicator of social class includes level of education, type of occupation, and the type of neighborhood a person lives in. Many consider social class a "richer" indicator than income or any of the individual social class components taken separately. They would argue that a lawyer and a plumber, for example, might have the same income but be members of different social classes. Because a person's social class—be it upper class or blue-collar working class—has a considerable influence on that person's choices in many product categories, companies frequently select one or two social classes as target markets and then develop a product and marketing mix to reach those segments.[5]

The ways in which segmentation bases can be combined is limited only by the imagination of the marketer and the availability of data. For example, an approach called geodemographic clustering is based on ZIP codes, demographic data available from the U.S. Census, and household data collected by the research firm Claritas. The trade name for the procedure is PRIZM (short for Potential Rating Index for ZIP Markets). Using Census data on education, income, occupation, housing, ethnicity, urbanization, and other variables, Claritas grouped the 36,000 U.S. ZIP codes into 62 similar clusters or segments. Each cluster then was further examined for similarities in life-styles and consumption behavior, and given descriptive names such as "kids and cul-de-sacs," "gray power," and "shotguns and pickups." Marketers use this information to identify ZIP codes for direct-mail promotions, to select locations for retail outlets, and to determine the best mix of products and brands to offer in particular stores.[6]

 www.claritas.com

Psychographic Segmentation

Demographics are used to segment markets because these data are related to behavior and because they are relatively easy to gather. However, demographics are not in themselves the causes of behavior. Consumers don't buy windsurfing equipment because they are young. They buy it because they enjoy an active, outdoor life-style, and it so happens that such people are also typically younger. Thus demographics often correlate with behavior, but they do not explain it.

Marketers often go beyond demographic attributes in an effort to better understand why consumers behave as they do. They engage in what is called **psychographic segmentation,** which involves examining attributes related to how a person thinks, feels, and behaves. Frequently included in a psychographic segmentation effort are personality dimensions, life-style characteristics, and consumer values.

Personality Characteristics

An individual's **personality** is usually described in terms of traits that influence behavior. Theoretically, they would seem to be a good basis for segmenting markets. Our experience tells us that compulsive people buy differently from cautious consumers, and quiet introverts do not buy the same things or in the same way as gregarious, outgoing people.

However, personality characteristics pose problems that limit their usefulness in practical market segmentation. First, the presence and strength of these characteristics in the general population are virtually impossible to measure. For example, how would you go about measuring the number of people in the U.S. who could be classified as aggressive? Another problem is associated with the accessibility condition of segmentation. There is no advertising medium that provides unique access to a particular personality type; that is, television reaches introverts as well as extroverts, aggressive people as well as timid people. So one of the major goals of segmentation, to avoid wasted marketing effort, is not likely to be accomplished using personality.

Nevertheless, firms often tailor their advertising messages to appeal to personality traits. Even though the importance of the personality dimension in a particular decision may be unmeasurable, the seller believes that it does play an influential role. Thus in its ads, Buckle suggests that you "make your own way," and Calvin Klein's says the user of Contradiction perfume is "always and never the same."

Life-Style

Life-style relates to activities, interests, and opinions. Your life-style reflects how you spend your time and what your beliefs are on various social, economic, and political issues. It is a broad concept that overlaps what some consider to be personality characteristics.

People's life-styles undoubtedly affect what products they buy and what brands they prefer. Marketers are aware of this and often design their strategies based on life-style segments. For example, Honda developed the S2000 sports car to appeal to baby boomers. With their children grown, and their earnings at a peak, Honda is betting that consumers in their fifties are ready to indulge themselves. At $30,000, the S2000 convertible goes from 0 to 60 in six seconds. It is designed to have the look and feel of a sports car, but still be compatible with a middle-aged life-style.

Although it is a valuable marketing tool, life-style segmentation has some of the same limitations as segmentation based on personality characteristics. For example, it is difficult to accurately measure the size of life-style segments in the population. The S2000 is targeted at consumers "looking to recapture their youth" and with the resources to make the attempt with an expensive car. Because Honda does not know how many people fit that description, it has taken a conservative position and produced only 20,000 cars a year.[7] Another problem is that a given life-style segment might not be accessible at a reasonable cost through a firm's usual distribution system or promotional program.

Values

According to psychologists, **values** are a reflection of our needs adjusted for the realities of the world in which we live. Researchers at the Survey Research Center at the University of Michigan have identified nine basic values that relate to purchase behavior.[8] The nine, which they call the list of values (LOV), are:

- Self-respect
- Security
- Excitement
- Fun and enjoyment in life
- Having warm relationships
- Self-fulfillment
- Sense of belonging
- Sense of accomplishment
- Being well respected

Although almost everyone would view all these values as desirable, their relative importance differs among people, and their relative importance affects behavior. For example, people who place a high value on fun and enjoyment are more likely to enjoy skiing, dancing, bicycling, and backpacking, whereas people who have high value for warm relationships tend to give gifts for no particular reason. Thus, the relative strength of values could be the basis for segmenting a market.

Behavioral Segmentation

Some marketers regularly attempt to segment their markets on the basis of product-related behavior—they utilize **behavioral segmentation.** In this section we briefly consider two of these approaches: the benefits desired from a product and the rate at which the consumer uses the product.

Benefits Desired

From a customer-oriented perspective, the ideal method for segmenting a market is on the basis of customers' desired benefits. Certainly, using benefits to segment a market is consistent with the idea that a company should be marketing benefits and not simply the physical characteristics of a product. After all, a carpenter wants a smooth surface (benefit), not a Black & Decker electric sander (the product). In many cases, however, benefits desired by customers do not meet the first condition of segmentation described above. That is, they are not easily measured because customers are unwilling or unable to reveal them. For example, what benefits do people derive from clothing that has the label on the outside? Conversely, why do others refuse to wear such clothing?

Performing benefit segmentation is a multistep process. First, the specific benefits consumers are seeking must be identified. This typically involves several research steps, beginning with the identification of all possible benefits related to a particular product or behavior through brainstorming, observing consumers, and listening to group discussions. Then more research is conducted to screen out unlikely or unrealistic benefits and to amplify and clarify the remaining possibilities. Finally, large-scale surveys are conducted to determine how important the benefits are and how many consumers seek each one.

To illustrate, Mobil Corp. conducted a market segmentation study of gasoline buyers to determine how to design its gasoline stations. The study identified five primary segments. Contrary to conventional wisdom, only one, accounting for about 20% of the buyers, consisted of price shoppers. To attract the four more profitable nonprice segments, Mobil has begun offering things that appeal to them—nicer snack foods, quick service, a personal touch, privileges for regular customers, and cleaner facilities.[9]

Usage Rate

Another basis for market segmentation is the rate at which people consume a product. A popular categorization of usage rates is nonusers, light users, medium users,

Is the Internet changing the shopper profile?

The marketers of most products continuously study their customers. They want to know who's buying their products, and why they buy. It is also important to detect any shifts in the customer profile that may suggest a need to alter strategy.

As companies move online and add the Internet as a method of promoting and selling their products, having a detailed description of who the customer is grows in significance for several reasons. First, Internet interaction is impersonal so the marketer has no opportunity to observe the customer directly. Second, a website must grab and hold attention. There is no sales person present to adjust the presentation if the prospect shows signs of disinterest. Finally, competition is intense. Firms may have only one chance to "get it right."

So who is the likely Internet customer? According to a recent study in Great Britain, men are taking a much more active role than women when it comes to shopping on the Internet. In fact, 13% of British men shop on the Internet, whereas the number for women is only 2%. A similar but less dramatic relationship exists in the U.S., where 53% of all online purchases are made by men. There are several (as yet unsubstantiated) explanations for this apparent role reversal. One is that many of the products currently offered via the Internet, such as CDs, computer software, cars, and insurance, may be more appealing to men than women. A second possibility is that the Internet offers what men want in shopping—speed, convenience, and simplicity.

Whatever the explanation, marketers cannot assume that the customer profile that exists in other methods of selling will carry over to the Internet. Nor can they assume that the Internet profile will remain unchanged. According to one researcher, the number of females shopping on the Internet will soon exceed the number of males because "Women view the Internet as a tool. Men view it as a toy."

Sources: Paul Taylor, "Men Set to Drive Internet Shopping Revolution," *Financial Times,* June 19 and 20, 1999, p.4; Cynthia Vespereny, "Women to Make 55% of Online Purchases in 2000," *St. Louis Business Journal,* Aug. 9–15, 1999, p. 71.

and heavy users. Normally a company is most interested in the heavy users of its product because fewer than 50% of all users of a product typically account for 80 to 90% of the total purchases. These heavy users are often referred to in an industry as the "heavy half" of the market. Many marketers aim their marketing efforts at retaining the consumers who make up the heavy half for their brand, and encouraging the heavy-half users of competitors' brands to switch. For example, Heinz's share of the ketchup market has declined because of inroads made by cheaper manufacturers' brands and by private-label brands of some supermarkets. To win back customers, Heinz is going after the heavy half of ketchup consumers—children and teenagers—with a $50 million worldwide advertising campaign. The goals of the campaign are to build a distinctive personality for Heinz ketchup and increase usage by suggesting new ways to use the product. A website describes some unusual uses in its "sin book," along with presenting a very positive image of the Heinz brand.[10]

www.ketchup.wonderland.org

Sometimes a marketer will select as a target market the nonuser or light user, intending to woo these customers into higher usage. Or light users may constitute an attractive niche for a seller simply because they are being ignored by firms that are targeting heavy users. Once the characteristics of these light users have been identified, management can go to them directly with an introductory low-price offer. Or a seller might get consumers to increase their usage rates by (1) describing new uses for a product (baking soda as a refrigerator deodorizer, chewing gum as an alternative to cigarettes); (2) suggesting new times or places for use (soup as an after-school snack, air fresheners in school lockers); or (3) offering multiple-unit packaging (a 12-pack of soft drinks).

Table 6.2	Segmentation Bases for Business Markets
Segmentation Basis	**Possible Market Segments**
Customer location	
Region	Southeast Asia, Central America, Upper Midwest, Atlantic Seaboard
Locations	Single buying site, multiple buying sites
Customer type	
Industry	Selected NAICS codes
Size	Sales volume, number of employees
Organization structure	Centralized or decentralized, group or individual decision
Purchase criteria	Quality, price, durability, lead time
Transaction conditions	
Buying situation	Straight rebuy, modified rebuy, new buy
Usage rate	Nonuser, light user, heavy user
Purchasing procedure	Competitive bidding, lease, service contracts
Order size	Small, medium, large
Service requirements	Light, moderate, heavy

Segmenting Business Markets

Even though the number of buyers in a business market may be relatively few compared to a consumer market, segmentation remains important. The reason is quite simple—a highly focused marketing effort directed at meeting the specific needs of a group of similar customers is both more efficient and more likely to be successful.

In Table 6.2 examples of business market segmentation bases are grouped by customer location, customer type, and transaction conditions. Notice that many of the bases are similar to ones used for segmenting consumer markets. To provide a feel for business market segmentation, several of these bases are described in more detail.

Customer Location

Business markets are frequently segmented on a geographic basis. Some industries are geographically concentrated. For example, businesses that process natural resources locate close to the source to minimize shipping costs. Other industries are geographically concentrated simply because newer firms either spun off from or chose to locate near the industry pioneers. For example, several brands of recreational vehicles, including Skyline and Holiday Rambler are manufactured in northern Indiana. A firm that sells to this industry, such as Viking Formed Products, has chosen to locate nearby and focus its efforts geographically.

Companies also segment international markets geographically. In considering developing countries, for example, a firm might consider the reliability of public utilities, the quality of the transportation system, and the sophistication of the distribution structure in deciding where to expand its operation.

Customer Type

Industry

Any firm that sells to business customers in a variety of industries may want to segment its market on the basis of industry. For example, a company that sells small electric motors would have a broad potential market among many different industries. However, this firm will do better by segmenting its potential market by type of customer and then specializing in order to more completely meet the needs of organizations in a limited number of these segments. The NAICS codes, described in Chapter 5, are particularly useful for this purpose because information published by the government and industry on such factors as the number of firms, their size, and their location is often organized according to this scheme.

Size

Business customer size can be estimated using such factors as sales volume, number of employees, number of production facilities, and number of sales offices. Many sellers divide their potential market into large and small accounts, using separate distribution channels to reach each segment. The seller's sales force may contact large-volume accounts directly, but to reach the smaller accounts, the seller may use a middleman or rely on the Internet or telemarketing.

Organization Structure

Firms approach buying in different ways. Some rely heavily on their purchasing departments to control the inflow of information, reduce the number of potential alternatives, and conduct negotiations. Selling to such companies would require a strong personal selling effort directed specifically at purchasing executives. It would also need excellent supporting materials if the product exceeded the technical expertise of the purchasing managers.

Other buyers opt for greater involvement in the purchase process by the people who will be directly affected by the purchase. These buyers tend to include many people in their decisions, hold meetings over a long period of time, and engage in a lot of internal communication. Government agencies are especially known for lengthy purchase decisions. For example, because of the extensive approval processes, obtaining an order to sell supplies to a prison often takes two or three years.[11] Selling to a market segment such as this requires many, varied contacts, and often involves several people from the selling firm.

Purchase Criteria

All buyers want good quality, low prices, and on-time delivery. However, within a market there are groups for which one of these or some other purchase criterion is particularly significant. Consider the automotive business. General Motors buys over $90 *billion* in components, machinery, and equipment a year. In selecting suppliers GM has a formal process that takes into account a prospect's technical capabilities, defect rates, and delivery schedule among other criteria.[12]

Transaction Conditions

The circumstances of the transaction can also be a basis for segmenting a market. Sellers may have to modify their marketing efforts to deal with different buying situations, usage rates, purchasing procedures, order sizes, or service requirements. To illustrate, three of these transaction conditions are described below.

Buying Situation

When United Airlines is faced with the decision of whether or not to buy the latest version of the Boeing 777 airplane, it is making a new buy. The decision is quite different from the modified rebuy that occurs when United purchases additional 737s, a plane it has flown successfully for years. These buying situations, along with the straight rebuy, are sufficiently unique that a business seller might well segment its market into these three buy-class categories. Or the seller could at least set up two segments by combining new buy and modified rebuy into one segment. Different marketing programs would be developed to reach each of these two or three segments.

Usage Rate

Markets for most products can be divided among heavy users, light users, and nonusers (prospects). Heavy users appear to be the most attractive because of the volume they purchase, but they also generate the most competition. As an alternative to pursuing heavy users, some firms have found it profitable to avoid the competition by concentrating on light users.

Purchase Procedure

Products can be leased, financed, or purchased outright. A price can be simply stated, negotiated, or submitted in a sealed bid. Consider how a bidding system affects a seller. Government agencies often buy on the basis of sealed bids; that is, each prospective seller submits a confidential bid in response to a detailed description of what the agency wants to buy. When the bids are opened, the agency is typically bound by law to accept the lowest bid unless it is clearly inappropriate. How is this different from a negotiated price? For one thing, the seller has only one chance to propose a price. Also, to compete in a sealed-bid market, it is essential to have low costs. And good industry knowledge is important in order to accurately predict what other firms will bid. These differences might cause a firm to treat the government as a distinct segment.

Segmentation identifies the opportunities that exist in a market. The next step is for a firm to decide which of those opportunities to target with a marketing effort.

• Target–Market Strategies

After a company has segmented a market, management must next select one or more segments as its target markets. The company can follow one of three strategies—market aggregation, single-segment concentration, or multiple-segment targeting.

Aggregation Strategy

By adopting a **market-aggregation strategy**—also known as a *mass-market strategy* or an *undifferentiated-market strategy*—a seller treats its total market as a single segment. An aggregate market's members are considered to be alike with respect to demand for the product. That is, customers are willing to make some compromises on less important dimensions in order to enjoy the primary benefit the product offers. In this situation, the total market is the firm's target. Therefore, management can develop a single marketing mix and reach most of the customers in the entire market. The company offers a single product for this mass audience; it designs one pricing structure and one distribution system for its product; and it uses a single promotional program aimed at the entire market. This is sometimes described as a "shotgun" approach (one program to reach a broad target).

When is an organization likely to adopt a market-aggregation strategy? In reality, the notion of an aggregate market is relatively uncommon. Even a commodity such as gasoline is provided at different octane levels, with or without ethanol, and with a variety of other additives. The total market for most types of products is too varied—too heterogeneous—to be considered a single, uniform entity. To speak of a market for vitamin pills, for example, is to ignore the existence of submarkets that differ significantly from one another. Because of these differences, One-A-Day vitamins are offered in 19 variations including the well-known regular formula for adults, a special women's formula, the Flintstones children's formula, and also separate formulations for energy, memory, tension and mood, as well as several others.[13]

Generally an aggregation strategy is selected after the firm has examined a market for segments and concluded that regardless of their differences, the majority of customers in the total market are likely to respond in very similar fashion to one marketing mix. This strategy would be appropriate for firms that are marketing an undifferentiated, staple product such as salt or sugar. In the eyes of many people, sugar is sugar, regardless of the brand, and all brands of table salt are pretty much alike.

The strength of a market aggregation strategy is cost minimization. It enables a company to produce, distribute, and promote its products very efficiently. Producing and marketing one product for the entire market means longer production runs at lower unit costs. Inventory costs are minimized when there is no (or a very limited) variety of colors and sizes of products. Warehousing and transportation are most efficient when one product is going to one market. Promotion costs are minimized when the same message is transmitted to all customers.

The strategy of market aggregation typically is accompanied by the strategy of product differentiation in a company's marketing program. **Product differentiation** occurs when, in the eyes of customers, one firm distinguishes its product from competitive brands offered to the same aggregate market. Through differentiation an organization creates the perception that its product is better than the competitors' brands, as when C&H Sugar advertises its product as "pure cane sugar from Hawaii." In addition to creating a preference among consumers for the seller's brand, successful product differentiation can also reduce price competition.

A seller differentiates its product either by (1) creating a distinctive appearance with the package or product shape, for example, or (2) using a promotional appeal that features a differentiating claim. For example, various brands of aspirin claim to be the most effective in relieving pain, although they all contain essentially the same ingredients.

Single-Segment Strategy

A **single-segment strategy**, also called a *concentration strategy*, involves selecting one segment from within the total market as the target market. One marketing mix is developed to reach this single segment. A company may want to concentrate on a single market segment rather than take on many competitors in the broader market. For example, Harley-Davidson concentrates only on the super-heavyweight motorcycle market. It does not produce small street bikes or off-road bikes. This strategy employs a "rifle" approach (a narrow program directed at a pinpointed target) in marketing activities. In contrast, Honda competes in all segments of the motorcycle market.

When manufacturers of foreign automobiles first entered the U.S. market, they typically targeted a single segment. The original Volkswagen Beetle was intended for the low-price, small-car market, and Mercedes-Benz targeted the high-income market. Today, of course, most of the established foreign car marketers have moved into a multisegment strategy. Consider, for example, the Volkswagen product line. Only a few, such as Rolls-Royce and Ferrari, continue to concentrate on their original single segment.

A single-segment strategy enables a seller to penetrate one market in depth and to acquire a reputation as a specialist or an expert in this limited market. Firms that pursue single segments are often referred to as **niche marketers** and their targeted segments as **niche markets.** Niche markets are often, but not always, relatively small. Some firms recently included in a list of fast-growing companies and their niches are Brass Eagle, an outfitter for the sport of paintball; Specialty Equipment, a maker of high-technology ranges for restaurants; and KV Pharmaceutical, a manufacturer of taste-masking products that make taking medicines less unpleasant.[14]

A company can initiate a single-segment strategy with limited resources. As long as the single segment remains a small market, large competitors are likely to leave it alone. However, if the small market should show signs of becoming a large

In existence since 1893, Wrigley sells 14 brands of gum in 140 countries. However, when U.S. sales flattened recently, the firm moved beyond a generic advertising effort to focusing on specific reasons why consumers should chew gum. In this ad, the company is suggesting the product as an alternative to smoking. In addition to smokers, are there other segments that Wrigley could pursue?

market, then the "big boys" may jump in. This is what appears to be happening to independent hardware stores. Despite the success of chains such as Lowe's and Home Depot, the independents have continued to serve a segment of the home improvement market that prefers to shop at smaller, neighborhood hardware stores. Home Depot, with $30 billion in sales, has taken notice. As described by Home Depot's CEO, there is ". . . a home improvement segment whose customers tend to be doing smaller jobs and prefer convenient store locations with quick in-and-out service." So Home Depot is introducing Villager Hardware stores to serve this market. With its buying power and sophisticated distribution system, Home Depot will be able to undercut the traditional neighborhood hardware store on price and, with these smaller stores, also provide convenience.[15] If Villager proves to be successful, the independents may be forced to redefine their segment.

The risk and limitation of a single-segment strategy is that the seller has "all its eggs in one basket." If the market potential of that single segment declines, the seller can suffer considerably. Also, a seller with a strong name and reputation in one segment may find it very difficult to expand into another segment. Sears, Roebuck, with an image as a retailer for the middle class, was not successful when it tried to move into the market for expensive furs and designer clothing. Gerber's, seen as a baby food company, was unable to market food in single-serving quantities to adults.

Multiple-Segment Strategy

Under a **multiple-segment strategy,** two or more different groups of potential customers are identified as target markets. A separate marketing mix is developed to reach each targeted segment. For example, the maker of Bayer aspirin offers seven variations of its pain relief product, each with its own marketing program.

How should a target market be defined?

Nestlé is the world's largest food marketer (did you know it is a Swiss company?). Among the product categories in which it is a global leader is bottled water. Nestlé's Perrier and San Pellegrino brands are well known and command premium prices. Per-capita consumption of bottled water in Europe hovers around 100 liters a year, and in the U.S. it is 45 liters. The typical consumers for these brands are adults with well above average incomes. For most people bottled water is a luxury, and for some it is even a status symbol. However, relatively few consumers see it as a necessity—at least not in the developed world.

Nestlé has budgeted $250 million over four years to introduce a new brand of bottled water, Pure Life, in areas of Asia where safe drinking water is difficult or impossible to find. The strategy is to draw the water from good quality wells in the local area, process and bottle it in a Nestlé or Perrier factory near where it will be consumed, and distribute it at an affordable price.

Nestlé sees at least 20 countries as attractive po-

tential markets. Pakistan was the first, with Pure Life introduced in 1998. A bottle sells for about 35 cents, and for many it is seen as essential. According to a Pakistani mother who buys Pure Life for her children, "We're always sick because the (water supply) is so terrible." Other Asian markets seen as having enormous potential are India and China. For example, a production facility was recently opened in Shanghai, an area with 69 million people, substandard water, and bottled water per capita consumption of only 10 liters per year.

So how is the market for bottled water defined? Clearly it depends on the part of the world under consideration. Like Nestlé, many companies must rethink their market definitions and adjust their marketing strategies as they explore global markets.

Sources: Ernest Beck, "Populist Perrier? Nestlé Pitches Bottled Water to World's Poor," *The Wall Street Journal*, June 18, 1999, pp. B1+; Joseph Lo, "Perrier Earmarks up to $250 M for Asia Bottling and Marketing," *South China Morning Post*, June 22, 1999, p. 3.

In a multiple-segment strategy, a seller frequently will develop a different version of the basic product for each segment. However, market segmentation can also be accomplished with no change in the product, but rather with separate distribution channels or promotional appeals, each tailored to a given market segment. Wrigley's, for example, targets smokers by promoting chewing gum as an alternative in situations where smoking is unwelcome. And Evian bottled water is attempting to broaden its market beyond athletes and fitness-oriented consumers with advertising aimed at other groups, including pregnant women and environmentalists.

A multiple-segment strategy normally results in a greater sales volume than a single-segment strategy. It also is useful for a company facing seasonal demand. Because of lower summer enrollments, many universities market their empty dormitory space to tourists—another market segment. A firm with excess production capacity may well seek additional market segments to absorb this capacity.

Multiple segments can provide benefits to an organization, but the strategy has some drawbacks with respect to costs and market coverage. In the first place, marketing to multiple segments can be expensive in both the production and marketing of products. Even with today's advances in production technology, it is obviously less expensive to produce mass quantities of one model and one color than it is to produce a variety of models, colors, and sizes. And a multiple-segment strategy increases marketing expenses in several ways. Total inventory costs grow, because adequate inventories of each style, color, and the like, must be maintained. Advertising costs go up because different ads may be required for each market segment. Distribution costs are likely to increase as efforts are made to make products available to various segments. Finally, general administrative expenses go up when management must plan and implement several different marketing programs.

Before selecting a strategy, management must determine the desirability of each of the segments it has identified. Some guidelines that are helpful in making that evaluation are discussed next.

Guidelines in Selecting a Target Market

Four guidelines govern how to determine whether a segment should be chosen as a target market. First, a target market should be compatible with the organization's goals and image. For years many manufacturers resisted distributing their products through Kmart because of the chain's discount image. However, as Kmart achieved a high level of acceptability with consumers, image concerns seemed to disappear.

A second guideline is to match the market opportunity represented by the target market with the company's resources. In examining the power tool and appliance markets, Black & Decker considered several options and chose as one of its targets the do-it-yourself home-improvement segment because of the marketing economies that could be achieved. The firm's name was well known to consumers, and the products could be sold through the retail outlets already selling Black & Decker products. Thus, entering this market was much less expensive than entering a market in which Black & Decker was inexperienced.

Over the long run, a business must generate a profit to survive. This rather obvious statement translates into our third market selection guideline. That is, an organization should seek markets that will generate sufficient sales volume at a low enough cost to result in a profit that justifies the required investment. Surprisingly, companies often have overlooked profit in their quest for high-volume markets. Their mistake is going after sales volume, not *profitable* sales volume. Seventh Generation, Inc., a manufacturer of environmentally friendly household products, found a market among hard-core environmentalists; however, the segment was not large enough to sustain the business. To reach a larger segment that is environmentally conscious but also expects competitive prices and good quality, the firm carefully evaluated its line. The result is that half its products have been replaced with items that are environmentally friendly and also are less expensive or of better quality than competing alternatives.[16]

Fourth, a company ordinarily should seek a market where competitors are few and/or weak. A seller should not enter a market that is already saturated with competition unless it has some overriding advantage that will enable it to take customers from existing firms. Nobel Learning Communities is a company that operates a chain of 140 privately owned primary schools. The schools are designed to appeal to families that are dissatisfied with public schools but are unable to afford fancy private schools. The objective is to provide a solid education without frills. The advantage of these schools over traditional private schools is a lower price, while their private status gives them greater control over the students than exists in public schools.[17] Despite these differences, Nobel Learning has had difficulty establishing itself in a market with many established competitors, notably public schools.

• Positioning

Having identified the potential segments and selected one or more to target, the marketer must next decide what position to pursue. A **position** is the way a firm's product, brand, or organization is viewed relative to the competition by current and prospective customers. To establish itself in a market that was dominated by firms appealing primarily to the preferences of children, Wendy's positioned its burgers as "hot and juicy," and therefore primarily for adults. If a position is how a product is viewed, then **positioning** is a firm's use of all the elements at its dis-

This ad for Wendy's suggests how the firm is positioning its sandwich relative to nutrition. Examine the websites of Wendy's, Burger King, and McDonald's and compare the accessibility, quantity, and quality of nutritional information provided. What observation would you formulate with regard to their respective positioning on nutrition? Does the fact that Wendy's is targeting adults while McDonald's appeals to kids play a role in their positioning on nutrition?

www.wendys.com
www.burgerking.com
www.mcdonalds.com

posal to create and maintain in the minds of a target market a particular image relative to competing products.

When positioning a product, the marketer wants to convey the benefit(s) most desired by the target market. A classic example of successful positioning is the original Head and Shoulders shampoo. As the first shampoo positioned as a dandruff remedy, the product's name implied the benefit, the medicinal fragrance suggested its potency, and the color (blue-green) and consistency (a paste rather than a liquid) indicated that it wasn't an ordinary shampoo.

To simplify decision making, individuals formulate mental positions for products, brands, and organizations. Often these positions are based on a single attribute and/or limited experience because consumers are seldom willing to invest much time and effort in the process. Because a product's position is critical to its evaluation, firms go to great lengths to influence how positions are formed.

There are three steps in a positioning strategy:

1. *Select the positioning concept.* To position a product or an organization, a marketer needs to first determine what is important to the target market. Marketers can then conduct positioning studies to see how members of a target market view competing products or stores on the important dimensions. The results of this research can be portrayed in a perceptual map that locates the brand or organization relative to alternatives on the dimensions of interest. A hypothetical example for jeans is shown in Figure 6.1. The length of the lines (or vectors) indicate the relative importance of the attributes, and the position of a brand relative to a vector indicates how closely the brand is associated with the attribute. For example, Calvin Klein jeans are perceived as more expensive than Gap jeans but not as comfortable, whereas Wranglers are seen as durable but low in status. This map suggests that a brand offering comfort and durability at a reasonable price would have little competition from these other brands. Thus it might be an attractive option.

Figure 6.1

A hypothetical perceptual map for jeans.

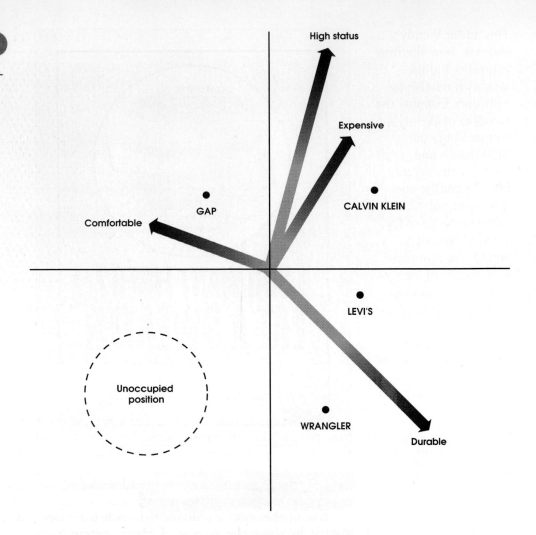

2. *Design the dimension or feature that most effectively conveys the position.* A position can be communicated with a brand name, a slogan, the appearance or other features of the product, the place where it is sold, the appearance of employees, and in many other ways. However, some features are more effective than others. It is important to not overlook details. According to a consultant, chairs for customers are vital in a retail environment because they signal that the seller "cares."[18] Because the marketer has limited resources, decisions have to be made on how best to convey the desired positioning concept.

3. *Coordinate the marketing mix components to convey a consistent position.* Even though one or two dimensions may be the primary position communicators, all the elements of the marketing mix—the product, price, promotion, and distribution—should complement the intended position. Many product failures are the result of inconsistent positioning that confuses consumers. For example, a compact car with a high price tag (Cadillac Cimarron), and Tetley Instant Iced Tea (in Britain, where the people take great pride in brewing tea) both flopped.

Over time a position may erode because of lack of attention, become less attractive to the market as needs or tastes change, or be usurped by a competitor. Hence positions must be regularly monitored and sometimes adjusted. Sensing a shift in outdoor interests away from shooting and hunting, and toward outdoor activities such as hiking, mountain biking, and kayaking, Hearst Corp. completely overhauled its *Sports Afield* magazine.[19]

Young people are an attractive market segment for many firms but they can be difficult to reach through traditional advertising media. Some marketers see schools as an ideal setting for reaching this target. Channel One is a 12-minute daily news program accompanied by commercials that is offered to schools free of charge. In exchange for guaranteeing that all their students watch the broadcasts, schools are given video monitors, VCRs, and satellite dishes by the sponsoring organization, Whittle Communications.

Although Channel One has been controversial since its beginning in 1989, it is just one of several ways marketers get into classrooms. Another is sampling. Packages of youth-oriented products are distributed at many schools. Also, magazines that focus on themes such as careers and sports and contain a large quantity of advertising are distributed to schools free with the provision that they are given to students. Another approach is corporate-sponsored teaching materials. By offering schools professionally produced, attention-getting posters, workbooks, and videos along with lesson plans for the teachers, companies are able to get their brands and products in front of students.

Is it ethical for marketers to pursue this hard-to-reach segment in such a fashion? Is it appropriate for money-starved school districts to use these tools to enhance their resources?

Sources: Pat Wechsler, "This Lesson Is Brought to You By . . . ," *Business Week,* June 30, 1997, pp. 68–69; the website of Consumers Union, www.consunion.org/other/selling/kids/March 2000.

When its position has eroded, and a firm attempts to reestablish its attractiveness, it is engaging in **repositioning.** Mercedes-Benz discovered that its target consumers rated the Mercedes at the top in safety, resale value, and overall performance, but only third or fourth on intent to purchase. Further research uncovered another critical dimension the firm had neglected. Consumers saw Mercedes-Benz as arrogant and aloof. It was not a company they wanted to do business with. As a result of this finding, Mercedes launched a seven-year program that includes major advertising changes and employee retraining to make the firm appear more youthful, friendlier, and more accessible.[20]

Forecasting Market Demand

Recall that one condition for useful segmentation is that the resulting segments be large enough to produce a profit. The potential of a segment is determined by forecasting how much it will buy. The process of forecasting demand is discussed next.

Demand forecasting estimates sales of a product during some defined future period. Forecasting is done to make various kinds of predictions. For example, a forecast can refer to an entire industry (such as apparel), to one firm's product line (Levi casual wear), or to an individual brand (Levi 501 jeans). Thus, for a forecast to be understood, it is important to make very clear what it describes.

Basic Forecasting Terms

In this section we'll explain some concepts so our discussion will be easier to follow.

Market Share

A term used frequently in business as a performance measure, **market share** is the proportion of total sales of a product during a stated period in a specific market that is captured by a single firm. If Almega Corp. sold $210 million worth of turbine engines in 1999, and total industry sales of turbine engines that year were $7 billion, Almega's market share was 3%.

Market share can refer to entire industries (aircraft), segments of industries (single-engine business jets), or particular geographic areas (Pacific Rim), and can also apply to past, present, or future periods. For example, the steel industry, which has a 95% market share for canned-food containers, is working to prevent a recurrence of the inroads in food packaging that were made by aluminum makers in the market for beverage cans.

Market Factor

A **market factor** is something that (1) exists in a market, (2) is measurable, and (3) is related to the demand for a product in a known way. To illustrate, the "number of cars three years old and older" is a market factor related to the demand for replacement tires. It's a market factor because the number of replacement tires that can be sold changes as the number of older cars changes.

In segmenting world markets geographically, McDonald's uses population, per capita income, and the number of people per store in the U.S. as market factors to obtain a rough forecast of the number of stores a country can support.[21] The formula looks like this:

$$\frac{\text{population of the country}}{\text{\# of people per McDonald's in U.S.}} \times \frac{\text{per capita income of the coutry}}{\text{per capita income of U.S.}} = \frac{\text{the number of stores the country can support}}{}$$

The formula, which produces a preliminary estimate that is adjusted for factors such as eating habits and competition, suggests the following:

Country	Market potential (no. of outlets)
China	784
Colombia	79
Pakistan	90
South Africa	190

Market Potential, Sales Potential, and Sales Forecast

Market potential is the total sales volume that *all organizations* selling a product during a stated period of time in a specific market could expect to achieve under ideal conditions. **Sales potential** is the portion of market potential that a *specific company* could expect to achieve under ideal conditions. For example, market potential applies to all refrigerators, but sales potential refers only to a single brand of refrigerators (such as Whirlpool).

With either of these measures of potential, the market may encompass whatever group or area interests the forecaster. It could be the world, one country, or a smaller market defined by income or some other basis. For example, Whirlpool may consider the market potential for refrigerators in the New England states, or the sales potential for Whirlpool refrigerators in households with incomes of $25,000 to $50,000.

The term *potential* refers to a maximum level of sales assuming that (1) all marketing plans are sound and effectively implemented and (2) all prospective customers with the desire and ability to buy do so. Of course, few industries or companies achieve their full potential. Therefore, potential should not be the final outcome of demand forecasting. It is an intermediate step. We must move from *potential* sales to *probable* sales, which are estimated by preparing forecasts.

A **sales forecast** is an estimate of probable sales for one company's brand of a product during a stated period in a specific market, assuming a defined marketing plan is used. Like measures of potential, a sales forecast can be expressed in dollars or product units. However, whereas market potential and sales potential are estimated on the basis of general factors and market assumptions, a sales forecast is made on the basis of a specific marketing plan for the product.

A sales forecast is best prepared after market potential and sales potential have been estimated. Sales forecasts typically cover a one-year period, although many firms review and revise their forecasts quarterly or even monthly. Forecasts of less than a year may be desirable when activity in the firm's industry is so volatile that it is not feasible to look ahead an entire year. As a case in point, many retailers and producers in the fashion industry prepare forecasts for only one fashion season at a time. Hence, they prepare three or four forecasts a year.

Once a sales forecast has been prepared, it affects all departments in a company. The sales forecast is the basis for deciding how much to spend on various activities like advertising and personal selling. Planning the necessary amount of working capital, plant utilization, and warehousing facilities is accomplished on the basis of anticipated sales. Scheduling production, hiring production workers, and purchasing raw materials also depend on the sales forecast.

Methods of Forecasting Sales

There are many methods of forecasting sales. Several of the more commonly used methods are described below.

Market-Factor Analysis

In many situations, future demand for a product is related to the behavior of certain market factors. When this is true, we can forecast future sales by studying the behavior of these market factors. Basically, **market-factor analysis** entails determining what these factors are and then measuring their relationship to sales activity.

Using market-factor analysis successfully requires that the analyst (1) select the best market factors and (2) minimize the number of market factors. The best factors are ones that vary in a consistent way with the demand for the product being forecast. Fewer factors are preferable in order to simplify the data collection and analyses.

We can translate market-factor behavior into a demand forecast with the **direct-derivation method.** To illustrate, suppose a producer of automobile tires wants to know the market potential for replacement tires in the U.S. in 2002. The primary market factor is the number and age of automobiles on the road. The first step is to estimate how many cars are prospects for new tires.

Assume that the producer's studies show (1) the average car is driven 10,000 miles per year and (2) the average driver gets 30,000 miles of use from a set of tires. This means that all cars that become three years old or multiples of three years old in 2002 can be considered as comprising the potential market for replacement tires during that year. From state and county auto license agencies as well as private organizations, the producer can obtain a reasonably accurate count of the number of cars that were sold in the U.S. in 1999 and therefore will be three years old in 2002. In addition, with a little digging the producer can determine how many cars will become 6, 9, and 12 years old and still be on the road in 2002, and therefore would also be ready for another set of tires.

The number of cars in these age brackets multiplied by four (tires per car) should give the approximate market potential for replacement tires in 2002. Of course, we are dealing in averages. Not all drivers will get 30,000 miles from their tires, and not all cars will be driven 10,000 miles per year.

The direct-derivation method is simple, inexpensive, and requires little statistical analysis. Executives who are not statisticians can understand it and interpret its results. This method's main limitation is that it can be used only when it is possible to identify an easily measured market factor that affects the product's demand in a stable way.

Correlation analysis is a statistical refinement of the direct-derivation method. It is a measure of the association between potential sales of the product and the market factor affecting its sales. Detailed explanation of this statistical technique is beyond the scope of this text. However, in general, a correlation analysis measures, on a scale of 0 (no association) to 1 (perfect association), the variation between two data series. For example, one data series might be the number of dogs registered in Boulder, Colorado, each year from 1980 to 2000, and the other the sales of canned dog food in Boulder in the corresponding years. If there is a reasonably strong historical relationship between these two series, a marketer might use current dog registrations to predict the demand for dog food.

Correlation analysis gives a more precise estimate of how well the market factor predicts market demand than does direct derivation. That's because in direct derivation, the association is assumed to be 1.0 (that is, perfect). But rarely is there a perfect association between a market factor and the demand for a product. Using a more sophisticated form of correlation analysis called **multiple correlation**, it is possible to include more than one market factor in the calculation.

Correlation analysis has two major limitations. For one thing, not all marketing executives understand it. For another, it can be used only when both of the following are available: (1) a sales history of the industry or firm consisting of at least 20 consecutive time periods, and (2) a corresponding history of the market factor being used to forecast demand. Last, correlation analysis depends on the assumptions, which can be quite unrealistic, that approximately the same relationship has existed between sales and the key market factor(s) during the entire period, and that this relationship will continue in the sales period being predicted.

Survey of Buyer Intentions

A **survey of buyer intentions** involves asking a sample of current or potential customers how much of a particular product they would buy at a given price during a specified future period. Some firms ask a sample of consumers from the target segment about their buying intentions and then extrapolate the result to the entire segment.

Selecting a representative sample of potential buyers can be a problem. For many consumer products, a large sample is needed because many groups with different buying patterns make up the market. Thus this method can be costly in terms of both money and time. This method has another serious limitation. Because it is one thing for prospects to *intend* to buy a product but quite another for them to *actually* buy it, surveys of buying intentions often show an inflated measure of market potential. Such surveys are probably most accurate in forecasting demand when (1) there are relatively few current or potential buyers, (2) the buyers are willing to express their buying intentions, and (3) their past records show a consistent relationship between their actual buying behavior and their stated intentions. These conditions are most likely to exist in a business market.

Test Marketing

In **test marketing** to forecast demand, a firm markets a new product in a limited geographic area, measures sales, and then—from this sample—projects the product's sales over a larger area. Test marketing is often used to determine whether there is sufficient demand for a new product to be viable. It also serves as a basis for evaluating new-product features and alternative marketing strategies. More details about test marketing, including its benefits and drawbacks, are presented in Chapter 7.

Past Sales and Trend Analysis

A popular method of forecasting is based entirely on past sales. Small retailers whose main goal is to "beat last year's figures" frequently use this technique. In **past sales analysis**, the demand forecast is simply a flat percentage change applied to the volume achieved last year or to the average volume of the past few years.

This technique is simple and inexpensive. For a firm operating in a stable market where its market share has remained constant for a period of years, past sales alone can be used to predict future volume. However, few companies operate in unchanging environments, making this method highly unreliable.

Trend analysis examines past sales data to calculate the rate of change in sales volume and uses it to forecast future sales. One type of trend analysis is a long-term projection of sales, usually computed with a statistical technique called regression. However, the statistical sophistication of long-term trend analysis does not offset the inherent weakness of basing future estimates only on past sales activity. A second type of trend analysis entails a short-term projection using a seasonal index of sales covering several months. Short-term trend analysis may be acceptable if a firm's sales follow a reliable seasonal pattern. For example, assume that the second quarter of the year historically produces sales about 50% higher than the first quarter. Hence, if sales reach 10,000 units in the first quarter, we can reasonably forecast sales of 15,000 units for the second quarter.

Sales-Force Composite

In sales forecasting, a **sales-force composite** consists of collecting from all sales people estimates of sales for their territories during the future period of interest. The total of all these estimates is the company's sales forecast.

A sales-force composite method can produce an accurate forecast if the firm has competent, well-informed sales people. Its strength is that it takes advantage of sales people's specialized knowledge of their own markets. Furthermore, it should make sales people more willing to accept their assigned sales quotas, because they participated in the process that produced the forecasts that serve as the basis for their quotas. A sales-force composite is most useful for firms selling to a market composed primarily of a few large customers where sales people work closely with them and are well informed about their plans. Thus this method would be more applicable to sales of large electrical generators to energy utilities than to sales of small general-use motors to many thousands of firms.

This method also has limitations. A sales force may not have the time or the experience to do the research needed for sales forecasting, and managers must guard against sales people who overestimate or underestimate future sales, depending on circumstances. For instance, sales people are by nature optimistic and therefore may overestimate future possibilities. Or, if compensation is based on meeting sales quotas, sales people may underestimate future sales.[22]

Executive Judgment

Basically, **executive judgment** involves obtaining opinions from one or more executives regarding future sales. If these are well-informed opinions, based on valid measures such as market-factor analysis, then executive judgment can produce accurate forecasts. However, forecasting by executive opinion alone is risky, because such opinions are sometimes simply intuition or guesswork. Executives at Gardenburger, Inc., the maker of a vegetarian burger, predicted sales of $200 million after annual sales more than doubled following the appearance of the firm's ad on the final episode of "Seinfeld" in 1998. However, their optimism now appears unfounded as sales have dropped to less than the preadvertisement level.[23]

One specialized form of executive judgment is the **Delphi method,** named after the location of an oracle in ancient Greece. Developed by the Rand Corporation for use in environmental forecasting, this technique can also be applied to sales forecasting. It is especially applicable to products that are truly innovative or are significant technological breakthroughs.

The Delphi method begins with a group of knowledgeable individuals anonymously estimating future sales. Each person makes a prediction without knowing how others in the group have responded. These estimates are summarized, and the resulting average and range of forecasts are fed back to the participants. Now, knowing how the group responded, they are asked to make another prediction on the same issue. Participants may change or stick to their original estimates. This process of estimates and feedback is continued for several rounds. In some cases—and usually in sales forecasting—the final round involves face-to-face discussions among the participants to produce a consensus sales forecast.

An advantage of the Delphi method is that the anonymity in the early rounds prevents one individual (for example, a top executive) from influencing others (a subordinate). And it permits each participant to consider the combined judgment of the group. If an individual's forecast is widely divergent from the group's average, the opportunity exists to justify or modify it in the next round. A potential disadvantage of the Delphi method—and of any executive judgment method—is that participants may lack the necessary information on which to base their judgments.

No method of sales forecasting is perfect. An executive's challenge is to choose an approach that is likely to produce the most accurate estimate of sales given the firm's particular circumstances. Because all techniques have limitations, companies should consider using a combination of forecasting methods and then reconciling any differences that are produced.

Summary

A market consists of people or organizations with wants, money to spend, and the willingness to spend it. However, within most markets the buyers' needs are not identical. Therefore, a single marketing program for an entire market is unlikely to be successful. A sound marketing program starts with identifying the differences that exist within a market, a process called market segmentation, deciding which segments will be pursued as target markets, and selecting a competitive position that will be conveyed to customers through the marketing mix.

Most marketers adopt some form of market segmentation as a compromise between the extremes of a strategy that treats the market as an aggregate, undifferentiated whole, and a strategy that views each customer as a different market. Market segmentation enables a company to make efficient use of its marketing resources. Also, it allows a small company to compete effectively by concentrating on one or two segments. The apparent drawback of market segmentation is that it will result in higher production and marketing costs than a one-product, mass-market strategy. However, if the market is correctly segmented, a better fit with customers' needs will actually result in greater efficiency. For segmentation to be effective: (1) the bases for segmentation must be measurable with obtainable data, (2) the segments identified must be accessible through existing marketing institutions, and (3) the segments must be large enough to be potentially profitable.

At the broadest level, most markets may be divided into two segments: ultimate consumers and business users. The four major bases used for further segmenting the consumer market are geographic, demographic, psychographic, and behavioral. The business market may be segmented on the basis of customer location, customer type, and transaction conditions. Normally, in either the consumer or business market, a seller will use a combination of two or more segmentation bases.

The three alternative strategies for selecting a target market are market aggregation and single-segment and multiple-segment strategies. Market-aggregation strategy involves using one marketing mix to reach a mass, undifferentiated market. With a single-segment strategy, a company still uses only one marketing mix, but it is directed at only one segment of the total market. A multiple-segment strategy entails selecting two or more segments and developing a separate marketing mix to reach each segment. The guidelines for selecting segments to target are compatibility with the firm's goals, fit with the firm's resources, profit potential, and the strength of the competition.

When targets have been selected, the organization must decide how to position the offering. Position is the way a brand or organization is viewed relative to the competition by current and prospective customers. A positioning effort should convey the benefits most desired by the target market. The three steps in positioning are (1) selecting the positioning concept, (2) designing the feature to convey the position, and (3) coordinating the marketing mix to consistently communicate the desired position.

Forecasting is essential in evaluating possible target segments. It involves estimating the demand of a market. Management usually estimates the total sales that could be expected under ideal conditions for all firms comprising the industry—market potential—and for its particular product—sales potential. The final step in estimating demand is a sales forecast, indicating probable sales for the company's brand of a particular product in a future time period and with a specified marketing program. The forecast normally covers one year.

Specific methods used to forecast sales are market-factor analysis, survey of buyer intentions, test marketing, past sales and trend analysis, sales-force composite, and executive judgment. Management's challenge is to select the techniques that are appropriate in a particular situation.

More about **NetJet**

In 1998 Warren Buffet, one of America's most successful investors, bought Executive Jet, the parent company of NetJet, for $725 million. The company immediately ordered 100 Cessna Citation Sovereign jets, and followed that up with a $2 billion order for 50 Raytheon Hawker Horizon jets in 1999. Clearly Buffet has big plans for NetJet's future.

In the U.S. there are 5,000 companies that own their own corporate jets, and another 120,000 companies with revenues of over $30 million that do not have corporate jets. According to a NetJet executive, they are all prospects.

Depending on the plane selected, fractional (such as one-eighth) ownership can cost from $330,000 to $3.5 million. NetJet estimates the break-even point for fractional ownership is 400 hours of flying. If a traveler flies more than 400 hours a year out of one location, then purchasing a jet outright makes more fiscal sense.

Two problems make responding to demand difficult and, as a result, are limiting NetJet's growth.

One is the lead time required in obtaining aircraft. Because the planes are made to order, delivery is typically one or even two years after orders are placed. The second is obtaining pilots. The hiring process is relatively slow, because the applicants must be carefully screened and properly certified. Fortunately for NetJet, its competitors face the same problems.

NetJet and its competitors are expanding their fleets to include larger planes that can travel greater distances and carry more passengers. There is an intense rivalry among firms in the industry to offer the newest planes and provide the fastest service. However, there may be other ways to differentiate the offerings. To seek some insights, FlexJet recently invited 100 of its fractional owners to a two-day brainstorming and pleasure trip in Pebble Beach, California.

Another concern is still more competition. In the not too distant future, there are likely to be reactions from the commercial airlines as they see fractional ownership cutting into their lucrative first-class business.[24]

1. What characteristics should NetJet use to segment the market for fractional ownership of airplanes?

 www.flexjet.com

Key Terms and Concepts

Market segments (150)
Target market (150)
Market segmentation (151)
Micromarketing (153)
Geographic segmentation (154)
Demographic segmentation (156)
Psychographic segmentation (157)
Personality (157)
Life-style (157)
Values (158)
Behavioral segmentation (158)
Market-aggregation strategy (162)

Product differentiation (163)
Single-segment strategy (163)
Niche marketers (163)
Niche markets (163)
Multiple-segment strategy (164)
Position (166)
Positioning (166)
Repositioning (169)
Demand forecasting (169)
Market share (169)
Market factor (170)
Market potential (170)
Sales potential (170)
Sales forecast (171)

Market-factor analysis (171)
Direct-derivation method (171)
Correlation analysis (172)
Multiple correlation (172)
Survey of buyer intentions (172)
Test marketing (172)
Past sales analysis (173)
Trend analysis (173)
Sales-force composite (173)
Executive judgment (173)
Delphi method (173)

Questions and Problems

1. Give two examples of goods or services whose market demand would be particularly affected by each of the following population factors:
   a. Regional distribution
   b. Marital status
   c. Gender
   d. Age
   e. Urban-rural-suburban distribution

2. From a recent "Survey of Buying Power" (from *Sales & Marketing Management* magazine), record the available data for the county in which you live and another county with which you are familiar (maybe the one in which your school is located). Comment on how differences you find may be useful to a fast-food franchisee seeking a location for a new outlet.

3. Using the psychographic bases discussed in this chapter, describe the segment likely to be the best market for:
   a. Ski resorts
   b. Online auto sales
   c. Power hand tools
   d. Donations to United Way
   e. PC that includes Internet access

4. What users' benefits would you stress in advertising each of the following three products to each of these three markets?

Product	Market
a. CD player	a. Schoolteachers
b. Toothpaste	b. Retired people
c. 10-day Caribbean cruise	c. Working women

5. What demographic characteristics would you think are likely to describe heavy users of the following?
   a. Online investment advice and stock trading
   b. Ready-to-eat cereal
   c. Videocassette recorders
   d. Laptop computers

6. How would you segment the market for copying machines such as Xerox or Canon photocopiers?

7. How might the following organizations implement the strategy of market segmentation?
   a. Manufacturer of personal computers
   b. American Heart Association
   c. Universal Studios (Hollywood movies)
   d. Internet-only retail banking service

8. Find a magazine advertisement that communicates the position for a product in each of the following categories:
   a. Household appliance
   b. Cellular phone service
   c. Airline
   d. Hotel or motel chain

9. What market factors might you use in estimating the market potential for each of the following products?
   a. Central home air-conditioning
   b. Electric milking machines
   c. First-class airline travel
   d. Printers to accompany personal computers

10. How would you determine (a) market potential and (b) a sales forecast for a textbook for an introductory marketing course?

Hands-On Marketing

1. Interview three friends or acquaintances who all own athletic shoes but differ on some demographic dimension (for example, education or age). Using the criteria of demographics, psychological variables, and behavioral variables, describe in as much detail as possible the market segment each represents.

2. Examine the annual reports (available in your library) of two consumer product marketers and two business product marketers to determine what target markets they are currently serving.

7

Marketing Research and Market Information

"Could properly designed and executed marketing research have prevented Iridium's failure? It is impossible to say. However, important questions could have been answered."

Could **Iridium**'s Flameout Have Been Prevented?

In the late 1970s Bell Labs (now known as Lucent Technologies) commissioned a market research study to investigate the potential of its invention, cellular phone service. When the results predicted only 800,000 subscribers by the year 2000, AT&T, then Bell Labs' parent company, decided to stay out of the business. Now, with over 80 *million* subscribers in the U.S. alone, that research appears terribly misguided. However, at that time the target was defined as business executives, cellular service could be used only from a car, the handsets were big and expensive, and the range was limited. Of course, all of that changed and the market experienced explosive growth.

More recently, the investors in another communications company, Iridium, may wish its managers had been equally conservative. Iridium set out to offer a global, wireless phone service, making use of earth-orbiting satellites to transmit calls. After over 10 years in development, $3 billion in debt, and only 20,000 subscribers, the company declared bankruptcy in 1999.

What went wrong? Several explanations have been offered. Some think the product was launched prematurely, before all the technological kinks were removed. Others criticize the large, unreliable phones the users had to lug around. Still others blame the initial price of the phone ($3,000), and the cost of the service (up to $7 a minute). There are accusations that the advertising campaign slogan used at the launch, "Anytime, anywhere," was misleading because the phone could not be used in buildings or cars, and service was not available in some countries. Finally, there was the issue of coordinating the international consortium of companies needed to finance and operate the system. For the system to function, each of the 15 switching systems located around the world had to operate at the same high level of efficiency.

Could properly designed and executed marketing research have prevented Iridium's failure? It's impossible to say. However, important questions could have been answered. For example, product tests could have indicated how well the product functioned and how closely that matched the expectations of the target market. Pricing research could have produced insights into the relative attractiveness of the satellite system versus the improving cellular alternative. Research monitoring the environment might have predicted how quickly the advantages of a satellite system were being displaced. And advertising copy research would have indicated what expectations the messages in the ads were likely to create.

Although we can only speculate how Iridium might have benefited from more or better marketing research, it appears at least one other company learned from monitoring Iridium's miscues. Globalstar, another satellite phone service, decided to initially target only North America and western Europe. With a smaller geographic market and fewer partners to manage, Globalstar's management believes it can offer better service at a lower cost than its more ambitious predecessor.[1]

1. If Iridium did conduct marketing research similar to what is described above, what are some possible explanations for why the company made so many marketing mistakes?

2. If you were considering launching a new product, what questions would you want answered?

 www.globalstar.com

The failure of Iridium's satellite phone venture illustrates one thing all organizations have in common—the risk of making decisions in an uncertain world. Firms attempt to reduce that uncertainty with information. To develop effective strategy, all marketing managers need current, accurate information about the macroenvironment affecting their particular industry, the markets they are trying to reach, and the internal and external forces that influence their specific market. We're about to examine how this information can be obtained and used.

After studying this chapter, you should be able to explain:

- What marketing research is, the need for it, and the variety of forms it takes.
- How information systems increase the usefulness of data.
- The growing role of technology in marketing research.
- The appropriate way to conduct a marketing research project.
- How firms gather and use information about competitors.
- How ethics enters into the performance of marketing research.
- Some threats to the future of marketing research.

The Marketing Research Function

Marketing research is needed before a product is introduced to the market, and on a regular basis throughout its life. Research is not limited to products; it is conducted to answer questions about potential market segments, entire stores, brand names, advertising, prices, and every other aspect of marketing. The challenges in every research project are to correctly define the issue to be studied, gather the appropriate data, and transform the raw data into useful information. To see how to do this, we will begin by briefly discussing where organizations use research. Then we will focus our attention on how research is performed and managed.

The Need for Marketing Research

Competitive pressure, the cost of making a strategic mistake, and the complexity of both domestic and foreign markets dictate that a firm must have access to timely information. Consider some of the marketing issues that are frequently researched:

- *Markets and market segments.* Experienced managers often suspect that a need exists in the market, but intuition is usually not sufficient to justify a decision that may require the investment of millions of dollars. Research can be used to clarify the need, identify and describe exactly who has it, and determine the strength of the need in various segments.

- *Products and brands.* Even when a marketer is confident that a need exists, it is not always clear what form a product should take to satisfy the need. Consider that several firms are designing and testing personal delivery units that are necessary if electronic shopping is to grow. These units are storage boxes that permit deliveries to a home or office when no one is present to personally accept the merchandise. The boxes must be accessible yet secure, large enough to hold a variety of different deliveries but not obtrusive, reasonably attractive, and easy to install. Having consumers evaluate alternative designs will help the makers. Some brand and company names are also extensively tested, and some are not but should have been. What does the company name Calyx & Corolla suggest to you? If you said "flowers," congratulations! You must have been paying attention during the boring part of your biology course. Unfortunately for Calyx & Corolla, most consumers don't make the association between these unfamiliar botanical terms and this merchant that sells fresh-cut flowers ordered by phone or the Internet.

www.calyxandcorolla.com

- *Advertising.* Before it ever appears in public, marketers want to determine if an ad can attract attention, effectively communicate the intended message, and be remembered. Advertising research is an industry in itself, with firms that specialize in everything from investigating ideas for ads to testing the final versions.

- *Expectations and satisfaction.* It is important to know what customers expect, which is influenced by what marketers have promised in their ads, and how well those expectations are being satisfied. Surprisingly few customers volunteer information to a firm. Research suggests that only 1 in 10 dissatisfied customers complain.[2] Firms need research to quickly identify problems and solve them before they result in lost business.

This is just a sample of the many types of marketing research. The 50 largest marketing research firms in the U.S. are paid nearly $6 *billion* a year by their clients from around the world for information to improve the quality of decision making.[3] Unaccounted for in this figure is the research done internally by firms and the hundreds of smaller marketing research companies. Obviously, research is an important part of marketing!

What Is Marketing Research?

Marketing research consists of all the activities that enable an organization to obtain the information it needs to make decisions about its environment, marketing mix, and present or potential customers. More specifically, **marketing research** is the development, interpretation, and communication of decision-oriented information to be used in all phases of the marketing process. This definition has two important implications:

- Research plays a role in all three phases of the management process in marketing: planning, implementation, and evaluation.

- It recognizes the researcher's responsibility to develop information, which includes defining problems, gathering and analyzing data, interpreting results, and presenting the information in such a way that it is useful to managers.

Scope of Marketing Research Activities

Depending on their needs and level of sophistication, marketing managers make use of four main sources of information. One is regularly scheduled reports that are produced and sold by research firms. These are called *syndicated services* because they are developed without a particular client in mind, but are sold to anyone interested. An example is National Total-Market Audit, produced by Audits & Surveys, Inc., a bimonthly national measure of total retail sales by brand. Subscribing to this service allows a marketer to regularly monitor retail sales of its own and competitors' products by type of outlet and geographic area.

www.surveys.com

The second source is a *marketing information system,* an internally coordinated activity that provides continuous, scheduled, or on-demand standardized reports. Most marketing information systems (MkIS) rely heavily on internal data such as sales reports, inventory amounts, and production schedules, but they also often include information purchased from research firms or trade associations. An MkIS is used by both managers and sales people. For example, a sales person sitting in a customer's office can use a laptop computer and an MkIS to check on the availability of current inventory and the schedule for producing more. Other frequent applications include tracking the sales performance of products and monitoring changing consumer tastes.

A *decision support system* is the third source. It is also internal, but it is interactive. It permits a decision maker to interact directly with data through a personal computer to answer specific questions. A manager, for example, might have a decision support system that will estimate the impact of various levels of advertising on sales of a product when given specific assumptions.

The fourth source is a nonrecurring, proprietary *marketing research project*, conducted by a company's own staff or by an independent research firm to answer a specific question. For example, Toro, a manufacturer of lawn mowers, might conduct a survey of retail dealers, consumers, or both to identify the most common problems customers have with power mowers.

There are many providers of syndicated research, the first source of information mentioned above. Detailing the topics and varied research methods of syndicated researchers goes beyond the scope of this discussion. (For more information and examples of syndicated research services, see the websites of Information Resources, Inc., and ACNielsen Corp.) Now, we will concentrate our discussion on the other three sources.

www.infores.com
www.acnielsen.com

Marketing Information Systems

As computers became common business tools in the early 1960s, firms were able to collect, store, and manipulate larger amounts of data to aid marketing decision makers. Out of this capability developed the **marketing information system**—an ongoing, organized procedure to generate, analyze, disseminate, store, and retrieve information for use in making marketing decisions. Figure 7.1 illustrates the characteristics and operation of an MkIS. The ideal MkIS:

- Includes real-time data.
- Generates regular reports and recurring studies as needed.
- Analyzes data using statistical analysis and mathematical models that represent the real world.
- Integrates old and new data to provide information updates and identify trends.

Designing a Marketing Information System

To build an effective MkIS, marketing managers must identify the information that will help them make better decisions. Working with researchers and systems analysts, managers then determine whether the data needed are available within the organization or must be procured, how the data should be organized, the form in which the data should be reported, and the schedule according to which the data will be delivered.

For example, the manager at Procter & Gamble who is responsible for Tide wants to know the retail sales of all detergent brands by geographic area on a weekly basis. The same manager may want monthly reports on the prices that competitors are charging and how much advertising they are doing. Less frequently, possibly once a year, this manager needs to know about developments in the marketplace such as demographic changes that might affect Tide in the long term. In addition to these (and probably other) regular reports, the manager may periodically request special reports that can be compiled from existing data. For example, while contemplating a proposal to introduce another version of Tide, the manager may want to see what share of the total market each detergent brand

Figure 7.1

The structure and function of a marketing information system.

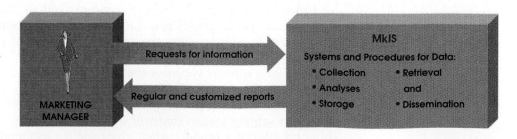

had by quarter over the last five years and a projection of how each is likely to perform over the next three years.

A well-designed MkIS can provide a continuous flow of this type of information for decision making. Collecting data on consumer purchases has been greatly facilitated by electronic cash registers and computer systems that connect retailers directly with their suppliers. The storage and retrieval dimensions of an MkIS allow a manager to examine data for trends and patterns over time. With this capability, managers can continually monitor the performance of products, markets, sales people, and other marketing units.

An MkIS is of obvious value in a large company, where information is likely to get lost or distorted as it becomes widely dispersed. However, experience shows that even relatively simple information systems can upgrade management's decision making in small and medium-sized firms. For example, a small manufacturer of electric motors that tracks sales by customer over time can use the information to divide its customers into good, better, and best categories, and allocate selling effort accordingly. How well an MkIS functions depends on three factors:

- The nature and quality of the data available.
- The ways in which the data are processed and presented to provide usable information.
- The ability of the operators of the MkIS and the managers who use the output to work together.

Global Marketing Information Systems

As firms expand their operations beyond national borders, their needs for information also grow. Centrally managed international organizations must be informed about what is happening around the world. Thus, many companies are creating global marketing information systems. However, establishing worldwide agreement on the types and forms of information to be maintained can be challenging. For example, to maintain its leadership in the personal grooming industry Gillette must keep thousands of technology-using employees in over 60 manufacturing and R&D facilities spread across 24 countries integrated into a single information system.

Clearly, designing and operating a global MkIS can be more complex than developing one at the domestic level. It requires convincing each unit of the value of timely and accurate information, accommodating differences in the operational definitions of terms, and adjusting for the use of different currencies and measures in reporting data.

Gillette has worldwide sales of nearly $10 billion. It manufactures products in 20 countries and has distribution in over 200 countries. It employs more than 39,000 people, nearly three-quarters of them outside the U.S. Gillette enjoys valuable economies of scale by marketing the same products in many markets. For example, the Mach 3 razor is sold virtually everywhere. To keep track of these far-flung operations and to share information, Gillette has invested heavily in a sophisticated global information system.

The features of an MkIS—a focus on preplanned, structured reports and centralized control over the information by computer specialists—resulted from the skills required to operate computers. Now, personal computers with greatly enlarged capacity and user-friendly software have reduced that dependency and led to the development of decision support systems.

Decision Support Systems

A **decision support system (DSS)** is a computer-based procedure that allows a manager to directly interact with data using various methods of analysis to integrate, analyze, and interpret information. Like an MkIS, the heart of a DSS is data—different types of data from a wide variety of sources. Typically, a DSS contains data describing the market, customers, competitors, economic and social trends, and the organization's performance. Also, like an MkIS, the DSS has methods for analyzing data. These methods range from simple procedures such as computing ratios or drawing graphs to sophisticated statistical techniques and mathematical models.

Where the MkIS and DSS differ is in the extent to which they permit managers to interact directly with the data. By combining personal computers and user-friendly software, the DSS allows managers to independently retrieve data, examine relationships, and even produce reports to meet their specific needs. This interactive capability makes it possible for managers to react to what they see in a set of data by asking questions and getting immediate answers. Figure 7.2 depicts the relationships in a DSS.

Consider this example: Midway through the month, the brand manager for Sunshine brand of frozen lemonade wants to compare actual sales of the product to what was forecast. Sitting down at her computer, she calls up the monthly forecast and the actual sales figures to date. Discovering that sales are slightly below the rate necessary to achieve the month's forecast, she commands the system to provide similar data for each of the four different package sizes of the product. Finding that three of the sizes are on target, she concludes that there is a problem with only one. Next, she asks the system to break down the total sales figure by geographic areas and discovers that the poor sales results occurred in only two of seven regions.

Suspecting competitive activity, she then has the system retrieve and compare couponing activity, advertising levels, and prices of Sunshine lemonade and competing brands in the markets where sales forecasts were achieved and where they weren't. Finding nothing out of the ordinary, she decides to examine distribution in the territories. Requesting data on stock-outs for all package sizes of the lemonade, she finds that in the two regions where sales have slipped the frequency of stock-outs is higher than elsewhere. Next, she checks production figures and ware-

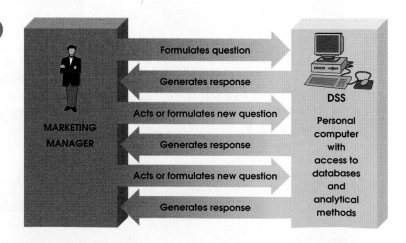

Figure 7.2

The structure and function of a decision support system.

house inventory levels and finds the problem is not due to internal shortages. Thus she concludes there must be a problem in the distribution of the product to the retail stores. As a result, she decides to investigate the performance of distributors in the problem regions.

Notice that, with an adequate DSS, this entire task was done in a short time by simply formulating a question, requesting information, analyzing the information, and moving on to another question suggested by the analysis. Note also that to function optimally the system requires current, accurate data that can be both costly and difficult to assemble and maintain.

The DSS adds speed and flexibility to the MkIS by making the manager an active part of the research process. The increased use of desktop computers, user-friendly software, and the willingness of suppliers and customers to link their computer systems (networking) have greatly enhanced the potential of DSS.

Databases, Data Warehouses, and Data Mining

An MkIS or a DSS uses data from a variety of sources both within the organization and from outside suppliers. Typically these data are organized, stored, and updated in a computer. The assembled data pertinent to a particular topic—customers, market segments, competitors, or industry trends, for example—is called a **database.**

Researchers probe databases with specific questions to uncover useful relationships and developments. For example, the managers of a retail supermarket chain might want to know which items are purchased most frequently in each of its stores. By having the computer sort through the electronic records of all completed transactions, this information can be compiled quickly. The resulting tallies can be used to customize each store's layout and improve customer convenience. Databases are not new. For years managers have been monitoring their customers and the environment. Computers, with their speed and capacity, have simply made the process more manageable, efficient, and accurate.

Analyzing databases has enabled marketers to better understand marketplace behavior and, as a result, address their customers' needs more specifically. Some believe that through the management of data, marketers will eventually reach the ultimate level of personalized marketing—targeting individuals. A move in that direction, called transactional segmentation, is being used by some banks to retain customers. By comparing an individual customer's transaction patterns to a database of all customers' transactions, a bank can often anticipate needs. With the information in hand, the bank can design individually tailored programs.[4]

It is clear that the development and use of databases in marketing will continue to grow. A recent national survey found that 85% of manufacturers and retailers believe databases will be essential in order to compete beyond the year 2000.[5]

Some organizations move beyond databases to create large and complex data repositories. Acknowledging that they are more than simply a "base" of data, these collections are called data warehouses. A **data warehouse** is an enormous collection of data, from a variety of internal and external sources, compiled by a firm that is conducting transactions with millions of customers. For example, American Express has a data warehouse consisting of over 500 *billion* bits of data describing how customers have used its 35 million charge cards to spend $350 billion since 1991.[6]

Data warehouses can be analyzed in the same way as databases, searching for predetermined patterns in the data. However, because of their size it would be a slow and cumbersome process. Fortunately, more advanced statistical and artificial intelligence techniques are now being applied to data warehouses.

Called **data mining,** these techniques have the capability to identify patterns and meaningful relationships in masses of data that would be overlooked or unrecognizable to researchers.[7] MCI WorldCom, for example, is especially concerned about losing long-distance telephone customers that have the greatest potential for future profits. Ideally the firm would like to identify attributes of buyers and the range of values on those attributes that are indicators of an imminent switch to another supplier. To evaluate its 140 million service subscribers, each with as many as 10,000 data points that include everything from income to calling habits, would take MCI months or even years with traditional methods. However using data mining techniques, MCI was able to develop 22 detailed profiles of customers on the verge of switching long-distance carriers. The firm then designed specially tailored programs to meet the particular concerns of each group.[8]

Major Data Sources

The data used by researchers and managers in databases and data warehouses are gathered from many sources. Internally, data can come from the sales force, marketing, manufacturing, and accounting. Externally, information is available from hundreds of research suppliers. Companies such as Market Facts, Inc., have developed computer systems to take the data captured from supermarket checkout systems to provide information on how well specific coupons work in various neighborhoods and which in-store displays are the most effective in generating sales.

Some sources provide a continuous flow—as when all transaction data for a retailer are fed into the system—whereas others are occasional or periodic providers—as when new demographic information on the population is released by the government. Some examples of especially useful data are described in more detail below.

Probably the most important data source for databases is **retail scanners,** the electronic devices at retail checkouts that read the bar code on each item purchased. Scanners were originally intended to speed up checkout and reduce errors in supermarkets. By matching an item's unique code with price information stored in a computer, the scanner eliminated the need for clerks to memorize prices and reduced mistakes from hitting the wrong cash register key. However, retailers quickly discovered scanners could also produce information on purchases that could be used to improve decisions about how much of a product to keep in inventory and the appropriate amount of shelf space to allocate to each product.[9]

Many retailers, including Kroger and Safeway, have taken scanning a step further by adding the customer's identity to the record of their purchases in what are called frequent shopper programs. Participants in the stores' frequent shopper programs are given special discounts if they permit the cashier to run their membership card through a reader when they check out. This allows the store to combine data stored on the card about household demographics and life-style with the shopper's scanned purchases. The store is then able to relate product choices to household characteristics and adjust the product assortment and store layout to make it more appealing. According to NCR Corp., a manufacturer of the computer equipment used in these systems, there are over 8,000 stores electronically collecting individual customer data in the U.S., and the number is growing rapidly.[10]

Linking household information to product purchases is even more valuable if you know what advertising the purchasers have been exposed to and the coupons they have used. Information Resources, Inc. (IRI), a marketing research firm, has created a database to provide this information. The firm maintains a sample of cooperating households for which it:

- Maintains an extensive demographic profile.
- Monitors television viewing electronically.
- Tracks the use of coupons.
- Records grocery purchases.

The result is that household demographics can be correlated to television advertising exposure, coupon usage, and product purchases. The output is called **single-source data** because all the information can be traced to individual households, providing a single source for the data.

Marketing Research Projects

Before MkIS and DSS, much of what was called marketing research consisted of projects to answer specific managerial questions. Projects, some that are nonrecurring and others that are repeated periodically, are still an important part of marketing research. The results of a project may be used to make a particular decision. They could also become part of a database to be used in an MkIS or a DSS. Examples of marketing research projects are described briefly in Table 7.1.

Most marketing research projects follow the procedure outlined in Figure 7.3. Let's examine what goes into conducting a marketing research project.

Define the Objective

Researchers need a clear idea of what they are trying to learn—the objective of the project. Usually the objective is to solve a problem, but this is not always so. Often the objective is to better understand or *define* a problem or opportunity.[11]

Sometimes the objective is simply to determine if there is a problem. To illustrate, a manufacturer of commercial air-conditioning equipment had been enjoying a steady increase in sales volume over a period of years. Management decided to conduct a sales analysis. This research project uncovered the fact that, although the company's volume had been increasing, its share of the market had declined because the industry was growing even faster. In this instance, marketing research uncovered a problem that management did not know existed. After specifying the objective, the researcher is ready for the second step—the situation analysis.

Conduct a Situation Analysis

Next, the researchers try to get a "feel" for the situation surrounding the problem. They analyze the company, its market, its competition, and the industry in general. The **situation analysis** is a background investigation that helps refine the research problem. This step involves obtaining information about the company and its business environment by means of library research and extensive interviewing of company officials.

In the situation analysis, researchers also try to refine the problem definition and develop hypotheses for testing. A research **hypothesis** is a tentative supposition that, if supported, would suggest a possible solution to a problem. An example of a testable hypothesis is: The appearance, quality and selection of produce is playing a larger role in the choice of a supermarket for consumers.[12] If research

Table 7.1	Typical Marketing Research Projects
Project	**Objective**
Concept test	To determine if a new-product idea is attractive to potential customers
Copy test	To determine if the intended message in an advertisement is being communicated effectively
Price responsiveness	To gauge the effect a price change would have on demand for a brand
Market-share analysis	To determine a firm's proportion of the total sales of a product
Segmentation studies	To identify distinct groups within the total market for a particular product
Customer satisfaction studies	To monitor how customers feel about an organization and its products

Figure 7.3

Marketing research pro-
cedure.

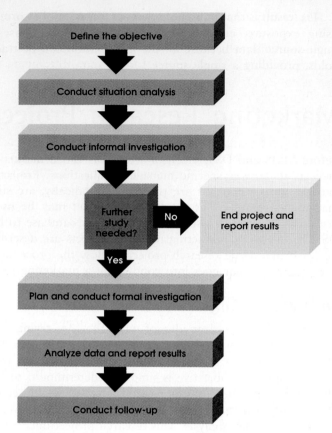

Define the objective

Conduct situation analysis

Conduct informal investigation

Further study needed? No → End project and report results

Yes

Plan and conduct formal investigation

Analyze data and report results

Conduct follow-up

supports this hypothesis, it would likely lead to changes in store layouts and the attention accorded the produce areas of a store. The project then turns to generating data that can be used to test the correctness of the hypotheses.

Conduct an Informal Investigation

Having developed a feel for the problem, the researchers are now ready to collect some preliminary data from the marketplace. This **informal investigation** consists of gathering readily available information from people inside and outside the company—middlemen, competitors, advertising agencies, and consumers.

The informal investigation is a critical step in a research project because it will determine whether further study is necessary. Decisions can frequently be made with information gathered in the informal investigation. For example, hotels hire professional "spies" to check in and act like typical guests when in fact they are evaluating the hotel's service. For as little as $1,500, a hotel can have its operation completely examined. And the examinations are thorough! For example, one hotel-rating company evaluates 50 items between a hotel's front door and the completion of check-in.[13] If the results of such a test are very positive, a hotel might decide that additional research is not needed. Alternatively, a poor result may dictate some immediate changes or more research.

Plan and Conduct a Formal Investigation

If the project warrants continued investigation, the researcher must determine what additional information is needed and how to gather it.

Select Sources of Information

Primary data, secondary data, or both can be used in an investigation. **Primary data** are new data gathered specifically for the project at hand. When researchers at a midwestern supermarket chain watched 1,600 shoppers move through the store, and discovered that 80% of the traffic was in 20% of the store (the produce, dairy, and meat sections), they were collecting primary data. **Secondary data** are available data, already gathered for some other purpose. For example, the data in a study by the Food Marketing Institute, an industry trade group, that reported the differences in food preference and shopping behavior of men and women, are secondary data.

One of the biggest mistakes made in marketing research is to collect primary data before exhausting what can be learned from information available in secondary sources. Ordinarily, secondary information can be gathered much faster and at far less expense than primary data. This is especially true today with so much data available over the Internet. For example, the U.S. Census Bureau has created the American FactFinder website to assist researchers in locating population data down to the community level. Statistics on housing, income, transportation, employment, and education are readily accessible at this site.[14]

www.census.gov

Sources of secondary data.   Excellent sources of secondary information are available to marketing researchers.[15] One source is the many records and reports *inside* the firm itself. For example, the daily call reports completed by sales people are used primarily to keep track of how they are spending their time. However, if they are examined over several months or years, they can provide a firm with important information on how its mix of customers is changing. Similarly, a contest with mail-in entries might be a good promotional tool. It also can be a source of information. Consumers who enter contests have indicated by their behavior that they are interested in particular products. Examining the geographic origins of these responses might indicate where the best potential markets are.

Outside the firm there are also a number of excellent secondary data sources. The federal government is the largest provider of demographic market information.

The U.S. Census Bureau gathers data from businesses and households in order to monitor social, economic, and demographic changes in the country. It is one of the primary sources of secondary data used by marketers. The Constitution mandates that a census of the population be conducted every 10 years, and all residents are legally required to participate. Even so, gaining cooperation is difficult. This ad was part of an extensive multimedia campaign to encourage residents to complete the 2000 census questionnaire.

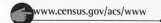

For example, the American Community Survey (ACS) being developed by the U.S. Census Bureau with nationwide implementation in 2003, will provide annual demographic, economic, and housing data on all communities in the country. Rather than rely on the decennial (once every 10 years) census of the population, community planners, businesspeople, and government officials will have current data on which to base decisions.[16] Other sources include the websites of firms and trade and professional organizations, private research firms, universities, business publications, and, of course, any good library. Some useful Web sources are described in Table 7.2.

Researchers must be aware that there is risk associated with using secondary data. Because the users have no control over how, when, by whom, or why the data were collected, they may not meet the objectives of the research. For example, some projects are undertaken to prove a preconceived point. The results of this so-called advocacy research often get considerable publicity, but may in fact be quite misleading. Thus researchers should check the source, motivation for the study, and definitions of key terms before relying on secondary data.

Sources of primary data. After exhausting all the available secondary sources considered pertinent, researchers may still lack sufficient data. If so, they must turn to primary sources and gather or purchase the information. In a company's research project, for instance, a researcher may interview the firm's sales people, middlemen, or customers to obtain the market information needed.

Table 7.2   Print and Electronic Sources of Secondary Data

Business and marketing publications

Sales & Marketing Management magazine <www.salesandmarketing.com> Survey of Buying Power

American Demographics magazine <www.marketingtools.com>

Advertising Age magazine <www.adage.com>

The New York Times: Business <www.nytimes.com/>

Business and marketing resource websites

Direct Contact Publishing's guide to over 3,000 trade and consumer publications <www.owt.com/dircom/mediajum.htm>

Academic Marketing Journals—directory of North American and European marketing journals <marketing.kub.nl/journal1.htm>

Executive Gateway to the Internet—links to dozens of useful sources in all areas of business and marketing <www.ceoexpress.com/>

Market research sources <www.vivamus.com/alphaurl.html>

Web Digest for Marketers—Summaries and reviews of marketing sites <www.wdfm.com>

Government agencies and publications

All U.S. government agencies <www.house.gov/house/govsites.html>

U.S. Census Bureau <http://www.census.gov>

Statistical Abstract of the U.S. <www.census.gov/statab/www/>

Federal Trade Commission <www.ftc.gov>

Marketing roundtables, discussion groups, and other resources

Marketing Tracks—sources and commentary on markets and marketing <NSNS.com/MouseTrack/>

Web Marketing Today Info Center <www.wilsonweb.com/webmarket/>

Professional association sources

American Marketing Association—professional association <www.ama.org/>

Direct Marketing Association <www.the-dma.org>

Sales and Marketing Executives International <www.smei.org>

Select a Primary Data-Gathering Method

There are three widely used methods of gathering primary data: observation, survey, and experimentation. Because each method has strengths and weaknesses, more than one may be used at different stages of a project. For example, observation may be used to develop hypotheses about shoppers' behavior and a survey may then be conducted to test the hypotheses. However, in many situations the researcher must select from among them. The choice of which to use depends on the nature of the problem, but it will also be influenced by how much time and money are available for the project.[17]

Observation method. The **observation method** involves collecting data by observing the actions of a person. In observation research there is no direct interaction with the subjects being studied.

Information may be gathered by *personal observation* or *mechanical observation*. In one kind of personal observation, the researcher poses as a customer. This technique is used by retailers to get information about the performance of sales people or to determine what brands the sales people emphasize. Mechanical observation takes many forms. One, described earlier, is the scanner used in retail stores to record purchases. Other, more dramatic forms are eye cameras that measure pupil dilation to record a person's response to a visual stimulus such as an ad, and brain wave monitors to test whether reactions to an object, such as a commercial, are primarily emotional or logical.

Internet "cookies" permit a special kind of observation. In Web jargon, a **cookie** is an inactive data file placed on a person's computer hard drive when that person visits a particular website. A cookie can record the visitor's activities while connected to the site. For example, it can keep track of which pages on the site are opened, how long the visitor remains at the site, the links the visitor makes to other sites, and the site from which the visitor came. If the site offers products for sale, purchases can also be recorded on a cookie. The cookie also allows the visitor (or more accurately, the visitor's computer) to be identified, so a profile of the individual's preferences can be created. The information from a cookie is used, for example, to welcome a website visitor by name or to offer particular products based on past purchases.[18] Through the cookies it places on visitors' computers, Amazon.com tracks the purchases of 4.5 million book-buying customers and offers suggestions about titles they might enjoy based on past purchases.[19]

The observation method has several merits. It can provide highly accurate data about behavior in given situations. Usually the parties being observed are unaware that they are being observed, so presumably they behave in a normal fashion. Thus the observation technique eliminates bias resulting from the intrusion of the research process into the situation. Also, because there is no direct interaction with the subject, there is no limit to how many times or for how long a subject can be observed. However, observation provides only information about *what* happens, it cannot tell *why*. Observation cannot delve into motives, attitudes, or opinions. To illustrate, what might explain why the ratio of shoppers' visits to purchases is much higher for the bakery department than for any other department in a supermarket? Interviews would be necessary to test your possible explanations.

Survey method. A **survey** consists of gathering data by interviewing people. Surveys may be conducted in person, or by telephone, by mail, or via the Internet. The advantage of a survey is that information comes directly from the people you are interested in. In fact, it may be the only way to determine the opinions or buying plans of a group. Surveys have several potential limitations:

- There are opportunities for error in the construction of the survey questionnaire and in the interviewing process.
- Surveys can be expensive and time-consuming.
- Desired respondents sometimes refuse to participate, and those who do respond often cannot or will not give true answers.

In some parts of the world, custom and/or technology dictate that marketing surveys be conducted in person. This interview, being conducted in Latin America, is an example. In situations where marketing research is uncommon, interviewers are treated with suspicion and gaining cooperation is difficult. As a result, the cost of data collection can vary dramatically depending on the location of the study.

As we will see below, careful design and execution of a survey can reduce the effects of these limitations.

Personal interviews are more flexible than phone or mail interviews because interviewers can probe more deeply if an answer is incomplete. Ordinarily, more information can be obtained by personal interviews than by other survey methods. They also have the advantage of being able to use various stimuli such as products, packages, and ads. Rising costs and other problems associated with door-to-door interviewing have prompted many market researchers to conduct surveys in locations that attract large numbers of people, such as shopping centers, airports, and parks. Because this approach was first used in shopping centers, it is generally called a *mall intercept* interview. However, there is growing concern about whether or not people interviewed in these settings are "typical" consumers.

In addition to their high cost and time-consuming nature, personal interviews also face the possible limitation of interviewer bias. An interviewer's appearance, style in asking questions, and body language can all influence a respondent's answers.

Another popular face-to-face type of personal interview is the **focus group.** In a focus group, a moderator leads 6 to 12 people in a discussion. Typically the participants are strangers before the session. They are contacted, screened for suitability, and invited to attend. Because focus group sessions require that participants gather at a particular time and place, and often last for two to three hours, participants are usually rewarded with cash or merchandise. General questions are posed by the moderator to prompt participants into freely discussing the topic of interest.

The strength of focus groups is found in the interaction of the participants. A comment by one person triggers thoughts and ideas in others, and the ensuing interaction can produce valuable insights. For example, gender-related feelings about food (men associate meat with high status and masculinity) and taste (women snack more, prefer sweets, and are willing to experiment, whereas men lean toward substantial meals, salty snacks, and familiar flavors) were uncovered in focus groups.[20] Focus groups generate ideas and hypotheses that can be tested using other research methods. However, when several independent focus group sessions conducted on the same topic produce a common theme, managers will sometimes act on the information without additional validation.

Telephone surveys can usually be conducted more rapidly than either personal or mail surveys. Because a few interviewers can make many calls from a central location, this method is easy to administer. A telephone survey can also be timely. For instance, to determine the impact of a particular TV commercial, viewers are contacted by phone within hours of the commercial's appearance, while the experience is still fresh. Telephone surveys have been used successfully with executives at work. When preceded by a letter introducing the study and a short call to make

Focus groups, such as the one shown in this photo with marketers observing the conversation, are an important tool for gathering in-depth insights. Besides providing the meeting facilities, research firms offer services such as recruitment of participants, moderators to conduct the sessions, a viewing area from which the session can be observed, audio and video taping, and equipment for presenting products, ads, and other discussion starters.

an appointment for the actual interview, these surveys can elicit a high cooperation rate.

One limitation of telephone surveys is that the interview must be short or the respondent becomes impatient. Also, about 30% of households have unlisted numbers, have moved since the latest directory was printed, or have no telephone. To lower the cost of telephone interviewing and reduce the problems of unlisted numbers and outdated directories, some surveys are done with the aid of computers. To ensure that all telephone owners, even those with unlisted numbers, have an equal chance of being called, researchers use a method called *random digit dialing* in which computers randomly select and dial numbers.

A **mail survey** involves sending a questionnaire to potential respondents, asking them to complete it, and having them return it. Traditionally mail surveys have used the post office to deliver and return questionnaires; however, e-mail is growing in popularity as a distribution method. Because interviewers are not used, this type of survey is not hampered by interviewer bias or problems connected with managing a team of interviewers. In addition, because there is no interviewer present, the respondent can remain anonymous. As a result, answers are more likely to be frank and honest.

A major problem with mail surveys is the compilation of an appropriate mailing list. In some cases lists are readily available. However, many studies require a sample for which there is no readily available mailing list. For example, if Amazon.com wants to survey a nationwide sample of consumers who have bought something at an auction in the last year, it might have a difficult time compiling a list. Fortunately, there are businesses, called list brokers that develop and maintain mailing lists. Another problem is the reliability of the information in the completed questionnaires. In a mail survey, researchers have no control over who actually completes the questionnaire or how carefully it is done.

One more problem is that a mail survey usually gets a low response rate, often less than 30 percent of those contacted. This is more than a numbers problem. If the respondents have characteristics that differentiate them from nonrespondents on important dimensions of the survey, the results will be invalid. For example, in a community survey about interest in the local PBS television station, the people willing to take the time to respond are likely to be highly interested in public television and therefore not representative of the entire community. Techniques for improving mail response rates include prenotification by phone, offering a reward, duplicate mailings and postcard reminders, and keeping the survey short and the questions simple.

Increasingly the Internet is being used to collect survey data. According to an article in *American Demographics,* "Almost every form of market research has been tried online, from the simplest demographic surveys to the most complex focus groups."[21] In an **Internet survey,** questionnaires can be posted on a firm's

How much confidence would you have in this research method?

Some marketing researchers are losing faith in focus groups (see the description of focus groups under the heading "Survey Method). They are concerned that focus group participants give less than candid responses in order to maintain a certain image and identify with the other members of the group. To avoid this "group effect," some researchers are examining individual consumers in their homes, at school, and at work. Listening in on conversations, inspecting pantries, and observing body language allows the researcher to "get in under the radar" according to an advertising executive.

MXG Media sells clothes and accessories targeted at teenage girls via the Internet. Teenage girls are an attractive market because they spend $70 billion a year. However, it is also an unpredictable market because a large portion of teen purchases are for items that are subject to fashion trends. What may be a best-selling nail polish or casual shoe style today, may be out of vogue tomorrow.

To stay on top of what's hot and to avoid what's not, MXG has an interesting research approach. At the beginning of each fashion season, the company lays out all the items being considered for its catalog. Then it hires 30 teenage girls to examine the items and make a hypothetical $150 in purchases. The choices the teens make determine what the company offers for sale. The reasoning of the owners is that no one cares more about fashion and entertainment than teenage girls, and the best way to stay in touch with their frequently changing tastes is to involve them directly.

Would you consider this an appropriate way to do research? How much confidence would you have in the results?

Sources: Caroline Waxler, "Guys with Moxie," *Forbes*, May 31, 1999, pp. 130–131; Melanie Wells, "New Ways to Get into Our Heads," *USA Today*, March 2, 1999, p. 1B.

www.MXGonline.com

website or e-mailed to a sample of individuals. Two of the most important advantages of this tool are speed and cost. An Internet survey can be done more quickly than any other method, and because all transmissions are electronic, there are significant personnel and material savings. Another important advantage is flexibility. JCPenney Co. was able to present 60 swimsuits to a sample of women, who viewed them on their PCs and indicated their likes and dislikes.[22]

Internet surveys have many of the same disadvantages as mail surveys, namely, verification of the identity of the respondent is not possible, good lists from which samples can be drawn are often difficult to find, and provision of an incentive to encourage response is difficult because there is not yet a reliable method of electronic delivery. Until Internet usage becomes more widespread, probably the greatest single concern in using the Internet for surveys is how well users represent the general population.[23]

Experimental method.   An **experiment** is a method of gathering primary data in which the researcher is able to observe the results of changing one variable in a situation while holding all other conditions constant. Experiments are conducted in laboratory settings or in the field. In marketing research, a "laboratory" is an environment over which the researcher has control.

Consider this example: A small group of consumers is assembled and presented with a brief product description (called a *product concept*) and proposed package for a new breakfast cereal. After they examine the package, the people are asked whether they would buy the cereal, and their responses are recorded. Next, a similar group of consumers is brought together and presented with the identical package and product information, except that a nutritional claim for the cereal is printed on the package. Members of this group are also asked if they would buy the product. The researcher has complete control over the test environment, and the only thing changed is the nutritional claim on the package. Therefore, any difference in buying intentions between the groups can be attributed to the claim.

Laboratory experiments can be used to test most components of marketing strategy. However, recognize that the laboratory setting is not an actual purchase, so consumers' responses may be influenced by the situation. To overcome this problem, some experiments are conducted outside the controlled conditions of the lab, or in the field. A *field experiment* is similar to a laboratory experiment but is conducted under more realistic conditions. For example, the owner of a chain of retail stores might try a traffic-building promotional program in one or two stores and then compare sales results with results in similar stores without the promotion. Certainly not everything in the stores can be controlled. However, if researchers believe all other conditions in the stores remained similar, any differences in sales can be credited to the promotion.

A common experiment is test marketing. In **test marketing** the researcher duplicates real market conditions in a limited geographic area to measure consumers' responses to a strategy before committing to a major marketing effort. Test marketing is undertaken to forecast sales for a particular marketing mix or to compare the performance of different marketing mixes. For example, McDonald's test-marketed pizza in selected areas for over two years before deciding not to add it to the menu of their traditional outlets.

The advantage of test marketing over a survey or a lab experiment is that it informs marketers how many people *actually buy* a product, instead of how many say they *intend to buy* it. However, duplicating the entire marketing effort on a small scale has several disadvantages. Test marketing is expensive; spending $500,000 to $1 million is not uncommon. It is also time-consuming. Testing frequently lasts 9 to 12 months. Lever Bros. kept Lever 2000 deodorant soap in test for two years before going national. Another problem is the researcher's inability to control the situation. Tests are impossible to keep secret from competitors, who may intentionally disrupt the test by temporarily changing their marketing mixes. When Pepsi tested Mountain Dew Sport drink in Minneapolis, Quaker Oats, the maker of Gatorade, flooded the market with coupons and advertising.

Because of the inherent limitations of the kind of test marketing just described, researchers have tried to find faster, less expensive alternatives. One of these is the *simulated test market,* in which an assembled group of volunteers is shown ads for the product being tested as well as for other products. The group is then allowed to shop in a test store that resembles a small grocery store and includes the product being tested. Interviews are conducted immediately thereafter with buyers and nonbuyers of the tested product. In addition, follow-up interviews are conducted with the buyers after they have consumed the product. The entire set of data then goes into a statistical model that forecasts sales for the product.

The potential benefits of simulated test marketing include:

- Costs are lower than for a traditional test market.
- Results are produced in as little as eight weeks.
- A simulated test can be kept secret.

The drawbacks of simulated test markets are:

- The accuracy for unique new products may be questionable, because the forecasting models are based on the historical sales of similar products.
- It is not possible to predict the response of competitors or retailers to the actual introduction of the product.
- It is not possible to test changes in marketing variables such as packaging or distribution because of the simulation's short duration.

Simulated test marketing has not replaced traditional test markets. In fact, the two methods are often used together, with the simulation results used to make marketing-mix modifications before beginning traditional test marketing.

International marketers sometimes use a few countries as a test market for a continent or even the world. Colgate-Palmolive introduced Palmolive Optims

Are databases an invasion of privacy?

The European Union (EU), the political and economic alliance of major western European countries, has demonstrated its concern about the collection and storage of personal data with a regulatory policy that impacts any firm doing research in any of the member countries. These regulations affect three areas:

- *Collection.* Consumers are often unaware that personal data are being collected for later use. Thus consumers must be informed when data are being collected.

- *Use.* Individuals must be informed in advance how data will be used and they must provide their consent.

- *Data sharing.* The transmission of data outside the EU to any country without "adequate" safeguards is banned.

The actual regulations are more liberal than some of the earlier proposals, but they are still viewed as vague and highly restrictive. The implications are significant for global marketers. First, the regulations will increase the cost of collecting personal data. Second, restrictions on transferring data will make it more difficult to obtain or even impossible to use information provided by third parties. For example, credit card companies routinely sell firms the names of likely prospects based on their past credit card purchases. Third, it will make developing and implementing global strategies much more difficult.

Sources: Jim Besson, "Riding the Marketing Information Wave," *Harvard Business Review,* September–October 1993, pp. 150–160; Greg Miller, "U.S. and Europe Hit a Snag in Debate over Consumer Privacy," *Los Angeles Times,* June 21, 1999, p. 3.

shampoo and conditioner in the Philippines, Australia, Mexico, and Hong Kong. When sales proved satisfactory, distribution was expanded to large portions of Europe, Asia, Latin America, and Africa.

Prepare Forms for Gathering Data

Whether interviewing or observing subjects, researchers use a questionnaire or form on which there are instructions and spaces to record observations and responses. It is not easy to design a data-gathering form that elicits precisely the information needed. Here are several fundamental considerations:

- *Question wording.* If a question is misunderstood, the data it produces are worthless. Questions should be written with the potential respondent's vocabulary, reading level, and familiarity with jargon in mind.

- *Response format.* Questions are designed for either check mark responses (such as yes-no, multiple-choice, agree-disagree scales) or open-ended replies. Open-ended questions are often easier to write and frequently produce richer answers, but they require more effort from the respondent and therefore lower the level of cooperation.

- *Questionnaire layout.* The normal procedure is to begin with easier questions and move to the more difficult or complicated questions. Possibly sensitive topics (for example, personal hygiene) or private matters (age, income) are normally placed at the very end of a questionnaire.

- *Pretesting.* All questionnaires should be pretested on a group of respondents to identify problems and make corrections and refinements prior to the actual study.

Complete books are available on questionnaire design. Extreme care and skill are needed to produce a questionnaire that maximizes the likelihood of getting a response while minimizing bias, misunderstanding, and respondent irritation.

Plan the Sample

It is unnecessary to survey or observe every person who could shed light on a research problem. It is sufficient to collect data from a sample if it is *representative* of the entire group. We all make use of sampling. For example, we often form opinions of people based on a few interactions. However, if the interactions include only one aspect of a person's life, for example work interactions, and ignore home life or recreation, they may not be representative. The key in these personal issues *and* in marketing research is whether the sample provides an accurate representation. Representativeness has been an issue in using the Internet to collect data. As attractive as it is for data collection, many researchers are concerned about how well Internet users represent the general population.[24]

The fundamental idea underlying sampling is that a small number of items— a sample—if properly selected from a larger number of items—a universe—will have the same characteristics and in about the same proportion as the larger number. Obtaining reliable data with this method requires the right technique in selecting the sample.

Improper sampling is a source of error in many studies. One firm, for example, selected a sample of calls from all the calls made to its 800 number and used the information to make generalizations about its customers. Would you be comfortable saying these callers are representative of all the firm's customers or even all the dissatisfied ones? Although numerous sampling techniques are available, only by using a random sample can a researcher confidently make generalizations about a universe. A *random sample* is selected in such a way that every member of the universe has an equal chance of being included.

All other (nonrandom) samples are known as *convenience samples*. Convenience samples are quite common in marketing research, for two reasons. First, random samples are very difficult to get. Even though the researcher may *select* the subjects in a random fashion, there is no guarantee that they all will participate. Some will be unavailable and others will refuse to cooperate. As a result, researchers often resort to carefully designed convenience samples that reflect the characteristics of the universe as closely as possible. Second, not all research is done with the objective of generalizing to a universe. For example, to confirm the judgment of the advertising department, a researcher may be satisfied with the finding that a small group of respondents all take a similar message away from an ad.

A common question regarding sampling is: How large should a sample be? With random methods, a sample must be large enough to be truly representative of the universe. Thus the size will depend on the diversity of characteristics within the universe. All basic statistics books contain general formulas for calculating sample size. In the case of nonrandom samples, because the objective is not to make generalizations, researchers can select any size sample they and the managers using the data feel comfortable with.

Collect the Data

Collecting primary data by interviewing, observation, or both can be done by people or machines. Unfortunately, it is often the weakest link in the research process. A research project can be designed with great care, but the fruits of these labors may be lost if the data gathering is inadequately conducted.

It is often difficult to motivate people who collect data. Because they frequently are part-time workers doing what is often a monotonous task for relatively low pay, proper training and supervision are essential to avoid problems. For instance, poorly trained data gatherers may fail to establish rapport with respondents or may change the wording of questions. In extreme cases, there have even been instances where interviewers faked the responses and filled out the questionnaires themselves!

Mechanical data collection includes such devices as retail scanners (described earlier), video cameras, audiotapes, and computer terminals (often found in malls, airport terminals, and hotel lobbies). The human element of the data collector is eliminated with these devices, but there are new issues that can affect data quality such as equipment reliability, how participants' responses and behavior are affected by the mechanical device, and the conversion of the raw data into useable form.

Analyze the Data and Present a Report

The value of research is determined by its results. And because data cannot speak for themselves, analysis and interpretation are key components of any project. Computers allow researchers to tabulate and process masses of data quickly and inexpensively. This tool can be abused, however. Managers have little use for reams of computer printouts. Researchers must be able to identify pivotal relationships, spot trends, and find patterns—that's what transforms data into useful information.

The end product of the investigation is the researcher's conclusions and recommendations. Most projects require a written report, often accompanied by an oral presentation to management. Here communication skill becomes a factor. Not only must researchers be able to write and speak effectively, they must adopt the perspective of the manager in presenting research results.

Conduct a Follow-up

Researchers should follow up their studies to determine whether their results and recommendations are being used. Management may choose not to use a study's findings for several reasons. The problem that generated the research may have been misdefined, become less urgent, or even disappeared. Or the research may have been completed too late to be useful. Without a follow-up, the researcher has no way of knowing if the project was on target and met management's needs or if it fell short. As a result, an important source of information for improving research in the future would be ignored.

Competitive Intelligence

A research area that is only recently receiving widespread, serious attention is competitive intelligence. U.S. marketers have learned from their foreign counterparts that closely monitoring competitors can be extremely useful. Japanese firms in particular have made a science out of watching and learning from their rivals.

Although it sounds intriguing, **competitive intelligence** is simply the process of gathering and analyzing available public information about the activities and plans of competitors. The data used to study competitors come from a variety of internal and external sources. The most common are databases created and sold by research firms. The simplest of these are newspaper and magazine clipping services that monitor a large number of publications for articles on particular industries or companies. There are several thousand of these competitive database services available today.

Another source is government reports, produced and made available by U.S. and foreign government agencies. For example, the Japan Center for Information and Cultural Affairs provides government documents, statistics on Japan, and information on various Japanese industries. Along the same line, the European Union provides competitive and financial information on European commerce.

Employees, particularly sales people, are the primary internal source of competitive data. It has become a standard practice for firms to incorporate space for competitive information in the reporting forms used by sales people. Other employees, such as engineers, service personnel, and purchasing agents, can pick up and report helpful information—if they are trained to be alert.

It is relatively common to use various observation techniques to collect competitive information. For example, representatives of consumer product manufacturers regularly shop retail stores to monitor competitors' prices and promotions. And it is not uncommon for a firm to buy a competitor's new product in order to examine and test it—called *reverse engineering.*

One of the newest sources of competitive intelligence is the Internet. In an attempt to please current or potential customers, firms put information on their websites that a few years ago would have been considered highly proprietary. Price lists, suppliers' and distributors' names, and new-product information are commonly posted. Other website information may be less direct but still valuable. For example, firms proud of their research and development efforts, often list research papers produced by their technical people. These papers can provide insights into the direction the firm is headed.[25] There are also firms that specialize in conducting intelligence gathering. For some, the information collected becomes the attraction that draws visitors to their websites. They, in turn, sell advertising space on the sites. An example is Company Sleuth.

 www.companysleuth.com

Clearly there is the potential for legal and ethical abuses in gathering competitive intelligence. Incidents of sifting through trash, electronic eavesdropping, and hiring competitors' employees to learn their plans are unfortunately not uncommon. Despite trade secret laws that make it illegal to acquire data through "improper means" such as theft, there are many unclear situations. Based on court opinions, attempts to get information when a competitor is taking reasonable care to conceal it from public exposure are unethical and may be illegal.

Many firms take elaborate precautions to protect the security of confidential information. Common techniques include the use of paper shredders, alerting employees to the importance of discretion, and limiting the circulation of sensitive documents. Of particular concern is the ease with which a thief can extract information from a careless sales person's or other employee's personal computer.

Ethical Issues in Marketing Research

As the desire for better information grows and the technology for gathering data improves, marketers are faced with an increasing variety of ethical issues related to the collection and use of research information. Typical of the growing concerns are the following:

- *Privacy in data collection.* It is possible to observe people with hidden cameras, identify an individual's purchase behavior by combining scanner data and credit card or check-cashing records, and track Internet activity with cookies. At what point does data collection became an invasion of privacy? The Federal Trade Commission has forced Liberty Financial Co. to stop presenting an Internet survey that claimed responses would be anonymous when in fact the company was retaining the names and addresses of respondents.[26] Although the company claims the respondents' identities were not used in any way, it's clear that responses were not anonymous.

- *Privacy in data use.* In the routine process of business, firms often gather a considerable amount of information about their customers. This information, if linked to an individual's name and address, could be highly valuable to other businesses. For example, airlines have information about travel behavior that a travel magazine publisher would find useful. Does the airline have the right to sell that information?

- *Intrusiveness.* All marketers want information. The problem is that gathering that information can be annoying and inconvenient for the respondent. Telephone surveys conducted around dinnertime, extraneous (to the transaction)

Online marketers use the information collected with cookies (see the text description of cookies under the heading "Observation Method") to develop individual as well as composite databases of visitors' preferences. Say, for example, you click on a bookseller's site and examine mystery thrillers. The next time you visit the site, you may see an unrequested banner ad for the latest Stephen King novel. How did that happen? The bookseller placed a cookie on your hard drive during the first visit, and attempted to match you and your preferences on the second visit. Online marketers contend that this matching benefits site visitors by providing them with useful information, such as special offers tailored to their preferences. In addition, they argue that without this information they would have a difficult time selling advertising on their sites because advertisers demand to know something about site visitors. Many websites, although they purport to be free, require that a visitor accept a cookie as a condition of access.

Are there situations in which it would be unethical to use a cookie to collect information about the preferences of website visitors? Is it unethical for a website operator to sell the information from cookies to others?

Sources: Greg Farrell, "Some Net Surfers Say Cookie Crummy," *USA Today,* Aug. 23, 1999, p. 7B; William M. Bulkeley, "We're Watching You," *The Wall Street Journal,* Nov. 22, 1999, pp. R32+.

data collected at the time of a purchase, and questionnaires sent to people at work can all be intrusive. The issue here is at what point does requesting information become excessively intrusive?

- *Deceptive implementation.* On occasion, researchers use deception to gather data. For example phoning a business and falsely representing oneself as a potential customer in order to collect data, or intentionally misleading respondents about the sponsor or objective of the research are deceptions. Some researchers intentionally don't disclose to respondents that they are research subjects participating in a study. For example, a researcher in a grocery store pretending to be a shopper and asking fellow shoppers their opinions of products or brands is nondisclosure. In most cases, these deceptions are harmless and are actually viewed by researchers as essential to gathering candid responses. However, at what point is extracting information from a person under false or misleading pretenses inappropriate?

- *False representation.* Practices called "sugging" (selling under the guise of research) and "frugging" (fund raising under the guise of research) are unfortunately so common that they are negatively affecting the ability of legitimate researchers to gain respondents' cooperation. Practitioners of these techniques use the ruse that they are researchers conducting a survey. After securing the cooperation of the unsuspecting consumer and posing a few questions, they attempt a sale or ask for a donation. Some argue that research and selling or fund raising should never be combined in the same presentation. Others contend that the issue is whether the consumer is misled, not what is presented.

There have been several reactions to practices such as these. One is efforts by professional associations such as the American Marketing Association and the Advertising Research Foundation to discourage such practices among their members and other practitioners. In some cases, laws have been passed to control research activity. For an illustration, see the Ethical Dilemma box in this section.

Status of Marketing Research

Significant advances have been made in both quantitative and qualitative research methodology, and researchers are making effective use of the behavioral sciences, mathematics, and statistics. Still, many companies invest very little in determining market opportunities for their products. Several factors account for the less-than-universal acceptance of marketing research:

- *Predicting behavior is inexact.* Because of the many variables involved, marketing research often cannot predict future market behavior accurately. AT&T's missed opportunity with cellular technology, described in the chapter-opening case, indicates that, even with information, firms still make misjudgments. When dealing with consumer behavior, the researcher may be hard pressed to determine present attitudes or motives (for reasons that were explained in Chapter 4), much less what they will be next year.

- *Conflicting objectives between researchers and managers.* The manager is frequently required to make quick decisions in the face of uncertainty, often with incomplete information. Researchers, on the other hand, are prone to approach problems in a cautious, scientific manner. This leads to disagreements about the research that should be conducted, how long it should take, and the way in which the results should be presented.

- *A project orientation to research.* Many managers do not treat marketing research as a continuous process. Too often marketing research is viewed in a fragmented, one-project-at-a-time manner. It is used only when management realizes that it has a marketing problem. The growth in the use of MkIS, DSS, and data mining will likely improve this situation.

Making research more "actionable," that is, on target and of value to managers, is a challenge. However, it is far from impossible. In examining the issue in interviews with both researchers and managers, communications proved to be the key.[27] When managers and researchers communicate continuously and consistently at every stage of the research process the likelihood of research leading to effective action increases greatly.

Summary

Competitive pressure, the cost of making a mistake, and the complexity of both domestic and foreign markets all contribute to the need for marketing research. For a company to operate successfully today, management must engage in marketing research: the development, interpretation, and communication of decision-oriented information. Three tools used in research are marketing information systems, decision support systems, and the research projects.

A marketing information system (MkIS) is an ongoing set of procedures designed to generate, analyze, disseminate, store, and retrieve information for use in making marketing decisions. An MkIS provides a manager with a regularly scheduled flow of information and reports. As firms develop global MkISs, they are faced with problems of timing, accuracy of data, and terminology and measurement differences. A decision support system (DSS) differs from an MkIS in that the manager, using a personal computer, can interact directly with data. The DSS adds speed and flexibility to the MkIS, but requires considerable investment to create and maintain.

Data used in an MkIS or DSS come from databases, which are organized sets of data pertinent to a particular topic stored and updated in a computer. Retail scanners are major sources of data that go into databases.

When data sets grow beyond simply a "base" of information, they are referred to as data warehouses. These enormous collections of data are probed for patterns and meaningful relationships in a process called data mining.

A marketing research project is undertaken to help resolve a specific marketing problem. The problem must first be clearly defined. Then a researcher conducts a situation analysis and an informal investigation. If a formal investigation is needed, the researcher decides which secondary and primary sources of information to use. Secondary data already exist. Primary data are gathered for the problem at hand.

Primary data are gathered using observation, surveys, or experiments. Observation is unintrusive, but cannot provide explanations for the behavior observed. Surveys are conducted in person, by phone or through the mail. The Internet and e-mail are growing in popularity as tools for doing surveys. The challenges in survey research are selecting a sample, designing a questionnaire, and generating an adequate response. The research project is completed when data are analyzed and the results reported. Follow-up provides information for improving future research.

Researchers have recently developed a stronger interest in competitive intelligence, or finding out what competitors are currently doing and forecasting what they are likely to do in the future. The news media, government, the Internet, and a company's own sales people are important sources of competitive intelligence information.

Among the ethical issues in marketing research are protecting the privacy of respondents when collecting and using data, being overly intrusive, deceiving respondents, and selling or fund raising under the guise of research.

Some managers are not highly supportive of research because its task, predicting behavior, is inexact and very difficult to accomplish; researchers and managers often operate with different objectives; and research is conducted sporadically. These problems can be reduced and research made actionable if there is more complete and

More about Iridium

The inspiration for the wireless, global phone service that became Iridium is said to have begun with a problem experienced by the wife of a Motorola executive. When she couldn't call home from a Caribbean beach, she asked her husband why a mobile phone that could be used anywhere on earth had not been developed. And, as they say, the rest is history. Motorola, famous for its engineering expertise (its founder invented the car radio), attacked the problem with typical enthusiasm. The proposed solution was 77 earth-orbiting satellites that would connect the entire globe (and serve as the inspiration for the company name—Iridium is the 77th element).

Not wanting to bear all the risk of such a major undertaking, Motorola joined forces with other investors around the world to form Iridium. In the 10+ years it took to go from an idea to a product, it appears that market knowledge and marketing research took a backseat. For example, the inconvenience of the 1-pound handset (described as a "brick") was ignored because that was the best

technology available. Likewise, the fact that operating the phone required complicated attachments and special training was downplayed as a problem.

Finally, the marketing effort of the worldwide partners was uneven. Differences in industry knowledge, culture, resources, and confidence in the project led to operating problems in a system that needed to be seamless in order to function properly. Clearly an effective global marketing information system was not in place.

Fearing the loss of "first-mover" advantage (several other firms were working on similar technology), and hoping that a large-scale advertising blitz (estimated to cost between $100 and $180 million) would produce a successful launch, Iridium chose to move ahead. The result, as reported in the chapter-opening portion of the case, was market rejection and bankruptcy.[28]

1. Which marketing research tools described in the chapter might have benefited Iridium's management?

2. If a company has a large investment of time and money in a project, can it afford to terminate it based on market research results?

Key Terms and Concepts

Marketing research (181)
Marketing information system (MkIS) (182)
Decision support system (DSS) (184)
Database (185)
Data warehouse (185)
Data mining (186)
Retail scanners (186)

Single-source data (187)
Situation analysis (187)
Hypothesis (187)
Informal investigation (188)
Primary data (188)
Secondary data (189)
Observation method (191)
Cookies (191)
Survey (191)

Personal interviews (192)
Focus group (192)
Telephone survey (192)
Mail survey (193)
Internet surveys (193)
Experiment (194)
Test marketing (195)
Competitive intelligence (198)

Questions and Problems

1. Explain how a marketing information system (MkIS) differs from a decision support system (DSS).

2. Should the task of marketing research go beyond providing data to marketing managers?

3. Evaluate surveys, observation, and experimentation as methods of gathering primary data in the following projects:
   a. A sporting goods retailer wants to determine college students' brand preferences for skis, tennis rackets, and golf clubs.
   b. A supermarket chain wants to determine shoppers' preferences for the physical layout of fixtures and traffic patterns, particularly around checkout counters.
   c. A manufacturer of conveyor belts wants to know who makes buying decisions for his product among present and prospective users.

4. Using the steps in the research process from the text, describe how you would go about investigating the feasibility of a copy shop adjacent to your campus.

5. Examine the procedure that Consumers Union uses in formulating the evaluations of automobiles presented in *Consumer Reports*. (The method is described in the magazine.) Based on the discussion of sampling in the chapter, comment on the procedure.

6. Shortly after a patient used a credit card to pay a bill at a dentist's office, she received a telephone solicitation for dental insurance. This suggests that the credit card company is developing a database using the specific purchasing activity of cardholders and selling it. Does this raise an issue of invasion of privacy?

7. If you were designing an academic program for the marketing researcher of the future, what areas of study would you include?

Hands-On Marketing

1. Assume you work for a manufacturer of a liquid glass cleaner that competes with Windex and Glass Wax. Your manager wants to estimate the amount of product that can be sold throughout the country. To help the manager in this project, prepare a report that shows the following information for your state and, if possible, your home city or county. Carefully identify the sources you use for this information.
   a. Number of households or families.
   b. Income or buying power per family or per household.
   c. Total retail sales in the most recent year for which you can find reliable data.
   d. Total annual sales of food stores, hardware stores, and drug stores.
   e. Total number of food stores.

2. Interview the manager of the bookstore that serves your school about the marketing information system it uses (keep in mind that it may be a very informal system).
   a. What are the data sources?
   b. What are the data collected?
   c. What reports are received and on what schedule?
   d. What problems arise with the MkIS?
   e. How could the MkIS be improved?

Cases for Part 2

Understanding and Responding to Customers

At the end of its 1999 fiscal year, the parent company of Cracker Barrel Old Country Stores was searching for a formula that would match the operation's past success. What began in 1969 as a small restaurant in a former gas station, had grown into a $1 billion operation called CBRL Group. From the mid-1980s until the mid-1990s, the firm had pleased customers with its offerings and investors with its performance. According to a former executive, Cracker Barrel has "been a quiet company just moving along." But growth has stalled. The difficulty of getting the company moving is reflected in the fact that between 1995 and 1999, Cracker Barrel had three different top executives.

Rolling Out the Barrel

Dan Evins opened the first Cracker Barrel along Interstate 40 near Lebanon, Tennessee. His concept was to combine a country atmosphere, "home-style" meals, and a retail gift shop specializing in collectibles. A key ingredient in his plan was locating the outlet along a major thoroughfare where it would have access to travelers as well as area residents. With generous servings, moderate prices, and good service, the operation was a success.

Cracker Barrel's corporate mission statement consists of only two words: Pleasing people. It is elaborated on the company's website as follows:

Pleasing people is about caring, about letting Guests forget about the lousy day they had as they sit down at a table near the fireplace and order up a favorite meal, getting a genuine smile from the server. All that is something special in the Cracker Barrel experience.

A walk through the Retail Store is the same kind of soft experience. It's not a fast hunt, but a slow tour around the displays. Pleasing people fits that experience, too.

Pleasing people recognizes that we have four different sets of people in our picture. And it is all of those people that we must strive to please: our Guests, our Employees, our Suppliers and our Shareholders.

Evins followed a conservative growth plan, ex-

panding slowly and avoiding debt. By 1996 the chain had grown to just over 200 units located in the lower Midwest and Southeast. Cracker Barrel customers are about equally divided between tourists and locals, just as Evins had anticipated. And because tourists tend to purchase souvenirs along with meals, the retail gift shops proved successful, generating about 25% of the chain's revenue.

Because of its location strategy, Cracker Barrel relies heavily on billboard advertising. It wasn't until 1998 that the firm did any network television advertising. Since the chain does not offer specials or discounts, all its ads are image-oriented to reinforce the Cracker Barrel brand. A typical theme is a nostalgic view of the values of country life associated with a visit to a Cracker Barrel. In another brand-building effort, the company sponsors a NASCAR race at the Atlanta Motor Speedway. An industry consultant praised the race sponsorship as "an extraordinary logical tie-in for them. Those folks are their folks."

The company continued to open new units, reaching 400 in 1999, but sales in outlets open more than a year flattened. Despite the fact that customers frequently had to wait up to 30 minutes for a table, the slower sales growth made investors nervous. What had been the darling of the restaurant industry became a cause for concern and sent management in a search of a solution.

The Barrel Gets a New Look

As the chain grew, it became increasingly difficult to find interstate locations in the South so Evins began opening units in other regions. He was careful to stick to his concept and, as a result, the chain was slow to adapt to local preferences. For example, grits, a staple in the South, were automatically served with breakfast at all Cracker Barrel restaurants. As a result, outlets in Wisconsin and Minnesota were able to generate only 60% of the revenue of southern restaurants, and in 1995, three outlets in the upper Midwest failed.

New executives, with experience in other restaurant chains, were brought on board. Soon a number of changes were implemented. When Cracker Barrel identified a potential new market, a team of managers would visit family restaurants in the area to identify and sample local dishes. Then, when a unit opened, it would have familiar items on the menu such as Reuben sandwiches in New York, eggs with salsa in Texas, and fried cheese curds in Wisconsin.

The merchandise in the gift shops was also adapted to local tastes. Items popular in the South are described by the VP of purchasing as "fluffier," whereas popular items in the North tend to be more "woodsy." For example, dishes with magnolia patterns were sold in the South. In the Northern states, a lighthouse motif proved more effective.

The chain also broke the mold on decorating. Although all the restaurants still have the look of a big, old barn, local touches have been added. For example, in Akron, Ohio, home of the national soapbox derby, the unit has a soapbox car suspended from the ceiling.

Even though some adjustments are being made in the concept, other elements remain unchanged. For example, because of their near-highway locations, Cracker Barrel restaurants are heavily dependent on billboard ads. Therefore, management does not foresee locating an outlet in Oregon because of the state's restrictions on billboards along interstates.

The new managers cut costs to improve financial performance. For example, the number of employees in the restaurants was reduced. In addition, prices were raised several times over a number of years. These moves were either immediately visible to customers, who saw the cost of a meal go up, or produced outcomes that were readily apparent. For instance, customers had to wait longer to be seated and served. Because of negative customer reactions, all these cost-cutting changes were later reversed. Coincidentally, new menu items were added to improve the customers' perceptions of value. The net result has been an increase in the number of customers but a decrease in the amount spent per customer in the restaurants.

Subtle changes were introduced to improve service. Rather than serve coffee in cups with saucers, Cracker Barrel switched to mugs. With mugs, one rather than two items needs to be handled when setting places and later washed. The size of beverage glasses was increased to reduce the number of requests for refills. The chain's signature cornbread and biscuits are now served right after an order is taken, rather than waiting until the customer's meal is ready. As a result, the food is served as soon as it is prepared. Individually these changes are minor, and probably aren't even noticed by customers, but collectively they are important. As a Cracker Barrel executive observed, "When you are as busy as we are, seconds count." As an indication, after the changes are introduced in a restaurant, Cracker Barrel finds improvements in measures of customer perceptions of service quality and satisfaction.

Another change that may not be apparent to customers but improves service is the introduction of technology. Although slower to act than most of its competitors, Cracker Barrel replaced order pads with automated point-of-sale systems. Having servers use an electronic touch system to record orders reduces kitchen errors and speeds up meal preparation. It also results in faster table turnover because customers are served more efficiently.

A Square Peg in a Round Barrel

Having done what it could to make the Cracker Barrel Old Country Stores more appealing to consumers, management continued looking for growth opportunities. One alternative is called home-meal replacement (HMR) or convenient meal solutions (CMS) in the food service industry. Consisting of ready-to-eat and ready-to-heat items in microwavable containers, this sector has been growing for several years. Single-parent and two-earner households have significantly reduced the time available for meal preparation. Time pressure and the desire for convenience are driving an increasing number of consumers to look for alternatives, and many have tired of fast-food outlets.

In an attempt to take advantage of this trend and capitalize on its brand name, the company opened an HMR outlet called Cracker Barrel Corner Market. However, it wasn't supported by advertising, and the name only confused consumers who associated it with the company's full-service restaurants rather than a carry-out operation. As a result, the idea never got beyond the test-market stage.

The Barrel Gets Bigger

In late 1998, Cracker Barrel Old Country Store formed a holding company called CBRL Group. The idea was to continue operating the 400 Cracker Barrel restaurants and gift shops, and also allow the company to explore and exploit other retail concepts. To some the move signaled that Cracker Barrel's management was concerned that the flagship operation was reaching market saturation.

So far, CBRL has made two moves. It acquired Logan's Roadhouse, a Nashville-based chain of mid-priced steakhouses with about 60 restaurants in place and plans for rapid growth. A second acquisition is Carmine Giardini's Gourmet Market, an upscale HMR operation, located in Palm Beach Gardens, Florida. Carmine's has just two outlets, each housing an Italian restaurant and a prepared-foods store. The stores have over 100 dishes from which to choose, including entrees such as lasagna and baked salmon. The average take-away item is priced around $6.

Most analysts view Logan's as a small but well-positioned operation with excellent growth potential.

Carmine's, on the other hand, is seen as another experiment in HMR for the company. Both chains will retain their names and their individual identities. CBRL Group hopes these moves will be enough to patch the leaks in the barrel.

Questions

1. What consumer characteristics contributed to the success of Cracker Barrel? What characteristics eventually constrained its growth?

2. Compare the demographics of Lebanon, Tennessee (the location of the first Cracker Barrel), with the demographics of Palm Beach Gardens, Florida (the location of Carmine's). A good source is *Sales & Marketing Management's* annual "Survey of Buying Power." What observations would you share with CBRL's management regarding the two locations?

3. What approaches would you suggest to segment the markets for Logan's and Carmine's?

www.crackerbarrel.com

www.giardinis.com

Sources: Cracker Barrel website January 2000; Gina LaVecchia, "Something in Store," *Restaurant Hospitality,* November 1999, pp. 48+; Ralph Raffio and Ben Van Houten, "Leaky Barrel," *Restaurant Business,* Sept. 15, 1999, pp. 33+; Andy Battaglia, "Cracker Barrel Scrambles to Regroup after Latest Management Exit," *Nation's Restaurant News,* Dec. 13, 1999, pp. 1+; Louise Kramer, "Cracker Barrel's Folksy Approach Hits Network TV," *Advertising Age,* Nov. 9, 1998, p. 10; Jack Hayes, "After Free Fall Cracker Barrel Rolls as a Top Contender in Family Segment," *Nation's Restaurant News,* Nov. 17, 1997, pp. 1+; and J. Alex Tarquinio, "King of Grits Alters Menu to Reflect Northern Tastes," *The Wall Street Journal,* Sept. 22, 1997, pp. B1+.

Case 2 • Covisint—Ford, General Motors, and DaimlerChrysler's E-marketplace

Manufacturers Adapting to Electronic Commerce

What began as a race turned into a team effort when Ford Motor Co., General Motors, and Daimler-Chrysler discovered they had more to gain than lose by working together on the Internet. The unprecedented cooperation among these car makers will be watched closely. If they successfully design and operate an Internet supply chain that produces seamless links from a car maker's suppliers to its final consumers, they will revolutionize automobile marketing. Equally important, such a system would become a model for many other industries, transforming the business potential of the Internet to a reality.

The Concept

U.S. auto manufacturers have made significant advances in procurement and manufacturing by taking advantage of technology. For example, robotics has made assembly more efficient, just-in-time delivery has reduced parts inventories, and sharing data with suppliers has lowered ordering costs. Despite these and other improvements, numerous opportunities remain.

Consider, for example, the path of the typical car order. If a consumer purchases a car with a particular set of features not on the retail dealership's lot, a search begins. First, the dealer checks the inventories of other dealers in the area. If the desired car can't be found, an order is submitted to the regional office. The order is combined with those from other dealerships and sent to the factory. At the factory, where a high priority is keeping the assembly line running as

efficiently as possible, the orders are organized into batches of similar cars to minimize assembly-line adjustments. Finally, the car is produced and shipped to the dealer. The result is an average of 64 days required from the time an order is placed until the car is delivered. In an attempt to reduce the waiting time, the manufacturers try to anticipate demand by building cars with various combinations of options and colors and placing them in dealers' inventories. However, because predicting consumer preferences is inexact, as much as $60 billion is tied up in the inventory of unsold cars at any time.

The ultimate alternative, described by Ford's chief executive, is a scenario in which a consumer configures a custom-designed car on the Internet. Then, with a click of a mouse, information goes to the suppliers that will provide all the parts, the factory that will assemble the car, the finance unit that will underwrite it, the dealer that will deliver it, and the designers that plan future models. This highly coordinated system then produces the car and puts the customer behind the wheel in less than a week.

What must change to make this happen? According to a major automotive executive who has studied the situation: Everything. Cars would have to be easier to build; car makers, suppliers, and consumers would have to be linked via the Internet; and finished cars would have to be shipped much more efficiently. More specifically, rather than assemble the 3,000 parts that now go into a car, the manufacturers and their suppliers would have to create as few as 30 "snap-together" modules that would produce a car.

As for suppliers, they would need to monitor consumers' orders and the manufacturer's production schedules via the Web so parts would be available when needed. Delivery would require a number of refinements. One would be "dynamic routing." That is, the company would need the capability to redirect a car on its way to a dealer's inventory if it matched the specifications of a customer's order someplace else in the country.

The Efforts

In mid-1999 a task force at Ford was assigned the job of finding out how the Internet might contribute to manufacturing improvements. As the team dug into the issues, they quickly discovered that the potential far exceeded the initial vision so they produced a computer simulation of the "auto company of the future" in order to demonstrate to Ford's senior management what they had discovered. In addition to cars being built to order and delivered in days rather than months, the simulation depicted dealerships reporting warranty and maintenance problems in real time so factories could correct problems immediately; suppliers directly managing the parts inventories at car makers' factories; and consumers paying a monthly fee to the manufacturer for a "portal on wheels" that would have Web access, satellite phone service, and e-mail capabilities.

Ford's chief executive, Jacques Nasser, described the ideas as "nothing short of reinventing the auto industry," and supported moving ahead quickly. The company created an organization called Consumer-Connect to oversee the initiative. In a matter of months, five business units were established:

- A business-to-business group to develop auto-xchange, a website to link Ford with its 30,000 suppliers and 6,900 dealers.

- A consumer e-business group to develop Buyer-Connection, a website where consumers can order custom-designed cars and trucks.

- A customer relationships group to develop Own-erconnection, a website to provide Ford owners with online assistance as well as gather information on customer problems.

- An auto technology group to equip cars with voice-activated telephones, online connection to emergency service, and e-mail.

- A financial services group to provide online financing and collections.

At the same time, General Motors had a team exploring the potential of e-commerce. What began as an effort to investigate how the Internet could improve purchasing snowballed into the identification of many Internet applications. To gather information, the GM team benchmarked the practices of firms such as Dell Computer, Federal Express, and United Parcel Service that are heavy users of the Internet. GM also sought advice from numerous software providers and systems designers.

Having developed a concept of a virtual market in cyberspace that would encompass all of GM's suppliers and customers, the team sought the support of the Automobile Strategy Board, the group that sets GM's future direction. The strategy board endorsed the concept called TradeXchange and, much like Ford, envisioned a time when GM—with the help of the Internet—would be able to build and deliver custom-designed cars in a few days.

Both firms moved ahead quickly. Within hours of each other, on November 2, 1999, they announced their initiatives. Beginning with Internet systems that would link their suppliers, the two rivals indicated that they foresaw enormous potential. They both teamed up with firms that could provide Internet experience and expertise. GM selected Commerce One Inc. as its initial partner. Ford teamed up with the following:

- Oracle Corp. to develop the computer software and databases needed to exchange information and conduct transactions.

- Cisco to provide networking expertise.

- Microsoft's CarPoint, an auto-sales website, to develop a build-to-order system.

- Yahoo! and Priceline.com to develop systems that will deliver personalized warranty, loan, and service information online.

In late February 2000, less than three months after squaring off to do battle over which firm could create the better Internet operation, Ford and General Motors dropped a bombshell. They announced that they had joined forces and added Daimler-Chrysler as a third partner to form a new company similar in concept to GM's TradeXchange and Ford's autoxchange. The new company will be operated independently from the automakers, and other car companies will be invited to join the system.

The Attraction

What do these car makers see in the Internet that caused them to act so quickly? The first attraction is the potential of moving all of their purchases online. Each firm has about 30,000 suppliers. GM purchases $87 billion a year in goods and services. Ford purchases a slightly smaller amount. If these transactions were made online, the automakers could pay lower prices in at least two ways. One way is to conduct what are known as reverse auctions. In these auctions the prospective buyer indicates what it would like to purchase, and potential sellers make bids over the Internet. Reverse auctions result in prices being bid down as sellers compete for the business. The other opportunity for lower prices occurs when firms combine their purchases to obtain a better price from a supplier. For example, Ford and several of its suppliers could consolidate their orders for office equipment to obtain better prices than would be possible if they buy separately. In Ford's case, analysts predict the annual savings that result from paying lower prices could be $8 billion a year.

Additional savings would result from changes in the procurement process. With online purchasing, time-consuming personal contacts and elaborate paper documentation would decrease dramatically. As a result, most of the approximately $100 it costs to process each of the hundreds of thousands of purchase orders the automakers issue each year would be eliminated. It is estimated that this change could save each company $1 billion in procurement costs annually.

The direct savings from moving purchases online may be just the tip of the iceberg. The automakers anticipate that the firms provisioning their suppliers will also join the system once they see the benefits. An example would be a gasket maker that sells its product to the company that produces air conditioners for Chrysler cars.

The newly created company would benefit by receiving a transaction fee charged for using the system. It's estimated that these fees would generate $1 to $3 billion in revenue in the first year alone. Beyond the savings and income generated from purchasing, there are other Web applications with potentially substantial benefits. For example, as more consumers order cars over the Internet, the need for inventory on dealers' lots would decrease. In addition, the need to offer discounts in order to sell unwanted cars would decline.

The Impact

The dollar estimates of the impact of these car makers going online are staggering. The move will affect all parties connected in the auto industry. Some examples are highlighted below:

Other auto manufacturers. Isuzu Motor Co. and Suzuki Motor Co. are placing all of their purchasing on the system. Making the company independent rather than an affiliate of either Ford or General Motors will reduce a major concern about the confidentiality of data expressed by Toyota in earlier negotiations. Building volume on an Internet purchasing network is important because it generates transaction fees, spreads the fixed overhead cost, and creates more opportunities to negotiate lower purchase prices. Thus there is likely to be considerable effort to attract other car makers to the system. Auto manufacturers that choose not to be involved risk being at a considerable competitive disadvantage.

Suppliers. Although the firms involved made it clear they will not attempt to force suppliers online, they have made it equally clear that they intend to do all of their purchasing online by the end of 2001. Many firms are suppliers to Ford, GM, DaimlerChrysler, and other car makers. These suppliers expressed concerns about working with two or possibly more separate systems. The consolidation will greatly facilitate their transition to a Web-based selling system. The auto makers contend suppliers that join will experience immediate benefits. Brian Kelly, head of Ford's ConsumerConnect business group, observed that suppliers will save two to three times the amount of the fee in inventory and selling costs alone. In addition, suppliers will be able to make use of the system to make their own purchases and/or to sell excess inventory.

Suppliers also have other concerns. Some feel the open-market, auction format common on the Internet will result in prices being bid down to unprofitable levels. Still another issue is differential pricing. In the past, suppliers have been able to charge smaller customers higher prices to make up for the discounts that big automakers demand. This is less likely to be possible if buyers consolidate their purchases. The purchasing vice president at a major automotive supplier describes it as "being between a rock and a hard place."

Dealers. If Internet purchasing reduces auto makers' costs, their dealers should benefit. In addition, efforts by car manufacturers on the Web to attract more customers should prove beneficial to dealers. For example, GM's chairman indicated that alliances with Internet sites such as Yahoo! are expected to generate 10 to 15 times more visits to GM's consumer website, resulting in 50,000 to 100,000 additional vehicle sales.

Currently all leads that are generated through the auto makers' websites are passed along to dealers. However, dealers are wary that the auto makers may eventually try to reduce their role in car sales. For example, some observers envision a time when most cars will be custom-designed and purchased on the Web by consumers who will know in advance the price of every component. There will be no haggling or negotiating. Financing, extended warranties, and other matters will all be handled on the Web. Car dealerships will have only a small inventory and a few vehicles available for test-drives. Their primary role will be to deliver the purchased cars to consumers.

Consumers. The business-to-business aspects of Ford, GM, and DaimlerChrysler going on the Internet affects consumers only in that it might reduce the cost and therefore the prices of cars. However, it remains to be seen how consumers will react to the broader Internet application. How many consumers will buy a car over the Internet? Will consumers add options such as e-mail, satellite-linked phones, navigation systems, and Web access from a car, along with the required $10 to $30 monthly fees? Most car buyers have become price shoppers, with little interest in establishing a relationship with a dealer. However, for many buyers a car is one of the largest purchases of their lives. And there is some comfort in knowing that if there is a problem, the seller is nearby.

Another consideration is the database a manufacturer can build from online purchases. By capturing information on how consumers configure cars, the manufacturers can reduce the number of possible combinations. For example, Ford's full-size F-150 pickup truck is currently offered in over 1,000 possible configurations of engine, transmission, body style, and color. With optional features added, the alternatives run into the millions. Also, by matching the choices consumers make with other data such as the individual's demographics, the car makers can do a better job planning parts procurement.

Hurdles

Clearly the first hurdle is developing the systems and software that will make using the Internet effective and efficient for members of the automotive supply chain. Other issues include the reactions of the labor union to any changes in how cars are assembled and delivered, the ramifications of strict state franchise laws that protect dealers, and the impact of these new methods of buying and selling on the industry's thousands of suppliers.

Will the auto industry move into cyberspace? The answer is yes. Will the move hit some bumps along the way? Almost certainly. Who will be the big winners? It's too soon to tell. However, it's quite likely that the losers will be the firms that get caught sitting on the sidelines while the rest of the supply chain gets involved.

Questions

1. How is the fact that business demand is derived likely to influence the use of the Internet by the auto industry?

2. How might the shift to Internet buying affect the relationship between auto makers and their suppliers?

3. In light of this development, what strategy would you recommend to an auto industry supplier? To an automobile dealer?

www.Ford.com

www.GeneralMotors.com

www.daimlerchrysler.com

Sources: Kathleen Kerwin, Marcia Stepanek, and David Welch, "At Ford, E-Commerce Is Job 1," *Business Week,* Feb. 28, 2000, pp. 74–78; Robert L. Simison, "GM Retools to Sell Custom Cars Online," *The Wall Street Journal,* Feb. 22, 2000, p. B23; Norihiko Shirouzu, "Toyota May Join Ford's Web System," *The Wall Street Journal,* Jan. 25, 2000, p. A13; Gregory L. White, "GM Supplier Site Expects $50 Billion of Business in 2000," *The Wall Street Journal,* Jan. 18, 2000, p. B14; Mary Connelly, "Ford Searches for E-Dollars," *Automotive News,* Jan. 17, 2000, pp. 1+; Diane Trommer, "Ford & GM Set to Ride the Internet Highway," *Electronic Buyers' News,* Dec. 6, 1999, p. 88; Gregory L. White, "How GM, Ford Think Web Can Make Splash on the Factory Floor," *The Wall Street Journal,* Dec. 3, 1999, pp. A1+; and "Riding the Storm," *The Economist,* Nov. 6, 1999, pp. 63–64.

Product

3

The planning, development, and management of the want-satisfying goods and services that are a company's products

In Part 2 we saw how markets are described and examined and how target markets are selected in keeping with the firm's marketing goals. We also considered why and how marketing research is conducted as well as how demand is forecasted. The next step is to develop a marketing mix that will achieve the company's goals in its target markets. The marketing mix is a strategic combination of four elements: the organization's products, prices, distribution, and promotion. All these variables are closely interrelated.

In Part 3 the spotlight is on the first element of the marketing mix—the product.

In Chapter 8 we define the term *product*, consider the importance of product planning and innovation, and discuss what needs to be done in developing new products. Chapter 9 deals mainly with product-mix strategies, management of the product life cycle, and a consideration of style and fashion. Chapter 10 discusses branding, packaging, and quality, among other features affecting a product's role in the marketing mix. And finally in Chapter 11, special consideration is given to intangible products and how they are marketed by both profit-seeking and nonprofit organizations.

" . . . an electric vehicle would help rebuild GM's reputation for technological innovation."

Should General Motors Pull the Plug on Its EV1?

General Motors—in fact, all automakers—seem to be schizophrenic about electric vehicles (EVs). Sometimes, they talk about progress in developing longer-lasting batteries or express enthusiasm about the sales prospects for electric-powered cars. More frequently, though, auto executives voice their opposition to state laws requiring the introduction of EVs or question whether this type of car can command a price that will allow manufacturers to cover their production and development costs. Recently, they have talked glowingly about vehicles powered by fuel cells or a combination of gas and electricity.

About 10 years ago, General Motors (GM) announced its intention to develop an EV, which eventually was named the EV1. The project sputtered, despite expenditures of at least $300 million. GM has not been alone in trying to successfully commercialize an electric car. The companies' interest in EVs was due, in part, to several states' new requirements that a small fraction of automakers' sales in the future would have to be "zero-emission" cars.

At the development stage, the EV1 was envisioned as having an aluminum skin, weighing no more than 2,200 pounds, and cruising at 55 miles per hour. The power would come from thirty-two 10-volt lead-acid batteries. Fully charged, the EV1 would have a driving range of at least 100 miles. Recharging would take about six hours on a normal 110-volt household outlet.

As an electric-powered car, the EV1 has some inherent drawbacks. Perhaps most serious are the limited driving range and the need to recharge the batteries frequently. Further, it seats only two people and is relatively expensive. According to the original estimates, the price of an EV1 would surpass the price of a similar gasoline-powered car by a minimum of $7,500 and perhaps as much as $20,000. Operating costs were gauged to be about twice those of a regular vehicle.

According to GM's original plan, the EV1 would strengthen the company's position in the U.S. market. Further, an electric vehicle would help rebuild GM's reputation for technological innovation. Because it relies on nonfossil fuels, the EV1 also could position GM as more sensitive to environmental concerns. And last but not least, the new model would help GM comply with a California law, which now requires that by 2003 at least 10% of the new cars each automaker sells in the state must be zero-emission (that is, nonpolluting) vehicles.

GM decided to introduce the EV1 in fall 1996. The company's chairman predicted that the innovative car would be "the first in a new generation of vehicles that redefined the limits of technology and efficiency." GM began distributing the new EV1 through Saturn dealers in Los Angeles, San Diego, Phoenix, and Tucson. The new model had a sticker price of $35,000, although the emphasis was placed on leasing the car for about $500 per month.

Sales and leases of the EV1—in fact, of all brands of EVs—were disappointing. GM sold or leased just over 500 EV1s to consumers in two years; other automakers sold or leased another 1,500 units. That level of sales is insignificant, considering that more than 16 million cars and light trucks are sold in the U.S. annually. Still, there's some optimism about the prospects for electric vehicles. In late 1998, one research firm predicted that over 100,000 EVs would be sold in the U.S. by 2003.

Over time, the EV1 has been upgraded in order to alleviate some of the product's drawbacks. Perhaps the most noteworthy development has been improved batteries. The 1999 version of the EV1 was equipped with 26 nickel-metal hydride batteries, which were intended to allow the car to go at least 140 miles before needing a recharge. Also, GM cut the one-time cost of a home recharger by two-thirds, to $500, and the monthly lease rate for an EV1 by 20%, to about $400 a month.[1]

Can General Motors' EV1 ultimately be a successful new product?

 www.gmev.com

Three factors stand out in the EV1 case. First, even giant companies like General Motors need to develop new products. Second, managing the product component of a marketing mix is a difficult, complex task. And third, success with new products is not guaranteed, as numerous failures (including the Merkur and the Yugo in the automotive field alone) indicate.

This chapter will provide you with insights regarding each of these important issues. Specifically, after studying this chapter, you should be able to explain:

chapter goals

- The meaning of the word *product* in its fullest sense.
- What a "new" product is.
- The classification of consumer and business products.
- The relevance of these product classifications to marketing strategy.
- The importance of product innovation.
- The stages in the new-product development process.
- Criteria for adding a product to a company's line.
- Adoption and diffusion processes for new products.
- Organizational structures for product planning and development.

The Meaning of Product

In a *narrow* sense, a product is a set of basic attributes assembled in an identifiable form. Each product is identified by a commonly understood descriptive (or generic) name, such as steel, insurance, tennis rackets, or entertainment. Features such as brand name and postsale service that appeal to consumer emotions or add value play no part in this narrow interpretation. According to this interpretation, an Apple and a Compaq would be the same good—a personal computer. And Disney World and Six Flags would be equivalent—both are amusement parks.

In marketing we need a broader definition of product to indicate that customers are not really buying a set of attributes, but rather benefits that satisfy their needs. Thus users don't want sandpaper; they really want a smooth surface. To develop a sufficiently broad definition, let's start with *product* as an umbrella term covering goods, services, places, persons, and ideas. Throughout this book, when we speak of products, we are using this broad connotation.

Thus a product that provides benefits can be something other than a tangible *good*. Red Roof Inn's product is a *service* that provides the benefit of a comfortable night's rest at a reasonable price. The Hawaii Visitors Bureau's product is a *place* that provides sun and sand, relaxation, romance, cross-cultural experiences, and other benefits. In a political campaign, the Democratic or Republican Party's product is a *person* (candidate) whom the party wants you to buy (vote for). The American Cancer Society is selling an *idea* and the benefits of not smoking. In Chapter 11 we discuss in more detail the marketing of intangible products such as services and ideas.

 www.visit.hawaii.org

To further expand our definition, we treat each *brand* as a separate product. In this sense, two Internet service providers, America Online and Mindspring for example, are different products. Squibb's aspirin and Bayer aspirin are also separate products, even though the only physical difference may be the brand name on the tablet. But the brand name suggests a product difference to the consumer, and this brings the concept of want-satisfaction into the definition. Going a step further, some consumers prefer one brand (Squibb's) and others favor a different brand (Bayer) of a similar product.

Any change in a feature (design, color, size, packaging), however minor, creates another product. Each such change provides the seller with an opportunity to use a new set of appeals to reach what essentially may be a new market. Pain

Figure 8.1

A product is much more than a set of physical attributes.

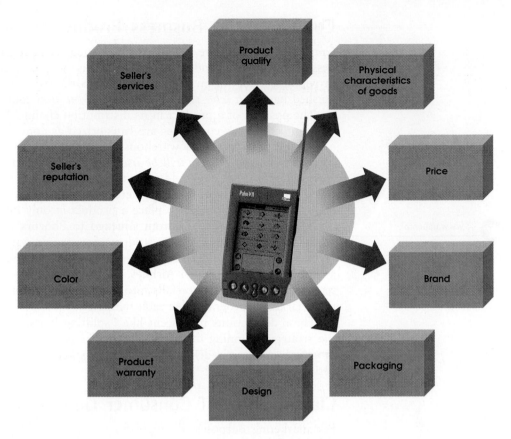

relievers (Tylenol, Anacin) in capsule form are a different product from the same brand in tablet form, even though the chemical contents of the tablet and the capsule are identical. Seemingly minor product changes can be the key to success (or failure) in international markets. For example, to satisfy Japanese consumers, two modified versions of Oreo cookies were developed. One has less sugar in the cookie batter, the other omits the cream filling.[2]

We can broaden this interpretation still further. A Sony TV bought in a discount store on a cash-and-carry basis is a different product than the identical model purchased in a department store. In the department store, the customer may pay a higher price for the TV but buys it on credit, has it delivered free of charge, and receives other store services. Our concept of a product now includes the services that accompany it when purchased. A prime example is the warranty that assures a buyer of free replacement or repair of a defective product during a specified period of time.

We're now ready for a definition that is useful to marketers. As shown in Figure 8.1, a product is a set of tangible and intangible attributes, which may include packaging, color, price, quality, and brand, plus the seller's services and reputation. A product may be a good, service, place, person, or idea. In essence, then, customers are buying much more than a set of attributes when they buy a product. They are buying want-satisfaction in the form of the benefits they expect to receive from the product.

Classifications of Products

To design effective marketing programs, organizations need to know what kinds of products they are offering to potential customers. Thus it's helpful to separate *products* into homogeneous categories. First we will divide all products into two categories—consumer products and business products—that parallel our description of the total market. Then we will subdivide each category.

Consumer and Business Products

Consumer products are intended for personal consumption by households. **Business products** are intended for resale, for use in producing other products, or for providing services in an organization. Thus the two types of products are distinguished based on *who will use them* and *how they will be used*.

The position of a product in its distribution channel has no bearing on its classification. Kellogg's cornflakes are categorized as consumer products, even if they are in the manufacturer's warehouses, in a freight line's trucks, or on retailers' shelves, *if ultimately they will be used in their present form by households*. However, Kellogg's cornflakes sold to restaurants and other institutions are categorized as business products no matter where they are in the distribution system.

Often it is not possible to place a product in only one class or the other. Seats on a United Airlines flight from Chicago to Phoenix may be considered a consumer product if purchased by students or a family going on vacation. But a seat on the same flight bought by a sales rep on a work-related trip is categorized as a business product. United Airlines, or any other company in a similar situation, recognizes that its product falls into both categories and therefore develops separate marketing programs for each market.

These distinctions may seem like "splitting hairs," but they are necessary for the strategic planning of marketing programs. Each major category of products ultimately goes to a distinctive type of market and thus requires different marketing methods.[3]

 www.ual.com

Classification of Consumer Goods

For marketing purposes, distinguishing consumer goods from business goods is helpful but only as a first step. The range of consumer goods is still too broad to be useful. Consequently, as shown in Table 8.1, they are further classified as convenience goods, shopping goods, specialty goods, and unsought goods. This classification is not based on intrinsic differences in the products themselves. Rather, it is based on how consumers go about buying a particular product. Depending on the buying behavior of different consumers, a single product—such as wine or software—can fall into more than one of the four categories.

Convenience Goods

A tangible product that the consumer feels comfortable purchasing without gathering additional information and then actually buys with a minimum of effort is termed a **convenience good.** Normally the advantages resulting from shopping around to compare price and quality are not considered worth the required time and effort. A consumer is willing to accept any of several brands and thus will buy the one that is most accessible. For most buyers, convenience goods include many food items, inexpensive candy, drug sundries such as aspirin and toothpaste, and staple hardware items such as light bulbs and batteries.

Convenience goods typically have a low unit price, are not bulky, and are not greatly affected by fad and fashion. They usually are purchased frequently, although this is not a necessary characteristic. Items such as Christmas tree lights or Mother's Day cards are convenience goods for most people, even though they may be bought only once a year.

Because a convenience good must be readily accessible when consumer demand arises, a manufacturer must be prepared to distribute it widely and rapidly. However, because most retail stores sell only a small volume of the total output of a convenience good (such as a particular brand of candy bar), it is not economical for the manufacturer to sell directly to all retail outlets. Instead the producer relies on wholesalers to sell the product to selected retailers.

Retailers usually carry several brands of the same type of convenience item because consumers frequently have a brand preference (even though they will

Table 8.1   Categories of Consumer Goods: Characteristics and Marketing Considerations

	Type of Product*		
	Convenience	**Shopping**	**Specialty**
Examples	Canned fruit	Furniture	Expensive suits
Characteristics			
Time and effort devoted by consumer to shopping	Very little	Considerable	As much as necessary to find desired brand
Time spent planning the purchase	Very little	Considerable	Considerable
How soon want is satisfied after it arises	Immediately	Relatively long time	Relatively long time
Are price and quality compared?	No	Yes	No
Price	Usually low	Usually high	Usually high
Purchase frequency	Usually frequent	Infrequent	Infrequent
Marketing considerations			
Length of channel	Long	Short	Short to very short
Retailer	Relatively unimportant	Important	Very important
Number of outlets	As many as possible	Few	Few; often only one in a market
Stock turnover	High	Lower	Lower
Gross margin	Low	High	High
Responsibility for advertising	Producer's	Joint responsibility	Joint responsibility
Point-of-purchase display	Very important	Less important	Less important
Brand or store name	Brand name	Store name	Both
Packaging	Very important	Less important	Less important

*Unsought products are not included. See text explanation.

accept a substitute). However, retail outlets are not inclined to advertise convenience goods because many other stores carry the same brands (such as General Electric and Sylvania light bulbs). Thus any advertising by one retailer would help its competitors. As a result, much of the advertising burden is shifted to the manufacturer.

Shopping Goods

A tangible product for which a consumer wants to compare quality, price, and perhaps style in several stores before making a purchase is considered a **shopping good.** Examples of shopping goods—at least for most consumers—are fashionable apparel, furniture, major appliances, and automobiles. The process of searching and comparing continues as long as the customer believes that the potential benefits from more information are worth the additional time and effort spent shopping. A *better* purchase might be saving several hundred dollars on the purchase of a new car or finally finding a software package that prepares financial statements in the manner desired by the buyer.

With shopping goods, buying habits affect the distribution and promotion strategies of both manufacturers and middlemen (such as retail stores). Shopping-goods manufacturers require fewer retail outlets because consumers are willing to look around for what they want. To facilitate comparison shopping, manufacturers often try to place their products in stores located near other stores carrying competing items. Similarly, department stores and other retailers that carry primarily shopping goods like to be near each other. Further, many retailers carry several brands of the same shopping good to allow shoppers to make in-store comparisons.

Manufacturers usually work closely with retailers in marketing shopping goods. Because manufacturers use fewer retail outlets, they are more dependent on those they do select. Retail stores typically buy shopping goods in large quantities, and it's common for manufacturers to distribute directly to retailers. To buyers of a shopping good, the reputations of the stores carrying the product often are more important than the images of the manufacturers. For example, a consumer may be more loyal to a Circuit City store than to various brands of audio and video equipment, such as JVC and Sanyo.

Specialty Goods

A tangible product for which a consumer has a strong brand preference and is willing to expend substantial time and effort in locating the desired brand is called a specialty good. The consumer is willing to forgo more accessible substitutes to search for and purchase the desired brand. Examples of products usually categorized as specialty goods include expensive men's suits, stereo sound equipment, health foods, photographic equipment, and, for many people, new automobiles and certain home appliances. Various brands, such as Armani, Nikon, and BMW, have achieved specialty-good status in the minds of some consumers.

Because consumers *insist* on a particular brand and are willing to expend considerable effort to find it, manufacturers can use few retail outlets. Ordinarily the manufacturer deals directly with these retailers. The retailers are extremely important, particularly if the manufacturer uses only one in each geographic area. And where the opportunity to handle the product is highly valued, the retailer may be quite willing to abide by the producer's policies regarding the amount of inventory that needs to be maintained, how the product should be advertised, or other marketing factors.

Because relatively few outlets are used *and* the product's brand name is important to buyers, both manufacturer and retailer advertise the product extensively. Often the manufacturer pays a portion of the retailer's advertising costs; and the name of the store carrying the specialty good frequently appears in the manufacturer's ads.

Attaining specialty-good standing in consumers' minds, as Nikon has done, is highly desirable. Shoppers exert added effort to locate a specialty good, and they tend to be less concerned about price than other features of this type of product. Of course, becoming a specialty good requires not just top quality or outstanding value but also large expenditures on advertising to create and sustain a special image for the brand.

 www.nikon.com

Unsought Goods

There's one more, quite different category of goods. In fact, it's so unlike the other three categories that we have not included it in Table 8.1. Nevertheless, because some firms sell unsought goods, this category deserves brief discussion.

An **unsought good** is a new product that the consumer is not yet aware of *or* a product that the consumer is aware of but does not want right now. Most people are unaware of interactive movies, in which the audience determines to some degree the plot and outcome of the show by means of an electronic voting device attached to each seat.[4] Currently unwanted products might include gravestones for those who have *not* lost a loved one and snow tires in the summer.

An electric car, as discussed in the chapter-opening case, might be an unsought good for most people, either because they are unaware of it or do not want one after learning about it. Bathroom tissue made strictly from cotton fiber, including the Cottonelle and Purely Cotton brands, would seem to be an unsought good. Despite ads in which various characters first state, "I don't use toilet paper," but then explain that they rely on Purely Cotton, few consumers know about the product and fewer still seek it out at the store.[5]

As the name suggests, a firm faces a very difficult, perhaps impossible, advertising and personal selling job when trying to market unsought goods. The best approach may be to make consumers aware of the product and continue to remind them of it so that they will buy the advertised brand when the need arises. Marketers of unsought goods try to build familiarity with their offerings by placing ads on bus–stop benches or in church bulletins.

Classification of Business Goods

As with consumer goods, the general category of *business goods* is too broad to use in developing a marketing program. Consequently, as shown in Table 8.2, we separate business goods into five categories: raw materials, fabricating materials and parts, installations, accessory equipment, and operating supplies. This classification is based on the product's broad *uses*. For example, a business good may be used in producing other products, in operating an organization, and in other ways we will discuss.

Raw Materials

Business goods that become part of another tangible product prior to being processed in any way (except as necessary to assist in handling the product) are considered raw materials. Raw materials include:

- Goods found in their natural state, such as minerals, land, and products of the forests and the seas.
- Agricultural products, such as cotton, fruits, livestock, and animal products including eggs and raw milk.

Because of their distinctive attributes, these two groups of raw materials usually are marketed differently. For instance, the supply of raw materials in their natural state is limited, cannot be substantially increased, and often involves only a few large producers. Further, such products generally are of a commodity nature, must be carefully graded, and, consequently, are highly standardized. Consider coal as an example; it is extracted in great quantities and then is graded by hardness and sulfur content.

The characteristics of raw materials in their natural state affect how they are marketed. For example:

- Prices are normally set by supply and demand, approximating the conditions of perfect competition. As a result, individual producers have little or no control over the prevailing market price.

Table 8.2   Categories of Business Goods: Characteristics and Marketing Considerations

	Type of Product				
	Raw Materials	**Fabricating Materials and Parts**	**Installations**	**Accessory Equipment**	**Operating Supplies**
Examples	Iron ore	Engine blocks	Blast furnaces	Storage racks	Paper clips
Characteristics					
Unit price	Very low	Low	Very high	Medium	Low
Length of life	Very short	Depends on final product	Very long	Long	Short
Quantities purchased	Large	Large	Very small	Small	Small
Frequency of purchase	Frequent delivery; long-term purchase contract	Infrequent purchase, but frequent delivery	Very infrequent	Medium frequency	Frequent
Standardization of competitive products	Very much; grading is important	Very much	Very little; custom-made	Little	Much
Quantity of supply	Limited; supply can be increased slowly or not at all	Usually no problem	No problem	Usually no problem	Usually no problem
Marketing considerations					
Nature of channel	Short; no middlemen	Short; middlemen only for small buyers	Short; no middlemen	Middlemen used	Middlemen used
Negotiation period	Hard to generalize	Medium	Long	Medium	Short
Price competition	Important	Important	Varies in importance	Not main factor	Important
Presale/postsale service	Not important	Important	Very important	Important	Very little
Promotional activity	Relatively little	Moderate	Sales people very important	Important	Not too important
Brand preference	None	Generally low	High	High	Low
Advance buying contract	Important; long-term contracts	Important; long-term contracts	Not usual	Not usual	Not usual

- Because of their great bulk, low unit value, and the long distances between producer and business user, transportation is an important consideration for natural raw materials.
- As a result of the same factors, natural raw materials frequently are marketed directly from producer to business user with a minimum of physical handling.
- Not much effort is expended on product differentiation for this type of product. It is tough, for example, to distinguish one producer's coal from that of another producer. However, some producers have been successful in developing and promoting their own brands of agricultural products (such as the famous Chiquita bananas).

Agricultural products are supplied by small producers as well as larger corporate farms, typically located some distance from their markets. The supply is largely controllable by producers, but it cannot be increased or decreased rapidly. The product is perishable and is not produced at a uniform rate throughout the year. Most citrus fruits, for example, ripen in late winter and thus are readily available at that time of year and become less available in subsequent months. Standardization and grading are commonplace for agricultural products. Also, transportation costs are likely to be high relative to the product's unit value.

Middlemen are ordinarily needed to market agricultural products because many producers are small and numerous and markets are distant. Transportation and warehousing greatly influence effectiveness *and* efficiency of distribution. Typically, there is relatively little promotional activity with agricultural products, as compared to other types of business goods.

Fabricating Materials and Parts

Business goods that become part of the finished product after having been processed to some extent fit into the category of fabricating materials and parts. The fact that they have been processed distinguishes them from raw materials. **Fabricating materials** undergo further processing; examples include pig iron going into steel, yarn being woven into cloth, and flour becoming part of bread. **Fabricating parts** are assembled with no further change in form; they include such products as zippers in clothing and semiconductor chips in computers.

Fabricating materials and parts are usually purchased in large quantities. Normally, buying decisions are based on the price and the service provided by the seller. To ensure an adequate, timely supply, a buyer may place an order a year or more in advance. Because consumers are concerned about price, service, and reliability of supply, most fabricating products are marketed directly from producer to user. Middlemen are used most often when the buyers are small in size and/or when buyers have small fill-in orders (after the large initial order) requiring rapid delivery.

Branding fabricating materials and parts is generally unimportant. However, some firms have successfully pulled their business goods out of obscurity by branding them. Talon zippers and the NutraSweet brand of sweeteners are examples.

www.nutrasweet.com

Installations

Manufactured products that are an organization's major, expensive, and long-lived equipment are termed **installations**. Examples are large generators in a dam, a factory building, diesel engines for a railroad, and blast furnaces for a steel mill. The characteristic of installations that differentiates them from other categories of business goods is that they directly affect the scale of operations in an organization producing goods or services. Adding 12 new Steelcase desks will not affect the scale of

Some products, including Talon zippers, are purchased by both business and consumer markets. For apparel makers, zippers are a fabricating part in a piece of clothing. Most consumers view a zipper as a convenience good, an item to be purchased as easily as possible. However, some consumers— perhaps those who sew their own clothes— consider a Talon zipper to be a specialty good. They will expend extra effort to locate and buy Talon rather than another brand.

ONE OF THE FEW THINGS
TALON DOESN'T MAKE A ZIPPER FOR.

operations at American Airlines, but adding 12 Boeing 757 jet aircraft certainly will. Therefore, jet aircraft are categorized as installations, but desks normally are not.

The marketing of installations presents a real challenge, because each unit sold represents a large dollar amount. Often each unit is made to the buyer's detailed specifications. Also, much presale and postsale servicing is essential. For example, an elevator or an escalator requires installation, maintenance, and—inevitably—repair service. Sales are usually made directly from producer to business user; no middlemen are involved. Because installations are technical in nature, a high-caliber, well-trained sales force is needed to market installations. Because installations require careful, detailed explanation, promotion emphasizes personal selling.

Accessory Equipment

Tangible products that have substantial value and are used in an organization's operations are called **accessory equipment**. This category of business goods neither becomes an actual part of a finished product nor has a significant impact on the organization's scale of operations. The life of accessory equipment is shorter than that of installations but longer than that of operating supplies. Some examples are point-of-sale terminals in a retail store, small power tools, forklift trucks, and office desks.

It is difficult to generalize about how accessory equipment should be marketed. For example, for some products in this category, it is suitable for a manufacturer to sell directly to a final customer. This is true particularly when an order is for several units or when each unit is worth a lot of money. A manufacturer of forklift trucks may sell directly to customers because the price of a single unit is large enough to make this form of distribution profitable. Normally, however, manufacturers of accessory equipment use middlemen—for example, office-equipment distributors. The reasons: Typically, the market is geographically dispersed, there are many different types of potential users, and individual orders may be relatively small.

Operating Supplies

Business goods that are characterized by low dollar value per unit and a short life and that contribute to an organization's operations without becoming part of the finished product are called **operating supplies**. Examples are lubricating oils, pencils and stationery, and heating fuel. Purchasers want to buy operating supplies with fairly little effort. Thus operating supplies are the convenience goods of the business sector.

As with the other categories of goods, the characteristics of operating supplies influence how they should be marketed. Because they are low in unit value and are bought by many different organizations, operating supplies—like consumer convenience goods—are distributed widely. Thus the producing firm uses wholesaling middlemen extensively. Also, because competing products are quite standardized and there is little brand insistence, price competition is normally stiff.

• Importance of Product Innovation

A business exists to satisfy customers while making a profit. Fundamentally, a company fulfills this dual purpose through its products. New-product planning and development are vital to an organization's success. This is particularly true now, given (1) rapid technological changes, which can make existing products obsolete, and (2) the practice of many competitors to copy a successful product, which can neutralize an innovative product's advantage. Thus, as emphasized by a top executive at Pillsbury, "In the end, the company with the most new products wins."[6] Of course, these new products must be satisfying to customers and profitable for the firm.

Requirement for Growth

Sooner or later, many product categories and individual brands become outdated. Their sales volumes and market shares drop because of changing consumer desires and/or superior competing products. Once successful products that are now in much less demand include fountain pens, audiocassettes, and electric typewriters. Some brands that no longer exist or have been relegated to remote locations in stores include Munsingwear shirts, White Cloud bathroom tissue, and Maypo cereal.[7]

Thus a guideline for management is "innovate or die." For many companies a substantial portion of this year's sales volume and net profit will come from products that did not exist 5 to 10 years ago. Introducing a new product at the right time can help sustain a firm. In fact, companies that are leaders in terms of profitability and sales growth obtain 39% of their revenues from products introduced during the preceding five years; the corresponding figure for the least successful companies is 23%.[8]

Some firms that were successful innovators for long periods—familiar names such as Rubbermaid, 3M, Nike, and Procter & Gamble—haven't maintained a steady flow of new products in recent years. Some of their competitors have been more successful. For example, Total toothpaste, which fights gum disease, helped Colgate-Palmolive surpass P&G's market share in this competitive market. Perhaps with this situation in mind, the head of P&G stated, "The core business is innovation. If we innovate well, we will ultimately win."[9]

High Failure Rates

For many years, the "rule of thumb" has been that about 80% of new products fail. However, because of dissimilar definitions of *new product* and *failure*, the statistics often vary from one study to another. One company that tracks new-product introductions placed the rate of failure at even higher than 80%. According to another study, even the best companies suffer 35% mortality for new products. And finally, an examination of 11,000 new goods and services discovered that 56% are still on the market 5 years after being introduced. Of course, some of those products still on the market undoubtedly are on the brink of failure whereas others are hugely successful.[10]

Why do new products fail? The most common problem is not being different than existing products. Among the numerous examples are Vaseline after-shave lotion, Pepsi A.M., and Farrah shampoo. A new product is also likely to fail if it does not deliver on its promise. Beech Aircraft's Starship plane was supposed to perform like a jet at the price of a propeller plane. Instead, the finished product wound up performing like a propeller plane (indeed it was a turboprop) at the price of a jet![11]

Further, a product is subject to failure if it is perceived as offering poor value in relation to its price. Priced at $4 to $7 apiece, the General Foods Culinova refrigerated dinners did not pass consumers' value tests. Other factors that can undermine new products include poor positioning and lack of marketing support.

Considering how vital new products are to a company's growth, the large number of new-product introductions, and the high failure rates, product innovation deserves special attention. Firms that are inattentive to their new products may face financial ruin because of the high cost of product failure—often more than $10 million per occurrence in a large company. Organizations that effectively manage product innovation can expect to reap a variety of benefits—differential advantage, higher sales and profits, and a solid foundation for the future.

Even successful companies have product failures. Pepsi A.M. was promoted for consumption in the morning, but consumers didn't discern how it was different than other colas. If the Vaseline name connotes petroleum jelly, then this well-known brand may have contributed to the failure of these after-shave lotions. Product failures even have their own museum, the New Products Showcase and Learning Center in Ithaca, New York, which contains 60,000 items—most of them huge flops.

• Development of New Products

It's often said that nothing happens until somebody sells something. This is not entirely true. First there must be something to sell—a good, service, person, place, or idea. And that "something" must be developed.

What Is a "New" Product?

Just what is a "new" product? Are the auto manufacturers' annual models new products? GM's electric vehicle? The Chevrolet Tahoe, which is sized between the Blazer and Suburban? Or, in other product categories, how about a supercaffeinated soft drink such as PepsiCo's Josta and Coca-Cola's Surge or a clear beer-like beverage such as Coors' Zima? Does an online auction of prospective employees that is being run by Monster.com qualify as new?[12] Or must a product be revolutionary, never before seen, before we can class it as *new*? How new a product is affects how it should be marketed.

There are numerous connotations of "new product," but we will focus our attention on three distinct categories of **new products:**

• Products that are *really innovative*—truly unique. Notable innovations during the 20th century range from the zipper to the photocopy machine and, of course, the computer. A recent example is a security device that electronically compares the shape of a person's hand with the image of a hand encoded on an identification card.[13] Still-to-be-developed products in this category would be a cancer cure and easily, inexpensively repaired automobiles. Any new product in this category satisfies a real need that is not being satisfied at the time it is introduced.

Are you—or any consumers—ready for paperless books?

The convergence of several technologies has created optimism about the commercial prospects for paperless books—better termed electronic books or e-books. This new product is, in effect, a scaled-down, single-purpose handheld computer, which is linked to the Internet. Several brands already are or soon will be on the market. The pioneers include SoftBook, Rocket eBook, and EveryBook.

An e-book actually has two parts, the storage unit and the content of the book. After purchasing the storage unit, a reader chooses content from a selection spanning best sellers, obscure or foreign-language books, journals, and textbooks. The content is delivered via the Internet. Some paperless books, notably the Rocket eBook, will be sold through book retailers; others will be sold directly to consumers.

E-books hold promise for both purchasers and publishers. A reader can store the contents of at least 10 books on a device that is about the same size as a hardcover paper book and also will be able to electronically underline content and write notes in the margin. Paperless books should pare various costs now incurred by publishers, including such costs as paper, printing, and shipping. Of course, e-books could create conflicts between publishers and book stores if publishers decide to bypass retailers and sell the content of books through their websites. Going a step further, authors might be tempted to sell their writing directly to readers.

Skeptics say few readers will abandon paper books. However, one e-book entrepreneur notes, "Paper ency-

clopedias are already gone." Price will affect the extent and rate of adoption of e-books. Presently, prices range from about $350 to $600, depending on the specific brand and its particular features. The content of a paperless book is priced separately, typically at or below the cost of a paper book. As with most forms of digital technology, prices should decline steadily as the underlying costs of an e-book are reduced.

Which groups of readers are most likely to embrace, or at least try, e-books? The primary target markets are likely to be pleasure readers for best sellers and romance novels, professionals for trade (technical) books, and students for textbooks. Rather than buying five or so separate paper textbooks, a college student might buy or lease an e-book that is loaded with all the textbooks needed for the upcoming term.

Thus far, though, there have been relatively few buyers of any kind. According to one estimate, only several thousand of the e-book storage units were purchased during the product's first year on the market. And some marketers of e-books have already failed. One person in this new field provided a status report, "These e-reader companies now have a pretty sober understanding that this market is going to take some time" before it's determined whether paperless books are here to stay.

Sources: Martha Mendoza, "Electronic Books Aren't Flying off the Screen," *St. Louis Post-Dispatch*, Aug. 31, 1999, p. C6; Alan Stewart, "Publishers Turn the E-Page," *Financial Times*, Apr. 21, 1999, p. 28; and Carol Vinzant, "Electronic Books Are Coming at Last!" *Fortune*, July 6, 1998, pp. 119–120, 122, 124.

- Replacements that are *significantly different* from existing products in terms of form, function, and—most important—benefits provided. Notable successes from the past century include cellophane, sterile bandage strips, and ballpoint pens. Johnson & Johnson's Acuvue disposable contact lenses and Kodak's and Fuji's new camera and film format, called Advanced Photo System, are replacing some traditional models. The electric vehicle also falls in this category.

- *Imitative* products that are new to a particular company but not new to the market. Usually, annual models of autos and new versions of cereals are appropriately placed in this category. In another situation, a firm may simply want to capture part of an existing market with a "me too" product. To maximize company-wide sales, makers of cold and cough remedies routinely introduce imitative products, some of which compete with a nearly identical product *from the same company*. That's the case with Dristan Sinus and CoAdvil, both put out by American Home Products.

 www.ahp.com

Ultimately, of course, whether or not a product is new depends on how the intended market perceives it. If buyers consider it to be significantly different from competitive products in some relevant characteristic (such as appearance or performance), then it is indeed a new product. Lately, marketers have found that anything labeled *digital* is especially appealing to numerous consumers. Thus "digital" has been attached to not just telephones and televisions, but also lights, music, and even a KitchenAid toaster priced at $89.99. Even though not all of these products are technically digital, many buyers prefer them to regular or analog versions.[14] As in other situations, *perception is reality!*

New-Product Strategy

To achieve strong sales and healthy profits, every producer of business goods or consumer goods should have an explicit strategy with respect to developing and evaluating new products. This strategy should guide every step in the process of developing a new product.

A **new-product strategy** is a statement identifying the role a new product is expected to play in achieving corporate and marketing goals. For example, a new product might be designed to protect market share, meet a specific return-on-investment goal, or establish a position in a new market. Or a new product's role might be to maintain the company's reputation for innovation or social responsibility. The last outcome appears to have been a primary aim of General Motors when it introduced the EV1 electric vehicle. Although EV1 may have helped GM rebut criticism about not being environmentally sensitive, it has failed with respect to achieving sufficient sales.[15]

A new product's intended role also will influence the *type* of product to be developed. To illustrate:

Company Goal	Product Strategy	Recent Examples
To defend market share.	➡ Introduce an addition to an existing product line or revise an existing product.	➡ Pizza Hut's "Big New Yorker" and "Stuffed Crust" pizzas.
To strengthen a reputation as an innovator.	➡ Introduce a *really* new product—not just an extension of an existing one.	➡ Digital cameras introduced by Sony, Canon, and other firms.

A new-product strategy can also help a firm avoid the problem of having numerous products under development but few actually becoming ready for the market.[16] The priorities in the strategy can be used to determine which prospective products should receive special attention, which should go on the "back burner," and which should be scrapped. Only in recent years have many companies consciously identified new-product strategies. The process of developing new products has become more efficient *and* more effective for firms with strategies because they have a better sense of what they are trying to accomplish.

Stages in the Development Process

Guided by a company's new-product strategy, a new product is best developed through a series of six stages, as shown in Figure 8.2. Compared to unstructured development, the formal development of new products provides benefits such as improved teamwork, less rework, earlier failure detection, shorter development times, and—most important—higher success rates.[17]

At each stage, management must decide whether to proceed to the next stage, abandon the product, or seek additional information.[18] Here's a brief description of what should happen at each stage of the **new-product development process:**

1. *Generating new-product ideas.* New-product development starts with an idea. A system must be designed for stimulating new ideas within an organization and then reviewing them promptly. In one study, 80% of companies pointed to customers as their best source for new-product ideas. A growing number of manufacturers are encouraging—in some cases, requiring—suppliers to propose innovations. And franchise systems frequently turn their owner-managers' ideas into

Identify the strategic role of new products, then . . . → 1. Idea generation → 2. Screening of ideas → 3. Business analysis → 4. Prototype development → 5. Market tests → 6. Commercialization

Figure 8.2

Major stages in the new-product development process.

highly successful products, such as the Egg McMuffin sandwich at McDonald's and annual club memberships at Moto Photo film-processing shops.[19]

2. *Screening ideas.* At this stage, new-product ideas are evaluated to determine which ones warrant further study.[20] Typically, a management team relies on experience and judgment, rather than on market or competitive data, to screen the pool of ideas.

3. *Business analysis.* A surviving idea is expanded into a concrete business proposal. During the stage of **business analysis,** management (a) identifies product features; (b) estimates market demand, competition, and the product's profitability; (c) establishes a program to develop the product; and (d) assigns responsibility for further study of the product's feasibility.

A Global Perspective

Can new-product ideas be found on other continents?

Seeking added sales and perhaps a differential advantage, a growing legion of companies are scanning foreign markets for new-product ideas. Various products introduced in the U.S.—including Whiskas cat food from Mars Inc., the Symphony chocolate bar from Hershey Foods, and Michelob Dry beer from Anheuser-Busch—originated in foreign markets.

Several factors prompt U.S. companies to look abroad for new-product ideas:

- Bored with mere imitations, consumers are willing to accept novel products.

- Truly innovative products, even potential breakthroughs, might be uncovered in foreign markets where problems are approached from a different perspective. For instance, Shaman Pharmaceuticals of San Francisco is tapping the knowledge of "medicine men" in Ecuador to identify tropical plants and trees that may contain curative compounds. This approach has helped the company develop several drugs.

- Marketing a foreign product in the firm's home country can be much cheaper than starting the development process from scratch. With that in mind, Prince, the sporting goods company, acquired the U.S. distribution rights for a high-tech tennis ball machine that can fire 10 types of shots at 8 degrees of difficulty.

- An existing foreign product may be the best way of satisfying an ethnic market segment in the home

country. For example, Colgate-Palmolive was confident that the lighter texture and pleasing smell of its Fabuloso cleaner, developed abroad, would appeal to Hispanics in the U.S.

An established foreign product is not guaranteed success here. The following guidelines can help:

- Stick to products that coincide with American trends. A greater interest in healthful foods helped Kellogg's achieve success in the U.S. with Mueslix, a cereal combining grains, nuts, and fruits that was invented in Switzerland.

- Don't just rely on the product's newness, but ensure it has a significant benefit.

- Concentrate on products that have achieved widespread success in foreign markets. In 1997, Häagen-Dazs saw that a very sweet, butterscotchlike flavor was wildly popular at its ice cream shop in Buenos Aires. Brought to the U.S., this flavor has been very well received in many markets. Häagen-Dazs next wondered if green tea, an appealing ice cream flavor in Japan, would suit American tastes.

Sources: David Leonhardt, "It Was a Hit in Buenos Aires—So Why Not Boise?" *Business Week,* Sept. 7, 1998, pp. 56, 58; Frederick C. Klein, "New Aussie Giant Serves Up Aces; Our Man Is Bushed," *The Wall Street Journal,* May 26, 1995, p. B8; Thomas M. Burton, "Drug Company Looks to 'Witch Doctors' to Conjure Products," *The Wall Street Journal,* July 7, 1994, p. A1; Michael J. McCarthy, "More Companies Shop Abroad for New-Product Ideas," *The Wall Street Journal,* Mar. 14, 1990, pp. B1, B6; and Bob Hagerty, "Unilever Scours the Globe for Better Ideas," *The Wall Street Journal,* Apr. 25, 1990, p. A11.

Virtually all products, ranging from Barbie dolls to Goodyear tires, undergo various tests before and also after being introduced to the market. Some producers do the testing themselves; others outsource the testing to specialized firms. Here, a new Goodyear tire is tested under simulated winter conditions in a laboratory. Such tests can lead to safer, more reliable products.

 www.goodyear.com

4. *Prototype development.* If the results of the business analysis are favorable, then a prototype (or trial model) of the product is developed. In the case of services, the facilities and procedures necessary to produce and deliver the new product are designed and tested. That certainly is a necessary step in developing a new roller-coaster ride for an amusement park!

In the case of goods, a small quantity of the trial model is manufactured to designated specifications. Technical evaluations are carried out to determine whether it is practical to produce the product. A firm may be able to construct a prototype of a new type of cellular telephone, but be unable to manufacture the new product in large quantities or at a cost that is low enough to stimulate sales and still yield a profit. Further, lab tests are conducted to judge whether the proposed product will endure normal—even abnormal—usage. Apple Computer puts new models through various durability tests that range from pouring a soft drink onto the computer to subjecting the screen to over 100 pounds of pressure.[21]

5. *Market tests.* Unlike the internal tests conducted during prototype development, **market tests** involve actual consumers. A new tangible product may be given to a sample of people for use in their households (in the case of a consumer good) or their organizations (a business good). Following the trial, users are asked to evaluate the product.

This stage in new-product development often entails test marketing, in which the product is placed on sale in a limited geographic area. Market test findings, including total sales and repeat purchases by the same customers, are monitored by the company that developed the product and perhaps by competitors as well. The product's design and production plans may be adjusted as a result of test findings. Following market tests, management must make a final "go–no go" decision about introducing the product.

6. *Commercialization.* In this stage, full-scale production and marketing programs are planned and then implemented. Up to this point in development,

As many as 80 firms in the U.S. tell inventors they will help them refine their ideas for new products, prepare patent applications and business plans, develop prototypes, and line up business deals with manufacturers and other producers. Typically, an inventor pays the "matchmaker" an up-front fee of $1,000 or more. Thousands of people have signed up with these invention-promotion firms.

Is it ethical for invention-promotion firms to charge substantial up-front fees? Would your opinion about whether or not this practice is ethical be changed if the invention-promotion firm received its fee later in the new-product development process?

Sources: Stephen Gregory, "Patently Dishonest?" *Los Angeles Times,* Nov. 18, 1998, p. C1; and "An Antidote for Patent Scams," *Machine Design,* Mar. 7, 1996, p. 192.

management has virtually complete control over the product. However, once the product is "born" and made available for purchase, the external competitive environment becomes a major determinant of its destiny.

Note that the overall new-product strategy guides the first two stages—idea generation and screening. This strategy can provide a focus for generating new-product ideas *and* a basis for evaluating them.

In the six-stage process, the first three stages are particularly critical because they deal with ideas and, as such, are the least expensive.[22] More important, many products fail because the idea or the timing is wrong—and the first three stages are intended to identify such situations. Each subsequent stage becomes more costly in terms of the dollars and human resources necessary to carry out the required tasks.

New-product development is a lengthy process, typically taking almost a year for minor revisions and more than three years to complete the process for a major breakthrough. Even with a mandate to get a new product to market rapidly, it took a team of 7-Eleven and Frito-Lay employees more than a year to develop a new "Frito pie" to the point where it was ready for test marketing. Because of competitive pressures and other factors such as globalization and rapid technological change, firms are trying to bring—in fact, are bringing—new products to market faster and faster. To do so, some companies skip stages in the development process. The most common omission is the fifth stage, market tests.[23] Without this stage, however, the company lacks the most telling reactions to the proposed product.

Historically, the marketing of goods has received more attention than the marketing of services. Thus it is not surprising that the new-product development process is not as advanced in services fields as it is in goods industries.[24] Service firms are almost starting with a clean slate as they devise a new-product development process that suits their distinctive circumstances.

www.fritolay.com

Producer's Criteria for New Products

When should a company add a new product to its current assortment of products? Here are guidelines that some producers use in answering this question:

- There must be *adequate market demand.* Too often management begins with the wrong question, such as, "Can we use our present sales force?" or "Will the new item fit into our production system?" The necessary first question is, "Do enough people really want this product?" A product is destined to fail if it fills a need that isn't important to consumers or doesn't even exist.[25]
- The product must *satisfy key financial criteria.* At least three questions should be asked: "Is adequate financing available?" "Will the new item reduce seasonal

and cyclical fluctuations in the company's sales?" And most critical, "Can we make a sufficient profit with the product?"

- The product must be *compatible with environmental standards.* Key questions include "Does the production process avoid pollution of air or water?" "Will the finished product, including its packaging, be friendly to the environment?" And, "After being used, does the product have recycling potential?"
- The product must *fit into the company's present marketing structure.* The Donna Karan firm probably would find it practical to add designer sheets and towels to its product mix that features clothing, whereas the Sherwin Williams paint company would likely find it more difficult to add sheets and towels to its mix. Specific questions related to whether or not a new product will fit the company's marketing expertise and experience include "Can the existing sales force be used?" "Can the present channels of distribution be used?"

Besides these four issues, a proposed product must satisfy other criteria. For instance, it must be in keeping with the company's objectives and image. The product also must be compatible with the firm's production capabilities. And it must satisfy any pertinent legal requirements.

Middleman's Criteria for New Products

In considering whether to buy a new product for resale, middlemen such as retailers and wholesalers should apply all the preceding criteria except those related to production. In addition, a middleman should apply the following guidelines:

- The middleman must have *a good working relationship with the producer.* By distributing a new product, a middleman should stand to benefit from (a) the producer's reputation, (b) the possibility of getting the right to be the only company to sell the product in a given territory, and/or (c) the promotional and financial help given by the producer.
- The producer and middleman must have *compatible distribution policies and practices.* Pertinent questions include "What kind of selling effort is required for the new product?" "How does the proposed product fit with the middleman's policies regarding repair service, alterations (for clothing), credit, and delivery?" "Does the product complement existing products?"
- As in the case of producers, the product must *satisfy key financial criteria.* One question is especially pertinent to middlemen: "If adding a new product necessitates eliminating another product because of a shortage of shelf or storage space, will the result be a net gain in sales?" And the fundamental question always is: "Can we make a sufficient profit with the product?"

New-Product Adoption and Diffusion

The likelihood of achieving success with a new product, especially a really innovative product, is increased if management understands the adoption and diffusion processes for that product. Once again, we stress that organizations need to understand how prospective customers behave. The **adoption process** is the set of successive decisions an *individual person or organization* makes before accepting an innovation. **Diffusion** of a new product is the process by which an innovation spreads throughout a *social system* over time.[26]

By understanding these processes, an organization can gain insight into how a product is or is not accepted by prospective customers and which groups are likely to buy a product soon after it is introduced, later on, or never. This knowledge of buying behavior can be valuable in designing an effective marketing program.

Stages in the Adoption Process

A prospective buyer goes through six stages in the adoption process—deciding whether to purchase something new:

Stage	Activity in That Stage
Awareness	Individual is exposed to the innovation; becomes a prospect.
Interest	Prospect is interested enough to seek information.
Evaluation	Prospect judges the advantages and disadvantages of a product and compares it to alternatives.
Trial	Prospect adopts the innovation on a limited basis. A consumer tries a sample, if the product can be sampled.
Adoption	Prospect decides whether to use the innovation on a full-scale basis.
Confirmation	After adopting the innovation, prospect becomes a user who immediately seeks assurances that the decision to purchase the product was correct.

Adopter Categories

Some people will adopt an innovation soon after it is introduced. Others will delay before accepting a new product, and still others may never adopt it. Research has identified five innovation adopter categories, based on when in the life of a product individuals adopt a given innovation. Nonadopters are excluded from this categorization. Characteristics of early and late adopters are summarized in Table 8.3. We should add that it's unlikely an individual will be in the same category, such as early adopter, for all products. It's possible a person may fit in one category for a specific product (like audio equipment) but go into another category for a much different product (like clothing).

Innovators

Representing about 3% of the market, innovators are venturesome consumers who are the first to adopt an innovation. In relation to later adopters, innovators are likely to be younger, have higher social status, and be in better financial shape.

Table 8.3	Characteristics of Early and Late Adopters of Innovations	
	Early Adopters	**Late Adopters**
Key characteristics		
Venturesome	Innovators	
Respected	Early adopters	
Deliberate	Early majority	
Skeptical		Late majority
Tradition-bound		Laggards
Other characteristics		
Age	Younger	Older
Education	Well educated	Less educated
Income	Higher	Lower
Social relationships: within or outside community	Innovators: outside Others: within	Totally local
Social status	Higher	Lower
Information sources	Wide variety; many media	Limited media exposure; limited reliance on outside media; reliance on local peer groups

Innovators also tend to have broad social relationships involving various groups of people in more than one community. They are likely to rely more on nonpersonal sources of information, such as advertising, rather than on sales people or other personal sources.

Early Adopters

Comprising about 13% of the market, **early adopters** purchase a new product after innovators but sooner than other consumers. Unlike innovators, who have broad involvements *outside* a local community, early adopters tend to be involved socially *within* a local community. Early adopters are greatly respected in their social system; in fact, other people are interested in and influenced by their opinions. Thus the early adopter category includes more opinion leaders than any other adopter group. Sales people are probably used more as information sources by early adopters than by any other category.

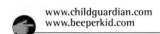

www.childguardian.com
www.beeperkid.com

In the process of diffusion, **a change agent** is a person who seeks to accelerate the spread of a given innovation. In business, the person responsible for introducing an innovative new product must be a change agent. Consider the electronic device that combines a microphone and a transmitter to allow a parent to keep track of a child's whereabouts. Marketers of this device, with different brands such as Child Guardian and Beeper Kid, must be effective change agents, convincing consumers that it is worthwhile to spend $50 or more for this type of added safety.[27]

A change agent focuses the initial persuasive efforts, notably targeted advertising campaigns, on people who fit the demographic profile of early adopters. Other consumers respect—often request—the opinions of early adopters and eventually will emulate their behavior. Thus, if a firm can get early adopters to buy its innovative product and they are satisfied by it, then they will say good things about the new offering. This is called *word-of-mouth communication*. In turn, the broader market eventually will accept the product as well. Of course, unlike advertising that is controlled by the firm, word of mouth can be influenced through advertising but is still largely uncontrolled. And sometimes, it turns out to be unfavorable and harmful rather than favorable and helpful.[28]

Early Majority

The **early majority**, representing about 34% of the market, includes more deliberate consumers who accept an innovation just before the "average" adopter in a social system. This group is a bit above average in social and economic measures. Consumers in the early majority group rely quite a bit on ads, sales people, and contact with early adopters.

Late Majority

The **late majority**, another 34% of the market, is a skeptical group of consumers who usually adopt an innovation to save money or in response to social pressure from their peers. They rely on members of the early and late majorities as sources of information. Advertising and personal selling are less effective with this group than is word-of-mouth communication.

Laggards

Laggards are consumers who are bound by tradition and, hence, are last to adopt an innovation. They comprise about 16% of the market. Laggards are suspicious of innovations and innovators; they wonder why anyone would pay a lot for a new kind of safety device, for example. By the time laggards adopt something new, it may already have been discarded by the innovators in favor of a newer concept. Laggards typically are older and usually are at the low end of the social and economic scales.

We are discussing only *adopters* of an innovation. For most innovations, there are many people who are *not* included in our percentages. They are **nonadopters;** they never adopt the innovation.

Characteristics Affecting Adoption Rate

The speed or ease with which a new product is adopted is termed its **adoption rate.** Five characteristics affect the adoption rate, especially in the case of truly innovative products:[29]

- *Relative advantage:* the degree to which an innovation is superior to currently available products. Relative advantage may be reflected in lower cost, greater safety, easier use, or some other relevant benefit. Safest Stripper, a paint and varnish remover introduced by 3M, has several advantages and thus scores high on this characteristic. The product contains no harmful chemicals, has no odor, and allows the user to refinish furniture indoors rather than having to work outdoors.

- *Compatibility:* the degree to which an innovation coincides with the values and life-styles of prospective adopters. Because many consumers want to save time *and* satisfy their desires now rather than later, microwave popcorn certainly satisfies this characteristic.

- *Complexity:* the degree of difficulty in understanding or using an innovation. The more complex an innovation is, the more slowly it will be adopted—if it is adopted at all. Combined shampoo and conditioners certainly are simple to use, so adoption of them was not impeded by complexity. However, some consumer electronics products and various services on the Internet have problems with this characteristic.

To gauge whether a sufficient number of consumers would adopt the Dryel Fabric Care System, Procter & Gamble tested the product, over five years, with thousands of consumers and even more loads of clothing. For Dryel to score high in terms of trialability and compatibility, consumers must feel confident that the product is safe, in the sense that its ingredients will not harm either the clothes or the environment.

 www.dryel.com

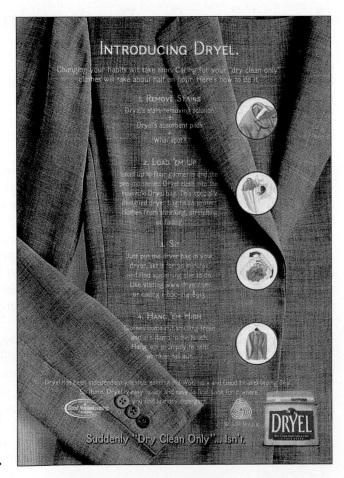

- *Trialability:* the degree to which an innovation may be sampled on some limited basis. Setting aside the other characteristics, the greater the trialability, the faster will be the adoption rate. For instance, a central home air-conditioning system is likely to have a slower adoption rate than a new seed or fertilizer, which may be tried on a small plot of ground. In general, because of this characteristic, costly products will be adopted more slowly than will inexpensive products. Likewise, many services, such as insurance, are difficult to use on a trial basis, so they tend to be adopted rather slowly.
- *Observability:* the degree to which an innovation actually can be demonstrated to be effective. In general, the greater the observability, the faster the adoption rate. For example, a new weed killer that works on existing weeds probably will be accepted sooner than a product that prevents weeds from sprouting. The reason? The latter product, even if highly effective, produces no dead weeds to show to prospective buyers!

A company would like an innovative product to satisfy all five characteristics discussed above. But few do. One-time cameras come close, however. Procter & Gamble hopes that a kit for dry cleaning clothes at home also does.[30] A moist cleaning cloth from the Dryel kit and the dirty clothes are placed in a nylon bag, then run through a heated cycle in the clothes dryer, a process that minimizes *complexity.* Considering that it can be used at home at any time, time-short consumers probably would give the product high marks for *compatibility.* Dryel and Custom Cleaner, a competing brand, cost about $10, a price level that contributes to *trialability.* Each manufacturer claims that its brand produces clean clothes at a fraction of the cost of so-called professional dry cleaning. If so, home dry-cleaning kits also possess *relative advantage* and *observability,* the final two characteristics that accelerate the adoption rate for new products.

Organizing for Product Innovation

For new-product programs to be successful, they must be supported by a strong, long-term commitment from top management. This commitment must be maintained even when some new products fail. To implement this commitment to innovation effectively, new-product efforts must be soundly organized.

Types of Organization

There is no "one best" organizational structure for product planning and development. Many companies use more than one structure to manage these activities. Some widely used organizational structures for planning and developing new products are:

- **Product-planning committee.** Members include executives from major departments—marketing, production, finance, engineering, and research. In small firms, the president and/or another top-level executive often serve on the committee.
- **New-product department.** These units are small, consisting of five or fewer people. The department head typically reports to the company president. In a large firm, this may be the president of a division.
- **Venture team.** This small group, with representatives from engineering, production, finance, and marketing research, operates like a separate small business. Typically the team reports directly to top management.[31]
- **Brand manager.** This individual is responsible for planning new products as well as managing established products. A large company may have many brand managers who report to higher marketing executives.

Product innovation is too important an activity to handle in an unorganized, nonchalant fashion, figuring that somehow the job will get done. What's critical is to make sure that some person or group has the specific responsibility for new-product development—and is backed by top management.

As the new product is completed, responsibility for marketing it usually is shifted either to an existing department or to a new department established just for this new product. In some cases the team that developed the product may continue as the management nucleus of the new unit.

Integrating new products into departments that are already marketing established products carries two risks, however. First, executives who are involved with ongoing products may have a short-term outlook as they deal with day-to-day problems of existing products. Consequently, they may not recognize the long-term importance of new products and, as a result, neglect them. Second, managers of successful existing products often are reluctant to assume the risks inherent in marketing new products.

Shifting Arrangements

Beginning in the 1950s, many companies—Procter & Gamble, Pillsbury, and General Foods, to name a few—assigned the responsibility for planning new products as well as coordinating the marketing efforts for established ones to a brand manager. Essentially, a brand manager, sometimes called a *product manager,* plans the complete marketing program for a brand or group of products. Specific tasks include setting marketing goals, preparing budgets, and drafting plans for advertising and personal selling activities. Developing new products along with improving established products may also be part of the job description.

The biggest drawback of this structure is that a company often saddles brand managers with great responsibility but provides them with little authority. For instance, brand managers are expected to develop the plan by which the sales force will market the product to wholesalers and retailers, but they have no real authority over the sales force. Their effectiveness depends largely on their ability to influence other executives to cooperate with their plans.

In the 1980s, many industries experienced slow growth in maturing markets, coupled with a trend toward strategic planning that stressed centralized managerial control. Subsequently, the pace of technological change placed a premium on rapid decision making. Because of these forces, one observer went so far as to state that brand managers were an "endangered species." Over time, the brand manager structure was modified in some companies. For instance, Procter & Gamble added *category managers* who oversee the activities of a related group of brand managers. Recently, though, several firms, notably General Motors and Ford, have turned to brand managers.[32]

Despite these prominent examples, many firms are now relying on team efforts—such as the product-planning committee or venture team discussed earlier—to develop new products. Typically, these are *cross-functional* teams, consisting of representatives from not only market research and marketing, but also product design, engineering, and manufacturing. The rationale has been explained as follows, "Cross-functional teams offer the benefits of different perspectives and skill sets, and . . . a functionally diverse team can improve the quality of products developed and reduce the cycle time necessary to launch new products."[33]

• Summary

The first commandment in marketing is "Know thy customer," and the second is "Know thy product." The relative number and success of a company's new products are a prime determinant of its sales, growth rate, and profits. A firm can best serve its customers by producing and marketing want-satisfying goods or services. The scarcity of some natural resources and a growing concern for our environment make social responsibility a crucial aspect of product innovation.

To manage its products effectively, a firm's marketers must understand the full meaning of *product*, which stresses that customers are buying want-satisfaction. Products can be classified into two basic categories—consumer products and business products. Each category is then subdivided, because a different marketing program is required for each distinct group of products.

There are many views as to what constitutes a *new* product. For marketing purposes, three categories of new products need to be recognized—innovative, significantly different, and imitative.

A clear statement of the firm's new-product strategy serves as a solid foundation for the six-stage development process for new products. At each stage, a firm must decide whether to proceed to the next stage or to halt the project. The early stages in this process are especially important. If a firm can make an early *and correct* decision to stop the development of a proposed product, a lot of money and labor can be saved.

In deciding whether or not to add a new product, a producer or middleman should consider if there is adequate market demand for it. The product also should fit in with the firm's marketing, production, and financial resources.

Management needs to understand the adoption and diffusion processes for a new product. A prospective user goes through six stages in deciding whether or not to adopt a new product. Adopters of an innovation can be divided into five categories, depending on how quickly they accept an innovation such as a new product. These categories are innovators, early adopters, early majority, late majority, and laggards. In addition, there usually is a group of nonadopters. Five characteristics of an innovation seem to influence its adoption rate: relative advantage, compatibility, complexity, trialability, and observability.

Successful product planning and development require a long-term commitment and strong support from top management. Furthermore, new-product programs must be soundly organized. Most firms use one of four organizational structures for new-product development: product-planning committee, new-product department, venture team, or brand manager. Recently, the trend has been away from brand managers and toward team efforts for development of new products.

More about General Motors

If all went well, a successful electric vehicle (EV) could help General Motors boost revenues, gain market share, and strengthen its reputation with respect to both technological leadership and environmental protection. But despite GM's abundant expenditures and dogged persistence, little has gone well with this new product.

One problem has been that despite frequent calls for environmental protection, relatively few consumers are enthusiastic about EVs. According to a 1997 survey, less than one-quarter of car owners would consider acquiring an EV. Further, virtually all consumers said they would use the same criteria in evaluating EVs and conventional cars. Low price and dependability were valued features, whereas favorable environmental impact wasn't in the top 10.

Recently, automakers have shown growing interest in other technologies for powering vehicles. One such method is a hybrid, which relies on both a gas engine and an electric motor. Toyota's hybrid vehicle, called the Prius, was introduced in Japan in late 1997. According to the company, the Prius will cost about $20,000, will get around 55 miles a gallon, and will go over 700 miles before needing more fuel. Toyota's schedule called for launching the Prius in the U.S. and Europe midway by mid-2001.

GM hoped to recoup all, or at least some, of its massive investment in electric vehicles by selling large numbers of EV1s at a profit. GM thought that battery improvements and lower prices would stimulate demand for the EV1. Besides aiming its electric-powered car at wealthy individuals, GM saw potential in the fleet market (beginning not surprisingly with electric utilities) and among environmentalists, auto enthusiasts, and consumers who like to buy innovative products.

Some automakers are pessimistic about EVs. In

fact, Honda gave up in 1999. Then the previously stubborn GM threw in the towel in early 2000. A top executive at GM admitted, "We recognize the limitations of a pure electric vehicle." Heading in the opposite direction, Ford Motor Co. introduced a two-seater EV, called the Th!nk, in several Scandinavian countries with plans to test the car in the U.S.

A consensus may be forming that the most plausible successor to the internal-combustion gasoline-powered engine is a low-emission fuel cell, which produces electricity by mixing oxygen with hydrogen. After saying it would stop production of the EV1, GM indicated its continuing interest in hybrid vehicles and, ultimately, in vehicles powered by fuel cells.[34]

1. a. How does the electric vehicle score with respect to the five characteristics affecting the rate at which innovations are adopted?
   b. On the basis of the preceding assessment, how rapidly will the EV be adopted by consumers?

2. What factors should GM have considered in deciding whether to continue its efforts to sell the EV1, to switch its efforts to fuel-cell or hybrid vehicles, or to concentrate all of its efforts on gasoline-powered vehicles?

www.toyota.com

Key Terms and Concepts

Product (215)
Consumer products (216)
Business products (216)
Convenience good (216)
Shopping good (217)
Specialty good (218)
Unsought good (219)
Raw materials (219)
Fabricating materials (221)
Fabricating parts (221)
Installations (221)
Accessory equipment (222)
Operating supplies (222)

New products (224)
New-product strategy (226)
New-product development process (226)
Business analysis (227)
Market tests (228)
Adoption process (230)
Diffusion (230)
Stages in the adoption process (231)
Innovation adopter categories (231)
Innovators (231)

Early adopters (232)
Change agent (232)
Early majority (232)
Late majority (232)
Laggards (232)
Nonadopters (233)
Adoption rate (233)
Product-planning committee (234)
New-product department (234)
Venture team (234)
Brand manager (234)

Questions and Problems

1. In what respects are the products different in each of the following cases?
   a. A Whirlpool dishwasher sold at an appliance store and a similar dishwasher sold by Sears under its Kenmore brand name. Assume that Whirlpool makes both dishwashers.
   b. A CD by the singer Jewel purchased online from Amazon.com and the same CD sold by a Blockbuster store.
   c. An airline ticket purchased through a travel agent and an identical ticket purchased directly from the airline via the Internet.

2. a. Explain the various interpretations of the term *new product*.

   b. Give some examples, other than those cited in this chapter, of products in each of the three new-product categories.

3. "Because brand preferences are well established with regard to many items of women's clothing, these items—traditionally considered shopping goods—will move into the specialty-goods category. At the same time, however, other items of women's clothing can be found in supermarkets and variety stores, thus indicating that some items are convenience goods."
   a. Explain the reasoning in these statements.
   b. Do you agree that women's clothing is shifting away from the shopping-goods classification? Explain.

4. Compare the elements of a producer's marketing mix for a convenience good with those of the mix for a specialty good.

5. In which of the five categories of business goods should each of the following be included? And which products may belong in more than one category?
   a. Trucks
   b. Medical X-ray equipment
   c. Typing paper
   d. Copper wire
   e. Printing presses
   f. Nuts and bolts
   g. Paper clips
   h. Land

6. In developing new products, how can a firm make sure that it is being socially responsible with regard to scarce resources and our environment?

7. Assume that the following organizations are considering additions to their product lines. In each case, does the proposed product meet the criteria for adding a new product? Explain your decisions.
   a. McDonald's—salad bar
   b. Safeway supermarkets—automobile tires
   c. Exxon—personal computers
   d. Banks—life insurance
   e. Amazon.com—life insurance

8. Several new products from foreign countries are described in the Global Perspective box. In your opinion, which ones will enjoy the greatest success in the U.S.? Explain your choices.

9. Describe the kinds of people who are most likely to be found in (a) the innovator category of adopters and (b) the late majority category.

10. Why are many firms relying more on cross-functional teams and less on product managers for new-product development?

Hands-On Marketing

1. Arrange a meeting with the manager of a large retail outlet in your community. Discuss two topics with the manager:
   a. What recently introduced product has been a failure or appears destined to fail?
   b. Did this product, in retrospect, satisfy the criteria for adding a new product? (Remember to consider not just the middleman's criteria, but also the applicable producer's criteria.)

2. Design, either in words or drawings, a new product that fits into one of the first two categories of newness—that is, a really innovative product or a significant replacement, not just an imitative product. Then evaluate how your proposed product rates with respect to the five characteristics of an innovation that influence the adoption rate.

Product-Mix Strategies

*"MindStorms may be the product that restores the
luster to the Lego brand name and, equally
important, boosts the company's sales."*

Will a New Product Line Help Lego Build Its Sales and Image?

You remember Legos. Bright, primary-colored building blocks that fit together in any shape you could imagine, they probably consumed some of your childhood playtime. Gaining widespread consumer loyalty, Legos dominated the construction-toy market around the world for many years. Indeed, at one time Lego Group AS of Denmark commanded 80% of this market.

Lately, however, the popularity of Legos has slipped. Total sales revenues of $1.2 billion in 1997 barely outpaced 1996, with discouraging results in the U.S. largely to blame. Then, despite an increase in global sales to $1.4 billion in 1998, Lego posted a loss of almost $50 million for the year.

It's been suggested that kids, especially those in the U.S., have been seduced by the electronic age. According to this line of thinking, basic construction toys were enjoyable for kids a generation ago. However, today's youth want the latest and greatest in digital technology and, as a result, they quickly become bored with toys that don't provide it. Even the head of Lego in the U.S., Peter Eio, admitted, "I think kids are a little more impatient today. They want instant gratification." Given the changes in children's interests (and perhaps their diminished attention spans), Lego's stubborn loyalty to its core product has been criticized.

To boost company sales and profits, and to recapture the U.S. market in particular, Lego developed a new product line, MindStorms. Introduced at the New York Toy Fair in February 1998, MindStorms combines high-tech gadgetry, including artificial intelligence, with traditional Lego architecture to allow kids or other users to build "smart toys." These designs can take the form of robots, trucks, animals, or any moving (and sometimes speaking) contraption you can dream up.

Although Lego's philosophy of mixing play with learning remains the same, the company's promotional strategy for MindStorms is markedly different from its past efforts. To promote its fledgling product line, Lego is employing television ads, animated and live-action television programs, films, videos, computer games and books, as well as LEGOLAND theme parks. The reliance on television is a particularly significant shift in strategy for the Danish firm. For years Lego blamed TV for changing the way kids play by decreasing their already limited attention spans.

In addition, Lego is licensing the MindStorms name to a wide variety of children's products, including bed sheets and clothing items. It is also seeking cross-marketing opportunities, such as a Star Wars robot package that was introduced to tie in with the latest *Star Wars* movie. Looking ahead to the year 2005, Kjeld Kirk Kristiansen, Lego's chief executive, stated, "It's our intention to have the most powerful brand among families with children."

In the meantime, Lego cannot forget the people that made the company the fifth largest toy manufacturer in the world, namely the parents of today's kids. These parents fondly remember Lego's basic line of building blocks. According to one brand researcher, "Lego needs to be extremely careful trying to broaden its market appeal. In doing so, it could reposition itself as a brand it doesn't really want to be." For the first time, for instance, Lego has introduced kits with gun-toting cowboys and other creatures that prospective customers could consider violent and, consequently, undesirable.

The first shipment of MindStorms, 80,000 sets priced at about $200 apiece, sold out before Christmas 1998. The new product generated a strong following not just among kids (and, of course, their parents who typically made the purchase) but also among two additional groups. According to Eio, the Lego executive, "MindStorms is helping us reach out to teenagers who think of Lego as just a construction toy." And, perhaps surprisingly, MindStorms is a hit with many employees in the so-called Silicon Valley of California and in other areas with concentrations of technology-oriented companies. The head of one such firm even had to ban MindStorms during work hours!

Based on the early results, MindStorms may be the product that restores the luster to the Lego brand name and, equally important, boosts the company's sales. Eio summed up the two-sided challenge and opportunity facing the company, "The trick for us is to be cool with kids as well as with adults."[1]

What factors will affect whether or not the new MindStorms product is a long-term success for Lego?

 www.lego.com

The Lego Group, like most firms, faces the challenge of sustaining its mature brand while building one or more new brands. This case illustrates that over time, a company must make numerous decisions about its array of products. Whether the correct decisions are made—and made at the right time—greatly affects a company's degree of success, not just for a single year but for many years to come.

At any given time, a firm may be marketing some new products and some old ones, while others are being planned and developed. This chapter covers a number of strategic decisions pertaining to an organization's assortment of products. After studying this chapter, you should be able to explain:

chapter goals

- The difference between product mix and product line.
- Major product-mix strategies—positioning, expansion, alteration, and contraction.
- Trading up and trading down.
- Managing a product throughout a life cycle.
- Planned obsolescence.
- Style and fashion.
- The fashion-adoption process.

Product Mix and Product Line

Red Hat Inc. markets only Linux software, Carma Labs Inc. sells only its lip balm, and WD-40 Co. concentrates on a single brand of spray lubricant. These examples notwithstanding, few firms rely on a single product; instead, most sell many products. A **product mix** is the set of all products offered for sale by a company. The structure of a product mix has both breadth and depth. Its **breadth** is measured by the number of product lines carried, its **depth** by the variety of sizes, colors, and models offered within each product line. A product-mix structure is illustrated in Figure 9.1.

A broad group of products, intended for essentially similar uses and having similar physical characteristics, constitutes a **product line.** Firms may delineate a product line in different ways. For Whitehall-Robins Healthcare, its various forms of Robitussin cough remedies (such as Pediatric and Maximum Strength syrups and cherry-flavored drops) represent a product line. However, for a large drugstore or supermarket, all brands of cough remedies—not just Robitussin products—comprise one of the store's many product lines.

Product-Mix Strategies

At one time, Anheuser-Busch Companies offered snack foods, baked goods, adventure-park entertainment, and about 25 brands of beer to consumers. Did this diverse assortment of products develop by accident? No—it reflected a planned strategy, as did the company's subsequent decision to dispose of the snack foods and baked goods divisions. To be successful in marketing, producers and middlemen need carefully planned strategies for managing their product mixes, as we'll see next.

Positioning the Product

Management's ability to bring attention to a product and to differentiate it in a favorable way from similar products goes a long way toward determining that product's revenues. Thus management needs to engage in *positioning*. Recall

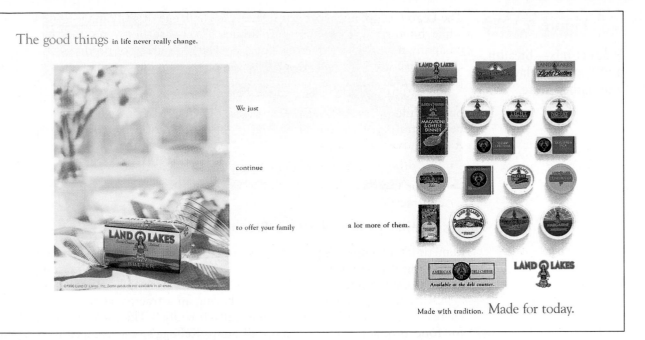

The good things in life never really change.

We just

continue

to offer your family

a lot more of them.

Made with tradition. Made for today.

Many consumers' perceptions of the Land O' Lakes brand go no further than butter. This ad is intended to inform prospective customers about the entire product mix, not only various forms of butter but also several types of cheese and some other products.

www.landolakes.com

www.saturn.com

from the discussion in Chapter 6 that positioning entails developing the image that a product projects in relation to competitive products and to the firm's other products.

Regardless of which positioning strategy is used, the needs of the target market always must be considered. For example, Holiday Inns has developed multiple (perhaps too many) offerings to satisfy diverse target markets. Thus, besides its traditional hotels, the lodging firm now has Holiday Inn Express, Select, and Sunspree Resort properties as well as Staybridge Suites and Inter-Continental and Crowne Plaza hotels and resorts. Likewise, to satisfy different consumers' desires regarding taste, Anheuser-Busch has both regular and light beers at five different price levels as well as two brands of nonalcoholic brews.

Marketing executives can choose from a variety of positioning strategies. Sometimes they decide to use more than one for a particular product. Here are several major positioning strategies.

Positioning in Relation to a Competitor

For some products the best position is directly against the competition. This strategy is especially suitable for a firm that already has a solid differential advantage or is trying to solidify such an advantage. After nine years of relying on a single (but successful) model, General Motors' Saturn division finally brought out larger models. The new L (for "larger") series is intended to attract customers from Saturn's primary competitors, Honda and Toyota. To fend off rival makers of microprocessors, Intel Corp. launched a campaign to convince buyers that its product is superior to competitors'. The company even paid computer makers to include the slogan, "Intel Inside," in their ads.[2]

For other products, head-to-head positioning is exactly what *not* to do, especially when a competitor has a strong market position. In women's professional basketball, the American Basketball League and Women's National Basketball Association competed directly against each other, including overlapping seasons. Ultimately, the ABL lost out to the WNBA, which had the financial backing of the men's NBA.[3]

One view is that underdogs should try to be the opposite of—or at least much different than—the market leader. Southwest Airlines has positioned itself effectively as the low-fare alternative to full-service airlines.[4]

Figure 9.1

Product mix—breadth and depth in a lawn and garden store.

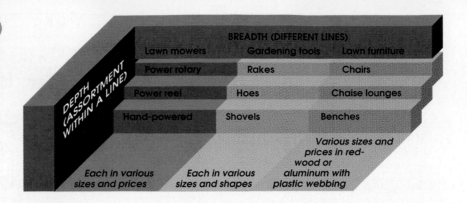

DEPTH (ASSORTMENT WITHIN A LINE)

BREADTH (DIFFERENT LINES)

Lawn mowers	Gardening tools	Lawn furniture
Power rotary	Rakes	Chairs
Power reel	Hoes	Chaise lounges
Hand-powered	Shovels	Benches
Each in various sizes and prices	*Each in various sizes and shapes*	*Various sizes and prices in redwood or aluminum with plastic webbing*

Positioning in Relation to a Product Class or Attribute

Sometimes a company's positioning strategy entails associating its product with (or distancing it from) a product class or attribute. For example, some companies try to place their products in a desirable class, such as "Made in the USA."

Other firms promote their wares as having an attractive attribute, such as "low energy consumption" or "environmentally friendly." This strategy is widely used for food products. Libby's, Campbell Soup, Kellogg's, and competing companies, for instance, have introduced lines of foods with one common denominator—they contain very little or no salt. These items are positioned against products that are packed with the conventional amounts of salt. Sometimes what's in, rather than left out of, the product is emphasized. That's the case with Volvo, which constructed a steel frame around the passenger compartment in order to be positioned as *the* safe automobile.

Positioning by Price and Quality

Certain producers and retailers are known for their high-quality products and high prices. In the retailing field, Saks Fifth Avenue and Neiman Marcus are positioned at one end of the price-quality continuum. Discount stores such as Kmart and Dollar General are at the other end. We're not saying that discounters ignore quality; rather, they stress low prices.

In recent years, both Ford and General Motors have sold large numbers of sport-utility vehicles (SUVs). Now, virtually every automaker has introduced or is preparing to launch its own SUV, most of which feature four-wheel drive and other high-quality, but expensive amenities. In a market filled with 25 models of SUVs, ranging from the familiar Ford Explorer and Chevy Suburban to the obscure Subaru Forester and Lexus RX300, producers are struggling to differentiate their particular model from all the others. Without differentiation, particularly with respect to positioning on the price-quality continuum, some models are likely to fail.

Product–Mix Expansion

Product-mix expansion is accomplished by increasing the depth within a particular line and/or the number of lines a firm offers to customers. Let's look at these options.

When a company adds a similar item to an existing product line with the same brand name, it is termed a **line extension.** For illustrations, pull the coupons insert out of your Sunday newspaper. You'll probably see examples such as Pillsbury promoting about 10 variations of its well-known biscuits and rolls; Vaseline announcing new versions of Intensive Care lotions; and Log Cabin advertising its sugar-free, as well as regular, syrups.

The line-extension strategy is also used by organizations in services fields. For example, universities now offer programs to appeal to prospective older students,

How many products are too many?

In a typical year, more than 25,000 new (using the term loosely) packaged goods are placed in front of consumers. In fact, the annual rate of introductions is 75% greater than 10 years ago. Just in the category of pain relievers, there were more than 400 new entries during the 1990s.

Does this flow of new offerings benefit consumers and retailers as well as manufacturers? A variety of evidence says "no." Many consumers cannot differentiate across the numerous alternatives—and get frustrated or angry in the process. Really, do you know the differences among the following remedies—Tylenol Flu, Tylenol Cold, Tylenol Sinus, and Tylenol Allergy Sinus, not to mention their different forms (tablets, caplets, and gel caps)?

The basic problem may be that almost three-quarters of so-called new products are line extensions within an existing product category, in which the new entry represents a different form or promises an added benefit. Only about one-quarter of new products are a mix or line extension outside the company's current category, and only 6% have truly new features. In the opinion of a manager for McKesson Drug Co., "The amount of duplication is staggering."

Supermarkets lack shelf space to add all or even most of the new products. According to a study conducted for the Food Marketing Institute, a trade association, the number of separate items (called stock-keeping units) carried by a supermarket can be reduced by 5 to 25% without reducing sales or causing consumers to think that the store offers a poor assortment of products.

How should a manufacturer decide how many separate items in a product line best serve the interests of consumers, retailers, and itself?

Sources: Michelle Wirth Fellman, "Number of New Products Sees Steady Rise over Past Decade . . . ," *Marketing News,* Mar. 29, 1999, p. 3; the "1995 Innovation Survey," conducted by Group EFO Limited of Weston, CT; Joseph Weber, "Painkillers Are about to O.D.," *Business Week,* Apr. 11, 1994, pp. 54+; and Ira Teinowitz and Jennifer Lawrence, "Brand Proliferation Attacked," *Advertising Age,* May 10, 1993, pp. 11+.

and the Roman Catholic church broadened its line of religious services by adding Saturday and Sunday evening masses.

There are many reasons for line extensions. The main one is that the firm wants to appeal to more market segments by offering a wider range of choices for a particular product. Line extensions were one of the more prominent—and debatable—trends during the 1990s. As discussed in the "You Make the Decision" box, line extensions have become so common that they raise questions about their effectiveness.

Another way to expand the product mix, referred to as mix extension, is to add a new product line to the company's present assortment. Jell-O pudding pops and Bic disposable lighters, both successes, and Bic pantyhose and Adidas colognes, both failures, are examples of mix extension. The maker of Swatch watches went far afield to create the very small and inexpensive Smart car in the European market. Perhaps recognizing that it had ventured into unknown territory, the Swiss company decided to allow DaimlerChrysler, its partner in the project, to proceed on its own.[5]

Johnson & Johnson's products illustrate the distinction between mix extension and line extension. When J&J introduced a line of Acuvue disposable contact lenses, that was *mix* extension because it added another product to the company's product mix. In contrast, line extension adds more items within the same product line. When J&J adds new versions of Tylenol pain reliever, that's *line* extension.

Under a mix-extension strategy, the new line may be related or unrelated to current products. Furthermore, it may carry one of the company's existing brand names or may be given an entirely new name.

Typically, the new line is related to the existing product mix because the company wants to capitalize on its strengths and experience. Given the success of Reese's peanut butter cups, Hershey's thinks the brand says "peanut butter" to consumers, so it introduced a line of Reese's peanut butters. Hunt-Wesson holds a similar view about its Swiss Miss brand in relation to chocolate, so it developed Swiss Miss puddings in chocolate and other flavors. In both cases, the new lines carry one of the company's popular brands to benefit from consumers' familiarity with and good feelings toward that brand. We'll consider this approach in more detail when *brand equity* is discussed in the next chapter.

Alteration of Existing Products

Rather than develop a completely new product, management might do well to take a fresh look at the organization's existing products. Often, improving an established product, termed **product alteration**, can be more profitable and less risky than developing a completely new one. The substitution of NutraSweet for saccharin in diet sodas increased sales of those drinks. Redesigning the product itself can sustain its appeal or even initiate its renaissance. For example, Kimberly-Clark redesigned its disposable diapers so that they are less bulky and also come in separate styles for girls and boys.

Product alteration is not without risks, however. When Coca-Cola Co. modified the formula for its leading product and changed its name to New Coke, sales plunged. As a result, the old formula was brought back three months later under the Coca-Cola Classic name.

Alternatively, especially for consumer goods, the product itself is not changed but its packaging is altered. For example, Pillsbury developed a unifying background for the packages of most of its dessert mixes, a royal blue field with small white polka dots.[6] To gain a small differential advantage, some companies are offering their sliced and shredded cheeses in packages that reseal using zipperlike devices. Thus packages can be altered to enhance appearance or to improve the product's usability.

Product-Mix Contraction

Another strategy, **product-mix contraction**, is carried out either by eliminating an entire line or by simplifying the assortment within a line. Thinner and/or shorter product lines or mixes can weed out low-profit and unprofitable products. The intended result of product-mix contraction is higher profits from fewer products. General Mills (Wheaties, Betty Crocker, Gold Medal flour) decided to concentrate on its food business and, consequently, sold its interest in Izod (the "alligator" apparel maker) and its lines of children's toys and games. In services fields, some travel agencies have shifted from selling all modes of travel to concentrate on specialized tours and trips to exotic places. And, to reduce their liability risks and insurance costs, many physicians have stopped offering obstetrical services.

During the early 1990s, most companies expanded—rather than contracted—their product portfolios. Numerous line extensions document this trend. Lately, some firms that wound up with an unmanageable number of products or multiple unprofitable items or lines engaged in product-mix pruning. As a result, many organizations now have fewer product lines, and the remaining lines are thinner and shorter. There are myriad examples of product-mix contraction, sometimes involving well-known firms. For example, Unilever PLC, an English-Dutch firm, decided to prune more than 1,000 brands from its total set of about 1,600. The company wants to concentrate its marketing resources on the 400 or so remaining brands—including Lipton teas, Lever soaps, and Elizabeth Arden cosmetics—that generate almost 90% of annual revenues.[7]

 www.unilever.com

Trading Up and Trading Down

The product strategies of trading up and trading down involve a change in product positioning *and* an expansion of the product line. **Trading up** means adding a higher-price product to a line in order to attract a broader market. Also, the

Home Depot has engaged in trading up by establishing separate Expo outlets to appeal to distinct market segments separately. This display of chandeliers is being set up in an Expo. In contrast, Lowe's intermingles expensive and economy models of the same product in its stores because the more expensive lines might entice shoppers to spend more than originally planned.

 www.homedepot.com

 www.lowes.com

seller intends that the new product's prestige will help the sale of its existing lower-price products.

Consider some examples of trading up. To its line of inexpensive sport watches, Swatch added an $80 Chrono stopwatch and other upgraded watches. Home-improvement retailers, including both Home Depot and Lowe's, are now offering more expensive products, all the way up to $39,500 chandeliers.[8] And even pet-food manufacturers have traded up to "superpremium" lines, as illustrated by Pedigree from Kal Kan and Purina One from Ralston Purina.

Trading down means adding a lower-price product to a company's product line. The firm expects that people who cannot afford the original higher-price product or who see it as too expensive will buy the new lower-price one. The reason: The lower-price product carries some of the status and some of the other more substantive benefits (such as performance) of the higher-price item.

The Marriott Corp. followed a trading-down strategy when it started (1) Courtyard by Marriott hotels, targeted at the mid-price market long dominated by chains such as Holiday Inn and Ramada Inn, and (2) Fairfield Inns, to compete in the economy-price market. Even some designers of highly fashionable women's clothing, such as Donna Karan and Bill Blass, are trading down by introducing lower-price lines. The new lines are priced between $100 and $900 per item, typically less than one-half the price of their top lines.[9]

Trading up and trading down are perilous strategies because the new products may confuse buyers, resulting in negligible net gain. It is equally undesirable if sales of the new item or line are generated at the expense of the established products. When *trading down,* the new offering may permanently hurt the firm's reputation and that of its established high-quality product. To reduce this possibility, new lower-price products may be given brand names unlike the established brands. That's why Hewlett-Packard Co. established a separate Apollo label for a new line of low-price printers, and Gap Inc. chose Old Navy Clothing Co. as the label for its lower-price outlets.[10] With this approach, a company forfeits the benefits of a well-known brand name but still can capitalize on its experience in distributing and promoting the successful product.

In *trading up,* on the other hand, the challenge depends on whether the new product or line carries the established brand or is given a new name. If the same name is used, the firm must change its image enough so that new customers will accept the higher-price product. At the same time, the seller does not want to lose its present customers. The new offering may cloud the established image, not attracting new customers but driving away existing customers. To avoid that problem, Sears used the Great Indoors name for a new store that sells comparatively expensive brands that are not found in Sears department stores.[11] If a different brand name is used, however, the company must create awareness for it and then stimulate consumers to buy the new product.

The Product Life Cycle

As we saw in Chapter 8, a product's life cycle can have a direct bearing on a company's survival. The life cycle of a product consists of four stages: introduction, growth, maturity, and decline. The concept of product life *applies to a generic category of product* (microwave ovens and microprocessors, for example) and not to specific brands (Sharp and Intel, respectively). A product life cycle consists of the aggregate demand over an extended period of time for all brands comprising a generic product category.

A life cycle can be graphed by plotting aggregate sales volume for a generic product category over time, usually years. It is also worthwhile to accompany the sales volume curve with the corresponding profit curve for the product category, as shown in Figure 9.2. After all, a business is interested ultimately in profitability, not just sales.

The *shapes* of these two curves vary from one product category to another. Still, for most categories, the basic shapes and the relationship between the sales and the profit curves are as illustrated in Figure 9.2. In this typical life cycle, the profit curve for most new products is negative (signifying a loss) through much of the introductory stage. In the latter part of the growth stage, the profit curve starts

With its "Intel Inside" branding strategy and extensive advertising program, Intel has been successful in convincing numerous manufacturers and buyers of personal computer that its microprocessor is superior to those of its competitors. In this ad, Intel stresses the benefits of its Pentium III processor in an Internet environment.

www.intel.com/PentiumIII

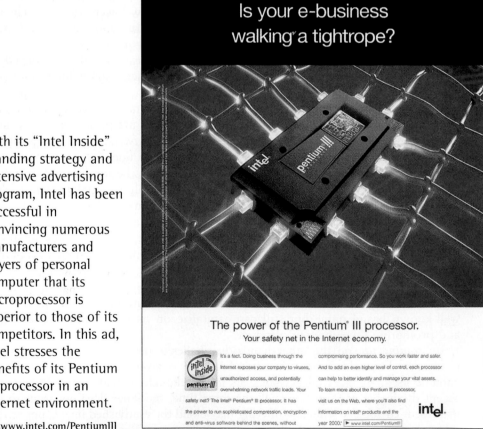

Figure 9.2

Typical life cycle of a product category.

During the introduction stage of a life cycle, a product category—and virtually all brands within it—is unprofitable. Total profits for the product category are healthy during the growth stage but then start to decline while a product's sales volume is still increasing.

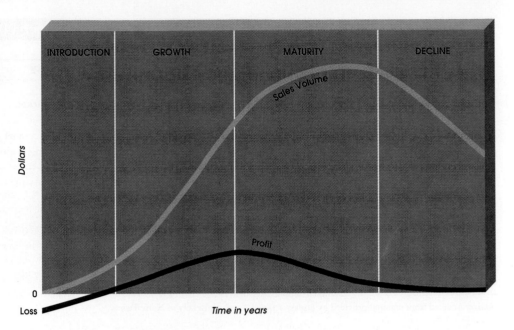

www.gillette.com

to decline while sales volume is still rising. Profits decline because the companies in an industry usually must increase their advertising and selling efforts and/or cut their prices to sustain sales growth in the face of intensifying competition during the maturity stage.

Introducing a new product at the proper time will help maintain a company's desired level of profit. Striving to maintain its dominant position in the wet-shaving market, the Gillette Company faces that challenge often. A while back, a large French firm cut into Gillette's market share by introducing the highly successful Bic disposable razors. After considerable research and development, Gillette counterattacked with the new Sensor razor, featuring independently suspended blades. The strategy worked, as many consumers left the convenience of low-price disposable razors in favor of the better shaves provided by the higher-price Sensor razor. More recently, Gillette traded up again, introducing the triple-blade Mach3 razor, which is priced about 35% higher than the Sensor.[12]

If a new product lacks competition and is particularly appealing to consumers, a firm can charge a fairly high price and achieve strong profits. That's been the case with Mach3, so Gillette is reaping healthy profits from the wet-shaving market. Intel Corp. has sought a measure of control over prices by introducing new generations of microprocessors only two or three years apart, even while demand is still growing for its current version. In recent years, though, Intel has had to rely more on price cuts to maintain its share of the market for microprocessors used in personal computers.[13]

The product life-cycle concept has been criticized as lacking empirical support and being too general to be useful in specific cases.[14] Admittedly, the product life cycle is not perfect and it must be adapted to fit different circumstances. Nevertheless, it is both straightforward and powerful. A company's marketing success can be affected considerably by its ability to determine and adapt to the life cycles for each of its product categories.

Characteristics of Each Stage

Management must be able to recognize what part of the life cycle its product is in at any given time. The competitive environment and marketing strategies that should be used ordinarily depend on the particular life-cycle stage. Table 9.1 contains a synopsis of all four stages. Each stage is highlighted below.

Table 9.1　Characteristics and Implications of Different Product Life-Cycle Stages

	Stage			
	Introduction	**Growth**	**Maturity**	**Decline**
Characteristics				
Customers	Innovators	Mass market	Mass market	Loyal customers
Competition	Little if any	Increasing	Intense	Decreasing
Sales	Low levels, then rising	Rapid growth	Slow/no annual growth	Declining
Profits	None	Strong, then at a peak	Declining annually	Low/none
Marketing Implications				
Overall strategy	Market development	Market penetration	Defensive positioning	Efficiency or exit
Costs	High per unit	Declining	Stable or increasing	Low
Product strategy	Undifferentiated	Improved items	Differentiated	Pruned line
Pricing strategy	Most likely high	Lower over time	Lowest	Increasing
Distribution strategy	Scattered	Intensive	Intensive	Selective
Promotion strategy	Category awareness	Brand preference	Brand loyalty	Reinforcement

Source: Adapted from material provided by Professor David Appel, University of Notre Dame.

Introduction

During the **introduction stage,** sometimes called the *pioneering stage,* a product is launched into the market in a full-scale marketing program. It has gone through product development, including idea screening, prototype development, and market tests. The entire product may be new, such as the zipper, the videocassette recorder, and the fat substitute for prepared foods. Or it may be well known but have a significant novel feature that, in effect, creates a new-product category; microwave ovens and in-line skates are examples.

For really new products, normally there is very little direct competition. However, if the product has tremendous promise, numerous companies may enter the industry early on. That has occurred in the multimedia-software field, where at least 1,000 firms are working to combine video, audio, and text on CD-ROMs that entertain and/or educate consumers. Because the industry is in its infancy, product-development costs are high—typically over $300,000 per program—but demand is meager. As Bill Gates of Microsoft observed, "There are more people pursuing this opportunity than can be sustained."[15] Many firms have failed, and—according to Gates—others will follow.

Because consumers are unfamiliar with the innovative product or feature, a pioneering firm's promotional program is designed to stimulate demand for the entire product category rather than a single brand. Introduction is the most risky and expensive stage because substantial dollars must be spent not only to develop the product but also to seek consumer acceptance of the offering. Many, perhaps most, new products are not accepted by a sufficient number of consumers and fail at this stage.

Growth

In the **growth stage,** or *market-acceptance stage,* sales and profits rise, frequently at a rapid rate. Competitors enter the market, often in large numbers if the profit outlook is particularly attractive. Mostly as a result of competition, profits start to decline near the end of the growth stage.

As part of firms' efforts to build sales and, in turn, market share, prices typically decline gradually during this stage. In high-tech fields, such as microprocessors, prices tend to fall sharply even as the industry is growing rapidly. According to a top executive at Eastman Kodak, "The only thing that matters is if the exponential growth of your market is faster than the exponential decline of your prices."[16] Appropriate marketing strategies for this stage, as well as the other three, are summarized in Table 9.1.

Maturity

During the first part of the **maturity stage**, sales continue to increase, but at a decreasing rate. When sales level off, profits of both producers and middlemen decline. The primary reason: intense price competition.

Seeking to differentiate themselves, some firms extend their product lines with new models; others come up with a "new and improved" version of their primary brand. During this stage, the pressure is greatest on those brands that trail the #1 and #2 brands. During the latter part of this stage, marginal producers, those with high costs or no differential advantage, drop out of the market. They do so because they lack sufficient customers and/or profits.

Decline

For most products, a **decline stage**, as gauged by sales volume for the total category, is inevitable for one of the following reasons:

- A better or less expensive product is developed to fill the same need. Microprocessors made possible many replacement products such as handheld calculators (which made slide rules obsolete) and video games (which may have pushed the category of board games, such as Monopoly and Clue, into the decline stage).
- The need for the product disappears, often because of another product development. For example, the broad appeal of frozen orange juice virtually eliminated the market for in-home mechanical or electrical fruit squeezers. (However, renewed interest in fresh foods has recently boosted sales of fruit squeezers.) Likewise, eight-track players were no longer needed once cassettes and compact discs supplanted eight-track tapes in the recorded music industry.
- People simply grow tired of a product (a clothing style, for instance), so it disappears from the market.

Seeing little opportunity for revitalized sales or profits, most competitors abandon the market during this stage. However, a few firms may be able to develop a small market niche and remain moderately successful in the decline stage. Some manufacturers of wood-burning stoves have been able to do this.

Length of Product Life Cycle

The total length of the life cycle—from the start of the introduction stage to the end of the decline stage—varies across product categories. It ranges from a few weeks or a short season (for a clothing fashion) to many decades (for autos or telephones). And it varies because of differences in the length of individual stages from one product category to the next. Furthermore, although Figure 9.2 suggests that all four life-cycle stages cover nearly equal periods of time, the stages in any given product's life cycle usually last for different periods.

Three variations on the typical life cycle are shown in Figure 9.3:

- In one, the product gains widespread consumer acceptance only after an extended introductory period (see part *a*). Fat substitutes, such as olestra, can be used in making foods ranging from potato chips to ice cream. However, this product category appears to be languishing in the introduction stage of its life cycle, perhaps because of shifts in consumer attitudes regarding fat in foods and/or concerns about possible side effects such as abdominal cramps.[17]
- In another variation, the entire life cycle begins and ends in a relatively short period of time (part *b*). This variation depicts the life cycle for a **fad**, a product or style that becomes immensely popular nearly overnight and then falls out of favor with consumers almost as quickly. Hula hoops and lava lamps are examples of past fads. Nasal dilators (such as Breathe Right strips), "virtual

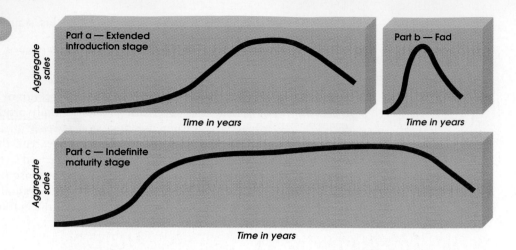

Figure 9.3

Product life-cycle
variations.

Part a — Extended introduction stage

Aggregate sales

Time in years

Part b — Fad

Time in years

Part c — Indefinite maturity stage

Aggregate sales

Time in years

pets," and "power bead" bracelets (which purport to provide benefits based on the bead colors) are likely to be classified as fads from the late 1990s.[18]

- In a third variation, the product's mature stage lasts almost indefinitely (part *c*). This life cycle is illustrated by canned, carbonated soft drinks, portable stereos (such as the Walkman),[19] and also the automobile with a gasoline-powered, internal-combustion engine. Electric- and solar-powered cars have been proposed or even introduced, but the automobile as we know it remains dominant.

Setting aside fads, which represent a special case, product life cycles are getting shorter generally. If competitors can quickly introduce a "me too" version of a popular product, it may move swiftly into the maturity stage. Or rapid changes in technology can make a product obsolete virtually overnight. Some said that would occur in the audio field, with digital audiotapes replacing compact discs (CDs), but that didn't happen. The latest forecast is that even newer formats, notably Super Audio CDs and DVD-Audio, will turn the CD into a dinosaur.[20]

Moreover, a number of product categories do not make it through all four stages of the life cycle. Some fail in the introductory stage. That appeared to be the case in the 1980s with a product that plays videodiscs rather than videotapes. Now the product is appearing again in a modified format, so perhaps it was just in a very extended introduction stage!

Also, because the life cycle refers to product categories rather than individual brands, not every brand proceeds through all four life-cycle stages. For instance, some brands fail early in the cycle. That's what happened with Cord and LaSalle, both of which failed during the introduction stage of the life cycle for automobiles. Other brands are not introduced until the market is in the growth or maturity stage. The Saturn is a very successful example in the automotive field.

Life Cycle Is Related to a Market

When we say a product is in a specific stage of its life cycle, implicitly we are referring to a specific market. A product may be well accepted (growth or maturity stage) in some markets but still be striving for acceptance in other markets. At the time Ortho Pharmaceuticals introduced Retin-A as a treatment for acne, existing products already served this purpose. Thus the acne-treatment category probably was in the maturity stage. However, it was discovered that Retin-A might be effective in reducing facial wrinkles. In effect, it created a new product category. Hence, Retin-A fit into both the acne-treatment category that was in the maturity stage among teenagers, and into the wrinkle-remover category that was in the introductory or perhaps early growth stage among middle-age people.

In terms of geographic markets, a product may be in its maturity stage in one country and its introductory stage or perhaps even unknown in another country.

Do all fads come from Japan?

Several popular products, which appear to be fads, have originated in Japan in recent years. The most notable include:

- "Virtual pets," egg-size objects with a liquid crystal screen that displays a pet, which requires constant care. Children anticipate the pets' needs, such as food, and satisfy the pets by pressing tiny buttons below the screen. Without proper care, the pets "die." After widespread success in Japan, millions more were sold in the U.S. several years ago.

- Pokémon role-playing video games, based on a collection of curious-looking cartoon characters. Born in Japan, there are now Pokémon trading cards, toys, TV show, movie, and, of course, video games in the U.S.

Why might Japan be the birthplace of more than its share of fads (or "wanna be" fads)? One possibility is that the Japanese have been innovative in developing low-price electronic gadgets.

Not all "hot" products in Japan translate to strong sales in the U.S. For example, a couple years ago, hundreds of thousands of Japanese adults bought "love beepers." The Lovegety (its real name) is carried by adults into crowded places such as bars. The beeper emits a signal when someone else who has a Lovegety is nearby. Then, using buttons, the two people can send a message such as "chat" to request the pleasure of a conversation. The Lovegety hasn't taken off in the U.S.—at least not yet.

Sources: John Lippman, "Pokémon's Invisible Champion," *The Wall Street Journal*, Aug. 16, 1999, p. B1; "Love Made Simple," *Columbia Daily Tribune*, June 3, 1998, p. 12A; and Joseph Pereira, "Toy Stores Bet 'Virtual Pets' Are Next Craze," *The Wall Street Journal*, May 2, 1997, pp. B1, B5.

For example, steel-belted radial tires were in their maturity stage in western Europe well before they were available across the U.S. In contrast, so-called fast foods are a mature product category in America, but are less common in some other parts of the world. And finally, chilled coffee in cans and bottles is widely accepted in Japan—at least $4 *billion* in annual sales. Yet sales of this beverage in the U.S. are paltry—not yet $200 *million*. In fact, Nestlé USA has already discontinued its line of Nescafe chilled coffees. However, seeing growth potential for this product in North America, PepsiCo and Starbucks Coffee have collaborated to market chilled coffee-based beverages. Frappuccino, a product of the joint venture, has been very well received by consumers.[21]

Life-Cycle Management

To some degree, the collective actions of firms offering competing products in the same category affect the shape of the sales and profit curves over the course of a life cycle. Even single companies can have an impact. A giant firm may be able to shorten the introductory stage by broadening the distribution or increasing the promotional effort supporting the new product.

Generally, however, companies cannot substantially affect the sales and profit curves for a product category. Thus their task is to determine how best to achieve success within the life cycle for a category. For an individual firm, successful life-cycle management depends on (1) predicting the shape of the proposed product's cycle even before it is introduced and (2) successfully adapting marketing strategies at each stage of the life cycle.

Entry Strategies

A firm entering a new market must decide whether to plunge in during the introductory stage. Or it can wait and make its entry during the early part of the growth stage, after innovating companies have proven there is a viable market.

www.palm.com

The strategy of entering during the introductory stage is prompted by the desire to build a dominant market position right away, and thus lessen the interest of potential competitors and the effectiveness of actual competitors. This strategy worked for Sony with the Walkman, Amana and Litton with microwave ovens, and recently USRobotics (now Palm, Inc.) with handheld personal digital assistants (PDAs) beginning with the Palm Pilot.

There is a benefit, called a **first-mover advantage** (also known as a *pioneer advantage*), to getting a head start in marketing a new type of product. The company that introduces a new product can target the highest potential market segments and can determine how to produce the good or service at lower and lower costs, to mention just a couple of specific benefits. However, pioneering requires a large investment, and the risks are great—as demonstrated by the high failure rate among new products. In fact, in the PDA category, Apple's Newton product was the pioneer, but soon failed.[22]

Large companies with the marketing resources to overwhelm smaller innovating firms are most likely to be successful with a delayed-entry strategy. In one such case, Coca-Cola introduced Tab and then Diet Coke, and Pepsi-Cola introduced Diet Pepsi, and the two giants surpassed Kirsch's No-Cal Cola, the pioneer.

A study of 50 product categories concluded that the first-mover advantage is temporary. The pioneer remains the market leader in only four of the categories (cola soft drink, color television, shortening, and telephone). In contrast, delaying entry until the market is proven can sometimes pay off. According to this same study, being an "early leader" can be advantageous over the long run. An early leader, which is a firm that enters a product category many years after the first mover but then gains market leadership during the growth stage of the cycle, is the current leader in more than one-half of the 50 product categories.[23]

Managing on the Rise

When sales are growing strongly and profits are robust in a product category, you might think marketing managers have little to do except tally up their anticipated bonuses. That's not the case. Decisions made during the growth stage influence (1) how many competitors enter the market and (2) how well the company's brand within a product category does in both the near and distant future.

During the growth stage of the life cycle, a company has to devise the right strategies for its brand(s) in that product category. Target markets have to be confirmed or, if necessary, adjusted. Product improvements must be formulated, prices assessed and perhaps revised, distribution expanded, and promotion enhanced.

www.nintendo.com

Home video games were introduced in the 1970s, but the more captivating (perhaps addictive) Nintendo brand, in effect, created a new product category in the 1980s. As the 1990s began, this product appeared to be in the growth stage of its life cycle. However, video game sales stagnated in the mid-1990s. Since then, to stimulate sales, Nintendo, Sony, and Sega have been engaged in "technological leap frog." That is, the three competitors are constantly striving to gain a differential advantage, even if only temporary, by building more video, audio, and graphics capabilities into their systems, while controlling prices.[24]

Managing during Maturity

Common strategies to maintain or boost sales of a product during the maturity stage of its life cycle include not just implementing line extension, but also modifying the product, designing new promotion, and devising new uses for the product.[25] Such steps may lead to added purchases by present customers and/or may attract new customers.

To reach a new market, Time Inc. extended its *Sports Illustrated* line, introducing a new edition for kids. As sales in the North American cruise industry flattened out, some cruise lines modified their services by adding fitness programs and offering special theme cruises (sometimes in conjunction with a professional sports team).[26]

DuPont's advertising is intended to create a preference among consumers for clothing that contains Lycra and to boost demand for this brand of spandex fiber. The company interviewed thousands of consumers in about 20 countries to determine if a single campaign would work around the world and for many kinds of clothing. The results were favorable, so the campaign (with necessary translations) is running globally. DuPont is the sole sponsor of some ads, including this one, and is the co-sponsor of other ads with clothing manufacturers.

 www.lycrashop.com

The DuPont Co. appears to be particularly adept at sustaining mature products, such as Teflon® protective coating and Lycra® fiber. Lycra is a brand of spandex, a fiber DuPont invented in 1959. DuPont's primary strategy to generate continuing interest in Lycra has been to develop improved versions of it. The product now is used in a variety of clothing, ranging from hosiery to women's and men's fashions to cycling shorts. DuPont also backs Lycra with aggressive promotion, such as a $40 million global ad campaign that was launched in 1999. With a theme of "Enjoy the Difference," the ads stress that clothes made with Lycra help consumers "look better, feel better."[27]

Surviving the Decline Stage

Perhaps it is in the decline stage that a company finds its greatest challenges in life-cycle management. For instance, condensed milk was developed prior to the Civil War when there was no electrical refrigeration to prevent food from spoiling. Now, with refrigerators in almost all U.S. homes, this product is in its decline stage. Borden sold its brand of condensed milk to Eagle Family Foods, which is trying to reinvigorate the product. Eagle launched a "Make Magic in Minutes" campaign to show consumers that condensed milk can help them make various food treats easily and year-round.[28]

When sales are declining, management has the following alternatives:

- Ensure that marketing and production programs are as efficient as possible.
- Prune unprofitable sizes and models. Frequently this tactic will *decrease* sales but *increase* profits.
- "Run out" the product; that is, cut all costs to the bare minimum to maximize profitability over the limited remaining life of the product.
- Best (and toughest) of all, improve the product in a functional sense, or revitalize it in some manner. Some publishers are working hard to maintain the appeal

of the dictionary. St. Martin's Press, for instance, has introduced a dictionary that includes workplace slang and also bios of celebrities. As part of a collaboration with Microsoft, the new dictionary will be available on a CD-ROM for use on personal computers and also in the traditional printed format.[29]

If one of these alternatives doesn't work, management will have to consider **product abandonment.** The expense of carrying profitless products goes beyond what shows up on financial statements. For example, there is a very real cost to the managerial time and effort that is diverted to terminally ill products. Management often is reluctant to discard a product, however, partly because it becomes attached to the product over the years. Knowing when and how to abandon products successfully may be as important as knowing when and how to introduce new ones.

Either before or after abandoning a declining product, a company may redefine its mission to concentrate on a more promising venture. That's what Fluke Manufacturing did when its traditional test and measurement devices started to become obsolete because of computing technology. Thus it was no fluke that the company came up with the following mission statement: "To be the leader in compact professional electronic test tools."[30]

Planned Obsolescence and Fashion

American consumers seem to be constantly searching for "what's new" but not "*too* new." They want newness—new products, new styles, new colors. However, they want to be moved gently out of their habitual patterns, not shocked out of them. Consequently, many manufacturers use a product strategy of planned obsolescence. The intent of this strategy is to make an existing product out-of-date and thus to increase the market for replacement products. Consumers often satisfy their thirst for newness through fashion. And producers of fashions rely heavily on planned obsolescence, as we'll see.

Nature of Planned Obsolescence

The term **planned obsolescence** is used to refer to either of two developments:

- **Technological obsolescence.** Significant technical improvements result in a more effective product. For instance, cassette tapes made phonograph records outmoded, and then compact discs rendered cassettes obsolete. This type of obsolescence is generally considered to be socially and economically desirable, because the replacement product offers more benefits and/or a lower cost.

- **Style obsolescence.** Superficial characteristics of a product are altered so that the new model is easily differentiated from the previous model. Style obsolescence, sometimes called "psychological" or "fashion" obsolescence, is intended to make people feel out-of-date if they continue to use old models. Products subject to this type of obsolescence include clothing, furniture, and automobiles.

Normally, when people criticize planned obsolescence, they mean style obsolescence. Still, technological (or functional) obsolescence is sometimes criticized. For example, Microsoft has been chided for its periodic revisions of Windows and related products. As one critic said sarcastically, "New versions of software are often little more than 'bug fixes,' . . . and you're given the privilege of paying for those fixes." To avoid such criticism (and gain more customers), Gateway offers customers who pay for their PCs over time the opportunity to upgrade to a new machine at the end of the contract.[31] In our discussion, when we speak of planned obsolescence, we will mean *only* style obsolescence, unless otherwise stated.

www.gateway.com

Nature of Style and Fashion

Although the words *style* and *fashion* are often used interchangeably, there is a clear distinction. A **style** is a distinctive manner of construction or presentation in any art, product, or endeavor (singing, playing, behaving). Thus we have styles in automobiles (sedans, station wagons), in bathing suits (one-piece, bikini), in furniture (early American, French provincial), and in music (jazz, rap).

A **fashion** is any style that is popularly accepted or purchased by successive groups of people over a reasonably long period of time. Not every style becomes a fashion. To be considered a fashion, or to be called "fashionable," a style must be accepted by many people. All styles listed in the preceding paragraph, except perhaps rap music, qualify as fashions. All societies, including ancient Egypt, medieval Europe, and contemporary America, have fashions.

Fashion is rooted in sociological and psychological factors. Basically, most of us are conformists. At the same time, we yearn to look and act a *little* different from others. We probably are not in revolt against custom; we simply wish to be a bit distinctive but not be accused of having bad taste or disregarding norms. Fashion furnishes the opportunity for self-expression.

Fashion–Adoption Process

The fashion-adoption process reflects the concepts of (1) cultural, social-class, and reference-group influences on consumer buying behavior, as discussed in Chapter 4, and (2) the diffusion of innovation, as explained in Chapter 8. People usually try to imitate others at the same or the next-higher socioeconomic level. One way of doing this is to purchase a product that is fashionable in the group you want to be like.

Thus the **fashion-adoption process** is a series of buying waves that arise as a particular style is popularly accepted in one group, then another group, and another, until it finally falls out of fashion. This movement, representing the introduction, rise, popular culmination, and decline of the market's acceptance of a style, is referred to as the **fashion cycle.** A case can be made that synthetic fibers such as polyester in clothing and the convertible model of automobile are two products that have run the full fashion cycle.

There are three theories of fashion adoption, as depicted in Figure 9.4:

* **Trickle-down,** where a given fashion cycle flows *downward* through several socioeconomic levels.
* **Trickle-across,** where the cycle moves *horizontally* and *simultaneously within* several socioeconomic levels.

Figure 9.4

Fashion-adoption processes.

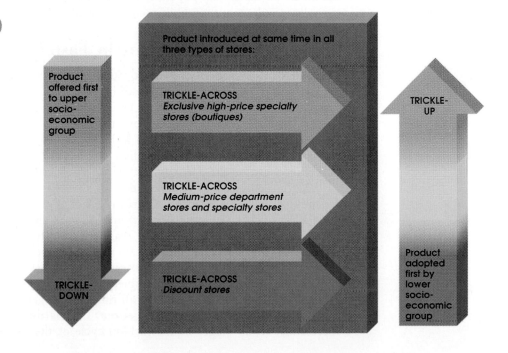

- **Trickle-up,** where a style first becomes popular at lower socioeconomic levels and then flows *upward* to become popular among higher levels.

Traditionally, the *trickle-down* theory has been used to explain the fashion-adoption process. As an example, designers of women's apparel first introduce a style to opinion leaders in the upper socioeconomic groups. If they accept the style, it quickly appears in leading fashion stores. Soon the middle-income and then the lower-income markets want to emulate the leaders, and the style is mass marketed. As its popularity wanes, the style appears in bargain-price stores and finally is no longer considered fashionable.

The *trickle-up* process also explains some product-adoption processes. Consider how styles of music such as jazz and rap became popular. Also look at blue denim pants and jackets, athletic footwear, and even pasta in the 1990s. They all had one thing in common: They were popular first with lower socioeconomic groups, and later their popularity "trickled up" to higher-income markets.

Today the *trickle-across* theory best explains the adoption process for most fashions. It's true that there is some flow downward, and obviously there is an upward flow. But, by means of modern production, communication, and transportation, companies can disseminate style information and products so rapidly that all social levels can be reached at about the same time. Now, designers of expensive fashions such as Yves Saint Laurent are even displaying their new offerings on the Internet. Recognizing this accelerated adoption process, most apparel manufacturers produce a wide *variety* of essentially one style. They also produce distinct *qualities* of the same basic style so as to appeal to different income groups.[32]

 www.yslonline.com

When an entire cycle may last only one season, sellers cannot afford to wait for style acceptance to trickle down. They must introduce it to many social levels simultaneously. For example, within a few weeks of the beginning of the fall season, the same style of dress (but at different quality levels) appears in (1) small, exclusive dress shops appealing to the upper social class, (2) large department stores aiming at the middle class, and (3) discount houses and low-price women's ready-to-wear chain stores, where the target is the portion of the lower class that has some disposable income.

Within each class, the dresses are purchased early in the season by the opinion leaders—the innovators. If the style is accepted, its sales curve rises as it becomes popular with the early adopters and then with the late adopters. Eventually, sales decline as the style loses popularity. This cycle is a horizontal movement, occurring virtually simultaneously within each of several socioeconomic levels.

Marketing Considerations in Fashion

Accurate forecasting is critical to success in fashion merchandising. This is extremely difficult, however, because the forecaster must deal with complex sociological and psychological factors. Frequently a retailer or manufacturer operates largely on intuition and inspiration, tempered by considerable experience. For example, noticing an upward trend in late-1998 sales for a T-shirt with a deep V-neck, a Banana Republic merchandiser emphasized this style in spring 1999. The hunch paid off, as the deep V-neck shirt became a hot seller.[33]

Accurate forecasting—indeed, effective marketing—has become increasingly difficult in women's fashions in recent years. One reason: Smaller numbers of female consumers are responding to annual style changes; many women are simply buying fewer clothes. Another reason: Many firms are allowing increasingly casual dress by workers. As a result, more and more often, T-shirts and stretch sweaters are in and jackets are out, especially for women.[34]

When a firm's products are subject to the fashion cycle, management must know what stage the cycle is in at all times. Managers must decide at what point to get into the cycle and when to get out. Ordinarily a retailer cannot participate successfully in all stages of the fashion cycle at the same time. Thus a specialty

It's not uncommon for a dress style created by a noted designer to be copied by other clothing firms or even retailers. Sometimes, in fact, "knockoffs" of new styles show up in department stores and discount houses *before* the original, high-price version reaches exclusive dress shops. This can happen if a competitor pays attention to the public fashion shows that some designers still use to announce their fall fashion lines, or otherwise obtains information about upcoming styles. Then the competing firm hurries through the production process, perhaps paying less attention to quality, and rushes the "knockoff" dresses into distribution channels.

Is it ethical or unethical for a firm to copy a style produced by a well-known designer and then to market this "knockoff"?

Sources: Mike Bosworth, "Gavels Pound on Knockoff Vendors," *Apparel Industry Magazine,* April 1999, pp. 86–90; and Teri Agins, "Fashion Knockoffs Hit Stores before Originals as Designers Seethe," *The Wall Street Journal,* Aug. 8, 1994, pp. A1, A4.

apparel store—whose stocks are displayed in limited numbers without price tags—should get in at the start of a fashion trend. And a department store appealing to the middle-income market should plan to enter the cycle in time to mass-market the style as it is climbing to its peak of popularity. For example, given its middle-income target market, Sears is striving to have its clothing stay within one year of the latest styles. Fundamentally, retail executives must keep in mind the product's target market in deciding at which stage(s) of the life cycle its stores should offer fashionable apparel.[35]

Summary

Many strategic decisions must be made to manage a company's assortment of products effectively. To start, a firm must select strategies regarding its product mix. One decision is how to position the product relative to competing products and other products sold by the firm.

Another strategic decision is whether or how to expand the product mix by adding items to a line and/or introducing new lines. Altering the design, packaging, or other features of existing products is still another option among the strategies of selecting the best mix. The product mix also can be changed by eliminating an entire line or by simplifying the assortment within a line. Alternatively, management may elect to trade up or trade down relative to existing products.

Executives need to understand the concept of a product life cycle, which reflects the total sales volume for a generic product category. Each of the cycle's four stages—introduction, growth, maturity, and decline—has distinctive characteristics that have implications for marketing. Managing a product as it moves through its life cycle presents a number of challenges and opportunities. Eventually, a product category may lack adequate acceptance; at that point, all or most companies should abandon their versions of this product.

Planned obsolescence is a controversial product strategy, built around the concepts of style, fashion, and the fashion cycle. Fashion—essentially a sociological and psychological phenomenon—follows a reasonably predictable pattern. With advances in communications and production, the fashion-adoption process has moved away from the traditional trickle-down pattern. Today the process is better described as trickle across. There also are examples of fashions trickling up. Managing a product, such as expensive apparel, through a fashion cycle may be even more challenging than adjusting another type of product's strategies during its life cycle.

More about **Lego**

Lego is relying on its new high-tech product, Mind-Storms, to regain a strong position in the construction-toy market. Meanwhile, a company named K'Nex Industries is challenging Lego in its more traditional product area. Introduced in 1992, K'Nex (pronounced "kuh-nex") allows children of all ages to construct items from brightly colored plastic tubes and connectors.

In contrast to the block design of Lego pieces, K'Nex are more fluid in appearance. With a basic kit, kids can construct a bridge or a Ferris wheel. More advanced sets feature pulleys and motors, but not the sort that would compete with the digital technology featured in the MindStorms product.

K'Nex attempted to fuel sales in the U.S. by obtaining a Star Wars license, but lost out to none other than Lego. After meager sales in the U.S., K'Nex switched its emphasis overseas. Thus, at this point, Lego and K'Nex are concentrating on different geographic markets. The Danish firm, Lego, is focused on the U.S. whereas the American company, K'Nex, has decided to pay primary attention to Europe. The young company's European sales are twice what they are in the U.S. In fact, K'Nex has already become the #2 construction-toy brand in Europe—behind Lego, of course. Says Joel Glickman, K'Nex's founder, "Europe has been our savior."

Glickman cites several cultural differences between American and European children in explaining the different levels of K'Nex sales on the two continents. For one thing, he says that kids in the U.S. often make the toy buying decisions in their households, and they are strongly influenced by TV commercials. European parents, however, play a larger role in such decisions, and are drawn to the educational element inherent in K'Nex products. Because of such cultural differences, and perhaps other factors as well, construction toys account for only 3% of toy sales in the U.S. versus about 10% in Europe.

Gradually, Lego Group and K'Nex Industries are competing more and more with each other. Lego has developed a new product line, called Znap. Looking like a high-tech erector set, Znap is compatible with Lego building blocks.

To counter Lego, K'Nex is implementing various strategies to get more of its products into European homes. For instance, the company has introduced cheaper versions of its product, with some selling for as little as $1.99. In addition, K'Nex is engaged in various cross-marketing arrangements, with K'Nex sets given away with everything from gasoline purchases in Belgium to newspaper subscriptions in Turkey.[36]

1. a. In what stage of the product life cycle are high-tech toys?
    b. What strategies should be used by the marketers of MindStorms and K'Nex, given the product category's life-cycle stage?

2. Could the makers of MindStorms or K'Nex use either technological or style obsolescence to stimulate sales over time?

Key Terms and Concepts

Questions and Problems

1. "It is inconsistent for management to follow concurrently the product-line strategies of *expanding* its product mix and *contracting* its product mix." Discuss.

2. "Trading up and trading down are product strategies closely related to the business cycle. Firms trade up during periods of prosperity and trade down during recessions." Do you agree? Why?

3. Name one category of goods and one category of services you believe are in the introductory stage of their life cycles. For each product, identify the market that considers your examples to be truly new.

4. Will the Internet accelerate or delay the movement of a new-product category through the introduction stage and into later stages of its life cycle?

5. What are two products that are in the decline stage of the life cycle? In each case, point out whether you think the decline is permanent. What recommendations do you have for rejuvenating the demand for either of these products?

6. How might a company's advertising strategies differ, depending on whether its brand of a product is in the introduction stage or the maturity stage of its life cycle?

7. What products, other than apparel and automobiles, stress fashion and style in marketing? Do styles exist among business products?

8. Is the trickle-across theory applicable to the fashion-adoption process in product lines other than women's apparel? Explain, using examples.

9. Planned obsolescence is criticized as a social and economic waste because we are urged to buy things we do not like and do not need. What is your opinion? If you object to planned obsolescence, what are your recommendations for correcting the situation?

Hands-On Marketing

1. Select a product category in which you are interested. Go to either the library or the Internet and identify the national or state trade association for this product category. Then obtain from the association sales figures for this product over its history and other information that will allow you to plot the life cycle for this product. What stage of the life cycle is this product in? Explain.

2. Arrange a meeting with a supermarket manager or a department manager in a supermarket. Discuss how the manager handles the challenge of line extensions. In which product category are line extensions most common? When new items are added to the line, how does the manager find space for the new entries—by giving more space to this category, dropping other items carrying this same brand, pruning other brands in this category, or some other means? What criteria are used in making this decision?

10

Brands, Packaging, and Other Product Features

"To combat the brand's stodgy image as well as the new entrants into the jeans market, Levi's developed an aggressive marketing campaign . . ."

Is the **Levi's** Brand Worn Out?

At one time, the Levi's brand name was synonymous with the word *cool*. Many celebrities, including James Dean and Marlon Brando, wore them. But Dean has been dead for more than four decades, and most young people today remember Brando as the paunchy, old guy who talked funny in the *Godfather* movies.

It's been quite awhile since a popular celebrity has been associated with Levi Strauss & Co. (LS), the once-dominant denim company. Besides, young people now need more than a pair of straight-leg blue jeans to express their individuality and perhaps their frustrations. As a result, the Levi's brand and, even more important, sales of its products have declined steadily, from a peak of $7 billion in 1996 to just over $5 billion in 1999.

The firm certainly faces a vastly different challenge than was faced by its founder, whose name was, of course, Levi Strauss. While selling canvas tents to the prospectors in the California gold rush almost 150 years ago, he found greater demand for durable pants made of cotton denim fabric. Denim pants steadily grew in popularity, eventually becoming "the uniform" of the American working class.

Then in the 1930s, *Vogue* magazine declared denim pants stylish. And in the 1960s, they represented a "statement," standing for freedom and individualism. By this time, the word *Levi's* had almost become the generic term for blue jeans. In the 1980s, Levi's faced tough competition from designer upstarts like Sergio Valente and Calvin Klein. LS responded with an innovative advertising campaign that focused on Levi's line of 501 blue jeans. The campaign's attitude was urban and gritty, and—most important—it was successful.

It seems the executives at LS could do no wrong. Perhaps they thought that too, because they became complacent, according to some critics. In 1990, the company commanded 31% of the jeans market in the U.S.; by 1999, that figure had plummeted to 17%. This decrease in market share can be attributed to many factors.

For one thing, middlemen's brands and designer jeans have taken large chunks of Levi's business. The Gap stopped selling Levi's and other brands and introduced its own line of jeans in 1991. Since then, other large chains, including Sears and The Limited, have done the same thing. J.C. Penney's brand of Arizona jeans, for instance, has been heavily marketed to teenagers through TV and print ads as well as a website. In 1997, Arizona was the third most popular jeans brand, right behind perennial leaders Levi's and Lee. Sears and J.C. Penney still carry the Levi's brand, but it is no longer the focus of their promotional efforts. Not only that, but many of these retailers' brands are typically less expensive than Levi's, sometimes $10 a pair cheaper.

In addition to competition from retailers' brands, Levi's is facing a revival of designer jeans. Tommy Hilfiger, Ralph Lauren, and supermodel Naomi Campbell are a few of the big names backing denim pants. These brands are typically cutting-edge fashion, and they react very quickly to the fickle tastes of teenagers who are willing to pay more (starting at $50 a pair) for the latest looks. And, according to a Lee executive, "It's very important that you attract this age group. By the time they're 24, they've adopted brands that they will use for the rest of their lives."

In recent years, teens have tended to associate Levi's with the jeans their parents wore. As one teenage girl commented, "Levi's styles are too tight and for the older generation, like middle-aged people." Levi's was slow to react to new trends in the marketplace, such as wide-leg and boot-cut jeans. "The company totally missed the significance of the inner city and the huge impact it has on trends," says one retail consultant. In just four years, the portion of teenage boys in the U.S. who considered Levi's a "cool" brand dropped from 21% to 7%.

LS was experiencing some success, however, with its Dockers line of cotton twill pants and related casual wear. However, Dockers consumed a considerable portion of the company's marketing resources.

To combat the brand's stodgy image as well as the new entrants into the jeans market, Levi's developed an aggressive marketing campaign in 1997 that trumpeted the brand name instead of its individual products. One set of outdoor ads tackled the designer competition directly by featuring the Levi's logo with copy that read, "Tommy wore them. Ralph wore them. Calvin wore them." Another ad showed Marilyn Monroe and Marlin Brando with the tag line, "Our models can beat up their models."[1]

What else, if anything, can Levi Strauss & Co. do to revitalize its Levi's brand?

 www.levi.com

As the Levi's case illustrates, a brand can be all important for many products. Otherwise, how do you account for some consumers wanting Bayer aspirin and others preferring or at least accepting Walgreen's brand, when both are physically and chemically the identical product? Other consumers' choices are influenced not only by the brand, but also by the package, design, or another product feature. Because these product features are important elements in a marketing program, we devote this chapter to them. After studying this chapter, you should be able to explain:

chapter goals

- The nature and importance of brands.
- Characteristics of a good brand name.
- Branding strategies of producers and middlemen.
- Why and how a growing number of firms are building and using brand equity.
- The nature and importance of packaging and labeling.
- Major packaging strategies.
- The marketing implications of other product features—design, color, and quality—that can satisfy consumers' wants.

Brands

The word *brand* is comprehensive; it encompasses other narrower terms. A **brand** is a name and/or mark intended to identify the product of one seller or group of sellers and differentiate the product from competing products.[2]

A **brand name** consists of words, letters, and/or numbers that can be vocalized. A **brand mark** is the part of the brand that appears in the form of a symbol, design, or distinctive color or lettering. A brand mark is recognized by sight but cannot be expressed when a person pronounces the brand name. Crest, Coors, and Gillette are brand names. Brand marks are the distinctively lined globe of AT&T and the Nike "swoosh." Green Giant (canned and frozen vegetable products) and Arm & Hammer (baking soda) are both brand names and brand marks. Sometimes the term *logo* (short for *logotype*) is used interchangeably with brand mark or even brand name, especially if the name is written in a distinctive, stylized fashion.

A **trademark** is a brand that has been adopted by a seller and given legal protection. (A trademark for a service has come to be called, not surprisingly, a *service mark*. Our use of *trademark* also covers *service mark*.) A trademark includes not just the brand mark, as many people believe, but also the brand name. The Lanham Act of 1946 permits firms to register trademarks with the federal government to protect them from use or misuse by other companies. The Trademark Law Revision Act, which took effect in 1989, is intended to strengthen the registration system to the benefit of U.S. firms. In Europe, companies can now submit a single application to obtain trademark registration and protections throughout the European Union.[3]

Companies strive vigorously, even filing law suits, to protect their trademarks. Recent instances include the makers of Bud Ice beer and Munsingwear battling over who has the rights to the penguin symbol; IBM and a small consulting firm arguing about the rights to a stylized "e" that the computer company uses to promote its various "e-business" products; and GoTo.com and Disney's Go Network both wanting to use a green traffic signal as part of logos for Internet enterprises.[4]

One method of classifying brands is on the basis of who owns them. Thus we have **producers' brands** and **middlemen's brands,** the latter being owned by retailers or wholesalers. Florsheim (shoes), Prozac (Eli Lilly & Company's antidepressant drug), Courtyard by Marriott (lodging), and Qantas (an Australian airline) are

 www.florsheim.com

Who's got the Bud?

A company trying to establish a global brand may find another firm using the same brand in some countries. For example, Anheuser-Busch Companies (A-B), the St. Louis-based brewery, isn't the only company placing the Budweiser brand on beer. A century-old brewery in the Czech Republic, Budejovicky Budvar, sells a Budweiser brew in parts of eastern Europe as well as Germany. The American brand is sold throughout most of the rest of the world. Further, the Czech brand is called "the beer of kings," and the American brand "the king of beers."

What's the problem? Essentially, both brewers lay claim to the Budweiser trademark. A-B began making Budweiser beer in the U.S. in 1876. Then in 1895, Czechs in a community called Budweis started a brewery to make and sell its own Budweiser beer. When the two enterprises began to expand into other countries, the dispute over the Budweiser trademark erupted.

Eventually, in 1939, the competing breweries agreed to divide up the world market with respect to where each concern could use the Budweiser brand. Thus A-B affixes various names on its product in European countries—the well-known Budweiser in some, but Bud, American Bud, and Anheuser Busch B in others. The only area in which both brewers use the Budweiser brand is Great Britain.

Wanting to develop its version of Budweiser as a global brand, A-B has persisted in seeking an agreement with Budvar. In late 1995, A-B offered to pay the Czech brewery $200 million and to purchase 10% of the Czech Republic's finest hops (a key ingredient in beer) for at least 10 years in exchange for the worldwide rights to the Budweiser name. Because the name is so well known, the Czech brewery saw added sales potential for its own Budweiser brand and, consequently, rejected A-B's proposal.

The two breweries continue to battle over the rights to the brand name in the courts of various countries. In mid-1999, after spotting the Czech brew being served in Maryland, A-B asked the federal government to examine whether Budvar was illegally importing its product into the U.S. The Czechs retaliated by requesting that the World Trade Organization declare that the only beer that can be called Budweiser has to be brewed in the Czech city that was named Budweis. And the dispute continues!

Sources: "Battle of the Buds," *St. Louis Post-Dispatch*, Nov. 28, 1999, p. E1; "A-B Sues Czech Budweiser Maker," *St. Louis Post-Dispatch*, July 13, 1999, p. C7; "Czechs Drop Attempt to End Bud War," *St. Louis Post-Dispatch*, Nov. 12, 1997, p. 1D; Robert L. Koenig, "Bud War," *St. Louis Post-Dispatch*, Oct. 22, 1995, p. 1A; and Roger Thurow, "The King of Beers and Beer of Kings Are at Lagerheads," *The Wall Street Journal*, Apr. 3, 1992, p. A1.

producers' brands; Lucerne (Safeway), Craftsman (Sears), and St. John's Bay (J.C. Penney) are middlemen's brands.

The terms *national* and *private* have been used to describe producer and middleman brand ownership, respectively. However, marketing people prefer the *producer-middleman* terminology. To say that a brand of poultry feed marketed in three states by a small Birmingham, Alabama, manufacturer is a *national* brand, or that the brands of Wal-Mart and Sears are *private* brands, stretches the meaning of these two terms.

Reasons for Branding

For consumers, brands make it easy to identify goods or services. They aid shoppers in moving quickly through a supermarket, discount outlet, or other retail store and in making purchase decisions. Brands also help assure consumers that they will get consistent quality when they reorder.

For sellers, brands can be promoted. They are easily recognized when displayed in a store or included in advertising. Branding reduces price comparisons. That is, because brands are another factor to be considered in comparing different products, branding reduces the likelihood of purchase decisions based solely on price. The reputation of a brand also influences customer loyalty among buyers of services as well as business and consumer goods. Finally, branding can differentiate

Despite the difficulty of differentiating a commodity, Morton International succeeded in creating a well-known, favored brand of salt. Some Morton ads, including this one, have been aimed at reinforcing the brand name. Realizing that salt is in the maturity stage of its life cycle, other Morton ads promote new uses for the product, ranging from eradicating ketchup stains from carpet to making panty hose resistant to runs by washing them in Morton Salt.

 www.mortonsalt.com

His teeth.

His ammo.

His wig.

His salt.

Which was stolen

from George Washington?

In 1777, British troops captured the lion's share of General Washington's all-important salt supply. For a time, this starved the upstart Americans of a nutrient absolutely vital to their health. It also served as a reminder that if victory is sweet, defeat is some-times very, very salty.
Salt has always made history, and Morton has always made salt.

When it rains, it pours.
www.mortonsalt.com

commodities (Sunkist oranges, Morton salt, and Domino sugar, for example). A wholesaler is even trying to establish a Hearts on Fire brand for diamonds.[5]

Not all brands are widely and favorably recognized by their target markets. And among those that are, many are unable to maintain a position of prominence. However, as a result of such activities as aggressive promotion and careful quality control, a few brands (Kodak film and Gillette razors) retain their leadership positions over a long time. Consequently, enormous amounts of money are spent to purchase companies that have widely recognized brands. Philip Morris paid $11 *billion* to acquire the Kraft Company, including its Velveeta cheese, Miracle Whip salad dressing, and other leading brands. Recently, Italy's Gucci Group bought another firm in order to acquire several well-known brands, including Yves Saint Laurent (luxury fashion accessories) and Van Cleef & Arpels (fragrances).[6]

Reasons for Not Branding

Two responsibilities come with brand ownership: (1) promoting the brand and (2) maintaining a consistent quality of output. Many firms do not brand their products because they are unable or unwilling to assume these responsibilities.

Some items remain unbranded because they cannot be physically differentiated from other firms' products. Clothespins, nails, and raw materials (coal, cotton, wheat) are examples of goods for which product differentiation, including branding, is generally unknown. The perishable nature of products such as fresh fruits and vegetables works against branding. However, well-known brands such as Dole pineapples and Chiquita bananas demonstrate that even agricultural products can be branded successfully.

 www.chiquita.com

Selecting a Good Brand Name

Some brand names are so good that they contribute to the success of products. Consider, for examples, DieHard batteries and the Roach Motel (which is a pest-eradication device, not a discount motel). But it takes more than a clever brand name to ensure success in the marketplace. Witness People Express, the discount airline that failed despite the apt name. Other brand names are so poor that they are a factor in product failures. Occasionally products achieve success despite poor brand names—consider Exxon, which had no meaning when it was first introduced.

Choosing a name for a product may appear trivial, but it's not. Al Ries, a well-known consultant, has gone so far (perhaps too far) as to say, "The most important element in a marketing program—and the one over which marketing managers can exert the most control—is the naming of a product."[7]

The Challenge

Nowadays, selecting a good brand name for a new product is especially challenging. The reason? We're running out of possibilities. On the one hand, about 10,000 new products are launched annually; on the other hand, only 50,000 words comprise the standard desk-size dictionary.[8] Further, many words either already adorn products (such as Pert Plus, Cascade, and Veryfine) or are unsuitable as brand names (such as obnoxious, hypocrite, and deceased).

One solution is to combine numbers with words, numbers, and/or letters to form a brand name. Examples include Net2Phone (an Internet telecommunications service), Formula 409 (household cleaner), WD-40 (lubricant and protectant), and Lotus 1-2-3 (software). Another possibility is to create a brand name that isn't part of the English language. Examples of so-called *morphemes* include Ameritrade stock brokerage, Lexus autos, Compaq computers, and Agilent Technologies (a subsidiary of Hewlett-Packard Co.). The naming process isn't cheap, costing $25,000 and up for the name itself and then much more to promote the new brand.[9]

Desirable Characteristics

Various characteristics determine the desirability of a brand name for either a good or a service.[10] It's difficult to find a brand name that rates well on every attribute.

Agilent Technologies was formed as a result of a corporate realignment at Hewlett-Packard Company in 1999. The new firm is a diversified technology company operating worldwide. The Agilent part of the name is a morpheme. Agilent is based on the word *agile* because it conveys the need for ongoing change and adaptation in order to serve customers well.

 www.agilent.com

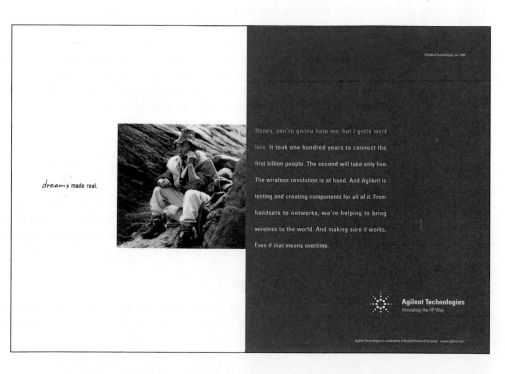

Still, a brand name should have as many of the following five characteristics as possible:

- *Suggest something about the product, particularly its benefits and use.* Names connoting benefits include Beautyrest, Mr. Goodwrench, Minute Rice, and—perhaps best of all—DieHard. Product use is suggested by Dustbuster, Ticketron, and La-Z-Boy chairs.
- *Be easy to pronounce, spell, and remember.* Simple, short, one-syllable names such as Tide, Ban, Aim, and Surf are helpful. However, even some short names, such as Aetna and Inacom, aren't easily pronounced by some consumers. Other brands that may not meet this criterion, at least not in the U.S., include Frusen-Glädje (ice cream), Au Bon Pain (bakeries), and Asahi (beer).
- *Be distinctive.* Brands with names like National, Star, Ideal, United, Allied, or Standard fail on this point. Many services firms begin their brand names with adjectives connoting strength and then add a description of the business, creating brands such as Allied Van Lines and United Parcel Service. But are these really distinctive?
- *Be adaptable to additions to the product line.* A family name such as Kellogg, Lipton, or Ford may serve the purpose better than a highly distinctive name suggesting product benefits. When fast-food restaurants added breakfasts to their menus, McDonald's name fit better than Burger King or Pizza Hut. Likewise, names like Alaska Airlines and Southwest Airlines may inhibit geographic expansion more than a name such as United Airlines.
- *Be capable of registration and legal protection.* Brand names are covered under the Lanham Act, its 1989 revision, and other laws.

Protecting a Brand Name

A firm with a well-known, successful brand name needs to actively safeguard it; otherwise, this valuable asset can be damaged—or even lost entirely—in either of two ways.

Product Counterfeiting

Some unscrupulous manufacturers engage in **product counterfeiting** by placing a highly regarded brand on their offering, disregarding the basic, yet critical fact that they do not own the rights to the brand. If you have ever been to Manhattan in New York City, you probably have been offered "genuine" Rolex or Gucci watches for $10 to $20 by a street vendor. Obviously, these are counterfeit products. Counterfeiting can be found in many categories, including leather goods, athletic footwear, software, toys (notably video games), and automobile replacement parts.

According to the latest estimates, imitation products cost American companies as much as $200 *billion* annually. Nintendo alone estimates that "video-game piracy" cost the company over $700 million in 1998. Because it's relatively easy to do and because law enforcement agencies do not vigorously pursue violators, a top FBI official called product counterfeiting "the crime of the 21st century."[11]

Counterfeiters can't be eliminated entirely. However, companies are not powerless in combating knockoffs. First, they need to be on the lookout for counterfeit goods carrying one of their brands. Second, when imitations and their producers are identified, legal action should be taken against the violators. Firms cannot afford to ignore this illegal practice because it can diminish the worth of a trademark owner's products.[12]

Generic Usage

Over a period of years, some brand names become so well accepted that they are commonly used instead of the generic names of the particular product categories.[13]

Branding on the Internet

There are basically two kinds of companies doing business on the Internet—existing companies and new start-ups. For all of them, especially the new enterprises, branding strategies and tactics are—or should be—receiving a great deal of attention.

Existing companies typically just add "dot com" to their company names when they go online. There's Nordstrom.com, USAToday.com, Revlon.com, and Coca-Cola.com. These firms are seeking to trade on the reputations developed over many years in business. Occasionally, an existing company will use a new brand name for an online product, especially if it wants to differentiate the product from its current offerings and perhaps appeal to consumers it is not presently serving. That's why CompUSA, the chain of computer superstores, chose cozone.com as the brand name for its new online sales site.

For new firms that are established specifically to seize business opportunities on the Internet, the branding decision is critical because this name creates a first impression in consumers' minds. It often serves as the company name as well. Internet-based brands that have become well known in recent years include Amazon.com, Yahoo!, America Online, and eToys.

Marketers are finding that what works in the real world may not be applicable to cyberspace. That's certainly true for branding. Notable differences include:

- Online, consumers ordinarily decide whether or not to view a promotional message. With traditional media, such as TV and magazines, ads are interspersed with other content that the consumer wants to see or hear. On the Internet, users decide what sites to visit and whether or not to look at a banner or some other type of ad.

- On the Internet, most consumers prefer so-called rational messages to emotional messages. That is, providing useful information and other help (such as financial-planning tools or fashion guidelines) appears to be most effective in keeping consumers at a particular website.

- The pool of potential brand names is more limited in cyberspace than in the real world. For one thing, although two or more companies can have the same word, such as *Express,* in their names, that word can be the basis for only one domain name in cyberspace. By the end of 1999, an organization that registers domain names had already given out over 5,000,000 "dot.com" addresses. There has been spirited bidding to acquire the rights to some simple names, such as *autos.com.* In fact, the rights to *business.com* sold for $7.5 million.

- The practice of "domain squatting," in which an individual or company registers famous names with the intent of selling the domain names at a later date, complicated Internet branding. A federal law banning domain squatting took effect in late 1999. In perhaps the first case tied to the new law, Heritage Carbide sued the sales manager of a competing firm for registering *heritagecarbide.com* as an Internet domain name. The small manufacturer of pump parts claimed that the competitor's actions represented unfair competition and trademark infringement.

Will the attention given to online branding subside soon? Probably not. In fact, an advertising agency head referred to branding on the Internet as "the biggest issue facing the marketing community in 25 years."

Sources: Christine Chen, "A Good Name Is Priceless—Some of the Time," *Fortune,* Feb. 7, 2000, p. 184; James Heckman, "Trademarks Protected through New Cyber Act," *Marketing News,* Jan. 3, 2000, p. 6; Rhonda L. Rundle, "Small Firm Sues Rival in Test on Cyberpiracy," *The Wall Street Journal,* Dec. 27, 1999, p. B6; Nick Wingfield, "The Game of the Name," *The Wall Street Journal,* Nov. 22, 1999, p. R14; Ellen Neuborne and Robert D. Hof, "Branding on the Net," *Business Week,* Nov. 9, 1998, pp. 76–78, 82, 84, 86; and Erica B. Garay, "Trademark Protection," *Marketing Management,* Fall/Winter 1998, pp. 54–56.

 www.cozone.com

Examples follow:

Generic Terms That Formerly Were Brand Names

aspirin	escalator	linoleum	thermos
brassiere	harmonica	nylon	yo-yo
cellophane	kerosene	shredded wheat	zipper

Originally these names were trademarks that could be used only by the owner. What happened? Well, a brand name can become generic in two primary ways:

- There is no simple generic name available, so the public uses the brand name as a generic name. This occurred with shredded wheat, nylon, and cellophane. The Formica Corporation wages an ongoing struggle, thus far successful, to retain the legal status of its Formica brand of decorative laminate.[14]

www.formica.com

- As contradictory as it appears, sometimes a firm is too effective in promoting a brand name. Although not yet legally generic, names such as Levi's, Band-Aid, Scotch Tape, and Kleenex are on the borderline. These brand names have been promoted so heavily and so successfully that many people use them generically. To illustrate, which terms do you use in conversation— adhesive bandage or Band-Aid, facial tissue or Kleenex? We suspect the latter in both cases.

There are various means to prevent the generic use of a brand name:

- Right after the brand name, place the ® symbol (if your brand is a registered trademark for a good), ™ (if it is not registered), or ℠ (for a service).
- Better yet, use the brand name together with the generic name—Dacron brand polyester, for instance.
- Call attention to and challenge improper use of your brand name. Rollerblade Inc. has gone so far as to sue competitors who use "rollerblade" as a generic word. Thus the maker of Rollerblades disdains a statement like "I broke my neck rollerblading" and prefers the term *in-line skating*.[15]

To protect its famous brand name, Xerox Corp. runs humorous ads to make a serious point, namely that Xerox is a brand name. The ads stress that Xerox is neither a verb nor a common noun. Also note how the ad indicates that Xerox should be used in conjunction with a noun, such as copier or duplicator.

www.xerox.com

"But Mr. Carruthers, you said you needed forty Xeroxes."

Mr. Carruthers used our name incorrectly. That's why he got 40 Xerox copiers, when what he really wanted was 40 copies made on his Xerox copier.

He didn't know that Xerox, as a trademark of Xerox Corporation, should be followed by the descriptive word for the particular product, such as "Xerox duplicator" or "Xerox copier."

And should only be used as a noun when referring to the corporation itself.

If Mr. Carruthers had asked for 40 copies or 40 photocopies made on his Xerox copier, he would have gotten exactly what he wanted.

And if you use Xerox properly, you'll get exactly what you want, too.

P.S. You're welcome to make 40 copies or 40 photocopies of this ad. Preferably on your Xerox copier.

XEROX

•Branding Strategies

Both producers and middlemen face strategic decisions regarding the branding of their goods or services.

Producers' Strategies

Producers must decide whether to brand their products and whether to sell any or all of their output under middlemen's brands.

Marketing Entire Output under Producer's Own Brands

Companies that rely strictly on their own brands usually are very large, well financed, and well managed. Maytag and IBM, for example, have broad product lines, well-established distribution systems, and large shares of the market. The reasons why a producer relies strictly on its own brands were covered in the earlier section on the importance of branding to the seller.

A small proportion of manufacturers rely strictly on this strategy, refusing to produce items to be sold as retailers' or wholesalers' brands. Gillette is one such company. The firm's top executive has said that manufacturing so-called private-label products would be "a sign of weakness." A company vice president was more blunt, "If any manager did that, he should be shot by the shareholders."[16] This stubbornness will not eliminate competition from middlemen, however. Many middlemen want to market under their own brands. If one manufacturer refuses to sell to them, they simply go to another.

It's particularly difficult for a new firm to produce strictly for its own brands. Only a minority of manufacturers employ this strategy, and the number seems to be decreasing. A primary reason is that there are lots of opportunities to make products to which middlemen apply their own brands.

Branding of Fabricating Parts and Materials

Some producers use a strategy of *branding fabricating parts and materials* (manufactured goods that become part of another product following subsequent manufacturing).[17] This strategy is used in marketing Dan River cottons, Acrilan fabrics, and many automotive parts such as spark plugs, batteries, and oil filters. DuPont has consistently and successfully used this strategy, notably with its Lycra spandex fiber and Stainmaster stain repellant for carpets.

With this strategy, the seller seeks to develop a market preference for its branded parts or materials. Dolby Labs seeks to create a market situation in which buyers insist that a stereo sound system include a Dolby noise-reduction component. This firm wants to convince manufacturers that their stereo sound systems will sell better if they contain Dolby noise-reduction units.

This strategy is most likely to be effective when the particular type of fabricating parts or materials has two characteristics:

- The product is also a consumer good that is bought for replacement purposes—Champion spark plugs and Delco batteries, for example.
- The item is a key part of the finished product—a microprocessor within a personal computer, for instance. Intel Corp. developed the slogan "Intel Inside" to strengthen its product's position. The campaign was so successful that some computer makers, including IBM and Compaq, feared that the brand of personal computer would become less important than the brand of microprocessor contained in the machine. For a while, IBM even stopped using the Intel slogan in order to emphasize its own brand, but eventually the computer maker restored the familiar "Intel Inside" in its ads.[18]

Marketing under Middlemen's Brands

A widespread strategy among manufacturers is to sell part or all of their output to middlemen for branding by these customers. Firms such as Borden, Keebler, and Reynolds Metals have their own well-known brands, and they also produce goods for branding by middlemen.

This approach allows a manufacturer to "hedge its bets." A company employing this strategy hopes its own brands will appeal to some loyal customers, whereas middlemen's brands are of interest to other, perhaps more cost-conscious shoppers.[19] Moreover, for a manufacturer, the output produced for middlemen's brands ordinarily represents additional sales. This strategy also helps a manufacturer fully utilize its plant capacity.

One drawback of this strategy is that the manufacturer may lose some customers for its own brands. Another drawback to marketing under middlemen's brands is that the producer's revenues depend on the strength of the middleman's marketing campaign for that brand. This problem grows as the proportion of a producer's output going to middlemen's brands increases.

Middlemen's Strategies

The question of whether to brand must also be answered by middlemen.

Carry Only Producers' Brands

Most retailers and wholesalers follow this policy. Why? They do not have the finances or other resources to promote a brand and maintain its quality.

Carry Both Producers' and Middlemen's Brands

Many large retailers and some large wholesalers stock popular producers' brands and also have their own labels. Sears, for instance, offers an assortment of manufacturers' brands such as Healthtex children's clothing and Firestone tires as well as its own brands such as Kenmore appliances and Craftsman tools. On its website, Sears even labels its own labels as the "brands you trust."

 www.sears.com

Middlemen may find it advantageous to market their own brands, in place of or in addition to producers' brands, because it increases their control over their target markets. A retailer's brand can differentiate its products. If customers prefer a given retailer's brand, sometimes called a *store brand,* they can get it only from that retailer. Examples include:

Some Retailers' Brands of Apparel

Nordstrom: Classiques Entier
Macy's: Charter Club, Austin Gray
Saks Fifth Avenue: The Works, SFA Collections

Prices on producers' brands sometimes are cut drastically when retail stores carrying these brands compete with each other. For an extended time, clothing carrying the labels of designers such as Ralph Lauren and Liz Claiborne was subject to price cutting. A retailer might avoid at least some of this price competition by establishing its own appealing brands. As a result, some large retailers (Saks Fifth Avenue and Nordstrom, for example) increased their stocks of upper-price apparel carrying the stores' brands. Some chains also cut their stocks of clothing carrying designer brands.[20]

Furthermore, middlemen usually can sell their brands at prices below those of producers' brands and still earn higher gross margins. For example, in dry cereals, a store brand may provide up to twice as much gross profits as a producer's brand.[21] This is possible because middlemen often can acquire merchandise carrying their own brands at lower costs than similar merchandise carrying producers' brands. Costs may be lower because manufacturers have to pay to advertise and sell their own brands, but these costs are not included in the prices of products sold for branding by middlemen. Also, producers may offer good prices in this situation because they are anxious to get the extra business. In some cases, the costs may be lower because the quality of the products carrying middlemen's brands is lower than the quality of competing products bearing producers' brands.

Middlemen have to be careful in pricing their own brands. According to one study, if store brands of groceries are not priced at least 10% below producers' brands, many consumers will not buy them. However, if the store brand is more than 20% lower in price, some consumers become suspicious about quality. In contrast, another study concluded that other factors such as relative quality are more important than price level in determining the success of middlemen's brands versus producers' brands.[22]

Middlemen's brands have had their greatest impact in the marketing of consumer packaged goods, such as groceries and personal-care products. The Safeway supermarket chain has long relied on Lucerne and other brands it owns. Loblaw's, the largest supermarket chain in Canada, has found great success with its President's Choice (PC) brand. In fact, Loblaw's has agreements with various American chains to distribute PC products in the U.S. Wal-Mart, the largest retailer, is multiplying its store brands as well, with the Sam's American Choice label attached to colas, cookies, and other products. Recently, Wal-Mart introduced its own laundry detergent, putting it in direct competition with one of its major suppliers, Procter & Gamble. According to observers, Wal-Mart's move was intended in part to pressure P&G into reducing its wholesale prices.[23]

In total, so-called private brands generate about $35 *billion* in annual sales, perhaps more, in the U.S. After leveling off in the mid-1990s, middlemen's brands are gaining share in supermarkets, now accounting for about one-sixth of total sales in this category of stores. They continue to expand their positions in drugstores and discount outlets as well. The outlook for middlemen's brands is strong, with one study indicating that 60% of retailers plan to place more emphasis on middlemen's brands. According to one forecast, the private-brand food business will account for $100 billion in volume in North America by 2005.[24]

Many retailers have also altered their private-brand strategies. In the past, stores introduced their own brands primarily to give shoppers lower-priced options and to boost profit margins. Now, to an increasing degree, major retailers are enhancing the quality of the middlemen's brands in their stores. Retailers see store brands as a way of differentiating their particular stores from competition. Some merchants are even offering "premium" private-brand products.

To counter middlemen's brands, some leading manufacturers, including Procter & Gamble and Philip Morris, have cut prices on a number of their well-known brands, including Pampers diapers, Tide detergent, and Marlboro cigarettes. Other manufacturers, including Gillette, have concentrated on convincing consumers of the superiority of their brands in relation to private brands. All factors considered, neither producers' brands nor middlemen's brands have demonstrated a convincing competitive superiority over the other in the marketplace. Consequently, the "battle of the brands" shows every indication of remaining intense.[25]

Carry Generic Products

In the late 1970s, several supermarket chains introduced products sold under their generic names. **Generic products** are simply labeled according to the contents, such as peanut butter, cottage cheese, or paper towels. These unbranded products generally sell for at least 20% less than producers' brands and 10 to 20% less than middlemen's brands. They appeal to the most price-conscious consumers. Although they are the nutritional or functional equivalent of branded products, generics may not have the color, size, and consistency of appearance of branded items.

For a while, generic products captured a large enough share of total sales in some product categories to be a major factor in the battle of the brands.

Generics' share of total grocery sales peaked at 2.5% in the early 1980s, but has been declining since then.[26] As supermarkets have improved and promoted their own brands, a growing number of shoppers apparently are choosing middlemen's brands as a compromise between generic products and producers' brands.

Strategies Common to Producers and Middlemen

Producers and middlemen alike must choose strategies with respect to branding their product mixes, branding for market saturation, and joint branding activity with another company.

Branding within a Product Mix

At least three different strategies are used by firms that sell more than one product:

- *A separate name for each product.* This strategy is employed by Lever Brothers and Procter & Gamble. Recently, Citigroup, the largest financial services firm in the U.S., decided to emphasize its individual brands (such as Travelers, Commercial Credit, and Citibank) rather than its overall corporate identity. Similarly, to reduce brand confusion, Bass Hotels & Resorts is removing the Holiday Inn name from its upscale Crowne Plaza and economy-priced Express establishments.[27]

- *The company name combined with a product name.* Examples include Johnson's Pledge and Johnson's Glo-Coat, and Kellogg's Rice Krispies and Kellogg's Corn Pops.

- *The company name alone.* Today few companies rely exclusively on this policy. However, it is followed for the most part by Heinz and Libby in the food field as well as by General Electric in various industries.

www.armorall.com

Using the company name for branding purposes, often termed **family branding,** makes it simpler and less expensive to introduce new, related products to a line.[28] Also, the prestige of a brand can be spread more easily if it appears on several products rather than on only one. Armor All Products took advantage of the smashing success of Armor All Protectant by adding other car-care products, such as Armor All Cleaner and Armor All Car Wax. A company name is best suited for marketing products that are related in quality, in use, or in some other manner.

Branding with the company name places a greater burden on the firm to maintain consistent quality among all products. One bad item can reflect unfavorably, even disastrously, on all other products carrying the same brand. For this reason, many companies prefer to let each individual product succeed or fail on its own—the first branding strategy in the list above.

Branding for Market Saturation

With increasing frequency, firms are employing a **multiple-brand strategy** to increase their total sales in a market. They have more than one brand of essentially the same product, aimed either at the same target market or at distinct target markets. Suppose, for example, that a company has built one type of sales appeal around a given brand. To reach other segments of the market, the company may use other appeals with other brands. Two Procter & Gamble detergents, Tide and Dreft, illustrate this point. Some people think that if Tide is strong enough to clean soiled work clothes, it should not be used on lingerie and other fine clothing. For these people P&G has Dreft, a detergent promoted as being more gentle than Tide.

Sometimes, multiple brands are necessary to penetrate separate target markets. For instance, Black & Decker (B&D) tools have strong appeal to do-it-yourselfers but not to professional tradespeople. Hence, B&D removed its company name

Not surprisingly, Church & Dwight Co. was interested in capitalizing on the widespread recognition of its Arm & Hammer brand. As indicated by this insert in Sunday newspapers, the Arm & Hammer name has been applied to several laundry products. Not all extensions succeed; Arm & Hammer deodorant was a failure—twice.

 www.armhammer.com

from power tools aimed at tradespeople and switched to DeWalt, the name of a maker of high-quality stationary saws that was acquired by Black & Decker years ago.[29]

Cobranding

More and more often, two separate companies or two divisions within the same company agree to place both of their respective brands on a particular product or enterprise. This arrangement is termed **cobranding,** or dual branding.

Cobranding is increasingly evident in the food products field and also in franchising. Boxes of Kellogg's Pop-Tarts proclaim that the product is made with Smucker's fruit filling. Heath Bars, Sunkist lemons, and Ocean Spray cranberries are all frequently promoted ingredients of other products, such as Nabisco's Fat Free Cranberry Newtons "with Ocean Spray cranberries." In franchising, cobranding occurs when two or more companies agree to share the same or adjacent retail space. Examples range from Church's Chicken and White Castle sharing space to MBE Business Express centers opening units in AmeriSuites hotels.[30]

As with any marketing strategy or tactic, cobranding has potential benefits and drawbacks. This form of cooperation can result in a differential advantage over competitors. Cobranding can provide added revenues for one or both of the participating firms, such as the fee paid to Sunkist Growers by General Mills in order to use the Sunkist name on packages of Betty Crocker lemon bar mix. When two franchises cooperate, they may ring up greater combined sales than if they were in separate locations. The biggest potential drawbacks to cobranding are possible overexposure of a brand name and, even more significant, the risk of damaging a brand's reputation if the cooperative endeavor fails.

Building and Using Brand Equity

In the minds of many consumers, just having a brand name such as Sony, Kenmore, Sheraton, or Hallmark adds value to a product. In particular, brands like these connote favorable attributes (such as quality or economy). What we're talking about is **brand equity**, which is the value a brand adds to a product.[31]

Brands rated the best in the U.S. and—for comparison purposes—in the United Kingdom and Argentina are shown in Table 10.1. There is little overlap across the top-10 lists. In fact, only four brands—Mercedes-Benz, BMW, Kodak, and Disney World—were on two of the three lists. Also note that only two services—Disney World and Sheraton—were on any of the lists, and both were given high marks by consumers in Argentina.

Brands are considered very important assets for a company. The former head of Quaker's food business stated it this way: "If this company were to split up, I would give you the property, plant and equipment and I would take the brands and the trademarks, and I would fare far better than you." Given the importance of brands, several methods have been developed to measure their value. One is consumer evaluations, which are reported in Table 10.1. Another method, developed by the Interbrand consulting firm, considers the worth of a particular brand to be the present value of future profits that will be derived from products carrying that brand. In Interbrand's latest ranking, all of the top-10 brands are part of U.S. companies, with Coca-Cola, Microsoft, and IBM at the top of the pack. The top-ranked brand from outside the U.S. is Nokia of Finland.[32]

If you're not convinced that a brand name by itself can have much value, consider some research results. In one study, the proportion of subjects choosing corn flakes cereal jumped from 47% when the brand was not known to 59% when the brand was identified as Kellogg's. In two mid-1990s studies, when samples of computer buyers were asked how much more or less they would pay for particular brands rather than the average computer brand, there was a range of $364. Brands commanding a premium included IBM, Compaq, Hewlett-Packard, and Dell. It's evident that Kellogg's, IBM, Compaq, and many other brands have substantial equity.[33]

www.compaq.com

We tend to think of brand equity as a positive aspect of a product. Occasionally a brand will lack equity or even have negative equity. In such a situation, a brand adds nothing or even detracts from the perceived ability of a product to do

Table 10.1	The Best Brands—According to Consumer Surveys		
Rank	**In the U.S.**	**In the United Kingdom**	**In Argentina**
1.	Craftsman tools (Sears)	Mercedes-Benz autos	Mercedes-Benz autos
2.	Crayola crayons	BMW autos	Alfa Romeo autos
3.	Kodak photographic film	Cadbury's chocolate bars	BMW autos
4.	Hallmark greeting cards	Disney World Florida	Land Rover sport-utility vehicles (SUVs)
5.	Reynolds Wrap aluminum foil	Lego toys	Havana pastries
6.	Waterford crystal	Duracell batteries	Jeep Grand Cherokee SUVs
7.	Chiquita bananas	Sony televisions	Disney World Florida
8.	M&M's candy	Fisher-Price toys	Sheraton hotels
9.	Ziploc plastic bags	Kodak photographic film	Nissan Pathfinder SUVs
10.	Hershey's chocolate bars	Kellogg's corn flakes	La Serenisima dairy products

Note: What constitutes "best" was based on a survey of consumers in each of the three nations. In the U.S., for example, "Consumers were asked to rate brands on a scale of zero to 10, with 10 representing extraordinary quality and zero poor or unacceptable quality."

Sources: The ratings were provided by Total Research Corporation (Princeton, NJ), the firm that conducts the periodic EquiTrend surveys of perceived brand quality.

what it's supposed to do. For example, in the research about computers, consumers typically indicated they would need a discount to select the Packard Bell brand. Not surprisingly, Packard Bell is now struggling to survive. In the services field, during the early 1990s, Trans World Airlines suffered from financial problems and uneven customer service. Therefore, in the minds of many air travelers, the TWA brand had negative equity. Seeking to establish positive equity as the 1990s ended, TWA promoted its improved performance with respect to on-time arrivals and frequent-traveler satisfaction, even running large ads in business periodicals.[34]

Building a brand's equity consists of developing a favorable, memorable, and consistent image—no easy task.[35] Product quality and advertising play vital roles in this endeavor. However, if substantial brand equity can be achieved, the organization that owns the brand can benefit in several ways:

- The brand itself can become an edge over competition, what we call a *differential advantage,* influencing consumers to buy a particular product. Examples include Craftsman (Sears' brand for hand tools and gardening equipment), BMW, and Häagen-Dazs.
- Because it is expensive and time-consuming to build, brand equity creates a barrier for companies that want to enter the market with a similar product.
- The widespread recognition and favorable attitudes surrounding a brand with substantial brand equity can facilitate international expansion. For example, a top executive at McDonald's has described what happens when the company brings the Golden Arches to a new country: "It is a huge event. It is a happening. . . . We time and again set new sales records."[36]
- Brand equity can help a product survive changes in the operating environment, such as a business crisis or a shift in consumer tastes.

Brand equity is often used to expand a product mix, especially by extending a product line. Examples include Ocean Spray drinks in flavors other than the original cranberry, and Wesson olive and canola oils. Similarly, all or part of a strong brand name can be applied to a new product line. For instance, there are now Olay cosmetics, Ann Taylor personal-care products, Starbucks ice cream, Courtyard by Marriott motels, and Marquis by Waterford crystal ware.[37] The rationale for using an existing, strong brand name on a new item or line is that the brand's equity will convey a favorable impression of the product and increase the likelihood that consumers will at least try it.

If a brand has abundant equity, that does not necessarily mean it should be applied to other products. Procter & Gamble decided its hugely successful Crest name could be used on different kinds of toothpaste but not on other product categories such as mouthwash. In developing a spaghetti sauce, Campbell determined its popular brand name would not convey an Italian image, so it selected Prego as the name for its new sauce. Also, strong equity does not guarantee success for new items or lines using the well-regarded brands. Even with their famous brand names, Harley-Davidson cigarettes, Levi's tailored men's clothing, Dunkin' Donuts cereal, and Swatch clothing did not pass the test of continuing consumer acceptance.

Trademark Licensing

Products with considerable brand equity have strong potential for **trademark licensing,** also called *brand licensing.* For example, Polo/Ralph Lauren licenses its popular brand to numerous companies for their use on various items of apparel. Under a licensing arrangement, the owner of a trademark grants permission (a license) to other firms to use its brand name and brand mark on their products. A licensee, which is the company that receives a license, ordinarily pays a royalty of about 5 to 10% of the wholesale price of each item bearing the licensed trademark. The royalty percentage varies depending on the amount of equity connected with the brand offered by a licensor, which is the company that owns it.

This branding strategy accounted for under $20 billion in retail sales in the early 1980s and now racks up about $75 *billion* in annual volume in the U.S. and Canada. However, sales of licensed merchandise have leveled off recently. One popular area for licensing is toys, especially those that feature the Poké-mon creatures, the *Star Wars* heroes, and other popular characters. But the biggest category of licensed merchandise is apparel. Recognizing that women account for the majority of purchases of licensed items, some manufacturers are designing licensed sports apparel to suit female sizes and tastes. Perhaps surprisingly, a growing area of licensing involves products displaying companies' brands and trademarks.[38]

Strategic decisions must be made by both the licensor and the licensee. For instance, a licensor such as Pierre Cardin must ask, "Should we allow other firms to use our designer label?" In turn, a potential licensee such as a manufacturer of eyeglass frames must ask, "Do we want to put out a line of high-fashion frames under the Pierre Cardin name?"

Owners of well-known brands are interested in licensing their trademarks for various reasons:

- *It can be very profitable.* There is little expense for the licensor. However, to protect the reputation of its trademark, the licensor must set criteria for granting licenses and monitoring licensing arrangements.

- *There is a promotional benefit.* The licensor's name gets circulation far beyond the original trademarked item. Coppertone's decision to allow its brand name to be placed on various outdoor products such as casual footwear and umbrellas was explained as follows: "The more Coppertone's name appears on the right kind of products in appropriate categories, the more it will reinforce the brand's position in the market."[39]

Licensing also offers promise to potential licensees. Specific reasons for acquiring a trademark license are:

- *The likelihood of new-product success may be improved.* It's a lot easier for an unknown firm to get both middlemen and consumers to accept its product if it features a well-known trademark.

- *Marketing costs may be reduced.* One licensee explained that licensing is "a way of taking a name with brand recognition and applying it to your merchandise without having to do the advertising and brand building that is so expensive."[40] Any savings may exceed the royalty fees paid to the licensor.

Packaging and Labeling

Even after a product is developed and branded, strategies must still be devised for other product-related aspects of the marketing mix. One such product feature, and a critical one for some products, is packaging. Closely related to packaging, labeling is another aspect of a product that requires managerial attention.

Purposes and Importance of Packaging

Packaging consists of all the activities of designing and producing the container or wrapper for a product. Packaging is intended to serve several vital purposes:

- *Protect the product on its way to the consumer.* A package protects a product during shipment. Furthermore, it can prevent tampering with products, notably medications and food products, in the warehouse or the retail store. The design and size of a package can also help deter shoplifting. That's why small items, such as compact discs, come in larger than needed packages.

- *Provide protection after the product is purchased.* Compared with bulk (that is, unpackaged) items, packaged goods generally are more convenient, cleaner,

When shopping in a supermarket or a discount store, have you ever noticed how similar the packages of some products are to the packages of their direct competitors? That's no coincidence. In fact, it's a common practice for retail chains to use "copycat" packaging. Essentially, the chains put their own brands of products, such as shampoos and liquid window cleaners, in packages with virtually identical shapes and colors to those used by the leading brands, such as Pert Plus and Windex. Middle-men hope that by having virtually identical packaging, the favorable attributes of the leading brand will carry over to the private brand, boosting its sales.

Is it acceptable behavior for chains to imitate the packaging of leading brands?

Sources: Justin Martin, "Is It Mr. Clean or Captain Shine?" *Fortune*, July 7, 1997, p. 206; and Bernice Kanner, "Send in the Clones, Some Courts Say," *St. Louis Post-Dispatch*, Sept. 17, 1995, p. 1E.

and less susceptible to losses from evaporation, spilling, and spoilage. Also, "childproof" closures thwart children (and sometimes adults) from opening containers of medications and other potentially harmful products.

- *Help gain acceptance of the product from middlemen.* A product must be packaged to meet the needs of wholesaling and retailing middlemen. For instance, a package's size and shape must be suitable for displaying and stacking the product in the store. An odd-shaped package might attract shoppers' attention, but if it doesn't stack well, the retailer is unlikely to purchase the product.
- *Help persuade consumers to buy the product.* Packaging can assist in getting a product noticed by consumers. Here's why that is important: "The average shopper spends 20 minutes in the store, viewing 20 products a second."[41] At the point of purchase—such as a supermarket aisle—the package can serve as a "silent sales person." In the case of middlemen's brands, which typically are not advertised heavily, packaging must serve as the means of communicating with shoppers.

Historically, packaging was intended primarily to provide protection. Today, with its marketing significance fully recognized, packaging is a major factor in gaining distribution and customers. For example, to get consumers to buy more Kleenex tissues, Kimberly-Clark developed a set of Expressions boxes featuring various designs such as Amish quilts. The company's rationale is that attractive boxes will encourage consumers to place Kleenex in various rooms of the house.[42] In the cases of convenience goods and operating supplies, most buyers consider one well-known brand about as good as another. Thus these types of products might be differentiated by a package feature—no-drip spout, reusable jar, or self-contained applicator (liquid shoe polish and glue, for example).

Ultimately, a package may become a product's differential advantage, or at least a significant part of it. That was certainly true with Coca-Cola and its distinctive contour glass bottle, so much so that the firm replicated the contour shape in bottles made of other materials such as plastic. Going a step further, the company placed a picture of the contour bottle on cans of Coca-Cola Classic. And, as 2000 began, the largest soft-drink firm even reintroduced the contour glass bottles on a limited basis.[43]

Packaging Strategies

In managing the packaging of a product, executives must make the following strategic decisions.[44]

Packaging the Product Line

A company must decide whether to develop a family resemblance when packaging related products. **Family packaging** uses either highly similar packages for all products *or* packages with a common and clearly noticeable feature. Campbell's

Soup, for instance, uses visually similar packaging for all of its condensed-soup cans, although minor changes (such as adding pictures of the prepared product) are made in the labels occasionally. When new products are added to a line, recognition and images associated with established products extend to the new ones. Family packaging makes sense when the products are of similar quality and have a similar use.

Multiple Packaging

For many years there has been a trend toward **multiple packaging**, the practice of placing several units of the same product in one container. Dehydrated soups, motor oil, beer, golf balls, building hardware, candy bars, towels, and countless other products are packaged in multiple units. Test after test has proved that multiple packaging increases total sales of a product.

Changing the Package

When detected, a company needs to correct a poor feature in an existing package, of course. Unless a problem was spotted, firms stayed with a package design for many years. Now, for competitive reasons, packaging strategies and tactics are reviewed annually along with the rest of the marketing mix.[45]

Firms need to monitor—and consider—continuing developments, such as new packaging materials, uncommon shapes, innovative closures, and other new features (measured portions, metered flow). All are intended to provide benefits to middlemen and/or consumers and, as a result, are selling points for marketers.

To increase sales volume, many companies find it costs much less to redesign a package than to conduct an expensive advertising campaign. To attract the teen market, Dean Foods Co. introduced a new single-serving "chug" container that can be resealed and fits in a car's drink holder. Although milk consumption didn't get a boost from the familiar "milk mustache" advertising campaign, milk sales jumped markedly following the introduction of the chug container.[46]

Redesign of packaging is neither easy nor inexpensive, however. This task can cost from $20,000 for a simple, single product to $250,000 for a project that

A package with an attractive appearance and a useful function can boost a product's sales, as Dean Foods' "chug" container has shown recently. The single-serving container has been used for pints of milk, other milk products, and even orange juice in various sizes. The package has helped make milk "cool" to teenagers, which is critical to the dairy industry in its constant battle with carbonated beverages, juices, and bottled water.

www.deanfoods.com/chugs

entails a product line and requires consumer research and testing. And these figures do not include the expense of promoting the new package design.[47]

Criticisms of Packaging

Packaging is in the public eye today, largely because of environmental issues. Specific concerns are:

- *Packaging that depletes natural resources.* This problem is magnified by firms that prefer larger-than-necessary containers. This criticism has been partially addressed through the use of recycled materials in packaging. A point in favor of packaging is that it minimizes spoilage, thereby reducing a different type of resource waste.

- *Forms of packaging that are health hazards.* Government regulations banned several suspect packaging materials, notably aerosol cans that used chlorofluorocarbons as propellants. Just as important, a growing number of companies are switching from aerosol to pump dispensers.

- *Disposal of used packages.* Consumers' desire for convenience in the form of throwaway containers conflicts with their stated desire for a clean environment. Some discarded packages wind up as litter, others add to solid waste in landfills. This problem can be eased by using biodegradable materials in packaging.

- *Deceptive packaging.* A common problem is that the package size conveys the impression of containing more than the actual contents. Government regulations plus greater integrity on the part of business firms regarding packaging have alleviated this concern to some extent.

- *Expensive packaging.* Even in seemingly simple packaging, such as for soft drinks, as much as one-half of the production cost is for the container. Still, effective packaging reduces transportation costs and spoilage losses.

Marketing executives are challenged to address these criticisms. At the same time, they must retain or even enhance the positive features of packaging, such as product protection, consumer convenience, and marketing support.

Labeling

A **label** is the part of a product that carries information about the product and the seller. A label may be part of a package, or it may be a tag attached to the product. Obviously there is a close relationship among labeling, packaging, and branding.

Types of Labels

There are three primary kinds of labels:

- A **brand label** is simply the brand alone applied to the product or package. Some oranges are stamped Sunkist or Blue Goose, and some clothes carry the brand label Sanforized.

- A **descriptive label** gives objective information about the product's use, construction, care, performance, and/or other pertinent features. On a descriptive label for a can of corn, there will be statements concerning the type of corn (golden sweet), style (creamed or in niblet kernels), can size, number of servings, other ingredients, and nutritional contents.

- A **grade label** identifies the product's judged quality with a letter, number, or word. Canned peaches are grade-labeled A, B, and C, and corn and wheat are grade-labeled 1 and 2.

Brand labeling is an acceptable form of labeling, but it does not supply sufficient information to a buyer. Descriptive labels provide more product information but not necessarily all that is needed or desired by a consumer in making a purchase decision.

Statutory Labeling Requirements

Labeling has received its share of criticism. Consumers have charged, for example, that labels contained incomplete or misleading information and there were a confusing number of sizes and shapes of packages for a given product. The public's complaints about false or deceptive labeling and packaging have led to a number of federal labeling laws.

The Food and Drug Act (1906) and its amendment, the Food, Drug, and Cosmetic Act (1938), provide explicit regulations for labeling drugs, foods, cosmetics, and therapeutic devices. Particularly noteworthy is the Fair Packaging and Labeling Act (1966). This law provides for (1) *mandatory* labeling requirements; (2) an opportunity for business to *voluntarily* adopt packaging standards that can limit the proliferation of the same product in different weights and measures; and (3) administrative agencies, notably the Food and Drug Administration and the Federal Trade Commission, with the *discretionary* power to set packaging regulations.

More recently, the Nutrition Labeling and Education Act (NLEA), which was passed in 1990 and enacted in 1994, established a set of **nutrition labeling** standards for processed foods. The intent of this law is to ensure full disclosure of foods' nutritional contents. Labels must clearly state the amount of calories, fat, cholesterol, sodium, carbohydrates, and protein contained in the package's contents. In addition, the amounts must be stated as a percentage of a daily intake of 2,000 calories. Vitamin and mineral content also must be expressed as a percentage of the recommended daily allowance.[48]

As part of the NLEA, the Food and Drug Administration issued standard definitions for key terms used in labeling, such as *light, lean,* and *good source.* To be labeled *light,* for example, a brand ordinarily has to contain one-half the fat or one-third fewer calories than standard products in this category. The NLEA allows firms to include on labels some health claims, such as fiber's value in preventing heart disease. And companies are permitted to list on labels endorsements of their products from health organizations such as the American Heart Association.

The nutrition labeling changes mandated by the NLEA apply to about 200,000 packaged foods, including meat and poultry products. Obviously, these changes represented an enormous one-time expense to food manufacturers, with estimates ranging from $2 billion to $6 billion. Nevertheless, supporters argue that the new labeling requirements promote improved nutrition, thereby reducing health care costs. Of course, these savings will occur only if consumers read the labels and use the information in choosing foods. The results of one study suggest that shoppers obtained and understood more nutrition information following the introduction of nutrition labeling.[49]

A 1992 amendment to the Fair Packaging and Labeling Act mandates metric labeling for selected products. Implemented in 1994, this law requires that metric weights and measures be shown on labels along with traditional American weights and measures, such as inches, pounds, and pints. Rather than replacing the American system, as many companies feared, the metric information is supplementary.[50]

Design, Color, and Quality

A well-rounded program for product planning and development will include strategies and policies on several additional product features. Design, color, and quality are covered in this chapter. Two more features, warranties and postsale service, are covered in Chapter 21 because they closely relate to the implementation of a company's marketing program.

Design

One way to satisfy customers and gain a differential advantage is through **product design**, which refers to the arrangement of elements that collectively form a good or service. Good design can improve the marketability of a product by making it easier to operate, upgrading its quality, improving its appearance, and/or reducing production costs. For instance, computer programmers are supposed to assure that any new software is very user-friendly.

According to an IBM executive, design has become "a strategic marketing tool."[51] Design is receiving more and more attention for several reasons:

- Rapidly advancing technologies are generating not only new products (such as desktop computer cameras for videoconferencing) that need attractive, yet functional designs but also new materials that can enhance design capabilities.

- A growing number of firms have turned to low prices as a competitive tool. In turn, designers have been asked to rework some of their companies' products and lower the costs of making them as one way of maintaining profit margins.

- A distinctive design may be the only feature that significantly differentiates a product. In the realm of business products, consider a cordless drill/driver that Black & Decker Corp. sells under the DeWalt brand. The product's design features a cushioned pistol grip, relatively light weight, and a powerful motor. The success of this drill/driver helped B&D reclaim its position of leadership in the market for professional power tools.[52]

www.blackanddecker.com

Companies are also being called upon to design products that are easily used by *all* consumers, including disabled individuals, the burgeoning number of senior citizens, and others needing special considerations. This approach is termed **universal design**. As one example, the Kohler Co. designed a bathtub with a door, eliminating the danger of having to climb into the tub. And home builders are featuring wider halls and doors in some models, in order to accommodate wheelchairs. Occasionally, products designed for the disabled or seniors are also appealing to other consumers. AT&T's Big Buttons telephone, for example, is a hit not just with the visually impaired but also with consumers who have small children and with those who like its playful styling.[53]

For most consumer and business goods, ranging from furniture to electronic equipment, design has long been recognized as important. According to estimates, design accounts for only 2% of the total cost of producing and marketing a product. As a result, a design that's a hit with consumers can produce a giant return on investment for a firm. There may be no better example than Volkswagen's Beetle. Decades ago, the car's odd shape generated a great deal of attention and attracted many buyers. It eventually fell out of favor, largely because of safety and environmental reasons. In 1998, Volkswagen of America introduced the New Beetle, featuring a familiar design including a front end that resembles a "happy face." This time around, a variety of new technology has been added to complement the Beetle's appealing design.[54]

Color

Like design, **product color** often is the determining factor in a customer's acceptance or rejection of a product, whether it is a dress, a table, or an automobile. In fact, color is so important that the U.S. Supreme Court confirmed in early 1995 that the color of a product or its packaging can be registered as part of a trademark under the Lanham Act. Color by itself can qualify for trademark status when, according to the Court's ruling, it "identifies and distinguishes a particular brand, and thus indicates its source." The case under review involved greenish-gold dry-cleaning press pads manufactured by the Qualitex Company. Other distinctive colors that help to identify specific brands are Owens-Corning's pink insulation and Kodak's gold color-film boxes.[55]

For some products, such as clothing, color is a critical ingredient. For others, such as personal computers, it would seem to be a less important feature. However, the image of Apple Computer and its iMac computers certainly got a boost from the use of bright, trendy colors. In fact, rainbow colors became a trend, or perhaps a fad, for a variety of electronic products, such as Nokia cellular phones and Samsung digital cameras and videocassette recorders.

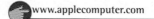
www.applecomputer.com

As with other marketing-mix elements, a differential advantage might be gained by identifying the most pleasing color and in knowing when to change colors. In the late 1990s, for example, Apple Computer used fruit-inspired colors, such as grape and tangerine, for its iMac PC. Apple's color decisions were backed by a survey indicating that over one-half of consumers disdained drab colors for high-tech products.[56] Of course, bright colors would probably be a disadvantage for PCs or other electronic products aimed at executives. Thus poor color choices can result in a differential *dis*advantage. For instance, if a garment manufacturer or the person responsible for purchasing merchandise for a retail store guesses wrong on what will be the fashionable color in women's clothing, disaster may ensue.

Color can be extremely important for packaging as well as for the product itself. Color specialists say it's no coincidence that Nabisco, Marlboro, Coca-Cola, Campbell's, and Budweiser are all top-selling brands. In each case, red is the primary color of their packaging or logo. Red may be appealing because it "evokes feelings of warmth, passion and sensuality." According to one color researcher, blue has overtaken red as the favorite color of American shoppers. For a while, blue seemed to be the color of choice for beverage bottles. In fact, so many vintners chose various shades of blue for their wine bottles that some of them have turned to other colors to be distinctive.[57]

Quality

There's no agreement on a definition of product quality, even though it is universally recognized as significant. One professional society defines **product quality** as the set of features and characteristics of a good or service that determine its ability to satisfy needs.[58] Despite what appears to be a straightforward definition, consumers frequently disagree on what constitutes quality in a product—whether it be a cut of meat or a performance by a rock musician. Personal tastes are deeply involved; what you like, another person may dislike. It is important to recognize, therefore, that quality—like beauty—is to a large extent "in the eyes of the beholder."

Besides personal tastes, individual expectations also affect judgments of quality. That is, a consumer brings certain expectations to a purchase situation. Sometimes you have high expectations, as with a movie about which you read rave reviews. Other times you have modest expectations, as with a course for next semester that is described to as "not too boring" by a current student. Your evaluation of a product's quality depends on whether the actual experience with the good or service exceeds, meets, or falls short of your expectations.

For some companies, *optimal* quality means that the product provides the consumer with an experience that meets, but does not exceed, expectations. The rationale is that there's no sense in incurring added costs to provide what amounts to *excessive* quality. Some firms that adopt this viewpoint supplement adequate product quality with superior customer service. According to one survey of personal computer users, this approach can be effective in generating repeat customers.[59] Other businesses, however, strive to exceed consumers' expectations in order to produce high levels of customer satisfaction and, in turn, brand loyalty.

For many years, there was substantial room for improved quality in many American-made products. For instance, German and Japanese automakers were beating their American competitors by turning out better-performing, more-reliable cars. Hence, since the 1980s, U.S. industry has paid more and more attention to product quality.[60] As will be discussed in Chapter 11, product quality should be a primary consideration not only for manufacturers of goods but also for producers of services.

Recently, quality was called "the single most critical factor for businesses to survive in the ever expanding and competitive global market place." General Motors found that to be true in China. The company discovered that Chinese consumers thought that products made in their own country were inferior to imports. Hence, GM's advertising in China stressed the high quality of Buicks that were made in Shanghai. So far, the cars are selling as fast as GM can make them.[61]

Because it is not easily duplicated, many organizations seek to build product quality to gain a differential *advantage*. In one survey of managers, quality was the most mentioned basis for a strong differential advantage.[62] At the least, an enterprise needs to avoid a differential disadvantage related to product quality.

To seize an advantage or avert a disadvantage, a number of businesses, government agencies, and nonprofit entities have implemented **total quality management** (TQM) programs. TQM entails not just specific policies and practices, but a philosophy that commits the organization to continuous quality improvement in all of its activities. In recent years, TQM has received some criticism for not improving financial performance as much as would be expected given the necessary investment of time and effort. However, according to one study, the stocks of firms with effective TQM programs performed much better than the stocks of other firms over a five-year period.[63]

Another noteworthy quality-related development is called ISO 9000 (pronounced ICE-o nine thousand). **ISO 9000** is a set of related standards of quality management that have been adopted by about 60 countries, including the U.S. Companies that meet ISO 9000 standards are awarded a certificate, which often puts them in a favorable position with large customers. Worldwide, tens of thousands of companies have earned ISO 9000 certification.

Some critics say that the standards place too much emphasis on documenting what a producer is doing and pay too little attention to whether what's being done results in satisfactory products. As one skeptic observed, "You can certify a manufacturer that makes life jackets from concrete, as long as those jackets are made according to the documented procedures." Perhaps with such criticism in mind, the new ISO 9001 standards are aimed at assuring customer satisfaction.[64]

• Summary

Effective product management involves developing and then monitoring the various features of a product—its brand, packaging, labeling, design, color, quality, warranty, and postsale service. A consumer's purchase decision may take into account not just the basic good or service, but also the brand and perhaps one or more of the other want-satisfying product features.

A brand is a means of identifying and differentiating the products of an organization. Branding aids sellers in managing their promotional and pricing activities. The dual responsibilities of brand ownership are to promote the brand and to maintain a consistent level of quality. Selecting a good brand name—and there are relatively few really good ones—is difficult. Once a brand becomes well known, the owner may have to protect it from product counterfeiting and from becoming a generic term.

Manufacturers must decide whether to brand their products and/or sell under a middleman's brand. Middlemen must decide whether to carry producers' brands alone or to establish their own brands as well. In addition, middlemen must decide whether to carry generic products. Both producers and middlemen must set policies regarding branding groups of products and branding for market saturation. The use of cobranding, placing two brands on a product or enterprise, is growing.

An increasing number of companies are recognizing that the brands they own are or can be among their most valuable assets. They are building brand equity—the added value that a brand brings to a product. Although it's difficult to build brand equity, doing so successfully can be the basis for expanding a product mix. Products with abundant brand equity also lend themselves to trademark licensing, a popular marketing arrangement.

Packaging is becoming increasingly important as sellers recognize the problems, as well as the marketing opportunities, associated with it. Companies must choose among strategies such as family packaging, multiple packaging, and changing the package. Labeling, a related activity, provides information about the product and the seller. Many consumer criticisms of marketing relate to packaging and labeling. As a result, there are several federal laws regulating these activities.

Companies are now recognizing the marketing value of both product design and quality. Good design can improve the marketability of a product; it may be the only feature that differentiates a product. Projecting the appropriate quality image and then delivering the level of quality desired by customers are essential to marketing success. In many cases, firms need to enhance product quality to eliminate a differential disadvantage; in others, firms seek to build quality as a way of gaining a differential advantage.

More about **Levi's**

After years of watching its brand equity diminish, Levi Strauss & Co. (LS) responded with a strategy that deviates drastically from its traditional emphasis on a single brand. LS decided to create a portfolio of brands to appeal to three distinct customer segments: urban opinion leaders, extreme sports, and regular youth. The brands within each segment will range from inexpensive to expensive, and from classic to designer looks. Each segment will have its own new-product development, brand management, and marketing teams within LS.

In late 1998, for example, LS introduced Red Line, a designer jean selling for about $100 a pair. This line was distributed through a small number of stores that cater to high-income consumers. LS has since broadened the line to encompass nondenim styles, including black leather jackets and also skirts made from the hottest fabrics. However, LS completely disassociated this new brand from its traditional brand; nowhere on the Red Line label does the name Levi's appear. Conversely, the Red Line brand isn't mentioned on the Levi's website. LS has also launched the Vintage collection, its most expensive line of designer jeans. This brand calls to mind the company's rich heritage while invoking a new, stylish edge.

Even if they do attract numerous buyers of designer jeans, Red Line and Vintage alone will still be too small to significantly help LS's bottom line. Not everyone believes that introducing new brands is the answer for LS. According to one observer, "If Levi's goes too far away from jeans, they'll fail."

Unfortunately, Levi's is also facing an overall decline in the popularity of denim, as new fabrics and trendy styles replace this one-time staple of the American closet. During the past few years, denim sales have been declining by more than 10% annually. Recognizing that trend, LS is broadening its nondenim lines, notably Dockers and Slates. Dockers, for instance, is being extended with the addition of Recode, a line of business-casual clothing using some stretch fabrics.

In response to these market conditions and in conjunction with its new multiple-branding strategy, LS is developing new lines of clothing aimed at the youth market, including nondenim styles in khakis, cargo pants, tops, and jackets. It is also reallocating its marketing resources to focus on activities, including product placement in movies and event sponsorships, that will attract younger consumers. For instance, the plan is for Levi's to try to entice young people by spending as much on music sponsorships as on traditional advertising. "We want to be a part of teens' lives," says Levi's vice president of youth marketing.

As part of their efforts to reinvigorate the brand, LS recently opened a 24,000-square-foot store in San Francisco. This showcase store features all of Levi's brands (including, interestingly, Red Line). Special emphasis is given to Levi's core brand of Red Tab jeans, which comprises more than 50% of the total assortment in the store. Customers can instantly shrink their jeans, if desired, by wearing them into a pool of water and then drying off in a glass booth filled with warm air. In addition, high-tech methods take measurements for alterations. Light beams are projected onto shoppers as they wait in a dark booth for computers to analyze the results.

LS intends to replicate its San Francisco store in prime urban locations across the country. The company's intention isn't to make a profit at these outlets. Instead, the goal is to create "shopper buzz" and build a hip, edgy image for the Levi's brand.

In late 1999, LS hired a new CEO, Philip Marineau, who came from PepsiCo. Marineau summarized what he discovered, "Levi's is a mythical brand, but our performance has been poor." The combination of new brands, broader product lines, and showcase stores is designed to restore Levi Strauss & Co., and its bellwether Levi's brand, to its former dominant position.[65]

1. Do you agree with LS's strategy to develop multiple brands of apparel? Why or why not?

2. How can LS increase the brand equity associated with the Levi's name, particularly with the teenage market?

Key Terms and Concepts

Brand (264)
Brand name (264)
Brand mark (264)
Trademark (264)
Producer's brand (264)
Middleman's brand (264)
Product counterfeiting (268)
Generic products (273)
Family branding (274)
Multiple-brand strategy (274)

Cobranding (275)
Brand equity (276)
Trademark licensing (277)
Packaging (278)
Family packaging (279)
Multiple packaging (280)
Label (281)
Brand label (281)
Descriptive label (281)
Grade label (281)

Nutrition labeling (282)
Product design (283)
Universal design (283)
Product color (283)
Product quality (284)
Total quality management (TQM) (285)
ISO 9000 (285)

Questions and Problems

1. Evaluate three of the brand names in Table 10.1 in relation to the characteristics of a good brand, indicating the strong and weak points of each name.

2. Do the following e-commerce brands possess the characteristics of a good brand?
   a. Fogdog Sports (sporting goods)
   b. CareerPath.com (job search and employee recruiting)
   c. Peapod, Webvan, and HomeGrocer.com (all of which are grocery shopping and delivery services)
   d. HotBot (search engine for the Web)
   e. FreeRealTime.com (stock quotes and financial information at no charge)

3. Identify one brand that is on the verge of becoming generic.
   a. Why should a company protect the separate identity of its brand?
   b. What course of action should a company take to do so?

4. In which of the following cases should the company use its name as part of the product's brand name?
   a. A manufacturer of men's underwear introduces women's underwear.
   b. A manufacturer of hair-care products adds a line of portable electric hair dryers.

5. A manufacturer of snow skis sold under a brand that has built up substantial equity acquires a company that markets ski boots carrying a brand that enjoys about the same amount of equity. What branding strategy should the acquiring organization adopt? Should all products (skis and boots) now carry the ski brand? The boot brand? Is there some other alternative that you think would be better?

6. Why do some firms sell identical products under more than one of their own brands?

7. Assume that a large department store chain proposed to the manufacturers of Maytag washing machines that Maytag supply the department store with machines carrying the store's brand. What factors should Maytag's management consider in making a decision? If the situation instead involved a supermarket chain and General Foods' Jell-O, to what extent should different factors be considered?

8. An American manufacturer plans to introduce its line of camping equipment (stoves, lanterns, ice chests) in several European Union countries. Should management select the same brand for all countries or use a different brand in each country? What factors should influence the decision? How should brand equity enter into the decision?

9. Select one product and indicate how you would improve its design.

10. Give examples of products for which the careful use of color has increased sales. Can you cite examples to show that poor use of color may hurt a product's salability?

Hands-On Marketing

1. Visit a large local supermarket and:
   a. Obtain the store manager's opinions regarding which products are excellently packaged and which are poorly packaged. Ask the manager for reasons.
   b. Walk around the store and compile your own list of excellent and poor packages. What factors did you use to judge quality of packaging?

2. Ask five students who are not taking this course to evaluate the following names for a proposed expensive perfume: Entice, Nitespark, At Risk, and Foreglow. For evaluation purposes, share with the students the characteristics of a good brand name. Also ask them to suggest a better name for the new perfume.

11

Services Marketing

"Wingspan is Bank One's answer to dramatic changes taking place in financial services marketing."

Will **Wingspan** Soar or Be Grounded?

By conventional measures, Bank One was doing just fine. In 1999 it was the fifth largest bank in the U.S., having acquired over 100 other banks in a 15-year period. It offered a full line of financial products, had 1,900 branches in 14 states, operated a highly successful credit card business (First USA), and even had an online banking service (www.bankone.com). Why then, would it introduce Wingspan, a "virtual" retail bank that is only accessible via the Internet?

Wingspan offers the normal array of retail banking services such as checking accounts, automatic bill paying, certificates of deposit, investment products, and various types of loans, but that's where the similarity to its parent, Bank One, ends: Wingspan has no "brick and mortar" locations. All interactions with customers are through its website.

Many of Wingspan's product lines are more extensive than similar offerings from Bank One. For example, Wingspan offers 7,000 mutual funds (to Bank One's 49), home mortgages from a number of different providers depending on current interest rates (to Bank One's internal home mortgage department), and five kinds of insurance from hundreds of providers (to Bank One's offering of only disability and life insurance). For several products Wingspan offers better rates than Bank One. For instance, its one-year certificate of deposit pays almost 1% more than a CD of the same duration offered by Bank One.

Finally, there has been no attempt to capitalize on Bank One's name or reputation. In fact, Wingspan marketers have made an effort to distance their company from the parent firm, even trying to lure away some of its customers.

Wingspan is Bank One's answer to dramatic changes taking place in financial services marketing. Consider these recent developments. Competitive pressure on banks from Internet-based, financial services firms is growing. Specialized mutual fund "supermarkets," investment brokers, and mortgage lenders can all be found on the Internet. The Internet is also redefining the traditional geographic boundaries of retail banking. Distant banks that once were not viewed by Bank One as a threat are now able to create "electronic branches" and pursue customers anywhere. Finally, nonfinancial organizations such as large retail chains view banking as a natural, and potentially very profitable, extension of their current operations. For example, Federated Department Stores has obtained regulatory approval to offer banking services in its retail stores.

Bank One's commitment to making this venture successful is reflected in the initial investment. It's estimated that the bank spent $150 million on advertising alone for Wingspan during the online venture's first year of operation.[1]

Should the approach to marketing this "virtual" bank be any different from marketing a conventional bank?

www.wingspan.com

Wingspan is marketing a service—retail banking. Recall that our definition of a product in Chapter 8 includes goods *and* services. This distinction is much more than a matter of semantics. Services are fundamentally different from goods in ways that affect their marketing. Recognizing what those differences are and understanding their implications are essential in developing effective services.

After studying this chapter, you should be able to explain:

- What services are and what they are not.
- The importance of services in advanced economies.
- The characteristics of services, and the marketing implications of these characteristics.
- The special situation of nonbusiness services marketing.
- How to plan the marketing mix for services.
- The challenges of managing services quality.
- The increasing productivity and performance expectations faced by services marketers.

Nature and Importance of Services

The U.S. has moved beyond the stage where goods production is its main economic activity to the stage where it has become the world's first services economy. Over two-thirds of the nation's gross domestic product (GDP) is accounted for by services, and just over one-half of all consumer expenditures are for services. Projections to the year 2005 indicate that services will attract an even larger share of consumer spending.

Services are also the major source of employment. More than 80% of the non-farm labor force is employed in service industries. According to U.S. Department of Labor predictions, virtually all the fastest-growing occupations between 1996 and 2006 are in services. The industries in which job growth will be the fastest are data and information management, health care, education, and financial services.[2]

That services account for over one-half of consumer expenditures is impressive, but it still grossly understates the economic importance of services. These figures do not include the vast amounts spent for business services. And by all indications, spending for business services will continue to grow. As commerce has become increasingly complex and competitive, managers have found that calling on specialized service providers is effective and efficient. The result is that many tasks formerly performed by regular employees, from research and training to advertising and distribution, are increasingly being "outsourced" to specialists.

Definition of Services

What should be classified as a service? The answer isn't always apparent because invariably services are marketed in conjunction with goods. Virtually all services require supporting goods (you need an airplane to provide air transportation service), and goods require supporting services (to sell even a shirt or a can of beans calls for at least a cashier's service). Furthermore, a company may sell a combination of goods and services. Thus, along with repair service for your car, you might buy spark plugs or an oil filter. Therefore, it may be helpful to think of every product as a mix of goods and services located on a continuum ranging from mostly goods to mostly services, as shown in Figure 11.1.

For marketing purposes, it is useful to separate services into two classes. In the first are services that are the main *purpose or object* of a transaction. Suppose you rent a car from Hertz. The company makes a car available (tangible good) to pro-

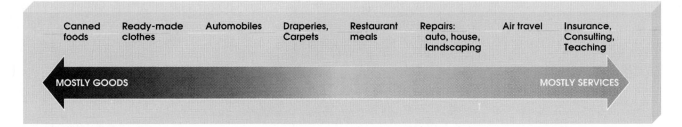

| Canned foods | Ready-made clothes | Automobiles | Draperies, Carpets | Restaurant meals | Repairs: auto, house, landscaping | Air travel | Insurance, Consulting, Teaching |

MOSTLY GOODS — MOSTLY SERVICES

Figure 11.1

A goods-services continuum.

vide the rental service. But you are buying the use of the car, not the car itself. In the second class are services that *support or facilitate* the sale of a good or another service. Thus, when you rent the car from Hertz, you can also obtain collision insurance, the use of a cellular phone, and an electronic navigational device. These are called supplementary or support services.

Considering these distinctions, we define **services** as identifiable, intangible activities that are the main object of a transaction designed to provide want-satisfaction to customers. This definition excludes supplementary services that support the sale of goods or other services. Even though we are excluding supplementary services from our discussion, we don't want to underestimate their importance. In industries where there are few differences among the primary products of competitors, supplementary services can be the basis for a differential advantage.

Scope of Services

Using a broad definition of transactions and customers, it is appropriate to recognize both for-profit and nonbusiness services organizations. **For-profit services firms** sell to consumers or other businesses with profitable operations as a primary goal. This category is reflected in the following examples, classified by industry:

- *Housing and other structures:* Rental of offices, warehouses, hotels, motels, apartments, houses, and farms.
- *Household operations:* Utilities, house maintenance and repairs, landscaping, and household cleaning.
- *Recreation and entertainment:* Theaters, spectator sports, amusement parks, participation sports, restaurant meals, and resorts.
- *Personal care:* Laundry, dry cleaning, personal grooming care, and spas.
- *Medical and health care:* Physical and mental medical services, dental, nursing, hospitalization, optometry, and physical therapy.
- *Private education:* Vocational schools, nursery schools, charter schools, and some continuing education programs.
- *Professional business services:* Legal, accounting, advertising, marketing research, public relations, and management consulting.
- *Financial services:* Personal and business insurance, banking, credit and loan service, brokerage service, and investment counseling.
- *Transportation:* Freight and passenger service on common carriers, automobile repairs and rentals, and express package delivery.
- *Communications:* Broadcasting, telephone, fax, computer, and Internet services.

These groups are not separated into business and consumer services as we did with goods because most of these services are purchased by both market groups.

Nonbusiness services organizations are of two types. One type is **not-for-profit (N-F-P) services organizations,** which have a profit goal because growth and continued existence depend on generating revenue in excess of its costs. However, profit (which may be referred to by a different name, such as "surplus") is secondary to the N-F-P's primary objective. In many cases N-F-Ps operate in a fashion very similar to for-profit businesses. These organizations generate and spend billions of dollars and employ thousands of people. Examples, organized by primary focus, include:

- *Educational:* Private grade schools, high schools, colleges, and universities.
- *Cultural:* Museums, opera and theater groups, zoos, and symphony orchestras.
- *Religious:* Churches, synagogues, temples, and mosques.
- *Charitable and philanthropic:* Charities, service organizations (Salvation Army, Red Cross), research foundations, and fund-raising groups (United Way).
- *Social concerns:* Organizations dealing with family planning, civil rights, termination of smoking, environmental concerns, the homeless, those for or against abortion, or those for or against nuclear energy.
- *Professional and trade:* Labor unions, certification groups, professional associations (American Marketing Association, American Medical Association), trade associations, and lobbying groups.
- *Social:* Fraternal organizations, civic clubs, special interest clubs.
- *Health care:* Hospitals, nursing homes, health research organizations (American Cancer Society, American Heart Association), health maintenance organizations.
- *Political:* Political parties, individual politicians.

You may note some overlap in the preceding two lists. For example, private education appears on both lists because some educational institutions are profit seeking, whereas others are not-for-profit. Also, most museums and hospitals are not-for-profit, but some are profit seeking.

Finally, the scope of services is further broadened by including a second type of nonbusiness organization. A **nonprofit organization** provides services but does not have a profit or surplus objective. Federal, state, and local government agencies fall into this category. They provide services, often charging for them, and may even operate in competition with for-profit businesses. For example, the U.S. National Park Service competes with private forms of outdoor recreation.

Many nonprofit organizations are heavily involved in marketing. For example, the U.S. Census Bureau uses a variety of marketing tools. To encourage citizens to complete and return their census forms in 2000, the Bureau spent $168 million on mass media advertising. Following the data collection, the Census Bureau will engage in a variety of marketing efforts to encourage utilization of the information it compiles.[3]

If nonbusiness organizations do an ineffective marketing job, the costs are high. Empty beds in hospitals and empty classrooms constitute a waste of resources a society can ill afford. There are additional social and economic costs of ineffective nonbusiness marketing. If the death rate from smoking rises because the American Cancer Society and similar organizations cannot persuade people that smoking is harmful, we all lose. When antilitter organizations fail to convince people to control their solid-waste disposal, society suffers. Thus, marketing by nonbusiness organizations should be treated as a serious undertaking with important consequences.

The Development of Services Marketing

Traditionally, many service industries—both business and nonbusiness—have not been market-oriented. There are several reasons why they lagged behind sellers of goods in accepting the marketing concept and in adopting marketing techniques.

Some services providers enjoy monopoly status. Until very recently most public utilities (telephone, electricity, water, natural gas) were operated as geographic monopolies under the supervision of government agencies. Quite naturally, when an organization is the only supplier of a necessity in a market, the focus of attention is on production and efficient operations, not marketing.

In some cases marketing activities are externally constrained. A number of large services industries are subject to substantial restrictions by federal and state governments or professional associations. Until recently, for example, banking and all major forms of interstate transportation services were severely restricted in marketing practices such as pricing, distribution, market expansion, and product introduction. In the fields of law, accounting, and health care, various state laws and professional-association regulations prevented and, to varying degrees, still prevent their members from engaging in advertising, price competition, and other marketing activities.

Many nonbusiness services providers are uncomfortable with a business image. These organizations attempt to distance themselves from business and its profit objective. As a result, they do not employ many business techniques, including marketing. In some professional-service industries, tradition suggests that the focus should be on producing the service, not on marketing it. Proud of their abilities to conduct an audit, diagnose an illness, or give legal advice, these professionals historically have not considered themselves businesspeople.

More recently, several developments have contributed to a growing awareness of marketing among services organizations:

- The success of services companies such as Marriott, Disney, and VISA serve as examples of the power of good marketing.
- Consumer protests, changes in laws, and court decisions have removed many of the governmental and professional-association restrictions on marketing in some services industries. These changes, along with increased competition, have generated a growing awareness of marketing challenges and opportunities.
- Reductions in federal aid, tax law changes that discourage gift giving, competition for funds from a new generation of social causes, and a slowdown in corporate contributions have squeezed the budgets of many nonbusiness services organizations. Consequently, many have begun to adopt modern business techniques, including marketing with a customer orientation.

Developing a Services Marketing Program

Marketing business and nonbusiness services includes the same basic elements as marketing goods. Whether its focus is goods or services, every organization should first define and analyze its markets, identify segments, and select targets. Then attention should turn to designing a coordinated marketing mix—the goods or services offering, the price structure, the distribution system, and the promotional activities—around a differential advantage that will create the position the organization desires. However, some important differences between goods and services influence these marketing decisions. The most important differences are described below.

Characteristics of Services

The four characteristics that differentiate services from goods—**intangibility, inseparability, heterogeneity,** and **perishability**—are major factors driving the differences between goods and services marketing.

Race car sponsorship is an example of association for a services marketer. The demographic profile of NASCAR fans—half with incomes over $50,000, 25% with college degrees, and more than 40% women—is attractive to marketers. However, most important is their loyalty. Research shows that once race fans associate a favored driver with a sponsor, they are more likely than fans of athletes in any other sport to purchase the products of the sponsor.

 www.nascar.com

Intangibility

Because services are intangible, it is impossible for prospective customers to sample—taste, feel, see, hear, or smell—a service before they buy it. Consequently, a company's promotional program must be explicit about the benefits to be derived from the service, rather than emphasizing the service itself. Four promotional strategies that may be used to suggest service benefits and reduce the effect of intangibility are:[4]

- *Visualization.* For example, Carnival Cruise Lines depicts the benefits of its cruises with ads that show people dancing, dining, playing deck games, and visiting exotic places.

- *Association.* By connecting the service with a tangible good, person, object, or place, a particular image can be created. Professional sports teams are linked with cities or regions to give them an identity. Prudential Insurance suggests stability and security with its Rock of Gibraltar. Merrill Lynch uses the symbol of a charging bull to imply strength and leadership.

- *Physical representation.* American Express uses color—gold or platinum—for its credit card services to symbolize wealth and prestige. Enterprise, the auto rental firm, depicts a car wrapped as a package in its TV ads to emphasize its unique delivery feature. The United Way depicts its role with a helping hand and a rainbow, the symbol of hope.

- *Documentation.* There are two forms of documentation—*past performance* and *capability.* Travel Air, a fractional ownership (time-share) aircraft company, highlights past performance by stating in its ads that it has been rated first in reliability by an independent research firm. Executive Jet, another firm in the industry, cites the number of planes in its time-share fleet as an indicator of its capability to provide high-quality service.

Websites are a valuable tool in reducing the intangibility of a service. They make it possible for marketers to present extensive information, use animation and sound, and answer a site visitor's specific questions via e-mail. By expanding the marketer's communications arsenal, the Web increases the quantity and quality of available information and thereby improves the customer's understanding of the service. An example is Royal Caribbean Cruise Line.

 www.rccl.com

How important is the size of a stadium seat?

New or renovated indoor sports arenas are important urban investments. In recent years, Atlanta, Denver, Miami, Boston, Washington, DC, and Portland, Oregon, are cities that have replaced aging facilities or undertaken major upgrades of existing stadiums. Among the features added are private boxes, cigar bars, valet parking, gourmet restaurants, and even boat docks at arenas on rivers. Publicity touts the luxurious surroundings fans will experience in the arenas. However, one feature appears to be common to most new arenas and upsetting to many fans: The general-admission seat sizes are getting smaller.

Although designers made the average seat more comfortable with added padding and improved back support, width and legroom have been reduced. In Boston's Fleet Center, some seats have 31 inches of legroom, 5 inches less than the typical movie-theater seat. And seats as narrow as 18 inches, or about the width of a computer keyboard, are common. This is happening at a time when the average American adult is getting larger.

Stadium owners argue that high construction and operating costs, combined with soaring players' salaries, force them to find ways to increase revenue. They point out that over the life of an arena, a single general-admission seat can generate $1 million in revenue at today's ticket prices.

Complaints from fans have led to some changes. For example, in the National Car Rental Center south of Miami that serves as the home of the Florida Panthers hockey team, 8,000 cup holders were removed to allow for more space between seat rows. Some fans are so disgruntled they revolt. When the Portland Trailblazers of the National Basketball Association moved to their new arena, a fan chose not to renew his tickets after 22 consecutive years as a season ticket holder. After testing the new seats, he said "I don't mind sitting on a wooden bench for $7, but if someone is going to charge me $60, I expect a certain comfort level."

In the purchase of entertainment, how important is a feature such as seat size in comparison to the game or show experienced by the consumer?

Source: Sam Walker, "Stadium Squeeze Play," *The Wall Street Journal,* Mar. 3, 1999, p. W1.

Inseparability

Services typically cannot be separated from the creator-seller of the service. Moreover, many services are created, dispensed, and consumed simultaneously. For example, dentists create and dispense almost all their services at the same time, *and* they require the presence of the consumer for the services to be performed. The same is true of a fast-food drive-up window employee, a physical therapist, and even an automatic teller machine.

A service's inseparability means that services providers are involved concurrently in the production and the marketing efforts. One physician can treat only so many medical patients in a day. This characteristic limits the scale of operation in a services firm. And the customers receive and sometimes consume the services at the production site—in the firm's "factory," so to speak. Consequently, customers' opinions regarding a service frequently are formed through contacts with the production-sales personnel and impressions of the physical surroundings in the "factory." In the case of education, this would be the teacher and the classroom.

From a marketing standpoint, inseparability limits distribution. It frequently means that direct sale is the only possible channel of distribution, and an individual seller's services can be sold only where direct contact is possible

There is an exception to the inseparability feature. Some services are sold by a person who is representing the creator-seller. A travel agent, insurance broker, or rental agent, for instance, represents, promotes, and sells services that will be provided at a later time by the institutions producing them. In these situations, the customer's opinion of the service can be influenced by the intermediary's appearance and behavior. Thus services marketers should be particularly careful in selecting agents and brokers.

Sporting events are an example of services in which the product cannot be standardized. Some spectators who watched the game in this photo, in which one team made no hits and scored no runs, would find it exciting and others would be bored by the lack of action. To offset the heterogeneity, sports marketers incorporate many other elements into an event including music and souvenir give-aways to avoid relying entirely on the game.

Heterogeneity

It is difficult if not impossible for a service firm, or even an individual seller of services, to standardize output. Each unit of the service is somewhat different from every other unit of the same service because of the human factor in production and delivery. Delta Airlines, for example, does not give the same quality of service on every flight, or even to each passenger on the same flight. All performances of the Boston Pops Orchestra, or all haircuts you get, are not of equal quality.

For the buyer this condition means it is difficult to forecast quality in advance of consumption. You pay a fixed amount to see the Atlanta Braves baseball team play without knowing whether it will be an exciting or a dull game. For some services it may even be difficult to judge the quality after it has been received, such as when you receive a diagnosis from a physician or get advice from a minister or rabbi.

To offset heterogeneity, services companies should pay special attention to the product-planning and implementation stages of their marketing programs. From the beginning, management must do all it can to ensure consistency of quality and to maintain high levels of quality control. Service quality will be given special attention later in this chapter.

Perishability

Services are highly perishable because the existing capacity cannot be stored or inventoried for future use. A cruise ship that sails with unoccupied staterooms, empty seats at a church service, and idle house painters represent available supply that is lost forever. Perishability creates potential imbalances in supply and demand. Furthermore, the demand for many services fluctuates considerably by season, by day of the week, and by hour of the day. Ski lifts can sit idle all summer, whereas golf courses in some areas go unused in the winter. The ridership of city buses fluctuates greatly during the day.

Perishability and the resulting difficulty of balancing supply with fluctuating demand poses promotion, product-planning, scheduling, and pricing challenges to services executives. Some organizations have developed new uses for idle capacity during off-seasons. During the summer, ski resorts operate their ski lifts for hikers and sightseers. Advertising and creative pricing are also used to stimulate demand during slack periods. Marriott Hotels, for example, offer lower prices and family packages on weekends.

The Service Customer

Service businesses define their market as present and potential customers. They then direct their marketing only in the direction of these prospective buyers.

In contrast, nonbusiness organizations must aim at two markets. One is the **provider market**—the contributors of money, labor, materials, or other resources to the organization. The second is the **client market**—the recipients of money or services from the organization. This recipient market is much like the customer market for a business. However, nonbusiness institutions—such as churches, hospitals, or universities—don't refer to their clients as customers. Instead, they call them parishioners, patients, or students. Because a nonbusiness organization must deal with two different markets, it must develop two different marketing programs—one directed at its resource providers, the other aimed at its clients.

Selecting Target Markets

Selecting target markets is essentially the same whether a firm is marketing goods or services. From Chapters 4 through 6, we know that services marketers need to understand how geographic and demographic factors of the market affect the demand for a service. Marketers also must try to determine their customers' buying behavior—their buying motives and patterns. The psychological determinants of buying behavior—motivation, perceptions, attitudes, personality—become more important when marketing services rather than goods. This is because we cannot touch, smell, or taste the service offered. For the same reasons, the sociological factors of social-class structure and reference groups are significant determinants of buying behavior in services markets.

In the course of selecting target markets, the concept of market segmentation has been adopted by many services marketers. We find apartment complexes for students, and others for the over-55 crowd. Some car-repair shops target owners of foreign cars. Limited-service motel chains (Motel 6, Days Inn) cater to the economy-minded segment. Hotels providing only suites (Embassy Suites, Residence Inns) seek to attract families and business travelers who prefer a "home away from home."

Segmentation strategies are also useful for nonbusiness marketers. Remember, they have two quite separate markets to analyze—resource providers and clients. Each of these two markets usually needs to be further segmented in some detail. A broad (nonsegmented) appeal to the provider market is likely to produce poor results. Likewise, trying to be all things to all people in the client market may mean being "nothing to anybody" and going broke in the process.

Many nonbusiness organizations segment their client markets, although they probably do not consider it market segmentation. For instance, country clubs develop different programs for golfers, tennis players, swimmers, and card players. Symphony orchestras design special programs for children, and arrange bus transportation and matinee performances for senior citizens.

Product Planning

The planning and development of goods has its counterpart in the marketing of services—by both business and nonbusiness organizations. The nonbusiness institution, however, requires one product-planning program for its provider market and one for its client market. Intangibility, inseparability, and high perishability present significant product-planning challenges in services marketing. In terms of product planning, a marketer of services must make strategic decisions concerning:

- What services to offer.
- What product-mix strategies to adopt.
- What features, such as branding and support service, to provide.

Services Offering

Many service firms have become successful by identifying—and then satisfying—a previously unrecognized or unsatisfied consumer want. Consider the cellular phone producers that have entered the expanding market for immediate access to communications. These firms provide a familiar service but overcome the constraint of the fixed-base telephone. In the process they had to create a signal transfer infrastructure and an easy-to-use, highly portable cellular phone.

Like goods marketers, service firms seek ways to *differentiate* their offerings. This is particularly important for services because of the intangibility characteristic. In the absence of physical differences, competing services may appear very similar to the customer. One option is to expand the product, preferably by adding noticeable, attractive physical features. For example, British Airways installed showers in its arrival and departure lounges in Heathrow Airport. However, an added feature should be one that cannot be easily duplicated by competitors or it will be quickly neutralized. In the case of Heathrow showers, American Airlines and United Airlines quickly followed the lead of British Airways. The net effect is none of the airlines has an advantage but all have increased costs.

The lesson here is that service features should be added with caution.[5] For example, a service feature that is difficult for competitors to duplicate is the Ritz-Carlton's "technology butler." Having a skilled computer technician available around the clock to assist guests with large and small software and hardware problems is viewed as highly valuable by traveling executives. However, finding people to fill the position and justifying the salaries will likely prevent most hotels from copying the Ritz.[6]

In most nonprofit organizations the "product" offered to *clients* typically is a service (education, health care, religion, culture), a person (in politics), a cause (stop smoking or don't do drugs), or a cash grant (research foundation). Some nonprofits offer goods such as food and clothing to clients, but these goods are incidental to the main services provided by the organization.

The key to selecting the services to offer is for an organization to decide (1) what "business" it is in and (2) what client markets it wants to reach. If a church views its mission only as providing religious services, its assortment will be limited. If this church views its mission broadly—as providing fellowship, spirituality, and personal development—it will offer more services to more markets. The church may then offer family counseling services, day-care services, religious education courses, and social activities for single people.

Planning the services offering to the *provider* market is more difficult. An organization asks people to contribute money, time, skills, or other resources to a cause. The contribution is the price paid in order to make the organization's services available. But what is the contributor getting for this price? What are the contributors buying with their donations? In the case of donations, the donors can receive an assortment of benefits that may include:

- Feeling good about themselves or relieving their guilt.
- Helping an organization provide a worthwhile service.
- Receiving a tax deduction.
- Contributing to their status in reference groups.
- Supporting their social or religious beliefs.

Product-Mix Strategies

Several of the product-mix strategies discussed in Chapter 9 can be employed by services marketers. Consider the strategy of *expanding the line*. Disney is adding parks in Tokyo and Paris and developing a theme park in Hong Kong, following on its success in the U.S., France, and Japan. Although none of the parks will be identical, they will be sufficiently similar to benefit greatly from the worldwide recognition of the Disney name.

 www.disney.com

In the nonprofit field, symphony orchestras expand their line by offering children's concerts and pop concerts for teenagers and college students. Universities have added adult night classes, TV programs, and concentrated between-semester courses.

Carnival Cruise Lines *contracted its services mix* by selling a casino hotel in the Bahamas—part of a series of moves designed to get the cruise ship company out of the resort business. Because of the high cost of malpractice insurance, some physicians have contracted their product mix by discontinuing the practice of obstetrics.

In response to the growing success of Internet brokerage firms such as Charles Schwab Corp., Merrill Lynch, the largest full-service securities firm in the U.S., is *altering its services offering.* The firm introduced online trading for its 5 million customers, a dramatic change for a firm that takes great pride in the personal service provided by its brokers.[7]

Managing the life cycle of a service is another strategy. Recognizing that the credit card industry is in the maturity stage, VISA sought ways to maintain its growth. The answer was new uses for the card, rather than issuing cards to more people. For starters, VISA targeted dentists, physicians, supermarkets, theaters, and even fast-food outlets, trying to get them to encourage their customers to pay with a VISA card. Likewise, amusement parks such as Knott's Berry Farm in California, Six Flags, and Great America have avoided the sales-decline stage of the life cycle by periodically adding new attractions.

Product Features

The emphasis in product planning is different for services than for goods. For example, packaging is nonexistent in services marketing. However, other features—branding and quality management, for instance—present greater challenges for services industries.

Branding of services is a problem because maintaining consistent quality, a responsibility of brand ownership, is difficult. Also, the intangibility characteristic means a brand cannot be physically attached to the service itself.

A services marketer's goal should be to create an effective brand image. The strategy to reach this goal is to develop a total theme that includes more than just

Goods marketers use color as part of a brand image. The yellow construction equipment of Caterpillar and the blue box of Morton's salt are familiar examples. Some service organizations have also made good use of color to convey an image and an identity. This photo at a college football game certainly suggests that these spectators share similar allegiances.

a good brand name. To implement this strategy, the following tactics frequently are employed:[8]

- Use a *tangible object* to communicate the brand image. The blanket of Nationwide Insurance, and the "Good Hands" of Allstate symbolize what these firms stand for.
- Develop a *memorable slogan* to accompany the brand. "Bring Data to Life" by Lucent Technologies and "Must See TV" by NBC are descriptive and easily remembered.
- Use a *distinctive color scheme* on all tangible aspects of the service. Avis's red and white or Hertz's black and gold office decor, counters, uniforms, and shuttle vans are highly recognizable.

Nonbusiness organizations have been slow to exploit branding. The little that has been done suggests that brands can provide effective marketing support. Colleges use nicknames (a form of brand name) primarily for their athletic teams, but also to identify their students and alumni. Most universities have school colors—another feature that helps increase the market's recognition of the school. Among health research organizations, the Lung Association has registered as a trademark its double-barred Christmas Seal cross. Likewise, the trademarks of the American Red Cross and the YMCA are readily recognized by many people.

Pricing Structure

In services marketing there is a great need for managerial skill in pricing. Because services are perishable, they cannot be stored, and demand for them often fluctuates considerably. Each of these features has significant pricing implications. To further complicate pricing, customers often have a "do-it-yourself" alternative, as in auto or home repairs. There are two tasks in designing a *pricing structure*: determine the base price and select strategies to adjust the base price.

Price Determination in For-Profit Firms

Services marketers set their prices by adding a markup to their costs (called cost plus) or by estimating what target customers are willing to pay, regardless of cost. Electric power and telephone companies, for example, use a cost basis to set prices that will generate a predetermined rate of return on investment. Painters, plumbers, and electricians frequently price their services on a cost-plus basis. Airlines, on the other hand, tend to meet competitors' prices, especially on routes served by two or more airlines, even if those prices result in a financial loss.

The perishability characteristic of services suggests that the demand for a service should influence its price. Interestingly enough, sellers often do recognize situations of strong demand and limited supply. For example, ticket prices are raised significantly for the final concert of a popular musical group, and hotels located near sports stadiums raise their room rates for the dates of championship events. The opposite situation, excess supply, has created an industry on the Internet.

www.priceline.com

Firms such as Priceline allow a buyer to specify a price he or she is willing to pay for a service such as a plane ticket on a particular day. If an airline flying the route is willing to sell a seat at that price, they have a deal. Other services offered on Priceline include hotel rooms, home mortgages, and personal loans.

Price Determination by Nonprofits

Pricing in nonbusiness organizations is different from pricing in a for-profit firm. In the first place, pricing becomes less important when profit making is not a goal. Also, a nonbusiness organization is faced with special forms of pricing in the provider market and in the client market.

In the *provider* market, nonbusiness organizations do not set the price—the amount of the resource contributed. That price is set by contributors when they decide how much they are willing to pay (donate) for the benefits they expect to receive. However, a price is often suggested—for example, donate one day's pay or volunteer for one day a month. And the suggested price is often translated into a client benefit (for example, the amount of food or clothing $100 will provide in an underdeveloped country) to provide the donor with a basis for valuing the contribution.

In the *client* market, some nonbusiness organizations face the same pricing situation, and can use the same methods, as profit-seeking firms. Museums and opera companies, for example, must decide on admission prices; fraternal organizations must set a dues schedule; and colleges must determine how much to charge for tuition. But most nonbusiness organizations cannot use the same pricing methods employed by business firms. These nonbusiness organizations know that they cannot cover their costs with prices charged to clients. The gap between anticipated revenues and costs must be made up by contributions. As yet, there simply are no real guidelines for nonbusiness pricing.

Also, some nonbusiness groups tend to believe there are no pricing considerations with regard to clients because there is no monetary charge to the client. Actually, the goods or services received by clients rarely are free—that is, without a price of some kind. The client almost always pays a price—in the form of travel and waiting time and, perhaps, embarrassment or humiliation—that a money-paying client would not have to pay.

Pricing Strategies

Several common pricing strategies are applicable in services marketing—in both profit-seeking and nonbusiness organizations. *Discounts,* for example, are widely used in marketing services. A season pass for the Metropolitan Opera or the Los Angeles Philharmonic Orchestra costs less per performance than tickets purchased for individual performances. Daily rates charged by Hertz or Avis are lower if you rent a car for a week or a month at a time. These are forms of quantity discount.

A *flexible-price* strategy is used by many service organizations. Museums and movie theaters offer lower prices for children and senior citizens. In some cities, bus transportation costs less during off-peak hours. The University of Colorado charges a higher tuition in its business and engineering colleges than in arts and sciences. On the other hand, the University of Notre Dame and many other universities typically follow a *one-price* strategy. That is, all students pay the same tuition for a full load of course work.

Databases that allow a company to examine an individual's purchase history, can be combined with real-time supply information that indicates how much of a service remains unsold. Using this information a firm can engage in *dynamic pricing,* or adjusting price to meet individual circumstances. For example, an airline can calculate the value of each of its customers based on their individual purchase histories. It can also compute the likelihood of selling the remaining inventory of seats on a particular flight at any time, using historical data. Combining the two pieces of information, an individual can be offered a price that considers the value of retaining the person's loyalty, maximizes the probability of a ticket being purchased, and optimizes the revenue from the flight.

Price competition among service providers varies by industry. Where it has become more common, the use of price competition seems to exist at three levels:

- Price is rarely mentioned as organizations attempt to compete on other dimensions. For example, a health maintenance organization (HMO) will run an ad explaining its services, but will not dwell much on price.
- The seller uses a segmentation strategy and targets a given market at a specific price. A law firm, for example, will prominently advertise its low prices for divorce proceedings or the preparation of a will.

- Intense price competition occurs as firms stress comparative prices in their advertising. Credit card companies and cellular phone service providers have engaged extensively in advertising that compares their prices with those of competitors.

Price competition is particularly intense in service industries where the products are viewed as highly interchangeable, such as fast food. Interestingly, in areas where the products should be fairly easy to differentiate, such as professional services, price competition seems to be increasing. This would suggest that professional services marketers are not effectively using the other components of the marketing mix to differentiate their offerings.

Distribution System

Designing a distribution system for a service (whether in the for-profit or non-business context) involves two tasks. One is to select the parties through which ownership will pass (called the channel of distribution), and the other is to provide facilities for physically distributing the services.

Channels of Distribution

The ownership channel for most services is short and quite simple because of the inseparability characteristic. That is, a service usually cannot be separated from its producer.

The only other frequently used channel includes one agent middleman. For example, an agent or broker often is used when marketing securities, travel arrangements, or housing rentals.

Short channels usually mean more control on the part of the seller. With direct distribution or only a single middleman, it would seem that service marketers should be able to reduce the heterogeneity or variance in the service from one transaction to another. However, because the service provider is also creating the service, a single firm may operate a large number of the same short channel. For example, McDonald's has over 24,000 outlets in 118 countries, all producing and distributing the product. Thus, the control problems are in the *number* of middlemen to be managed, not the length of the channel.

Distribution Facilities

A good location is essential when the distribution of a service requires personal interaction between producer and consumer, especially today because consumers are so convenience-oriented. Some services marketers have broadened their distribution by extending their accessibility, thus offsetting to some extent the limitations imposed by the inseparability factor. Zoots, a dry-cleaning chain, is using technology to increase customer convenience. By providing customers with bar-coded garment bags, soiled clothing can be dropped off at a drive-through window with no employee interaction. The clothes are cleaned, and preapproved charges are made to the customer's credit card, so no paper changes hands. Finally, customers can pick up their cleaned items after hours from lockers outside the outlet.[9]

The Internet has greatly broadened the distribution of some services, making it easier for buyers and sellers to establish contact. As described in the opening case, the Internet has expanded the geographic reach of banks. Bank One and other U.S. banks are faced with competition from Canadian banks that can offer consumers Internet-based accounts virtually anywhere in North America the banking laws permit. Like Bank One, all services retailers need to examine how the Internet impacts the inseparability characteristic of their businesses.

Not-for-profit organizations try to provide arrangements to make donor contributions easy and convenient. Besides cash and checks, charities use payroll deductions, installment plans, and credit cards. If you are contributing used goods, the Disabled American Veterans may collect them at your residence.

What determines the growth of Internet retailing?

Two conditions are necessary for the Internet to function as a retail shopping medium. First, consumers must have access, which in most cases means having a PC and subscribing to an Internet service. Second, consumers must have credit cards and be willing to use them to make online purchases. In the U.S., 45% of households have Internet access, and that figure is projected to grow to 65% by 2003. American consumers are also frequent credit card users, with the average annual charges amounting to $6,500. Thus, the conditions are conducive to Internet retailing in the U.S. However, in Japan only about 13% of the population use the Internet, and credit cards are much less popular. In fact, the average volume of purchases using credit cards in Japan is less than one-third the U.S. average.

Although Japan may not sound like an attractive Internet shopping market, that may be changing. The answer could be found in Japanese convenience stores. In the 1970s the convenience store concept was transferred from the U.S. to Japan, where it grew rapidly. Called *combini* in Japan, the stores are a mainstay in Japanese retailing, with over 50,000 in operation.

The largest chain is 7-Eleven Japan. It has formed an agreement with a Tokyo computer and Internet firm to initially sell books and videos over the Internet. Consumers will order the desired items over the Internet, go to a combini and pay cash for the item, and then visit the store again to pick up the merchandise. To serve people without access to the Internet, 7-Eleven is installing terminals in some stores. The partnership, called eShopping!Books, allows consumers to pay for a purchase at any 7-Eleven, and then select the outlet where they want their order delivered.

Combinis, in an intensely competitive environment, are constantly looking for ways to differentiate their operations. They pioneered utility bill payment in the stores a dozen years ago. Now 7-Eleven records over $4.7 billion in utility payments annually. Most combinis are also in the process of installing automated teller machines, a rarity in Japan. It seems whatever they can do to generate consumer traffic is explored. In this case, two retail operating models, one for a retail store and the other for an Internet service, have been modified to accommodate local market conditions.

Source: Peter Landers, "In Japan, the Hub of E-Commerce Is a 7-Eleven," *The Wall Street Journal*, Nov. 1, 1999, pp. B1+.

Location is also critical when dealing with nonbusiness client markets. Libraries have branches; blood banks conduct blood drives on location in factories and schools; Goodwill Industries locates its stores in low-income neighborhoods; and big-city museums arrange for portable exhibits to be taken to small towns.

Promotional Program

Several types of promotion are used extensively in services marketing—in both profit-seeking and nonprofit organizations. In fact, promotion is the one part of the marketing mix with which services marketers are most familiar and adept. Unfortunately, many services firms, especially nonbusiness organizations, believe that promotion and marketing are the same thing.

Personal Selling

Because of the inseparability characteristic, personal selling plays a pivotal role in promotional programs for most services. Face-to-face contact between buyer and seller is required in order to make a transaction. Thus, it is important that a service employee be skilled at customer relations as well as capable of producing a quality service.

Personal selling is frequently employed by not-for-profit organizations in soliciting donations. Potentially large donors may be approached by fundraisers (sales people). Many nonprofit organizations also use personal selling to reach their clients. For example, all branches of the military make use of recruiters. For centuries, religious missionaries recruited new members by personal contact. Colleges send admissions officers, alumni, and current students to talk to high school students, their parents, and their counselors. These representatives may not be called sales people, but that is exactly what they are.

Whether they realize it or not, all employees of a service provider who come in contact with a customer are, in effect, part of that organization's sales force. In addition to a regular sales force, customer-contact personnel might include airline counter attendants, law office receptionists, package delivery people, bank tellers, ticket takers, and ushers at ballparks or theaters.

The term **service encounter** is used to describe a customer's interaction with any service employee, or with any tangible element such as a service's physical surroundings (bank, theatre, medical office). A large part of a customer's evaluation of an organization and its service is made on the basis of service encounters. Consequently, management must prepare its contact personnel and physical surroundings. The approach to this preparation is often called *internal marketing* to emphasize the idea that a services organization should view its employees as customers to whom it markets customer-contact jobs. When an organization adopts this perspective, it will go to great lengths to make these jobs interesting and fulfilling. The net effect is satisfying service encounters for customers and success for the organization. Many service organizations do not think in these terms and, as a result, have not developed the orientation necessary to produce outstanding customer-contact employees.[10]

Advertising

For years, advertising has been used extensively in many service fields—transportation, recreation, and insurance, for example. At one time, advertising by professional-services providers including attorneys, physicians, and accountants was

Cause-related marketing can be a substantial part of the marketing efforts of businesses and not-for-profit organizations. The Breast Cancer Crusade sponsored by Avon raises funds through the sale of special Crusade fundraising products and through a series of six three-day, sixty-mile fundraising walks such as the one shown here. Although the business benefits of cause-related marketing are sometimes difficult to measure directly, few would argue with the value of the goodwill generated.

 www.avoncrusade.com

Cause-related marketing (see text description) gives nonbusiness organizations a way to extend their promotional reach by teaming up with for-profit corporations. A typical example is America Online's support of Special Olympics. Corporations also find these joint efforts attractive since research shows that they influence consumers' evaluations of a product and enhance employee morale. However, some of these alliances have taken a form that has raised eyebrows. That is, in exchange for a fee, some charities have allowed their logos to be used in the advertising of businesses. For example, the American Cancer Society's logo has appeared in ads for a nicotine-control product, and the American Lung Association's logo has been presented in connection with a carbon monoxide detector. The concern is that the presence of the logo implies an endorsement of the product, and therefore has the potential to mislead consumers into believing that the product is superior to alternatives.

Is it unethical for a business to capitalize on the reputation of a nonprofit organization?

Sources: "Charities' Selling of Logos," *Consumers' Research Magazine,* June 1999, p. 7; Rachel Fox and Jeanie Casison, "Employees and Consumers Like Cause Marketing," *Incentive,* September 1999, p. 16.

prohibited by their professional associations on the grounds that it was unethical. However, the Supreme Court has ruled that prohibiting a professional firm from advertising is restraint of trade and thus a violation of antitrust laws. Some associations still try to limit and control advertising, but the restrictions continue to be eased.[11]

Nonbusiness organizations use advertising extensively to reach their donor markets. Mass media (newspapers, television, radio) frequently are used in annual fund-raising drives. Direct mail can be especially effective in reaching particular donor-market segments, such as cash contributors, religious or ethnic groups, or college alumni. The relatively low cost of a website on the Internet has provided nonprofits such as colleges and universities, and organizations like the Special Olympics and Mother Against Drunk Driving (MADD) with an opportunity to share much more information than was possible in the past.

 www.specialolympics.org

 www.madd.org

Forming an alliance with a for-profit organization can be another valuable source of promotion for nonbusiness organizations. Called *cause-related marketing,* it involves developing a relationship that generates sales for the firm and publicity (along with donations) for the nonprofit organization. A recent survey of young people found that two-thirds consider the causes that may be affected when they shop for clothing and other items. And more than one-half would switch to a brand or retailer that is associated with a good cause if price and quality are equal.[12] A recent example of cause-related marketing is Avon's Breast Cancer Awareness Crusade in conjunction with the National Alliance of Breast Cancer Organizations.

 www.avon.com

Large and small nonbusiness groups also can communicate with client markets through advertising. To offset declining enlistments, the military branches are heavy users of all forms of mass media advertising. The Navy has been successful with a campaign that includes ads directed by filmmaker Spike Lee.[13] After carefully developing a marketing plan, a midwestern women's religious order used advertising to help attract prospective members.[14]

Other Promotional Methods

Various forms of sales promotion are frequently used by services marketers. Laundry and dry-cleaning firms, opticians, and auto-repair shops include reduced-price offers in coupon books mailed periodically to local households. Travel agents, ski resorts, and landscaping services have displays at sports shows or home shows. These displays show the beneficial results of using the service. The United Way,

Salvation Army, and other charitable organizations frequently have booths in shopping malls.

Many service firms, especially in the recreation and entertainment fields, benefit considerably from free publicity. Sports coverage by newspapers, radio, and television provides publicity, as do newspaper reviews of movies, plays, and concerts. Travel sections in newspapers help sell transportation, housing, and other services related to the travel industry.

Managing Service Quality

In Chapter 10, we noted the elusiveness of product quality. Service quality is particularly difficult to define, measure, control, and communicate. Yet in services marketing, the quality of the service is critical to a firm's success. Two airlines each fly Boeing 747s and charge the same fare; two auto-repair shops each use factory-authorized parts and charge the same price; and two banks make home mortgage loans at identical interest rates. Assuming similar times and locations, quality of the service is the only factor that differentiates what is offered by these firms.[15]

Services providers must understand two attributes of **service quality:** First, quality is defined by the customer, not by the producer-seller. Your hairstylist may be delighted with the job done on your hair, but if you think your hair looks terrible, then the service quality is poor. Second, customers assess service quality by comparing their expectations to their perceptions of how the service is performed. In this process, there is no guarantee that expectations will be reasonable, nor is there any assurance that a customer's perception of performance will be based on more than a single experience.

Consequently, to effectively manage quality, a services firm should:

1. Help customers formulate expectations.

2. Measure the expectation level of its target market.

3. Strive to maintain consistent service quality at or above the expectations level.

Expectations are based on information from personal and commercial sources, promises made by the service provider, and experience with the particular service as well as other similar services. Firms have an opportunity through their formal and informal communications to influence customers' expectations. Because of the intangibility of services, providers tend to exaggerate performance. Extravagant claims for education programs, weight-loss regimens, and vacation packages that contribute to unrealistic expectations are unfortunately too commonplace. A services firm must do some research to measure expectations. Gathering data on the target market's past behavior, existing perceptions and beliefs, and exposure to information can provide the basis for estimating expectations.

With the desired level of service keyed to expectations, the next challenge is standardizing service performance—that is, maintaining consistency in service output. Service performance typically varies even within the same organization. This is true in such diverse fields as opera, legal services, landscaping, baseball, hospital care, and marketing courses. The reason is simple: services are most often performed by people and their behavior is very difficult to standardize.

As part of managing service quality, an organization should design and operate an ongoing quality-improvement program. The foundation of quality improvement is monitoring the level and consistency of service quality. Holding to the idea that service quality is defined by customers, a firm must regularly measure customer satisfaction—that is, customers' perceptions of the quality of an organization's services.[16] The Ritz-Carlton hotel chain, a two-time winner of the Malcolm Baldrige National Quality award, emphasizes employee training and measuring customer satisfaction.

 www.ritzcarlton.com

One proposal for standardizing the quality of service delivery is to substitute machines for people whenever possible. At least in theory, an ATM machine or a website on the Internet treats every interaction in the same fashion. Although it's a fact that a machine will not suffer from fatigue, forgetfulness, or stress, this argument ignores the variability on the customer side of the exchange. If a consumer is not adept at surfing the Internet, forgets the required ATM personal identification number, or gets impatient with the branching process on a recorded telephone answering system, the quality of the service encounter is not standardized. Despite this possible shortcoming, the consistency and reliability of machines is one factor that is contributing to the growing popularity of Internet shopping sites.[17]

To standardize the quality of their local operations, some nonbusiness organizations are copying the operating structures used by commercial franchise systems. For example, Camp Fire Girls and Boys and United Way provide local units with managerial expertise, performance evaluation, marketing guidance, and purchasing assistance in exchange for a fee. This arrangement provides the local unit with policies to achieve consistency in all its operations, a high level of managerial expertise, and valuable operating economies.

The Future of Services Marketing

Until recently, many services industries enjoyed growth, supported by government and professional-association regulations, the absence of significant foreign competition, and a strong economy. But the environment is changing, bringing with it a focus on increasing productivity and customer-satisfying performance.

The Impact of Technology on Services

Technology has dramatically changed some services industries and created others. The most immediate impact is being felt by firms that act as agents or brokers for services providers. The Internet offers firms in the travel, accommodations, recreation, and insurance industries a cost-effective way to bypass intermediaries. As a result, travel agents, insurance brokers, and other types of middlemen are being confronted with a new type of competition.[18] In another industry, interactive telecommunications technology has created a distance learning capability that is changing the way training and education are distributed. These and other developments on the horizon will force many services firms to redefine what they do. For example, facsimile machines have diminished the need for overnight delivery of documents, causing FedEx to reinvent itself as an information company rather than a delivery service.[19]

Need for Increased Productivity

The changing services environment has exposed inefficiency and poor management in many services industries, clearly demonstrating the need for restructuring. At the same time, inefficiency provides competent services firms with a tremendous opportunity to increase productivity. This opportunity is being seized by services chains and franchise systems that are replacing small-scale, independent services firms and professionals in many fields. Examples include Kaiser Permanente and Humana in health care; Midas Muffler and Jiffy Lube in auto repairs and maintenance; Pearle Vision and LensCrafters in vision improvement; and Re/Max and Century 21 in real estate.

Not long ago, attempts to increase services productivity were focused on a manufacturing-based approach. For example, Burger King and McDonald's adopted assembly line techniques and increased their output per worker. The most

If viewers talk back, what can advertisers learn?

Interactive television, technology that converts a TV set from a one-way communication device into a dynamic, two-way medium, has been eagerly anticipated for several years. More specifically, it allows viewers to request information and make purchases with a click of the remote control.

Most of the interest comes from marketers who perceive that interactive TV (ITV) provides two "front-end" benefits. First, it gives each viewer the opportunity to tailor the information in a commercial message. By clicking on icons in an ad, a consumer can request coupons, additional details on specific topics, or even product samples. A second benefit is that ITV allows the viewer to purchase items directly through the set using a credit card. So the decision to buy a product can be acted upon immediately, not delayed until the consumer visits a store.

A second function of ITV, referred to as a "back-end" feature, gets less attention but may prove to be more valuable to marketers. ITV can provide specific tracking of viewers' behavior. A company called Wink Communications has developed a system that permits it to determine how many viewers responded to specific shows and commercials, and in what ways they responded. For example, Wink's system is able to track the number of households tuned to a channel, the number that stay tuned, and precisely when those that change channels did so. Thus, an advertiser is able to get a measure of the attention-holding strength of an ad and the types of requests and sales it generates.

ITV is only in a limited number of homes because of the equipment required. However, AT&T, Ford, and Charles Schwab are among the advertisers experimenting with it. According to an AT&T advertising executive, "We (AT&T) wanted to see how this interaction happened (at this early stage) a lot more than we wanted to get new customers."

Source: Yochi J. Dreazen, "Investors Bat Eyes at TV Pioneer Wink," *The Wall Street Journal,* July 21, 1999, p. B8.

 www.wink.com

widely adopted technology was some form of computer-based information system that increased the efficiency of operations. And for several years this manufacturing-based model for increasing service productivity was successful.

However, the basic premise of the manufacturing model is that machines and technology are the primary keys to increased productivity, that the people who deliver the services are not as important. But this premise no longer works in the services environment. Instead, a model is needed that combines technology and customer-contact workers, and designs the business operations around the needs of the customer.

Performance Measurement

Profit-seeking service firms can evaluate their performances by using quantitative measures such as profitability, market share, or return on investment, and then can compare these figures with industry averages and trends. However, for most nonbusiness organizations, because their objectives are so varied, there are few generally accepted performance measures. Consequently, measuring marketing performance in the nonbusiness sector requires some imagination and creativity.

Nonbusiness organizations can quantify the contributions they receive, but the result reflects only their fund-raising abilities. It does not measure the services rendered to their clients. How do you quantitatively evaluate the performance of, say, the Red Cross? Perhaps by the number of people the organization houses and feeds after a hurricane or some other natural disaster. Or by the number of people trained in first aid and life-saving techniques. Churches, museums, and YMCAs can count their attendance, but how do they measure the quality of the services and benefits they provide to their clients?

The analysis and management of customer complaints is an evaluation tool that can be used by both nonbusiness and profit-seeking organizations. The complaint-management process involves keeping track of (1) customer complaints, (2) how they are resolved, and (3) whether the complaint handling was satisfactory, so the complaining customer ends up as a returning customer.

Prospects for Growth

Services will continue to take an increasing share of the consumer dollar, just as they have done over the past 40 years. Time pressure and a reevaluation of priorities are contributing factors. As one New Jersey entrepreneur observed, "Life has become so compressed that I decided my time with my family is worth more than money."[20] This forecast seems reasonable even for periods of economic decline. History shows that the demand for services is less sensitive to economic fluctuations than the demand for goods.

The demand for commercial services should also continue to expand as business becomes more complex and as management further recognizes its need for specialized support services. In professional services especially, the use of marketing programs is expected to increase considerably during the coming decade. This expansion will occur as physicians, lawyers, and other professionals come to understand the economic benefits they can derive from an effective marketing program.

The significance of nonbusiness marketing will increase as the people in these organizations understand what marketing is and what it can do for them. As noted earlier in this chapter, nonbusiness organizations typically have a limited concept of marketing, even though they engage in some efforts without calling it marketing. The marketing activities they do perform (usually promotion) often are not well coordinated, and the people in charge of them usually have other duties and titles. In a university, for example, personal selling may be managed by the director of admissions, fund raising coordinated by a director of development, and advertising done through an office of public information. For a more effective marketing job, most nonbusinesses need a more formal, recognizable marketing structure.

Summary

The scope of services marketing is enormous. About 50% of what consumers spend goes for services, and more than 80% of nonfarm jobs are in services industries. Services purchased by businesses constitute another major segment of the economy. The nonbusiness services field includes thousands of organizations spanning educational, cultural, religious, charitable, social, health care, and political activities. Services marketers can be divided into for-profit businesses and nonbusiness organizations, made up of not-for-profits and nonprofits. The not-for-profit organizations have a profit (or surplus) objective, but it is secondary to some other goal. Nonprofits do not have a profit objective.

Most product offerings are a mix of tangibles (goods) and intangibles (services), somewhere between pure goods and pure services. To distinguish between goods and services, we define services as separately identifiable, intangible activities that are the main object of a transaction designed to provide want-satisfaction.

Services are intangible, usually inseparable from the seller, heterogeneous, highly perishable, and widely fluctuating in demand. These characteristics that differentiate services from goods have several marketing implications.

The growth in services has not been matched by service management's application of the marketing concept. Monopoly status, external constraints, and a nonbusiness orientation have caused many services marketers to be slow in adopting marketing techniques that, in goods marketing, have brought satisfaction to consumers and profits to producers and middlemen. However, that is changing as constraints and restrictions are removed, and service producers observe the benefits of effective marketing.

Developing a program for marketing services is much the same as for goods, but takes into account the characteristics of services. Management first identifies its target market, making use of market segmentation strategies, and then designs a marketing mix around a differential advantage to provide want-satisfaction for the market.

Many nonbusiness services organizations must deal with two markets: donors, the contributors to the organization; and clients, the recipients of the organization's money or services. Consequently, a nonbusiness organization must develop two separate marketing programs: one to attract resources from donors and one to provide services to clients.

In the product-planning stage, services enterprises use various product-mix strategies, and they should try to brand their services. Service firms must determine base prices and select appropriate pricing strategies. Pricing in nonbusiness organizations often is quite different from pricing in profit-seeking businesses.

Channels of distribution are quite simple in services marketing, and middlemen are not often used. The main physical distribution challenge is to locate the services organization where it can most effectively serve its markets. Regarding promotion, services firms often use personal selling and advertising extensively and quite effectively. These organizations are recognizing the importance of service encounters and the need to engage in internal marketing directed at customer-contact personnel.

Consistently maintaining a level of quality that the customer expects is critical to a company's success. Managing customers' expectations is an important services issue.

The expanding services arena has exposed inefficiency in services industries. Key issues in improving services marketing are the effective use of technology, the need to increase productivity, and the development of useful performance measures.

More about **Wingspan**

About 10 million consumers are using Internet banking. But of that group, less than 5% are customers of Internet-only banks. Some believe that banking exclusively over the Internet is too radical for most consumers. According to one Dallas-based bank consultant, Bank One is "way out in left field" in its estimate of the market potential.

The biggest drawback to this mode of banking is that the Internet cannot directly accept or deliver cash. Customers have to use ATM machines to get cash. For now, Wingspan refunds to its customers the charges associated with using another system's ATM machine. Another problem is the elimination of paper records. One of Internet banking's cost savings comes from paper reduction. However, many bank customers want a physical record of their transactions. Finally, the issue of Internet security is still on many consumers' minds.

Other major banks, such as Wells Fargo and Bank of America, also offer services over the Internet. However, these other major banks have thus far avoided creating Internet-only electronic branches similar to Wingspan. Critics of this cautious approach have suggested that traditional bankers like their "bricks and mortar." They also recall how slow banks were in responding to competition from thrift institutions, credit unions, and insurance companies in the 1960s and 1970s.

Wingspan will face immediate competition from Canadian banks seeking growth opportunities in the U.S. Royal Bank of Canada has linked two of its U.S. operations online, an Internet bank in Atlanta and a discount investment brokerage firm. Also entering the market is Canadian Imperial Bank of Commerce. It is following Canadian "snowbirds" to Florida with an Internet bank in Orlando.

Possibly offering some insight into its move, a Bank One executive noted that in Internet book selling, market shares were determined quickly, and only the most assertive firms have survived. It's been predicted that over 85% of U.S. banks will offer Internet banking by 2003, up from just 6% in 1998.[21]

1. How important is it for a firm to quickly establish itself in a market in which transactions are conducted electronically?

2. What can Wingspan do to adapt to the service characteristics of intangibility, inseparability, heterogeneity, and perishability?

Key Terms and Concepts

Services (293)
For-profit services firms (293)
Not-for-profit services organiza-
tions (N-F-P) (293)
Nonprofit organization (294)

Intangibility (295)
Inseparability (295)
Heterogeneity (295)
Perishability (295)
Provider market (299)

Client market (recipients) (299)
Service encounter (306)
Service quality (308)

Questions and Problems

1. a. What are some marketing implications of the fact that services possess the characteristic of intangibility?
   b. How can an organization's website be used to reduce intangibility?

2. Services are highly perishable and are often subject to fluctuations in demand. In marketing an amusement park, how can a company offset these factors?

3. Cite some examples of large services firms that seem to be customer-oriented, and describe what these firms have done to create this impression.

4. Identify the various segments of the donor market for your school.

5. Present a brief analysis of the market for each of the following service firms. Make use of the components of a market discussed in Chapters 4 and 5, and the concepts of market segmentation in Chapter 6.
   a. Hospital in your city
   b. Hotel near a large airport
   c. Indoor tennis club
   d. Regional airline

6. What are some ways in which each of the following service firms might expand its product mix?
   a. Certified public accountant (CPA)
   b. Hairstyling salon
   c. Bank

7. A financial consultant for a private university suggested a change in the school's pricing methods. He recommended that the school discontinue its present one-price policy, under which all full-time students pay the same tuition. Instead, he recommended that the tuition vary by departments within the university. Thus, students majoring in high-cost fields of study, such as engineering or a laboratory science, would pay higher tuition than students in lower-cost fields, such as English or history. Should the school adopt this recommendation?

8. Explain how the components of the marketing mix (product, price, distribution, promotion) are applicable to marketing the following social causes:
   a. The use of returnable bottles, instead of the throwaway type
   b. The prevention of heart ailments
   c. A campaign against smoking
   d. Obeying the speed limit

9. "When used by consumers for making purchases, the Internet seems to offset the service characteristics of inseparability and heterogeneity." Explain whether or not that statement is true in the case of:
   a. eBay.com
   b. eToys.com
   c. bicworldusa.com

10. How would you measure the marketing performance of each of the following?
    a. adidas website
    b. Your school
    c. The Republican Party
    d. A group in favor of gun control

Hands-On Marketing

1. Grade the marketing performance of a sample of five profit-seeking services firms in your college community by asking 10 of your friends to rate each of them on a scale of 10 (excellent performer) to 1 (very poor performer). Compute an average "performance score" for each firm. On the basis of your survey, identify those that are doing a good marketing job and those that are not. In your report, explain briefly the reasons that contribute to the ratings of the best and worst performers.

2. Examine the websites of three nonbusiness services organizations (for example, a charity, a college or university, and a professional or trade association). Report the evidence you find that indicates the organizations are focused on a need, have identified a target market, and have developed a complete marketing mix.

Cases for Part 3

Case 1 • Sega versus Nintendo versus Sony

Positioning a New Product for a Big Score

In 1993, Sega commanded almost 60% of the U.S. video game market. The industry, once dominated by rival Nintendo, had been turned upside down by Sega. The product that made Sega so popular with video gamers was Genesis, which means beginning. Unfortunately for Sega, it seemed like the beginning of the end. Their next product introduction, the Saturn, was a dismal failure and was blown away by Nintendo 64 and Sony's PlayStation.

By 1999, Sega's share of the $7 billion home video game market in the U.S. was 1%, compared to 42% for Nintendo and 56% for Sony. Instead of calling it quits, Sega designed a new game machine called the Dreamcast that had an impressive product launch during the 1999 holiday season, giving Sega reason for hope in the new century. Sega's latest introduction continues a high-stakes game of "technological leap frog" as the three companies strive to improve the capabilities of their brands of video game machines in order to win the favor of consumers.

The Industry's Top Three Players

The home video game market was born in 1976 when Fairchild introduced the Video Entertainment System, which featured 21 different games including Pong. Enthusiasm for home video games soared in 1977, when Atari introduced the Video Computer System. In 1978, hardware and software sales totaled $200 million. In 1979, Atari bought the rights to Space Invaders, a tremendously successful arcade game. Within three years, Atari was a $2 billion international company. However, intense competition from other video game companies and a lack of product innovation eventually led to Atari's demise.

The rise of personal computers in the mid-1980s spurred interest in computer games, which caused a crash in the home video game market. Video games rebounded when a number of different companies developed hardware consoles that provided graphics superior to the capabilities of computer games. By 1990, the Nintendo Entertainment System dominated the product category. The introduction of Genesis in the early 1990s made Sega one of the most recognized brand names among American kids. It also gave Sega a 60% share of the market. The company's success was short-lived. Sega launched the Saturn system, a new 32-bit system (bit is a unit of computer memory) in 1995, but it was a dismal failure. Largely because of this flop, Sega lost $361 million in the 1997 fiscal year.

The Saturn system failed to capture the imagination of devoted video game players for several reasons:

- Sega acted as the primary software developer for Saturn. As a result, it was difficult for third-party developers to create additional games that could be played on the console.

- Too often, Sega was late delivering its own software to retailers. Consequently, there were few interesting games that could be played on the Saturn.

- The price of the Saturn system was high compared to other video machines with similar capabilities.

Nintendo and Sony benefited greatly from Saturn's weaknesses. Unveiled in late 1994, Sony's PlayStation was installed in 70 million homes worldwide by the end of 1999. Its "open design" encouraged the efforts of third-party software developers. The outcome was an astonishing number of compatible game titles for the PlayStation—almost 3,000 in all. When the PlayStation was released, its 32-bit graphics capabilities were considered sophisticated, and appealed to an older audience. More than 30% of PlayStation owners are over 30 years old, and only 17% are in grade school. In contrast, most of Nintendo's users are between the ages of 6 and 13 and, because the company exercises more control over software development, Nintendo had only one-tenth the number of games compared to PlayStation.

Nintendo 64, introduced in 1996, had eye-popping 64-bit graphics and was able to lure some customers away from both Sony and Sega. In 1999, more than 28 million homes owned Nintendo 64. However, having introduced its console first, Sony held the majority of market share at the end of the 20th century, with Nintendo in second place. Sega was struggling just to remain a player in the competitive world of home video games.

Sega Gets Back in the Game

Sega either had to concede defeat or introduce an innovative video game machine that would ring up huge sales. And it was equally important that Sega bring a new product to the market before rival companies did. Sega spent $100 million to promote the September 1999 launch of Dreamcast. The massive effort created such a "buzz" that 300,000 video gamers placed advance orders for the new product. In addition, many retailers opened their doors for business at midnight on September 9, when Dreamcast was first available for sale.

So what was all the fuss about? For starters, the Dreamcast boasts a 128-bit system capable of generating 3-D visuals. Within three months of Dreamcast's introduction, 40 different games were available on CD-ROMs, with more on the way. It appears Sega learned from its mistakes with the Saturn, because the company made a concerted effort to support outside development efforts and promised substantial financial incentives for games that became big hits.

For the hard-core players, several optional features such as the plug-in Visual Memory Unit and the LCD screen allow users to play games away from the console. In addition, there's a microphone for voice control and a video camera for those who desire to truly insert themselves into the action.

The early reviews for Dreamcast, as a video game machine, were highly favorable. Questions were raised, however, as to whether or not the added built-in capabilities were worthwhile and effective. Nevertheless, because it was first and foremost a marvelous game-playing machine, the launch of the Dreamcast was a blazing success. Sega sold 1.5 million Dreamcast machines and 4.5 million games in less than four months, beating the company's own forecast by two months and setting new industry records. By year-end 1999, Sega had boosted its market share to 15%. This gain is particularly impressive considering that home video game sales grew a modest 11% in 1999, compared to 24% in 1998.

More Than Just Fun and Games

Besides its impressive game capabilities, the Dreamcast includes a 56K modem, which runs through a user's phone line, and a Web browser. These were promoted as allowing access to the Web so users could play each other online. However, to many people's disappointment, that feature wasn't immediately available. Purchasers did have access to the Web (for a monthly surcharge) and the Dreamcast Network, which provides product information and playing tips. Unfortunately, many technology buffs reported that the quality of the television display was poor and the controller was unwieldy when navigating the Web.

Sega isn't alone in this strategy of adding functionality beyond games. Sony and Nintendo have altered their next generation of game consoles to include additional features. Nintendo describes its new Neptune system, scheduled for release in late 2000, as being built on a DVD (digital video disc) platform with a 128-bit processor and a modem. Analysts applaud the move to DVD, because it is less expensive to produce and allows more storage than CDs. It also gives purchasers the ability to use the machine as a CD music player and a DVD movie player. Nintendo said the company is developing its own Neptune games first and will release third-party titles later.

Sony's PlayStation 2, available in the U.S. in fall 2000, also uses DVD technology. PlayStation 2 is able to play games developed for its predecessor, which was CD-based. This "backward-compatible" feature is exciting news for current PlayStation owners. Like the competing machines, PlayStation 2 has a 128-bit main chip.

The new PlayStation seems to be the most aggressive step in pursuing technology for functions other than games. PlayStation 2 features a high-speed modem so users can access the Internet through digital cable as well as over telephone lines. This will give Sony the ability to distribute movies, music, and games directly to its PlayStation 2 customers. The new machine not only will be able to hook up to the Internet, but also will offer applications for a variety of electronic devices such as digital camcorders. "We're positioning this as an all-around entertainment player," said Ken Kutaragi, president of Sony Computer Entertainment Inc.

The Price of Winning the Video Game Wars

When released, Dreamcast was competing only against Nintendo 64 and the original PlayStation. Sony and Nintendo were at least a year away from introducing their next generation of game machines. "Compared to existing machines, Dreamcast beats them in every respect," remarked Jyunichi Nagai, publicity manager for Capcom, a major software manufacturer.

Dreamcast carried a price tag of $199, with compatible games selling for about $50 each. In response to the new-product introduction, both Nintendo and Sony lowered the prices of their existing systems to an all-time low of $99, and classic game titles were discounted, some to as low as $19.99.

Nintendo did not divulge the suggested retail price of the Neptune system prior to introducing it. The new PlayStation has a price tag of $360. That's considerably higher than Dreamcast, but Sony expects (or hopes) that consumers will pay the higher price because PlayStation 2 can act as a DVD and CD player as well as a video game machine. In fact, Sony's Kutaragi sees the PlayStation 2 as nothing less than "a new entertainment platform for the home." The head of a company that supplies software to Sony considers the new PlayStation to be an historic breakthrough, describing it as "a mass-market appliance that fundamentally changes society in the way the printing press did." That remains to be seen, of course!

Other Players Enter the Fray

The video game industry has just three main players—Nintendo, Sega, and Sony. Because of strong brand loyalty and high product-development costs, newcomers have had great difficulty entering this industry. But one company thinks it can attain a foothold in the video games market, perhaps even achieve a dominant position. Microsoft has indicated that it may invest billions of dollars in a home video game console, nicknamed the X-Box. Some observers believe this move is a response to Sony's PlayStation 2, which has functions that rival Microsoft's WebTV system and even some lower-end PCs. The X-Box would be much like a basic PC that connects to a TV to play games and DVD videos; it would also provide access to the Internet. With PC component prices falling rapidly, the X-Box may be able to offer even more advanced capabilities than PlayStation 2, and one software executive described it as "a console machine with PC innards."

In addition to the threat of new game machines, manufacturers of video game consoles still consider computer video games significant competition. In 1997, $1.8 billion worth of PC-based games were sold, compared to $3.3 billion of console games. However, sales of software for consoles increased by 65% over the previous year, compared to a meager 5% for PC game software. Clearly, video game fanatics enjoy the superior graphics provided by game machines.

Additional competition in the video game industry may come from upstart Internet companies that offer consumers the opportunity to play new games at their websites. As many traditional manufacturers are now discovering, the Web is changing the rules of the game at a rapid pace, with online enterprises coming out of nowhere to score big, even in established markets.

Although Sega is facing a variety of existing and potential competition, it has the advantage of introducing its 128-bit console one year earlier than Nintendo, Sony, and even Microsoft. That strategy paid off big for Sony in the 1990s. However, if Dreamcast doesn't remain a winner in the video game wars, it may be "Game Over" for Sega.

Questions

1. Should video game companies continue to alter their products to include functions besides games?

2. a. Where do video game machines fall in the product life cycle?
   b. What are the marketing implications of being in that life-cycle stage?

3. Does Dreamcast have the desired attributes of a brand name?

www.sega.com

www.playstation.com

www.nintendo.com/n64

Sources: Steven Levy, "Here Comes PlayStation 2," Newsweek, March 6, 2000, pp. 54–59; Robert A. Guth, "Inside Sony's Trojan Horse," The Wall Street Journal, Feb. 25, 2000, pp. B1, B4. Dean Takahashi, "'Sonic' Boom Marks Sega's Comeback in Video Games," The Wall Street Journal, Jan. 13, 2000, p. B6; Janet Rae-Dupree and Irene M. Kunii, "Can Dreamcast Make Sega's Dreams Come True?" Business Week, Dec. 27, 1999, p. 62; Tracy Collins, "PlayStation, Nintendo or Dreamcast?" St. Louis Post-Dispatch, Dec. 12, 1999, p. EV8; Dean Takahashi, "With Sony in Its Sights, Microsoft Weighs Entry into Game Machines," The Wall Street Journal, Oct. 26, 1999, pp. B1, B6; Stephen H. Wildstrom, "Boy, Can This Box Play Games," Business Week, Oct. 11, 1999, p. 22; Jonathan Takiff, "Sega's Dreamcast . . . A Dream Come True for Video Gamers," St. Louis Post-Dispatch, Sept. 26, 1999, p. EV7; "Dreamcast Wires Next Jolt of Future Shock," St. Louis Post-Dispatch, Sept. 26, 1999, p. EV7; Irene M. Kunii and Janet Rai-Dupree, "Sega's Dream Machine," Business Week, Sept. 13, 1999, p. 60; Rachel Beck, "Dreamcast Goes on Sale Today; Players Already Seem to Love It," St. Louis Post-Dispatch, Sept. 9, 1999, p. C1; Ben Pappas, "From Pong to Kingpin," Forbes, May 31, 1999, p. 54; Maryanne Murray Buechner, "The Battle Has Just Begun," Time Digital, Apr. 12, 1999, pp. 28–31; Benjamin Fulford, "Killer Sequel," Forbes, Apr. 5, 1999, pp. 52–53; Reiji Yoshida, "Sega Plays Survival Game with Dreamcast," Japan Times Weekly International Edition, Dec. 14–20, 1998, p. 13; "The Interactive Digital Software Association Report on Video and Compute Game Software," Billboard, Apr. 4, 1998, p. 56; and information from <www.emuunlim.com>.

Putting Forth Its Own Brands of Hospitality

Although Marriott opened its first hotel in Arlington, Virginia, in 1957, its experience in the service industry dates back to 1927. That's when J. W. and Alice Marriott opened a small root beer stand in Washington, DC, that later became known as the Hot Shoppe restaurant. The family aggressively expanded the business to include 70 Hot Shoppes in the district and seven states. They also began the very first in-flight catering service and later purchased several well-known restaurant chains. In 1953, the company went public; J. W. Marriott remained president, succeeded by his son Bill in 1964.

Marriott expanded its hotel business by building a variety of new properties and by acquiring successful, existing chains. In the process, the Marriott family name became one of the best-known brands in the entire world. Marriott later divested itself of the restaurant business, and eventually spun off its burgeoning food-service business in order to concentrate primarily on lodging. The moves seem to have paid off. In 1999, Marriott International was the largest hotel company in *Fortune* magazine's ranking of the 500 biggest U.S. firms. It was also one of the "Most Admired Companies in America," according to a poll conducted by *Fortune*.

Checking Out Marriott's Product Mix

Marriott International operates and franchises lodging properties that offer business and pleasure travelers an array of products from which to choose. Marriott's eight primary brands are described below, in approximate order of their room rates:

- *Ritz-Carlton Hotels*—about three dozen hotels, intended to be synonymous with luxury and among the finest in the industry; purchased by Marriott as an established chain.

- *Marriott Hotels, Resorts and Suites*—the company's flagship brand, providing upscale, full-service lodging.

- *Renaissance Hotels and Resorts*—strategically located in major cities to attract upscale business and pleasure travelers at about the same price levels as the flagship properties.

- *Residence Inn by Marriott*—moderately priced, spacious suites with kitchens for people who need a place to stay for an extended period of time.

- *Courtyard by Marriott*—a moderately priced brand that emphasizes consistency in fulfilling the needs of business travelers.

- *SpringHill Suites by Marriott*—the company's upper-moderate, all-suite brand, targeted at business and leisure travelers, with an emphasis on women and families.

- *TownePlace Suites by Marriott*—another extended-stay chain in the lower moderate-price range.

- *Fairfield Inn by Marriott*—the company's upper-economy chain, targeting both business and pleasure travelers.

Keying In on a Successful Branding Strategy

Several different product-mix and branding strategies are evident in the hotel industry. For instance, Choice Hotels International has seven brands, each targeting a different market segment. To keep them distinctive, none of the brands mentions the name Choice and each brand has its own toll-free reservation number. According to a Choice Hotels senior vice president, these strategies help the company avoid market conflicts.

Hilton is at the other end of the branding spectrum. With a primary focus on the upscale and midrange markets, every property owned by the company carries the Hilton name as part of the brand. The company recently launched a new brand, Hilton Garden Inn, to compete in the moderate-price segment. Hilton strategically places these new hotels in suburban areas to ensure they will not compete with existing Hilton properties. Despite this decision to target an additional market segment in the hotel industry, Hilton has no plans to downscale further. "We would not go into the budget arena," stated a corporate vice president. "We can't stretch the Hilton name further down the market."

Marriott falls somewhere between Choice and Hilton on this dimension of branding. Even with a broad product mix, Marriott displays its name on most of its hotels, although sometimes in a secondary position. The brands that don't contain the company name were acquired and already possessed strong, well-known brands. "We have the Marriott name on all our products except for Renaissance Hotels and Ritz-Carlton," explained a vice president who oversees branding. "We feel there is great equity in the name, particularly when a traveler seeks out a room on short notice."

Some critics contend that this strategy might create confusion. After all, some consumers might connect the Marriott name with Fairfield and its limited amenities and economy price, and others might associate it with the more luxurious and higher-price Marriott resorts. That's why Marriott places such a high premium on providing a dependable level of service at every one of its 1,800 different locations. As a result, the company doesn't worry that the lesser brands will detract from its overall image. Rather, it believes that using the Marriott name creates more value by giving travelers an array of lodging options and an assurance of consistent quality.

Bill Marriott further explains the company's strategy, using one particular metropolitan area as an example. "Atlanta is a tight market, but if a customer calls us, we can usually get him a room because we have 50 properties in the area. They have a better chance of getting their needs satisfied by us than they would by calling an individual hotel." To help Marriott serve its customers in this manner, it offers one toll-free reservations number for all of its lodging brands. This strategy seems to be paying off; Marriott's occupancy rates are the highest in the industry in each market segment it serves.

Making Room for International Expansion

In addition to blanketing the U.S. with Marriott properties, the company is seeking growth internationally. It already has more than 350 locations in over 50 countries. Now, Marriott is looking at Europe and Latin America to further globalize the brand.

Courtyard by Marriott, which had no European hotels until several years ago, opened 10 in Germany and one in both France and Austria in 1998. This division of Marriott intends to open up to 10 hotels a year in Europe. According to this plan, Marriott will take advantage of the equity of the Marriott name by placing new Courtyards in cities that already have at least one Marriott hotel.

By the end of the 20th century, Marriott had also established hotels in every capital city in Latin America, with the exception of Caracas. In many of these countries, Marriott has a more visible presence than any other hotel company. Seeking to capitalize on this strong position, Marriott announced plans to build new Renaissance and Ritz-Carlton hotels throughout Latin America.

These plans for international expansion seem to make sense even in a city like Moscow. Despite a sagging Russian economy, depressed hotel occupancies, and falling hotel rates, the three Moscow Marriotts are faring much better than their competitors. Approximately 80% of the hotels' guests are from the U.S. or western Europe, for whom the Marriott name and its Western style of management are strong at-

tractions. The hotels' employees are also impressed by the Marriott firm, so turnover is low, which is essential in providing a high quality of service.

Marriott is hoping to further leverage its global brand name as the Official Lodging Supplier for the 2002 Olympic Winter Games and for all of the U.S. Olympic Teams through 2004. "The Olympic Games provide a tremendous opportunity for Marriott International as a new marketing effort to reinforce our growing presence around the world," explained Bill Marriott.

Accommodating Other Products

In addition to its eight primary hotel brands, Marriott International operates time-share villas, conference centers, and corporate housing facilities. In total, these products comprise the broadest selection of lodging in the world, with more than 325,000 rooms and time-share units. Below is a description of the additional four brands:

- *Marriott Vacation Club International*—as the world's largest vacation ownership company, offers time-share units at 38 resorts.

- *Marriott Conference Centers*—designed to accommodate group business meetings by providing meeting space and support, dining facilities, and recreational options.

- *ExecuStay by Marriott*—provides corporate housing for business travelers who require lodging for very extended stays.

- *Marriott Executive Apartments*—upscale apartments in major cities outside the U.S., featuring hotel amenities designed for business executives on an international assignment for an extended period of time.

Marriott also operates a national network of food distribution centers and a company that offers contracting and procurement services to the hospitality industry. In addition, it has developed more than 150 senior-living communities throughout the U.S. You might think the only segment Marriott hasn't targeted is the toddler set. Well, you would be wrong!

Creating Loyalty without Reservation

In service industries, maintaining consistent and high levels of quality is very important, which makes employee retention a primary priority. This is particularly difficult in the hotel industry. Consider the demographics of Marriott's employee population. Almost 85% of its 135,000 U.S. employees are hourly workers, and many are single women trying to balance work with raising a family on a limited wage.

Typically, turnover and absentee rates are high, which in turn can damage service quality.

As a result, Marriott has experimented with employer-sponsored child-care centers. The first such joint venture, based in Atlanta, was funded by several hotels, including two Marriotts. Its goal is to provide affordable (and in some cases subsidized) child care during the hours worked by hotel employees. Although participation hasn't been as high as anticipated, Marriott is considering revising the program and expanding it to other cities in the U.S.

In 1991, Marriott launched another innovative program, called Pathways, which offers welfare recipients the training and support necessary to become productive employees. It has been so successful that President Clinton based his Welfare to Work initiative on it. For Marriott, such programs are designed to do much more than garner favorable public relations. Graduates of Pathways have a first-year turnover rate that is much lower than that of other hotel employees. Marriott also believes it has achieved a good return on its investment in a confidential hotline for employees who need assistance with everything from immigration issues to help with babysitters or care for elderly family members.

Marriott strives to build loyalty among its employees *and* its customers. With 12 million members, the Marriott Rewards program is the largest frequent-guest program in the hotel industry. It gives Marriott customers the opportunity to obtain a variety of travel awards in exchange for points that are based on the amount of money spent at Marriott properties. When it was first introduced in 1983, the program was limited to Marriott Hotels, Resorts, and Suites. Some frequent travelers were displeased that they could not earn points from (or redeem them for prizes at) other Marriott properties. In 1997, the program was revamped to include all of Marriott's lodging brands. In 1999, readers of *Business Traveler International* magazine selected it as the "Best Hotel Reward Program in the World" for the third consecutive year.

With a broad product mix and a number of innovative programs to satisfy both customers and employees, not to mention more than $8 billion in annual sales, Marriott is certainly providing a wake-up call that the rest of the industry can't afford to ignore.

Questions

1. The Marriott company evolved from providing a variety of services (restaurants and in-flight catering in addition to lodging) to focusing on lodging. Recently it has expanded its product mix once again by adding conference centers and apartments. What factors should enter into a decision to contract or expand an organization's product mix?

2. Do you agree with Marriott's strategy to brand some, but not all, of its properties with the Marriott name?

3. Considering the desirable attributes of a brand name, which of the Marriott properties has the best brand name?

4. How does Marriott's marketing plan take into account the unique challenges and opportunities posed by the four distinguishing characteristics of a service?

www.choicehotels.com

www.marriott.com

www.hilton.com

Sources: Ellen Graham, "Marriott's Bid to Patch the Child-Care Gap Gets a Reality Check," *The Wall Street Journal,* Feb. 2, 2000, p. B1; "Interstate Braves the Cold," *Hotels,* May 1999, pp. 30+; Onelia Collazo, "Chain Reaction," *LatinFinance,* April 1999, p. S11; "Courtyard Eyes Corporate Travellers across Europe," *Travel Trade Gazette Europa,* Nov. 26, 1998, p. 11; Christina Binkley, "Marriott Outfits an Old Chain for New Market," *The Wall Street Journal,* Oct. 13, 1998, pp. B1, B4; Robert Selwitz, "MultiBranding Opportunities Need Special Strategies," *Hotel & Motel Management,* May 18, 1998, pp. 34+; Shannon Stevens, "Brand Builders," *Brandweek,* Mar. 16, 1998, pp. 19+; Edward Watkins, "Bill Marriott Speaks," *Lodging Hospitality,* September 1997, pp. 22+; Jeffrey P. Berlind, "Talking with Bill Marriott," *Restaurant Business,* July 1, 1997, pp. 160+; and several press releases and historical information from Marriott International's home page.

Price

The development of a pricing structure and its use as part of the marketing mix

We are in the process of developing a marketing mix to reach our target markets and achieve our marketing goals. Having completed product planning, we turn now to pricing, where we face two tasks. First, we must determine the base price for a product that is consistent with our pricing objectives; this endeavor is covered in Chapter 12. Second, we must decide on strategies (such as discounts and value pricing) to employ in modifying and applying the base price; these strategies are discussed in Chapter 13.

*According to Jay Walker, the founder of
Priceline.com Inc., his company's approach
to pricing and selling products is "absolutely
revolutionary."*

With **Priceline.com**, Is the Price Always Right?

You've probably seen or heard the ads in which William Shatner, the former star of *Star Trek,* urges consumers to visit Priceline.com to "name their own price" for various products, including airline tickets, cars, and hotel rooms. According to Jay Walker, the founder of Priceline.com Inc., his company's approach to pricing and selling products is "absolutely revolutionary."

Walker raised more than $100 million in venture capital to launch Priceline, his vision of "buyer-driven commerce." Priceline began by selling otherwise vacant airline seats to price-conscious leisure travelers who were willing to fly at inconvenient times in exchange for a price they deemed acceptable.

Walker developed and patented a business process that begins when a prospective traveler logs on to Priceline.com. The consumer fills out a form specifying desired departure and arrival cities and travel dates as well as the maximum acceptable ticket price. A person submitting a bid agrees to accept any departure time between 6 a.m. and 10 p.m. on the stipulated travel date. The information submitted by a hopeful traveler is then compared against a database maintained by Priceline to determine whether or not a match is available. The information contained in the database includes prices the airlines are willing to accept for unsold seats. If there's a match (that is, the desired travel dates and cities at a mutually acceptable price), the customer is notified by e-mail. If a match is made, the traveler has to purchase the ticket.

At the request of participating airlines, Priceline has instituted a number of other restrictions to ensure that it sells tickets to people, typically leisure travelers, who probably would not purchase an airline ticket without a special inducement. Thus the consumer cannot pick a particular airline, ask to change the flight schedule, or receive frequent-flier miles. Often, the flights include a change of planes with one or more stops. A customer who cannot take the flight is not allowed to request a refund.

In Priceline's first year of business, only 7% of the requests submitted by prospective travelers wound up in a match. A big reason for the low match rate was that only two airlines, TWA and America West, initially signed up for the service. In addition, Priceline subsidized many of the bids and wound up losing about $30 on each ticket it sold. Priceline makes its money by keeping the difference between the consumer's bid and the amount it paid for the product. Nevertheless, the costly subsidies were deemed necessary to build a customer base.

In August 1998, Priceline added three more airlines—Delta, Northwest, and Continental. Consequently, Priceline had more airline seats to match with consumers' bids. Priceline's match rate rose to 24% of all bids it received, and 42% of what it termed reasonable offers. The firm's chief executive believes the latter figure must rise to at least 50% for Priceline to be successful. In late 1999, Priceline signed up three more airlines—American, United, and US Airways—giving it access to about 90% of the U.S. leisure travel market.

Thus far, Priceline has shown an ability to ring up more and more sales, but not profits. In fact, by the end of 1999, Priceline had accumulated losses of over $250 million. Despite these losses, Priceline held an initial public offering (IPO) of its stock on March 30, 1999. It was successful, to say the least. The stock rocketed from an opening price per share of $16 to $69 by the end of the day.

Besides its mounting losses, Priceline faces other problems. First, two entrepreneurs sued Walker and his firm, claiming that they developed the basic business model underlying Priceline and that Walker stole the concept from them. Next, Microsoft announced that it intended to allow consumers to name their own prices for travel services, starting with hotel rooms, on its Expedia website. This dispute wound up in court, because Priceline believes it holds the patent for "reverse auctions." If Microsoft prevails, Priceline can expect added competition as other companies initiate various forms of reverse auctions.[1]

In this situation, who actually determines the price for the airline seats offered through Priceline? Is it the consumer, Priceline, or the airlines that contract with Priceline?

www.priceline.com

"How much should we charge for airline seats?" "How does price fit into our marketing mix?" Airlines—in fact, all organizations—face these questions constantly. These kinds of questions are asked any time an enterprise introduces a new product or considers changing the price of an existing one.

In this chapter we cover the role of price in the marketing mix—what price is, how it can be used, and how it is set relative to such factors as product costs, market demand, and competitors' prices. After studying this chapter, you should be able to explain:

chapter goals

- The meaning of price.
- The significance of price in our economy, in a consumer's mind, and to an individual firm.
- The concept of value and how it relates to price.
- Major pricing objectives.
- Key factors influencing price.
- The types of costs incurred in producing and marketing a product.
- Approaches to determining prices, including cost-plus pricing, marginal analysis, and setting prices in relation only to other prices in the market.
- Break-even analysis.

In this chapter we will discuss major methods used to determine a price. Before being concerned with actual price determination, however, executives—and you—should understand the meaning and importance of price.

Meaning of Price

Some pricing difficulties occur because of confusion about the meaning of *price*, even though the concept is easy to define in familiar terms. Simply, **price** is the amount of money and/or other items with utility needed to acquire a product. Recall that *utility* is an attribute with the potential to satisfy wants.

Thus price may involve more than money. To illustrate, the price of a rare Mark McGwire baseball card may be (1) $500; (2) the rookie cards for 10 players, includ-

Barter First Inc., which operates a trade exchange in the Dallas area, brings together organizations that want to engage in barter. According to Barter First, "Clients of an exchange use trade dollars, instead of cash, to handle their transactions. If a hotel trades $1,000 worth of rooms to another client, the hotel receives $1,000 in trade dollars which it can use to purchase what it needs from other exchange clients."

www.barterfirstinc.com

ing Barry Bonds and Pedro Martinez; or (3) some combination of dollars and baseball cards. Exchanging goods and/or services for other products is termed **barter.** Because our economy is not geared to a slow, ponderous barter system, we typically state price in monetary terms and use money as our medium of exchange.

In socially undesirable situations, there are prices called blackmail, ransom, and bribery. Here are prices under various names and the products with which they are associated in normal situations:[2]

Price Is What You Pay . . .		For What You Get
Tuition	→	Education
Interest	→	Use of money
Rent	→	Use of living quarters or a piece of equipment.
Fare	→	Taxi ride or airline flight
Fee	→	Services of a physician or lawyer
Retainer	→	Lawyer's or consultant's services over a period of time
Toll	→	Long-distance phone call or travel on some highways
Salary	→	Services of an executive or other white-collar worker
Wage	→	Services of a blue-collar worker
Commission	→	Sales person's services
Dues	→	Membership in a union or a club

Practical problems arise when we try to state simply the price of a product. Suppose you paid $395 for a desk, but your instructor paid only $295 for one of similar size. At first glance, it looks as if the instructor taught the student a lesson! But consider this: Your desk—which has a beautiful finish—was delivered to your apartment, and you had a year to pay for it. The instructor, a do-it-yourself buff, bought a partially assembled, unfinished desk. It had to be put together and then stained and varnished. The seller provided neither delivery nor credit. Now, even with the differences in price, who got the better deal? The answer is not as easy as it first appeared.

This example indicates that the definition depends on determining exactly what is being sold. A seller usually is pricing a combination of (1) the specific good or service that is the object of the transaction, (2) several supplementary services (such as a warranty), and (3) in a very real sense, the want-satisfying benefits provided by the product. Sometimes it is difficult even to define the price of the predominant good or service itself. On one model of automobile, a stated price may include radio, power steering, and power brakes. For another model of the same brand, these three items may be priced separately. So, to know the real price of a product you need to look at the identifiable components that make up that product.

Importance of Price

Price is significant in our economy, in the consumer's mind, and in an individual firm. Let's consider each situation.

In the Economy

A product's price influences wages, rent, interest, and profits. Price is a basic regulator of the economic system because it influences the allocation of the factors of production: labor, land, and capital. High wages attract labor, high interest rates attract capital, and so on. As an allocator of resources, price determines what will be produced (supply) and who will get the goods and services produced (demand).

Criticism of the American system of reasonably free enterprise and, in turn, public demand for added restraints on the system are often triggered by negative reactions to prices or pricing policies. To reduce the risk of government intervention,

Who's determining prices in China?

Often, U.S. firms find it difficult to arrive at suitable prices for the domestic market and, of course, various foreign markets. But they are not alone in facing pricing challenges. Worldwide, companies must deal with various circumstances to set prices for their products. Lately, pricing decisions have been particularly challenging for Chinese enterprises.

After decades of communist limitations on commerce, Chinese leaders allowed various aspects of a free-market economy. The overriding reasons for doing so were to sustain economic growth, bolster employment levels, and build per capita income. Even state-owned enterprises were given some autonomy in making business decisions covering pricing and other aspects of marketing.

In the late 1990s, however, many Chinese industries had excess production capacity and faced growing competition from imported products. Various manu-

facturers cut prices to stimulate demand, starting price wars in some industries. Fearful that aggressive price competition would put some companies out of business, thereby swelling unemployment, government officials in Beijing intervened by setting minimum prices in 21 industries. As a result, Chinese managers in various industries, including autos, sugar, and TVs, once again have less latitude in pricing.

The price controls may protect profit margins and employment, at least for a while. However, this form of government intervention certainly curtails efforts to improve efficiency and competitiveness. Even some Chinese officials question the action to set minimum prices. As one stated, "The outcome of price controls is to protect the backward and frustrate the advanced."

Sources: Dexter Roberts, "So Much for Competition," *Business Week,* Nov. 30, 1998, pp. 56, 58; and Volker Pasternak, "The Right Price," *China Business Review,* September/October 1998, pp. 40–43.

businesses need to establish prices in a manner and at a level that consumers and government officials consider socially responsible.

In the Customer's Mind

Some prospective customers are interested primarily in low prices, whereas another segment is more concerned with other factors, such as service, quality, value, and brand image. It's safe to say that few, if any, customers are attentive to price alone *or* are entirely oblivious to price. One study identified four distinct segments of shoppers: *brand loyals* (relatively uninterested in price), *system beaters* (prefer certain brands but try to buy them at reduced prices), *deal shoppers* (driven by low prices), and *uninvolveds* (seemingly not motivated by either brand preferences or low prices).[3]

An important question is whether consumer price sensitivity can be predicted. There is no clear-cut answer. The four shopper segments mentioned above are not distinguished by demographic factors. Rather, according to the study's results, the segments' differing degrees of price sensitivity are more likely to be related to psychographic factors, such as life-style, or to which product categories are involved. In contrast, a major study of sales data for 18 product categories in a chain of 83 supermarkets concluded that consumers' relative interest in price does vary across demographic groups. According to this research, consumers with particular attributes—such as low income level, small house, or large family—are likely to be price sensitive.[4]

Another consideration is that some consumers' perceptions of product quality vary directly with price. Typically, the higher the price, the better the quality is perceived to be. In the words of an engineering consultant, "Many consultants have told me that when they raised their prices, their sales went up." The explanation was that with higher prices, clients felt more comfortable regarding the quality of the advice.[5]

Haven't you been concerned about product quality—such as when you are looking at ads for compact disc players—if the price is unexpectedly low? Or, at the other

In a major advertising campaign, Extended Stay America (ESA) told "road warriors" (also known as frequent travelers) that its hotels are a better value than higher-price alternatives. The ads announced ESA's prices as well as various amenities, including a kitchen in the room and free local calls. ESA also mentioned its other brands, StudioPLUS and Crossland. Other ads in this campaign featured Gen. George Patton and Napoleon Bonaparte as "road warriors."

 www.extstay.com

extreme, have you selected a restaurant for a special dinner because you heard it was fairly high priced so you expected it to be very nice? Consumers' perceptions of quality may be influenced not just by price but also by such factors as store reputation and advertising.

Price is also important as a component of value. During the 1990s, more and more prospective customers, both in consumer and business markets, expected better value in the goods and services they purchased. **Value** is the ratio of perceived benefits to price and any other incurred costs. Examples of *other incurred costs* for consumers include time associated with shopping for the product, time and gasoline used traveling to the place of purchase, and time and perhaps aggravation assembling the product. Online shopping can reduce some of these other costs, such as the effort of traveling from one store to another; however, it may amplify some costs, such as the perceived risk of buying a product without seeing it in person.

When we say a product has ample value, we don't necessarily mean it is inexpensive or has a very low price. Rather, good value indicates that a particular product has the kinds and amounts of potential benefits—such as quality, image, and purchase convenience—consumers expect at a particular price level.

Many businesses are responding to calls for more value by devising new products. For instance, during the latter half of the 1990s, the number of extended-stay hotels grew tremendously. The target market for this product consists of people who need or want to stay in the same locale for several days, weeks, or even months. Given the surging demand for this type of lodging as well as the success of Residence Inns by Marriott, many new chains—Summerfield Suites, Candlewood Hotels, and Extended Stay America, to mention several—entered this field. They offer value by providing relatively low rates as well as amenities that are important to extended-stay guests, such as spacious rooms, kitchenettes, and free buffet breakfasts. To pare expenses, this type of hotel reduces or eliminates less important amenities, such as room service and daily housekeeping.[6]

Other businesses are striving for better value with existing products. Asea Brown Boveri, a manufacturer of power transformers and other large, expensive equipment, has worked hard to enhance product quality *and* pare production costs. With lower costs, the urge to increase prices in order to maintain profits is lessened. Another avenue to enhanced value is to give customers more at the same price. Although they are dissimilar in many respects, both Little Caesars and California Pizza Kitchen have used that approach by providing larger portions and holding the line on prices.[7]

Attention to value was certainly heightened by the recession of the early 1990s. However, the increased emphasis on value probably reflects a more fundamental shift in attitudes. Consumers' greater interest in the ratio of benefits to price has created a new approach to pricing, not surprisingly called "value pricing," which we will discuss in Chapter 13.

In the Individual Firm

A product's price is a major determinant of the market demand for it. Through prices, money comes into an organization. Thus price affects a firm's competitive position, revenues, and net profits. According to a McKinsey consultant, "Pricing is extremely important because small changes in price can translate into huge improvements in profitability." In fact, in a study of 1,000 companies, McKinsey found that a 1% increase in price would improve profits by 7%, assuming no change in sales volume.[8]

Some businesses use higher prices to convey an image of superior quality. This approach will have a positive impact only on consumers who consider quality important. It's most likely to work well in the case of services and certain goods for which consumers have difficulty judging quality on an objective basis. To be highly effective in signaling superior quality, the high price should be combined with other conspicuous elements of the marketing mix, such as a compelling advertising message and an appealing package design.[9]

Prices are important to a company most of the time—but not always. Several factors can limit how much effect pricing has on a company's marketing program. Differentiated product features, a favorite brand, high quality, convenience, or some combination of these and other factors may be more important to consumers than price. As we saw in Chapter 10, one object of branding is to *decrease* the effect of price on the demand for a product. Thus we need to put the role of pricing in a company's marketing program in its proper perspective: It is only one of four marketing-mix elements that must be skillfully combined—and then adapted over time—to achieve business success.

• Pricing Objectives

Every marketing activity—including pricing—should be directed toward a goal. Thus management should decide on its pricing objective before determining the price itself.[10] Yet, as logical as this may sound, few firms consciously establish a pricing objective.

To be useful, the pricing objective management selects must be compatible with the overall goals set by the firm and the goals for its marketing program. Let's assume that a *company's goal* is to increase return on investment from its present level of 15% to 20% within three years. It follows that the primary *pricing goal* during this period should be to achieve some stated percentage return on investment. It would be questionable, in this case, to adopt a primary pricing goal of maintaining the company's market share or of stabilizing prices.

We will discuss the following **pricing objectives:**

- Profit-oriented:
  - To achieve a target return
  - To maximize profit

- Sales-oriented:
  - To increase sales volume
  - To maintain or increase market share
- Status quo–oriented:
  - To stabilize prices
  - To meet competition

Recognize that all these objectives can be sought—and hopefully attained—through pricing that is coordinated with other marketing activities such as product design and distribution channels. And all these objectives are ultimately aimed at satisfactory performance over the long run. For a business, that requires ample profits.

Profit-Oriented Goals

Profit goals may be set for the short or long term. A company may select one of two profit-oriented goals for its pricing policy.

Achieve a Target Return

A firm may price its product to *achieve a target return*—a specified percentage return on its *sales* or on its *investment*. Many retailers and wholesalers use a target return *on sales* as a pricing objective for short periods such as a year or a fashion season. They add an amount to the cost of the product, called a *markup*, to cover anticipated operating expenses *and* provide a desired profit for the period. Safeway or Kroger, for example, may price to earn a net profit of 1% on a store's sales. A chain of men's clothing stores may have a target profit of 6% of sales, and price its products accordingly. (Markup and other operating ratios are discussed fully in Appendix A following this chapter.)

www.kroger.com

Achieving a target return *on investment* is measured in relation to a firm's net worth (its assets minus its liabilities). This pricing goal is often selected by the leading firm in an industry. Target-return pricing is used by industry leaders such as DuPont, Alcoa, and Exxon because they can set their pricing goals more independently of competition than smaller firms in the industry. The leaders may price so that they earn a net profit that is 15 or 20% of the firm's net worth.

www.alcoa.com

Maximize Profits

The pricing objective of making as much money as possible is probably followed more than any other goal. The trouble with this goal is that to some people, *profit maximization* has an ugly connotation, suggesting profiteering, high prices, and monopoly. Where prices are unduly high and entry into the field is severely limited, public criticism can be expected. If market conditions and public opinion do not bring about reasonable prices, government may intervene.

In both economic theory and business practice, however, there is nothing wrong with profit maximization. Theoretically, if profits become high in an industry because supply is short in relation to demand, new capital will be attracted to increase production capacity. This will increase supply and eventually reduce profits. In the marketplace it is difficult to find many situations where profiteering has existed over an extended period of time. Substitute products are available, purchases are postponable, and competition can increase to keep prices at a reasonable level.

A profit-maximization goal is likely to be far more beneficial to a company if it is pursued over the *long term*. To do this, however, firms may have to accept modest profits or even losses over the short term. For example, a company entering a new geographic market or introducing a new product frequently does best by initially setting low prices to build a large clientele. Repeat purchases from this large group of customers may allow the firm to maximize its profits over the long term.

Periodically, pharmaceutical companies introduce drugs to fight AIDS or the HIV virus. Inevitably, the firms are criticized for charging excessive prices. Some years ago, Burroughs Wellcome Co. set AZT's price equivalent to about $8,000 for a one-year supply per patient. Following outcries from AIDS patients and their supporters, the company cut the price of AZT by 20%. More recently, DuPont Pharma brought Sustiva to the market at a price that converts to about $4,800 per year. The companies respond to the criticism by saying that high prices are necessary in order to recover the enormous costs of developing the complex drugs.

Is it ethical to charge a seemingly high price for a product that could be a life or death necessity?

Sources: Charles W. Henderson, "AIDS Groups Protest Pricing of New DuPont Drug," *AIDS Weekly Plus,* Oct. 5, 1998; and Marilyn Chase, "Burroughs Wellcome Cuts Price of AZT under Pressure from AIDS Activists," *The Wall Street Journal,* Sept. 19, 1989, p. A3.

The goal should be to maximize profits on *total output* rather than on each single product. In fact, a company may maximize total profit by setting low, relatively unprofitable prices on some products in order to stimulate sales of others. The Gillette Company frequently promotes razors at very low prices. The firm hopes that once customers acquire Gillette razors, they will become loyal customers for Gillette blades, which generate healthy profits for the company.

Sales-Oriented Goals

In some companies, management's pricing is focused on sales volume. The pricing goal may be to increase sales volume or to maintain or increase the firm's market share.

Increase Sales Volume

This pricing goal of *increasing sales volume* is typically adopted to achieve rapid growth or to discourage other firms from entering a market. The goal is usually stated as a percentage increase in sales volume over some period, say, one year or three years.

Management may seek higher sales revenues by discounting or by some other aggressive pricing strategy. Periodically, the Monsanto Co. has lowered the prices of its popular Roundup brand of herbicide. The intent of these price cuts seemingly has been to stimulate more farmers to use the product, and on more acres of land, thereby augmenting Monsanto's revenues.[11]

Occasionally companies are willing to incur a loss *in the short run* to expand sales volume or meet sales objectives. Clothing stores run end-of-season sales, and auto dealers offer rebates and below-market loan rates on new cars. Many vacation spots, such as golf courses and resorts, reduce prices during off-seasons to increase sales volume.

Maintain or Increase Market Share

In some companies, both large and small, the pricing objective is to *maintain or increase market share*. Why is market share protected or pursued so vigorously? In growing fields, such as computers and other technology-based products, companies want large shares in order to gain added clout with vendors, drive down production costs, and/or project a dominant appearance to consumers. In order to gain a foothold in the marketplace, many electronic-commerce firms are emphasizing market share or sales volume over profits, at least in the short run.[12]

Most industries today are not growing much, if at all, *and* have excess production capacity. Many firms need added sales to utilize their production capacity more fully and, in turn, gain economies of scale and better profits. Because the size of the "pie" isn't growing in most cases, businesses that need added volume have to grab a bigger "slice of the pie"—that is, greater market share. The U.S. auto and retail grocery industries illustrate these situations.

Other firms are also intent on maintaining their market shares. In the mid-1990s, for instance, the Japanese yen rose considerably in relation to the American dollar, making Japanese products more expensive in American dollars. To maintain their market shares, Toyota, Nissan, and Honda accepted smaller profit margins and reduced their costs so that they could lower the selling prices of their autos in the U.S. More recently, Intel Corp. slashed prices in order to sustain its share of the market for personal computer microprocessors. The company was also aggressive in cutting prices of network adapters, devices that link PCs to networks, in order to take market share from the leading firm in this field.[13]

Status Quo Goals

Two closely related goals—*stabilizing prices* and *meeting competition*—are the least aggressive of all pricing goals. They are intended simply to maintain the firm's current situation—that is, the status quo. With either of these goals, a firm seeks to avoid price competition.

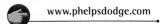
www.phelpsdodge.com

Price stabilization often is the goal in industries where (1) the product is highly standardized (such as steel or bulk chemicals) *and* (2) one large firm, such as Phelps Dodge in the copper industry, historically has acted as a leader in setting prices. Smaller firms in these industries tend to "follow the leader" when setting their prices. What is the reason for such pricing behavior? A price cut by any one firm is likely to be matched by all other firms in order to remain competitive; therefore, no individual firm gains, but all may suffer smaller profits. Conversely, a price boost is unlikely to be matched. But the price-boosting firm faces a differential disadvantage, because other elements of a standardized product such as gasoline are perceived to be fairly similar.

Even in industries where there are no price leaders, countless firms deliberately price their products to meet the prevailing market price. This pricing policy gives management an easy means of avoiding difficult pricing decisions.

Firms that adopt status quo pricing goals to avoid price competition are not necessarily passive in their marketing. Quite the contrary! Typically these companies compete aggressively using other marketing-mix elements—product, distribution, and especially promotion. This approach, called *nonprice competition*, will be discussed in Chapter 13.

Factors Influencing Price Determination

Knowing the objective of its pricing, a company can move to the heart of price management: determining the base price of a product. **Base price**, or *list price*, refers to the price of one unit of the product at its point of production or resale. This price does not reflect discounts, freight charges, or any other modifications such as leader pricing, all of which will be discussed in the next chapter.

The same procedure is followed in pricing both new and established products. Pricing an established product usually is less difficult than pricing a new product, however, because the exact price or a narrow range of prices may be dictated by the market.[14]

According to an Arthur Andersen consultant, failing to consider the various interrelated factors that affect pricing is "the most common mistake made by small businesses."[15] Thus other factors, besides objectives, that influence price determination are discussed next.

Estimated Demand

In pricing, a company must estimate the total demand for the product. This is easier to do for an established product than for a new one. The steps in estimating demand are: (1) determine whether there is a price the market expects and (2) estimate what the sales volume might be at different prices.

The **expected price** of a product is the price at which customers consciously or unconsciously value it—what they think the product is worth. Expected price usually is expressed as a *range* of prices rather than as a specific amount. Thus the expected price might be "between $250 and $300" or, for another product, "not over $20."

A producer must also consider a middleman's reaction to price. Middlemen are more likely to promote a product if they approve its price. Sometimes they don't. For instance, retailers—notably Wal-Mart—complained when Rubbermaid Inc. tried to raise prices in the mid-1990s. The manufacturer thought it needed to, after the cost of resin (a major ingredient in its various plastic housewares and toys) more than doubled. However, rather than antagonize retailers, Rubbermaid settled for smaller increases, which hurt the company's profits.[16]

www.loreal.com

It's possible to set a price too low. If the price is much lower than what the market expects, sales may be lost. For example, it probably would be a mistake for L'Oreal, a well-known cosmetics maker, to put a $1.49 price tag on its lipstick or to price its imported perfume at $3.49 an ounce. In all likelihood, shoppers would be suspicious about product quality, or their self-concept would not let them buy such low-priced products.

After raising a product's price, some organizations have experienced a considerable increase in sales. When this occurs, it indicates that customers infer better quality from the higher prices. This situation is called **inverse demand**—the higher the price, the greater the unit sales. Inverse demand usually exists only within a given price range and only at low price levels. At some point (see Figure 12.1), inverse demand ends and the usual-shaped curve is evident. That is, demand declines as prices rise.

How do sellers determine expected prices? One restaurant in London, rather than putting prices in its menus, lets patrons decide how much to pay after they have completed their meals. With this unconventional approach, customers pay an amount they think is equal to the value received from the dining experience. The restaurant owner claims that patrons pay about 20% more than he would charge![17]

Typically, to gauge expected prices, sellers may submit products to experienced retailers or wholesalers to gauge the selling price the market will accept for a particular item. Or they may go to customers. A business goods manufacturer, for instance, might get price estimates by showing models or blueprints to engineers working for prospective customers. Another alternative is to ask a sample of consumers what they would expect to pay for the product, or which item in a list of alternatives with known prices is most similar to the test product. Using such methods, a seller can determine a reasonable range of prices.

It is extremely helpful to estimate what the sales volume will be at several different prices. By doing this, the seller is, in effect, determining the demand curve for the product. Moreover, the seller is gauging *price elasticity of demand,* which refers to the responsiveness of quantity demanded to price changes. (Price elasticity of demand is covered in more detail in Appendix A following this chapter.)

Sellers can choose from several methods to estimate sales at various prices. Recall some of the demand-forecasting methods discussed in Chapter 6— survey of buyer intentions, test marketing, executive judgment, and sales-force composite, for example. These methods can be used in this situation as well.[18]

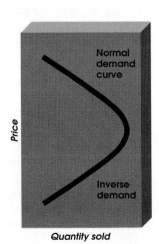

Figure 12.1

Inverse demand.

Competitive Reactions

Competition greatly influences base price. A new product is distinctive only until competition arrives, which is inevitable. The threat of potential competition is greatest when the field is easy to enter *and* profit prospects are encouraging. Competition can come from these sources:

- *Directly similar products:* Nike versus adidas or Reebok running shoes.
- *Available substitutes:* DHL air express versus Consolidated Freightways truck shipping or Union Pacific rail freight.
- *Unrelated products seeking the same consumer dollar:* Videocassette recorder (VCR) versus a bicycle or a weekend excursion.

For directly similar products, it is important to learn what consumers think about competing products. Thus a marketer at DuPont stressed, "Understanding customer perceptions of the organization's and competitors' offerings is the first step in developing good pricing decisions."[19]

For similar or substitute products, a competitor may adjust its prices. In turn, other firms have to decide what price adjustments, if any, are necessary to retain their customers. In the photographic-film industry, for instance, Fuji used lower prices to build its market share at the expense of Kodak. Although it still holds a 70% share of the market, Kodak decided to cut its prices to combat Fuji.[20]

Other Marketing-Mix Elements

A product's base price is influenced considerably by the other ingredients in the marketing mix.

Product

We've already observed that a product's price is affected by whether it is a new item or an established one. Over the course of a life cycle, price changes are necessary to keep the product competitive. A product's price is also influenced by whether (1) it may be leased as well as purchased outright, (2) a trade-in is involved, and (3) it may be returned by the customer to the seller for a refund or an exchange. For example, a firm that has a liberal return policy may compensate by having higher initial prices.

The end use of the product must also be considered. For instance, there is little price competition among manufacturers of packaging materials or producers of industrial gases, so their price structure is stable. These business products are only an incidental part of the final article, so customers will buy the least expensive product consistent with the required quality.

Distribution Channels

The channels and types of middlemen selected will influence a producer's pricing. A firm selling both through wholesalers and directly to retailers often sets a different factory price for these classes of customers. The price to wholesalers is lower because they perform services that the producer would have to perform—such as providing storage, granting credit to retailers, and selling to small retailers.

Promotion

The extent to which the product is promoted by the producer or middlemen and the methods used are added considerations in pricing. If major promotional responsibility is placed on retailers, they ordinarily will be charged a lower price for a product than if the producer advertises it heavily. Even when a producer promotes heavily, it may want retailers to use local advertising to tie in with national advertising. Such a decision must be reflected in the producer's price to retailers.

Cost of a Product

Pricing of a product also should consider its cost. A product's total unit cost is made up of several types of costs, each reacting differently to changes in the quantity produced. In many industries, especially those based on leading-edge technologies such as microprocessors and optic fibers, a product's costs are viewed—and treated—in much different ways than they were just a decade or so ago.

Consider a couple of examples. In the software field, there are substantial upfront research and development costs, but the costs of producing each unit of the finished product are relatively small. Thus some software developers give away hundreds of thousands of copies of their product when it is introduced in order to gain favorable word-of-mouth publicity and, in turn, sales of related software and future upgrades of this product. Red Hat Inc. essentially gives away Linux operating-system software but then sells technical support services to Linux users. In another industry, Teleport Communications installs more optic fibers than a customer requests—and does so without additional charge. Why? As technology surely advances, the customer will want more capacity. Therefore, the company installs more capacity than is needed because the cost of extra fibers is far less than the cost of labor to do the job again in the future.[21]

The following cost concepts are fundamental to our discussion of pricing:

Various Kinds of Costs

- A **fixed cost,** such as rent, executive salaries, or property tax, remains constant regardless of how many items are produced. Such a cost continues even if production stops completely. It is called a fixed cost because it is difficult to change in the short run (but not in the long run).
- **Total fixed cost** is the sum of all fixed costs.
- **Average fixed cost** is the total fixed cost divided by the number of units produced.
- A **variable cost,** such as labor or materials, is directly related to production. Variable costs can be controlled in the short run simply by changing the level of production. When production stops, for example, all variable production costs become zero.
- **Total variable cost** is the sum of all variable costs. The more units produced, the higher is this cost.
- **Average variable cost** is the total variable cost divided by the number of units produced. Average variable cost is usually high for the first few units produced. And it decreases as production increases because of such things as quantity discounts on materials and more efficient use of labor. Beyond some optimum output, it increases because of such factors as crowding of production facilities and overtime pay.
- **Total cost** is the sum of total fixed cost and total variable cost for a specific quantity produced.
- **Average total cost** is total cost divided by number of units produced.
- **Marginal cost** is the cost of producing and selling one more unit. Usually the marginal cost of the last unit is the same as that unit's variable cost.

These concepts and their interrelationships are illustrated in Table 12.1 and Figure 12.2. The interrelationships among the various *average costs per unit* from the table are displayed graphically in the figure. It may be explained briefly as follows:

- The **average fixed cost curve** declines as output increases, because the total of the fixed costs is spread over an increasing number of units.
- The **average variable cost curve** usually is U-shaped. It starts high because average variable costs for the first few units of output are high. Variable costs per unit then decline as the company realizes efficiencies in production. Eventually the average variable cost curve reaches its lowest point, reflecting optimum output with respect to variable costs (not total costs). In Figure 12.2 this point is at three units of output. Beyond that point the average variable cost rises, reflecting the increase in unit variable costs caused by overcrowded facilities and other inefficiencies. If the variable costs per unit were constant, then the average variable cost curve would be a horizontal line at the level of the constant unit variable cost.

Table 12.1   An Example of Costs for an Individual Firm

Total fixed costs do not change in the short run, despite increases in quantity produced. Variable costs are the costs of inputs—materials and labor, for example. Total variable costs increase as production quantity rises. Total cost is the sum of all fixed and variable costs. The other measures in the table are simply methods of looking at costs per unit; they always involve dividing a cost by the number of units produced.

(1) Quantity Produced	(2) Total Fixed Costs	(3) Total Variable Costs	(4) Total Costs (2) + (3)	(5) Marginal Cost per Unit	(6) Average Fixed Cost (2) ÷ (1)	(7) Average Variable Cost (3) ÷ (1)	(8) Average Total Cost (4) ÷ (1)
0	$256	$ 0	$256		Infinity	Infinity	Infinity
				$ 84			
1	256	84	340		$256.00	$84	$340.00
				28			
2	256	112	368		128.00	56	184.00
				32			
3	256	144	400		85.33	48	133.33
				80			
4	256	224	480		64.00	56	120.00
				176			
5	256	400	656		51.20	80	131.20

Figure 12.2

Unit cost curves for an individual firm.

This figure is based on data in Table 12.1. Here we see how *unit* costs change as quantity increases. Using cost-plus pricing, two units of output would be priced at $184 each, whereas four units would sell for $120 each.

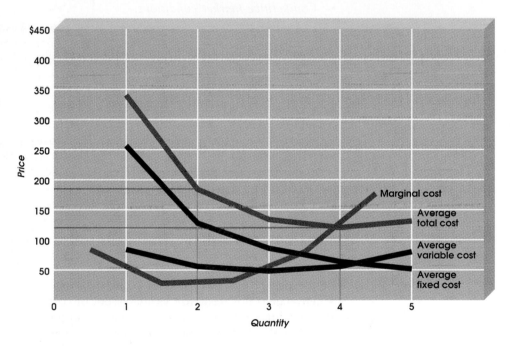

- The **average total cost curve** is the sum of the first two curves—average fixed cost and average variable cost. It starts high, reflecting the fact that total *fixed* costs are spread over so few units of output. As output increases, the average total cost curve declines because unit fixed cost and unit variable cost are decreasing. Eventually the point of lowest total cost per unit is reached (four units of output in the figure). Beyond that optimum point, diminishing returns set in and average total cost rises.
- The **marginal cost curve** has a more pronounced U-shape than the other curves in Figure 12.2. The marginal cost curve slopes downward until the second unit of output, at which point the marginal costs start to increase.

Note the relationship between the average total cost curve and the marginal cost curve. The average total cost curve slopes downward *as long as the marginal cost is less than the average total cost*. Even though marginal cost increases after the second unit, the average total cost curve continues to slope downward until the fourth unit. This occurs because marginal cost—even when going up—is still less than average total cost.

The two curves—marginal cost and average total cost—intersect at the lowest point of the average total cost curve. Beyond that point (the fourth unit in the example), the cost of producing and selling the next unit is higher than the average cost of all units. The data in Table 12.1 show that producing the fifth unit reduces the average fixed cost by $12.80 (from $64 to $51.20), but causes the average variable cost to increase by $24. From then on, therefore, the average total cost rises. This occurs because the average variable cost is increasing faster than the average fixed cost is decreasing.

Cost-Plus Pricing

We are now at the point in price determination to talk about setting a *specific* selling price. Most companies establish their prices based on:

- *Total cost plus a desired profit,*
- *Marginal analysis*—a consideration of both market demand and supply, and/or
- *Competitive market conditions.*

According to a survey that examined the approaches used to price new products, 9% of companies "guesstimate" what the base price for a new product should be, whereas 37% match what competitors charge for similar offerings. One-half the responding firms charge what the market will bear, if conditions allow. The most common approach, used by 52% of the companies, is to choose a price that is intended to cover costs and provide a fair profit.[22] Because the total is more than 100%, evidently most firms use more than one approach.

Let's first discuss the most popular method, **cost-plus pricing**, which means setting the price of one unit of a product equal to the total cost of the unit plus the desired profit on the unit. Suppose that King's Kastles, a contractor, figures that the labor and materials required to build and sell 10 condominiums will cost $750,000, and other expenses (office rent, depreciation on equipment, management salaries, and so on) will be $150,000. The contractor wants to earn a profit of 10% on the total cost of $900,000. This makes cost plus desired profit $990,000. So, using the cost-plus method, each of the 10 condos is priced at $99,000.

Although it is an easily applied method, cost-plus pricing has limitations. One is that it does not recognize various types of costs or the fact that these costs are affected differently by changes in level of output. In our housing example, suppose that King's Kastles built and sold only eight condos at the cost-plus price of $99,000 each. As shown in Table 12.2, total sales would then be $792,000. Labor and materials chargeable to the eight condos would total $600,000 ($75,000 per unit). Because the contractor would still incur the full $150,000 in overhead expenses, the total cost would be $750,000. This would leave a profit of $42,000, or $5,250 per condominium instead of the anticipated $9,000. On a percentage basis, profit would be only 5.6% of total cost rather than the desired 10%.

A second limitation of this pricing approach is that market demand is ignored. That is, cost-plus pricing assumes that cost determines the value of a product, or what customers are willing to pay for it. But what if the same number of units could be sold at a higher price? Using cost-plus pricing, the seller would forgo some revenues. Conversely, if fewer units are produced, each would have to sell for a higher price to cover all costs and show a profit. But if business is slack and output must be cut, it's not wise to raise the unit price. Another limitation of this method is that it doesn't recognize that total unit cost changes as output expands or contracts. However, a more sophisticated approach to cost-plus pricing can consider such changes.

Table 12.2	King's Kastles: An Example of Cost-Plus Pricing		
Actual results often differ from planned outcomes because various types of costs react differently to changes in output.			
		Number of Condominiums Built and Sold by King's Kastles	
King's Kastles' Costs, Selling Price, and Profit		Planned = 10	Actual = 8
Labor and materials costs ($75,000 per condo)		$750,000	$600,000
Overhead (fixed) costs		150,000	150,000
Total costs		$900,000	$750,000
Total sales at $99,000 per condo		990,000	792,000
Profit: Total		$ 90,000	$ 42,000
Per condo		$9,000	$5,250
As percent of cost		10%	5.6%

Prices Based on Marginal Costs Only

Another approach to cost-plus pricing is to set *prices based on marginal costs only*, not total costs. Refer again to the cost schedules shown in Table 12.1 and Figure 12.2, and assume that a firm is operating at an output level of three units. Under marginal cost pricing, this firm could accept an order for one more unit at $80 or above, instead of the total unit cost of $120. The revenue from a unit sold at $80 would cover its variable costs. However, if the firm can sell for a price above $80—say, $85 or $90—the balance contributes to the payment of fixed costs.

Not all orders can be priced to cover only variable costs. Marginal cost pricing may be feasible, however, if management wants to keep its labor force employed during a slack season. It may also be used when one product is expected to attract business for another. Thus a department store may price meals in its café at a level that covers only the marginal costs. The reasoning is that the café will bring shoppers to the store, where they will buy other, more profitable products.

Pricing by Middlemen

At first glance, cost-plus pricing appears to be widely used by retailing and wholesaling middlemen. A retailer, for example, pays a given amount to buy products and have them delivered to the store. Then the merchant adds an amount, called a markup, to the acquisition cost. This markup is estimated to be sufficient to cover the store's expenses and provide a reasonable profit. Thus a building materials outlet may buy a power drill for $30 including freight, and price the item at $50. The $50 price reflects a markup of 40% based on the selling price, or 66⅔% based on the merchandise cost. Of course, in setting prices, middlemen also should take into account the expectations of their customers.

Various types of retailers require different percentage markups because of the nature of the products handled and the services offered. A self-service supermarket has lower costs and thus can have a lower average markup than a full-service delicatessen. Figure 12.3 shows examples of markup pricing by middlemen. (Markups are discussed in more detail in Appendix A.)

Is cost-plus pricing really used by middlemen? For the following reasons, it's safe to say that cost-plus pricing is *not* used widely by middlemen:

- Most retail prices are really just offers. If customers accept the offer, the price is fine. If they reject it, the price usually will be changed quickly, or the product may even be withdrawn from the market. Prices thus are always on trial.
- Many retailers don't use the same markup on all the products they carry. A supermarket, for instance, may have a markup of 10 to 15% on sugar and

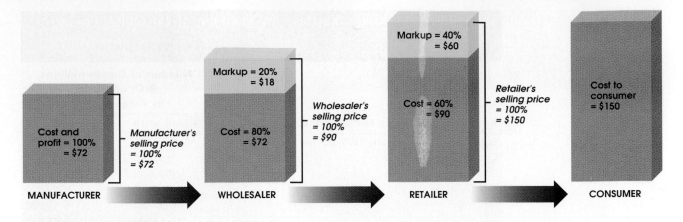

Figure 12.3

Examples of markup pricing by retailers and wholesalers.

soap products, 15 to 25% on canned fruit and vegetables, and 10 to 45% on fresh meats and produce, depending on the particular item. These different markups for distinctive products reflect competitive considerations and other aspects of market demand.

- A middleman usually doesn't actually set a base price but only adds a percentage amount to the price already set by the producer. The producer's price is set to allow each middleman to add a reasonable markup and still sell at a competitive retail price. The key price is set by the producer, with an eye on the final market. Thus what seems to be cost-plus pricing by middlemen is usually market-influenced pricing.

Evaluation of Cost-Plus Pricing

A firm should be market-oriented and cater to consumers' wants, so why are we considering cost-plus pricing? Simply, cost-plus pricing must be understood because it is referred to often in business. Further, it is used by numerous firms because it is straightforward and easy to explain.[23]

The traditional perspective has been that costs should be a determinant of prices, but not the only one. Costs are a floor for a company's prices. If goods are priced below this floor for a long time, the firm will be forced out of business.

In recent years, inflation has diminished and firms have had great difficulty raising prices. As a result, a new perspective is that price should determine costs. That is, a firm may not have much flexibility in setting its price so costs must be reduced if profits are to be realized. If this perspective is accepted, production processes and marketing activities must be revamped to squeeze out costs wherever possible. After cutting prices in its battle with Fuji, Eastman Kodak started a major effort to cut costs by about $750 million.[24] The appropriate conclusion is that used by itself, cost-plus pricing is a weak and unrealistic method because it ignores market conditions, notably demand and competition.

www.fujifilm.com

Break-Even Analysis

One way to consider both market demand and costs in price determination is by using **break-even analysis** to calculate break-even points. A **break-even point** is that quantity of output at which total revenue equals total costs, *assuming a certain selling price*. There is a different break-even point for every selling price. Sales exceeding the break-even point result in a profit on each additional unit. The more sales are above the break-even point, the larger will be the total and unit profits. Sales below the break-even point result in a loss to the seller.

Table 12.3	Futon Factory: Computation of Break-Even Point

At each of several prices, we wish to find out how many units must be sold to cover all costs. At a unit price of $100, the sale of each unit contributes $70 to cover overhead expenses. The Futon Factory must sell about 357 units to cover its $25,000 in fixed costs. See Figure 12.4 for a depiction of the data in this table.

(1) Unit Price	(2) Unit Variable Costs	(3) Contribution to Overhead (1) − (2)	(4) Overhead (Total Fixed Costs)	(5) Break-even Point (Rounded) (4) ÷ (3)
$ 60	$30	$ 30	$25,000	833 units
80	30	50	$25,000	500 units
100	30	70	$25,000	357 Units
150	30	120	$25,000	208 units

Determining the Break-Even Point

The method of determining a break-even point is illustrated in Table 12.3 and Figure 12.4. In our example, Futon Factory's fixed costs are $25,000, and variable costs are constant at $30 per unit. In our earlier example (Table 12.1 and Figure 12.2), we assumed that unit variable costs are *not* constant but fluctuate. To simplify our break-even analysis, we now assume that variable costs *are* constant.

The total cost of producing one unit is $25,030—Futon Factory obviously needs more volume to absorb its fixed costs! For 400 units, the total cost is $37,000 ($30 multiplied by 400, plus $25,000). In Figure 12.4 the selling price is $80 a unit and variable costs of $30 per unit are incurred in producing each unit. Consequently, any revenue over $30 contributes to covering fixed costs (sometimes termed *overhead*). When the price is $80, that would be $50 per unit. At a price of $80, the break-even point is 500 units, because a $50 per-unit contribution will just cover overhead of $25,000.

Stated another way, variable costs for 500 units are $15,000 and fixed costs are $25,000, for a total cost of $40,000. This amount equals the revenue from 500 units sold at $80 each. So, at an $80 selling price, the break-even volume is 500 units. Figure 12.4 shows a break-even point for an $80 price. However, it is highly desirable to calculate break-even points for several different selling prices.

Figure 12.4

Break-even chart for Futon Factory with an $80 selling price.

If this company sells 500 units, total costs are $40,000 (variable cost of 500 × $30, or $15,000, plus fixed costs of $25,000). At a selling price of $80, the sale of 500 units will yield $40,000 revenue, and costs and revenue will equal each other. At the same price, the sale of each unit above 500 will yield a profit.

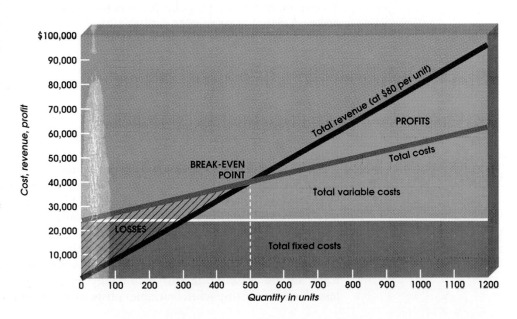

The break-even point may be found with this formula:

$$\text{Break-even point in units} = \frac{\text{total fixed costs}}{\text{unit contribution to overhead}}$$

Because unit contribution to overhead equals selling price less the average variable cost, the working formula becomes:

$$\text{Break-even point in units} = \frac{\text{total fixed costs}}{\text{selling price} - \text{average variable cost}}$$

Evaluation of Break-Even Analysis

A drawback of break-even analysis is that it cannot tell us whether or not we *can* actually sell the break-even amount. Table 12.3, for example, shows what revenue will be at the different prices *if* the given number of units can be sold at these prices. The amount the market will buy at a given price could be below the break-even point. If that happens, the firm will not break even—it will show a loss.

Two basic assumptions underlie simple break-even analysis: (1) Total fixed costs are constant, and (2) variable costs remain constant per unit of output. Actually, fixed costs may change (although usually not in the short term) and average variable costs normally fluctuate.

Despite these limitations, management should not dismiss break-even analysis as a pricing tool. Even in its simplest form, break-even analysis is helpful because in the short run many firms experience reasonably stable cost and demand structures.[25]

Prices Based on Marginal Analysis

Another pricing method, marginal analysis, also takes account of both demand and costs to determine the best price for profit maximization. Firms with other pricing goals might use *prices based on marginal analysis* to compare prices determined by different means.

Determining the Price

To use marginal analysis, the price setter must understand the concepts of average and marginal revenue as well as average and marginal cost. **Marginal revenue** is the income derived from the sale of the last unit. **Average revenue** is the unit price at a given level of unit sales; it is calculated by dividing total revenue by the number of units sold.

Referring to the hypothetical demand schedule in Table 12.4, we see that Limos for Lease can sell one unit (that is, lease one limousine for a two-hour period on a weekend night) at $80. To attract a second customer and thereby lease two limos on the same night, it must reduce its price to $72 for each unit. Thus the company receives an additional $64 (marginal revenue) by selling a second unit. After the fourth unit, total revenue declines each time the unit price is lowered in order to sell an additional unit. Hence, there is a negative marginal revenue.

Marginal analysis is illustrated in Figure 12.5. We assume that a company—a services firm, like Limos for Lease, or a manufacturer—will continue to produce and sell its product as long as revenue from the last unit sold exceeds the cost of producing this last unit. That is, output continues to increase as long as marginal revenue exceeds marginal cost. At the point where they meet, production theoretically should cease. Ordinarily a company will not want to sell a unit at a price less than its out-of-pocket (variable) costs of producing it. The optimum volume

Table 12.4	Limos for Lease: Demand Schedule for an Individual Firm		
At each market price a certain quantity of the product—in this example, a two-hour rental of a limousine on a weekend night—will be demanded. Marginal revenue is simply the amount of additional money gained by selling one more unit. Limos for Lease gains no additional marginal revenue after it has rented its fourth limo at a price of $53.			
Units Sold (Limos Leased)	Unit Price (Average Revenue)	Total Revenue	Marginal Revenue
1	$80	$ 80	$64
2	72	144	45
3	63	189	23
4	53	212	-2
5	42	210	-6
6	34	204	

of output is the quantity level at which *marginal cost equals marginal revenue,* or quantity Q in Figure 12.5*a.*

Thus the unit price is determined by locating the point on the average revenue curve that represents an output of quantity Q—the level at which marginal cost equals marginal revenue. Remember that average revenue represents the unit price. Referring to Figure 12.5*b,* in which the average revenue curve has been added, the unit price at which to sell quantity Q is represented by point C—that is, price B.

The average total cost curve has been added in Figure 12.5*c.* It shows that for output quantity Q, the average unit cost is represented by point D—that is, unit cost A. Thus, with a price of B and an average unit cost of A, the company enjoys a unit profit given by B minus A in the figure. Total profit is quantity Q times the unit profit.

Evaluation of Marginal Analysis Pricing

Marginal analysis has been used sparingly as a basis for price setting. According to businesspeople, it can be a help in studying past price movements. However, many managers think marginal analysis *cannot* serve as a practical basis for setting prices unless accurate, reliable data can be obtained for plotting the curves.

On the brighter side, management's knowledge of costs and demand is improving. Computerized databases are bringing more complete and detailed information to management's attention all the time. And experienced management can do a fairly accurate job of estimating marginal and average costs and revenues.

Figure 12.5

Price setting and profit maximization through marginal analysis.

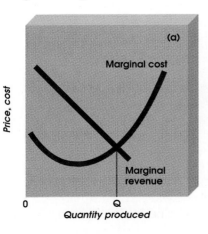

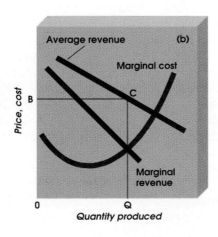

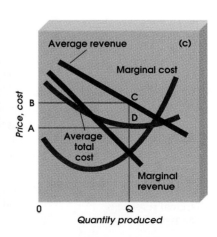

Prices Set in Relation to Market Alone

Cost-plus pricing is one extreme among pricing methods. At the other extreme is *price set in relation to the market alone*. The seller's price may be set right at the market price to meet the competition, or it may be set above or below the market price.

Pricing to Meet Competition

Pricing to meet competition is simple to carry out. In a situation with multiple suppliers, a firm should ascertain what the prevailing market price is and, after allowing for customary markups for middlemen, arrive at its own selling price. To illustrate, a manufacturer of women's shoes knows that retailers want to sell the shoes for $70 a pair and have an average markup of 40% of their selling price. Consequently, after allowing $28 for the retailer's markup, the producer's price is $42. This manufacturer then has to decide whether $42 is enough to cover costs and provide a reasonable profit. Sometimes a producer faces a real squeeze if its costs are rising but the market price is holding firm.

One situation in which management might price a product right at the market level is when competition is keen and the firm's product is not differentiated significantly from competing products.[26] To some extent, this pricing method reflects the market conditions of **perfect competition**. That is, product differentiation is absent, buyers and sellers are well informed, and the seller has no discernible control over the selling price. Most producers of agricultural products and small firms marketing well-known, standardized products use this pricing method. As explained in the Marketing in the Information Economy box, the Internet is moving some industries toward perfect competition.

The sharp drop in revenue occurring when the price is raised above the prevailing market level indicates that the individual seller faces a **kinked demand** (see Figure 12.6). The prevailing price is at A. Adjusting this price is not beneficial to the seller for the following reasons:

- Above the prevailing price, demand for the product drops sharply, as indicated by the fairly flat average revenue curve beyond point P. Above price A, demand is highly elastic and, as a result, total revenue declines.

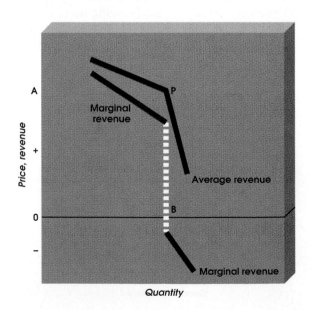

Figure 12.6

Kinked demand curve.

This type of curve faces firms selling well-known, standardized products as well as individual firms in an oligopolistic market structure. The kink occurs at the point representing the prevailing price, A. At prices above A, demand declines rapidly. A price set below A results in very little increase in volume, so revenue is lost; that is, marginal revenue is negative.

Has the Internet placed the customer in charge?

The Internet has already had a tremendous impact on pricing and prices, perhaps affecting this element of marketing more than any other. With so many sellers and buyers coming together electronically in cyberspace, the balance of power may be shifting toward customers. In a real sense, the Internet fosters conditions approaching perfect competition. That is, nearly identical products are available from numerous suppliers, and prospective buyers have ample information for making purchase decisions.

Through the Internet, online shoppers can examine the offerings of vendors around the world, including their comparative prices. Further, they are better able to influence prices in electronic commerce than in traditional transactions. In fact, the Internet facilitates **dynamic pricing**, in which prices are adjusted instantly and frequently in line with what the market will bear. In online transactions, prices are less likely to be fixed and more likely to result from negotiation, popularly termed "haggling."

Dynamic pricing is evident in various forms of electronic commerce. The most visible example of dynamic pricing is online auctions. The auction can be initiated by a seller, who places a product up for sale online, or by a buyer, who announces the desire to purchase a particular good or service online. To learn about variations on the basic method, review the eBay, FreeMarkets, and Priceline.com cases at the beginnings of Chapter 1, Chapter 5, and this chapter, respectively.

It's widely believed that dynamic pricing, as found in online auctions, will result in lower prices. In fact, an early study concluded that prices for the two products examined, books and music CDS, were 9 to 16% lower online than at conventional retailers.

The reasons for lower prices? First and foremost, comparison shopping is easier on the Internet, helped greatly by "shopping robots" (more on this type of electronic search engine in Chapter 15). Of course, consumers may gather price information through the Internet and then use it to negotiate a lower price from a conventional "offline" seller such as a retail store. In addition, online buyers may be able to design a product to meet their particular needs, thereby assuring maximum value from the purchase. Dell Computer stressed that advantage in order to build its online sales volume.

However, the Internet also should, or could, benefit sellers' pricing activities. The reasons? For one thing, it's much easier for a seller to change prices online than to retag every item in an actual retail store. In addition, because shoppers have to provide various information in order to make an online purchase and their transactions can be compiled and analyzed, e-commerce firms can tailor special offerings for individual customers. For example, if a customer's several purchases of decorating accessories at MyHome.com were all related to the living room, the company could provide the customer with a special incentive (such as a 25% discount) for a purchase related to a different room in the home.

Surprisingly, dynamic pricing may not always result in lower prices. Sometimes a winning bid may be at a higher figure than what the seller would have charged as a fixed price. That's consistently been the case at AucNet, an online auction for used autos.

It's too early to conclude what effect e-commerce on the Internet will ultimately have on prices. Here's one plausible scenario, "The Internet may turn out to be more of a price leveler than a price cutter. To economic theorists, perfect market information tends to make prices converge."

Sources: David Bank, "A Site-Eat-Site World," *The Wall Street Journal*, July 12, 1999, p. R8; Robert D. Hof, "Going, Going, Gone," *Business Week*, Apr. 12, 1999, pp. 30–32; Robert D. Hof, "'The Buyer Always Wins,'" *Business Week E.Biz*, Mar. 22, 1999, pp. EB26, EB28; and Amy E. Cortese, "Good-Bye to Fixed Pricing?" *Business Week*, May 4, 1998, pp. 71–73+. The concluding statement is from Bernard Wysocki, Jr., "The Outlook: Internet Is Opening Up a New Era of Pricing," *The Wall Street Journal*, June 8, 1998, p. A1.

- Below price A, demand for the product increases very little, as shown by the steeply sloping average revenue curve and the negative marginal revenue curve below point P. Demand is highly inelastic and, as a result, total revenue still declines.

In the case of kinked demand, total revenue decreases each time the price is adjusted from the prevailing price, A in Figure 12.6. The prevailing price is well established. Consequently, when a single firm reduces its price, its unit sales will not increase very much—certainly not enough to offset the loss in average revenue.

Can you deal with a kinked demand curve?

Intense price competition has characterized the airline industry in the U.S. since it was deregulated. In an attempt to increase the number of passengers, an airline such as United may cut its price on a heavily traveled route—New York to Los Angeles, for example. However, competitors on this route, such as American, Delta, and Trans World Airlines, usually match that lower fare immediately. As a result, there is no signifi-cant shift in the market share held by each airline on that route. But another result is that the market price settles—at least temporarily—at the lower level. Unless the number of passengers increases substantially, the profits of all airlines flying this route and matching the cut-rate prices are likely to suffer.

What marketing strategies might an airline use to avoid having to match a competitor's price cut?

So far in our discussion of pricing to meet competition, we have observed market situations that involve *many* sellers. Oddly enough, this same pricing method is often used when the market is dominated by a *few* firms, each marketing similar products. This type of market structure, called an **oligopoly,** exists in such industries as copper, aluminum, soft drinks, breakfast cereals, auto tires, and even among barber shops and grocery stores in a small community. When the demand curve is kinked, as in Figure 12.6, oligopolists should simply set prices at a competitive level and leave them there. Typically they do.

Pricing below Competition

A variation of market-based pricing is to set a price *below* the level of your main competitors. **Pricing below competition** is done by discount retailers, such as Wal-Mart, Target, and Drug Emporium, which stress small markups, high volume, and few customer services (including sales people). They price heavily advertised, well-known brands 10 to 30% below the suggested list price, which is normally charged by full-service retailers. Even retailers that offer an assortment of customer services may price below the competitive level by eliminating some services. Some gas stations offer a discount to customers who pay with cash instead of a credit card, for instance.

The risk in pricing below competition is that consumers begin to view the product (or an entire retail store) as an undifferentiated commodity, such as coal and bulk salt, with the entire focus on price differences. If that happens, and some would say it already has in fields such as personal computers, then consumers choose the brand with the lowest price. In turn, competing firms are likely to wind up in a price war that diminishes or eliminates profits. One observer asked a question that applies to any industry in which firms rely on price as a way to gain an edge over competitors: "How can restaurant chains ever expect to charge top dollar again after relentlessly pushing value [low] prices?"[27]

Pricing above Competition

Producers or retailers sometimes set their prices *above* the prevailing market level. Usually, **pricing above competition** works only when the product is distinctive or when the seller has acquired prestige in its field. Most communities have an elite clothing boutique and a prestigious jewelry store where prices are noticeably above the level set by other stores with seemingly similar products. However, a gas station that has a strong advantage based on a superior location (perhaps the only such station for many miles on an interstate highway) may also be able to use above-market pricing.

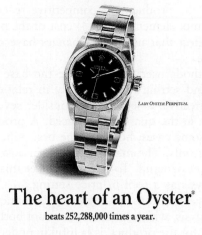

LADY OYSTER PERPETUAL

The heart of an Oyster®

beats 252,288,000 times a year.

As appealing to the eye as this Lady Oyster Perpetual is, it's even more appealing and impressive on the inside. Consider, for example, the tiny balance wheel that is the heart of the Oyster, and oscillates more than a quarter of a billion times a year.

Every balance wheel is individually equalized for weight, matched with its ideal hairspring by computer and individually calibrated. No wonder this splendid $2,175 Lady Oyster Perpetual can perform in the most trying conditions without missing a beat.

Rolex Lady Oyster Perpetual in stainless steel with matching Oyster bracelet. For the name and location of an Official Rolex Jeweler near you, please call 1-800-36ROLEX. Rolex, ®, Oyster Perpetual and Oyster are trademarks.

ROLEX ♔

Rolex positions its watches as top quality. This ad emphasizes three aspects of quality—accuracy, durability, and appearance. The company reinforces the image of its watches with high prices (this model is priced at $2,175) and limited distribution. Retailers that sell this brand will be expected to provide superior service, especially knowledgeable sales people.

 www.rolex.com

 www.patekphilippe.com

Above-market pricing often is employed by manufacturers of prestige brands of high-cost goods such as autos (Ferrari, Mercedes), crystal (Waterford), leather products (Gucci, Fendi), and watches (Breguet, Rolex). Patek Philippe, a Swiss firm, makes only about 15,000 watches per year, but they are priced from $5,000 to $400,000—per watch! Above-market pricing also is used for business goods. Sometimes it can be effective for relatively low-cost goods. Premier Industrial, for example, prices its fasteners and tubing at least 10% higher and occasionally much higher than competing products. Premier, an industrial distributor, can do this because—unlike competitors—it accepts small orders and ships an order within 24 hours.[28]

Some services firms also price above their competitors. In the hotel industry, the Ritz Carlton and Fairmont chains have used this approach successfully. In the airline industry, the supersonic Concorde may be the best example. This aircraft flies at about twice the speed of sound, over 1,300 miles per hour, which is more than two times the average speed of a regular commercial jet. As a result, a flight between Paris and New York takes about 3½ hours, compared to a regular flight time of 8 hours. The reduced travel time comes with a steep price, with a round-trip fare typically costing at least $7,500. Perhaps because of the price, there is very limited demand for travel on the Concorde. In fact, British Airways flies the Concorde only between London and New York, and Air France operates this aircraft between Paris and New York.[29]

Summary

In our economy, price influences the allocation of resources. In individual companies, price is one significant factor in achieving marketing success. And in many purchase situations, price can be of great importance to consumers. However, it is difficult to define price. A general definition is: Price is the amount of money and/or other items with utility needed to acquire a product.

Before setting a product's base price, management should identify its pricing objective. Major pricing objectives are to (1) earn a target return on investment or on net sales, (2) maximize profits, (3) increase sales, (4) hold or gain a target market share, (5) stabilize prices, and (6) meet competition's prices.

Besides the firm's pricing objective, other key factors that influence price setting are: (1) demand for the product, (2) competitive reactions, (3) strategies planned for other marketing-mix elements, and (4) cost of the product. The concept of elasticity refers to the effect that unit-price changes have on the number of units sold and on total revenue.

Three major methods used to determine the base price are cost-plus pricing, marginal analysis, and setting the price only in relation to the market. For cost-plus pricing to be effective, a seller must consider several types of costs and their reactions to changes in the quantity produced. A producer usually sets a price to cover total cost. In some cases, however, the best policy may be to set a price that covers marginal cost only. The main weakness in cost-plus pricing is that it completely ignores market demand. To partially offset this weakness, a company may use break-even analysis as a tool in price setting.

In actual business situations, price setting is influenced by market conditions. Hence, marginal analysis, which takes into account both demand and costs to determine a suitable price for the product, is helpful in understanding the forces affecting price. Price and output level are set at the point where marginal cost equals marginal revenue. The effectiveness of marginal analysis in setting prices depends on obtaining reliable cost data.

For many products, price setting is relatively easy because management simply sets the price at the level of competition. Pricing at prevailing market levels makes sense for firms selling well-known, standardized products and sometimes for individual firms in an oligopoly. Two variations of market-level pricing are to price below or above the levels of primary competitors.

More about **Priceline.com**

After establishing its website as a place to bid on airline tickets, Priceline.com added hotel rooms to its product mix. According to Jay Walker, the company's founder, the hotel industry was a natural area of expansion for Priceline. "Our service will be a giant plus," he said. "Until now, hotels have faced the worst of two possible worlds. If they lower prices for some rooms, they risk angering guests who paid higher prices. If they keep prices static, there is the opportunity risk where rooms go unsold." By allowing consumers to name their own price, Walker claims Priceline sells rooms to travelers who otherwise wouldn't book rooms with the participating hotel chains.

Because there is more customer service involved in a hotel stay than in an airline flight, it's been suggested that Priceline customers might not be treated as well as guests who paid full price at a hotel. Consumers seemed unconcerned by this possibility, however. Just months after its launch, Priceline was booking more than 4,000 rooms per month in 200 cities.

However, Walker and Priceline's chief executive officer, Richard Braddock, agreed that the company had to expand beyond the travel business, which accounted for 84% of Priceline's volume. As a result, the company added home mortgages and rental cars to its product mix as well as Perfect YardSale, an auction site that is being tested in Atlanta. In early 2000, Priceline's website indicated that "name your own price" gasoline and long-distance calling time were coming soon.

The company's most aggressive expansion perhaps has been into groceries. Many consumers apparently consider it reasonable to go online and make a bid for an airline ticket or a hotel room. But what about cereal, soft drinks, and other groceries that consumers typically buy in a nearby supermarket? Starting out in the New York metro area, consumers will have the opportunity to do just that, according to Priceline's new venture, WebHouse Club Inc.

Much like the original concept that fueled Priceline's early success, grocery shoppers will be able to go online to name their own price for items in 140 different categories. After obtaining a plastic card with a unique number and a magnetic strip at their local supermarket, a grocery shopper enters the card number on WebHouse's Internet site to activate an account. For a $3 monthly fee, a consumer can make bids and instantly find out if the bids are acceptable to the products' manufacturers. After paying online with a credit card, the customer then goes to one of the 600 participating local supermarkets, walks the aisles, and picks out the items purchased.

Bidding on grocery items and then collecting them in the store might sound like a time-consuming process for participating consumers. Walker points out, however, that numerous grocery shoppers spend a great deal of time clipping, organizing, and redeeming manufacturer's coupons from newspaper inserts.

Manufacturers also must participate in Web-House because, much like couponing, they need to reimburse the grocery stores for the difference between the accepted price and the full price of the item in the store where the shopper picks up the order. To ensure that a variety of items are available for purchase, WebHouse supplements some of its customers' bids so they meet minimums established by the manufacturers. WebHouse makes its money from the monthly fees paid by consumers and transaction fees paid by manufacturers.

WebHouse plans to expand the service across the entire country by the end of 2000. And success with WebHouse could lead to a number of other ventures for Priceline. According to Walker, "There is no category we won't be in."[30]

1. Which pricing objective(s) does it appear Priceline is pursuing?

2. What other product categories might be suitable for Priceline's business model?

 webhouse.priceline.com

Key Terms and Concepts

Price (324)
Barter (325)
Value (327)
Pricing objectives (328)
Base price (list price) (331)
Expected price (332)
Inverse demand (332)
Fixed cost (334)
Total fixed cost (334)
Average fixed cost (334)
Variable cost (334)

Total variable cost (334)
Average variable cost (334)
Total cost (334)
Average total cost (334)
Marginal cost (334)
Average fixed cost curve (334)
Average variable cost curve (334)
Average total cost curve (335)
Marginal cost curve (335)
Cost-plus pricing (336)
Break-even analysis (338)

Break-even point (338)
Marginal revenue (340)
Average revenue (340)
Pricing to meet competition (342)
Perfect competition (342)
Kinked demand (342)
Dynamic pricing (343)
Oligopoly (344)
Pricing below competition (344)
Pricing above competition (344)

Questions and Problems

1. a. Explain how a firm's pricing objective may influence the promotional program for a product.
   b. Which of the six pricing goals involves the largest, most aggressive promotional campaign?

2. What marketing conditions might logically lead a company to set "meeting competition" as a pricing objective?

3. What is your expected price for each of the following articles? How did you arrive at your estimate in each instance?

a. An Internet service that would send you, via e-mail, daily news from two cities of your choosing (such as your hometown, a city where you might like to live in the future).

b. A new type of cola beverage that holds its carbonation long after it has been opened; packaged in 12-ounce (355-milliliter) and 2-liter bottles.

c. A nuclear-powered 23-inch table-model television set, guaranteed to run for 10 years without replacement of the original power-generating component; requires no battery or electric wires.

4. Name three products, including at least one service, for which you think an inverse demand exists. For each product, within which price range does this inverse demand exist?

5. In Figure 12.2, what is the significance of the point where the marginal cost curve intersects the average total cost curve? Explain why the average total cost curve is declining to the left of the intersection point and rising beyond it. Explain how the marginal cost curve can be rising while the average total cost curve is still declining.

6. What are the merits and limitations of the cost-plus method of setting a base price?

7. In a break-even chart, is the total *fixed* cost line always horizontal? Is the total *variable* cost line always straight? Explain.

8. Referring to Table 12.3 and Figure 12.4, what would be Futon Factory's break-even points at prices of $50 and $90, if variable costs are $40 per unit and fixed costs remain at $25,000?

9. A small manufacturer sold ballpoint pens to retailers at $8.40 per dozen. The manufacturing cost was 50 cents for each pen. Expenses, including all selling and administrative costs except advertising, were $19,200. How many dozen must the manufacturer sell to cover these expenses and pay for an advertising campaign costing $6,000?

10. In Figure 12.5, why would the firm normally stop producing at quantity Q? Why is the price set at B rather than at D or A?

Hands-On Marketing

1. Select three goods (new or used nonfood items in the price range of $10 to $100) that you are considering buying. Determine the price of each of the items in your local community by checking with one or more retail outlets. Then go to an online auction site such as eBay.com or Amazon.com, and check the prices of each of the items. Which are cheaper—the online or in-store prices? Where would you buy each item? What reasons underlie your decisions?

2. Identify one store in your community that generally prices *below* the levels of most other firms and one that prices *above* prevailing market levels. Arrange an interview with the manager of each store. Ask both managers to explain the rationale and procedures associated with their pricing approaches. Also ask the manager of the store with below-market prices how profits are achieved with such low prices. Ask the manager of the store with above-market prices how customers are attracted and then satisfied with such high prices.

Appendix A

Marketing Math

Marketing involves people—customers, middlemen, and producers. Much of the business activity of these people is quantified in some manner. Consequently, knowledge of certain concepts in economics, accounting, and finance is essential for decision making in many areas of marketing. With that in mind, this appendix presents an overview—or, for many of you, a review—of (1) price elasticity of demand, (2) the operating statement, (3) markups, and (4) analytical ratios.

Price Elasticity of Demand

Price elasticity of demand refers to the responsiveness of quantity demanded to price changes. Specifically, it gauges the effect that a change in the price of a product has on amount sold and on total revenue. (Total revenue—that is, total sales in dollars—equals the unit price times the number of units sold.)

We say demand is **elastic** when (1) reducing the unit price causes an increase in total revenue *or* (2) raising the unit price causes a decrease in total revenue. In the first case, the lower price results in a boost in quantity sold that more than offsets the price cut—hence, the increase in total revenue. In the second case, the higher price results in a large drop in quantity sold that more than counters the potential gain from the price rise—hence, the decrease in total revenue.

These elastic demand situations are illustrated in Figure A.1. We start with a situation where, at $5 a sandwich, the Campus Sandwich Company sells 100 units and the total revenue (TR) equals $500. When the firm lowers the price to $4, the quantity sold increases to 150 and total revenue also goes up—to $600. When the price is boosted to $6, however, the quantity sold drops off so much (to 70 sandwiches) that total revenue also declines (to $420). Thus demand is *elastic* when the price change (either up or down) and total revenue change move in the *opposite* direction.

Demand is **inelastic** when (1) a price cut causes total revenue to decline *or* (2) a price rise results in an increase in total revenue. In each of these situations, the changes in unit price more than offset the relatively small changes in quantities sold. That is, when the price is cut, the increase in quantity sold is not enough to offset the price cut, so total revenue goes down. And when the unit price is raised, it more than counters the decline in quantity sold, so total revenue goes up. Simply, demand is *inelastic* when the price change and the resulting change in total revenue go in the *same* direction.

Inelastic demand situations are illustrated in Figure A.2. Again we start with a unit price of $5, Paperbacks and More sells 100 units, and total revenue is $500. When the store lowers the unit price

Figure A.1

Elastic demand.

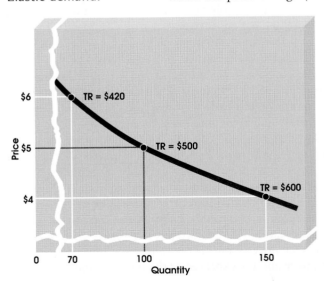

Inelastic demand.

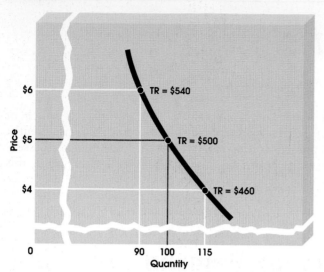

to $4, the quantity of books sold increases to 115. But this is not enough to off-set the price cut, so total revenue declines to $460. When the unit price is raised to $6, the quantity sold falls off to 90. But the price increase more than offsets the drop in quantity sold, so total revenue goes up to $540.

In general, the demand for necessities (salt, sugar, gasoline, telephone service, gas and electric service) tends to be inelastic. If the price of gasoline goes up or down, say 10 or 15 cents a gallon, the total num-ber of gallons sold does not change very much. Sim-ply, consumers need gasoline for their cars. Con-versely, the demand for products purchased with discretionary income (luxury items, large appliances, furniture, autos) typically is much more elastic. That is why the demand for new electronics products often soars as prices decline in the early stages of the life cycle.

Moreover, the demand for individual *brands* is more elastic than is the demand for the broader *product* category. If consumers encounter an unsat-isfactory price on an individual brand, they ordinar-ily can purchase an alternative brand. However, if they are displeased with the prices in an entire product category, they may not be able to find an alternative type of product to meet their needs. Thus the demand for Continental Airlines or Hertz rental cars is far more elastic (price-sensitive) than is the demand for air travel or rental cars in general.

Price elasticity of demand is not just a theoretical concept in economics. It has practical value. By gauging whether demand for a product is elastic or inelastic, marketing executives are better able to establish suitable prices for their products.

The Operating Statement

A company prepares two main financial statements—a balance sheet and an oper-ating statement. A **balance sheet** shows the assets, liabilities, and net worth of a company at a given time—for example, at the close of business on December 31, 2000.

The focus of our attention here, however, is the operating statement. Often called a *profit-and-loss statement* or an *income statement,* an **operating statement** is a summary of the firm's income and expenses over a period of time—for exam-ple, the 2000 calendar year. The operating statement shows whether the business earned a net profit or suffered a net loss during the period covered.

An operating statement can cover any period of time. To fulfill income tax requirements, virtually all firms prepare a statement covering operations during a calendar year or another 12-month period called a fiscal year. It is also common for businesses to prepare monthly, quarterly, and/or semiannual operating state-ments.

Table A.1 is an operating statement for a hypothetical firm, the Alpha-Zeta Company, which could be either a wholesaler or a retailer. The major differ-ence between the operating statement of a middleman and that of a manufac-turer is the cost-of-goods-sold section. A manufacturer shows the cost of goods *manufactured,* whereas the middleman's statement shows net *purchases.*

The essence of business is very simple. A company buys or makes a product and then (hopefully) sells it for a higher price. From the sales revenue, the seller intends to cover the cost of the merchandise and the expenses of the business and have something left over, which is called **net profit**. These relationships form the basic structure of an operating statement:

- Sales minus cost of goods sold equals gross margin.
- Gross margin minus expenses equals net profit.

An example based on the Alpha-Zeta Company in Table A.1 follows:

	Sales	$80,000
less	Cost of goods sold	48,000
equals	Gross margin	32,000
less	Expenses	27,200
equals	Net profit	$ 4,800

Now let's look at the primary components in an operating statement.

Table A.1   An Operating Statement for a Wholesaler or a Retailer

The Alpha-Zeta Company
Operating Statement for Month Ending December 31, 2000

Gross sales		$87,000	
Less: Sales returns and allowances	$ 5,500		
Cash discounts allowed	1,500	7,000	
Net sales			$80,000
Cost of goods sold			
Beginning inventory, December 1 (at cost)		$18,000	
Gross purchases	$49,300		
Less: Cash discounts taken on purchases	900		
Net purchases	$48,400		
Plus: Freight in	1,600		
Net purchases (at delivered cost)		50,000	
Cost of goods available for sale		$68,000	
Less: Ending inventory, December 31 (at cost)		20,000	
Cost of goods sold			48,000
Gross margin			$32,000
Expenses			
Sales force salaries and commissions		$11,000	
Advertising		2,400	
Office supplies		250	
Taxes (except income tax)		125	
Telephone and fax		250	
Delivery expenses		175	
Rent		800	
Heat, light, and power		300	
Depreciation		100	
Insurance		150	
Interest		150	
Bad debts		300	
Administrative salaries		7,500	
Office salaries		3,500	
Miscellaneous expenses		200	
Total expenses			27,200
Net profit before taxes			$ 4,800

Sales

The first line in an operating statement records **gross sales**—the total amount sold by an organization, stated in dollars. From this figure the Alpha-Zeta Company (hereafter, A-Z) deducts sales returns and sales allowances. A-Z also deducts discounts granted to employees when they purchase merchandise or services.

In virtually every firm, at some time during an operating period, customers want to return or exchange merchandise. In a **sales return,** the customer is refunded the full purchase price in cash or credit. In a **sales allowance,** the customer keeps the merchandise but is given a reduction from the selling price because of some dissatisfaction. The income from the sale of returned merchandise is included in a company's gross sales, so returns and allowances must be deducted to calculate net sales.

Net Sales

The most important figure in the sales section of the statement is **net sales,** which represents the net amount of sales revenue, out of which the company will pay for the products and all its expenses. The net sales figure is also the one on which many operating ratios are based. It is designated as 100% (of itself), and the other items are then expressed as a percentage of net sales.

Cost of Goods Sold

As we work toward determining A-Z's net profit, we deduct from net sales the cost of the merchandise. To calculate the **cost of goods sold** in a retail or wholesale operation, we start with the value of any merchandise on hand at the beginning of the period. To this we add the net cost of what is purchased during the period. From this total we deduct the value of whatever remains unsold at the end of the period.

In Table A.1 the firm started with an inventory worth $18,000, and during the course of the month, it purchased goods that cost $50,000. Thus A-Z had a total of $68,000 worth of goods available for sale. If all were sold, the cost of goods sold would have been $68,000. At the end of the month, however, there was still $20,000 worth of merchandise on hand. Thus, during the month, A-Z sold goods that cost $48,000.

We just spoke of merchandise *valued at* a certain figure or *worth* a stated amount. Actually, the problem of inventory valuation is complicated and sometimes controversial. The rule of thumb is to value inventories at cost or market, whichever is lower. The application of this rule in the real world may be difficult. Assume that a store buys six beach balls at $5 each and the following week buys six more at $6 each. The company places all 12, jumbled, in a basket display for sale. Then one is sold, but there is no marking to indicate whether its cost was $5 or $6. Thus the inventory value of the remaining 11 balls may be $60 or $61. If we multiply this situation by thousands of purchases and sales, we begin to see the depth of the problem.

A figure deserving some comment is the **net cost of delivered purchases.** A company starts with its gross purchases at billed cost. Then it must deduct any purchases that were returned or any purchase allowances received. The company should also deduct any discounts taken for payment of the bill within a specified period of time. Deducting purchase returns, allowances, and discounts gives the net cost of purchases. Freight charges paid by the buyer (called **freight in**) are added to net purchases to determine the net cost of *delivered* purchases.

In a manufacturing concern, the cost-of-goods-sold section has a slightly different form. Instead of determining the cost of goods *purchased,* the firm determines the cost of goods *manufactured,* as in Table A.2. Cost of goods manufactured ($50,000) is added to the beginning inventory ($18,000) to ascertain the total goods available for sale ($68,000). Then, after the ending inventory of finished goods has been deducted ($20,000), the result is the cost of goods sold ($48,000).

Table A.2 Cost-of-Goods-Sold Section of an Operating Statement for a Manufacturer

Beginning inventory of finished goods (at cost)			$18,000
Cost of goods manufactured:			
Beginning inventory, goods in process		$24,000	
Plus: Raw materials	$20,000		
Direct labor	15,000		
Overhead	13,000	48,000	
Total goods in process		$72,000	
Less: Ending inventory, goods in process		22,000	
Cost of goods manufactured			50,000
Cost of goods available for sale			$68,000
Less: Ending inventory, finished goods (at cost)			20,000
Cost of goods sold			$48,000

To find the cost of goods *manufactured*, a company starts with the value of goods partially completed (beginning inventory of goods in process—$24,000). To this beginning inventory figure is added the cost of raw materials, direct labor, and factory overhead expenses incurred during the period ($48,000). The resulting figure is the total goods in process during the period ($72,000). By deducting the value of goods still in process at the end of the period ($22,000), management finds the cost of goods manufactured during that span of time ($50,000).

Gross Margin

Gross margin is determined by subtracting cost of goods sold from net sales. Gross margin, sometimes called *gross profit*, is a key figure in the entire marketing program. When we say that a certain store has a *margin* of 30%, we are referring to the gross margin.

Expenses

Operating expenses are deducted from gross margin to determine net profit. The operating expense section includes marketing, administrative, and miscellaneous expenses. It does not, of course, include the cost of goods purchased or manufactured, because these costs have already been deducted.

Net Profit

Net profit is the difference between gross margin and total expenses. Obviously, a negative net profit is a loss.

• Markups

Many retailers and wholesalers use markup percentages to determine the selling price of an article. Normally the selling price must exceed the cost of the merchandise by an amount sufficient to cover operating expenses and still leave the desired profit. The difference between the selling price of an item and its cost is the **markup,** sometimes referred to as the *mark-on.*

Typically, markups are expressed in percentages rather than dollars. A markup may be expressed as a percentage of either the cost or the selling price. Therefore, we must first determine which will be the *base* for the markup. That is, when we speak of a 40% markup, do we mean 40% of the *cost* or 40% of the *selling price*?

To determine the markup percentage when it is based on *cost*, we use the following formula:

$$\text{Markup \%} = \frac{\text{dollar markup}}{\text{cost}}$$

When the markup is based on *selling price*, the formula to use is:

$$\text{Markup \%} = \frac{\text{dollar markup}}{\text{selling price}}$$

All interested parties must know which base is being used in a given situation. Otherwise there can be considerable misunderstanding. To illustrate, suppose that Allan Aaron runs a clothing store and claims he needs a 50% markup to make a small net profit. Blanche Brister, who runs a competitive store, says she needs only a 33⅓% markup and that Aaron must be either inefficient or a big profiteer.

Actually, both merchants are using identical markups, but they are using different bases. Each seller buys hats at $6 apiece and sets the selling price at $9. This is a markup of $3 per hat. Aaron is expressing his markup as a percentage of cost—hence the 50% figure ($3 ÷ $6 = 0.5, or 50%). Brister is basing her markup on the selling price ($3 ÷ $9 = 0.333, or 33⅓%).

It would be a mistake for Aaron to try to get by on Brister's 33⅓% markup, as long as Aaron uses cost as his base. If Aaron used the 33⅓% markup, but *based it on cost*, the markup would be only $2. And the selling price would be only $8. This $2 markup, averaged over the entire hat department, would not enable Aaron to cover his usual expenses and make a profit. *It is conventional to state markup percentages as a percentage of selling price.*

Markup Based on Selling Price

The following diagram shows the relationships among selling price, cost, and markup. It can be used to calculate these figures regardless of whether the markup is stated in percentages or dollars, and whether the percentages are based on selling price or cost:

		Dollars	Percentage
	Selling Price		
less	Cost	___	___
equals	Markup		

As an example, suppose a merchant buys an article for $90 and knows the markup based on selling price must be 40%. What is the selling price? By filling in the known information in the diagram, we obtain:

		Dollars	Percentage
	Selling Price		100
less	Cost	90	___
equals	Markup		40

The percentage representing cost must then be 60%. Thus the $90 cost is 60% of the selling price. The selling price is then $150. That is, $90 equals 60% of the selling price. Then $90 is divided by 0.6 (or 60%) to get the selling price of $150.

A common situation facing merchants is to have competition set a ceiling on selling prices. Or possibly the sellers must buy an item to fit into one of their price lines. Then they want to know the maximum amount they can pay for an item and still get their normal markup. Assume that the selling price of an article is set at $60—set by competition or by a $59.95 price line. The retailer's normal markup is 35%. What is the most the retailer should pay for this article? Again let's fill in what we know in the diagram:

		Dollars	Percentage
	Selling Price	60	100
less	Cost	___	___
equals	Markup		35

The dollar markup is $21 (that is, 35% of $60). So by simple subtraction we find that the maximum cost the merchant will want to pay is $39.

Series of Markups

Markups are figured on the selling price at *each level of business* in a channel of distribution. A manufacturer applies a markup to determine its selling price. The manufacturer's selling price then becomes the wholesaler's cost. The wholesaler must determine its own selling price by applying its usual markup percentage based on its—the wholesaler's—selling price. The same procedure is carried out by the retailer, using the wholesaler's selling price as its—the retailer's—cost.

The following calculations illustrate this point:

Producer's cost $ 7 } Producer's markup = $3, or 30%
Producer's selling price $10

Wholesaler's cost $10 } Wholesaler's markup = $2, or 16⅔%
Wholesaler's selling price $12

Retailer's cost $12 } Retailer's markup = $8, or 40%
Retailer's selling price $20

Markup Based on Cost

If a firm customarily deals in markups based on cost—and sometimes this is done among wholesalers—the same diagrammatic approach may be employed. The only change is that cost will equal 100%. The selling price will be 100% plus the markup based on cost. As an example, a firm bought an article for $70 and wants a 20% markup based on cost. The markup in dollars is $14 (in other words, 20% of $70). The selling price is $84 (that is, $70 + $14):

		Dollars	Percentage
	Selling Price	84	120
less	Cost	70	100
equals	Markup	14	20

The relationship between markups on cost and markups on selling price is important. For instance, if a product costs $6 and sells for $10, there is a $4 markup. This is a 40% markup based on selling price, but a 66⅔% markup based on cost. The following may be helpful in understanding these relationships and in converting from one base to another:

If selling price = 100%   If cost = 100%

$10 = 100%   { 60% → Cost = $6.00 ← 100% } $10 = 166⅔%
       40% → Markup = $4.00 ← 66⅔%

The relationships between the two bases are expressed in the following formulas:

$$\% \text{ markup on selling price} = \frac{\% \text{ markup on cost}}{100\% + \% \text{ markup on cost}}$$

$$\% \text{ markup on selling price} = \frac{\% \text{ markup on selling price}}{100\% - \% \text{ markup on selling price}}$$

To illustrate the use of these formulas, let's say a retailer has a markup of 25% on *cost*. This retailer wants to know what the corresponding figure is, based on selling price. In the first formula we get:

$$\frac{25\%}{100\% + 25\%} = \frac{25\%}{125\%} = 0.2, \text{ or } 20\%$$

A markup of 33⅓% based on *selling price* converts to 50% based on cost, according to the second formula:

$$\frac{33\frac{1}{3}\%}{100\% - 33\frac{1}{3}\%} = \frac{33\frac{1}{3}\%}{66\frac{2}{3}\%} = 0.5, \text{ or } 50\%$$

The markup is closely related to gross margin. Recall that gross margin is equal to net sales minus cost of goods sold. Looking below gross margin on an operating statement, we find that gross margin equals operating expenses plus net profit.

Normally the initial markup in a company, department, or product line must be set a little higher than the overall gross margin desired for the selling unit. The reason? Some reductions will be incurred before all the articles are sold. Because of one factor or another, certain items will not sell at the original price. They will have to be marked down—reduced in price from the original level. Some pilferage, damages, and other shortages also typically occur.

Analytical Ratios

From a study of the operating statement, management can develop several ratios to evaluate the results of its marketing program. In most cases net sales is used as the base (100%). In fact, unless specifically mentioned to the contrary, all ratios reflecting gross margin, net profit, or any operating expense are stated as a percentage of net sales.

Gross Margin Percentage

The ratio of gross margin to net sales is termed simply **gross margin percentage**. In Table A.1 the gross margin percentage for A-Z is $32,000 ÷ $80,000, or 40%.

Net Profit Percentage

The ratio called **net profit percentage** is determined by dividing net profit by net sales. For A-Z this ratio is $4,800 ÷ $80,000, or 6%. This percentage may be calculated either before or after federal income taxes are deducted, but the result should be labeled to show which it is.

Operating Expense Ratio

When total operating expenses are divided by net sales, the result is the **operating expense ratio.** Using the figures in Table A.1, this ratio for A-Z is $27,000 ÷ $80,000, or 34%. In similar fashion we may determine the expense ratio for any given cost. Thus we note in the table that rent expense was 1%, advertising 3%, and sales force salaries and commissions 13.75%.

Stockturn Rate

Management often measures the efficiency of its marketing operations by means of the **stockturn rate.** This figure represents the number of times an amount equal to the average size of the firm's inventory is *turned over,* or sold, during the period under study. The rate is calculated on either a cost or a selling-price basis. Both the numerator and the denominator of the fraction must be expressed in the same terms, either cost or selling price.

On a *cost* basis, the formula for stockturn rate is:

$$\text{Stockturn rate} = \frac{\text{cost of goods sold}}{\text{average inventory at cost}}$$

The average inventory is determined by adding beginning and ending inventories and dividing the result by 2. In Table A.1 the average inventory is ($18,000 + $20,000) ÷ 2 = $19,000. The stockturn rate then is $48,000 ÷ $19,000 = 2.53. Inventories usually are abnormally low at the first of the year in anticipation of taking physical inventory so a single average may not be representative. Consequently, some companies find their average inventory by adding the book inventories at the beginning of each month and then dividing this sum by 12.

Now let's assume inventory is recorded on a *selling-price* basis, as is done in most large retail organizations. Then the stockturn rate equals net sales divided by average inventory at selling price. Sometimes the stockturn rate is computed by dividing the number of *units* sold by the average inventory expressed in *units.*

Wholesale and retail trade associations in many types of businesses publish figures showing the average stockturn rate for their members. A firm with a low rate of stockturn is not generating sufficient sales volume or is carrying too much inventory. In either case, it is likely to be spending too much on storage and inventory. The company runs a higher risk of obsolescence or spoilage.

If the stockturn rate gets too high, the company's average inventory may be too low. Often a firm in this situation is using hand-to-mouth buying (that is, buying small quantities and selling all or most of them before replenishing inventory). In addition to incurring high handling and billing costs, the company is likely to be out of stock on some items.

Markdown Percentage

Sometimes retailers are unable to sell products at the originally stated prices. When this occurs, they often reduce these prices to move the products. A **markdown** is a reduction from the original selling price. The size of an individual markdown is expressed as a percentage of the original sales price. To illustrate, a retailer purchases a hat for $6 and marks it up 40% to sell for $10. The hat does not sell at that price, so it is marked down to $8. Now the seller may advertise a price cut of 20% (which is $2 ÷ $10).

Management frequently finds it helpful to determine the markdown percentage. Then the size and number of markdowns and the reasons for them can be analyzed. Retailers, particularly, analyze markdowns.

Markdown percentage is calculated by dividing total dollar markdowns by total net sales during a given period. Two important points should be noted. First, the markdown percentage is determined in this fashion whether the markdown items were sold or are still in the store. Second, the percentage is calculated with respect to total net sales, and not only in connection with sales of marked-down articles. As an example, assume that a retailer buys 10 sports hats at $6 each and prices them to sell at $10. Five hats are sold at $10. The other five are marked down to $8, and three are sold at the lower price. Total sales are $74 and total markdowns are $10. The retailer has a markdown ratio of $10 ÷ $74, or 13.5%.

Markdowns do not appear on the operating statement because they occur *before* an article is sold. The first item on an operating statement is gross sales. That figure reflects the actual selling price, which may be the selling price after a markdown has been taken.

Return on Investment

A commonly used measure of managerial performance and of the operating success of a company is its rate of return on investment. We use both the balance sheet and the operating statement as sources of information. The formula for calculating **return on investment** (ROI) is as follows:

$$\text{ROI} = \frac{\text{net profit}}{\text{sales}} \times \frac{\text{sales}}{\text{investment}}$$

Two questions may come to mind. What do we mean by "investment"? Why do we need two fractions? It would seem that the sales component in each fraction would cancel out, leaving net profit divided by investment as the meaningful ratio.

To answer the first query, consider a firm whose operating statement shows annual sales of $1,000,000 and a net profit of $50,000. At the end of the year, the balance sheet reports:

Assets	$600,000	Liabilities		$200,000
		Capital stock	$300,000	
		Retained earnings	100,000	400,000
	$600,000			$600,000

The ROI figure is obviously affected by which figure we use. But is the investment $400,000 or $600,000? The answer depends on whether we are talking to the stockholders or to the company executives. Stockholders are more interested in the return on what they have invested—in this case, $400,000. The ROI calculation then is:

$$\text{ROI} = \frac{\text{net profit } \$50,000}{\text{sales } \$1,000,000} \times \frac{\text{sales } \$1,000,000}{\text{investment } \$400,000} = 12\frac{1}{2}\%$$

Management, on the other hand, is more concerned with total investment, as represented by total assets ($600,000). This is the amount that the executives must manage, regardless of whether the assets were acquired by stockholders' investment, retained earnings, or loans from outside sources. Within this context the ROI computation becomes:

$$\text{ROI} = \frac{\text{net profit } \$50,000}{\text{sales } \$1,000,000} \times \frac{\text{sales } \$1,000,000}{\text{investment } \$600,000} = 8\frac{1}{3}\%$$

Regarding the second question, we use two fractions because we are dealing with two separate elements—the rate of profit on sales and the rate of capital turnover. Management really should determine each rate separately and then multiply the two. The rate of profit on sales is influenced by marketing considerations—notably, sales volume, price, product mix, and advertising effort. Capital turnover is a financial consideration that is not involved directly with costs or profits—only with sales volume and assets managed.

To illustrate, say our company's profits doubled with the same sales volume and investment because of an excellent marketing program this year. In effect, we doubled our profit rate with the same capital turnover:

$$\text{ROI} = \underbrace{\frac{\text{net profit } \$100,000}{\text{sales } \$1,000,000}}_{10\%} \times \underbrace{\frac{\text{sales } \$1,000,000}{\text{investment } \$600,000}}_{1\frac{2}{3}} = 16\frac{2}{3}\%$$
$$= 16\frac{2}{3}\%$$

As expected, this $16\frac{2}{3}\%$ is twice the ROI calculated above.

Now assume that we earned our original profit of $50,000 but did it with an investment of only $500,000. We cut the size of our average inventory, and we closed some branch offices. By increasing our capital turnover from 1.67 to 2, we raised the ROI from $8\frac{1}{3}\%$ to 10%, even though sales volume and profits were unchanged:

$$\text{ROI} = \underbrace{\frac{\$50,000}{\$1,000,000}}_{5\%} \times \underbrace{\frac{\$1,000,000}{\$500,000}}_{2} = 10\%$$
$$= 10\%$$

Finally, let's say that we increased our sales volume—we doubled it—but did not increase our profit or investment. The cost-profit squeeze has brought us "profitless prosperity." The following results occur:

$$\text{ROI} = \underbrace{\frac{\$50,000}{\$2,000,000}}_{2\frac{1}{2}\%} \times \underbrace{\frac{\$2,000,000}{\$600,000}}_{3\frac{1}{3}} = 8\frac{1}{3}\%$$
$$= 8\frac{1}{3}\%$$

The profit rate was cut in half, but this was offset by a doubling of the capital turnover rate. The result was that the ROI was unchanged.

Questions and Problems

1. Construct an operating statement from the following data and compute the gross margin percentage:

Purchases at billed cost	$15,000
Net sales	30,000
Sales returns and allowances	200
Cash discounts given	300
Cash discounts earned	100
Rent	1,500
Salaries	6,000
Opening inventory at cost	10,000
Advertising	600
Other expenses	2,000
Closing inventory at cost	7,500

2. Prepare a retail operating statement from the following information and compute the markdown percentage:

Rent	$ 9,000
Closing inventory at cost	28,000
Sales returns	6,500
Cash discounts allowed	2,000
Salaries	34,000
Markdowns	4,000
Other operating expenses	15,000
Opening inventory at cost	35,000
Gross sales	232,500
Advertising	5,500
Freight in	3,500
Gross margin as percentage of sales	35

3. What percentage markups *on cost* correspond to the following percentages of markup on selling price?
   a. 20%
   b. 37½%
   c. 50%
   d. 66⅔%

4. What percentage markups *on selling price* correspond to the following percentages of markup on cost?
   a. 20%
   b. 33⅓%
   c. 50%
   d. 300%

5. A hardware store bought a gross (12 dozen) of hammers, paying $602.40 for the total order. The retailer estimated operating expenses for this product to be 35% of sales, and wanted a net profit of 5% of sales. The retailer expected no markdowns. What retail selling price should be set for each hammer?

6. Competition in a line of sporting goods limits the selling price on a certain item to $25. If the store owner thinks a markup of 35% is needed to cover expenses and return a reasonable profit, what is the most the owner can pay for this item?

7. A retailer with annual net sales of $2 million maintains a markup of 66⅔% based on cost. Expenses average 35%. What are the retailer's gross margin and net profit in dollars?

8. A company has a stockturn rate of five times a year, a sales volume of $600,000, and a gross margin of 25%. What is the average inventory at cost?

9. A store has an average inventory of $30,000 at retail and a stockturn rate of five times a year. If the company maintains a markup of 50% based on cost, what are the annual sales volume and cost of goods sold?

10. From the following data, compute the gross margin percentage and the operating expense ratio:
    Stockturn rate = 9
    Average inventory at selling price = $45,000
    Net profit = $20,000
    Cost of goods sold = $350,000

11. A ski shop sold 50 pairs of skis at $90 a pair, after taking a 10% markdown. All the skis were originally purchased at the same price and had been marked up 60% on cost. What was the gross margin on the 50 pairs of skis?

12. A women's clothing store bought 200 suits at $90 each. The suits were marked up 40%. Eighty were sold at that price. The remaining suits were each marked down 20% from the original selling price, and all were sold. Compute the sales volume and markdown percentage.

13. An appliance retailer sold 60 portable cassette players at $40 each after taking markdowns equal to 20% of the actual selling price. Originally all the cassette players had been purchased at the same price and were marked up 50% on cost. What was the gross margin percentage earned in this situation?

14. An appliance manufacturer produced a line of small appliances advertised to sell at $30. The manufacturer planned for wholesalers to receive a 20% markup, and retailers a 33⅓% markup. Total manufacturing costs were $12 per unit. What did retailers pay for the product? What were the manufacturer's selling price and percentage markup?

15. A housewares manufacturer produces an article at a full cost of $4.80. It is sold through a manufacturers' agent directly to large retailers. The agent receives a 20% commission on sales, the retailers earn a margin of 30%, and the manufacturer plans a net profit of 10% on the selling price. What is the retail price of this article?

16. A building materials manufacturer sold a quantity of a product to a wholesaler for $350, and the wholesaler in turn sold it to a lumberyard. The wholesaler's normal markup was 15%, and the retailer usually priced the item to include a 30% markup. What is the selling price to consumers?

17. From the following data, calculate the return on investment, based on a definition of *investment* that is useful for evaluating managerial performance:

Net sales	$800,000
Gross margin	280,000
Total assets	200,000
Cost of goods sold	520,000
Liabilities	40,000
Average inventory	75,000
Retained earnings	60,000
Operating expenses	240,000
Markup	35%

13

Pricing Strategies

"Apple needed to examine what happened to its once-polished image and then plant some seeds for future growth. A key step was reevaluating pricing strategy."

Can a New Pricing Strategy Restore the Shine to **Apple**?

For many years, Apple Computer Inc. followed a relatively simple marketing formula: Offer technologically advanced, user-friendly personal computers, disdain price competition, and promote the products by building an image as "the hippest box in the business." The formula worked very well, elevating Apple to one of the 100 largest industrial firms in the U.S., and making its Macintosh computers both wildly popular and highly respected.

By the mid-1990s, however, the company had lost substantial market share and its stock price was spiraling downward. There were several reasons why Apple was bruised:

- The introduction of Microsoft Windows meant that Apple computers were no longer the most user-friendly PCs in the marketplace.

- Steve Jobs, one of Apple's founders who became a visionary and charismatic leader, removed himself from day-to-day leadership of the firm.

- The company suffered through one organizational upheaval after another.

Once accounting for almost 10% of PC sales, Apple's market share sank to 7% in 1995, representing almost $3 billion in lost revenue. Not surprisingly, Apple's stock price fell. Apple needed to examine what happened to its once-polished image and then plant some seeds for future growth. A key step was reevaluating pricing strategy.

For many years, Apple priced its computers according to its own standards and did not engage in price competition with other PC makers. It was able to do this by manufacturing high-quality, easy-to-use products that required far less customer service than other PCs.

But Microsoft Windows changed all that. Now, every PC was easier to operate, eliminating Apple's technological edge. As a result, computer buyers were no longer willing to pay more for an Apple.

The company could no longer stay out of the pricing fray. After all, every lost customer for Apple was potentially gone forever, because the software they would buy for their new PCs was incompatible with Apple models.

Apple was losing the confidence of software developers and even its most loyal customers. Software developers were important to Apple because without compatible software, Apple PCs would be significantly less attractive than other types of machines. In addition, large corporations and government agencies that were interested in building large networks of PCs were shying away from investing in Apples. The company needed to boost sales—and quickly.

As a result, in late 1995 Apple slashed PC prices up to 25%, which cut its gross profit margin by almost one-half. This drastic measure failed to increase sales, however, and Apple went through several downsizings during the next several months. What followed were more management restructurings, unclear product and pricing strategies, billion-dollar losses, and continued drops in market share. The company's sales continued to plummet from a high of $11 billion in 1995 to an eventual low of $6 billion in 1998. Apple seemed destined to wither away unless drastic measures were taken.

Apple's board of directors agreed and, in a radical move, reinstated Jobs as acting chairman and CEO in mid-1997. After a 12-year absence, Jobs brought his vision and zeal back to the company. Jobs challenged employees to refocus Apple on its core business by developing a new version of the most successful product in Apple's history—the Macintosh.[1]

What advice would you give Apple regarding the pricing of its new Macintosh product?

 www.apple.com

Fundamentally, in managing the price element of a company's marketing mix, management first must decide on its pricing goal and then set the base price for a good or service. The final task, as shown in Figure 13.1, is to design pricing strategies that are compatible with the rest of the marketing mix. Many strategic questions related to price must be answered—not just by Apple as in the preceding case, but by all firms. These questions include: Will our company compete primarily on the basis of price, or on other factors? What kind of discount schedule should be adopted? Will we occasionally absorb shipping costs? Are our approaches to pricing ethical and legal?

In this chapter we primarily discuss ways in which a firm adjusts a product's base price to coincide with its overall marketing program. After studying this chapter, you should be able to explain:

chapter goals

- Price competition, notably value pricing, and nonprice competition.
- Pricing strategies for entering a market, especially market skimming and market penetration.
- Price discounts and allowances.
- Geographic pricing strategies.
- Special pricing situations, notably one-price and flexible-price approaches, leader pricing, everyday low pricing and high-low pricing, and reactive and proactive changes.
- Legal issues associated with pricing.

We will use the term *strategy* frequently in this chapter, so let's explain its meaning. A **strategy** is a broad plan of action by which an organization intends to reach a particular goal. To illustrate, a company may adopt a strategy of offering quantity discounts to achieve the goal of a 10% increase in sales this year.

Price versus Nonprice Competition

In developing a marketing program, management has to decide whether to compete primarily on the basis of price or the nonprice elements of the marketing mix. This choice obviously affects other parts of the firm's marketing program.

Figure 13.1

The price-determination process.

The first two steps were discussed in Chapter 12. The third step is the subject of this chapter.

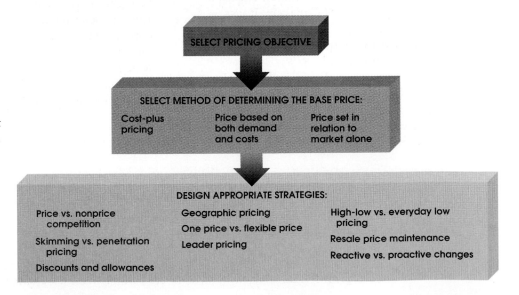

Dollar Tree Stores, Inc., which has almost 1,000 outlets, sells all of its merchandise for $1 per item. To make a profit, "deep discounters" such as Dollar Tree must control both operating expenses and cost of goods sold. One approach is finding suppliers willing to sell closeout merchandise and excess inventory at very low costs.

 www.dollartree.com

 www.familydollar.com

Price Competition

A company engages in **price competition** by regularly offering products priced as low as possible and accompanied by a minimum of services. Consumer electronics, computers, and air travel are just several of the myriad industries characterized by rigorous price competition at the present time. In the retail sector, large discount chains, such as Target and Wal-Mart, compete largely on the basis of price. Smaller chains, such as Dollar General and Family Dollar Stores, offer so-called "deep discounts" and thus depend still more on low prices. In the late 1990s, even though the economy was flourishing, deep discounters were expanding rapidly by "enticing consumers with a wide range of food and household products in clean, well-organized and heavily stocked stores."[2]

Price competition has been spreading to other parts of the world as well. For example, price reductions are becoming more common throughout Europe. This switch in competitive strategy was due to the elimination of various trade barriers and, for a while, the continent's economic woes. E-tailers have used price competition to lure buyers and establish a foothold in the market.

In Chapter 12 we discussed how more and more consumers are seeking better value in their purchases. In response, many companies in diverse industries are using what's called **value pricing**. This form of price competition aims to improve a product's value—that is, the ratio of its benefits to its price and related costs. To implement value pricing, a firm typically (1) offers products with lower prices but the same, or perhaps added, benefits; and (2) at the same time seeks ways to slash expenses so profits do not suffer.

Value also can be improved by introducing a much better product with a somewhat higher price than competing entries. Gillette's Mach 3 razor, Intel's Pentium III microprocessor chip, and Goodyear's Aquatred radial tire all illustrate this approach. Despite these notable examples, this approach is not that common today.

During the 1990s, value pricing became a pivotal marketing trend in fields as diverse as air travel, groceries, personal computers, and fast food. Consider an example. Taco Bell trimmed prices on some of its mainstays such as tacos and burritos and tried, but then dropped, cheaper snack-size items. Equally important, the chain attacked its cost structure, particularly labor costs. Its employees "assemble" tacos and other items from meats and vegetables that are cooked, sliced, and otherwise prepared by outside suppliers and delivered to the outlets.[3]

Value pricing certainly emphasizes the price element of the marketing mix. But that's not enough. A top executive of a computer company stated it in this way: "If all you have to offer is price, I don't think it's a successful long-term strategy."[4]

How is a new currency affecting pricing in Europe?

As explained in Chapter 3, all but 4 of the 15 countries comprising the European Union have adopted a common currency called the euro. The new bills and coins are scheduled to be introduced in 2002. In the meantime, the exchange rates of the participating countries have been linked together.

The advent of a common currency has significant implications for firms doing business in these 11 countries, which collectively have about 300 million citizens. The implications include:

- European companies will not have to use financial maneuvers in order to deal with various exchange rates, as existed previously in these 11 countries. However, U.S. firms will still have to worry about the dollar–versus–euro exchange rate.

- With a single currency, marketers will find it more difficult to use different price levels in different countries because consumers will easily detect these price variations. Prior to the euro, companies would vary prices from country to country, taking into account such factors as competition and consumers' price sensitivity in a particular region. For example, in 1998, a bottle of Gatorade cost almost four times as much in Germany as in Spain. Now, with the euro, such a wide range of prices is less likely to occur. In fact, a recent European Commission study found that the range of prices for identical models of the same new car has already narrowed across the European Union region.

- With the prospect of added price competition, retailers and wholesalers are likely to seek lower prices from their suppliers.

Given the introduction of the euro, companies are already considering whether or how to modify their pricing strategies. Here are some common steps:

- Examining individual markets to determine whether a single "pan-European" price is necessary or whether price differences are still plausible. As one executive commented, "The common currency doesn't erase 2,000 years of historical and cultural differences."

- Designing innovative products that address specific needs and, as a result, are not subject to constant price comparisons.

- Considering whether the single currency provides an opportunity to establish a pan-European marketing program, consisting of a common product, package, price, and promotional program across this entire region of the world. Procter & Gamble is very interested in this approach.

Firms, whether European or American, that are able to assess the impact of the euro and modify their pricing strategies accordingly will gain a differential advantage, at least temporarily.

Sources: "Euro Narrows Differences in New-Car Sticker Prices," *The Wall Street Journal,* Feb. 8, 2000, p. A23; Andrea Know, "Pricing in Euroland," *World Trade,* January 1999, pp. 52–56, and Maricris G. Briones, "The Euro Starts Here," *Marketing News,* July 20, 1998, pp. 1, 39.

Consequently, value pricing depends on creatively combining all elements of the marketing mix in order to maximize benefits in relation to price and other costs.

With a value-pricing strategy, products often have to be redesigned to expand benefits and/or shave costs. Relationships with customers have to be strengthened to generate repeat sales. Steps toward this end include frequent-buyer programs, toll-free customer service lines, and hassle-free warranties. And advertising has to be revamped to provide more facts and fewer emotional appeals. Finally, firms that desire to stress value need to negotiate aggressively with suppliers. What was said about one deep discounter applies rather well to all firms relying on value pricing, ". . . to sell merchandise at Family Dollar's low price points, you had to first buy it at the right price."[5]

Nonprice Competition

In **nonprice competition,** sellers maintain stable prices and attempt to improve their market positions by emphasizing other aspects of their marketing programs. Of course, competitors' prices still must be taken into consideration, and price changes will occur over time. Nevertheless, in nonprice competition, the emphasis is on something other than price.

Using terms familiar in economic theory, we can differentiate price and nonprice competition. In *price* competition, sellers attempt to move up or down their individual demand curves by changing prices. In *nonprice* competition, sellers attempt to shift their demand curves to the right by means of product differentiation, promotional activities, or some other technique. In Figure 13.2, the demand curve faced by the producer of a given model of skis is DD. At a price of $350, the producer can sell 35,000 pairs a year in the European market. On the basis of price competition alone, sales can be increased to 55,000 if the producer is willing to reduce the price to $330. The demand curve is still DD. However, the producer is interested in boosting sales without any decrease in selling price. Consequently, the firm embarks on a fresh promotional program—a form of nonprice competition. Suppose that enough new customers are persuaded to buy at the original $350 price that unit sales increase to 55,000 pairs a year. In effect, the firm's entire demand curve has been shifted to position D'D'.

With price competition, many consumers "learn" to buy a brand only as long as it has the lowest price. There is little customer loyalty when price is the only feature differentiating products from each other. As one consultant advised retailers, "Long-term price competition can take a devastating toll on profits."[6] With nonprice competition, however, a seller retains some advantage through its differentiation on other features (such as stylish design), even when another company decides to undersell it. Thus many firms stress nonprice competition, and others would like to rely on it rather than price competition. Wanting to be masters of their own destinies, companies believe they have more control in nonprice competition.

The best approach in nonprice competition is to build strong—if possible, unassailable—brand equity for the firm's products. Two methods of accomplishing this are to develop distinctive, hopefully unique, products and to create a novel, appealing promotional program. In addition, some firms emphasize the variety and quality of the supplementary services they offer to customers.[7]

Market-Entry Strategies

In preparing to enter the market with a new product, management must decide whether to adopt a skimming or a penetration pricing strategy.

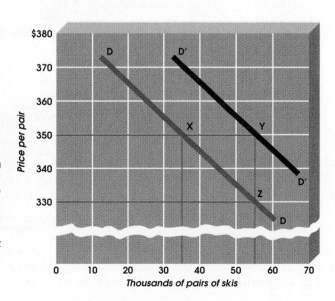

Figure 13.2

Shift in demand curve for skis.

Nonprice competition can shift the demand curve for a product. A company selling skis in the European market used a promotional program to sell more skis at the same price, thereby shifting DD to D'D'. Volume increased from 35,000 to 55,000 units at $350 (point X to point Y). Besides advertising, what other devices might this firm use to shift its demand curve?

Market-Skimming Pricing

Setting a relatively high initial price for a new product is referred to as **market-skimming pricing.** Ordinarily the price is high in relation to the target market's range of expected prices. That is, the price is set at the highest possible level that the most interested consumers will pay for the new product. For example, L'Oreal started with a relatively high price for innovative cosmetics such as Niosôme, a wrinkle-fighting facial cream.[8]

Market-skimming pricing has several purposes. Because it should provide healthy profit margins, it is intended primarily to recover research and development costs as quickly as possible. Lofty prices can be used to connote high quality. Market-skimming pricing is likely to curtail demand to levels that do not outstrip the firm's production capacities. Finally, it provides the firm with flexibility, because it is much easier to lower an initial price that meets with consumer resistance than it is to raise an initial price that has proven to be too low to cover costs. Even though the price may be lowered gradually, the high initial prices associated with market skimming are subject to criticism from consumers and government officials.

Market-skimming pricing is suitable under the following conditions:

- The new product has distinctive features strongly desired by consumers.
- Demand is fairly inelastic, most likely the case in the early stages of a product's life cycle. Under this condition, lower prices are unlikely to produce greater total revenues.
- The new product is protected from competition through one or more entry barriers such as a patent.

www.bellagiolasvegas.com

Market skimming is used for various products, notably in pricing new technological goods such as high-definition TVs. Some new hotels and resorts, such as the Bellagio in Las Vegas, use market-skimming pricing. And in a much different industry, the recently developed LASIK vision-correction procedure started with a price of about $2,000 per eye. As a result of growing competition, LASIK prices are already dropping, however.

The EV Warrior was promoted as "the first mass-produced street-legal electric vehicle of any type in the modern era." It could be pedaled like a regular bicycle, or the rider could rely on the built-in electric power. The suggested retail price for different models of the EV Warrior ranged from $1,399 to $1,899. Does the situation justify the Electric Bicycle Company's market-skimming pricing strategy? Possibly not, given that the company has gone out of business!

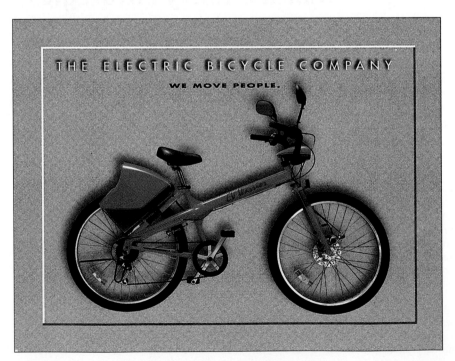

THE ELECTRIC BICYCLE COMPANY
WE MOVE PEOPLE.

Market-Penetration Pricing

In **market-penetration pricing,** a relatively low initial price is established for a new product. The price is low in relation to the target market's range of expected prices. The primary aim of this strategy is to penetrate the mass market immediately and, in so doing, generate substantial sales volume and a large market share. At the same time, it is intended to discourage other firms from introducing competing products.

Market-penetration pricing makes the most sense under the following conditions:

- A large mass market exists for the product.
- Demand is highly elastic, typically in the later stages of the life cycle for a product category.
- Substantial reductions in unit costs can be achieved through large-scale operations. In other words, economies of scale are possible.
- Fierce competition already exists in the market for this product or can be expected soon after the product is introduced.

In the mid-1990s, some software companies used the ultimate in penetration pricing—they gave away their products for a limited time or up to a stipulated quantity. Computer Associates, for example, gave away the first million copies of its Simply Money accounting program! Now various enterprises are not charging for their Internet-based services. Intranets.com, to mention one company, is giving away software that allows small companies to set up internal computer networks. What motivates the giveaways? Some firms want to create favorable word of mouth to motivate later buyers and to stimulate purchases of upgrades and complementary software by the recipients of the giveaways. Others intend to generate revenue from such sources as training, technical support, and even advertising at their websites for various firms.[9]

Referring to penetration pricing, two consultants stated, "Extended use of this offensive tactic inevitably leads to kamikaze pricing and calamity in markets as competitors respond, cost savings disappear, and customers learn to ignore value."[10] Thus, to avoid triggering intense price competition that erodes profits, firms typically need to use penetration pricing selectively.

In an extreme case, penetration pricing might violate federal antitrust laws. If a company gives away its products or charges a far below-the-market price with the intention of driving competitors out of the marketplace, such *predatory pricing* is likely to be illegal. Microsoft has been accused of this practice when it gave away its Web browser, Internet Explorer, in order to obtain a dominant position in the market. Critics charge that predatory pricing can result in a monopoly, in which case the surviving firm can raise prices substantially. Other observers say that low prices, whatever the seller's purpose, benefit buyers. In any event, it's very difficult to prove predatory pricing in a court case.[11]

www.intranets.com

Discounts and Allowances

Discounts and allowances result in a deduction from the base (or list) price. The deduction may be in the form of a reduced price or some other concession, such as free merchandise or advertising allowances. Discounts and allowances are common in business dealings.

Quantity Discounts

Quantity discounts are deductions from a seller's list price intended to encourage customers to buy in larger amounts or to buy most of what they need from the seller offering the deduction. Discounts are based on the size of the purchase, either in dollars or in units.

A **noncumulative discount** is based on the size of an *individual order* of one or more products. A retailer may sell golf balls at $2 each or at three for $5. A manufacturer or wholesaler may set up a quantity discount schedule such as the following, used by a manufacturer of industrial adhesives:

Boxes Purchased in a Single Order	% Discount from List Price
1–5	None
6–12	2.0
13–25	3.5
Over 25	5.0

Noncumulative quantity discounts are intended to encourage large orders. Many expenses, such as billing, order filling, and salaries of sales people, are about the same whether the seller receives an order totaling $10 or one totaling $500. Consequently, selling expense as a percentage of sales decreases as orders grow in size. With a noncumulative discount, a seller shares such savings with a purchaser of large quantities.

A **cumulative discount** is based on the total volume purchased *over a specified period*. This type of discount is advantageous to a seller because it ties customers closely to that firm. The more total business a buyer gives a seller, the greater the discount.

Cumulative discounts can be found in many industries. Airline frequent-flyer and hotel frequent-guest programs are one example. In a much different field, the Monsanto Co. offered a form of cumulative discount in order to gain more purchases of Posilac, a drug that stimulates milk production in cows. To qualify for the discount, farmers had to agree to purchase the drug for at least six months.[12] Cumulative discounts also are common in selling perishable products. These discounts encourage customers to buy fresh supplies frequently, so that the buyer's merchandise will not become stale.

Quantity discounts can help a producer achieve real economies in production as well as in selling. On the one hand, large orders (motivated by a noncumula-

The Monsanto Co. used this off-beat ad to draw attention to one of its products, Posilac. To build customer loyalty, Monsanto offered a cumulative discount to customers. A noncumulative discount encourages a single large purchase, but a cumulative discount builds loyalty by giving customers another reason (besides satisfaction with the product) to purchase a good or service on a consistent basis.

www.monsanto.com

POSILAC HELPS MAKE COWS MORE PROFITABLE REGARDLESS OF AGE, COLOR, OR BREED.

Heifers, Holsteins, lazy cows, or top producers, POSILAC does not discriminate. Neither should you. For best results treat all eligible cows beginning during the ninth week after calving. To learn more call 1-800-233-29

tive discount) can result in lower production and transportation costs. On the other hand, frequent orders from a single customer (motivated by a cumulative discount) can enable the producer to make much more effective use of production capacity. Thus the producer might benefit even though individual orders are small and do not generate savings in marketing costs.

Trade Discounts

Trade discounts, sometimes called *functional discounts,* are reductions from the list price offered to buyers in payment for marketing functions the buyers will perform. Storing, promoting, and selling the product are examples of these functions. A manufacturer may quote a retail price of $400 with trade discounts of 40 and 10%. The retailer pays the wholesaler $240 ($400 less 40%), and the wholesaler pays the manufacturer $216 ($240 less 10%). The wholesaler is given the 40 and 10% discounts. The wholesaler is expected to keep the 10% to cover costs of wholesaling functions and pass on the 40% discount to retailers. Sometimes, however, wholesalers keep more than the 10%—and it's not illegal for them to do so.

Note that the 40 and 10% discounts do not constitute a total discount of 50% off list price. They are not additive because the second discount (in this case, 10%) is computed on the amount remaining after the preceding discount (40%) has been deducted.

Cash Discounts

A **cash discount** is a deduction granted to buyers for paying their bills within a specified time. The discount is computed on the net amount due after first deducting trade and quantity discounts from the base price. Every cash discount includes three elements, as indicated in Figure 13.3:

- The percentage discount.
- The period during which the discount may be taken.
- The time when the bill becomes overdue.

Let's say a buyer owes $360 after other discounts have been granted and is offered terms of 2/10, n/30 on an invoice dated October 8. This means the buyer may deduct a discount of 2% ($7.20) if the bill is paid within 10 days of the invoice date—by October 18. Otherwise the entire (net) bill of $360 must be paid in 30 days—by November 7.

There are almost as many different cash discounts as there are industries. For example, in women's fashions, large discounts and short payment periods have been common; thus a cash discount of 5/5, n/15 would not be surprising. Such differences persist not so much for business reasons but because of tradition in various industries.

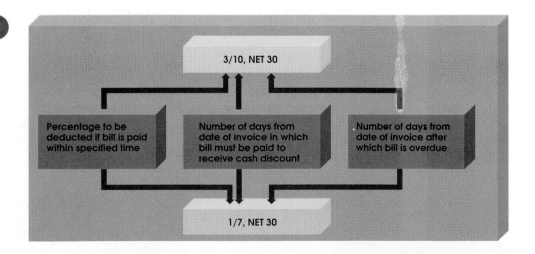

Figure 13.3

Parts of a cash discount.

3/10, NET 30

Percentage to be deducted if bill is paid within specified time

Number of days from date of invoice in which bill must be paid to receive cash discount

Number of days from date of invoice after which bill is overdue

1/7, NET 30

Most buyers are eager to pay bills on time to earn cash discounts. The discount in a 2/10, n/30 situation may not seem like very much. But this 2% is earned just for paying 20 days in advance of the date the entire bill is due. If buyers fail to take the cash discount in a 2/10, n/30 situation, they are, in effect, borrowing money at a 36% annual rate of interest. Here's how we arrived at that rate: In a 360-day business year, there are 18 periods of 20 days. Paying 2% for one of these 20-day periods is equivalent to paying 36% for an entire year.

Other Discounts and Allowances

To stimulate sales, some sellers offer rebates to prospective customers. A **rebate** is a discount on a product that a customer obtains by submitting a form or certificate provided by the seller. There are two kinds of rebates. In a *mail-in rebate*, the customer fills out a short form, encloses proof of the purchase, and sends the items to a specified address. If all goes well, a rebate check arrives in the mail a short while later. The second kind of rebate is a *coupon*, which is a small printed certificate that the customer presents when purchasing the product in order to obtain a discount equal to the value shown on the certificate. As the 1990s ended, the use of coupons was dropping but the use of mail-in rebates was growing. Marketers favor mail-ins not only because they stimulate sales and can be offered for quite short periods, but also because few consumers, seldom more than 10%, actually submit them for redemption.[13]

The intent of **price customization** is to establish various prices on the basis of how much different people value a product. It's important, though, to build a "fence" to keep customers who value a product highly from taking advantage of low prices. Quantity discounts are one fencing mechanism that can be used in conjunction with price customization. Others include multiperson pricing (such as "companion fares" offered by airlines) and a less expensive alternative (which involves developing a lower-price line of products).[14]

A manufacturer of goods such as air conditioners or toys purchased on a seasonal basis may consider granting a **seasonal discount.** This discount of, say, 5, 10, or 20% is given to a customer who places an order during the slack season. Off-season orders enable manufacturers to better use their production facilities and/or avoid inventory-carrying costs. Many services firms also offer seasonal discounts. For example, Club Med and other vacation resorts lower their prices during the off-season.

www.clubmed.com

A **promotional allowance** is a price reduction granted by a seller as payment for promotional services performed by buyers. To illustrate, a producer of builders' hardware gives a certain quantity of free goods to dealers who prominently display its line. Or a clothing manufacturer pays one-half the cost of a retailer's ad featuring its product.

The Robinson–Patman Act and Price Discrimination

The discounts and allowances discussed here may result in various prices for different customers. Such price differentials represent **price discrimination.** In certain situations price discrimination is prohibited by the Robinson-Patman Act, one of the most important federal laws affecting a company's marketing program. (Any federal law regulating pricing is applicable only in cases where there is *interstate* trade. However, many states have pricing statutes that cover sales *within* the state—that is, *intrastate* trade.)

Main Provisions of the Act

The **Robinson-Patman Act,** passed in 1936, was intended to curb price discrimination by large retailers. It was written in very general terms, so over the years it has also become applicable to manufacturers.

Not all price differentials are illegal under the act. Price discrimination is unlawful only when the effect *may be* to substantially injure competition. In other words, a price difference is allowed if it does not substantially reduce competition. This law does *not* apply to sales to ultimate household consumers, because presumably they are not in business competition with each other.

Defenses and Exceptions

Price discrimination is legal in response to changing conditions that affect the marketability of products. For instance, differentials are allowed in cases of seasonal obsolescence (for products such as Christmas decorations), physical deterioration (fruits and vegetables), and going-out-of-business sales. Competitive considerations also are relevant. As one example, retailers accused pharmaceutical companies of illegal discrimination, claiming the prices hospitals and health maintenance organizations (HMOs) pay are often only a small fraction of what retail pharmacies must pay for identical products. Each manufacturer said the differentials are necessary—and legal—because hospitals and HMOs choose other manufacturers' products if they are not given significant price concessions.[15] That is, typically a price differential is allowable if it is needed to meet competitors' prices.

Price differentials also are permissible if they do not exceed differences in the cost of manufacture, sale, or delivery of the product (see Figure 13.4). Cost differences may result from (1) variations in the quantity sold or (2) various methods of sale or delivery of the product. Thus, if selling a large quantity of a product directly to Safeway is more efficient than selling a small quantity through wholesalers to a neighborhood grocery store, the producer can legally offer Safeway a lower price per unit of the product. Such differentials are allowable even though there is a reasonable probability of injuring competition.

Under the Robinson-Patman Act, a buyer is as guilty as the seller if the buyer *knowingly* induces or receives an unlawful price differential. This provision is intended to restrain large buyers from demanding discriminatory prices. The American Booksellers Association filed a lawsuit alleging that the two largest retail book chains place "pressure on publishers to make secret and illegal deals that put independent bookstores at a serious competitive disadvantage." According to the trade association, Barnes & Noble and Borders obtain discounts from publishers that violate federal laws. From a practical standpoint, however, it is difficult to prove that the buyer coerced or knowingly received an unlawful price differential from a supplier. Thus, in the book-retailing case, one attorney said the independent bookstores face an uphill battle in the case because they have to prove that they were discriminated against *and* that the two chains caused the publishers to act in a discriminatory manner.[16]

Quantity discounts result in different prices to various customers. Consequently, these discriminatory prices could be illegal under the Robinson-Patman

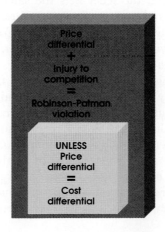

Figure 13.4

The Robinson-Patman Act.

Price differential + Injury to competition = Robinson-Patman violation

UNLESS Price differential = Cost differential

Act if it is shown that they injure competition. To justify price differentials stemming from its quantity discount schedule, a firm must rely on the cost defense provided in the act. In a nutshell, quantity discounts are legal if the resulting price differentials do not exceed differences in the cost of manufacturing, selling, or delivering the product.

Trade discounts are not addressed in the Robinson-Patman Act or in its predecessor, the Clayton Act. However, court cases many years ago established that separate discounts could be given to distinct classes of buyers. That is, one discount could be granted to wholesalers and another to retailers, as long as all buyers within a given group were offered the same discount.

Various types of promotional allowances are lawful *only* if they are offered to all competing customers on proportionally equal terms. For example, assume that a large chain receives promotional support valued at $15,000 when it purchases $750,000 of goods from a manufacturer. Another retailer should not expect the same dollar amount of support on a much smaller—say, $40,000—order. However, the second retailer is entitled to the same percentage amount of support as given to the large chain—2% in this case. The $40,000 order should yield promotional services and materials valued at $800. Despite the straightforward math, disputes frequently arise over what is meant by "proportionally equal terms." This concept and its legal implications are examined further in Chapter 17, in connection with a firm's promotional program.

Geographic Pricing Strategies

In pricing, a seller must consider the costs of shipping goods to the buyer. These costs grow in importance as freight becomes a larger part of total variable costs. Pricing policies may be established whereby the buyer pays all the freight expense, the seller bears the entire cost, or the seller and buyer share this expense. The strategy chosen can influence the geographic limits of a firm's market, locations of its production facilities, sources of its raw materials, and its competitive strength in various geographic markets.

Point-of-Production Pricing

In a widely used geographic pricing strategy, the seller quotes the selling price at the point of production, and the buyer selects the mode of transportation and pays all freight costs. Usually referred to as **FOB factory pricing** (or *FOB mill pricing*), this strategy is the only one of the four discussed in this section in which the seller does not pay any of the freight costs. The seller pays only for loading the shipment aboard the freight carrier—hence the term *FOB*, which stands for *free on board*.

Under FOB factory pricing, the seller nets the same amount on each sale of similar quantities. The delivered price to the buyer varies according to the freight costs. In purchasing goods from a manufacturer in Columbia, Missouri, differences in freight costs surely will provide a customer in St. Louis with a lower delivered price than a customer in Pittsburgh.

The Federal Trade Commission has considered FOB factory pricing to be legal. However, this pricing strategy has serious marketing and financial implications. In effect, FOB factory pricing makes a given seller more attractive to nearby customers and much less attractive to distant customers. The reason? Because the customers bear the freight costs, they prefer to deal with suppliers located close to them, rather than far away. Thus the firm in Pittsburgh mentioned above probably would seek suppliers in Pennsylvania or nearby Ohio and West Virginia as alternatives to the supplier in Missouri. Of course, this assumes that alternative suppliers are comparable with respect to other important factors, such as product quality.

Uniform Delivered Pricing

Under **uniform delivered pricing**, the same delivered price is quoted to all buyers regardless of their locations. This strategy is sometimes referred to as *postage stamp pricing* because of its similarity to the pricing of first-class mail service. Of course, just like first-class mail, freight costs go up as weight of the shipment increases. Using our same example, if the Missouri-based manufacturer adopted uniform delivered pricing, the delivered cost of goods would be the same for the businesses in Pittsburgh and St. Louis, and elsewhere across the country, assuming of course that the shipments weigh the same amounts.

Uniform delivered pricing is typically used where freight costs are a small part of the seller's total costs. This strategy is also used by many retailers who believe "free" delivery is an additional service that strengthens their market position.

With a uniform delivered price, the net revenue to the seller varies depending on the freight cost involved in each sale. In effect, buyers located near the seller's factory pay some of the costs of shipping to more distant locations. Critics of FOB factory pricing usually favor a uniform delivered price. They maintain that the freight cost should not be charged separately to customers any more than other single marketing or production expenses.

Zone-Delivered Pricing

Zone-delivered pricing divides a seller's market into a limited number of broad geographic zones and then sets a uniform delivered price for each zone. The freight charge built into the delivered price is an average of the charges to all points within a zone. An eastern firm that quotes a price and then says "Slightly higher west of the Rockies" is using a two-zone pricing system. Zone-delivered pricing is similar to the *distance-based pricing* used by package-delivery services, notably UPS and Federal Express. In switching from flat-rate to distance-based prices, FedEx divided the U.S. into eight zones.[17] It's important to remember that even with zone-delivered pricing, freight costs will vary based on weight of the shipment.

 www.fedex.com/US/rates/

When using this pricing strategy, a seller must be careful to avoid charges of illegal price discrimination. Under a strict interpretation, the zones must be drawn so that all buyers who compete for a particular market are in the same zone. This condition is almost impossible to meet in densely populated areas, such as the East and Midwest, which means that zone-delivered pricing is not practical everywhere.

Freight-Absorption Pricing

To penetrate distant markets, a seller may be willing to pay part of the freight cost. Thus, under **freight-absorption pricing**, a manufacturer will quote to the customer a delivered price equal to its factory price *plus* the shipping costs that would be charged by a competitive seller located near that customer. In our continuing example, let's assume the manufacturing firm in Missouri agreed to freight absorption. Then the customer in Pittsburgh would not be charged full freight costs, but only the costs that would be charged by a competing supplier located close to the customer—say, in Youngstown, Ohio.

A freight-absorption strategy is adopted to offset competitive disadvantages of FOB factory pricing. With an FOB factory price, a firm is at a price disadvantage when trying to sell to buyers located in markets near competitors' plants. The reason? Because buyers pay the shipping costs under FOB factory pricing, these charges will grow as the distance between supplier and customer increases. A nearby supplier has an advantage over more distant suppliers—at least with respect to shipping costs. Freight absorption erases any price advantages that are due to differences in shipping costs.

A seller can continue to expand its geographic market as long as its net revenue after freight absorption is larger than its marginal costs for units sold. If a manufacturer's costs of producing, selling, and shipping one more unit—that is, its marginal cost—is $75, then freight-absorption pricing makes sense so long as the revenue received by the manufacturer exceeds $75. The firm's revenue would consist of the selling price of the product plus any freight costs charged to the buyer.

Freight absorption is particularly useful to a firm that has (1) excess capacity, (2) high fixed costs, and (3) low variable costs per unit of product. In these cases, management must constantly seek ways to cover fixed costs. Freight-absorption pricing is one means of generating additional sales volume to do that.

Freight absorption is legal if it is used independently and not in collusion with other firms. Also, it must be used only to meet competition. In fact, if it is practiced properly, freight absorption can strengthen competition by breaking down geographic monopolies.

Special Pricing Strategies and Situations

To be effective in setting initial prices, evaluating existing prices, and adjusting them as necessary, a firm needs to be aware of a variety of special pricing strategies and situations.[18]

One-Price and Flexible-Price Strategies

Early in its pricing deliberations, management should decide whether to adopt a one-price or a flexible-price strategy. Under a **one-price strategy,** a seller charges the *same* price to all similar customers who buy identical quantities of a product. Under a **flexible-price strategy** (also called a *variable-price strategy*), similar customers may pay *different* prices when buying identical quantities of a product. Although you may think otherwise, this practice is normally legal.

In the U.S., the one-price strategy is more common than the variable-price strategy. Most retailers, for example, follow a one-price policy. This strategy shifts the focus from price to other factors, such as product quality. A one-price strategy can build customer confidence in a seller—whether at the manufacturing, wholesaling, or retailing level—because the buyer does not have to worry that other customers paid lower prices. Thus, with a one-price strategy, weak bargainers need not think they are at a disadvantage.

Several airlines, Continental and TWA for example, have used aggressive flexible pricing to enter new markets and to increase their market shares on existing routes. (However, this strategy hasn't produced consistent profits for these two enterprises.) Their new business comes from two sources—passengers now flying on other airlines and passengers who would not fly at higher prices. Especially in the second group, demand for air travel is highly elastic. The trick is to keep apart the segment of pleasure travelers (in which demand tends to be elastic) and the segment of business travelers (in which demand is typically inelastic). Airlines separate these segments by placing restrictions on lower-price tickets—requiring advance purchase and a Saturday night stay in the destination city, for example. Flexible pricing is also used in many other fields.

A variable-price strategy abounds in buying situations involving trade-ins. With flexible pricing, buyer-seller bargaining often determines the final price.[19] Both factors, trade-ins and bargaining, are common in automobile retailing. Thus, even though window-sticker prices may suggest a one-price policy, variable pricing has been the norm in selling cars.

Pricing strategies change over time. For instance, during the 1990s, a growing number of car companies switched to—or experimented with—a one-price strategy. In launching the Saturn model, General Motors urged its dealers to set fixed prices so as to minimize haggling between consumer and sales person. Automakers have found it's difficult to implement this approach, however. The reason: Dealers, as independent firms, can decide whether to use a single-price ("no-haggle") strategy or a variable-price ("let's make a deal") strategy.[20]

Used-car superstores, particularly AutoNation USA and CarMax, also employ a one-price strategy. Interestingly, there's growing evidence that purchase prices of used cars are higher if there is a superstore in the vicinity. Apparently, other used-car retailers, such as new-car dealers and independent car lots, look at the superstores' prices and then stay close to them. According to a consultant, "the superstores have set both a ceiling and a floor for prices in their areas."[21] Previously, used-car retailers were more likely to compete with each other through a series of price cuts in order to make a sale.

Flat-rate pricing, a variation of the one-price strategy, has been receiving some attention lately. Under such an arrangement, a purchaser pays a stipulated single price and then can consume as little or as much of the product as desired. An example of highly successful flat-rate pricing is the single admission fee charged by the Walt Disney Co. at its amusement parks. Several years ago, America Online switched to a flat rate of $19.95 per month for unlimited time online. Flat-rate pricing should be used only for products with a low marginal cost and, as one writer stated, "for which there's a natural limit to demand—like all-you-can-eat salad. Or bus trips."[22]

A **single-price strategy** is an extreme variation of the one-price strategy. Not only are all customers charged the same price, but all items sold by the firm carry a single price! This approach originated many decades ago. Then, in the early 1990s, chains such as Everything's $1.00 grew rapidly by offering frugal shoppers a variety of merchandise ranging from grocery items to cosmetics at a single price of $1. Other chains such as Simply 6 attracted customers with assorted clothing at a single price.

Typically a store that adopts a single-price strategy purchases discontinued products as well as production overruns from a variety of sources at a small fraction of their original costs. Low prices cannot sell unappealing merchandise for long; therefore, single-price stores cannot get by with merchandise that is outdated and/or shoddy. After a slump in the mid-1990s, single-price stores are enjoying a resurgence. Several chains, including 99¢ Only and Everything for a Buck, are growing rapidly because they provide shoppers with exceptional values.[23]

www.disneyland.com

www.99only.com

Price Lining

Price lining involves selecting a limited number of prices at which a business will sell related products. It is used extensively by retailers of apparel. The Athletic Store, for instance, sells several styles of shoes at $39.88 a pair, another group at $59.95, and a third assortment at $79.99.

For the consumer, the main benefit of price lining is that it simplifies buying decisions. For the retailer, price lining helps in planning purchases. The buyer for The Athletic Store can go to market looking for shoes that can be sold at one of its three price points.

Rising costs can put a real squeeze on price lines. That's because a company hesitates to change its price line every time its costs go up. But if costs rise and prices are not increased accordingly, profit margins shrink and the retailer may be forced to seek products with lower costs.

Odd Pricing

Earlier, we briefly discussed pricing strategies that might be called *psychological* pricing: pricing above competitive levels, raising an unsuitably low price to increase sales, and price lining. All these strategies are intended to convey desirable images about products.

Odd pricing, another psychological strategy, is commonly used in retailing. **Odd pricing** sets prices at uneven (or odd) amounts, such as 49¢ or $19.95, rather than at even amounts. Autos are priced at $13,995 rather than $14,000, and houses sell for $119,500 instead of $120,000. Odd pricing is often avoided in prestige stores or on higher-priced items. Expensive men's suits, for example, are priced at $750, not $749.95.

The rationale for odd pricing is that it suggests lower prices and, as a result, yields greater sales than even pricing. According to this reasoning, a price of 98¢ will bring in greater revenue than a $1 price for the same product. Research has indicated that odd pricing can be an effective strategy for a firm that emphasizes low prices. According to another study, many consumers look only at the first two digits in a price. If so, companies should choose a price such as $1.99, rather than $1.95 or $2.09, in order to maximize sales and profits for a particular product.[24]

Leader Pricing and Unfair-Practices Acts

Many firms, primarily retailers, temporarily cut prices on a few items to attract customers. This strategy is called **leader pricing.** The items on which prices are cut are termed **leaders;** if the leader is priced below the store's cost, it's a **loss leader.**

Leaders should be well-known, heavily advertised products that are purchased frequently. Amazon.com reduces the base price of best-selling books by as much as 50%. As stated in one article, "Amazon may be able to treat best-selling books as loss leaders that attract customers into its online store where they can be tempted by other merchandise that isn't priced so cheaply."[25]

More than 20 states have **unfair-practices acts,** sometimes called *unfair-sales acts,* to regulate leader pricing. Typically, these laws prohibit a retailer or wholesaler from selling an item below invoice cost *plus* some stipulated amount. Varying from state to state, "cost plus" is usually defined as either a markup of several percent or the firm's cost of doing business.

In a widely publicized test of this type of law, three Arkansas drugstores charged that Wal-Mart's pharmacies sold some prescription drugs below cost in order to drive small competitors out of business. The giant discounter admitted it sold some products below cost but did so to provide value to customers rather than to destroy competitors. Originally, a court ruled for the drugstores, concluding that Wal-Mart did in fact engage in predatory pricing. Ultimately, the Arkansas Supreme Court overturned the decision. The court stated, "Drugstores are far from destroyed. There is simply enhanced competition in the area."[26]

According to their supporters, unfair-practices acts eliminate price cutting intended to drive other products or companies out of business. However, such laws permit firms to use leaders—if their prices are *above* the stipulated minimum. According to critics, these laws reduce retailers' freedom to set prices. Going a step further, the purpose of a business is to make a profit on the *total* enterprise, not necessarily on each transaction. Thus unfair-practices acts limit retailers' ability to determine how best to generate profits. Also, the minimum prices stipulated by these laws may result in higher prices, which hurts consumers' pocketbooks. In some states these laws have been declared unconstitutional.

High-Low Pricing and Everyday Low Pricing

Many retailers, especially supermarkets and department stores, that want to engage in price competition rely on **high-low pricing.** This strategy entails alternating between regular (high) and "sale" (low) prices on the most visible products offered by a retail firm. Frequent price reductions are combined with aggressive promotion to convey an image of very low prices. By starting with relatively high prices, retailers can boost their profits through sales to that segment of shoppers that really wants the product and is not very price sensitive. Then prices can be cut by various amounts, based on the quantities of remaining inventory for various products.[27] J.C. Penney, with its numerous and heavily promoted sales, is a prime example of a retailer that relies on high-low pricing.

Are "free" PCs worth the price?

Some people don't have, but desire, personal computers (PCs) and Internet access. Conversely, some firms that sell products through the Internet don't have, but want, sufficient information about online shoppers. Whenever two parties have unmet needs, there's an opportunity for a mutually satisfying exchange. In this situation, both parties' needs might be met by a free PC.

Sensing an opportunity, Bill Gross, who has started over 20 Internet-related ventures, launched Free-PC.com in early 1999. The company gave qualified consumers a basic Compaq computer and Internet access—both for free. In exchange, recipients agreed to provide Free-PC with personal profiles, including demographic data, shopping patterns, and media preferences. As part of the deal, they also committed to use their PCs and Internet service for at least 10 hours monthly, which assures exposure to a constant stream of advertising that appears on the right side of the computer screen. Each participant's stream of advertising was based on the personal profile given to Free-PC.

Was this arrangement satisfying to both parties? To Gross, the pricing strategy was entirely sensible. "In this new economy, all the world has loss leaders. . . . Here the loss leader is the PC." Free-PC intended to generate revenues by selling the advertising space on the computer screen, perhaps at premium prices because an advertiser could reach consumers who possess the attributes of the firm's target market.

Consumers who entered into the deal got a PC and Internet service with no out-of-pocket payment. However, the arrangement was not free of costs to recipients. For starters, they had less usable space on their computer screens and they could not avoid a constant

barrage of Internet advertising. Further, and perhaps more important, they sacrificed privacy by providing personal information to Free-PC. A consumer advocate wondered, "What guarantee is there that the data that's gathered . . . will not be used sometime in the future for law enforcement investigations, insurance purposes, employment, decision making?" Free-PC stated that advertisers would not be given the personal information about participants. Concerns about privacy or other matters did not seem to hurt demand; 1.2 million consumers submitted applications to Free-PC in the first couple of months of the program.

Other technology-related firms are also using this type of leader pricing. For quite a while, cellular phone companies have given away or charged very little for the equipment in order to sell the monthly service.

Some Internet service providers are offering "free" PCs in exchange for a multiyear commitment to use that firm's service—for a monthly fee, of course. And, in a case of "man bites dog," some PC makers are bundling free or almost-free Internet access with new computers. Now the future of "free" PCs may be clouded given that Gross, the originator of the concept, sold Free-PC to eMachines, the maker of bare-bones computers in late 1999. Quickly, eMachines announced that it would not give away PCs but was considering other strategic options related to the new acquisition.

Sources: "'Free PC' Strategy Is Set for Launch across U.S.," *The Wall Street Journal,* Jan. 26, 2000, p. A6; Peter Lewis, "Free PCs Come with Strings," *The Arizona Republic,* Aug. 2, 1999, p. E1; "Compaqs Exchanged for Consumer Information," *Marketing News,* Mar. 15, 1999, p. 9; and David Kirkpatrick, "The $0.00 PC," *Fortune,* Mar. 1, 1999, p. 36.

Given the need to change prices frequently, high-low pricing can be costly. It also may cause some consumers to not purchase products at regular prices, but always wait for reduced prices. Further, some consumer advocates have criticized high-low pricing, asserting that it misleads shoppers. The concern is that most transactions are made at decreased prices, which means that the so-called low prices are normal rather than real bargains.[28]

For a retailer that intends to compete on the basis of price, the alternative to high-low pricing is everyday low pricing (EDLP). Basically, **everyday low pricing** involves consistently low prices and few if any temporary price reductions. This strategy is featured by some large discounters, such as Wal-Mart and Family Dollar, and warehouse clubs, such as Costco. Recently it has been adopted by a growing group of retailers, including such diverse chains as Linens 'n Things, Stein Mart, and Men's Wearhouse. In 1998, "Jeden Tag Tiefpreise!" signs proclaiming everyday low prices were starting to appear in German retail outlets that had just been acquired by Wal-Mart.[29]

 www.steinmart.com

When it moved into Germany, Wal-Mart Stores brought the marketing strategies and tactics that worked well in the U.S. A key strategy is "Jeden Tag Tiefpreise," which is German for everyday low pricing. Wal-Mart promotes its approach to pricing on its plastic bags and on large banners hung in its stores.

There are several reasons for EDLP. Retailers expect (or at least hope) that it will improve their profit margins because the average sales price will be higher than would be the case with high-low pricing. Further, retailers can point to their use of EDLP when negotiating lower purchase prices from suppliers. Also, operating expenses should be lessened, and profits boosted, because of lower levels of advertising.[30]

The arena for EDLP expanded in the 1990s. A manufacturer ordinarily gives retailers a variety of discounts and allowances to stock and promote its brands. In addition, it often provides short-term "special deals" involving larger deductions and perhaps even free merchandise. However, Procter & Gamble (P&G) switched course and eliminated most special deals on about one-half its products, ranging from Jif peanut butter to Oxydol detergent. P&G replaced the deals with consistently lower prices. There were two reasons for the shift, according to P&G: First, stable selling prices tend to even out supermarket orders, which improves production efficiency. Second, with steady retail prices, consumers might be less price-oriented and more loyal to P&G's well-known brands.

Supermarkets said EDLP hurt their profits because special discounts and allowances were less available to them. However, because P&G has a great deal of power in its distribution channels (a topic covered in the next chapter), the giant manufacturer has been able to stick with EDLP. Moreover, P&G instituted EDLP in several European markets. As in the U.S., some grocery chains have complained about the elimination of special deals.[31]

Which is better—EDLP or high-low pricing? A controlled experiment compared the effects of the two pricing strategies on 26 product categories in a chain of 86 grocery stores. EDLP increased sales somewhat, whereas high-low pricing resulted in slightly lower volume. More important, though, profits fell 18% with EDLP but jumped almost as much with high-low pricing.[32] Despite this evidence, it appears that an increasing number of firms are adopting everyday low pricing.

Resale Price Maintenance

Some manufacturers want to control the prices at which middlemen resell their products; this is termed **resale price maintenance**. Manufacturers seek to do this to protect the brand's image. Publicly, they state that their control of prices—and avoidance of discounted prices—provides middlemen with ample profit margins. In turn, consumers should be able to expect sales help and other services when they buy the manufacturers' products from middlemen. Critics, however, claim that control over prices leads to inflated prices and excessive profits.

One way in which producers can gain a bit of control, and perhaps provide guidance to retailers, is with a **suggested list price**. This price is set by a manufacturer at a level that provides retailers with their normal markups. To illustrate, a producer sells to, say, a hardware store a certain product for $6 a unit. It recommends a retail price of $9.95, which would furnish the store with its normal markup of 40% of selling price. This is only a *suggested* retail price. Retailers have the right to sell the product for less or more than the suggested price.

Other manufacturers try even harder to control their products' retail prices. Such effort is worthwhile only for a producer selling to relatively few retailers that want very much to carry the product. A manufacturer may even threaten to stop shipment of products to retailers that price products substantially below suggested list prices.

Is it legal to act aggressively in order to control retail prices? From about 1930 to 1975, a set of state and federal laws permitted manufacturers to set minimum retail prices for their products. The state laws became known as *fair-trade laws*. However, such price controls were prohibited by the federal Consumer Goods Pricing Act of 1975. According to this law, a producer no longer can set resale prices and impose them on resellers.[33]

The struggle over resale price maintenance never seems to end, however. Recently, the focus has been on whether or not a supplier can set a *maximum* price without violating antitrust laws. In what turned out to be a significant case, the owner of a Unocal 76 gas station charged that the supplier stipulated the maximum retail price, thereby limiting the station owner's ability to compete and be profitable. After hearing this case, the U.S. Supreme Court ruled that a supplier's setting maximum prices was not automatically illegal but had to be considered on a case-by-case basis. The key issue is whether or not fixing a maximum price enhances or inhibits competition.[34] This ruling did not affect the fixing of *minimum* prices, a practice that remains automatically illegal.

Sometimes manufacturers are charged with violating antitrust laws as a result of their efforts to control resale prices. For example, Ty Inc., maker of the popular Beanie Babies, was charged with forcing retailers to adhere to a $5 price. To resolve a lawsuit, Ty Inc. consented to pay a $50,000 fine and to cease its efforts to have a standard price for Beanie Babies. In an earlier, and much larger case, Reebok agreed to abandon certain price-control practices and to pay a total of $9.5 million in fines.[35]

Reactive and Proactive Changes

After an initial price is set, a number of situations may prompt a firm to change its price. As costs increase, for instance, management may decide that raising price is preferable to maintaining price and either cutting quality or promoting the product aggressively. According to a pricing consultant, "Small companies are more reluctant to raise prices than their large counterparts."[36] Obviously, it's wise to raise prices gradually and with little fanfare. The "art" of raising pricing is discussed further in the nearby You Make the Decision box.

Temporary price cuts may be used to sell excess inventory or to introduce a new product. Also, if a company's market share is declining because of strong competition, its executives may react initially by reducing price. Small firms' price cuts typically are not matched by large competitors, unless they significantly diminish the larger firm's sales. Decreasing price makes the most sense when enough new customers are attracted to offset the smaller profit margin per sale.[37] Nevertheless, for many products, a better long-term alternative to a price reduction is improving the overall marketing program.

Any firm can safely assume that its competitors will change their prices—sooner or later. Consequently, every firm should have guidelines on how it will

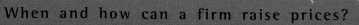
When and how can a firm raise prices?

Snorkel Stove Co., which manufactures kits for hot tubs, increases the product's price only when suppliers increase their prices. The head of the firm fears that if prices are raised, "our business will drop dramatically." In contrast, Quality Cleaners, a small chain of dry-cleaning outlets, raised prices by 6% when a new 2% environmental tax was imposed by the state. Quality's president explained that the company seized the opportunity to recoup "all the environmental costs that we'd been absorbing."

These firms' vastly different approaches indicate that decisions about the frequency and amount of price increases ordinarily are based on several factors, including likely reactions of the target market and the degree to which executives are comfortable taking risks. It's particularly difficult to boost prices when inflation is very low, as is the case at the start of the new century.

Customers are more likely to accept higher prices if firms conform to several guidelines:

- *Explain the reason for the increase.* The owner of the Roasterie, Inc., a wholesaler of gourmet coffees, sent a detailed letter to 300 customers announcing that a price increase was necessary because the cost of "green" (unroasted) coffee beans had risen sharply.

- *If possible, improve the product's value.* The best opportunity for doing this, of course, is by introducing a "new and improved" version of the product. The Gillette Co. is a master at doing this, as evidenced most recently by its Oral-B Cross Action toothbrush, which was priced about 50% higher than the leading toothbrush. Gillette has used the same approach with razor blades and batteries.

- *Provide advance warning of the increase.* Many customers will appreciate being able to take final advantage of the lower price.

Even when these guidelines are followed, some customers may be lost when prices are increased. Nevertheless, periodic price increases can be necessary or desirable in order to augment or maintain profit margins.

When are occasional price increases worth the risk of lost customers?

Sources: Howard Scott, "The Tricky Art of Raising Prices," *Nation's Business,* February 1999, pp. 30+; Mark Maremont, "New Toothbrush Is Big-Ticket Item," *The Wall Street Journal,* Oct. 27, 1998, p. B1; and Roberta Maynard, "Taking Guesswork out of Pricing," *Nation's Business,* December 1997, pp. 27–29.

react. If a competitor *boosts* price, a short delay in reacting probably will not be perilous. However, if a competing firm *reduces* price, a prompt response normally is required to avoid losing customers.

In the absence of collusion, occasional price reductions occur even in an oligopoly with relatively few firms, because the actions of all sellers cannot be controlled. Every so often some firm will cut its price, especially if sales are flat. From a seller's standpoint, the big disadvantage in price cutting is that competitors will retaliate—and not let up. A **price war** may begin when one firm decreases its price in an effort to increase its sales volume and/or market share. The battle is on if other firms retaliate, reducing price on their competing products. Additional price decreases by the original price cutter and/or its competitors are likely to follow until one of the firms decides it can endure no further damage to its profits. Most businesses would like to avoid price wars.

Always part of business, price wars were epidemic in the 1990s. Low prices often were the primary weapon in numerous disparate fields, such as computer microprocessors, cigarettes, air travel, and ready-to-eat cereals. Even ski resorts, at least those in Colorado, are competing intensely through low prices. Various resorts are offering "buddy passes" and other discounts that bring lift-ticket prices down to levels of 25 years ago. According to one consultant, price wars often are "overreactions to threats that either aren't there at all or are not as big as they seem."[38]

Price wars can be harmful to a firm, especially one that is financially weak. One article listed the damages as follows: "Customer loyalty? Dead. Profits? Imploding. Planning? Up in smoke." In the music retailing business, for example,

Many retailers use electronic systems in which a check-out clerk scans bar codes on products to automatically ring up prices. Now, as described in the You Make the Decision box in Chapter 4, some stores are experimenting with similar self-scanning systems that allow shoppers to check out on their own.

Both systems have the potential for ethical problems, but let's focus here on store-controlled (as contrasted with self-scanning) electronic systems. According to a mid-1990s survey in California, overcharges outnumber undercharges by a ratio of 1.5 to 1. A similar study in Michigan revealed a 4-to-1 ratio in favor of stores. However, a more recent study conducted by the Federal Trade Commission indicated that 2.58% of the items were scanned at a price that was lower than the actual price

and 2.24% at an incorrect high price. Thus the error ratio was 1:15 to 1, in favor of consumers.

Retailers say any mispricing is due to human error, specifically clerks failing to put price changes into the scanning system's computer. Some consumers and their advocates charge retailers put price increases into the system before price decreases. That means the store is in an advantageous position compared to consumers when price changes are made.

Have retail chains acted unethically with their electronic checkout scanning systems?

Sources: "Sum Comfort," *St. Louis Post-Dispatch,* Oct. 23, 1996, p. C1; and Catherine Yang, "Maybe They Should Call Them 'Scammers,'" *Business Week,* Jan. 16, 1995, pp. 32, 33.

---

www.bestbuy.com

consumer-electronics chains such as Best Buy decided to use compact discs as leaders to attract shoppers. Record store chains such as Camelot and Musicland retaliated with price cuts of their own. The consumer electronics retailers could afford leader pricing because they earned profits on other items like TVs and CD players, but the record stores didn't have another major generator of profits. As a result, a number of record store chains either shut down or had to reorganize under bankruptcy laws.[39] After extended price wars, companies in other industries as different as groceries and personal computers have gone out of business.

In the short term, consumers benefit from price wars through sharply lower prices. But over the longer term, the net effects on consumers are not clear-cut. Ultimately, a smaller number of competing firms might translate to fewer product choices and/or higher prices for consumers.

Summary

After deciding on pricing goals and setting the base (or list) price, marketers must establish pricing strategies that are compatible with the rest of the marketing mix. A basic decision facing management is whether to engage primarily in price or nonprice competition. Price competition establishes price as the primary, perhaps the sole, basis for attracting and retaining customers. A growing number of businesses are adopting value pricing to improve the ratio of benefits to price and, in turn, win customers from competitors. In nonprice competition, sellers maintain stable prices and seek a differential advantage through other aspects of their marketing mixes. Common methods of nonprice competition include offering distinctive and appealing products, promotion, and/or customer services.

When a firm is launching a new product, it must choose a market-skimming or a market-penetration pricing strategy. Market skimming uses a relatively high initial price, market penetration a low one.

Strategies also must be devised for discounts and allowances—deductions from the list price. Management has the option of offering quantity discounts, trade discounts, cash discounts, and/or other types of deductions. Decisions on discounts and allowances must conform to the Robinson-Patman Act, a federal law regulating price discrimination.

Freight costs must be considered in pricing. A producer can require the buyer to pay all freight costs (FOB factory pricing), or a producer can absorb all freight costs (uniform delivered pricing). Alternatively, the two parties can share the freight costs (freight absorption).

Management also should decide whether to charge the same price to all similar buyers of identical quantities of a product (a one-price strategy) or to set different prices (a flexible-price strategy). Many organizations, especially retailers, use at least some of the following special strategies: price lining—selecting a limited number of prices at which to sell related products; odd pricing—setting prices at uneven (or odd) amounts; and leader pricing—temporarily cutting prices on a few items to attract customers. Some forms of leader pricing are illegal in a number of states. A company must also choose between everyday low pricing, which relies on consistently low prices and few if any temporary price reductions, and high-low pricing, which involves alternating between regular and "sale" prices on the most visible products offered by a firm.

Many manufacturers are concerned about resale price maintenance, which means controlling the prices at which middlemen resell products. Some approaches to resale price maintenance are more effective than others; moreover, some methods may be illegal.

Market opportunities and/or competitive forces may motivate companies to initiate price changes or, in other situations, to react to other firms' price changes. A series of successive price cuts by competing firms creates a price war, which can harm the profits of all participating companies.

More about **Apple**

When he returned as head of Apple Computer, Steve Jobs decided the company should concentrate on the consumer market. Therefore, he wanted the updated Macintosh to be exceedingly simple to use, extremely stylish, and—most important—inexpensive. No longer could Apple afford to price its products above the competition and rely on its user-friendly operating system to attract buyers. After the advent of Windows, all PCs had a relatively easy-to-use operating system.

In response to Jobs's challenge, the iMac was born. Apple touted the fact that the iMac was completely set up and Internet-ready as soon as it was taken out of the box and plugged into the wall. Attracting considerable publicity, the iMac's sleek styling and translucent bluish-green color signaled a new era for Apple. Finally, and very important, the iMac was competitively priced at $1,299, and lowered to $1,199 a few months later.

Introduced in August 1998, the iMac was an instant hit with PC buyers. The new machine doubled Apple's market share and increased the sales of other

Apple products by 20%. The iMac not only appealed to die-hard Macintosh users but also attracted new fans, some of whom had never owned a PC. According to Jobs, 29% of iMac buyers were computer novices, and about 12% switched from another PC brand. For the 1999 fiscal year, Apple recorded $6.1 billion in sales (up just 3% over 1998) and $600 million of profit (up a resounding 94%). The company projected accelerated sales at the start of the century.

Jobs has continued to push Apple to improve iMac and further expand its market appeal. Thus iMac computers are now available in five fruit-inspired colors and the priced has been pared still further to $999. Apple also launched two more powerful models, the iMac DV priced at $1,299 and the iMac DV Special Edition with a price tag of $1,499. Apple next introduced the iBook, a laptop computer that features the same stylish design of the desktop iMac and includes an AirPort that gives users wireless access to the Internet. Apple promotes the iBook as one of the fastest portable computers.

Although most reviews have been favorable, the iMacs have received some criticism. For one thing, users find the mouse difficult to handle. For another, the iBook weighs a relatively heavy 6 pounds. Despite these minor shortcomings, Apple has certainly succeeded in recapturing the attention of the computer industry and PC buyers. As a result, the iMac has helped Apple take a bite out of the competition's market share.

Now the question is whether or not Apple's turnaround can be sustained. The revitalization was based largely on snazzy designs and competitive prices. What's next? Apple has been challenged to retain its shrinking number of small-business customers and even to recapture some of the lost Apple loyalists in this market segment. In early 2000, Jobs indicated that Apple will become a player on the Internet, offering such services as e-mail and online greeting cards. Suc-cesses in one or more of these new thrusts will be needed in order to keep the restored shine on Apple Computer.[40]

1. a. Prior to introducing the iMac, which pricing strategies were being used by Apple?
   b. Which pricing strategies is Apple using for the iMac?

2. When introducing new products, such as the iMac line of PCs or any new products for the small-business market, should Apple rely on market-skimming or market-penetration pricing?

Key Terms and Concepts

Strategy (364)
Price competition (365)
Value pricing (365)
Nonprice competition (366)
Market-skimming pricing (368)
Market-penetration pricing (369)
Quantity discount (369)
Noncumulative discount (370)
Cumulative discount (370)
Trade (functional) discount (371)
Cash discount (371)
Rebate (372)
Price customization (372)

Seasonal discount (372)
Promotional allowance (372)
Price discrimination (372)
Robinson-Patman Act (372)
FOB factory (mill) pricing (374)
Uniform delivered pricing (375)
Zone-delivered pricing (375)
Freight-absorption pricing (375)
One-price strategy (376)
Flexible-price (variable-price) strategy (376)
Flat-rate pricing (377)
Single-price strategy (377)

Price lining (377)
Odd pricing (377)
Leader pricing (378)
Leaders (378)
Loss leader (378)
Unfair-practices (unfair-sales) acts (378)
High-low pricing (378)
Everyday low pricing (379)
Resale price maintenance (380)
Suggested list price (381)
Price war (382)

Questions and Problems

1. For each of the following products, should the seller adopt a market-skimming or a market-penetration pricing strategy? Support your decision in each instance.
   a. High-fashion dresses styled and manufactured by Yves Saint Laurent.
   b. An exterior house paint that lasts twice as long as any competitive brand.
   c. A by-subscription website that sends you daily e-mails containing information about up to five topics of your choosing.
   d. A tablet that converts a gallon of water into a gallon of automotive fuel.

2. As economic unification is being attained and trade barriers are being removed throughout the multination European Union (EU), numerous companies are deliberating how best to achieve sales and profits in all or part of this huge market. Name two U.S. brands that might benefit from adopting a market-skimming pricing strategy in the EU, and two others that should use a market-penetration strategy.

3. Carefully distinguish between cumulative and noncumulative quantity discounts. Which type of quantity discount has the greater economic and social justification? Why?

4. A manufacturer of appliances quotes a list price of $800 per unit for a certain model of refrigerator and grants trade discounts of 35, 20, and 5%. What is the manufacturer's selling price? Who might get these various discounts?

5. The Craig Charles Company (CCC) sells to all its customers at the same published price. One of its sales managers discerns that Jamaican Enterprises is offering to sell to one of CCC's customers, Rocky Mountain Sports, at a lower price. CCC then cuts its price to Rocky Mountain Sports but maintains the original price for all other customers. Is CCC's price cut a violation of the Robinson-Patman Act?

6. "An FOB point-of-production price system is the only geographic price system that is fair to buyers." Discuss.

7. An eastern firm wants to compete in western markets, where it is at a significant disadvantage with respect to freight costs. What pricing alternatives can it adopt to overcome the freight differential?

8. Under what conditions is a company likely to use a variable-price strategy? Can you name kinds of firms that employ this strategy other than when a trade-in is involved?

9. On the basis of the topics covered in this chapter, establish a set of price strategies for the manufacturer of a new glass cleaner that is sold through a middleman to supermarkets. The manufacturer sells the cleaner at $15 for a case of a dozen 16-ounce bottles.

10. Friends of yours are entering the world of electronic commerce, intent on selling college-related merchandise and memorabilia on the Internet. On the basis of your reading in this chapter, what three points of advice would you offer them about pricing strategies?

Hands-On Marketing

1. Talk to the owner or a top executive of a firm in your community regarding whether the company emphasizes price or nonprice competition and the reasons for following this course. Also ask whether its approach is similar to or dissimilar from the normal approach used by competitors to market the primary product sold by this firm.

2. Identify a firm in your community that is selling products online. Arrange an interview with the person who directs the company's marketing. Ask the executive which of the following pricing strategies the online firm is using as well as the rationale for the choices:
   a. Price or nonprice competition
   b. Market-skimming or market-penetration pricing
   c. Noncumulative or cumulative discounts
   d. One-price or flexible-price strategy
   e. Everyday low pricing or high-low pricing

Cases for Part 4

Keeping Prices Grounded

In 1999, Southwest Airlines posted its 26th consecutive year of profitability—a feat unmatched in the airline industry. Adhering to a basic strategy of providing no-frills service at low fares to pleasure travelers (rather than business travelers) on relatively short flights, Southwest has maintained its position as the predominant low-cost airline in the U.S. While other airlines are trying to imitate or improve upon this strategy, Southwest is gradually expanding its operations to include new regions of the U.S. and also longer flights.

Taking Off with a New Business

Southwest started service in 1971, with four planes that served three Texas cities—Dallas, Houston, and San Antonio. When it outgrew the in-state market, the airline began interstate service in 1978. By 1999, Southwest had spread its wings far enough to serve more than 50 cities and become the fourth-largest carrier of domestic passengers. The company's revenues in 1999 are expected to top $4.7 billion, it is twice as profitable as United Airlines, and its stock has increased in value by an average of 29% each year during the past decade. In a survey conducted by *Fortune* magazine, executives ranked Southwest as the sixth most admired company in the U.S.

How has Southwest achieved such phenomenal success in the face of stiff competition? Says Southwest's charismatic CEO, Herb Kelleher, "We're always very cost-conscious and we're constantly looking for ways to be more productive." In addition, Southwest boasts legendary customer service and an employee-friendly work environment that landed the company the top spot on *Fortune*'s list of the "100 Best Companies to Work for in America."

The core of Southwest's marketing strategy is short-flight domestic routes. Despite its recent expansion into longer routes and even nonstop cross-country flights, 80% of its flights are 750 miles or less. In addition, Southwest serves airports that are readily accessible, rather than large, crowded international airports. In this way, the airline reduces long delays that arise because of congested air traffic.

Avoiding Soaring Costs

In order to offer low prices and earn healthy profits, Southwest works hard to control expenses. For ex-ample, it emphasizes keeping planes in the air. Its average turnaround time (the elapsed time from arriving at the airport gate to backing away from the gate with a new load of passengers) is about 20 minutes, which is shorter than the industry average. Rapid turnaround allows Southwest's planes to be in the air an average of 11 hours per day, compared to 8 hours for other airlines.

By using only a single type of aircraft, the Boeing 737, Southwest has reduced employee training costs and spare parts inventories. Further, the carrier does not offer many typical airline services, such as assigned seating, a first-class section, interairline luggage transfers, or in-flight meals. When you consider that the average cost per passenger for a standard airline meal is about $5 versus 20¢ for Southwest's usual snack and beverage, that's a big savings.

Southwest has maintained its price leadership position by curtailing expenses. On the basis of what's called cost per available seat-mile (ASM), an efficiency measure in which lower is better, the company has a sizable advantage over much larger airlines. Southwest's cost per ASM was just over 7¢ in 1998 for 500-mile flights; in contrast, Delta, United, Continental, and US Airways all had figures of almost 12¢. Southwest has also taken steps to protect its cost advantage over competitors. For example, even when demand increases in a market, Southwest adds more flights instead of increasing its prices.

Fueling Its Differential Advantage

By keeping prices low, the airline attracts customers who otherwise might not be able to afford air travel. A shareholder once asked Kelleher why Southwest didn't raise prices by even a few dollars for a particular route where it was $47 cheaper than competitors. Kelleher replied, "We're not competing with other airlines. We're competing with ground transportation."

Southwest continually looks for ways to reduce costs and at the same time improve customer service. In 1995, the airline was the first to introduce ticketless travel. In less than a year, 30% of its passengers were using this service, saving the company $25 million. Further, to strengthen loyalty and to reduce customer service labor costs, Southwest encourages travelers to use the Internet to check flight information and buy tickets.

Southwest enjoys a splendid working relationship with its 25,000 employees. It was the first airline to develop a profit-sharing initiative, beginning in 1973. Moreover, Kelleher challenges a widely held business axiom. When asked, "Aren't customers always right?" Kelleher replied they are not. "And I think that's one of the biggest betrayals of employees a boss can possibly commit. The customer is sometimes wrong." Kelleher has been known to personally answer customer complaints, sometimes defending the airline and its employees. To one woman who complained about almost everything on each flight she took with Southwest, Kelleher replied, "Dear Mrs. Grump. We'll miss you."

Southwest employees are encouraged to have fun on their jobs. Humor (such as attendants' funny comments during preflight announcements) is encouraged. Employees' uniforms are more casual than on other airlines, and Southwest reports noteworthy accomplishments of individual employees in its in-flight magazine. High employee morale means low turnover, which in turn helps maintain low costs. The combination of these factors explains why more than 150,000 people apply for jobs at Southwest each year.

A friendly work environment often pays off in high-quality customer service. Colleen Barret, Southwest's executive vice president of customers, explains, "We are not an airline with great customer service. We are a great customer service organization that just happens to be in the airline business." Southwest employees are famous for going above and beyond the call of duty, such as a pilot helping to unload bags to keep the airline on schedule. On another occasion, a customer service rep invited an 87-year-old female customer to stay at her home after the passenger missed a connecting flight. Company policy even dictates, "No employee will ever be punished for using good judgement and good old common sense when trying to accommodate a customer—no matter what our rules are."

Altering Its Course

Southwest's most significant recent action probably was to add longer flights to its schedule. Kelleher once said that longer flights would not grow to more than 10% of Southwest's total flights. However, according to Kelleher, a federal ticket tax that was levied in 1997 forced Southwest to look at the addition of longer routes to its system. Most of the other major airlines pushed for the new per-passenger fee instead of the previous tax that was a percentage of the ticket price. Kelleher believes the per-passenger fee, which is particularly harmful to low-cost carriers, was a direct attack on Southwest Airlines.

To accommodate coast-to-coast travel, the company responded by adding one-stop flights through such cities as Nashville and Kansas City. It has aggressively expanded eastward, adding such cities as Providence, Rhode Island; Raleigh-Durham, North Carolina; and New York (through Islip airport on Long Island). Southwest has even experimented with a nonstop flight from Baltimore, Maryland, to Oakland, California. One industry analyst believes that Southwest's addition of longer flights "will really rewrite the economics of the airline industry."

Whereas Southwest's cost per ASM for flights under 500 miles is just over 7¢, that figure drops to about 6¢ for flights over 1,500 miles. The other carriers still average between 8 and 9¢ in cost per ASM on longer flights. Southwest maintains this advantage by remaining true to its strategy. It has not added seat assignments, a full meal service, or movies. Passengers are invited to bring their own food onboard, and snacks are offered regularly.

Once it has gained a foothold in the eastern region of the U.S., the next target on Southwest's radar screen might be the international market. It presently has an arrangement with Icelandair that allows passengers to book connections using the two airlines. Southwest will closely monitor the Icelandair experiment. As Dave Ridley, Southwest's vice president of marketing and sales, stated, "If it goes well, maybe we can say we've got a model here and do something in Mexico or the Caribbean."

Making It a Fare Fight

During the 1980s, a number of airlines were launched with the intent of copying Southwest's successful strategy. The start-ups borrowed some of Southwest's cost-saving ideas, but failed to duplicate its success. As a result, most of them are now out of business or are struggling.

Some large, established airlines are now supplementing their regular air service with low-fare, no-frills, low-cost service. Delta Airlines, for example, launched Delta Express in 1995, with lower prices but still reserved seating. Armed with concessions from its pilots' union that included lower pay, more flight hours, and more efficient work rules, the airline has a goal of making Delta Express's ASM cost comparable to Southwest's. Within two years, Delta Express had expanded to 19 cities, although only a very small percentage of its flights now overlap with Southwest routes.

Shuttle by United, launched in 1994, flies to 20 cities. It has, however, abandoned four routes served by Southwest. It offers first-class and reserved seating, and serves as a feeder to United flights in Los Angeles and San Francisco. The latest entry into the low-fare airline market is US Airways. It launched MetroJet in 1998 to compete with Southwest's expansion into East Coast markets. US Airways' ASM costs are about 70% more than Southwest's, but MetroJet is committed to matching Southwest's fares.

It hopes to lure customers with its frequent-flier program and reserved seating.

These "airlines within an airline" may be in for a bumpy ride. Continental Airlines abandoned Continental Lite, when the low-price entry could not sustain a half-price fare sale long enough to gain a foothold in the market. To counter Continental Lite, Southwest dropped its fares still further. It also replaced its "Just Plane Smart" slogan with "The Low Fare Airline," leaving little doubt that Southwest knows what its target market wants.

These major airlines are clearly worried about Southwest's new long-haul flights. But some airlines have not pursued the low-cost strategy. For instance, Alaska Airlines has positioned itself as offering the best value in terms of price and service. This airline's promotion campaign uses the slogan, "For the same price, you just get more!"

Booking Sales Online

With ticket price a major consideration for most pleasure travelers, the rise of the Internet has given consumers a powerful tool for finding cheap fares. Ticket consolidators, such as Cheaptickets.com and Lowestfare.com, buy tickets in bulk at discount prices, add a small markup, and then offer them to individual consumers. The flights have restrictions, however, and scheduling flexibility is limited. Priceline.com allows consumers to bid on tickets between the destination and arrival cities of their choice (see the Chapter 12 case for more about Priceline).

Many online travel agencies are attracting customers by promoting their travel expertise and outstanding customer service. Sites such as Travelocity.com tack on a fixed fee (about $10) for each domestic ticket it sells, as opposed to the traditional 8 to 10% commission (up to $50) most traditional travel agencies charge. These online agents have the added benefit of being able to secure exclusive discount arrangements with most of the major airlines. These arrangements allow the online firms to offer prospective travelers favorable rates on selected routes that would otherwise be unavailable to the average consumer.

In 1998, revenue from travel booked on the Web exceeded $2 billion. Industry analysts expect travel sites to account for almost 8% of the travel business by the year 2002. Travelocity, which has 6.5 million subscribers, recently unveiled a new service called Best Fare Finder that allows consumers to compare fares with minimal effort. To compete with online travel services, Southwest has established its own easy-to-use site, requiring just 10 clicks from sign-on to a completed ticket purchase. The airline has a superior "look-to-book" ratio, which is the percentage of site visitors who actually buy a ticket. Southwest's ratio of 14% is twice Travelocity's rate, for instance.

Flying into the Future

In the turbulent world of low-fare airline competition, Southwest is certainly facing new challenges posed by other major airlines and online ticketing services. Despite these competitive threats, the firm continues to lead the industry in on-time performance, and the addition of new and longer routes should fuel the company's growth. So long as Kelleher is in the pilot's seat, Southwest Airlines appears to have clear skies ahead.

Questions

1. What pricing strategies does Southwest Airlines employ to compete against other airlines?

2. What types of costs must Southwest and other airlines control to remain competitive?

3. How will online ticket discounters affect Southwest Airlines and its bid to remain the industry's most successful low-cost airline?

www.southwest.com

www.cheaptickets.com

www.travelocity.com

Sources: Geoffrey Colvin, "America's Most Admired Companies," *Fortune,* Feb. 21, 2000, pp. 108–111+; "10 Companies That Get It," *Fortune,* Nov. 8, 1999, p. 115; Karen Walker, "The King of Low-Cost," *Airline Business,* June 1999, p. 38; "How Herb Keeps Southwest Hopping," *Money,* June 1999, pp. 61–62; J. C. Conklin, "That's the Ticket," *The Wall Street Journal,* July 12, 1999, p. R45; Wendy Zellner, "Southwest's New Direction," *Business Week,* Feb. 8, 1999, pp. 58–59; Alan Rosenspan, "Airline Soars to New Heights," *Direct Marketing,* December 1998, pp. 18–21; Wendy Zellner, "Will This Short-Hauler Fly," *Business Week,* June 8, 1998, p. 39; and Danna K. Henderson, "Winning Ugly," *Air Transport World,* September 1997, p. 66.

Lowering Prices and Raising Eyebrows

Where can you go to find "the lowest prices on Earth?" According to the tag line of e-tailer Buy.com, all you need to do is visit the company's website. There you can find everything from CDs to books to golf equipment at cut-rate prices that are sometimes below what Buy.com actually paid for the products. It's an aggressive—and perhaps risky—new business model that has made Buy.com one of the fastest-growing companies in U.S. history.

Bargain Shop 'til You Drop

In 1996, Scott Blum founded BuyComp.com and began selling computer products at discounted prices. Items were shipped directly from wholesalers to customers in order to keep operating costs down. Blum soon began looking for ways to expand the business. A year later, he purchased an e-tailer of books and videos. At that time, he decided to establish Buy.com as an e-commerce portal, with plans to ultimately become the largest portal on the Internet. He continued selling computers through BuyComp.com, and added several new websites, including BuyBooks.com and BuyVideos.com.

With sales of $125 million in 1998, Buy.com is believed to have broken Compaq's first-year sales record of $111 million. However, the company was also losing several million dollars each month. But according to Blum, that was all part of the strategic plan! Buy.com set out to build a large customer base by offering some products below cost and others slightly above cost. According to the plan, these customers would return again and again to make purchases. Buy.com eventually would turn a profit by selling advertising space and additional services, including warranties and equipment leases. Many prominent companies, including the Gap, Lexus, and Pepsi, have placed ads on Buy.com.

"My goal is to reach $10 billion in revenue with 1% gross margin on product sales," stated Blum, when asked where he wanted the company to be financially by 2003. Toward that end, the company has purchased thousands of Internet domain names that start with the word "buy," including BuyStuff.com, BuyInsurance.com, and BuyCars.com. It even owns the rights to 10percentoffamazon.com, which isn't surprising, considering that one of Blum's 10 goals for 1999 was "Beat Amazon." By 1999, Buy.com was selling travel, gifts, books, software, games, music, computers, videos, golf items, and electronics. It even established a site called BuyClearance.com for selling closeout merchandise at "rock-bottom" prices.

Maintaining the lowest prices on Earth requires tight controls over costs. Buy.com does this by inhabiting inexpensive office space and limiting the number of employees by outsourcing various functions, including customer service. The company has absolutely no product inventory, relying instead on distributors to fulfill orders. The only department that is spared from pinching pennies is advertising. Buy.com advertises heavily to attract traffic to its site and to establish the company's brand name.

Is a Lower Price Always Right?

Buy.com is not the only e-tailer basing its entire marketing strategy on the promise of low prices. OnSale Inc. sells personal computing equipment without marking it up by even a dime. Instead, it charges a small order-handling fee, offers service contracts and equipment leases, and sells advertising on its website.

OnSale, Buy.com, and other price-oriented e-tailers are changing the way business is conducted and products are priced, not only computers but books and music as well. And the ramifications reach far beyond just the Internet. "We're not going to put stores out of business," explains Jerry Kaplan, president and CEO of OnSale. "But we think the Internet creates a new form of retailing that is inherently more efficient. We want to take that to its logical extreme." One venture capitalist commented that the logical—or illogical—outcome would be for an Internet site to sell dollars for 85¢ and make up the difference and more through revenues from the sale of ads on the site.

Despite the fact that other Internet companies are attracting customers by emphasizing low prices, Buy.com is committed to being the lowest-priced option in every category it serves. It does this with technology that continually searches other websites to evaluate their prices and ensure that Buy.com offers the best deals on the Web. In July 1999, *The Wall Street Journal* selected 10 best-selling books and 10 other titles, and compared prices at five different websites, including Borders.com, Amazon.com, Barnesandnoble.com, Books.com, and Buy.com. Overall, Buy.com had the best prices, slightly better than Books.com, and about 8% lower than the other three booksellers.

Numerous observers wonder if price alone is a durable foundation on which to build a long-lasting enterprise. Some industry analysts contend that when you're talking about business on the Internet, the answer is yes. After all, consumers may be reluctant to drive an extra 20 or 30 minutes in order to save a few bucks. But they can go virtually anywhere in the world in a matter of seconds just by visiting the World Wide Web to find the lowest available prices.

Some of the largest, best-known e-tailers are already being squeezed by Buy.com. Amazon.com has experienced a new kind of pressure as shoppers visited the site to take advantage of the wealth of information it supplies, such as book reviews, and then placed their orders at Buy.com. In response, Amazon lowered its prices on best-sellers to 50% below list price in May 1999. "Every company is vulnerable, every company is under attack," states Blum. "The Internet is going to shrink your margins to the point where you will not survive" strictly on revenue from merchandise sales.

But are the majority of consumers willing to make buying decisions on the basis of price alone? Assuming one market segment is driven solely by price, Buy.com's business model still might be considered a risky proposition. One industry analyst stated, "These guys are setting themselves up to be price leaders, and so that's all their customers are going to care about. As they raise prices, those customers will leave."

According to a study conducted in May 1999, price is not the most important factor for most Internet shoppers. Instead, according to the research, consumers are more swayed by such factors as branding, awareness, and trust. For instance, Amazon commands more than 80% of the online book market, but its prices are higher than other e-tailers. "On the Internet, there is a separation between when the customer buys and gets the order," explains one of the researchers. "Customers don't really know if they're going to get the products, so they will want to go with a company that they trust." This is one reason why e-commerce companies are spending millions of dollars to advertise and turn their sites into familiar brand names.

Cheap Pricing Tactics or Honest Mistakes?

Enticing consumers to visit a website and place an order is only part of an e-tailer's challenge, however. In order to retain customers, it is essential to provide a favorable shopping experience, and this aspect of the sales cycle has been more difficult for Buy.com. In early 1999, a monitor worth $566 was inadvertently advertised for $165. Before Buy.com caught its mistake, hundreds of customers had placed orders for the monitor. Claiming its distributor, Ingram Micro, didn't have enough monitors in stock, Buy.com refused to fulfill the orders. Dozens of lawsuits were filed to force Buy.com to honor the original price. The company later changed its online terms and conditions to disavow responsibility for any typographical errors leading to incorrect prices.

Later in the year, some customers began to allege that Buy.com was charging credit cards for items not in stock. Again caught in the cross fire, Ingram Micro said this was an avoidable situation because Buy.com receives real-time inventory reports showing which products are not currently in stock. This snafu led to a Buy.com backlash on the Internet, as several irate customers created their own "anti-Buy.com" websites. In response, Greg Hawkins, Buy.com's new CEO, invited a select group of disgruntled customers to the company's California headquarters to air their grievances and to hear how Buy.com was prepared to address their complaints. One customer who refused the invitation because she didn't believe the company had changed its ways nevertheless said, "I hope he is sincere about wanting to clean it up."

A few weeks later, the company sent its customers an e-mail that read, "All DVDs $14.99 or less." Unfortunately, when shoppers visited the site, they discovered that some of the more popular movies cost a great deal more. When they complained, their e-mails and phone calls went unanswered or they were told that the offer had expired.

After appointing Hawkins CEO in March 1999, Blum remained Buy.com's chairman. Later that same year, however, Blum departed to start a new company, called ThinkTank.com, which would help launch new Internet companies. His resignation came just months before the company planned to go public. Blum's departure probably was necessary prior to the initial public offering (IPO), because some investors had voiced their concerns about his previous involvement with a company that was investigated by the Securities and Exchange Commission. Although Blum remained Buy.com's largest shareholder with 60% of the company's stock, he resigned his seat on the board, ending his direct involvement with the dot-com he founded.

Hackers Teach Buy.com an Expensive Lesson

On February 8, 2000, Buy.com announced its IPO of 14 million shares of common stock at a price of $13 per share. Despite the fact that Buy.com had lost $603 million in 1999, compared to sales of $597 million, the stock price climbed to $35 within a few hours. Then disaster struck that same day, as Buy.com fell victim to a rash of "cyber-assaults" by hackers who also targeted eBay, Amazon, and Yahoo!.

Because of the IPO, there were more visitors to Buy.com than usual when the attack began. Basically, the hackers bombarded the site with 800 megabits of data per second, which is about eight times the site's capacity. Soon, Buy.com's stock retreated to its initial offering price. Whereas some analysts blamed the attack for the disappointing IPO results, others cited a lack of faith in the Buy.com business model.

For now, it is unclear whether the firm's unique pricing strategy will pay off in the long run. But in the meantime, savvy online shoppers will surely benefit from deep discounts as e-commerce sites battle for online supremacy.

Questions

1. a. Which pricing objectives is Buy.com pursuing?
   b. What type of long-term impact will Buy.com's pricing strategy have on Internet commerce?

2. a. Does Buy.com engage in price or nonprice competition?
   b. Will this strategy be effective over the long run?

www.buy.com

www.buycomp.com

www.buyclearance.com

www.onsale.com

Sources: Yahoo! Finance website, Feb. 21, 2000; Shawn Langlois, "Why Buy.com? Investors Swept Up in Heat of IPO," *CBS MarketWatch.com,* Feb. 18, 2000; Robert Lemos and Jennifer Mack, "Attack Hit List: eBay, Buy.com, Yahoo!," *Yahoo! News,* Feb. 8, 2000; George Anders, "Buy.com's Blum Leaves to Launch ThinkTank.com," *The Wall Street Journal,* Oct. 22, 1999, p. B9; David Bank, "A Site-Eat-Site World," *The Wall Street Journal,* July 12, 1999, pp. R8, R10; Lisa Bransten, "The Bottom Line," *The Wall Street Journal,* July 12, 1999, pp. R8, R10; Scott Campbell, "Buy.com Loses One in Court, but Precedent Is Unclear," *Computer Reseller News,* July 12, 1999, p. 6; Ed Foster, "Dubious Marketing Ploys at Buy.com Expose the Seamy Side of E-Commerce," *Infoworld,* May 3, 1999, p. 99; Scott Campbell, "Buy.com: Not All It's Cracked Up to Be," *Computer Reseller News,* Apr. 19, 1999, p. 7; Eric Nee, "Meet Mister Buy(Everything).com," *Fortune,* Mar. 29, 1999, pp. 119–124; George Anders, "Web Seller Asks: How Low Can PC Prices Go?" *The Wall Street Journal,* Jan. 19, 1999, p. B1; and William Gurley, "Buy.com May Fail, but If It Succeeds, Retailing May Never Be the Same," *Fortune,* Jan. 11, 1999, pp. 150–151.

Distribution

The arrangements necessary to transfer ownership of a product and transport the product from where it is produced to where it is finally consumed

We are in the process of developing a marketing program to satisfy the firm's target markets. So far, we have considered the product and price elements in the marketing mix. Now we turn our attention to the distribution system—the means of getting the product to the market.

The distribution part of the marketing mix encompasses several broad topics: (1) strategies for selecting and operating distribution channels; (2) the retail market and the major retailing institutions used in distribution; and (3) the wholesale market, the major wholesaling institutions used in distribution, and the primary arrangements for physically distributing materials and supplies to production facilities and then moving finished products to target markets. These topics are covered in Chapters 14, 15, and 16, respectively.

14

Channels of Distribution

"The challenge for the direct-selling firm has been to update its corporate image and reach the estimated 20 to 30 million women who don't know an Avon rep and have never used an Avon product—without alienating its current sales force and customers."

Will **Avon**'s Distribution Be More Attractive after a Makeover?

Avon Products, Inc., was founded in 1886 when David McConnell hired a housewife to sell perfume door to door in Winchester, New Hampshire. For the next 100 years the company's marketing formula remained essentially the same: Hire housewives who want flexible hours and extra income to sell cosmetics to their neighbors. The concept was successful, largely because of the personal contact in the sales process. With her regular visits to homebound women, the "Avon lady" made friends who became loyal customers. Avon's U.S. sales force grew to more than 450,000, and annual revenues surpassed $5 billion by the late 1990s.

However, times change. As the number of working women has increased, fewer potential customers can be found at home. These same women have more disposable income to spend on beauty products, but less time to do so. The challenge for the direct-selling firm has been to update its corporate image and reach the estimated 20 to 30 million women who don't know an Avon rep and have never used an Avon product—without alienating its current sales force and customers.

Avon started by adopting a more contemporary logo as well as classier product packaging and sales brochures. Next, it more than doubled the budget for advertising that used slogans like "Dare to change your mind about Avon." But by far, the company's boldest decision was to sell its products through channels other than independent sales reps.

In 1995, Avon began giving customers other options for ordering its products. The firm distributed a direct-mail catalog and started accepting mail, telephone, and fax orders directly from consumers. Soon after, it added a website for two purposes—to generate online sales and to help its reps manage their businesses. By the end of 1998, the website had 300,000 registered users and $8 million in sales. Although this sales figure is tiny when compared to the company's total revenues, it's viewed as an encouraging start. Consumers who visit the website can also request a visit from an Avon salesperson.

To complete its facelift, Avon decided to open some company-owned stores around the country, including a glitzy showcase in the Trump Tower in midtown New York City. Next, about 50 Beauty Center kiosks popped up in malls. The new outlets are reaching women who hadn't considered Avon for their cosmetic purchases. In fact, new customers account for over 90% of sales at the stores and kiosks. As one convert at a mall in Peabody, Massachusetts, explained, "I wouldn't take the time to order out of an Avon brochure, but I'll buy it if it's here." Avon can also recruit new reps at these outlets.

Avon's former chief executive officer, Jim Preston, remarked, "We've proven that broader access works in many markets around the world. The more we can get our face and name out there, the better it is for our representatives." Not all of Avon's reps agree with the strategy, however. This is troubling news, considering that they accounted for 98% of Avon's sales volume in 1998. According to a senior executive at the firm, "Managing channel conflict is probably our number one concern right now." To placate its sales force, Avon limited the number of products it sells online and at its kiosks to less than 10% of its 5,000-product assortment. Further, discounts and promotions are not offered at either of these channels, but the reps can boost sales through these means.

Initial results from the website and retail outlets may be encouraging for Avon's reps. Numerous consumers visiting the kiosks and Avon.com have requested a call from an Avon rep. In addition, market research reveals that brand awareness has increased and the company's image has improved in areas where there is an Avon Beauty Center.

In late 1999, Andrea Jung was named CEO of Avon, only the second woman to head a *Fortune* 500 company, a move that—at least initially—should please the predominantly female sales force. However, Jung is committed to the new channels and, in her words, "a far more significant move into retail." Thus, while implementing the new distribution arrangements, Jung may also have to reassure the Avon reps that she is looking out for their best interests.[1]

What are the advantages and disadvantages of Avon's using multiple ways to reach consumers?

 www.Avon.com

Even before a product is ready for market, management should determine what methods and routes will be used to get it there. This means establishing strategies for the product's distribution channels and physical distribution. Then, as illustrated by Avon's situation, distribution activities and relationships need to be monitored and adjusted over time.

The area of distribution is in a state of flux, perhaps even transformation, in large part because of widespread use of the Internet and the resulting surge of electronic commerce. Consider, for instance, the titles of two recent articles: "Defining the Seller in On-Line Market" and "Merrill Lynch Shakes Up Industry by Going Online."[2] Given the dynamic—some would say chaotic—situation in distribution, this element of the marketing mix should command substantial attention from business owners and executives.

Managing a distribution channel often begins with a producer. Therefore, we will discuss channels largely from the vantage point of a producer. As you will see, however, the problems and opportunities that middlemen face in managing their channels are similar to those faced by producers. After studying this chapter, you should be able to explain:

- The nature and importance of middlemen and distribution channels.
- The sequence of decisions involved in designing a channel.
- The major channels for goods and services.
- Vertical marketing systems.
- How to choose specific channels and middlemen.
- Intensity of distribution.
- The nature of conflict and control within distribution channels.
- Legal considerations in channels.

Middlemen and Distribution Channels

Ownership of a product has to be transferred somehow from the individual or organization that makes it to the consumer who needs and buys it. Goods also must be physically transported from where they are produced to where they are needed. Services ordinarily cannot be shipped but rather are produced and consumed in the same place. As explained in Chapter 2, all the companies that add value to a product that is eventually bought by an individual or an organization comprise a *value chain*. In this chapter and the following two, we pay special attention to the role of middlemen and selected other facilitating organizations as members of the value chain.

Distribution's role within a marketing mix is getting the product to its target market. The most important activity in getting a product to market is arranging for its sale and the transfer of title from producer to final customer. Other common activities (or functions) are promoting the product, storing it, and assuming some of the financial risk during the distribution process.

A producer can carry out these functions in exchange for an order—and payment—from a customer. Or producer and customer can share these activities. Typically, however, firms called middlemen perform some of these activities on behalf of the producer or the customer.

A **middleman** is a business firm that renders services related *directly* to the sale and/or purchase of a product as it flows from producer to consumer. (Note that in business, *middleman* is an accepted, gender-neutral term.) A middleman either owns the product at some point or actively aids in the transfer of own-

As this ad stresses, the aim of Elgrande is to link manufacturers and consumers around the world through electronic commerce. Basically, a manufacturer places information about its inventory on Elgrande's online database; in turn, consumers shop at the Elgrande website. According to the firm, the price of an order is the wholesale cost plus a flat rate of $1.50 per item. The manufacturer fulfills the order or arranges for a channel member to do so.

 www.elgrande.com

ership. Often, but not always, a middleman takes physical possession of the product.

Middlemen are commonly classified on the basis of whether or not they take title to the products being distributed. **Merchant middlemen** actually take title to the products they help to market. The two groups of merchant middlemen are wholesalers and retailers. **Agent middlemen** never actually own the products, but they do arrange the transfer of title. Real estate brokers, manufacturers' agents, and travel agents are examples of agent middlemen.

How Important Are Middlemen?

Critics say prices are high because there are too many middlemen performing unnecessary or redundant functions. Some manufacturers draw this conclusion, especially during a recession, and seek to cut costs by eliminating wholesaling middlemen. Although middlemen can be eliminated from channels, a practice called **disintermediation,** lower costs may not always be achieved.[3] The outcome is not predictable because of a basic axiom of marketing: *You can eliminate middlemen, but you cannot eliminate the essential distribution activities they perform.*

Activities such as creating assortments and storing products can be shifted from one party to another in an effort to improve efficiency. However, someone has to perform the various activities—if not a middleman, then the producer or the final customer.[4] It is usually not practical for a producer to deal directly with ultimate consumers. Think for a moment how inconvenient your life would be if there were no retail middlemen—no supermarkets, gas stations, or ticket sales outlets, for instance.

Middlemen may be able to carry out distribution activities better or more cheaply than either producers or consumers. Even huge firms sometimes conclude that using middlemen is better than a "do-it-yourself" approach to distribution. For example, Kmart Corp. decided to use two large distributors, Supervalu Inc. and Fleming Companies, to supply grocery products to its over 2,000 stores. As a result of this arrangement, Kmart expects to improve its grocery assortments,

Figure 14.1

Typical activities of a middleman.

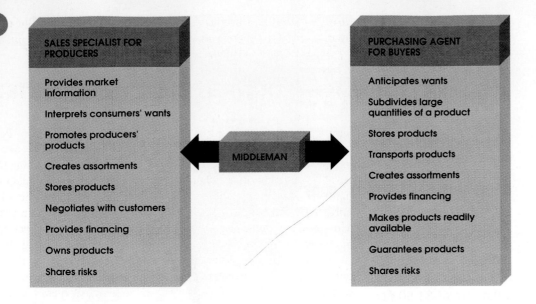

SALES SPECIALIST FOR PRODUCERS	PURCHASING AGENT FOR BUYERS
Provides market information	Anticipates wants
Interprets consumers' wants	Subdivides large quantities of a product
Promotes producers' products	Stores products
Creates assortments	Transports products
Stores products	Creates assortments
Negotiates with customers	Provides financing
Provides financing	Makes products readily available
Owns products	Guarantees products
Shares risks	Shares risks

MIDDLEMAN

boost sales, obtain lower wholesale prices, and free up warehouse space for its other lines.[5]

Middlemen act as sales specialists for their suppliers. Conversely, they serve as purchasing agents for their customers. Consider the sales role performed by Lotus Light Enterprises, a distributor that represents about 400 companies and their 7,500 different teas, herbal products, and related items. According to a Lotus Light manager, "Our most important service is providing a forum for our customers' products. We show their products to retailers and exhibit them at trade shows."[6] As illustrated in Figure 14.1, middlemen also provide financial services for both suppliers and customers. And their storage services, capability to divide large shipments into smaller ones for resale, and market knowledge benefit suppliers and customers alike.

www.lotuslight.com

What Is a Distribution Channel?

A **distribution channel** consists of the set of people and firms involved in the transfer of title to a product as the product moves from producer to ultimate consumer or business user. A channel of distribution always includes both the producer and the final customer for the product in its present form as well as any middlemen such as retailers and wholesalers.

The channel for a product extends only to the last person or organization that buys it without making any significant change in its form. When its form is altered and another product emerges, a new channel is started. When lumber is milled and then made into furniture, two separate channels are involved. The channel for the *lumber* might be lumber mill → broker → furniture manufacturer. The channel for the *finished furniture* might be furniture manufacturer → retail furniture store → consumer.

Besides producer, middlemen, and final customer, other institutions aid the distribution process. Among these *intermediaries* are banks, insurance companies, storage firms, and transportation companies. However, because they do not take title to the products and are not actively involved in purchase or sales activities, these intermediaries are not formally included in the distribution channel.

This chapter focuses on the flow (or transfer) of *ownership* for a product, whereas part of Chapter 16 examines the *physical* flow of goods. These flows are distinct; consequently, different institutions may carry them out. For example, a contractor might order roofing shingles from a local distributor of building materials. To minimize freight and handling costs, the product might be shipped directly—that is, shingles manufacturer → contractor. But the channel for title (and ownership) would be manufacturer → distributor → contractor.

Designing Distribution Channels

Similar firms often have dissimilar channels of distribution. For instance, large sellers of auto insurance use different channels. To reach prospective customers, Aetna uses independent agents who typically sell several brands of insurance. In contrast, State Farm markets through agents who sell only its brand of insurance products. Like virtually all firms, insurance providers are trying to determine whether or how to incorporate the Internet into their distribution strategies. Some are proceeding slowly for fear of alienating long-time middlemen. State Farm, for example, quotes rates online but refers these prospects to its agents rather than closing the sale via the Internet.[7]

www.statefarm.com

A company wants a distribution channel that not only meets customers' needs but also provides a differential advantage. With that in mind, Caterpillar uses construction equipment dealers that provide customers with many valued services, ranging from rapid fulfillment of orders for repair parts to advice about equipment financing. Installers' Service Warehouse, which sells auto parts, seeks an advantage by employing former mechanics to provide expert advice to parts managers or mechanics at dealerships or repair shops who call to place orders or ask questions about a particular part.[8]

To design channels that satisfy customers and outdo competition, an organized approach is required. As shown in Figure 14.2, we suggest a sequence of four decisions:

1. *Specify the role of distribution.* A channel strategy should be designed within the context of the entire marketing mix. First, the firm's marketing objectives are reviewed. Next, the roles assigned to product, price, and promotion are specified. Each element may have a distinct role, or two elements may share an assignment. For example, a manufacturer of pressure gauges may use both middlemen and direct-mail advertising to convince prospective customers that it is committed to servicing the product following the sale.

Figure 14.2

Sequence of decisions to design a distribution channel.

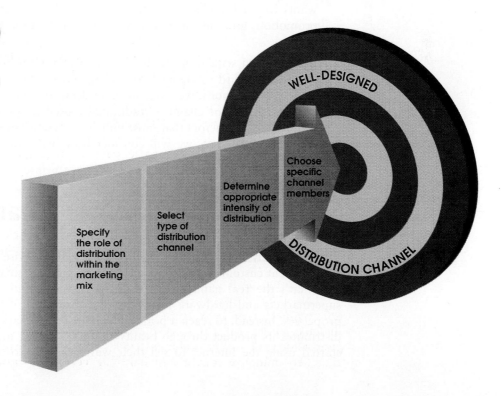

2. *Select the type of channel.* Once distribution's role in the overall marketing program has been agreed on, the most suitable type of channel for the company's product must be determined. At this point in the sequence, a firm needs to decide whether middlemen will be used in its channel and, if so, which types of middlemen.[9]

To illustrate the wide array of institutions available, as well as the difficulty of channel selection, consider a manufacturer of compact disc (CD) players. If the firm decides to use middlemen, it must choose among many different types. At the retail level, the range of institutions includes specialty audio-video outlets, department stores, discount outlets, and mail-order firms.

3. *Determine intensity of distribution.* The next decision relates to intensity of distribution—that is, the number of middlemen used at the wholesale and retail levels in a particular territory. As we will see later, the target market's buying behavior and the product's nature have a direct bearing on this decision. Because of the desires of prospective customers, Goodyear found it necessary to intensify its distribution and, as a result, started selling most of its tire lines through Sears and various discount outlets.

4. *Choose specific channel members.* The last decision concerns the selection of specific firms to distribute the product. Sometimes, a company—often a small one trying to market a new product—has little choice regarding which channel members to use. In this case, the company has to go with those middlemen that are willing (and hopefully able) to distribute the product. Typically, though, a company that is designing a channel has various companies from which to choose for each type of institution that will form the channel.

Assume that the manufacturer of CD players prefers two types of middlemen: department stores and specialty outlets. If the CD players will be sold in Chicago, the producer must decide which department stores—Marshall Field and/or Montgomery Ward & Co.—will be asked to distribute its product line. Also, one or more consumer electronics chains—from a group including United Audio Centers and Circuit City—might be selected. Similar decisions must be made for each territory in the firm's market.

When selecting specific firms to be part of a channel, a producer should consider whether the middleman sells to the customers that the manufacturer wants to reach and whether the middleman's product mix, pricing structure, promotion, and customer service are all compatible with the manufacturer's needs.

In this design sequence, the first decision relates to broad marketing strategy, the second and third to channel strategies, and the last to specific tactics. In the next two major sections, we cover in more detail these channel strategies. First we will look at the major channels traditionally used by producers and at two special channels. Then factors that most influence a company's choice of channels can be discussed. After that, we will consider how many middlemen should be used by a firm.

Selecting the Type of Channel

Firms may rely on existing channels, or they may devise new channels to better serve current customers and to reach new prospects. A small company named New Pig (that's the real name) decided not to use conventional middlemen such as supermarkets and hardware stores to sell a dust cloth with special dirt-attracting properties. Instead, to reach a primarily female target market, this enterprising firm distributes its product through beauty salons.[10] Lately, many manufacturers have started using the Internet to sell their wares directly to customers. For instance,

Clinique Laboratories, Inc., has a website to entice consumers to "shop online" as shown on the computer screen. Note how Clinique has tried to make its website "user friendly" by clearly displaying various options, "tips," and new products. Although the site accounts for less than 0.2% of Clinique's annual sales of over $4 billion, the company is pleased that almost one-fifth of the online shoppers are not previous Clinique users.

www.clinique.com

besides selling through various types of retailers, Clinique is selling its cosmetics and hair-care products online.

Most distribution channels include middlemen, but some do not. A channel consisting only of producer and final customer, with no middlemen providing assistance, is called **direct distribution**. ServiceMaster uses a direct approach to sell its building cleaning services to both residential and commercial customers. Displeased with slow sales of its NetFinity line of personal-computer servers, IBM switched to direct distribution from an indirect approach involving distributors. Thus IBM's own sales force started to call on some big customers in 1998.[11]

A channel of producer, final customer, and at least one level of middlemen represents **indirect distribution**. TWA, Delta, and most other airlines depend heavily on an indirect approach, involving travel agents, to market air travel services to consumers. One level of middlemen—retailers but no wholesaling middlemen, for example—or multiple levels may participate in an indirect channel. (For consumer goods, sometimes a channel in which wholesalers are bypassed but retailers are used is termed *direct,* rather than indirect, distribution.) With indirect distribution a producer must determine the type(s) of middlemen that will best serve its needs. The range of options at the wholesale and retail levels will be described in the next two chapters.

Major Channels of Distribution

Diverse distribution channels exist today. The most common channels for consumer goods, business goods, and services are described next and summarized in Figure 14.3.

Distribution of Consumer Goods

Five channels are widely used in marketing tangible products to ultimate consumers:

- *Producer → consumer.* The shortest, simplest distribution channel for consumer goods involves no middlemen. The producer may sell from door to door or by mail. For instance, the Southwestern Company uses college students to market its books on a house-to-house basis.

Figure 14.3

Major marketing channels for different categories of products.

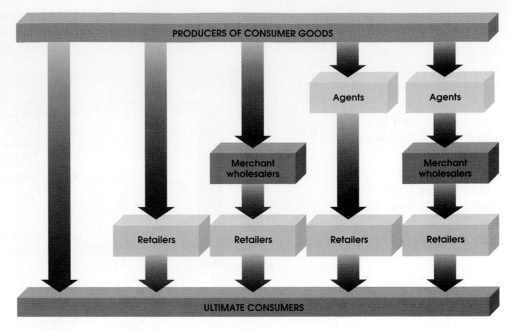

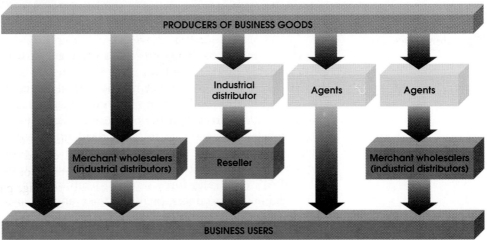

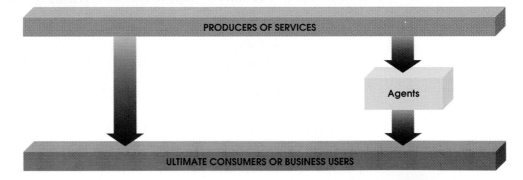

- *Producer → retailer → consumer.* Many large retailers buy directly from manufacturers and agricultural producers. To the chagrin of various wholesaling middlemen, Wal-Mart has increased its direct dealings with producers.
- *Producer → wholesaler → retailer → consumer.* If there is a traditional channel for consumer goods, this is it. Small retailers and manufacturers by the thousands find this channel the only economically feasible choice.
- *Producer → agent → retailer → consumer.* Instead of using wholesalers, many producers prefer to rely on agent middlemen to reach the retail market, espe-

cially *large-scale* retailers. For example, Clorox uses agent middlemen (such as Acosta, a food broker) to reach retailers (such as Dillon's and Schnucks, both large grocery chains), which in turn sell Clorox's cleaning products to consumers.

www.acosta.com

- *Producer → agent → wholesaler → retailer → consumer.* To reach *small* retailers, producers often use agent middlemen, who in turn call on wholesalers that sell to large retail chains and/or small retail stores. Working as an agent on behalf of various grocery products manufacturers, Acosta sells to some wholesalers (such as Supervalu) that distribute a wide range of products to retailers (such as Dierberg's, a supermarket chain in the St. Louis area). In turn, Dierberg's offers its assortment of products to final consumers.

Distribution of Business Goods

A variety of channels is available to reach organizations that incorporate the products into their manufacturing process or use them in their operations.[12] In the distribution of business goods, the terms *industrial distributor* and *merchant wholesaler* are synonymous. The four common channels for business goods are:

- *Producer → user.* This direct channel accounts for a greater *dollar* volume of business products than any other distribution structure. Large installations, such as jet engines, air-conditioning systems, and elevators (all of which are made by divisions of United Technologies), are usually sold directly to users.
- *Producer → industrial distributor → user.* Producers of operating supplies and small accessory equipment frequently use industrial distributors to reach their markets. Manufacturers of building materials and air-conditioning equipment are two examples of industries that make heavy use of industrial distributors.
- *Producer → industrial distributor → reseller → user.* This channel has been common for computer products and related high-tech items. Distributors, which usually are large, national companies, buy various products from manufacturers and then bundle them with related products for resale. Resellers, which usually are smaller, local firms, work closely with end users to meet the buyers' needs. With direct distribution growing, particularly sales through the Internet, distributors and resellers are seeking new ways to add value through their roles. Resellers of computer products, for example, are offering technology solutions such as network installation.[13]
- *Producer → agent → user.* Firms without their own sales departments find this a desirable channel. Also, a company that wants to introduce a new product or enter a new market may prefer to use agents rather than its own sales force.
- *Producer → agent → industrial distributor → user.* This channel is similar to the preceding one. It is used when, for some reason, it is not feasible to sell through agents directly to the business user. For example, the order size may be too small to justify direct selling. Or decentralized inventory may be needed to supply users rapidly, in which case the storage services of an industrial distributor are required.

Distribution of Services

The intangible nature of services creates special distribution requirements. There are only two common channels for services:[14]

- *Producer → consumer.* Because a service is intangible, the production process and/or sales activity often require personal contact between producer and customer. Thus a direct channel is used. Direct distribution is typical for many professional services, such as health care and legal advice, and personal services, such as weight-loss counseling and hair cutting. However, other services, including travel and insurance, may also be sold and distributed directly.
- *Producer → agent → consumer.* Although direct distribution often is necessary

for the performance of a service, producer-customer contact may not be required for distribution activities. Agents frequently assist a services producer with transfer of ownership (the sales task). Many services, notably travel, lodging, advertising media, entertainment, and insurance, are sold through agents. However, various advances in computing and communications technologies have made it easier for customers to deal directly with service providers, thereby threatening the role of agents.[15]

Multiple Distribution Channels

Many, perhaps most, producers are not content with only a single distribution channel. Instead, for reasons such as reaching two or more target markets or avoiding total dependence on a single arrangement, they employ **multiple distribution channels.** For example, Sherwin-Williams paints and Goodyear tires are distributed through wholesalers, independent retailers, large retail chains, and the manufacturers' own stores. Thus far, neither firm has added the Internet as another channel. (Similarly, many companies establish multiple *supply* channels to ensure that they have products when needed.)

Use of multiple channels occurs in several distinct situations.[16] A manufacturer is likely to use multiple channels to reach *different types of markets* when selling:

- The same product (for example, sporting goods or insurance) to both consumer and business markets.[17]
- Unrelated products (education and consulting; rubber products and plastics).

Multiple channels are also used to reach different segments within a single market when:

- Size of the buyers varies greatly. An airline may sell directly to travel departments in large corporations, but rely on travel agents to reach small businesses and ultimate consumers.
- Geographic concentration differs across parts of the market. A manufacturer of industrial machinery may use its own sales force to sell directly to customers that are located close together, but may employ agents in sparsely populated markets.

A significant trend involves selling the *same brand to a single market* through channels that compete with each other; this is sometimes called *dual distribution.* Many independent insurance agents are concerned, even angry, because insurance companies (including Allstate Corp.) are arranging for banks to sell their products and/or are experimenting with Internet selling.[18] When they are not satisfied with the market coverage provided by existing retail outlets, producers may open their own stores, thereby creating dual distribution. Or they may establish their own stores primarily as testing grounds for new products and marketing techniques.

 www.allstate.com

Although multiple distribution channels provide benefits to the producer, they can aggravate middlemen—as Avon has learned. In another industry, many owners of franchised Carvel Ice Cream Bakery Stores rebelled when faced with multiple channels. The franchisees (who are middlemen) claimed their marketing efforts were undermined and sales and profits reduced when the producer decided to sell its ice cream in supermarkets as well as in franchised stores.[19]

Sometimes it is possible to arrange multiple channels in such a way that a firm's middlemen do not get upset. One approach, which is difficult to achieve, is to develop separate marketing strategies for each different channel. For example, the Scotts Company sells some of its lawn-care products to large discount chains but reserves other products only for smaller stores.[20]

Vertical Marketing Systems

Historically, distribution channels stressed the independence of individual channel members. That is, a producer used various middlemen to achieve its distribution objectives. However, the producer typically was not concerned with middlemen's

Pizzeria Uno's restaurants, featuring "original Chicago-style deep dish pizza," have been quite successful. In fact, some customers prefer this brand of pizza so much that they want to prepare it at home. As a result, the company developed a line of products for sale in grocery stores, notably supermarkets. Now, Pizzeria Uno reaches consumers through multiple distribution channels centered on its restaurants and also grocery stores.

 www.pizzeriauno.com

needs. Conversely, wholesalers and retailers were more interested in maintaining their freedom than in coordinating their activities with a producer. These priorities of conventional distribution channels provided an opportunity for a new type of channel.

During the past several decades, the vertical marketing system has become *the* dominant form of distribution channel. A **vertical marketing system** (VMS) is a tightly coordinated distribution channel designed specifically to improve operating efficiency and marketing effectiveness. A VMS illustrates the concept of function shifting that was discussed earlier in this chapter. In a VMS no marketing function is sacred to a particular level or firm in the channel. Instead, each function is performed at the most advantageous position in the channel.

The high degree of coordination or control characterizing a VMS is achieved through one of three means: common ownership of successive levels of a channel; contracts between channel members; or the market power of one or more members. Table 14.1 shows these three distinct forms of vertical marketing systems.

In a **corporate vertical marketing system,** a firm at one level of a channel owns the firms at the next level or owns the entire channel. Nike (athletic shoes and sports wear) and Swatch (watches), for example, own retail outlets. Even the automakers, notably General Motors and Ford, have been buying back and operating some of their previously franchised dealerships.[21]

Middlemen may also engage in this type of vertical integration. For example, many grocery chains, including Kroger, own food-processing facilities, such as dairies, which supply their stores. And various large retailers, including Sears, own all or part of manufacturing facilities that supply their stores with many products.

In a **contractual vertical marketing system,** independent producers, wholesalers, and retailers operate under contracts specifying how they will try to improve the effectiveness and efficiency of their distribution. Three kinds of contractual systems have developed: wholesaler-sponsored voluntary chains (for example, Supervalu grocery stores); retailer-owned cooperatives (True Value hardware stores); and franchise systems (Domino's pizza and Midas automotive maintenance and repairs). All will be discussed in Chapter 15.

An **administered vertical marketing system** coordinates distribution activities through (1) the market and/or economic power of one channel member or (2) the willing cooperation of channel members. Sometimes the brand equity possessed by a manufacturer's product is strong enough to gain the voluntary cooperation of retailers in matters such as inventory levels, advertising, and store display. This situation is illustrated by Corning in ovenware, Rolex in watches, and Kraft in food products. It's important to note that retailers, especially giant ones such as Wal-Mart, are more likely to dominate channel relationships now than in prior years. To satisfy Wal-Mart, Procter & Gamble has established an office in Bentonville, Arkansas, the location of the largest retailer's headquarters.[22]

In the distant past, competition in distribution usually involved two different conventional channels. For instance, two producer → retailer → consumer channels tended to compete with each other. More recently, competition pitted a conventional channel against some form of VMS. Thus a traditional producer → retailer → consumer channel, such as Van Heusen shirts sold through various department stores, battled an administered VMS for business, such as cooperative merchandising efforts between Arrow and a specific chain of department stores.

Increasingly, the most common competitive battles are between different forms of vertical marketing systems. For example, a corporate system (stores owned by Goodyear) competes with a contractual system (Firestone's franchised dealers).

www.truevalue.com

www.rolex.com

Table 14.1	Types of Vertical Marketing Systems	
Type of System	**Control Maintained by**	**Examples**
Corporate	Ownership	Singer (sewing machines), Goodyear (tires), Tandy Corp. (electronics)
Contractual:		
Wholesaler-sponsored voluntary chain	Contract	Western Auto stores, IGA stores
Retailer-owned cooperative	Stock ownership by retailers	True Value hardware stores
Franchise systems:	Contract	
Manufacturer-sponsored retailers		Ford, DaimlerChrysler, and other auto dealers
Manufacturer-sponsored wholesalers		Coca-Cola and other soft drink bottlers
Marketers of services		Wendy's, Midas Muffler, Holiday Inn, National car rentals
Administered	Economic power	Hartman luggage, General Electric, Kraft dairy products

Considering the potential benefits of vertical marketing systems with respect to both marketing effectiveness and operating efficiencies, they should continue to grow in number and importance.

Factors Affecting Choice of Channels

If a firm is customer-oriented (and it better be, if it hopes to prosper), its channels are determined by consumer buying patterns. As the coauthor of a study about the insurance industry commented, "It's time to stop battling about distribution channels and listen to what the customer wants."[23] Thus the nature of the market should be the key factor in management's choice of distribution arrangements. Other considerations are the product, the middlemen, and the company itself.

Market Considerations

A logical starting point is to consider the target market—its needs, structure, and buying behavior:

- *Type of market.* Because ultimate consumers behave differently than business users, they are reached through different distribution channels. Retailers, by definition, serve ultimate consumers, so they are not in channels for business goods.
- *Number of potential customers.* A manufacturer with few potential customers (firms or industries) may use its own sales force to sell directly to ultimate consumers or business users. Boeing uses this approach in selling its jet aircraft. If it has a large number of customers, a manufacturer would likely use middlemen. Reebok relies on numerous middlemen, notably retailers, in trying to reach the millions of consumers in the market for athletic footwear. A firm that uses middlemen does not need as large a sales force as a company, such as Avon, that sells directly to final consumers.
- *Geographic concentration of the market.* When most of a firm's prospective customers are concentrated in a few geographic areas, direct sale is practical. This is the situation in the textile and garment manufacturing industries. When customers are geographically dispersed, direct sale is likely to be impractical because of high travel costs. Sellers may establish sales branches in densely populated markets and use middlemen in less concentrated markets. Some small American manufacturers turn to specialized middlemen, called *trade intermediaries,* to crack foreign markets. Manufacturers sell their goods to trade intermediaries at lower-than-normal wholesale prices in exchange for the intermediaries' ability to secure distribution in markets around the globe.[24]
- *Order size.* When either order size or total volume of business is large, direct distribution is economical. Thus a food products manufacturer would sell directly to large supermarket chains. The same manufacturer, however, would use wholesalers to reach small grocery stores, whose orders are usually too small to justify direct sale.[25]

Product Considerations

Although there are numerous product-related factors to consider, we will highlight three:

- *Unit value.* The price attached to each unit of a product affects the amount of funds available for distribution. For example, a company can afford to use its own employee to sell a printing-press part that costs more than $10,000. But it would not make sense for a company sales person to call on a household or a business firm to sell a $2 ballpoint pen. Likewise, Minnesota Mining and Manufacturing Co. (3M, for short) thus far has avoided online sales because the typically low unit value and small quantity ordered would make the transaction unprofitable for the firm.[26] Thus products with low unit values usually

www.3m.com

Why do gray markets give producers and middlemen gray hair?

Occasionally items are sold through distribution channels that are not authorized by the manufacturer. This practice, typically called *gray marketing* or sometimes *export diversion,* accounts for about $10 billion in sales annually in the U.S. It usually involves products made in one country and destined for sale in another country.

Gray marketing takes many forms. In one form, a wholesaling middleman purchases a product made in one country and agrees to distribute it in a second country, but instead diverts the product to a third country (often the U.S.). Because the product typically is sold at a discount in a reputable outlet, not on the "black market" or from the trunks of cars, it isn't apparent that normal distribution has not been used.

Cameras, computer disk drives or entire PCs, perfumes, cars, and liquor are among the diverse products sold through gray markets. Ordinarily, gray marketing arises when a product with a well-known brand name carries different prices under different circumstances. For example, a product's wholesale price may vary depending on the country in which it is sold or the quantity purchased.

So what's wrong with gray marketing? After spending time and money to promote the product, authorized distributors lose sales to the gray market. Manufacturers then have to placate their authorized distributors. Gray marketing also disrupts a producer's distribution and pricing strategies. Moreover, when consumers buy products through the gray market, they may wind up without warranties or service contracts.

Still, some parties (but definitely not authorized distributors) see benefits in gray marketing. Unauthorized distributors are able to sell products they normally cannot acquire. To sell excess output, some manufacturers allow gray marketing. Consumers pay lower prices for popular products and may also find them at more outlets.

Some manufacturers have concluded that it's too difficult and costly to fight gray marketing. But other producers try to minimize it by revising price schedules and distribution policies and taking unauthorized distributors to court. Further, some law enforcement agencies, at least in the U.S., have stepped up their efforts to prosecute individuals and firms engaged in export diversion or other forms of gray marketing. Because it continues, no doubt because of the lure of "easy money," gray marketing represents one more challenge for both producers and wholesaling middlemen.

Sources: David Champion, "The Bright Side of Gray Markets," *Harvard Business Review,* September–October 1998, pp. 19–22; Amy Borrus, "Exports That Aren't Going Anywhere," *Business Week,* Dec. 4, 1995, pp. 121, 124; Gert Assmus and Carsten Wiese, "How to Address the Gray Market Threat Using Price Coordination," *Sloan Management Review,* Spring 1995, pp. 31–41; and Robert E. Weigand, "Parallel Import Channels—Options for Preserving Territorial Integrity," *Columbia Journal of World Business,* Spring 1991, pp. 53–60.

are distributed through one or more levels of middlemen. There are exceptions, however. For instance, if order size is large because the customer buys many units of a product at the same time from the company, then a direct channel may be economically feasible.

- *Perishability.* Some goods, including many agricultural products, physically deteriorate fairly quickly. Other goods, such as clothing, perish in a fashion sense. As was discussed in Chapter 11, services are perishable because of their intangible nature. Perishable products require direct or very short channels.

- *Technical nature.* A *business* product that is highly technical is often distributed directly to business users. The producer's sales force must provide considerable presale and postsale service; wholesalers normally cannot do this. *Consumer* products of a technical nature pose a real distribution challenge. Ordinarily, because of other factors discussed in this section, producers cannot sell highly technical products directly to the consumer. As much as possible, they sell them directly to retailers, but even then product servicing often poses problems.

    For a variety of technical products, such as golf clubs (which, believe it or not, are technical because of the myriad sizes, materials, grips, and features),

some consumers do some preliminary shopping in "bricks and mortar" stores. Then they go to the Internet to seek the lowest price for the clubs they want. The purchase might be made online or from the store, often depending on whether the store is willing to match an online vendor's lower price.

Middlemen Considerations

Here we begin to see that a company may not be able to arrange exactly the channels it desires:

- *Services provided by middlemen.* Each producer should select middlemen offering those marketing services that the producer either is unable to provide or cannot economically perform. For instance, firms from other countries seeking to penetrate business markets in the U.S. commonly utilize industrial distributors. This is because they furnish needed capabilities such as market coverage, sales contacts, and storage of inventories.[27]

- *Availability of desired middlemen.* The middlemen preferred by a producer may not be available. They may carry competing products and, as a result, not want to add another line. Famous Amos Chocolate Chip Cookie Corp. faced this challenge. The company was unable to get its product on the shelves of a sufficient number of supermarket chains. Hence, Famous Amos boosted sales by relying on alternative middlemen—warehouse clubs, vending machines, and even Burger King restaurants.[28]

- *Producers' and middlemen's policies.* When middlemen are unwilling to join a channel because they consider a producer's policies to be unacceptable, the producer has fewer channel options. Some retailers or wholesalers, for example, will carry a producer's line only if they receive assurance that no competing middlemen will carry the line in the same territory. A growing number of small manufacturers have become very frustrated with the demands for lower prices and other concessions that are placed on them by giant retailers such as Wal-Mart and Home Depot. Thus makers of various products ranging from children's clothing to garden products decided—very reluctantly—to not do business with these retailers.[29]

Company Considerations

Before choosing a distribution channel for a product, a company should consider its own situation:

- *Desire for channel control.* Some producers establish direct channels because they want to control their product's distribution, even though a direct channel may be more costly than an indirect channel. By controlling the channel, producers can achieve more aggressive promotion, assure the freshness of merchandise stocks, and set their products' retail prices. Wanting to deal one-on-one with both prospective and repeat customers, Dell Computer has used various direct channels, such as mail-order sales. Now the emphasis is on its website, which by the end of 1999 was ringing up $30 million in sales *daily* (compared to sales of $3.5 million daily at the more publicized Amazon.com site).[30]

- *Services provided by seller.* Some producers make decisions about their channels based on the distribution functions desired (and occasionally demanded) by middlemen. For instance, numerous retail chains will not stock a product unless it is presold through heavy advertising by the producer.

- *Ability of management.* The marketing experience and managerial capabilities of a producer influence decisions about which channel to use. Many companies lacking marketing know-how turn the distribution job over to middlemen.

- *Financial resources.* A business with adequate finances can establish its own sales force, grant credit to its customers, and/or warehouse its own products. A financially weak firm uses middlemen to provide these services.

In the mid-1990s, Michael Dell, the founder of Dell Computer Corp., saw the Internet as a way to deal directly with computer buyers. The company's site is organized for different groups of customers. Note that shoppers can place an order online or by calling a toll-free number. Dell may be the most successful Internet merchant, with 2 million visitors to its site each month and, more importantly, as much as $10 billion in annual online sales.

www.dell.com/us

In a few cases, virtually all factors point to a particular length and type of channel. However, there often is not a single "best" channel. In most cases the guiding factors send mixed signals. If a company with an unproven product having low profit potential cannot place its product with middlemen, it may have no other option but to try to distribute the product directly to its target market.

Determining Intensity of Distribution

At this point in designing a channel, a firm knows what role has been assigned to distribution within the marketing mix, and which types of middlemen will be used (assuming indirect distribution is appropriate). Next the company must decide on the **intensity of distribution**—that is, how many middlemen will be used at the wholesale and retail levels in a particular territory. Optimal intensity, from the standpoint of a producer, is just enough middlemen to meet the desires of the target market. Extra intensity boosts the producer's marketing expenses, but does not really help the firm. Of course, like so many tasks in marketing (and life), achieving this optimum is easier said than done.[31]

There are many degrees of intensity. As shown in Figure 14.4, we will consider the three major categories—ranging from *intensive* to *selective* to *exclusive*. Distribution intensity ordinarily is thought to be a single decision. However, if the channel has more than one level of middlemen (wholesaler and retailer, for example) or the firm is using multiple channels, the appropriate intensity must be selected for each level and channel.

Different degrees of intensity may be appropriate at successive levels of distribution. A manufacturer can often achieve intensive retail coverage with selective, rather than intensive, wholesale distribution. Or selective intensity at the retail level may be gained through exclusive intensity at the wholesale level. Of course, the wholesaling firm(s) will determine which retail outlets actually receive the product. Despite this lack of control, a producer should plan the levels of intensity needed at both the wholesale and retail levels.

Will the rise of the Internet be the demise of middlemen?

Many producers of diverse goods and services are trying to reach customers through the Internet. Tupperware, Dell Computer, Merrill Lynch, and virtually all airlines are among the legion of firms that have established websites as one more way to sell their products. Will this direct contact with end users eliminate middlemen?

The potential benefits of bypassing middlemen and perhaps even a company's own sales force through online selling can be captivating. According to one estimate, selling through a website can cut expenses related to sales commissions and paperwork by as much as 15%. Perhaps with these figures in mind, CarsDirect.com is dealing directly with prospective car buyers, even closing the sale online. Then CarsDirect obtains the specified auto from an existing dealer and, in turn, delivers the new purchase to the customer's home or office.

Some companies, such as CarsDirect, locate on the Internet to gain a differential advantage. Others, such as Merrill Lynch, go online to avoid a disadvantage. Seeing a substantial number of its customers switching to online brokers, the firm decided to allow online trading of stocks even at the risk of jeopardizing or angering its network of 14,000 investment brokers. And still other firms add the Internet as a channel in order to reach new customers. Tupperware, for instance, launched a website for this purpose.

But let's not write off middlemen, even in this Internet era. Most companies continue to use middlemen. For one thing, few manufacturers are geared up to ship very small quantities to numerous buyers. Middlemen are. Further, many consumers and end users still want to see the actual product, or at least talk with a real person, prior to making a purchase. Various types of wholesaling middlemen and retailers offer these services to prospective customers.

Most firms that establish an Internet presence don't discard middlemen but instead strive to placate, or at least not alienate, them. Thus some companies have limited their Internet activities by providing information only (Scotts in lawn-care products), different merchandise (Mattel with its Barbie dolls), or just a limited assortment (Tupperware) on their websites. Going a step further, numerous organizations are incorporating middlemen into their Internet activities. A common arrangement is for manufacturers to pay retailers to deliver bulky merchandise that has been ordered online. Another tactic is for producers to somehow provide middlemen with a share of the revenues from Internet sales.

It's quite possible that middlemen will benefit, rather than suffer, from the move to online sales. Their services will be needed to provide the services that producers with online enterprises either cannot or do not want to provide. Consider a prominent example. Most large "bricks and mortar" bookstores use a publisher → retailer → consumer channel. In contrast, Amazon.com tends to rely on a longer channel of publisher → wholesaler → retailer → consumer.

Sources: Fara Warner, "Racing for Slice of a $350 Billion Pie, Online Auto-Sales Sites Retool," *The Wall Street Journal,* Jan. 24, 2000, pp. B1, B6; Andrea Isabel Flores, "Tupperware to Launch Online Sales, Creating Rival to Own Representatives," *The Wall Street Journal,* Aug. 10, 1999, p. B8; "Merrill Lynch Shakes Up Industry by Going Online, *St. Louis Post-Dispatch,* June 2, 1999, pp. C1, C2; and George Anders, "Some Big Companies Long to Embrace Web but Settle for Flirtation," *The Wall Street Journal,* Nov. 4, 1998, pp. A1, A14.

 www.carsdirect.com

Intensive Distribution

 www.haagendazs.com

Under **intensive distribution,** a producer sells its product through every available outlet in a market where a consumer might reasonably look for it. Ultimate consumers demand immediate satisfaction from convenience goods and will not defer purchases to find a particular brand. Thus intensive distribution is often used by manufacturers of this category of product. Ice cream makers, such as Carvel and Häagen-Dazs, eventually decided they needed intensive, rather than more selective, distribution. Likewise, shortly after acquiring the Iams brand of pet food, Procter & Gamble concluded that sales were being lost by relying only on veterinary clinics and pet store chains at the retail level of the channel. As a result, P&G added supermarkets and discount stores, such as Wal-Mart, to its retail channel members.[32]

Figure 14.4

The intensity-of-distribution continuum.

Retailers often control whether a strategy of intensive distribution actually can be implemented. For example, a new manufacturer of toothpaste or a small producer of potato chips may want distribution in all supermarkets, but these retailers may limit their assortments to, say, four fast-selling brands.

Except when they want to promote low prices, retailers are reluctant to pay to advertise a product that is sold by competitors. Therefore, intensive distribution places much—perhaps most—of the advertising and promotion burden on the producer. Many producers offer cooperative advertising, in which they reimburse middlemen for part of the cost of ads featuring the producer's product.

Selective Distribution

In **selective distribution,** a producer sells its product through multiple, but not all possible, wholesalers and retailers in a market where a consumer might reasonably look for it. Selective distribution is appropriate for consumer shopping goods, such as various types of clothing and appliances, and for business accessory equipment, such as office equipment and handheld tools. The relative ease of online selling has prompted firms in many industries to shift from selective to more intensive distribution.

In contrast, a company may choose to be more selective after some experience with intensive distribution. The decision to change usually hinges on the high cost of intensive distribution or the unsatisfactory performance of middlemen. Certain middlemen perennially order in small, unprofitable amounts; others may be poor credit risks. Eliminating such marginal middlemen may reduce the number of outlets *but* increase a company's sales volume. Many companies have found this to be the case simply because they were able to do a more thorough selling job with a smaller number of accounts.

A firm may move toward more selective distribution to enhance the image of its products, strengthen customer service, improve quality control, and/or maintain some influence over its prices. For instance, Step 2, a manufacturer of large, plastic toys, decided not to distribute through discount stores in order to protect its image and profit margins.[33] Of course, whether or not Step 2's efforts to control its prices at the retail level are fruitful is open to question.

Exclusive Distribution

Under **exclusive distribution,** the supplier agrees to sell its product only to a single wholesaling middleman and/or retailer in a given market. At the wholesale level, such an arrangement is normally termed an exclusive *distributorship* and, at the retail level, an exclusive *dealership*. A manufacturer may prohibit a middleman that holds an exclusive distributorship or dealership from handling a directly competing product line. That type of restriction is becoming less common. Thus, even under an exclusive distributorship, many middlemen handle directly competing products or, at least indirectly competing products (for example, high-price and economy-price power mowers).

Producers often adopt an exclusive distribution strategy when it is essential that the retailer carry a large inventory. Thus exclusive dealerships are frequently used in marketing consumer specialty products such as expensive suits. This strategy is also desirable when the dealer or distributor must furnish installation and repair service. For this reason, manufacturers of farm machinery and large construction equipment grant exclusive distributorships.

Exclusive distribution helps a manufacturer control the last level of middleman before the final customer. A middleman with exclusive rights is usually willing to promote the product aggressively. Why? Interested customers will have to purchase the product from this middleman because no other outlets in the area carry the same brand. However, a producer suffers if its exclusive middlemen in various markets do not serve customers well. Essentially a manufacturer has "all its eggs in one basket."

An exclusive dealer or distributor has the opportunity to reap all the benefits of the producer's marketing activities in a particular area. However, under exclusive distribution, a middleman may become too dependent on the manufacturer. If the manufacturer fails, the middleman also fails (at least for that product). Another risk is that once sales volume has been built up in a market, the producer may add other dealers or, worse yet, drop all dealers and establish its own sales force.

Conflict and Control in Channels

Distribution should be—and occasionally is—characterized by goals shared by suppliers and customers and by cooperative actions. But conflicts as well as struggles for control are increasingly common in this Internet age. To manage distribution channels effectively requires an understanding of both conflict and control, including techniques to (1) decrease conflict, or at least its negative effects, and (2) increase a firm's control within a channel.

Channel conflict exists when one channel member perceives another channel member acting in a way that prevents the first member from achieving its distribution objectives. Firms in one channel often compete vigorously with firms in other channels; this represents horizontal conflict. Even within the same channel, firms disagree about operating practices and try to gain control over other members' actions; this illustrates vertical conflict.

A by-product of the rise of the Internet has been added channel conflict, both horizontal and vertical in nature. For example, Home Depot has stated that its suppliers should not sell their products online. A letter from the chain to suppliers stated, "We, too, have the right to be selective in regard to vendors we select, and . . . a company may be hesitant to do business with its competitors." Perhaps trying to win favor with these same vendors, Lowe's encouraged its suppliers to go online. Lowe's stated its interest in linking websites and maybe even sharing revenues with its suppliers.[34]

 www.lowes.com

Horizontal Conflict

Horizontal conflict occurs among firms on the same level of distribution. The cellular telephone field provides an excellent example. Cell phone equipment and services can be bought seemingly everywhere. Consider the range of competitors: office-supply outlets, department stores, warehouse clubs, and consumer electronics retailers as well as the telecommunications providers (such as Sprint) with their own outlets, toll-free telephone lines, and websites.

Basically, horizontal conflict is a form of business competition. It may occur among:

- *Middlemen of the same type:* Maryvale Hardware (an independent retailer) versus Fred's Friendly Hardware (another independent retailer), for example.
- *Different types of middlemen on the same level:* Fred's Friendly Hardware (an independent retailer) versus Dunn Edwards Paint (a store within a large chain) versus Kmart (a single department in a store within a giant chain).

The Casino supermarket chain obtained over 300 Daewoo autos intended for export to central and eastern Europe. Casino priced the autos 30,000 francs (almost $5,000) below the price charged by Daewoo's authorized dealers. Undercut on price, the dealers were upset not only with Casino but also with Daewoo's distributor.

A primary source of horizontal conflict is **scrambled merchandising,** in which middlemen diversify by adding product lines not traditionally carried by their type of business. Supermarkets, for instance, expanded beyond groceries by adding health and beauty aids, small appliances, records, snack bars, and various services. Retailers that originally sold these product lines became irritated both at supermarkets for diversifying and at producers for using multiple distribution channels. Banks selling insurance, mutual funds, and trust services is another example of scrambled merchandising in the previously tradition-bound world of financial services.

Scrambled merchandising and the resulting horizontal competition may stem from consumers, middlemen, or producers. Many *consumers* prefer convenient, one-stop shopping, so stores broaden their assortments to satisfy this desire. *Middlemen* constantly strive for higher gross margins and more customer traffic, so they increase the number of lines they carry. Perhaps with that in mind, a supermarket chain in France began to sell Korean-made Daewoo autos at discount prices in its stores, much to the chagrin of regular Daewoo dealers.[35] *Producers* seek to expand their market coverage and reduce unit production costs (through economies of scale), so they add new means of distribution. Such diversification intensifies horizontal conflict.

Vertical Conflict

Perhaps the most severe conflicts in distribution involve firms at different levels of the same channel. **Vertical conflict** typically occurs between producer and wholesaler *or* producer and retailer.

Producer versus Wholesaler

A producer and a wholesaler may disagree about aspects of their relationship. For instance, in the late 1990s, Anheuser-Busch instituted a set of incentives to encourage its wholesalers to stock only A-B products and, conversely, to drop other brands of alcoholic and nonalcoholic beverages. Channel friction is likely to develop between A-B and any wholesaler that desires to carry other profitable brands but does not want to miss out on the new financial incentives offered by A-B.[36]

Why do conflicts arise? Basically, manufacturers and wholesalers have differing points of view. On the one hand, manufacturers think that wholesalers neither promote products aggressively nor hold sufficient inventories. And they contend that wholesalers' services cost too much. On the other hand, wholesalers believe that producers either expect too much (such as requiring an extensive inventory of the product) or do not understand the wholesaler's primary obligation to customers.

Channel conflict sometimes stems from a manufacturer's attempts to bypass wholesalers and deal directly with retailers or consumers. Direct sales occur because either producers or customers are dissatisfied with wholesalers' services or because market conditions invite or require this approach. With the rise of the Internet, battles about direct sales are increasingly common.

To bypass wholesalers, a producer has two alternatives:

- *Sell directly to consumers.* Producers may employ door-to-door, mail-order, or online selling. They may also establish their own distribution centers in various areas or even their own retail stores in major markets. Many clothing makers, such as Van Heusen and Harve Benard, own and operate numerous factory outlets. Sunbeam Corp. has also tried this type of store (more on factory outlets in the next chapter).[37] Typically, manufacturers use this approach as a supplementary, rather than sole, form of distribution.

- *Sell directly to retailers.* Under certain market and product conditions, selling directly to retailers is feasible and advisable. An ideal retail market for this option consists of retailers that buy large quantities of a limited line of products. Luxottica Group of Italy, which makes more eyeglass frames than any other company, eliminated most of its wholesale distributors. According to the firm, doing so not only boosted its profit margins but also improved service to its customers, mainly optical shops in Italy, the U.S., and other countries.[38]

Direct distribution—a short channel—places a financial and managerial burden on the producer. The manufacturer must operate its own sales force and handle physical distribution of its products. Further, a direct-selling manufacturer faces competition from its former wholesalers, which no doubt will begin distributing competitive products.

To avoid being bypassed in channels or to respond when they are bypassed, wholesalers need to improve their competitive positions. Their options include:

- *Improve internal performance.* Many wholesalers have modernized their operations. Functional, single-story warehouses have been built outside congested downtown areas, and mechanized materials-handling equipment has been installed. Computers have improved order processing, inventory control, and billing.

- *Provide management assistance to retailers.* Wholesalers have realized that improving retailers' operations benefits all parties. Wholesalers help meet certain retailers' needs, such as store layout, merchandise selection, promotion, and inventory control.

www.igainc.com

- *Form a voluntary chain.* In this form of vertical marketing system, a wholesaler contractually agrees to furnish management services and volume buying power to a group of retailers. In turn, the retailers promise to buy all, or almost all, their merchandise from the wholesaler. Examples of wholesaler-sponsored voluntary chains include IGA (groceries) and Western Auto (automotive products).

www.supervalu.com

- *Develop middlemen's brands.* Some large wholesalers have successfully established their own brands. Supervalu has developed its Flavorite brand for groceries and Chateau for personal-care products. A voluntary chain of retailers provides a built-in market for the wholesaler's brands.

Producer versus Retailer

Conflict between manufacturers and retailers—in fact, between any two parties—is likely to intensify during tough economic times. Conflict is also bound to occur when producers compete with retailers by selling through producer-owned stores or over the Internet. A number of apparel makers—including Levi's, Polo, and Liz Claiborne—have opened retail outlets. Their doing so aggravated department stores and specialty retailers that also carry their brands.[39]

Producer and retailer may also disagree about terms of sale or conditions of the relationship between the two parties. In recent years large retail chains, particularly department stores and discount houses, have demanded not only lower prices but also more service from suppliers. Producers sometimes find it costly, if not nearly impossible, to comply with the retailers' new policies. The policies cover the gamut, including automatic deductions in place of returning damaged merchandise, larger contributions to advertising and other promotion expenses, and even the quality of hangers on which apparel is hung (so that the retailer doesn't have to pay for hangers and rehang the merchandise when it is received at the store).[40]

Conflict also has occurred as some large retailers, especially in the grocery field, have demanded a **slotting fee** (also called a *slotting allowance*) to place a manufacturer's product on store shelves. In some cases, companies with new products are required to pay a fee of $100 to over $1,000 per store for each version of the product. Manufacturers with popular brands typically do not have to pay these fees. According to one estimate, the slotting fees paid by manufacturers total about $9 billion annually. Because supermarkets' profit margins are very small on the products they sell, these payments probably account for about 30% of grocery chains' profits. Given the controversy (see the Ethical Dilemma box), the U.S. Congress started to examine slotting fees in late 1999.[41]

Both producers and retailers have methods to gain more control. Manufacturers can:

- *Build strong consumer brand loyalty.* Meeting and surpassing customers' expectations is a key in creating such loyalty.
- *Establish one or more forms of vertical marketing system.* Procter & Gamble uses the administered type of VMS, dedicating special teams to work with key customers, such as Wal-Mart and Target.
- *Refuse to sell to uncooperative retailers.* This tactic may not be defensible from a legal standpoint.
- *Arrange alternative retailers.* Squeezed by large retail chains, some producers are building their distribution strategy around smaller specialty stores.

An Ethical Dilemma?

In exchange for shelf space in their stores, many supermarket chains require manufacturers to pay slotting fees (as discussed above). Part or all of the revenues a chain receives from this policy might be passed on to consumers in the form of lower prices. Or the chain could retain these revenues to cover added labor costs associated with shelving new products and/or to boost profits. Critics charge that slotting fees stifle the introduction of new products, particularly those developed by small companies. Further, some small producers cannot afford them. Supermarkets contend they must find a way to recoup the costs of reviewing the flood of new products, stocking some of them, and removing failures.

Assume that you are a supermarket chain vice president who is responsible for establishing policies regarding relationships with suppliers. Is it ethical for your chain to demand slotting fees from manufacturers?

Sources: Paul N. Bloom, Gregory T. Gundlach, and Joseph P. Cannon, "Slotting Allowances and Fees: Schools of Thought and the Views of Practicing Managers," *Journal of Marketing,* April 2000, pp. 98–108; Holman W. Jenkins, Jr., "We ♥ Slotting Fees," *The Wall Street Journal,* Sept. 22, 1999, p. A23; and Nahal Toosi, "Congress Looks at the Selling of Shelf Space," *St. Louis Post-Dispatch,* Sept. 15, 1999, p. C1.

Although risky, a number of apparel makers, such as Dion-Jones Ltd., have taken this course of action.[42]

Effective marketing weapons are also available to retailers. They can:

- *Develop store loyalty among consumers.* Skillful advertising and strong store brands are means of creating loyal customers.
- *Improve computerized information systems.* Information is power. Knowing what sells and how fast it sells is useful in negotiating with suppliers.
- *Form a retailer cooperative.* In this type of vertical marketing system, a group of retailers (usually fairly small ones) band together to establish and operate a wholesale warehouse. The primary intent is to gain lower merchandise costs through volume buying power. Examples of retailer cooperatives include True Value hardware stores and Associated Wholesale Grocers.

Who Controls Channels?

Every firm would like to regulate the behavior of the other members in its distribution channel. When a company is able to do this, it has **channel control.** In many situations, including distribution channels, power is a prerequisite for control. **Channel power** is the ability to influence or determine the behavior of another channel member. There are various sources of power in distribution channels. They include:

- *Expertise*—for example, possessing vital technical knowledge about the product or valuable information about customers.
- *Rewards*—providing financial benefits to cooperative channel members.
- *Sanctions*—removing uncooperative firms from the channel.

Interestingly, power doesn't have to be exercised to provide control. A firm might be able to gain control just by making other channel members aware that it has, for example, sanctioning power. Not surprisingly, the types of power used to influence distributors have a strong effect on their levels of satisfaction.[43]

Traditionally, manufacturers have been viewed as in control of channels—that is, they make the decisions regarding types and number of outlets, participation of individual middlemen, and business practices to be followed by a channel. But with the enormous size and strong customer loyalty that some middlemen—particularly retailers—now possess, this is a one-sided, outdated point of view.

Middlemen now control many channels. Certainly the names Safeway, Target, and Nordstrom mean more to consumers than the names of many producers' brands sold in these stores. Large retailers are challenging manufacturers for channel control, just as many manufacturers seized control from wholesalers years ago. As one article explained, "Powerful chains—May and Dillard in particular—drive hard bargains with vendors, requiring them to pay a bigger share of advertising and promotional expenses."[44] Even small retailers can be influential in local markets because their reputations may be stronger than their suppliers' prestige.

Manufacturers contend they should assume the leader's role in a channel because they create the new products and need greater sales volume to benefit from economies of scale. Conversely, retailers also stake a claim for leadership, because they are closest to ultimate consumers and, as a result, are best able to know consumers' wants and to design and oversee channels to satisfy them. Various factors have contributed to retailers' growing ability to control channels. Perhaps most notably, many retailers have implemented electronic scanning devices, giving them access to more accurate, timely information about sales trends of individual products than producers have.[45]

A Channel Viewed as a Partnership

Sometimes, members see a channel as a fragmented collection of independent, competing firms. This is a myopic viewpoint. Instead, suppliers and middlemen should think of channels as partnerships aimed at satisfying end users' needs rather than as something they "command and control." The head of Sutter Home Winery attributes his firm's success to its good distributors and cooperative working relationship with them: "I have always felt it was a real partnership."[46]

Partnerships within channels can entail a variety of cooperative activities that are most effective when they benefit both parties. A supplier may be asked to get involved in a customer's new-product development efforts. Bailey Controls, a division of ABB Automation that makes control systems for large manufacturing plants, even allowed one of its suppliers, Arrow Electronics, to have a warehouse at Bailey's factory. An increasingly common occurrence is for a firm to provide a supplier with information about past or projected sales and/or existing inventory levels so the supplier can better schedule its production and fill the customer's orders in a timely manner. For example, Wal-Mart allows each of its over 7,000 suppliers to examine two years of sales figures for that supplier's products across the giant retail chain.[47] In Chapter 16, we'll discuss *collaborative planning, forecasting, and replenishment* systems, which emphasize this type of data sharing in a channel.

Developing and sustaining partnerships in a distribution channel require communication beyond a sales person and a purchasing agent. Typically, a supplier's top executives also meet with their counterparts in customer organizations. For example, the Baxter hospital supply firm uses the information about the customer's mission and strategies that comes out in such meetings to develop means to better serve that customer and to cut costs. The company has discovered (happily) that strong partnerships with customers yield a differential advantage over competitors.[48]

There are other potential benefits of partnering. Lower inventory and operating costs, improved quality of products and service, and more rapid filling of orders are all possible, but by no means assured. There are risks as well. A close working relationship often requires sharing sensitive information, which may be misused by the other party; worse yet, it may wind up in a competitor's hands. Because firms entering into a partnership often reduce the number of other suppliers or customers with which they do business, they may have fewer options to turn to if the relationship doesn't work out.[49]

To increase coordination and facilitate partnerships within channels, many large firms have pared the number of suppliers with which they do business. Some observers suggest, however, that the resulting "preferred vendor" lists are a means for sizable customers to dominate relatively small suppliers. As implied, channel partners are not necessarily equals. Still, given the potential sales volume that comes with being a preferred vendor, most suppliers are willing to meet the demands of powerful customers.[50]

Many channel partnerships really are part of a broader, significant trend called *relationship marketing* (introduced in Chapter 1). In the context of distribution channels, relationship marketing refers to a concerted effort by a company not only to work closely with customers to better understand and satisfy their needs but also to develop long-term, mutually beneficial relationships with them. Conversely, customers can seek to engage in relationship marketing with their suppliers.[51]

Legal Considerations in Managing Channels

Attempts to control distribution are subject to legal constraints. We will now discuss legal aspects of four control methods sometimes employed by suppliers, usually manufacturers. Each method is limited by the Clayton Antitrust Act, Sherman Antitrust Act, or Federal Trade Commission Act. None of the four methods is illegal by itself. Distribution control becomes unlawful when it is judged to (1) substantially lessen competition, (2) create a monopoly, or (3) restrain trade.

Exclusive Dealing

A manufacturer that prohibits its dealers from carrying products of its competitors is engaged in **exclusive dealing.** If a manufacturer stipulates that any store carrying its Perfecto Gas Grill *not* carry competing brands of outdoor barbecue grills, this is exclusive dealing. Such an arrangement is likely to be *illegal* when:

- The manufacturer's sales volume is a substantial portion of total volume in a given market. Competitors are thus excluded from a major part of the market.

- The contract is between a large manufacturer and a much smaller middleman, the supplier's power is considered inherently coercive, and is thus in restraint of trade.

However, some court decisions have held that exclusive dealing is *permissible* when:

- Equivalent products are available in a market or the manufacturer's competitors have access to equivalent dealers. In these cases exclusive dealing may be legal if competition is not lessened to any large degree.

- A manufacturer is entering a market, or its total market share is so small as to be negligible. An exclusive-dealing agreement may actually strengthen the producer's competitive position if the middlemen decide to back the product with a strong marketing effort.

Likewise, a middleman that uses its clout to force a manufacturer to stop selling products to another middleman may be guilty of illegal exclusive dealing. In fact, Toys "R" Us was accused first by the Federal Trade Commission and later by state agencies of coercing large manufacturers, such as Mattel and Hasbro, to withhold popular toys from warehouse clubs, such as Costco and Sam's Club, that would sell the toys at discount prices. Although Toys "R" Us argued that the practice was not illegal, the chain eventually agreed to pay $50 million to settle the state claims.[52]

Tying Contracts

When a supplier sells a product to a middleman only under the condition that the middleman also buy another (possibly unwanted) product from the supplier, the two companies have entered into a **tying contract.** If Paramount Products requires middlemen to buy unpopular, old models of cassette players in order to be able to buy popular, new models of compact disc players, that's a tying contract.

A manufacturer pushes for a tying agreement in several situations. When there are shortages of a popular product, a supplier may see an opportunity to unload other, less desired products. When a supplier relies on exclusive dealers or distributors (in appliances, for example), it may want them to carry a full line of its products. Or when a company grants a franchise (as in fast foods), it may see the franchisees as captive buyers of all the equipment and supplies needed to operate the business. Both Domino's and Little Caesar's franchisees claimed that a tying contract resulted in their paying excessive prices for dough and other supplies. According to the franchisees, their franchise rights were tied to a requirement that they purchase only from the parent company or approved vendors.[53]

In general, tying contracts are considered violations of antitrust laws. There are exceptions, however. Tying contracts may be *legal* when:

- A new company is trying to enter a market.

- An exclusive dealer or distributor is required to carry the manufacturer's full product line, but is not prohibited from carrying competing products.

Refusal to Deal

To select—and perhaps control—its channels, a producer may refuse to sell to certain middlemen. This practice is called **refusal to deal.** A 1919 court case established that manufacturers can select the middlemen to whom they will sell, so long as there is no intent to create a monopoly. In the mid-1990s, independent service companies charged Eastman Kodak Co. with trying to monopolize the business of repairing its brand of photocopiers. A federal jury agreed, deciding that Kodak illegally refused to sell parts for its photocopiers and related equipment to independent service companies. Under the verdict, the 11 companies were awarded more than $70 million in damages from Kodak.[54]

A manufacturer's decision to end or diminish a relationship with a wholesaler or retailer may not be legal. Generally it is *illegal* to drop or withhold products from a middleman for (1) carrying competitors' products, (2) resisting a tying contract, or (3) setting prices lower than desired by the manufacturer. Several years ago, the New York attorney general charged that Stride Rite Corp. held back Keds shoes from retailers that did not abide by the manufacturer's "suggested" retail prices. Eventually, Stride Rite agreed to pay over $7 million to resolve the claim.[55]

Exclusive-Territory Policy

Under an **exclusive-territory policy**, a producer requires each middleman to sell *only* to customers located within an assigned territory. In several court cases, exclusive (also called *closed*) sales territories were ruled unlawful because they lessened competition and restrained trade. The courts sought to encourage competition among middlemen handling the *same* brand.

Exclusive territories may be *permitted* when:

- A company is small or is a newcomer in the market.
- A producer establishes a corporate vertical marketing system and retains ownership of the product until it reaches the final buyer.
- A producer uses independent middlemen to distribute the product under consignment, in which a middleman does not pay the supplier until after the merchandise is sold.

As you can see, these conditions certainly are subject to interpretation. Thus it is not uncommon for conflicts to be settled by the courts.

• Summary

The role of distribution is getting a product to its target market. A distribution channel carries out this assignment, with middlemen performing some tasks. A middleman is a business firm that renders services directly related to the purchase and/or sale of a product as it flows from producer to consumer. Middlemen can be eliminated from a channel, but some organization or individual still has to carry out their essential functions.

A distribution channel is the set of people and firms involved in the flow of title to a product as it moves from producer to ultimate consumer or business user. A channel includes producer, final customer, and any middlemen that participate in the process.

Designing a channel of distribution for a product occurs through a sequence of four decisions: (1) delineating the role of distribution within the marketing mix; (2) selecting the proper type of distribution channel; (3) determining the appropriate intensity of distribution; and (4) choosing specific channel members.

A variety of channels are used to distribute consumer goods, business goods, and services. Firms often employ multiple channels to achieve broad market coverage, although this strategy can alienate some middlemen. Because of deficiencies in conventional channels, vertical marketing systems have become widespread in distribution. There are three forms of vertical marketing systems: corporate, contractual, and administered.

Numerous factors need to be considered in selecting a distribution channel. The primary consideration is the nature of the target market. Others relate to the product, the middlemen, and the company itself.

Distribution intensity refers to the number of middlemen a producer uses at the wholesale and retail levels in a particular territory. It ranges from intensive to selective to exclusive. To increase distribution intensity, some channel members have set up Internet sites that sell products to current and/or new customers.

Firms that distribute goods and services sometimes clash. There are two types of conflict: horizontal (between firms at the same level of distribution) and vertical (between firms at different levels of the same channel). Scrambled merchandising is a prime cause of horizontal conflict. Vertical conflict typically pits producer against wholesaler or retailer. Manufacturers' attempts to bypass middlemen, perhaps through online selling, are a prime cause of vertical conflict.

Channel members frequently strive for some control over one another. Depending on the circumstances, either producers or middlemen can achieve the dominant position in a channel. The firms comprising a particular channel are served best if they all view their channel as a partnership requiring coordination of distribution activities. Partnerships in channels are part of a significant trend called relationship marketing.

Attempts to control distribution may be subject to legal constraints. In fact, some practices, such as exclusive dealing and tying contracts, may be ruled illegal.

More about **Avon**

Avon Products, Inc., has moved aggressively into many countries beyond the U.S. In fact, 60% of Avon's sales are generated outside the U.S.

The cosmetics maker markets its products through 2.8 million representatives in 135 different countries. The Asia-Pacific region is especially important to Avon, accounting for 16% of its total sales. The company is also intent on making Avon a global brand. Toward that end, the cosmetics marketer launched a $100 million advertising campaign to promote the brand. The campaign's theme was "Let's Talk." The total budget was split about 50-50 between the U.S. and foreign markets.

In the U.S., Avon is trying channels besides independent sales reps. In China, it must use other channels because of a 1998 ban on direct selling in that country. The edict of China's State Council forbidding all forms of direct selling threatens the interests of a number of U.S. firms, including Avon.

Several factors prompted the ban on direct selling. Ever since the protests that ignited riots in Tiananmen Square in Beijing in 1989, the Chinese government has been wary of large-scale sales meetings, viewing them as potentially inflammatory. In addition, the government takes a dim view of civil servants working for companies such as Avon in order to supplement their incomes.

U.S. Trade Representative Charlene Barshefsky pointed out that American firms should not be penalized for successful operations in China. Avon alone has invested more than $90 million in its Chinese operations. With at least 20 million Chinese citizens engaged in direct selling, partly as a result of the country's rising unemployment rate, it may be difficult for the government to enforce the ban. Nevertheless, Avon decided it had no choice but to halt direct selling in China, which included severing ties with its many sales reps. The cosmetics firm has resorted to another channel, opening company-opened retail outlets in China and agreeing to supply Chinese retail stores with its brand of products.[56]

1. What other channels should Avon consider using in China?

2. In what other countries, if any, might Avon not be able to rely on direct selling?

Key Terms and Concepts

Middleman (396)
Merchant middleman (397)
Agent middleman (397)
Disintermediation (397)
Distribution channel (398)
Direct distribution (401)
Indirect distribution (401)
Multiple distribution channels (404)
Vertical marketing system (VMS) (405)

Corporate vertical marketing system (405)
Contractual vertical marketing system (406)
Administered vertical marketing system (406)
Intensity of distribution (410)
Intensive distribution (411)
Selective distribution (412)
Exclusive distribution (412)
Channel conflict (413)

Horizontal conflict (413)
Scrambled merchandising (414)
Vertical conflict (414)
Slotting fee (416)
Channel control (417)
Channel power (417)
Exclusive dealing (419)
Tying contract (419)
Refusal to deal (419)
Exclusive-territory policy (420)

Questions and Problems

1. Which of the following institutions are middlemen? Explain.
   a. Girl Scout cookie seller
   b. Electrical wholesaler
   c. Real estate broker
   d. Railroad
   e. Advertising agency
   f. Grocery store
   g. Stockbroker
   h. Bank

2. Which of the channels illustrated in Figure 14.3 is most apt to be used for each of the following products? Defend your choice in each case.
   a. Fire insurance
   b. Single-family residences
   c. Farm hay balers
   d. Washing machines
   e. Hair spray
   f. An ocean cruise

3. "The great majority of business sales are made directly from producer to business user." Explain why this occurs, first in terms of the nature of the market, and then in terms of the product.

4. "You can eliminate middlemen, but you cannot eliminate essential distribution activities." Discuss how this statement is supported or refuted by vertical marketing systems.

5. A small manufacturer of fishing lures is faced with the problem of selecting its channel of distribution. What reasonable alternatives does it have? Consider particularly the nature of its product and the nature of its market.

6. Is a policy of intensive distribution consistent with consumer buying habits for convenience goods? For shopping goods? Is intensive distribution normally used in the marketing of any type of business goods?

7. From a producer's viewpoint, what are the competitive advantages of exclusive distribution?

8. A manufacturer of a well-known brand of men's clothing has been selling directly to one dealer in a southern city for many years. For some time the market has been large enough to support two retailers very profitably. Yet the present dealer objects strongly when the manufacturer suggests adding another outlet. What alternatives does the manufacturer have in this situation? What course of action would you recommend?

9. "Manufacturers should always strive to select the lowest-cost channel of distribution." Do you agree? Should they always try to use the middlemen with the lowest operating costs? Why or why not?

10. A new company is designing and making stylish—in fact, very trendy—women's clothing. Should the firm establish a website to sell its products?

Hands-On Marketing

1. Arrange an interview with either the owner or a top-level manager of a small manufacturing firm. Inquire about (a) the distribution channel(s) the company uses for its primary product, (b) the factors that were the greatest influences in arriving at the channel(s), (c) whether the company would prefer some other channel, and (d) the firm's strategy regarding online selling.

2. Visit with either a supermarket manager or a buyer for a supermarket chain to learn more about slotting fees and any other charges they levy on manufacturers. Inquire whether such charges have led to channel conflict and how the supermarket chain is handling this type of situation. Also ask whether any grocery products manufacturers refuse to pay slotting fees and whether the chain ever waives the fees.

Retailing

"To serve the pet owners' market, PETsMART is pioneering a new model of online retailing . . . to combine the advantages of an Internet business and a retailer with physical stores."

Can **PETsMART** Sniff Retail Success on the Internet?

In just a few years, the Internet has become a viable—in fact, a desirable—option in the world of retailing. It has changed the buying habits of millions of consumers and stimulated the creation of thousands of "clicks-and-modem" stores. As a result, many traditional "bricks-and-mortar" retailers are rethinking the way they do business.

Almost anything can be purchased online. The leading product categories in cyberspace include computer hardware and software (which had estimated Internet sales exceeding $3 billion in 1999), and consumer electronics, books, and apparel (each just over $1 billion). Since early 1999, the competition has been heating up in pet supplies as well. The attractions of this product category are compelling: About 60% of American homes have pets. Pet owners tend to buy the same brands and desire convenience. And, in the U.S. alone, annual expenditures on pet supplies are at least $23 *billion*. Only $300 million of this amount was spent online in 1999, but that figure is projected to rise to $2.5 billion in just three years.

To serve the pet owners' market, PETsMART is pioneering a new model of online retailing. Labeled a "clicks-and-mortar" enterprise, this new model seeks to combine the advantages of an Internet business and a retailer with physical stores. PETsMART.com began as PetJungle.com, which was started by idealab!, an Internet incubator that has launched a variety of online ventures such as eToys.

In May 1999, PETsMART Inc., a chain with about 500 pet stores, announced it would invest $16 million in PetJungle, and the online retailer's name was changed to PETsMART.com. The retail chain had previously experimented with its own website, but thought it needed to acquire Internet expertise. PETsMART's CEO, Phil Francis, explained the joint venture, "There's been a lot of talk about brick-and-mortar companies being unable to cope with the dot-coms. But we think the old paradigm has been supplanted by a new one

that's better—a virtual company and a big-box retailer teaming up to attack a category."

Pet supplies quickly became a popular product category in cyberspace. At least a dozen companies launched new sites in 1999. PETsMART.com's primary competitors are the similarly named Pets.com and Petopia.com. Pets.com is partially funded by Amazon.com. Petopia is another clicks-and-mortar joint venture, with the physical presence being provided by Petco, the nation's #2 retailer of pet products. Other entrants in this field include Petstore.com, allpets.com, and the oldest pet site, acmepet.com.

Launched in July 1999, PETsMART.com is an integral part of PETsMART's strategy to sell its products through three different channels—in stores, by catalog, and on the Web. The company "cross-promotes" the three channels and has vowed to overcome the inevitable conflicts that arise among them. "We've explained that there will be promotions for the stores on the Web site," says Francis. "By showing some reciprocity, we've overcome the conflicts before they started."

PETsMART's existing base of 575 retail stores and its established catalog division give PETsMART.com an edge in brand awareness on the Web. These units also provide PETsMART.com with merchandise buying and pricing expertise as well as order-fulfillment and warehousing systems. Distribution, in particular, is a significant concern for pet supply e-tailers. After all, how efficient is shipping a 40-pound bag of dog food? Many online pet stores are charging negligible amounts for shipping and handling, raising questions about whether they will be able to turn a profit.

PETsMART.com appears to be off to a good start. But it remains to be seen whether the clicks-and-mortar venture will succeed over the long run in the dog-eat-dog world of online retailing.[1]

What will be the keys to long-term success for PETsMART.com and other online pet supply retailers?

www.petsmart.com

www.pets.com

www.petco.com

Distribution of consumer products begins with the producer and ends with the ultimate consumer. Between the two, there is usually at least one middleman—a retailer. The many types of retailing institutions and their marketing activities are the subjects of this chapter.

You have abundant experience with retailing—as a consumer. And perhaps you also have worked in retailing. This chapter builds on that experience and provides insights about retail markets, different types of retailers, and key strategies and trends in retailing, notably the growing volume of retail sales through the Internet. After studying this chapter, you should be able to explain:

chapter goals

- The nature of retailing.
- What a retailer is.
- Types of retailers classified by form of ownership.
- Types of retailers classified by marketing strategies.
- Forms of nonstore retailing, including online sales to final consumers.
- Trends in retailing.

Nature and Importance of Retailing

For every successful large retailer like Publix supermarkets, Crate & Barrel stores, and of course Wal-Mart, thousands of tiny retailers serve consumers in very small areas. Despite their differences, all have two common features: They link producers and ultimate consumers, and they perform valuable services for both. In all likelihood, all of these firms are retailers, but not all of their activities may qualify as retailing. Let's see how that can be.

Retailing and Retailers

If a Winn-Dixie supermarket sells floor wax to a gift shop operator to polish the shop's floor, is this a retail sale? Can a wholesaler or manufacturer engage in retailing? When a service such as Aamco transmission repair is sold to an ultimate consumer, is this retailing? Obviously, we need to define some terms, particularly *retailing* and *retailer*, to answer these questions and to avoid misunderstandings later.

Retailing (or *retail trade*) consists of the sale, and all activities directly related to the sale, of goods and services to ultimate consumers for personal, nonbusiness use. Although most retailing occurs through retail stores, it may be done by any institution. A Tupperware rep selling plastic containers at lunchtime meetings at a factory is engaged in retailing, as is a farmer selling vegetables at a roadside stand.

Any firm—manufacturer, wholesaler, or retailer—that sells something to ultimate consumers for their nonbusiness use is making a retail sale. This is true regardless of *how* the product is sold (in person, online, or by telephone, mail, or vending machine) or *where* it is sold (in a store, at the consumer's home, or on the Internet). However, a firm engaged *primarily* in retailing is called a **retailer**. In this chapter we will concentrate on retailers rather than on other types of businesses that make only occasional retail sales.

In the past couple of years, it has become common to differentiate *bricks-and-mortar* retailers (that is, those with physical stores) from *clicks-and-modem* retailers (those that operate online). The latter type, also referred to as *e-tailers*, is covered at various places in the chapter. Further, although this chapter focuses primarily on retailers of *goods*, much of what is said—particularly regarding marketing strategies—also applies to retailers of *services* (as covered in Chapter 11).

Economic Justification for Retailing

As discussed in Chapter 14, all middlemen basically serve as purchasing agents for their customers and as sales specialists for their suppliers. To carry out these roles, retailers perform many activities, including anticipating customers' wants, developing assortments of products, acquiring market information, and financing.

It is relatively easy to become a retailer. No large investment in production equipment is required, merchandise can often be purchased on credit, and store space can be leased with no "down payment" or a simple website can be set up at relatively little cost. Considering these factors, perhaps it's not surprising that there are just over 1.1 million retail firms in the U.S., operating a total of about 1.5 million establishments.[2] This large number of companies, many of which are trying to serve and satisfy the same market segments, results in fierce competition and better values for shoppers.

To enter retailing is easy; to fail is even easier! To survive in retailing, a firm must do a satisfactory job in its primary role—catering to consumers. Stanley Marcus, the former chairman of Neiman Marcus, described a successful retailer as "a merchant who sells goods that won't come back to customers who will."[3] Of course, a retail firm also must fulfill its other role—serving producers and wholesalers. This dual role is both the justification for retailing and the key to success in retailing.

www.neimanmarcus.com

Size of Market and Firms

Retail sales in 1997 (the latest year for which this statistic is available) totaled almost $2.5 *trillion* (see Figure 15.1). The increase in total sales volume has been tremendous—nearly sixfold from the early 1970s to the late 1990s. Even adjusting for the rise in prices, total retail sales and per-capita retail sales have gone up considerably.

There is a high degree of concentration in retailing. As depicted in Figure 15.2, three-quarters of retail firms have fewer than 10 employees. These small merchants ring up about one-eighth of all sales to consumers. Conversely, a small number of companies account for a large share of retail trade. Just 0.3% of all retailers had at least 500 employees, but these firms accounted for about 45% of total retail sales.

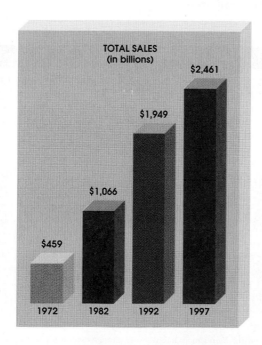

Figure 15.1

Total retail trade in the United States.

Retail sales have increased steadily over the past 25 years.

Note: The *Economic Census* is conducted every five years; hence, this is the latest available figure.

Sources: 1997 *Economic Census*, Retail Trade-Geographic Area Series, U.S. Census Bureau, Washington, DC, 2000, p. United States 7; and corresponding censuses from prior years. The 1997 statistic was found on the U.S. Census Bureau website: <www.census.gov/prod/ec97/97r44-US.pdf>.

TOTAL SALES
(in billions)

- $459 — 1972
- $1,066 — 1982
- $1,949 — 1992
- $2,461 — 1997

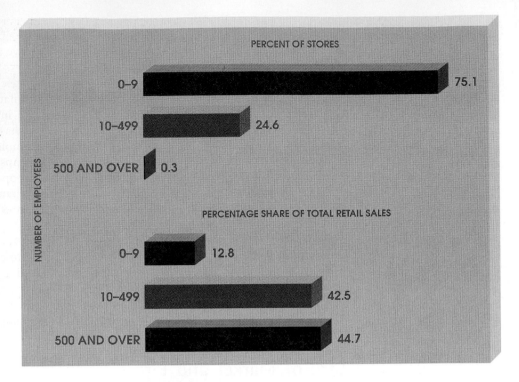

Figure 15.2

Distribution of retail stores and sales by number of employees.

Source: Statistical Abstract of the United States: 1999, 119th edition, U.S. Bureau of the Census, Washington, DC, 1999, p. 556.

Figure 15.2 does not tell the full story of large-scale retailing because it represents a tabulation of individual *store* sales and not *company* sales volume. A single company may own many stores, as in the case of chains. When retail sales are analyzed by companies, the high degree of concentration becomes even more evident. As shown in Table 15.1, the combined sales of the 10 largest retailers make up about 15% of total retail trade.

Stores of different sizes face distinct challenges and opportunities. Buying, promotion, staffing, and expense control are influenced significantly by whether a store's sales volume is large or small. Size of a retail business creates certain advantages and disadvantages, several of which are described in Table 15.2. Considering these factors, large stores ordinarily—but not always—have a competitive advantage over small stores.

Table 15.1   Total Sales of 10 Largest Retailers Based in the United States

Retailer	1998 sales (billions)	% change in sales, 1997–1998	1998 net profit as % of sales
1. Wal-Mart	$137.6	+16.7	3.2
2. Sears, Roebuck	41.3	+0.1	2.5
3. Kmart	33.7	+4.6	1.5
4. Dayton Hudson	31.0	+11.5	3.0
5. J.C. Penney	30.7	+0.4	1.9
6. Home Depot	30.2	+25.1	5.3
7. Kroger	28.2	+6.2	1.5
8. Safeway	24.5	+8.9	3.3
9. Costco	24.3	+11.0	1.9
10. Amercian Stores	19.9	+3.8	1.2
Total sales volume	401.4		
Average for top 10 firms		+8.8	2.4

Notes: Dayton Hudson is now named Target. In some cases, total sales may include non-retail revenues.

Sources: "American Express Top Retailers," as presented on the *Stores* magazine website: <http://www.stores.org/eng/archives/1999top100_1.html>.

Table 15.2 Competitive Positions of Large and Small Retailers

Selected Bases for Evaluation	Who Has the Advantage?
Division of labor and specialization of management	Large-scale retailers—their biggest advantage.
Flexibility of operations—merchandise selection, services offered, store design, reflection of owner's personality	Small retailers—their biggest advantage.
Buying power	Large retailers buy in bigger quantities and thus get lower wholesale prices.
Access to desirable merchandise	Large retailers promise suppliers access to large numbers of customers, whereas a single small retailer may be viewed as insignificant.
Development and promotion of retailer's own brand	Large retailers.
Efficient use of advertising, especially in city-wide media	Large retailers' markets match better with media circulation.
Ability to provide top-quality personal service	Small retailers, if owners pay personal attention to customers and also to selecting and supervising sales staff.
Opportunity to experiment with new products and selling methods	Large retailers can better afford the risks.
Financial strength	Large retailers have resources to gain some of the advantages noted above (such as private brands and experimentation).
Public image	Small retailers enjoy public support and sympathy. However, the public often votes with its wallet by shopping at big stores.

Small retailers face a variety of difficulties, and many fail. The strong economy during the second half of the 1990s helped small merchants hold their own, however. In fact, the number of retail failures in 1998 was one-sixth lower than the prior year and just below the level at the start of the decade.[4]

How do small retailers succeed? They understand their target markets very well. Then, in seeking to satisfy their consumers, they need to differentiate themselves from large retailers.[5] Here are two possible avenues not just to survival but to success:

- Many consumers seek benefits that small stores often provide better than large stores. For instance, some people seek high levels of shopping convenience. Small outlets located near residential areas offer such convenience. Other consumers desire abundant personal service. A small store's highly motivated owner-manager and customer-oriented sales staff may surpass a large store on this important shopping dimension.

- Numerous small retailers have formed or joined contractual vertical marketing systems, as explained in Chapter 14. These entities—called retailer cooperatives, voluntary chains, or franchise systems—give members some of the advantages of large stores, such as specialized management, buying power, and a well-known name.

Operating Expenses and Profits

Total operating expenses for retailers average 28% of retail sales. In comparison, wholesaling expenses run about 11% of *wholesale* sales or 8% of *retail* sales.[6] Thus, roughly speaking, retailing costs are about 2½ times the costs of wholesaling when both are stated as a percentage of the sales of the specific type of middleman.

Higher retailing costs are the result of dealing directly with ultimate consumers—answering their questions, showing them different products, and so on. Compared to wholesale customers, ultimate consumers typically expect more convenient locations with nicer decor, both of which drive up retailers' costs. Also, relative to wholesalers, retailers typically have lower total sales and lower rates of merchandise turnover. Retailers buy smaller quantities of merchandise, again compared to wholesalers, so their overhead costs are spread over a smaller base of operations. Furthermore, retail sales people often cannot be used efficiently because customers do not come into stores at a steady rate.

Retailers' costs and profits vary depending on their type of operation and major product line. Assorted kinds of retailers earn wide-ranging gross margins—the difference between net sales and cost of goods sold. For instance, gross margins for auto dealers and gasoline service stations are in the vicinity of 15%, whereas margins for retailers of clothing, shoes, and jewelry are around 40%.

Healthy gross margins do not necessarily translate into the highest levels of net profits. Some retailers have large gross margins but incur heavy operating expenses, resulting in meager profits. Conversely, other retailers with small gross margins are able to serve customers well with low operating expenses, thereby winding up with substantial net profits. For example, e-tailers have substituted new technology for physical stores and, to a large extent, for retail sales people. As a result, online stores should have lower operating expenses compared to traditional stores, if they can reach a point where they do not have to advertise so heavily in order to attract customers.

Just as retail firms' gross margins range widely, so do their net profits. Supermarkets typically earn a profit of less than 1% of sales, compared to as much as 10% for some specialized retailers. In general, retailers' net profits average about 3% of sales. This modest figure may surprise people who suspect that retailers make enormous profits.

Physical Facilities

Later in this chapter we will classify retailers according to their product assortments, price strategies, and promotional methods. Here, we'll look at **physical facilities,** which represent the distribution element of a retailer's marketing mix.

Some firms engage in *nonstore* retailing—by selling online or through catalogs or door to door, for example—but many more firms rely on retail *stores*. Firms that operate retail stores must consider four aspects of physical facilities:

- *Location.* It is frequently stated that there are three keys to success in retailing: location, location, and location! Although overstated, this axiom does suggest the importance that retailers attach to location. Thus a store's site should be the first decision made about facilities. Considerations such as surrounding population, traffic, and cost determine where a store should be located.
- *Size.* This factor means the total square footage of the physical store, not the magnitude of the firm operating the store. These are much different factors. A firm may be quite large with respect to total sales, but each of its outlets may be only several thousand square feet in size. Even though a 7-Eleven store is quite small, the nearly 20,000 of them together ring up over $6 billion in annual sales.[7]
- *Design.* This factor refers to a store's appearance, both exterior and interior.
- *Layout.* The amount of space allocated to various product lines, specific locations of products, and a floor plan of display tables and racks comprise the store's layout.

 www.7-eleven.com

As would be expected, the location, size, design, and layout of retail stores are based on where consumers live and how they like to go about their shopping. Consequently, the bulk of retail sales occur in urban, rather than rural, areas. And suburban shopping areas have become more and more popular, whereas many downtown areas have declined.

Shopping centers are the predominant type of retail location in most suburban areas. A **shopping center** consists of a planned grouping of retail stores that lease space in a structure that is typically owned by a single organization. Shopping centers can be classified by such attributes as size, market served, and types of tenants. In order of increasing size, there is the *convenience center, neighborhood center,* and *community center.*

A new kind, a *power center*, grew rapidly in the early 1990s. A power center can be of various sizes, but its distinguishing attribute is a tenant mix that includes several large, popular limited-line stores that stress value (such as Circuit City, Home Depot, and Toys "R" Us), but not a department store anchor. The rise of power centers subsided in the late 1990s because of saturation in some markets.[8]

The largest kind of shopping center, a *regional center*, is anchored by one or more department stores and complemented by many smaller retail outlets. Typically enclosed, climate-controlled malls, many regional shopping centers are gigantic. The biggest, Mall of America in suburban Minneapolis, opened in 1992. Under one roof, it combines about 400 retail stores with a theme park, miniature golf course, two lakes, and more than a dozen movie theaters—all adjacent to 17,000 free parking spaces. Surprising many skeptics, this "megamall" draws over 40 million shoppers, including many tourists, annually. Even more important, most retailers with stores there are generating satisfactory levels of sales. Plans are underway to double the size of Mall of America![9]

www.mallofamerica.com

Starting in the mid-1950s, regional centers became the hub of shopping and social activities in many communities. Eventually, though, many shoppers grew too time conscious to spend much time shopping or socializing at a huge mall. Between 1980 and 1998, the average amount of time consumers spent in malls on a monthly basis dropped from 12 hours to under 4 hours. Some observers are pessimistic about the future of regional centers, especially those that were constructed several decades ago. One real estate executive went so far as to predict that the number of malls in the U.S. would drop from a peak of 2,000 in the mid-1990s to 1,200 prior to 2010.[10]

With such forecasts, it's not surprising that relatively few regional centers were built in the late 1990s. Instead, many enclosed malls are being renovated and modernized to enhance their appeal to shoppers. Some are even locating competitors (such as Gap Kids, Gymboree, and other children's clothing stores) close to each other to make shopping more convenient and efficient for time-starved consumers. Often, entertainment is taking center stage in today's malls, both renovated and new ones. Another common approach among the limited number of new centers is a Main Street theme, which tries to evoke memories of historic downtown areas; some of these new centers are open-air, rather than enclosed.[11]

Some retailers, such as Sterling Optical, are locating new outlets in the heart of cities that many merchants abandoned years ago. Tax breaks offered by government and/or by falling crime rates in the urban core may influence these decisions. The overriding consideration should be whether or not the outlet can be successful in an urban, rather than the more popular suburban, location.

The growth of suburban shopping, especially in regional malls, led to vacant stores and decreased retail sales in many urban areas. Now some retail firms see opportunities in the urban core. For example, Sterling Optical and Athlete's Foot are both opening nonmall locations in urban neighborhoods. Some cities have

www.sterlingoptical.com

worked to revitalize their downtown shopping districts. Enclosed shopping centers featuring distinctive designs—including Water Tower Place in Chicago—and new open-air projects—including the Denver Pavilions (in Colorado) and the Block at Orange (in California)—are successful in some downtown areas.[12]

Wherever they are located, most retail stores have been getting larger and larger—perhaps because the overhead of operating a store doesn't vary much based on size. Many outlets such as Sports Authority, Lowe's, and Best Buy are called "big boxes," alluding to their enormous sizes as well as their rather plain designs. Because some consumers do not want to devote the necessary time and energy to shop at very large stores, a few chains are experimenting with smaller formats. Home Depot is trying a new "hardware convenience store," called Villager Hardware, about one-third the size of the chain's normal 100,000-square-foot outlet. And Wal-Mart is looking at Neighborhood Markets, each about 40,000-square-feet, or one-fifth the size of the chain's supercenters.[13]

Classification of Retailers

To understand how retailers serve both suppliers and customers, we will classify retailers on two bases: form of ownership and marketing strategies. Any retail firm can be classified according to both bases. For example, Sears is a corporate chain of department stores with broad, relatively deep assortments, moderate prices, and levels of personal service that vary across departments. In contrast, a neighborhood paint store operates as an independent limited-line store that has narrow, relatively deep assortments, tries to avoid severe price competition, and provides extensive personal service.

Retailers Classified by Form of Ownership

The major forms of ownership in retailing are corporate chain, independent, and contractual vertical marketing system (VMS). The VMS category includes several different types.

Corporate Chains

A **corporate chain** is an organization of two or more centrally owned and centrally managed stores that generally handle the same lines of products. Three factors differentiate a chain from an independent store and the contractual form of VMS:

- Technically, two or more stores constitute a chain. Many small merchants that open several stores in shopping centers and newly populated areas do not think of themselves as chains, however. Perhaps with that in mind, the U.S. Census Bureau considers 11 stores to be the minimum size for a chain.

- A corporate chain has central ownership; as we'll soon see, a contractual VMS does not.

- Because of centralized management, individual units in a chain typically have little autonomy. Strategic decisions are made at headquarters, and operations typically are standardized for all the units in a chain. Standardization assures consistency, but it often results in inflexibility. And that means a chain sometimes cannot adjust rapidly to local market conditions.

Corporate chains continue to increase their share of total retail trade. During a recent 15-year period, the proportion of retail sales made by chains with 11 or more stores rose from 37% to 40%. In the same period, chains grabbed a larger share of sales in all major areas of retail trade except variety stores and eating places.[14]

Chains are more common in some kinds of retailing than in others. Chains dominate the department store business, accounting for 99% of sales for this type of retailer. But chains are not very significant among auto and home supply stores or eating places, generating just 36% and 24% of sales, respectively.[15] Essentially, chains are large-scale retailing institutions. As such, they possess the comparative strengths and weaknesses outlined in Table 15.2.

Independent Stores

An **independent retailer** is a company with a single store that is not affiliated with a contractual vertical marketing system. Most retailers are independents, and most independents are quite small. Independents usually have the characteristics of small retailers presented in Table 15.2.

Independent retailers typically are viewed as having higher prices than chain stores. However, because of differences in merchandise and services, it is difficult to compare the prices of chains and independents directly. For instance, chains often have their own private brands that are not sold by independents. Also, independents and chain stores frequently provide customers with different levels—and perhaps quality—of services. Many customers are willing to pay extra for services they consider valuable, such as credit, delivery, alterations, installation, a liberal return policy, and friendly, knowledgeable personal service.

Contractual Vertical Marketing Systems

In a **contractual vertical marketing system**, independently owned firms join together under a contract specifying how they will operate. The three types of contractual VMS are discussed below.

Retailer Cooperatives and Voluntary Chains

The main difference between these two types of systems is who organizes them. A **retailer cooperative** is formed by a group of small retailers that agree to establish and operate a wholesale warehouse. In contrast, a **voluntary chain** is sponsored by a wholesaler that enters into a contract with interested retailers.

Historically these two forms of contractual VMS have been organized for defensive reasons—to enable independent retailers to compete effectively with large, strong chains. They do this by providing their retail members with volume buying power and management assistance in store layout, employee and management training programs, promotion, accounting, and inventory control systems.

Retailer cooperatives are declining, but still have strong representatives in groceries (Certified Grocers) and hardware (True Value). Voluntary chains are prevalent in the grocery field (IGA, Supervalu); they are also found in hardware (Ace) and auto supplies (Western Auto) stores.

www.acehardware.com

Franchise Systems

Franchising involves a continuing relationship in which a parent company provides management assistance and the right to use its trademark in return for payments from the owner of the individual business unit. The parent company is called a *franchisor,* whereas the owner of the unit is called a *franchisee.* The combination of franchisor and franchisees comprises a *franchise system.*

This type of contractual VMS is growing steadily, generating $1 *trillion* in annual sales and accounting for over one-third of all retail sales in the U.S. According to the International Franchise Association, roughly 600,000 units are affiliated with about 2,500 franchise systems.[16]

There are two kinds of franchising:

- **Product and trade name franchising.** Historically the dominant kind, product and trade name franchising is prevalent in the automobile (Ford, Honda) and petroleum (Chevron, Texaco) industries. It is a distribution agreement under which a supplier authorizes a dealer to sell a product line, using the parent company's trade name for promotional purposes. The franchisee agrees to buy from the franchisor and also to abide by specified policies. The focus in product and trade name franchising is on *what is sold*.

- **Business format franchising.** Much of franchising's growth and publicity over the past three decades has involved the business format kind (used by firms such as Kentucky Fried Chicken, Midas, and H&R Block). This kind of franchising covers an entire method (or format) for operating a business. A successful retail business sells the right to operate the same business in another geographic area. The franchisee expects to receive from the parent company a proven method of operating a business; in return, the franchisor receives from each business owner payments and also conformance to policies and standards. The focus here is on *how the business is run*.

www.littleprofessor.com

In business format franchising, the franchisor may be a manufacturer that provides franchisees with merchandise. However, typically this is not the case. For example, Little Professor Book Centers, Inc., does not sell books to its franchised stores; rather, the stores buy their inventory from wholesalers. The franchisor is supposed to provide management assistance, especially marketing expertise, to franchisees.

Selling franchises can be attractive to a successful retail business that wants to expand. Among the advantages:

- Rapid expansion is expedited, because franchisees provide capital when they purchase franchises. Ambitious, successful retailers and service firms, such as Berlitz in language training, are employing franchising as an offensive tool.
- Because they have an investment at risk, franchisees typically are highly motivated to work hard and adhere to the parent company's proven format.

Buying a franchise can offer protection to a prospective new retail store or to an independent store that faces stiff competition from chains. Among the benefits:

- Franchisees can use the parent company's well-known trade name, which should help attract customers. Nestlé's franchised coffee bars should have good name recognition.
- Various forms of management assistance are provided to franchisees prior to as well as after opening the store, including site-selection and store-layout guidance, technical and management training, promotional programs, and inventory control systems.

Franchising is not without problems. Some franchises are based on poor products or unsound business practices and consequently fail. Further, a number of franchisees criticize franchisors for practices such as the following: (1) enticing prospective franchisees by projecting unrealistically high revenues or unrealistically low operating costs, (2) not providing franchisees with the promised levels of business support, (3) locating too many of the company's outlets in the same market, or (4) unjustifiably terminating or not renewing the franchise agreement. Franchisors have their own complaints, notably that some franchisees deviate from the system's policies and practices.

Despite some challenges, continued growth in franchising is expected. For one thing, 92% of existing franchisees consider themselves successful, a statistic that is widely publicized by franchisors. (Of course, this statistic ignores franchisees that fail.) Further, some franchisors are working more closely with their franchisees. Burger King, for instance, is allowing its franchisees to request an impact study before a new unit is opened nearby.[17]

Numerous products, especially services, lend themselves to franchising. Growth areas in franchising often coincide with demographic and social trends. At this time, therefore, services designed to aid either an aging population or time-starved

Would you buy a retail franchise?

Many products reach consumer markets through franchised retail outlets. Consider these examples:

Product Category	Sample Franchises
Fast food and other prepared food	McDonald's, Domino's, Subway, Popeyes
Automotive repairs	Midas, Maaco, Mr. Transmission
Clothing	T-Shirts Plus, Just Pants, Fashions under $10, The Athlete's Foot
Hair care	Fantastic Sams, Supercuts
Groceries and other food products	7-Eleven, Candy Bouquet, Gloria Jean's Gourmet Coffees
Education Programs	Sylvan Learning Center, Computertots
Home decorating products	Wallpapers to Go, Decorating Den, Stained Glass Overlay

The total cost of buying a franchise varies greatly. As the following samples illustrate, some are inexpensive and others are steep. Of course, total start-up costs for "bricks-and-mortar" enterprises can vary widely depending upon whether or not the franchisee owns the physical facility.

Brand Name	Type of Franchise	Approximate Up-Front Franchise Fee	Approximate Total Start-Up Costs
Mr. Goodcents	Sandwiches and pastas	$12,500	$127,000
Hardee's	Fast-food restaurant	$35,000	$912,000
Mr. Rooter	Sewer and drain cleaning	$19,500	$80,000
Rainbow International	Carpet dyeing and cleaning	$23,400	$65,000

Most, but certainly not all, franchise systems are successful. And, typically, franchisees work long hours weekly to build sales and contain expenses in order to earn a reasonable profit.

If you were going to open a retail business, would you do it as an independent or would you purchase a franchise?

Source: Estimated costs provided by Jeff Kolton, Frandata Corp., Washington, DC.

individuals and families have potential as franchises. One such franchise is Take Home Instead, which provides companionship and assistance to senior citizens.[18]

Retailers Classified by Marketing Strategies

Whatever its form of ownership, a retailer must develop marketing-mix strategies to succeed in its chosen target markets. In retailing, the marketing mix emphasizes product assortment, price, location, promotion, and customer services designed to aid in the sale of a product. They include credit, delivery, gift wrapping, product installation, merchandise returns, store hours, parking, and—very important—personal service.

We will now describe the major types of retail stores, paying particular attention to the following three elements of their marketing mixes:

- Breadth and depth of product assortment.
- Price level.
- Amount of customer services.

Table 15.3 classifies retail stores on the basis of these three elements.

Some types of retail stores, such as category-killer stores, are relatively new and have grown rapidly. Others, such as variety stores, are diminishing in importance. Still others, particularly department stores, are under competitive pressure to modify some strategies. We will see that certain retailers are similar to others because new or modified institutions have filled the "strategic gaps" that once separated different types of retail institutions.

Table 15.3 Retail Stores Classified by Key Marketing Strategies

Type of Store	Breadth and Depth of Assortment	Price Level	Amount of Customer Services
Department store	Very broad, deep	Avoids price competition	Wide array
Discount store	Broad, shallow	Emphasizes low prices	Relatively few
Limited-line store	Narrow, deep	Traditional types avoid price competition; new kinds emphasize low prices	Vary by type
Specialty store	Very narrow, deep	Avoids price competition	At least standard; extensive in some
Off-price retailer	Narrow, deep	Emphasizes low prices	Few
Category-killer store	Narrow, very deep	Emphasizes low prices	Few to moderate
Supermarket	Broad, deep	Some emphasize low prices; others avoid price competition	Few
Convenience store	Narrow, shallow	High prices	Few
Warehouse club	Very broad, very shallow	Emphasizes very low prices	Few (open only to members)

Department Stores

www.mayco.com

Long a mainstay of retailing in the U.S., a **department store** is a large-scale retailing institution that has a very broad and deep product assortment, tries not to compete on the basis of price, and provides a wide array of customer services. The combination of distinctive, appealing merchandise and numerous customer services, such as alterations, various credit plans, and bridal registry, is supposed to allow the stores to charge full (or nondiscounted) prices. Familiar department store names include Filene's, Dillard's, Foley's, Rich's, May, Marshall Field's, Sears, J.C. Penney, and Montgomery Ward.

Department stores face serious challenges.[19] Because of their prime (that is, busy but expensive) locations and abundant customer services, their operating expenses are considerably higher than most other retailers. Many producers' brands that used to be available exclusively through department stores are now widely distributed and are often available at discounted prices in other outlets or on the Internet. And the quality of personal service, especially knowledgeable sales help, has deteriorated in many department stores.

Intense horizontal competition also tests department stores. Other retail institutions—such as discount houses and "off-price" retailers—are aggressively trying to lure shoppers away from department stores by offering lower prices. To varying degrees, retail chains such as Target, Wal-Mart, Circuit City, and Home Depot vie with traditional department stores. The convenience of buying from catalogs or online represents still more competition. Overall, department stores' share of total retail trade has dropped about 5 percentage points in recent years.[20]

Striving to gain an advantage or at least remain competitive, many department stores have modified their target markets and/or elements of their marketing mixes. Some department store chains, for example, have dropped several lines of hard goods, including major appliances and sporting goods. Instead, they are placing greater emphasis on clothing, jewelry, cosmetics, and other product lines that appeal to more upscale shoppers. Most department stores are also trying to be more price competitive. They do not need to match the lower prices of rivals that lack extensive assortments and a variety of customer services. However, it's essential that they provide good value.

Is the department store a "dinosaur"? Probably not. Despite their problems, department stores as a group still account for a huge amount of retail sales. Moreover, there are recent success stories, perhaps none more prominent than Kohl's.

Similar in many respects to other department stores, Kohl's excels in the area of implementation. Computer-based inventory-control systems help Kohl's stores stock the right types and amounts of merchandise to satisfy customers and, at the same time, avoid the costs of excess inventories.[21]

Discount Stores

Discount retailing involves comparatively low prices as a major selling point combined with reduced costs of doing business. Several institutions, including off-price retailers and warehouse clubs, which are discussed later in this chapter, rely on discount retailing as their main marketing strategy.

The prime example of discount retailing is the **discount store**, a large-scale retailing institution that has a broad, shallow product assortment, low prices, and few customer services. A discount store normally carries a broad assortment of soft goods (particularly apparel) and hard goods (including popular brands of appliances and home furnishings) and advertises them heavily. Wal-Mart, Kmart, and Target are the largest discount store chains. In recent years, other discount chains with smaller stores, including Dollar General and Family Dollar, have been growing rapidly. Discount stores have had a major impact on retailing, prompting many merchants to lower their prices.

www.familydollar.com

The leading discount chains are also committing substantial resources to a much expanded discount store, called a **supercenter**. Basically, it is a combined discount store and grocery store. Wal-Mart's more than 700 supercenters are different from discount stores in several noteworthy ways: larger size, wider aisles, more attractive decor, broader assortment of merchandise, and added customer services. Demonstrating its commitment to this format, Wal-Mart set a goal of opening 150 supercenters annually for five years. A company executive even surmised that all or most regular Wal-Mart stores could become supercenters in the future.[22]

Limited-Line Stores

Much of the "action" in retailing in recent years has been in **limited-line stores**. This type of institution has a narrow but deep product assortment and selected customer services. Traditionally, limited-line stores selling products such as clothing, baked goods, and furniture sought to maintain full, or nondiscounted, prices.

Increasingly, retailers are expanding globally. Wal-Mart Stores took its first international step in 1991, opening a store in Mexico City. As described in the Global Perspective box, Wal-Mart moved aggressively into Europe during 1999. Considering that the world's largest chain operates in only about 10 countries, including China, it has substantial room for further expansion.

www.walmartstores.com

Is Wal-Mart receiving a warm welcome in Europe?

In becoming the world's largest retailer, Wal-Mart adhered to a basic formula—selling consumables (health and beauty aids, for example), soft goods (such as apparel), and hard goods (such as gas-powered outdoor grills) at sharply discounted prices. To keep prices down and still earn satisfactory profits, the huge chain pares operating expenses wherever possible and also negotiates hard—some say mercilessly—with suppliers to obtain low merchandise costs.

The Wal-Mart formula has been phenomenally effective in the U.S. However, the company has found it more difficult to attain success, much less blockbuster performance, in other countries. For example, Wal-Mart struggled to earn a profit for its first several years in South American countries, notably Brazil and Argentina.

In its latest, and boldest, international move, Wal-Mart entered Europe. The American chain started slowly, purchasing two German firms that operated about 100 *hypermarkets,* which are even larger than supercenters. But then in 1999, Wal-Mart acquired Asda Group, the third-largest chain of supermarkets in Great Britain. And the competition began in earnest!

Many European consumers are pleased about the broad collections of merchandise and low prices that can be found in Wal-Mart stores. But some consumers, executives, and government officials are not enthused about the newcomer. A common refrain is that small retailers will be forced out of business as a result of stepped-up price competition. Large British retailers have stated their intentions to match the new entrant's low prices. In Germany, the arrival of Wal-Mart precipitated a price war (*preiskrieg,* in German).

Wal-Mart's move into Europe also appears to be causing consolidation among the continent's retailers. For instance, Metro AG, the largest retail firm in Germany, acquired two small chains of hypermarkets in order to bolster its market position. And Carrefour bought another French merchant, Promodés, to create the largest European retail firm. Carrefour, which has 8,800 stores in 26 countries, intends to compete vigorously with Wal-Mart, not just in France and surrounding countries, but all around the globe.

Wal-Mart's ultimate success in Europe is far from assured. For starters, it must satisfy consumers with wide-ranging cultural backgrounds. The American chain also must clear hurdles in each country. For example, in Germany it must deal with trade unions and also with regulations prohibiting prices that are "too low." In addition, Wal-Mart must change consumers' buying habits and overcome some formidable competitors. Given its size and successful track record, the company founded by Sam Walton probably has a better chance for retail success than any other foreign invader. One outcome is assured: With Wal-Mart's arrival, retailing in Europe in the early 21st century will be much different than it was during the last part of the 20th century.

Sources: Ernest Beck and Emily Nelson, "As Wal-Mart Invades Europe, Rivals Rush to Match Its Formula," *The Wall Street Journal,* Oct. 6, 1999, pp. A1, A6; Carol Matlack, "En Garde, Wal-Mart," *Business Week,* Sept. 13, 1999, pp. 54–55; Jonathan Friedland and Louise Lee, "The Wal-Mart Way Sometimes Gets Lost in Translation Overseas," *The Wall Street Journal,* Oct. 8, 1997, pp. A1, A12.

As discussed in relation to off-price retailers and category-killer stores, new types of limited-line retailers have gained a foothold by emphasizing low prices.

The breadth of assortment varies somewhat across limited-line stores. A store may choose to concentrate on:

- Several related product lines (shoes, sportswear, and accessories).
- A single product line (shoes).
- Part of one product line (athletic footwear).

We identify limited-line stores by the name of the primary product line—furniture store, hardware store, or clothing store, for example. Some retailers such as grocery stores and drugstores that used to be limited-line stores now carry much broader assortments because of scrambled merchandising, a strategy we described in the preceding chapter.

Specialty Stores

A very narrow and deep product assortment, often concentrating on a specialized product line (baked goods) or even part of a specialized product line (cinnamon rolls), is offered to consumers by a **specialty store**. Examples of specialty stores are donut shops, furriers, athletic footwear stores, meat markets, and dress shops. (Specialty *stores* should not be confused with specialty *goods*. In a sense, specialty stores are misnamed, because they may carry not just specialty goods but any of the categories of consumer goods that were discussed in Chapter 8.)

Most specialty stores strive to maintain manufacturers' suggested prices, although they may offer their own store brands at lower prices. Typically, they provide at least standard customer services. Some specialty retailers, however, emphasize extensive customer services, particularly knowledgeable and friendly sales help. The prosperity of specialty stores depends on their ability to attract and then satisfy consumers who especially want deep assortments and extensive, top-quality services.

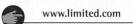
www.limited.com

Successful specialty store chains include Noodle Kidoodle (now part of Zany Brainy Inc.), which concentrates on learning toys that stimulate children's creativity and thinking; Batteries Plus, which specializes in various types of batteries; and The Limited, Inc., which consists of clothing chains such as Express and Limited Stores. Sunglass Hut International stuffs 1,000 different pairs of sunglasses into its tiny outlets, typically kiosks of about 300 square feet. When the chain faltered in the late 1990s, one part of the remedy was to complement the array of sunglasses with a collection of watches. The plan is to attract new customers and reduce the seasonality of demand.[23]

Forecasts for specialty stores are mixed. Those selling clothing in malls face a twofold challenge—apparel sales in general have been stagnant, and many malls are experiencing reduced shopper traffic. However, some theme-oriented specialty chains are prospering. For example, the Container Store is attracting numerous consumers who want to have "a place for everything."[24]

Off-Price Retailers

When some discount stores started to trade up during the 1980s, **off-price retailers** positioned themselves below discount outlets with lower prices on selected product lines. This type of institution features a narrow, deep product assortment,

To survive and—better yet—prosper, small retailers must satisfy consumers' unfilled needs. At Petroglyph Ceramic Lounge outlets in northern California, customers pay to sit and paint a piece of ceramic ware. The final step, kiln-firing, occurs right at the store. Petroglyph combines convenience (because customers do not have to take the time to work with the clay) and entertainment (because customers can enjoy the painting part of the process).

low prices, and few customer services. Off-price retailers are most common in the areas of apparel and footwear. Store names such as Ross Dress for Less and Payless ShoeSource are known to consumers in many locales.

To the extent possible, off-price retailers concentrate on well-known producers' brands. They often buy manufacturers' excess output, inventory remaining at the end of a fashion season, or irregular merchandise (called *seconds*) at lower-than-normal wholesale costs. In turn, their prices are much lower than prices for regular, in-season merchandise sold in other stores. Customers are attracted by the low prices and fairly current fashions.

Factory outlets are a special type of off-price retailer. They usually sell a single company's merchandise. This type of institution gives manufacturers another channel for their products—one over which they have complete control. Factory outlets used to stock mainly clearance items and seconds. Now they are likely to feature the same merchandise that can be found on other retailers' shelves, typically at lower prices than charged by other retailers. Many popular brands, such as Corning, Van Heusen, Bass, Royal Doulton, and Dansk, are featured in factory outlets.

Not everyone has been pleased by the emergence of factory outlets. In particular, other retailers do not like their suppliers competing directly with them. Therefore, to avoid aggravating retailers that distribute the same products, factory outlets typically locate together in a shopping center some distance from major malls and downtown shopping areas. From their inception in the early 1980s, outlet centers grew rapidly until the mid-1990s. At that time, some factory outlet shoppers started to have second thoughts when a growing number of retailers in regional shopping centers turned to value pricing.[25]

Category-Killer Stores

A phenomenon of the 1980s, a **category-killer store** has a narrow but very deep assortment, low prices, and few to moderate customer services. This type of store aims to capture a large portion of sales in a specific product category and, in so doing, "kill" the competition. Successful category killers include Ikea in home furnishings, Circuit City in consumer electronics, Home Depot and Lowe's in building supplies, Staples in office supplies, and Toys "R" Us. Other product areas with category killers are housewares, recorded music, and sporting goods.[26]

www.ikea.com

A category killer concentrates on a single product line or several closely related lines. What distinguishes a category killer is the combination of low prices *and* many different sizes, models, styles, and colors of the products. For example, a Borders or a Barnes & Noble bookstore ordinarily exceeds 30,000 square feet, about 10 times the size of the typical mall bookstore, and carries over 100,000 titles.[27] Category-killer stores are taking sales and customers away from long-standing retailers, especially specialty stores and department stores.

Recently, the format has been tried with other products. For example, CarMax and AutoNation established "megastores" featuring an inventory of around 1,000 not-too-used cars and trucks. However, neither chain was able to sustain its initial high sales or earn a consistent profit. Other category-killer chains have also stumbled. In sporting goods, Jumbo Sports wound up in bankruptcy, and Sports Authority has had strong sales but weak profits because of intense price competition from other types of retailers. One executive went so far as to predict that category killers "will be a diminishing force," largely as a result of the size and effectiveness of discount chains such as Wal-Mart. Still, the combination of deep assortments and low prices is appealing to many consumers. Thus the impact of this type of retail store is expected to expand.[28]

Supermarkets

As with *discount,* the word *supermarket* can be used to describe a method of retailing *and* a type of institution. As a method, **supermarket retailing** features several related product lines, a high degree of self-service, largely centralized checkout, and competitive prices. Supermarket retailing is used to sell various kinds of merchandise, including building materials, office products, and—of course—groceries.

The term *supermarket* usually refers to an institution in the grocery retailing field. In this context a **supermarket** is a retail institution that has a moderately broad, moderately deep product assortment spanning groceries and some nonfood lines, and offers relatively few customer services. Most supermarkets emphasize price. Some use price *offensively*, featuring low prices to attract customers. Others use price *defensively*, relying on leader pricing to avoid a price disadvantage. Having very thin gross margins, supermarkets need high levels of inventory turnover to achieve satisfactory returns on invested capital.

Stores using the supermarket *method* of retailing now dominate grocery retailing. Because these stores added more products and more selling space, some were called *superstores* and *combination stores*. Like the new *supercenters* discussed in the section on discount stores, superstores and combination stores are expanded versions of supermarkets.

For many years the supermarket has been under siege from competitors. A grocery shopper can choose among not only many brands of supermarkets (Publix, Safeway, Albertson's, and Kroger, to name several), but also various types of institutions (warehouse clubs, meat and fish markets, and convenience stores). Competition has intensified further as Wal-Mart and the other giant discount chains have made major moves into grocery retailing, opening supercenters and/or regular-size supermarkets.[29]

www.publix.com

Typically, supermarkets have reacted to competitive pressures in either of two ways: Some cut costs and stressed low prices, offering more private brands and generic products and few customer services. Others expanded their store sizes and assortments, adding more nonfood lines and groceries—ethnic foods, for example—attuned to a particular market area. They also added various service departments, including video rentals, delicatessens, financial institutions, and pharmacies. Loblaw dominates grocery retailing in Canada, with one differential advantage being wide-ranging supplementary services—to the point of putting a fitness club in one of its new supermarkets. Most supermarket chains are also trying to build customer loyalty through frequent-shopper programs.[30]

Convenience Stores

To satisfy increasing consumer demand for convenience, particularly in suburban areas, the **convenience store** emerged several decades ago. This retail institution concentrates on selected groceries and nonfoods (especially beverages, snacks, and cigarettes), typically has higher prices than other grocery stores, and offers few customer services. Gasoline, fast foods, and selected services, such as car washes and automated teller machines, can also be found in many convenience stores.

Its label reflects the institution's appeal and explains how its higher prices are justified. Convenience stores are typically located near residential areas and are open extended hours; in fact, some never close. Examples of convenience store chains are 7-Eleven (originally open from 7 a.m. to 11 p.m. but now open 24 hours daily in most locations), Circle K, and Convenient Food Mart.

Convenience stores compete to some extent with both supermarkets and fast-food restaurants. Furthermore, petroleum companies have modified many of their service stations by phasing out auto repairs and adding a convenience section. For instance, Arco has AM/PM Mini Marts and both Shell Oil and Texaco have Food Marts. In some cases, they are including fast-food counters in these outlets. As one example, Mobil Corp. is partnering with both Blimpie and Taco Bell.[31]

To boost their competitiveness, convenience stores are adjusting their marketing strategies. To do this (and to enlarge profit margins), the 7-Eleven chain is adding more fresh foods. A consulting firm recommends that convenience stores rely more on technology to better satisfy customers and boost sales. Under this scenario, when a consumer uses a credit card and starts pumping gas, coupons for beverages or other products the customer had purchased in the past would appear on a screen near the pump. Also, convenience stores could better live up to their names by accepting e-mails from consumers and then having their orders, including groceries, rental videos, and perhaps dry cleaning, ready for pick up at a designated time. Another possibility is for convenience stores to serve as secure drop-off points for shipments of online purchases when customers are not at home to accept delivery.[32]

Warehouse Clubs

Another institution that has mushroomed since the mid-1980s is the **warehouse club,** sometimes called a *wholesale club.* A combined retailing and wholesaling institution, it has very broad but very shallow product assortments, extremely low prices, and few customer services. Warehouse clubs are open only to members who pay an annual fee of about $25 to $100. Their target markets are small businesses (some purchasing merchandise for resale), select groups (such as government personnel and credit union members), and—to an increasing degree—individual consumers.[33]

A warehouse club carries about the same breadth of assortment as a large discount house but in much less depth. For each item, the club stocks only one or two brands and a limited number of sizes and models. It is housed in a warehouse-type building with tall metal racks that display merchandise at ground level and store it at higher levels.

The primary advantage of a warehouse club is its extremely low prices. (Prices for household consumers typically are about 5% higher than prices offered to business members.) This institution has some limitations. Customers ordinarily must pay cash and handle their own merchandise, even heavy, bulky items. Moreover, some shoppers prefer a deeper assortment of products and smaller quantities or packages.

 www.costco.com

The leading warehouse clubs are Sam's Club (owned by Wal-Mart), Costco, and BJ's Wholesale. As with other retailing institutions, warehouse clubs continue to modify and refine their strategies. For example, Costco has been expanding its array of products, often adding "big ticket" items such as diamond engagement rings and its own Kirkland brand of appliances. In the words of a Costco executive, "We want to surprise people at every turn. Even if you don't buy the Waterford crystal, it makes an impact on you."[34]

An Ethical Dilemma?

The owner of a small independent bookstore runs short of "best-sellers" during the peak Christmas season. Obtaining more inventory from the store's normal supplier, a wholesaler in another city, takes several days. In the meantime, thousands of dollars of sales could be lost. A warehouse club about 5 miles from the bookstore carries a limited selection of books; in fact, they are priced at about the bookstore's wholesale cost. By buying best-sellers at the warehouse club, substituting

new price stickers for the warehouse club's stickers, and getting the books on the store's shelves within a couple of hours rather than several days, the independent bookstore builds sales during this critical selling period and satisfies its customers.

Considering that customers do not know the bookstore acquired some of its best-sellers from a warehouse club and then resold them, is this ethical business behavior on the part of the bookstore owner?

Nonstore Retailing

A large majority—about 80%—of retail transactions are made in stores. However, a growing volume of sales is taking place away from stores. Retailing activities resulting in transactions that occur away from a physical store are called **nonstore retailing**. It is "guesstimated" that sales volume through nonstore retailing is in the vicinity of $475 billion annually.[35] Based on this figure, nonstore sales account for almost 20% of total retail trade.

We will consider five types of nonstore retailing: direct selling, telemarketing, automatic vending, online retailing, and direct marketing. (Rather than worrying about the confusing names, focus on the features and competition across the five types.) Each type may be used not just by retailers but by other types of organizations as well.

Direct Selling

In the context of retailing, **direct selling** is defined as personal contact between a sales person and a consumer away from a retail store. This type of retailing has also been called *in-home selling*, but the changing roles of women made this term less accurate. Annual volume of direct selling in the U.S. was about $25 billion at the beginning of the 21st century. These transactions were rung up by about 10 million independent sales people, only 10% of whom devote full time to direct selling.[36]

www.shaklee.com

Like other forms of nonstore retailing, direct selling is utilized in most countries. It's particularly widespread in Japan, which accounts for about 35% of the worldwide volume of direct selling. The U.S. represents almost 30% of the total, and all other countries the rest.[37]

The two kinds of direct selling are door to door and party plan. There are many well-known direct-selling companies, including Mary Kay, Amway, Shaklee, Pampered Chef, Creative Memories, and Excel Communications. Diverse products are marketed through direct selling. This channel is particularly well suited for products that require extensive demonstration. Thus it's not surprising that home/family care (such as cookware and cleaning products) and personal care (such as cosmetics) account for the largest volumes of direct selling.[38]

With so many women—more than half—now working outside the home, direct-selling firms have had to find new ways to meet prospective customers.

The Pampered Chef, Ltd., markets a wide variety of kitchen tools using party-plan direct selling. Each year, independent sales reps hold about 1 million Pampered Chef "kitchen shows" in the homes of friends and neighbors to present the company's line of products, such as a measuring cup that has a built-in plunger to remove the contents. Using only direct selling, Pampered Chef rings up about $500 million in annual sales.

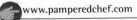
www.pamperedchef.com

For instance, many reps call on employees in the workplace or give sales parties at lunchtime in offices. As you might suspect, some employers take a dim view of such selling in the workplace. As discussed in the Chapter 14 case, to reach new customers and win back former clients, Avon has turned to new channels. So too has Tupperware, which is distributing its products not only by direct selling, but also at kiosks in shopping malls, through television infomercials, and on the Internet.[39]

www.tupperware.com

Direct selling has drawbacks. Sales commissions run as high as 40 to 50% of the retail price; of course, they are paid only when a sale is made. Recruiting, training, motivating, and retaining sales people—most of whom are part-timers— are difficult tasks. Moreover, some sales reps use "high-pressure" tactics or are fraudulent. To minimize this problem, nearly all states have "cooling-off" laws that permit consumers to nullify a party-plan or door-to-door sale within several days of the transaction.

Direct selling also offers significant benefits. Consumers have the opportunity to buy at home or at another convenient nonstore location that provides the opportunity for personal contact with a sales person. For the seller, direct selling offers the boldest method of trying to persuade ultimate consumers to make a purchase. The seller takes products to the shopper's home or workplace and even demonstrates them for the consumer.

Telemarketing

Sometimes called *telephone selling,* **telemarketing** refers to a sales person initiating contact with a shopper and closing a sale over the telephone. Telemarketing may entail cold canvassing from the phone directory. Or it may rely on prospects who have requested information from the company or whose demographics match those of the company's target market. Many products that can be bought without being seen are sold over the telephone. Examples are pest control services, magazine subscriptions, credit cards, and athletic club memberships. One estimate places the total annual volume of telemarketing in the retail sector at about $200 billion.[40]

Telemarketing is not problem free. Often encountering hostile people on the other end of the line and experiencing many more rejections than closed sales, few telephone sales reps last very long in the job. It's not uncommon for annual turnover to average 100%. Further, some telemarketers rely on questionable and/or unethical practices. For instance, firms may place calls at almost any hour of the day or night. This tactic is criticized as violating consumers' right to privacy (and uninterrupted meals). In addition, some telemarketing involves outright fraud— for example, attempts to obtain a person's credit card number for illegal use. It's estimated that such fraud costs consumers $40 *billion* annually.[41]

Reacting to telemarketing abuses, two federal agencies and a growing number of states have enacted rules to constrain telemarketers' activities. One rule, for instance, bans calls before 8 a.m. and after 9 p.m. These rules also empower federal and state officials to seek stiff fines against fraudulent operators.[42]

Despite these problems, telemarketing sales have increased in recent years. Fundamentally, some people appreciate the convenience of making a purchase by phone. Costs have been reduced by computers that automatically dial a telephone number, even deliver a taped message and record information the buyer gives to complete the sale. The future of telemarketing is sure to be affected by the degree to which the problems above can be addressed *and* by the surge of online retailing.

Automatic Vending

The sale of products through a machine with no personal contact between buyer and seller is called **automatic vending.** The appeal of automatic vending is convenient purchase. Products sold by automatic vending are usually well-known, presold brands with a high rate of turnover. The large majority of automatic vending sales comes from the "4 C's": cold drinks, coffee, candy, and cigarettes. It is estimated that vending rings up approximately $30 billion in annual sales, which represents just over 1% of all retail trade.[43]

Vending machines can expand a firm's market by reaching customers where and when they cannot come to a store. Thus vending equipment is found almost everywhere, particularly in schools, workplaces, and public facilities. Automatic vending has high operating costs because of the need to replenish inventories frequently. The machines also require maintenance and repairs.

The outlook for automatic vending is uncertain. The difficulties mentioned above may hinder future growth. Further, occasional vending-related scams may scare some entrepreneurs away from this business.

Vending innovations give reason for some optimism. For starters, there is a flow of new products for vending machines, including movie soundtracks (sold in theater lobbies), freshly squeezed orange juice, heatable diet dinners, office supplies, and even live bait for fishing. Debit cards that can be used at vending machines are becoming more common. When this card is inserted into the machine, the purchase amount is deducted from the credit balance. Technological advances also allow operators to monitor vending machines from a distance, thereby reducing the number (and lost revenues) of out-of-stock or out-of-order machines. Coca-Cola is even testing a vending machine with two-way communication capabilities, which would allow long-distance price changes based on supply and demand considerations. Of course, these advances are costly.[44]

Online Retailing

When a firm uses its website to offer products for sale and then individuals or organizations use their computers to make purchases from this company, the parties have engaged in *electronic transactions* (also called *online selling* or *Internet marketing*). Many electronic transactions involve two businesses, but this chapter focuses on sales by firms to ultimate consumers. Thus we are interested in **online retailing,** which consists of electronic transactions in which the purchaser is an ultimate consumer.

Online retailing is being carried out by a rapidly increasing number of new firms, such as Fogdog Sports, Buy.com, and CDNow.com. It has also attracted existing retailers, such as Nordstrom, Lands' End, and PETsMART, operating either on their own or in alliances with Internet firms.[45] Some websites feature broad assortments, especially those launched by general-merchandise retailers such as Wal-Mart and Target. Some Internet-only firms, notably Amazon.com, are using various methods to broaden their offerings. However, most e-tailers concentrate on one or two categories that are often reflected in their names—garden.com, 1–800-Flowers.com, and Furniture.com are several examples.

 www.garden.com

Whatever their differences, e-tailers are likely to share an attribute: They are unprofitable or, at best, barely profitable. Of course, there are substantial costs in establishing an online operation. Aggressive efforts to attract shoppers and retain customers through extensive advertising and low prices are also expensive. The head of Pets.com attributed the firm's mounting losses to necessary efforts to gain market share, "We're building ahead of the curve." The substantial losses racked up by online enterprises used to be accepted, perhaps even encouraged, by investors and analysts. The rationale was that all available funds should be used to gain a foothold in this growing market. As the new century began, this attitude was changing. For instance, Value America's stock plunged as the company struggled to come up with a profitable approach to e-tailing.[46]

Besides figuring out how to turn a profit, online merchants must address the dual challenges of order fulfillment and customer service. The situation in early 2000 was underscored by the results of a test of the top 50 retail websites. The conclusion: "Shoppers were unable even to place an order 25% of the time; 20%

Will "bots" change how products are priced on the Internet?

Online shopping robots, nicknamed "bots," made their debut in 1995. They were devised to help consumers do comparison shopping on the Internet. Bots do this by searching the Web for a particular item and then furnishing the interested consumer with a list of merchants who offer it, including the prices they charge. Initially, most e-tailers' prices were higher than physical stores', but bots have forced online merchants to lower their prices in order to be competitive. In 1998, Ernst & Young examined 30 consumer products and determined that the online price was the same as or lower than the price charged by retail stores in 87% of the cases.

Now some e-tailers are investing in shopping robots. Amazon, for example, spent $180 million to purchase All Product Search. Questions have been raised as to whether merchant-owned bots will be unbiased. Critics have pointed to instances where All Product Search has ignored books that are available at lower prices through Amazon's biggest rival, Barnesandnoble.com.

Many bots, like mySimon.com, are completely independent. Unfortunately, they don't have access to every online merchant's prices. Some e-tailers are blocking bots from their sites because they are con-cerned about being forced into a price war with competitors. In addition, a few online merchants don't disclose hidden costs, such as shipping and handling. These circumstances make it difficult for potential buyers to make informed purchase decisions, even with price comparisons from bots.

Bots are becoming more sophisticated. Wireless Dimension, for instance, is designed to help buyers determine which product best fits their needs, and mySimon.com can e-mail potential buyers when a merchant is offering a product at a price they are willing to pay. NexTag.com allows shoppers to actually negotiate prices with online merchants. Bots are forcing e-tailers, and also traditional retailers, to monitor and adjust their prices more frequently. As a professor stated, "After all, fixed prices have been around only for a couple of hundred of years."

Sources: Janet Rae-Dupree and Diane Brady, "Let the Buyer Be in Control," *Business Week,* Nov. 8, 1999, p. 100; Chris Taylor, "Bot Till You Drop," *Time,* Oct. 11, 1999, pp. 52–53; Scott Kirsner, "The Bots Are Back," *CIO Web Business,* May 1, 1999, pp. 26–28; Michelle Rafter, "New Sites Troll Net for Products, Prices," *St. Louis Post-Dispatch,* Feb. 24, 1999, p. C8; and Heather Green, "A Cybershopper's Best Friend," *Business Week,* May 4, 1998, p. 84.

 www.mySimon.com

 www.nextag.com

of packages arrived late or never; and 36% of sites had busy or unhelpful customer-service numbers."[47]

Despite these challenges, online retailing is expected to grow, rapidly and significantly for the foreseeable future. Online sales represented about 1% of retail spending in 1999, but one research firm estimates that consumer purchases on the Internet will top $185 billion by the year 2004. If that occurs, online retailing will account for about 6% of all Internet sales (the rest being business-to-business transactions) and about 5% of total retail trade. Although online retail sales will rise, the number of e-tailers probably will decline. One research firm predicted a "shakeout," with most online retailers going out of business by 2002.[48]

Which product categories are consumers most likely to buy on the Internet in the future? Consumers' shopping intentions in 1999 placed the following goods and services at the top of the list: books, music and videos, computer hardware and software, travel, and apparel. Of course, given that change on the Internet occurs at warp speed, these categories soon may be surpassed by others—perhaps groceries, toys, health and beauty aids, auto parts, or pet supplies.[49]

Direct Marketing

There is no consensus on the exact nature of direct marketing. In effect, it comprises all types of nonstore retailing other than direct selling, telemarketing, automatic vending, and online retailing. In the context of retailing, we define **direct marketing** as using print or broadcast advertising to contact consumers who, in turn, buy products without visiting a retail store. (A caution: Be careful to distinguish among the terms direct *marketing,* direct *selling,* and direct *distribution*!) As denoted by the preceding section, we have chosen to treat online retailing, which involves computer contact, as a separate type of nonstore retailing.

Direct marketers contact consumers through one or more of the following media: radio, TV, newspapers, magazines, catalogs, and mailings (direct mail). Consumers order by telephone or mail. Direct marketers can be classified as either general-merchandise firms, which offer a variety of product lines, or specialty firms, which carry only one or two lines such as books or fresh fruit. Direct marketing is big business, accounting for perhaps $200 billion in annual retail sales![50]

Under the broad definition, the many forms of direct marketing include:

- *Direct mail,* in which firms mail letters, brochures, and even product samples to consumers, and ask them to purchase by mail or telephone. This form of direct marketing is best for selling a variety of services, such as credit cards and athletic club memberships, and well-known goods, such as magazines and recorded music. Some small retailers use direct mail in creative and effective ways. For example, Zane's Cycles, in Branford, Connecticut, sends postcards to selected customers offering a special price on a child's bike. The bicycle shop has a database on its 19,000 customers, including their past purchases. Thus this particular promotion is directed only at customers who purchased a baby seat for a bicycle three years earlier.[51]

- *Catalog retailing,* in which companies mail catalogs to consumers or make them available at retail stores. After expanding at an annual rate of 10% during the 1980s, the growth of catalog retailing flattened out during the 1990s. Retailers relying on catalogs can't be faulted for lack of effort, though, as the number of catalogs distributed in the U.S. nearly doubled during this two-decade period—to about 15 *billion* each year. The slowdown hurt giant retailers (such as Penney's and Ward's) and established catalog retailers (such as Spiegel and J. Crew). Now prospects are better for catalog firms because some of their competencies, such as maintaining large customer databases and shipping small orders, transfer very well to online retailing. In fact, according to one research firm, two catalog retailers (Lands' End and L.L. Bean) quickly earned the top ratings in online apparel retailing.[52]

- *Televised shopping,* in which various categories of products are promoted on dedicated TV channels and through *infomercials,* which are TV commercials that run for 30 minutes or even longer on an entertainment channel. The leading shopping channels, QVC and the Home Shopping Network, sell jewelry, consumer electronics, home decor, and other products at relatively low prices. Infomercials have been used to sell various items, including cutlery, sprays to color and disguise thinning hair, and home-based businesses. Televised shopping burgeoned during the 1980s, but has slowed down in recent years, with infomercials being the stronger of the two forms.[53]

Direct marketing has drawbacks. Consumers must place orders without seeing or touching the actual merchandise (although they may see a picture of it). To offset this, direct marketers must offer liberal return policies. Furthermore, catalogs and, to some extent, direct-mail pieces are costly and must be prepared long before they are issued. Price changes and new products can be announced only through supplementary catalogs or brochures.

On the plus side, like other types of nonstore retailing, direct marketing provides shopping convenience. In addition, direct marketers enjoy comparatively low operating expenses because they do not have the overhead of physical stores. Direct marketing's future is difficult to forecast, given the rise of the Internet. The issue is whether or not firms relying on direct marketing can achieve and sustain a differential advantage in a growing competition with online enterprises.

Institutional Changes in Retailing

As consumers change, so do forms of retailing. Executives would like to anticipate major changes before they occur. When the change is as revolutionary as the sudden, dramatic emergence of online retailing, that's difficult to do. However, evolutionary changes in retailing often follow a pattern in which an established retail institution trades up to attract a broader market, achieve higher margins, and gain more status. Sooner or later, high costs and, ultimately, high prices (as perceived by its target markets) make the institution vulnerable to new retail types, most likely a low-cost, low-price store.[54]

To illustrate, discount stores have been trading up recently. Target has been successful in becoming, as contradictory as it sounds, an "upscale discounter."[55] If trading up by discount stores is pervasive, an opening may be created for a new low-cost, low-price institution. Maybe that's already here, in the form of e-tailers such as Amazon.com, which continues to broaden its offerings while emphasizing low prices.

What will be the retailing innovations of the next 10 years? Given the surge in Internet usage, perhaps various kinds of e-tailing? Some other form of nonstore retailing? Or a new type of low-cost, low-price store such as supercenters, or giant specialty retailers that dwarf even category killers?

Retail firms must identify and respond to significant trends that affect retailing by developing—and, as necessary, modifying—their need-satisfying marketing strategies. According to a retailing expert, merchants that prosper in the future will (1) provide consumers with a distinctive bundle of benefits, (2) stress value not just low prices, (3) save their customers time and energy, and (4) make shopping fun. Many retailers and even entire large malls, in fact, are stressing entertainment-based selling. Of course, as the saying goes, being distinctive and effective in implementing one or more of these four strategies is "easier said than done."[56]

Regional shopping centers are trying to make shopping more convenient and efficient for time-conscious shoppers. One method being tested in late 1999 is YourSherpa.com. A shopper provides credit-card information in exchange for an electronic wand that records bar codes of products of interest when the consumer visits different stores. At the end of shopping, the consumer goes to a kiosk in the mall and pays for the products that have been scanned by the wand. Later, the merchandise is delivered to the customer's home.

 www.yoursherpa.com

Summary

Retailing is the sale of goods and services to ultimate consumers for personal, non-business use. Any institution (such as a manufacturer) may engage in retailing, but a firm engaged primarily in retailing is called a retailer. Retailers serve as purchasing agents for consumers and as sales specialists for producers and wholesaling middlemen. They perform many specific activities, such as anticipating customers' wants, developing product assortments, and financing.

There are about 1.5 million retail establishments in the U.S.; collectively they generated about $2.5 trillion in sales during 1997. Most retail firms are small—either single stores or several stores under common ownership. Small retailers can survive—and even prosper—if they remain flexible and pay careful attention to personally serving customers' needs. Retailers' operating expenses run about 28% of retail sales. Their profits are usually a tiny fraction of sales, generally about 3%.

Besides product, price, promotion, and customer services, retailers also must make strategic decisions regarding physical facilities. Specific decisions concern location, size, design, and layout of the store. Downtown shopping areas declined as suburban shopping centers grew. Now regional shopping centers are feeling competitive pressures from many sources, including Internet firms.

Retailers can be classified by (1) form of ownership, including corporate chain, independent store, and various kinds of contractual vertical marketing systems (notably franchising), and (2) key marketing strategies. Also, types of retailers, distinguished according to product assortment, price levels, and customer service levels, include department stores, discount stores, limited-line stores (notably specialty stores, off-price retailers, and category-killer stores), supermarkets, convenience stores, and warehouse clubs. Mature institutions such as department stores, discount stores, and supermarkets face strong challenges from new competitors, particularly chains of category-killer stores in various product categories.

Although the large majority of retail sales are made in physical stores, perhaps 20% occur away from stores. And this proportion is growing steadily. Five major forms of nonstore retailing are direct selling, telemarketing, automatic vending, online retailing, and direct marketing. Each type has advantages as well as drawbacks. Online retailing, in particular, is growing dramatically.

Retail owners and executives must try to anticipate changes in retail institutions. Often, evolutionary change begins when one type of institution begins to trade up. To succeed, retailers need to identify significant trends and ensure that they develop marketing strategies to satisfy consumers.

More about **PETsMART**

With so many e-tailers vying to be "top dog" in online pet supply sales, these companies are going to great lengths to create brand awareness and then customer loyalty. Capable of carrying a broader array of products than tradiitonal pet supply stores, cyberstores entice shoppers with better selection and greater convenience.

Online pet supply retailers can also provide pet owners with a wealth of information. This is an important factor for pet owners, 70% of whom think of their pets as children. Most pet supply websites offer advice about pet health and also have set up chat rooms so owners can discuss pet issues and trade helpful tips. To illustrate how the online firms are competing, Petstore.com has an exclusive agreement with a large group of veterinarians to promote its site, and Pets.com offers a list of "pet friendly" hotels as well as a nationwide directory of veterinarians. PETsMART.com uses its website to sponsor pet photo contests and to raise funds for national animal charities.

With pet supply e-tailers providing similar types of services, marketing is likely to be a differentiating factor. PETsMART.com should benefit from PETsMART's $100 million annual marketing budget, which includes TV and print ads. It has also arranged a prime spot on America Online's site, and an exclusive arrangement with Disney's Go Network. However, Petopia.com and Petstore.com also have marketing agreements with AOL and other Internet portals. Of course, because it's partially owned by Amazon, Pets.com gets special exposure to the leading e-tailer's 17 million customers.

In a unique cross-promotional arrangement, PETsMART.com and Big Dog Holdings are marketing each other's products. Big Dog, which sells casual sportswear through nearly 200 retail stores, catalog operations, and a website, promotes PETsMART.com through each of these channels and also directly to members of its Big Dog Club. In

exchange, PETsMART.com has established a Big Dog Boutique in its cyberstore to sell this brand of merchandise and also will incorporate the Big Dog brand in its advertising efforts.

Despite aggressive promotion strategies, pet owners are still basing many of their online buying decisions solely on price, resulting in a frenzy of online offers. Tom McGovern, CEO of PETsMART.com says, "In the early stages of a business . . . we cannot let ourselves be at a disadvantage on price." In one price promotion, PETsMART.com allowed shoppers to buy any pet food item and get a second identical item free. Petstore.com has provided free shipping for orders less than 50 pounds. And, in January 2000, Petco.com gave consumers $10 off any order. Although pet products carry a gross margin of 20% to 35%, price discounting is one reason why very few online retailers have yet to turn a profit.[57]

1. Can PETsMART.com prevent its success from taking sales away from PETsMART bricks-and-mortar stores?

2. Can online retailers compete with bricks-and-mortar stores with respect to customer service?

Key Terms and Concepts

Retailing (retail trade) (426)
Retailer (426)
Physical facilities (430)
Shopping center (430)
Corporate chain (432)
Independent retailer (433)
Contractual vertical marketing system (433)
Retailer cooperative (433)
Voluntary chain (433)
Franchising (433)

Product and trade name franchising (433)
Business format franchising (434)
Department store (436)
Discount retailing (437)
Discount store (437)
Supercenter (437)
Limited-line store (437)
Specialty store (439)
Off-price retailer (439)
Category-killer store (440)

Supermarket retailing (440)
Supermarket (441)
Convenience store (441)
Warehouse club (wholesale club) (442)
Nonstore retailing (443)
Direct selling (443)
Telemarketing (444)
Automatic vending (444)
Online retailing (445)
Direct marketing (446)

Questions and Problems

1. In each of the following situations, is the seller a *retailer* and is the transaction a *retail sale*?
   a. Independent contractor selling lawn-care services door to door.
   b. Farmer selling produce door to door.
   c. Farmer selling produce at a roadside stand.
   d. Sporting goods store selling uniforms to a professional baseball team.
   e. Fogdog.com selling running shoes to a college student.

2. What recommendations would you offer a department store chain that wants to reduce retailing costs? What would you recommend to discount houses in this regard?

3. Support or refute the following statements, using facts and statistics where appropriate:
   a. "Retailing is typically small-scale business."
   b. "There is a high degree of concentration in retailing today; the giants control the field."

4. The ease of entry into retailing undoubtedly contributes to the high failure rate among retailers, which—in the view of some—creates economic waste. Should entry into retailing be restricted? If so, how could this be done?

5. Do you agree that there are three keys to success in retailing—location, location, and location? How do you reconcile this with the fact that there is so much price competition in retailing at the present time?

6. What can department stores do to strengthen their competitive positions?

7. "The supermarket, with its operating expense ratio of 20%, is the most efficient institution in retailing today." Do you agree with this statement? In what ways might supermarkets further reduce their expenses?

8. "Door-to-door selling is the most efficient form of retailing because it eliminates wholesalers and retail stores." Discuss.

9. What new retail institutions might we see in the future?

10. Of the types of retail stores discussed in the chapter, which ones do you think have been or would be most successful in foreign countries? Which ones have been or would be unsuccessful in other countries? Explain your answers.

Hands-On Marketing

1. Arrange an interview with a small retailer. Discuss with this merchant the general competitive positions of small and large retailers, as covered in this chapter. Which, if any, of these points does the small retailer disagree with, and why? Also ask what courses of action this merchant takes to achieve or maintain a viable competitive position. Interview a second small retailer, ask the same questions, and compare their answers.

2. Write to the headquarters of two retail franchise systems with which you are familiar and request information provided to prospective purchasers of a franchise. (Local units of the franchise systems should be able to supply you with the headquarters' mailing addresses; or go to the International Franchise Association website to obtain franchisors' names and addresses.) Once you have received the information, evaluate whether you would like to own either of these franchises. What criteria did you use in making this evaluation?

 http://www.franchise.org

"Supervalu no longer concentrated on making money by raising the prices of goods purchased from manufacturers . . . seeking instead to generate profits on a variety of value-added services."

Is There a **Supervalu** Advantage in Grocery Distribution?

With annual sales of about $23 billion following a mid-1999 acquisition, Supervalu Inc. is the leading grocery wholesaling company in the U.S. Headquartered just outside Minneapolis, Supervalu is a wholesaler-sponsored voluntary chain that is the primary supplier of merchandise and management services to more than 4,800 independent grocery stores in 48 states. Supervalu also operates about 475 retail outlets that contribute 29% of the organization's total sales.

In 1995, trying to position itself for the future, Supervalu launched a new program, labeled Advantage. According to Michael Wright, the chain's chairman and CEO, the goals of Advantage include lower cost of goods, more efficient distribution, added market share, and new business opportunities. The Advantage program has three main elements: (1) providing more support to Supervalu's primary customers; (2) enhancing relationships with suppliers and retailers in its channels; and (3) restructuring the physical flow of goods. Wright stressed that Advantage should strengthen its customers, which in turn would benefit Supervalu. Implementing the new program took longer than originally anticipated. But the early results were favorable. And good news was needed in the wholesale grocery industry, which was losing a collective $1 billion annually.

A key element of Advantage was the restructuring of Supervalu's business. Previously, the company was divided into 25 operating divisions. The revamped arrangement consolidated formerly dispersed activities into seven marketing regions and four distribution regions. The new marketing structure is intended primarily to enhance services provided to Supervalu's customers, whereas the revised distribution structure is aimed mainly at reducing expenses and, in turn, wholesale prices. Supervalu expects profits to improve steadily as well.

Decentralization enabled Supervalu to employ category management, which entails organizing promotional programs around clusters of stores that would benefit from similar types of marketing activities. Typically, promotions are at least partially funded by manufacturers. Supervalu's category management department develops the strategies for spending these funds, which adds value to the wholesaler's relationship with its member stores. "Each department and each category must be considered individually when strategy is concerned," explained Leland Dake, vice president of merchandising. "What is the retailer's strategy in regard to merchandising? Is it to generate sales, to generate profits or to compete with retailers?" Supervalu is committed to helping its clients answer these questions.

The Advantage program changed Supervalu's business model and its relationship with member stores. Supervalu no longer concentrated on making money by raising the prices of goods purchased from manufacturers. Instead, it passed these prices on to the member stores, seeking instead to generate profits on a variety of value-added services. As a result, Supervalu's emphasis switched from making shrewd buying decisions to helping its customers sell more. "We are really focused on driving retailers' sales and profitability," said Dake. "If they are successful, they will . . . buy more products from us. They will become more efficient and we will too."[1]

Does the Advantage program assure Supervalu Inc. of maintaining a position of leadership in grocery wholesaling?

 www.supervalu.com

Although consumers shop regularly at the stores of retailers, they rarely see the establishments of wholesaling middlemen. Also, beyond noticing transportation carriers such as trucks and trains, consumers have little exposure to how products actually are moved from the point of production to the point of final sale. As a result, wholesaling and physical distribution are too often ignored or misunderstood by consumers.

Nevertheless, wholesaling middlemen can be essential members of a distribution channel, and physical distribution is an integral aspect of marketing most goods. And with the rise of the Internet, all aspects of distribution are receiving more attention as online enterprises try to figure out how to procure merchandise for sale and then deliver it to customers after it's sold. This chapter will provide you with insight into how wholesale markets, wholesaling institutions, and physical distribution activities relate to marketing. After studying this chapter, you should be able to explain:

chapter goals

- The nature and economic justification of wholesaling.
- The role of wholesaling middlemen in the distribution process.
- Differences across three categories of wholesaling middlemen.
- Major types of merchant wholesalers, agent wholesaling middlemen, and manufacturers' sales facilities, and the services they render.
- What physical distribution is.
- The systems approach to physical distribution.
- How physical distribution can strengthen a marketing program and reduce marketing costs.
- The five subsystems within physical distribution: order processing, inventory control, inventory location and warehousing, materials handling, and transportation.

Nature and Importance of Wholesaling

Wholesaling and retailing enable what is produced to be purchased for consumption. We already know retailing involves sales to ultimate consumers for their personal use. Now we'll see what the role of wholesaling is in the marketing system.

Wholesaling and Wholesaling Middlemen

Wholesaling (or *wholesale trade*) is the sale, and all activities directly related to the sale, of goods and services to businesses and other organizations for (1) resale, (2) use in producing other goods or services, or (3) operating an organization. When a business firm sells shirts and blouses to a clothing store that intends to resell them to final consumers, this is wholesaling. When a mill sells flour to a large bakery for making bread and pastries, this is also a wholesale transaction. And when a firm sells uniforms to some organization for its employees to wear in carrying out their duties, this is wholesaling as well.

Sales made by one producer to another are wholesale transactions, and the selling producer is engaged in wholesaling. Likewise, a discount store is involved in wholesaling when it sells calculators and office supplies to a business firm. Thus wholesaling includes sales by any firm to any customer *except* an ultimate consumer who is buying for personal, nonbusiness use. From this perspective, all sales are either wholesale or retail transactions—distinguished only by the purchaser's intended use of the good or service.

In this chapter we will focus on firms engaged *primarily* in wholesaling. This type of company is called a **wholesaling middleman.** We will not be concerned with retailers involved in occasional wholesale transactions. And we will not focus on manufacturers and farmers because they are engaged primarily in production rather than wholesaling. Keep in mind, then, that *wholesaling* is a business *activity* that can be carried out by various types of firms, whereas a *wholesaling middleman* is a business *institution* that concentrates on wholesaling.

Economic Justification for Wholesaling

Most manufacturing firms are small and specialized. They don't have the capital to maintain a sales force to contact the many retailers or final users that are (or could be) their customers. Even for manufacturers with sufficient capital, some of their products or lines generate such a small volume of sales that it would not be cost-effective to establish a sales force to sell them.

At the other end of the distribution channel, most retailers and final users buy in small quantities and have only a limited knowledge of the market and sources of supply. Thus there is often a gap between the seller (producer) and the buyer (retailer or final user).

A wholesaling middleman can fill this gap by providing services of value to manufacturers and/or retailers. For example, a wholesaling middleman pools the orders of many retailers and/or final users, thereby creating a market for the small producer. At the same time, a wholesaling middleman selects various items from among many alternatives to form its product mix, thereby acting as a buying service for small retailers and final users. Essentially, as we will see at several points in this chapter, the activities of a wholesaling middleman create time, place, and/or possession utility.

Let's look at two situations, one very specific and the other very broad and significant, to see how wholesaling middlemen serve producers and retailers. A manufacturer of modular office dividers, Pleion Corp., decided to replace most of its sales force with independent dealers. The switch allowed Pleion to expand into new regions quicker and halved the company's marketing expenses. Taking a broader perspective, there were numerous predictions that the rise of electronic commerce would harm distributors, perhaps even eliminate many of them. Thus far, many wholesaling middlemen are thriving by furnishing needed services to online enterprises. For instance, e-tailers are calling upon distributors to fill and, in some cases, even ship customers' orders.[2]

From a broad point of view, wholesaling brings to the total distribution system the economies of skill, scale, and transactions:

- Wholesaling *skills* are efficiently concentrated in a relatively few hands. This saves the duplication of effort that would occur if many producers had to perform wholesaling functions themselves. For example, one wholesaler's warehouse in Memphis, Tennessee, saves many manufacturers from having to build their own warehouses to provide speedy service to customers in this area.

- Economies of *scale* result from the specialization of wholesaling middlemen performing functions that might otherwise require several small departments run by producing firms. Wholesalers typically can perform wholesaling functions more efficiently than can most manufacturers.

- *Transaction* economies come into play when retailers and/or wholesaling middlemen are introduced between producers and their customers. Let's assume that four manufacturers want to sell to six retailers. As shown in Figure 16.1, *without* a middleman, there are 24 transactions; *with* one wholesaling middleman, the number of transactions is cut to 10. Four transactions occur when all the producers sell to the middleman, and another six occur when the middleman sells to all the retailers.

Figure 16.1

The economy of trans-
actions in wholesaling.

Four producers each sell directly to six retailers, resulting in 24 transactions:

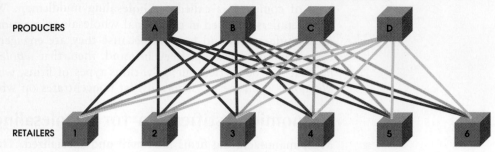

Four producers use the same wholesaling middleman, reducing the number of transactions to 10:

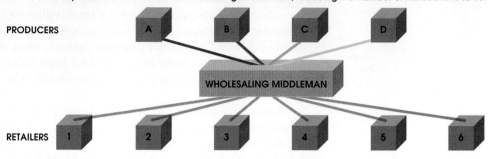

Size of the Wholesale Market

The total annual sales volume of wholesaling middlemen was more than $4.2 *tril-lion* in 1997 (the year of the last published national census of wholesale trade). As shown in Table 16.1, this level of wholesale sales represents an increase of 60% over 1987 and almost 800% over 1967. Even if the effects of inflation are taken into account, these figures still reflect a major increase in wholesale trade.

You might be surprised to see in Table 16.1 that total wholesale trade exceeds total retail trade by a wide margin. How can this be, especially considering that a product's retail price is higher than its wholesale price? We can find an explanation by considering the customers of wholesaling middlemen. About 70% of the sales of wholesaling middlemen are made to organizations *other than* retailers.[3] For example, some products sold to nonretailers are *business* goods (such as large printing presses or iron ore) that, by definition, are never sold at retail. Others may be *consumer* goods (such as groceries or toys) that are sold more than once

Table 16.1	Total Wholesale Trade versus Total Retail Trade in the United States
	Total wholesale sales (in current dollars) increased 60% between 1987 and 1997. Compare these figures with the growth in retail sales over the same period.

Year	Number of Wholesaling Middlemen	Wholesale Sales (billions)	Retail Sales (billions)
1997	453,000	$4,058	$2,461
1987	470,000	2,525	1,540
1977	383,000	1,258	723
1967	311,000	459	310

Sources: 1997 *Economic Census,* Wholesale Trade—Geographic Area Series, U.S. Census Bureau, Washington, DC, 2000, p. United States 7 <www.census.gov/prod/ec97/97w42-US.pdf>; and 1997 *Economic Census,* Retail Trade—Geographic Area Series, U.S. Census Bureau, Washington, DC, 2000, p. United States 7 <www.census.gov/prod/ec97/97r44-US.pdf>; and corresponding censuses from prior years.

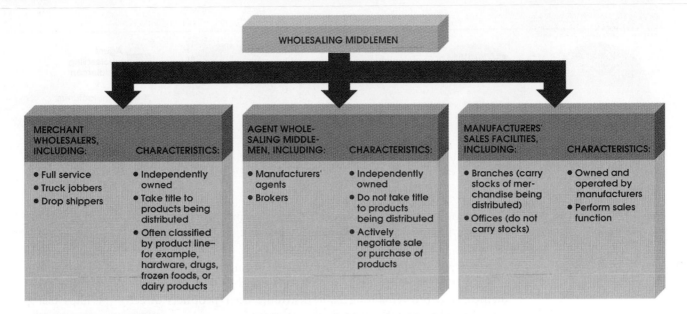

WHOLESALING MIDDLEMEN

MERCHANT WHOLESALERS, INCLUDING:	CHARACTERISTICS:
• Full service • Truck jobbers • Drop shippers	• Independently owned • Take title to products being distributed • Often classified by product line—for example, hardware, drugs, frozen foods, or dairy products

AGENT WHOLE-SALING MIDDLE-MEN, INCLUDING:	CHARACTERISTICS:
• Manufacturers' agents • Brokers	• Independently owned • Do not take title to products being distributed • Actively negotiate sale or purchase of products

MANUFACTURERS' SALES FACILITIES, INCLUDING:	CHARACTERISTICS:
• Branches (carry stocks of merchandise being distributed) • Offices (do not carry stocks)	• Owned and operated by manufacturers • Perform sales function

Figure 16.2

Types of wholesaling institutions.

at the wholesale level, with all such transactions counted as part of total wholesale trade. Thus total wholesale trade is greater than total retail trade because wholesale trade includes sales of business goods and successive sales of consumer goods at the wholesale level.

At last count, 453,000 wholesaling middlemen were conducting business in the U.S. According to Table 16.1, the number of such establishments rose substantially—by one-half, in fact—between 1967 and 1987 but has declined since then. These statistics document that wholesaling middlemen remain viable members of distribution channels.

Profile of Wholesaling Middlemen

A producer or retailer considering the use of wholesaling middlemen must know what options are available, whom these middlemen serve, and how they operate.

Major Categories

Wholesaling middlemen vary greatly in products carried, markets served, and methods of operation. We will discuss about 10 different types of wholesaling middlemen. Nevertheless, all fit into three categories developed by the U.S. Bureau of the Census (see Figure 16.2). Brief descriptions of the categories follow, with more details presented later in the chapter:

- A **merchant wholesaler** is an independently owned firm that engages primarily in wholesaling and takes title to (that is, owns) the products being distributed. Sometimes these firms are referred to simply as *wholesalers, jobbers,* or *industrial distributors.*[4] Merchant wholesalers form the largest segment of wholesaling firms when measured by either number of establishments or sales volume.

- An **agent wholesaling middleman** is an independently owned firm that engages primarily in wholesaling by actively negotiating the sale or purchase of products on behalf of other firms but that does *not* take title to (that is, does not own) the products being distributed.

- A **manufacturer's sales facility** is an establishment that engages primarily in wholesaling and is owned and operated by a manufacturer but is physically separated from manufacturing plants.[5] Manufacturers' sales facilities are common in fields ranging from major appliances to plumbing equipment to electrical supplies. The two major types are similar except in one important respect.

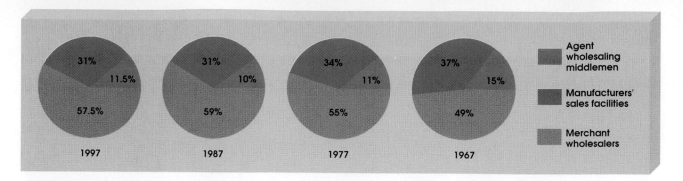

Figure 16.3

Share of wholesale trade, by category of institution.

Sources: 1997 Economic Census, Wholesale Trade, Geographic Area Series, U.S. Census Bureau, Washington, DC, 2000, p. United States 7 <www.census.gov/prod/ec97/97w42-US.pdf}>; and corresponding censuses from prior years.

A **manufacturer's sales branch** carries an inventory of the product being sold, but a **manufacturer's sales office** does not.

Although wholesaling middlemen are not part of every distribution channel, they are present in most. According to one survey, 32% of business goods manufacturers rely on merchant wholesalers. Another 42% use agent wholesaling middlemen, and the remaining 26% distribute their products directly (perhaps using sales branches or offices) to final customers.[6]

The statistics in Figure 16.3 (the latest available census data) indicate that merchant wholesalers account for the majority of sales made through wholesaling middlemen. Between 1967 and 1987, merchant wholesalers continually increased their share of wholesale trade, whereas the other two categories declined. Since then, manufacturers' sales facilities have taken a small amount of market share from merchant wholesalers.[7]

Operating Expenses and Profits

Total operating expenses for wholesaling middlemen average about 11% of *wholesale* sales; operating expenses for retailers run about 28% of *retail* sales. Therefore, generally speaking, the expenses of wholesaling middlemen take about 8% of the ultimate consumer's dollar.[8]

Operating expenses vary widely across the several categories of wholesaling middlemen:

- Merchant wholesalers have the highest average operating expenses, at 14% of sales. However, the range is wide. For example, operating expenses for wholesalers of a complete assortment of grocery products typically are below 10% of sales, compared with as much as 30% for office equipment wholesalers.

- Agent wholesaling middlemen have fairly low costs, around 4.5% of sales, largely because they do not have to carry inventories.

- The two types of manufacturers' sales facilities generally have much different cost structures. Sales offices' operating expenses are about 4% of sales; sales branches' expenses are around 11%, because of the costs incurred in storing merchandise.

These costs need to be interpreted carefully. We should not conclude that agent wholesaling middlemen are highly efficient and merchant wholesalers inefficient because of the disparity in their expenses. The differences in costs are partially traceable to differences in the services they provide. Also, because of factors such as perishability, value in relation to bulk, and special storage requirements, there are tremendous variations in the expenses connected with wholesaling various products. For example, jewelry has much higher value in relation to bulk than furniture, so this factor would suggest lower storage costs for jewelry as a percentage of value. However, any savings on this factor might be offset by the added expenses of providing ample security for jewelry in inventory.

Net operating profit expressed as a percentage of net sales is rather modest for wholesaling middlemen and is considerably lower than net profit for retailers (except for large grocery stores). Generally, wholesaling profits range from 1.5 to 4% of sales.

Merchant Wholesalers

Wholesaling middlemen that take title to products—that is, merchant wholesalers—are common in the marketing of both consumer goods and business goods. We'll examine several types next.

Full-Service Wholesalers

An independent merchant middleman that performs a full range of wholesaling functions is a **full-service wholesaler.** This type of middleman may handle consumer and/or business products that may be manufactured or nonmanufactured (such as grown or extracted), and are imported, exported, or made and sold domestically.

www.fleming.com

The forms of assistance offered by full-service wholesalers are summarized in Table 16.2. The Fleming Companies, Supervalu's primary competitor, exemplifies how a full-service wholesaler operates. As one of the largest wholesaler of groceries and related products, Fleming helps independent grocery stores remain viable by providing them with the business tools that grocery chains have. Fleming offers dozens of different services to its customers. These services include demographic studies, development of marketing plans for grocery stores, advertising support, and shelf-space allocation guidelines.[9]

Individual manufacturers in various industries have begun to distribute their products directly, thereby eliminating wholesalers in their channels. Amana Refrigeration, a maker of home appliances, decided to end its relationships with merchant wholesalers and deal directly with appliance retailers. Obviously, this action displeased—and perhaps devastated—many wholesalers that had carried the Amana line.[10]

To maintain their competitiveness and boost profits, full-service wholesalers are striving to improve their own operations. Two common avenues are enhanced quality and advanced technology. Further, to remain an integral part of distribution channels by better satisfying customers, many distributors have expanded their services. Some assist manufacturers with warranty claims, whereas others offer

Table 16.2	Full-Service Wholesalers' Typical Services to Customers and to Producers
Service	**Description**
Buying	Act as purchasing agent for customers.
Creating assortments	Buy from many suppliers to develop an inventory that matches customers' needs.
Subdividing	Buy in large quantities (such as a truckload) and then resell in smaller quantities (such as a dozen).
Selling	Provide a sales force for producers to reach small retailers and other businesses, at a lower cost than producers would incur by having their own sales forces.
Transportation	Make quick, frequent deliveries to customers, reducing customers' risks and investment in inventory.
Warehousing	Store products in facilities that are nearer customers' locations than are manufacturing plants.
Financing	Grant credit to customers, reducing their capital requirements. Aid producers by ordering and paying for products before purchase by customers.
Risk taking	Reduce a producer's risk by taking title to products.
Market information	Supply information to customers about new products and producers' special offers and to producer-suppliers about customers' needs and competitors' activities.
Management assistance	Assist customers, especially small retailers, in areas such as inventory control, allocation of shelf space, and financial management.

training for customers' employees on how to use or resell products. As a specific example, Sales Systems Ltd., a distributor of industrial fasteners located in Portsmouth, Virginia, built its own product-testing labs so that it can help customers with quality control.[11]

Partnerships between wholesalers and either producers or customers are increasingly common. Ordinarily, these arrangements represent the administered type of vertical marketing system (discussed in the two preceding chapters). To cite one example, Safety Equipment Co. formed a partnership with a major customer, Tampa Electric Co. To become the utility's sole supplier of safety items, the Tampa-based distributor agreed to provide special services, such as a customized catalog, and to meet stringent performance standards, such as guaranteed next-day delivery of orders.[12]

Full-service wholesalers comprise the majority of merchant wholesaling middlemen. They have held their own in competitive struggles with other forms of indirect distribution, including manufacturers' sales facilities and agent middlemen. Although full-service wholesalers have gained in some industries, they have lost ground in others.[13]

At some point, the total number of merchant wholesalers may decline because of increasing mergers and acquisitions. In grocery wholesaling, for instance, there have been several hundred mergers and acquisitions during the past two decades.[14] A growing number of distributors believe they need to be bigger to maintain their competitive edge. Smaller wholesalers will have to decide whether they intend to acquire, be acquired, or somehow insulate themselves from this trend—perhaps by serving small market niches.

Other Merchant Wholesalers

Two types of merchant wholesalers with distinctive operations also warrant brief description:

- A **truck jobber,** also called a *truck distributor,* carries a limited line of perishable products (such as candies, dairy products, potato chips, or tobacco products) and delivers them by truck to stores. Jobbers furnish fresh products so frequently that retailers can buy perishable goods in small amounts to minimize the risk of loss. But truck jobbers are saddled with high operating costs, caused primarily by the small order size and inefficient use of their trucks (for example, only during parts of the day).

- A **drop shipper,** also known as a *desk jobber,* sells merchandise for delivery directly from the producer to the customer. Drop shippers do not physically handle the product. They are common in only a few product categories, including coal, lumber, and building materials, that are typically sold in very large quantities and that have high freight costs in relation to their unit value.

Agent Wholesaling Middlemen

As distinguished from merchant wholesalers, agent wholesaling middlemen (1) do *not* take title to products and (2) typically perform fewer services. As shown in Table 16.3, product characteristics and market conditions determine whether a distribution channel should include agent or merchant wholesaling middlemen. For their assistance, agent middlemen receive a commission, which is a percentage of sales volume, to cover their expenses and to (hopefully) provide a profit. Commission rates vary from about 1 to 10%, depending mainly on the nature of the product and the services performed.

Agent wholesaling middlemen lost more than one-fourth of their share of wholesale trade between 1967 and 1977. In the case of agricultural products, agent middlemen were replaced by merchant wholesalers or by direct sales to food-processing companies and grocery stores. Likewise, for manufactured goods, agent middlemen were supplanted by merchant wholesalers or direct distribution. Since then, agents have fought back. In fact, their share of total wholesale trade has been relatively constant since 1977.[15]

On the basis of sales volume, the most significant types of agent wholesaling middlemen are manufacturers' agents and brokers. Each is described next.

Manufacturers' Agents

An independent agent wholesaling middleman that sells part or all of a manufacturer's product mix in an assigned geographic territory is a **manufacturers' agent,** or *manufacturers' representative.* According to one estimate, about 35,000 manufacturers' reps operate in the U.S.[16] Agents are not employees of the manufacturers; they are independent business firms. Although technically independent, agents have little or no control over prices and terms of sale, which are established by the manufacturers they represent.

Table 16.3	Factors Suggesting Which Type of Wholesaling Middlemen Should Be Used in a Channel	
Factors	**Favoring Agent Wholesaling Middlemen**	**Favoring Merchant Wholesalers**
Nature of product	Nonstandard, perhaps made to order	Standard
Technicality of product	Simple	Complex
Product's gross margin	Small	Relatively large
Number of customers	Few	Many
Concentration of customers	Concentrated geographically and in a few industries	Dispersed geographically and in many industries
Frequency of ordering	Relatively infrequently	Frequently
Time between order and receipt of shipment	Customer satisfied with relatively long lead time	Customer requires or desires shorter lead time

Source: Adapted from Donald M. Jackson and Michael F. d'Amico, "Products and Markets Served by Distributors and Agents," *Industrial Marketing Management,* February 1989, pp. 27–33.

Because a manufacturers' agent sells in a limited territory, each producer uses multiple agents to fully cover its total market. Manufacturers' reps have year-round relationships with the companies (often called *principals*) they represent. Each agent usually serves several noncompeting manufacturers of related products. For example, a manufacturers' agent may specialize in toys and carry an assortment of noncompeting lines in board games, dolls, learning materials, and outdoor play equipment.

Manufacturers' agents are used extensively in distributing many types of consumer and business goods, ranging from sporting goods to heating and air-conditioning vents and ductwork. Their main service to manufacturers is selling. Because a manufacturers' agent does not carry nearly as many lines as a full-service wholesaler, an agent can be expected to provide knowledgeable, aggressive selling.

Manufacturers' agents are most helpful to:

- A small firm that has a limited number of products and no sales force.
- A business that wants to add a new, possibly unrelated line to its existing product mix, but its present sales force either is not experienced in the new line or lacks familiarity with the new market.
- A firm that wants to enter a new market that is not yet sufficiently developed to warrant the use of its own sales force.

A manufacturers' agent can be cost-effective because its major expenses (travel and lodging) are spread over a number of manufacturers' lines. Also, because producers pay them a commission, reps are paid only for what they actually sell. Some agents operate on a commission as low as 2% of net sales; others earn as much as 20%. Depending on how difficult the product is to sell and whether it is stocked by the agent, operating expenses of reps can vary greatly. However, they average about 6% of sales.[17]

There are limitations to what manufacturers' agents do. Agents usually do not carry an inventory of merchandise, do not install machinery and equipment, and typically are not equipped to furnish customers with repair service. However, to remain viable, manufacturers' reps are adding new marketing services. Because they have direct contact with customers, some are able to assist their principals in developing new products. Others offer telemarketing and direct-mail programs.[18]

Brokers

A **broker** is an independent agent wholesaling middleman that brings buyers and sellers together and provides market information to one party or the other. It furnishes information about many topics, including prices, products, and general market conditions. In recent years, manufacturers' agents and brokers have become more similar with respect to attributes and services. Typically, they do not physically handle the products being distributed.

Most brokers work for sellers, although some represent buyers. Brokers have no authority to set prices. They simply negotiate a sale and leave it up to the seller to accept or reject the buyer's offer.

Brokers are used in selling real estate and securities, but they are most prevalent in the food field. For example, a seafood broker handles the output from a salmon cannery, which operates only about three months each year. The canner employs a broker to find buyers among retail stores, wholesalers, and other institutions such as government agencies.

Brokers receive relatively small commissions, normally less than 4% of sales. They provide limited services and, as a result, incur fairly low expenses—about 3% of sales.[19]

Other Agent Wholesaling Middlemen

Three additional types of agent wholesaling middlemen account for smaller shares of wholesale trade than do manufacturers' reps and brokers. Nevertheless, they are very important for certain products and in specific markets. These middlemen are:

As explained in Chapter 14, through gray marketing, products wind up being distributed outside a manufacturer's authorized distribution channels. For example, an export agent (or some other type of wholesaling middleman) may establish a relationship with a European manufacturer to distribute its line of stereo equipment in South America, but not in the U.S. However, without the manufacturer's knowledge, the agent diverts a large shipment for sale in the U.S. Assume that you're the stereo equipment buyer for a chain of discount houses. The export agent contacts you about purchasing some stereos at prices substantially below the normal wholesale price.

Would it be ethical to buy these stereos for resale in your stores? Would your view depend on whether you knew for sure that the stereos were indeed gray market goods?

- A **selling agent** essentially substitutes for a marketing department by marketing a manufacturer's entire output. Selling agents transact only about 1% of wholesale trade, but they play a key role in distributing textile products and coal and, to a lesser extent, apparel, food, lumber, and metal products.
- An **auction company** helps assembled buyers and sellers complete their transactions. Traditional auction companies provide auctioneers who do the selling, and physical facilities for displaying the sellers' products. Although they make up only about 1% of total wholesale trade, this type of auction company is extremely important in the wholesaling of used cars and certain agricultural products such as tobacco, livestock, and fruit. In the mid-1990s, Internet-based auction companies started to appear, providing cyberspace in which sellers offer products for sale and a website at which both consumers and organizations search for bargains or rare products. Now, according to one estimate, there are 1,500 Internet-based auction sites, including FreeMarkets, OneMediaPlace, and others focused on business markets.[20]

www.onemediaplace.com

- An **import-export agent** brings together sellers and buyers from different countries. Export agents work in the country in which the product is made; import agents are based in the country where the product will be sold.

Nature and Importance of Physical Distribution

After a company establishes its channels of distribution, it must arrange for actually moving its tangible products through these channels. **Physical distribution**, which we use synonymously with *logistics*, consists of all the activities concerned with moving the right amount of the right products to the right place at the right time. According to one estimate, total annual spending on logistics is about $1 *trillion* in the U.S., or 10% of the gross domestic product; worldwide, the total is approximately $2 trillion. For an individual firm, the cost of logistics can be equivalent to 10 to 15% of sales.[21]

In its full scope, physical distribution for manufacturers includes the flow of *raw materials* from their sources of supply to the production line *and* the movement of *finished goods* from the end of the production line to the final users' locations. Middlemen manage the flows of goods *onto* their shelves as well as *from* their shelves to customers' homes, stores, or other places of business.

The activities comprising physical distribution are order processing, inventory control, inventory location and warehousing, materials handling, and transportation.

A decision regarding any one of these activities affects all the others. The location of a warehouse influences the selection of transportation methods and carriers; the choice of a carrier influences the optimum size of shipments.

Increasing Attention to Physical Distribution

As described in one article, "Virtually the entire economy depends on the arcane and complex science of logistics to get billions of parts and supplies into U.S. manufacturing plants on time and to distribute finished products efficiently to consumers."[22] Thus a business faces a problem (or maybe it's an opportunity) when it has a warehouse full of patio furniture in Atlanta but unsatisfied customers in New Orleans, or too many ski parkas in Phoenix and too few in Missoula, Montana. These examples underscore that the appropriate assortment of products must be in the right place at the right time to maximize the opportunity for profitable sales. Further, the movement of goods from one place to another must be accomplished in a cost-effective manner.

Physical distribution may be the last marketing area with substantial opportunities for cost cutting. And the potential savings are great. For some products, such as furniture and building materials, physical distribution represents the largest operating expense. Profits are paper-thin for many businesses, so any savings are appreciated. A supermarket, for instance, typically earns a net profit of 1% of sales. Thus every $1 a supermarket saves in physical distribution costs has the same effect on profit as a $100 increase in sales!

Effective logistics also can be the basis by which a firm gains and sustains a differential advantage. On-time delivery, which requires competent physical distribution, can provide an edge. With that in mind, Caterpillar is able to deliver replacement parts within 72 hours for 99.7% of all orders.[23]

Opportunities to better satisfy customers, cut costs, and/or gain a competitive edge expanded greatly in 1980. During that year, two new federal laws (the Motor Carrier Act and the Staggers Act) completed the deregulation of marketing activities related to *interstate* transportation. Previously, pricing by railroads, airlines, and trucking companies had been subject to restrictive regulations. By the beginning of 1995, *intrastate* trucking was basically deregulated as well.

Since deregulation, transportation firms have been able to decide which rates (prices) and levels of service would best satisfy their target markets. For example,

From this "nerve center" at the headquarters of Schneider National, Inc., about 450 employees use satellite technology to keep track of the company's more than 20,000 pieces of trucking equipment. This system has cut Schneider's internal costs by nearly one-quarter and boosted on-time deliveries from under 90% to almost 99%.

 www.schneider.com

Can the locations of over 50,000 truck tractors and trailers be pinpointed?

In years past, trucking companies and other freight carriers were not able to monitor the locations of their equipment (trucks, railcars). As one manager admitted, "We didn't know where trucks were, in Florida or Tennessee." As a result, carriers could not inform customers about the status of their shipments. Or at least they could not do so with much reliability.

That has changed. Most transportation firms can pinpoint the locations of their equipment, and many monitor shipments on a real-time basis. Schneider National, based in Green Bay, Wisconsin, started this movement in 1988. Today Schneider, the largest trucking company, knows within 100 feet where all of its over 10,000 tractors (the front part of the truck that contains the engine) are at any time.

How is this done? Schneider and some other carriers have equipped their tractors with tracking devices and onboard computers that permit two-way communication between truck and company office through a satellite. Recently, Schneider decided to add similar tracking devices to all of its trailers. By doing so, it would know where they are even when they are not tethered to a tractor—in trailer staging areas or on railcars, for example. Tracking systems are also used by railroads and other modes of transportation.

Real-time monitoring should satisfy customers because they can know not only the precise location of a shipment but also its expected arrival time. A carrier benefits too. For instance, a tracking system helps a trucking company reroute rigs to avoid bad weather or other delays and to locate empty trailers when extra capacity is needed. Such steps increase the efficiency of expensive transportation equipment. As a Schneider executive commented, "Most of the payback will come from greater asset utilization." Tracking both tractors and trailers could produce annual savings of $5 billion, according to one consultant.

Sources: Wendy Leavitt, "Relocating the Edge," *Fleet Owner,* July 1999, p. 110; Daniel Machalaba, "Schneider National to Outfit Trailers with Tracking Devices to Map Locations," *The Wall Street Journal,* May 7, 1999, p. A2; and Warren Cohen, "Taking to the Highway," *U.S. News & World Report,* Sept. 18, 1995, pp. 84–87.

Landair Transport Inc. gained recognition by promising on-time deliveries; in fact, 99% of shipments arrived within 15 minutes of the scheduled time.[24] Deregulation has also benefited shippers, who are now better able to shop around for rates and service levels that best meet their needs.

In the past several years, the surge of electronic commerce has underscored the importance of physical distribution. The challenge relates to **fulfillment,** which entails having the merchandise that is ordered by a customer in stock and then packing and shipping it in an efficient, timely manner. Many manufacturers are adept at filling large orders for a small number of customers. But some, or even most, are encountering difficulties in filling small orders for a large number of customers. Traditional retailers are used to shoppers coming to their "bricks and mortar" stores and then carrying home their purchases. And purely Internet retailers "are discovering that if they don't control their own warehouses and shipping, their reliability ratings with customers can turn dismal."[25] If there are problems with fulfillment, the likelihood of repeat purchases drops sharply. Some firms engaged in electronic commerce are doing their own fulfillment, but many—perhaps most—are outsourcing the fulfillment task.

Supply Chain Management

Occasionally we have referred to marketing as a *total system* of business activities rather than a series of fragmented operations. **Supply chain management** represents a total system perspective of distribution, combining distribution channels and physical distribution. The core of supply chain management (SCM) is coordinated logistics.

Internet merchants can turn fulfillment over to a specialized firm such as SubmitOrder.com, Inc. This company provides "e-fulfillment" services, including inventory management, order filling, shipping, and management of customer data. According to SubmitOrder.com, its clients will benefit in several ways, such as getting purchases to customers quicker and reducing fulfillment costs.

 www.submitorder.com

Traditionally, logistics activities were fragmented and, in many firms, they still are. If you ask, "Who's in charge of physical distribution?" too often the answer is "No one." Responsibility for it is delegated to various units that may have conflicting goals. The production department, for instance, is interested primarily in long production runs to minimize unit manufacturing costs, even though the result may be high inventory costs. In contrast, the finance department wants a minimum of funds tied up in inventories. At the same time, the sales department wants to have a wide assortment of products available at locations near customers.

Uncoordinated conditions like these make it impossible to achieve a flow of products that satisfies the firm's goals. To alleviate this problem, a number of firms are establishing separate departments responsible for all logistics activities. Even when this occurs in large firms, physical distribution usually is separated from the marketing department. This separation causes problems when a company is trying to formulate and implement coordinated marketing strategies, including logistics. With supply chain management, individual logistics activities are brought together in a unified way.

The **total cost concept** is integral to effective supply chain management. A company should determine the set of activities that produces the best relationship between costs and profit for the *entire* physical distribution system. This approach is superior to focusing strictly on the separate costs of individual distribution activities.

Sometimes a company attempts to minimize the cost of only one aspect of physical distribution—transportation, for example. Management might be upset by the high fees for air freight. But the expense of air freight may be more than offset by savings from (1) lower inventory costs, (2) less insurance and interest expense, (3) lower crating costs, and (4) fewer lost sales because of out-of-stock conditions. The point is not that air freight is the best mode of transportation; which mode is best varies with the situation. The key point is that physical distribution should be viewed as a *total* process, with all of the related costs and benefits analyzed.

Effective supply chain management can improve several aspects of performance. A consultant estimated that superior SCM can (1) improve on-time deliveries by about 20%, (2) reduce necessary inventory levels by about 50%, and (3) boost the firm's profits by an amount equal to 3 to 6% of sales.[26]

As part of supply chain management, some companies are contracting out, or *outsourcing,* their physical distribution function. It's more and more common for logistics companies to manage firms' distribution processes under a multiyear contract. The growth of **contract logistics,** also called *third-party logistics* or simply

3PL, reflects a broader trend in the U.S. whereby firms are outsourcing various business tasks ranging from payroll to public relations.

The scope of contract logistics is evident in the following two examples. Caliber Logistics (now part of FedEx Corp.) operated a warehouse for a unit of Hewlett-Packard that produces computer printers. Besides handling the storage function, Caliber employees delivered needed parts and materials to the nearby H-P manufacturing plant. Recently, Ford Motor Co. signed up United Parcel Service to track new cars as they move from factories to dealerships. The intent is to reduce shipping times by as much as 40%.[27]

www.fedex.com

Companies are turning to contract logistics for essentially the same reasons they are outsourcing other business tasks. Basically, by turning the physical distribution function over to a third party, a firm can concentrate on its core business (for example, producing power hand tools or fine lingerie). Further, it expects to become more effective (as indicated by greater customer satisfaction) and/or more efficient (as indicated by lower costs and greater return on investment) in the area of logistics. At the start of the new century, contract logistics comprises about a $50 billion business annually, three times its size in 1994. Almost two-thirds of large American manufacturers are outsourcing part of their physical distribution activities. Compared to annual growth rates of about 15% in the U.S., contract logistics is expanding at least twice as fast in Europe.[28]

Strategic Use of Physical Distribution

The strategic use of physical distribution may enable a company to strengthen its competitive position by providing more customer satisfaction and/or by reducing operating costs. The management of physical distribution can also affect a firm's marketing mix—particularly distribution channels. Each opportunity is described below.

Improve Customer Service

A well-run logistics system can improve the service a firm provides its customers—whether they are middlemen or ultimate users. Furthermore, the level of customer service directly affects demand. This is true especially in marketing undifferentiated products (such as chemicals and most building materials) where effective service may be a company's only differential advantage. For example, Hillenbrand Industries Inc. is set up to deliver any one of 300 casket models to its funeral home customers, ordinarily within 48 hours.[29]

To ensure reliable customer service, management should set standards of performance for each subsystem of physical distribution. These standards should be quantitatively measurable. Here are some hypothetical examples:

- *Electronics manufacturer:* Make delivery within five days after receiving an order, with no more than 20% of the shipments by air.
- *Sporting goods wholesaler:* Fill 99.5% of orders accurately, without increasing the size of the order-fulfillment staff.
- *Industrial distributor:* Fulfill at least 85% of orders received from inventory on hand, but maintain a stockturn of 30 days.

Reduce Distribution Costs

Many avenues to cost reductions may be opened by effective physical distribution management. For example, inventories—and their attendant carrying costs and capital investment—may be reduced through more accurate forecasting of demand for various goods. According to one estimate, better demand forecasts could reduce total inventory in the U.S. by 25%, which would pare inventory levels by over $150 *billion.*[30]

When National Semiconductor applied the total cost concept, it committed to a major investment, building a distribution center in Singapore. The company decided that all computer chips assembled in East Asia would be shipped to this facility, sorted there, and then sent by air freight to customers around the world. National Semiconductor contracted with FedEx Corp. to manage this distribution process. Over a two-year period, logistics costs shrank from 2.6% to 1.9% of sales. On a sales base of a couple of *billion* dollars, that's a considerable savings.[31]

Create Time and Place Utilities

Storage, which is part of warehousing, creates *time utility.* Storage is essential to correct imbalances in the timing of production and consumption. An imbalance can occur when there is *year-round consumption* but only *seasonal production,* as in the case of agricultural products. For instance, time utility is created and value is added when apples are harvested and stored in the fall for sale and consumption months later. In other instances warehousing helps adjust *year-round production* to *seasonal consumption.* A manufacturer may produce lawn mowers on a year-round basis; during the fall and winter, the mowers are stored for sale in the spring and summer.

Transportation adds value to products by creating *place utility.* A fine suit hanging on a manufacturer's rack in New York City has less value than an identical suit ready for sale in a retailer's store in Baltimore. Transporting the suit from New York to Baltimore creates place utility and adds value to it.

Stabilize Prices

Careful management of warehousing and transportation can help stabilize prices for an individual firm or for an entire industry. If a market is temporarily glutted with a product, sellers can store it until supply and demand conditions are better balanced. Such use of warehousing facilities is common in the marketing of agricultural products and other seasonally produced goods.

The judicious movement of products from one market to another may enable a seller to (1) avoid a market with depressed prices or (2) take advantage of a market that has a shorter supply and higher prices. If demand for heating oil is stronger in Akron, Ohio, than in Des Moines, Iowa, a producer should be able to achieve greater revenues by shifting some shipments from Des Moines to Akron.

Influence Channel Decisions

Decisions regarding inventory management have a direct bearing on a producer's selection of channels and the location of middlemen. Logistical considerations may become paramount, for example, when a company decides to decentralize its inventory. In this case management must determine (1) how many sites to establish and (2) whether to use wholesalers, the company's own warehouses, or public warehouses. One producer may select merchant wholesalers that perform storage and other warehousing services. Another may prefer to use a combination of manufacturers' agents, to provide aggressive selling, and public warehouses, to distribute the products ordered.

Control Shipping Costs

Managers with shipping responsibilities need to ensure that their companies enjoy the best combination of delivery times *and* shipping rates for whatever methods of transportation they deem to use. The pricing of transportation services is one of the most complicated parts of American business. The rate, or tariff, schedule is the carrier's price list. Typically it is complex. To cite one example, shipping rates vary for different types of goods, depending on many factors including not only distance to the destination but also the bulk and weight of the products. Therefore, being able to interpret a tariff schedule properly is a money-saving skill for a manager with shipping responsibilities.

Tasks in Physical Distribution Management

Physical distribution refers to the actual physical flow of products. In contrast, **physical distribution management** is the development and operation of processes resulting in the effective and efficient physical flow of products.

Irrespective of whether a firm is part of a logistics alliance or handles this function on its own, effective physical distribution management requires careful attention to five interrelated activities:

- Order processing
- Inventory control
- Inventory location and warehousing
- Materials handling
- Transportation

Each of these activities must be carefully coordinated with the others.

Order Processing

The starting point in a physical distribution system is *order processing*, which is a set of procedures for receiving, handling, and filling orders promptly and accurately. This activity should include provisions for billing, granting credit, preparing invoices, and collecting past-due accounts. Customer ill will results if a company makes mistakes or is slow in filling orders. In addition, inefficient order processing can lead to unnecessarily large inventories. That's why more and more firms have turned to computers to execute most of their order processing activities. At the same time, some suppliers are even providing customers with computer technology to use in placing orders.

There have been various computer-based advances in order processing, most notably **electronic data interchange (EDI)**. Under EDI, orders, invoices, and perhaps other business information as well are transmitted by computer rather than by mail. As such, EDI speeds up the process and markedly reduces the associated paperwork. Originally, the EDI process required a direct computer link between supplier and customer. Now EDI is being adapted for Internet usage, which could lower the costs of the process and, in turn, expand the number of firms that could engage in computer-to-computer transmission of orders and other distribution-related information. Small retailers are even using e-mail to place orders with some suppliers.[32]

www.covisint.com

Some of the largest manufacturers intend to use the Internet for virtually all of their purchasing. In early 2000, Ford, General Motors, and DaimlerChrysler announced that they would jointly establish an Internet site, named Covisint, to handle the bulk of their $240 billion in annual purchases. Suppliers will be expected to use the automakers' new site to bid on parts and services contracts. Online auctions will be part of the new purchasing arrangement. Likewise, Boeing and Oracle Corp. started a joint venture to establish an online parts-supply website for the aircraft firm. Giant manufacturers anticipate that Internet-based purchasing will lower purchase prices, as a result of increased competition among suppliers, and will reduce the cost of order processing significantly.[33]

Inventory Control

Controlling the size and composition of inventories, which represent a sizable investment for most companies, is essential to any physical distribution system. The goal of *inventory control* is to satisfy the order-fulfillment expectations of customers while minimizing both the investment and fluctuations in inventories.

Customer–Service Requirements

Inventory size is determined by balancing costs and desired levels of customer service. Different customers have varying needs regarding order fulfillment. In today's acutely competitive environment, most individuals or organizations expect the order to be completely filled almost immediately. The rare customer is one that is not demanding and will accept an occasional out-of-stock item or a slight delay in receiving an order. Management must identify and respond to differences in expected levels of customer service.

When a company knows its customers' expectations regarding order fulfillment, it then must decide what percentage of orders it intends to fill promptly from inventory on hand. Out-of-stock conditions result in lost sales, loss of goodwill, even loss of customers. Yet to be able to fill 100% of orders promptly may require an exceedingly large and costly inventory.

Economic Order Quantity

Management must establish the optimal quantity for reorder when it is time to replenish inventory stocks. The **economic order quantity (EOQ)** is the volume at which the sum of inventory-carrying costs and order-processing costs are at a minimum. Typically, as order size increases, (1) inventory-carrying cost goes up (because the average inventory is larger) and (2) order-processing cost declines (because there are fewer orders).

In Figure 16.4, point EOQ represents the order quantity having the lowest total cost. Actually, the order quantity that a firm considers best (or optimal) often is larger than the EOQ. That's because management must try to balance the sometimes conflicting goals of low inventory costs and responsive customer service. For various reasons, such as gaining a differential advantage, a firm may place a higher priority on customer service than on inventory costs. To completely fill orders in a timely manner may well call for a larger order quantity than the EOQ—for example, quantity X in Figure 16.4.

Just-in-Time

First widely used in Japan, **just-in-time (JIT)** integrates inventory control, purchasing, and production scheduling. Applying JIT, a firm buys in small quantities that arrive *just in time* for production and then it produces in quantities *just in time* for sale. When effectively implemented, the just-in-time concept has many

Figure 16.4

Economic order quantity.

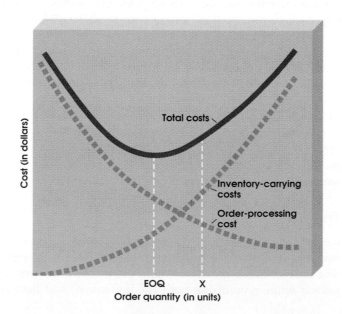

benefits. By purchasing in small quantities and maintaining low inventory levels of parts and finished goods, a company can achieve dramatic cost savings because fewer items are damaged, stolen, or otherwise become unusable. Production and delivery schedules can be shortened and made more flexible and reliable. The Japanese found that quality improves with JIT purchasing. When order quantities are small and deliveries frequent, a company can quickly spot and correct a quality problem in the products received.[34]

An organization that relies on JIT tends to use fewer suppliers because a high level of coordination is needed. Just-in-time was adopted slowly in the U.S., largely because of long-standing business practices. Many American firms, for instance, were more secure with a large inventory of parts and supplies. Eventually, during the 1980s, the JIT philosophy was adopted in the American auto industry and then was implemented by other leading firms such as IBM and General Electric. Often, the results are quite dramatic. For example, Xerox eliminated 4,700 suppliers in one year, and Black & Decker cut more than 50% of its suppliers in two years.[35] JIT puts pressure on a supplier to meet a manufacturer's needs in a very timely fashion. In some instances, it has created friction between vendor and customer.

An updated version of JIT, labeled *JIT II,* stresses closer working relationships between manufacturers and suppliers. Under JIT II, a company provides a supplier with sales forecasts and other useful information, some of which may be confidential. In turn, a supplier often places one of its employees at the customer's plant to handle all or part of the purchasing function.[36]

As with any business practice, there are potential problems with JIT II, such as sharing of confidential data. Hence, some companies are applying JIT or JIT II, whereas many others are not convinced the improvements in customer service are sufficient to justify the additional costs. Channel members, even entire channels, that employ JIT or JIT II effectively can gain a differential advantage. Firms or channels that ignore it risk a differential disadvantage.[37]

Market-Response Systems

JIT's focus tends to be on production and the relationship between a producer and its suppliers. There's a parallel trend, however, involving producers or wholesalers of finished goods and their customers. Several labels have been used to describe this counterpart to JIT; we prefer **market-response system.** The central idea is that expected or actual purchases by final customers, those who intend to consume the product, should activate a process to produce and deliver replacement items. In this way, a product is pulled through a channel on the basis of demand rather than on short-term price reductions or other inducements, which often result in excess inventories.

The intent of a market response system is similar to that of JIT, namely to have just the right amount of goods in stock to satisfy demand and then to replenish exhausted stocks rapidly. By minimizing the quantity of inventory that languishes in middlemen's warehouses, a market response system can shrink the funds that channel members have tied up in inventory and also reduce their operating expenses. Consumer prices may also drop—or at least not rise as much.

Under *automatic replenishment,* one kind of market response system, a retail store's computer, knows when a product is sold and, in turn, notifies the supplier's computer that a replacement item is needed. VF Corp., an apparel maker based in Greensboro, North Carolina, has its computers linked to those of various retailers, including Penney's and Wal-Mart. Each night a store's computer sends to VF's computer precise information about which of the manufacturer's products, including Lee and Wrangler jeans and Vanity Fair women's underwear, were sold that day. Then VF ships replacement items, either from existing inventory or as soon as they are produced. Store shelves can be replenished as soon as two days later.[38]

www.vfc.com

The grocery industry's version of a market response system has been labeled *efficient consumer response (ECR)*. Originating in the early 1990s, ECR is focused on developing and implementing improved practices in four areas of marketing: new-product introductions, product assortments, replenishment (a combination of order processing and inventory control), and trade promotions. Projected savings from ECR are $30 billion a year.[39]

In the past few years, arrangements—actually systems—that extend beyond automatic replenishment have been developed. **Collaborative planning, forecasting, and replenishment** (CPFR) is a method by which a producer or a wholesaler and a customer, ordinarily a retail chain, jointly and interactively develop sales forecasts through a shared website. The intent of CPFR is to supply the right amount of products—neither too many nor too few—in response to demand. The outcomes of CPFR are not just decision rules related to replenishment but also a full plan for marketing a specific product. CPFR requires sharing of confidential information between the participating channel members, so it depends on trust in the relationship.

www.warnerlambert.com

A pilot test of CPFR involving Warner-Lambert, Inc., which makes Listerine mouthwash, and Wal-Mart produced very promising results. Of particular interest was a 25% reduction in inventories of Listerine. Subsequent tests, involving other firms, generated sales gains and reductions in out-of-stock situations. These results notwithstanding, sophisticated, yet user-friendly software that facilitates the electronic interactions is needed to make CPFR practical on a widespread basis. For this to happen, leading firms from both the manufacturing and distribution sectors must agree on a common set of standards for the collaborative software. Thus much work needs to be done if CPFR is to become an enduring part of physical distribution management.[40]

CPFR is very much related to company-wide initiatives that are intended to integrate by means of computer programs the various business functions of an organization. The functions include sales, manufacturing, purchasing, distribution, financial management, and human resources. These efforts are commonly called **enterprise resource planning systems,** or simply *ERP* or *enterprise software*. As the new century began, ERP was paying increased attention to what has been labeled *supply chain optimization* and *customer relationship management,* both of which are directly linked to distribution.[41]

Inventory Location and Warehousing

Management must make critical decisions about the size, location, and transportation of inventories. These areas are interrelated, often in complex ways. The number and locations of inventory sites, for example, influence inventory size and transportation methods. One important consideration in managing inventories is *warehousing*, which embraces a range of functions, such as assembling, dividing (bulk-breaking), and storing products and preparing them for reshipping.

Types of Warehouses

Any producer, wholesaler, or retailer has the option of operating its own private warehouse or using the services of a public warehouse. A **private warehouse** is more likely to be an advantage if (1) a company moves a large volume of products through a warehouse, (2) there is very little, if any, seasonal fluctuation in this flow, and (3) the goods have special handling or storage requirements.

A **public warehouse** offers storage and handling facilities to individuals or companies. Public warehousing costs are a variable expense. Customers pay only for the space they use, and only when they use it. Public warehouses can also provide office and product display space, and accept and fill orders for sellers. Furthermore, warehouse receipts covering products stored in certain types of public warehouses may be used as collateral for bank loans.

Distribution Centers

An effective inventory-location strategy may involve the establishment of a **distribution center,** or perhaps more than one. This type of facility, typically very large in size, is planned around markets rather than transportation requirements. The idea is to develop under one roof an efficient, fully integrated system for the flow of products—taking orders, filling them, and preparing them for delivery to customers.

www.nintendo.com

Distribution centers have been established by many well-known firms. Nintendo of America has a 380,000-square-foot distribution center in North Bend, Washington, where products are received in large sealed containers from Japan. From there, video games and related accessories are shipped to 10,000 stores nationally. Orders are filled with a 99.996% accuracy rate, which translates to less than one mis-shipped item per every 10,000 items shipped. Given the intense competition in the video game market, efficiency and accuracy are key goals at Nintendo's distribution center. Recently, leading e-commerce firms such as Amazon, eToys, and Webvan are building distribution centers at carefully selected locations around the U.S. Amazon, for example, is constructing centers in Kansas, Kentucky, and Nevada to serve as the hubs of its physical distribution system.[42]

Distribution centers can cut costs by reducing the number of warehouses, pruning excessive inventories, and eliminating out-of-stock conditions. Considering that companies are in business to sell goods, not to store or ship them, warehousing and delivery times must be cut to a minimum. Distribution centers can help in this regard as well.

Materials Handling

Selecting the proper equipment to physically handle products, including the warehouse building itself, is the *materials handling* subsystem of physical distribution management. Equipment that is well matched to the task can minimize losses from breakage, spoilage, and theft. Efficient equipment can reduce handling costs as well as time required for handling.

Modern warehouses are huge one-story structures located in outlying areas where land is less expensive and loading platforms are easily accessed by trucks and trains. Conveyor belts, forklift trucks, and other mechanized equipment are used to move merchandise. In some warehouses the order fillers are even outfitted with in-line skates!

Containerization is a cargo-handling system that has become standard practice in physical distribution. Shipments of products are enclosed in large metal or wood containers. The containers are then transported unopened from the time they leave the shipper's facilities (such as a manufacturer's plant) until they reach their destination (such as a wholesaler's warehouse). Containerization minimizes physical handling, thereby reducing damage, lessening the risk of theft, and allowing for more efficient transportation.

Transportation

A major function of the physical distribution system in many companies is *transportation*—shipping products to customers. Management must decide on both the mode of transportation and the particular carriers. In this discussion we will focus on *intercity* shipments.

In arranging transportation, firms are trying to satisfy customers while controlling expenses. To do so, numerous small companies are forming or joining *shippers cooperatives*. This type of organization, which is run by the members, pools the shipping needs of many firms in order to obtain volume discounts from various carriers, such as railroads. One small business, Marshmallow Products Inc. of Cincinnati, was pleased that its shipping costs dropped 40% after joining a shippers cooperative. Other companies are going to a website, such as iShip.com, to use software that allows them to display the current rates charged by various trans-

www.iship.com

portation firms for different types of service. This service is particularly valuable for small Internet merchants and also for customers of online auctions.[43]

Major Modes

Railroads, trucks, pipelines, water vessels, and airplanes are the leading modes of transportation. In Table 16.4 these five methods are compared on the basis of criteria likely to be used by physical distribution managers in selecting a mode of transportation. Of course, the ratings of alternative modes of transportation can vary from one manager to the next, even within the same buying center in an organization.[44]

The relative use of each of the five major modes, along with trends in use, are shown in Table 16.5. Virtually all intracity shipping is done by motor truck. As indicated in the table, the use of trucks has expanded greatly since 1950. Even as the relative position of railroads slipped between 1950 and 1970, the absolute amount of rail freight increased considerably. The railroads' position has stabilized since 1970.

The future of railroads is clouded as a result of both operating problems and environmental factors. In recent years, notably 1997 and 1998, freight trains often ran late or didn't even move for days at a time because of congested tracks and poor monitoring systems. Aggravated by these problems, a number of shippers turned to other modes of transportation, most often trucks. In terms of the environment, the rise of e-commerce favors modes that are adept at handling small shipments and delivering them directly to consumers. Trucking firms and air-freight companies do that well; in contrast, railroads specialize in large shipments.[45]

Intermodal Transportation

Using two or more modes of transportation to move freight is termed **intermodal transportation**. The intent of this approach is to seize the advantages of multiple forms of transportation. Continued strong growth is forecasted for intermodal transportation, largely because of the ongoing globalization of business, stimulated by compacts such as the North American Free Trade Agreement.[46]

Table 16.4	Comparison of Transportation Methods				
	Transportation Method				
Selection Criteria	**Rail**	**Water**	**Highway**	**Pipeline**	**Air**
Speed (door-to-door time)	Medium	Slowest	Fast	Slow	**Fastest**
Cost of transportation	Medium	**Lowest**	High	Low	Highest
Reliability in meeting delivery schedules	Medium	Poor	Good	**Excellent**	Good
Variety of products carried	**Widest**	**Widest**	Medium	Very limited	Somewhat limited
Number of geographic locations served	Very many	Limited	**Unlimited**	Very limited	Many
Most suitable products	Long hauls of carload quantities of bulky products, when freight costs are high in relation to product's value	Bulky, low-value non-perishables	Short hauls of high-value goods	Oil, natural gas, slurried products	High-value perishables, where speed of delivery is all-important

Table 16.5	Distribution of Intercity Freight Traffic in the United States Based on Ton Miles		
	% of Total		
Specific Mode	**1997**	**1970**	**1950**
Railroads	40	40	56
Trucks	29	21	16
Oil pipelines	17	22	12
Water vessels	14	17	15
Air	*	*	*
Total	100	100	100

*Less than 1% of total.

Notes: A *ton mile* refers to 1 ton of freight being transported 1 mile. The 1950 column does not total to 100% because of rounding. The latest available data are for 1997. These statistics do not cover *intracity* freight traffic or ocean coastal traffic between U.S. ports.

Source: Railroad Facts, Association of American Railroads, Washington, DC, 1999, p. 32.

So-called *piggyback service* involves carrying truck trailers on railroad flatcars. For example, a shipment of auto glass is loaded on J. B. Hunt Transport trucks at the Libbey-Owens-Ford plant near Toledo, Ohio. The truck trailers are placed on a Burlington Northern Santa Fe train in Chicago for a trip to Los Angeles. There, Hunt trucks take the auto glass to its destination in Fontana, California. This form of intermodal transportation provides (1) more flexibility than railroads alone can offer, (2) lower freight costs than trucks alone, and (3) less handling of goods.[47] Another form of intermodal transportation, *fishyback service,* combines ships or barges with either railroads or trucks, or both.

With the trend toward intermodal transportation, more companies that have goods to move are interested in **one-stop shipping,** which consists of one transportation firm offering multiple modes of transportation to customers. Typically, the carrier owns the various modes (such as a truck line, cargo ships, and even airplanes); sometimes, however, they will turn to an outside firm if they need to use a mode of transportation they don't own.[48]

Freight Forwarders

A specialized marketing institution serving firms that ship in less-than-full-load quantities is called a **freight forwarder.** Its main function is to consolidate less-than-carload or less-than-truckload shipments from several shippers into full-load quantities. The complexities of foreign shipments have prompted many companies to rely on forwarders.

The freight forwarder picks up the merchandise at the shipper's place of business and arranges for delivery to the buyer's door. A small shipper benefits from the speed and minimum handling associated with large shipments. It may also cost less to use a freight forwarder than to deal directly with a carrier because of the volume discounts that forwarders can obtain from airlines, railroads, and other carriers. A freight forwarder also provides its customers with traffic management services, such as selecting the best transportation methods and routes.

Package-Delivery Firms

For more than 30 years, **package-delivery firms** have been on the rise. These companies deliver shipments of small packages and high-priority mail. The movement toward just-in-time purchasing certainly has contributed to the continuing growth of this type of transportation company.

Why are packages flying around the world overnight?

Package-delivery services, including those that provide next-day delivery, are well established in the U.S. They are also expanding rapidly in other parts of the world, with growth rates substantially higher than in the U.S. Despite the region's financial crisis in 1997–1998, especially strong demand is projected for East Asia.

A wide variety of products are flowing from Asia to the U.S. and Europe. The contents of shipments include fresh cherries and Pokémon dolls from Japan, cashmere sweaters from Tibet, and athletic footwear from China. The most common shipment probably is computer parts, made in various Asian nations and sent to customers in the U.S. and beyond.

Three factors, in particular, help explain the expanding global market for package-delivery services:

- Simply, more and more goods are being produced in one country and sold in another. In fact, total world exports are now in the vicinity of $8 *trillion* per year.

- A growing number of companies are adopting a just-in-time philosophy. With continuing efforts to reduce inventory levels, manufacturers and middlemen are relying on overnight-delivery firms to ship products as soon as they are produced and just before they are needed by the customer.

- Many foreign markets have greater potential for strong sales and ample profits than does the U.S. Intense competition and widespread adoption of substitute technologies (such as e-mail for delivering documents almost instantaneously) have made it difficult for package-delivery firms to sustain their prior rates of growth in the U.S.

Given the strong potential in East Asia, FedEx Corp. constructed a major hub in the Philippines. FedEx is expecting burgeoning revenues in East Asia, particularly China, where the firm holds exclusive rights to the cargo routes into and out of this emerging market. United Parcel Service is ready for the competition in foreign markets, with its chairman describing the company as "a global conveyor belt," especially for just-in-time deliveries. Although not as well known as FedEx and UPS, DHL Worldwide Express is the leader in Asia, with a 35% market share compared to 20% for FedEx and 10% for UPS. To sustain its position, DHL decided to move its Asian hub from the Philippines to Hong Kong, which is the busiest market for package-delivery services in this region of the world.

DHL is launching an electronic system, called a "landed-cost generator," that will calculate tariffs and duties for shipments among 12 nations that are leaders in world trade. The new system should facilitate e-commerce and aid relatively small companies that have long been perplexed by complex and changing tariffs and duties on shipments to foreign countries. DHL hopes its landed-cost generator will both generate added revenues and provide the firm with a differential advantage over its primary competitors in global markets.

Sources: Douglas A. Blackmon, "DHL Plans to Launch System to Compute Duty, Tariff Fees," *The Wall Street Journal,* Dec. 15, 1999, p. A4; Robert Frank, "U.S. Express Carriers Deliver the Goods as Asia Bounces Back," *The Wall Street Journal,* Dec. 21, 1999, p. A18; Douglas A. Blackmon, "Overnight, Everything Changed for FedEx; Can It Reinvent Itself?" *The Wall Street Journal,* Nov. 4, 1999, pp. A1, A16; and Erick Schonfeld, "Greasing the Wheels of World Trade," *Fortune,* Oct. 28, 1996, p. 228.

You surely are familiar with such package-delivery firms as United Parcel Service (UPS), FedEx, and Airborne Express. All of these companies compete vigorously not only among themselves but also with the U.S. Postal Service. The competition is particularly intense in the overnight-delivery market, where FedEx and UPS go head-to-head. Each giant tries to surpass the other with respect to delivery times, technology that helps customers prepare and then track their shipments, and—of course—low prices.[49]

In contrast to freight forwarders, which do not own their own transportation equipment, package-delivery firms do. Companies such as UPS and FedEx are essentially combined cargo airlines and trucking companies. Furthermore, package-delivery firms, in effect, use intermodal transportation. Consider FedEx, for example. A package is picked up by truck, shipped intercity or overseas by plane, and delivered locally by truck.

The boom in e-commerce, particularly where the shipment is headed to a consumer, has generated still more business for package-delivery firms. It has also

Here, a FedEx employee uses a hand-held device to record data that will enable the tracking of a customer's shipment. Some technological advances pose threats for FedEx. For instance, many documents previously shipped overnight are now being transmitted via e-mail. But technology also brings opportunities. For example, the boom in e-commerce has markedly increased the quantity of small packages being shipped from seller to buyer.

 www.kozmo.com

spawned small start-ups, such as Kozmo.com Inc., which delivers convenience items (groceries and movie rentals, for example) *within one hour* in several metropolitan areas. In a new alliance, Amazon.com contracted with Kozmo.com to provide one-hour delivery of purchases to customers in some areas. Rather than outsourcing this function, other e-tailers have chosen to use their own employees to make deliveries. Webvan Group Inc., an online supermarket, has so-called Internet couriers, each of whom delivers groceries to about 20 customers' homes per day.[50]

Summary

Wholesaling consists of the sale, and all activities directly related to the sale, of goods and services for resale, use in producing other goods or services, or operating an organization. Firms engaged primarily in wholesaling, called wholesaling middlemen, provide economies of skill, scale, and transactions to other firms involved in distribution.

Three categories of wholesaling middlemen are merchant wholesalers, agent wholesaling middlemen, and manufacturers' sales facilities. The first two are independent firms; the third is owned by a manufacturer. Merchant wholesalers take title to products being distributed; agent wholesaling middlemen do not. In recent years, the shares of total wholesale trade captured by the three categories have stabilized, with merchant wholesalers accounting for the majority share.

Merchant wholesalers, which account for the majority of wholesale trade, include both full-service and limited-service wholesalers. Of the three major categories of wholesaling middlemen, merchant wholesalers offer the widest range of services and thus incur the highest operating expenses.

Agent wholesaling middlemen lost ground to merchant wholesalers for at least a couple decades. The main types of agent middlemen are manufacturers' agents and brokers. Because they perform more limited services, agent middlemen's expenses tend to be lower than merchant wholesalers'.

Physical distribution is the flow of products from supply sources to the firm and then from the firm to its customers. The goal of physical distribution is to move the right amount of the right products to the right place at the right time. Physical distribution costs are a substantial part of total operating costs in many firms. Moreover, physical distribution is probably the only remaining source of possible cost reductions in many companies.

Physical distribution activities are still fragmented operationally and organizationally in many firms. To overcome these shortcomings, supply chain management takes a total-system perspective toward distribution. The total cost concept should be applied to physical distribution. That is, management should strive *not* for the lowest total cost of a single physical distribution activity, but for the best balance between customer service and total cost. Effective management of physical distribution can help a company gain an advantage over competitors through better customer service and/or lower operating costs. To improve their physical distribution, some firms are turning to contract logistics.

The operation of a physical distribution system requires management's attention and decision making in five areas: order processing, inventory control, inventory location and warehousing, materials handling, and transportation. They should not be treated as individual activities but as interrelated components within a physical distribution system. Effective management of these five activities requires an understanding of electronic data interchange, economic order quantity, just-in-time processes, market-response systems such as collaborative planning, forecasting, and replenishment (CPFR), distribution centers, and intermodal transportation.

More about **Supervalu**

Even though it is the nation's largest grocery wholesaler, Supervalu Inc. believes it must continue to grow in order to gain economic power that is essential not only when competing with other wholesalers, but also when negotiating with giant manufacturers. At the same time, the chain recognizes that it must become increasingly efficient. The Advantage program is intended to help on both fronts. In addition, Supervalu is exploring a number of other strategies that could pay dividends in terms of growth and/or efficiency.

Mainly dedicated to serving smaller, independent grocery chains, Supervalu wants to supply huge retail chains that traditionally have been "self-distributing," meaning they dealt directly with manufacturers. As a major step down this business path, Supervalu recently entered into an agreement to supply Kmart with over $2 billion in groceries and related merchandise each year. This deal should benefit both companies. Rather than trying to master the wholesale business, Kmart can focus on its retail activities. The added sales volume gives Supervalu more clout when negotiating purchase prices with manufacturers.

To boost efficiency, Supervalu is opening new distribution centers for merchandise that sells relatively slowly, such as health and beauty aids. This approach allows its other distribution centers to concentrate on faster-moving products. Both moves, which are part of the Advantage program, should lower the costs of getting goods from manufacturers to member stores.

Not content to focus solely on wholesaling, Supervalu has also invested heavily in almost 500 corporate-owned stores. These stores have several different banners (including Save-A-Lot, Cub Foods, Shop 'n Save, and bigg's), and they serve distinct market segments. Despite these differences, Supervalu has formulated one overall marketing plan and standard operating procedures to guide all of its own grocery stores. Previously these stores operated completely apart from each other. The new approach allows Supervalu's grocery stores to share ideas, streamline technology, and take advantage of economies of scale.

As more manufacturers decide to bypass wholesalers and deal directly with supermarket chains, Supervalu believes a larger retail presence will protect the company against erosion in its wholesale business. Further, profit margins in retailing are typically twice those in wholesaling. One unresolved issue is whether Supervalu's retail operations help or hurt its member stores and, subsequently the relationship between Supervalu and these customers.[51]

1. Can Supervalu continue to increase the number of company-owned retail stores without jeopardizing its relationships with the independent grocery stores that are its customers?

2. Which of Supervalu's new distribution-related strategies has the most promise? The most risk?

Key Terms and Concepts

Wholesaling (454)
Wholesaling middleman (455)
Merchant wholesaler (457)
Agent wholesaling middleman (457)
Manufacturer's sales facility (457)
Manufacturer's sales branch (458)
Manufacturer's sales office (458)
Full-service wholesaler (459)
Truck jobber (460)
Drop shipper (461)
Manufacturers' agent (461)

Broker (462)
Selling agent (463)
Auction company (463)
Import-export agent (463)
Physical distribution (463)
Fulfillment (465)
Supply chain management (465)
Total cost concept (466)
Contract logistics (466)
Physical distribution management (469)
Electronic data interchange (EDI) (469)
Economic order quantity (EOQ) (470)

Just-in-time (JIT) (470)
Market-response system (471)
Collaborative planning, forecasting, and replenishment (CPFR) (472)
Enterprise resource planning (ERP) systems (472)
Private warehouse (472)
Public warehouse (472)
Distribution center (473)
Containerization (473)
Intermodal transportation (474)
One-stop shipping (475)
Freight forwarder (475)
Package-delivery firms (475)

Questions and Problems

1. Which of the following are wholesaling transactions?
   a. Color Tile sells wallpaper to an apartment building contractor and also to the contractor's wife for her home.
   b. General Electric sells motors to Whirlpool for its washing machines.
   c. A shrimp "farmer" sells shrimp to a local restaurant.
   d. A family orders carpet from a friend, who is a home decorating consultant, at 50% off the suggested retail price. The carpet is delivered directly to the home.

2. As shown in Figure 16.3, agent wholesaling middlemen and manufacturers' sales facilities lost part of their combined share of wholesale trade to merchant wholesalers over the past several decades. But then this erosion stopped. What could the two types of wholesaling middlemen do to combat merchant wholesalers in the future?

3. Why is it that manufacturers' agents often can penetrate a market faster and at a lower cost than a manufacturer's sales force?

4. Which type of wholesaling middleman, if any, is most likely to be used by each of the following firms? Explain your choice in each instance.
   a. A small manufacturer of a liquid glass cleaner to be sold through supermarkets.
   b. A small canner in Vermont packing a high-quality, unbranded fruit product.
   c. A small-tools manufacturing firm that has its own sales force selling to the business market and now wants to add backyard barbecue equipment to its product mix.
   d. A North Carolina textile mill producing unbranded towels, sheets, pillowcases, and blankets.

5. Looking to the future, which types of wholesaling middlemen do you think will increase in importance, and which ones will decline? Explain.

6. "The goal of a modern physical distribution system in a firm should be to operate at the lowest possible *total* costs." Do you agree?

7. Name some products for which you think the cost of physical distribution constitutes at least one-half of the total price of the goods at the wholesale level. Can you suggest ways of decreasing the physical distribution cost of these products?

8. "A manufacturer follows an inventory-location strategy of concentration rather than dispersion. This company's inventory size will be smaller, but its transportation and warehousing expenses will be larger than if its inventory were dispersed." Do you agree? Explain.

9. "The use of public warehouse facilities makes it possible for manufacturers to bypass wholesalers in their channels of distribution." Explain.

10. For each of the following products, determine the best transportation method for shipment to a distribution center in the community where your school is located. In each case the buyer (not the seller) will pay all freight charges and, unless specifically noted, time is not important. The distribution center has a rail siding and a dock for loading and unloading trucks.
    a. Disposable diapers from Wisconsin. Total shipment weight is 112,000 pounds.
    b. A replacement memory card for your computer, which is now inoperative. Weight of the shipment is 1.5 pounds, and you need this card in a hurry.
    c. Blank payroll checks for your company. (There is a sufficient number of checks on hand for the next two weekly paydays.) Shipment weight is 100 pounds.
    d. Ice cream from St. Louis. Total shipment weight is 42,000 pounds.

Hands-On Marketing

1. Interview the owner or a manager at a firm that is a type of merchant wholesaler (such as a full-service wholesaler). Ask the owner or manager to describe the firm's activities, its differential advantage or disadvantage at the present time, and the company's prospects for the future. Conduct a similar interview with the owner or a manager at a firm that is a type of agent wholesaling middleman (such as a broker). How do you explain any discrepancies between the interview results and the content of this chapter (other than saying that the chapter must be wrong)?

2. A manufacturer of precision lenses used in medical and hospital equipment wants to ship a 5-pound box of these lenses from your college town to a laboratory in Stockholm, Sweden. The lab wants delivery in five days or less. The manufacturer wants to use a package-delivery service but is undecided as to which shipper to choose. Compile and compare the types of services provided and prices charged by FedEx, United Parcel Service, and one other package-delivery firm.

Cases for Part 5

Not Just Playing Around with Different Distribution Strategies

When the Internet was in its infancy (just several years ago), a few companies jumped into e-commerce and got a significant head start. One of those "first movers" was eToys Inc., which opened for business in October 1997 with Toby Lenk as head of the firm. The start-up was funded in part by idealab!, an incubator for various e-commerce enterprises. Relying solely on the Internet as its method of distribution, eToys built up a loyal customer following and quickly became one of the Web's most well-known e-tailers.

eToys' fast start certainly caught the attention of Toys "R" Us, the largest specialty toy retailer in the U.S. with almost $12 billion in annual sales. Toys "R" Us (TRU) launched its own website, Toysrus.com, in 1998. Compared to eToys' pure Internet focus, TRU's "clicks-and-mortar" approach (meaning the company has physical stores as well as an Internet sales channel) has led to inevitable conflicts between the stores and its website. But it has also given TRU the advantage of having two channels, immediate brand recognition, and tremendous buying power. In the ensuing battle for market share, both firms are playing for keeps.

The Original Toy Story

During the 1980s, a new type of retail outlet evolved. Labeled *category killer*, this type of merchant concentrated on one type of product and built huge stores to showcase an enormously deep assortment. Nationwide chains of category killers sprang up in product categories such as sports equipment, pet supplies, and home improvement items. The man credited with the category-killer concept was Charles Lazarus, founder of Toys "R" Us.

Throughout the 1980s, TRU expanded at a phenomenal pace, averaging 30% growth per year. As TRU became the largest toy seller in the U.S., its two primary competitors, Child World and Lionel, went into bankruptcy. Eventually though, TRU's stores became run down, and customer service eroded. In addition, TRU was very late to recognize the potential in the fast-growing subcategory of educational toys. As TRU took its eye off the ball, its market share fell from 25% to 17%, and its stock lost more than one-half of its value in the late 1990s. To make matters worse, Wal-Mart overtook TRU as the retailer that sold the largest volume of toys in the U.S., and then eToys became the premier toy merchant on the Internet.

A Giant eToybox

Lenk, who formerly was a Disney executive, explained eToys' approach: "We pioneered a new channel and thought about it, from the ground up, from a new perspective." But all the preparation didn't prevent the new company from making mistakes along the way, beginning on day one. eToys' first "customer" was an executive from TRU who placed an order for five different products. Unfortunately, eToys' inventory tracking system wasn't yet in place, and four of the items were unavailable. "Our first customer—and we just totally blew it," Lenk said.

The fulfillment issue was remedied quickly, and Lenk began to focus on adding products to enhance eToys' selection. According to Lenk, eToys' philosophy is to "give the customer what they want and let them choose. . . . In the physical world, merchants have only so much shelf space—they can't afford to let the customer choose." He began by offering about 1,000 toys from 100 different manufacturers, and later expanded the e-tailer's product mix to include music, videos, software, and books. eToys also acquired BabyCenter, an Internet firm that provides information about raising babies and, of course, sells baby-related items. By 1999, the company's assortment had grown to include more than 100,000 items, and Lenk declared that it was his goal to make eToys the #1 e-tailer of merchandise for kids aged 12 and younger.

Besides offering an enormous selection of children's items, eToys is known for providing special touches to please both parents and children. Its site is attractive, simple to use, and includes an advanced search engine that helps customers find items or product ideas based on one or more traits specified by the shopper. Packages are shipped in plain, unlabeled boxes so kids don't peek. Multiple gifts with separate destinations can be ordered at one time and individually gift wrapped, each with its own unique card.

eToys was the only online toy store open for business in 1997. That year, it registered just $500,000 in sales, but gained valuable experience in dealing with the holiday rush. The next holiday season, it was responsible for 50% of total online toy sales. eToys' revenues soared to $32 million in 1998. Although that amount represents much less than 1% of TRU's annual revenue, eToys was rewarded with a highly successful initial public offering (IPO.) On the offering day, the eToys stock rocketed from $20 to $76 per share, making the company's estimated market capitalization $7.7 *billion*—35% more than TRU's capitalization.

Toying with a New Channel

The success of Wal-Mart and eToys forced TRU to reevaluate its business strategy. In mid-1999, TRU committed millions of dollars to renovate its stores, increase the number of products in each store from 10,000 to approximately 17,000, and revamp its supply chain to reduce inventory and add distribution centers.

To keep pace with eToys, TRU set up a separate e-commerce entity in 1998. However, the unit's first CEO was forced out when he said Toysrus.com needed to discount its prices in order to compete more effectively with eToys and other online toy vendors. His request was denied because the company was fearful of confusing customers by having one set of prices in the stores and another set online. The new site was also criticized for being difficult to use and for providing low levels of customer service. In late November, Toysrus.com's server was overloaded with orders and "crashed" (that is, quit working) for a short while. Sporadic service outages during the next four weeks, combined with order-fulfillment problems, led to a disastrous 1998 holiday season for Toysrus.com.

A new, more user-friendly site was launched in April 1999, and John Barbour was appointed CEO later that same year. His first order of business was to arrange for TRU's physical stores to accept returns of purchases made at Toysrus.com. Barbour believes this approach gives Toysrus.com a distinct advantage over eToys: "Customers are finding they like the convenience of being able to walk down to the local Toys 'R' Us and exchange a toy." In addition, Barbour plans to take advantage of TRU's buying clout to ensure adequate supplies of Furbys, Pokémons, or whatever happens to be the hottest toy of the season.

These changes *and* a hefty advertising campaign helped Toysrus.com become the fourth-most visited e-commerce site during the 1999 holiday season, with 1.7 million separate customers. eToys attracted 1.9 million visitors, but both companies lagged behind Amazon.com. In July 1999, Amazon began selling toys online. A week later Amazon's founder and CEO, Jeff Bezos, declared, "I believe we're already the largest seller of children's products online."

Online Retailing Isn't All Fun and Games

During the 1999 holiday season, the number of customers who made online purchases grew by 37% over the prior year, which caused a variety of customer service and fulfillment problems for both eToys and Toysrus.com. Despite shipping 96% of its orders on time in November and December, eToys thought its level of customer service had declined somewhat, and offered $10 coupons to dissatisfied shoppers. A company spokesperson summarized the situation, "We were not perfect this year. But we won't rest until we are."

eToys' top management may have been distracted by efforts to establish an online toy store in the United Kingdom. Although some European toy manufacturers were already selling their own products through their companies' websites, eToys was the first e-tailer to supply toys from a variety of suppliers to consumers in the U.K. Doing so required the establishment of a distribution center in London. The first-year projections were modest, but the company wanted to build early market share and awareness of the eToys brand in the U.K.

Toysrus.com's fulfillment difficulties were widely publicized. The firm launched a big ad campaign to kick off the 1999 holiday season and offered free shipping and $10 off each first-time order. The enticements were effective, as site traffic jumped by 300%—causing the site to crash for a short period of time. Then, several days before Christmas, Toysrus.com announced it would be unable to guarantee on-time delivery, which infuriated shoppers who had trusted the Toys "R" Us brand name when placing their online orders. Despite investing in a large distribution center in Memphis to handle online fulfillment, inventory shortages arose. To make matters worse, the company told angry customers they would have to pay extra for priority shipping. Toysrus.com later gave dissatisfied shoppers a coupon worth $100, but this did little to placate angry parents who were forced to desperately search elsewhere for items they had already promised to their kids.

Whereas TRU seems to have paid for its holiday transgressions with bad publicity and perhaps lost customers, eToys suffered on Wall Street. Its stock hit a high of $86 per share, but began to fall during the holiday season as Amazon, Toysrus.com, and about 15 other online toy merchants lured customers away. Eventually eToys' stock plummeted to $5, below its initial offering price of $20.

One thing Amazon knows is how to keep its customers happy, fulfilling 99% of its 1999 holiday orders according to schedule. To prevent future problems, Amazon is investing $300 million in additional warehouse space, with competitors also investing significant amounts in new warehouses.

eToys, in fact, revamped its approach to fulfillment. Beginning in mid-1999, Fingerhut, a catalog company owned by Federated Department Stores, handled all of eToys' fulfillment. This arrangement was ended abruptly in early 2000, however. eToys decided it would drastically expand its own distribution centers and handle its own fulfillment, with the goals of reducing shipping costs and streamlining operations.

For now it's unclear which distribution strategy will be more effective in the long run. eToys' founder, Lenk, insists, "What history has shown so far is that the land-based companies in general have found it very difficult to adapt their brand, skills and culture to the Web." The chairman of TRU, Michael Goldstein, disagrees: "The combination of bricks-and-mortar operation with a Web component is the best formula." Both companies intend to prove they know the best way to sell kids' stuff.

Questions

1. a. Which approach to e-commerce will be more effective at attracting and satisfying customers—Toys "R" Us' clicks-and-mortar strategy or eToys' pure Internet focus?

    b. Which approach will promote better relationships with toy manufacturers and wholesalers?

2. How can Toysrus.com compete effectively with eToys' discount pricing without reducing sales in its physical stores?

 www.etoys.com

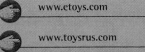 www.toysrus.com

Sources: Lisa Bannon, "EToys' Strategy to Stay in the Game," *The Wall Street Journal,* Apr. 25, 2000, pp. B1, B4; Abigail Goldman and Charles Piller, "Chronic Losses Take the Fun Out of eToys, Other E-Retailers," *The Miami Herald,* Jan. 29, 2000, pp. 1C, 3C; Lisa Bannon, "eToys Meets Expectation but Stock Falls," *The Wall Street Journal,* Jan. 28, 2000, p. B2; Katrina Brooker, "The Nightmare before Christmas," *Fortune,* Jan. 24, 2000, pp. 24–25; Rebecca Smith, "eToys Lured Holiday-Season Shoppers but Concern about Service Hurts Stock," *The Wall Street Journal,* Dec. 28, 1999, p. A3; Maryanne Murray Buechner and Marc Hequet, "Clicks and Bricks: E-tailers Don't Own the World Yet," *Time,* Dec. 27, 1999, pp. 88+; Rachel Beck, "Toysrus.com Will Miss Some Deliveries," *Columbia Missourian,* Dec. 23, 1999, p. 8A; Matt Krantz, "Stocking a Giant Toybox," *USA Today,* Nov. 24, 1999, pp. 1B, 2B; George Anders, "Amazon, eToys Make Big, Opposing Bets; Which One Is Right?" *The Wall Street Journal,* Nov. 2, 1999, pp. A1, A10; Lisa Bannon, "eToys Raises Holiday Budget for Marketing," *The Wall Street Journal,* Oct. 29, 1999, p. B9; Lisa Bannon, "'Tis the Season for eToys' $20 Million Blitz," *The Wall Street Journal,* Sept. 27, 1999, p. B10; Katrina Brooker, "Toys Were Us," *Fortune,* Sept. 27, 1999, pp. 145+; Lisa Bannon, "eToys Plans to Launch U.K. Web Site in Time for Holiday Shopping Season," *The Wall Street Journal,* Sept. 1, 1999, p. B7; Joseph Pereira, "Toys 'R' Us CEO, Nakasone, Resigns," *The Wall Street Journal,* Aug. 27, 1999, p. A3; Joseph Pereira, "On the Internet, Toys 'R' Us Plays Catch-Up," *The Wall Street Journal,* Aug. 19, 1999, pp. B1, B4; Larry Armstrong, "This Toy War Is No Game," *Business Week,* Aug. 9, 1999, pp. 86–87; Jason Fry, "eToys Story," *The Wall Street Journal,* July 12, 1999, p. R38; Betty Liu, "Toys R Us Set to Revamp 525 Stores," *Financial Times,* June 9, 1999, p. 17; Clinton Wilder, "Companies Rush for Online Market Share," *InformationWeek,* May 24, 1999, pp. 18, 20.

Case 2 • United Parcel Service

Delivering New Products and Channels

United Parcel Service (UPS) was founded in 1907 by Jim Casey after he borrowed $100 from a friend to start a parcel-delivery and messenger service in Seattle, Washington. Hired to deliver packages from local department stores to shoppers' homes, UPS's early "fleet" of delivery vehicles included a Model T and a few motorcycles.

From this humble beginning, UPS grew to become one of the largest companies in the world. At the end of the 20th century, the company that is nicknamed "Big Brown" employed 326,000 people worldwide. It had a fleet of 150,000 trucks and 610 planes, and was responsible for transporting 6% of the gross domestic product. UPS, which serves every company in *Fortune* magazine's list of the 1,000 largest companies in the U.S., reported earnings of $2.3 billion on revenues of $27.2 billion in 1999.

Although it is already one of the most ubiquitous and successful companies in the U.S., UPS is constantly looking for ways to better serve its existing customers and to further expand its client base. Fueled by the emergence of the Internet and the promise of international expansion, Big Brown is refining and rethinking its service offering. As explained by the company's chief executive officer, James Kelly, "We want to increase our global footprint across the entire supply chain."

Boxing Up the Competition

Just as it was in 1907, the core of UPS's business is ground transportation. No other company, or even the United States Postal Service (USPS), is as adept, reliable, and economical at moving packages to any address, residential or commercial. For years, UPS relied on a tightly defined business model that prescribes everything from how the firm's drivers should dress (for example, shirts can't be unbuttoned below the top button) to how they should walk (briskly, but without running). UPS drivers are paid an average of $22 per hour for following these requirements (and, of course, delivering lots of packages). Big Brown has achieved an employee retention rate that tops 90%. Most of UPS's executives began their careers in the driver's seat. That includes Kelly, who got his start as a part-time driver in New Jersey before being promoted to a variety of positions in operations.

UPS moves over 12,000,000 packages each day, most of them entirely by ground transportation. But Big Brown has also been expanding its air express business to compete head-to-head with FedEx Corporation, which has dominated that market for many years. FedEx was the first delivery firm to utilize scanning equipment that provides the capability of tracking packages shipped on a priority basis. UPS implemented its own tracking system and recently upgraded it significantly so that as a customer signs to accept a delivery, the information is immediately transmitted to UPS's computers. Senders can go online to receive real-time status reports about their shipments, including the time of delivery.

UPS now delivers 2 million air express packages each day, compared to 3 million for FedEx. However, whereas FedEx grew this part of its business by less than 5% in 1999, UPS's volume in this segment increased by about 10%.

FedEx is fighting back by challenging UPS on the ground. In early 1999, FedEx bought RPS, a delivery company with trucking operations, and renamed it FedEx Ground. Drivers are independent contractors who deliver only to business addresses. FedEx is supplementing its ground business with a new division called FedEx Home Delivery. Until these new divisions take off for FedEx, however, UPS is able to seamlessly serve all of its clients by offering ground and air express delivery, as well as discounts on the volume of combined purchases. But both companies may have to contend with the USPS in the near future. To facilitate on-time delivery of important parcels, the USPS is in the process of developing its own tracking system.

In the meantime, Big Brown is looking for ways to attract more residential and small-business customers. To this end, in early 2000 UPS opened its first store where customers can ship packages, pick them up if they are not home at the time of attempted delivery, purchase office supplies, make copies, and rent mailboxes. There are already about 11,000 pack-and-send stores in the U.S., some with well-known names such as Mail Boxes Etc. and Pak Mail. These companies were understandably upset to hear that UPS would soon become a competitor, especially because they routinely supply UPS with a good deal of business. A UPS spokesman reacted by saying, "This is all a test to see where it might play out."

Being on Time with an Internet Strategy

Earlier, in 1998, UPS launched what may be an even more significant method of distribution, this time using the Internet. The new service, called Document Exchange, allows customers to electronically transmit documents via a secure website. Encryption technology is used so that only the document's sender and recipient can access it, an attractive feature for companies such as law offices and brokerage houses that often need to send "sensitive" materials. In contrast to faxes and traditional e-mail, users are assured complete confidentiality. And considering the price is between $1 and $10 per document, it is considerably less expensive than overnight delivery.

In addition, customers use the Internet to print shipping labels and track their packages. It costs approximately $2 for UPS to service a request received via telephone versus about 10¢ if a customer uses the Internet. Considering that UPS receives more than 2 million online tracking queries each day, the potential savings for the company are enormous. Big Brown can also receive shipping orders electronically, a feature used by more than one-half of its clients, which represents additional savings.

A large number of UPS clients using the Web to place and track orders are e-commerce companies. With enormous growth potential in the world of e-tailing, UPS is well positioned to capture a significant share of Internet companies' shipments of purchases to consumers. In 1999, about $25 billion worth of goods were ordered online; analysts predict that figure will jump to $180 billion by 2004. During this same period, it's projected that the number of shipments will increase several fold, if not more.

The rise of e-tailing is one reason why FedEx decided to augment its ground transportation services. But UPS was able to establish an early foothold by capturing 55% of this line of business in 1998, followed by the USPS with 30% and FedEx with only 10%. Once its tracking system is completed, the USPS will be a more formidable competitive threat to UPS considering that the USPS already delivers to every residence and business in the U.S. on a daily basis.

Fulfilling Customer Needs

Besides shipping packages for e-tailing enterprises, UPS has begun to help these same clients streamline their operations by handling a variety of their physical distribution tasks. Big Brown formed a subsidiary, UPS Worldwide Logistics Group, that is capable of handling warehousing, picking and packing, product repair, and customer service. And that's a mix of services the USPS can't duplicate.

To support its Internet ventures, Worldwide Logistics Group, and other technological endeavors, UPS invested over $11 *billion* in technology during the 1990s. Said Kelly, "The Net, and electronic commerce in general, is causing us all to rethink the entire business model, and certainly the supply chain as it relates to UPS."

Kelly says there is $1 *trillion* worth of inventory sitting in companies' warehouses, a figure that can be cut in half with sophisticated physical distribution management systems. Part of the investment UPS has made in technology has been in software that links its clients with its own networks. According to Kelly, "We're becoming a logistics company because we have many customers who don't want to do certain things themselves any longer, customers who are saying, 'I want to produce a product, and after that I want you to take care of it.'"

UPS is now performing functions that go way beyond just moving goods. For instance, it hired professional musicians to tune Fender guitars before sending them to the instrument manufacturer's clients. It is also taking customer orders for Nike.com at a call center in San Antonio and fulfilling orders for Nike shoes and apparel out of a warehouse in Louisville, Kentucky. UPS has even struck an agreement with Ford to track its vehicles as they are being delivered to dealerships, a move both companies believe will reduce delivery time by 40%.

UPS is facing competitive pressure from rival FedEx in the rapidly growing area of contract logistics. With a goal of reducing inventory costs, Cisco Systems chose FedEx (over UPS) to deliver computer routers to customers in a precise and timely manner in order to reduce inventory expenses. Despite that particular lost sale, UPS predicts its Worldwide Logistics Group will attain 40% growth over the next several years, with a good portion of it coming from the e-commerce market. "Logistics became a very hot topic for the e-commerce industry as people realized that the connection between logistics and customers' satisfaction hit the bottom line," commented a UPS spokeswoman. In 2000, to fortify its position in e-commerce, UPS created a subsidiary called eVentures. The new unit was formed to test Internet-based services, in an environment that is a bit less rigid than the traditional UPS culture.

Trucking into International Markets

In addition to its expansion into cyberspace, UPS is increasing the scope of its international operations. Although the company began doing business in Europe in 1976, it wasn't until 1998 that it made a profit overseas. FedEx first began doing business in Europe in the 1980s, but stopped in 1992 because it was losing an estimated $1 million each day. Now it has begun to increase its European network.

Both package-delivery firms are facing stiff competition from national postal agencies in France, the Netherlands, and the U.K. In particular, the German post office, Deutsche Post, set its sights on the European shipping market, and acquired a 24% stake in DHL International (the leading European shipping company).

The fact that these national postal agencies have the benefit of monopolistic protection rankles Kelly. In his view, these agencies can subsidize their package-delivery operations with revenues from first-class mail.

Asia, another key international target for UPS, represents a $3 billion express-shipping market with double-digit growth projections. The recovery of Asian markets after the financial problems of the late 1990s has led to an export boom. In fact, in some cases, shipping companies have been forced to turn away business. "We're filled to the roof on most of our flights," says UPS's top executive in Asia. DHL is the current market leader in Asia, with a 35% share, followed by FedEx with 20% and UPS with 10%. UPS is scrambling to increase its network of employees, trucks, and warehouses to gain ground in this part of the world.

Recently, UPS made an impressive move on Wall Street. In November 1999, the employee-owned company sold 10% of its stock in a widely publicized initial public offering (IPO) that turned out to be the largest in U.S. history. It raised $5.5 billion by offering the stock at a price of $50 per share. Before the day of the offering ended, the stock price soared to $74. UPS's IPO came after a number of e-commerce companies had impressive debuts with their own IPOs. Most of those companies show little promise of turning a profit for years to come, whereas UPS has demonstrated that it's capable of delivering results— for both customers and the company's owners.

Questions

1. What factors might have affected UPS's decision to open retail outlets in regard to the market, products, middlemen, and the company itself?

2. How can UPS maintain its advantage over its competition in serving e-commerce companies?

www.ups.com

www.fedex.com

www.dhl.com

Sources: Rick Brooks, "UPS Seeks to Chip Away at FedEx's Big Lead in China," *The Wall Street Journal,* May 16, 2000, p. B4; Rick Brooks, "UPS Is Planning Pack-and-Ship Stores in Test Aimed at Luring New Customers," *The Wall Street Journal,* Feb. 17, 2000, p. B2; Rick Brooks, "UPS's New eVentures Unit Plans to Expand Logistics Business," *The Wall Street Journal,* Feb. 7, 2000, p. A4; Brian O'Reilly, "They've Got Mail," *Fortune,* Feb. 7, 2000, pp. 100–101+; David Rynecki, "Net Effects," *Fortune,* Feb. 7, 2000, p. 104; "Ford Expects to Cut Delivery Time in Pact with UPS Logistics," *The Wall Street Journal,* Feb. 3, 2000, p. A8; Kelly Barron, "Logistics in Brown," *Forbes,* Jan. 10, 2000, pp. 78–83; Robert Frank, "U.S. Express Carriers Deliver the Goods as Asia Bounces Back," *The Wall Street Journal,* Dec. 21, 1999, p. A18; Scott Malone, "Package Firms See E-Commerce Delivering Big Bucks," *WWD,* Dec. 8, 1999, p. 18; "UPS: Will This IPO Deliver?" *Business Week,* Nov. 15, 1999, p. 41; Douglas A. Blackmon, "FedEx Plans European Expansion," *The Wall Street Journal,* Sept. 23, 1999, p. A3; "Secure E-Mail Delivery Poised to Take Off," *Computerworld,* Aug. 23, 1999, p. 38; Karen E. Nussel, "UPS.com," *Business Marketing,* Aug. 1, 1999, p. 34; J. P. Donlon, "Big Brown Boots Up," *Chief Executive,* March 1999, pp. 30+; and "UPS Sees 'Huge' Impact from Online Retailing," *HFN,* Feb. 1, 1999, p. 4.

Promotion

6

Informing, persuading, and reminding current and potential customers

We have examined three of the four marketing-mix elements used by an organization to serve its target markets and achieve its marketing goals. To complete the marketing mix, we now turn our attention to designing and managing the fourth element, promotion.

Chapter 17 provides an overview of integrated marketing communication, including the various types of promotion, how promotion works, and management issues in developing a promotion program. Chapter 18 looks at the personal selling process and sales-force management. Advertising, sales promotion, and public relations are the subjects of Chapter 19.

17

Integrated Marketing Communications

PacSun must engage in a variety of promotional activities to maintain its position with targeted customers.

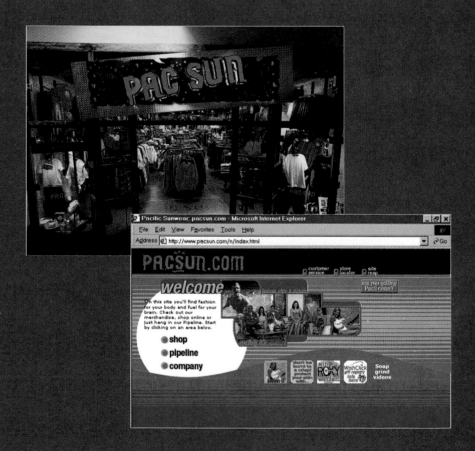

Is **Pacific Sunwear** Riding the Crest of a Fashion Wave?

From a Newport Beach surf shop to a chain of 450 stores, it has been an exhilarating ride for Pacific Sunwear of California, better known as "PacSun." It began in the winter of 1980, when the cool weather kept surfers away, and the chain's founder began searching for something to do. He hit on the then novel idea of a year-round, indoor surf shop, with a heavier emphasis on clothes, and opened a store in a Santa Monica mall.

The idea proved successful, and by 1987 the company had grown to 21 stores located in southern California malls from Thousand Oaks to West Los Angeles. The original target market was 12-to-22-year-old males who prefer a casual, "surfer" look. As the chain grew, merchandise lines for females were added.

The first PacSun store outside California was opened in 1989. As the chain grew into the Midwest and Northeast, it became apparent that the merchandise assortment needed adjusting. The shorts and T-shirts made popular by the California surfing culture were not as popular in colder climates. To serve these markets, the firm began looking to skateboarding and snowboarding, as well as surfing, for its fashion direction. As a result, long-sleeved shirts and long pants became part of the basic merchandise.

The chain was successful in identifying and stocking popular brands earlier than most other retailers. For example, it caught the baggy jeans fashion wave before it crested. By 1993 PacSun had expanded to 60 stores. The next few years saw continued increases in the number of stores, expansion of the prototype store size to accommodate a growing assortment of product lines including shoes, and the opening of the first nonmall store in New York's Greenwich Village.

PacSun is marketing its stores as a key fashion resource for the casual teen wardrobe. It is positioned by a carefully defined selection of popular and emerging brands such as Billabong, Quicksilver, and Rusty. Staying on top of trends is critical to its success. To that end, the chain holds a "vendor open house" at its headquarters every Wednesday. Any vendor with merchandise it thinks is appropriate for PacSun can make a presentation to the company's buyers and get a decision on the spot.

PacSun must engage in a variety of promotional activities to maintain its position with targeted customers. The firm's advertising budget of $9.3 million for 2000 doubled the amount spent in 1999. Its advertising includes television spots on youth-oriented cable channels such as ESPN, ESPN2, Comedy Central, and MTV, and ads in magazines such as *Spin, Seventeen, Teen People,* and *Sports Illustrated.* The company is also a sponsor of ESPN's X Games. The exterior signs on all of its stores are being changed from Pacific Sunwear to PacSun, the abbreviated name its customers have given it. Its website offers free e-mail, a wide variety of vendor-sponsored contests, teen-oriented news, a "wish list" gift registry, and interviews with surfing and boarding celebrities. In 1999 the site was expanded to permit online shopping.

In 1999 another 109 stores were opened, bringing the total to 450 in 47 states. Sales in stores open at least a year, a key measure of health for retailers, is growing at a solid 5%. Total sales in 1999 were over $320 million. With growth at more than 30% a year, PacSun appears to be well positioned for a long, exciting ride.[1]

What should Pacific Sunwear try to accomplish with its promotion program?

 www.pacsun.com

Like all marketers, Pacific Sunwear is faced with deciding how much and what types of promotion to undertake on behalf of its stores. These decisions are complicated by the fact that there are many forms of promotion and no two marketing situations are exactly alike. This chapter will help you understand how the various forms of promotion can be brought together in an integrated marketing communications effort that contributes to a firm's total marketing program. After studying this chapter, you should be able to explain:

chapter goals

- The role of promotion.
- The forms promotion can take.
- The concept of integrated marketing communications.
- How the process of communicating relates to effective promotion.
- The considerations in developing a promotion mix.
- Alternative promotional budgeting methods.
- The major types of promotion regulation.

The Role of Promotion in Marketing

One of the attributes of a free-market system is the right to use communication as a tool of influence. In our socioeconomic system, that freedom is reflected in the promotional efforts by businesses to influence the feelings, beliefs, and behavior of prospective customers. Let's examine how promotion works from an economic perspective and from a marketing perspective.

Promotion and Imperfect Competition

The American marketplace operates under conditions of imperfect competition, characterized by product differentiation, emotional buying behavior, and incomplete market information. A company uses promotion to provide information for the decision maker's buying-decision process, to assist in differentiating its product, and to persuade potential buyers.

In economic terms, the role of promotion is to change the location and shape of the demand (revenue) curve for a company's product. (See Figure 17.1 and recall the discussion of nonprice competition in Chapter 13.) Through promotion a company strives to increase its product's sales volume at any given price (Figure 17.1a);

Figure 17.1

The goal of promotion is to change the pattern of demand for a product.

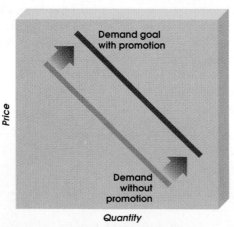

a. A shift in the demand curve to the right.

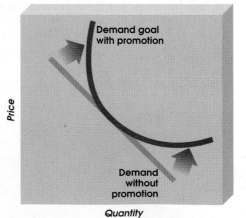

b. Changing the shape (or elasticity) of the demand curve.

Are Internet and bricks-and-mortar retailers friends or enemies?

Alliances between online services and traditional retailers, frequently depicted as bitter rivals for consumer spending, came as a surprise to many observers. Recently teaming up are America Online with Wal-Mart, Yahoo! with Kmart, and Microsoft with Best Buy.

Although the details of the programs differ, the overriding motivation is an opportunity to communicate with millions of potentially new customers. Here's how they work:

- *America Online (AOL) and Wal-Mart.* AOL provides a low-priced Internet access service that includes the Wal-Mart brand name. In addition, Wal-Mart's Internet store is promoted by AOL to its 19 million online subscribers. In return, Wal-Mart promotes AOL's service in its stores and through its television advertising, encouraging its 92 million customers to sign up for the service and shop online.

- *Yahoo! and Kmart.* Yahoo! provides free Internet access to users of Kmart's website. This has the potential of opening a new segment of the market for Yahoo! because many Kmart customers are not currently Internet users. In return, Kmart provides links from its site to Yahoo!

- *Microsoft and Best Buy.* Best Buy stores will promote Microsoft's Internet service and prominently display other Microsoft products in exchange for special consideration by the Internet provider.

Investors are betting the number of consumers using the Internet will continue to grow, and as a result the service providers will generate profits from electronic retailing and the sale of advertising. Thus, firms such as AOL and Yahoo! constantly need more subscribers, and gaining access to millions of new customers through retail stores is very attractive. At the same time, traditional retailers see the sales potential of the Internet and are looking for ways to improve their Web presences. Gaining a priority position on the site of an Internet service with millions of regular visitors is a quick way to establish a position.

Sources: Andrew Edgecliffe-Johnson, Louise Kehoe, and Andrew Heavens, "Wal-Mart, AOL in Low-Cost Net Move," *Financial Times,* Dec. 17, 1999, p. 24; Kara Swisher and Nick Wingfield, "Behind the Wedding of Brick and Clicks: Need to Woo New Customers," *The Wall Street Journal,* Dec. 17, 1999, pp. B1+.

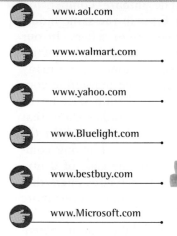

www.aol.com

www.walmart.com

www.yahoo.com

www.Bluelight.com

www.bestbuy.com

www.Microsoft.com

that is, the firm seeks to shift its demand curve to the right. Simply stated, promotion is intended to make a product more attractive to prospective buyers.

A firm also hopes that promotion will affect the demand elasticity for its product (Figure 17.1b). Recall from Appendix A that elasticity is the responsiveness of demand to a change in price. The intent is to make the demand more inelastic when price increases, and more elastic when price decreases. In other words, management wants promotion to increase the attractiveness of a product so the quantity demanded will decline very little if price goes up (inelastic demand), and sales will increase considerably if price goes down (elastic demand).

Promotion and Marketing

From a marketer's perspective, promotion serves three essential roles—it informs, persuades, and reminds prospective and current customers and other selected audiences about a company and its products. The relative importance of these roles varies according to the circumstances faced by a firm.

The most useful product or brand will be a failure if no one knows it is available! Because distribution channels are often long, a product may pass through many hands between a producer and consumers. Therefore, a producer must *inform* middlemen as well as the ultimate consumers or business users about the product. Wholesalers, in turn, must inform retailers, and retailers must inform consumers. As the number of potential customers grows and the geographic dimensions of a market expand, the problems and costs of informing the market increase.

The website for J.C. Penney's *Noise* magazine for teens includes a questionnaire that asks visitors their opinions of the magazine and the store. Sears Roebuck is also trying to connect with the youth market. At the Sears website, the retailer describes its Pulse Card, which qualifies a holder for discounts for special merchandise in Sears stores and its Fashion 411 guide to popular styles and fashions.

 www.noiseonline.com

 www.sears.com/pulse

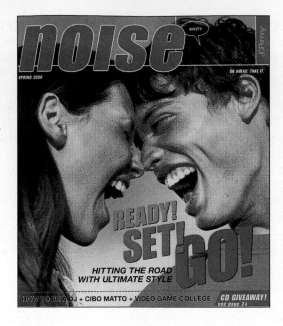

Few teens view J.C. Penney as a place to buy stylish clothing. The retailer is concerned that if Generation Y gets in the habit of shopping elsewhere now, they'll be even more difficult to attract later on. As a first step in attracting teenagers, Penney's must inform them that it is "hip" and offers stylish clothes and popular brands. To that end, the retailer has launched a quarterly magazine called *Noise*. Available free both online and in printed form, the magazine's editorial content is described by its publisher as "edgy." With a planned circulation for the print version of 3.5 million copies, Penney's hopes *Noise* will change its image among teens.[2]

Another purpose of promotion is *persuasion*. The intense competition among different industries, as well as among different firms in the same industry, puts tremendous pressure on the promotional programs of sellers. In our economy of abundance, even a product designed to satisfy a basic physiological need requires strong persuasive promotion, because consumers have many alternatives to choose from. Campbell Soup Company has been marketing condensed soup for over 100 years, and accounts for 80% of all soup sales in the U.S. It is one of the most recognized brands in the country. Studies show that virtually every U.S. household has some Campbell's soup in the pantry. Yet the firm spends over $60 million a year advertising soup because of strong competition from other firms offering easy-to-prepare food.[3] In the case of a luxury product, for which sales depend on the ability to convince consumers that the product's benefits exceed those of other luxuries, persuasion is even more important.

Consumers also must be *reminded* about a product's availability and its potential to satisfy. Sellers bombard the marketplace with thousands of messages every day in the hope of attracting new consumers and establishing markets for new products. Given the intense competition for consumers' attention, even an established firm must constantly remind people about its brand to retain a place in their minds. It is unlikely that a day goes by, for example, in which you don't see some form of promotion (an ad, in-store display, counter sign, billboard, or imprinted T-shirt) for Coca-Cola. In fact, the company spends over $150 million a year on advertising for Coca-Cola Classic alone. Thus, much of a firm's promotion may be intended simply to offset competitors' marketing activity by keeping its brand in front of the market.[4]

Promotion Methods

Promotion, in whatever form it takes, is an attempt to influence. There are four forms of promotion: personal selling, advertising, sales promotion, and public relations. Each has distinct features that determine the role it can play in a promotion program:

- **Personal selling** is the direct presentation of a product to a prospective customer by a representative of the organization selling it. Personal selling takes place face-to-face or over the phone, and it may be directed to a business person or a final consumer. We list it first because, across all organizations, more money is spent on personal selling than on any other form of promotion.

- **Advertising** is nonpersonal communication paid for by a clearly identified sponsor promoting ideas, organizations, or products. The most familiar outlets for ads are the broadcast (TV and radio) and print (newspapers and magazines) media. However, there are many other advertising vehicles, from billboards to T-shirts and, more recently, the Internet.

- **Sales promotion** is demand-stimulating activity designed to supplement advertising and facilitate personal selling. It is paid for by the sponsor and frequently involves a temporary incentive to encourage a sale or purchase. Many sales promotions are directed at consumers. The majority, however, are designed to encourage the company's sales force or other members of a distribution channel to sell products more aggressively. When sales promotion is directed to the members of the distribution channel, it is called *trade promotion*. Included in sales promotion are a wide spectrum of activities, such as event sponsorships, frequency programs, contests, trade shows, in-store displays, rebates, samples, premiums, discounts, and coupons.

- **Public relations** encompasses a wide variety of communication efforts to contribute to generally favorable attitudes and opinions toward an organization and its products. Unlike most advertising and personal selling, it does not include a specific sales message. The targets may be customers, stockholders, a government agency, or a special-interest group. Public relations can take many forms, including newsletters, annual reports, lobbying, and support of

Oscar Mayer Wienermobiles have traveled America's highways promoting the company's products since 1936. The latest version is 27 feet long and 10 feet high. Nine identical Wienermobiles tour the U.S. Wienermobiles can also be found in Hawaii, Puerto Rico, Canada, Spain, and Japan. The vehicles are driven by recent college graduates who spend a year as "hot dog ambassadors of goodwill." Virtual tours are available at the Oscar Mayer website.

www.kraftfoods.
oscarmayer.com

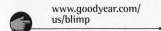
charitable or civic events. The Goodyear blimps and the Oscar Mayer Wiener-mobiles are familiar examples of public relations devices.

Publicity is a special form of public relations that involves news stories about an organization or its products. Like advertising, it consists of an impersonal message that reaches a mass audience through the media. But several features distinguish publicity from advertising: It is not paid for, the organization that is the subject of the publicity has little or no control over it, and it appears as news and therefore has greater credibility than advertising. Organizations actively seek good publicity and frequently provide the material for it in the form of news releases, press conferences, and photographs. When a picture of a company's CEO appears on the cover of a business publication and is accompanied by a flattering article in the magazine, it is often attributable to the efforts of the firm's public relations department. There also is, of course, bad publicity, which organizations try to avoid or deflect.

Integrated Marketing Communication

Marketers have a variety of promotional tools at their disposal. To make effective use of them, a company's personal selling, advertising, and other promotional activities should form a coordinated promotional program within its total marketing plan. However, these activities are fragmented in many firms, with potentially damaging consequences. For example, advertising directors and sales-force managers may come into conflict over resources, or the sales force may not be adequately informed about the details of a sales promotion effort. This wouldn't happen if the elements comprising promotion were part of an integrated marketing communication (IMC) effort, a strategic business process used to plan, develop, execute, and evaluate coordinated communication with an organization's public.[5]

IMC begins with a strategic planning effort designed to coordinate promotion with product planning, pricing, and distribution, the other marketing-mix elements. Promotion is influenced, for instance, by how distinctive a product is and whether its planned price is above or below the competition. A manufacturer or middleman must also consider its promotional links with other firms in the distribution channel. For example, DaimlerChrysler recognizes that its success is closely tied to the performance of its dealers. Therefore, in addition to advertising its automobiles directly to consumers, the firm trains the dealers' sales people in how to show a car effectively and conduct a test drive, and offers cash incentives to dealers with high customer satisfaction scores.

An Audience Perspective

An IMC approach adopts the position that a customer or prospect is exposed to many bits and pieces of information about a company or brand. Certainly some of these are designed and presented by the marketer, but others, possibly the majority, come from other sources. These sources can include personal experiences, the opinions of others, and comparisons made by competitors in their advertising. On the basis of all this information, an individual makes an evaluation and forms a judgment. With so little control over the information an audience uses, or how the information is used, a marketer's promotional efforts must be highly coordinated and complementary to have an impact. That means anticipating the opportunities when the target audience will be exposed to information about the company or brand, and effectively communicating the appropriate message in those "windows of opportunity." Usually this involves utilizing several promotional methods, and requires a high degree of coordination.

IMC Elements

The use of an IMC approach to promotion is reflected in how managers think about the information needs of the message recipients. Organizations that have adopted an IMC philosophy tend to share several characteristics, notably:

- An awareness of the target audience's information sources, as well as their media habits and preferences.
- An understanding of what the audience knows and believes that relates to the desired response.
- The use of a mix of promotional tools, each with specific objectives but all linked to a common overall goal.
- A promotional effort in which personal selling, advertising, sales promotion, and public relations are coordinated in order to communicate a consistent message.
- A carefully timed, continuous flow of information adapted to the audience's information needs.

Implementing IMC

By definition, IMC embraces the entire promotional program. In developing integrated communications, a company coordinates its advertising, personal selling, sales promotion, public relations, and direct marketing to accomplish specific objectives. For example, in the early 1990s, IBM's promotional efforts had become highly fragmented. The company was using over 80 advertising agencies around the world, and its ads were sending mixed messages. To rectify the problem and coordinate its efforts:

- The 80 agencies were replaced by one.
- All packaging, brochures, and trade show booths were standardized to present a unified image.
- Sports sponsorships were consolidated in a few big events such as the Olympics in order to better showcase IBM technology.
- Internet home pages with a consistent look and content were developed for 77 countries in their native languages.

Promotion at IBM is now built around the theme of being a technology innovator that is accessible and responsive.[6]

An IMC program may incorporate several different promotional campaigns, with some even running concurrently. Depending on objectives and available funds, a firm may undertake simultaneous local, regional, national, and international programs. Moreover, a firm may have one campaign aimed at consumers, and another at wholesalers and retailers.

Evaluating IMC

The last step in an IMC program is evaluation. A program can be evaluated in a number of ways. One approach is to examine how it is implemented. For example, if the promotion by a large manufacturer of consumer goods is being carried out in a manner consistent with the notion of IMC, we would expect to find:

- An advertising program consisting of a series of related, well-timed, carefully placed ads that reinforce personal selling and sales promotion efforts.
- A personal selling effort that is coordinated with the advertising program. The firm's sales force would be fully informed about the advertising portion of the campaign—the theme, media used, and the schedule for the appearance of ads. The sales people would be able to explain and demonstrate the product benefits stressed in the ads, and be prepared to transmit the promotional message and supporting material to middlemen so they can take part in the campaign.

Is the world's most populous country receptive to Western-style promotion?

China has almost 20 years of experience with the kind of promotion associated with capitalism. Beginning in the late 1970s, consumer products and brands familiar in the rest of the world began appearing on Chinese billboards and in newspaper and television ads. Based simply on its population of 1.3 billion, China seemed to be a market with enormous potential.

However, results have fallen short of expectations. Some of the reasons follow:

- *The market is smaller than expected.* The number of consumers able to afford products such as Crest toothpaste or Gatorade (two brands marketed there) is now estimated to be one-third of earlier estimates. An annual income of $1,000 may make a person middle class in China's urban areas, but it is not enough to afford many consumer goods.

- *Competition is intense.* Some U.S. firms thought the quality and allure of Western consumer products would be irresistible to the Chinese. However, satisfying Chinese tastes is not always easy, as Quaker Oats discovered when two of its breakfast cereals, Cap'n Crunch and hot oatmeal, failed in this huge foreign market. There is also competition for attention. Chinese firms spend three to five times more on advertising than foreign firms. The most heavily advertised products in China are Gai Zhong Gai, a calcium drink, and Yandi, a cough medicine. All but one of the 10 most advertised products in the country are Chinese.

- *Consumers object to the quantity and quality of advertising.* Television advertising in China is shown in blocks up to 10 minutes in length. Besides the length of the interruptions, consumers object to the total amount of advertising. Viewers have criticized the content of advertising, finding it often too violent or graphic. Some products, such as undergarments, are considered inappropriate for television advertising. These and other complaints have led to consumer-initiated suits accusing advertisers of violating Chinese laws.

What's to be learned from this? Probably the most basic lesson is that nothing is as easy as it may first appear. From a strategic point of view, however, it appears that U.S. marketers hoping to be successful in China should avoid an opportunistic approach in favor of a focused, integrated marketing communications approach.

Sources: Paul Wiseman, "Tidal Wave of TV Ads Overwhelm Some Chinese," *USA Today*, Oct. 18, 1999, p. 7B; Michael Flagg, "For U.S. Advertisers in China, It's Time for a Bracing Reality Test," *The Wall Street Journal*, Jan. 3, 2000, pp. A11+.

- Sales promotional devices, such as point-of-purchase display materials, that are coordinated with other aspects of the program. Incentives for middlemen would be clearly communicated and understood. Retailers would be briefed about consumer promotions and adequate inventories would be in place.
- Public relations efforts scheduled to coincide with the other mix components and emphasizing the same theme.

More rigorous evaluation examines the results of the program. The outcome of each promotional component is compared with the objectives set for it to determine if the effort was successful. Listed below are some typical promotion objectives and some common measures associated with each of them:[7]

- *Awareness of a company or a brand:* competitive brand position studies, focus groups with distributors at trade shows, and website "hits."
- *Interest in a product or brand:* number of brochures or other company publications distributed, attendance at company-sponsored seminars, and website traffic on specific pages.
- *Action:* usage of sales support tools by distributors and retailers, responses to direct mail, customer inquiries or store visits, and sales.

According to an *Exhibitor* magazine survey, only 36% of firms evaluate participation in a trade show with a formal return on investment analysis. Other measures used include cost per visitor (to the exhibit) and cost per sales lead generated. Some firms refine the cost-per-sales lead measure by adding factors such as position titles of the leads and the eventual outcomes. Qualitative measures include media coverage of the exhibit and customer problems discovered.

 www.exhibitormagazine.com

 www.gap.com

To be meaningful, most of these measures need to be taken before and after the promotional effort, with the difference between the two measures indicating its effect. For example, The Gap did not experience a meaningful increase in store traffic and sales during and after some recent TV ad campaigns. One in particular, featuring young people in khakis dancing the swing, was particularly disappointing because it was lauded by industry observers as an outstanding ad. As a result, the retailer deemphasized the TV component of its promotional strategy, shifting more funds to in-store promotion, print advertising, and online advertising.[8] After an appropriate amount of time, the performance of these promotional tools will also be evaluated.

Barriers to IMC

Despite its intuitive attractiveness, an IMC approach to promotion is not universally supported. In some organizations the promotional functions are in different departments. For example, the sales force may be in a unit apart from where advertising decisions are made. As a result, there is a lack of internal communication and coordination. In other companies there is a belief that promotion is such an imprecise activity that efforts to carefully design objectives and coordinate efforts would be unproductive. In still other firms there is a history of relying on a particular form of promotion and a resistance to consider alternatives.

Fully utilizing an IMC approach would likely require a firm to make several changes. One involves restructuring internal communication to ensure that all relevant parties involved in promotion are working together. Some firms have approached this by creating a marketing communications (or marcom) manager who oversees the planning and coordination of promotional efforts. A second change entails conducting research to gather the necessary information about the target audience. Firms utilize extensive customer databases for this purpose, but they are costly to create and expensive to maintain. Finally, and most important, top management must support the effort to integrate promotion. Strong leadership is essential in order to gain commitment from the entire organization.

Next we'll examine how communication, the core of promotion, actually works. Then we'll move to the key managerial issues in a promotion program.

The Communication Process and Promotion

Communication is the verbal or nonverbal transmission of information between someone wanting to express an idea and someone else expected or expecting to get that idea. Because promotion is a form of communication, much can be learned about structuring effective promotion by examining the communication process.

Fundamentally, communication requires only four elements: a message, a source of the message, a communication channel, and a receiver. In practice, however, important additional components come into play. Figure 17.2 illustrates these components of a communication process, and relates them to promotion activities.

Consider this hypothetical example of what happens when a teenager sees an ad for the U.S. Army.

- The information that the sending source wants to share must first be *encoded* into a transmittable form. In marketing this means translating an idea ("You can achieve your full potential as a member of the U.S. Army") into words ("Be all that you can be"), or pictures (a soldier leading others in accomplishing a mission), or a combination of the two.

- Once the message has been *transmitted* through some communication channel, the symbols must be *decoded*, or given meaning, by the receiver. The received message may be what the sender intended ("The Army is a place to develop valuable life skills") or something else that is possibly less desirable ("The Army is overpromising in order to get recruits"), depending on the recipient's frame of reference.

- If the message has been transmitted successfully, there is some change in the receiver's knowledge, beliefs, or feelings. As a result of this change, the receiver formulates a *response*. The response could be nonverbal (making a mental note to ask a high school counselor about the opportunities that exist in the military), verbal (asking friends if they have ever considered joining), or behavioral (visiting a recruiting office).

- The response serves as *feedback*, telling the sender whether the message was received and how it was perceived by the recipient. Through feedback the

Figure 17.2

The communication process in promotion.

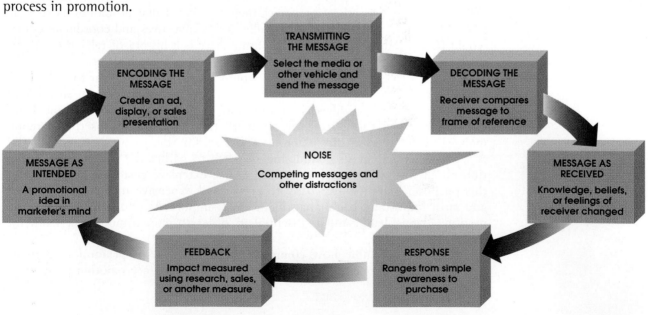

To offset increasing costs, colleges and universities are constantly on the alert for new sources of revenue other than tuition. At the same time, advertisers are looking for ways to reach students who are relatively light users of mass media. One approach is to allow firms to serve as sponsors of universities' websites. For example, at more than 500 institutions, when students log into the school's system to learn about upcoming campus events, financial aid, or next semester's class schedule, they see small banner ads for such things as textbook sellers, housing providers, and educational testing services. By clicking on the banners, which are not identified as paid ads, students can go directly to the advertisers' websites.

Permitting advertising on a college or university's website is viewed by some as an inappropriate intrusion. One professor describes it as "... throwing our freshmen to the wolves." Others suggest that the ads, which offset the hundreds of thousands of dollars it costs to construct and maintain a website, are a relatively painless way of providing students with needed information at no out-of-pocket cost.

Is it ethical for a nonbusiness service provider (such as a university) to further its objectives by assisting others who want to gain access to its clientele (such as students)?

Source: Lisa Guernsey, "Colleges Give Advertising Access to Web Sites," *St. Louis Post-Dispatch*, Aug. 17, 1999, p. C7.

---

sender can learn what a communication accomplished. Then a new message can be formulated and the process begun again.

- All stages of the process can be affected by *noise*—that is, any external factor that interferes with successful communication. (Anything competing for the attention of the prospect, but particularly messages about career opportunities, are noise for the U.S. Army.)

Introduced in 1981, "Be all that you can be" has been rated one of the most familiar advertising lines of the century. However, because enlistments are down, it was dropped. According to the Secretary of the Army, "The question is whether it is the right slogan for today's 18-to-24-year-olds."[9] Even though the words remained the same, it's quite possible that the message as received changed in 20 years.

What does the communication process tell us about promotion? First, the act of encoding reminds us that messages can take many forms. Messages can be physical (a sample, a premium) or symbolic (verbal, visual), and there are a myriad of options within each of these categories. For example, the form of a verbal message can be factual, humorous, or even threatening.

Second, the number of channels or methods of transmitting a message are limited only by the imagination and creativity of the sender. Consider that promotional messages are transmitted by the voice of a sales person, the airwaves of radio, the mail, the side of a bus, a website on the Internet, and the lead-in to a feature in a movie theater. Each channel has its own characteristics in terms of audience reach, flexibility, permanence, credibility, and cost. In selecting a channel, a marketer must have clearly defined objectives and a familiarity with the features of the many alternatives. For example, how would you promote a greeting card company? Blue Mountain Arts, competing with firms such as Hallmark and American Greeting Cards, uses free electronic greetings to promote its brand. A visitor to the Blue Mountain Arts website can send an electronic card to anyone with an Internet connection. Along with the electronic card, the recipient gets information about Blue Mountain Arts. The result? Blue Mountain attracts 4.2 million unique visitors a month who learn about its products. This approach, spreading information about a company from one person to another with little input from the firm, is called **viral marketing.**[10] It is most often utilized by the smaller firms in an industry.

www.bluemountain.com

In an apparent response to the success of Blue Mountain Arts' strategy of providing free electronic greeting cards, the industry leader Hallmark introduced a similar program that can be found at its website. Since Hallmark is a well-known brand name already associated with greeting cards, what does it gain from providing free electronic greetings?

 www.hallmark.com

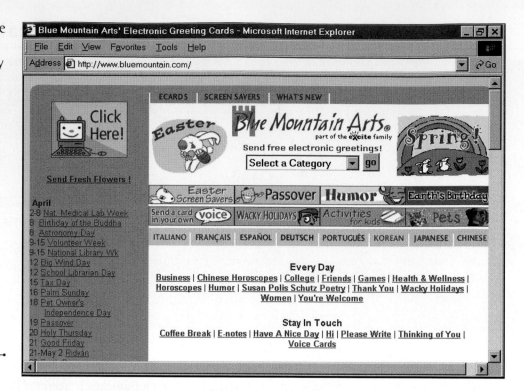

Third, how the message is decoded or interpreted depends on its form (encoding and transmission) and the capability and interest of the recipient. In designing and sending messages, marketers must be sensitive to the audience. What is their vocabulary and level of verbal sophistication? What other messages have they received? What experiences have they had? What will get and hold their attention?

Finally, every promotion should have a measurable objective. The response and feedback provided by the recipients can be used to determine if the objective is accomplished. Feedback may be collected in many forms—changes in sales, recall of advertising messages, more favorable attitudes, increased awareness of a product or an organization—depending on the objective of the promotion. For some promotional activities the objective may be modest—for example, an increase in the audience's awareness of a brand. For others, such as a direct-mail solicitation, the objective would be a particular level of sales. Without objectives, there is no way of evaluating the effectiveness of a message.

Determining the Promotional Mix

A **promotion mix** is an organization's combination of personal selling, advertising, sales promotion, and public relations. An effective promotional mix is a critical part of virtually all marketing strategies. Product differentiation, market segmentation, trading up and trading down, and branding all require effective promotion. Designing an effective promotional mix involves a number of strategic decisions about five factors: (1) target audience, (2) objective of the promotion effort, (3) nature of the product, (4) stage in the product's life cycle, and (5) amount of money available for promotion.

Target Audience

As is true for most areas of marketing, decisions on the promotional mix will be greatly influenced by the target audience. The target may be final consumers, who could be further defined as existing customers or new prospects. Some marketers (notably toy and fast-food firms) direct much of their efforts at decision makers rather than the actual purchasers. In some cases the target consists of middlemen in order to gain their support in distributing a product, or in the case of a company about to make a stock offering, the investment community.

Final consumers and middlemen sometimes buy the same product, but they require different promotion. To illustrate, 3M Company sells its computer diskettes to final consumers through computer and office-supply stores. Promotion to dealers includes sharing the cost of yellow pages ads and advertising in specialized business magazines such as *Office Products Dealer.* Different ads aimed at final consumers are run in magazines such as *Personal Computing, Fortune,* and *Business Week.*

A promotion program aimed primarily at middlemen is called a **push strategy,** and a promotion program directed primarily at end users is called a **pull strategy.** Figure 17.3 contrasts these two strategies.

Using a push strategy means a channel member directs its promotion primarily at the middlemen that are the next link forward in the distribution channel. The product is "pushed" through the channel. Take the case of a hardware producer that sells its tools and replacement parts to household consumers through wholesalers and retailers such as Ace and True Value. The producer will promote heavily to wholesalers, which then also use a push strategy to retailers. In turn, the retailers promote to consumers. A push strategy usually involves a lot of personal selling and sales promotion, including contests for sales people and displays at trade shows. This promotional strategy is appropriate for many manufacturers of business products, as well as for consumer goods that are undifferentiated or do not have a strong brand identity.

With a pull strategy, promotion is directed at end users—usually ultimate consumers. The intention is to motivate them to ask retailers for the product. The retailers, in turn, will request the product from wholesalers, and wholesalers will order it from the producer. In effect, promotion to consumers is designed to "pull" the product through the channel. This strategy relies on heavy advertising and sales promotion such as premiums, samples, or in-store demonstrations.

Retailers have little incentive to provide shelf space for minor variations of existing brands unless they are confident the products will sell. So manufacturers of consumer packaged goods often use a pull strategy to get new products stocked on supermarket shelves. For example, to introduce Sportz, a new cheese-and-cracker ready-to-eat snack, Nabisco ran 18 weeks of TV spots, 3 months of print ads,

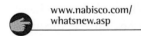
www.nabisco.com/
whatsnew.asp

Figure 17.3

Push and pull promotional strategies.

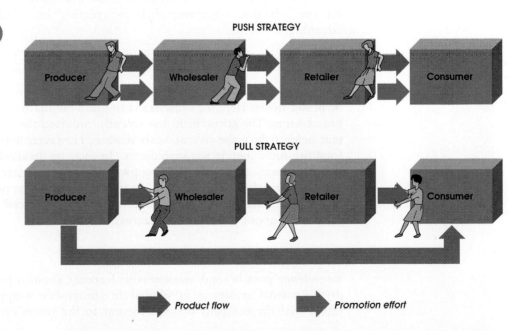

Consumer discount coupons are often part of a pull strategy. However, coupons appearing in magazines and newspapers have very low redemption rates. Consumers can search websites such as couponpages.com and find coupons for grocery products as well as other types of merchandise. Many of the coupons available on these sites are for new or repositioned products.

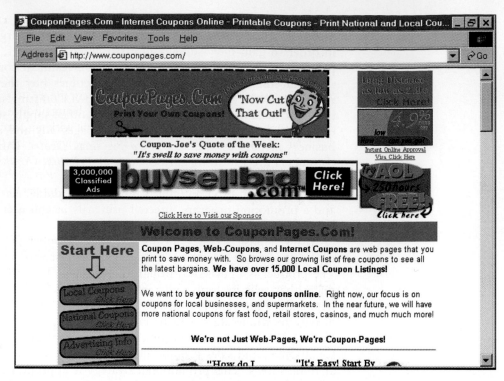

www.couponpages.com

newspaper coupons, in-store sampling with coupons, a contest for kids, and gave the product a featured position on the Nabisco website.[11] With this level of support, retailers have some assurance that the brand has a reasonable chance of success.

Promotion Objective

A target audience can be in any one of six stages of buying readiness. These stages—awareness, knowledge, liking, preference, conviction, and purchase—are called the **hierarchy of effects** because they represent stages a buyer goes through in moving toward a purchase, and each describes a possible objective or effect of promotion. The goal of promotion is to get the prospect to the final, or purchase stage, but in most cases that is not possible until the person has moved through the earlier stages. Thus, a promotion effort may have what appears to be a modest but essential objective, such as creating knowledge about a product's advantages.

Awareness

At the *awareness* stage the seller's task is to let the buyers know that the product or brand exists. Here the objective is to build familiarity with the product and the brand name. The government has recently endorsed the health claim that soy protein helps reduce the risk of heart disease. However, few consumers know what food products contain soy ingredients. To increase awareness, Archer Daniel Midland Company, the world's leading processor of soy, is forming alliances with food makers to mark products containing its soy protein. The promotion will make use of a logo similar to the NutraSweet swirl that appeared on packages to inform consumers about the artificial sweetner.[12]

Knowledge

Knowledge goes beyond awareness to learning about a product's features. Enterprise Rent-A-Car uses as its symbol an automobile wrapped up as a package to signal that the company delivers the car to the renter's home. In a market with several well-established brands, Enterprise had to find a way to quickly and easily inform consumers how its service is unique.

Liking

Liking refers to how the market feels about the product. Promotion can be used to move a knowledgeable audience from being indifferent to liking a brand. A common technique is to associate the item with an attractive symbol or person. An online sporting goods retailer, MVP.com, has Michael Jordan, John Elway, and Wayne Gretzky as investors and spokespersons. The firm is hopeful that the celebrity appeal of three of the world's best-known athletes, even though they are recently retired, will create a favorable impression among consumers.[13]

www.MVP.com

Preference

Creating *preference* involves distinguishing among brands such that the market finds your brand more attractive than alternatives. It is not uncommon to like several brands of the same product, but the customer can't make a decision until one brand is preferred over the alternatives. Ads that make direct comparisons with the competition are intended to create a preference. In the competition for long-distance customers, MCI compares its price to AT&T's, whereas AT&T compares its service reputation to MCI's.

Conviction

Conviction entails the actual decision or commitment to purchase. A student may prefer the IBM PC over a clone, but not yet be convinced to buy a computer. The promotion objective here is to increase the strength of the buyer's need. Trying a product and experiencing the benefits that come from using it are very effective in strengthening the conviction to own it. Radio Shack encourages consumers to visit its stores and try its computers, and auto dealers invite consumers to test-drive new cars.

Purchase

Purchase can be delayed or postponed indefinitely, even for customers who are convinced they should buy a product. The inhibitor might be a situational factor such as not having enough money at the moment, or a natural resistance to change. Action may be triggered through a temporary price reduction or the offer of additional incentives. For example, for a Web portal, having a visitor stay online is equivalent to a purchase, because the portal earns its income from advertisers who are buying access to the visitors. To encourage Web surfers to stay online, some sites are paying them incentives of 50 cents or more for every hour they remain connected. Visitors can surf anywhere on the Internet and still earn the incentive as long as they keep a special advertising window open on the screen. Advertisers pay the website operator to have their messages appear in the window. One such firm, AllAdvantage.com, ranks ahead of MTV.com and CBS.com in popularity with Web surfers.[14]

www.AllAdvantage.com

Promotional efforts are also aimed at obtaining repeat purchases or building loyalty among customers who have purchased a product. A credit card company's database that indicates a cardholder has not made a purchase using the credit card for an unusual length of time might trigger a direct-mail piece or a personal phone call.

Nature of the Product

Several product attributes influence the promotion mix. We will consider three that are especially significant: unit value, customization, and service requirements.

Unit Value

A product with low unit value is usually relatively uncomplicated, involves little risk for the buyer, and must appeal to a mass market to survive. As a result, advertising would be the primary promotional tool. In contrast, high–unit value products often are complex and expensive. These features suggest the need for personal selling. BMW dealers are being encouraged to have sales people get out of the showroom and call on prospects. By increasing the personal selling effort through techniques such as delivering cars to potential customers for test-drives, BMW hopes to stimulate declining U.S. sales.

Degree of Customization

If a product must be adapted to the individual customer's needs, personal selling is necessary. Thus you would expect to find an emphasis on personal selling for something like home remodeling or an expensive suit of clothing. However, the benefits of most standardized products can be effectively communicated in advertising. Although this principle holds true for many products, it is being challenged by firms implementing mass customization. Levi Strauss, for example, produces individual, custom-fit jeans for women. A customer's measurements are taken in a retail store, transmitted by computer to a Levi factory, and a custom-fit pair of jeans is produced and sent to the store.

Presale and Postsale Service

Products that must be demonstrated, for which there are trade-ins, or that require frequent servicing to stay in good working order lend themselves to personal selling. Typical examples are riding lawn mowers and powerboats.

Stage in the Product Life Cycle

Promotion strategies are influenced by a product's life-cycle stage. When a new product is introduced, prospective buyers must be informed about its existence and its benefits, and middlemen must be convinced to carry it. Thus both advertising (to consumers) and personal selling (to middlemen) are critical in a product's introductory stage. At introduction a new product also may be something of

Earth's Best, founded by Arnie and Ron Koss in 1984, was sold to H.J. Heinz in 1998. Heinz continues to distribute the product in grocery stores, while the Hain Food Group distributes the brand in health food stores. How would you explain the fact that Earth's Best website makes no mention of its Heinz connection?

www.earthsbest.com

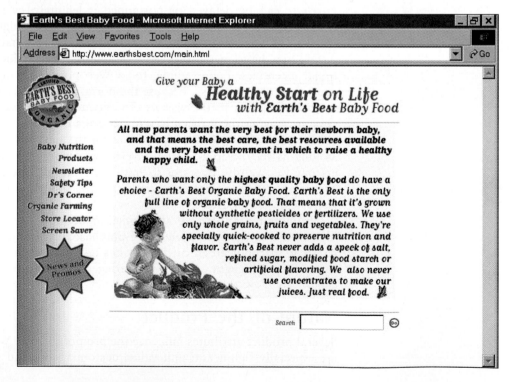

Table 17.1　Promotional Strategies for Different Product Life-Cycle Stages

Market Situation	Promotional Strategy
Introduction Stage	
Customers are not aware of the product's features, nor do they understand how it will benefit them.	Inform and educate potential customers that the product exists, how it might be used, and what want-satisfying benefits it provides.
	In this stage, a seller must stimulate primary demand—the demand for a type of product—as contrasted with selective demand—the demand for a particular brand. For example, producers had to sell consumers on the value of compact discs in general before they considered it feasible to promote a particular brand.
	Normally, heavy emphasis must be placed on personal selling. Exhibits at trade shows are also used extensively in the promotional mix. A trade show gives a new product broad exposure to many middlemen. Manufacturers also rely heavily on personal selling to attract middlemen to handle a new product.
Growth Stage	
Customers are aware of the product's benefits. The product is selling well, and middlemen want to handle it.	Stimulate selective (brand) demand as competition grows. Increase emphasis on advertising. Middlemen share more of the total promotional effort.
Maturity Stage	
Competition intensifies and sales level off.	Advertising is used more to persuade rather than only to provide information. Intense competition forces sellers to devote larger sums to advertising and thus contributes to the declining profits experienced in this stage.
Decline Stage	
Sales and profits are declining. New and better products are coming into the market.	All promotional efforts are cut back substantially. The focus moves to reminding remaining customers.

a novelty, offering excellent opportunities for publicity. Later, if a product becomes successful, competition intensifies and more emphasis is placed on persuasive advertising. Table 17.1 shows how promotional strategies change as a product moves through its life cycle.

Funds Available

Regardless of the most desirable promotional mix, the amount of money available for promotion is often the ultimate determinant of the mix. A business with ample funds can make more effective use of advertising than a firm with limited financial resources. For example, television advertising can carry a particular promotional message to far more people and at a lower cost per person than most other media. Yet a firm may have to rely on less expensive media, such as yellow pages advertising, because it lacks the funds to take advantage of television's efficiency.

Smaller brands or economically efficient companies are likely to rely on personal selling, dealer displays, or joint manufacturer–retailer promotions. For example, Earth's Best, a manufacturer of organic baby food that sells at a price 40% higher than mainstream brands like Gerber's, is a relatively small brand with a focused promotional budget. To achieve maximum efficiency of its promotional resources, Earth's Best uses a highly targeted newsletter to maintain contact with interested consumers; reduced-price coupons to gain trial; and a website providing information about its products, a locator to find retailers that carry the brand, and links to other baby product firms that stress high health and safety standards.[15] Earths' Best is a division of The Food Group, Inc.

www.earthsbest.com

The Promotion Budget

Establishing promotion budgets is extremely challenging because management lacks reliable standards to determine how much to spend altogether on advertising, personal selling, and the remainder of the promotion mix, or how much of the total budget to allocate to each mix component. A firm may have the alternative of adding three sales people or increasing its trade show budget by $200,000 a year, but it cannot determine precisely what increase in sales or profits to expect from either expenditure.

Promotional activities generally are budgeted as current operating expenses, implying that their benefits are used up immediately. However, it's been suggested that advertising (and presumably other promotional efforts) should be thought of as a capital investment, even if it must be treated as an expense for accounting purposes. The reason is that the benefits and returns on promotional expenditures are like investments, often not immediately evident, instead accruing over several years. For example, slogans such as "Like a rock" (Chevrolet trucks), "It works for me" (Apple computers), and "Bringing data to life" (Lucent Technologies) may build awareness and familiarity for years through advertising before actual sales are realized. Taking a longer-term, investment perspective on promotion would likely lead to greater consistency in the amounts spent, and the manner in which the budget is allocated across the types of promotion.

Rather than one generally accepted approach to promotion budgeting, there are four common **promotional budgeting methods:** percentage of sales, all available funds, following the competition, and budgeting by task or objective. These methods are frequently discussed in connection with the advertising budget, but they may be applied to any promotional activity as well as being used to determine the total promotional budget.

Percentage of Sales

The promotional budget may be related in some way to company income, as a percentage of either past or anticipated sales. A common approach for determining the sales base is to compute an average between the previous year's actual sales and expected sales for the coming year. Some businesses prefer to budget a fixed amount of money per unit of past or expected future sales. Manufacturers of products with a high unit value and a low rate of turnover (automobiles or appliances, for example) frequently use the unit method.

Because the percentage-of-sales method is simple to calculate, it is probably the most widely used budgeting method. Moreover, it sets the cost of promotion in relation to sales income, making it a variable rather than a fixed expense.

There are two important limitations to basing promotional expenditures on past sales. First, management is effectively making promotion a result of sales when, in fact, it is a cause of sales. Second, using the percentage-of-past-sales method reduces promotional expenditures when sales are declining—just when promotion usually is most needed.

All Available Funds

A new company or a firm introducing a new product frequently plows all available funds into its promotional program. The objective is to build sales and market share as rapidly as possible during those early, critical years. This is the strategy utilized by many Internet start-ups.[16] After a time, management generally finds it necessary to invest in other things, such as new equipment, expanded production capacity, or warehouses and distribution centers (as Internet marketing firms are now doing), so the method of setting the promotional budget is changed.

Following Competition

A weak method of determining the promotional budget, but one th[...]ed occasionally, is to match the promotional expenditures of competitors [...] spend in proportion to market share. Sometimes only one competitor is follo[...] in other cases, if management has access to industry average expenditures [...] omotion through a trade association, these become company benchmarks.

There are at least two problems with this approach. First, a firm's competitors may be just as much in the dark regarding how to set a promotional budget. Second, a company's promotional goals may be quite different from its competitors' because of differences in strategic marketing planning.

Task or Objective

The best approach for establishing the promotional budget is to determine the tasks or objectives the promotional program must accomplish and then decide what they will cost. The task method forces management to realistically define the goals of its promotional program and view them outside the confines of a defined budgetary period.

This is often called the buildup method because of the way the budget is constructed. For example, a company may elect to enter a new geographic market. Management determines this venture will require five additional sales people. Compensation and expenses of these people will cost a total of $350,000 per year. Salary for an additional sales supervisor and expenses for an extra office and administrative needs will cost $80,000. Thus in the personal selling part of the promotional mix, an extra $430,000 must be budgeted. Similar estimates can be made for the anticipated costs of advertising, sales promotion, and other promotional tools. The promotional budget is built up by summing the costs of the individual promotional tasks needed to reach the goal of entering the new territory.

Regulation of Promotion

Because a primary objective of promotion is to sell something through persuasion, the potential for abuse always exists. As a result, some firms must be discouraged or prevented from intentional or unintentional misrepresentation. In addition, some consumers, because they lack particular knowledge or skills, need protection from being misled. Thus, there is a need for regulation to discourage the occurrence of abuses and to correct those that do occur.

Regulations have been established by the federal government and most state and local governments in response to public demand. In addition, professional associations and individual businesses have established promotion guidelines.

Federal Regulation

Federal regulation of promotional activities applies to firms engaged in interstate commerce. It is authorized by three major pieces of legislation: the Federal Trade Commission Act and the Robinson-Patman Act, both administered by the Federal Trade Commission (FTC), and the Lanham Trademark Act.

The measure that has the broadest influence on promotional mes ages is the **Federal Trade Commission Act.** The act prohibits unfair methods of competition. And, according to FTC and federal-court decisions, one area of unf ir competition is false, misleading, or deceptive advertising.

Under the original Federal Trade Commission Act, false or misle ding advertising had to injure a competitor before a violation could be charge This loophole led to the enactment of the **Wheeler-Lea Amendment** to the FTC Act in 1938.

This amendment considerably strengthened the original act by specifying that an unfair competitive act violates the law if it injures the public, regardless of the effect it may have on a competitor.

The FTC has plenty of clout—particularly in cases of possibly false or deceptive advertising. For example, the commission may require a company to *substantiate* its advertising claims by submitting test results or other supporting research. Furthermore, this supporting information may be made public even if it could embarrass the company.

If the FTC determines advertising is deceptive, it requests that the advertiser sign a *consent* decree, which amounts to an agreement to stop making the deceptive claim. Another FTC regulatory tool is the *cease-and-desist* order. If an ad or a claim is deemed deceptive, and the advertiser refuses to sign a consent decree, the FTC may compel a firm to remove it from circulation. A cease-and-desist order may be appealed to the FTC and even fought in federal court, during which time the advertising is allowed to continue.

Probably the FTC's most potent remedy is corrective advertising. A consent decree or a cease-and-desist order may force a firm to stop running a deceptive ad, but that does not rectify the incorrect impressions already made by the ad. *Corrective advertising*, paid for by the offending firm, and with the content and schedule approved by the FTC, is intended to correct misinformation resulting from the allegedly false ads. Among the products for which corrective ads have been run are Hawaiian Punch, Profile Bread, STP motor oil additive, Listerine mouthwash, and Ocean Spray cranberry juice.

Because corrective ads have proved to be only marginally successful in eliminating false impressions, they have been used sparingly. In fact, none had been run in 25 years. However, the FTC recently ordered Novartis Consumer Health to run $8 million in corrective ads for Doan's Pills. The FTC contends that from 1987 until 1996, Doan's ads falsely presented the brand as better for back pain than other remedies. The ruling is being challenged by the company, and the outcome of the appeal will likely determine the future use of corrective advertising.[17]

The FTC also has the authority to order *restitution* to compensate consumers for damages resulting from a false ad. However, because of the severe damage it could do to a company, the FTC has seldom resorted to requiring restitution.

The **Robinson-Patman Act**, which is best known for outlawing price discrimination, has two sections relating to promotional allowances offered to wholesalers and retailers. These sections state that a seller must offer promotional services or payments for them, on a proportionally equal basis to all competing wholesalers or retailers. Thus, if a manufacturer wants to furnish in-store demonstrators, advertising support, or any other type of promotional assistance, it must make it available proportionally to all firms competing in the resale of the product. "Proportionally equal" has sometimes been hard to define. Generally the courts have accepted the amount of the product purchased as a basis for allocation. Say, for example, that Martin's, a regional supermarket chain, buys $150,000 worth of merchandise per year from a grocery wholesaler, and Hank's, a neighborhood grocery store, purchases $15,000 worth from the same wholesale firm. The wholesaler may legally offer Martin's promotional allowances valued at 10 times those offered to Hank's.

The 1946 **Lanham Trademark Act** made false claims about one's own products illegal. It was broadened in 1988 by the **Trademark Law Revision Act** to encompass comparisons made in promotional activity. Under this law, a firm can seek damages if a competitor in its advertising or promotions makes false comparisons. For example, if a firm compared the price of its lesser-quality product to the price of a competitor's superior-quality product without disclosing the quality differences, it would be engaging in a false comparison. In a precedent-setting case, Jartran was required to pay U-Haul $40 million for misleading comparisons of the rental fees and sizes of their trucks.

You Make the Decision

Should there be restrictions on where promotional messages can be placed?

The conventional media (radio, television, magazines, newspaper) are very important outlets for promotion, as are some newer vehicles such as e-mail and the Internet. But marketers are constantly looking for new ways and places to put their messages in front of consumers. You may be familiar with Channel One, the mix of news and advertising broadcast daily in many schools, or the television monitors in airport waiting areas. You've also seen ads on buses, on grocery shopping carts, in sports arenas, on racing cars, and on the clothing of professional golfers. Even the uniforms of college athletes carry the logos of sponsoring athletic equipment makers.

Marketers continue to look for sites that are unconventional (so people will notice the ad), have heavy traffic, and require little competition for attention. Some recent examples include:

- Otis Elevator is placing video screens in elevators to display news and advertising.

- AT&T tried playing prerecorded ads for AT&T services to long-distance callers before connecting them with their parties.

- Firms are stenciling messages on sidewalks.

- Ads are appearing between the previews and the feature films in movie theatres, and even on the popcorn bags.

- Ads are on air-sickness bags in airplanes, on automatic pinsetters in bowling alleys, and on the stall doors of public restrooms.

- Universities are selling the naming rights of their sports arenas.

- For the first time, the official Olympic website will carry ads in conjunction with the 2000 games in Sydney.

- Gasoline pumps have small television monitors that present news and ads.

- Ads appear on ATM screens during the 15 seconds a transaction is being processed.

- Brand names of soft drinks are placed in the bottom of the cups used for the holes on a golf course.

- A roller towed behind a tractor makes minibillboard impressions in the sand on a beach.

What should govern where an ad can be placed?

Sources: Sam Walker, "University of Maryland Gives Comcast Naming Rights to Basketball Arena," *The Wall Street Journal,* Jan. 6, 1999, p. B13; Karen Jacobs, "Elevator Maker to Add Commercial Touch," *The Wall Street Journal,* Dec. 7, 1999, p. B8; Skip Wollenberg, "Ads Turning Up Everywhere," *South Bend Tribune,* May 26, 1999, pp. B8+; Teri Agins, "Battle of the Golf Shirts," *The Wall Street Journal,* Jan. 6, 1999, pp. B1+; and Mary Kuntz, Joseph Weber, and Heidi Dawley, "The New Hucksterism," *Business Week,* July 1, 1996, pp. 76–84.

 www.fcc.gov

www.fda.gov

Several other federal agencies are involved in the regulation of promotion. The Federal Communications Commission (FCC) licenses radio and television stations. Its mandate, to ensure that public interest is considered, combined with its authority to remove or deny the renewal of licenses, gives the FCC considerable power over the content of advertising. In addition, the FCC oversees the telephone industry, giving it jurisdiction over telemarketing.

The Food and Drug Administration (FDA) is responsible for the regulation of labeling, packaging, branding, ingredient listing, and advertising of packaged food and drug products. The FDA is responsible for warning labels that appear in food and drug ads, and it has established legal definitions for terms such as "natural," "light," and "low fat" when they are used in advertising and promotion.

The U.S. Postal Service regulates advertising done through the mail. Of particular concern is the use of the mail to commit fraud or distribute obscene material. The Postal Service also oversees sales promotions such as premiums, contests, coupons, and samples that are sent through the mail.

The **Telephone Consumer Protection Act** requires telemarketers to keep a "do-not-call" list of consumers who request that they not receive telephone solicitations, and it restricts the indiscriminant use of automatic telephone dialing systems. The law also prohibits marketers from sending advertising to a facsimile machine without first obtaining the recipient's permission. It has not yet been resolved whether unsolicited e-mail ads are included under the law.

State and Local Regulation

Legislation at the state level is intended to regulate promotional activities in intrastate commerce. Most of these state statutes are patterned after a model developed by *Printers' Ink* magazine in 1911 to establish truth in advertising. Today 44 states have what are known as **Printers' Ink statutes** to punish "untrue, deceptive, or misleading" advertising. Several states have also established separate state agencies to handle consumer protection, and some states' attorneys general have taken a very proactive stance in regulating promotional activity. For example, recent lawsuits against tobacco manufacturers to recover medical costs incurred by 46 states as a result of alleged false or misleading advertising claims resulted in a financial settlement requiring the companies to pay $206 billion over 25 years.[18]

A general type of local legislation that affects personal selling is the so-called **Green River ordinance** (so-named because Green River, Wyoming, was one of the first towns to enact such a law). Green River ordinances restrict sales people who represent firms located outside the affected city and who sell door-to-door or call on business establishments. To operate in a community with a Green River ordinance, a sales person is typically required to register locally and purchase a license. Supposedly passed to protect local citizens from fraudulent operators, the measures also serve to insulate local businesses from outside competition.

Regulation by Private Organizations

www.caru.org

Numerous private organizations exert considerable control over the promotional practices of business. For example, the Council of Better Business Bureaus and several advertising trade associations joined forces to create a self-regulation process. Two agencies have come out of this collaboration: the National Advertising Division (NAD) and the Children's Advertising Review Unit (CARU). Both investigate complaints of false and misleading advertising brought by competitors, consumers, and local Better Business Bureaus. If NAD or CARU find an ad unsatisfactory, they negotiate with the advertiser to discontinue or modify the ad. Despite the fact that neither NAD nor CARU can force compliance or sanction an advertiser in any way, they have been very successful in getting objectionable ads changed or dropped.

The media also serve a regulatory role. Virtually all publications and broadcasters have established standards for acceptable advertising. Some standards affect an entire industry; for example, hard liquor ads are banned by broadcasters. Others deal with the specifics of how a product can be advertised. For example, in ads directed at children, the three major networks have specified that the words "just" and "only" cannot be used in reference to price. Standards in the print media tend to vary by the size and type of publication. Some are quite strict. For example, *Good Housekeeping* and *Parent* magazines test products to substantiate the claims before ads are accepted. Finally, some professional associations have established codes of ethics that include standards for communications. For example, the American Marketing Association specifies that the promotional efforts of its members avoid using false or misleading advertising, high-pressure or misleading sales tactics, and sales promotions that use deception or manipulation.[19]

Summary

Promotion is the fourth component of a company's total marketing mix. In economic terms, the role of promotion is to change a firm's demand curve—either shifting it to the right or changing its shape to make demand inelastic when prices increase and elastic when prices decrease. In marketing terms it means informing, persuading, and reminding existing or prospective customers. The primary methods of promotion are personal selling, advertising, sales promotion, and public relations.

Integrated marketing communication (IMC) describes a coordinated promotional effort that includes planning, developing, executing, and evaluating communication with an organization's publics. An IMC approach to promotion adopts a customer perspective, selects from the alternative promotional tools to produce a defined response, coordinates all promotional efforts, and evaluates the effectiveness of promotion activity.

Promotion is communication. Fundamentally, the communication process consists of a source sending a message through a channel to a receiver. The success of communication depends on how well the message is encoded, how easily and clearly it can be decoded, and whether any noise interferes with its transmission. Feedback, the response created by a message, is a measure of how effective a communication has been.

When deciding on the promotional mix (the combination of advertising, personal selling, and other promotional tools), management should consider (1) the target audience, (2) the objective of the promotion effort, (3) the nature of the product, (4) the stage of the product's life cycle, and (5) the funds available for promotion.

There are several methods involved in setting a total promotional budget. The most common method is to set the budget as a percentage of past or anticipated sales. Other methods include using all available funds and following the competition. The best approach is to set the budget by establishing the promotional objectives and then estimating how much it will cost to achieve them.

In response to the desire to protect consumers and curb abuses, there are a number of federal laws and agencies regulating promotion. Promotional practices also are regulated by state and local legislation, by private organizations, and by industry.

More about **Pacific Sunwear**

Pacific Sunwear is selling fashions, or what some might even call fads. And it is selling them to a fickle audience that is very conscious of trends. Consistently staying a step ahead of the market is critical, but certainly not easy. Thus far, Pac-Sun has been successful at identifying popular brands and styles early in the fashion cycle. According to one analyst who follows the company, "Pacific Sunwear has built a reputation among consumers as the (retail) authority of the surf-and-skate lifestyle." The challenge is how to continue riding the crest of that wave.

By dramatically increasing its promotion budget, the firm is generating 300 million advertising impressions a year on its target market. With a coordinated, consistent communications strategy, PacSun intends to move more of its target customers from holding a positive image (the knowledge and prefer-

ence stages of the hierarchy of effects, reflected in the quotation above) to seeing it as the best place to shop for casual clothes (the conviction and purchase stages).

In 1998 the company opened 15 new stores under the trade name d.e.m.o., and added 40 more in 1999. This chain's target audience is 14-to-24-year-old males and females. Hoping to capitalize on what it has learned in developing PacSun, Pacific Sunwear's management has positioned these stores as the place to get trendy, casual clothes, but with a fashion influence that comes from hip-hop music, music personalities, and mainstream sports celebrities. There are no overlapping brands or merchandise between PacSun stores and d.e.m.o. stores. Interestingly, d.e.m.o. is not mentioned on the PacSun website.[20]

1. Why is promotion important in the marketing mix of a fashion retailer like Pacific Sunwear?

2. From a promotional perspective is there a reason for keeping PacSun and d.e.m.o. separate?

Key Terms and Concepts

Promotion (491)
Personal selling (493)
Advertising (493)
Sales promotion (493)
Public relations (493)
Integrated marketing communi-
  cation (IMC) (494)
Communication (498)
Viral marketing (499)

Promotion mix (500)
Push strategy (501)
Pull strategy (501)
Hierarchy of effects (502)
Promotional budgeting methods
  (506)
Federal Trade Commission
  Act (507)
Wheeler-Lea Amendment (507)

Robinson-Patman Act (508)
Lanham Trademark Act (508)
Trademark Law Revision Act
  (508)
Telephone Consumer Protection
  Act (509)
Printers' Ink statutes (510)
Green River ordinance (510)

Questions and Problems

1. Integrated marketing communications is just another way to say, "Keep everyone informed
   about what is going on." Comment.

2. Relate each of the components of the communication process model to the following situations:
   a. A college student trying to convince her fa-
      ther to buy her a used car.
   b. A sales person describing the same car to the
      college student.

3. How might the message on a company's website
   differ from the message it would use in a magazine advertisement?

4. The promotional budget for many products
   would be divided between a push strategy and
   a pull strategy. For the product below, give an
   example of who might be in the push strategy
   audience and who might be in the pull strategy
   audience:
   a. Contact lenses
   b. Golf balls
   c. Home insulation
   d. Personal computers
   e. Frozen pizza

5. Would it be appropriate for a firm to use advertising to create awareness of its brand at the same
   time that it uses sales promotion to stimulate

purchase? Explain using an Internet portal such
as America Online as an example.

6. Explain how the nature of the following products would likely affect its promotional mix.
   a. Automobile tires
   b. Use of a tanning salon
   c. Light bulbs
   d. Ten-minute automobile oil changes
   e. College education
   f. Individual Retirement Account (IRA)

7. How does the life-cycle stage of the automobile
   industry explain the promotional efforts carried
   out on behalf of most brands?

8. Assume you are marketing a liquid that removes
   creosote (and the danger of fire) from chimneys
   in home fireplaces. Briefly describe the roles you
   would assign to advertising, personal selling,
   sales promotion, and direct marketing in your
   promotional campaign.

9. Do you think additional legislation is needed to
   regulate advertising? To regulate personal selling? If so, explain what you would recommend.

Hands-On Marketing

1. An ad should have a particular objective that should be apparent to a careful observer. For each of the following promotional objectives, find an example of a print ad:
   a. Primarily designed to inform.
   b. Primarily designed to persuade.
   c. Primarily designed to remind.

2. An integrated promotional program is a coordinated series of promotional efforts built around a single theme and designed to reach a predetermined goal. It often includes several of the promotional methods described in the chapter. For an important event at your school (such as a homecoming, the recruitment of new students, or a fund-raising effort), describe the promotional tools used and evaluate their appropriateness based on the criteria in the chapter for designing a promotional mix.

18

Personal Selling and Sales Management

Johnson Controls, in its ASG division, views personal selling as much more than generating transactions.

What Does It Take to Keep
Johnson Controls in the Driver's Seat?

Johnson Controls, Inc., is a diversified company with annual sales of $12.5 billion. It produces batteries, security systems, heating and air-conditioning regulators, and plastic bottles, among other products. The company's largest and most successful division, the Automotive Systems Group (ASG), is a supplier to automobile and truck manufacturers.

The way firms in the auto industry deal with their suppliers has gone through a drastic change. Car makers used to order individual parts from a large number of suppliers, and then assemble the parts to produce a vehicle. The suppliers focused on building quality parts as specified by the car makers, and delivering the parts on time. However, as the competitive pressure in the automotive business grew, this approach was no longer satisfactory. Increasingly complex cars, combined with the need for lower costs, forced some changes. For instance, suppliers were asked to provide integrated systems, not individual parts. So Johnson went from being a seat maker to providing preassembled interiors (dashboard, instrument panel, seats, and headliner) that could be bolted into a car.

But a product change isn't enough to explain ASG's 20% annual growth rate since 1995. Its success can only be accounted for by a more fundamental revision in the way the division approaches marketing and sales. It begins with a recognition that success demands more than just meeting requirements. As one Johnson executive put it, "Our expertise used to be in manufacturing and delivery, but it is a completely different industry today. We are much more customer driven." This orientation is reflected in several ways:

- Rather than rely on the car makers for direction on auto interiors, ASG goes directly to the final customers and does extensive consumer research. Drivers and passengers are interviewed, videotaped, and probed in focus groups. Consumers are given cameras and asked to photograph the interior features they like and dislike in their cars, and they are asked to keep diaries about how they spend time in the car on trips. As a result, the company develops new products, supported by extensive data for its sales people to present to the auto manufacturers. Its research has produced a child-activity table (developed jointly with Lego) that folds out of the rear seat, a voice recorder concealed in a sun visor, an instrument panel device to indicate if a tire is losing air, and a flip-down screen on which rear seat passengers can watch videotapes.

- ASG has redefined the role of its sales people. With few potential customers (because there are only a handful of auto makers), and very large purchases, it is important that ASG sales people have the confidence and trust of the manufacturers. Success requires that they be viewed as partners, playing a consultative role. To do their jobs, ASG sales people need to combine their knowledge of the customer with information about the markets' needs and solid new-product ideas. In other words, ASG needs to have its marketing team and sales people working closely together. To encourage this collaboration, ASG combines sales and marketing under one executive.

- ASG has broken down a major barrier between sales people and other employees by eliminating sales commissions. Sales people are paid year-end performance bonuses, whereas engineers, marketing managers, and product designers receive bonuses based on the division's performance. Because everyone benefits from the division's common success, support of the sales effort is undertaken with enthusiasm.

- At ASG there is a realization that everyone serves the customer. Some companies place all the customer-contact responsibility on their sales people. Because of its market focus, ASG recognizes that sales people need to develop relationships with customers. However, there is also an awareness of the value of interaction at various levels. For example, it's not uncommon for representatives from sales, engineering, product design, and marketing to visit a customer, or for a similar group to host a customer team when they visit ASG to see a product test or discuss a new concept.

Johnson Controls, in its ASG division, views personal selling as much more than generating transactions. Its broader, integrated approach to the sales function is characteristic of a growing number of firms. On the basis of the success of ASG and others that have adopted a similar perspective, this may be the model that puts organizations in the fast lane.[1]

How do selling activities at Johnson Controls' ASG division differ from selling at a more traditional firm?

The importance of personal selling and the need for its integration with marketing can seldom be understated. The cooperation fostered at Johnson Controls and the success it has produced certainly support this position. ASG's innovations in sales-force management have established a new standard in its industry and left the competition scrambling to catch up.

After studying this chapter, you should be able to explain:

chapter goals

- The role that personal selling plays in our economy and in an organization's marketing program.
- The variety of personal selling jobs.
- The changing patterns of personal selling.
- The personal selling process.
- The strategic role of sales-force management.
- The major tasks in staffing and operating a sales force.
- Key issues in evaluating a sales person's performance.

Nature of Personal Selling

The goal of all marketing effort is to increase profitable sales by providing want-satisfaction to consumers over the long run. **Personal selling,** the personal communication of information to persuade somebody to buy something, is by far the major promotional method used to reach this goal. To illustrate, the number of people employed in advertising is about 500 *thousand*. In personal selling, the number is close to 15 *million*.[2] In many companies, personal selling is the largest single operating expense, often equaling 8 to 15% of sales. In contrast, advertising costs average 1 to 3% of sales.

In Chapter 17 we discussed five factors that influence an organization's promotional mix—the target market, the objective, the product, the product's life-cycle stage, and the money available for promotion. Referring to those five factors, personal selling is likely to carry the bulk of the promotional load when:

- The market is concentrated geographically, in a few industries, or in several large customers.
- The value of the product is not readily apparent to the prospect.
- The product has a high unit cost, is quite technical in nature, or requires a demonstration.
- The product must be fitted to an individual customer's need, as in the case of securities or insurance.
- The product is in the introductory stage of its life cycle.
- The organization does not have enough money to sustain an adequate advertising campaign.

Merits of Personal Selling

Personal selling is the direct, *personal* communication of information, in contrast to the mass, *impersonal* communication of advertising, sales promotion, and other promotional tools. This means that personal selling can be more flexible than these other tools. Sales people can tailor their presentations to fit the needs and behavior of individual customers. They can see their customers' reactions to a particular sales approach and make adjustments on the spot.

Also, personal selling can be focused on individuals or firms that are known to be prospective customers if an organization has done an adequate job of segmenting and targeting its market. As a result, wasted effort is minimized. In contrast, advertising messages are often wasted on people who are not realistic prospects.

Another advantage of personal selling is that its goal is to actually make a sale. Advertising usually has a less ambitious goal. It is often designed to attract attention, provide information, and arouse desire, but seldom does it stimulate buying action or complete the transfer of title from seller to buyer.

On the other hand, a full-fledged personal selling effort is costly. Even though personal selling can minimize wasted effort, the cost of developing and operating a sales force is high. Another disadvantage is that a company may find it difficult to attract the quality of people needed to do the job. At the retail level, many firms have abandoned their sales forces and shifted to self-service for this very reason.

Scope of Personal Selling

Personal selling is involved when a student buys a Honda motorcycle or an Ann Taylor store sells a dress to a businesswoman. But you should recognize that some personal selling also occurs when (1) Citicorp recruits a graduating senior who majored in marketing or, conversely, a student tries to convince Citicorp to hire her; (2) a minister talks to a group of students to encourage them to attend church services; (3) a lawyer tries to convince a jury that her client is innocent; or even (4) a boy persuades his mother to buy him something from eToys. The point is that a form of personal selling occurs in nearly every human interaction.

In business situations, there are two kinds of personal selling, as shown in Figure 18.1. One is where the customers come to the sales people. Called **inside selling**, it primarily involves retail sales. In this group, we include the sales people in stores and the sales people at catalog retailers such as Lands' End or L.L. Bean, who take telephone orders. Also included are the telephone order takers at manufacturers and wholesalers, most of whom take existing customers' routine orders over the telephone. By far, most sales people in the U.S. fall into this first category, but some are being replaced by purchasing done over the Internet.

In the other kind of personal selling, known as **outside selling**, sales people go to the customer. They make contact by telephone or in person. Most outside sales forces usually represent producers or wholesaling middlemen, selling to business users and not to household consumers. However, in our definition of an outside sales force, we also include (1) producers whose representatives sell directly to household consumers—for example, insurance companies such as State Farm or Northwestern Mutual and in-home sellers such as Kirby Vacuum cleaner distributors; (2) representatives of retail organizations who go to consumers' homes to demonstrate a product, give advice, or provide an estimate,

Figure 18.1

Scope of personal selling.

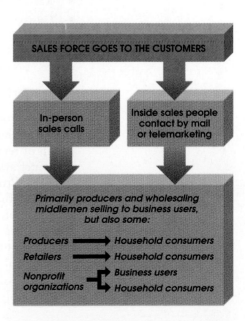

Table 18.1	America's Best Sales Forces in 1999*
Company	**Industry**
Enron Corporation	Energy management
Dell Computer Corp.	Computers
Cisco Systems	Computer networking equipment
GE Capital Services	Financial services
Pfizer	Pharmaceuticals

*In some cases the winning sales organization is from one division of the company.

Source: "Here's to the Winners," *Sales & Marketing Management*, July 1999, pp. 46–70.

such as sales people for some furniture stores and home heating and air-conditioning retailers; and (3) representatives of nonprofit organizations—for example, charity fund raisers, religious missionaries, and workers for political candidates.

Nature of Sales Jobs

As suggested by the opening case, the sales job of today is quite different from the stereotype of the past. The images of high pressure, false friendship, and glibness are largely outdated, as is the notion of a price-cutting order chaser. Even the stereotype of the sales *man* is much less evident as more and more women enter professional selling.

The Professional Sales Person

A new type of sales rep has emerged—the professional sales person. Today these reps are typically managers of a designated market, which may be a geographic area or a category of customers. They frequently engage in a total selling job identifying prospects, servicing their customers, building goodwill, selling their products, and training their customers' sales people. Today's reps are supposed to act as a mirror of the market by relaying market information back to the firm. They organize much of their own time and effort. They often take part in recruiting new sales people, sales planning in their territories, and other managerial activities.

Whose sales forces best reflect this professionalism? *Sales & Marketing Management* magazine conducted a multistage survey to identify America's best sales forces. The criteria used were:

- *Results:* Superior sales performance over the past three years.
- *Customer satisfaction:* A reputation for taking care of customers.
- *High morale:* A satisfied sales force.

The top five sales forces for 1999 are presented in Table 18.1.

Wide Variety of Sales Jobs

The types of sales jobs and the activities involved in them cover a wide range. Consider the job of a Coca-Cola driver–sales person who calls routinely on a group of retail stores. That job is in another world from the IBM rep who sells a computer system for managing reservations to Delta Airlines. Similarly, a sales rep for Avon Products selling door to door in Japan or China has a job only remotely related to that of a Cessna airplane rep who sells executive-type aircraft to Dow Chemical and other large firms in the U.S.

The types of sales jobs differ in terms of the creative selling skills required, from the simple to the complex. The six categories that follow are updated and adapted from several sales-job classification schemes that have been proposed over the years:[3]

- *Driver–sales person.* In this job the sales person primarily delivers the product—for example, soft drinks or fuel oil—and services the account. The sell-

L.L. Bean is one of several firms, including Eddie Bauer and Norm Thompson, that successfully market upscale sportswear and outdoor products using catalogs delivered through the mail. Recently most of these companies have added electronic catalogs that allow customers to purchase via the Web. Does traditional catalog selling utilizing inside order takers offer any advantages over selling on the Web?

 www.llbean.com

ing responsibilities are secondary, although most of these sales people are authorized to and rewarded for finding opportunities to increase sales to existing accounts.

- *Inside order taker.* This is a position in which the sales person takes orders and assists customers at the seller's place of business—for example, a retail clerk on the sales floor at a J.C. Penney store or a telephone representative at a catalog retailer such as Eddie Bauer or L.L. Bean. Most customers have already decided to buy. The sales person's job is to serve them efficiently and engage in suggestion selling.

- *Outside order taker.* In this position the sales person goes to the customer in the field and requests an order. An example is a John Deere sales person calling on a farm equipment dealer, or a sales rep for a radio station selling advertising time to local businesses. The majority of these sales are repeat orders to established customers, and much of the sales person's time is devoted to support activities such as assisting the distributors with promotion and training their sales people. These sales people are assigned goals that require them to seek new customers and introduce new products to existing customers.

- *Missionary sales person.* This type of sales person is expected to provide information and other services for existing or potential customers, perform promotional activities, and build goodwill. A missionary sales person does not solicit orders. An example of this job is a detail sales person for a pharmaceutical firm such as Merck or Lilly.

- *Sales engineer.* In this position the major emphasis is on the sales person's ability to explain the product to a prospective customer, and also to adapt the product to the customer's particular needs. The products involved here typically are complex, technically sophisticated items. A sales engineer usually provides technical support and works with another sales rep who calls regularly on a given account.

- *Consultative sales person.* This involves the creative selling of goods and services. This category contains the most complex, difficult selling jobs—especially the creative selling of services, because you can't see, touch, taste, or smell them. Customers often are not aware of their need for a seller's product. Or they may not realize how that product can satisfy their wants better than the product they are now using. Consultative selling requires that a relationship of trust be established with the customer. It often involves designing a system to fit the needs of a particular customer. For example, to win the contract for the new Houston Astros ballpark, the sales team from Enron, the energy management company, must design a system that convinces the owners it can do everything related to providing and managing energy for the facility.

In summary, the above six types of sales jobs fall into three groups: order takers (categories 1, 2, and 3), sales-support personnel (categories 4 and 5), and order getters (category 6). Order takers, unless they can find ways to provide added value to their customers, are the sales positions most threatened by electronic commerce over the Internet.

A classification with several categories of jobs helps dispel the notion that all sales jobs are alike. However, it is worth noting that some richness is lost in the creation of any classification. In fact, there is considerable diversity in sales because firms design jobs to fit their particular situations. A study in the 1980s identified over 120 specific and reasonably exclusive tasks performed by at least some sales people.[4] A more recent study identified nearly 50 more tasks, many associated with the use of technology in selling.[5] So even though it is possible to classify sales jobs in a general way, it's important to note that specific sales jobs are tailored to the needs of the market and the sales organization.

The Cost of Personal Selling

The cost of a sales call depends on the sales approach used. For firms selling commodities and emphasizing price, the cost is about $85. On the other hand, when the sales approach is to identify and design solutions for customers' problems, the cost of a call is $190.[6] Add to this the fact that it typically takes from three to six calls to make a sale to a new customer, and it becomes apparent that personal selling is expensive.

The Uniqueness of Sales Jobs

The features that differentiate sales jobs from other jobs follow:
- The sales force is largely responsible *for implementing a firm's marketing strategies.* Moreover, it's the sales reps who generate the revenues that are managed by the financial people and used by the production people.
- Sales people are typically the most *visible representatives of their company* to customers and to society in general. Many sales jobs require the rep to socialize with customers who frequently are upper-level executives in their companies. Opinions of the firm and its products are formed on the basis of impressions made by sales people in their work and in outside activities. The public ordinarily does not judge a company by its factory or office workers, and customers can't judge products until after they are purchased and used.
- Sales reps operate with *limited direct supervision.* For success in selling, a sales rep must work hard physically and mentally, be creative and persistent, and show considerable initiative. This all requires a high degree of motivation.
- By the nature of the job, sales people *have more rejections than acceptances;* that is, more prospects choose not to buy than to buy. A sales person who internalizes the rejection will quickly become discouraged.
- Sales jobs frequently involve considerable *traveling and time away from home.* To reduce sales travel time, some firms redesign sales territories, route sales trips better, and rely more on telemarketing and electronic ordering. Nevertheless, being in the field, sales people deal with a seemingly endless stream of customers who may seem determined not to buy their products. These stresses,

Do sales executives need coaching prior to foreign assignments?

Virtually all large firms and many small businesses either buy or sell products beyond their home country borders. As a result, it has become commonplace for sales executives to communicate with foreign customers. And international trips to build relationships or close deals are not unusual.

Traveling on business is very different from pleasure travel. Schedules are often tight, certain protocol is expected, and precise communication is essential. Even though English is considered the language of international business, a sales person cannot assume that it is "business as usual" when dealing with a foreign client.

There are many ways inexperienced executives can send the wrong message. Some potentially disastrous examples are:

- Body language.
  - Standing with hands on hips in the U.S. signals intensity or frustration; in many parts of Asia it suggests aggressiveness.
  - Shaking the head from side to side means "no" in most places, but in Bulgaria and Sri Lanka it means "yes."
  - Patting someone on the back in the U.S. is a sign of affection or congratulations; in Japan it is seen as condescending.
  - Pointing out an object or even a person with the index finger in the U.S. is generally acceptable, but it is considered rude in India, Israel, and Belgium.
- The spoken and written word.
  - A word can have different meanings depending on where you are. In Portugal, an "escoba" is a toothbrush, but in Spain it is a broom. Americans might be surprised to find that in England a lift, a flat, a bonnet, and the first floor of a building are not what they might expect. In England a lift is an elevator, a flat is an apartment, a bonnet is the hood of a car, and the first floor of a building is what Americans call the second floor.
  - Many different words may describe the same things. Arabs have 1,000 words for a camel, so it pays to be precise.
- Social customs. Knowing how to greet a stranger, when to stand or sit at a social gathering, what dress is appropriate, when to arrive for an appointment, and the correct level of formality in a meeting vary from culture to culture.

In travel, as in other areas, the Internet can be of assistance. The meaning of body language around the world can be found at the Web of Culture. The value of any country's currency in any other currency can be found with the Universal Currency Converter. A message can be typed in English or any of several European languages, and it will be instantly translated into the language of choice at the Foreign Language Translator. The time anywhere on earth is available from the Time Zone Converter.

Sources: Mark Wexler, "Translating Body Language," *Modern Maturity,* January–February 2000, p. R; Stephen Williams, "Send the Right Signal: A Guide to International Body Language," *Travel & Leisure,* March 1997, p. 118; Cristina Pelayo, "The Tongue-Tied Traveler," *US Airways Magazine,* March 1997, pp. 78–82.

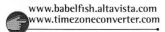

www.webofculture.com
www.xe.net/currency

www.babelfish.altavista.com
www.timezoneconverter.com

coupled with long hours and traveling, require mental toughness and physical stamina. Personal selling is hard work!

Changing Patterns in Personal Selling

Traditionally, personal selling was a face-to-face, one-on-one situation between a sales person and a prospective buyer. This situation existed both in retail sales involving ultimate consumers and also in business-to-business transactions. In recent years, however, some very different selling patterns have emerged. These new patterns reflect a growing purchasing expertise among consumers and business buyers, which, in turn, has fostered more professionalism in personal selling. Several of these patterns are described as follows.

Selling Centers

To match the expertise of the buying center (described in Chapter 5) in business markets, an increasing number of firms on the selling side have adopted the organizational concept of a **selling center**. A selling center is a group of people representing a sales department as well as other functional areas in a firm such as finance, production, and research and development brought together to meet the needs of a particular customer. This is sometimes called a *sales team* or *team selling*.

Team selling is expensive, and is therefore usually restricted to accounts that have a potential for high sales volume and profit. Procter & Gamble, for example, has selling teams assigned to large retailers such as Wal-Mart. The opening case described how Johnson Controls uses sales teams. When AT&T sells to a large multinational firm such as Nestlé, AT&T will send a separate selling team to deal with each of Nestlé's major divisions.

Most sales teams are ad hoc groups, assembled to deal with a particular opportunity. Except for the sales person, the team members have other responsibilities in the firm. This creates several managerial issues. For example, who directs a team—the most senior person involved, the sales person who organizes the team, or the most experienced member? What happens if the buying center decides it prefers to work with a senior manager on the team or the technical expert who "speaks their language" rather than the sales person? Also, how should team members be evaluated and compensated? Despite these challenges, the increasing complexity of sales has made team selling increasingly popular.

Systems Selling

The concept of **systems selling** means selling a total package of related goods and services—a system—to solve a customer's problem. The idea is that the system will satisfy the buyer's needs more effectively than selling individual products separately. Xerox, for example, originally sold individual products, using a separate sales force for each major product line. Today, using a systems-selling approach, Xerox studies a customer's office information and operating problems. Then Xerox provides a total automated system of machines and accompanying services to solve that customer's office problems.

System selling has several benefits. The most obvious is that it produces a larger initial sale because a system rather than a product is purchased. Second, it reduces compatibility problems because all parts of the system come from the same supplier. Third, it often means that the supplier is also retained to service the system because of its familiarity with it. Finally, if the system performs effectively, the system provider is in an excellent position to propose upgrades as they are needed.

Systems selling is not right for every situation. For example, the components that make up some systems, such as Internet routing equipment, are so complex they require the expertise of several firms.

Global Sales Teams

As companies expand their operations to far-flung corners of the globe, they expect their suppliers to do the same. Having products readily available, understanding local conditions, and providing quick service are essential to maintaining global customers. To service their largest and most profitable global customers, sellers are forming **global sales teams**. Such a unit is responsible for all of a company's sales to an account anywhere in the world. For example, AMP Inc., a $3.5 billion supplier of connection systems, uses a global sales team to serve the needs of IBM worldwide. The team manager is located close to the customer's headquarters, and the team members are prepared to deal with issues and opportunities wherever they may occur.

Relationship Selling

Developing a mutually beneficial relationship with selected customers over time is **relationship selling**. It may be an extension of team selling, or it may be developed by individual sales reps in their dealings with customers. In relationship selling, a seller discontinues the usual practice of concentrating on maximizing the number and size of individual transactions. Instead, the seller attempts to develop a deeper, longer-lasting relationship built on trust with key customers—usually larger accounts.

Unfortunately, often there is little trust found in buyer–seller relationships, either in retailer–consumer selling or in business-to-business selling. In fact, in some circles selling is viewed as adversarial, with one side winning and the other side losing. For example, a buyer may try to squeeze the last penny out of the seller in price negotiations, even with the knowledge that the agreed-on price may make it difficult for the seller to perform adequately.

How do sellers build trust? First and foremost, there must be a customer orientation. The seller must place the customers' needs and interests on a par with its own. From that will follow a shared vision of success, an expanded time horizon that looks beyond the immediate sale, and a perspective that the parties to a transaction are partners not adversaries.

Many large companies—Procter & Gamble, Hyatt Hotels, RJR Nabisco, and Kraft General Foods to name just a few—have realigned their sales forces to engage in relationship selling.

Telemarketing

Telemarketing is the innovative use of telecommunications equipment and systems as part of the "going to the customer" category of personal selling. Under certain conditions, telemarketing is attractive to both buyers and sellers. Buyers placing routine reorders or new orders for standardized products by telephone use less of their time than with in-person sales calls.

Many sellers find that telemarketing increases selling efficiency. With the high costs of keeping sales people on the road, telemarketing reduces the time they spend on routine order taking. Redirecting routine reorders to telemarketing allows the field sales force to devote more time to creative selling, major account selling, and other more profitable selling activities.

Here are examples of selling activities that lend themselves nicely to a telemarketing program:

- Seeking leads to new accounts and identifying potentially good customers that sales reps can follow up with in-person calls.
- Processing orders for standardized products. Some customers of Baxter International (a seller of hospital supplies) have prepared their computers to communicate directly with Baxter's computers to place orders when inventories reach certain levels.
- Dealing with small-order customers, especially where the seller would lose money if field sales calls were used.

Some companies hoped that online self-service would replace traditional call centers like the one shown in the photo. However, it has been estimated that businesses lose over $3 billion a year in potential sales due to poor online service. In response, companies are linking their websites and their call centers despite the fact that an online service inquiry costs a company 5 to 7¢ per minute whereas a person taking the call costs about $3.50 a minute.

- Improving relations with middlemen. Manufacturers use telemarketing to answer dealers' questions about inventory management, service, and replacement parts. This gives the dealers an immediate source for assistance, saving them the time and effort of trying to track down a sales person.

Internet Selling

Most sales efforts over the Internet would not be considered personal, and therefore would not be part of a discussion about *personal* selling. For example, when W.W. Grainger posted its 4,000-page catalog of repair and maintenance parts on its website so customers could order items electronically, the resulting transactions were impersonal. In fact, the impersonal nature of the process is one of its strengths, because it speeds up purchasing and reduces the frequency of errors. However, one category of **Internet selling,** the business-to-business auction, qualifies as personal selling because of its interactive nature.[7]

www.purchasepro.com

Using the traditional auction format, a seller (working through an intermediary such as PurchasePro.com that provides the linking technology) notifies potential bidders of a product available for sale. Typically the item for sale is a discontinued model of a product or excess inventory of some raw material. According to a predetermined schedule, bids are submitted electronically in round-robin fashion in real time. Both the seller and all the bidders see each bid and have the opportunity to respond.

www.freemarkets.com

Another version is called a reverse auction. (Recall the Freemarkets.com description at the beginning of Chapter 5.) The prospective buyer notifies potential sellers of its willingness to purchase a specified product and an electronic auction is held to select a seller. In both auction formats, there is an interchange of information between buyers and sellers, negotiation of terms, and intense price competition.

Thus far, Internet auctions have been limited to commodities or standardized goods. For example a state bought salt for use on icy roads, and a computer memory chip maker sold microprocessors. However, there is little doubt that the technology will improve and become more widespread. As it does, the Internet will become an increasingly significant sales tool.

Sales-Force Automation

Equipping sales people with laptop computers, cellular phones, fax machines, and pagers in order to give them access to databases, the Internet, e-mail, and other information and communication tools is called **sales-force automation** (SFA). The

Although sales people have become comfortable with faxes, cellular phones, and pagers, using sales presentation software and laptops as shown here is still relatively uncommon. Explanations for nonuse include a high degree of comfort with existing techniques, problems with learning the new technology, and a fear of the technology being used to monitor activities.

Is it possible to have too much of a good thing?

Technology is quickly becoming an indispensable tool for sales people. It comes in many forms and assists with many tasks. For example:

- Linked to headquarters through the Internet, an outside sales person can make sure a particular product is available before a customer places an order, check on the status of a shipment, and verify prices, all in real time.

- Equipped with a laptop computer, a sales person representing a company with hundreds of products can show a customer a 3-D picture of a particular item with just a few key strokes.

- Software is available that will ensure accuracy when a sales person places an order. The program makes it impossible to accept an invalid product or model number; calculates prices taking into consideration shipping, taxes, and any discounts or special promotions; and notifies a sales person when individual customers should be contacted.

- Cellular phones, pagers, and e-mail have made sales people accessible at any time, day or night.

- Private intranets allow sales people in the field to tap into their company database and get a customer's complete history while preparing for a sales call.

According to a sales technology consultant, "At the end of the day, it really comes down to making the sales person more productive."

As technology and the information it provides threaten to engulf the sales person, a key question is: How much is enough? According to a study by Pitney-Bowes, an office equipment maker, the average U.S. white-collar worker sends or receives over 200 messages of all kinds each day. To ensure technology produces a return on the investment, an organization must: (1) set priorities among the many available technology resources, (2) make sure the sales person benefits as well as the company, and (3) keep in mind that the ultimate test of any innovation is how much value it adds for the customer.

Sources: Megan Doscher, "Death of the Off-Line Salesman," *The Wall Street Journal,* June 21, 1999, pp. R16+; Libby Estill, "Wait'll You Hear This," *Sales & Marketing Management,* March 1999, pp. 57–61.

---

concept is quite simple. Tools are available to help sales people manage information about their accounts and prospects, generate proposals, submit reports, and manage their time and territories more efficiently. For example, JVC, a video equipment manufacturer, found its sales force was spending time every morning tracking down information about customers' purchase orders. To reduce the search time, the company designed a system that allows the sales force to download the information from the company's main database to their laptops every day. Now the information sales people need is available immediately.[8]

Automating a sales force can be expensive, depending on the level and the degree of customization. For example, providing sales people with pagers so they can keep in touch with customers would be a modest investment compared to a system that permitted access to corporate databases. Implementing SFA involves several challenges:

- Identifying the parts of the sales process that can benefit the most from automation.
- Designing a system that accomplishes the objectives and is user friendly.
- Gaining the cooperation of the sales force in changing the way they do their jobs to incorporate the technology.[9]

Experiences with automation have been mixed. According to a firm that installs programs, 55% fail to meet expectations.[10] However, many of the problems result from inadequate planning or implementation. Despite these difficulties, increasingly sales forces are being automated. The average growth in revenue from the sale of SFA equipment is expected to be about $1 billion a year.[11] On the basis of a recent survey in which 83% of the responding companies indicated plans to upgrade their systems, it is safe to say the sales role of the future will include a significant electronic component.[12]

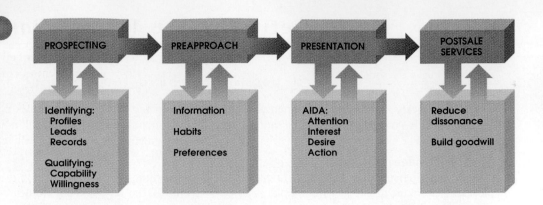

Figure 18.2

The personal selling
process.

PROSPECTING → PREAPPROACH → PRESENTATION → POSTSALE SERVICES

Identifying:
Profiles
Leads
Records

Qualifying:
Capability
Willingness

Information

Habits

Preferences

AIDA:
Attention
Interest
Desire
Action

Reduce
dissonance

Build goodwill

The Personal Selling Process

The **personal selling process**, depicted in Figure 18.2, is a logical sequence of four steps that a sales person takes in dealing with a prospective buyer. This process is designed to produce some desired customer action, and ends with a follow-up to ensure customer satisfaction. The desired action usually is a purchase by the customer.

The same four-step process also is used in other marketing situations, seeking different outcomes. For example, RJR Nabisco persuades Safeway to give Oreo cookies a good shelf location in a special promotion program; or Northwestern University persuades alumni to contribute to a special fund-raising effort; or BMW wants its dealers to do some local advertising of their automobiles.

Prospecting

The first step in the personal selling process is really two related steps. Prospecting consists of identifying possible customers and then qualifying them—that is, determining whether they have the necessary potential to buy. They are combined as a single step because they are typically done at the same time.

Identifying Prospective Customers

The identification process is an application of market segmentation. By analyzing the firm's database of past and current customers, a sales rep can determine characteristics of an ideal prospect. Comparing this profile to a list of potential customers will produce a set of prospects.

A list of potential customers can be constructed using suggestions from current customers, trade associations and industry directories, the customer lists of related but noncompeting businesses, and mail-in or telephone responses to ads.

A little thought often will suggest logical prospects. Homestead House (a furniture store chain) and US West (a telephone company) find prospects in lists of building permits issued. Insurance companies (Northwestern Mutual or Prudential), real estate firms (Re/Max, Century 21), and even local diaper services use marriage and birth announcements in newspapers as sources.

Qualifying Prospects

After identifying prospective customers, a seller should qualify them—that is, determine whether they have the necessary willingness, purchasing power, and authority to buy. To determine willingness to buy, a seller can seek information about any changes in the prospect's situation. For example, a business firm or a household consumer may have had a recent problem with an insurance provider.

www.dnb.com

In this case there may be an opportunity for a sales person from a competing insurer to get that prospect's business.

To determine a prospect's financial ability to pay, a seller can refer to credit-rating services such as Dun & Bradstreet. For household consumers or small businesses in an area, a seller can get credit information from a local credit bureau. Identifying who has the authority to buy in a business or a household can be difficult, as we saw back in Chapters 4 and 5. In a business, the buying authority may rest with a committee or an executive in a distant location. Besides determining the buying authority, a seller also should identify the one or more persons who influence the buying decision. A purchasing agent may have buying authority, but what he or she buys may depend on the recommendation of an office secretary, a factory engineer, or a vice president.

Preapproach to Individual Prospects

Before calling on prospects, sales people should conduct a preapproach—learning all they can about the persons or companies to whom they hope to sell. This might include finding out what products the prospects have used in the past, what they are now using, and their reactions to these products. In business-to-business selling, a sales person or selling team should find out how buying decisions are made in the customer's organization. A sales rep can target the right people if he or she knows who is the gatekeeper, who influences and/or makes the buying decision, and who actually makes the purchase.

Finding out something about the prospect's personal life—interests, activities, and habits—as well as gathering some insights into the preferred business practices of the prospect can be useful. Sales people should try to get all the information they can, so they will be able to tailor their presentations to individual buyers.

Presenting the Sales Message

With the appropriate preapproach information, a sales person can design a sales presentation that will attract the prospect's attention. The sales person will then try to hold the prospect's interest while building a desire for the product and, when the time is right, attempt to stimulate action by closing the sale. This approach, called **AIDA** (an acronym formed by the first letters of Attention, Interest, Desire, and Action), is used by many organizations.

Attract Attention—the Approach

The first task in a sales presentation is to attract the prospect's attention and to generate curiosity. In cases where the prospect is aware of a need and is seeking a solution, simply stating the seller's company and product may be enough. However, more creativity often is required.

For instance, if the sales person was referred to the prospect by a customer, the right approach might be to start out by mentioning this common acquaintance. Or a sales person might suggest the product benefits by making some startling statement. One sales training consultant suggests greeting a prospect with the question, "If I can cut your selling costs in half, and at the same time double your sales volume, are you interested?"

Hold Interest and Arouse Desire

After attracting the prospect's attention, the challenge for the sales rep is to hold it and stimulate a desire for the product with a sales presentation. There is no universal format here, but when it is practical, a product demonstration is invaluable. Whatever format is followed in the presentation, the sales person must always show how the product will benefit the prospect.

Some companies train their sales people to use a canned sales talk—a memorized presentation designed to cover all points determined by management to be important. Companies engaging in telemarketing typically use scripted sales talks. They may be appropriate if the sales person is inexperienced or knows very little about the customer, but a presentation with more flexibility can be personalized and tailored to individual customers' needs.

Meet Objections and Close the Sale

After explaining the product and its benefits, a sales person should try to close the sale—that is, obtain action on the customer's part. Periodically in a presentation, the sales person may venture a trial close to test the prospect's willingness to buy. One method is posing an "either-or" question that presumes the prospect has decided to buy. For example, "Would you prefer that the installation be done immediately or would it be better to have it done next week?"

The trial close tends to uncover the buyer's objections. The toughest objections to answer are those that are unspoken. Thus, a sales person should encourage buyers to state their objections. Then the sales person has an opportunity to meet the objections and bring out additional product benefits or reemphasize previously stated points.

Postsale Services

An effective selling job does not end when the order is written up. The final stage of a selling process is a series of postsale activities that can build customer goodwill and lay the groundwork for future business. An alert sales person will follow up sales to ensure that no problems occur in delivery, financing, installation, employee training, and other areas that are important to customer satisfaction.

Postsale service reduces the customer's postpurchase cognitive dissonance—the anxiety that usually occurs after a person makes a buying decision (discussed in Chapter 4). In this final stage of the selling process, a sales person can minimize the customer's dissonance by (1) summarizing the product's benefits after the purchase, (2) repeating why the product is better than alternatives not chosen, (3) describing how satisfied other buyers have been with the product, and (4) emphasizing how satisfied the customer will be with the product.

Strategic Sales-Force Management

Managing the personal selling function is a matter of applying the three-stage management process (planning, implementation, and evaluation) to a sales force and its activities. Sales executives begin by setting sales goals and planning sales-force activities. This involves forecasting sales, preparing sales budgets, establishing sales territories, and setting sales quotas. Then a sales force must be organized, staffed, and operated to implement the strategic plans and reach the goals that were set. The final stage involves evaluating the performance of individual sales people as well as appraising the total sales performance.

Effective sales-force management starts with a qualified sales manager. Finding the right person for this job is not easy. In many organizations the common practice when a sales management position becomes available is to reward the most productive sales person with a promotion. The assumption is that, as a manager, an effective sales person will be able to impart the necessary wisdom to make others equally successful.

However, the qualities that lead to effective sales management are often the opposite of the attributes of a successful sales person. Probably the biggest difference in the positions is that sales people tend to be self-motivated and self-reliant.

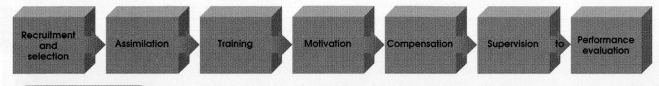

Figure 18.3

Staffing and operating a sales force.

They often work independently, receiving all the credit or blame for their successes or failures. In contrast, sales managers must work through and depend on others, and must be prepared to give recognition rather than receive it.

It is an unusual person who can be a successful sales manager without previous selling experience. To be effective, a sales manager must understand customers, appreciate the role of the sales person, and have the respect of the sales force. These attributes can only be acquired by spending time in sales. The resolution may come in not using the sales management position as a reward for outstanding sales performance. Rather, the criteria for sales management should be respectable sales performance coupled with the necessary attributes of management.

Staffing and Operating a Sales Force

Because most sales executives spend the bulk of their time in staffing and operating their sales forces, we will discuss these activities in some detail. Figure 18.3 shows what's involved.

Recruitment and Selection

Selecting personnel is the most important management activity in any organization. This is true whether the organization is an athletic team, a college faculty, or a sales force. No matter what the caliber of sales management, if a sales force is distinctly inferior to that of a competitor's, the rival firm will win.

Sales-force selection involves three tasks:

1. Determining the type of people needed by preparing a written job description.
2. Recruiting an adequate number of applicants.
3. Selecting the most qualified persons from among the applicants.

Determining Hiring Specifications

There have been many attempts to identify a general set of personality attributes that explain selling success.[13] However, these lists tend to be of little practical value because they consist of common sense characteristics such as assertiveness and empathy, don't account for motivation, and fail to recognize the differences in sales jobs.

Some companies analyze the personal histories of their existing sales representatives in an effort to determine the traits common to successful (and unsuccessful) performers. Even when a firm thinks it knows what the important attributes are, measuring the degree to which each quality should be present or the extent an abundance of one can offset the lack of another is difficult.

A better approach is to identify the specifications for the particular job, just as if the company were purchasing equipment or supplies rather than labor. This calls for a detailed job analysis and a written job description. The description then becomes the basis for identifying the aptitude and skills a person needs to perform the job. Later, this written description will be invaluable in training, compensation, and supervision.

Qualified sales people are hard to find, especially experienced sales people who are familiar with a recruiter's industry. One way to get such people is to aggressively recruit them from a competitor's sales force. Not only do these reps know the business, they might also bring along some of their customers. Competitors object strongly to this "pirating," as they call it. They have spent much money and effort training these reps, and they now want to benefit from the reps' sales productivity. The recruiting companies believe that taking sales people from competitors is no different than taking customers. They call it competition.

Is it ethical for a sales manager to directly approach a competitor's sales rep with a job offer?

Recruiting Applicants

A planned system for recruiting a sufficient number of applicants is the next step in selection. A good recruiting system:

- Operates continuously, not only when sales-force vacancies occur.
- Is systematic in reaching all appropriate sources of applicants.
- Provides a flow of more qualified applicants than is needed.

To identify recruits, large organizations often use placement services on college campuses or professional employment agencies. Smaller firms that need fewer new sales people may place classified ads in trade publications and daily newspapers. Many firms solicit recommendations from company employees, customers, or suppliers.

Matching Applicants with Hiring Specifications

Sales managers use a variety of techniques—including application forms, interviews, references, credit reports, psychological tests, aptitude tests, and physical examinations—to determine which applicants possess the desired qualifications. Virtually all companies ask candidates to fill out application forms. In addition to providing basic screening information, the application indicates areas that should be explored in an interview.

No sales person should be hired without at least one personal interview. And it is usually desirable to have several interviews conducted by different people in different physical settings. Pooling the opinions of a number of people increases the likelihood of discovering any undesirable characteristics and reduces the effects of one interviewer's possible bias.

The individuals involved in the selection process need to be aware of the laws against discrimination in order to avoid inadvertent violations. For example, it is illegal to ask on an application or in an interview a person's age or marital status. Testing for intelligence, attributes, or personality, although legal under the proper conditions, is somewhat controversial. Some companies avoid testing for fear that they will be accused of discrimination. However, employment tests are legitimate selection tools as long as the attributes measured can be shown to predict job performance.

Assimilating New Sales People

After sales people are hired, management should integrate them into the company. Because selling by its nature involves a considerable amount of rejection by prospects, the new sales person needs support in order to avoid becoming discouraged. A wise sales manager will recognize that the new people must be made comfortable with the details of the job, their fellow workers, and their status in the firm if they are to be successful.

Traditional sales training is often divided into classroom lectures, interactive exercises, and supervised field experience. Some companies such as Land Rover North America enrich the training experience. At Land Rover University, sales people can put the company's SUVs through their paces on off-road training courses. Stories about the experiences are the sales peoples' most valuable selling tools.

 www.landrover.com

Training a Sales Force

Virtually all companies put new and inexperienced sales people through an orientation and sales training program, often lasting weeks or months. Recognizing that the recent college graduates it hires into its sales force are unlikely to have much experience with its appliances, Whirlpool devised an unusual training experiment.[14] Eight new hires spent two months living in a house together, using the products the company sells. Under the supervision of trainers, they cooked, cleaned, baked, and washed using their employer's products. At the end of the program the trainees had the experience and confidence to go out into the field and teach retail sales clerks how to sell Whirlpool appliances.

Even experienced sales people need continual training to improve their selling skills, learn about new products, and improve their time- and territory-management practices. One of the primary training areas for experienced sales people is in the use of sales-force automation tools described earlier in the chapter.

Motivating a Sales Force

Sales people, especially outside sales forces, require a high degree of motivation. Think back to our earlier discussion about the uniqueness of sales jobs—how sales people often work with little or no direct supervision and guidance from management, and how they must deal with frequent rejection by customers. In addition, outside sales people work most of the time away from the support and comfort of home office surroundings.

Consequently, management faces a challenge in motivating sales people. One key is to determine what motivates the sales reps—is it a need for money, status, control, accomplishment, or something else? People differ in what motivates them, and the motivations change over a person's life. A young sales person is more likely to be motivated by money, whereas an older sales person may be more interested in recognition.

Sales executives can draw from a wide assortment of specific motivational tools. Financial incentives—compensation plans, expense accounts, fringe benefits—serve as basic motivators, but they don't always push people to exceptional performance. Nonfinancial rewards—job enrichment, praise from management, recognition and honor awards (pin, trophy, certificate)—may stimulate some reps. Sales meetings and sales contests are often-used alternatives. Many firms provide cruises, resort trips, and other travel incentives as rewards to top-performing sales

Which incentive is the best motivator?

Companies use all types of incentives to motivate their sales forces. The only limits seem to be the imagination of the sales manager and the budget. Some incentives are directed at the employee—for example, a gold watch or a salesperson-of-the-year plaque. Others include the spouse or family, such as a night out on the town or a visit to an amusement park. However, the one used most often, by 63% of firms according to a survey conducted by the Incentive Federation, is cash. Yet most experts suggest that cash alone is not the best motivator.

Other incentives that have been used to motivate sales people include:

- A CEO who agreed to let his sales people shave his head in public if they exceeded an annual sales goal.

- An all-expenses-paid trip to Germany that included picking out a new Mercedes to bring home.

- A $20,000 donation in the sales person's name to the charity of his/her choice.

- Autographed sports memorabilia.

- Posting the photos of the top performers for all to see.

- Posting the photos of the worst performers for all to see.

  Clearly the dollar value of an incentive has to be in line with the magnitude of the results, but what else should guide the manager in deciding what to offer?

Sources: Diane Sanchez, "Putting Motivation Back in Sales Incentives," *Sales & Marketing Management,* August 1999, pp. 24+; Vincent Alonzo, "An Incentive to Embrace Family Values," *Sales & Marketing Management,* July 1999, pp. 28+; Erin Strout, "Just Rewards," *Sales & Marketing Management,* May 1999, pp. 37–42.

reps. The importance of finding ways to motivate sales people is reflected in the attention it receives in the sales management literature.[15]

Compensating a Sales Force

Financial rewards are by far the most widely used tool for motivating sales people. Consequently, designing and administering an effective sales compensation plan is a big part of a sales manager's job. Financial rewards may be direct monetary payments (salary, commission) or indirect monetary compensation (paid vacations, pensions, insurance plans).

Establishing a compensation system calls for decisions concerning the level of compensation as well as the method of compensation. The level refers to the total dollar income that a sales person earns over a period of time. Level is influenced by the type of person required for the job and the competitive rate of pay for similar positions. The method is the system or plan by which the sales person will reach the intended level.

The three widely used **methods of sales-force compensation** are straight salary, straight commission, and a combination plan. A *salary* is a fixed payment for a period of time during which the sales person is working. A *salary-only plan* (called a straight salary) provides security and stability of earnings for a sales rep. This plan gives management control over a rep's effort, and the reps are likely to spend time on nonselling activities that cater to the customer's best interests. The main drawback of a straight salary is that it does not offer an incentive for sales people to increase their sales volume. Also, a straight salary is a fixed cost for the firm, unrelated to sales volume or gross margin.

Straight-salary plans typically are used when:

- Compensating new sales people or missionary sales people.
- Opening new territories.
- Selling a technical product that requires a lengthy period of negotiation.

A *commission* is a payment tied to a specific unit of accomplishment. Thus a rep may be paid 5% of every dollar of sales or 8% on each dollar of gross margin. A *straight-commission plan* (commission only) tends to have just the opposite merits and limitations of a straight salary. A straight commission provides considerable incentive for sales people to sell, and it is a variable cost related directly to a rep's sales volume or gross margin. On the other hand, it is difficult to control straight-commission people. And it is especially difficult to get them to perform tasks for which no commission is paid.

Straight-commission plans may work well when:

- A strong incentive is needed to generate sales.
- Very little nonselling work is required, such as setting up displays in retail stores.
- The company is financially weak and must relate its compensation expenses directly to sales or gross margins.

A heavy emphasis on commissions can cause employees to lose sight of the importance of the customer. Kirby Company, for example, has sold vacuum cleaners door to door for 65 years using distributors paid on straight commission. The company is highly successful, selling about $1 billion worth of machines a year. Its long history suggests that most of its distributors are ethical. However, recent complaints to a number of consumer protection agencies suggest the lure of commissions has caused some distributors to take advantage of elderly and disadvantaged consumers.[16]

The ideal method of compensation is a *combination plan* that has the best features of both the straight-salary and the straight-commission plans, with as few of their drawbacks as possible. To reach this ideal, a combination plan must be tailored to a particular firm, product, market, and type of selling. Today about three-quarters of the firms in the U.S. use some kind of combination plan.

Supervising a Sales Force

Supervising a sales force is difficult because sales people often work independently at far-flung locations where they cannot be continually observed. And yet supervision serves both as a means of ongoing training and as a device to ensure that company policies are being carried out.

An issue that management must resolve is how closely to supervise. If too close, it can unduly constrain the sales person. One of the attractions of selling is the freedom it affords sales people to develop creative solutions to customers' problems. Close supervision can stifle that sense of independence. Conversely, too little supervision can contribute to a lack of direction. Sales people who are not closely supervised may not understand what their supervisors and companies expect of them. They may not know, for example, how much time to spend servicing existing accounts and how much developing new business.

The most effective supervisory method is personal observation in the field. Typically, at least half a sales manager's time is spent traveling with sales people. Other supervisory tools are reports, e-mail, and sales meetings.

Evaluating a Sales Person's Performance

Managing a sales force includes evaluating the performance of sales people. Sales executives must know what the sales force is doing in order to reward them or make constructive proposals for improvement. By establishing performance standards and studying sales people's activities, managers can develop new training programs to upgrade the sales force's efforts. And, of course, performance evaluation should be the basis for compensation decisions and other rewards.

Performance evaluation can also help sales people identify opportunities for improving their efforts. Employees with poor sales records know they are doing something wrong. However, they may not know what the problem is if they lack objective standards by which to measure their performance.

Both quantitative and qualitative measures should be used to formulate a complete picture of performance. **Quantitative evaluation bases** generally have the advantage of being specific and objective. **Qualitative evaluation bases,** although often reflecting broader dimensions of behavior, are limited by the subjective judgment of the evaluators. For either type of appraisal, management faces the difficult task of setting standards against which a rep's performance can be measured.

Quantitative Bases

Sales performance should be evaluated in terms of inputs (efforts) and outputs (results). Together, inputs such as number of sales calls per day or direct selling expenses, and outputs such as sales volume or gross margin, provide a measure of selling effectiveness.

Useful quantitative input measures include:

- Call rate—number of calls per day or week.
- Number of formal proposals presented.
- Nonselling activities—number of promotion displays set up or training sessions held with distributors or dealers.

Some quantitative output measures useful as evaluation criteria are:

- Sales volume by product, customer group, and territory.
- Sales volume as a percentage of quota or territory potential.
- Gross margin by product line, customer group, and territory.
- Orders—number and average dollar amount.
- Closing rate—number of orders divided by number of calls.
- Accounts—percentage of existing accounts retained and number of new accounts opened.

An increasing number of firms, among them IBM and Hallmark, are using customer satisfaction as a performance indicator. Satisfaction is measured a number of different ways, from detailed questionnaires that customers complete to counting the number of complaints received from customers.

Assessing satisfaction reflects a recognition by companies that there is more to selling than making a sale. Firms have discovered that finding a new customer is much more difficult and expensive than keeping an existing one. As a result, they have shifted their emphasis from a single-minded focus on sales volume to satisfaction. This allows a sales person to nurture a small account with considerable potential rather than always go for the big order. And it discourages sales people from engaging in detrimental actions such as loading up customers with unneeded inventory in order to meet a sales quota.

Qualitative Bases

In some respects, performance evaluation would be much easier if it could be based only on quantitative criteria. The standards would be absolute, and the positive and negative deviations from the standard could be measured precisely. Quantitative measures would also minimize the subjectivity and personal bias of the evaluators. However, many qualitative factors must be considered because they influence a sales person's performance. Some commonly used factors are:

- Knowledge of products, company policies, and competitors.
- Time management and preparation for sales calls.
- Customer relations.
- Personal appearance.

A successful evaluation program will appraise a sales person on all the factors that can be related to performance. Otherwise management may be misled. A high daily call rate may look good, but it tells us nothing about how many orders are being written up. A high closing rate may be camouflaging a low average order size or a high sales volume on low-profit items.

Summary

Personal selling is the main promotional method used in American business, regardless of whether it is measured by number of people employed, by total expenditures, or by expenses as a percentage of sales. The total field of personal selling comprises two broad categories. One covers selling activities where the customers come to the sales people—primarily retail store or retail catalog selling, but also includes the order takers at manufacturers and wholesalers. The other includes all selling situations where the sales people go to the customer—primarily outside sales forces.

The sales job has evolved. A new type of sales rep—a professional sales person—has been developing over the past few decades. But this new breed of sales rep still faces the unique characteristics of selling: implementing the firm's marketing strategy, representing the company, little direct supervision, frequent rejection by prospects, and considerable travel.

Sales jobs today range from order takers through support sales people (missionary sellers, sales engineers) to order getters (consultative sellers). Some changing patterns in personal selling have emerged in recent years—patterns such as selling centers (team selling), systems selling, global sales teams, relationship selling, telemarketing, Internet selling, and sales force automation.

The personal selling process consists of four steps, starting with prospecting for potential buyers and then preapproaching each prospect. The third step is the sales presentation, which includes attracting attention, arousing buyer interest and desire, meeting objections, and then hopefully closing the sale. Finally, postsale activities involve follow-up services to ensure customer satisfaction and reduce dissonance regarding the purchase.

The sales management process involves planning, implementing, and evaluating sales-force activities within the guidelines set by the company's strategic marketing plan. The tasks of staffing and operating a sales force present managerial challenges in several areas. The key to successful sales-force management is to do a good job in selecting sales people. Then plans must be made to assimilate these new people into the company and to train them. Management must set up programs to motivate, compensate, and supervise a sales force. The final stage in sales-force management is to evaluate the performance of the individual sales people.

More about **Johnson Controls**

Competition to supply auto makers is fierce. The manufacturers want low prices, innovative products, and outstanding service. Suppliers, in order to survive, must be creative.

In the case of Johnson Controls' Automotive Systems Group (ASG), that means serving the entire value chain, not just the next link in the channel. As described by the division's marketing president, "Our market research helps us learn, understand, and translate consumer needs and wants into innovative products for our auto maker customers." The firm uses what it has learned to make its sales people more valuable. When the ASG reps can provide a manufacturer with vital information it did not already have about its product or the market, they are adding value.

Doing things right, however, does not always guarantee success. Despite efforts by ASG and one of its major competitors, Lear Corp., to win the seat assembly contract for the global car that will serve as the platform for five General Motors models, the contract was awarded to Faurecia, a French firm. Some contend that the business, estimated at $500 million a year, went to Faurecia because General Motors wants another strong competitor in the industry to keep prices down. Thus, the outcome may have been beyond the control of ASG.

Johnson Controls continues to search for ways to make the selling task easier. The company is now looking at a consumer pull strategy by taking a lesson from the marketing of a parts supplier in the computer industry. Through its branding and promotion efforts, Intel convinced consumers that its microprocessor differentiates a computer. As a result, PC makers added value to their machines by touting "Intel Inside." Johnson Controls believes it can produce a similar outcome for auto makers. The challenge is to effectively promote the benefits of its innovative components to consumers, and then have its sales force convince the auto makers that using the components can translate into value for them.[17]

How important are sales people to Johnson Controls' success in the auto industry?

Key Terms and Concepts

Personal selling (516)
Inside selling (517)
Outside sales (517)
Selling center (522)
Systems selling (522)
Global sales teams (522)
Relationship selling (522)

Telemarketing (523)
Internet selling (524)
Sales force automation (SFA) (524)
Personal selling process (526)
AIDA (527)

Methods of sales-force compensation (532)
Quantitative evaluation bases (534)
Qualitative evaluation bases (534)

Questions and Problems

1. The cost of a two-page, four-color advertising spread in one issue of *Sports Illustrated* magazine is more than the cost of employing two sales people for a full year. A sales-force executive is urging her company to eliminate a few of these ads and, instead, to hire more sales people. This executive believes that for the same cost, a single good sales person working for an entire year can sell more than one ad in an issue of *Sports Illustrated*. How would you respond?

2. Would systems selling make more sense for a soft drink bottler or a plumbing supplies distributor? Why?

3. Refer to the classification of sales jobs from driver–sales person to creative seller and answer the following questions:
   a. In which types of jobs are sales people most likely to be free from close supervision?
   b. Which types are likely to be the highest paid?
   c. For which types of jobs is the highest degree of motivation necessary?

4. What type of business should consider replacing inside telephone sales people with a Web-based ordering system?

5. What are some sources you might use to acquire a list of prospects for the following products?
   a. Bank accounts for new area residents
   b. Dental X-ray equipment
   c. Laptop computers
   d. Contributors to the United Way
   e. Baby furniture and clothes

6. If you were preparing a sales presentation for the following products, what information about a prospect would you seek as part of your preparation?
   a. Two-bedroom condominium
   b. New automobile
   c. Carpeting for a home redecorating project

7. What sources should be used to recruit sales applicants in each of the following firms? Explain your choice in each case.
   a. A Marriott Hotel that wants companies to use the hotel for conventions
   b. IBM, for sales of mainframe (large) computers
   c. Johnson Controls' Automotive Systems Group

8. Compare the merits of straight-salary and straight-commission plans of sales compensation. What are two types of sales jobs in which each plan might be desirable?

9. How might a firm determine whether a sales person is using high-pressure selling tactics that might damage customer satisfaction?

10. How can a sales manager evaluate the performance of sales people in getting new business?

Hands-On Marketing

1. Review your activities of the past few days and identify those in which:
   a. You did some personal selling.
   b. People tried to sell something to you.

   Select one situation in each category where you thought the selling was particularly effective, and explain why.

2. Interview three students from your school who recently have gone through the job interviewing process conducted by companies using your school's placement office. Use the personal selling process described in the chapter to evaluate the students' sales efforts. Prepare a report covering your findings.

Advertising, Sales Promotion, and Public Relations

Although technology has been critical to Intel's success, advertising has played a large part as well.

How Can **Intel** Go from Being Inside to Staying Ahead?

In the late 1960s two engineers left Fairchild Semiconductor, a Silicon Valley technology company. They started a new business to produce computer memory chips, and called the firm Intel, a shortened version of "integrated electronics." In response to a request from a customer, the fledgling firm developed the first microprocessor, an invention that greatly enhances the capability of a computer by minaturizing the memory component.

The firm's owners believed they had something special in the microprocessor. To develop a market they had to inform the broader engineering community of its potential. Because the company was small, their initial promotional efforts were very modest, consisting of some seminars and a few ads in publications such as *Electronic News*.

Demand for standard memory chips grew as applications were developed. However, so did competition as more firms developed chip-making capability. Foreign and domestic competitors bid down the price so much the business was no longer attractive. So in 1986 Intel quit making chips and began concentrating totally on microprocessors. Since then, the firm has focused on developing and marketing successive generations of more powerful microprocessors, a strategy that has proven highly successful. Intel has annual sales of over $25 billion and profits of $6 billion.

Although technology has been critical to Intel's success, advertising has played a large part as well. In 1989, Intel was searching for a way to get PC owners to upgrade from its existing 286 model microprocessor to the faster 386. The firm attempted a "pull" strategy by concentrating its advertising on consumers. Using Denver as a test, Intel conducted a print, radio, billboard, and in-store campaign that "Xed" out the 286 and promoted the 386. The market response was favorable, increasing awareness of the Intel brand and stimulating demand for PCs with the more powerful memory component. Encouraged by the Denver test, the advertising was expanded and the "Intel Inside" tagline was developed.

The major portion of the Intel processor advertising program is a cooperative arrangement that was begun in 1991. Cooperative advertising involves firms sharing advertising costs. Intel sets aside 5% of what PC manufacturers pay for its processors for co-op advertising, and pays 60% of the cost of ads by PC makers that include the "Intel

Inside" logo. Intel has invested more than $4 billion in the co-op program since it began. It is so successful that nearly 90% of all print advertising pages for PCs include the Intel slogan. In 1989 Intel had 56% of the microprocessor market. After 10 years of co-op promotion, its share has grown to 83%.

The corporate campaign featuring the "Intel Inside" line, and the associated co-op program, has been ranked by *Advertising Age* as the second best U.S. business-to-business ad campaign of the 20th century. The campaign is credited with creating a brand preference for microprocessors where there had been little knowledge that they even existed.

Intel also is using the Internet in its advertising. Banner ads appear on several search engines as well as on other websites. To make fuller use of the Internet, a traditional media campaign for its latest generation microprocessor, the Pentium III, includes a TV ad directing viewers to the firm's website for additional information. Getting prospects to the website is highly desirable because much more information can be transmitted than is possible in a 30-second TV ad or with a one-page print ad. The ad campaign featuring the Web address has doubled Intel's website traffic.

Similar to its experience in the chip market in the 1970s, Intel is witnessing a transition in PCs. The growth in microprocessor capability has exceeded the needs of most of the market. The majority of consumers just want a PC that provides e-mail capability and access to the Internet, which can be purchased for $1,000. As a result, there is decreasing demand for more powerful microprocessors. In addition, the competition has intensified. For example, Advanced Micro Devices, with ads aimed at sophisticated consumers and small business owners, claims its processor outperforms Intel's Pentium III.

Intel has been a major force in the spread of PCs. However, that business appears to be losing momentum. If it is to maintain its 30% annual growth rate, Intel needs to identify the next technology driver of the information economy and become as important in that development as it has been with PCs. So management is searching for another marriage of technology and advertising as successful as "Intel Inside."[1]

Other than the advertising methods mentioned in the case, what are some additional ways Intel might use promotion in its marketing strategy?

Advertising, sales promotion, and public relations are the mass-communication tools available to marketers. As the name suggests, *mass* communication uses the same message for everyone in an audience. The mass communicator trades off the advantage of personal selling, the opportunity to deliver a tailored message in person, for the advantage of reaching many people at a lower cost per contact.

The term mass communication does not imply indiscriminate efforts to reach large audiences. As we shall see, marketers are constantly seeking refinements that will allow them to present their messages to more specifically defined target audiences.

This chapter examines *nonpersonal*, mass-communication promotional tools—advertising, sales promotion, and public relations. After studying this chapter, you should be able to explain:

chapter goals

- The nature and scope of advertising, sales promotion, and public relations.
- Characteristics of the major types of these mass communication tools.
- How advertising campaigns are developed and advertising media are selected.
- The alternative ways firms organize their advertising efforts.
- How sales promotion is managed to maximize its effectiveness.
- The role of public relations in the promotional mix.

Nature and Scope of Advertising

All advertisements (ads, for short) have four features:
- A verbal and/or visual message.
- A sponsor who is identified.
- Delivery through one or more media.
- Payment by the sponsor to the medium carrying the message.

Advertising, then, consists of all the activities involved in presenting to an audience a nonpersonal, sponsor-identified, paid-for message about a product or organization.

Advertising in one form or another is used by most organizations. The significance of advertising is indicated by the amount of money spent on it. In 1999, total U.S. advertising expenditures were over $215 *billion*, nearly four times the amount spent in 1980. A slightly larger amount, $216 *billion*, was spent in the rest of the world during 1999. Table 19.1 shows the relative importance of the major U.S. advertising media over the past 30 years. Throughout most of this period newspapers have been the most widely used medium, based on total advertising dollars spent. However, television exceeded newspaper in 1999. As newspapers' share has declined, the proportions accounted for by direct-mail advertising and the newcomer, the Internet, have increased.

Advertising as a Percentage of Sales

The amounts businesses spend on advertising can seem daunting. For example, Procter & Gamble spends more than $4.5 *billion* a year on advertising worldwide, and Coca-Cola's global advertising budget is over $1.5 *billion*.[2] Table 19.2 shows the 10 companies with the largest dollar expenditures for advertising in the U.S. Not surprisingly, these are companies with which we are all familiar.

To gauge advertising spending, however, we should measure it against some benchmark rather than simply look at the totals. For example, advertising expenses frequently are expressed as a percentage of a company's sales. Similar figures, except by industry rather than firm, are presented in Table 19.3. Notice how much variation exists across industries.

Table 19.1 Advertising Expenditures in the United States by Medium

Advertising expenditures declined in 1991, the first decrease in half a century, but began increasing again in 1992. In 1999, television overtook newspapers as the most heavily used medium. The Internet, at only 1% of the total, is expected to grow very rapidly.

Medium	1999 Expenditures (in billions)	1999 (%)	1990 (%)	1980 (%)	1970 (%)
Newspapers	47	22	25	28	29
Television	48	22	22	21	18
Direct Mail	42	19	18	14	14
Radio	17	8	7	7	7
Yellow pages	13	6	7	—	—
Magazines	11	5	5	6	7
Internet	2	1	—	—	—
Other*	36	17	15	24	25
Total percentage**		100	100	100	100
Total dollars (in billions)	$216		$128	$55	$20

*Before 1988 this category included yellow pages. Also includes outdoor, transportation advertising, weekly newspapers, regional farm publications, and point-of-sale advertising.

**Percentages have been rounded.

Sources: Robert J. Coen, "McCann's Insider's Report," Universal McCann Erickson, Dec. 6, 1999; Robert J. Coen, "More Gains Forseen for '95 Ad Spending," *Advertising Age,* May 8, 1995, p. 36; 1980 figures from *Advertising Age,* Mar. 22, 1982, p. 66. Others adapted from *Advertising Age,* Nov. 17, 1975, p. 40.

Industry averages can be misleading. How much an individual firm spends on advertising is influenced by its resources and objectives more than by what other firms in the industry are doing. In the U.S., Ford Motor Co. spends an amount equal to about 1.5% of its sales on advertising, whereas Mazda's U.S. ad budget is nearly 5% of its sales. Despite this proportional difference, Ford spends about $6 on advertising for every dollar spent by Mazda.[3]

Advertising Cost versus Personal Selling Cost

Although there are no accurate figures for the cost of personal selling, we do know it far surpasses advertising expenditures. Only a few manufacturing industries, such as drugs, toiletries, cleaning products, tobacco, and beverages, spend more

Table 19.2 Top 10 National Advertisers in 1998, Based on Total Expenditures in the United States

Company	Advertising Expenditures Dollars (in millions)	As Percentage of U.S. Sales
1 General Motors	2,940	2.6
2. Procter & Gamble	2,650	14.0
3. Philip Morris Cos.	2,049	5.7
4. DaimlerChrysler	1,647	2.1
5. Sears, Roebuck	1,578	4.2
6. Ford Motor Co.	1,521	1.5
7. AT&T	1,428	2.7
8. Walt Disney Co.	1,359	7.5
9. PepsiCo.	1,263	8.2
10. Diageo	1,206	13.0

Source: "100 Leading National Advertisers," *Advertising Age,* Sept. 27, 1999, pp. S1+.

Table 19.3	Advertising as a Percentage of Sales for Selected Industries	
Industry	**Advertising as Percentage of Sales**
Candy and confectionery	17.4
Watches and clocks	15.9
Games and toys	13.1
Books	10.7
Perfumes and cosmetics	8.5
Apparel	5.8
Farm machinery	1.0
Construction machinery and equipment	0.3

Source: "1997 Advertising to Sales Ratios for the 200 Largest Ad Spending Industries," *Advertising Age,* June 30, 1997, p. 35.

on advertising than on personal selling. Advertising runs 1 to 3% of net sales in many firms, whereas the expenses of recruiting and operating a sales force are typically 8 to 15% of sales.

At the wholesale level, advertising costs are very low. Personal selling expenses for wholesalers, however, may run 10 to 15 times more than their expenditures for advertising. Even among many retailers, including some with self-service operations, the total cost of their customer-contact employees is substantially higher than what they spend on advertising.

Types of Advertising

Advertising can be classified according to (1) the target audience, either consumers or businesses; (2) the objective sought, the stimulation of primary or selective demand; and (3) what is being advertised, a product versus an institution. To fully appreciate the scope and types of advertising, it is essential to understand these three classifications.

Consumer and Business-to-Business Advertising

An ad is directed at consumers or businesses; thus it is either **consumer advertising** or **business-to-business advertising**. Retailers by definition sell only to consumers; therefore, they are the only organizations that are not faced with this choice. The publisher of *Money* magazine, for example, must decide what portion of its advertising budget will be used to attract businesses to advertise in the magazine, and what portion will go toward selling magazines.

Primary-Demand and Selective-Demand Advertising

Primary-demand advertising is designed to stimulate demand for a generic category of a product such as coffee, electricity, or garments made from cotton. In contrast, **selective-demand advertising** is intended to stimulate demand for individual brands such as Folger's coffee, American Electric Power electricity, and Liz Claiborne sportswear.

Primary-demand advertising is used in either of two situations. The first is when the product is in the introductory stage of its life cycle. This is called *pioneering advertising*. The objective of pioneering advertising is to inform, not to persuade, the target market. Recall from Chapter 4 that a consumer must first be made aware of a product before becoming interested in or desiring it. To inform engineers about microprocessors, Intel ran pioneering ads.

The other use of primary-demand advertising occurs throughout the product life cycle and therefore is considered *demand-sustaining advertising*. It is usually done by trade associations trying to stimulate or sustain demand for their industry's product. Thus, the National Fluid Milk Processor Promotion Board encourages us to consume more milk with its campaign depicting celebrities with milk "mustaches."

Selective-demand advertising is essentially competitive advertising. It pits one brand against the rest of the market. This type of advertising is employed when a product is beyond the introductory life-cycle stage and is competing for market share with several other brands. Selective-demand advertising emphasizes a brand's special features and benefits—its differential advantage.

Selective-demand advertising that makes reference to one or more competitors is called **comparative advertising.** In this kind of advertising, the advertiser either directly (by naming a rival brand) or indirectly (through inference) points out differences between the competing brands. The chapter-opening case mentioned the comparative advertising done by Advanced Micro Devices in its attempt to gain ground on Intel. Comparative advertising is encouraged by the Federal Trade Commission as a means of stimulating competition and disseminating useful information to consumers.

Product and Institutional Advertising

All selective advertising may be classified as product or institutional. **Product advertising** focuses on a particular product or brand. It is subdivided into direct-action and indirect-action product advertising:

- *Direct-action* advertising seeks a quick response. For instance, a magazine ad containing a coupon or an 800 number may urge the reader to send or call immediately for a free sample, or a supermarket ad in a local newspaper stresses this week's specials.

- *Indirect-action* advertising is designed to stimulate demand over a longer period of time. It is intended to inform or remind consumers that the product exists and to point out its benefits. Dave Thomas, appearing in ads as a spokesperson for Wendy's, is an example. Most network television advertising is indirect action, whereas much local television advertising is direct action.

Institutional advertising presents information about the advertiser's business or tries to create a favorable attitude—that is, build goodwill—toward the organization. In contrast to product advertising, institutional advertising is not intended to sell a specific product. Its objective is to create a particular image for a company. United Airlines, for example, spent millions over the years communicating its corporate philosophy with the "Fly the Friendly Skies" campaign.

•Developing an Advertising Campaign

An **advertising campaign** consists of all the tasks involved in transforming a theme into a coordinated advertising program to accomplish a specific goal for a product or brand. Typically a campaign involves several different advertising messages, presented over an extended period of time, using a variety of media. For example, after a seven-year run, Coca-Cola replaced its "Always Coca-Cola" campaign with a message intended to be more of an invitation than a command. Using the slogan "Coca-Cola.enjoy," the company is suggesting that the soft drink goes along with relaxing. The new campaign was introduced in the U.S. in early 2000, and rolled out globally with ads in a variety of media.[4]

DaimlerChrysler's Dodge division used potatoes, fishing lures, shirts, ants, and other everyday items in print and television teaser ads to kick off a campaign. The objective, to position Dodge cars and trucks as nonconformist vehicles, is accomplished in part by having a car ad without a picture of a car. The campaign continues with model-specific ads that prominently display the "Different" theme along with details about the particular vehicle. The campaign, with various executions, is expected to run for 5–7 years.

Dodge Different.

An advertising campaign is planned within the framework of the overall strategic marketing plan and the broader promotional program. The framework is established when management:

- Identifies the target audience.
- Establishes the overall promotional goals.
- Sets the total promotional budget.
- Determines the overall promotional theme.

With these tasks completed, the firm can begin formulating an advertising campaign. The steps in developing a campaign are defining objectives, establishing a budget, creating a message, selecting media, and evaluating effectiveness.

Defining Objectives

The purpose of advertising is to sell something—a good, service, idea, person, or place—either now or later. This goal is reached by setting specific objectives that can be expressed in individual ads incorporated into an advertising campaign. For example, as mentioned in the Chapter 14 case, Avon recently launched a $100 million global ad campaign in 26 markets worldwide with a goal of providing support for its sales force of 2.8 million "Avon ladies." The specific objectives were to heighten awareness of its brand and introduce some new cosmetic products.[5]

Typical advertising objectives are to:

- *Support personal selling.* Advertising may be used to acquaint prospects with the seller's company and products, easing the way for the sales force, as Avon is doing.
- *Improve dealer relations.* Wholesalers and retailers like to see a manufacturer support its products with advertising.
- *Introduce a new product.* Consumers need to be informed even about line extensions that make use of familiar brand names.

Who are the world's major advertisers?

About one-half of all advertising is done outside the U.S. A look at which firms do the most advertising in the rest of the world indicates that U.S. firms are among the leaders, but other well-known names also appear among the biggest spenders. The table below of the top 10 advertisers includes each company and its headquarters location, the amount spent on media advertising outside the U.S., and the amount spent on media advertising in the U.S. during 1998.

Examination of the table provides an indication of where these leading firms focus their efforts. For example, although Ford and General Motors spend about the same amount on advertising outside the U.S., General Motors outspends Ford by a billion dollars in the U.S.

Company (Location)	Ad Spending outside the U.S. (millions of $)	Ad Spending in the U.S. (millions of $)
Procter & Gamble (U.S.)	3,018	1,729
Unilever (Netherlands/U.K.)	2,737	691
Nestlé (Switzerland)	1,559	274
Volkswagen (Germany)	1,070	255
Ford Motor Co. (U.S.)	1,050	1,180
General Motors (U.S.)	1,039	2,154
Toyota (Japan)	1,035	658
Coca-Cola (U.S.)	1,012	316
Peugeot Citroen (France)	855	—
L'Oreal (France)	841	403

Source: "Top 100 Marketers by Media Ad Spending Outside the U.S.," *Advertising Age International*, Nov. 8, 1999, pp. 1+.

- *Expand the use of a product.* Advertising may be used to lengthen the season for a product (as Lipton did for iced tea); increase the frequency of replacement (as Fram did for oil filters); or increase the variety of product uses (as Arm & Hammer did for baking soda).

- *Counteract substitution.* Advertising reinforces the decisions of existing customers and reduces the likelihood that they will switch to alternative brands.

Establishing a Budget

Once a promotional budget has been established (discussed in Chapter 17), it must be allocated among the various activities comprising the overall promotional program. In the case of a particular brand, a firm may wish to have several ads, as well as sales promotion and public relations activities, directed at different target audiences all at the same time. To introduce the redesigned 2000 Taurus, Ford used displays at 150 shopping malls; sweepstakes tied to Nascar racing and college football broadcasts; a custom-published magazine sent to subscribers of both *Road & Track* and *Car & Driver*; and print, television, outdoor, and Internet advertising. The budget for the promotional effort exceeded the $110 million campaign that accompanied the last Taurus redesign in 1996.[6] Because all these efforts must be paid for from the promotional budget, the potential value of each must be weighed and allocations made accordingly.

One method that firms use to extend their budgets is **cooperative advertising,** which is a joint effort by two or more firms intended to benefit each of the participants. There are two types of cooperative ads—vertical and horizontal. *Vertical cooperative advertising* involves firms on different levels of distribution. For example, a manufacturer and a retailer share the cost of the retailer's advertising of that manufacturer's product. Frequently the manufacturer prepares the actual ad, leaving space for the retailer's name and address. Then the manufacturer and retailer share the media cost of placing the ad. Many local retail ads in newspapers and on radio and television involve co-op funds.[7]

Another type of vertical cooperation is an *advertising allowance,* or cash discount offered by a manufacturer to a retailer, to encourage the retailer to advertise or prominently display a product. In cooperative advertising the manufacturer has control over how the money is actually spent, but that is not the case with an advertising allowance.

Cooperative arrangements benefit retailers by providing them with extra funds for promotion. Manufacturers also benefit because cooperative advertising provides them with local identification for their products. In addition, a manufacturer's ad dollars go farther because rates charged by local media (such as a daily newspaper) are typically lower for ads placed by local firms than for ads placed by national advertisers.

Horizontal cooperative advertising is joint advertising in which two or more firms on the same level of distribution, such as a group of retailers, share the costs. For example, all the stores in a suburban shopping center may run a joint newspaper ad. Intel, described in the opening case, illustrates how manufacturers engage in horizontal cooperative advertising. The principal benefit is that by pooling their funds, the firms achieve greater exposure or impact than if they advertised individually.

Creating a Message

Whatever the objective of an advertising campaign, the individual ads must accomplish two things: get and hold the *attention* of the intended audience, and *influence* that audience in the desired way. Attention can be achieved in many ways. (Recall our discussion of perception in Chapter 4.) Television makes possible special visual effects, as for example the flying cans in the Mountain Dew ads and the talking lizards in the Anhueser-Busch ads. Radio can use listeners' imaginations to create mental images that would be impossible to actually produce. Surprising, shocking, amusing, and arousing curiosity are all common techniques to gain attention. Thus a print ad might be mostly white space, or a billboard might show the product in an unusual setting.

If the ad succeeds in getting the audience's attention, the advertiser has a few seconds to communicate a message intended to influence beliefs and/or behavior. The message has two elements, the *appeal* and the *execution*. The appeal in an ad is the reason or justification for believing or behaving. It is the benefit that the individual will receive as a result of accepting the message.

Some advertisers mistakenly focus their appeal on product features or attributes. They either confuse attributes with benefits, or assume that if they present the product's attributes, the audience will infer the correct benefits. Telling consumers that a breakfast cereal contains fiber (an attribute) is much less meaningful than telling them that because it contains fiber, consuming it reduces the likelihood of colon cancer (the benefit).

Execution is combining in a convincing, compatible way the feature or device that gets attention with the appeal. An appeal can be executed in different ways. Consider the ways you could communicate the desirability of fast food—showing people enjoying it, describing the taste, or emphasizing the value with a comparison to competing products are all possibilities. Rather than any of these, Taco Bell opted for an execution that featured a Chihuahua that is obsessed with the

Recognized as a no-nonsense performance shoe by serious runners, in the 1980s Saucony was reasonably successful. Eventually, the company lost ground to more stylish brands. Now the firm hopes to capitalize on its reputation for quality to gain a larger market share. This ad is aimed at knowledgeable runners who are likely to know that Saucony's Grid model received a high rating from a major running magazine.

It is commonly accepted that advertisers engage in "puffery" or exaggeration. Such boasts, which may actually reflect the opinion of some people but which cannot be factually proven, are treated as part of presenting an advocate position. For example, claiming that a musical review is the "greatest show on earth," would be considered puffery. However, at some point puffery becomes deception.

A type of promotion, cash sweepstakes that are accompanied by offers to purchase magazine subscriptions or other products, has been criticized for some time. The questionable claims in the sweepstakes attracted heightened attention when several elderly consumers traveled to Tampa, Florida, to claim an $11 million prize they mistakenly thought they had won in an American Family Publishers sweepstake.

Some of the practices the promoters use include:

- Making the envelope containing the sweepstakes

information look like a letter from a government agency.

- Stating in a mailing that the recipient is a "guaranteed" prize winner.

- Presenting magazine ordering information in bold detail, but making information that a purchase is not required to enter the contest much harder to find.

Magazine publishers argue that people know most advertising is somewhere between the truth and lies, and that any deceptiveness criterion for ads should be designed with the normal, not the especially vulnerable, person in mind.

Is this an ethical criterion for judging whether or not advertising is deceptive?

Sources: "Sweeping Changes," *The Economist*, May 1, 1999, pp. 62–63; Tom Lowery, "Criticism of Sweepstakes Grows," *USA Today*, June 24, 1999, p. 3B.

company's product. After a two-year campaign and $200 million of advertising, the company decided to reduce the dog's role in its ads and focus more on the food. According to a Taco Bell franchisee, the dog, which had become a pop-culture icon, appearing on the cover of *TV Guide* magazine and in a music video, became the focus. Meanwhile, the food was receiving too little attention. The evidence was in the results. Although many people are familiar with the Taco Bell Chihuahua, sales in the stores increased only 2% during the campaign.[8]

Selecting Media

In describing the steps involved in developing an advertising campaign, we discussed the creation of an advertising message before selection of the **advertising media** in which to place the ad. In reality these decisions are made simultaneously. Both the message and the choice of media are determined by the appeal and the target audience.

Advertisers need to make decisions at each of three successive levels in order to select the specific advertising medium to use:

1. Which *type(s)* will be used—newspaper, television, radio, magazine, or direct mail? What about the less prominent media of billboards, the Internet, and yellow pages?

2. Which *category of the selected medium* will be used? Television has network and cable; magazines include general-interest *(Newsweek, People)* and special-interest *(Popular Mechanics, Runner's World)* categories; there are national as well as local newspapers; and the Internet offers portals as well as individual websites.

3. Which *specific media vehicles* will be used? An advertiser that decides first on radio and then on local stations must determine which stations to use in each city.

Here are some general factors that will influence media choice:

- *Objectives of the ad.* The purpose of a particular ad and the goals of the entire campaign influence which media to use. For example, if the campaign goal is to generate appointments for sales people, the company may rely on direct mail. If an advertiser wants to induce quick action, newspaper or radio may be the medium to use.

- *Audience coverage.* The audience reached by the medium should match the geographic area in which the product is distributed. Furthermore, the selected medium should reach the desired types of prospects with a minimum of wasted coverage—that is, only reach people who are prospects for the product. Many media, even national and other large-market media, can be targeted at small, specialized market segments. For example, *Time* magazine publishes regional editions with different ads in the East, Midwest, and West. Large metropolitan newspapers publish suburban editions as well as regional editions within the city.

- *Requirements of the message.* The medium should fit the message. For example, magazines provide high-quality visual reproductions that attract attention along with printed messages that can be carefully read and evaluated. As a result, they are well suited to business-to-business advertising.

- *Time and location of the buying decision.* If the objective is to stimulate a purchase, the medium should reach prospective customers when and where they are about to make their buying decisions. This factor highlights one of the strengths of point-of-purchase advertising (such as ads placed on shopping carts and in the aisles of supermarkets), which reach consumers at the actual time of purchase.

- *Media cost.* The cost of each medium should be considered in relation to the amount of funds available to pay for it and its reach or circulation. For example, the cost of network television exceeds the available funds of many advertisers. To compare various media, advertisers use a measure called **cost per thousand** (CPM), which is the cost of reaching a thousand people, one time each, with a particular ad.

Beyond these general factors, management must evaluate the advertising characteristics of each medium it is considering. We have carefully chosen the term *characteristics,* instead of advantages and disadvantages, because a medium that works well for one product is not necessarily the best choice for another product. To illustrate, a characteristic of radio is that it makes its impressions through sound and imagination. The roar of a crowd, the rumbling of thunder, or screeching tires can be used to create mental images quickly and easily. But radio will not do the job for products that require a specific visual image. Let's examine the characteristics of the major media.

Newspapers

As an advertising medium, newspapers are flexible and timely. Ads can be inserted or canceled on very short notice and can vary in size from small classifieds to multiple pages. Pages can be added or dropped, so the space in newspapers is not limited in the way time is constrained on TV and radio. Newspapers can be used to reach an entire city or, where regional editions are offered, selected areas. Cost per thousand is relatively low.

On the other hand, the life of newspapers is very short. Typically, they are discarded soon after being read. A metropolitan newspaper provides coverage of about one-half the households in a local market. However, in many large cities, circulation of daily newspapers is decreasing. Also, the growth of the Internet has created a new source of competition for newspapers. Especially hard hit is classified advertising which accounts for about 40% of newspaper ad revenue.[9] Finally, because newspapers don't offer much format variety, it is difficult to design ads that stand out.

Television

Virtually every U.S. household has a television and the typical viewer watches more than seven hours a day.[10] Television combines motion, sound, and special visual effects. Products can be demonstrated as well as described on TV. It offers wide geographic coverage and flexibility in when the message can be presented. However, TV ads lack permanence, so they must be seen and understood immediately. As a result, TV does not lend itself to complicated messages.

Television can appear to be a relatively expensive medium, but it has the potential to provide a large audience. For example, a single 30-second spot on the 2000 Super Bowl telecast cost $2 million, but it reached an audience of 125 million viewers. Table 19.4 shows how the cost of a network ad in prime time has increased over the years. Television ads are also expensive to produce. It's not unusual for a firm to spend $500,000 to create a 30-second commercial. As a result, fewer ads are being made, and they are being kept on the air longer.

The share of the television audience in prime time that is held by the networks has declined from 90% in 1980 to less than 50% today.[11] The major reason is the growing popularity of cable television. Over 65% of American homes (80% with household incomes over $50,000) have cable, with an average of 30 stations per household.[12] The result is more fragmented markets and specialized programming, making it difficult to reach a mass market. On the positive side, the specialization of cable channels such as MTV, CNBC, and ESPN offers an advertiser a more homogeneous group of viewers at a lower price (because the audience is smaller) than broadcast networks.

Advertisers are also using *place-based* television to attract target audiences—young professionals, teenagers, working women—who have become less accessible through traditional media. Firms such as Whittle Communications and CNN are putting TVs in classrooms, waiting rooms, supermarkets, airports, health clubs, and other places where there are "captive audiences."

Direct Mail

Over 60 *billion* pieces of direct-mail advertising are distributed in the U.S. each year.[13] It can be sent in the traditional fashion, using the Postal Service or an overnight delivery, or electronically by fax or e-mail.

Table 19.4	The Cost of Prime-Time Advertising on Network Television		
Year	**Program**	**Type of Ad**	**Cost**
1970	Bewitched	60 seconds	$ 5,200
	Best of Everything	60 seconds	4,000
1972	Bonanza	30 seconds	26,000
	Peyton Place	30 seconds	27,500
1980	M*A*S*H	30 seconds	150,000
	Dallas	30 seconds	145,000
1992	Murphy Brown	30 seconds	310,000
	Roseanne	30 seconds	290,000
1995	Seinfeld	30 seconds	490,000
	Home Improvement	30 seconds	475,000
1999	Ally McBeal	30 seconds	450,000
	ER	30 seconds	750,000

Sources: "50 Years of TV Advertising: The Buying and Selling," *Advertising Age,* Spring 1995, p. 29; Joe Mandese, "Seinfeld Is NBC's $1M/Minute Man," *Advertising Age,* Sept. 18, 1995, pp. 11; and personal contacts.

Direct mail has the potential of being the most personal and selective of all media. Highly specialized direct-mail lists can be developed from a firm's own customer database or purchased from list suppliers (among the thousands available are lists of air traffic controllers, wig dealers, college professors, pregnant women, and disc jockeys). Because direct mail goes only to the people the advertiser wishes to contact, there is almost no wasted coverage. Traditional direct mail also allows for the distribution of product samples. Printing and postage fees make the cost per thousand of direct mail quite high compared with other media. On the other hand, electronic direct mail is less expensive to send.

Reaching the prospect does not ensure that the message is communicated. Direct mail is pure advertising. It is not accompanied by editorial matter (unless the advertiser provides it). Therefore, a direct-mail ad must attract its own readers. This is critical when you consider that the average American home receives more than 10 direct-mail pieces a week, and that the recipient of a direct-mail ad decides in four seconds whether to discard or open it.[14]

Radio

When interest in television soared after World War II, radio audiences (especially for network radio) declined so dramatically that some people predicted radio's demise. However, radio has enjoyed a rebirth as an advertising and cultural medium, with the number of stations increasing at a steady rate. Today there are over 11,000 stations in the U.S. (60% of them FM).[15]

Radio is a low cost-per-thousand medium because of its broad reach. Nearly 80% of Americans listen to the radio daily and, on average, adults 18 years of age and over listen more than 20 hours a week. With programming ranging from all-talk to sports to country music, certain target markets can be pinpointed quite effectively. Radio commercials can be produced in less than a week, at a cost far below television.

Because radio makes only an audio impression, it relies entirely on the listener's ability to retain information heard and not seen. Also, audience attention is often at a low level, because radio is frequently used as background for working, driving, studying (Is your radio on now?), or some other activity.

Yellow Pages

A printed directory of local business names and phone numbers organized by type of product, the yellow pages directory has been around since the late 1800s. The breakup of the Bell System telephone monopoly in 1983 led to an increase in the number of yellow pages directories. Today there are over 6,000 in the U.S., with large metropolitan areas commonly having four or five competing directories.[16] The yellow pages are a source of information with which most consumers are familiar. And they are used by consumers at or very near the buying decision. On the negative side, yellow page ads are difficult to differentiate, and an advertiser's message is surrounded by the messages of competitors.

Magazines

Magazines are the medium to use when high-quality printing and color are desired in an ad. Magazines can reach a national market at a relatively low cost per reader. In recent years, the rapid increase in special-interest magazines and regional editions of general-interest magazines has made it possible for advertisers to reach a selected audience with a minimum of wasted circulation. Business and trade magazines, many of which are given away to readers, can be effective in reaching specialized industry audiences. The number of different magazines in the U.S. has increased from just over 14,000 in 1993 to more than 18,000 today.[17]

Magazines are usually read in a leisurely fashion, in contrast to the haste in which other print media are read. This feature is especially valuable to the advertiser with a lengthy or complicated message. A variety of production innovations make it possible to introduce variety in magazine ads. Oversized foldouts, pullout sections, and poly-wrapped samples are becoming common. Magazines have a relatively long life, anywhere from a week to a month, and a high pass-along readership.

With less flexible production schedules than newspapers, magazines require that ads be submitted several weeks before publication. In addition, because they are published weekly or monthly, it is difficult to use timely messages. Magazines are often read at times or in places—on airplanes or in doctors' offices, for instance—far removed from where a buying impulse can be acted on.

Out-of-Home Advertising

Spending on out-of-home advertising is growing at about 10% a year, amounting to $4.8 billion in 1999.[18] At one time, the category was dominated by billboards, and was called outdoor advertising. However, *out-of-home* is more descriptive today because billboards now are in malls, arenas, airports, and other indoor locations as well as outdoors.

There have been other changes in billboards as well. One is the computer-painting technology that makes it possible to create high-quality visual reproductions. Another development is the capability built into the boards themselves, including three-dimensional structures, digital tickers, and continuous motion. Low cost per thousand is the chief advantage of out-of-home media, although prices vary by the volume of traffic passing a site. Apple, Gap, and Disney pay $100,000 a month for billboards in New York's Times Square and along Sunset Strip in Los Angeles.[19]

Most out-of-home advertising is for local businesses, but it is increasingly being used for national brand-building ads. Because it is seen by people "on the go," billboard advertising is appropriate only for brief messages. The rule of thumb is six words or less.

Billboards can provide intense market coverage within an area. However, unless the advertised product is a widely used good or service, considerable wasted circulation will occur, because many of the passersby will not be prospects. Finally, the landscape-defacing criticism of outdoor advertising may be a consideration for some advertisers.

Interactive Media

Interactivity refers to a feature that permits the advertising message recipient to respond immediately using the same medium. For example, a person receiving an e-mail message can reply with the click of a mouse. The fastest-growing interactive medium is the Internet. A subsystem of the Internet, known as the World Wide Web, gives millions of organizations and individuals direct electronic access to one another.

Until recently access to the Web required a personal computer. Now "Internet appliances" are available. Less sophisticated and less expensive than a PC, Internet appliances provide only the capability to traverse the Internet and to exchange e-mail messages. These devices are likely to contribute to an even faster diffusion of the Internet among consumers around the world.

The opportunity the Web has created has not been lost on marketers who can use it to communicate advertising messages. This medium requires the recipient to take the initiative and tap into the sender's message. Once the connection is established, the recipient controls the flow of information, selecting with mouse clicks which pages to examine and how long to remain connected. For example, a consumer interested in buying a car might begin by using the Internet to find out which companies make minivans. From there, the consumer could move on to information about performance, safety features, technical specifications, and

At Ford's website, vehicle owners can get information about warranties and service and shoppers can examine all the company's makes and models, shop for pre-owned vehicles, and configure a new vehicle. If the visitor chooses, the information will be electronically supplied to a local dealer who will provide a price quote by phone or e-mail. Ford also plans to use interactive television, which will allow consumers to do many of the same things using a TV set.

www.ford.com

www.grillparts.com

prices of specific makes. The next step might be to locate a page that identifies dealers in the area, their respective inventories, and financing alternatives.

As an advertising medium, the Internet is particularly popular with companies selling products that involve extensive decision making. Ford Motor Co. recently shifted a significant portion of its national advertising from magazines to interactive media, including the Internet. According to Ford's manager of media services, the move was made because interactive media allow the firm to "have a dialogue with existing and prospective customers."[20]

Some small companies with limited promotional budgets have discovered that the Internet allows them to reach a broader geographic market. For example, Barbecue Renew, a Kirkland, Washington, retailer of barbecue-grill replacement parts, turned to the Internet after local newspaper ads proved unsuccessful. It now generates sales from all over the U.S. from its website.[21]

Interactivity creates a very different environment for advertisers. On the plus side, the audience has demonstrated its interest by logging on, and the technology makes it easy to track the number of visitors to the site, how long they stay connected, and what pages they visit. On the minus side, using this medium requires some proficiency with the technology on the part of recipients. Also, with hundreds of thousands of websites only a mouse click away, holding a visitor's attention is difficult.

Media decision makers abroad are faced with different conditions that require local knowledge. For example, the move toward greater democracy has created new media options in some eastern European countries, where private radio and television stations now can carry up to four times as much advertising as was permitted on state-owned stations. On the other hand, print media in most of the world cannot offer the special editions and narrowly targeted audiences available in highly-developed countries.

Evaluating the Advertising Effort

Top executives want proof that advertising is worthwhile. They want to know whether dollars spent on advertising are producing as many sales as could be

The use of virtual advertising in television broadcasting is evolving quickly. Early efforts, including a soccer match in Greece during which viewers saw giant spray cans of deodorant floating over the playing field, were often awkward and annoying. However, the technology has evolved to the point that inserts of all kinds can be made seamlessly.

Princeton Video Images, a firm that places computer-generated electronic images into live broadcasts, inserted virtual advertisements in the international feed of the National Football League's 2000 Super Bowl game for a number of firms. Virtual signs for General Motors, Kodak, Canadian Tire, Charles Schwab, Tecate beer, and others appeared on either side of the goalposts during breaks in the game action. The Super Bowl, which was seen live on ABC by 125 million viewers in the U.S., had a worldwide audience of nearly 800 million. By selectively inserting virtual signs in signals sent around the world, an advertiser was able to have its message seen by consumers only in the countries where it does business.

In addition to signs, Princeton Video is able to create virtual product placements. This makes it possible to alter the scene in a previously filmed show. For example, a can of a particular brand of soft drink could be made to appear on a table in a rerun of a *Seinfeld* episode.

The use of virtual messages has become quite common in live sporting events. In addition to the NFL, it is used on broadcasts of Major League Baseball, professional soccer matches, motor sports, and horse races. Some organizations have regulated the use of virtual advertising. For example, the governing body of professional soccer, the FIFA, does not permit superimposing virtual images on certain areas of the field during play, and bans entirely virtual messages on players or spectators.

Sources: "Virtual Advertising," *The Economist,* Jan. 15, 1999, p. 68; "Kodak Added to Sponsor List Using Princeton Video Image System to Insert Virtual Ads in the International Feed of Super Bowl XXXIV," *Business Wire,* Jan. 28, 2000; Joe Mulich, "Imagine Gilligan in Ray-Bans," *Business Journal,* Nov. 26, 1999, p. 31.

reaped from the same dollars spent on other marketing activities. On the other hand, advertisers promise only that a certain number of people will be exposed to an ad. They do not guarantee a certain level of sales and, in most instances, would even find it impossible to indicate the portion of sales that are attributable to advertising.

Difficulty of Evaluation

It is hard to measure the sales effectiveness of advertising. By the very nature of the marketing mix, all elements—including advertising—are so intertwined that it is nearly impossible to measure the effect of any one by itself. Factors that contribute to the difficulty of measuring the sales impact of advertising are:

- *Different objectives.* Although all advertising is ultimately intended to increase sales, individual ads may not be aimed at producing immediate results. For example, some ads simply announce new store hours or service policies. Other ads are designed to build corporate goodwill or contribute to a brand's position.

- *Effects over time.* Even an ad designed to have an immediate sales impact may produce results weeks or months after it appears. An ad may plant in the prospect's mind a seed that doesn't blossom into a sale for several weeks.

- *Measurement problems.* Consumers cannot usually say when or if a specific ad influenced their behavior, let alone if it caused them to buy. Human motivation is too complicated to be explained by a single factor.

In spite of these problems, advertisers try to measure advertising effectiveness because they must—and some knowledge is better than none. An ad's effectiveness may be tested before it is presented to the target audience, while it is being presented, or after it has completed its run.

Methods Used to Measure Effectiveness

Ad effectiveness measures are either direct or indirect. **Direct tests,** which compile the responses to an ad or a campaign, can be used only with a few types of ads. Tabulating the number of redemptions of a reduced-price coupon incorporated in an ad, for example, will indicate its effectiveness. Coupons frequently are coded so they can also be traced to the publications in which they were run. Another direct test of an ad's effectiveness is the number of inquiries received from an ad that offers additional information to prospects who call or write in.

Most other measures are **indirect tests** of effectiveness, or measures of something other than actual behavior. One of the most frequently used measures is advertising recall. Recall tests are based on the premise that an ad can have an effect only if it is perceived and remembered. Three common recall tests are:

- *Recognition*—showing people an ad and asking if they have seen it before.
- *Aided recall*—asking people if they can recall seeing any ads for a particular brand.
- *Unaided recall*—asking people if they can remember seeing any ads within an identified product category.

Refinements are constantly being made in advertising testing. Developments in areas such as laboratory test markets and computer simulations hold promise for the future. However, the complexity of decision making, combined with the multitude of influences on the buyer, will continue to make measuring the effectiveness of advertising a difficult task.

Organizing for Advertising

There are three ways a firm can manage its advertising:

- Develop an internal advertising department.
- Use an outside advertising agency.
- Use a combination of an internal department and an outside advertising agency.

Regardless of which alternative is selected, generally the same specialized skills are necessary to do the advertising job. Creative people are needed to prepare the copy, generate audio and/or video material, and design the formats. Media experts are required to select the appropriate media, buy the time or space, and arrange for the scheduled appearance of the ads. And managerial skills are essential to plan and administer the entire advertising program.

Internal Departments

All these advertising tasks, some of them, or just overall direction can be performed by an internal department. A company whose advertising is a substantial part of its marketing mix will usually have its own advertising department. Large retailers, for example, have their own advertising departments, and many do not use advertising agencies at all. If a company has adopted the marketing concept, the advertising department head will report to the organization's top marketing executive.

Advertising Agencies

Many companies, especially producers, use advertising agencies to carry out some or all of their advertising activities. An **advertising agency** is an independent company that provides specialized advertising services. Many large agencies have expanded the services they offer to include sales promotion, public relations, and even broader marketing assistance. As a result, they are frequently called upon to assist in strategic planning, marketing research, new-product development, package design, and selection of product names.

Can you recall any Motel 6 ad messages? Consistency and repetition are important if an advertiser intends to make an impression and have its message recalled. Since 1986, Motel 6 has relied on humorous appeals to economy-minded travelers with radio commercials featuring Tom Bodett and the tagline "We'll leave the light on for you." This print ad makes use of another medium but also uses humor and incorporates another message common to all Motel 6 ads—the lowest price of any national chain.

The motel of choice for the serious traveler.

After a day of sightseeing caverns or mountains carved up into presidents, nothing makes more sense than Motel 6. You'll get just what you need for the lowest price of any national chain. Which should free up some money for the Hillbilly Wax Museum.

Advertising agencies plan and execute entire advertising campaigns. They employ more advertising specialists than their clients do, because they spread the cost over many accounts. A client company can benefit from an agency's experience gained from other products and campaigns.

Inside Department and Outside Agency

Many firms have their own advertising department and also use an advertising agency. The internal department acts as a liaison with the agency, giving the company greater control over this major expenditure. The advertising department approves the agency's plans and ads, is responsible for preparing and administering the advertising budget, and coordinates advertising with personal selling. It may also handle direct marketing, dealer displays, and other promotional activities if they are not handled by the agency.

Sales Promotion

Sales promotion is one of the most loosely used terms in the marketing vocabulary. We define **sales promotion** as demand-stimulating devices designed to supplement advertising and facilitate personal selling. Examples of sales promotion devices are coupons, premiums, in-store displays, sponsorships, trade shows, samples, in-store demonstrations, and contests.

Sales promotions are conducted by producers and middlemen. The target for producers' sales promotions may be middlemen, end users—households or business users—or the producers' own sales forces. Middlemen direct sales promotion at their sales people or prospects further down the channel of distribution.

Nature and Scope of Sales Promotion

Sales promotion is distinct from advertising or personal selling, but these three forms of promotion are often used together in an integrated fashion. For example, prospective customers may be generated from people who enter a contest to win a copier at the Canon website and at a Canon exhibit at an office equipment trade show. These prospects might be sent some direct-mail and e-mail advertising and then be contacted by a sales person.

There are two categories of sales promotion: *trade promotions,* directed to the members of the distribution channel, and *consumer promotions,* aimed at consumers. It may surprise you to learn that manufacturers as a group spend about twice as much on trade promotion as they do on advertising, and an amount about equal to their advertising on consumer promotions.[22]

The magnitude of sales promotion activities is mind boggling. Although no statistics are available on total expenditures, the trade publication *PROMO Magazine,* compiles an annual estimate that places the figure at about $85 billion in 1998, and growing at more than 5% a year.[23]

Several factors in the marketing environment contribute to the popularity of sales promotion:

- *Short-term results.* Sales promotions such as couponing and trade allowances produce quicker, more measurable sales results. However, critics of this strategy argue that these immediate benefits come at the expense of building brand equity. They believe that an overemphasis on sales promotion may undermine a brand's future.

- *Competitive pressure.* If competitors offer buyers price reductions, contests, or other incentives, a firm may feel forced to retaliate with its own sales promotions.

- *Buyers' expectations.* Once they are offered purchase incentives, consumers and channel members get used to them and soon begin expecting them.

- *Low quality of retail selling.* Many retailers use inadequately trained sales clerks or have switched to self-service. For these outlets, sales promotion devices such as product displays and samples often are the only effective promotional tools available at the point of purchase.

Sales promotion should be included in a company's promotion plans, along with advertising and personal selling. This means setting sales promotion objectives and strategies, determining a sales promotion budget, and selecting appropriate sales promotion techniques.

One problem management faces is that many sales promotion techniques are short-run, tactical actions. Coupons, premiums, and contests, for example, are designed to produce immediate (but short-lived) responses. As a result, they tend to be used as stopgap measures to reverse unexpected sales declines rather than as parts of an integrated marketing communications program.

Determining Objectives and Strategies

Three broad objectives of sales promotion were suggested when the term was defined in Chapter 17:

- Stimulating business user or household demand for a product.
- Improving the marketing performance of middlemen and sales people.
- Supplementing advertising and facilitating personal selling.

A single sales promotion technique may accomplish one or two—but probably not all—of these objectives.

Determining Budgets

The sales promotion budget should be established as a specific part of the budget for the total promotional mix. If sales promotion is included in an advertising or public relations budget, it may be overlooked or poorly integrated with the other

How should a promotion be evaluated?

To stimulate sales of its Healthy Choice brand of grocery items, Conagra Inc. offered an incentive of frequent flyer miles. Between May and the end of December, a consumer could earn 500 free miles for every 10 labels from a Healthy Choice product sent in. Double miles (1,000 miles for 10 labels) could be earned for labels submitted by the end of May. An enterprising civil engineer, David Phillips, noticed the offer on a Healthy Choice frozen entrée and decided it was too good to pass up—but with a slight modification from what Conagra had in mind.

At a supermarket chain that specializes in buying excess inventory and reselling it as a discount, Phillips found Healthy Choice pudding cups for 25 cents apiece. He paid $3,140 for 12,560 of the desserts. He then donated the puddings to a local food bank in exchange for having volunteers remove the labels. With the help of the food bank, he was able to meet the May 31 deadline, and collected 1.2 million frequent flyer miles!

A spokesperson for Conagra commented that the frequent flyer offer had "met and even exceeded expectations." It's probably safe to say it at least met the expectations of David Phillips.

What factors should enter into a firm's evaluation of the effectiveness of a sales promotion effort?

Source: Jane Costello, "Shopper Turns Lots of Pudding into Free Miles," *The Wall Street Journal*, Jan. 24, 2000, pp. B1+.

components of promotion. Setting a separate budget for sales promotion forces a company to recognize and manage it.

Within the concept of developing an integrated marketing communications strategy, the amount budgeted for sales promotion should be determined by the task or objective method. This forces management to identify specific objectives and the sales promotion techniques that will be used to accomplish them.

Directing the Sales Promotion Effort

Many marketers plan and implement their sales promotion efforts internally. Others rely on specialized agencies. Sales promotion agencies fall into two primary categories. The first category is called *promotional service agencies*. They specialize in executing sales promotion programs such as sampling and couponing.

The other type of organization, called a *promotional marketing agency,* provides management advice and strategic planning of sales promotion as well as execution of the resulting program. As the use of sales promotion has increased, more organizations have turned to promotional marketing agencies for guidance. Rather than treat sales promotion as a periodic, single-shot sales stimulator, more firms are now integrating it into a planned strategy with long-term goals.

Selecting the Appropriate Techniques

A key step in sales promotion management is deciding which devices will help the organization reach its promotional goals. Factors that influence the choice of promotional devices include:

- *Nature of the target audience.* Is the target group loyal to a competing brand? If so, a high-value coupon may be necessary to disrupt customers' purchase patterns. Is the product bought on impulse? If so, an eye-catching point-of-sale display may be enough to generate sales.
- *Nature of the product.* Does the product lend itself to sampling, demonstration, or multiple-item purchases?
- *Cost of the device.* Sampling to a large market may be prohibitively expensive.

Table 19.5   Major Sales Promotion Devices, Grouped by Target Audience

Business Users or Households	Middlemen and Their Sales Forces	Producers' Own Sales Forces
Coupons	Trade shows and exhibitions	Sales contests
Cash rebates	Point-of-purchase displays	Sales training manuals
Premiums (gifts)	Free goods	Sales meetings
Free samples	Advertising allowances	Packets with promotional materials
Contests and sweepstakes	Contests for sales people	Demonstration model of product
Point-of-purchase displays	Training middlemen's sales forces	
Product demonstrations	Product demonstrations	
Trade shows and exhibitions	Advertising specialties	
Advertising specialties		

- *Current economic conditions.* Coupons, premiums, and rebates are good options during periods of recession or inflation, when consumers are particularly price conscious.

Common sales promotion techniques are shown in Table 19.5, where they are divided into three categories based on the target audience: business users or households, middlemen, and producers' sales forces. To illustrate the significance of sales promotion, several of these techniques are described below.

Sampling. Sampling is the only sure way of getting a product into the hands of potential customers. And it would seem to be a powerful motivator. In a national survey of consumers, 71% said they would try a sample, and 70% said they would switch brands if they liked the product.[24]

Sampling is not a new technique. A New Jersey promotions firm has been assembling samples of relevant products and distributing them to new mothers for over 45 years. However, in order to get the product into the right hands, creativity has increased. For example, a promotion for milk included a sample of items to be consumed with milk. The items, in a "goodie bag," were distributed in supermarkets to customers buying a gallon of milk. Nutella, a chocolate spread, was one of the sampled items. Its sales increased 75% during the promotion.[25] S.C. Johnson, the maker of Off! insect repellent, placed samples of its product in a million new Sunbeam barbecue grills. And snack food makers have joined with Blockbuster to give video renters samples of new products.

Sampling is most commonly done through the mail. Other methods include newspaper inserts and direct person-to-person handouts on the street or in stores or malls. Some firms are experimenting with sampling through their websites on the Internet. The advantage is that the people requesting a sample are most likely very interested in the product. However, the interest could wane while they wait for the requested sample to be delivered.

The cost per thousand of sampling is much higher than advertising. However, the conversion rate (the proportion of people exposed who buy the product) is typically around 10% for sampling, which is considerably better than advertising.[26]

Couponing. Coupons are the most frequently used form of consumer sales promotion by manufacturers. And consumers like them. In 1998 consumers saved between $3.1 billion and $3.6 billion by using coupons.[27] The volume of couponing is staggering. Over 275 *billion* coupons are distributed a year, and about 5 billion (less than 2%!) are redeemed by consumers.[28]

Freestanding inserts (FSI) in newspapers account for more than 80% of all coupons.[29] Other methods of distribution are direct mail, in magazines, and coupons packaged in or on products. An increasing number of coupons are being distributed in retail stores. One technique is to offer coupons in a dispenser attached to the retail shelf where a product is displayed. The rationale is that con-

Catalina Marketing Corp. produces "checkout coupons" for over 11,000 super-markets. If a product scanned at the checkout is a competitor to a Catalina client, a store-specific, short-dated coupon is automatically printed for the client's product. Catalina also collects data on the other purchases the customer makes on the same shopping trip, allowing retailers to identify the shopping profile of their most profitable customers.

 www.coolsavings.com

sumers, at the point of purchase, may be influenced to select a particular brand if a coupon is readily available. Not surprisingly, these coupons have redemption rates as much as nine times higher than coupons included in newspapers. Another method growing in popularity is to electronically dispense coupons at the checkout counter on the basis of the items a consumer purchases. Thus, when a shopper buys a particular brand of a product, a coupon might be issued for a competing alternative. This approach is designed to encourage brand switching on the consumer's next shopping trip. Also, consumers who are members of retailers' frequent-shopper programs are given coupons when they make purchases.

A small but growing number of coupons are being distributed on the Internet. Combining the Internet and coupons provides access to hard-to-reach audiences. For example, college students can log onto coolsavings.com, become registered members, and download coupons for redemption at campus-area restaurants and retail stores.

Although most coupons are for frequently-purchased convenience items, they are used by marketers of other products as well. When its share of the new car sales failed to improve in 1999, GM mailed millions of $500 coupons to U.S. consumers, a tactic the firm used successfully in 1998 to provide a sales boost.

Critics of coupons point out that they are expensive. The average face value of a coupon for a packaged good is 70 cents.[30] Another problem is that they may undermine brand loyalty. Coupons may teach consumers to seek out the best bargains rather than consistently select a particular brand.

Couponing has increased in other parts of the world, but the methods of distribution are different from those in the U.S. Whereas the bulk of coupons in the U.S. are FSIs, in Canada coupons are most often included as part of ads. Spanish and Italian marketers place coupons in or on packages. And in several other European countries, coupons are distributed door to door.

Sponsorships and Event Marketing.   Corporate sponsorship of events has become a major promotional activity. Worldwide expenditures exceed $12 billion, with nearly $7 billion of the total spent in North America.[31] Most corporate sponsorships are for sports events and charitable causes. Auto racing draws the greatest amount of corporate sponsorships, estimated at $1.35 billion in 2000.[32] The remainder includes concerts and entertainment tours, festivals and fairs, and the arts. Considering that there are over 50,000 festivals and events in the U.S. each year, the range of sponsorship opportunities is almost unlimited.

Sponsorship is typically viewed as a long-range image-building activity, such as when adidas sponsored the Women's World Cup soccer tournament in 1999. But it can also have an effect on sales. When Eddie Cheever won the Indianapolis 500 race in a car sponsored by Rachel's Gourmet Snacks, the small Minnesota firm was able to sign up new distributors all over the country.[33]

Unlike advertising time or space in which the advertiser is in complete control, sponsorship is sometimes shared. As a result, a sponsor has to be very explicit about what will be provided and what is expected. Reebok withdrew its $6.4 million sponsorship of the 2000 Sydney Olympics when organizers arranged for other sportswear firms to provide hats and rugby shirts.[34]

The principal difficulty in justifying sponsorship expenditures is measuring their effectiveness. Because sales are usually not the primary objective, the value of a sponsorship is frequently determined by the amount of publicity it generates for the sponsor (and comparison of that to the cost of an equivalent amount of advertising). An alternative approach is a survey of attendees before and after an event to determine awareness and brand preference.

Trade Shows. Associations in industries as diverse as computers, sporting goods, food, and broadcasting sponsor trade shows. There are 5,000 trade shows a year in Canada and the U.S. alone. About half restrict attendance to business representatives, whereas the remainder allow consumers to attend. In a typical year, trade shows host about 1.3 million exhibitors and attract 85 million visitors.[35]

The appeal of a trade show is efficiency. In one place and in a compressed amount of time, trade shows allow buyers and sellers to see and interact with many of their counterparts. They also tend to attract decision makers. In a survey of trade show attendees, 26% made a purchase at the show, and 51% asked that a sales representative be sent to their company.[36]

On the other hand, trade shows are expensive for exhibitors. In addition to the cost of the booth and the living expenses of the company representatives during the show, transporting equipment and display material is costly. As a result, firms are selective about the trade shows they attend, often requiring the sponsors to provide demographic profiles of the attendees.

The trade show industry grew by over 70% during the 1980s, and is on track to continue growing at a fast pace.[37] Much of the growth has come from offshoots of existing broad-based events. Like advertising, trade shows are seeking out narrower market segments and offering more specialized topics.

Product Placements. For many years firms have paid fees to have their products used as props in movies, and the practice is growing. On TV shows, paid placements must be disclosed to the audience, so networks generally disapprove of their use unless the product is central to the story. Some examples of product placements are shown in Table 19.6. Product placements also occur in novels and video games.

Placements have proved very beneficial to some products, taking them from virtual obscurity to national prominence. You may have noticed product placements, but if you're like most consumers these props simply added to the realism of the experience, and that is the strength of product placement. It displays the product in a noncommercial way, sometimes linking it with the show's characters and creating a positive association for the audience.

Technology has made "virtual product placement" in films possible. That is, nonexistent props can be electronically inserted in movie or television scenes. This greatly increases opportunities for product placements. For example, newer products can replace older ones or simply be added to remakes of movies or syndicated television shows. Or different brands can be displayed in a show broadcast in different parts of the country or the world. Advertisers, concerned with the implications of video recorders that can be programmed to automatically eliminate commercials during playback, are enthusiastic about this development.[38]

Table 19.6	Examples of Product Placements
Movie or TV Show	**Product(s)**
E.T.	Reese's Pieces
GoldenEye	IBM computers, BMW, Perrier, and Omega
Baywatch	Hawaiian Tropic suntan products
Seinfeld	TV Guide, Snapple, Mars candy bars, Junior Mints
You've Got Mail	America Online
Deep Impact, Object of My Affections, 3rd Rock from the Sun	Avalon bottled water
The Horse Whisperer	EquiSearch.com
Risky Business, Men in Black	RayBan sunglasses
Flubber, He Got Game	RAM Sports (balls)
Chicago Hope	Heartstream Inc. (heart defibrillator)

Sources: Dale D. Buss, "Making Your Mark in Movies and TV," *Nation's Business,* December 1998, pp. 28+; Wayne Friedman and Jean Halliday, "BMW's MGM Promotional Deal Puts 007 in Z8 Driver's Seat," *Advertising Age,* Mar. 1, 1999, p. 8.

Public Relations

Public relations is a management tool designed to favorably influence attitudes toward an organization, its products, and its policies. It is an often-overlooked form of promotion. In most organizations this promotional tool is typically a stepchild, relegated far behind personal selling, advertising, and sales promotion. There are several reasons for management's lack of attention to public relations:

- *Organizational structure.* In most companies, public relations is not the responsibility of the marketing department. If there is an organized effort, it is usually handled by a small public relations department that reports directly to top management.
- *Inadequate definitions.* The term public relations is used loosely by both businesses and the public. There are no generally accepted definitions of the term. As a result, what actually constitutes an organized public relations effort often is not clearly defined.
- *Unrecognized benefits.* Only recently have many organizations come to appreciate the value of good public relations. As the cost of promotion has gone up, firms are realizing that positive exposure through the media or as a result of community involvement can produce a high return on the investment of time and effort.

Nature and Scope of Public Relations

Public relations activities typically are designed to build or maintain a favorable image for an organization with its various publics—customers, prospects, stockholders, employees, labor unions, the local community, and the government. We're aware that this description is quite similar to our definition of institutional advertising. However, unlike advertising, public relations need not use the media to communicate its message.

Good public relations can be achieved in many ways. Some examples are supporting charitable projects (by supplying volunteer labor or other resources), participating in community service events, sponsoring nonprofessional athletic teams, funding the arts, producing an employee or customer newsletter, and disseminating information through exhibits, displays, and tours. Major firms such as ExxonMobil and Johnson & Johnson sponsor shows on public television (PBS) as part of their public relations effort.

Publicity as a Form of Public Relations

Publicity is any communication about an organization, its products, or policies through the media not paid for by the organization. Publicity usually takes the form of a news story appearing in the media or an endorsement provided by an individual, either informally or in a speech or interview. This is good publicity.

There is also, of course, bad publicity—a negative story about a firm or its product appearing in the media. In a society that is increasingly sensitive about the environment and in which news media are quick to report mistakes, organizations tend to focus on this negative dimension of publicity. As a result, managers are so concerned with avoiding bad publicity that they overlook the potential of good publicity.

There are three means for gaining good publicity:

- *Prepare and distribute a story (called a news release) to the media.* The intention is for the selected newspapers, television stations, or other media to report the information as news.

- *Personal communication with a group.* A press conference will draw media representatives if they think the subject or speaker has news value. Company tours and speeches to civic or professional groups are other forms of individual-to-group communications.

- *One-on-one personal communication, often called lobbying.* Companies lobby legislators or other powerful people in an attempt to influence their opinions, and subsequently their decisions.

Publicity can help accomplish any communication objective. It can be used to announce new products, publicize new policies, recognize employees, describe research breakthroughs, or report financial performance. But to receive coverage, the message, person, group, or event being publicized must be viewed by the media as newsworthy. This is what distinguishes publicity from advertising—publicity is not "forced" on the audience. This is also the source of its primary benefit. The credibility of publicity typically is much higher than advertising. If an organization tells you its product is great, you may well be skeptical. But if an independent, objective third party says on the evening news that the product is great, you are more likely to believe it.

Other benefits of publicity are:

- *Lower cost.* Publicity usually costs less than advertising or personal selling because there are no media space or time costs for conveying the message and no sales people to support.

- *Increased attention.* Many consumers are conditioned to ignore advertising or at least pay scant attention to it. Publicity is presented as editorial material or news, so it is more likely to be watched, listened to, or read.

- *More information.* Because it is presented as editorial material, publicity can contain greater detail than the usual ad. More information and persuasive content can be included in the message.

- *Timeliness.* A company can put out a news release very quickly when some unexpected event occurs.

Of course, publicity has limitations:

- *Loss of control over the message.* An organization has no guarantee that a news release will appear in the media. In addition, there is no way to control how much or what portion of a story the media will print or broadcast.

- *Limited exposure.* The media will typically use news releases to fill space when there is a lack of other news and only use them once. If the target audience misses the message when it is presented, there is no second or third chance.

- *Publicity is not free.* Even though there are no media time and space costs, there are expenses in generating ideas for publicity and in preparing and disseminating news releases.

Recognizing the value of publicity, some organizations have one or more staff members who generate news releases. These stories are sent to the media and are typically made available to anyone via the company's website. For example, Microsoft provided an extensive collection of releases useful in learning about the company's perspective on its recent antitrust case as well as other issues.

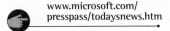
www.microsoft.com/
presspass/todaysnews.htm

• Summary

Advertising, sales promotion, and public relations are the nonpersonal, mass-communications components of a company's promotional mix. Advertising consists of all the activities involved in presenting to an audience a nonpersonal, sponsor-identified, paid-for message about a product or organization. The total advertising expenditure in a firm is typically 1 to 3% of sales, considerably less than the average cost of personal selling. Most advertising dollars are spent on television, newspapers, and direct mail. Other frequently used media are radio, magazines, yellow pages, and out-of-home displays. The Internet is increasing in importance as an ad medium.

Advertising can be directed to consumers or businesses. Ads are classified according to whether they are intended to stimulate primary or selective demand. Primary demand ads introduce new products and sustain demand for a product throughout its life cycle. Selective-demand ads emphasize a particular brand or company. They are divided into product ads, that focus on a brand, or institutional ads, that focus on an organization. Product ads are further subdivided into direct action ads, which call for immediate action, and indirect-action ads, which are intended to stimulate demand over a longer period of time. A selective-demand ad that makes reference to one or more competitors is called a comparative ad.

An advertising campaign involves transforming a theme into a coordinated advertising program. Designing a campaign includes defining objectives, establishing a budget, creating new messages, selecting media, and evaluating the effort. Objectives can range from creating awareness of a brand to generating sales. Advertising budgets can be extended through vertical and horizontal cooperative arrangements. An advertising message—consisting of the appeal and the execution of the ad—is influenced by the target audience and the media used.

A major task in developing a campaign is to select the advertising media—the general type, the particular category, and the specific vehicle. The choice should be based on the characteristics of the medium, which determine how effectively it conveys the message, and its ability to reach the target audience. Each of the media that carry advertising has characteristics that makes it more or less suitable for a particular advertising objective.

A difficult task in advertising management is evaluating the effectiveness of the advertising effort—both the entire campaign and individual ads. Some methods of advertising allow for direct measures of effect, but most can only be evaluated indirectly. A commonly used technique measures recall of an ad. To carry out an advertising program, a firm may rely on its own advertising department, an advertising agency, or a combination of the two.

Sales promotion consists of demand-stimulating devices designed to supplement advertising and facilitate personal selling. The amount of sales promotion increased considerably in the past two decades, as management sought measurable, short-term sales results.

Sales promotion should receive the same strategic attention that a company gives to advertising and personal selling, including setting objectives and establishing a budget. Sales promotion can be directed toward final consumers, middlemen, or a company's own employees. Management can choose from a variety of sales promotion devices. Some of the most common are samples, coupons, sponsorships, trade shows, and product placements. Like advertising, sales promotion performance should be evaluated.

Public relations is a management tool designed to favorably influence attitudes toward an organization, its products, and its policies. It is a frequently overlooked form of promotion. Publicity, a part of public relations, is any communication about an organization, its products, or policies through the media that is not paid for by the organization. Typically these two activities are handled in a department separate from the marketing department in a firm. Nevertheless, the management process of planning, implementation, and evaluation should be applied to these activities in the same way it is applied to advertising, sales promotion, and personal selling.

More about **Intel**

The situation at Intel has been likened to a three-legged stool:

- Microprocessors, where Intel has been the leader, is the first leg. More than 80% of the firm's revenue and all of its profits come from this source. However, as described in the opening part of this case, this market is in decline as the demand for increasingly powerful microprocessors shrinks.
- The second leg of the stool consists of the hardware components for the network era. Just as Intel has been the primary provider of the core or memory for PCs, now it would like to create the building blocks that will link the yet-to-be-developed memory chips, switching gear, and software that will make networks function.
- Finally, the third leg is a Web-based service that will handle global network traffic.

To develop the second and third legs, Intel once again needs a blend of technology and promotion. Consumers have to think of Intel as more than a firm that makes microprocessors, so the firm has begun some fundamental changes in its promotion program.

The first element of its strategy is a $150 million global advertising effort that positions Intel as a powerful Internet enabler. The campaign demonstrates how Intel with its Pentium III processor provides a richer, more engaging Internet experience. The campaign also carries a new slogan to emphasize Intel's capability on the Web, "Don't just get onto the Internet, get into it."

The next phase of the campaign targets business leaders with ads in publications such as *Business Week, Fortune,* and *The Wall Street Journal,* describing Intel's broadened activity. The ads emphasize Intel's own e-commerce efforts, its Internet data service, and the firm's involvement in developing a networking processor. The reader is informed that Intel's own e-commerce business has grown into a $1-billion-a-month operation in only 18 months. The objective is to transform Intel from being viewed as a building block for PCs to a building block for the Internet.

Recognizing the global nature of the networking business, Intel has taken its advertising messages to China, Taiwan, South Korea, and Australia. The messages are adapted to the local markets. For example, Intel's message in Australia is designed to help consumers find, design, and buy PCs on the Internet. In Asia, buyers of PCs with the Pentium III are offered a special service called the WebOutfitter. Users get free software that provides an enhanced Internet experience and "sneak previews" of future sites.

Intel discovered the power of advertising in building a strong, profitable technology-based company. "Intel Inside" is an example of ingredient branding. The strategy is an application of the concept of derived demand. Recognizing that the demand for its microprocessors depends on the demand for PCs that include them as components, Intel sought to stimulate demand for the PCs that contain Intel products. The strategy is not new. DuPont does it with nylon and other synthetic fibers, and Nutrasweet does it for artificial sweetener. However, Intel was the first to do it in the technology area.

"Intel Inside" became symbolic of what could be accomplished with the merger of a meaningful message and excellent execution. The company now faces the challenge of adapting to the next generation of the information age. Its success will once again depend on having a message to share and finding ways to share it.[39]

1. Why is it important that Intel communicate to consumers its shift in focus from being primarily a microprocessors producer to being an Internet enabler?

2. a. How could Intel use sales promotion and public relations in revamping its image and in boosting sales for its network products?

   b. Would the same promotional tools be appropriate both in the U.S. and in foreign markets?

Key Terms and Concepts

Advertising (540)
Consumer advertising (542)
Business-to-business advertising (542)
Primary-demand advertising (542)
Selective-demand advertising (542)

Comparative advertising (543)
Product advertising (543)
Institutional advertising (543)
Advertising campaign (543)
Cooperative advertising (545)
Advertising media (547)
Cost per thousand (CPM) (548)

Direct tests (554)
Indirect tests (554)
Advertising agency (554)
Sales promotion (555)
Public relations (561)
Publicity (562)

Questions and Problems

1. How do you account for the variation in advertising expenditures as a percentage of sales among the different companies in Table 19.2?

2. Select a general type of advertising medium for each of the following products and explain your choice.
   a. Internet-based investment service
   b. Hanes pantyhose
   c. Tax-preparation service
   d. Mortuary
   e. Toys for young children
   f. Plastic clothespins

3. Many grocery product and candy manufacturers earmark a good portion of their advertising budgets for use in magazines. In contrast, department stores use newspapers more than local radio stations as an advertising medium. Are these media choices wise for these industries and firms? Explain.

4. Why is it worthwhile to test ads before they appear in the media? How could a test market be used to test an ad? (You may want to refresh your memory with a review of test marketing in Chapter 7.)

5. What procedures can a firm use to determine how many sales dollars resulted from a direct-mail ad?

6. What type of sales promotion would be effective for selling expensive consumer products such as houses, automobiles, or cruise trips? How about expensive business products?

7. What advantage would sampling have over advertising for a new brand of sunscreen lotion?

8. Should virtual product placement raise any ethical concerns for the media?

9. Bring to class an article from a daily newspaper that appears to be the result of a firm's publicity efforts. Summarize the points made in the article that may benefit the firm. Could advertising create the same benefits?

Hands-On Marketing

1. Common appeals or benefits and examples of product categories in which they are frequently used include:
   - Physical well-being (food, nonprescription drugs)
   - Social acceptance (cosmetics, health and beauty aids)
   - Material success (automobiles, investments)
   - Recognition and status (clothing, jewelry)
   - Sensory pleasure (movies, candy)
   - Time savings (websites)
   - Peace of mind (insurance, tires)

   Find print ads that make use of five of these appeals.

2. Visit a supermarket, drugstore, or hardware store, and make a list of all the sales promotion tools you observe. Describe how each one relates to the sales promotion objectives described in the chapter. Which do you think are particularly effective, and why?

Cases for Part 6

Promoting a Mature Product

Americans love pizza, averaging 11.5 million pizza purchases a day, or 4.2 billion a year! Retail sales of fresh and frozen pizza total $25 billion annually. These numbers explain why pizza restaurants are so plentiful, and they also suggest that pizza marketing is a highly competitive business in which only the strong can survive.

Who's Selling and Who's Eating Pizza

The fresh pizza industry includes three groups of firms: national chains, regional chains, and local independents. National chains, made up of company-owned and franchised outlets, dominate the industry. The largest of these is Pizza Hut with 22% of the total market, followed by Domino's (11%), Little Caesar's (7%), and Papa John's (5%). These operations rely on scale economies to keep their costs down. For example, they buy components in large quantities to get lower prices, prepare ingredients at central locations to gain efficiencies, and carefully manage portions in the preparation of the final products. They all compete on price, relying heavily on coupons and other promotions to generate traffic.

Regional chains include firms such as East of Chicago and Donatos (recently acquired by McDonald's) in the Midwest, Foodee's in New England, and Pittsburgh-based Pizza Outlet. The differential advantages that allow these firms to survive in this intensely competitive market range from offering many alternative crusts to using more and/or exotic ingredients. These firms also achieve some economies of scale in promotion and pizza assembly that are common to the national chains.

Typically, a local pizza business with no more than one or two restaurants got started before the chains entered its market area. The pizzeria developed a small but very loyal customer base and was able to withstand the competitive pressure. Independents tend to provide a difference—for example, using only fresh ingredients—that cannot be matched by the chains. However, they also have higher prices and seldom offer discounts.

Four broad segments of fresh pizza consumers can be identified:

- The first is a price-sensitive segment that has little if any brand loyalty. It includes heavy coupon users who view pizza as just another way to fill hungry mouths. Little Caesar's is targeted at this segment.

- A second segment is convenience-oriented. Price is important, but secondary to getting the pizza quickly and easily. Domino's focuses on this market.

- A third segment places a higher priority on quality and variety, but is also receptive to an attractive price. Pizza Hut and Papa John's vie for this segment.

- Finally, there is a segment willing to pay a premium price for a specialized product. These consumers are most likely to patronize the independent, local pizzerias.

The Battle Goes to Court

The intensity of the competition in the pizza industry is reflected in a recent conflict between two of the national chains. Papa John's has sought to position itself as having the best pizza among the national pizza chains. Considering the firm's rapid growth, the positioning appears to be quite successful. Since becoming a public company in 1993, Papa John's has grown to 2,000 units and over $1 billion in sales. And it continues to grow at about 10% a year.

In the execution of its quality appeal, Papa John's adopted the slogan "Better ingredients. Better pizza." Taking issue with the claim and the ads in which it was portrayed, Pizza Hut sued in federal court. The suit asked that Papa John's be barred from using the slogan, and that it pay damages for disparaging Pizza Hut. Papa John's defense was that the slogan was no more than commonly used puffery. The firm sees it in the same category as Burger King's claim that its hamburgers "just taste better," or Snapple's line that its products are "made from the best stuff on earth."

Pizza Hut countered that puffery is acceptable as long as it isn't directed at a particular competitor. In this instance, Pizza Hut claimed, Papa John's was making it clear that its slogan was a comparison to Pizza Hut. The judge apparently agreed, ruling that Papa John's must quit using the claim and remove it from all ads, boxes, napkins, employee uniforms, and delivery cars. Papa John's is appealing the ruling, which may take years to resolve. In the meantime, the firm was required to eliminate a slogan and ad campaign that it used for five years in building its competitive position.

Pizza Hut's Origin

As the oldest and largest of the national chains, Pizza Hut provides an interesting example of how a company uses promotion as part of an integrated marketing communications strategy. Today the firm has more than 10,000 outlets (about one-half are franchised units), consisting of restaurants, delivery/carryout units, and kiosks, located in 86 countries. In getting to this point, Pizza Hut has experienced solid growth, but also a number of bumps along the way.

Pizza Hut was founded in Wichita, Kansas, by brothers Frank and Dan Carney. In 1958 the two struggling college students borrowed $600 from their mother to start the business. Because many people were unfamiliar with pizza, they initially gave out samples to educate consumers about the new product.

The Carneys pizza quickly became popular. In 1959 they opened their first franchised Pizza Hut restaurant in Topeka, Kansas. Ten years later, the firm had 300 locations. International expansion began in the late 1960s. At the same time, the firm adopted the red roof motif as a common theme for all its restaurants.

In 1977, when Pizza Hut had grown to 2,000 units, it was acquired by PepsiCo, along with Taco Bell and Kentucky Fried Chicken (now called KFC). Supported by PepsiCo's resources, the pace of growth picked up. In two years, the number of Pizza Hut units doubled to 4,000. However, PepsiCo began to feel the financial burden of building and operating retail stores. So, in 1997, PepsiCo created a new company called Tricon Global comprised of the three restaurant chains. The head of the newly created firm, David Novak, mandated that the three chains use a strategy of product innovations to attract new customers.

Pizza Hut's New-Product Legacy

New products had long been part of Pizza Hut's strategy. As competition in the pizza business intensified, the company recognized the necessity of a dynamic and integrated marketing program of locations, products, and promotion. Fundamental to its efforts was a steady stream of innovations that attract new patrons and provide the variety that keeps regular customers coming back. Examples of Pizza Hut's successful new products and the date when each was introduced are shown below:

Thin 'n Crispy Crust (1970)	BIG FOOT Pizza (1993)
Thick and Chewy (1975)	Chunky-style Pizza (1993)
Super Supreme (1977)	Stuffed Crust Pizza (1995)
Sicilian Pan Pizza (1979)	Italian Chicken Pizza (1996)
Personal Pan Pizza (1980)	The Edge Pizza (1997)
Priazza and Calizza (1985)	The Sicilian Pan Pizza (1998)
Hand Tossed Traditional Pizza (1988)	Big New Yorker (1999)

The value of new products is reflected in what the Big New Yorker has accomplished. Introduced with ads during the 1999 Super Bowl telecast, the Big New Yorker (a 16-inch pizza for $9.99) was tried by 40 million consumers in its first three months. After only nine months, 70 million had been sold. That's an average of over 30 a day for every Pizza Hut outlet.

An integrated strategy was required in order to achieve such success in a mature market. First, Pizza Hut had to come up with an appealing product, which isn't easy in the pizza business. There are only a limited number of product features with which to work. Plus any new menu item must be compatible with the existing equipment and the ability of the company's pizza makers in every outlet. Equally important, a new product must be able to grab the attention of the target market. Added to all of this was Pizza Hut's desire to come up with an item that would be an everyday product, not just for weekends or special occasions.

In the case of the Big New Yorker the new-product team spent two years exploring various combinations of ingredients and sizes, searching for a pizza with a broad but distinctive appeal. After test marketing three versions—all of which produced unsatisfactory results—they hit on the idea of returning to pizza's roots. Research showed that many people associate pizza with New York. More specifically, they picture New Yorkers eating a foldable slice of cheesy pizza. By linking this concept with a basic product, Pizza Hut believed it could meet its goal of a moderate price and still provide a generous-sized pizza. At the same time, it had a promotable image—the New York name and its connection to pizza, along with the touch of "attitude" frequently associated with New Yorkers.

Ad executions featuring celebrity spokespersons Fran Drescher, Donald Trump, and Spike Lee provided the New York connection. In addition, Pizza Hut ran joint promotions with Blockbuster (a coupon for a rental movie with a Big New Yorker pizza purchase) and Mountain Dew (a 2-liter bottle with a purchase) to introduce the product. The result has been the most successful product launch in the industry's history.

Sales Promotion Generates Traffic

As with many other restaurants, sales promotion is an important aspect of Pizza Hut's overall promotional strategy. Coupons that offer price discounts, extra toppings, or additional items (such as soft drinks) are a staple of the pizza business.

A firm that does not offer coupons can be at a competitive disadvantage because a large portion of the market is price sensitive. However, balancing the type of offer, coupon value, and frequency of distribution in order to generate the best results has largely been a process of trial and error. Using database marketing, Pizza Hut found a solution.

By bar coding coupons and tracking redemption rates, Pizza Hut has been able to reduce the number of different promotional offers from 650 to the 16 that produce the best responses. Taking the data a step further, the company was able to cluster the different markets around the country on the basis of customer demographics and coupon redemption rates. Then, for each cluster, it was able to identify the best method of coupon distribution and most effective offers. The result is a 40% reduction in the cost of couponing and a 50% increase in redemptions.

Other popular sales promotions are tie-ins with movies snd other events of interest to the target audience. In 1989, for example, Pizza Hut restaurants sold 9.5 million hand puppets in a promotion linked to the movie *Land before Time*. In another successful tie-in, this time with the National Collegiate Athletic Association, 3.7 million basketballs were sold by Pizza Hut outlets in conjunction with the 1994 Final Four college tournament. Other promotions have been carried out in connection with *The Care Bear Movie*, *ET*, and *Beauty and the Beast*.

Like ads, promotions must be carefully selected. Pizza Hut, through its parent Tricon, found that out in a disappointing movie tie-in. When the three chains were still part of PepsiCo, a deal had been struck for a tie-in promotion with the three-film *Star Wars* sequel. Following the spin-off, Tricon retained the rights to a tie-in with the first in the series, *Star Wars: Episode 1—The Phantom Menace*. The promotion involved 28 Star Wars toys and a dozen drink cups in the shape of characters from the movie. Unfortunately for Pizza Hut and its sister chains, the primary audience for the movie (teens, young adults, and some older adults nostalgic about the earlier films) was older than the market for a toy promotion. As a result, a sales promotion effort linked to one of the most hyped movies of all times failed.

PR as an Integral Part of Promotion

Pizza Hut engages in various public relations (PR) efforts. For example, the firm participated in raising funds for Easter Seals. Further, it has redesigned its pizza boxes to reduce the amount of cardboard used, thereby reducing its consumption of trees. The firm also sponsors a program called BOOK IT!, a national incentive program that rewards school children with coupons for Personal Pan pizzas when they achieve reading goals.

Pizza Hut has also enjoyed some interesting publicity:

- During an attempted political coup in 1991, Russian president Boris Yeltsin ordered Pizza Hut pizzas for himself and his beleaguered staff when they were under siege in the Russian Parliament Building.

- In 1992 the firm set up trailers in Florida to provide 120,000 free meals to relief workers and victims of Hurricane Andrew.

- U.S. service personnel serving as peacekeepers in Somalia were air shipped 600 pepperoni pizzas in 1993.

These events all produced good publicity for Pizza Hut, but it has had its share of bad publicity as well. The firm has had battles with franchisees and has encountered employee disputes that have been covered by the media. A recent experiment with charging a small fee for delivery has also generated some negative news. The firm quietly added delivery charges of 50 cents to $1 in a few markets with the intent of comparing the effect on demand with markets without a delivery charge. However, when the media heard about the project, they were able to secure statements from Pizza Hut competitors who were quick to criticize the idea.

Aiming High for an Advantage

The company is in the midst of a multiyear brand-repositioning effort that includes remodeling restaurants, adding a new, hand-drawn logo of the trademark red roof, and improving both order taking and order fulfillment to provide speedier service. According to a company executive, "Pizza Hut turned 40 last year, and many of the chain's assets look their age." The program involves closing 600 underperforming stores, spending $500 million to modernize the 2,000+ company-owned restaurants, and providing an incentive in the form of reduced royalty fees for franchisees who undertake substantial remodeling.

To draw attention to its updated image, Pizza Hut paid $1 million to have its new logo painted on a Russian space rocket. The 30-foot-high version of the logo was to be on the fuselage of a rocket, launched as part of the 16-country International Space Station initiative. Pizza Hut's intention was that its logo would be seen by most of the 500 million TV viewers around the world watching the launch. Complications prevented the promotion from occurring, but

Pizza Hut received plenty of media coverage when the plan for putting a "pie in the sky" was announced.

Questions

1. What does the success of the Big New Yorker suggest about how promotional activities should be developed?

2. Given the life-cycle stage of the pizza industry and the nature of past promotional efforts, which promotional tools should Pizza Hut emphasize in the future?

3. What challenges does Pizza Hut face in developing integrated marketing communications?

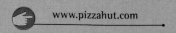 www.pizzahut.com

Sources: Pizza Hut website, January 2000; Jacqueline Kochak, "Pie Chart," *Restaurant Business,* Nov. 15, 1999, pp. 49+; Amy Zuber, "Pizza Hut Logo Launch Fuels Chain's Reimaging Strategy," *Nation's Restaurant News,* Oct. 11, 1999, p. 4; Amy Zuber, "Pizza Hut Delivery Fee: Future Unclear at Company, Segment," *Nation's Restaurant News,* Oct. 4, 1999, pp. 4+; Richard Gibson, "For Pizza Hut, a New Pie-in-the-Sky Ad Strategy," *The Wall Street Journal,* Sept. 30, 1999, pp. B1+; Theresa Howard, "Attitude, Not Anchovies," *BrandWeek,* Aug. 23, 1999, pp. 24–25; Theresa Howard, "Raising the Roof," *BrandWeek,* Aug. 9, 1999, p. 3; "Episode II: Promo Doom," *Advertising Age,* July 12, 1999, p. 24; Louise Kramer, "Tricon Enlists Force of Three for 'Star Wars,'" *Advertising Age,* Mar. 1, 1999, pp. 1+; Carol Krol, "Pizza Hut's Database Makes Its Couponing More Efficient," *Advertising Age,* Nov. 30, 1998, p. 27.

Case 2 • Nike, Inc.

Promotion Strategies in an Evolving Market

The U.S. market for athletic footwear has grown to over $14 billion. That's approximately 325 million pairs of shoes. A market of this size, with purchase motives that range from fashion to function, is a good candidate for stiff competition. To be successful, a firm must have a clever and well-coordinated marketing program that includes effective promotion.

Nike, Inc., has been the leader in the athletic footwear industry for nearly 20 years. It dominates the category with a 40% market share. The company's cofounder, Phil Knight, was an honorable mention in *Fortune* magazine's selection of the business persons of the century, and Nike was named one of the 100 most powerful corporate brands of the century. In 1999 *Popular Mechanics* awarded Nike's Gauntlet running shoe a design and engineering award, *Business Week* named the Nike Air Zoom M9 soccer boot one of the best products of the year, and the Nike Triax 300 sport wristwatch was given the design of the decade award by the Industrial Design Society of America. Certainly the record suggests this organization is on the right track. However, despite its successes, Nike faces stiff challenges.

How the Race Got Started

An understanding of the athletic shoe market requires a look at the past 40 years. In the 1960s, there were few choices for those buying athletic shoes. Function was the main attribute considered by consumers. Converse's Chuck Taylor All Stars and Keds were the dominant brands of sneakers. In addition, a few manufacturers (for example, adidas and Puma) marketed specialized shoes for track and football.

Market conditions changed dramatically in the 1970s when the adult physical fitness movement began. A large market, composed of people in their twenties and thirties, developed for jogging and running shoes. In addition, "wanna-bes" (people who

weren't actually involved in jogging and running but wanted to convey a sporting image) began to wear sneakers as a fashion statement. The switch from function to fashion started a race that upstarts and well-known manufacturers alike wanted to win. A Sporting Goods Manufacturers survey in the late 1980s indicated that over 90% of the U.S. population owned at least one pair of athletic shoes, and over 70% bought a new pair each year.

Just Doing It

In 1964, Phil Knight and his former track coach at the University of Oregon, Bill Bowerman, launched Blue Ribbon Sports. Their objective was to provide competitive athletes with a high-performance shoe, and, by so doing, unseat adidas as the market leader for running shoes. Knight's initial strategy was to bring the Tiger brand, a Japanese-made running shoe, to the U.S. Later, believing they could design a better shoe for the serious runner, Knight and Bowerman formed Nike. The company name was taken from Greek mythology in which Nike is the goddess of victory.

Because they had limited resources and unlimited confidence in their product, Knight and Bowerman did very little marketing. Early efforts consisted of Knight, formerly a college track athlete, persuading several of the top American distance runners to try the new shoes, and Bowerman encouraging fellow coaches to give the shoes a try.

Athletes liked the shoes, word spread, and sales grew. As money became available, Nike began advertising. Following the 1972 Olympic marathon trials, Nike boasted that "four of the top seven finishers" ran in Nike shoes. When it was later pointed out that the three winners had worn adidas shoes, it had little effect on a brand that was headed for the front of the pack.

Nike's sales grew rapidly, reaching $14 million by 1976. During the next five years, sales and profits surged at an astonishing rate of 75% per year. The growth over this period was fueled by athletic shoes becoming a wardrobe staple. By the early 1980s, 80% of athletic footwear was purchased for nonathletic purposes.

Everything seemed to be going Nike's way. Then, in the 1980s the competitive landscape changed when the aerobics boom took off. Thinking aerobic exercise was a fad, Nike didn't take it seriously. When the company finally did produce a shoe for aerobics, it was highly functional but not attractive.

Although these missteps may appear minor, they reflect a fundamental marketing error. Nike was not in touch with the market and therefore missed a major development. In addition, it defined the motivation for athletic shoes in terms of function only, ignoring other reasons people were buying. As a result, firms such as Reebok and L. A. Gear were able to establish a foothold in the market. Meanwhile, Nike's market share of athletic shoes declined from 50% in 1980 to 22% by 1986.

To reverse the trend, Nike had to become more market-oriented. Its revamped strategy recognized consumer desires for appearance, style, and image, as well as functional performance. As Knight said at the time, "We've come around to saying that Nike is a marketing-oriented company. The design elements and functional characteristics of the product itself are just part of the overall marketing process."

Nike's new sense for the market was best reflected in signing Michael Jordan to an endorsement contract in 1985. The company developed Air Jordans, a shoe focused on the basketball category, which eventually accounted for 25% of the total sales of athletic footwear. Equally important, ads for the shoe emphasized fashion and life-style along with performance, redefining how sporting goods would be marketed. Nike's subsequent advertising also reflected an understanding of consumer motivations for purchasing athletic shoes. For example, the "Just Do It" campaign, which debuted in 1988, appealed to every person's desire to improve regardless of his or her athletic abilities.

The mid-1990s was a period of dramatic growth at Nike. The product mix was expanded to include apparel, equipment, and accessories as well as shoes specially designed for many different athletic endeavors. Nike also added new forms of promotion. It began sponsoring events from soccer matches to golf tournaments. In addition to signing famous athletes to endorsement contracts, the company became a sponsor of professional and collegiate teams. With the Nike "swoosh" logo on uniforms as well as shoes, the company was highly visible to the TV audiences of many sports contests. As a measure of Nike's effectiveness in promotion, its swoosh was recently rated as one of the best-known corporate symbols of all time. The result of these efforts was a sales explosion, from $3.8 billion in 1994 to $9.2 billion in 1997.

During this period Nike helped give birth to a tactic now known as *guerrilla marketing*. By running ads in and around events it hadn't paid to sponsor, Nike was able to garner much of the goodwill that sponsorship generates. It became so adept at this technique that at the 1998 Winter Olympics, 73% of people surveyed thought Nike was an official sponsor, even though it wasn't.

A Victim of Its Own Success

While Nike was experiencing this spectacular success, several converging events spelled trouble. For example:

- Factories in Southeast Asia, where many of Nike's shoes are made, were targeted for human rights violations. Nike initially denied the claims but later acknowledged that factories operated by independent contractors had mistreated employees and had permitted unhealthy working conditions to exist.

- Fashion preferences began moving toward hiking boots and casual leather shoes and away from athletic shoes. Nike discovered how fickle fashion can be. As teens' tastes switched from denim to khaki, their preferences in shoes also changed. Nike was not the only athletic shoe firm to suffer. Reebok and other companies in the industry experienced sales declines that resulted in management shake-ups and cost cutting. Nike continued to dominate the category, but athletic shoe sales as a proportion of all shoe sales declined substantially. The results of an annual Young & Rubicam survey of teens' preferred brands is symptomatic of the change in preference. For years Nike regularly showed up as one of the top firms, but it dropped off in 1997 and hasn't reappeared.

- Nontraditional "extreme" sports became increasingly influential with teens. Similar to the way it overlooked the growing importance of aerobics in the 1980s, Nike was unprepared for the impact of sports such as snowboarding, skateboarding, and mountain biking. The antiestablishment aura surrounding extreme sports struck a nerve with teens. As a result, the participants have become fashion trendsetters. Unfortunately for Nike, the company had neither a presence nor credibility with this group.

- Nike went years without a major technological advance in its athletic shoes, even though both the number of styles and prices continued to increase.

Nike comes up with as many as 350 new shoe designs a year, but in the minds of many consumers its last significant improvement was installing cushioning air bags in shoes, introduced in 1987. According to an industry consultant, "Nike stopped selling shoes and began selling cool in the late 1980s."

- As the firm increased its product lines, it experienced a number of highly publicized blunders that damaged its image. Nike's position on new products is to only enter areas where it can provide a significant innovation. In athletic equipment, however, innovators must contend with tradition and the performance trade-offs a new design or material can produce. For example, some ill-fated Nike efforts include a baseball glove made of synthetic material (too unconventional), a lighter hockey stick (that split because of poor glue), and in-line roller skates (with wheels that disintegrated). All of these problems reflected poorly on Nike as it sought to establish a reputation as a sports equipment leader.

- There was a growing disenchantment with the high salaries and behavior of some athletes, tarnishing the images of organizations and institutions associated with them. Certainly Nike has benefited from its association with Michael Jordan. However, there have been questions raised about why a man who reportedly makes over a $100 million a year in endorsements alone isn't doing more for society. Eyebrows were also raised when it was reported that Tiger Woods was being paid $60 to $80 million over five years by Nike. There appeared to be a sense of "it serves them right" in many media reports that the initial line of Tiger golf apparel by Nike, with shirts priced from $65 to $80, had performed poorly.

The result of these developments was a precipitous drop in performance for Nike. Sales declined by 8% from 1997 to 1998, and increased only slightly in 1999. On top of these weak performances, the company projected results for the foreseeable future that were less than industry observers expected. When investors responded by selling its stock, dropping Nike's value 25%, Knight recognized that the problems were serious.

The company made a number of adjustments, including trimming its work force by 1,600 employees, creating a nontraditional sports division, and developing an automatic replenishment distribution system to smooth out deliveries to retailers and reduce the frequency of stock outs. Many of the strategic moves either involve promotion or have promotional efforts associated with them.

Getting Back in the Race

Phil Knight has acknowledged that overconfidence may have contributed to Nike's recent problems. The firm's success had caused it to become complacent about costs, insular when it came to product development, and insensitive to public opinion.

Knight and his top managers are immersed in an effort to change the culture at Nike as well as the way marketing is performed. First and foremost, Nike is now listening more closely to the market. The Sporting Goods Manufacturers of America reports that three of the four activities with the greatest growth in participation between 1993 and 1997 were in-line skating, snowboarding, and roller hockey. Yet it wasn't until after a number of smaller competitors had become firmly entrenched that Nike responded with its ACG (for All Conditions Gear) brand of footwear, apparel, and equipment for extreme sports. The unit is located in a building separate from the main footwear operation at Nike headquarters, and has its own staff, budgets, and marketing plan. These moves were made to create a fresh start and to signal that this will not be "business as usual."

Intending not to be outflanked again, Nike has signed NASCAR Winston Cup champion Dale Jarrett and several other drivers to endorse a new shoe designed for race car drivers and their crews. Because the number of drivers and crew members is quite small, the Air Zoom Drive Pro DJ Nike apparently is intended to attract a following among the fans of the fastest-growing spectator sport in America.

The company is also responding to the increased participation of women in team sports. Nike has made running shoes designed for women for years, and began a strong marketing effort with Air Swoopes (a women's basketball shoe endorsed by Sheryl Swoopes) in 1995. However, the market for women's soccer shoes was too small to attract special attention. Women participating in soccer simply bought ill-fitting, small-sized men's soccer shoes. Recently, Nike has taken the lead in both product development in women's soccer shoes and in their promotion. After carefully studying the stresses created by the motions in the sport, Nike determined that in addition to size, there are fundamental differences in men's and women's feet that require alterations in shoe design. As a result, the firm has produced a shoe made specifically for women. To promote the shoes, Nike signed Mia Hamm, considered one of the top players in the U.S. Hamm and her teammates didn't hurt Nike's cause when they won the Women's World Cup in 1999.

The vehement and persistent criticism about working conditions in Asian factories that make athletic shoes surprised Nike management. Having been an icon for so long, it was difficult for the firm to internalize the accusations. Knight's first reaction was to deflect responsibility to the independent contractors that operated the plants. However, critics pointed out that Nike paid Michael Jordan more in one year to endorse Air Jordans than its subcontractors paid the 35,000 Vietnamese who made them.

When it was clear the problems were real and Nike shared responsibility for them, the firm began to act. A vice president for corporate responsibility was hired, and a staff of 95 was soon in place. The company insisted on better working conditions in the plants making its shoes and in the plants supplying shoe pieces to its subcontractors, tougher rules to ensure workers were receiving appropriate wages, and more oversight of subcontractors' production operations by Nike employees. Nike also invited some independent monitoring of the manufacturing plants.

To counteract the bad publicity, Nike has made good use of public relations. For example, it has publicized the changes in the production facilities that are described above. In addition, Nike has undertaken other efforts to improve its image. For example, the firm initiated a literacy program for workers in Indonesia, and invited two independently selected students from the University of Arizona, a locus of criticism, to make an all-expenses-paid tour of overseas factories. Nike committed to posting on its website the students' unedited reports on what they had learned.

Several Nike ads have drawn acclaim. From its "Just Do It" campaign to the recent "I Can" series, the ads have attempted to go beyond product function and relate to the values of the audience. However, in attempting to reach today's younger generation, Nike had to get over some hurdles. One was its lack of a presence on the Web. In the summer of 1998, Knight brought together a group of Internet experts to begin the education of Nike employees. Now the firm has an effective website that it uses to communicate its updated positioning, display its full range of products, and sell personalized apparel to consumers.

To reach the Web-savvy consumers in its audience, Nike developed ads that integrate television with the Web in a new way. The TV ads, featuring sprinter Marion Jones, baseball star Mark McGwire, and snowboarder Rob Kingwill, are seen from the viewer's perspective. The action ends in a cliff-hanger situation, and viewers are urged to go to "www.whatever.nike.com" to see the ending.

Visitors to the site can select from seven possible outcomes. According to the ad agency's creative director, the ads are trying to "take a 30-second experience and turn it into a 15-to-20-minute experience" where the consumers can receive a strong selling message for Nike products.

Another problem in reaching the youth market stemmed from Nike's success over the years. The Nike swoosh logo simply became too common. According to a marketing consultant, "Generation Y wants a sense of having discovered [a product] themselves." When they see the swoosh everywhere, and especially when they see it on their parents' and grandparents' clothes, they are likely to reject the brand as not for them. To counteract this effect, Nike is using the swoosh more selectively.

Will these efforts bring Nike back to the glory years? One analyst contends that athletic shoemakers "may have to come to grips with the fact that prospects for long-term growth are fairly modest." If she is correct, and the industry has hit the mature stage in its life cycle, then promotion will certainly play a major role in determining which firms succeed in the bell lap.

Questions

1. What is the role of promotion in a consumer-product company such as Nike?

2. What are some appropriate promotional objectives for Nike?

3. Are there other promotional methods Nike should consider in order to reassert itself in the athletic shoe industry?

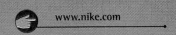 www.nike.com

Sources: Louise Lee, "Can Nike Still Do It?" *Business Week,* Feb. 21, 2000, pp. 120–128; James Pilcher, "Extreme Sports Dominate Gear Market," *Associated Press Online,* Feb. 11, 2000; Lee Gomes, "Nike Forecasts Disappointing Sales as Outlets for Sneakers Dwindle," *The Wall Street Journal,* Feb. 9, 2000, p. B10; Matt Carmichael, "Nike Integration on TV, Online a Strong Lesson," *Advertising Age,* Jan. 31, 2000, p. 74; Pila Martinez, "Nike Asks UA Protesters to Tour Overseas Shoe Factories," *The Arizona Daily Star,* Nov. 7, 1999, p. 4B; Julie Schmit, "Nike's Image Problem after Global Outcry, Company Makes Strides to Improve," *USA Today,* Oct. 4, 1999, p. 1B; William C. Symonds and Louise Lee, "They're Running as Fast as They Can," *Business Week,* July 12, 1999, pp. 106–108; Joan O'C. Hamilton, "A Shoe of One's Own," *Business Week,* May 24, 1999, pp. 62–64; and Dottie Enrico, "Nike Hopes to Regain Sales Footing with New Ads," *USA Today,* Dec. 29, 1997, p. 3B.

Managing the Marketing Effort

Planning and then implementing a company's marketing program, evaluating its performance, and examining the two-way connection between marketing and the information economy as well as the impact of information technology on marketing

Up to this point, we have dealt separately with how a firm selects its target markets and then develops and manages the four elements of its marketing mix for those markets. Now we bring those separate areas together as we present an overview of an organization's *total* marketing program.

We will apply the basic management process to a company's marketing program. The planning stage, including various types

and methods of planning, will be covered in Chapter 20. Then the implementation and evaluation stages of the management process will be discussed in Chapter 21. In the final chapter, we will consider the role of marketing in the new information economy as well as the impact of burgeoning information and advancing technologies on marketing, with particular attention given to the Internet and electronic commerce.

Strategic Marketing Planning

The company's mission is "to establish Starbucks as the premier purveyor of the finest coffee in the world while maintaining our uncompromising principles as we grow."

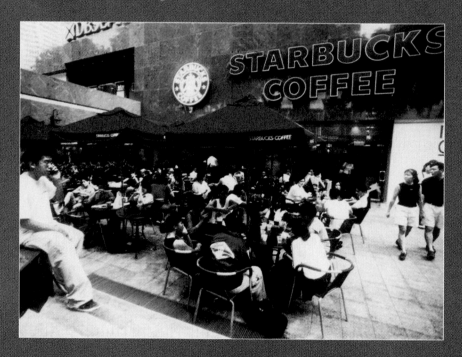

Can **Starbucks** Continue to Brew Plans for Profitable Growth?

Seattle has long been known for its rainy weather. Recently, it has developed a reputation for "grunge" bands and the best coffee in America. That last distinction is due in no small part to Starbucks, which opened its first coffee bar in Seattle in 1971. Named after the first mate in *Moby Dick,* the chain attacked the retail coffee market with all the enthusiasm of the original Starbuck and his fellow crew members. Within 10 years, it had expanded to five outlets, a roasting plant, and a wholesaling business. The outlets feature a variety of coffees, including blends of the day, lattés, mochas, and cappuccinos. The coffee can be iced or flavored with syrups, whatever suits the customer.

In 1982, Starbucks hired Howard Schultz to manage retail sales and marketing. Not long after, he left to open his own coffee bars. After acquiring more operating experience and financial resources, he bought Starbucks for $4 million, and became its chairman and CEO.

The company's mission is "to establish Starbucks as the premier purveyor of the finest coffee in the world while maintaining our uncompromising principles as we grow." Those principles relate to high standards for its coffee, a great work environment, diversity, satisfied customers, profitability, and giving back to the community and the environment. In addition, the company set the objective of being the most recognized and respected brand in the world. To achieve this ambition, Starbucks plans to increase its number of locations and develop new products and channels that capitalize on the Starbucks name.

To fulfill its mission, Schultz guided the company in a number of different ways. He began by creating an enviable package of training and benefits, including a free pound of coffee per week, all available to every worker. Schultz believes that happy employees lead to satisfied customers and repeat business. This must be true because according to one analyst, "Ten percent of their customers come in twice a day. That's a pretty remarkable figure for a retailer."

Starbucks aimed to capture the majority of a city's retail coffee market before moving on to the next locale. Schultz could have expanded Starbucks more quickly. For instance, he had inquiries from hundreds of people eager to own a Starbucks franchise. "We turned them down so we would not dilute the integrity of the product and our people," he said. Some critics thought Starbucks was moving too slowly, particularly on the East Coast where competitors were becoming entrenched. But Schultz stuck to his plan for careful growth.

While spreading gradually throughout North America, Starbucks began overseas expansion, beginning with East Asia. It opened its first locations in Tokyo and Singapore in 1996 and had almost 400 foreign outlets by the late 1990s. Starbucks acquired the United Kingdom's leading specialty coffee retailer, Seattle Coffee Company, in 1998, and announced plans to establish 500 stores in Europe by 2003. At the end of the century, 2,200 Starbucks around the world produced sales exceeding $1.5 billion and net income over $100 million.

Over the years, Starbucks slowly added new channels of distribution. In 1988, it debuted a mail-order catalog. Through a partnership with Host Marriott, Starbucks opened its first airport location at Sea-Tac International in 1991. Starbucks also created relationships with hotels and airlines to serve its coffee, established coffee bars in Barnes & Noble bookstores, and announced its intention to open outlets in more than 100 Albertson's supermarkets. Further, Starbucks formed a partnership with Kraft Foods to sell its whole-bean and ground coffee through grocery stores. Schultz explained the company's strategy by saying, "Our goal is to make our coffee available where people shop, travel, play, and work so it bursts into the national consciousness." Some critics said the brand was being diluted.

Starbucks was slow to develop its Internet strategy. In 1998, it introduced its website but did very little to promote it. A year later, Starbucks said it would invest millions of dollars to create a "life-style portal" that would link to a number of other Web pages selling everything from gourmet foods to home furnishings. Citing the $100 billion opportunity in these categories, Schultz explained that the website would use Starbucks' brand equity to attract customers and sell merchandise that complemented their life-styles.[1]

Over the years, has Starbucks developed sound and consistent plans?

 www.starbucks.com

In this chapter we'll examine how a company, including Starbucks, plans its total marketing program. After studying this chapter, you should be able to explain:

- The nature and scope of planning and how it fits within the management process.
- Similarities and differences among mission, objectives, strategies, and tactics.
- The essential difference between strategic company planning and strategic marketing planning.
- The steps involved in strategic marketing planning.
- The purpose and contents of an annual marketing plan.
- Similarities and differences as well as weaknesses and strengths across several models used in strategic planning.

As the Starbucks case suggests, success for any organization requires skillful marketing management. The *marketing* part of the term *marketing management* was defined in Chapter 1, but what about the *management* part? **Management** is the process of planning, implementing, and evaluating the efforts of a group of people working toward a common goal. In this chapter we provide an overview of the management process and examine planning in some detail. In the next chapter, we will cover implementation and evaluation, the other two steps in the management process.

Planning as Part of Management

The management process, as applied to marketing, consists basically of (1) planning a marketing program, (2) implementing it, and (3) evaluating its performance. This process is illustrated in Figure 20.1.

The *planning* stage includes setting goals and designing strategies and tactics to reach these goals. The *implementation* stage entails forming and staffing the marketing organization and directing the actual operation of the organization according to the plan. The *evaluation* stage consists of analyzing past performance in relation to organizational goals.[2] This third stage indicates the interrelated, ongoing nature of the management process. That is, the results of this stage are used in *planning* goals and strategies for future periods. So the cycle continues.

The Nature of Planning

"If you don't know where you're going, any road will get you there." The point of this axiom is that all organizations need both general and specific plans to be successful. Management should first decide what it intends to accomplish as a total organization and develop a strategic plan to achieve these results. Based on this

Figure 20.1

The management process in marketing.

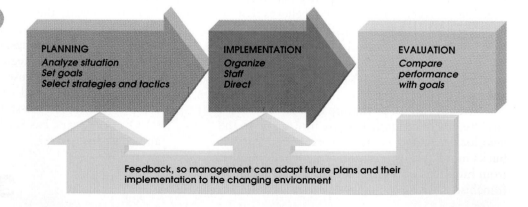

PLANNING
Analyze situation
Set goals
Select strategies and tactics

IMPLEMENTATION
Organize
Staff
Direct

EVALUATION
Compare performance with goals

Feedback, so management can adapt future plans and their implementation to the changing environment

A small firm, Idus Howard Inc., used advertising and personal selling to market custom logo merchandise and then received orders by phone and fax. But then it changed its name and approach to marketing. Now, as eCompanyStore.com, it focuses on larger accounts and sells online. Potential customers are presented two options for ordering merchandise, depending on the size of their companies.

www.ecompanystore.com

overall plan, each division of the organization should determine what its own plans will be. Of course, the role of marketing in these plans needs to be considered.

If planning is so important, exactly what is it? Quite simply, **planning** is deciding now what we are going to do later, including how and when we are going to do it. Without a plan, we cannot get things done effectively and efficiently, because we don't know what needs to be done or how to do it. In **strategic planning,** managers match an organization's resources with its market opportunities over the long run.

The fact that strategic planning has a long-run perspective does not mean that plans can be developed or executed in a sluggish manner. Years ago, the term **strategic window** was suggested to describe the limited amount of time in which a firm's resources coincide with a particular market opportunity.[3] Typically, the "window" is open only temporarily. Thus a firm must be able to move rapidly and decisively when a strategic window opens.

Recently, an online enterprise, eCompanyStore.com, saw a strategic window in which it could multiply its sales volume. The firm, which sells promotional products such as clothing and glassware with company logos imprinted on them, had switched from traditional methods to a reliance on online selling. To concentrate on large customers, eCompanyStore.com even made the painful decision to not serve its existing small customers. In two years, the firm secured 30 customers for which it has built websites that each customer uses to purchase substantial quantities of various promotional products displaying its own logo.[4]

Essential Planning Concepts

Besides the terms introduced above, you also need to become familiar with other basic terms used in discussing marketing management, especially in the planning phase.

Mission

An organization's **mission** states what customers it serves, what needs it satisfies, and what types of products it offers. A mission statement indicates, in general terms, the boundaries for an organization's activities.

A mission statement should be neither too broad and vague nor too narrow and specific. To say that a firm's mission is "to benefit American consumers" is too vague; to state that its purpose is "to make tennis balls" is too narrow. Neither statement outlines meaningful benefits for customers or provides much guidance to management. Unless the firm's purpose is clear to executives, strategic planning will likely result in disagreement and confusion.

Traditionally, companies stated their missions in product-oriented terms, such as "We make furnaces" (or telephones, or tennis rackets). Today, firms abiding by the marketing concept express their mission in customer-oriented terms. Executives should think about the needs they are satisfying and the benefits they are providing. Thus, instead of "We make furnaces," Lennox Company's statement of mission should be "We provide home climate control." Recall that Table 1.1 illustrated market-oriented ways of stating a company's mission.

Objectives and Goals

We treat *objectives* and *goals* as synonyms. An **objective** is simply a desired outcome. Effective planning must begin with a set of objectives that are to be achieved by carrying out plans. To be worthwhile and workable, objectives should be:

- Clear and specific.
- Stated in writing.
- Ambitious, but realistic.
  Consider these examples:

- Consistent with one another.
- Quantitatively measurable when possible.
- Tied to a particular time period.

Weak (too general)		Workable
Increase our market share.	→	Increase our market share to 25% next year from its present 20% level.
Improve our company's public image.	→	Receive favorable recognition awards next year from at least three consumer or environmental groups.

Strategies and Tactics

The term *strategy* was originally applied to the art of military generalship. In business, a **strategy** is a broad plan of action by which an organization intends to reach its objectives and, in turn, to fulfill its mission. In marketing, the relationship between objectives and strategies may be illustrated as follows:

Objectives		Possible Strategies
Increase sales next year by 10% over this year's figure.	→	1. Intensify marketing efforts in domestic markets. 2. Expand into foreign markets.

Two organizations might have the same objective but use different strategies to reach it. For instance, both firms might aim to increase their market shares by 20% over the next three years. To do that, one firm in, say, the packaged-foods industry might intensify its efforts in household markets; a competing firm might concentrate on expanding into institutional markets (for example, food service organizations). Conversely, two organizations might have different objectives but select the same strategy to reach them.

A **tactic** is a means by which a strategy is implemented. A tactic is a more specific, detailed course of action than a strategy. Also, tactics generally cover shorter time periods than strategies. Here's an illustration:

Strategy		Tactics
Direct our promotion to males, ages 25–40.	→	1. Advertise in magazines read by this group of people. 2. Sponsor events attended and watched on TV by this group.

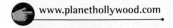
www.planethollywood.com

To be effective, a tactic must coincide with and support the strategy with which it is related. That's sometimes difficult to do, as Planet Hollywood found out. A key strategy for the restaurant chain was a theme built around celebrities, many of whom were investors in the business. A related tactic was frequent appearances at the restaurants by stars and other well-known personalities. However, most celebrities didn't want to interact with the public. Equally damaging, the restaurants' food was generally poor. As a result, Planet Hollywood is in danger of disappearing from this planet.[5]

Key Questions for an Organization

The concepts of mission, objectives, strategies, and tactics raise important questions that must be answered by an organization seeking success in business or, more specifically, in marketing. These questions can be summarized as follows:

Concept		Question
Mission	→	What business are we in?
Objectives	→	What do we want to accomplish?
Strategies	→	In *general* terms, how are we going to get the job done?
Tactics	→	In *specific* terms, how are we going to get the job done?

Scope of Planning

Planning may cover long or short periods. Strategic planning is usually long range, spanning 3, 5, 10, or (infrequently) even more years. It requires the participation of top management and often involves a planning staff.

Long-range planning deals with company-wide issues such as expanding or contracting production, markets, and product lines. For example, all firms in the home appliance industry must look ahead for at least a decade to identify key markets, plan new products, and update production technologies.

Short-range planning typically covers one year or less and is the responsibility of middle- and lower-level managers. It focuses on such issues as determining which target markets will receive special attention and the specific composition of the marketing mix. Looking again at the home appliance industry, Whirlpool annually decides which target markets it will concentrate on and whether its marketing mixes for each of these markets need to be changed. Naturally, short-range plans must be compatible with the organization's long-range intentions.

Planning the marketing strategies in a firm should be conducted on three different levels:

- *Strategic company planning.* At this level management defines an organization's mission, sets long-range goals, and formulates broad strategies to achieve these goals. Company-wide goals and strategies then become the framework for planning in the firm's different functional areas, such as production, finance, human resources, research and development, *and* marketing.

- *Strategic marketing planning.* The top marketing executives set goals and strategies for an organization's marketing effort. Strategic *marketing* planning obviously should be coordinated with *company-wide* planning.

- *Annual marketing planning.* Short-term plans should be prepared for a firm's major functions. Covering a specific period, usually one year, the annual marketing plan is based on the firm's strategic marketing planning.

Attitudes toward strategic planning seem to run in cycles. From the mid-1960s through the 1970s, strategic planning was highly valued in large corporations. Then, during the 1980s and most of the 1990s, the focus shifted to implementation and evaluation—especially efforts to boost efficiency and profitability. Now strategic planning seems to be back in favor—especially as it relates to global

Figure 20.2

Three levels of organizational planning.

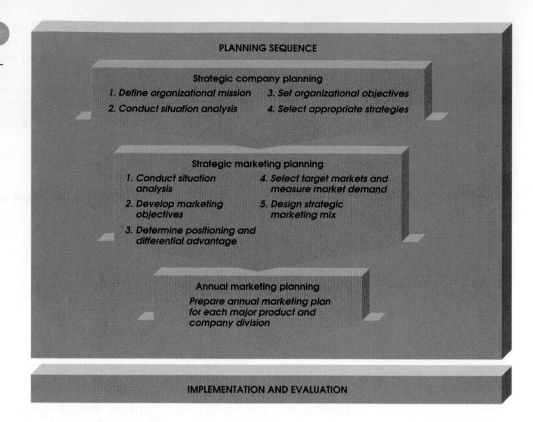

expansion. In fact, in a recent survey, 27% of high-level corporate executives ranked strategic planning as the most important business function. Only product development, placed on top by 29% of the participants, ranked higher.[6]

Strategic Company Planning

Strategic company planning consists of four essential steps:

1. Define the organizational mission.
2. Analyze the situation.
3. Set organizational objectives.
4. Select strategies to achieve these objectives.

The process is shown in the top part of Figure 20.2. The first step, *defining the organizational mission,* influences all subsequent planning. For some firms, this step requires only reviewing the existing mission statement and confirming that it is still suitable. Still, this straightforward step is too often ignored.

Conducting a situation analysis, the second step, is vital because strategic planning is influenced by many factors beyond and within an organization. By **situation analysis,** we simply mean gathering and studying information pertaining to one or more specified aspects of an organization. We'll talk more about conducting a situation analysis in an upcoming section.

The third step in strategic company planning, *deciding on a set of objectives,* guides the organization in fulfilling its mission. Objectives also provide standards for evaluating an organization's performance.

By this point in its strategic planning, the organization has determined where it wants to go. The fourth step, *selecting appropriate strategies,* indicates how the firm is going to get there. **Organizational strategies** represent broad plans of action by which an organization intends to achieve its goals and fulfill its mission. Strategies are selected either for the entire company if it is small and has only a single product, or for each division if the company is large and has multiple products or units.

Do companies actually engage in strategic planning and then prepare a written plan? The results of one survey indicated that almost 70% of firms had strategic plans in place; among them, nearly 90% believed their strategic plans had been effective. However, according to a more recent survey, only 12% of small firms (those with fewer than 500 employees) had a long-range plan in writing. In fact, almost 60% of these companies had no written plans.[7]

• Strategic Marketing Planning

After conducting strategic planning for the organization as a whole, management needs to lay plans for each major functional area, such as marketing or production. Of course, planning for each function should be guided by the organization-wide mission and objectives.

Strategic marketing planning is a five-step process:

1. Conduct a situation analysis.
2. Develop marketing objectives.
3. Determine positioning and differential advantage.
4. Select target markets and measure market demand.
5. Design a strategic marketing mix.

These five steps are shown in the middle of Figure 20.2, indicating how they relate to the four steps of strategic company planning. Each step is discussed below.

Situation Analysis

The first step in strategic marketing planning, **situation analysis,** involves analyzing where the company's marketing program has been, how it has been doing, and what it is likely to face in the years ahead. Doing this enables management to determine if it is necessary to revise the old plans or devise new ones to achieve the company's objectives.

Situation analysis normally covers external environmental forces and internal nonmarketing resources that were discussed in Chapter 2. A situation analysis also considers the groups of consumers served by the company, the strategies used to satisfy them, and key measures of marketing performance. Due attention should be given to identifying and assessing competitors. In particular, a firm should study competitors serving the same markets it serves. Also, as stressed by two consultants, it's important to "get out of the box"—that is, to develop new perspectives on the organization's core activities and to question assumptions about how the organization does business (assumptions such as "we must offer competitive prices").[8]

As the basis for planning decisions, situation analysis is critical. But it can be costly, time-consuming, and frustrating. For example, it is usually difficult to extract timely, accurate information from the "mountains" of data compiled during a situation analysis. Moreover, some valuable information, such as sales or market-share figures for competitors, is often unavailable.

As part of a situation analysis, many organizations perform a **SWOT assessment.** In this activity, a firm identifies and evaluates its most significant *s*trengths, *w*eaknesses, *o*pportunities, and *t*hreats. To fulfill its mission, an organization needs to capitalize on its key strengths, overcome or alleviate its major weaknesses, avoid significant threats, and take advantage of the most promising opportunities.

We're referring to strengths and weaknesses in an organization's own capabilities. For example, a strength of Sears is its large size, which gives it—among other things—clout in dealing with suppliers. However, a weakness is its comparatively high operating expenses, which makes it difficult for Sears to compete on the basis of low prices.

Opportunities and threats often originate outside the organization. According to Radio Shack's chief executive, advances in computing and telecommunications technologies give the chain the opportunity to become the "home connectivity store." Radio Shack intends to sell consumers various high-tech products and also provide installation and support services. But a threat is the variety of competitors, ranging from competing chains such as CompUSA to telecommunications giants such as AT&T, that have similar intentions.[9]

www.radioshack.com

Marketing Objectives

The next step in strategic marketing planning is to *determine marketing objectives*. Marketing goals should be closely related to company-wide goals and strategies. In fact, a *company strategy* often translates into a *marketing goal*. For example, to reach an organizational objective of a 20% return on investment next year, one organizational strategy might be to reduce marketing costs by 15%. This company strategy would become a marketing goal. In turn, converting all sales people from salaried compensation to a commission basis might be one of the marketing strategies adopted to achieve this marketing goal.

We already know that strategic planning involves matching an organization's resources with its market opportunities. With this in mind, each objective should be assigned a priority based on its urgency and potential impact on the marketing area and, in turn, the organization. Then resources should be allocated in line with these priorities.[10]

Positioning and Differential Advantage

The third step in strategic marketing planning actually involves two complementary decisions: *how to position a product in the marketplace* and *how to distin-*

In contrast to large cruise ships, Windjammer Barefoot Cruises positions its product as a more informal, less crowded vacation. Windjammer's "tall ships," each an actual working ship with a unique history, accommodate either 64 or 128 vacationers. The ships meander throughout the Caribbean Sea, sailing primarily at night and stopping at various islands in the region during the day.

www.windjammer.com

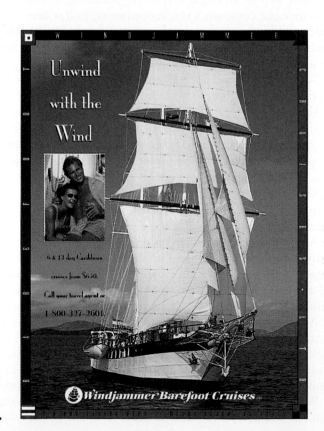

Each year in the U.S., the average person consumes 65 to 70 pounds of beef. Is this good news for beef producers? Not really. Per-capita consumption of beef, depending on the statistics you look at, either was stagnant throughout the 1990s or rose slightly from 1993 on. However, demand for pork has risen to about 55 pounds per person annually, although the rate of growth has slowed recently. Even more significant, demand for chicken has skyrocketed to nearly 80 pounds per person, an increase of 70% since 1980.

Clearly, beef producers face a marketing challenge. The pork industry was at a similar crossroads in the 1980s. Following extensive consumer research, pork producers decided to reposition their product as "the other white meat." The campaign successfully positioned pork closer to chicken, which has a healthful image in the minds of consumers, and further away from beef, which is perceived less favorably. The only problem was that the campaign didn't give much of a boost to pork consumption. So now, in an updated cam-paign, pork producers are promoting pork's pleasing taste.

Coming up with a real differential advantage for beef is more difficult, however. The latest strategy, backed by a new $30 million marketing campaign, is to emphasize convenience and nutrition. At the same time, the beef industry is in the test kitchen working on new easy-to-prepare products. How about a cheeseburger loaf that can be sliced, or veal bacon? Would you try strips of all-beef hot dogs that are dipped in batter, deep fried, and served with condiments? If beef producers have their way, new products such as these will be in supermarkets and concession stands soon.

What is—or could be—beef's differential advantage in relation to pork and chicken?

Sources: "Love That Steak!" *Business Week*, Feb. 14, 2000, p. 10; Howard Riell, "Convenience & Nutrition," *Supermarket Business*, Dec. 15, 1999, p. 90; Gary Strauss, "Stewing in a Tough Market," *USA Today*, July 8, 1999, p. 1B; and Daniel Rosenberg, "Pork Is Tasty, Say National Ads That Shift Focus from Nutrition," *The Wall Street Journal*, Aug. 13, 1997, p. B5.

guish it from competitors. As described in Chapters 6 and 9, **positioning** refers to a product's image in relation to directly competitive products as well as other products marketed by the same company. For example, a Canadian company is trying to win over U.S. consumers by promoting the dreadful taste of its cough syrup! Because Buckley's Mixture doesn't use sugar or alcohol to overcome the chemical taste, it uses the slogan: "It tastes awful. And it works."[11]

www.buckleys.com

After the product is positioned, a viable differential advantage has to be identified. **Differential advantage** refers to any feature of an organization or brand perceived by customers to be desirable and different from those of the competition. Some dry cleaning outlets have sought an advantage by using petroleum-based solvents rather than the traditional cleaning agent, which is toxic and may cause cancer.[12]

Besides striving for a differential advantage, a company has to avoid a **differential disadvantage** for its product. Returning to the dry cleaning example, the outlets using the cleaning agents that are less harmful to the environment have to offer competitive prices. Otherwise, they risk having a price *dis*advantage, which could negate the advantage gained by using an alternative cleaning method.

The concepts of differential advantage and differential disadvantage apply to both goods and services and, in some areas such as retailing, to entire firms. One consultant believes that retailers can gain a differential advantage by developing one or more of four *est* dimensions—that is, the cheap*est* prices, the bigg*est* assortments, the hott*est* (most fashionable) merchandise, the easi*est* store to shop in. Nordstrom doesn't compete based on low prices but it excelled in the other three areas, although it has stumbled a bit in recent years. Conversely, a firm risks a differential *dis*advantage if it is only average or "pretty good" on these four dimensions.[13]

Target Markets and Market Demand

Selecting target markets is the fourth step in marketing planning. As covered in earlier chapters, a **market** consists of people or organizations with needs to satisfy, money to spend, and the willingness to spend it. For example, many people favor air travel, and are both able and willing to pay for it. However, this large group is made up of a number of segments (that is, parts of markets) with various preferences. Because an organization typically cannot satisfy all segments with different needs, it is wise to concentrate on one or more of these segments. Thus a **target market** refers to a group of people or organizations at which a firm directs a marketing program.

To analyze its opportunities, a firm must forecast demand (that is, sales) in its target markets, as discussed in Chapter 6. The results of demand forecasting indicate whether the firm's targets are worth pursuing, or whether alternative segments need to be considered.

Marketing Mix

For each target market, management must design a **marketing mix,** which is the combination of multiple aspects of the following four elements: a product, how it is distributed and promoted, and its price. These four elements, which were covered in detail in Chapters 8 through 19, are intended to please the target market(s) and, equally important, achieve the organization's marketing objectives.

Each marketing-mix element contains countless alternatives. Further, decisions regarding one element affect the others. Marketing decision makers need to consider these options and interactions when designing a marketing mix that will be directed to a particular target market. Here's an illustration of a customer satisfying marketing mix. Founded in the mid-1980s, Midwest Express Airlines focuses on business travelers. Midwest's basic product is air travel, of course, but it offers several enhancements, including leather seats with no more than two on a side, full in-flight dinners, and fresh-baked chocolate chip cookies served on afternoon flights. Midwest uses the industry's standard methods for promoting and distributing its service, and it matches competitors' coach fares—while providing what amounts to business-class service. As a result, since it was founded in the mid-1980s, Midwest has grown steadily to become the 17th largest carrier in the U.S.[14]

www.midwestexpress.com

Annual Marketing Planning

Besides strategic planning for several years into the future, more specific, shorter-term planning is also vital. Thus strategic marketing planning in an organization leads to the preparation of an annual marketing plan, as shown in the bottom part of Figure 20.2. An **annual marketing plan** is the master blueprint for a year's marketing activity for a specified organizational division or major product. It is a written document.

A separate plan normally should be prepared for each major product and company division. Sometimes, depending on a company's circumstances, separate plans are developed for key brands and important target markets. As the name implies, an annual marketing plan usually covers one year. There are exceptions, however. Because of the seasonal nature of some products or markets, it may be advisable to prepare plans for shorter time periods. For fashionable clothing, plans are made for each season, lasting just several months. The planning horizon is even shorter in today's information economy. As noted in a recent article, "On the Internet, companies have to be ready to change goals or strategies virtually overnight."[15]

Purposes and Responsibilities

An annual marketing plan serves several purposes:

- It summarizes the marketing strategies and tactics that will be used to achieve specified objectives in the upcoming year. Thus it becomes the "how-to-do-it" document that guides executives and other employees involved in marketing.

- The plan also points to what needs to be done with respect to the other steps in the management process—namely, implementation and evaluation of the marketing program.

- Moreover, the plan outlines who is responsible for which activities, when they are to be carried out, and how much time and money can be spent.

The executive responsible for the division or product covered by the plan typically prepares it. Of course, all or part of the task may be delegated to subordinates. Preparation of an annual marketing plan may begin nine months or more before the start of the period covered by the plan. Early work includes necessary research and arranging other information sources. The bulk of the work occurs one to three months prior to the plan's starting date. The last steps are to have the plan reviewed and approved by upper management. Some revision may be necessary before final approval is granted. The final version of the plan, or relevant parts of it, should be shared with all employees who will be involved in implementing the agreed-upon strategies and tactics.

Recommended Contents

Annual marketing planning follows a sequence similar to strategic marketing planning. However, annual planning has a shorter time frame and is more specific—both with respect to the issues addressed and to the plans laid. Still, as shown in Table 20.1, the major sections in an annual plan are similar to the steps in strategic marketing planning.[16]

In an annual marketing plan, more attention can be devoted to tactical details than is feasible in other levels of planning. As an example, strategic marketing

---

Table 20.1 Contents of an Annual Marketing Plan

1. **Executive Summary.** In this one- or two-page section, the thrust of the plan is described and explained. It is intended for executives who desire an overview of the plan but need not be knowledgeable about the details.

2. **Situation Analysis.** Essentially, the marketing program for a major division of a company (called a strategic business unit) or product covered by the plan is examined within the context of pertinent past, present, and future conditions. Much of this section might be derived from the results of strategic marketing planning. Additional information of particular relevance to a one-year planning period may be included in this section.

3. **Objectives.** The objectives in an annual plan are more specific than those produced by strategic marketing planning. However, annual objectives must help achieve organizational goals and strategic marketing goals.

4. **Strategies.** As in strategic marketing planning, the strategies in an annual plan should indicate which target markets are going to be satisfied through a combination of product, price, distribution, and promotion.

5. **Tactics.** Specific activities, sometimes called action plans, are devised for carrying out each major strategy included in the preceding section. For ease of understanding, strategies and tactics may be covered together. Tactics specifically answer the questions of *what, who,* and *how* for the company's marketing efforts.

6. **Financial Schedules.** This section normally includes two kinds of financial information: projected sales, expenses, and profits in what's called a pro forma financial statement; and the amounts of resources dedicated to different activities in one or more budgets.

7. **Timetable.** This section, often including a diagram, answers the question of *when* various marketing activities will be carried out during the upcoming year.

8. **Evaluation Procedures.** This section addresses the questions of *what, who, how,* and *when* connected with measuring performance against goals, both during and at the end of the year. The results of evaluations during the year may lead to adjustments in the plan's strategies and/or tactics or even the objectives to be achieved.

planning might stress personal selling within the marketing mix. If so, the annual plan might recommend increased college recruiting as a source of additional sales people.

An annual marketing plan actually relates to all three steps of the management process, not just planning. That is, sections 5 through 7 deal with implementation and section 8 is concerned with evaluation. To increase the likelihood of careful review, some firms limit annual marketing plans to a certain specified length, such as 20 pages.

Selected Planning Models

Over the past three decades, a number of frameworks or tools—we'll call them *models*—have been designed to assist with strategic planning. Most of these models can be used with both strategic company planning *and* strategic marketing planning. In this section, therefore, we briefly discuss several planning models that have received ample attention in recent years. First, however, you need to be familiar with a form of organization, the strategic business unit, that pertains to these planning models.

Strategic Business Units

Most large and medium-sized companies—and even some smaller firms—consist of multiple units and produce numerous products. In such diversified firms, company-wide planning cannot serve as an effective guide for executives who oversee the organization's various divisions. The Philip Morris Company provides an example. The mission, objectives, and strategies in its tobacco division are—and must be—quite different from those in the Miller Brewing or Kraft Foods divisions.

Consequently, for more effective planning and operations, a multibusiness or multiproduct organization should be divided according to its major markets or products. Each such entity is called a **strategic business unit (SBU)**. Each SBU may be a major division in an organization, a group of related products, or even a single major product or brand.

To be identified as an SBU, an entity should:

- Be a separately identifiable business.
- Have a distinct mission.
- Have its own competitors.
- Have its own executive group with profit responsibility.

The McGraw-Hill Companies, as suggested by this ad, serves a variety of markets, ranging from executives to school children. Its business, simply stated, is "keeping the world up to speed" by providing customers with needed information in various forms, including print, CD-ROM, online, and television. As you may have noticed, this textbook is a product of Irwin/McGraw-Hill, a division of the McGraw-Hill Companies.

 www.mcgraw-hill.com

Some very important financial people depend on us for information. Not to mention your 9-year-old.

Around the world, teachers of all levels depend on us to help shape curricula. But it hardly stops there. From online learning to business news to the latest credit ratings and financial analyses, The McGraw-Hill Companies gives people the knowledge to be their best at any age.

The McGraw-Hill Companies
Keeping the world up to speed.®

www.mcgraw-hill.com

The trick in setting up SBUs in an organization is to arrive at the *optimum* number. Too many can bog down top management in details associated with planning, operating, and reporting. Too few SBUs can result in each one covering too broad an area for managerial planning. SBUs for two giant companies and a nonprofit organization are as follows:

- *PepsiCo, Inc.:* Soft drinks (Pepsi-Cola Company), snack foods (Frito-Lay Company), and juices (Tropicana Products, Inc.). Several years ago, PepsiCo spun off its restaurant SBUs—consisting of KFC, Pizza Hut, and Taco Bell—to become a free-standing enterprise, named Tricon Global Restaurants, Inc.

- *The McGraw-Hill Companies, Inc.:* Educational and professional publishing, financial services, and information and media services.

- *Your university or college:* Different schools (such as business and engineering) *or* different delivery systems (such as on-campus curricula and televised courses).

Let's now consider several well-known planning models.

Product–Market Growth Matrix

Most organizations' statements of mission and objectives focus on growth—that is, a desire to increase revenues and profits. In seeking growth, a company has to consider *both* its markets and its products. Then it has to decide whether to continue doing what it is now doing—only do it better—*or* establish new ventures. The **product-market growth matrix,** first proposed by Igor Ansoff, depicts these options.[17]

Essentially, as shown in Figure 20.3, there are four product-market growth strategies:

- *Market penetration.* A company tries to sell more of its present products to its present markets. Supporting tactics might include greater spending on

Figure 20.3

Product-market growth
matrix.

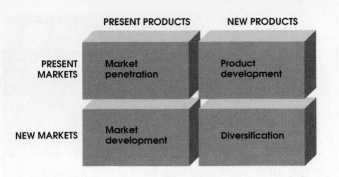

	PRESENT PRODUCTS	NEW PRODUCTS
PRESENT MARKETS	Market penetration	Product development
NEW MARKETS	Market development	Diversification

advertising or personal selling. For example, the William Wrigley Jr. Co. relies on this strategy, encouraging smokers to chew gum where smoking is prohibited. Or a company tries to become a single source of supply by offering preferential treatment to customers who will concentrate all their purchases with that company.

- *Market development.* A firm continues to sell its present products, but to a new market. About a decade ago, for instance, when the defense market softened, McDonnell Douglas devoted more resources to selling its helicopters in the commercial market. In a much different industry, cruise lines such as Carnival and Royal Caribbean are concentrating their marketing efforts on the 89% of Americans who have never taken a cruise.[18]

- *Product development.* This strategy calls for a company to develop new products to sell to its existing markets. Some ski resorts, for example, built steep, dangerous slopes in order to appeal to thrill-seeking "extreme" customers. The Wrigley company is also using this strategy by introducing mint-flavored gum aimed at teenagers. The Medical Center Pharmacy in Scottsbluff, Nebraska, expanded by offering new product lines—first, wheelchairs and hospital beds for in-home use and, subsequently, on-site repair and even custom building of these products. These moves better satisfied, and generated more revenues from, existing customers. Next, the firm moved into new geographic markets by means of a mobile showroom and repair shop.[19]

- *Diversification.* With this strategy, a company develops new products to sell to new markets. This approach is risky because it doesn't rely on either the company's successful products or its position in established markets. Sometimes it works, but sometimes it doesn't. As one example of diversification, the maker

With huge cruise ships, this industry can serve about 200,000 customers at the same time. To fill their ships, cruise lines are engaging in market development. To entice first-time customers, the cruise lines are competing more with marketers of other leisure activities than with each other.

Is international expansion a desirable growth strategy?

One of the four product-market growth strategies is to offer the firm's goods and services for sale in new markets. In this context, the additional market could be a demographic group, type of organization, or country or region of the world not served by the company.

According to one assessment, globalization is one of the most promising growth strategies at the start of the new century. Not surprisingly, therefore, that writer believes that globalization is the growth strategy that is receiving the most attention from companies at the present time. Recall that in Chapter 15, "A Global Perspective" box discussed Wal-Mart's invasion of Europe and other parts of the world, while also noting that many other retailers—such as Carrefour, the French firm—are moving far beyond their home territories. In virtually all industries, there are similar examples of international expansion and the resulting intense competition. In the auto industry, for instance, many Japanese firms are making cars, or at least key components of cars, in the U.S. Conversely, American automakers that have been selling in foreign markets for a long time are concentrating now on establishing more manufacturing facilities in other countries, most notably China.

As firms expand internationally, or consider doing so, what conditions are they likely to face around the world? A recent Delphi study (see Chapter 6 for an overview of this research technique) asked a worldwide panel of experts to predict changes in the international business environment over the next 10 years. Some of the key findings could help companies decide whether or not to adopt globalization as a growth strategy and, if so, how they should proceed:

- The Asia Pacific region is most promising in terms of growth potential. China's emergence as a major force in global business was labeled "the economic event of the decade."

- The opportunities for growth may be affected by political and/or social issues that persist or develop in specific nations.

- Services is the business sector that expects to experience the greatest change. A key cause of the transformation of the services sector is the continuing rise of the information economy, which supplies service providers with new methods of communicating with customers.

- The "hottest" issue will be the role of intellectual property. It is a growing challenge to adequately protect copyrights, patents, and trademarks, considering that it is increasingly easy to transfer technology and that many countries lack adequate laws or enforcement mechanisms. However, given that intellectual property is often a significant asset for an organization, efforts must be increased to protect intellectual property rights across national boundaries.

Sources: Anul G. Karnani, "Five Ways to Grow the Market and Create Value," *Financial Times,* Oct. 18, 1999, p. 8; and Michael R. Czinkota and Ilkka A. Ronkainen, "International Business and Trade in the Next Decade: Report from a Delphi Study," *Journal of International Business Studies,* Winter 1997, pp. 827+.

of Swatch timepieces decided to design and produce a car, nicknamed the "Swatchmobile." However, perhaps concerned about diversifying into unknown territory, the Swiss company sold its interest back to its partner, DaimlerChrysler, in early 2000.[20]

As market conditions change over time, a company may shift product-market growth strategies. For example, when its present market is fully saturated, a company may have no choice other than to pursue new markets. That's the path followed by Liz Claiborne Inc., which earned a reputation for making stylish clothing for women engaged in professional careers. Recently, the company has added new brands in order to serve a variety of target markets, especially more budget-conscious female shoppers. Today, Claiborne labels, such as Villager and Crazy Horse, can be found in a wide range of retail outlets, including Sears and Wal-Mart.[21]

 www.lizclaiborne.com

In pursuing one or more product-market growth strategies, a company seeks to build its sales and profits, of course. However, in the case of product development, it's possible that revenues rung up by new products may come at the expense of other products sold by that firm. This situation is called **cannibalization**. Eastman Kodak Co. realized that sales of its traditional films might suffer when it introduced digital-imaging products. The case introducing Chapter 8 deals with potential cannibalization—the prospect of electric vehicles taking sales away from autos powered by internal-combustion engines. And the Claiborne clothing firm, discussed above, accepted some degree of cannibalization.

Why do companies take actions that result in cannibalization? Very simply, if they don't introduce new products or channels to better serve existing customers, competitors will. If that occurs, the passive firm will lose customers and, in turn, revenues. One study focused on high-tech industries casts a favorable light on cannibalization, concluding that success with truly innovative new products requires a willingness to cannibalize in order to achieve substantial gains in the future.[22]

BCG Matrix

Developed by a management consulting firm, the Boston Consulting Group, the **BCG matrix** dates back more than 25 years.[23] Using this model, an organization classifies each of its SBUs (and, sometimes, major products) according to two factors: its market share relative to competitors, and the growth rate of the industry in which the SBU operates. When the factors are divided simply into high and low categories, a 2 × 2 grid is created, as displayed in Figure 20.4.

In turn, the four quadrants in the grid represent distinct categories of SBUs or major products. The categories differ with respect not only to market share and industry growth rate, but also to cash needs and appropriate strategies:

- *Stars*. High market shares and high industry growth rates typify SBUs in this category. However, an SBU that falls into this category poses a challenge for companies because it requires lots of cash to remain competitive in growing markets. Aggressive marketing strategies are imperative for stars to maintain or even build market share. Microsoft's Windows software package and Palm, Inc.'s "personal digital assistant" exemplify this category.

www.palm.com

Figure 20.4

The BCG matrix.

COMPANY'S MARKET SHARE

- *Cash cows.* These SBUs have high market shares and do business in mature industries (those with low growth rates). When an industry's growth diminishes, stars move into this category. Because most of their customers have been with them for some time and are still loyal, a cash cow's marketing costs are not high. Consequently, it generates more cash than can be reinvested profitably in its own operations. As a result, cash cows can be "milked" to support other SBUs that need more resources. Marketing strategies for cash cows seek to defend market share, largely by reinforcing customer loyalty. As examples, consider Bausch & Lomb's sunglasses (such as its Ray-Ban brand) and Campbell's canned soups.

- *Question marks* (sometimes called *problem children*). SBUs characterized by low market shares but high industry growth rates fit in this category. A question mark has not achieved a strong foothold in an expanding, but highly competitive, market. The question surrounding this type of SBU is whether it can gain adequate market share and be profitable. If management answers "no," then the SBU should be divested or liquidated. If management instead answers "yes," the firm must come up with the cash to build market share—more cash than the typical question mark generates from its own profits. Appropriate marketing strategies for question marks focus on creating an impact in the market by displaying a strong differential advantage and, thereby, building customer support. As will be discussed in next chapter's case, the Walt Disney Co. has been trying to attract sufficient visitors to its Go Network website. When it couldn't overtake popular general-interest portals such as Yahoo!, Disney decided to reposition Go as an entertainment and leisure Internet portal.[24]

- *Dogs.* These SBUs have low market shares and operate in industries with low growth rates. A company normally would be unwise to invest substantial funds in SBUs in this category. Marketing strategies for dogs are intended to maximize any potential profits by minimizing expenditures *or* to promote a differential advantage to build market share. The company can instead say "Enough's enough!" and divest or liquidate a dog. Even Wal-Mart has had to deal with some dogs, eventually selling its Deep Discount Store and Helen's Arts and Crafts divisions.

The portfolios of most organizations with numerous SBUs or major products include a mix of stars, cash cows, question marks, and dogs. Consider one company's situation. In the late 1990s, Pepsi-Cola's flagship brands—Pepsi, Diet Pepsi, and Mountain Dew—could be described as cash cows. A joint venture with Lipton produced a line of stars, Lipton bottled and canned iced teas. Pepsi's brand of sports drink, All Sport, was a question mark as it battled the well-entrenched Gatorade for a larger share of a growing market. Finally, Pepsi's Crystal was a

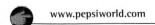
www.pepsiworld.com

dog—a failure, in fact—because demand for clear colas was sluggish and Crystal attracted few customers. In late 1998, Pepsi-Cola introduced a new diet cola, Pepsi One. Backed by a $100 million marketing campaign, the company hoped the new product would become a cash cow.[25]

In the financial arena, an investor needs a balanced portfolio with respect to risks and potential returns. Likewise, a company should seek a balanced portfolio of SBUs. Certainly, cash cows are indispensable. Stars and question marks are also integral to a balanced portfolio because products in growing markets determine a firm's long-term performance. Although dogs are undesirable, it's a rare company that doesn't have at least one.

One firm typically cannot affect the growth rate for an entire industry, however. (An exception might be the dominant firm in a fairly new, rapidly growing industry. Well-known examples are Microsoft, in operating-systems software, and Rollerblade, Inc., in the in-line roller skating market.) If growth rate cannot be influenced, companies must turn to the other factor in the BCG matrix—market share. Hence, marketing strategies based on the BCG matrix tend to concentrate on building or maintaining market share, depending on which of the four SBU categories is involved. Various strategies require differing amounts of cash, which means that management must continually allocate the firm's limited resources (notably cash) to separate marketing endeavors.

www.rollerblade.com

GE Business Screen

On the surface, the **GE business screen** appears to be very similar to the BCG matrix. This planning model, developed by General Electric with the assistance of the McKinsey consulting firm, also involves two factors and results in a grid.[26] But, as we shall see, the two models are different in significant respects.

Management can use the GE business screen to classify SBUs or major products on the basis of two factors: market attractiveness and business position. Each factor is rated according to several criteria. *Market attractiveness* should be judged with respect to market growth rate (similar to the BCG matrix), market size, degree of difficulty in entering the market, number and types of competitors, technological requirements, and profit margins, among other criteria. *Business position* encompasses market share (as in the BCG matrix), SBU size, strength of differential advantage, research and development capabilities, production capacities, cost controls, and strength of management, among others.

The criteria used to rate market attractiveness and business position are assigned different weights because some criteria are more important than others. Then each SBU is rated with respect to all criteria. Finally, overall ratings (usually numerical scores) for both factors are calculated for each SBU. On the basis of these ratings, each SBU is labeled as high, medium, or low with respect to (1) market

Figure 20.5

The GE business screen.

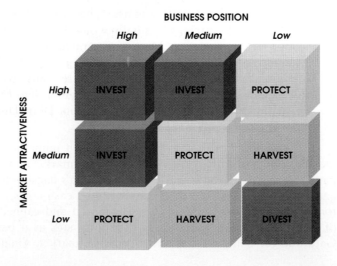

attractiveness and (2) business position. For example, an SBU may be judged as having high market attractiveness but medium business position.

Following the ratings, an organization's SBUs are plotted on a 3 × 3 grid, as illustrated in Figure 20.5. The best location for an SBU is the upper left cell because it points to (1) the most attractive market opportunity and (2) the best business position to seize that opportunity. In contrast, the worst location is the lower right cell, for the opposite reasons. The nine cells have implications with respect to how resources are allocated and, in turn, what marketing strategies are suitable.

Every organization has to make decisions about how to use its limited resources most effectively. That's where these planning models can help—determining which SBUs or major products should be stimulated for growth, which ones maintained in their present market position, and which ones eliminated. An SBU's evaluation, as indicated by its location on the GE business screen, suggests how it should be treated:

- *Invest strategy.* SBUs in the three cells in the upper left of the grid should receive ample resources. To strengthen and build these kinds of SBUs, bold, well-financed marketing efforts are needed. In late 1999, Silicon Graphics Inc. announced that it would concentrate on producing powerful server computers that are well suited for challenging technical and Internet applications. SGI's decision seemed to be based on an assessment indicating high market attractiveness and a mid-range business position. Eastman Kodak Co. is following this strategy with respect to digital cameras.[27]

- *Protect strategy.* Resources should be allocated selectively to SBUs along the diagonal running from the lower left to the upper right of the grid. This somewhat defensive approach helps an SBU maintain its present market position because it generates cash needed by other SBUs. For example, while investing in digital cameras, Kodak has also spent large sums on marketing, especially for extensive advertising campaigns, to protect its position in the color film industry.[28]

- *Harvest strategy.* Because they lack an attractive market and a strong business position, SBUs in the two cells just below the three-cell diagonal should not receive substantial new resources. Instead, expenditures should be curtailed to maximize any remaining profits. An alternative is to sell these SBUs. A case can be made that General Motors has been following this strategy with some of its brands, such as Buick and Oldsmobile, or even some models, such as full-size sedans.[29]

- *Divest strategy.* SBUs in the lower right cell do not have much going for them. Hence, an SBU in this location should not receive any resources. The best approach probably is to eliminate it from the organization's portfolio by selling it or, failing that, shutting it down. When the Gerber Products Company failed to convince adults of the benefits of Singles, pureed single-serving meals such as turkey in mornay sauce, it dropped the line.[30]

Firms typically employ more than one of these four strategies. To illustrate, after assessing its portfolio, the Kraft Foods unit of the Philip Morris Company employed a *harvest* strategy by selling some businesses that had small profit margins and/or did not fit into its core activities. Divisions sold by Kraft have included specialty oils, food service, and baking (with such brands as Entenmann's and Oroweat). The chairman of this gigantic firm labeled the divested businesses "hippopotamuses" rather than the preferred "greyhounds." Philip Morris is using the resources derived from the sales to support a *protect* strategy for key brands such as Maxwell House, Oscar Mayer, and Jell-O.[31]

Assessment of the Planning Models

Each of these planning models has been praised and criticized.[32] Although each is somewhat distinctive, all share some common limitations and benefits.

The primary limitation is probably oversimplification. Each model bases its assessment of market opportunities and subsequent decisions on only two or three key factors. In this regard, the GE business screen, with its multiple criteria for assessing market attractiveness and business position, is an improvement over the BCG matrix. Still, the GE model reflects a lack of precision, in that what constitutes *high*, *medium*, and *low* for each of the two factors is largely a matter of judgment.

Another shortcoming is the possibility of placing an SBU on a grid or choosing a strategy without relevant, reliable information. For example, whether market share is critical to a product's profitability is still debated. A third potential limitation is that the results from one of the models might be used to override the critical business judgments made by line managers such as a marketing vice president. A better approach to decision making is to take into account the results from the model *and* the judgments of executives and managers who are well informed about the particular situation.

However, these models also produce noteworthy benefits. Most important is that they encourage careful, consistent assessment of opportunities, allocation of resources, and formulation of strategies. Without planning models, these activities might be haphazard—for example, using one set of criteria this month and, with no good reason, another set next month. Another value of the models is straightforward classification. That is, each model permits an organization to examine its entire portfolio of SBUs or major products in relation to criteria that influence business performance. Another benefit is that the models can point to attractive business opportunities and suggest ventures to avoid.

The search for helpful planning aids is ongoing. Recently, two researchers in France advocated *value innovation*. Focusing on value "places the buyer, not the competition, at the center of strategic thinking." According to them, too many organizations merely try to be slightly better than competitors, whereas an "emphasis on innovation pushes managers to consider totally new ways of doing things."[33]

In the mid-1990s, two consultants urged firms to develop their organizational strategies in terms of *value disciplines*. According to this framework, a firm must increase the value offered to customers by cutting prices, improving products, or enhancing service. Doing so requires choosing—and effectively implementing—one of three value disciplines: operational excellence, product leadership, or customer intimacy. Dell Computer and Wal-Mart exemplify operational excellence, whereas Nike footwear and Acuvue disposable contact lenses illustrate product leadership. Customer intimacy emphasizes delivering precisely what specific customers really want and cannot find elsewhere. Cable & Wireless, a long-distance telephone carrier, avoids price competition with the industry giants by serving well small businesses that want a combination of services to meet their particular needs.[34]

www.acuvue.com

Overall, we believe planning models can help management allocate resources and also develop sound business and marketing strategies. Of course, any planning model should supplement, rather than substitute for, managers' judgments and decisions.

Summary

The management process consists of planning, implementation, and evaluation. Planning is deciding now what we are going to do later, including when and how we are going to do it. Planning provides direction to an organization. Strategic planning is intended to match an organization's resources with its market opportunities over the long run.

In any organization, there should be three levels of planning: strategic company planning, strategic marketing planning, and annual marketing planning. In strategic company planning, management defines the organization's mission, assesses its operating environment, sets long-range goals, and formulates broad strategies to achieve the goals. This level of planning guides planning in different functional areas, including marketing.

Strategic marketing planning entails five steps: conduct a situation analysis, develop marketing objectives, determine positioning and differential advantage, select target markets and measure market demand, and design a marketing mix. Based on strategic marketing plans, an annual marketing plan lays out a year's marketing activities for each major product and division of an organization. An annual plan includes tactics as well as strategies. It is typically prepared by the executive responsible for the division or product.

Management can rely on one or more of the following models for assistance with strategic planning: the product-market growth matrix, the BCG matrix, and the GE business screen. In seeking growth through new products, an organization may need to deal with the matter of cannibalization. A planning model helps management see how best to allocate its resources and to select effective marketing strategies.

More about **Starbucks**

Starbucks has continued to filter additional opportunities for growth, at one point rejecting a coffee-scented tanning oil. Still the firm has developed some new products that leverage its brand name and loyal customer following. In 1995 it began selling compact discs featuring the background music played at its stores. A year later, the coffee purveyor formed an alliance with Dreyer's to create Starbucks ice cream, which quickly became the best-selling brand of coffee ice cream in the U.S.

Starbucks also partnered with Pepsi-Cola to produce and market Frappuccino, a bottled version of its popular, low fat, iced-coffee beverage. In 1998, Starbucks started selling tea-based drinks at its retail stores and later purchased Tazo, a company that produces premium tea products.

One aspect of Starbucks' business that perplexes management is food. Although the coffee bars have served baked goods for years, the quality has not been particularly good because they are not baked on-site. Although food is not a primary product for Starbucks, it can help increase coffee sales, particularly after 11 a.m. By that time, the typical Starbucks outlet has rung up 50% of its daily sales. Thus the chain is looking for ways to attract more customers at lunchtime and later in the day.

To increase its experience with prepared foods, Starbucks opened several Café Starbucks that offer full-meal service at breakfast, lunch, and dinner. The cafés generate steady sales throughout the day. In addition, Starbucks has been experimenting with boxed lunches and salads supplied by outside caterers at a small number of stores in Washington, DC, and Seattle. Sales at each of these test outlets jumped an average of $75,000 on an annual basis, causing

Starbucks to launch a full-scale effort to add lunch menus to every one of its existing retail sites.

Starbucks received a reminder about the importance of its core business, namely sales of coffee at its own outlets. After unveiling plans for its Internet portal, industry analysts poured on the criticism, contending that the company didn't know beans about e-tailing or any of the products (other than coffee, of course) that comprised the new site. At the same time, Starbucks' in-store sales were slumping and new outlets were delayed, causing concerns about expected earnings. Investors thought Howard Schultz (then CEO and now chairman of Starbucks) was spending too much time on a questionable Internet strategy instead of building the core business. Starbucks' stock price fell 28% the day after weak earnings were announced in 1999.

In response, Starbucks scaled back its Internet endeavors to a few partnerships. An Internet firm, Kozmo.com, agreed to pay $150 million to partner with Starbucks. Under the agreement, Starbucks outlets will promote the one-hour delivery service and serve as collection points for rental videotapes returned by Kozmo customers. Starbucks also decided to increase capital spending by 15% to allow for more new locations. Schultz declared, "Our management team is 100% focused on growing our core business without distraction or dilution from any other initiative." Perhaps this is a sign that Starbucks woke up and smelled the coffee.[35]

1. Where in the product-market growth matrix does Starbucks' expansion into grocery stores fall? What about ice cream? Airport locations? In-flight service? Café Starbucks?

2. Which of the above ventures is/are in line with Starbucks' mission statement: "to establish Starbucks as the premier purveyor of the finest coffee in the world while maintaining our uncompromising principles as we grow"?

Key Terms and Concepts

Management (578)
Planning (579)
Strategic planning (579)
Strategic window (579)
Mission (579)
Objective (580)
Strategy (580)
Tactic (580)
Strategic company planning (581)
Situation analysis (582)

Organizational strategies (582)
Strategic marketing planning (583)
Situation analysis (583)
SWOT assessment (583)
Positioning (585)
Differential advantage (585)
Differential disadvantage (585)
Market (586)
Target market (586)

Marketing mix (586)
Annual marketing plan (586)
Strategic business unit (SBU) (588)
Product-market growth matrix (589)
Cannibalization (592)
BCG matrix (592)
GE business screen (594)

Questions and Problems

1. Should a small firm (a manufacturer, a traditional retailer, or an online enterprise) engage in formal strategic planning? Why or why not?

2. Every organization needs to define its mission. Using a customer-oriented approach (benefits provided or wants satisfied), answer the question "What business are we in?" for each of the following companies:
   a. Holiday Inn
   b. Amazon.com
   c. Dell Computer
   d. Universal (movie) Studios
   e. Goodyear Tire and Rubber Co.

3. In the situation-analysis step of strategic marketing planning, what specific external environmental factors should be analyzed by a firm that manufactures equipment used for backpacking in the wilderness?

4. Can a product have a differential advantage and a differential disadvantage at the same time?

5. Identify and explain the differential advantage or disadvantage for the primary product for one of the following organizations:
   a. Trans World Airlines
   b. Your university or college

   c. Victoria's Secret
   d. The United Way in your community
   e. Major-league baseball
   f. eBay

6. For one of the six organizations listed immediately above, describe its target market(s).

7. Use an example to explain the concept of a strategic business unit.

8. a. What's the basic difference between the BCG matrix and the GE business screen?
   b. Which do you think is better, and why?

9. If you were the vice president of marketing for a large airline, which of the three planning models would you find most useful? Why?

10. "The European Union (EU), which seeks the economic unification of Europe, means absolute chaos for American firms targeting consumers in countries that belong to the EU. For a number of years, the situation will be so dynamic that U.S. executives should not waste their time on formal strategic planning related to European markets." Do you agree with this statement?

Hands-On Marketing

1. Either go online or go to your school's library and obtain a copy of an annual report for a major corporation. On the basis of your examination of the year-end review, which of the following product-market growth strategies is being used by this company: market penetration, market development, product development, and/or diversification?

2. Talk with the owner or manager of a local firm about its marketing strategies. Considering the information you have obtained, determine the differential advantage or disadvantage for the firm's primary product. Then indicate how the advantage could be strengthened or how the disadvantage could be alleviated.

Marketing Implementation and Evaluation

Eisner saw Disney as competing against the other successful Internet portals, notably Yahoo! and America Online, and also helping realize the ultimate goal of Disney to become a multimedia conglomerate.

Has Disney's **Go.com** Come to a Stop Sign?

Once upon a time, a magical kingdom called Disney made films and operated theme parks, following a formula created by Walt Disney. The kingdom was very successful for many years. When Michael Eisner became chief executive officer in 1984, the company was producing $1.6 billion in revenue.

The next 15 years were mostly golden for Disney. The firm invested billions to acquire ABC and ESPN, expand its theme parks, add a cruise line, and venture into "tomorrowland" with an ambitious Web portal called the Go Network. By the end of the century, the company was a $23 billion empire. However, the company was so large that it was unable to boost earnings simply by premiering a new movie or rereleasing a classic on video. In the late 1990s, Disney stock rode a roller-coaster, partly because of faltering earnings as well as the decision to go online.

In 1998, Disney purchased 43% of Infoseek, a popular search engine. The two companies jointly launched the Go Network in January 1999. Besides providing search services, the Go Network was designed to be a portal to other websites, including those of Disney, ABC, and ESPN. Eisner's vision for Disney's Internet business was to create the ultimate site where anybody could search the Internet, shop, and check sports scores or news. Eisner saw Disney as competing against the other successful Internet portals, notably Yahoo! and America Online, and also helping realize the ultimate goal of Disney to become a multimedia conglomerate. Eisner wanted to position the Go Network as a vehicle for distributing music, games, films, and even television programming. "When broadband [substantial capacity for transmitting and receiving digital data] hits, the Internet is going to be the place for streaming video, for streaming audio, movies, all those things," he explained.

In mid-1999, Disney and Infoseek agreed to combine a number of Internet sites under the umbrella of Go.com. Several months later, Go.com launched the Go Network Auction to capitalize on the popularity of other Internet auction sites, such as eBay. Go.com also announced that it would add Go Network Shopping, which would offer 5 million products from 300 different merchants. Further, it planned to develop Go Network Sites and Stores to act as a "cybermall" for small businesses.

Go.com then introduced football fans to Enhanced Television. Viewers of National Football League games on ABC and ESPN were encouraged to go online during games to get statistics and play-by-play reports, answer trivia questions, and participate in polls and chat rooms. This ambitious effort was intended to integrate television with the Internet, creating new revenue streams from sales of sports-related merchandise and online ads.

Unfortunately, these new ventures did little to help the Go Network overtake AOL and Yahoo!. In November 1999, Disney acquired the rest of Infoseek and issued a new class of common stock for Go.com. The move eliminated the problem of having two companies run one business and gave Disney extra capital for expanding its online interests.

By the end of 1999, the Go Network was still only the sixth ranked Internet portal, despite constant promotional efforts by Disney on ABC, on ESPN, and in its theme parks. The company's Internet endeavors generated only $200 million in revenue, but lost more than $1 *billion,* for the year. In December 1999, the Go Network attracted 16 million visitors, compared to over 40 million apiece for AOL and Yahoo! It also lagged behind MSN, Excite, and Lycos, prompting Disney to look for new ways to create magic for its Internet kingdom.[1]

1. What factors should Disney consider in evaluating the performance of the Go Network?

2. Who within the Disney Co. should assess the performance of the Go Network?

www.go.com

www.yahoo.com

www.aol.com

The Go.com case illustrates not just inventive strategic plans but also ongoing implementation of strategies and tactics and periodic evaluation of results. In Chapter 20 we defined the management process as planning, implementing, and evaluating marketing in an organization. Most of this book has dealt with **planning** a marketing program. For example, we discussed how to select target markets and how to design an integrated marketing program to deliver want-satisfaction to those markets.

Now in this chapter we discuss the implementation and evaluation of a marketing program. **Implementation** is the operational stage during which an organization attempts to carry out its strategic plan. At the end of an operating period (or even during the period), management should conduct an **evaluation** of the organization's performance. This stage involves determining how well the organization is achieving the goals set in its strategic planning and then, as necessary, preparing new or modified plans.

After studying this chapter, you should be able to explain:

Implementation in Marketing Management

There should be a close relationship among planning, implementation, and evaluation. Without strategic planning, a company's operational activities—its implementation tactics—can go off in any direction, like an unguided missile. As stressed recently, "Implementation . . . is a critical link between the formulation of marketing strategies and the achievement of superior organizational performance."[2]

A couple of decades ago, there was tremendous interest in strategic planning, sparked by management consulting firms. Then disenchantment set in, as many companies came to realize that strategic *planning* alone was not enough to ensure success. These plans had to be *effectively implemented*. Experience has shown that good planning cannot overcome poor implementation, but effective implementation sometimes can overcome poor planning.

In recent years, therefore, much more attention has been devoted to implementing a company's strategies. Consider airlines and hotels that set objectives and develop strategies related to prices. They are likely to be interested in the degree of price competition, the percentage of seats or rooms sold, and total revenue. Computer programs can assist service firms in this area of yield management. Omni Hotels Corp., for example, uses a program called OmniCharm (Centralized Hotel Automated Revenue Management) to estimate demand based on historical sales patterns. The demand estimates, along with data about the number of unsold rooms for different dates, are helpful in setting specific prices that are consistent with the firm's pricing objectives and strategies.[3]

Implementation comprises three activities:

- *Organizing the marketing effort.* Once a company has developed its strategic marketing plan, an early activity is to organize the people who will implement

Omni Hotels Corp., with 40 hotels in the U.S., Canada, and Mexico, uses a computer program called OmniCharm to set room rates. The hotel chain varies its prices to maximize revenue for specified periods of time, such as an entire week. For a particular Omni hotel, prices might range from $59 to $199 depending on expected demand.

 www.omnihotels.com

it. The relationship between marketing and the other functional divisions of the firm must be defined. Then, within the marketing department, management must design an organization that will implement both strategies and tactics.

- *Staffing the organization.* For plans to produce the intended results, an organization needs skilled, dedicated employees to carry them out well. Thus selection of people is all-important—no matter the type of organization that is being staffed. A college football coach's success depends greatly on his ability to recruit the right players. According to one article, the most common reason for failure among top executives is not putting the right people in the right jobs. Thus a CEO who intends to be successful should adopt the motto, "People first, strategy second."[4] Likewise, a sales manager's success depends in great measure on the sales people the manager selects. In most marketing organizations, the sales force plays a vital role in implementing a company's plans. Consequently, in Chapter 18 we discussed a process for selecting sales people.

- *Directing the execution of marketing plans.* In this third phase of implementation, revenues are generated by carrying out the firm's strategies and tactics. To do so, management needs to direct the work of the people who have been selected and organized as the company's marketing team. Success in this phase depends to a large extent on four important aspects of managing employees—delegation, coordination, motivation, and communication.

Detailed discussion of staffing and directing an organization is beyond the scope of this marketing text. In-depth coverage of these topics can be found in management books. However, it is appropriate to consider how organizational structures are used to implement marketing programs.

Organizing for Implementation

Organizational structures are receiving increasing attention in companies—both American and foreign—as management recognizes that yesterday's arrangements may hinder operations in today's dynamic environment. Satisfying customers profitably requires talking with—and listening to—customers. Teamwork across business functions such as marketing and production is also essential. Traditional organizational structures, however, isolate different business functions and have

A big question for numerous companies is how best to implement a marketing effort aimed at college students, who typically are very busy and are besieged by various forms of communication. The answer, for some firms, is to involve students in devising and carrying out marketing programs, often paying them for doing so. Examples of on-campus student-focused sales programs follow:

- VarsityBooks.com hires students who use various tactics to entice fellow students to order their textbooks from the online firm.

- A growing number of companies "sponsor" classes, providing funds for class projects in which students

develop and implement promotions and other marketing activities for the firms' products.

Is it ethical or unethical for businesses to pay students or to sponsor classes with the intention of selling or otherwise promoting the companies' goods and services to the college market? Do you see any ethical problems in university departments receiving some compensation in conjunction with this type of project?

Sources: Jeffrey A. Tannenbaum, "Marketers on Campus: A New Bag of Tricks," *The Wall Street Journal,* Jan. 31, 2000, pp. B1, B8; and Anne Marie Chaker, "Pitching Saturns to Your Classmates—for Credit," *The Wall Street Journal,* Jan. 31, 2000, pp. B1, B4.

---

many managerial layers between customers and decision makers. Recognizing these contradictions, General Motors, AT&T, Xerox, Siemens (the huge German electronics concern), and Donna Karan International (the clothing maker) are among many firms that have made significant organizational changes fairly recently.[5]

In a very real sense, traditional vertical structures are being replaced by horizontal organizations.[6] Several specific trends are noteworthy:

- *Fewer organizational levels.* The intent is to facilitate communication among executives who develop strategic plans, the employees who have continuing contact with the market, and the firm's customers.

- *Employee empowerment.* Granting more authority to middle-level executives in decentralized locations can stimulate innovation and generate faster responses to market shifts. And empowering customer-contact personnel can boost both customer satisfaction and repeat business. With that in mind, the Ritz-Carlton hotel chain allows any employee who hears that a customer has a problem to spend up to $2,000 on a solution.[7]

 www.ritzcarlton.com

- *Cross-functional teams.* By having personnel from various departments work on a project, not only are barriers among functions broken down but the best combination of expertise and experience can be focused on the assignment. Empowering cross-functional teams is a recommended approach for developing new products, particularly in high-technology industries.[8]

Revising an organizational structure is challenging, because doing so requires that employees give up long-standing, comfortable arrangements. But the results often justify the effort. Modicon Inc., a manufacturer of automation-control equipment, used to consider product development strictly as an engineering task. Now the process is carried out by a 15-person team representing marketing, manufacturing, and finance in addition to engineering. Under the new arrangement, the time required to develop software packages has been cut by two-thirds.[9]

Company-Wide Organization

In Chapter 1 we stated that one of the three components of the marketing concept is to coordinate all marketing activities. In firms that are product-oriented or sales-oriented, typically we find fragmented marketing activities. The sales force is separate from advertising, and sales training may be under the human resources department.

In a market-oriented enterprise, all marketing activities are coordinated under one executive, as shown in Figure 21.1. The top marketing executive, who usually is at the vice presidential level, reports directly to the president and is on an equal level with top executives in finance, production, and other major functions. One consultant has called for *concurrent marketing* in order to integrate product management, sales management, and field service operations. In the consultant's view, these are the three areas "that now must interact more often, more quickly, and in more depth across more products, markets, and accounts."[10]

Another aspect of organizational coordination is to establish effective working relationships between marketing and each of the other major functional areas. Marketing can help production, for example, by providing accurate sales forecasts. Production can return the favor with desired quality products precisely when needed to fill customers' orders. Marketing and finance people can work together to establish pricing and credit policies. Over time, new organizational structures emerge in response to changing environments.[11]

Organization within the Marketing Department

Within the marketing department—especially in medium-size or large firms—the sales force frequently is specialized in some organizational fashion. This is done to effectively implement the company's strategic marketing plan. Most often, the sales force is organized in one of three forms of specialization: geographic territory, product line, or customer type. Sometimes a hybrid form is created by combining the best features of two standard forms.

Geographic Specialization

Perhaps the most widely used method of specializing selling activities is on the basis of **geographic specialization**. Each sales person is assigned a specific geographic area—called a territory—in which to sell. Several sales people representing contiguous territories are placed under a territorial sales executive, who reports directly to the general sales manager. These territorial executives usually are called district or regional sales managers, as shown in Figure 21.2A.

A geographic organization usually ensures better implementation of sales strategies in each local market and better control over the sales force. Customers can be serviced quickly and effectively, and local sales reps can respond better to competitors' actions in a given territory. As its major drawback, a geographic organization

Figure 21.1

Company organization embracing the marketing concept.

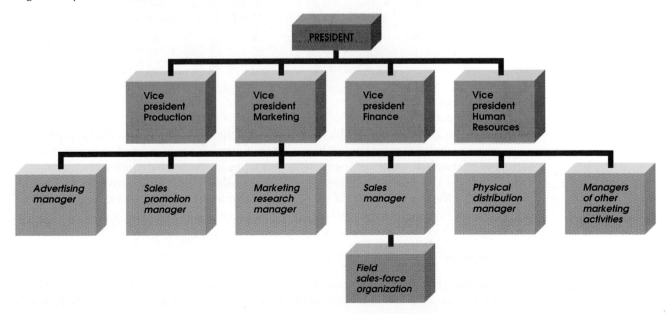

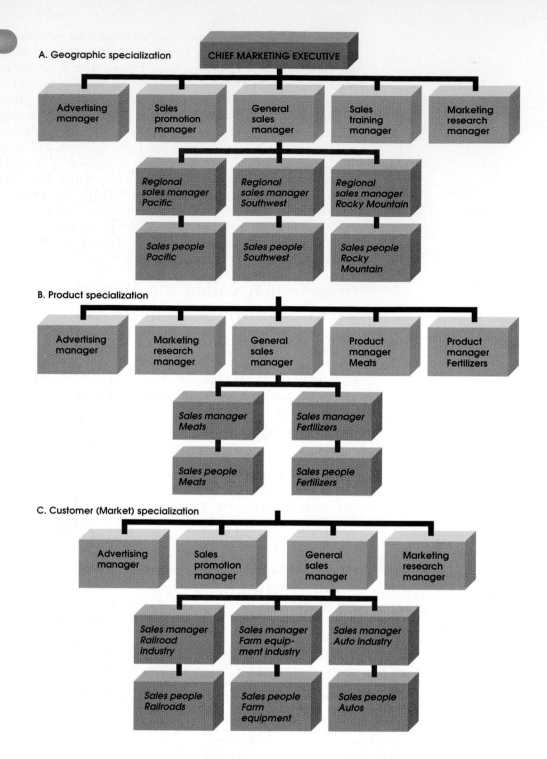

Figure 21.2

Major forms of sales organization.

does not provide the product expertise or other specialized knowledge that some customers may want. To address that problem, the professional imaging division of Eastman Kodak Company switched from a geographic alignment of its sales force to one that also takes into account sales people's expertise and customer needs. Rather than call on all kinds of customers in a territory, say Atlanta, a Kodak rep now works with certain types of customers, say commercial color labs or professional resellers, in a somewhat larger geographic area.[12]

Product Specialization

Another basis for organizing a sales force is **product specialization,** as illustrated in Figure 21.2B. A company such as a meat packer may divide all its products into two lines—meat products and fertilizers. One group of sales reps sells only the line of meats, whereas another group sells the fertilizer line. Each group reports to its own product sales manager who, in turn, reports to the general sales manager.

This type of organization is very well suited for companies that are marketing:

- Complex technical products—a manufacturer of several electronic products.
- Unrelated or dissimilar products—a company marketing luggage, folding tables and chairs, and toy building blocks.
- Thousands of items—a hardware wholesaler.

The main advantage of a product-specialized sales organization is the attention each product line can get from the sales force. A drawback is that more than one sales rep from the same company may call on the same customer. This duplication not only is costly, but also may irritate and confuse customers. In early 2000, FedEx Corp. switched from separate sales groups for its FedEx and RPS delivery services to a single unified sales force. The move was made in order to reduce various forms of duplication and to facilitate cross-selling of FedEx's airfreight and ground delivery services.[13]

www.fedexcorp.com

Customer Specialization

In recent years, many companies have divided their sales departments on the basis of **customer specialization.** Customers may be grouped by type of industry or channel of distribution. An oil company may divide its markets by industries, such as railroads, auto manufacturers, and farm equipment producers, as shown in Figure 21.2C. A firm that specializes its sales operations by channel of distribution may have one sales force selling to wholesalers and another dealing directly with large retailers.

As more companies fully adopt the marketing concept, the customer specialization type of organization is likely to increase. Certainly the basis of customer specialization is consistent with the customer-oriented philosophy that underlies the marketing concept. That is, the organizational emphasis is on customers and markets rather than on products. In this regard, one author maintains that an organization must be structured around customer groups if integrated marketing communications are to be effective.[14]

A variation of customer specialization is the **major accounts organization.** Many companies are adopting this structure as a better way to deal with large, important customers. A major accounts organization usually involves team selling—a concept introduced in Chapter 18. A selling team, consisting perhaps of a sales rep, a sales engineer, a financial executive, and a manufacturing person, will negotiate with a buying team from the customer's organization. Procter & Gamble, for example, has established a series of selling teams, each specializing in a broad product category (cleaning products, food products) to better service key accounts such as Wal-Mart.

Postsale Follow-Through

It is shortsighted to think that marketing ends when a sale is made. In line with the marketing concept, a firm should be committed to ensuring that customers are fully satisfied. If that is accomplished, organizational objectives (including desired levels of profits) probably will be achieved *and* loyal customers will be created, thereby contributing to the future vitality of the company.

Some specific elements of a marketing program are implemented largely after a sale is made. Customer satisfaction—as well as future revenues—require that a company provide its customers with suitable warranties and other desired postsale services. Thus we should consider important aspects of each of these marketing activities.

Warranties

The purpose of a **warranty,** which we use interchangeably with *guarantee,* is to assure buyers they will be compensated if the product does not perform to reasonable expectations. In the U.S., companies decide on the terms and length of their product warranties. In contrast, the 15 countries comprising the European Union agreed jointly that the length of guarantees must be at least two years. EU member countries that stipulate longer mandatory lengths (six years in the United Kingdom, for example) can maintain them.[15]

Years ago, courts seemed to recognize only an **express warranty**—one stated in written or spoken words. Usually this form of reassurance was quite limited in its coverage and seemed mainly to protect the seller from buyers' claims. As a result, the following caution was appropriate: "Caveat emptor," which means "Let the buyer beware."

But times change! Consumer complaints led to a governmental campaign to protect the consumer in many areas, including product warranties. Courts and government agencies have broadened the scope of warranty coverage by recognizing **implied warranty.** This means a warranty was *intended,* although not actually stated, by the seller. Furthermore, producers are being held responsible, even when the sales contract is between the retailer and the consumer. Now the caution is: "Caveat venditor," or "Let the seller beware."

Product Liability

Passage of the Consumer Product Safety Act (1972) reflected the changed attitude regarding product liability and injurious products. This federal legislation created the Consumer Product Safety Commission (CPSC), which has the authority to establish mandatory safety standards for many consumer products not covered by separate laws or other agencies. The CPSC can publish information regarding injurious products—naming brands and producers. It can ban the distribution of these products without a court hearing. And top management of offending companies may face criminal—not just civil—charges.

Product liability is a legal action asserting that an illness, accident, or death resulted from the named product because it was harmful, faulty, or inadequately labeled. Basically, liability results from one or more of three problems: a flaw in the product design, a defect in production, or a deficiency in warning the customer about proper use and potentially harmful misuse of the product.[16]

In the past 15 years, some product-liability claims involved entire categories of goods, including asbestos insulation and breast implants. Other cases focused on specific brands of toys, tampons, pharmaceuticals, birth control devices, tires, and chain saws, among others. Claims have also been filed against firms offering services such as auto repairs and weight loss programs. For example, Nutri/System Inc. was sued by a group of consumers who alleged that their gallbladders were damaged as a result of the company's weight loss services.

In many product-liability cases, juries have granted very large settlements to the plaintiffs—sometimes tens or hundreds of millions of dollars. The most significant recent cases have involved the tobacco industry. Some of these lawsuits went in favor of the tobacco companies, whereas others ended in awards to the plaintiffs. The major cigarette makers have been concerned about potentially catastrophic judgments from lawsuits filed on behalf of a large group of harmed smokers. Thus they have been willing to accept marketing restrictions and make large payments to the government (beyond normal taxes) in exchange for some limits on product-liability lawsuits. In late 1998, tobacco companies agreed to pay a total of about $250 *billion* to the states over 25 years. In return, the industry received protection at the state level. A similar arrangement at the federal level has not come about.[17]

Thousands of product-liability claims are filed every year in the U.S. Thus this issue is of great consequence to companies because of the financial risk as well as the adverse publicity connected with consumers' damage claims. It has proved to be difficult to write a federal law that (1) curbs lawsuits related to allegedly defective products and (2) is also considered fair and acceptable by groups on both sides of the issue. A recent attempt in Congress sought to place limits on product-liability judgments against small companies, specifically those with fewer than 25 employees.[18]

Lawsuits charging harm from failed products are not limited to the U.S. In fact, product-liability problems are likely to increase for companies marketing in western Europe. European laws now provide compensation to consumers in cases of demonstrated bodily injury or property damage from products—even when there has been no negligence on the part of the seller.

To ward off product-liability claims, many manufacturers are placing expanded labels on their goods to tell consumers not to misuse the product and to inform them of almost every conceivable danger associated with using it. Such **warning labels** go so far as to state: "Do not use ladder in front of unlocked doors." Or for another product: "Do not iron clothes while on body." And, believe it or not, on a chain saw: "Do not attempt to stop chain with hands or genitals." Producers hope such blatant, seemingly obvious warnings protect them against charges that they did not properly inform consumers about a product's use, misuse, and potential dangers.[19]

Benefits versus Costs

There's no denying that warranties can be costly if numerous buyers must be compensated when a product fails or is unsatisfactory. In another sense, deficient warranties and warning labels that do not protect companies from product-liability claims can also be very expensive.

Rather than considering only costs, some organizations see marketing benefits in their warranties. Many sellers, for example, use their warranties as promotional devices to stimulate first-time *and* repeat purchases by reducing consumers' risks. With that in mind, more companies are making their warranties understandable and comprehensive—and, therefore, customer friendly. Others are extending the length of the warranty period for their products. In 1999, for instance, the Korean car manufacturer Hyundai announced a full warranty that lasts for five years or 60,000 miles, whichever comes first.[20]

It is common practice among manufacturers, retailers, and especially service firms (given the intangible nature of services) to offer a full refund of the purchase price to a dissatisfied buyer. A number of hotel chains, for example, give a free night's stay to any customer who experiences and reports a problem. For decades, L.L. Bean, which sells outdoor clothing and related gear through catalogs and now online, has offered an unconditional guarantee: "If at any time you are not completely satisfied, return the product for a full refund or exchange." Occasionally, a customer may abuse a full-refund guarantee (by returning a worn-out jacket, for example), but the benefits in terms of avoiding customer dissatisfaction and building customer loyalty are compelling.[21]

It's already evident that customer-friendly warranties are vital in the online environment. According to one study, offering a money-back guarantee is the biggest step an Internet merchant can take in order to reduce the risk that consumers associate with online shopping. In mid-1999, after numerous fulfillment problems in prior months, Shopping.com tried to improve its image by instituting a "125% satisfaction guaranteed" program, meaning that any disgruntled customer would be refunded the full purchase price plus an additional 25%.[22]

www.llbean.com

Automakers can differentiate their particular brands in various ways—through styling, fuel economy, and/or interior roominess, for example. Seeking a differential advantage, Hyundai announced the longest warranty in the auto industry in 1999. Most "bumper-to-bumper" warranties extend for three years or 36,000 miles, whichever comes first; Hyundai added two years and 24,000 miles to its warranty. Hyundai believes this warranty will attract new customers and will not prove to be costly because its cars are quite reliable now.

 www.hyundaiusa.com

Other Postsale Services

Many companies have to provide **postsale service**, notably maintenance and repairs, to fulfill the terms of their warranties. Other firms offer postsale services to gain a differential advantage over competitors, or at least to fully satisfy their customers. Some businesses use postsale services to augment their revenues. For instance, companies such as Otis and Montgomery, both of which sell elevators, rely on service contracts for a substantial portion of their sales and profits.

Some manufacturers consider the postsale service market so lucrative they want to keep it to themselves. To do so, they might limit availability of replacement parts. As discussed in Chapter 13, Eastman Kodak Co. was found guilty of refusing to supply independent service companies with replacement parts for its photocopiers and related equipment.[23]

With more complex products, increasingly demanding and vocal consumers, and now the Internet environment, postsale service has become essential. There are distinctive challenges, however, in attaining both efficiency and effectiveness when providing such services. To illustrate, brief profiles of several postsale services follow.

Merchandise Returns

The best way to handle returns is to minimize the need for them by selling a satisfying product to a customer and, in situations where delivery is involved, getting the shipment to its destination on time. Even under the best of circumstances, however, some customers want or need to return their purchases. Thus a firm needs to consider how stringent or generous its conditions for accepting merchandise

A Global Perspective

Can a guarantee be legal in all countries but one?

Like many firms, Lands' End reassures its American customers by offering a no-questions-asked, money-back guarantee. The guarantee, also permissible in numerous other countries around the world, ran into legal problems in Germany. Soon after the clothing marketer started doing business there, competitors complained to the government about the intruder's warranty. A German agency ruled that the company had engaged in unfair advertising. According to the country's laws, additional services cannot be offered when merchandise is advertised. The German Supreme Court upheld the ruling, concluding that the guarantee was "economically unfeasible" and consequently represented unfair competition.

What could Lands' End do? Shut down its German operations? Drop or dilute the guarantee? The direct marketer stopped promoting the guarantee directly.

However, on the Lands' End website in Germany, there's a link to the U.S. site where the warranty is detailed.

Lands' End also ran an ad in Germany that alluded to the guarantee and mocked the ban. The ad pictured a fly, a washing machine, and the Lands' End logo accompanied by a caption that said the guarantees for the three objects were, respectively, one day, six months, and "advertisement forbidden in Germany." Presumably the ad was intended to bring even more attention to the guarantee and, by so doing, attract additional customers (and perhaps raise the ire of both competitors and the government in Germany).

Sources: "Lands' End's Guarantees Are Too True to Be Good for Competitors in Germany," *St. Louis Post-Dispatch*, Sept. 26, 1999, p. E6; and "Lands' End Ads Run Afoul of German Law," *Advertising Age*, Nov. 2, 1998, p. 48.

www.landsend.com

returns should be. Stringent conditions may curtail costs but are unlikely to gain favor with customers; the opposite is true for generous conditions.

Merchants that sell through an Internet site and also operate retail stores or wholesale branches face the decision of whether or not to accept returns at the physical outlets. Most retailers either accept returns at their stores or are preparing to do so. If a firm prohibits its bricks-and-mortar outlets from accepting returns of online purchases, it forfeits a built-in advantage it has over strictly online competitors. Companies that only sell online are discovering that making the return process convenient for customers is a special challenge. Typically, customers are asked to send the returns to a warehouse or office operated by the company or to a separate business that handles fulfillment of orders for the online firm. Based on its studies, a research agency recommended that one of the top three ways to improve online service is to establish a simple return process. As with many matters, that's easier said than done.[24]

Maintenance and Repairs

A recurring concern among consumers is that manufacturers and retailers do not provide adequate maintenance and repair services for the products they sell. A manufacturer can shift the main burden for such services to middlemen, compensate them for their efforts, and possibly even train their technicians and customer-support staff members. This approach is evident in the automobile and personal computer industries. Or a manufacturer can establish regional factory service centers, staff them with well-trained company employees, and strive to make product servicing a separate profit-generating activity. This approach is found in the appliance industry. To process customers' requests for repairs, Otis established a center that handles over 1 million calls a year, ranging from a broken escalator to people trapped in an elevator.[25]

www.otis.com

Some manufacturers of costly computers, office equipment, and medical diagnostic equipment have developed "smart" products. With built-in sensors and microcomputers, such products can diagnose themselves and/or allow a technician to conduct a diagnosis from a distance by means of either wired or wireless telecommunications. This innovation expedites repairs and, by so doing, cuts aggravating "down time" for valuable products. Further, labor costs associated with repairs may be reduced, thereby improving the manufacturer's profit margins on service contracts.[26]

Complaint Handling

The most common gripes among consumers, as determined by one study, are deficient product quality, deceptive sales methods, and poor repair work. Consumers become even more frustrated if they cannot voice their complaints and get their problems solved. According to research, "A majority of consumers are dissatisfied with the way their complaints are resolved."[27] Ignored or mishandled complaints can have dire consequences with respect to lost business and negative word-of-mouth communication.

Prompt, effective handling of complaints can increase or, if necessary, restore a customer's confidence in a firm, irrespective of whether it operates in physical space or cyberspace. With that in mind, a number of responsive producers have established toll-free telephone lines to their customer service departments. Holiday Inn posts its 800 number in each room, in case guests aren't satisfied by a call to the front desk. A toll-free line for complaints apparently is a wise move. Research indicates that about 85% of phoned-in complaints are satisfied in a single call; less than 35% of complaints conveyed by e-mail or another electronic means are resolved so readily.[28]

Many Internet marketers now realize that the quality of customer service is at least as important as website design, product assortment, and competitive prices in attracting and then keeping buyers. Further, many online customers strongly prefer to interact with an actual person. Companies that engage in online selling can provide this type of customer service on their own or they can outsource this task by contracting with a vendor such as LivePerson.

 www.liveperson.com/tips

Does impersonal online customer service send the wrong message?

Most online firms have been so busy establishing and then improving the sales capabilities of their websites that customer service has received comparatively little attention. Of course, this kind of service is important both before and after a sale is made. Consequently, Internet merchants are seeking the optimal way of dealing with questions and comments from shoppers who are considering a purchase as well as customers who are happy and those who are not so happy for some reason. As in other business endeavors, an optimum would be the most efficient way of achieving a level of effectiveness that is consistent with the company's goals.

Numerous, perhaps most, online enterprises encourage input via e-mail and/or via a toll-free telephone line. There are reports that too many e-mails go unanswered or are not answered promptly and that toll-free lines are busy or not "open for business" when a consumer wants information from the business.

Advancing technology is improving customer service in cyberspace. New software can scan customers' e-mails for key words. Then, depending on the key word, the e-mail might be routed to the department that is best able to respond to the customer, or a standard reply is automatically sent back via e-mail (an electronic "form letter"). A drawback of e-mail, besides any delayed response, is the lack of actual human interaction. Research conducted in 1999 indicated that 90% of online customers want to interact with a real person—now.

Another relatively new technology allows real-time electronic dialogue between an online shopper and a firm's customer service agent. The consumer initiates the "chat," typically through an icon on the website that has a label such as "Live Help." Then one or more e-mail iterations ensue. The online agent can even synchronize screens with the customer so they are looking at the same images or information. Typically, the agents are expected to chat with several customers at the same time; of course, effectiveness and customer satisfaction may drop as a result of this attempt at boosting efficiency.

In late 1999, the predominant form of online customer service interaction was e-mail, used by 70% of cybershoppers. In contrast, only 5% of consumers had participated in a live chat with a firm's customer service rep. About 5% of the 2,000 largest commercial websites offer this service, but the percentage is expected to increase rather quickly to 90%. This is good news to Net Effect Systems and LivePerson, both of which sell and support such chat systems.

Looking ahead, an emerging technology has the capability of combining a live chat and a toll-free telephone call. Using voice-over-IP (the "IP" stands for Internet protocol), an online shopper whose computer has a built-in microphone would click an icon to initiate a telephone call to a customer service rep. The same telephone line would be used for Internet access and the call.

As the founder of Net Effect Systems observed, "the irony is that the primary benefit of online shopping—convenience—is being undermined by a lack of real-time purchasing assistance." Thus effective real-time customer service will be essential for online firms if they are to establish and maintain a differential advantage over traditional businesses *and* their online competitors.

Sources: "Retailers Use Online Chats for Customer Service," *St. Louis Post-Dispatch,* Dec. 6, 1999, p. A6; "Online Customer Service: Guiding Consumers through the Maze," *Financial Service ONLINE,* November 1999, pp. 24–27+; and Bill Meyers, "Service with an E-Smile," *USA Today,* Oct. 12, 1999, pp. 1B, 2B.

Postsale follow-through, like other more visible elements of the marketing mix, can be either a differential advantage or a disadvantage for an organization. Thus the various forms of follow-through certainly should be on the list of matters managers need to heed constantly.

• Evaluating Marketing Performance

Soon after a firm's plans have been set in operation, the process of evaluation should begin. Without evaluation, management cannot tell whether a plan is working or which factors are contributing to its success or failure. Evaluation logically follows planning and implementation. Planning sets forth what *should* be done.

Figure 21.3

The circular relationship among management tasks.

Evaluation shows what *really was* done. A circular relationship exists, as illustrated in Figure 21.3. Plans are made, they are put into action, the results of those actions are evaluated, and new plans are prepared on the basis of this evaluation.

Previously we discussed evaluation as it relates to individual parts of a marketing program—the product-planning process, the performance of the sales force, and the effectiveness of the advertising program, for instance. Now let's look at the evaluation of the *total marketing effort*.

The Marketing Audit

A marketing audit is an essential element in a total evaluation program. An audit implies a review and evaluation of some activity. Thus a **marketing audit** is a comprehensive review and evaluation of the marketing function in an organization— its philosophy, environment, goals, strategies, organizational structure, human and financial resources, and performance.[29]

It's true that a marketing audit involves evaluation. But it's more than that. As suggested by Figure 21.3, the results of any evaluation—including a marketing audit—represent vital input to an organization's planning. In advocating the value of marketing audits in the banking industry, one writer stressed, "Simply stated, a [strategic] marketing plan should only be written after the completion of an intensive, objective marketing audit."[30]

A complete marketing audit is an extensive and difficult project. That's why it is conducted infrequently—perhaps every several years. However, a company should not delay a marketing audit until a major crisis arises.

The rewards of a marketing audit can justify the effort. Management can identify problem areas in marketing. By reviewing its strategies, the firm is likely to keep abreast of its changing marketing environment. Successes can also be analyzed so the company can capitalize on its strong points. The audit can spot lack of coordination in the marketing program, outdated strategies, or unrealistic goals. Furthermore, an audit should anticipate future situations. It is intended for "prognosis as well as diagnosis. . . . It is the practice of preventive as well as curative marketing medicine."[31]

Misdirected Marketing Effort

One of the benefits of evaluation is that it helps correct **misdirected** (or misplaced) **marketing effort**.

The 80–20 Principle

In most firms, a large proportion of the total orders, customers, territories, or products accounts for only a small share of total sales or profit. Conversely, a small proportion produces a large share of sales or profit. This relationship has been characterized as the **80–20 principle**. That is, the large majority (say, 80%) of the orders, customers, territories, or products contribute only a small fraction (say, 20%) of sales or profit. On the other hand, relatively few of these selling units account for the large majority of the volume or profit. We use the 80–20 figure simply to highlight the misplacement of marketing effort. In reality, of course, the percentage split varies from one situation to another; for example, in another situation, just 5% of customers might provide 90% of an organization's sales.

The basic reason for the 80–20 (or similar) split is that almost every marketing program includes some misdirected effort. Marketing endeavors and costs are proportional to the *numbers* of territories, customers, or products, rather than to their actual sales volume or profit. For example, approximately the same order-filling, billing, and delivery expenses are involved whether a $500 suit or a $25 necktie is sold in a May Company department store. Or a manufacturer such as Xerox may assign one sales person to each territory. Yet usually there are differences in the actual sales volume and profit among the territories. In each example the marketing effort (cost) is not in line with the actual return.

Reasons for Misdirected Effort

Frequently, executives cannot uncover their misdirected effort because they lack sufficient information. The **iceberg principle** is an analogy that illustrates this situation. Only the small tip of an iceberg is visible above the water's surface, and the huge submerged part represents the hidden danger. The figures representing total sales or total costs on an operating statement are like the visible tip of an iceberg. The detailed figures representing sales, costs, and other performance measures for each territory or product correspond to the dangerous submerged part.

Total sales or cost figures are too general to be useful in evaluation; in fact, they often are misleading. A company may show satisfactory overall sales and profit figures. But when these totals are subdivided by pertinent factors such as geographic territories, individual products, or various time periods, serious weaknesses often are discovered. A manufacturer of audio equipment showed an overall increase of 12% in sales and 9% in net profit on one product line in one year. But management wasn't satisfied with this "tip of the iceberg." In analyzing the figures more closely, the executives found that the sales change within territories ranged from an increase of 19% to a decrease of 3%. Profit increased as much as 14% in some territories, but was down 20% in one.

A more basic cause of misplaced marketing effort is that executives must make decisions on the basis of inadequate knowledge of the exact nature of marketing costs. In other words, management often lacks knowledge of (1) the disproportionate spread of marketing effort, (2) reliable standards for determining what should be spent on marketing, and (3) the results that should be expected from these expenditures.

As an illustration, a company may spend $250,000 more on advertising this year than last year. But management ordinarily cannot state what the resulting increase in sales volume or profit should be. Also, the executives do not know what would have happened if they had spent the same amount on (1) new-product development, (2) management training seminars for middlemen, or (3) some other aspect of the marketing program.

The Evaluation Process

The evaluation process—whether a complete marketing audit or only an appraisal of individual components of the marketing program—involves three steps:

1. Find out *what* happened. Get the facts; compare actual results with goals and budgets to determine where they differ.

2. Find out *why* it happened. Determine which specific factors in the marketing program accounted for the results.

3. Decide *what to do* about it. Plan the next period's program so as to improve on unsatisfactory performance and capitalize on the aspects that were done well.

To evaluate a total marketing program, we need to analyze results. To do this, two tools are available—sales volume analysis and marketing cost analysis. We'll discuss both of these tools using the Great Midwest Company ("the other GM"), a firm that markets office furniture. This company's 14-state market is divided into four sales districts, each with seven or eight sales people and a district sales manager. The company sells to office equipment wholesalers and directly to large business users. GM's product mix is divided into four groups: desks, chairs, filing equipment, and office accessories (wastebaskets and desk sets, for example). Some of these products are manufactured by GM and some are purchased from other firms.

Analyses of Sales Volume and Market Share

Management should analyze its sales volume in total and by relevant subdivisions such as geographic territories and product lines. These sales figures should be compared with company goals and industry performance. But that's not enough. A firm also needs to measure its sales against the entire industry in which it competes. Each of these methods is described now.

Sales Volume Analysis

We start with an analysis of Great Midwest's total sales, as shown in Table 21.1. A **sales volume analysis** is a detailed study of the *net sales* section of a company's profit and loss statement (operating statement). Annual sales doubled from $18 million to $36 million during the 10-year period ending with fiscal year 2000. Furthermore, sales increased each year, with the exception of 1997. In most years, planned sales goals were met or surpassed. Thus far in our analysis, the company's situation is encouraging.

A study of total sales volume alone is usually insufficient and may even be misleading. Remember the analogy of an iceberg! To learn what is going on in the "submerged" parts of the market, we need to analyze sales volume by other relevant dimensions—sales territories, for example.

Table 21.2 is a summary of the planned sales goals and actual sales results in Great Midwest's four sales districts. A key measurement is the *performance index* for each district—that is, actual sales divided by sales goal. An index of 100 means that the district did exactly what was expected. From the table we see that Great Lakes and Heartland did just a little better than was expected, and Delta passed its goal by a wide margin, but High Plains was quite a disappointment.

So far in our evaluation, we know a little about *what* happened in GM's districts. Now management has to figure out *why* it happened and *what should be done* about it. These are the difficult steps in evaluation. GM's executives need to determine *why* the High Plains district did so poorly. The fault may lie in some aspect of the marketing program, or competition may be especially strong in that

Table 21.1	Annual Sales Volume of Great Midwest Company, Industry Volume, and Company's Share in 14-State Market		
Year	**Company Volume (in millions of dollars)**	**Industry Volume in Company's market (in millions of dollars)**	**Company's Percentage Share of Market**
2000	36.0	900	4.0
1999	34.7	825	4.2
1998	33.1	765	4.3
1997	30.4	660	4.6
1996	31.7	705	4.5
1995	28.0	600	4.7
1994	24.5	510	4.8
1993	22.5	465	4.8
1992	21.8	450	4.8
1991	18.0	360	5.0

Table 21.2

	Sales Goals (in millions of dollars)	Actual Sales (in millions of dollars)	Performance Index (actual ÷ goal)	Dollar Variation (in millions)
District	**District Sales Volume in Great Midwest Company, 2000**			
Delta	$10.8	$12.5	116	+1.7
Great Lakes	9.0	9.6	107	+0.6
Heartland	7.6	7.7	101	+0.1
High Plains	8.6	6.2	72	−2.4
Total	$36.0	$36.0		

district. They also should find out the reasons for Delta's success, and whether this information can be used in the other districts.

This brief examination of two aspects of sales volume analysis shows how this evaluation tool may be used. However, for a more useful evaluation, GM's executives should go much further. They should analyze their sales volume by individual territories within districts and by product lines. Then they should carry their territorial analysis further by examining volume by product line and customer group *within* each territory. For instance, even though Delta did well overall, the iceberg notion may apply here. The fine *total* performance in this district may be covering up weaknesses in an individual product line or territory.

Market-Share Analysis

Comparing a company's sales results with its goal is a useful evaluation, but it does not indicate how the company is doing relative to its competitors. We need a **market-share analysis** to compare the company's sales with the industry's sales. The company's share of the market should be analyzed in total, as well as by product line and market segment.

Probably the major obstacle encountered in market-share analysis is obtaining industry sales information in total and in sufficient detail. Trade associations and government agencies are possible sources for industry sales volume statistics in many fields.

Great Midwest Company is a good example of the value of market-share analysis. Recall from Table 21.1 that GM's total sales doubled over a 10-year period, with annual increases in nine of those years. But, during this span, the annual sales for all competing firms in this geographic area increased from $360 million to $900 million (a 150% increase). Thus the company's market share actually *declined* from 5 to 4%. Although GM's annual sales increased 100%, its market share declined 20%.

The next step is to determine *why* Great Midwest's market position declined. The number of possible causes is quite large—and this is what makes management's task so difficult. A weakness in almost any aspect of GM's product line, distribution system, pricing structure, or promotional program may have contributed to the loss of market share. Or the culprit might have been competition. There may be new competitors in the market that were attracted by the rapid growth rates. Or competitors' marketing programs may be more effective than Great Midwest's.

• Marketing Cost Analysis

An analysis of sales volume is helpful in evaluating and controlling a company's marketing effort. A sales analysis, however, does not tell us anything about the *profitability* of this effort. Management needs to assess costs to determine the relative profitability of its territories, product lines, or other marketing units. A **marketing cost analysis** is a detailed study of the *operating expenses* section of a company's profit and loss statement. As part of this analysis, management should establish budgetary goals, and then study the variations between budgeted costs and actual expenses.

Types of Marketing Cost Analyses

A company's marketing costs may be analyzed:

- As they appear in its ledger accounts and profit and loss statement.
- After they are grouped into activity classifications.
- After these activity costs have been allocated to territories, products, or other marketing units.

Analysis of Ledger Expenses

The simplest and least expensive approach is a study of the *object of expenditure* costs as they appear in the firm's profit and loss statement. These figures come from the company's accounting ledger records. The simplified operating statement for the Great Midwest Company on the left side of Table 21.3 is the model we shall use in this discussion.

The procedure is to analyze each cost item (salaries and media space, for example) in detail. We can compare this period's total with the totals for similar periods in the past, and observe the trends. In addition, we can examine actual costs with budgeted expense goals. We should also compute each expense as a percentage of net sales. Then, we should compare these expense ratios with industry figures, which are often available through trade associations.

Analysis of Activity Costs

Total costs should be allocated among the various marketing activities, such as advertising or warehousing, for more effective control. Management then can analyze the cost of each of these activities.

The procedure here is first to identify the major activities, and then to allocate each ledger expense among those activities. As indicated in the expense distribution

| Table 21.3 | Profit and Loss Statement and Distribution of Natural Expenses to Activity Cost Groups, Great Midwest Company, 2000 |

Profit and Loss Statement (in $000)			colspan		**Expense Distribution Sheet (in $000)**			
Net sales		$36,000			**Activity (Functional) Cost Groups**			
Cost of goods sold		23,400	**Personal Selling**	**Advertising**	**Warehousing and Shipping**	**Order Processing**	**Marketing Administration**	
Gross margin		12,600						
Operating expenses:								
Salaries and commissions	$2,710	→	$1,200	$ 240	$ 420	$ 280	$ 570	
Travel and entertainment	1,440	→	1,040				400	
Media space	1,480	→		1,480				
Supplies	440	→	60	35	240	70	235	
Property taxes	130	→	16	5	50	30	19	
Freight out	3,500	→			3,500			
Total expenses		9,700	$2,316	$ 1,760	$ 1,760	$ 380	$ 1,024	
Net profit		$ 2,900						

sheet on the right-hand side of Table 21.3, we have decided on five activity cost groups in our Great Midwest example. Some items, such as the cost of media space, can be apportioned entirely to one activity (advertising). For other expenses, the cost must be spread among several activities. So management must decide on some reasonable basis for allocation among these activities. For example, property taxes may be allocated according to the proportion of total floor space occupied by each activity. The warehouse accounts for 46% of the total square feet of floor space in the firm, so the warehousing and shipping activity is charged with $60,000, which is 46% of the property taxes.

An analysis of marketing costs gives executives more information than they can get from an analysis of ledger accounts alone. Also, an analysis of activity expenses in total provides a starting point for management to analyze costs by territories, products, or other marketing units.

Analysis of Activity Costs by Product or Market

The third and most beneficial type of marketing cost analysis is a study of the expenses and profitability of specific components of a product assortment or total market. This type of analysis breaks out a product assortment by lines or individual items or divides up a market by territories, customer groups, or order sizes.

By combining a sales volume analysis with a marketing cost study, a researcher can prepare a complete operating statement for each product or market component. These statements can then be analyzed to determine how they affect the total marketing program. Cost analysis by product or market enables management to pinpoint trouble spots much more effectively than does an analysis of either ledger account expenses or activity costs.

The procedure for a cost analysis by product or market is similar to that used to analyze activity costs. The total cost of each activity (the right-hand part of Table 21.3) is allocated on some basis to each product or market segment being studied. Let's walk through an example of a cost analysis, by sales districts, for the Great Midwest Company, as shown in Tables 21.4 and 21.5.

First, for each of the five GM activities, we select an allocation basis for distributing the cost of that activity among the four districts. These bases are shown in the top part of Table 21.4. Then we determine the number of allocation "units"

Table 21.4 Allocation of Activity Costs to Sales Districts, Great Midwest Company, 2000

Activity		Personal Selling	Advertising	Warehousing and Shipping	Order Processing	Marketing Administration
		Allocation Basis				
Allocation basis		Direct expense to each district	Number of pages of advertising	Number of orders shipped	Number of invoice lines	Equally among districts
Total activity cost		$2,316,000	$1,760,000	$4,220,000	$380,000	$1,024,000
Number of allocation units			88 pages	10,550 orders	126,667 lines	4 districts
Cost per allocation unit			$20,000	$400	$3	$256,000
		Allocation of Costs				
Delta district <	units	—	27 pages	3,300 orders	46,000 lines	—
	cost	$650,000	$540,000	$1,320,000	$138,000	$256,000
Great Lakes district <	units	—	19 pages	2,850 orders	33,000 lines	—
	cost	$606,000	$380,000	$1,140,000	$99,000	$256,000
Heartland district <	units	—	22 pages	2,300 orders	26,667 lines	—
	cost	$540,000	$440,000	$920,000	$80,000	$256,000
High Plains district <	units	—	20 pages	2,100 orders	21,000 lines	—
	cost	$520,000	$400,000	$840,000	$63,000	$256,000

that make up each activity cost, and we find the cost per unit. This completes the allocation method, which tells us how to assign costs to the four districts:

- Personal selling expenses pose no problem because they are direct expenses, chargeable to the district in which they are incurred.
- Advertising costs are allocated on the basis of the number of pages of advertising run in each district. GM purchased the equivalent of 88 pages of advertising during the year, at an average cost of $20,000 per page ($1,760,000 ÷ 88).
- Warehousing and shipping expenses are apportioned on the basis of the number of orders shipped. Because 10,550 orders were shipped during the year at a total activity cost of $4,220,000, the cost per order is $400.
- Order processing expenses are allocated according to the number of invoice lines typed during the year. Because there were 126,667 lines, the cost per line is $3.
- Marketing administration—a totally indirect expense—is divided equally among the four districts, with each district being allocated $256,000.

The final step is to calculate the amount of each activity cost to be allocated to each district. The results are shown in the bottom part of Table 21.4. We see that $650,000 of personal selling expenses were charged directly to Delta, for example. Regarding advertising, the equivalent of 27 pages of advertising was run in Delta, so that district is charged with $540,000 (27 pages × $20,000 per page). Regarding warehousing and shipping expenses, 3,300 orders were shipped to customers in the Delta district, at a unit allocation cost of $400 per order, for a total allocated cost of $1,320,000. To allocate order-processing expenses, management determined that 46,000 invoice lines went to customers in the Delta district. At $3 per line (the cost per allocation unit), Delta is charged with $138,000.

After the activity costs have been allocated among the four districts, we can prepare a profit and loss statement for each district. These statements are shown in Table 21.5. Sales for each district are determined from the sales volume analysis (Table 21.2). Cost of goods sold and gross margin for the respective districts are obtained by assuming that the company's gross margin of 35% ($12,600,000 ÷ $36,000,000) was maintained in each district.

Table 21.5 subdivides Great Midwest's total results into operating statements for each of the company's four districts. For example, we note that Delta's net profit was 11.8% of sales ($1,471,000 ÷ $12,500,000). In sharp contrast, High Plains did rather poorly, earning a net profit of only 1.5% of net sales ($91,000 ÷ $6,200,000).

Table 21.5	Profit and Loss Statements for Sales Districts (in $000), Great Midwest Company, 2000				
	Total	**Delta**	**Great Lakes**	**Heartland**	**High Plains**
Net sales	$36,000	$12,500	$9,600	$7,700	$6,200
Cost of goods sold	23,400	8,125	6,240	5,005	4,030
Gross margin	12,600	4,375	3,360	2,695	2,170
Operating expenses:					
Personal selling	2,316	650	606	540	520
Advertising	1,760	540	380	440	400
Warehousing and shipping	4,220	1,320	1,140	920	840
Order processing, billing	380	138	99	80	63
Marketing administration	1,024	256	256	256	256
Total expenses	9,700	2,904	2,481	2,236	2,079
Net profit (in dollars)	$ 2,900	$ 1,471	$ 879	$ 459	$ 91
Net profit (as percentage of sales)	8.1%	11.8%	9.2%	6.0%	1.5%

At this point in our performance evaluation, we have completed the *what happened* stage. The next stage is to determine *why* the results are as depicted in Table 21.5. As mentioned earlier, it is difficult to answer this question. In High Plains, for example, the sales force obtained only about two-thirds as many orders as in Delta (2,100 versus 3,300). Was this because of poor selling, inadequate sales training, more severe competition in High Plains, or some other reason among a multitude of possibilities?

After a performance evaluation has determined why district results came out as they did, management can move to the third stage in its evaluation process. That final stage is *what should management do about the situation?* This stage will be discussed briefly after we review two major challenges in marketing cost analysis.

Challenges in Cost Analysis

Marketing cost analysis can be expensive in time, money, and labor. In particular, the task of allocating costs is often quite difficult.

Allocating Costs

The challenge becomes evident when total activity costs must be apportioned among individual territories, products, or other marketing units. Operating costs can be divided into direct and indirect expenses. **Direct costs,** also called *separable expenses,* are incurred totally in connection with one market segment or one unit of the sales organization. Thus salary and travel expenses of the sales representative in the Delta district are direct expenses for that territory. The cost of newspaper space to advertise the company's line of desks is a direct cost of marketing that product. Allocating direct expenses is easy. They can be charged entirely to the marketing unit that incurred them.

The allocation challenge arises in connection with **indirect costs,** also called *common costs* or *overhead.* These expenses are incurred jointly for more than one marketing unit. Therefore, they cannot be charged totally to one market segment.

Within the category of indirect costs, some expenses are *variable* and others are *fixed.* (These two types of costs were introduced in Chapter 12.) Order filling and shipping, for example, are largely variable. They would *decrease* if some territories or products were eliminated; conversely, they would *increase* if new products or territories were added. On the other hand, marketing administrative expenses are more fixed. The cost of the chief marketing executive's staff and office would remain about the same whether or not the number of territories or product lines was changed.

Any method selected for allocating indirect expenses has weaknesses that can distort the results and mislead management. Two commonly used allocation methods are to divide these costs (1) equally among the marketing units being studied (territories, for instance) or (2) in proportion to the sales volume in each marketing unit. But each method gives a different result for the total costs for each marketing unit.

Full Cost versus Contribution Margin

In a marketing cost analysis, two means of allocating indirect expenses are (1) the contribution-margin (also called contribution-to-overhead) method and (2) the full-cost method. A controversy exists regarding which of these two approaches is better for purposes of evaluation.

In the **contribution-margin approach,** only direct expenses are allocated to each marketing unit being analyzed. These costs presumably would disappear if that marketing unit were eliminated. When direct expenses are deducted from the gross margin of the marketing unit, the remainder is the amount that unit is contributing to cover total indirect expenses (or overhead).

In the **full-cost approach**, all expenses—direct and indirect—are allocated among the marketing units under study. By allocating *all* costs, management can estimate the net profit of each territory, product, or other marketing unit.

For any specific marketing unit, these two methods can be summarized as follows:

Contribution Margin	Full Cost
Sales $	Sales $
less	*less*
Cost of goods sold	Cost of goods sold
equals	*equals*
Gross margin	Gross margin
less	*less*
Direct expenses	Direct expenses
equals	*less*
Contribution margin (the amount available to cover indirect expenses plus a profit)	Indirect expenses
	equals
	Net profit

Proponents of the *full-cost* approach contend that a marketing cost analysis is intended to determine the net profitability of the units being studied. They believe that the contribution-margin method does not fulfill this purpose and may be misleading. A given territory or product may be showing a contribution to overhead. Yet, after indirect costs are allocated, this product or territory may actually have a net loss. In effect, say the full-cost proponents, the contribution-margin approach is the iceberg notion in action. That is, the visible tip (the contribution margin) looks good, whereas the submerged part may be hiding a net loss.

Contribution-margin supporters contend that it is not possible to accurately allocate indirect costs among product or market segments. Furthermore, these costs (such as the salary of the vice president of marketing or the expenses associated with the company's marketing research department) are not all related to any *one* territory or product, but rather pertain to the entire organization. Therefore, the marketing units should not bear any of these costs. Advocates of the contribution-margin approach also say that a full-cost analysis may show a net loss for a product or territory, but this unit may be contributing something to overhead. If the losing product or territory is eliminated, the unit's contribution to overhead would then have to be borne by other units. With the contribution-margin approach, there would be no question about keeping this unit as long as there is no better alternative.

Use of Findings from Volume and Cost Analyses

So far we have been dealing with the first two stages of marketing performance evaluation—finding out *what happened* and *why it happened*. Now we're ready to see some examples of how management might use the results from a combined sales volume analysis and marketing cost analysis to *improve* performance.

Territories

Knowing the net profit (or contribution to overhead) of territories in relation to their potential gives management several possibilities for action. It may decide to adjust (expand or contract) territories to bring them into line with current sales potential. Or, if territorial problems stem from weaknesses in the distribution system, changes related to distribution may be needed. Firms that use manufacturers' agents may find it advisable to establish their own sales forces in growing markets, for instance. Or technology may be applied to bring about automatic replenishment and/or reordering via the Internet. If intense competition is the cause of unprofitable volume in some districts, modifications in the promotional program may be necessary.

Of course, a losing territory might be abandoned completely. An abandoned region may have been contributing something to overhead, however, even though a net loss was shown. Management must recognize that this contribution must now be carried by the remaining territories.

Products

When the profitability of each product or group of products is known, unprofitable models, sizes, or colors can be eliminated. Sales people's compensation plans may be altered to encourage the sale of high-margin items. Channels of distribution may be changed. Instead of selling all of its products directly to business users, for instance, a machine tools manufacturer shifted to industrial distributors for standard products of low unit value. The company thereby improved the profitability of these products.

Management may decide to discontinue a losing product. But it should not do so without first considering the effect this decision will have on other items sold by the company. Often a low-volume or unprofitable product must be carried simply to round out the product assortment. Supermarkets, for example, carry salt and sugar even though these are profitless for a store. Customers expect a grocery store to carry those items. If they are not available at one store, that seller will lose business because shoppers will go to other stores that do carry a full complement of grocery products.

Customer Classes and Order Sizes

By combining a sales volume analysis with a cost study, executives can determine the profitability of each group of customers.[32] If one market segment is unprofitable or generates too little profit, then changes may be required in the pricing structure when selling to these customers. Or perhaps customers that have been sold to directly by a producer's sales force should be turned over to wholesaling middlemen. A manufacturer of air conditioners made just such a move when it found that direct sales to individual building contractors were not profitable.

A difficulty plaguing many firms today is the **small-order problem.** Many orders are below the break-even point. Revenue from each of these orders is actually less than allocated expenses. This problem occurs because several costs, such as billing or direct selling, are essentially the same whether the order amounts to $10 or $10,000. Management's immediate reaction may be that no order below the break-even point should be accepted. Or small-volume accounts should be dropped from the customer list. Such decisions may be harmful, however. Some of those small-order customers may, over time, grow into large, profitable accounts.

Management should first determine *why* certain accounts are small-order problems and then figure out how to correct the situation. Proper handling can often turn a losing account into a satisfactory one. For example, a small-order handling charge, which some customers would willingly pay, might change the profit picture entirely.

• Summary

The management process in marketing is the planning, implementation, and evaluation of the marketing effort in an organization. Implementation is the stage in which an organization attempts to carry out its strategic planning. Strategic planning is virtually useless if it is not implemented effectively.

Implementation includes three activities—organizing, staffing, and directing. In organizing, the company should first coordinate all marketing activities into one department whose top executive reports directly to the president. Then, within the marketing department, the company should choose some form of organizational specialization based on geographic territories, products, or customer types.

Two elements of a marketing program, warranties and other postsale services, are implemented largely after a sale is made. Warranties require considerable management attention these days because of consumer complaints and governmental regulations. Product liability is an issue of great consequence to companies because of the financial risk associated with consumers' claims of injuries caused when using a firm's product.

Many companies provide postsale service, such as merchandise returns, maintenance and repairs, and complaint handling, to fulfill the terms of their warranties and/or to augment their revenues. To promote customer satisfaction, a number of firms are improving their methods of inviting and responding to consumer complaints.

The evaluation stage in the management process involves measuring performance results against predetermined goals. Evaluation enables management to determine the effectiveness of its implementation and to plan corrective action where necessary. A marketing audit is a key element in a total marketing evaluation program.

Most companies are victims of at least some misdirected marketing effort. That is, the 80–20 and iceberg principles are at work in most firms because marketing costs are expended in relation to the number of marketing units (territories, products, customers), rather than to their profit potential. Too many companies do not know how much they should spend for marketing activities, or what results they should get from these expenditures.

The financial results of marketing endeavors should be analyzed in terms of sales volume, market share, and marketing costs. One challenge in marketing cost analysis is allocating costs—especially indirect costs—to the marketing units. Given detailed analyses, management can study sales volume and marketing costs by territories, product lines, customer classes, and/or order sizes. The findings from these analyses can be helpful in shaping decisions regarding a company's marketing program.

More about **Go.com**

It seems that Disney's strategy of creating the best and biggest portal on the Internet was more wishful than realistic. Disney learned quickly that competitors had a significant head start in building their portals and creating loyal customer bases. The Go Network's disappointing showing in 1999 caused Go.com to rethink its strategy. In January 2000, the Disney subsidiary announced that it would refocus the Go Network. Instead of trying to appeal to the broadest possible audience, the Go Network would concentrate on the areas of entertainment and leisure. Although the site would still provide comprehensive search capabilities, it would scale back significantly on its other offerings, and stick to areas with which Disney was very familiar—and successful.

Industry analysts were enthusiastic about the news. One commented, ". . . it was inevitable. For Disney to be banging their head against the wall called AOL and Yahoo! didn't make any sense." Many pointed out that there isn't much need for more than a few comprehensive portals, which are very difficult to develop and maintain. Some analysts speculated that to be successful, new entrants would have to focus on a specific area in order to build a loyal following from a particular market segment or audience. Such sites would then attract more advertisers willing to pay higher rates to reach well-defined target markets.

Despite representing a substantial shift in strategy, the announcement still seemed to support Eisner's ultimate vision for the Go Network as an entertainment distributor. The chairman and CEO of Go.com said the revamped Go site would be a "fantastic aggregator" of information and links pertaining to music, movies, sports, and other recreational topics such as travel. All of these topics related to Disney's traditional strengths.

As the transition of the Go Network began, Go.com announced plans to expand its online offerings. Go.com formed an alliance with StreamSearch.com, which will allow Go visitors to search for and then play or download audio and video files.

In addition, a new Go.com Internet site, EXPN.com, is designed to appeal to teens and twentysomethings, particularly those with an interest in extreme sports. EXPN.com, in the thinking of Go.com's management, would complement ESPN's coverage of the semiannual X (for Extreme) Games, which feature competitors in a variety of sports, including skateboarding, snowboarding, and surfing. The new site would provide information about not only the events, but also other aspects of the "ex-treme" culture, including fashion, music, and travel. To support the new site, Go.com established links to related Internet sites and even agreed to cover the Gravity Games, which are partially owned and broadcast by NBC.

With so many successful "offline" entertainment enterprises, Disney possesses a wealth of experience and material to fuel its refocused Go Network. However, it remains to be seen whether Disney can live happily ever after in cyberspace.[33]

1. Did Disney's initial Internet marketing strategy (that is, trying to create a full-service, general-audience portal) exhibit misdirected effort?

2. After EXPN.com has been operating for a year, how should Go.com assess the performance of this Internet site—with respect to sales volume, market share, and/or marketing costs?

 www.expn.com

Key Terms and Concepts

Planning (602)
Implementation (602)
Evaluation (602)
Geographic specialization (605)
Product specialization (606)
Customer specialization (607)
Major accounts organization (607)
Warranty (608)
Express warranty (608)

Implied warranty (608)
Product liability (608)
Warning label (609)
Postsale service (610)
Marketing audit (614)
Misdirected marketing effort (614)
80–20 principle (614)
Iceberg principle (615)

Sales volume analysis (616)
Market-share analysis (617)
Marketing cost analysis (618)
Direct costs (621)
Indirect costs (621)
Contribution-margin approach (621)
Full-cost approach (622)
Small-order problem (623)

Questions and Problems

1. "Good implementation in an organization can overcome poor planning, but good planning cannot overcome poor implementation." Explain, using examples from business periodicals, such as *Business Week, Forbes, Advertising Age, BrandWeek,* and *The Wall Street Journal.*

2. Give some examples of companies that are likely to organize their sales forces by product groups.

3. A manufacturer of small aircraft designed for executive transportation, Cessna for example, has decided to implement the concept of a selling center. Who should be on this company's selling teams? What problems might this manufacturer encounter when it uses team selling?

4. Explain the relationship between a warranty on small electric appliances and the manufacturer's distribution system for these products.

5. a. Should the primary role of postsale services be to assure customer satisfaction or to generate added revenues for the firm?

   b. Would the way in which postsale services are carried out vary depending on the role given to this element of marketing by the firm's executives?

6. a. What are several ways in which providing postsale services would vary between an e-tailer and a retailer that has physical stores?

   b. Do online-only firms have any advantages with respect to carrying out postsale services?

7. A sales volume analysis by territories indicates that a manufacturer's sales of roofing materials have increased 12% a year for the past three years in the territory comprising South Carolina, Georgia, and Florida. Does this indicate conclusively that the company's sales volume performance is satisfactory in that territory?

8. A manufacturer found that one product accounted for 35 to 45% of the company's total sales in all but 2 of the 18 territories. In each of those two territories, this product accounted for only 14% of the company's volume. What factors might explain the relatively low sales of this article in the two districts?

9. What effects might a sales volume analysis by product have on training, supervising, and compensating a company's sales force?

10. Should a company stop selling to an unprofitable customer? Why or why not? If not, then what steps might the company take to make the account a profitable one?

Hands-On Marketing

1. Interview a sales executive (a) in a manufacturing company and (b) in either a securities brokerage or a real estate brokerage firm to find out how they motivate their sales forces. As part of your report, give your evaluation of each motivational program.

2. Interview a marketing executive to find out how the total marketing performance is evaluated in that particular company. As part of your report, include your appraisal of this firm's evaluation program.

22

Marketing and the Information Economy

"Although service is one of Grainger's hallmarks, management recognized that in the emerging information economy, outstanding service would not be enough to keep the company competitive."

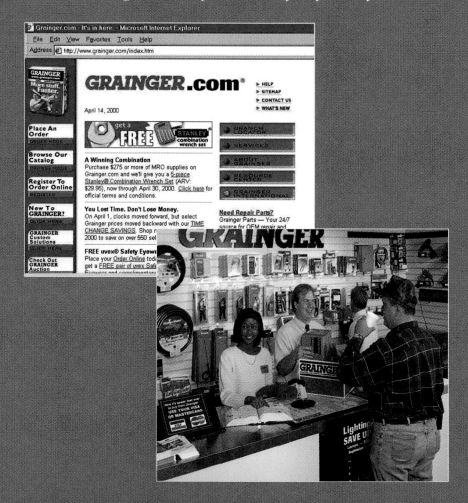

Is the Transformation of **W. W. Grainger** the Model for the Future?

In 1927, Chicago businessman William Grainger spotted an overlooked opportunity. When a firm needed a replacement electric motor for one that was damaged or worn out, the only option was to order a new one and wait days or even weeks for delivery. To solve the problem, Grainger started a wholesale business that stocked an inventory of electric motors of various sizes made by a number of different manufacturers. To advertise the motors, he created and distributed an eight-page catalog. Seventy years later W. W. Grainger, Inc., has become a $4 billion business with 12,000 employees and an inventory of over 200,000 products. It has nine regional distribution centers and 500 outlets that put its products within 20 minutes of 70% of U.S. businesses.

Grainger retains its focus, stocking only maintenance, repair, and operations (MRO) products and reselling them to other businesses. Its inventory includes hand and power tools, cleaning equipment, light bulbs of all sizes and shapes, every kind of fastener, and almost anything else you can imagine that would be used to keep a business operating. Its customers range from factories to military bases and schools. And yes, it still sells electric motors, but now they are included in a 4,000-page catalog.

The success of the company is attributed to its outstanding reputation for customer service. Grainger has a corporate commitment to surpass customers' expectations. To reach that goal the firm has created a "no excuses" guarantee that empowers its employees to take responsibility for ensuring customer satisfaction.

Although service is one of Grainger's hallmarks, management recognized that in the emerging information economy, outstanding service would not be enough to keep the company competitive. Thus, in 1995 the board of directors, following one of the firm's core values of "challenging the status quo and being open to new ideas," approved an exploratory move into electronic commerce.

The first effort was to create the firm's website. It allows buyers to quickly search for specific items and compare prices using product descriptions, brand names, or model numbers. Developing a user-friendly online catalog is a valuable addition to Grainger's marketing program. Buyers report that they can place their orders more quickly, saving time and money. They also note that there are fewer ordering mistakes when they log on and enter the parts numbers themselves rather than order verbally over the phone. In examining its online orders, Grainger made two other discoveries. Online orders are on average 85% larger than phone orders, and nearly 25% of the online volume comes in after Grainger distribution outlets are closed for the day.

W. W. Grainger's vision for electronic business is to have more than a toll-free ordering line. The company foresees that the Internet will change the way it does business by improving the effectiveness and the efficiency of both its customers and itself.[1]

What can Grainger do to more fully utilize the potential of the Internet?

 www.grainger.com

Information has always played a major role in marketing. Today, both the quantity and quality of information is increasing at the fastest rate in history. Much of this growth is due to improvements in information technology and the ability of marketers to find creative ways to make use of it. The result is that marketers are entering an information economy in which new ways of doing business are being designed and some existing ways are being reconfigured.

The company described in the chapter-opening case is a good example. W. W. Grainger is a wholesaler, founded on the concept of having a ready supply of inventory on hand. For most of its history, inventory has been a foundation of its success. Now it is evolving into a firm that relies much more heavily on information to serve its customers. Although it still maintains an extensive inventory, Grainger uses information technology to make searching, comparison shopping, and buying easier and more efficient for its customers. Some analysts predict that instead of bricks and mortar (and inventory) defining a business, information and how it is used will be the key attributes of success in the near future.

In this chapter the goal is to examine the role of marketing in this emerging information economy. More specifically, we will look at how information technology is creating new opportunities and challenges and some of the ways marketers are trying to seize these opportunities. On completing this chapter you should:

chapter goals

- Appreciate the role of information in marketing.
- Be familiar with the importance of information technology and electronic networking.
- Understand how the Internet has changed how markets function.
- Appreciate some of the ways the Internet is affecting marketing strategy.
- Recognize challenges and opportunities marketers are addressing as they enter the information economy.

The Importance of Information in Marketing

The Industrial Revolution, beginning in the second half of the 19th century, marked the beginning of the widespread application of technology to business. Steam and electric power made it possible to operate large machinery and equipment, conveyors moved products along assembly lines and then into and out of inventory, and individual workers were taught to perform specialized tasks very efficiently. As a result, businesses began to experience substantial improvements in manufacturing productivity. However, the impact of manufacturing technology on marketing was not nearly as dramatic. Although it did result in lower costs and therefore lower prices, the job of the marketer remained largely unchanged, requiring considerable personal interaction before, during, and after most sales.

Significant increases in marketing productivity required a different kind of technology. The job of marketing is to direct the organization in how to most effectively satisfy customers. Providing direction entails learning as much as possible about the customer, and using that information to design need-satisfying strategies. In short, marketing is driven by information. Sellers must learn what buyers like and dislike by monitoring their behavior, asking them questions, and inviting their comments. And all marketers must gather data on current or potential markets to determine their status and to anticipate how they are likely to change.

The effective utilization of information improves the performance of marketing in ways that have been discussed throughout this book. For example, it results in:

- *Better products.* A refined understanding of the buyer allows a marketer to develop products that more closely fit the buyer's needs, requiring fewer compromises and greater satisfaction.

- *Better prices.* What customers are willing to pay for a product depends on how much they value it. Knowing how important a product is to a customer and what resources the customer has available to purchase it helps sellers set attractive prices.
- *Better distribution.* The likelihood of having a product available when and where a customer wants to find it is enhanced if the seller knows the shopping habits and preferences of the buyer.
- *Better promotion.* A product and its benefits can be communicated in many ways. Both the form and the content of advertisements and other promotions can be improved if the marketer understands the buyer's motivations and expectations.

But recognizing the importance of information and using it effectively are two different things. Except in the smallest businesses, utilization requires technology. In the case of marketing, gathering, analyzing, and storing large amounts of data about markets, competitors, media, distribution, and customer behavior wasn't practical before the widespread availability of computers.

Consider, for example, a supermarket chain with several stores, each with 30,000 different items on its shelves. Without computers, keeping track of the performance of each item, deciding which to keep and which to drop, and determining when and how much to reorder would be an enormous task. However, by today's standards, a relatively small computer can compile a record of all the transactions made at every checkout lane for each store. Utilizing predetermined programs, the computer can use the data to signal when individual items need to be reordered, given more or less shelf space, or even dropped.

Computers can also be used to carry out very complex tasks. Recall the example of data mining in Chapter 7. Firms use sophisticated analytical techniques and powerful computers to sift through millions of bits of customer-related data in search of patterns that wouldn't be apparent to human observers no matter how much time and effort they invested. Thus the marriage of information and technology has become a fact of life in marketing.

Information Technology in Marketing

Numerous technological developments have had a significant impact on marketing. Certainly television (which provides a mass-market advertising medium), household telephones (which permit easy interaction between buyers and sellers), and personal computers (which increase individual productivity of marketing managers) are examples. Rather than try to discuss all the information technology that impacts marketing, we will focus on the Internet, a development that has created such a stir that some have described it as the most important invention since the printing press.[2] We will then examine the impact it has had on an activity fundamental to the information economy, electronic networking.

The Internet

In the early 1970s the **Internet** was created as part of a U.S. government project. Its original purpose was to link researchers at many different sites and allow them to exchange information. The procedure for using the Internet served the purposes of the researchers, but it was too cumbersome for broad commercial applications. Then, in 1989 the **World Wide Web** (now simply referred to as the Web) was developed. The Web provided access to a portion of the larger Internet, making it possible for users to share a full range of communications from text to graphics and audio messages. Any individual or organization can create and register a **website**, a collection of Web files beginning with a home page, that is accessible through a unique address.

The Web opened the door to an array of commercial developments. The most basic is the Web browser. A **browser** provides an Internet visitor with the necessary application program to look at and interact with individual websites. Two of the best known browsers are Netscape Navigator and Microsoft's Internet Explorer. Because a browser acts as a visitor's starting site on any visit to the Web, it has a significant influence on the subsequent sites a Web surfer will visit.

As the number of websites grew, it became apparent that an electronic **directory** (similar in concept to a phone book) was needed. What has become one of the largest and best-known directories was initiated by two graduate students who began compiling a list of sites organized by topics and subtopics. They called it Yahoo! (The letters in the name stand for "Yet another hierarchical officious oracle," reflecting the youthful exuberance of the founders!) It now consists of hundreds of thousands of websites and millions of Web pages.

Even with directories, finding your way around the Web can be difficult. To assist Web visitors, the browser developers and others have created gateway or portal websites. A **portal** is an entrance and a guide to the rest of the Web. Typically a portal offers a directory of websites, a search engine to look for information and other websites, access to e-mail service, news, weather forecasts, and other information designed to attract visitors. Some of the better-known portals are Netscape, Lycos, Excite, and America Online.

Browsers, directories, and portals permit easy access to the Web for virtually anyone with a PC and a telephone line connection. The Internet and its supporting commercial developments opened up an entirely new communication vehicle that permits significant advances in electronic networking to occur.

Electronic Networking

Networks are individuals or organizations linked together to share data, exchange information and ideas, and perform tasks. Some networks are simple, requiring no technology. People have social networks, professional networks, and work group networks. You've probably been advised to develop personal networks and

Yahoo! was the first navigational guide for the Web and has become one of the most recognized brands associated with the Internet. Services available on Yahoo! include e-mail, shopping, classified ads, financial services, auctions, chat rooms, and news. Worldwide Yahoo! has 145 million individual users and records an average of 625 million page views per day. Including both work and home connections, Yahoo! reaches over 60% of the U.S. population.

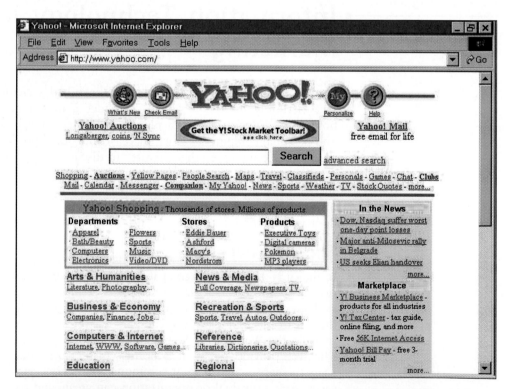

use them when looking for a job. **Electronic networks** are created when the individuals or organizations are linked via some form of telecommunications.

In business, when the personal computers of individuals in a company or department are linked together a local electronic network or **intranet** is created. For example, at an appliance manufacturer, an intranet of designers, engineers, and marketers may be created to share input as a new product is developed. The power of these networks is expanded when they include a server, which is a central, more powerful computer that can store large databases and perform sophisticated analyses. With access to the server through their PCs, the participants in a network can perform tasks not possible on individual PCs. Several levels of electronic networking exist in the information economy.

Electronic Data Interchange

When electronic networking moves outside the firm, it is known as **electronic data interchange** (EDI), which is a proprietary system in which data are exchanged between trading partners, to be used for standardized, preapproved transactions.[3] For example, Kmart stocks Procter & Gamble's Tide detergent in its stores. When the inventory of Tide reaches a predetermined level in Kmart's distribution center, its computer automatically transmits an order to P&G's computer. The P&G computer confirms the order and sets in motion the activities to fill it. Transactions similar to this are carried out thousands of times daily between firms and their suppliers. Doing it electronically saves time, minimizes order-processing expenses, and reduces clerical errors.

Early EDI made use of long-distance telephone lines that allowed the computer in one firm to dial up and "talk" to a supplier's computer. EDI is limited to large firms because of the costs involved in implementation. Because it cannot quickly adjust to price or product availability changes, it is also somewhat inflexible.

Electronic Information Transfer

The Web ushered in another level of networking for marketers. Called **electronic information** (or e-information), this form of networking involves creating a corporate website and posting information on it. Firms are able to make vast amounts of information available on their websites. The information ranges from product descriptions and invitations to suppliers to submit bids on planned purchases to product operating instructions and information about contacting sales personnel. Some e-information websites are open—that is, freely accessible to anyone. Others are restricted—that is, accessible only to those in possession of a password. By applying restrictions, a firm can make the information on its Web site available selectively to customers, distributors, and/or suppliers.

Many consumer product manufacturers and retailers view an e-information website as a necessary form of communication—like an ad with much more information than possible with traditional media. These sites often include special inducements to attract visitors, such as electronic coupons and contests. For business-to-business marketers, e-information reduces the need for paper-based communication and lowers the costs of working with suppliers and serving distributors because much of the information a customer or supply chain member needs is available 24 hours a day, 7 days a week. As a result, e-information has become the most common use of the Internet for business-to-business marketers.

The postings on an e-information website typically fall into five categories:

- *Background and general information*—primarily the company's history, its mission, corporate philosophy, and general orientation. This category includes financial performance and investor information, the structure of the firm if it is global or has several divisions, and profiles of top managers. Employment opportunities with the firm also are frequently posted here, as are recent press releases. Background and general information pages would be accessible to anyone visiting the site.

- *Current business operations*—for existing and potential business partners. This category typically has information for suppliers (how to contact corporate buyers, invitations to bid on planned purchases, payment terms and conditions, delivery requirements) and customers (product descriptions, dealer contact information, credit terms). Because some of this information is considered confidential, access may be restricted and require a password.

- *Links*—connections to other related sites. For example, a furniture manufacturer's site might make it possible for consumers to link to the website of a retailer located in their area that carries the manufacturer's products. By simply clicking on an icon that describes the related site, the visitor is transferred to it.

- *Attraction and entertainment features*—tools and techniques for engaging site visitors. Attempts to attract and hold visitors to a site often involve weaving the desired promotional message into entertaining features. For example, McDonald's website includes an electronic coloring book, visual tours of McDonald's restaurants around the world, special promotion and contest information, overviews of the firm's environmental efforts, and many more attractions. Entertainment is much more common on the websites of consumer product marketers than business-to-business marketers, but all sites must be attractive and easy to navigate to hold visitors.

- *Contact point*—providing an e-mail link for visitors, permitting them to ask questions or make comments. This opportunity for interaction is a major distinguishing feature for Internet communications in comparison to traditional media advertising. It also requires a high level of attention on the part of the site owner because unanswered inquiries or form letter responses can create substantial ill will.

The benefits marketers are seeking through a website depend on the nature of the organization. The primary benefit to business-to-business firms is greater efficiency in dealing with suppliers and customers. *If* current and potential suppliers and customers can be convinced to search a firm's website, answers to many of their routine questions can be found. When Cisco Systems, a giant maker of routers, switches, and other technical networking equipment, reduced its personal selling effort and moved much of its sales to the Web, it ran into a technical service problem. Customers phoning the service center tied up service engineers regardless of whether the issue was routine or a significant technical challenge. To relieve the pressure, Cisco put answers to customers' most frequently asked questions (FAQs) on its website. The company found customers liked the approach because they could get answers quickly, 24 hours a day. For Cisco, service engineers now focus on the more serious problems. Even though its technical staff has grown along with sales, the company estimates its savings as a result of automating much of its sales support at $75 million a year.[4]

A website (or portion of a business website) designed for final consumers is intended to build goodwill and strengthen relationships. It is comparable to brand-building advertising, except the opportunity exists to provide much more content and to interact with individual site visitors through e-mail. Most large consumer packaged-goods firms such as Kellogg's, Coca-Cola, and Procter & Gamble maintain e-information sites, as do durable-goods manufacturers such as Whirlpool and Ford Motor Co.

A firm typically attracts visitors through ads placed in other media and by publicizing its website address (called its URL) on its letterhead and on executives' business cards. For both business and consumer marketers, websites offer flexibility, because the content can be changed as frequently as desired, and broad geographic reach, because anyone in the world with access to the Internet is potentially reachable.

www.kelloggs.com

www.whirlpool.com

Electronic Transactions

Note that e-information sites provide information but they are not designed to make transactions. Creating the capability of making purchases directly from a firm's website is known as **electronic transactions** (or e-transactions), the next higher level of electronic networking. E-transactions involve more interaction and feedback than e-information. Both consumer product marketers and business-to-business sellers make use of e-transactions. Because of media coverage, most people are familiar with consumer buying via the Web—estimated at $19 billion in 1999, and expected to grow to about $80 billion by 2003.[5] However, the dollar volume of so-called B2C (business-to-consumer) transactions is dwarfed by B2B (business-to-business) transactions. Business purchases on the Web totaled nearly $110 billion in 1999, and the forecast for 2003 is $1.4 *trillion*.[6]

For firms that already have telephone-ordering desks and 1-800 phone lines, adding e-transactions may not be a major adjustment. In many cases it simply offers existing customers another contact point with the firm. For example, when W. W. Grainger put its catalog of MRO supplies on its website, it was inviting e-transactions. However, many firms with e-information sites have avoided moving to e-transactions because of the negative impact selling directly can have on their existing channel members. Another reason for avoiding e-transactions is that even if one or more levels of distribution are removed from a channel, the functions must still be performed. Thus many firms opt to stick with their existing arrangements rather than create the necessary processing, shipping, and service operations required to deal with large numbers of individual orders. According to an industry consultant, "Manufacturers are very good at shipping in bulk to a few distribution points. That's very different than shipping one unit to a person."[7]

There are two categories of firms that conduct transactions over the Web: (1) new businesses seeking an effective way to reach the market, and (2) existing businesses expanding their access to the market or replacing their current channel. This is an important distinction because the Web has allowed new business models to be created that would be impossible using traditional channels. An example is Fineartlease, a company that leases expensive works of art to individuals and businesses that want to display the art but don't want to buy it. The art is actually owned by various galleries and museums around the world. What Fineartlease does is match the galleries and museums with the prospective customers who are also geographically dispersed. According to the founder, "Without the Internet, you couldn't create an effective way to distribute this (service)."[8] The online auctions such as eBay (the opening case in Chapter 1), and the reverse auctions organized by FreeMarkets (described at the beginning of Chapter 5) are additional examples of new business models made possible by the Internet.

www.Fineartlease.com

www.ebay.com

www.freemarkets.com

The other category consists of existing firms, both small and large, that want to expand their market access. For example, Prairie Frontier, a wildflower seed company, sold its products only through garden centers near its Waukesha, Wisconsin, location before going online. Now the firm sells seeds to consumers all over the country from a site that attracts visitors with wildflower photographs and gardening instructions.[9] Large firms are moving to the Internet as well. Here we find businesses of all types including travel agents, industrial goods suppliers such as W. W. Grainger, and cosmetics firm such as Avon (the subject of the Chapter 14 case). Wal-Mart, Kmart, Allstate, Toyota, and Office Depot are just a few of the other well-known firms that have broadened their marketing reach through websites designed for e-transactions.

Electronic Commerce

When a firm reconfigures its marketing operations around the interactions made possible by its Web connections, it is engaging in **electronic commerce** (or e-commerce). This is a sophisticated network that can link a large number of firms at different levels of a distribution channel in what is called an **extranet.** For example, a firm

The Web has greatly extended the reach of small firms such as Prairie Frontier. Unlike Prairie Frontier, many firms have created websites with inadequate business models. Forrester Research, a firm specializing in the Internet, predicts that many will fail because of insufficient financial resources, a lack of differentiation from competitors, or a decrease in the optimism and confidence of investors.

 www.prairiefrontier.com

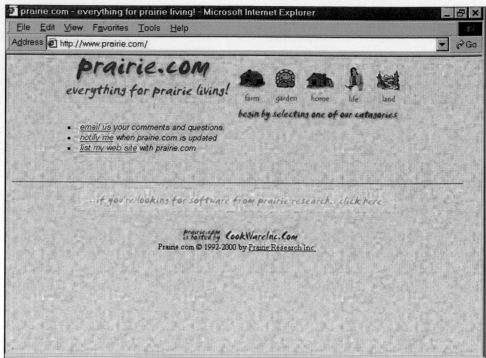

may create customized Web pages for individual customers, as Grainger does with specialized catalogs for firms that qualify for discounts. It might also involve suppliers in the design of products on the website, monitor orders from the time they are taken until the finished products are delivered, and permit customers to examine and make suggestions about the firm's production schedule.

Extranets allow business partners access to highly sensitive data about current operations as well as future plans. Thus they require strong relationships and a high level of trust. In return, they speed up decision making with the result that products get to market more quickly and at a lower cost.[10]

Electronic networking is not necessarily in the future of all firms. However, its growth is unmistakable. For example, just the number of firms that use services to assist them in making purchases on the Internet has gone from 0 in 1994 to 600,000 in 1999, and it is expected to grow to 250 million by 2003.[11] The Internet and electronic networking are impacting firms and consumers in many ways. In the next section we will describe how the relationships and functions of markets are being affected.

The Impact of the Internet on Markets

Use of the Internet by consumers as well as businesses has grown very rapidly.[12] In 1996, only about 14% of U.S. households had access to the Web. By 2000, that figure grew to an estimated 50%. Among the *Fortune* 500, the largest firms in the U.S., 98% have some type of Internet presence. When the head of IBM, Louis Gerstner, describes the Internet as the "ultimate medium for business," firms of all sizes and types are compelled to at least investigate its potential impact on customer expectations and behavior. Several fundamental developments in how markets have been affected by the Internet are described below.[13]

CSX Corp., with railroads, ships, and trucks, is one of the world's largest suppliers of transportation services. Its data management system handles 7 million transactions a day, coordinates 100,000 rail cars over 24,000 miles of track, and directs 27,000 shipping containers on land and at sea. Yet the company, through the Internet, enables customers to track their individual shipments day or night.

 www.csx.com

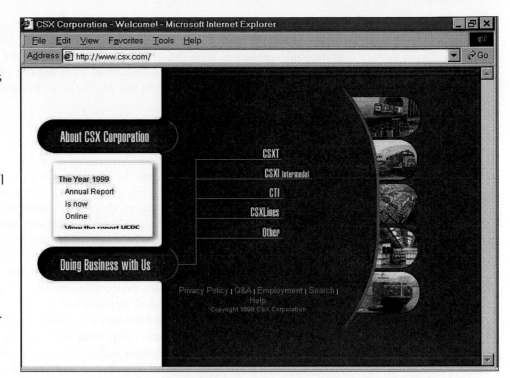

Control of Information Flow

The traditional model of marketing communication has the seller largely in control of the flow of information. Consumer product firms decide when and where to advertise their products, and business marketers design the messages their sales people will present and plan their visits to clients. Clearly these choices are made with the customer in mind, but they are made by sellers.

In the online environment, the information flow is controlled by the customer. It is the customer who must sit down at a computer, search for a website, and decide what pages to examine or ignore. If a marketer fails to provide information valued by customers, it will lose them as an audience. On its website, the maker of Mentadent toothpaste offers product information, a chance to order a sample, a $1-off coupon, specific oral-care information, and the opportunity to ask a dental hygienist questions. In contrast, much of the mass media advertising for the same brand offers very little but reinforcement of the brand name to a passive audience. The net effect of this shift in control is that websites must be enticing and informative.

 www.mentadent.com

Opportunity for Comparisons

One of the features of the Internet is convenience. Customers of CSX Corp., one of the nation's largest freight railroads, can book shipments, get prices quotes, or determine the exact location of goods in transit any time, day or night, from the railroad's website. Likewise, consumers can shop from home without worrying about whether a retailer is open or closed. That convenience has been greatly enhanced by the development of search engines designed to facilitate product comparisons. By integrating information from many online marketers, a site such as Junglee (part of Amazon) can provide a visitor with a one-stop source of information on product features and prices for dozens or even hundreds of alternatives.

Clearly the ability to make comparisons on the Internet forces online firms to be aware of and responsive to the prices charged by other Web marketers. However, it has another implication. Customers can now gather comparison information from the Internet and use it in negotiations with traditional marketers. In the past, many firms had a "geographic monopoly" because they had little or no local competition, and customers were uninformed about the cost of the same product elsewhere. Now there is no reason why a small firm buying printing services or a consumer buying a car need approach the purchase without comparative information.

Customized Products

Customization has been relatively common in business-to-business marketing, although it is generally limited to "big-ticket" purchases with high margins. On the other hand, nearly all consumer products are highly standardized. The reason for the difference is quite simple—the flow of information. Getting the customization details from the buyer to the seller, arranging to have suppliers provide the necessary parts, and sharing the information internally with manufacturing and other functions took too much time. The Internet speeds up that flow and makes customization not only possible but practical. Ford and General Motors have joined Toyota in a commitment to provide customized cars within five days of receiving an order.[14] And the expectation is that customization will quickly spread to consumer electronics and appliances.

One of the advantages of customization is eliminating the investment in inventory. Imagine an automobile dealership with only enough cars and trucks on its lot to permit test-drives. In the auto industry, studies indicate that shifting from mass production of standardized vehicles to customized sales could reduce prices by as much as 30%.[15]

Fewer Fixed Prices

Fixed prices are the norm in consumer markets, with only a few exceptions. In business-to-business marketing, negotiated prices are more common, but many prices are fixed there as well. This is likely to change. As the Internet makes real-time auctions possible, fixed prices for business and consumer sales may become rarities. eBay, the dominant firm in consumer Internet auctions, has nearly 8 million registered users bidding on 3 million items.[16] Products as diverse as a retired Russian submarine and Barbie dolls are offered on the eBay site. In business markets, firms such as TradeOut.com conduct online auctions of surplus and discontinued equipment and merchandise.

 www.tradeout.com

The reverse auction, as described in the opening case for Chapter 5, is also increasing in popularity. In this situation, the buyer specifies what is desired, and prospective sellers make offers, bidding the price down. Reverse auctions are expected to expand beyond standard, commodity items purchased by businesses to include a wide variety of consumer goods.

Traditional online auctions expand the market, giving sellers access to many more potential buyers. Reverse auctions also give buyers access to more sellers. In both scenarios, prices are determined in real time by the interactions of buyers and sellers.

Delivering Products

In a traditional arrangement, a manufacturer produces a product and sells it to the next level in the distribution channel (possibly a wholesaler or a retailer). As was described in Chapter 14, firms further down the channel maintain an inventory of the product, promote it locally, provide credit to buyers, take and process orders, distribute the product in smaller quantities to other firms or consumers, and provide a variety of services to the buyers. Many of these activities are related to filling orders, and are captured by the term **fulfillment.**

When a firm sells on the Web and therefore skips one or more channel levels, it must create the systems to provide fulfillment. Even a traditional retailer that goes on the Web must arrange to process orders and get the product to the buyer. One option is to perform these tasks internally. For example, a manufacturer that formerly shipped truckloads of products to wholesalers might start packaging and shipping individual units to consumers. Another option is to outsource fulfillment. For example, recall the description of how Wal-Mart is working with Fingerhut, a catalog retailer, to support its online operation. Fingerhut provides order processing, warehousing, shipping, and customer service for Wal-Mart's Web sales.[17] Fingerhut has a similar fulfillment arrangement with eToys.

www.sears.com

The challenge of fulfillment is reflected in the intended strategy of Sears. Seeking a way to blend its online effort with its stores, Sears plans to have customers visit its stores to pick up purchases made on its website.[18] This defeats one of the primary reasons for online buying, the convenience of not having to leave home.

Buyer Communication

Word of mouth is recognized by marketers as a potent force because objective assessment of a trusted third party is very influential in a purchase decision. Of course, word of mouth can be negative as well as positive. Thus firms go to considerable effort to encourage positive word of mouth and to resolve any unfavorable impressions that might lead to negative word of mouth.

The Internet has magnified both the speed and the reach of word of mouth. Forums, chat rooms, and individual sites provide a nearly unlimited source of opinions about products and experiences. Even if none of your friends have taken a Carnival cruise, purchased from an L. L. Bean's catalog, or stayed in a hotel in London, you can quickly gather opinions and recommendations of people who have.

A form of buyer communication that mimics the consumer cooperatives of the 1970s is reflected online buyer cartels such as Mercata, Inc., where consumers can pool their spending power to buy certain items. With the leverage of bulk buying, the site operators are able to negotiate discounts from sellers.[19]

Mercata illustrates how the Web can overcome the constraints of distance and lack of information by providing a way for consumers to create buying groups. A seller putting merchandise on Mercata's website specifies a price and the length of time the offer will remain available. The seller also agrees to lower the price for all buyers as the number of individuals agreeing to buy increases.

 www.mercata.com

It's been suggested that many companies have taken advantage of customer ignorance about alternative prices and the relative performance of substitute products. However, the Internet makes information exchange among buyers much easier, shifting power from the sellers to the customers.

The Impact of the Internet on Marketing Strategy

The Internet has created opportunities for firms to create their own websites to communicate with other businesses and consumers, and to conduct transactions. As discussed above, the objectives of these sites are to reduce costs, generate revenue, or both.

In addition to creating new businesses, the Web has changed existing ways of doing business. For example, it has stimulated some unlikely alliances between traditional retailers and Web access providers. America Online and Wal-Mart, Yahoo! and Kmart, and Microsoft and Best Buy have forged agreements in which the stores promote the Web access provider to their customers in return for promotion of the retailer's online store on the portals.[20] This is just one example of how the Internet has influenced marketing strategy. As the following discussion suggests, many areas have been affected.

Market Research

Like all good marketers, firms making use of the Internet want to segment markets and then concentrate on selected targets. Gathering data about website visits and visitors and relating that data to other information about visitors is a useful place to begin. Online research firm Media Matrix illustrates this approach.[21] It records the Internet activity of 50,000 individuals who have agreed to permit monitoring devices to be attached to their computers. The firm tracks which sites each person visits, how much time they spend at a site, and the banner ads they click on. This information is combined with individual demographics, psychographics, preferences, and consumption data provided by the respondents to form profiles and define targets. With consumer product makers selecting sites on which to place their ads (expected to total $1.2 billion by 2003), information such as this is helpful. For example, a simple finding by Media Matrix that cola drinkers are more likely to visit travel sites, whereas noncola drinkers prefer kids and entertainment sites, can be useful to a soft drink firm deciding where to place its Web advertising.

In another effort to gain greater insight into Web visitors, Media Matrix has joined with Information Resources, Inc., to form e-Scan. This effort links Internet usage with buying behavior from offline sources of a large sample of households over time. The firms hope the results will identify patterns useful to marketers in deciding where to advertise, and what links to other websites they should provide. Among their early findings: Dog food buyers are more likely to browse www.ESPN.com, and cookie buyers tend to surf www.MTV.com.[22]

There are other research techniques to identify segments that involve gathering data through electronic observation of site visitors. One approach, called **clustering**, tracks the pages visited, amount of time at a page, and items purchased by individuals while they navigate a site. It then creates groups or clusters of visitors with very similar patterns. When subsequent visitors display behavior similar to a particular cluster, they can be steered in real time to content or merchandise they are most likely to buy.

Amazon developed a similar technique called **collaborative filtering** that allows it to recommend books or tapes to an individual based on a comparison of the person's selections and the purchases of previous visitors. So, for example, assume a number of visitors who purchased books on gardening from Amazon.com also examined books on home repairs. When you click on home repairs, in addition to giving you that information, the site would suggest some popular gardening titles.[23]

As the competition intensifies, Internet marketers recognize the importance of segmentation and targeting. As one research analyst observed, "Online services have mostly been competing on selection and price, but now that the playing field is growing, the smart ones are realizing they need to differentiate themselves by offering a relevant, personalized experience to the customer."[24]

Rather than just offering a lower price, Internet marketers are learning to use the technology to improve service. For example, NextCard has linked its website to the databases of the major consumer credit bureaus, which allows it to make the process of applying for a Visa credit card much quicker and easier.[25] Another example is the effort of General Motors to add an Internet link to its Onstar system, which combines a car phone and global-positioning equipment to offer travel information and emergency help. The added service will allow a driver to listen to an individually designed mix of news, customized traffic reports, and personal e-mail messages.[26]

Channel Relationships

The attraction of the Web for manufacturers is a closer link with the final customer. By selling over the Web and eliminating middlemen, both business and consumer product makers are able to decide which of their products to present, how they will be presented, and what level of service will accompany them. Equally important, the direct connection of the Internet permits manufacturers to obtain unfiltered feedback from the buyers who actually use their products. According to an advertising executive, "They (manufacturers) never owned that customer relationship before."[27] Firms as diverse as Mattel, Timex, Clinique, Sony, and Polaroid are using websites to sell their products.

For an established firm (other than a retailer), selling on the Web usually means bypassing one or more channel members or even a manufacturer's own sales force. In most instances, this is a source of tension. For example, when General Motors floated the idea of selling cars via the Web in response to the competition of sites such as Autobytel and Cars.com, there was an immediate negative response from its dealers. Closer to home, a firm's own sales force can be affected by Web sales. When Merrill Lynch announced it would offer online trading to its existing clients, its brokers were quick to ask how their commissions would be affected.

The issue is simple. Changing the way a product is sold and distributed has an impact on the individuals and organizations currently selling the product. Anticipating their reaction and insuring they are treated fairly is not as obvious. By moving some of its sales to the Web, a firm risks losing the loyalty and commitment of its existing channel. W. W. Grainger dealt with this by guaranteeing its sales people commissions on all sales made on the Web by customers in their territories. However, paying commissions to sales people or distributors not actually involved in a sale eliminates at least some of the cost savings of selling on the Web.

Because the majority of sales for most manufacturers are still made through traditional channels, the risk of alienating important business partners has affected Web strategies. Some of the approaches used by manufacturers to avoid Internet-related channel conflict are:[28]

- *Use the Web as a lead generator only.* Some manufacturers, notably the auto companies, use their websites to collect sales leads, and then direct potential customers to dealers located near them.
- *Offer different products online.* Mattel offers collectibles online that are not available in stores.

The market has changed since Mattel had success with brand names such as Barbie, Hot Wheels, and Fisher-Price. Many think the future for toy makers is in customized toys (as shown here) and in games and puzzles for kids online. Revenue comes from firms that attach ads to the online material. With over 22 million young people between 2 and 18-years-old already online, advertisers see "online toys" as a way to reach this attractive audience.

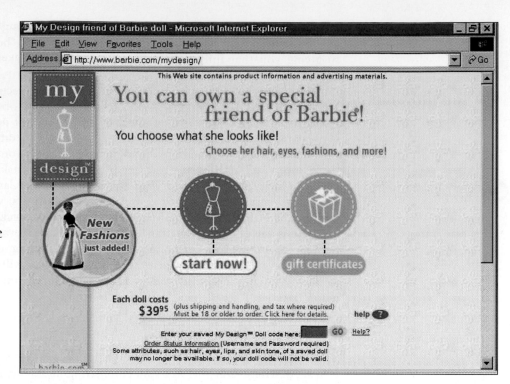

www.mattel.com

www.quixtar.com

• *Sell online at the retail list price.* To avoid undercutting retail stores, Polaroid sells its digital cameras and photo printers online at the same price consumers find in stores.

• *Involve middlemen in online sales.* Some manufacturers have designed their systems to have buyers visit retail stores to pick up their online purchases. This is appealing to the merchants because it gets consumers in the store, but it negates one of the primary benefits of online buying. When Amway started selling online, it devised a plan to engage and protect its 3 million sales representatives. Representatives are encouraged to sign up customers for Amway's website. The sales person then gets a commission for any online purchases made by customers they have registered.[29]

• *Target a different market segment.* Clinique, which offers customized cosmetics and hair-care products on its website, targets consumers who avoid the cosmetics counters in department stores.

Middlemen have devised strategies of their own to add value to their positions in the supply chain.[30] One approach is to take over the final assembly role for products purchased online. The manufacturer ships the product to the distributor in semifinished form, and the distributor completes the assembly and, if appropriate, tests the product before delivery. Called **channel assembly,** this approach allows products to be customized for customers and at the same time shortens the delivery time because many manufacturers, preferring not to disrupt their production processes, postpone custom projects. Another strategy, termed *co-location,* has employees of the distributor stationed at the manufacturer's site to arrange shipment of the finished product to the customer. Because the product is handled fewer times, co-location shortens delivery time.

The Internet has also created a new breed of electronic middlemen. These firms make or facilitate transactions through the Internet, but their only investment is a website. The model for this type of operation was created by eBay, the online auction. It has since been copied, modified, and extended to insurance, travel, long-distance phone calls, home repair services, and other industries. Without existing distribution systems, these firms are unconcerned about upsetting established

www.ecoverage.com

relationships. An example is eCoverage, a San Francisco-based company that sells insurance online, with the insurance provided by Pacific Specialty Insurance. A customer can buy a policy on eCoverage's website in five minutes. Because it has no local offices or sales people, the firm's costs are 10 to 20% below those of traditional insurance firms.[31]

One thing is clear. When a firm uses the Internet for transactions, it has an impact on channel relationships. The resulting channel adjustment may be moderate (redefining the role of middlemen) or drastic (eliminating middlemen).

Promotion

A website without visitors is a waste of money. Equally ineffective is a site without the right visitors—the target audience of the organization. This is a concern of online consumer marketers because 1 out of 10 U.S. households shop online,[32] but only about 2% of site visitors make a purchase.[33] Part of the problem is simply the number of websites and the fact that the search engines can't keep track of them all. Imagine going to a mall with thousands of stores and looking for a particular one using an incomplete directory.

Another complicating factor is that visits to websites are always initiated by the visitor—a customer, supplier, or even a competitor. There is no passive exposure, as occurs with mass media such as television or radio, and very little incidental exposure, as occurs with billboards or walking past a store. These characteristics of the Internet have resulted in some adjustments in how website promotion is carried out.

The first issue is *attracting* the right audience to a website. Several approaches are being used:

- *Banner ads on other websites.* A **banner ad** is a boxed-in promotional message, often appearing at the top of a Web page. A site visitor who clicks on a banner ad is transported to the advertiser's home page. As Web visitors become familiar with banner ads, they tend to ignore them and their effectiveness diminishes. Banner ads are also the least targeted ads. Despite these shortcomings, they account for about one-half of all advertising dollars spent online. The reason is probably the relatively low cost. On average, a banner ad costs about $10 per thousand exposures.[34]

- *Portal arrangements.* For a fee, portals give a site a prominent position when a visitor undertakes an appropriately directed search. For example, if eToys has a portal arrangement with AltaVista, a consumer who uses AltaVista's search engine to find toy marketers will find eToys at or near the top of the list.

- *Sponsorship.* For a sponsorship fee, an advertiser is given a permanent place on the host's site. For example, iVillage, a site targeted at women, lists 47 sponsors, including AT&T, First USA, and Kellogg's.[35] Each sponsor has special offers and advice for the target audience. For example, Ford invites visitors to design a "dream car" for women.

- *Targeted e-mail.* With this method, a firm directs e-mail to current or potential customers, inviting them to visit its site. When this approach is not properly targeted, it becomes electronic "junk mail" and can create ill will among the recipients.

- *Affiliate promotion.* Under this approach, a firm includes on its site a link to related sites, usually in exchange for a commission on any sales the arrangement produces. For example, a site selling sporting goods might have as affiliates a sports magazine, a camping equipment site, and a sports memorabilia site. Affiliates are typically identified as such on the site. A recent survey reported that affiliate promotion outperformed all other forms of promotion except targeted e-mail.[36]

Following a broad study of consumer information on the Internet, the Consumer Federation of America announced that consumers may be misled by the tactics employed on many websites. Among their conclusions:

- Searches on some portals are influenced by paid advertisers who are able to purchase preferred positions in the list of search results.

- Some sites offer different prices for the same item, depending on how visitors enter the site.

- Well-known brands are omitted from some searches.

- Prices are often quoted without shipping and handling charges, which in some cases can be substantial.

Under what conditions would these practices raise ethical concerns?

Sources: Richard Wolfe, "Websites Mislead Shoppers," *Financial Times,* Nov. 5, 1999, p. 7; and Consumer Federation of America website.

www.consumerfed.org

All of these promotion methods use the Internet in one way or another. According to Forrester Research, total expenditures for this type of advertising amounted to about $2.8 billion in 1999.[37] Nearly as much, $2.5 billion, was spent in traditional media (television, radio, newspapers, magazines, and billboards) by Internet marketers in an attempt to attract visitors.[38]

Attracting visitors is only half the battle. The second objective of promotion is *holding* visitors once they click on a site. Internet users are generally viewed as impatient—not surprising, because speed and convenience are major attractions. With a simple mouse click, they can disappear as quickly as they arrived. Thus Internet marketers look for ways to make their sites "sticky."[39]

www.cherrycoke.com

The holding power of a site is measured in terms of time spent per visit. For example, when Coca-Cola Co. found that visitors spent only an average of 90 seconds at cherrycoke.com, it redesigned the site. In contrast, a site can have excellent holding power but not meet a firm's objective, as Bell Atlantic found out. The firm created an online "soap opera" about a newlywed couple. Episodes were run weekly, and they attracted large audiences, even receiving positive reviews from entertainment critics. However, when consumer surveys showed no change in Bell Atlantic's brand awareness, the feature was discontinued.

Another measure combines attraction and hold. It is the number of minutes per month a person spends at a site. For example, Amazon.com visitors spend an average of 13 minutes a month at the site, while eBay visitors average 105 minutes a month.[40] This may help explain why Amazon added an online auction similar to eBay's.

There is still much to learn about attracting visitors to online sites and about marketing to them once they arrive. As firms gain experience and more research is conducted, firms will develop more savvy about online efforts. In the meantime, some online marketers are willing to go to almost any length to attract customers. For example, more.com, an online drugstore, allows customers to lock in forever the price of an item they buy now, as long as they purchase the item at least once a year. According to a more.com executive, "We'll invest what it takes to be competitive in building a large customer base and maintaining a large share of the market."[41]

www.more.com

Issues and Opportunities in the Information Economy

The information economy and the Internet pose major challenges for marketers. Not only are some traditional strategies and tactics obsolete or quickly becoming so, but entirely new issues are frequently discovered. As always, the firms that find ways to overcome these obstacles are likely to be the most successful in the long run.

Information Quality and Quantity

The Internet demonstrates how valuable information can be. A prospective car buyer who can compare the prices of several sellers has an advantage in negotiations. Similarly, a component supplier to a manufacturer kept informed of the manufacturer's production schedule can minimize inventory costs. However, as the Internet grows, the issues of the quality and quantity of the information provided is becoming a larger issue.

For a little as $75, anyone can register a Web address and create a website. As a result, there are millions of websites in existence and the number is expanding daily. A recent estimate suggests that there are over 800 million documents available on the Internet.[42] Visiting the Web is equally easy, requiring only access to a PC and a willingness to pay a monthly connection fee. The problem is that Web users are in danger of being buried by the onslaught of information, and websites risk being lost in the clutter. For example, do consumers want to sift through the terms and conditions of over 300 insurance providers, even if the information is conveniently provided on one website?

Another information issue is quality. There is very little regulation of the Internet and virtually no standards except voluntary guidelines set by professional organizations such as the American Marketing Association. As a result, fraud is quite common. According to the International Chamber of Commerce, online retail sales of counterfeit products may total $25 billion worldwide.[43] Hardest hit are designer brands like Cartier, Gucci, Chanel, and Coach.

The Web also creates instant critics. Anyone with a website can offer a critique of a company, a product, a book, or anything else, and there is nothing to ensure the credentials of the reviewer or the accuracy of the comments. Some evaluations are given credibility by the sites on which they appear. For example, Amazon has professional critics who review and recommend books and compact discs. Even in this controlled environment, however, issues of objectivity have been raised. For example, About.com, which provides expert reviews in 650 subject areas, also includes links to many shopping services. If a visitor follows a link from a review to a shopping site and buys something, the author of the review is paid a commission.[44]

The challenge for marketers using the Internet is to understand their target markets well enough to provide them with the right amount of useful information. Doing any less will frustrate customers in the short term and possibly alienate them in the long run.

Customer Service

Infatuated with the technology and the ability to conduct transactions, some online marketers overlook the importance of service. Presale information, operating instructions, and postsale problem resolution frequently receive too little attention. According to a consumer seeking renter's insurance on the Web, "It was quite a nightmare," because of difficulty in navigating the sites and the lack of follow-up by the companies.[45]

In some cases the Web may replace the retail store for a consumer or the sales person for a business-to-business customer. However, it's not likely to eliminate the services provided by these middlemen. Thus online marketers must address challenges such as returned merchandise, payment problems, and performance complaints. For example, when Amazon began its auction site, it offered a customer satisfaction guarantee. Even though the transactions are between the buyers and sellers, and Amazon only brings them together, Amazon is attempting to avoid the problems eBay experienced when customers were dissatisfied and had nowhere to turn.

Providing service may be the single biggest hurdle for firms comtemplating a move to the Internet. According to one analysis, surviving in the information economy will require flawless service simply because customers will demand it.[46]

Security and Privacy

The factor that keeps nearly two-thirds of all online consumers from making purchases over the Internet is the fear of disclosing credit card information, according to a study by Ernst & Young.[47] After years of being advised to guard against having credit card numbers stolen, consumers are now asked to freely give those numbers to strangers over the Internet. Creating a climate of trust on the Internet is difficult. The challenge is compounded by the newness and intangibility of the Internet. Without stores or employees to talk to face-to-face, consumers' hesitancy to share personal or financial information is not surprising.

To overcome the fears of potential customers, online buying must develop a reputation as being safe. That means the customers must perceive the system over which they make the transaction and the seller as trustworthy. Trust is created when a customer believes that the seller is legitimate and that everything possible has been done to provide a secure environment.[48]

A seller can create an image of legitimacy in several ways. One approach is to transfer an existing reputation earned in another selling format to electronic commerce. For example, Lands' End, with a proven record as a catalog retailer, simply states on its website, "You have no credit card risk. Period." Another approach is to create associations with trusted brands or firms. For example, a less-well-known firm can increase its credibility and trust by selling only well-established brands on its site. Finally, by having a well-known partner or recognizable sponsors, an unknown online merchant can give its site legitimacy.

Online security systems, which involve encryption, digital certification, authentification, and other sophisticated technology are not likely to be understood by consumers. However, what they can understand is the assurance of the seller. Net-market.com, for example, briefly describes its elaborate security system and then offers an absolute guarantee of safe shopping.

Privacy concerns focus on how data about Internet visitors are collected and used. Data about Web visitors are gathered in several ways. Some data are provided by visitors when they register on a website. Registration is frequently required in order to gain access to specialized information, games, contests, and other attractive features. Consumers also provide information at the time of a purchase. In

A primary concern of consumers shopping on the Internet is security. On its site, Lands' End points out that since going online in 1995 it has not had a confirmed case of credit card fraud. The firm further reassures consumers by promising that whatever happens on its site, there is no risk to the customer. If fraud occurs, Lands' End vows it will correct the problem and guarantees the customer will suffer no loss.

 www.landsend.com

Do dot-coms need more substance?

With the rapid growth of business websites and the scramble for attention, traditional media are inundated with advertising for firms that have ".com" at the end of their names. Even network television advertising rates were pushed up as much as 20% in 1999 as the demand for time slots exceeded the supply. Several Internet firms, including Monster.com and HotJobs.com, bought ad space on the 2000 Super Bowl, where 30 seconds cost $3 million.

The dot-com suffix has been a simple shorthand to identify that a company does business on the Web. However, as it becomes a staple in the names of more businesses, they risk creating confusion rather than understanding. For example, there are now firms named Pets.com, Petstore.com, PETsMART.com, and Petopia.com. (Quick, can you recall which one was the subject of the Chapter 15 case?)

One firm has taken a different approach. Bigstar.com, which sells movies online, has its name on delivery trucks—230 in all—in New York, Dallas, San Francisco, and Los Angeles. According to the company's senior vice president of marketing, the objective is to "create a sense of permanence." None of the trucks carry Bigstar products, but they give the firm the look of being a "real" company with "real" assets.

What communication objectives is Big Star trying to accomplish? What else could Big Star, or another "dot-com" do to achieve these objectives?

Sources: Suein L. Hwang, "A New Spin for Web Firms 'Not.com,'" *The Wall Street Journal,* Nov. 11, 1999, pp. B1+; Daniel Eisenberg, "The Net Loves Old Meida," *Time,* Nov. 1, 1999, pp. 60–61.

addition to some demographic data, the information requested to register on a site or make a purchase often includes a short survey with questions about activities, interests, and other purchase behavior. Data are also gathered without the direct involvement of the visitor. An online firm does this by using a **cookie,** a file placed on the hard drive of the visitor's computer that automatically records where the person goes online, the frequency of visits to a site, and the duration of each visit.

Internet marketers collect the data to better understand their current and potential markets. However, a number of consumer protection concerns have been raised:[49]

- *Gathering information.* Should marketers ever gather information without the express consent of the consumer? Even if permission is granted, should there be limits on the information considered appropriate to gather? Recognizing that children are especially vulnerable, Congress passed the Children's Online Privacy Protection Act, which requires that commercial websites obtain consent from a parent before asking children under 13 years of age for their names, addresses, telephone numbers, or other identifying information.[50] Another challenging question is whether customers should be compensated for the information they provide because it obviously has value to the organizations collecting it.[51]

- *Using information.* Once consumer information is gathered, should its application be constrained? For example, Amazon uses a consumer's profile to suggest books, which few people find objectionable. But should a search engine, assumed by most users to be an objective directory, tailor its recommendations to a searcher's demographics or past purchases? In the U.S. there are few regulations; but in the European Union consumers must be given explicit explanations about how any information they provide will be used.

- *Selling, exchanging, or combining information.* Is it acceptable for a website that has gathered information legitimately to sell it to another firm? For example, an online investment broker or insurance agency would find information about an online bank's customers very valuable. What about combining catalog purchase behavior with online shopping behavior, as several research firms are planning to do? Although these profiles will initially be anonymous, as marketers search for patterns of behavior and target segments, there are questions about what might happen in the future when individuals can be specifically identified.

Marketers prefer self-regulation. However, there are calls for provision of greater control of Internet security and privacy by the government.[52] Clearly these are issues that must be addressed as use of the Internet grows.

International Markets

Theoretically, electronic commerce knows no boundaries. A customer in Taiwan can use the Internet to make a purchase from Chicago-based W. W. Grainger as easily as can a firm in Milwaukee. The only physical constraint is delivery, and that has been greatly simplified by shipping companies. However, a variety of other issues must be overcome as marketers expand globally.

The model for Web-based marketing has been created in the U.S., relying on the infrastructure that's in place, but many parts of the world lack one or more critical components that have contributed to the rapid growth of online marketing. For example, only 1 in 10 Latin Americans have the telephone lines necessary to carry Internet signals, compared to 9 out of 10 people in the U.S.[53] Also, few developing countries have national credit card systems, so there is no convenient method of paying for online purchases.

And there's the issue of PC ownership. In countries where per capita income is only a few thousand dollars or less, few people can afford a PC. For example, in China with a population of 1.2 billion, only 7 million people have Internet access.[54] In some countries, notably Brazil, entrepreneurs are trying to reduce this problem by making the Web accessible in supermarket kiosks for consumers who lack computers.[55]

There are also cultural barriers to the rapid expansion of the Internet. Although English is the standard language for business-to-business transactions, many small-business people are able to communicate only in their native languages. In terms of consumers, local Internet portals have been more successful than larger imported counterparts such as AOL because they provide a rich mix of local content. There have also been some notable cultural blunders. For example, when eBay entered Great Britain, its first foreign market, the prices on its auction site were listed only in U.S. dollars. It later changed the price quotes to the local currency, but not before alienating some potential customers.[56]

Specific legal restrictions imposed by individual governments have added complications to international e-commerce. For example, there is a French requirement that all contracts be written in French, a ban in Finland on mentioning speed as a feature of a car, and a restriction in Sweden on advertising directed at children under 12 years of age. According to one executive who has learned from experience, international online marketing can "really turn into a can of worms" for the uninitiated.[57]

In a somewhat surprising turn of events, some laws have actually encouraged international online sales. For example, German consumers find it's cheaper to buy books from websites in Great Britain, and British consumers can get better deals on cars purchased from online dealers in Belgium.[58] In both cases, consumers are reacting to laws that attempt to protect domestic businesses by creating artificially high prices.

Because Web-based commerce is so new, there has been very little progress in developing legislation that facilitates its growth. However, it appears marketers are not waiting for governments to catch up. Despite problems with customs regulations and import duties, 75% of electronic purchases made by Latin Americans are with businesses outside the region. Although that amounted to only about $120 million in 1999, it is expected to grow to $8 billion by 2004.[59]

There are other issues such as sales tax that will face online marketers. Presently, no taxes are charged, but many states want to collect sales taxes on purchases made by residents from online firms located elsewhere.

A Global Perspective

What hurdles are on the track to global e-commerce?

The impediments to global electronic trade are substantial. Resolving them takes time, effort, and cooperation. One unsuccessful and one successful example illustrate the challenge.

The Organization for Economic Cooperation and Development of the European Union has been unsuccessful in developing safeguards against fraud in electronic commerce. After months of negotiation, the committee recommended that contract disputes in electronic commerce transactions be dealt with in the customer's national courts. Some believe this is an unnecessary government intrusion into the marketplace that will discourage small businesses from participating in the Internet economy. Rather than risk costly legal actions anywhere in the EU where they have customers, firms with limited resources may choose not to do business online. Some possible alternatives—codes of conduct, national ombudsmen, and better-informed buyers—might achieve the same objective but keep the Internet accessible to small companies.

In contrast, the United Nations and members of a computer industry group called OASIS (Organization for the Advancement of Structured Information Standards) that includes Microsoft, Boeing, Oracle, IBM, Fuji, and others have devised a standard Web-based electronic business procedure for paperless trading. The initiative enables companies to deal online with suppliers and customers anywhere in the world. It also provides documentation for customs, insurance companies, and banks. A major advantage of the new protocol—called electronic business XML or ebXML—is the access it will give small and medium-sized businesses to the Internet by making electronic transactions easier and cheaper. Currently 99% of international sales use paper invoices, which cost an average of $75 each to process. A comparable online transaction using the new system will cost about 50 cents.

Sources: Frances Williams, "Web Standards Promise Big Boost for Global Commerce," *Financial Times*, Nov. 30, 1999, p. 5; and "Cybershopping," *Financial Times*, Nov. 4, 1999, p. 14.

The Future

The growth of electronic networking in all forms is remarkable. Networks have energized managers, stimulated the development of new business models, and caught the attention of nearly everyone. In the business-to-business sector, electronic networking has added to efficiency and contributed to bottom-line performance. It has been less successful in generating profits for firms that sell to consumers because Internet retailers tend to reinvest any surplus to build brand names and market shares.[60]

Thus far, the most successful Internet marketing sites deal in information, such as online investment brokers for consumers and Cisco Systems in the business-to-business market. Because all aspects of the transaction are conducted over the Internet, maximum benefits are achieved. Next in line are the sites that market services such as airline seats or hotel rooms. These marketers have an inventory that becomes obsolete at a definable time—for example, when a plane takes off. The challenge is to develop a yield-management program that adjusts fares over time to fill the largest number of seats at the highest possible price. The most challenging Internet businesses are those handling physical goods that must be inventoried, stored, and distributed. Examples are online marketers of groceries, clothing, furniture, and automobiles. The logistics problems in these businesses consume much of the gains achieved from the online transactions.[61]

Despite its expanding impact, electronic commerce will not replace traditional marketing as we know it. Jeff Bezos, the founder of Amazon.com and one of the leaders of the e-commerce movement, predicts that Internet sellers can attract at most 15% of the world's $5 trillion retail market.[62] Although $750 billion is hardly a trifling amount, Bezos contends that stores will always be around because people enjoy the interaction shopping provides, and some needs must be met more quickly than is possible over the Internet.

Clearly the information economy has arrived. What is yet to be determined is how it will impact each individual industry and business. The challenge for marketers is to determine how information can be most effectively utilized to meet the needs of the customer and satisfy the objectives of the organization. Not surprisingly, determining its value brings us back once again to the marketing concept.

• Summary

Information has always played a major role in marketing. The effective utilization of information leads to better products, prices, distribution, and promotion. Technology combined with information is especially powerful.

Although many forms of technology have influenced marketing, the Internet is currently having a major—perhaps unprecedented—impact. The commercial application of the Internet required the development of the World Wide Web and several tools to make it accessible, including browsers, directories, and portals. Now the Web is available to virtually anyone with a PC.

Electronic networks are created when individuals or organizations are linked via some form of telecommunications. Internal electronic networks are called intranets. There are several types of external electronic networks, including electronic data interchanges, electronic information transfer, electronic transactions, electronic commerce, and extranets. All of these now make use of the Internet.

Internet marketing changes the dynamics in markets. Customers gain greater control of information flows and have the opportunity to compare products and prices. More products are customized, and fewer prices are fixed. New ways are developed to deliver products to buyers, and buyers share more information. The Internet also influences marketing strategy. Areas most affected are marketing research, channel relationships, and promotion.

The information economy poses both challenges and opportunities for marketers. Among the most significant are managing the quality and quantity of information, providing customer service, ensuring the security of transactions and the privacy of customers, and developing international electronic commerce.

The Internet will continue to grow and evolve. At this point companies dealing in information are best able to take advantage of the economies provided by the Internet, whereas those selling goods face the most challenges. Although its impact will be felt by all businesses, it's not likely that the Internet will entirely replace traditional marketing.

More about **W. W. Grainger**

Grainger has made good use of the Internet in creating an electronic catalog. However, the firm is committed to changing its "business model." That means looking for other ways to make use of this tool to improve its performance and its customers' performance. The firm has looked at every aspect of its business and identified several other applications. For example, Grainger has:

- Designed an electronic database to keep track of products in its own system.
- Linked its distribution centers and local branches with a satellite network to quickly find products for customers.
- Created Orderzone, a site featuring six other companies that offer thousands of MRO products

that Grainger doesn't stock. Grainger gets a commission for any purchases made from these companies through the site. More important, when customers use Orderzone, they are buying items that Grainger doesn't offer, but doing it through Grainger.

- Initiated an auction site that allows customers to bid on discontinued or excess inventory. The customer gets a good price, and Grainger frees up cash.

- Developed a search engine called Findmro that allows its customers to check the product assortments of several other MRO suppliers (with a total inventory of over 5 million items). Customers can search for items Grainger doesn't carry and/or can check prices.

- Produced customized electronic catalogs for customers that qualify for discounts. That way all buyers from B. F. Goodrich, for example, automatically see the Goodrich discount when they log on to the site. This reduces the amount of negotiation and allows the buyers to see the price they will pay without any additional calculations.

- Made its database interactive allowing online buyers to see if particular items in the catalog have been purchased by companies similar to their own, to ask for suggestions about products for specific or unusual applications, and to examine their previous purchases.

Grainger has also provided its 1,500 sales representatives a measure of income protection. Specifically, Grainger guarantees them a commission on all electronic purchases made by their accounts.

W. W. Grainger has discovered that a 70-year-old company selling unglamorous products to customers primarily interested in saving money can be energized and possibly even transformed by new technology.[63]

1. Why is W. W. Grainger, in effect, assisting actual and potential competitors through Orderzone.com and Findmro.com?

2. If it works for a business such as Grainger, should all firms be engaged in electronic commerce?

www.orderzone.com

www.findmro.com

Key Terms and Concepts

Internet (631)
World Wide Web (631)
Website (631)
Browser (632)
Directory (632)
Portal (632)
Networks (632)

Electronic networks (633)
Intranet (633)
Electronic data interchange (EDI) (633)
Electronic information (633)
Electronic transactions (635)
Electronic commerce (635)

Extranet (635)
Fulfillment (638)
Clustering (640)
Collaborative filtering (640)
Channel assembly (642)
Banner ad (643)
Cookie (647)

Questions and Problems

1. Two examples of information technology that have had a significant impact on marketing are radio and television. How does the Internet differ from these breakthroughs as a marketing tool?

2. Examine the e-information sites of a fast-food restaurant and a traditional manufacturer (such as Whirlpool or Ford Motor Co.). Using the five categories of information described in the chapter, compare the sites.

3. What key strategic issues are faced by traditional "bricks-and-mortar" retailers such as Wal-Mart,

Kmart, and Office Depot when they go online to sell products?

4. Describe one possible marketing implication of each of the following effects of the Internet:
   a. Information flow controlled by customers
   b. Greater opportunity for product and price comparisons
   c. Fewer fixed prices
   d. New product-delivery methods
   e. More buyer communication

5. Why should firms such as Mattel, Timex, and Sony be concerned about their existing channels when they begin selling products to consumers via the Web?

6. Go to one of the Web portals (Netscape, Alta Vista, Lycos), and click through several links. Note the banner ads on each link. What appears to be the objective of the banner ads? What are some factors that may make them effective or ineffective?

7. Providing customer service appears to be one of the primary challenges for Internet marketers. What implications does this have for their "bricks-and-mortar" competitors?

8. There are concerns about Internet marketers using "cookies" to gather data about online customer behavior. Is this different than observing customers as they shop in retail stores?

Hands-On Marketing

1. Interview five students who have shopped on the Web within the last week. Gather the following information:
   a. Why did they choose the Web as a place to shop?
   b. Did they make a purchase? Why or why not?
   c. In the process of shopping, did they make any unplanned site or page visits?
   d. How long did their shopping "trip" take?

   On the basis of this information as well as your own experiences, what do you see as the strengths and weaknesses of the Web as a marketing tool?

2. Talk to the owner or manager of a retail store in a category where online marketing is growing (such as books, recorded music, groceries, videos, or toys). Determine how serious a threat the person considers online marketing to be, and what changes have been made or are planned in response.

Cases for Part 7

Developing and Implementing Strategy

During the 1980s and most of the 1990s, Coca-Cola's performance was excellent. With the exception of the embarrassing failure of "New Coke," a reformulation of its flagship cola's flavor in 1985, the company's strategy was on target. During the period, Coca-Cola had annual earnings increases that averaged at least 15%. As an investment, Coca-Cola was generally considered one of the economy's premier growth companies. In fact, from 1982 to 1998, Coke's stock rose a dazzling 3,500%. But by mid-1998, sales had flattened, earnings were declining, and Coca-Cola was facing serious challenges on several fronts.

The Lure of Globalization

Probably no product epitomized the attraction and potential of globalization better than Coke. By the 1950s, Coke and the hourglass bottle were familiar to consumers all over the world. In 1971, Coca-Cola produced an ad that served as a public statement of its belief that a product, more specifically its product, could have global appeal. Ranked as one of the 50 most memorable in television history, the ad depicted 200 children of all races and nationalities standing on a hilltop in Italy singing "I'd like to teach the world to sing." Besides creating a pop music hit, the ad ushered in the era of globalization.

Coca-Cola's actions reflect its confidence in the universal potential of its product. Long before it was common practice, the company was expanding abroad at a rapid rate. With investments on every continent, Coke now spends about 75% of its $1.3 billion advertising budget outside the U.S., and generates a similar proportion of its $18 billion in revenue from foreign sources.

The company has always taken a long-term view of overseas markets. For example, despite limited short-run potential in China and Russia, Coca-Cola invested heavily in bottling and distribution facilities in both countries. In fact, the company's management team in China put together what may be an unprecedented 100-year strategic plan for Coke in that country. The approach is summed up in a 1998 statement by the then CEO: "We have two guiding principles: We're everywhere. And we stay forever. We never look at one-year returns."

In countries with economic problems, Coke implemented a number of tactics to stimulate sales, including switching from plastic to returnable glass bottles, lowering the price of a serving by using 6.5-ounce bottles, and engaging in consumer promotions such as bundling a candy bar with its half-liter bottles in Poland. In Mexico, the company's second-largest market after the U.S., Coca-Cola discovered that many small-store owners were single mothers and retirees who could not afford health insurance. In response, the firm created an incentive that ties the volume of a store's Coke sales to reduced rates in a group insurance plan. The program contributed to a 13% increase in sales in one year.

Counting on depressed economies to recover, Coca-Cola invested heavily in Brazil, Russia, and Indonesia. And looking to the future, the company has committed to invest $1 billion in Africa. Coke is also doubling its investment in China, despite the very slow growth in sales in that country and the Chinese government's pronouncement that it will restrict the firm's growth.

Developments in the Domestic Market

U.S. consumers guzzle more soft drinks per capita than consumers in any other country except Mexico, and 45% of what they drink is made by Coca-Cola. The company's U.S. product line includes soft drinks (Coca-Cola Classic, Diet Coke, Sprite, Fanta, Barq's, Mello Yello, and Surge), Dasani bottled water, Minute Maid juices, Nestea, POWERaDE sports drink, Hi-C, and Fruitopia, and accounts for 13% of all fluid intake in the U.S., including tap water. Despite its success, Coke has set an even higher goal of a 25% increase in per-capita U.S. consumption. That means, on average, every person in the country would consume two eight-ounce servings of Coca-Cola products every day.

To breathe more life into the U.S. market, Coca-Cola is experimenting with a number of concepts. One is a vending machine that would automatically adjust the price for the product based on the outdoor temperature. Other ideas include vending of U.S. postage stamps and Coca-Cola products from the same machine, and connecting a Coke vending machine to a gasoline pump. Coke has also added new products, including citrus-flavored Surge, as well as juices, teas, and bottled water.

Recognizing that soft drink loyalties are often established at an early age, Coke has sought arrangements to distribute its products in schools. In one Michigan school district a Coke bottler paid $28.5 million for an exclusive 10-year contract.

Coke Loses Some Fizz

Economic problems hurt sales in several countries in which Coca-Cola had invested heavily. In 1998 sales were flat in Brazil and Japan, two major markets for Coke. The situation in Russia, where Coca-Cola invested $700 million, was even worse. Following the economy's collapse, Russian bottlers were able to operate at only 50% of capacity.

Then there were regulatory problems in some foreign markets. Attempts to purchase the popular French brand Orangina and the rights to Cadbury Schweppe's brands (including Canada Dry and Dr. Pepper) in 120 markets outside the U.S. ran into snags. The French government, which had fined Coke for anticompetitive practices in 1997, the same year the company announced its plans to purchase Orangina, blocked that deal. Although some believed the government's move was more a reaction to the timing than a substantive legal issue, it still prevented the sale.

In the Cadbury Schweppe's brand acquisition effort, nearly 100 of the markets were approved. However, some key ones met with opposition. Regulators in Mexico and Australia rejected the plan because Coke's soft drink market share exceeded 50% in both countries. In Europe, Coke attempted to circumvent approval by the European Union in the purchase, generating an immediate negative response. The EU's competition commissioner said of Coke, "They should learn to respect the rules like everyone else. They thought we would be too naive or not determined enough to stop them."

Then came what may have been the most serious problem. In 1999 Coke faced two health scares that resulted in 14 million cases of its products being pulled from the shelves in four European countries. The crisis began with some Belgian schoolchildren complaining of headaches, stomachaches, and vomiting after drinking Coke. Coming on the heels of another food scare in Belgium in which meat products were removed from store shelves after some were found to be contaminated with cancer-causing dioxin, the news spread rapidly.

It was discovered that the Coke the children consumed was from a bottling plant in Dunkirk, France. However, before a cause of the problem could be uncovered, another outbreak of illnesses was traced to a Coke plant in Antwerp, Belgium. Unnerved by the events, officials in France, Belgium, the Netherlands, and Luxembourg removed Coke products from stores served from the suspect plants.

Coke's explanations for the illnesses suggested that the occurrences, even though close together in time and location, were unrelated. The cause of one situation was reported to be contaminated carbon dioxide, the gas that puts the fizz in soft drinks. The other, according to Coca-Cola, resulted from a fungicide that had been sprayed accidentally on some wooden pallets and rubbed off onto some cans. Both were easily corrected. And the illnesses proved to be minor. In fact, in the case of the Belgian schoolchildren, a doctor who examined them suggested the nausea might have had more to do with the national school exams going on at the time than the Coke they drank.

However, when the stories first broke, Coke's management underestimated the magnitude of the issue, and was slow to react. When it did respond, Coke referred to the problems as "quality issues," not contaminated products, and denied that the fungicide or bad carbon dioxide would make anyone sick. Eventually the company acknowledged that the products might have caused the problem and publicly apologized in a letter published in European newspapers. The company even offered to pay the medical costs of any affected consumers.

When looked at from the point of view of the enormous quantity of Coca-Cola products that are consumed around the world every day with few if any problems, this was indeed a minor issue. According to some marketers, this highly rational view is the problem. Coke fails to understand the strong feelings consumers have for the product and the trust they place in the brand. A former high-ranking Coca-Cola manager said, "Coke executives think of the company as a money machine, but it's a gestalt that happens to make money."

The Challenge from Pepsi

Coke has consistently held a domestic market-share lead of 10 to 15 percentage points over Pepsi (currently 44% to 31%). However, sensing some weakness because of Coke's problems, Pepsi has increased its pressure in an attempt to gain market share or at least force Coke to spend more money. It apparently has adopted a strategy of challenging Coke at every turn. For example, when Coke's Burger King fountain contract came up for renewal in 1998, an offer from Pepsi forced Coke to lower its price to the fast-food giant by $25 million, or more than 10% of its 1997 contract, in order to keep the business.

In other developments, Pepsi introduced a new diet drink, Pepsi One. Pepsi also doubled its advertising spending to $300 million a year, and committed to spend $2 billion over 6 years in a tie-in promotion program with three *Star Wars* movies. In addition, Pepsi is adding vending machines at a faster rate than Coke. Although Coke has about one-third more in place (1.4 million to 1 million), the battle for locations has intensified.

Pepsi has taken the rivalry into another arena. It has sued Coke for unfair competitive practices, most recently in the U.S., Venezuela, France, and India. Some argue the suits have little merit, and are intended primarily to position Pepsi as the underdog in the eyes of the public.

Leadership at Coca-Cola

In the recent history of Coca-Cola, the hero was Roberto Goizueta. He was the company's CEO for 16 years until his death from lung cancer in 1997. Douglas Ivester, the chief operating officer under Goizueta, was selected to replace him. Ivester had a strong record of implementing programs. He was the architect of a program to spin off Coke's ownership of bottling operations, freeing the company of many fixed assets. Although his management style was much more hands-on, Ivester vowed to continue the strategy of investing overseas for the long run and working to expand sales at home.

According to Ivester, Coke was immune to global economic problems. In 1999, he observed, "We're dealing with human thirst. There's nothing about economic change that is going to change people's thirst." However, many people found a cheaper way to quench their thirst! For example, Coke lost 10% of its 50% market share in Brazil to lower-cost local drinks.

The problems that occurred during Ivester's tenure as CEO may have been the result of ineffective management or simply bad timing. Whichever, by late 1999 Ivester had seen enough and resigned. His replacement, Australian Douglas Daft, had previously directed the company's Africa, Middle East, and Far East divisions. In his first public statements, Daft endorsed the company's strategy of focusing on long-term growth; however, he was quick to make some fundamental changes in how the firm would go about it. In January 2000, he announced that 6,000 employees, 20% of Coke's corporate work force, would be eliminated. The move was explained as equivalent to the number of new positions that had been added over the period when Coke experienced unprecedented success, before its recent problems.

Next Daft announced that Coke would forge partnerships with governments overseas and become a "valued citizen" in the areas where it invests. As an example, he noted that Coke was investigating how its distribution network in India could be used to get polio vaccine into rural areas on behalf of the government. To reinforce Coke's commitment, Daft announced he would periodically move his office from Atlanta to other countries for a month or more at a time in order to get directly involved in local issues.

Under Daft, Coke intends to develop and introduce more locally targeted brands in foreign markets. Its most successful product in India, for example, is not Coke but a locally acquired brand called Thums Up. According to Daft, "We [Coca-Cola] need more of a balance between global and local brands." To get closer to local markets Daft reconfigured Coke's international regions. For example, the Middle and Far East Group, which consisted of a vast geographic area of highly diverse markets, has been divided into two more homogeneous groups, the Africa and the Middle East Group and the Asia Pacific Group. Daft also seems intent on reducing Coke's dependence on cola, announcing that the company will diversify into more noncarbonated drinks.

At this point, it appears Coca-Cola is moving away from a reliance on global products and even a global brand to a strategy described by Daft as "Think local, act local." As Daft prepares Coca-Cola for the 21st century, he predicts, "Ten years from now, people will look back and say the local model, decentralization, emphasis on people, emphasis on innovation, and emphasis on marketing was absolutely right."

Questions

1. Could the problems experienced by Coke have been avoided by better planning?

2. How does the Coca-Cola experience illustrate the need for effective implementation of plans?

3. Is there a place for electronic commerce in Coke's strategy for the future?

www.coke.com

www.pepsi.com

Sources: Betty Liu and Andrew Edgecliffe-Johnson, "Coke Unveils 'World Citizen' Policy," *Financial Times,* Feb. 1, 2000, p. 1; Andrew Edgecliffe-Johnson, "Coke's Chairman Tries Chinese Recipe," *Financial Times,* Feb. 1, 2000, p. 19; Richard Tomkins, "Fallen Icons," *Financial Times,* Feb. 1, 2000, p. 12; Betsy McKay, "Coke's Daft Makes Two More Key Appointments," *The Wall Street Journal,* Jan. 10, 2000, pp. A3+; John Abbott, "Crunch Time," *Fortune,* July 19, 1999, pp. 72–78; William Echison and David Rocks, "The Name Coke Now Scares People," *Business Week,* July 5, 1999, p. 32; James R. Hagerty and Amy Barrett, "France, Belgium Reject Pleas to Lift Ban," *The Wall Street Journal,* June 18, 1999, pp. B1+; Nikhil Deogun, "Besieged CEO Jets to Brussels amid PR Fiasco," *The Wall Street Journal,* June 18, 1999, pp. B1+; Nikhil Deogun, James R. Hagerty, Steve Stecklow, and Laura Johannes, "Anatomy of a Recall: How Coke's Controls Fizzled Out in Europe," *The Wall Street Journal,* June 6, 1999, pp. A1+; Dean Foust, Geri Smith, and David Rocks, "Man on the Spot," *Business Week,* May 3, 1999, pp. 142–151.

Marketing Strategy for an Internet Start-Up

Will consumers change the way they buy groceries? Webvan founder Louis Borders, one-half of the brother team that started Borders Bookstores, thinks so. However, he knows consumers will need a good reason, or maybe several good reasons, to change. That's why he developed a detailed marketing plan before trying to implement his idea. Apparently the plan is appealing; it attracted $122 million in initial venture capital when the average for a start-up is about $20 million.

The Idea Sprang from a Box

Borders got the idea for Webvan Group, Inc., while opening a FedEx package that had been delivered to his home. He knew that delivery companies such as UPS and FedEx prefer business clients to residential customers. The reasons are simple. Businesses do a greater volume of shipping, typically send larger packages, and, most important, can be delivered to less expensively. It occurred to him that if online retailing were to be successful, it would be necessary to develop a less costly and more efficient way to deliver goods to consumers' homes.

Intrigued by the idea, he applied the same design skills he had used to develop a state-of-the-art ordering and inventory management systems for Borders Bookstores. The result is Webvan, a full-service, online grocery and drugstore that provides free delivery for orders over $50. Webvan offers 50,000 perishable and nonperishable items ranging from produce to packaged goods, and fresh meat to fine wine. The customer selects a 30-minute delivery window up to seven days in advance, and the selections are hand-delivered by one of the company's couriers. All of this is done, according to Webvan, at prices that are comparable to local grocery stores. On top of that, the couriers are not permitted to accept tips.

Borders wasn't the first entrepreneur to be struck by the potential for home delivery of grocery and sundry items ordered on the Internet. Peapod, for example, had been in business for 10 years before Webvan got started. What intrigued investors about Webvan was the system Borders designed and the marketing plan he developed to support it.

Internet Retailing

Internet retailing requires two components: a website that makes it easy for consumers to place orders, and a fulfillment operation that delivers the orders on time and in good condition. Much of the excitement of electronic retailing has been centered on the novelty of creating effective websites. Sellers are intrigued by the challenges of attracting and holding site visitors, helping visitors navigate around a site, and reducing the fear consumers might have about Web-based transactions.

Fulfillment, on the other hand, draws far less attention. Most of the logistical challenges appear to be solved. Catalog retailers had shown, for example, that it is possible to maintain inventory, fill orders, and ship goods to meet the requests of thousands of customers all over the world. Thus, the reasoning goes, Internet retailers should focus their energies and programming skills on marketing and sales (the front end of the operation), and fulfillment (the back end) can be delegated to subcontractors. This model allows online merchants to meet the needs of customers without the investment and infrastructure of traditional retailers such as Wal-Mart.

It wasn't long before Borders and other Internet retailers discovered the fallacy in this approach. What they found was that no matter how many customers a website attracts, a fulfillment deficiency can be fatal. Consumers who try a Web retailer and are disappointed usually do not give the firm a second chance. An industry consultant put it this way: "Customer acquisition costs are quite high for these companies, and the only way to get a payoff is if you get a lot of repeat business from people. One bad experience, and you've blown it forever." As a result, increasingly online merchants are opting to control their order processing, warehousing, and shipping.

Assembling Orders

Fortunately, Borders had the vision and technical skill to design a fulfillment system. First, he divided fulfillment into two components: a distribution center and the actual physical delivery of the purchases. His concept for a distribution center is a highly automated warehouse. The 330,000-square-foot prototype in Oakland, California, is the size of eight typical supermarkets, but can serve the same number of customers as 20 supermarkets. It incorporates 4.5 miles of conveyor belts and temperature-sensitive rooms to protect such items as fresh vegetables, dairy products, and wine. The facility houses about 50,000 different items, compared to 30,000 in a typical supermarket. The mix includes 300 varieties of fresh fruit, 500 types of cereals, and 700 cuts of fresh meat and fish.

As impressive as the facility is, Borders is more proud of the order-assembly process. Workers, called "pickers," assemble orders in plastic boxes called "totes." Pickers need walk no more than 20 feet to reach any item because rotating carousels bring 8,000 bins of goods to them. At full capacity the system can handle 8,000 twenty-five-item orders a day, which translates to $300 million in annual revenue. In comparison, a conventional supermarket brings in about $12 million annually. The warehouse and its equipment, which cost $35 million, are designed to serve customers within an area of about 40 square miles. Assuming the facility can be fully utilized, Webvan estimates it will spend less than 1% of its revenue on physical facilities, whereas conventional stores spend about 6%.

Delivering Orders

As for delivering the purchases, Borders considered this the most important online retailing component. Referred to in the business as "the critical last mile," delivery is highly dependent on the ability of employees to meet schedules and effectively interact with customers. At Webvan the process is made more difficult by the 30-minute delivery window customers are asked to specify. If a driver arrives late, Webvan refunds $3 to the customer.

From the Oakland distribution center, Webvan has trucks that take assembled orders to 1 of 12 docking stations around the Bay area. There the orders are loaded into one of the firm's 120 vans for final delivery. Route planning software is designed to produce a schedule that permits a courier to make a delivery every 10 to 20 minutes without driving more than 10 miles from the docking station.

In addition to the driving, lugging the heavy boxes of groceries, and meeting deadlines, a Webvan courier is likely to be the only human contact customers have with the company. Hence, delivery personnel need good people skills. Webvan's CEO describes them as "our ambassadors of reliability." The couriers are put through a week of classroom training before they hit the streets. Among the topics covered are avoiding saying anything about a customer's home, even if it is beautiful, because a stranger making such comments makes some people uneasy. The classes also role-play various delivery problems. The bottom line, according to a Webvan manager, is that a courier should "do whatever it takes" to please customers.

Generating Orders

Another critical element of the plan was to gain trial and repeat usage by consumers. The Webvan concept is built on what is known as the "milkman principle." Home delivery of milk was feasible because the milkman stopped at nearly every house on a street. Thus the cost of delivery was shared by all the households in a small geographic area. If Webvan couriers must drive long distances between deliveries, the cost goes up dramatically. Because most consumers are unwilling to pay substantial delivery charges, to be successful the service must have large individual orders and/or many deliveries in the same geographic area. To develop a "critical mass" of customers quickly, Webvan's plan called for investing heavily in advertising. In the San Francisco area the firm spent $10 to $20 million to introduce the service. As it rolls out nationally, Webvan is spending $150 to $200 million annually on advertising.

Focusing on Growth

Growth is a key feature in the Webvan plan because it will give the firm buying power with suppliers. Fundamental to the firm's growth plan was to get a prototype operating and quickly work out any unforeseen problems. What appeared to be ideal solutions on paper had to be implemented effectively. For example, Borders calculated the optimal distance a picker should walk in the distribution center to assemble an order, how large the delivery boxes should be, how many items each box should hold, and the greatest distance a van can travel from the docking station to a customer's home and still be cost-effective. However, the system had to be put in place and tested with real people and real orders. That was accomplished with the Oakland facility.

According to the company's CEO, if Webvan's distribution system is effective, the competition will quickly copy it. To be successful, therefore, Webvan has to grow very rapidly, establishing a loyal customer base before competitors can react. Its plan is to open 26 distribution centers, all modeled after the Oakland unit, to serve major metropolitan areas around the country by 2003. The estimated total construction cost is $1 billion.

Webvan is not the first firm to attempt online grocery sales. Several other organizations with different operating and growth scenarios exist. For example:

- NetGrocer.com has its headquarters in North Brunswick, New Jersey. The firm does not offer perishables, and requires a lengthy delivery time. Purchases from NetGrocer are delivered by FedEx anywhere in the U.S. two to four days after an order is placed.

- HomeGrocer.com is backed by Amazon. The company is based in Kirkland, Washington, and also has distribution facilities in Portland, Oregon, and Orange County, California. HomeGrocer charges $9.95 for delivery of orders under $75. It defines the feasible delivery area around one of its distribution sites more narrowly than does Webvan in order to ensure on-time delivery. The company has plans to expand into several new markets.

- Peapod.com, with headquarters in Skokie, Illinois, has been in operation since 1989. The company serves about 100,000 customers in eight metropolitan areas. One if its strengths is the customer database it has developed. Peapod's initial business model had grocery items shipped by outside vendors directly to consumers. However, when too many orders were delivered with missing items because the vendors were out of stock, the firm began building and operating its own distribution centers.

- Streamline.com is based in Boston. To use its service, customers pay a monthly registration fee of $30. In return, they get a special refrigerator—usually installed in the garage—so deliveries can be made when no one is at home. In addition to dropping off groceries, Streamline picks up items to be dry cleaned, film for processing, and rental videos. Compared to Webvan, Streamline has small warehouses serving areas with only about 11,000 households. A day's deliveries might include 60 stops in a very small geographic zone. A typical customer places 42 orders a year, and spends more than $5,000 a year with the company.

- Kroger, Albertson's, Schnucks, and other traditional bricks-and-mortar supermarket chains are experimenting with home delivery. However, none has made a major investment in online grocery retailing.

Early Results

Clearly the investment community is impressed with Webvan. The firm was able to raise $275 million from venture capitalists, and then a November 1999 public offering of the company's stock produced another $375 million. Apparently investors have confidence in the concept and the management team's ability to implement it.

One influential factor may be the addition of George Shaheen as CEO. As former head of Andersen Consulting, Shaheen has had many opportunities to run companies. He declined all the offers until Webvan came along with the plan devised by Borders. Shaheen observed, "Webvan was all about leveraging technology and reinventing the grocery business, just as Andersen had reinvented consulting."

Webvan has also been acknowledged by industry sources. *InfoWorld* magazine named the firm its "Realtailer" of the year for 1999. Explaining the designation, the magazine noted the term describes real-time Internet retailing, which is "extraordinarily tough and costly." The magazine went on to say, "The last mile is a space that's completely up for

grabs, and Webvan is positioning itself to deliver." Gomez Advisors, a leading provider of Internet research and analysis, evaluated the websites of 11 online grocers and ranked Webvan's site #1. The Gomez spokesperson observed, "The site combines features that save customers time and help them make food decisions, as well as offering robust services and products."

Webvan began taking orders in 1999. Third-quarter sales were $4.2 million, and sales for the year were $13.3 million. Cost of goods sold for the year amounted to $11.3 million. However, with operating expenses at $156 million, the firm had a net loss for the year (after adjustments) of $145 million. Borders has predicted that one of Webvan's distribution centers should be profitable within nine months after it opens. However, with its aggressive growth plans, analysts expect the firm to have operating losses for the foreseeable future.

At the end of 1999, Webvan had 47,000 active customers, more than double the number it had just three months earlier. Repeat orders as a percentage of all orders were up, as was the average order size. According to Shaheen, the results "reflect the great progress we have made in our effort to develop the infrastructure for the last mile of e-commerce."

What Lies Ahead

Estimates for the size of the grocery industry vary, depending on what is included. The Food Marketing Institute sets the figure at $435 billion a year. The current online portion of the total is about $350 million, or less than one-tenth of 1%. A research firm in the industry predicts the online portion will grow to $3.5 billion by 2002.

So despite being a small part of the total, online grocery retailing could account for a substantial amount of business. Will it happen? A securities analyst who follows e-commerce points out three key areas of concern for grocery e-tailing services:

- Lower-than-expected gross margins because of (1) a lack of volume purchasing from suppliers and (2) a limited merchandise mix.

- Higher-than-expected order-assembly costs. The fragility of some merchandise, the need for physical inspection of perishables, the need for temperature control throughout the assembly process, and the variability of sizes across products have all contributed to slowing down the process, which raises the costs.

- High delivery expenses. The full cost of a delivery van and driver is about $27 an hour.

These are the areas that the Webvan plan has tried to address. One optimistic investment analyst describes Webvan as "melding the latest in Internet retailing with the latest in retail distribution. They are redefining the entire retail sales process over the Internet." Recognizing the revolutionary nature of the effort, a less effusive observer notes, "The consumer adoption rate is probably the key variable and the biggest unknown."

Questions

1. From a marketing evaluation perspective, how would you react to Webvan's losses in 1999?

2. Once Webvan has its infrastructure in place, what other products could be added to its product mix? How would that benefit the firm?

3. Should the fact that Webvan is an online operation change the way the marketing effort is managed?

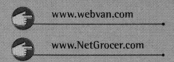

www.webvan.com

www.NetGrocer.com

www.Peapod.com

www.Streamline.com

www.HomeGrocer.com

Sources: Webvan website, February 2000; Sean M. Dugan, "Internet Commerce Winners for 1999 Kept in Mind How to Please Customers," *Info-World,* Jan. 17, 2000, p. 78; Douglas A. Blackmon, "The Milkman Returns—with Much More," *The Wall Street Journal,* Dec. 15, 1999, pp. B1+; George Anders, "How Webvan Conquers E-Commerce's Last Mile," *The Wall Street Journal,* Dec. 15, 1999, pp. B1+; David Wellman, "Are We On?" *Supermarket Business,* Dec. 15, 1999, pp. 35+; Scott Thurm, "Getting the Goods," *The Wall Street Journal,* Nov. 22, 1999, p. R39; Robert Whiddon, "Webvan's Wait Has Just Begun," *IPO Reporter,* Nov. 15, 1999, p. 3; Alice C. Cuneo, "Milkman of Cyberspace," *Advertising Age,* Nov. 1, 1999, p. 22; Robert Lenzer, "Bagging Groceries," *Forbes,* Oct. 18, 1999, p. 80; Angela Dawson and John Voight, "Online Grocers Deliver New Tasks," *Adweek,* Oct. 4, 1999, p. 88; George Anders, "Virtual Realty: Web Firms Go on Warehouse Building Boom," *The Wall Street Journal,* Sept. 8, 1999, pp. B1+; Linda Himelstein and David Leonhardt, "Can You Sell Groceries Like Books?" *Business Week,* July 26, 1999, pp. EB44+.

Appendix B

Careers and Marketing

A college education is many things. It's a gateway to new ideas and a lifetime of learning, an opportunity to develop new skills and test your abilities, and a springboard to independence. For most people college is also preparation for a job. But your goal should be more than just finding employment. Your first full-time job after graduation should serve as a launching pad to a successful career. To provide yourself with every opportunity, you should begin your preparation as early as possible in college. Assuming you want to begin working shortly after completing your degree, you should begin your actual job search at least nine months before graduation.

To get you thinking about your postgraduation ambitions and upcoming job search, this appendix first discusses choosing a career. Then a variety of career opportunities in marketing are described. Finally, guidelines on obtaining a postgraduation job are presented in a section that is relevant to all students regardless of major.

Choosing a Career

One of the most significant decisions you will ever make is choosing a career. This career decision will influence your future happiness, self-fulfillment, and well-being. Yet, unfortunately, career decisions often seem to be based on insufficient information, analysis, and evaluation of alternatives.

Early in the career decision process, everyone should spend some time in introspection. Introspection is the process of looking into yourself and honestly assessing what you want and what you have to offer.

What Do You Want?

Perhaps a better way to ask the question is, "What's important to you in life?" To answer this broad question, you must answer several more specific ones, such as the following:

- Do you want your career to be the main event in your life? Or do you see a career only as the means of financing leisure-time activities?

- How important are money and other financial rewards?

- How important are the social surroundings, climate, and other aspects of the environment in which you live?

- Would you prefer to work for a large company or a small organization?

- Would you prefer living and working in a small town or in an urban area?

- Are you willing to relocate to another part of the country? How often would you be willing to move?

- How important is the social prestige of your career?

- Do you prefer work that is evenly paced or occasionally hectic? How do you deal with the pressure of deadlines?

- Do you need tangible signs of results on a job to feel fulfilled?
- Do you prefer to work alone or as part of a team?

Another way to approach the question of what you want from a career is to identify—in writing—your goals in life. List both your intermediate-term goals (three to five years from now) and your long-term goals (10 years or more).

Still another approach is to simply describe yourself in some detail. By writing a description of your personality, likes and dislikes, and hopes and fears, you may be able to identify various careers that would (or would not) fit your self-image.

What Can You Offer?

Next you need to identify in some detail your strong and weak points. Why would anyone want to hire you? What skills have you developed? What experience—work, education, and extracurricular activities—do you have that might be attractive to prospective employers?

An important consideration is your work experience. Employers are less concerned with where you have worked than they are with the initiative you demonstrate in finding a job and your performance on the job. To gain some exposure to what goes on in business, consider a job with a temporary help agency. Manpower Inc., for example, employs 100,000 people in the summer. Another option is a summer internship. Many students make an extra effort to find an internship in the summer before their last year of college. Increasingly, firms are using these positions as a primary source of permanent employees. Over the course of an internship, many companies give interns exposure to several functional areas and different business units with the organization.

Because the attributes sought by business aren't acquired overnight, you should start developing them early in your college program. However, keep in mind that prospective employers are much more interested in what a person *accomplished* in various roles than how many different titles he or she had. One tangible way to demonstrate accomplishments is to carry out a project that ends with a written report. Ask your internship employer if you can use the report in your search for a permanent job. (It may be necessary to delete confidential information.) This type of evidence of an accomplishment is very persuasive in an interview.

Information on Careers and Internships

It may be useful to learn more about the career opportunities in business and how to plan for them. There are a number of publications available, including:

- Richard Nelson Bolles, *What Color Is Your Parachute?*, 30th edition, Ten Speed Press, 1999.

- J. Michael Farr, *America's Top Jobs for College Graduates*, 3rd edition, JIST Works, Inc., 1999.

- Carol Carter, *Majoring in the Rest of Your Life*, 3rd edition, Farrar Straus & Giroux, 1999.

There are also some useful websites. For example:

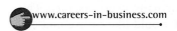

- Careers in Business. Here you will find a wealth of resources including career descriptions, recommended books, and other sites on introspection and career evaluation.

www.career-index.com

- Career Index. This site contains a compilation of jobs and career-related resources. It includes links to professional associations, career tools, employer sites, resume services, and newspapers with job listings.

There are also a variety of sources of information about internships. The place to begin is your campus career center. Many schools participate in an online database called the Internship Exchange that provides up-to-date information on internships around the country as well as information about various companies and organizations that provide internships. Other sources include:

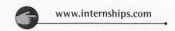 www.internships.com

- National Internships. Here you will find 18 regionally focused directories that describe positions in the for-profit and not-for-profit sectors. It includes information on the organization, position descriptions, contact information. There is a fee for the directories.

www.PrincetonReview.com

- Princeton Review. At this site a book by Mark Oldman and Samer Hamadeh, *America's Top Internships*, is described by *The Princeton Review*. The book, which is updated annually, provides extensive information about internships in all fields of business. Information about it can be found by clicking through to the "Careers" page.

- Professional associations. There are thousands of professional associations representing most of the industries in the U.S. Many business and not-for-profit organizations publicize their internships through trade and professional associations. A publication that describes over 7,600 professional organizations, *National Trade and Professional Associations of the United States*, is probably available in your school's library or career services office. A similar publication, published by a different organization, is called the *Associations Yellow Book*. It provides profiles of over 2,000 firms, government groups, and not-for-profit operations.

What Are the Marketing Jobs?

In Chapter 1 we noted that about one-quarter to one-third of all civilian jobs are in the field of marketing. These jobs cover a wide variety of activities and a great range of qualifications and aptitudes. For instance, jobs in personal selling call for a set of qualifications that are different from those in marketing research. A person who is likely to be successful in advertising may not be a good prospect in physical distribution. Consequently, the aptitudes and skills of different individuals make them candidates for different types of marketing jobs.

In this section we shall briefly describe the major jobs in marketing, grouping them by title or activity. The initial positions that are most often available to recent graduates are summarized in Table B.1.

Personal Selling

Sales jobs are by far the most numerous of all the jobs in marketing. Personal selling spans a broad array of activities, organizations, and titles. Consider the following people: a driver–sales person for Coca-Cola, a sales clerk in a department store, a sales engineer providing technical assistance in sales of hydraulic valves, an IBM representative coordinating the sales effort to provide information management for an appliance manufacturer, and a pharmaceutical representative visiting physicians and pharmacists to introduce new drugs. All these people are engaged in personal selling, but each sales job is different from the others.

Sales jobs of one sort or another are available in virtually every locality. This means that you can pretty well pick the area where you would like to live and still get involved in personal selling.

There are opportunities to earn a very high income in personal selling. This is especially true when the compensation plan is straight commission, or is a combination of salary plus a significant incentive element.

A sales job is the most common entry-level position in marketing. Furthermore, as illustrated in Figure B.1, a sales job is a widely used stepping-stone to a management position. There is no better way to learn about a company's products or its customers!

Table B.1   Eight Entry-Level Marketing Jobs for College Graduates

Job Title	Comments
Sales representative	Responsible for selling the organization's goods or services to customers. Customers may be ultimate consumers, middlemen, or other organizations.
Sales (or marketing) support person	Assists sales manager and staff in implementing programs, such as trade shows and dealer or sales-force incentive programs. Marketing support position involves broader responsibility, including assisting in product development and distribution.
Customer service representative	Assists customers after the sale, often by handling complaints and requests for information or service. Common in the business goods sector, and growing in importance in e-commerce.
Retail management executive trainee	Position is common in department store chains. After training, usually moves through rotating assignment in buying and management of selling department. Ultimately, person focuses on either buying or store management.
Assistant store manager	Position is common in chains that have small specialty stores in shopping centers. Assists in overseeing day-to-day activities of the store, especially staffing and display. In effect, is a trainee position.
Assistant media buyer	Common starting position in an advertising agency. Assists buyer in purchasing advertising space and time for firms that are the agency's clients. Another entry-level position, working for either an agency or an advertiser, is junior copywriter.
Research trainee	Found in various large organizations and in marketing research firms. After or during training, assists with one or more phases of the research process, such as data collection, data analysis, database management, or report preparation.
Assistant product manager	Assists in planning and, especially, implementing marketing program for a specific brand or product line. Most commonly found in large companies that sell consumer goods or services.

Many companies recruit people for sales jobs with the intention of promoting some of these people into management positions. Personal selling and sales management jobs are also a good route to the top in a firm because it is relatively easy to measure a person's performance and productivity in selling.

A sales job is different from other jobs in several significant ways that are discussed in Chapter 18. Sales people represent their company to customers and to the public in general. The public ordinarily does not judge a firm by its factory or office personnel. Also, outside sales people (those who go to the customers) operate with little or no direct personal supervision. They must have considerable creativity, persistence, and self-motivation. Johnson Controls, the subject of the opening case in Chapter 18, suggests what a professional sales position involves. Furthermore, sales jobs often involve traveling and some require considerable time away from home and family. Among white-collar jobs, personal selling generally rates low in social status and prestige.

All in all, selling is hard work, but the potential rewards are immense. Certainly no other job contributes as much to the success of an organization. Remember—nothing happens until somebody sells something!

Retail Management

Retailing is second only to personal selling in terms of number of job opportunities for new college graduates. The two primary areas of opportunity in department store, specialty, and discount chains are in merchandising or buying (described in the section on buying and purchasing) and store management.

Store managers have a great deal of responsibility and authority. A store manager's authority related to acquiring merchandise (the buying function) varies

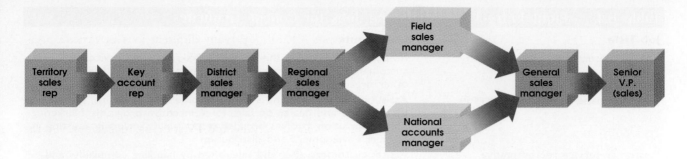

Typical career path starting in personal selling.

greatly from one firm to the next. However, once the merchandise arrives in the store, the manager has the responsibility and authority for displaying, selling, and controlling the inventory. Store managers in most companies, either directly or indirectly through department heads, oversee personal selling, promotion, credit, personnel management, and store security.

The entry-level position for store management is typically assistant department manager, department manager, or assistant store manager, depending on the size of the store. The performance of a store or department manager is directly measurable in terms of sales or profits. Therefore, speed of advancement into higher positions is determined primarily by the quality and quantity of results produced by the manager.

Electronic Commerce

Consisting of both B2B organizations and "e-tailing," electronic commerce could well be one of the primary growth areas in marketing. FreeMarkets Inc. (introducing Chapter 5) and PETsMART.com (Chapter 15) are good examples of the developments that are occurring. Managers in electronic commerce have many of the same challenges as conventional marketers. For example, they have to select the correct merchandise and price it appropriately. However, they also have some unique challenges such as developing attractive websites, filling orders taken electronically, and ensuring that customers who they may never actually see are satisfied.

Buying and Purchasing

Most medium-sized and larger organizations employ people who specialize in buying, as opposed to selling, goods and services. In one type of position, people select and acquire merchandise for resale. In another type of position, people purchase goods and services not for resale but for use in a manufacturing process or in operating an organization.

Every retail organization needs people to buy merchandise for resale. Frequently the route to the top in retailing is through the buying (also called merchandising) division of the business. Large retailers have many positions for buyers and assistant buyers. Each merchandise department normally has a buyer. Consequently, you often have a chance to work with particular products that interest you.

A purchasing agent is the business market counterpart of the retail store buyer. Virtually all firms in the business market have purchasing departments. People in these departments buy raw materials and supplies for the production, office, and sales departments in their firms. Many firms are taking all or a substantial portion of their purchasing online. That has created an entire new breed of brokers that provide the technical skills that bring electronic buyers and sellers together. In addition, they must be able to persuasively market these new methods of making transactions to buyers and sellers.

Retail buyers and purchasing agents need many of the same skills. They must be able to analyze markets, determine merchandise needs, and negotiate with sellers. It is also necessary to have some knowledge of credit, finance, and physical distribution.

Advertising

Opportunities in advertising can be found in many different jobs in various organizations. The three primary areas of opportunity are:

- Advertisers, including manufacturers, retailers, and service firms. Many of these organizations prepare and place their own ads. In some of these firms the advertising department is a large one.

- Various media (including newspapers, radio and TV stations, magazines, and the Internet) that carry ads.

- Advertising agencies that specialize in creating and producing individual ads and entire promotion campaigns.

Jobs in advertising encompass a number of aptitudes and interests—artistic, creative, managerial, research, and sales. The advertising field holds real opportunity for the artistic or creative person. Agencies and advertising departments need copywriters, artists, photographers, layout designers, printing experts, and others to create and produce ads.

Account executive is a key position in advertising agencies. People in this position are the liaisons between the agency and its clients (the advertisers). Account executives coordinate the agency's efforts with the clients' marketing programs.

Another group of advertising jobs involves the placement of ads. On the advertisers' side, this entails allocating the advertising budget by planning an advertising schedule and selecting the media. On the media side, every TV and radio network and station, all newspapers and magazines, websites, and every other advertising outlet employ sales people. Advertisers and agencies also often need people who can conduct buyer-behavior studies and other marketing research.

Sales Promotion

The main function of sales promotion is to tie together the activities in personal selling and advertising. Effective sales promotion requires imagination and creativity, coupled with a sound foundation in marketing fundamentals.

One aspect of sales promotion is the design and creation of retailers' in-store displays and window displays. Another aspect deals with trade shows and other company exhibits. Sales promotion activities also include the development and management of premium giveaways, contests, product sampling, and other types of promotion.

Marketing Research

Marketing research jobs cover a broad range of activities that are outlined in Chapter 7. People are hired for marketing research jobs by manufacturers, retailers, services marketers, government agencies, and other organizations. There are also a large number of specialized marketing research companies. Generally, however, there are fewer jobs in marketing research than in personal selling or in retailing.

Marketing researchers are problem solvers. They collect and analyze masses of information. Thus they need an aptitude for precise, analytical work. Some quantitative skills are needed, particularly an understanding of statistics. In progressive firms, marketing researchers also work with marketers to define problems and interpret research results, so an understanding of marketing is important.

Product/Brand Management

In Chapter 8 we discuss briefly the position of product manager in connection with the organizational structure for new-product planning and development.

Product managers (sometimes called brand managers) are responsible for planning and directing the entire marketing program for a given product or group of products.

Early on, product managers make decisions about packaging, labeling, and other aspects of the product itself. Product managers are also responsible for the marketing research necessary to identify the market. They plan advertising, personal selling, and sales promotional programs for their products. Product managers are concerned with pricing, physical distribution, and legal issues of the product.

In many respects, being a product manager is like running your own business. Product managers must have good analytical skills to keep abreast of what competitors are doing and what is happening in the market. They also need to be tactful and persuasive to gain the cooperation of functional areas such as manufacturing and sales.

Physical Distribution

Many jobs exist in the field of physical distribution, and the prospects are even brighter as we look ahead to the year 2000 and beyond. More and more firms are expected to adopt the systems approach in physical distribution (described in Chapter 16) to control the huge expenses involved in materials movement and warehousing.

Manufacturers, retailers, and all other goods-handling firms have jobs that involve two stages of physical distribution. First the product must be moved to the firm for processing or resale. Then the finished products must be distributed to the markets. These physical distribution tasks involve jobs in transportation management, warehousing, and inventory control. In addition, many transportation carriers and warehousing firms also provide a variety of jobs that may interest you.

Public Relations

The public relations department is a valuable connection between an organization and its various publics. The department must deal with, or go through, the news media to reach these publics. Public relations people must be especially good in communications. In fact, these people often have college degrees in communications or journalism, rather than in marketing.

In essence, the job of public relations is to project the desired company image. More specifically, public relations people are responsible for telling the public about the company—its products, community activities, social programs, environmental improvement activities, labor policies, and views regarding controversial issues. Public relations specialists are particularly important—and very visible—when a company responds to adverse publicity. Such publicity may come from a governmental investigation such as the antitrust case involving Microsoft, or a charge of unethical or inappropriate practices, as when Nike responded to charges of selling athletic shoes made in unhealthy factories. Whether disseminating favorable publicity or responding to adverse publicity, the company's position must be stated in a clear, understandable, and—above all—believable fashion.

Consumer Affairs and Protection

The broad area of consumer affairs and protection encompasses several activities that provide job and career opportunities. Many of these jobs are an outgrowth of the consumer movement. Many companies have a consumer affairs department to handle consumer complaints. Several federal and state agencies keep watch on business firms and provide information and assistance to consumers. Grocery product manufacturers and gas and electric companies regularly hire college graduates to aid consumers in product use. Government and private product-testing agencies hire people to test products for safety, durability, and other features.

Other Career Areas

In this short appendix it is not possible to list all the careers that stem from marketing. We have, however, covered the major areas. You may get additional career ideas from the sources listed below:

- Networking in the Public Interest. Through its service called ACCESS, Networking in the Public Interest provides a means to find opportunities in the not-for-profit sector.

- Careers in Marketing. This website includes information on jobs in various areas of marketing including retailing, advertising, product management, and marketing research. There is also a list of recommended reading, and links to additional websites that focus on careers in marketing.

- Marketing Jobs. Here you will find job openings in inside sales, technical sales, Internet sales, product-line management, and technical support. The site also includes other resources for finding a job in marketing including professional associations and periodicals that publicize job openings.

- Best Jobs USA. This website includes job listings by type (marketing/advertising, for example) and geographic location. It includes a career guide section to help individuals make good career matches. Assistance with résumé preparation is also available.

Where Are the Marketing Jobs?

In this section we briefly describe the types of companies and other organizations that provide jobs in marketing. This section also includes comments on jobs in international marketing and a comparison of job opportunities in large versus small organizations.

Types of Organizations

Literally millions of organizations provide jobs and career opportunities in marketing. The organizations can be grouped into the following categories.

Manufacturing

Most manufacturing firms provide career opportunities in all the activities discussed in the previous section. In their promotional mix, some manufacturers stress personal selling, whereas others rely more on advertising. Even small manufacturing companies offer job opportunities in most of the categories we have mentioned.

Everyone has heard of IBM, Ford Motor Co., and Nabisco. However, because most manufacturers make products that are used by other businesses, their names are not familiar to the general public. Unfortunately, many college graduates overlook some of these potentially excellent employers just because they don't recognize their corporate names. Starting salaries are often higher in manufacturing firms than in retailing and the other organizations described next.

Retailing

Retailing firms provide more marketing jobs by far than does any other organizational category, but most of these jobs are not intended for college graduates. Careers in retailing are not well understood by college students, who may equate retailing with clerking in a department store or filling shelves in a supermarket.

Students often perceive that retail pay is low and that retail work-hours include a lot of evenings and weekends.

Actually a career in retailing offers many attractive features for college graduates. There are opportunities for very rapid advancement for those who display real ability. Performance results, such as sales and profits, are quickly and highly visible. If you can produce, management will generally note this fact in a hurry.

Although the starting pay in many (but not all) stores is lower than in manufacturing, the compensation in higher-level retailing jobs typically is excellent. There are good retailing jobs in virtually every geographic area. Also, large retail chains (such as the May Company and Wal-Mart) generally have excellent management-training programs for newly hired college graduates.

Perhaps the main attractions in retailing are less tangible. Retailing can be an exciting field. You are constantly involved with people—customers, suppliers, and other workers. And there are challenges in merchandise buying, especially finding out what will sell well—what customers really want.

It is easier to start a career in retailing than in many other fields. In large stores there are jobs involving personnel management, accounting controls, and store operations (receiving, credit, and customer service departments). However, the lifeblood of retailing is the buying and selling of merchandise or services. Thus the more numerous and better-paying positions are in merchandising and store management. A typical career path is presented in Figure B.2. Note that after several years of experience in both areas, a retail manager often decides to concentrate on merchandising or store management.

Wholesaling

Career opportunities in wholesaling generally are less well understood and appreciated than those in retailing or manufacturing. Wholesaling firms typically do not recruit on college campuses, and they generally have a low profile among students.

Yet opportunities are there. Wholesalers of consumer products and industrial distributors provide many jobs in buying, personal selling, marketing research, and physical distribution. Manufacturers' agents, brokers, and the other agent middlemen discussed in Chapter 16 also offer jobs and careers. Consider the success of W. W. Grainger, the case that begins Chapter 22, to see how this function is being transformed. Wholesaling middlemen are increasing in numbers and in sales volume, and their future is promising.

Services Marketing

The broad array of service industries discussed in Chapter 11 provides a bonanza of job and career opportunities in marketing. Many of these fields are expected to experience rapid growth. The travel, hospitality, education, finance, entertainment, health care, communications, and professional services fields are prime examples. Recognizing the importance of marketing, most of these industries and the organizations within them employ marketing-related personnel. Many of these firms really are retailers of services. Consider, for example, Wingspan, the case that introduces Chapter 11. Though its parent organization, Bank One, may have had some problems, services marketing via the Internet will certainly continue to grow. Consequently, many of the statements we made earlier about retailing careers are relevant here.

Other Business Areas

Besides the general types of organizations just described, more specialized business firms hire college graduates for marketing-related positions. Entry-level opportunities can be found with communications media (such as TV stations), advertising agencies, franchise systems, participation and spectator sports organizations, public utilities, and transportation firms (such as truck lines).

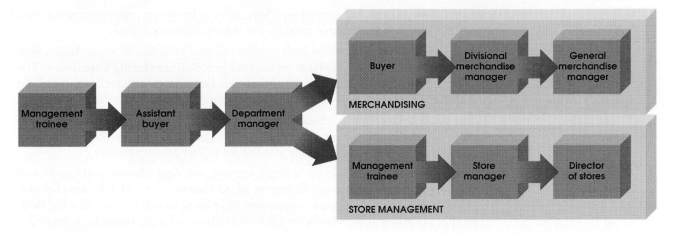

Buyer → **Divisional merchandise manager** → **General merchandise manager**

MERCHANDISING

Management trainee → **Assistant buyer** → **Department manager** →

Management trainee → **Store manager** → **Director of stores**

STORE MANAGEMENT

Figure B.2

Typical career path in a department store chain.

Not-for-Profit Organizations

As described in Chapter 11, not-for-profit organizations are realizing that marketing is a key to their success. Consequently, it is likely that jobs and careers in many not-for-profit organizations will open up in large numbers. Consider the wide variety of such organizations—hospitals, museums, educational institutions, religious organizations, foundations, charities, and political parties, among others. Given this diversity, you can expect to find a wide range of marketing-related positions in not-for-profit organizations.

Government

Countless federal and state government organizations hire people for marketing positions. Here we include the major cabinet departments—agriculture, defense, human services, and the others. We also include all the regulatory agencies. Government organizations employ people in purchasing, marketing research, public relations, physical distribution, consumer affairs and protection, and even advertising and sales promotion. Sometimes students tend to overlook the many marketing career opportunities in government.

International Careers

Students who like to travel and experience different cultures may want to work at least part of the time in foreign countries. They may be interested in careers in international marketing, and they may even major in international business in college. Typically, however, companies do not hire college graduates and immediately assign them to jobs in international marketing. People are normally hired for entry-level positions in the domestic divisions of a company's operations. Then, after some years of experience with the firm, an employee may have an opportunity to move into the firm's international divisions. If you have international aspirations, begin looking for companies that have or are developing international markets. You would also be wise to study a second language and take advantage of opportunities to learn about other cultures.

Large versus Small Companies

Should you go to work for a large company or a small firm? Or should you go into business for yourself upon graduation? For over a decade now, more and more students have been saying that they want to work for a small company. They think that there is more freedom of action, more rapid advancement, and fewer constraints on their life-styles in smaller firms.

Perhaps so. And certainly no one should discourage you from a career in small business. *But* we typically recommend to students (who ask for advice) that they start their careers in a big company. Then, after a few years, they can move into a smaller firm. There are three reasons for this recommendation:

- A large firm is more likely to have a good training program in your chosen field of activity. Many students have little or no practical marketing experience. The fine training programs provided by numerous large manufacturers, retailers, and major services marketers can be critical in launching a career.

- You can learn something about how a big company operates. After all, when you go into a smaller firm, large companies will be your competitors. So the more you know about them, the better able you will be to compete with them.

- After working for a while for a big company, you may change your mind and decide to stay with the larger firm after all. On the other hand, let's say that you want to go to a small company after you have worked a few years at a big firm. At that point it will be relatively easy to move from a large company to a smaller one. If you start in a small firm, however, and later want to move into big business, it is not so easy to move.

We have discussed various career fields and types of organizations that hire people in these fields. Now let's take a brief look at how you should go about getting a job with one of these organizations.

How Do You Search for a Job?

This book and your entire course are designed to teach you the fundamentals involved in developing and managing a marketing program. These fundamentals are applicable regardless of whether you are marketing a good, service, idea, person, or place.

Now let's see whether we can apply these fundamentals to a program designed to market a person—*you*! We shall discuss a marketing approach that you can use to get a job and to start a career. Although we are focusing on a marketing career, this same approach can be used in seeking jobs and careers in any field.

Identify and Analyze the Market

The first step in building a marketing program is to identify and analyze the market. In this case the market consists of prospective employers. Right now you don't know exactly who comprises that target market. So you must research several possible markets and then eventually narrow down your choice. In effect, we are talking about "choosing a career." Much of what we discussed in the first section of this appendix is applicable here, as are the listed reference sources.

You should initially get as much information as you can regarding various career opportunities in marketing. For information sources you might start with one or two professors whom you know reasonably well. Then turn to the career services office in your school, or wherever postgraduation jobs are listed. Many companies prepare recruiting brochures for students that describe the company and explain its career opportunities.

For many, the Internet has become the primary source of career information. However, don't overlook newspapers and business journals. *The Wall Street Journal* and the business sections of large-city newspapers can be useful. Periodicals such as *Business Week, Marketing News, Advertising Age,* and trade publications in many individual industries are helpful. You should exchange information with other students who are also in the job market. Use course assignments such as term projects and papers to investigate various industries and firms.

In summary, learn all you can about a broad cross section of firms and industries. Then, from this information search, zero in on one or two industries and a few companies that are your leading choices. You will now be ready to develop the marketing mix that will be effective in marketing yourself to your target markets.

Product

In this case the "product" you are planning and developing is yourself and your services. You want to make yourself as attractive as possible to your market—that is, prospective employers.

Start your product planning by listing in some detail your strong and weak points. These will lead to another list—your qualifications and achievements. This introspection is something we discussed in the first section of this appendix in connection with choosing a career.

When you are considering your qualifications, it may help to group them into broad categories such as these:

- Education—schools attended, degree earned, grade-point average, major, favorite subjects.

- Work experience—part-time and full-time responsibilities.

- Honors and awards.

- Technical skills—computer programming, software proficiency, foreign languages.

- Extracurricular activities and accomplishments—offices, memberships, committees, volunteer activities.

- Hobbies.

Later we will discuss the presentation of your qualifications in a personal data sheet. An important aspect of product planning is product differentiation. How can you differentiate yourself from all the other college grads? What have you done that is different, unusual, or exceptional? This doesn't have to be earthshaking—just something that shows a trait such as initiative, imagination, or perseverance.

Another part of product planning is packaging. When you go for an interview, be sure that the external package looks attractive. People do judge you by your appearance, just as you judge products by the way they look. This means paying attention to what you wear and how you are groomed. A good impression starts with prospective employers' first meetings with you.

Price

"What salary do you expect?" "How much do you think we should pay you?" These are two of the questions a prospective employer might ask in a job interview. If you have not done some research and thinking in advance regarding the price you want for your services, these questions may throw you.

As part of your marketing program, find out what the market price is for people entering your field. Talk with career services officers, career counselors, professors, and other students who are in the job market. From these sources you should get a pretty good idea of starting salaries in entry-level positions. Use this information to decide *before* the interview on a range of salaries for yourself. Remember that income can be stated in several different ways. For example, there may be a base salary, the possibility of a bonus, and fringe benefits such as the use of a company-supplied car.

Distribution Channel

There are only a few major channels you are likely to use in marketing yourself to prospective employers. The most accessible channel is your career services office, assuming that there is one on your campus. Most colleges, through their career services, host and assist companies that send job recruiters to do on-campus interviewing.

Another channel is help-wanted ads in business journals, trade journals, and newspapers. Perhaps the most difficult, but often the most rewarding, channel is going directly to firms in which you are especially interested—knock on doors or write letters seeking a job interview. Many employers look favorably on people who display this kind of initiative in their job search.

Promotion

Other than planning and developing an excellent product, the most important ingredient in your marketing mix is a good promotion (or communications) program. Your promotion will consist primarily of written communications (a form of advertising) and interviewing (a form of personal selling).

To stand out from the crowd and be noticed, job applicants have tried everything from singing telegrams to skywriting. One enterprising student rented the sides of an 18-wheeler. Soon after his name, phone number, and plea for a job began cruising the nation's highways, he received dozens of calls.

Most applicants use more conventional approaches. Frequently your first contact with a prospective employer is a cover letter in which you state briefly why you are writing to that company and what you have to offer. You enclose a personal résumé, and you request an appointment for an interview.

Cover Letter

In the opening paragraph of your cover letter, you should indicate why you want to work for the firm. Mention a couple of key points regarding the firm—points you learned from your research. In the second paragraph, you can present a few highlights of your own experience or personality that make you an attractive prospect. In the third paragraph, state that you are enclosing your résumé, and request an appointment for an interview, even suggest some dates and a time when you will telephone to arrange the meeting.

Résumé

A résumé (also called a curriculum vitae or personal data sheet) is really a brief history of yourself. Personal computers and word processing packages make it possible to design a distinctive and very professional-appearing résumé. You can start with biographical information such as your name, address, and phone number. Then divide your résumé into sections, including education, work experience, and activities that were described in the product section.

You will need some references—people who know you well and can speak to your personal attributes or professional capabilities. Family friends, former employers or supervisors, and college instructors are typically used. To save space, one approach is simply to state at the end of the résumé, "References furnished upon request." An alternative is to list your references by name (along with their titles, addresses, and phone numbers) at the bottom of your résumé or on a separate sheet. The thinking behind this approach is that you should make it as easy as possible for a prospective employer to check your references. Of course, you should obtain permission before you use a person as a reference.

It is difficult to overstate the value of a persuasive cover letter and a distinctive résumé. They are critically important elements in your job search. They certainly are two of the most important ads you will ever write. Useful advice on preparing résumés can be found in the books cited earlier, and at most of the recommended websites.

Interview

Rarely is anyone hired without one or more interviews. In some cases, as when recruiters visit your campus, the interview is your initial contact with the firm. In other situations the interviews come as a result of your letter of introduction and résumé.

The interview is an exercise in personal selling—in this case, you are selling yourself. People are often uncomfortable and uptight in interviews, especially their first few, so don't be surprised or disappointed if you are. One way to reduce your anxiety and increase the likelihood of impressing the interviewer is to prepare yourself to answer tough questions that may be asked:

- Why should we hire you?
- What are your distinctive strengths?
- Do you have any weaknesses and how do you plan to overcome them?
- What challenges have you successfully overcome?
- What kind of job do you expect to have in five years?

Your performance in an interview often determines whether or not you get the job. So be on your toes—be honest in your answers, and try to look more relaxed and confident than you may feel!

After interviews with a company have been completed, it is worthwhile to write a letter to each of the interviewers. Thank them for the opportunity to learn about their company and, if appropriate, restate your interest in the job.

Evaluating Job Offers

You are likely to receive multiple job offers *if:*

- The economy is fairly healthy.
- You have at least an acceptable academic record.
- You conduct an aggressive job search.
- You develop a persuasive cover letter and professional résumé.
- You perform well in job interviews.

You should evaluate the suitability of a single job offer or compare multiple job offers against a set of criteria that are important to you. The criteria you select and the importance you place on them require some careful thought. Below are examples of criteria you might consider.

- *Will you be happy in your work?* It is no accident that we frequently hear about "Blue Monday" (the weekend of freedom is finished and I have to go back to work) and "TGIF" (Thank God It's Friday). Many people in society are not happy with their jobs. Normally, half or more of your waking hours will be spent at work, commuting to and from work, or doing job-related work at home. So you should look for a job and career that you will enjoy.

- *Does the career fit your self-image?* Are the job and career in line with your goals, dreams, and aspirations? Will they satisfy you? Will you be proud to tell people about your job? Will your spouse (and someday your teenage children) be proud of you in that career?

- *What demands or pressures are associated with the career?* Some people thrive on pressure. They constantly seek new challenges in their work. Other people look for a more tranquil work experience. They do not want a job with constant demands and deadlines to meet.

- *Do the financial factors meet your needs?* How does the starting salary compare with those of other jobs? Consider what the job is likely to pay after you have been there three to five years. Some engineering jobs, for example, have high starting salaries, but soon hit a salary ceiling. In contrast, some marketing jobs have lower starting salaries but no upper limits.

- *Are there opportunities for promotion?* You should evaluate the promotion patterns in a job or in a firm. Try to find out how long it normally takes to reach a given executive level. Study the backgrounds of presidents of a number of large companies in the industry. Did they come up through engineering, the legal department, sales or marketing, accounting, or some other area?

- *Are the travel considerations suitable?* Some jobs involve a considerable amount of travel whether you are an entry-level worker or an executive. Other jobs are strictly in-house, with no travel at all.

- *Is there job or career "transportability"?* Are there similar jobs in many other geographic areas? If both you and your spouse are career-oriented, what will happen to you if your spouse is transferred to another city? One nice thing about careers such as teaching, retailing, nursing, and personal selling is that generally these jobs exist in considerable numbers in many different locations.

- *What is the supply-and-demand situation in this field?* Determine generally how many job openings currently exist in a given field, as compared with the supply of qualified applicants. At the same time, study the future prospects regarding this supply-and-demand condition. Determine whether a present shortage or overcrowding of workers in a field is a temporary situation or is likely to exist for several years.

What Next?

We encourage you to keep in mind the questions and guidelines presented in this appendix as you take this course and progress through your academic program. We have included several sources of additional advice and guidance, and there are many more both in print form and on the Internet. We encourage you to get started. It's never too soon to start thinking about—and planning—your search for a postgraduation job!

Notes and References

Chapter 1

1. Saul Hansell, "Hackers' Bazaar," *The New York Times*, Apr. 2, 1998, pp. D6+; George Anders, "Amazon.com Will Go Head-to-Head with eBay, OnSale in Online Auctions," *The Wall Street Journal*, Mar. 3, 1999, p. A3; Roger Taylor, "Going, Going, Gone.com," *Financial Times*, Apr. 10 and 11, 1999, p. 7.

2. George Anders and Thomas E. Weber, "Latest Chat Topic at AOL: Links with eBay," *The Wall Street Journal*, Feb. 17, 1999, p. B1.

3. Robert J. Keith, "The Marketing Revolution," *Journal of Marketing*, January 1960, p. 37.

4. Geraldine E. Williams, "High Performance Marketing: An Interview with Nike's Phil Knight," *Harvard Business Review*, July–August 1992, pp. 91–101.

5. Tony Jackson, "Reflections of a Knowledge Worker," *Financial Times*, Apr. 27, 1999, p. 12.

6. Most of the following market-oriented descriptions are extracted from the Internet sites and publications of the respective companies. Kodak—We help preserve beautiful memories; Amazon.com—We use the Internet to offer products that educate, inform, and inspire; Hewlett-Packard—We improve the effectiveness of individuals and organizations by helping customers acquire, display, analyze, communicate, store, and manage information <http://www.hp.com>; Levi—We offer comfort, fashion, and durability in wearing apparel; Steelcase—We design and manufacture work environments that help people perform more effectively; Caterpillar—We help build the world's infrastructure <http://www.cat.com>.

7. Jim Wetherbe, "Federal Express Corporation: An Overnight Success," *Hemisphere*, December 1996, pp. 33+.

8. I. Jeanne Dugan, "The Barons of Books," *Business Week*, June 29, 1998, pp. 109+.

9. Kathy Kranhold, "Selling Power to the People Like Soap Suds," *The Wall Street Journal*, Mar. 17, 1998, p. B1.

10. Sonya S. Hamilton, "You Don't Say," *Sales & Marketing Management*, October 1994, pp. 111–112.

11. Sathnam Sanghera, "Making Continuous Improvement Better," *Financial Times*, Apr. 21, 1999, p. 28.

12. Christopher W. Hart and Michael D. Johnson, "Growing the Trust Relationships," *Marketing Management*, Spring 1999, pp. 9–24.

13. Stan Rapp and Thomas L. Collins, "The New Marketing: Sell and Socialize," *The New York Times*, Feb. 20, 1994, p. 11.

14. Robert D. Hof, "Now It's Your Web," *Business Week*, Oct. 5, 1998, pp. 164–178.

15. For more information see Michael W. Cox and Richard Aim, "America's Move to Mass Customization," *Consumers' Research Magazine*, June 1999, pp. 15+.

16. Paul Roberts, "John Deere Runs on Chaos," *Fast Company*, November 1998, pp. 164–173.

17. Frederick E. Webster, Jr., "Defining the New Marketing Concept," *Marketing Management* 2, no. 4 (1993), pp. 22–31.

18. Charles Fishman, "This Is a Marketing Revolution," *Fast Company*, May 1999, pp. 204–218.

19. "Report on ROI," *Marketing News*, Apr. 12, 1999, pp. 1+.

20. Jefery Ball, "Auto Makers Are Racing to Market 'Green' Cars Powered by Fuel Cells," *The Wall Street Journal*, Mar. 15, 1999, p. A1.

21. For a complete discussion of ethics in marketing, see Gene R. Laczniak and Patrick E. Murphy, *Ethical Marketing Decisions: The Higher Road*, Allyn & Bacon, New York, 1993.

22. Robert Berner, "Pharmacies Say Rates Paid by Rite Aid Unit Are Doing Them In," *The Wall Street Journal*, June 30, 1999, pp. A1+.

23. D. Kirk Davidson, "High Stakes Cause Ethical Problems," *Marketing News*, May 22, 1995, p. 8.

24. "Online Bids Amused Teen, Horrified Parents," *The South Bend Tribune*, Apr. 30, 1999, p. A3.

Chapter 2

1. Amy Barrett, "Just Like Mom Used to Engineer," *Business Week*, Dec. 21, 1998, pp. 82, 84; Vanessa O'Connell, "How Campbell Saw a Breakthrough Menu Turn into Leftovers," *The Wall Street Journal*, Oct. 6, 1998, pp. A1, A12; Vanessa O'Connell, "Changing Tastes Dent Campbell's Canned-Soup Sales," *The Wall Street Journal*, Apr. 28, 1998, p. B1; Joseph Weber, "Now, Campbell's Makes House Calls," *Business Week*, June 16, 1997, pp. 144, 146; and Michael J. McCarthy, "Food Companies Hunt for a 'Next Big Thing' but Few Can Find One," *The Wall Street Journal*, May 6, 1997, pp. A1, A6.

2. A set of "10 trend commandments" is contained in Laurie Freeman, "Marketers, Too, Can Keep Ahead of the Curve," *Marketing News*, June 21, 1999, p. 8.

3. Ram Subramanian, Nirmala Fernandes, and Earl Harper, "Environmental Scanning in U.S. Companies: Their Nature and Their Relationship to Performance," *Management International Review* 33, no. 3, 1993, pp. 271–286.

4. Melanie Wells, "Iced Coffee Market May Get Steamy," *USA Today*, Apr. 24, 1996, p. 2B.

5. Robert Steyer, "Monsanto Marks the Early Success of Celebrex," *St. Louis Post-Dispatch*, July 21, 1999, p. C1.

6. "Resident Population of the United States: Middle Series Projections, 2015–2030, by Sex, Race, and Hispanic Origin, with Median Age," U.S. Bureau of the Census, Washington, DC, March 1996 <http://www.census.gov/population/projections/nation/nsrh/nph1530.txt>; and "Resident Population of the United States: Middle Series Projections, 1996–2000, by Sex, Race, and Hispanic Origin, with Median Age," U.S. Bureau of the Census, Washington, DC, March 1996 <http://www.census.gov/population/projections/nation/nsrh/nprh9600 txt>.

7. Gary L. Berman, "The Hispanic Market: Getting Down to Cases," *Sales & Marketing Management*, October 1991, p. 66.

8. "Ever-Elusive Inflation," *The Economist*, June 19, 1999, p. 24. The statement by Jack Welch was contained in David Bank, "A Site-Eat-Site World," *The Wall Street Journal*, July 12, 1999, p. R8.

9. Christopher Farrell and Zachary Schiller, "Stuck!" *Business Week*, Nov. 15, 1993, pp. 146–148+. For an essay that describes price deflation in retailing

and recommends strategies for coping with deflation, see Walter K. Levy, "Beware, the Pricing Genie Is out of the Bottle," *Retailing Issues Letter,* November 1994, pp. 1–4.

10. Rachel Beck, "Web Site Helps to Calm the Frenzy of Toy Shopping," *St. Louis Post-Dispatch,* Nov. 11, 1998, p. C7; and Joseph Pereira, "Toys 'R' Us Grows Up, Finds Life Isn't All Fun, Games," *The Wall Street Journal,* Mar. 20, 1995, p. B6.

11. James R. Hagerty, "Carpet Makers Confront Era That Extols Wood Floors," *The Wall Street Journal,* Mar. 31, 1998, p. B1.

12. This point and the diskettes and crayons examples are drawn from Jacquelyn Ottman, "Environmental Winners Show Sustainable Strategies," *Marketing News,* Apr. 27, 1998, p. 6.

13. The statistic related to consumers buying environmentally friendly products comes from Laura Litvan, "Going 'Green' in the '90s," *Nation's Business,* February 1995, p. 31. The Roper input was contained in Kevin Goldman, "'Green' Campaigns Don't Always Pay Off, Survey Finds," *The Wall Street Journal,* Apr. 11, 1994, p. B8.

14. The contradiction between attitudes and buying behavior was reported in C. Mitchell Adrian and Michael D. Richard, "An Examination of Purchase Behavior versus Purchase Attitudes for Environmentally Friendly and Recycled Consumer Goods," *Southern Business Review,* Spring 1995, pp. 1–15. The plastic cup example was described in Stephen Budiansky, "Being Green Isn't Always What It Seems," *U.S. News & World Report,* Aug. 26, 1996, p. 42.

15. Peter Stisser, "A Deeper Shade of Green," *American Demographics,* March 1994, p. 28.

16. Joseph Pereira, "Women Jump Ahead of Men in Purchases of Athletic Shoes," *The Wall Street Journal,* May 26, 1995, p. B1.

17. The statistic regarding working women comes from John Merli, "Working Women Use Radio Heavily," *Broadcasting & Cable,* Aug. 3, 1998, p. 34. The Leo Burnett study was reported in Stephanie Thompson, "Spin City: 18–49 Women," *Brandweek,* May 10, 1999, pp. S16–S18.

18. Thompson, loc. cit.; and Teri Agins, "Many Women Lose Interest in Clothes, to Retailers' Dismay," *The Wall Street Journal,* Feb. 28, 1995, p. A1.

19. Joan O'C. Hamilton, "A Shoe of One's Own," *Business Week,* May 24, 1999, pp. 62–64.

20. Maria Mallory, Dan McGraw, and Jill Jordan Sieder, "Women on a Fast Track," *U.S. News & World Report,* Nov. 6, 1995, pp. 60+, and Cyndee Miller, "Study Dispels '80s Stereotypes of Women," *Marketing News,* May 22, 1995, p. 3.

21. Diane Crispell, "The New World of Men," *American Demographics,* January 1992, pp. 38–43.

22. Lorrie Grant, "Grocery Chore No More," *USA Today,* July 21, 1999, p. 1B; Nick Wingfield, "Products to Watch," *The Wall Street Journal,* July 12, 1999, p. R34; and David Leonhardt, "Checking Out the Corner Cyberstore," *Business Week,* May 10, 1999, p. 130.

23. Leonhardt, loc. cit.

24. Nikhil Deogun, "Fat-Free Snacks Aren't Wowing Frito Customers," *The Wall Street Journal,* Sept. 12, 1998, pp. B1, B4.

25. Fred Faust, "Smaller Bookstores Challenge Two Chains," *St. Louis Post-Dispatch,* Mar. 19, 1998, p. B1; and Bryan Gruley, "Booksellers Sue Random House on Price Practices," *The Wall Street Journal,* Jan. 15, 1996, p. B10.

26. Gary McWilliams, "At Compaq, a Desktop Crystal Ball," *Business Week,* Mar. 20, 1995, pp. 96–97.

27. Vanessa O'Connell, "Campbell Decides Its IQ Health Meals May Be Ahead of the Curve for Foods," *The Wall Street Journal,* Apr. 27, 1998, p. B2; O'Connell, "How Campbell"; O'Connell, "Changing Tastes"; Weber, loc. cit.; and McCarthy, loc. cit.

Chapter 3

1. Charles P. Wallace, "adidas Back in the Game," *Fortune,* August 18, 1997, pp. 176+; Julia Day, "Adidas to focus on Brand Strength," Marketing Week, Dec. 10. 1998, pp. 21+; Mark Tedeschi, "Rough Riders," *Sporting Goods Business,* Jan. 8, 1999, pp. 36+; Adidas corporate material.

2. *Economic Indicators,* U.S. Government Printing Office, Washington, DC, May 1999.

3. Bruce Upbin, "Beyond Burgers," *Forbes,* Nov. 1, 1999, pp. 218–223.

4. Douglas A. Blackmon and Diane Brady, "Just How Hard Should a U.S. Company Woo a Big Foreign Market?" *The Wall Street Journal,* Apr. 6, 1998, pp. A1+.

5. Nikhil Deogun and Jonathan Karp, "For Coke in India, Thums Up Is the Real Thing," *The Wall Street Journal,* Apr. 29, 1998, pp. B1+.

6. Miriam Jordan, "Pillsbury Presses Flour Power in India," *The Wall Street Journal,* May 5, 1999, pp. B1+.

7. Bob Ortega, "Wal-Mart Is Slowed by Problems of Price and Culture in Mexico," *The Wall Street Journal,* July 29, 1994, p. A1.

8. Amy Louise Kazmin and Nikki Tait, "U.S. Carmakers Take Lessons from the Indian Consumer," *Financial Times,* Nov. 22, 1999, p. 5.

9. Alec Klien, "Kodak Losing U.S. Market Share to Fuji," *The Wall Street Journal,* May 5, 1999, p. A3.

10. "Cybershopping," *Financial Times* editorial, Nov. 4, 1999, p. 14.

11. Amy Borrus, Keith Naughton, and Laxmi Nakarami, "Now Detroit's Heavy Artillery Is Trained on Seoul," *Business Week,* Sept. 25, 1995, p. 78.

12. Neal E. Boudette, "In Europe, Surfing a Web of Red Tape," *The Wall Street Journal,* Nov. 29, 1999, pp. B1+.

13. Helene Cooper and Michael Williams, "U.S. Scales Down Hopes for APEC Talks," *The Wall Street Journal,* Nov. 16, 1995, p. A17.

14. Robert Frank, "Indonesia Chaos Has Its Rewards for the U.S.," *The Wall Street Journal,* June 1, 1999, p. A16; William Flannery, "Fast-Growing Southeast Asia Is a Land of Opportunity," *The St. Louis Post-Dispatch,* June 27, 1994, pp. 6BP+.

15. Joel Millman and Geoff Winestock, "EU and Mexico Reach Free-Trade Pact," *The Wall Street Journal,* Nov. 26, 1999, p. A9.

16. Mark M. Nelson and Brian Coleman, "U.S. and EU Sign Trade, Security Pact, Boosting Trans-Atlantic Cooperation," *The Wall Street Journal,* Dec. 4, 1995, p. A11.

17. Amy Borrus, Pete Engardio, and Dexter Roberts, "The New Trade Superpower," *Business Week,* Oct. 16, 1995, pp. 56–57.

18. Christopher Cooper and Stephanie Gruner, "U.S. Internet Firms Must Hustle to Catch Up in Europe," *The Wall Street Journal,* Nov. 11, 1999, pp. A25+.

19. Tara Parker-Pope, "Nonalcoholic Beer Hits the Spot in the Mideast," *The Wall Street Journal,* Dec. 6, 1995, pp. B1+.

20. *Statistical Abstract of the United States: 1999,* 119th ed., U.S. Bureau of the Census, Washington, DC, 1999, pp. 794 and 797.

21. Raymond Colitt, "Cola War Is Stepped Up," *Financial Times,* May 27, 1999, p. 19.

22. "Ford Unit to Launch Car for India Market," *Journal of Commerce,* Mar. 22, 1999, p. 7A.

23. Emily DeNitto, "Pepsi, Coke Think International for Future Growth," *Advertising Age,* Oct. 3, 1994, p. 44.

24. Michael Skapinker, "Airlines Bent on Bigamy Ruffle Alliances," *Financial Times,* June 23, 1999, p. 8.

25. "Hold My Hand," *The Economist,* May 15, 1999, pp. 73+.

26. Keith Naughton, "Ford's Global Gladiator," *Business Week,* Dec. 11, 1995, pp. 116–117.

27. Paulette Thomas, "Cosmetic Makers Offer World's Women an All-American Look with Local Twist," *The Wall Street Journal,* May 5, 1995, pp. B1+.

28. Nancy Dunne, "U.S. Steelmakers Press New Dumping Claims," *Financial Times,* May 25, 1999, p. 7; "Dump, Counterdump," *The Economist,* May 15, 1999, p. 66.

29. Helene Cooper, "The Euro: What You Need to Know," *The Wall Street Journal,* Jan. 4, 1999, pp. A5+.

30. Fara Warner, "GM Tests E-Commerce Plans in Emerging Markets," *The Wall Street Journal,* Nov. 25, 1999, p. B6.

31. Matthew Rose and Ernest Beck, "How Coke Got Snared by Gray Goods," *The Wall Street Journal,* July 6, 1999, p. A12.

32. Leslie Kaufman, "Avon's New Face," *Newsweek,* Nov. 16, 1998, pp. 59–60.

33. Lisa Bannon and Laura Bird, "Toyota Irritates Italians by Using Corruption Theme," *The Wall Street Journal Europe,* Jan. 24, 1994.

34. "Coty Targets Sporty Males," *Retail World,* Oct. 12 & 25, 1998, p. 25; Wallace, loc. cit.; Adidas corporate material.

Chapter 4

1. Kathleen Kerwin and Keith Naughton, "Can Detroit Make Cars that Baby Boomers Like?" *Business Week,* Dec. 1, 1997, pp. 134–148; John Griffin, "The Clean, Mean Electric Machine," *Financial Times,* Mar. 29, 1999, p. 12; Jeffery Ball, "But How Does It Make You Feel?" *The Wall Street Journal,* May 3, 1999, pp. B1+; Keith Naughton and Karen Lowery Miller, "From the New Beetle to a VW Pickup," *Business Week,* Aug. 9, 1999, pp. 37–38; Bill Vlasic, "Beeltemania to the Rescue," *Business Week,* Jan. 12, 1998, pp. 46–47.

2. Unless otherwise noted, this and the other demographic statistics in this chapter come from *Statistical Abstract of the United States: 1999,* 119th ed., U.S. Bureau of the Census, Washington, DC, 1999.

3. Brad Edmonson, "The Rural Rebound Keeps Rolling," *Forecast,* newsletter by Intertec Publishing, June, 1997; Brad Edmonson, "A New Era for Rural America," *American Demographic,* September 1997, pp. 30–31.

4. Diane Crispell, "The Hottest Metros," *American Demographics,* April 1995, pp. 4–6.

5. Michael Porter and Anne Habiby, "A Window on the New Economy," *Inc.,* May 1999, pp. 48–49.

6. Sandi Schlueter, "Maturing Market Offers an Opportune Niche," *Marketing News,* Aug. 31, 1998, p. 12; Charles D. Schewe and Geoffrey E. Meredith, "Digging Deep to Delight the Mature Adult Consumer," *Marketing Management,* Winter 1994, p. 22; and Stanley Kranczer, "Outlook for U.S. Population Growth," *Statistical Bulletin* (Metropolitan Life Insurance Co.), October 1994, p. 181.

7. A number of family life-cycle models have been developed with marketing implications. Several are compared with suggestions for modification in Charles M. Schaninger and William D. Danko, "A Conceptual and Empirical Comparison of Alternative Household Life Cycle Models," *Journal of Consumer Research,* March 1993, pp. 580–594.

8. Jon Berry, "Forever Single," *Adweek's Marketing Week,* Oct. 15, 1990, pp. 20–24.

9. Paul Gray, "Adding Up the Under-Skilled," *Time,* Sept. 20, 1993, p. 75.

10. Leah Rickard and Jeanne Whalen, "Retail Trails Ethnic Changes," *Advertising Age,* May 1, 1995, p. 11.

11. Melissa Campanelli, "The African-American Market: Community, Growth, and Change," *Sales & Marketing Management,* May 1991, pp. 75–81.

12. Peter Kerr, "Cosmetic Makers Read the Census," *The New York Times,* Aug. 29, 1991, p. C11.

13. Chris Taylor, "Bot Till You Drop," *Time,* Oct. 11, 1999, pp. 52–53.

14. *Advertising Age* website, <www.adage.com>, June 1999.

15. Michael McCarthy, "Mind Probe," *The Wall Street Journal,* Mar. 22, 1991, p. B2.

16. A good source of cultural trends is *American Demographics* magazine and its website <www.americandemographics.com>. See, for example, Richard Cimino and Don Lattin, "Choosing My Religioin," *American Demographics,* April 1999, pp. 60–65.

17. For an update on the Coleman and Rainwater classification, see Richard P. Coleman, "Continuing Significance of Social Class to Marketing," *Journal of Consumer Research,* December 1983, pp. 265–280.

18. A. H. Maslow, *Motivation and Personality,* Harper & Row, New York, 1954, pp. 80–106. There are numerous other need classification schemes that are described in most basic psychology texts.

19. Steven Reiss and Susan M. Havercamp, "Toward a Comprehensive Assessment of Fundamental Motivation: Factor Structure of the Reiss Profile," *Psychological Assessment,* June 1998, pp. 97–106.

20. There are some researchers who believe that consumers have hidden or subconscious motives for many activities, from skiing to wearing a necktie. For a compilation of observations about motivation derived from psychoanalytic techniques, see Ernest Dichter, *The Handbook of Consumer Motivation,* McGraw-Hill, New York, 1964.

21. Kristin Eddy, "The Nose Knows," *The South Bend Tribune,* Feb. 2, 1997, p. F6.

22. Yumiko Ono, "Marketers Seek the 'Naked' Truth in Consumer Psyches," *The Wall Street Journal,* June 30, 1997, pp. B1+.

23. Fred R. Bleakley, "Why Shoppers Think Food Is a Rip-Off," *The Wall Street Journal,* Mar. 6, 1997, pp. B1+.

24. McCarthy, loc. cit.

25. A description of learning theories as they apply to marketing can be found in books on consumer behavior. An especially good discussion is presented in William L. Wilkie, *Consumer Behavior,* 3d ed., Wiley, New York, 1994.

26. Kathleen Kerwin and Keith Naughton, loc. cit.

27. This classic definition is from Gordon W. Allport, "Attitudes," in C. A. Murchinson, ed., *A Handbook of Social Psychology,* Clark University Press, Worcester, MA, 1935, pp. 798–844.

28. Joe Schwartz, "Climate-Controlled Customers," *American Demographics,* March 1992, pp. 24–32.

29. Ronald E. Millman, "Using Background Music to Affect the Behavior of Supermarket Shoppers," *Journal of Marketing,* Summer 1982, pp. 86–91.

30. "U.S. Ranks No. 1 among Developed Nations in Believing It Is Headed in the Right Direction" and "Americans Lead the Industrial World in Bullishness for '99," website of Roper Starch Worldwide *<www.roper.com>,* Dec. 2, 1999.

31. Kerwin and Naughton, loc. cit.; Keith Naughton and Bill Vlasic, "The Nostalgia Boom," *Business Week,* Mar. 23, 1998, pp. 58–64; Keith Naughton, Emily Thornton, Kathleen Kerwin, and Heidi Dawley, "Can Honda Build a World Car?" *Business Week,* Sept. 8, 1997, pp. 100–108.

Chapter 5

1. Timothy Aeppel "A Web Auctioneer Roils the Rust Belt," *The Wall Street Journal,* Jan. 5, 2000, pp. B1+; Sharon Machlis, "Auction Site Woos Corporate Bidders," *Computerworld,* Dec. 7, 1998, p. 45; Paul Gillin, "Going Once, Twice . . . ," *Computerworld,* July 5, 1999, p. 30; Sarah Lorge, "Online Bidding Keeps Suppliers in Line," *Sales & Marketing Management,* August 1998, p. 16.

2. The statistics on the business market cited in this chapter come from U.S. Bureau of the Census publications. A particularly useful source is the *Statistical Abstract of the United States,* an annual publication that summarizes a myriad of facts.

3. Kathryn Barry Stelljes, Don Comis, and Marcia Wood, "From Sky to "Earth . . . Researchers Capture 'Ground Truth,'" *Agricultural Research,* March 1999, pp. 4–8.

4. Rhonda L. Rundle, "PurchasePro.com in Marketing Deal with Office Depot to Promote e-Business," *The Wall Street Journal,* Oct. 21, 1999, p. B15.

5. Robert D. Hof, "The Buyer Always Wins," *Business Week E.Biz,* Mar. 22, 1999, pp. 26–28; Eric J. Smith, "Online Auction Role-Reversal," *American Metal Market,* July 13, 1999, p. 2.

6. George Anders, "Buying Frenzy," *The Wall Street Journal,* July 12, 1999, pp. R6+.

7. Therese Eiben, "U.S. Exporters on a Global Roll," *Fortune,* June 29, 1992, pp. 94–95.

8. De'Ann Weiner, "Navistar: Gunning the Engines," *Business Week,* Feb. 2, 1998, pp. 135–138.

9. Hof, loc. cit.

10. For a description of the Standard Industrial Classification system and a complete listing of all SIC numbers and classifications, see *Standard Industrial Classification Manual,* U.S. Government Printing Office, Washington, DC, 1972, and also the *1987 Supplement.* Also see "SIC: The System Explained," *Sales & Marketing Management,* Apr. 22, 1985, pp. 52–53.

11. More information "Nakes") is available in *North American Industry Classification System—United States, 1997,* U.S. Government Printing Office, Washington, DC, 1997.

12. For over 30 years the U.S. Census Bureau has conducted a census of all domestic manufacturers every 5 years (on years ending in 2 and 7). The survey results, organized according to the Standard Industrial Classification (SIC) system, are compiled into hundreds of reports describing the locations, revenue, employees, payroll, and other information about firms. The output is reported in the *Census of Manufactures.* Similar surveys and reports are conducted for mining, construction, and agriculture. In 2000, the federal government began reporting economic data using the North American Industry Classification System (NAICS) under the general title *The Economic Census, 1997.* More information can be found on the Census Bureau website <www.census.gov>.

13. Tim Minihan, "What Makes a Supplier World-Class?" *Purchasing,* Aug. 13, 1998.

14. Robert D. McWilliams, Earl Naumann, and Stan Scott, "Determining Buying Center Size," *Industrial Marketing Management,* February 1992, pp. 43–49.

15. For more on building business relationships see Christopher W. Hart and Michael D. Johnson, "Growing the Trust Relationship," *Marketing Management,* Spring 1999, pp. 9–22.

16. John Dodge, "Shifting Gears," *The Wall Street Journal,* July 12, 1999, pp. R40+.

17. To see the way this process can work, see Timothy Aeppel, "Bidding for E-nuts and E-bolts on the Net," *The Wall Street Journal,* Mar. 12, 1999, p. B1.

18. Michael Hickens, "It's an E-Buyer's Market," *Management Review,* June 1999, p. 6; "Why FreeMarkets Excites Buyers," *Purchasing,* Oct. 21, 1999, pp. S48+; Helen Atkinson, "Shippers Buy Transport Tickets at Auction," *The Journal of Commerce,* June 30, 1999, p. 6.

Chapter 6

1. Paula Szuchman, "Time-Share in the Air for Execs," *Condé Nast Traveler,* August 1997, p. 30; Louis Lavelle, "Executive Jet Expanding Fleet, Time Share Taking Off," *The* (New Jersey) *Record,* May 14, 1997, p. B1; Lorraine Woellert, "Bombardier Zeroes in on Buffett," *Business Week,* May 3, 1999, p. 6.

2. Paul Beckett, "American Express Starts Online Bank, an Increasingly Competitive Business," *The Wall Street Journal,* July 23, 1999, p. B8.

3. Gabriella Stern, "Attempt to Cut Candy Calories Sours for P&G," *The Wall Street Journal,* Aug. 25, 1995, p. B11.

4. Brian Steinberg, "Toyota Plans Ads Aimed at Those in 20s, 30s," *The Wall Street Journal,* June 21, 1999, p. B13.

5. A good description of the role of social class in marketing can be found in Richard P. Coleman, "The Continuing Significance of Social Class to Marketing," *Journal of Consumer Research,* December 1983, pp. 267–280.

6. Christina De Valle and Jon Berry, "They Know Where You Live—and How You Buy," *Business Week,* Feb. 7, 1994, p. 89.

7. Robert L. Simison, "The Vroom-Vroom Toy of the Baby Boomer—a Honda?" *The Wall Street Journal,* July 14, 1999, pp. B1+.

8. Lynn R. Kahle, Sharon E. Beatty, and Pamela Homer, "Alternative Measurement Approaches to Consumer Values: The List of Values (LOV) and Values and Lifestyles (VAL)," *Journal of Consumer Research,* December 1986, pp. 405–409.

9. Allanna Sullivan, "Mobil Bets Drivers Pick Cappuccino over Low Prices," *The Wall Street Journal,* Jan. 30, 1995, p. B11.

10. Richard Tomkins, "Shaking Out the Last Dollop of Growth," *Financial Times,* June 12 and 13, 1999, p. 7.

11. Kevin Helliker, "Expanding Prison Population Captivates Marketers," *The Wall Street Journal,* Jan. 9, 1995, p. B1.

12. David C. Smith "Inside GM Purchasing, Part II," *Ward's Auto World,* May 1995, p. 69.

13. One-A-Day's other formulations include vitamins for men, women, garlic, maximum, antioxidant, 50 plus, calcium plus, energy, memory and concentration, bedtime and rest, bone strength, menopause, tension and mood, joint health, cold season, cholesterol, and prostate.

14. Amy Barrett, "Here's Our Ranking of 1999's Best Small Corporations," *Business Week,* May 31, 1999, pp. 86+.

15. Andrew Edgecliffe-Johnson, "U.S. Retail Giants Try Thinking Small," *Financial Times,* June 6, 1999, p. 18.

16. Laura M. Litvan, "Going 'Green' in the '90s," *Nation's Business,* February 1995, pp. 30–32.

17. Lisa Gubernick, "Midmarket Schools," *Forbes,* July 31, 1995, pp. 46–48.

18. Holly Finn, "Thinking Smart in the Retail Jungle," *Financial Times,* July 17 and 18, 1999, p. IX.

19. Patrick Reilly, "Venerable Hunting Magazine Disarms, Tries Kayaking," *The Wall Street Journal,* July 6, 1999, pp. A17+.

20. Based on an advertisement for *The Wall Street Journal* appearing in *The Wall Street Journal,* July 23, 1999, p. B9.

21. Andrew E. Serwer, "McDonald's Conquers the World," *Fortune,* Oct. 17, 1994, pp. 103–116.

22. For more information on the role of sales people in forecasting, see William Keenan, Jr., "Numbers Racket," *Sales & Marketing Management,* May 1995, pp. 64–76.

23. Jim Carlton, "Where's the Beef? Gardenburger Inc. Posts Wider Loss," *the Wall Street Journal,* July 26, 1999, p. A10.

24. Szuchman, loc. cit.; Lavelle, loc. cit.; Woellert, loc. cit.; "Bombardier Aerospace (Special Advertising Section)," *Business Week,* Mar. 29, 1999.

Chapter 7

1. Leslie Cauley, "Iridium's Downfall: The Marketing Took a Back Seat to Science," *The Wall Street Journal,* July 18, 1999, pp. A1+; Christopher Price, "Iridium: Born on a Beach but Lost in Space," *Financial Times,* Aug. 20, 1999, p. 16; Jagdish N. Sheth and Rajendra Sisodia, "Why Cell Phones Succeed Where Iridium Failed," *The Wall Street Journal,* Aug. 23, 1999, p. A14.

2. Karl Albrecht and Ron Zemke, *Service America! Doing Business in the New Economy,* Dow Jones–Irwin, Homewood, IL, 1985.

3. Jack Honomichl, "The Honomichl 50," *Marketing News,* June 7, 1999, pp. H1–H39.

4. Michael M. Pearson and Gary H. Gessner, "Transactional Segmentation to Slow Customer Defections," *Marketing Management,* Summer 1999, pp. 16–23.

5. Jonathan Berry, John Verity, Kathleen Kerwin, and Gail DeGeorge, "Database Marketing," *Business Week,* Sept. 5, 1994, pp. 56–62.

6. Laurie Hays, "Using Computers to Divine Who Might Buy a Gas Grill," *The Wall Street Journal,* Aug. 8, 1994, p. B1.

7. A two-part article exploring the process of and prospects for data mining is Peter R. Peacock, "Data Mining in Marketing: Part 1," *Marketing Management,* Winter 1998, pp. 8–18; and Peter R. Peacock, "Data Mining in Marketing: Part 2," *Marketing Management,* Spring 1998, pp. 14–25.

8. John Verity, "Coaxing Meaning out of Raw Data," *Business Week,* Feb. 3, 1997, pp. 134–138.

9. Thomas C. Boyd, Timothy C. Krehbiel, and James M. Stearns, "The Impact of Technology on Marketing Research," *The Journal of Marketing Management,* Spring/Summer 1998, pp. 24–34. this article describes how new research methods can complement and supplement traditional data-gathering and analysis methods.

10. Robert O'Harrow, Jr., "Buying Patterns Turn into Directed Advertising," *The Washington Post* as reported in *The Idaho Statesman,* Jan. 1, 1999, p. 3D.

11. Lawrence D. Gibson, "Defining Marketing Problems." *Marketing Management,* Spring 1998, pp. 5–14.

12. In fact, the support of this hypothesis is reported in Robert Berner, "A Battle Fought with Kiwis and Kale," *The Wall Street Journal,* Mar. 15, 1999, p. B1.

13. Neal Templin, "Undercover with a Hotel Spy," *The Wall Street Journal,* May 12, 1999, pp. B1+.

14. American FactFinder, a website supported by the U.S. Census Bureau, can be found at <http://www.census.gov/dads/www>.

15. The Gale Group publishes several useful reference sources. *The Encyclopedia of Major Marketing Campaigns* (1999) describes 500 major marketing and advertising campaigns including the target markets, objectives, competition, marketing strategy, and outcomes. *Gales Guide to Industry* (2000), and *Gale's Guide to the Media* (2000) provide information on associations, directories, periodicals, databases and online services, and leading companies.

16. Information on the American Community Survey developed by the U.S. Census Bureau can be found at <http://www.census.gov.acs/www>.

17. Researchers are constantly searching for more effective methods for understanding behavior. For some examples of what might be considered unconventional research techniques such as storytelling (used by Kimberly-Clark to develop a new line of diapers), deprivation diaries (used in the "Got Milk?" ads), disguised data gathering, and hypnosis see Ronald B. Lieber, "Storytelling: A New Way to Get Close to Your Customer," *Fortune,* Feb. 3, 1997, pp. 102–108; Yukimo Ono, "Marketers Seek the 'Naked' Truth in Consumer Psyches," *The Wall Street Journal,* May 30, 1997, pp. B1+.

18. For a comprehensive description of Internet marketing see Judy Strauss and Raymond Frost, *Marketing on the Internet,* Prentice Hall, 1999.

19. O'Harrow, Jr., loc. cit.

20. Focus groups in research are quite common. Recently focus groups have been used by Campbell Soup Co. to understand what women want for lunch (Shelly Branch, "Campbell's New Soup-to-Go Ads Are Directed at Working Women," *The Wall Street Journal,* Nov. 18, 1999, p. B4), by Toys "R" Us to develop new store layouts (Lisa Bannon, "Why Girls and Boys Get Different Toys," *The Wall Street Journal,* Feb. 14, 2000, pp. B1+), and by Thomson Electronics to learn how people integrate music into their daily activities (Melanie Wells, "New Ways to Get into Our Heads," *USA Today,* Mar. 2, 1999, pp. 1B+).

21. Brad Edmonson, "The Wired Bunch: Online Surveys and Focus Groups Might Solve the Toughest Problems in Market Research," *American Demographics,* June 1997, pp. 10–15.

22. Roy Furchgott, "If You Like the Suit, Click Here," *Business Week,* Nov. 17, 1997, p. 8.

23. An experiment comparing mail, fax, e-mail, and the Web for collecting data is reported in Rick Weible and John Wallace, "Cyber Research," *Marketing Research,* Fall 1998, pp. 19–24.

24. "Net Working," *St. Louis Post-Dispatch,* Sept. 16, 1998, p. 61, reports a study comparing a sample of Internet users with a sample from the general population on product ownership, shopping behavior, and health care. The researchers concluded there were no significant differences.

25. Adam L. Penenberg, "Is There a Snoop on Your Site?" *Forbes,* May 17, 1999, pp. 322–325.

26. Aaron Lucchetti, "FTC Tackles an 'Anonymous' Web Survey," *The Wall Street Journal,* May 7, 1999, p. B2.

27. Diane H. Schmalensee and A. Dawn Lesh, "How to Make Research More Actionable," *Marketing Research,* Winter 1998/Spring 1999, pp. 23–36.

28. Leslie Cauley, "Iridium's Downfall: The Marketing Took a Back Seat to Science," *The Wall Street Journal,* July 18, 1999, pp. A1+; Christopher Price, "Iridium: Born on a Beach but Lost in Space," *Financial Times,* Aug. 20, 1999, p. 16; Jagdish N. Sheth and Rajendra Sisodia, "Why Cell Phones Succeed Where Iridium Failed," *The Wall Street Journal,* Aug. 23, 1999, p. A14.

Chapter 8

1. Based on Frederic M. Biddle, "A Little Gas Fuels Hope for a New Type of Electric Car," *The Wall Street Journal,* July 9, 1999, p. B1; Andrea Adelson, "GM Tries to Boost the Appeal of Its EV1 Electric Car," *Star Tribune* (Minneapolis, MN), Jan. 2, 1999, p. 2M; Kenneth Cole, "Electric Cars Unlikely to Take Center Stage," *The Detroit News,* Dec. 21, 1998, p. F15; "Business Bulletin," *The Wall Street Journal,* Oct. 22, 1998, p. A1; Keith Naughton, "Can You Have Green Cars without the Red Ink?" *Business Week,* Dec. 29, 1997, p. 50; "GM's First Electric Cars Head West," *St. Louis Post-Dispatch,* Nov. 15, 1996, p. 3C; and David Woodruff, "GM: All Charged Up over the Electric Car," *Business Week,* Oct. 21, 1991, pp. 106, 108.

2. Yumiko Ono, "Some Kids Won't Eat the Middle of an Oreo," *The Wall Street Journal,* Nov. 20, 1991, p. B1.

3. For a different classification scheme that provides strategic guidelines for management by relating products and prices, along with an excellent bibliography on product classification, see Patrick E. Murphy and Ben M. Enis, "Classifying Products Strategically," *Journal of Marketing,* July 1986, pp. 24–42. Also see Ernest F. Cooke, "The Relationship between a Product Classification System and Marketing Strategy," *Journal of Midwest Marketing,* Spring 1987, pp. 230–240.

4. Jeffrey A. Trachtenberg, "Interactive Movies: Hot Medium or Smell-O-Vision, Part Three?" *The Wall Street Journal,* Jan. 16, 1995, p. B1.

5. Rodney Ho, "In a Crowded Market, Two Ambitious Brothers Try Bathroom Humor," *The Wall Street Journal,* Aug. 6, 1999, p. B1; and J. Taylor Buckley, "Starting at the Bottom," *USA Today,* July 14, 1998, p. 28.

6. Kathleen Deveny, "Failure of Its Oven Lovin' Cookie Dough Shows Pillsbury Pitfall of New Products," *The Wall Street Journal,* June 17, 1993, p. B1.

7. Stuart Elliott, "The Famous Brands on Death Row," *The New York Times,* Nov. 7, 1993, p. 1F.

8. Barton G. Tretheway, "Everything New Is Old Again," *Marketing Management,* Spring 1998, p. 7.

9. Durk Jager, as quoted in Katrina Brooker, "Can Procter & Gamble Change Its Culture, Protect Its Market Share, and Find the Next Tide?" *Fortune,* Apr. 26, 1999, p. 149. For more about Rubbermaid's varied troubles, see Geoffrey Colvin, "How Rubbermaid Managed to Fail," *Fortune,* Nov. 23, 1998, pp. 32–33. For a description of 3M's successes and problems related to product innovation, see Thomas A. Stewart, "3M Fights Back," *Fortune,* Feb. 5, 1996, pp. 94–99. For perspectives about Nike's trials and tribulations, see William J. Holstein, "From Swoosh to Clank," *U.S. News & World Report,* Mar. 30, 1998, p. 42, and Patricia Sellers, "Nike's Not Cool," *Fortune,* Mar. 30, 1998, pp. 26–27.

10. Respectively, Marketing Intelligence, Inc., as cited in Deveny, loc. cit.; Tretheway, loc. cit.; and Kuczmarski & Associates, as described in Christopher Power, "Flops," *Business Week,* Aug. 16, 1993, pp. 76–77.

11. The reasons for failure are drawn from the "1995 Innovation Survey," conducted by Group EFO Limited of Weston, CT. The two examples are drawn from Ted Anthony, "Where's Farrah Shampoo? Next to the Salsa Ketchup," *Marketing News,* May 6, 1996, p. 13, and Alan Farnham, "It's a Bird! It's a Plane! It's a Flop!" *Fortune,* May 2, 1994, pp. 108–110.

12. Jerry Useem, "*Sold! Elvis Impersonator for $61.23 an Hour,*" *Fortune,* Aug. 16, 1999, p. 36.

13. Eugene Carlson, "Some Forms of Identification Can't Be Handily Faked," *The Wall Street Journal,* Sept. 14, 1993, p. B2.

14. Evan Ramstad, "Products Go Digital . . . Whether They Are or Not," *The Wall Street Journal,* Sept. 7, 1999, p. A11A.

15. Richard Gibson, "Too Skinny a Burger Is a Mighty Hard Sell, McDonald's Learns," *The Wall Street Journal,* Apr. 15, 1993, pp. A1, A6.

16. As stressed by a consultant, Philip Himmelfarb, in Roberta Maynard, "The Heat Is On," *Nation's Business,* October, 1997, pp. 16, 18.

17. These benefits and a "stage gate system" for new-product development are described in Robert G. Cooper and Elko J. Kleinschmidt, "Stage Gate Systems for New Product Success," *Marketing Management,* Vol. 1, No. 4, 1993, pp. 20–29. For an approach for managing multiple new-product development projects, see Steven C. Wheelwright and Kim B. Clark, "Creating Project Plans to Focus Product Development," *Harvard Business Review,* March—April 1992, pp. 70–82.

18. For a report on the criteria used in making "go–no go" decisions in the product-development process, see Ilkka A. Ronkainen, "Criteria Changes across Product Development Stages," *Industrial Marketing Management,* August 1985, pp. 171–178.

19. The information about customers, suppliers, and franchisees comes, respectively, from "Study: Launching New Products Is Worth the Risk," *Marketing News,* Jan. 20, 1992, p. 2; Neal Templin and Jeff Cole, "Manufacturers Use Suppliers to Help Them Develop New Products," *The Wall Street Journal,* Dec. 19, 1994, pp. A1, A6; and Jeffrey A. Tannenbaum, "Role Model," *The Wall Street Journal,* May 23, 1996, p. R22.

20. For more on the first two stages, termed *opportunity identification,* see Linda Rochford, "Generating and Screening New Product Ideas," *Industrial Marketing Management,* November 1991, pp. 287–296.

21. Faye Rice, "Secrets of Product Testing," *Fortune,* Nov. 29, 1994, pp. 166–171.

22. Cooper and Kleinschmidt, op. cit., pp. 22–23.

23. Development times are discussed in Maynard, op. cit., pp. 15, 22. For an in-depth look at the development of the Frito Pie, see Emily Nelson, "Product Development Is Always Difficult; Consider the Frito Pie," *The Wall Street Journal,* Oct. 25, 1999, pp. A1, A22. For a discussion of automakers' efforts to dramatically reduce the time required to develop new models, see Valerie Reitman and Robert L. Simison, "Japanese Car Makers Speed Up Car Making," *The Wall Street Journal,* Dec. 29, 1995, pp. B1, B13. The omission of market tests was described in "Study: Launching New Products Is Worth the Risk," loc. cit.

24. Robert G. Cooper and Scott J. Edgett, "Critical Success Factors for New Financial Services," *Marketing Management,* Fall 1996, pp. 26–37; and Howard Schlossberg, "Services Development Lags behind New Products," *Marketing News,* Nov. 6, 1989, p. 2.

25. "No Yen for Chocolate Salsa? You've Got Company," *St. Louis Post-Dispatch,* Dec. 20, 1994, p. 5C.

26. For foundations of diffusion theory and a review of landmark studies on diffusion of innovations, see Everett M. Rogers, *Diffusion of Innovations,* 3d ed., Free Press, New York, 1983.

27. Susan Chira, "High-Tech Safety: Will Parents Buy It?" *The New York Times,* Feb. 17, 1994, p. C1.

28. Denise Smith Amos, "Are You an 'Influential'? Advertisers Want You," *St. Louis Post-Dispatch,* Aug. 6, 1995, pp. E1, E9.

29. Rogers, loc. cit.

30. Tara Parker-Pope, "P&G Puts Two Cleaning Products on Its New Marketing Fast Track," *The Wall Street Journal,* May 18, 1999, p. B6; and Yumiko Ono, "Novel P&G Product Brings Dry Cleaning Home, *The Wall Street Journal,* Nov. 19, 1997, p. B1.

31. See Frank G. Bingham and Charles J. Quigley, Jr., "Venture Team Application to New Product Development," *Journal of Business and Industrial Marketing,* Winter–Spring 1989, pp. 49–59.

32. The quote about brand managers being an "endangered species" is drawn from Rance Crain, "Brand Management's Decline May Haunt GM," *Advertising Age,* Nov. 6, 1995, p. 16. Jolie Solomon and Carol Hymowitz, "P&G Makes Changes in the Way It Develops and Sells Its Products," *The Wall Street Journal,* Aug. 11, 1987, pp. 1, 12. For more about P&G's challenges moving into the new century, see Brooker, loc. cit. Raymond Serafin, "Ford Taps Insiders As Brand Managers," *Advertising Age,* Jan. 1, 1996, p. 3.

33. Various arrangements are discussed in Eric M. Olson, Orville C. Walker, Jr., and Robert W. Ruekert, "Organizing for Effective New Product Development: The Moderating Role of Product Innovativeness," *Journal of Marketing,* January 1995, pp. 48–62. The favorable comment comes from Steve McDougal and Jeff Smith, "Wake up Your Product Development," *Marketing Management,* Summer 1999, pp. 24–30.

34. Gregory L. White, "GM Stops Making Electric Car, Holds Talks with Toyota," *The Wall Street Journal,* Jan. 12, 2000, p. A14; Tim Burt, "Ford Launches Electric Car," *Financial Times,* Nov. 8, 1999, p. 15; Sue Zesiger, "Reinventing the Wheel," *Fortune,* Oct. 25, 1999, pp. 184–186+; "Honda Gives Up on Expensive, Unpopular Electric Cars," *St. Louis Post-Dispatch,* Apr. 30, 1999, p. C1; Ian P. Murphy, "Charged Up: Electric Cars Get Jolt of Marketing," *Marketing News,* Aug. 18, 1997, p. 1; Naughton, loc. cit.; Biddle, loc. cit.; and Woodruff, loc. cit.

Chapter 9

1. Adam Feuerstein, "Lego Robots Marching on Marin County," *San Francisco Business Times,* June 11, 1999, p. 1; Cora Daniels, "Lego's Star Wars Robot: Another Great Way to Kill Time in Silicon Valley," *Fortune,* June 7, 1999, p. 190; Clare Macarthy, "Lego Builds on Its Values Despite the High-Tech Toys," *The Financial Times,* Jan. 22, 1999, p. 27; Joseph Pereira and Cacilie Rohwedder, "Block by Block, Lego Is Building a Strategy for the Interactive Age," *The Wall Street Journal,* Feb. 2, 1998, pp. A1, A12.

2. Kathleen Kerwin and Keith Naughton, "A Different Kind of Saturn," *Business Week,* July 5, 1999, pp. 28–29, and Russell Mitchell, "Intel Isn't Taking This Lying Down," *Business Week,* Sept. 30, 1991, pp. 32–33.

3. Michael Goldstein, "Few Leagues of Their Own," *Business Week,* Jan. 18, 1999, pp. 74–76.

4. For more on this approach, see Jack Trout and Al Ries, "*Don't* Follow the Leader," *Sales & Marketing Management,* February 1994, pp. 25–26; and William Keenan, Jr., "Drawing the Line," *Sales & Marketing Management,* August 1993, pp. 32–36.

5. Carol Matlack, "Swatch: Ready for Net Time?" *Business Week,* Feb. 14, 2000, p. 61; and Brandon Mitchener, "Can Daimler's Tiny 'Swatchmobile' Sweep Europe?" *The Wall Street Journal,* Oct. 2, 1998, p. B1.

6. Laura Bird, "Romancing the Package," *Adweek's Marketing Week,* Jan. 21, 1991, pp. 10–11, 14.

7. Ernest Beck, "Unilever to Cut More than 1,000 Brands," *The Wall Street Journal,* Sept. 22, 1999, p. A17.

8. James R. Hagerty, "Gilding the Drill Bit? Hardware Giants Go High-End," *The Wall Street Journal,* July 28, 1998, pp. B1, B7.

9. Bianca Riemer and Laura Zinn, "Haute Couture That's Not So Haute," *Business Week,* Apr. 22, 1991, p. 108.

10. Lee Gomes, "H-P to Create a New Subsidiary to Sell Cheap 'Apollo' Brand of Ink-Jet Printers," Jan. 6, 1999, p. B4; and Susan Caminiti, "Will Old Navy Fill the Gap?" *Fortune,* Mar. 18, 1996, p. 59.

11. Hagerty, loc. cit.

12. William C. Symonds, "Would You Spend $1.50 for a Razor Blade?" *Business Week,* Apr. 27, 1998, p. 46; and Mark Maremont, "Gillette Finally Reveals Its Vision of the Future, and It Has 3 Blades," *The Wall Street Journal,* Apr. 14, 1998, pp. A1, A10.

13. Dean Takahashi, "Intel to Unveil Speedier Chips on Monday," *The Wall Street Journal,* Oct. 22, 1999, p. B6; and Andy Reinhardt, "Intel Is Taking No Prisoners," *Business Week,* July 12, 1999, p. 38.

14. The criticisms are summarized in Geoffrey L. Gordon, Roger J. Calantone, and C. Anthony diBenedetto, "Mature Markets and Revitalization Strategies: An American Fable," *Business Horizons,* May–June 1991, pp. 39–50. Alternative life cycles are proposed in Edward D. Popper and Bruce D. Buskirk, "Technology Life Cycles in Industrial Markets," *Industrial Marketing Management,* February 1992, pp. 23–31; and C. Merle Crawford, "Business Took the Wrong Life Cycle from Biology," *The Journal of Product & Brand Management,* Winter 1992, pp. 51–57.

15. Don Clark, "Multimedia's Hype Hides Virtual Reality: An Industry Shakeout," *The Wall Street Journal,* Mar. 1, 1995, pp. A1, A6.

16. Neil Gross and Peter Coy, "The Technology Paradox," *Business Week,* Mar. 6, 1995, p. 77.

17. John Nolan, "Maker Says Its Fake Fat Is Losing to the Real Thing," *St. Louis Post-Dispatch,* Aug. 6, 1999, p. C16.

18. Emily Nelson, "In a Rainbow of Hues, Bracelets Bring a Pot of Gold," *The Wall Street Journal,* Dec. 6, 1999, pp. B1, B4.

19. Eric Adler, "The Walkman at 20: Portable Stereo Has Changed the World," *St. Louis Post-Dispatch,* Sept. 2, 1999, p. G1.

20. Kevin Coughlin, "Are CDs' Days Numbered? Two New Technologies Join the Battle for the World's Ear," *St. Louis Post-Dispatch,* Sept. 5, 1999, p. E1; and Robert A. Starrett, "Burning Down the House: Home Recorders Are Here," *EMedia Professional,* May 1999, p. 50.

21. David Wellman, "Young Brews," *Supermarket Business,* December 1998, pp. 29–33; Gerry Khermouch, "Nestlé Suddenly Kills Ready-to-Drink Nescafe Coffee, Cosmo Chocolate," *Brandweek,* Nov. 23, 1998, p. 4; and "RTD Coffee: Grounds for Encouragement," *Beverage World,* Mar. 15, 1998, p. 65.

22. Jim Carlton, "Newton's Fate Is Lesson for PC Industry," *The Asian Wall Street Journal,* Mar. 2, 1998, p. 8.

23. The concept of "pioneer advantage" and the historical study of the 50 product categories are described in Gerard J. Tellis and Peter N. Golder, "Pioneer Advantage: Marketing Logic or Marketing Legend," *USC Business,* Fall/Winter 1995, pp. 49–53.

24. Reiji Yoshida, "Sega Plays Survival Game with Dreamcast," *Japan Times Weekly International Edition,* Dec. 14–20, 1998, p. 13.

25. Ten distinct strategies are described in Joel R. Evans and Gregg Lombardo, "Marketing Strategies for Mature Brands," *Journal of Product & Brand Management,* Vol. 2, No. 1, 1993, pp. 5–19. For a discussion of four strategies—recapture, redesign, refocus, and recast—that are particularly applicable to *business* products, see Paul C. N. Michell, Peter Quinn, and Edward Percival, "Marketing Strategies for Mature Industrial Products," *Industrial Marketing Management,* August 1991, pp. 201–206.

26. Martha Brannigan, "Cruise Lines Look to the Land to Get Boomers on Board," *The Wall Street Journal,* Dec. 6, 1999, p. B4.

27. Becky Ebenkamp, "Lycra Streeetches," *Brandweek,* July 5, 1999, p. 3; Elaine Gross, "New York Markets," *Textile World,* May 1999, p. 24; and Monica Roman, "How DuPont Keeps 'Em Coming Back for More," *Business Week,* Aug. 20, 1990, p. 68.

28. Dana James, "Rejuvenating Mature Brands Can Be Stimulating Exercise," *Marketing News,* Aug. 16, 1999, p. 16.

29. Hardy Green, "The Last Word in New Words," *Business Week,* Aug. 30, 1999, p. 6.

30. Bill Saporito, "How to Revive a Fading Firm," *Fortune,* Mar. 22, 1993, p. 80.

31. The criticism of Microsoft and other software firms comes from Joel Dreyfuss, "Planned Obsolescence Is Alive and Well," *Fortune,* Feb. 15, 1999, p. 192P; the Gateway example is drawn from "Gateway: Buy Now, Upgrade Later," *Business Week,* June 8, 1998, p. 46.

32. William Echikson, "Designers Climb onto the Virtual Catwalk," *Business Week,* Oct. 11, 1999, pp. 164, 168. For an example of producing multiple variations of a style, see Riemer and Zinn, loc. cit.

33. Wendy Bounds, Rebecca Quick, and Emily Nelson, "In the Office, It's Anything Goes," *The Wall Street Journal,* Aug. 26, 1999, pp. B1, B4.

34. Bounds et al., loc. cit.; Teri Agins, "The Fall of the Jacket Leaves Retailers Torn over Fashion's Future," *The Wall Street Journal,* Aug. 26, 1999, pp. A1, A6; and Teri Agins, "Many Women Lose Interest in Clothes, to Retailers' Dismay," *The Wall Street Journal,* Feb. 28, 1995, pp. A1, A8.

35. Veronica Chambers and Alisha Davis, "Direct from Paris . . . to the Mall," *Newsweek,* Apr. 13, 1998, pp. 64–65.

36. Roger Trapp, "Playing with the Big Boys," *The Independent,* Oct. 11, 1998, p. 24; and Joseph Pereira, "Slighted in U.S., Whimsical Toy Is a Wow in Europe," *The Wall Street Journal,* May 21, 1998, pp. B1, B2.

Chapter 10

1. Joan Voight, "Red, White and Blue: An American Icon Fades Away," *Adweek,* Apr. 26, 1999, pp. 28–35; Becky Ebenkamp, "Less Emphasis on Image, More Focus on the Product," *Brandweek,* June 15, 1998, p. S20; Linda Himelstein, "Levi's Is Hiking Up Its Pants," *Business Week,* Dec. 1, 1997, pp. 70–75; Ralph T. King, Jr., and Wendy Bounds, "Its Share Shrinking, Levi Strauss Lays Off 6,395," *The Wall Street Journal,* Nov. 4, 1997, p. B1; "Dueling Denim," *Marketing News,* Sept. 15, 1997, p. 1; and Ellen Neuborne and Stephanie Anderson Forest, "Look Who's Picking Levi's Pocket," *Business Week,* Sept. 8, 1997, pp. 68–72.

2. Adapted from Peter D. Bennett, ed., *Dictionary of Marketing Terms,* American Marketing Association, Chicago, 1988, p. 18.

3. The European procedure is described in Maxine Lans Retsky, "Who Needs the New Community Trademark?" *Marketing News,* June 3, 1996, p. 11. For a description of changes in trademark law and court decisions on trademarks as well as their marketing implications, see Dorothy Cohen, "Trademark Strategy Revisited," *Journal of Marketing,* July 1991, pp. 46–59.

4. Bruce Orwall, "Judge Tells Disney and Infoseek to Stop Using Logo That Led to GoTo.com Suit," *The Wall Street Journal,* Nov. 15, 1999, p. B8; Tim Bryant, "Bud Ice Trademark Suit Won't Be Tried Here," *St. Louis Post-Dispatch,* Jan. 29, 1999, p. B1; and Raju Narisetti, "IBM Battles Start-Up over 'e-business,'" *The Wall Street Journal,* July 2, 1998, p. B10.

5. Rodney Ho, "Brand-Name Diamonds: A Cut Above?" *The Wall Street Journal,* June 1, 1998, p. B1; and Betsy Morris, "The Brand's the Thing," *Fortune,* Mar. 4, 1996, pp. 72–75+.

6. Thomas Kamm, "Rivalry in Luxury Goods Heats Up as Gucci and LVMH Unveil Deals," *The Wall Street Journal,* Nov. 16, 1999, p. A22.

7. Al Ries, "What's in a Name?" *Sales & Marketing Management,* October 1995, p. 36. This article also discusses eight attributes of a desirable brand name.

8. Material in this paragraph and the following one are drawn from Suein L. Hwang, "Picking Pithy Names Is Getting Trickier as Trademark Applications Proliferate," *The Wall Street Journal,* Jan. 14, 1992, p. B1.

9. For more about *morphemes,* see Teresa Pavia and Janeen A. Costa, "The Winning Number: Consumer Perceptions of Alpha-Numeric Brand Names," *Journal of Marketing,* July 1993, pp. 85–98; and Casey McCabe, "What's in a Name?" *Adweek's Marketing Week,* Apr. 16, 1990, p. 22.

10. See also Kim Robertson, "Strategically Desirable Brand Name Characteristics," *The Journal of Product & Brand Management,* Summer 1992, pp. 62–72. For a good discussion of the special opportunities and challenges associated with services branding, see Vicki Clift, "Name Service Firms for the Long Haul," *Marketing News,* Dec. 6, 1993, p. 10. Some of the examples in this section are drawn from Leonard L. Berry, Edwin F. Lefkowith, and Terry Clark, "In Services, What's in a Name?" *Harvard Business Review,* September–October 1988, pp. 28–30.

11. Dean Takahashi, "In Pursuit of Poké-mon Pirates," *The Wall Street Journal,* Nov. 8, 1999, pp. B1, B4; and David Stipp, "Farewell, My Logo," *Fortune,* May 27, 1996, p. 130.

12. Russell E. Brooks and Gila E. Gellman, "Combating Counterfeiting," *Marketing Management,* Vol. 2, No. 3, 1993, pp. 49–51.

13. An excellent summary of this challenge and a list of safeguards are contained in Maxine S. Lans, "On Your Mark: Get Set or It May Go," *Marketing News,* Sept. 26, 1994, p. 12.

14. Jack Alexander, "What's in a Name? Too Much, Said the FTC," *Sales & Marketing Management,* January 1989, pp. 75, 78.

15. Carrie Goerne, "Rollerblade Reminds Everyone That Its Success Is Not Generic," *Marketing News,* Mar. 2, 1992, p. 1.

16. Patricia Sellers, "Brands: It's Thrive or Die," *Fortune,* Aug. 23, 1993, p. 53.

17. For an excellent discussion of the nature and benefits of this strategy, see Donald G. Norris, "Ingredient Branding: A Strategy Option with Multiple Beneficiaries," *Journal of Consumer Marketing*, Summer 1992, pp. 19–31.

18. Morris, op. cit., p. 82, and Bradley Johnson, "IBM, Compaq Tire of 'Intel Inside' Track," *Advertising Age*, Sept. 19, 1994, p. 52.

19. Gabriella Stern, "Big Companies Add Private-Label Lines That Vie with Their Premium Brands," *The Wall Street Journal*, May 21, 1993, p. B1.

20. Teri Agins, "Big Stores Put Own Labels on Best Clothes," *The Wall Street Journal*, Sept. 26, 1994, p. B1.

21. Greg Burns, "A Froot Loop by Any Other Name," *Business Week*, June 26, 1995, p. 72.

22. The study was conducted by Raj Sethuraman of the University of Iowa, and reported in Richard Gibson, "Store-Brand Pricing Has to Be Just Right," *The Wall Street Journal*, Feb. 14, 1992, p. B1. The second study was summarized in Stephen J. Hoch, "Private Label a Threat? Don't Believe It," *Advertising Age*, May 24, 1993, p. 19.

23. Wal-Mart's approach is summarized in Peter Galuszka and Wendy Zellner, "Soap Opera at Wal-Mart," *Business Week*, Aug. 16, 1999, p. 44; and Emily Nelson, "For Wal-Mart, a Soap War Looms against Mighty P&G," *The Wall Street Journal*, Aug. 6, 1999, p. B1. The other examples come from Clyde H. Farnsworth, "Quality: High. Price: Low. Big Ad Budget? Never," *The New York Times*, Feb. 6, 1994, p. F10.

24. The estimate of current volume is based on statistics in Emily DeNitto, "Back into Focus," *Brandweek*, May 29, 1995, pp. 22–26. The proportion of supermarket sales volume accounted for by middlemen's brands and the proportion of retailers intending to place more emphasis on such products come from Susan Zimmerman, "A Rosy Future," *Progressive Grocer*, November 1998, pp. 45–52. The $100 billion forecast was made by Destination Products International, as reported in Stephanie Thompson, "The New Private Enterprise," *Brandweek*, May 3, 1999, pp. 36+.

25. Recommendations as to how manufacturers can sustain their brands are presented in Susan R. Ashley, "How to Effectively Compete against Private-Label Brands," *Journal of Advertising Research*, January–February 1998, pp. 75+. The examples of price cutting are drawn from Gabriella Stern, "As National Brands Chop Prices, Stores Scramble to Defend Private-Label Goods," *The Wall Street Journal*, Aug. 23, 1993, p. B1.

26. The 2.5% market-share figure for generics comes from Gerard P. Prendergast and Norman E. Marr, "Generic Products: Who Buys Them and How Do They Perform Relative to Each Other?" *European Journal of Marketing*, January–February 1997, pp. 94+. The downward trend in sales of generics is reported in Thompson, loc. cit.

27. Scheherazade Daneshkhu, "Awareness Becomes the Name of the Game," *Financial Times*, Sept. 9, 1999, p. II; and Paul Beckett and Suzanne Vranica, "Citigroup Spotlights Its Member Brands," *The Wall Street Journal*, June 25, 1999, p. B2.

28. There are potential disadvantages as well as advantages to introducing new products under the family brand. For more on this, see Barbara Loken and Deborah Roedder John, "Diluting Brand Beliefs: When Do Brand Extensions Have a Negative Impact?" *Journal of Marketing*, July 1993, pp. 71–84.

29. Norton Paley, "Back from the Dead," *Sales & Marketing Management*, July 1995, pp. 30+.

30. Gabrielle Solomon, "Co-Branding Alliances: Arranged Marriages Made by Marketers," *Fortune*, Oct. 12, 1998, p. 188[N]; and Richard Gibson, "Co-branding Aims to Double the Appeal," *The Wall Street Journal*, Aug. 3, 1993, pp. B1, B8.

31. This definition is drawn from the comprehensive examination of brand equity in Peter H. Farquhar, "Managing Brand Equity," *Journal of Advertising Research*, August/September 1990, pp. RC 7–RC 12. For more on brand equity, see David A. Aaker, *Managing Brand Equity: Capitalizing on the Value of a Brand Name*, Free Press, New York, 1991.

32. The quote is from Roger Baird, "Asset Tests," *Marketing Week*, Oct. 1, 1998, pp. 28–31. The information about Interbrand's ranking of brands comes from Jane Bainbridge, "The World's Biggest Brands," *Marketing*, June 24, 1999, p. 22; and Richard Tomkins, "Assessing a Name's Worth," *Financial Times*, June 22, 1999, p. 12.

33. The Kellogg's example was described by Farquhar, "Managing Brand Equity," op. cit., p. RC-7. The 1993 study of personal computers was summarized in Kyle Pope, "Computers: They're No Commodity," *The Wall Street Journal*, Oct. 15, 1993, p. B1; the 1995 update was described in Jim Carlton, "Marketing Plays a Bigger Role in Distributing PCs," *The Wall Street Journal*, Oct. 16, 1995, p. B4.

34. Packard Bell's travails are reported in "Packard Bell Pulls PCs off U.S. Market," *Columbia Daily Tribune*, Nov. 4, 1999, p. 6B; TWA's improved performance is covered in Christopher Carey, "TWA Boasts Best On-Time Record," *St. Louis Post-Dispatch*, Oct. 7, 1999, p. C2.

35. Farquhar, "Managing Brand Equity," op. cit., pp. RC-8 to RC-10.

36. Morris, op. cit., p. 84.

37. The efforts of Oil of Olay and Ann Taylor to capitalize on their strong brand equities by introducing new lines are described, respectively, in Tara Parker-Pope, "P&G's Cosmetics Makeover," Apr. 12, 1999, pp. B1, B3; and Pam Weisz, "'Trying to Move from the Wardrobe to the Bathroom," *Brandweek*, Apr. 24, 1995, pp. 36, 38. For more on the rationale for the Marquis by Waterford line, see Judith Valente, "A New Brand Restores Sparkle to Waterford," *The Wall Street Journal*, Nov. 10, 1994, p. B1.

38. Statistics in this paragraph come from "Entertainment, Trademark/Brand Sectors Drive 4% Increase to Record $74.15 Billion," *The Licensing Letter*, Jan. 3, 2000, pp. 1+. Other material is drawn from "Fashion Plays in Licensing," *Discount Store News*, June 7, 1999, pp. A6–A7.

39. "Coppertone Gives More Products a Place in the Sun," *Sales & Marketing Management*, May 1990, p. 40.

40. Dale D. Buss, "Hot Names, Top Dollars," *Nation's Business*, August 1995, p. 17.

41. Eliot Schreiber, "Retail Trends Shorten Life of Package Design," *Marketing News*, Dec. 5, 1994, p. 7.

42. Raju Narisetti, "Plotting to Get Tissues into Living Rooms," *The Wall Street Journal*, May 3, 1996, pp. B1, B12.

43. The Coca-Cola Classic example is drawn from Betsy McKay, "Coke to Open New Old-Bottle Campaign," *The Wall Street Journal*, Jan. 5, 2000, p. B8; Paul Lukas, "If It Ain't Got Glass, It Ain't Got *Class*," *Fortune*, Apr. 12, 1999, p. 40; and Nikhil Deogun, "Coke to Test Curvy Can in South, Midwest," *The Wall Street Journal*, Feb. 6, 1997, pp. B1, B5. For recommendations on managing the packaging aspect of a company's

marketing mix, see Richard T. Hise and James U. McNeal, "Effective Packaging Management," *Business Horizons,* January–February 1988, pp. 47–51.

44. For further discussion of package-design strategies that can boost sales and profit, see Sue Bassin, "Innovative Packaging Strategies," *Journal of Business Strategy,* January–February 1988, pp. 38–42.

45. Schreiber, loc. cit.

46. David Leonhardt, "The Hip New Drink: Milk," *Business Week,* Feb. 16, 1998, p. 44.

47. Laura Bird, "Romancing the Package," *Adweek's Marketing Week,* Jan. 21, 1991, p. 10.

48. Information about the National Labeling and Education Act is drawn from the Food and Drug Administration website: <http://vm.cfsan.fda.gov/~dms/fdnewlab.html>.

49. John Sinisi, "New Rules Exact a Heavy Price as Labels Are Recast," *Brandweek,* Dec. 7, 1992, p. 3. For a study that examines the impact of the NLEA on consumers' processing of nutrition information, see Christine Moorman, "A Quasi Experiment to Assess the Consumer and Informational Determinants of Nutrition Information Processing Activities: The Case of the Nutrition Labeling and Education Act," *Journal of Public Policy & Marketing,* Spring 1996, pp. 28–44. This issue of the journal contains several other articles examining various aspects of nutrition labeling.

50. Laura M. Litvan, "Sizing Up Metric Labeling Rules," *Nation's Business,* November 1994, p. 62.

51. Bruce Nussbaum, "Is In-House Design on the Way Out?" *Business Week,* Sept. 25, 1995, p. 130.

52. The Target example comes from Bruce Nussbaum, "The Best Product Designs of the Year: Winners 1999," *Business Week,* June 7, 1999, pp. 84+; and Joseph Weber, "A Better Grip on Hawking Tools," *Business Week,* June 5, 1995, p. 99.

53. Joshua Harris Prager, "People with Disabilities Are Next Consumer Niche," *The Wall Street Journal,* Dec. 15, 1999, pp. B1, B6; "Business Bulletin," *The Wall Street Journal,* Feb. 23, 1995, p. A1; and Bruce Nussbaum, "What Works for One Works for All," *Business Week,* Apr. 20, 1992, pp. 112–113. For a description of a related notion, termed *user-centered design,* see Artemis March, "Usability: The New Dimension," *Harvard Business Review,* September–October 1994, pp. 144–149.

54. The Beetle's comeback was described in Bill Vlasic, "Bug-Eyed over the New Beetle," *Business Week,* May 25, 1998, p. 88. The figure pertaining to cost of design comes from Brian Dumaine, "Design That Sells and Sells and . . . ," *Fortune,* Mar. 11, 1991, pp. 86, 88.

55. Nancy Arnott, "Shades of Distinction," *Sales & Marketing Management,* June 1995, p. 20; Paul M. Barrett, "Color in the Court: Can Tints Be Trademarked?" *The Wall Street Journal,* Jan. 5, 1995, p. B1; and Junda Woo, "Rulings Clash over Colors in Trademarks," *The Wall Street Journal,* Feb. 25, 1993, p. B1.

56. Cindy Waxer, "Computer Couture," *Yahoo! Internet Life,* November 1999, pp. 144–145, and "Banish the Beige," *USA Weekend,* Oct. 8–10, 1999, p. 25.

57. Meera Somasundaram, "Red Packages Lure Shoppers Like Capes Flourished at Bulls," *The Wall Street Journal,* Sept. 18, 1995, p. A13B; and Elizabeth Jensen, "Blue Bottles, Gimmicky Labels Sell Wine," *The Wall Street Journal,* July 7, 1997, p. B1.

58. Ross Johnson and William O. Winchell, *Marketing and Quality Control,* American Society for Quality Control, Milwaukee, 1989, p. 2.

59. Scott McCartney, "Middling Quality as a Marketing Plus? Survey Finds a Link," *The Wall Street Journal,* May 16, 1994, p. B6.

60. For a list of reasons why product quality is so important and for a discussion of the marketing function's role in quality management, see Neil A. Morgan and Nigel F. Pierce, "Market Led Quality," *Industrial Marketing Management,* May 1992, pp. 111–118.

61. T. S. Raghunathan, S. Subba Rao, and Luis S. Solis, "A Comparative Study of Quality Practices: USA, China and India," *Industrial Management & Data Systems,* May–June 1997, p. 192.

62. As reported in D. A. Aaker, "Managing Assets and Skills: The Key to a Sustainable Competitive Advantage," *California Management Review,* Winter 1989, pp. 91–106.

63. As reported in "TQM Is Alive," *Quality,* February 1999, p. 12.

64. ISO 9000 is covered in Ronald Henkoff, "The Hot New Seal of Quality," *Fortune,* June 28, 1993, pp. 116–118, 120. ISO 9001 is described in Tito Conti, "Vision 2000: Positioning the New ISO 9000 Standards with Respect to Total Quality Management Models," *Total Quality Management,* July 1999, pp. S454–S464. A critical look at the ISO standards is contained in James Lamprecht, "Is ISO 9001: 2000 the Beginning of the End? *Quality Progress,* July 1999, pp. 47–52.

65. Carol Emert, "When a Store Is More than a Store," *The San Francisco Chronicle,* Aug. 14, 1999, p. D1; Elizabeth Church, "Personal Pair Didn't Fit into Levi Strauss' Plans," *The Globe and Mail,* May 27, 1999, p. B13; Julian Lee, "Can Levi's Ever Be Cool Again?" *Marketing,* Apr. 15, 1999, pp. 28–29; Nina Munk, "How Levi's Trashed a Great American Brand," *Fortune,* Apr. 12, 1999, pp. 83–90; Lee, loc. cit.; and Voight, loc. cit.

Chapter 11

1. Carol Power, "On-Line Banking: Internet Banks Dominate in Ranking of Bank Web Sites," *American Banker,* Oct. 25, 1999, p. 15; Julie Johnsson, "Taking Flight with Wingspan," *Crain's Chicago Business,* Aug. 2, 1999, pp. 3+; Chris Costanzo, "Bank One's Wingspan," *American Banker,* Oct. 13, 1999, pp. 1+; Rick Brooks, "Bank One's Strategy as Competition Grows: New, Online Institution, *The Wall Street Journal,* Aug. 25, 1999, pp. A1+; Jerry Useem, "Internet Defense Strategy: Cannibalize Yourself," *Fortune,* Sept. 6, 1999, pp. 121–134.

2. Economic statistics are from the *Statistical Abstract of the United States: 1998,* 118th ed., U.S. Bureau of the Census, Washington, DC, 1998.

3. Walter Shapiro, "Census' Promotion Is the American Way," *USA Today,* Nov. 5, 1999, p. 4A.

4. Based on Leonard L. Berry and Terry Clark, "Four Ways to Make Services More Tangible," *Business,* October–December 1986, p. 53.

5. Michael Skapinker, "Airline's Reputation for Service Comes Down with a Bump," *Financial Times,* May 27, 1999, p. 9.

6. Neal Templlin, "For Hotel Guests with Glitches, High-Tech Room Service," *The Wall Street Journal,* Aug. 30, 1999, pp. B1+.

7. Rebecca Buckman, "Wall Street Is Rocked by Merrill's Online Move," *The Wall Street Journal,* June 2, 1999, pp. C2+.

8. Based on Allan C. Reedy, Bruck D. Buskirk, and Ajit Kaicker, "Tangibilizing the Intangibles: Some Strategies for Services Marketing," *Journal of Services Marketing,* Vol. 7, No. 3, 1993, pp. 13–17.

9. Paulette Thomas, "Staples Executives Now Aim to Reinvent Dry Cleaning," *The Wall Street Journal*, Apr. 27, 1999, pp. B1+.

10. For more details on developing service employees see Leonard L. Berry, *Discovering the Soul of Service*, Free Press, New York, 1999.

11. Paul H. Rothschild, "New Advertising Regs Change the Rules for Lawyers," *Business West*, October 1999, p. 65.

12. Melinda Ligos, "Mall Rats with a Social Conscience," *Sales & Marketing Management*, November 1999, p. 115; Aja Whitaker, "Cause Marketing Gaining Ground," *Management Review*, September 1999, p. 8.

13. Andrea Stone, "Rich Economy Leads to Poor Recruiting," *USA Today*, June 24, 1999, p. 4A.

14. Meera Louis, "Modern Marketing Helps Sell Life as a Nun," *The Wall Street Journal*, May 11, 1999, pp. B1+.

15. For more on service quality see Roland T. Rust, Anthony J. Zahorik, and Timothy L. Keiningham, *Service Marketing*, HarperCollins, New York, 1996.

16. Measuring service quality is more complex than it may first appear. More information can be found in Albert Caruana, "The Role of Service Quality and Satisfaction in Customer Loyalty," *Proceedings of the 1999 Summer Educators Conference*, American Marketing Association, 1999, pp. 139–145.

17. George Anders, "Buying Frenzy," *The Wall Street Journal*, July 12, 1999, pp. R6+.

18. Paul Richer, "Agents Must Adapt or Pack Their Bags," *Financial Times*, Nov. 18, 1999, p. vii.

19. Douglas A, Blackmon, "Overnight, Everything Changed for FedEx; Can It Reinvent Itself?" *The Wall Street Journal*, Nov. 4, 1999, pp. A1+.

20. June Fletcher, "Extreme Nesting," *The Wall Street Journal*, Jan. 7, 2000, pp. W1+.

21. Power, loc. cit.; Johnsson, loc. cit.; Costanzo, loc. cit.; Brooks, loc. cit.; Useem, loc. cit.

Chapter 12

1. Nick Wingfield, "Priceline Adds 3 Airlines to System, Resulting in a Charge of $1.1 Billion," *The Wall Street Journal*, Nov. 17, 1999, p. B2; Nick Wingfield, "Priceline.com Posts Wider Loss on Airline-Partnership Charges," *The Wall Street Journal*, Oct. 29, 1999, p. B8; Paul Davidson, "Priceline.com: Microsoft Violated Patent," *USA Today*, Oct. 14, 1999, p. 3B; Mike France, "A Net Monopoly No Longer?" *Business Week*, Sept. 27, 1999, p. 47; Peter Elkind, "The Hype Is Big, Really Big, at Priceline," *Fortune*, Sept. 6, 1999, pp. 193–194+; Shari Weiss, "Internet Offers Priceless Marketing, Booking Opportunities," *Hotel & Motel Management*, June 3, 1999, pp. 58, 60; and Heather Green, "Priceline's Bid for the Big Time," *Business Week*, Jan. 18, 1999, p. 43.

2. This list was suggested in part by John T. Mentzer and David J. Schwartz, *Marketing Today*, 4th ed., Harcourt Brace Jovanovich, San Diego, 1985, p. 599.

3. David Meer, "System Beaters, Brand Loyals, and Deal Shoppers: New Insights into the Role of Brand and Price," *Journal of Advertising Research*, May/June 1995, pp. RC2–RC7.

4. Stephen J. Hoch, Byung-Do Kim, Alan L. Montgomery, and Peter E. Rossi, "Determinants of Store-Level Price Elasticity," *Journal of Marketing Research*, February 1995, p. 28.

5. Roberta Maynard, "Taking Guesswork out of Pricing," *Nation's Business*, December 1997, p. 28. For in-depth discussions of the relationship between price levels and perceived quality, see David J. Curry and Peter C. Riesz, "Prices and Price/Quality Relationships: A Longitudinal Analysis," *Journal of Marketing*, January 1988, pp. 36–51, and Valarie A. Zeithaml, "Consumer Perceptions of Price, Quality, and Value: A Means-End Model and Synthesis of Evidence," *Journal of Marketing*, July 1988, pp. 2–22.

6. Marty Whitford, "Extended-Stay Properties Push 'More for Less' Motif," *Hotel & Motel Management*, Sept. 7, 1998, pp. 46–47; and Anne Faircloth, "Toward a Finer Flophouse," *Fortune*, July 20, 1998, pp. 34–36.

7. Dean Takahashi, "Little Caesar's Plans 'Big! Big!' Pizzas, While Keeping Price Structure the Same," *The Wall Street Journal*, Sept. 2, 1997, p. B6; and Rahul Jacob, "Beyond Quality and Value," *Fortune* (special issue), Autumn/Winter 1993, pp. 8, 10.

8. Gary H. Anthes, "The Price Had Better Be Right," *Computerworld*, Dec. 21, 1998, pp. 65–66.

9. Frank Alpert, Beth Wilson, and Michael T. Elliott, "Price Signaling: Does It Ever Work?" *Journal of Product & Brand Management*, Vol. 2, No. 1, 1993, pp. 29–41.

10. For a list of 21 pricing objectives and a discussion of objectives as part of a strategic pricing program for industrial firms, see Michael H. Morris and Roger J. Calantone, "Four Components of Effective Pricing," *Industrial Marketing Management*, November 1990, pp. 321–329.

11. Robert Steyer, "Monsanto Slashes Roundup Prices," *St. Louis Post-Dispatch*, Sept. 2, 1998, p. C1.

12. George Anders, "Buying Frenzy," *The Wall Street Journal*, July 12, 1999, pp. R6, R10.

13. Andy Reinhardt, "Intel Is Taking No Prisoners," *Business Week*, July 12, 1999, p. 38.

14. For a discussion of new-product pricing, taking into account the product's perceived benefits and entry time, see Eunsang Yoon, "Pricing Imitative New Products," *Industrial Marketing Management*, May 1991, pp. 115–125.

15. Maynard, op. cit., p. 27.

16. Zachary Schiller, "The Revolving Door at Rubbermaid," *Business Week*, Sept. 18, 1995, pp. 80–83.

17. Imogen Wall, "It May Be a Dog-Eat-Dog World, but This Restaurant Won't Prove It," *The Wall Street Journal*, Dec. 11, 1998, p. B1.

18. For a report on how this is done in the business market, see Michael H. Morris and Mary L. Joyce, "How Marketers Evaluate Price Sensitivity," *Industrial Marketing Management*, May 1988, pp. 169–176.

19. George E. Cressman, Jr., "Snatching Defeat from the Jaws of Victory," *Marketing Management*, Summer 1997, p. 15

20. Chanoine Webb, "The Picture Just Keeps Getting Darker at Kodak," *Fortune*, June 21, 1999, p. 206; and Tobi Elkin, "Momentous Shifts," *Brandweek*, June 1, 1998, pp. 26–30.

21. Steve Hamm, "The Wild and Woolly World of Linux," *Business Week*, Nov. 15, 1999, pp. 130, 134; James Aley, "Give It Away and Get Rich!" *Fortune*, June 10, 1996, pp. 90- 92+; and Neil Gross and Peter Coy, "The Technology Paradox," *Business Week*, Mar. 6, 1995, pp. 76–81, 84.

22. "Pricing Gets Easier (Sort Of)," *Inc.*, November 1993, p. 124.

23. Morris and Calantone, op. cit., p. 323.

24. The perspective that price dictates cost levels is presented in Christopher Farrell and Zachary Schiller, "Stuck!" *Business Week*, Nov. 15, 1993, pp. 146, 148. The magnitude of Kodak's cost-cutting efforts is from Webb, loc. cit.

25. For an approach to break-even analysis that includes semifixed costs and is of more practical value in situations typically faced by marketing executives, see Thomas L. Powers, "Breakeven Analysis with Semifixed Costs," *Industrial Marketing Management,* February 1987, pp. 35–41.

26. G. Dean Kortge and Patrick A. Okonkwo, "Perceived Value Approach to Pricing," *Industrial Marketing Management,* May 1993, p. 134.

27. Dan Koeppel, "Fast Food's New Reality," *Adweek's Marketing Week,* Mar. 30, 1992, pp. 22–23.

28. Margaret Studer, "Switzerland's Luxury-Watch Industry Continues to Defy Economic Downturn," *The Wall Street Journal,* Aug. 10, 1992, p. A5B; and Thomas T. Nagle, "Managing Price Competition," *Marketing Management,* Vol. 2, No. 1, 1993, p. 41.

29. "Air France Celebrates Supersonic Summer," *PR Newswire,* May 19, 1999; and Frederic Tomesco, "Air France to Drop Concorde in 2007," *The Seattle Times,* March 22, 1999, p. C6.

30. Nick Wingfield, "Priceline Prepares to Launch Web Site for Online 'Yard Sales,'" *The Wall Street Journal,* Dec. 27, 1999, p. B8; Nick Wingfield, "New Battlefield for Priceline Is Diapers, Tuna," *The Wall Street Journal,* September 22, 1999, p. B1; France, loc. cit; and Weiss, loc. cit.

Chapter 13

1. Peter Burrows, "Can Apple Take Its Game to the Next Level?" *Business Week,* Dec. 20, 1999, p. 52; Cathy Booth, David S. Jackson, and Valerie Merchant, "Steve's Job: Restart Apple," *Time,* Aug. 18, 1997, pp. 28+; and Kathy Rebello, Peter Burrows, and Ira Sager, "The Fall of an American Icon," *Business Week,* Feb. 5, 1996, pp. 34–42.

2. Gary Strauss, "99¢ Only Started Trend," *USA Today,* June 22, 1998, pp. 1B, 2B.

3. Patricia Sellers, "Look Who Learned about Value," *Fortune,* Oct. 18, 1993, p. 75; and Bill Saporito, "Why the Price Wars Never End," *Fortune,* Mar. 23, 1992, pp. 68+.

4. Stratford Sherman, "How to Prosper in the Value Decade," *Fortune,* Nov. 30, 1992, p. 98.

5. Anne Faircloth, "Values Retailers Go Dollar for Dollar," *Fortune,* July 6, 1998, p. 166.

6. Albert D. Bates, "Pricing for Profit," *Retailing Issues Newsletter,* September 1990, p. 1.

7. For three recommended forms of non-price competition for retailers, see Bates, op. cit., p. 4.

8. William Echikson, "Aiming at High and Low Markets," *Fortune,* Mar. 22, 1993, p. 89.

9. The Computer Associates scenario is described in Neil Gross and Peter Coy, "The Technology Paradox," *Business Week,* Mar. 6, 1995, pp. 76–77; the Intranets.com example comes from Timothy Hanrahan, "Free for All," *The Wall Street Journal,* Nov. 15, 1999, pp. R8, R10.

10. Reed K. Holden and Thomas T. Nagle, "Kamikaze Pricing," *Marketing Management,* Summer 1998, p. 39.

11. Mike France and Steve Hamm, "Does Predatory Pricing Make Microsoft a Predator?" *Business Week,* Nov. 23, 1998, pp. 130, 132.

12. Robert Steyer, "Monsanto *Offers* Discounts to Dairy Farmers," *St. Louis Post-Dispatch,* Oct. 22, 1995, p. 1E.

13. William M. Bulkeley, "Rebates' Secret Appeal to Manufacturers: Few Consumers Actually Redeem Them," *The Wall Street Journal,* Feb. 10, 1998, pp. B1, B6.

14. For more about this approach, see Hermann Simon and Robert J. Dolan, "Price Customization," *Marketing Management,* Fall 1998, pp. 10–17.

15. Joseph Weber, "Can a 1,245% Markup on Drugs Really Be Legal?" *Business Week,* Nov. 1, 1993, p. 34.

16. G. Bruce Knecht, "Independent Bookstores Are Suing Borders Group and Barnes & Noble," *The Wall Street Journal,* Mar. 19, 1998, p. B3.

17. Douglas A. Blackmon, "FedEx Is to Adopt Rate Structure Based on Distance Package Travels," *The Wall Street Journal,* Jan. 23, 1997, p. B4.

18. For further discussion of pricing strategies and policies, see Gerard J. Tellis, "Beyond the Many Faces of Price: An Integration of Pricing Strategies," *Journal of Marketing,* October 1986, pp. 146–160.

19. For a theoretical model of flexible pricing and discussion of its managerial implications, see Kenneth R. Evans and Richard F. Beltramini, "A Theoretical Model of Consumer Negotiated Pricing: An Orientation Perspective," *Journal of Marketing,* April 1987, pp. 58–73.

20. Brian S. Akre, "Restructure of Dealer Networks Will Change Retailing," *Marketing News,* Oct. 26, 1998, p. 10.

21. Joann Muller, "Old Carmakers Learn New Trick," *Business Week,* Apr. 12, 1999, pp. 116, 118; Steven D. Kaye, "Goodbye to Haggling," *U.S. News & World Report,* Oct. 20, 1997, p. 57; and Gabriella Stern and Rebecca Blumenstein, "GM, Happy with 'No Haggle' Pricing, Is Expected to Extend Plan to More States," *The Wall Street Journal,* Apr. 24, 1996, p. A3.

22. Peter Coy, "Are Flat Rates Good Business?" *Business Week,* Feb. 10, 1997, p. 108.

23. Strauss, loc. cit.

24. A recent study of the beneficial effects of odd pricing, if used on a very limited basis, is mentioned in "Why That Deal Is Only $9.99," *Business Week,* Jan. 10, 2000, p. 36. Previously the effectiveness of odd pricing was described in Robert M. Schindler and Lori S. Warren, "Effects of Odd Pricing on Price Recall," *Journal of Business,* June 1989, pp. 165–177. Consumers' paying attention to just the first two digits in a price is examined in Mark Stiving and Russell S. Winer, "An Empirical Analysis of Price Endings with Scanner Data," *Journal of Consumer Research,* June 1997, pp. 57–67.

25. George Anders, "Amazon Plans to Offer 50% Discounts on Hardcover, Paperback Bestsellers," *The Wall Street Journal,* May 17, 1999, p. B11.

26. "Wal-Mart Wins Suit over Low-Price Strategy," *St. Louis Post-Dispatch,* Jan. 10, 1995, p. 7C; and Bob Ortega, "Wal-Mart Loses a Case on Pricing," *The Wall Street Journal,* Oct. 13, 1993, p. A3.

27. "Consumers' Reference Prices: Implications for Managers," *Stores,* April 1996, p. RR4.

28. Patrick J. Kaufmann, N. Craig Smith, and Gwendolyn K. Ortmeyer, "Deception in Retailer High-Low Pricing: A 'Rule of Reason' Approach," *Journal of Retailing,* Summer 1994, pp. 15+.

29. For an overview of how one chain, Family Dollar Stores, switched from high-low pricing to EDLP, see Michael Friedman, "A Contented Discounter," *Progressive Grocer,* November 1998, pp. 39–41. For information about other chains' use of EDLP, see Duke Ratliff, "Variations on the Theme," *Discount Merchandiser,* March 1996, pp. 24–25. The appearance of EDLP in German is covered in Jennifer Negley, "Jeden Tag Tiefpreise—Sprechen sie EDLP?" *Discount Store News,* June 8, 1998, p. 17.

30. Stuart Hirshfield, "The Squeeze," *Apparel Industry Magazine,* August 1998, pp. 60–64.

31. Roberta Gerry, "Stain, Stain Go Away," *Chemical Market Reporter,* Jan. 27, 1997, pp. SR3, SR4; and

Claire Murphy, "Will P&G's Bravery Pay Off?" *Marketing*, Dec. 12, 1996, p. 23.

32. Stephen J. Hoch, Xavier Drèze, and Mary E. Purk, "EDLP, Hi-Lo, and Margin Arithmetic," *Journal of Marketing*, October 1994, pp. 16–27.

33. For a discussion of the legal status of resale price maintenance, plus some steps that manufacturers can take to avoid legal problems when establishing resale price maintenance programs, see Mary Jane Sheffet and Debra L. Scammon, "Resale Price Maintenance: Is It Safe to Suggest Retail Prices?" *Journal of Marketing*, Fall 1985, pp. 82–91.

34. Joel M. Cohen and Arthur J. Burke, "Antitrust: Supreme Court Acts on Maximum Pricing," *International Commercial Litigation*, December 1997/January 1998, p. 43; and Susan B. Garland, "You'll Charge What I Tell You to Charge," *Business Week*, Oct. 6, 1997, pp. 118, 120.

35. "Beanie Babies Maker Settles Price-Fixing Case," *St. Louis Post-Dispatch*, Sept. 12, 1997, p. 10C; and Viveca Novak and Joseph Pereira, "Reebok and FTC Settle Price-Fixing Charges," *The Wall Street Journal*, May 5, 1995, p. B1.

36. Michael Selz, "Small Firms Use Variety of Ploys to Raise Prices," *The Wall Street Journal*, June 17, 1993, p. B1.

37. Thomas T. Nagle, "Managing Price Competition," *Marketing Management*, Vol. 2, No. 1, 1993, p. 45.

38. "Chipmakers Spark a PC Price War," *Business Week*, Sept. 6, 1999, p. 42; Robert Weller, "Colorado Ski Resorts Give In to Need for Deep Discounts," *St. Louis Post-Dispatch*, Sept. 4, 1999, p. 33OT. The statement about price wars was made by Michael Marn, a McKinsey consultant, as contained in David R. Henderson, "What Are Price Wars Good for? *Absolutely Nothing*," *Fortune*, May 12, 1997, p. 156.

39. The description of price-war damages is from Andrew E. Serwer, "How to Escape a Price War," *Fortune*, June 13, 1994, pp. 82+. The example about music retailing is drawn from Tim Carvell, "These Prices Really Are Insane," *Fortune*, Aug. 4, 1997, pp. 109–110+.

40. Brent Schlender, "Steve Jobs' Apple Gets Way Cooler," *Fortune*, Jan. 24, 2000, pp. 66–72+; Peter Burrows, "Apple's Core Employee," *Business Week*, Jan. 17, 2000, p. 44; Stephen H. Wildstrom, "Giving Small Biz Short Shrift," *Business Week*, Dec. 20, 1999, p. 32; David P. Hamilton, "Apple Computer Unveils Three iMacs, Including Its First Sub-$1,000 Model," *The Wall Street Journal*, Oct. 6, 1999, p. B8; Chris Mark, "Apple Unveils iBook, Filling Its Last Hole," *The Wall Street Journal*, July 22, 1999, p. B4; Lucas Graves, "The iMac," *Mc Technology Marketing Intelligence*, January 1999, pp. 34–35; James Heckman, "Don't Let the Fat Lady Sing," *Marketing News*, Jan. 4, 1999, pp. 1, 32; and Burrows, loc. cit.

Chapter 14

1. Janet Ginsburg, "Deck the Malls with Kiosks," *Business Week*, Dec. 13, 1999, pp. 86–88; Laura Klepacki, "Avon to Make Stronger Move into Retailing," *WWD*, Dec. 8, 1999, p. 2; Carolyn Edy, "Avon Malling," *American Demographics*, April 1999, pp. 38–40; Leslie Kaufman, "Avon's New Face," *Newsweek*, Nov. 16, 1998, pp. 59–60; Sharon Machlis, "Beauty Product Sites Facing Channel Clash," *Computerworld*, Nov. 9, 1998, p. 24; Tara Parker-Pope, "Avon Is Calling with a New Way to Make a Sale," *The Wall Street Journal*, Oct. 27, 1997, pp. B1, B4; and James E. Preston, "Not Your Mother's Avon," *Chief Executive*, October 1997, pp. 74–76.

2. Sara Nathan, "Defining the Seller in On-Line Market," *USA Today*, Aug. 26, 1999, p. 3B; and "Merrill Lynch Shakes Up Industry by Going Online," *St. Louis Post-Dispatch*, July 22, 1999, p. B13. For a discussion of the contention that the Internet is the biggest influence on distribution since the Industrial Revolution, see Leyland Pitt, Pierre Berthon, and Jean-Paul Berthon, "Changing Channels: The Impact of the Internet on Distribution Strategy," *Business Horizons*, March/April 1999, pp. 19–28.

3. For insight regarding whether the Internet will eliminate middlemen in two industries, air travel and groceries, see Eric Clemons, "When Should You Bypass the Middleman?" *Financial Times*, Feb. 22, 1999, p. 14. The term *disintermediation* is explained further in "On-Line Commerce Business Trends," *The Wall Street Journal*, Dec. 12, 1996, p. B4.

4. The concept of shifting activities, the possibility of manufacturers shifting some functions away from their firms, and the opportunity for small wholesalers to perform added functions to maintain their economic viability are all discussed in Ronald D. Michman, "Managing Structural Changes in Marketing Channels," *The Journal of Business and Industrial Marketing*, Summer/Fall 1990, pp. 5–14.

5. Calmetta Y. Coleman, "Kmart Expands Grocery-Supply Pacts with Distributors Supervalu, Fleming," *The Wall Street Journal*, July 22, 1999, p. B13.

6. Julie Candler, "How to Choose a Distributor," *Nation's Business*, August 1993, p. 46.

7. Diane Brady, "Insurers Step Gingerly into Cyberspace," *Business Week*, Nov. 22, 1999, p. 160.

8. Karen Roche and Bill O'Connell, "Dig a Wider Channel for Your Products," *Marketing News*, Nov. 9, 1998, p. 10.

9. For more on selecting channels for international markets, especially the decision of whether to use middlemen, see Saul Klein, "Selection of International Marketing Channels," *Journal of Global Marketing*, Vol. 4, 1991, pp. 21–37.

10. The New Pig example is drawn from "Unconventional Channels," *Sales & Marketing Management*, October 1988, p. 38.

11. Craig Zarley and Edward F. Moltzen, "IBM Takes Direct Route to Small Firms," *Computer Reseller News*, Mar. 1, 1999, p. 2.

12. An excellent discussion of distribution channels for business goods and services is found in Michael D. Hutt and Thomas W. Speh, *Business Marketing Management*, 6th ed., Dryden Press, Ft. Worth, TX, 1998, pp. 375–410.

13. Maricris G. Briones, "Resellers Hike Profits through Service," *Marketing News*, Feb. 15, 1999, pp. 1, 14; and Maricris G. Briones, "What Technology Wrought: Distribution Channel in Flux," *Marketing News*, Feb. 1, 1999, pp. 1, 15.

14. For an instructive discussion of this topic, see Donald H. Light, "A Guide for New Distribution Channel Strategies for Service Firms," *The Journal of Business Strategy*, Summer 1986, pp. 56–64.

15. J. C. Conklin, "That's the Ticket," *The Wall Street Journal*, July 12, 1999, p. R45; and George Anders, "Some Big Companies Long to Embrace Web but Settle for Flirtation," *The Wall Street Journal*, Nov. 4, 1998, p. A14.

16. Rowland T. Moriarty and Ursula Moran, "Managing Hybrid Marketing Systems," *Harvard Business Review*, November–December 1990, pp. 146–155.

17. For extensive discussion of this approach to serving distinct markets, see Wim G. Biemans, "Marketing in the Twilight Zone," *Business Horizons*, November–December 1998, pp. 69–76;

and John A. Quelch, "Why Not Exploit Dual Marketing?" *Business Horizons,* January–February 1987, pp. 52–60.

18. Deborah Lohse, "Allstate to Launch Online Sales of Car and Home Insurance," *The Wall Street Journal,* Nov. 11, 1999, p. B18. Samuel Schiff, "Agency System Lives but Continued Survival Will Require Adapting to Changes," *Rough Notes,* February 1999, pp. 14–16; and "Dramatic Shift to Multiple Distribution Channels for Property-Casualty Insurance Industry," *Limra's Marketfacts,* March/April 1998, p. 6.

19. Milford Prewitt, "Franchisees' Lawsuits: Chains' Nontraditional Growth Paths Lead to New Encroachment Battles," *Nation's Restaurant News,* Oct. 9, 1995, pp. 118–120; and Jack Hayes, "Carvel, Franchisees Lock Horns over Retail Program," *Nation's Restaurant News,* Sept. 4, 1995, pp. 3, 82.

20. The Scotts example comes from Valerie Reitman, "Manufacturers Start to Spurn Big Discounters," *The Wall Street Journal,* Nov. 30, 1993, p. B1. For further discussion of the advantages and disadvantages of multiple channels as well as ways to minimize conflict resulting from multiple channels, see Martin Everett, "When There's More than One Route to the Customer," *Sales & Marketing Management,* August 1990, pp. 48–50+.

21. Carol Matlack, "Swatch: Ready for Net Time?" *Business Week,* Feb. 14, 2000, p. 61; Gregory L. White, "Ford Resarting Move to Buy Stakes in Its Dealers, Albeit More Cautiously," *The Wall Street Journal,* Nov. 22, 1999, p. B22; and Joann Muller, "Meet Your Local GM Dealer: GM," *Business Week,* Oct. 11, 1999, p. 48.

22. Allison Lucas, "Can You Sell to Wal-Mart?" *Sales & Marketing Management,* August 1995, p. 14.

23. "Dramatic Shift to Multiple Distribution Channels . . . ," loc. cit.

24. Michael Selz, "More Small Firms Are Turning to Trade Intermediaries," *The Wall Street Journal,* Feb. 2, 1993, p. B2.

25. For more on the idea that market considerations should determine a channel structure, see Louis W. Stern and Frederick D. Sturdivant, "Customer-Driven Distribution Systems," *Harvard Business Review,* July–August 1987, pp. 34–41.

26. Anders, op. cit., pp. A1, A14.

27. Bert Rosenbloom and Trina L. Larsen, "How Foreign Firms View Their U.S. Distributors," *Industrial Marketing Management,* May 1992, pp. 93–101.

28. "Putting the Aim Back into Famous Amos," *Sales & Marketing Management,* June 1992, p. 31.

29. Reitman, op. cit., pp. B1, B2; and Christina Duff, "Nation's Retailers Ask Vendors to Help Share Expenses," *The Wall Street Journal,* Aug. 4, 1993, p. B4.

30. Daniel Roth, "Dell's Big New Act," *Fortune,* Dec. 6, 1999, pp. 152–154+.

31. For an in-depth discussion of differences in distribution intensity, as well as a study of this factor in the context of the consumer electronics industry, see Gary L. Frazier and Walfried M. Lassar, "Determinants of Distribution Intensity," *Journal of Marketing,* October 1996, pp. 39–51.

32. Shelly Branch, "P&G Is Out to Fetch Distribution Gains for Iams Pet Food," *The Wall Street Journal,* Jan. 6, 2000, p. A6.

33. Reitman, op. cit., pp. B1, B2.

34. Nathan, loc. cit.

35. Stephane Farhi, "Eggs, Bread—and a Discount Daewoo," *Automotive News,* June 28, 1999, p. 46.

36. Rick Desloge, "Report Card: A-B Grading Distributors on Loyalty," *St. Louis Business Journal,* Nov. 18–24, 1996, p. 8A.

37. "Two Outlet Stores Open in Distribution Strategy," *The Wall Street Journal,* Mar. 11, 1997, p. B6; and Teri Agins, "Apparel Makers Are Refashioning Their Operations," *The Wall Street Journal,* Jan. 13, 1994, p. B4.

38. Bill Saporito, "Cutting Out the Middleman," *Fortune,* Apr. 6, 1992, p. 96.

39. "Levi's Plans Own Stores," *Marketing News,* Jan. 30, 1995, p. 1.

40. Laura Bird and Wendy Bounds, "Stores' Demands Squeeze Apparel Companies," *The Wall Street Journal,* July 15, 1997, pp. B1, B12.

41. Holman W. Jenkins, Jr., "We ♥ Slotting Fees," *The Wall Street Journal,* Sept. 22, 1999, p. A23; Nahal Toosi, "Congress Looks at the Selling of Shelf Space," *St. Louis Post-Dispatch,* Sept. 15, 1999, p. C1; and Richard Gibson, "Supermarkets Demand Food Firms' Payments Just to Get on the Shelf," *The Wall Street Journal,* Nov. 1, 1988, pp. 1, 14.

42. Christina Duff, "Big Stores' Outlandish Demands Alienate Small Suppliers," *The Wall Street Journal,* Oct. 27, 1995, pp. B1, B5.

43. James E. Zemanek, Jr., and James W. Hardin, "How the Industrial Salesperson's Use of Power Can Affect Distributor Satisfaction: An Empirical Examination," *Journal of Marketing Channels,* Vol. 3, No. 1, 1993, pp. 23–45.

44. Agins, loc. cit.

45. The emerging dominance of gigantic retailers and their dictates to manufacturers are described in Zachary Schiller and Wendy Zellner, "Clout!" *Business Week,* Dec. 21, 1992, pp. 66–69+.

46. For a model showing a range of channel relationships, see John T. Gardner, W. Benoy Joseph, and Sharon Thach, "Modeling the Continuum of Relationship Styles between Distributors and Suppliers," *Journal of Marketing Channels,* Vol. 2, No. 4, 1993, pp. 11+. The Sutter situation was described in Candler, op. cit., p. 45.

47. The Wal-Mart example comes from "Wal-Mart Expands Access to Product Sales History," *The Wall Street Journal,* Aug. 18, 1999, p. B8; the Bailey-Arrow arrangement was summarized in Myron Magnet, "The New Golden Rule of Business," *Fortune,* Feb. 21, 1994, pp. 60–64.

48. For a discussion of attributes of successful alliances in channels, based on a study of computer dealers, see Jakki J. Mohr and Robert E. Spekman, "Perfecting Partnerships," *Marketing Management,* Winter/Spring 1996, pp. 35–43. Baxter's efforts were described in B. G. Yovovich, "Partnering at Its Best," *Business Marketing,* March 1992, pp. 36–37.

49. Magnet, loc. cit. For further ideas on how to build a good producer-middleman relationship, see James A. Narus and James C. Anderson, "Distributor Contributions to Partnerships with Manufacturers," *Business Horizons,* September–October 1987, pp. 34–42.

50. Agins, loc. cit.

51. John R. Nevin, "Relationship Marketing and Distribution Channels: Exploring Fundamental Issues," *Journal of Marketing Channels,* Vol. 23, No. 4, 1995, pp. 327–334.

52. "Toys R Us, Two Toymakers Settle Discounting Suit," *St. Louis Post-Dispatch,* May 26, 1999, p. C9.

53. Jeffrey A. Tannenbaum, "Franchisees Balk at High Prices for Supplies from Franchisers," *The Wall Street Journal,* July 5, 1995, pp. B1, B2.

54. Jennifer E. Gully, "Image Technical Services, Inc. v. Eastman Kodak Co.," *Berkeley Technology Law Journal,* 1998, pp. 339–353; and Wendy Bounds, "Jury Finds Kodak Monopo-

lized Markets in Services and Parts for Its Machines," *The Wall Street Journal,* Sept. 19, 1995, p. A4.

55. Joseph Pereira, "Stride Rite Agrees to Settle Charges It Tried to Force Pricing by Retailers," *The Wall Street Journal,* Sept. 28, 1993, p. B5.

56. Erin White, "Ding-Dong, Avon Calling (on the Web, Not Your Door)," *The Wall Street Journal,* Dec. 28, 1999, p. B4; "Avon Calling Up $100 Mil for Global Branding Push," *Advertising Age,* Dec. 13, 1999, p. 3; Melinda Ligos, "Direct Sales Die in China," *Sales & Marketing Management,* August 1998, p. 14; Donald A. Davis, "China Game," *Drug & Cosmetic Industry,* June 1998, p. 8; "U.S. Firms Hurt by China Ban," *Direct Marketing,* June 1998, p. 6; Dexter Roberts, "Ultimatum for the Avon Lady," *Business Week,* May 11, 1998, p. 33; and Preston, loc. cit.

Chapter 15

1. Arlene Weintraub, "For Online Pet Stores, It's Dog-Eat-Dog," *Business Week,* Mar. 6, 2000, pp. 78, 80; Eric J. Savitz, "Profitless Prosperity," *The Industry Standard,* Nov. 22–29, 1999, p. 127; Maryann Jones Thompson, "Customer Feeding Frenzy: E-Retailers Vie for $185 Billion," *The Industry Standard,* Nov. 22–29, 1999, p. 167; Melanie Warner, "10 Companies That Get It," *Fortune,* Nov. 8, 1999, p. 115; Jennifer Negley, "Partnership at Warp Speed," *Discount Store News,* Sept. 20, 1999, p. 13; Evantheia Schibsted, "K9 Commerce," *Business 2.0,* August 1999, pp. 29–31; Clinton Wilder, "The Partnership: PetSmart," *Informationweek,* July 26, 1999, p. 52; Nick Wingfield, "Products to Watch," *The Wall Street Journal,* July 12, 1999, p. R34; and Clinton Wilder, "Companies Rush for Online Market Share," *Informationweek,* May 24, 1999, pp. 18, 20.

2. *Statistical Abstract of the United States: 1999,* 119th ed., U.S. Bureau of the Census, Washington, DC, 1999, p. 770.

3. As quoted in Lou Grabowsky, "Globalization: Reshaping the Retail Marketplace," *Retailing Issues Letter,* November 1989, p. 4.

4. *Statistical Abstract of the United States: 1999,* op. cit., p. 561.

5. For specific ways in which small retailers can remain competitive, see Dale D. Buss, "The Little Guys Fight Back," *Nation's Business,* July 1996, pp. 18–24; and Stanley N. Logan, "The Small Store—A Struggle to Survive," *Retailing Issues Letter,* January 1995, pp. 1–6.

6. *1992 Census of Retail Trade,* Subject Series, U.S. Bureau of the Census, Washington, DC, 1996, p. 2-7; and *1992 Census of Wholesale Trade,* Geographic Area Series—U.S., U.S. Bureau of the Census, Washington, DC, 1995, p. US-9. The 8% figure was calculated by multiplying the 11% representing wholesale operating expenses by 72%, the remainder after the 28% representing retailing operating expenses is subtracted from the 100% representing retail sales (or the consumer's dollar).

7. 7-Eleven, Inc. home page: <http:// www.7-eleven.com/investor/press/dec99sales.html>.

8. "The Plug Gets Pulled on Power Centers," *Building Design & Construction,* April 1997, p. 9; and Ellen Neuborne, "Stores Siphon Shoppers from Regional Malls," *USA Today,* June 13, 1995, p. 1B.

9. Richard Gibson, "Mall of America Considers Expansion That Would More Than Double Space," *The Wall Street Journal,* Dec. 30, 1999, p. B8.

10. Calmetta Y. Coleman, "Making Malls (Gasp!) Convenient," *The Wall Street Journal,* Feb. 8, 2000, pp. B1, B4. The pessimistic forecast was contained in Ellen James Martin, "Mall Blues," *Institutional Investor,* February 1997, p. 119.

11. Emphasizing convenience, entertainment, or a Main Street theme is described in Coleman, loc. cit.; John McCloud, "U.S. Shopping Centers Thrive as Hubs of Entertainment," *National Real Estate Investor,* May 1999, pp. 42–55; and Sunil Taneja, "Reinventing the Experience," *Chain Store Age,* November 1998, pp. 153–156.

12. Gabrielle Solomon, "Striking Gold in the Nation's Urban Core," *Fortune,* May 10, 1999, p. 152[J]. Downtown developments are covered in Beverly Vasquez, "Denver Pavilions Energizes Downtown Retail," *Denver Business Journal,* Apr. 23, 1999, p. 12B; and Ann Carrns, "Malls Are Going Topless," *The Wall Street Journal,* Mar. 31, 1999, pp. B1, B12.

13. Emily Nelson, "Wal-Mart's 'Small-Marts' May Make It Biggest Grocer," *The Wall Street Journal,* June 21, 1999, p. B4; and Mark Tosh, "Downsizing the Depot," *Progressive Grocer,* November 1998, p. 32.

14. *Statistical Abstract of the United States: 1995,* 115th ed., U.S. Bureau of the Census, Washington, DC, 1995, p. 783.

15. Ibid.

16. Dale D. Buss, "New Dynamics for a New Era," *Nation's Business,* June 1999, pp. 45–48.

17. Dan Morse and Jeffrey A. Tannenbaum, "Poll on High Success Rate for Franchises Raises Eyebrows," *The Wall Street Journal,* Mar. 17, 1998, p. B2; "Survey Reports 92 Percent of Franchisees Say They Are Successful," *Franchising World,* May/June 1998, pp. 34–36; and Nicole Harris and Mike France, "Franchisees Get Feisty" *Business Week,* Feb. 24, 1997, pp. 65–66.

18. Growth areas for franchising are suggested in Dan Morse, "Follow the Demographics, Franchising Experts Advise," *The Wall Street Journal,* Dec. 21, 1999, p. B2; and Dennis Chaplin, "New Partnerships for Franchising," *The Financial Times,* June 22, 1999, p. 2. Factors contributing to franchising's continued growth are outlined in Bruce J. Walker, "Retail Franchising in the 1990s," *Retailing Issues Letter,* January 1991, pp. 1–4.

19. David Rachman and Keith J. Fabes, "The Decline of the Traditional American Department Store," *Journal of Marketing Channels,* Vol. 1, No. 3, 1992, pp. 39+.

20. David Moin, "Differentiate or Die—Retail," *WWD,* June 8, 1998, p. 10.

21. Emily Nelson and Calmetta Y. Coleman, "America Is Shopping with Abandon—Just Not at J.C. Penney," *The Wall Street Journal,* Jan. 14, 2000, pp. A1, A7.

22. Wendy Zellner, "Look Out, Supermarkets—Wal-Mart Is Hungry," *Business Week,* Sept. 14, 1998, pp. 98, 100; and Nelson, loc. cit.

23. "Sunglass Hut Net Rises 10% in 2nd Period," *WWD,* Aug. 23, 1999, p. 20; and Gail DeGeorge, "Sunglass Hut Is Feeling the Glare," *Business Week,* June 9, 1997, pp. 89–91.

24. Gary E. Hoover, "What's in a Store?" *Across the Board,* September 1998, pp. 11+; and Alina Matas, "Specialty Store Sales Slumping at Nation's Malls," *Knight-Ridder/Tribune Business News,* Jan. 15, 1997, p. 115.

25. Glen Creno, "Outlet Bloom Is Off," *The Arizona Republic,* Aug. 1, 1999, p. 1; and Fred Faust, "Outlet Mall Industry Feels Growing Pains," *St. Louis Post-Dispatch,* Jan. 24, 1999, pp. E1, E7.

26. Sometimes category killers are referred to as *superstores.* Using this term in this context can create confusion, however, because it is also applied to very large supermarkets. For more

about the Home Depot versus Lowe's battle, see Patti Bond, "Lowe's vs. Foe," *The Atlanta (Georgia) Journal-Constitution,* Apr. 18, 1999, p. R1.

27. Babette Morgan, "Borders Enters Big Bookstore Competition Here," *St. Louis Post-Dispatch,* Mar. 20, 1995, p. 3BP.

28. William M. Bulkeley, "'Category Killers' Go from Lethal to Lame in the Space of a Decade," *The Wall Street Journal,* Mar. 9, 2000, pp. A1, A8; Joseph B. White, "AutoNation Says Earnings to Fall Short," *The Wall Street Journal,* Dec. 14, 1999, p. A3; and Andrea Isabel Flores, "Sports Authority Takes Steps to Whip Itself into Shape," *The Wall Street Journal,* Aug. 3, 1999, p. B4.

29. Len Lewis, "Markets in Motion," *Progressive Grocer,* April 1999, pp. 9–14.

30. Joel A. Baglole, "Loblaw Supermarkets Add Fitness Clubs to Offerings," *The Wall Street Journal,* Dec. 27, 1999, p. B4; and Lewis, loc. cit.

31. Wendy Zellner, "How Classy Can 7-Eleven Get?" *Business Week,* Sept. 1, 1997, pp. 74–75.

32. "Business Bulletin," *The Wall Street Journal,* Mar. 9, 2000, p. A1; Joe Dwyer III, "Retail Systems Group Sees Convenience Store of Future," *St. Louis Business Journal,* Feb. 8–14, 1999, p. 32; and Zellner, loc. cit.

33. Amy Trollinger, "Sam's Eases Up," *Kansas City Business Journal,* Mar. 20–26, 1998, p. 13.

34. Shelly Branch, "Inside the Cult of Costco," *Fortune,* Sept. 6, 1999, pp. 184–186+.

35. This estimate (perhaps better labeled a "guesstimate") of the total annual volume of nonstore retailing represents a sum of the estimates for the five types that are discussed in subsequent sections.

36. The sales estimate and number of sales people are drawn from the "1999 Direct Selling Growth & Outlook Survey" and the "1999 National Salesforce Survey," both available on the website of the Direct Selling Association, Washington, DC: <http://www.dsa.org/facsht.stm>. For seven articles covering various aspects of direct selling, see the *Journal of Marketing Channels,* Vol. 2, No. 2, 1992.

37. The worldwide sales figures are drawn from an international statistical survey on the website of the Worldwide Federation of Direct Selling Associations, Washington, DC: <http://www.wfdsa.org/statsurvey.stm>

38. "1999 Direct Selling . . . ," loc. cit.

39. Dennis Berman, "Is the Bell Tolling for Door-to-Door Selling?" *Business Week E.Biz,* Nov. 1, 1999, pp. EB58, EB60; and "Tupperware Pops Up in Unfamiliar Places," *St. Louis Post-Dispatch,* Mar. 7, 1999, p. E8.

40. Catherine Romano, "Telemarketing Grows Up," *Management Review,* June 1998, pp. 31+.

41. Dana Milbank, "Telephone Sales Reps Do Unrewarding Jobs That Few Can Abide," *The Wall Street Journal,* Sept. 23, 1993, pp. A1, A8. The estimated cost of telemarketing fraud is from Romano, loc. cit.

42. "FTC Adopts Rules to Combat Fraud in Telemarketing," *The Wall Street Journal,* Aug. 17, 1995, p. A10; and Mary Lu Carnevale, "FCC Adopts Rules to Curb Telemarketing," *The Wall Street Journal,* Sept. 18, 1992, p. B1.

43. Rodney Ho, "Vending Machines Make Change," *The Wall Street Journal,* July 7, 1999, pp. B1, B4.

44. Ibid.; "Coke Tests Machine That Adjusts Prices," *St. Louis Post-Dispatch,* Oct. 28, 1999, p. C2; and "Coke Machine Modems Send Distress Signals," *Marketing News,* Oct. 9, 1995, p. 2.

45. For more on established retailers' methods of going online, see Greg Farrell, "Clicks-and-Mortar World Values Brands," *USA Today,* Oct. 5, 1999, pp. 1B, 2B; and Wendy Zellner and Stephanie Anderson Forest, "The Big Guys Go Online," *Business Week,* Sept. 6, 1999, pp. 30–32.

46. James R. Hagerty and Greg Jaffe, "Value America to Slash Jobs, Limit Focus," *The Wall Street Journal,* Dec. 30, 1999, pp. A3, A4.

47. Ellen Neuborne, "E-tail: Gleaming Storefronts with Nothing Inside," *Business Week,* May 1, 2000, pp. 94–98. The test results are from Christine Y. Chen and Greg Lindsay, "The Straight Dope on Web Retailers: Which Ones Passed the Test?" *Fortune,* Feb. 21, 2000, pp. 280+. For more on e-tailers' shortcomings, see Jodi Mardesich, "The Web Is No Shopper's Paradise," *Fortune,* Nov. 8, 1999, pp. 188–190+.

48. "Emarketplaces Boost B2B Trade," from the Forrester Research website <http://www.forrester.com>, February 2000. Greg Wiles, "E-tailers Are Facing Doom, Survey Finds," *St. Louis Post-Dispatch,* April 12, 2000, p. B7.

49. Zellner and Forest, loc. cit.; and Cristina Lourosa-Ricardo, "Picking the Product," *The Wall Street Journal,* Nov. 22, 1999, pp. R8, R10.

50. Based on figures contained in *Economic Impact: U.S. Direct & Interactive Marketing Today,* Direct Marketing Association, Inc., New York, 1999, pp. 33, 34. The estimated sales refer only to direct orders, not to subsequent sales that were based on leads and store traffic generated by telemarketing. Although we considered it separately, telemarketing is sometimes included under the umbrella of direct marketing. Another term often associated with direct marketing, *mail order,* actually refers to the way an order is placed and/or delivered, whereas the types we describe focus on the way contact is made with consumers.

51. Chad Kaydo, "Planting the Seeds of Marketing," *Sales & Marketing Management,* August 1998, p. 73.

52. Philana Patterson, "Catalog Companies See Growing Portion of Their Business Shift to the Internet," *The Wall Street Journal,* Apr. 19, 2000, p. B9A. The number of catalogs and the rankings of apparel e-tailers are drawn, respectively, from Calmetta W. Coleman, "Retailers Strive for Shopping Synergy," *The Wall Street Journal,* Dec. 20, 1999, pp. B1, B6; and "Lands' End, Bean Lead Pack," *Daily News Record,* Nov. 3, 1999, p. 12. The tribulations of various firms engaged in catalog retailing are covered in Cyndee Miller, "It Was the Worst of Times," *Marketing News,* Mar. 15, 1993, p. 1.

53. "Nonstore Retailing Gains Favor with Consumers," *Chain Store Age,* August 1999, pp. A29–A32; and Ted Duncombe, "TV Sales Pitchers See Long Game," *St. Louis Post-Dispatch,* July 26, 1995, p. 8C.

54. A theory of institutional change, called the wheel of retailing, was first described in M. P. McNair, "Significant Trends and Developments in the Postwar Period," in A. B. Smith, ed., *Competitive Distribution in a Free, High-Level Economy and Its Implications for the University,* The University of Pittsburgh Press, Pittsburgh, 1958, pp. 17–18.

55. Gary Strauss, Lorrie Grant, and Michael McCarthy, "Dayton Hudson Hopes Name Change Hits Bull's-Eye," *USA Today,* Jan. 14, 2000, p. 5B.

56. Janet Ginsburg, "Xtreme Retailing," *Business Week,* Dec. 20, 1999, pp. 120–124+; and Leonard L. Berry, "Stores with a Future," *Retailing Issues Letter,* March 1995, pp. 1–4.

57. Debra Aho Williamson, "How Low Can They Go?" *The Industry Standard,* Nov. 22–29, 1999, pp.

224–229; Frederic M. Biddle, "Big Pet-Supply Retailers Try to Tame the Competition," *The Wall Street Journal,* Aug. 20, 1999, p. B4; Weintraub, loc. cit.; Negley, loc.cit.; Schibsted, loc.cit.; and Wingfield, loc. cit.

Chapter 16

1. Sue Hurley, "Save-A-Lot Makes Its Mark in the Low-Cost Marketplace," *St. Louis Post-Dispatch,* Nov. 29, 1999, pp. BP10, BP11; Mark Tosh, "Linking the Chain," *Progressive Grocer,* January 1999, pp. 32–34; Mark Tosh, "Wholesale Changes," *Progressive Grocer,* January 1999, pp. 29–30; Steve Weinstein, "Taking the Right Course," *Progressive Grocer,* January 1999, pp. 40–41; Steve Weinstein, "The Cluster Approach," *Progressive Grocer,* January 1996, pp. 45–49; Ryan Mathews, "A Spirit of Cooperation," *Progressive Grocer,* January 1996, pp. 61–62; and Steve Weinstein, "The Reinvention of Supervalu," *Progressive Grocer,* January 1996, pp. 26+.

2. J. William Gurley, "Why Online Distributors—Once Written Off—May Thrive," *Fortune,* Sept. 6, 1999, p. 270; and "Making the Switch from Direct to Dealer Sales," *Nation's Business,* July 1996, p. 10.

3. *1992 Census of Wholesale Trade,* Subject Series—Miscellaneous Subjects, U.S. Bureau of the Census, Washington, DC, 1995, p. 42.

4. The terms *merchant wholesaler* and *wholesaler* are sometimes used synonymously with *wholesaling middleman.* This is not accurate, however. *Wholesaling middleman* is the all-inclusive term, covering the three major categories of firms engaged in wholesale trade, whereas *wholesaler* is more restrictive, applying to only one category, namely, merchant wholesaling middlemen.

5. Because manufacturers' sales facilities are owned by manufacturers rather than being truly independent, they could be viewed as a *direct* distribution channel, rather than as distinct middlemen used in indirect distribution. Although this view has merit, we treat manufacturers' sales facilities as a category of middlemen because the Census Bureau does and also because they are separate from manufacturing firms by location, if not by ownership.

6. Donald M. Jackson and Michael F. d'Amico, "Products and Markets Served by Distributors and Agents," *Industrial Marketing Management,* February 1989, p. 28.

7. *1997 Economic Census,* Wholesale Trade, Geographic Area Series, U.S. Census Bureau, Washington, DC, 2000, p. United States 7 <www.census.gov/prod/ec97/97w42-US.pdf>; and corresponding census from prior years. For a comprehensive historical analysis of wholesaling, see Robert F. Lusch, Deborah Zizzo, and James M. Kenderine, *Foundations of Wholesaling: A Strategic and Financial Chart Book,* Distribution Research Program, University of Oklahoma, Norman, 1996.

8. Average operating expenses in this paragraph and the following one are based on the *1992 Census of Wholesale Trade,* Geographic Area Series—U.S., U.S. Bureau of the Census, Washington, DC, 1995, p. US-9; and the *1992 Census of Retail Trade,* Subject Series, U.S. Bureau of the Census, Washington, DC, 1996, p. 2-7. The 8% figure was calculated by multiplying the 11% representing wholesale operating expenses by 72%. The remainder after the 28% representing retail operating expenses is subtracted from the 100% representing retail sales (or the consumer's dollar).

9. For a brief overview of the challenges the Fleming Companies has been experiencing recently, see Emily Nelson, "Fleming to Take Charge of $550 Million in the First Step of Long-Term Overhaul," *The Wall Street Journal,* Dec. 7, 1998, p. B2.

10. Jeffrey A. Tannenbaum, "Cold War: Amana Refrigeration Fights Tiny Distributor," *The Wall Street Journal,* Feb. 26, 1992, p. B2.

11. The steps taken by Sales Systems Ltd., which is now part of Pentacon Inc., were described in Michael Selz, "Firms Innovate to Get It for You Wholesale," *The Wall Street Journal,* July 23, 1993, pp. B1, B2. For recommendations on how wholesalers can compete effectively with chains of category-killer stores and warehouse clubs that tend to buy directly from manufacturers, see Robert F. Lusch and Deborah Zizzo, *Competing for Customers,* Distribution Research and Education Foundation, Washington, DC, 1995, pp. 80–108.

12. Selz, op. cit., p. B1.

13. For an in-depth profile of 10 high-performing wholesalers plus financial and operating statistics summaries for 291 U.S. and Canadian wholesalers, see Lusch, Zizzo, and Kenderine, loc. cit.

14. Ken Partch, "Grocery Wholesaling Now Efficient? Yes, But Is It Competitive?" *Supermarket Business,* April 1993, pp. 21–26.

15. *1997 Economic Census,* Wholesale Trade, loc. cit.; and corresponding censuses from prior years.

16. Dan Balaban, "Swarms of Reps Zigzag Country to Push Product," *Kansas City Business Journal,* Jan. 24–30, 1997, p. 18.

17. *1992 Census of Wholesale Trade,* Subject Series—Miscellaneous Subjects, op. cit., p. 4-74.

18. Melissa Campanelli, "Agents of Change," *Sales & Marketing Management,* February 1995, pp. 71–75.

19. *1992 Census of Wholesale Trade,* Subject Series—Miscellaneous Subjects, op. cit., p. 4-76.

20. "Little Ads Can Be Big Trouble, Experts Say," *South Bend Tribune,* Jan. 5, 2000, p. D8.

21. The estimate of total spending is from Bill Fahrenwald, "Supply Chain: Managing Logistics for the 21st Century," *Business Week,* Dec. 28, 1998, p. 45. The cost of logistics to an individual firm was estimated by the head of the North American Logistics Association, as reported in Francis J. Quinn, "Logistics' New Customer Focus," *Business Week,* Mar. 10, 1997, p. 54.

22. Jon Bigness, "In Today's Economy, There Is Big Money to Be Made in Logistics," *The Wall Street Journal,* Sept. 6, 1995, pp. A1, A9.

23. Anil Kumar and Graham Sharman, "We Love Your Product, but Where Is It?" *Business Edge,* October 1992, p. 21. For a discussion of how firms can achieve a differential advantage through superior physical distribution, see Donald W. Bowersox, John T. Mentzer, and Thomas W. Speh, "Logistics Leverage," *Journal of Business Strategies,* Spring 1995, pp. 36–49.

24. Bruce G. Posner, "Growth Strategies," *Inc.,* December 1989, p. 125.

25. The quote is from George Anders, "Virtual Reality: Web Firms Go on Warehouse Building Boom," *The Wall Street Journal,* Sept. 8, 1999, pp. B1, B8. Also see Scott Thurm, "Getting the Goods," *The Wall Street Journal,* Nov. 22, 1999, p. R39; and Anne Pollak, "E-Retailers' Biggest Headache Is Fulfillment," *St. Louis Post-Dispatch,* Oct. 1, 1999, p. C2.

26. Fahrenwald, op. cit., p. 34.

27. "Ford and UPS Deliver a Deal," *Business Week,* Feb. 14, 2000, p. 54; and Bigness, loc. cit.

28. The motives for contract logistics are drawn from Quinn, op. cit., p. 69. The statistics about the extent of contract logistics come from Robert J. Bowman,

"Pick and Choose," *World Trade,* January 1999, pp. 82–84; James Aaron Cooke, "Third Party Logistics Grows Up," *Logistics Management & Distribution Report,* November 1998, pp. 65–68; and "Outsourcing to Drive Growth in Contract Logistics Market," *Logistics Focus,* September 1997, p. 16.

29. Tom Murray, "Just-in-Time Isn't Just for Show—It Sells," *Sales & Marketing Management,* May 1990, p. 64.

30. John W. Verity, "Clearing the Cobwebs from the Stockroom," *Business Week,* Oct. 21, 1996, p. 140.

31. Heidi Elliott, "Delivering Competition," *Electronic Business Today,* May 1997, pp. 34–36; and Ronald Henkoff, "Delivering the Goods," *Fortune,* Nov. 28, 1994, pp. 64+.

32. Amy Zuckerman, "Should You Do EDI or Internet?" *Transportation & Distribution,* June 1999, pp. 40–42, and "Internet to Play Bigger Role in Distribution," *Purchasing,* Apr. 22, 1999, pp. 47–50.

33. Robert L. Simison, Fara Warner, and Gregory L. White, "Big Three Car Makers Plan Net Exchange," *The Wall Street Journal,* Feb. 28, 2000, pp. A3, A16; and "Boeing and Oracle Are in Talks for an Online Parts Venture," *St. Louis Post-Dispatch,* Dec. 22, 1999, p. C2.

34. For further discussion of JIT, see Marvin W. Tucker and David A. Davis, "Key Ingredients for Successful Implementation of Just-in-Time: A System for All Business Sizes," *Business Horizons,* May–June 1993, pp. 59–65; and Gary L. Frazier, Robert E. Spekman, and Charles R. O'Neal, "Just-in-Time Exchange Relationships in Industrial Markets," *Journal of Marketing,* October 1988, pp. 52–67.

35. The Xerox and Black & Decker results are described by Earnest C. Raia, "Journey to World Class (JIT in USA)," *Purchasing,* Sept. 24, 1987, p. 48.

36. Brian Milligan, "What's It Going to Take to Make It Work?" *Purchasing,* Sept. 2, 1999, pp. 40–44; and Fred R. Bleakley, "Some Companies Let Suppliers Work on Site and Even Place Orders," *The Wall Street Journal,* Jan. 13, 1995, pp. A1, A6.

37. Implications of JIT for channels are discussed in Steve McDaniel, Joseph G. Ormsby, and Alicia B. Gresham, "The Effect of JIT on Distributors," *Industrial Marketing Management,* May 1992, pp. 145–149.

38. Eryn Brown, "VF Corp. Changes Its Underware," *Fortune,* Dec. 7, 1998, pp. 115–118; and Joseph Weber, "Just Get It to the Stores on Time," *Business Week,* Mar. 6, 1995, pp. 66–67.

39. Richard J. Sherman, "Collaborative Planning, Forecasting and Replenishment (CPFR): Realizing the Promise of Efficient Consumer Response through Collaborative Technology," *Journal of Marketing Theory and Practice,* Fall 1998, pp. 6–9; and Jerri Stroud, "Big Savings Seen in Food Handling," *St. Louis Post-Dispatch,* Dec. 11, 1994, pp. E1, E8.

40. Penelope Ody, "Sharing Data Is Just the Beginning of the Process," *Financial Times,* Sept. 1, 1999, p. VI; and John Verity, "Collaborative Forecasting: Vision Quest," *Computerworld,* Nov. 10, 1997, pp. S12–S14. For an extended discussion of CPFR, see the article by Sherman, loc. cit.

41. Rod Newing, "Industry Is About to Reinvent Itself," *Financial Times,* Dec. 15, 1999, p. I.

42. Nintendo's distribution center is detailed in Michael Lear-Olimpi, "More than Just Games," *Warehousing Management,* September 1999, pp. 22–30. The new warehouses and centers of e-commerce firms are described in Robert D. Hof, "What's with All the Warehouses?" *Business Week e.biz,* Nov. 1, 1999, p. EB88.

43. Nick Wingfield, "Iship.com Hopes to Make Shipping Simpler for E-Stores," *The Wall Street Journal,* Sept. 2, 1999, p. B6; and Ken Cottrill, "A Way to Lower Shipping Costs," *Nation's Business,* December 1998, pp. 33–34.

44. For research results indicating that perceptions of different modes vary across members of a buying center, see James H. Martin, James M. Daley, and Henry B. Burdg, "Buying Influences and Perceptions of Transportation Services," *Industrial Marketing Management,* November 1988, pp. 305–314.

45. David Rocks, "Transportation," *Business Week,* Jan. 10, 2000, p. 134; and Daniel Machalaba, "Delays and Snafus Grip Rail Freight," *The Wall Street Journal,* May 29, 1998, pp. B1, B2.

46. Sarah Stone, "Intermodal at Global Watershed Point," *Purchasing,* May 20, 1999, pp. 103–105; and David Hage, "On the Right Track," *U.S. News & World Report,* Mar. 21, 1994, pp. 46+.

47. Joseph Weber, Seth Payne, Kevin Kelly, and Stephanie A. Forest, "The Great Train Turnaround," *Business Week,* Nov. 2, 1992, pp. 56–57; and Sally Solo, "Every Problem Is an Opportunity," *Fortune,* Nov. 16, 1992, p. 93.

48. Anna Wilde Mathews, "More Firms Rely on 'One-Stop' Shipping," *The Wall Street Journal,* Apr. 29, 1997, p. A2.

49. "Out of the Box at UPS," *Business Week,* Jan. 10, 2000, p. 76; and Douglas A. Blackmon, "Overnight, Everything Changed for FedEx; Can It Reinvent Itself?" *The Wall Street Journal,* Nov. 4, 1999, pp. A1, A16.

50. "E-Retailers Seek to Speed Delivery of Their Web Products," *St. Louis Post-Dispatch,* Mar. 21, 2000, p. C2; and George Anders, "How Webvan Conquers E-Commerce's Last Mile," Dec. 15, 1999, pp. B1, B6.

51. Richard Merli, "Supply Agreement to Grow Kmart Frozens," *Frozen Food Age,* September 1999, pp. 8, 50; Len Lewis, "Leap of Faith," *Progressive Grocer,* January 1999, p. 62; Len Lewis, "Forging a New Supply Chain," *Progressive Grocer,* January 1999, pp. 36–38; "Wholesalers Are Bringing the Benefits of ECR to Independent Grocers," *Chain Store Age Executive,* February 1997, pp. 54–56; and Tosh, "Linking the Chain," loc. cit.

Chapter 17

1. Greg Hardesty, "California Clothing Retailer to Target Teens with Advertising Campaign," *The Orange County Register,* Dec. 16, 1999; Pacific Sunwear, Inc. website <http://www.pacsun.com>.

2. Emily Nelson, "Penney to Launch Free Teen Magazine," *The Wall Street Journal,* Apr. 6, 1999, p. B2.

3. Caroline E. Mayer, "Campbell's Reshuffles, Ponders Profit Recipe," *The Washington Post,* June 26, 1999, p. E1.

4. Beth Snyder, Louise Kramer, and Laura Petrecca, "Seismic Shift: Coke Sets Return to Classic Lineup," *Advertising Age,* July 12, 1999, pp. 1+.

5. This is a condensed version of the definition offered by Don E. Shultz and Heidi F. Shultz, "Transitioning Marketing Communications into the Twenty-First Century," *Journal of Marketing Communications,* March 1998, pp. 9–26.

6. This example is based on information in Bradley Johnson, "Abe Kohnstann: IBM," *Advertising Age,* June 26, 1995, p. S-4; and Sloane Lucas, "One on One," *Brandweek,* Sept. 20, 1999, pp. 16+.

7. Russ Green, "Making Measuring Simple: Plan Marcomm, Evaluate Criteria," *Advertising Age's Business Marketing,* September 1999, p. 49.

8. Alice Z. Cuneo, "Bridging the Gap," *Advertising Age,* Dec. 13, 1999, p. 22.

9. Jim Abrams, "Army Thinks about Changing Its Tune, Tag," *Marketing News,* Sept. 27, 1999, p. 48.

10. Jane Weaver, "Marketing Secrets for the New Economy," *PC Computing,* January 2000, pp. 90+.

11. Stephanie Thompson, "Nabisco Maps Out Major Ad Blitz to Back New Cookie, Cracker Lines," *Advertising Age,* Dec. 6, 1999, p. 3+.

12. Deborah L. Cohen, "ADM Makes Branding Plan for Soy," *Advertising Age,* Dec. 6, 1999, p. 30.

13. George Anders, "A Dream Team Online—Elway, Gretzky, Jordan," *The Wall Street Journal,* Dec. 21, 1999, p. B1+.

14. Thomas E. Weber, "With Cash for Clicks, Web Marketers Turn Advertising on Its Head," *The Wall Street Journal,* Nov. 1, 1999, p. B1.

15. Information obtained from the website of Earth's Best Organic Food <http://www.earthsbest.com>.

16. Lisa Bransten, "Buying the Buyers," *The Wall Street Journal,* Nov. 22, 1999, p. R42.

17. Ira Teinowitz, "Doan's Decision Worries Marketers," *Advertising Age,* May 31, 1999, p. 74.

18. Marianne Lavelle, "Tobacco Checks in the Mail," *U.S. News & World Report,* Dec. 20, 1999, p. 26.

19. American Marketing Association website <http://www.ama.org>.

20. Greg Hardesty, "California Clothing Retailer to Target Teens with Advertising Campaign," *The Orange County Register,* Dec. 16, 1999; Pacific Sunwear, Inc. website <http://www.pacsun.com>.

Chapter 18

1. Andy Cohen, "In Control," *Sales & Marketing Management,* June 1999, pp. 32–38; Robert Sherefkin, "GM Seat Deal Would Create New Player," *Automotive News,* Aug. 2, 1999, p. 1; Mark Savage, "Johnson Control, Lego Team Up with Play Seat," *Milwaukee Journal Sentinel,* Jan. 4, 1999, p. 3; Mark Savage, "Johnson Controls Expects Auto Unit to Grow Rapidly," *Milwaukee Journal Sentinel,* Jan. 28, 1999, p.1.

2. *Statistical Abstract of the United States: 1999,* 119th ed., U.S. Bureau of the Census, Washington, DC, 1999, adapted from pp. 424–425.

3. Robert N. McMurray, "The Mystique of Super-Salesmanship," *Harvard Business Review,* March–April 1961, pp. 113–122; Derek A. Newton, *Sales Force Performance and Turnover,* Marketing Science Institute, Cambridge, MA, 1973.

4. William C. Moncrief, "Selling Activity and Sales Position Taxonomies for Industrial Salesforces," *Journal of Marketing Research,* Aug., 1986, pp. 261–270.

5. Greg W. Marshall, William C. Moncrief, and Felicia G. Lassk, "The Current State of Sales Force Activities," *Industrial Marketing Management,* 28(1), 1998, pp. 87–98.

6. Michele Marchetti, "The Cost of Doing Business," *Sales & Marketing Management,* September 1999, pp. 56–57. The figures are derived from an annual study commissioned by *S&MM* magazine, and include compensation, benefits, and travel and entertainment costs.

7. Firms that arrange business-to-business auctions include www.freemarkets.com, www.e-steel.com, and www.metalsite.com. Visit their websites to learn more about how they operate. Also see Sarah Lorge, "Online Bidding Keeps Suppliers in Line," *Sales & Marketing Management,* August 1998, p. 16.

8. Erika Rasmusson, "The 5 Steps to Successful Sales Force Automation," *Sales & Marketing Management,* March 1999, pp. 34–40.

9. To see an example of a Web-based sales force management system designed for small companies, visit <http://www.salesforce.com>.

10. Rasmusson, loc. cit.

11. Andrea Petersen, "Making the Sale," *The Wall Street Journal,* Nov. 15, 1999, p. R16.

12. "Get Plugged In," *Sales & Marketing Management,* March 1999, p. 33.

13. Erika Rasmusson, "The 10 Traits of Top Salespeople," *Sales & Marketing Management,* August 1999, pp. 34–37.

14. Rekha Balu, "Whirlpool Gets Real with Customers," *Fast Company,* December 1999, pp. 74–76.

15. Andy Cohen, "Eyes on the Prize," *Sales & Marketing Management,* November 1999, pp. 98+; Erin Stout, "Just Rewards," *Sales & Marketing Management,* May 1999, pp. 37–42; Chris Glass, "Success Sure Is a Lot of Fun," *Sales & Marketing Management,* January 1999, pp. 54–58. In addition to feature articles such as these, the publication runs a monthly column entitled "Motivating Matters."

16. Joseph B. Cahill, "How Kirby Persuades Consumers to Buy a $1,500 Vacuum," *The Wall Street Journal,* Oct. 4, 1999, pp. A1+.

17. Gerry Kobe, "The Demise of Brand X," *Automotive Industries,* May 1999, pp. 53+; Cohen, loc. cit.; Sherefkin, loc. cit; Savage, "Johnson Control, Lego Team Up with Play Seat," loc. cit.

Chapter 19

1. Elizabeth Corcoran, "Reinventing Intel," *Forbes,* May 3, 1999, pp. 154–159; "50 Greatest B-to-B Ads," *Advertising Age's Business Marketing,* September 1999, pp. 34+; Steven J. Stark, "Reaching 'Joe Consumer,'" *Electronic Media,* June 28, 1999, pp. 28+; Tobi Elkins and Bradley Johnson, "Co-op Crossroads," *Advertising Age,* Nov. 15, 1999, pp. 1+.

2. Laurel Wentz, "P&G Tops $3 Billion Mark in Non–U.S. Ad Spending," *Advertising Age,* Nov. 8, 1999, p. 12; Betty Liu, "Coca-Cola Aims to Recapture the Real Thing," *Financial Times,* Jan. 14, 2000, p. 19.

3. "100 Leading National Advertisers," *Advertising Age,* Sept. 27, 1999, p. S3.

4. Liu, loc. cit.

5. Mercedes M. Cardona, "Avon Calling Up $100 Million for Global Brand Push," *Advertising Age,* Dec. 13, 1999, pp. 3+.

6. Jean Halliday, "Non-Traditional Tactics Back Ford Revamp of Taurus," *Advertising Age,* Dec. 13, 1999, p. 4.

7. If you examine an issue of your local newspaper, you may notice different local retailers featuring the same item (such as La-Z-Boy recliners, 7-Up, or Fuji film). This is a good sign that co-op funds are being used to pay for the ads.

8. Kathryn Kranhold, "Taco Bell Ads to Focus on Food, Not Dog," *The Wall Street Journal,* Oct. 11, 1999, p. B10.

9. "Newspaper," *Media Facts: A Comprehensive Media Guide,* Radio Advertising Bureau, October 1999, p. 16.

10. Wendy Bounds, "Magazines Seek to Demonstrate Efficacy of Ads," *The Wall Street Journal,* Apr. 12, 1999, pp. B1+.

11. "Broadcast TV," *Media Facts: A Comprehensive Media Guide,* Radio Advertising Bureau, October 1999, p. 7.

12. "Cable Television," *Media Facts: A Comprehensive Media Guide*, Radio Advertising Bureau, October 1999, p. 9.

13. "Direct Mail," *Media Facts: A Comprehensive Media Guide*, Radio Advertising Bureau, October 1999, p. 10.

14. Ibid.

15. Personal correspondence from the Radio Advertising Bureau, February 2000.

16. "Yellow Pages," *Media Facts: A Comprehensive Media Guide*, Radio Advertising Bureau, October 1999, pp. 24–25.

17. "Sweeping Changes," *The Economist*, May 1, 1999, pp. 62–63.

18. Marc Gunther, "The Great Outdoors," *Fortune*, Mar. 1, 1999, pp. 150–157.

19. Ibid.

20. Charlotte W. Craig, "Ford Cuts Budget for Magazine Spending, Turns toward Direct Marketing," *Knight-Ridder/Tribune Business News*, July 26, 1999.

21. Nancy J. Wagner, "Picking a Medium for Your Message," *Nation's Business*, February 1999, pp. 56–57.

22. Scot Hume, "Trade Promos Devour Half of All Marketing $," *Advertising Age*, Apr. 13, 1992, p. 3.

23. Kerry J. Smith, "Up. Up, and Away," *Sparkling Innovation, The 1999 Annual Report of the Promotion Industry*, supplement to *PROMO Magazine*, July 1999, p. S3.

24. A study conducted by the firm Target Marketing and Research and reported in Claire Mahoney, "Because It's Worth It," *Soap, Perfumery & Cosmetics*, July 1999, pp. 61+.

25. Allison Wellmer, "Try It—You'll Like It," *American Demographics*, August 1998, pp. 42+.

26. Ibid.

27. "Dollars Up, Redemption Down," *Sparkling Innovation, The 1999 Annual Report of the Promotion Industry*, supplement to *PROMO Magazine*, July 1999, pp. 517–518.

28. Ibid.

29. Ibid.

30. Ibid.

31. Harvey Meyer, "And Now, Some Words about Sponsors," *Nation's Business*, March 1999, pp. 38+.

32. "Business Bulletin," *The Wall Street Journal*, Feb. 24, 2000, p. A1.

33. Meyer, loc. cit.

34. Shawn Donnan and Matthew Garrahan, "Reebok Quits as Olympics Sponsor," *Financial Times*, Dec. 9, 1999, p. 8.

35. William Dunn "On with the Show," *Marketing Tools*, July/August 1995, pp. 46–55.

36. Ibid.

37. Ibid.

38. "Virtual Advertising," *The Economist*, Jan. 15, 2000, p. 68.

39. Elizabeth Corcoran, "Reinventing Intel," *Forbes*, May 3, 1999, pp. 155–159; Tobi Elkins and Bradley Johnson, "Co-op Crossroads," *Advertising Age*, Nov. 15, 1999, pp. 1+; Normandy Madden, "Internet Focus: Hong Kong/China," *Advertising Age International*, Nov. 8, 1999, pp. 46+; Tobi Elkin, "$150 Million Push; Intel inside the Internet," *Advertising Age*, Sept. 13, 1999, pp. 1+.

Chapter 20

1. Bruce Horovitz, "Java King Crowns Successor," *USA Today*, Apr. 7, 2000, p. 3B; Louise Lee, "Now, Starbucks Uses Its Bean," *Business Week*, Feb. 14, 2000, pp. 92, 94; "Starbucks-Albertson's Partner for In-Store Coffee Bar Development," *Nation's Restaurant News*, Dec. 6, 1999, p. 22; Tim Carvell, "Double-Tall, Skinny, Decaf Web Portal," *Fortune*, Aug. 2, 1999, pp. 31–32; Nelson D. Schwartz, "Still Perking after All These Years," *Fortune*, May 24, 1999, pp. 203–210; Tim Moran, "How Starbucks Plunged into Grocery Competition," *Supermarket News*, Apr. 19, 1999, p. 55; Susan Kuchinskas, "Wake Up and Smell the Coffee: Starbucks Unveils E-comm Site," *Brandweek*, Oct. 12, 1998, p. 28; David Benady and Lucy Killgren, "Caffeine Hits," *Marketing Week*, May 7, 1998, pp. 28–29; Normandy Madden, "Starbucks Ships Its Coffee Craze to Pacific Rim," *Advertising Age*, Apr. 27, 1998, p. 28; "Making Customers Come Back for More," *Fortune*, Mar. 16, 1998, p. 156[L]; and Ingrid Abramovitch, "Miracles of Marketing," *Success*, April 1993, pp. 22–27.

2. Many writers and executives use the terms *control* and *evaluation* synonymously. We distinguish between them. To speak of control as only one part of the management process is too restrictive. Rather than being an isolated managerial function, control permeates virtually all other organizational activities. For example, management *controls* its operations through the goals and strategies it selects. Also, the type of organizational structure used in the marketing department determines the degree of *control* over marketing operations.

3. Derek F. Abell, "Strategic Windows," *Journal of Marketing*, July 1978, pp. 21–26.

4. Rodney Ho, "Forsaking Sentiment, Small Clients, a Business Grows," *The Wall Street Journal*, Jan. 3, 2000, pp. A11, A13.

5. Richard Gibson, "Fame Proves Fleeting at Planet Hollywood as Fans Avoid Reruns," *The Wall Street Journal*, Oct. 7, 1998, pp. A1, A6.

6. The survey results are reported in Ellen Neuborne, "Mad Ave: A Star Is Reborn," *Business Week*, July 26, 1999, pp. 54–56+. For more on changing attitudes toward strategic planning, see John A. Byrne, "Strategic Planning," *Business Week*, Aug. 26, 1996, pp. 46–52.

7. Dan Morse, "Many Small Businesses Don't Devote Time to Planning," *The Wall Street Journal*, Sept. 7, 1999, p. B2; and *Pulse of the Middle Market—1990*, BDO Seidman, New York, 1990, pp. 12–13.

8. For one approach to competitive analysis, see Bruce H. Clark, "Managing Competitive Interactions," *Marketing Management*, Fall/Winter 1998, pp. 8–20. For more about the consultants' recommended reflection process, see Michael Hammer and Steven A. Stanton, "The Power of Reflection," *Fortune*, pp. 291+.

9. Stephanie Anderson Forest, "Cable, Phone, Internet . . . Who Ya Gonna Call?" *Business Week*, Mar. 1, 1999, pp. 64, 66.

10. Malcolm H. B. McDonald, "Ten Barriers to Marketing Planning," *The Journal of Business and Industrial Marketing*, Winter 1992, p. 15.

11. Joel A. Baglole, "Cough Syrup Touts 'Awful' Taste in U.S.," *The Wall Street Journal*, Dec. 15, 1999, p. B10.

12. Stacy Kravetz, "Dry Cleaners' New Wrinkle: Going Green," *The Wall Street Journal*, June 3, 1998, pp. B1, B15. Differential advantage in the context of services industries is examined in Sundar G. Bharadwaj, P. Rajan Varadarajan, and John Fahy, "Sustainable Competitive Advantage in Service Industries: A Conceptual Model and Research Proposition," *Journal of Marketing*, October 1993, pp. 83–99.

13. Norman H. McMillan, "EST Retailing: How to Stay out of the Black Hole," *International Trends in Retailing*, Winter 1993, pp. 60–75.

14. David Leonhardt, "Big Airlines Should Follow Midwest's Recipe," *Business Week,* June 28, 1999, p. 40.

15. Marcia Stepanek, "How Fast Is Net Fast?" *Business Week E.Biz,* Nov. 1, 1999, pp. EB52–EB54. An excellent source of information on how various companies prepare their marketing plans is Howard Sutton, *The Marketing Plan,* The Conference Board, New York, 1990.

16. One of many guidebooks for preparing an annual marketing plan is Roman G. Hiebing, Jr., and Scott W. Cooper, *The Successful Marketing Plan,* brief edition, NTC/Contemporary Publishing Group, Lincolnwood, IL, 2000.

17. See H. Igor Ansoff, *The New Corporate Strategy,* John Wiley & Sons, New York, 1988, pp. 82–85. In this updated discussion, Ansoff substituted the term *mission* for *market* in the matrix. We still prefer, and thus retain, the original term.

18. Martha Brannigan, "Cruise Lines Look to the Land to Get Boomers on Board," *The Wall Street Journal,* Dec. 6, 1999, p. B4; and Adam Goodman, "McDonnell Puts Spin on Commercial Helicopters," *St. Louis Post-Dispatch,* Sept. 2, 1991, p. 4BP.

19. Janet Ginsburg, "Not the Flavor of the Month," *Business Week,* Mar. 20, 2000, p. 128; and "Targeting Customer Needs Unveils New Opportunities," *Nation's Business,* September 1998, p. 12.

20. Carol Matlack, "Swatch: Ready for Net Time?" *Business Week,* Feb. 14, 2000, p. 61.

21. Teri Agins, "Claiborne Patches Together an Empire," *The Wall Street Journal,* Feb. 2, 2000, pp. B1, B4.

22. Rajesh K. Chandy and Gerard J. Tellis, "Organizing for Radical Product Innovation: The Overlooked Role of Willingness to Cannibalize," *Journal of Marketing Research,* November 1998, pp. 474+.

23. *The Experience Curve Reviewed: IV. The Growth Share Matrix of the Product Portfolio,* Boston Consulting Group, Boston, 1973.

24. Bruce Orwall, "Disney Plans to Narrow Portal Focus," *The Wall Street Journal,* Jan. 28, 2000, p. A3.

25. Nikhil Deogun, "Pepsi Takes Aim at Coke with New One-Calorie Drink," *The Wall Street Journal,* Oct. 5, 1998, p. B4; and Laura Zinn, "Does Pepsi Have Too Many Products?" *Business Week,* Feb. 14, 1994, pp. 64+.

26. Discussed in Derek F. Abell and John S. Hammond, *Strategic Marketing Planning,* Prentice Hall, Englewood Cliffs, NJ, 1979.

27. Alec Klein, "Kodak Plans Strategy Shift in Digital Area," *The Wall Street Journal,* Mar. 23, 2000, p. B14; and Lee Gomes, "Silicon Graphics Sets Designs to Ride High-End Computer Line to Turnaround," *The Wall Street Journal,* Nov. 15, 1999, p. B6.

28. Laurie Freeman, "Shooting for Share," *Supermarket Business,* February 1999, pp. 47+.

29. Kathleen Kerwin, "Reviving GM," *Business Week,* Feb. 1, 1999, pp. 114–120, 122.

30. Paul Lukas, "The Ghastliest Product Launches," *Fortune,* Mar. 16, 1998, p. 44.

31. Steven Lipin and Yumiko Ono, "Philip Morris's Bakery Unit Is for Sale; Asking Price Is Put at about $1 Billion," *The Wall Street Journal,* July 17, 1995, p. A3.

32. Improvements worth considering are suggested in the following articles: R. A. Proctor and J. S. Hassard, "Towards a New Model for Product Portfolio Analysis," *Management Decision,* Vol. 28, No. 3, 1990, pp. 14–17; and Rick Brown, "Making the Product Portfolio a Basis for Action," *Long Range Planning,* February 1991, pp. 102–110.

33. W. Chan Kim and Renée Mauborgne, "When 'Competitive Advantage' Is Neither," *The Wall Street Journal,* Apr. 21, 1997, p. A18.

34. Michael Treacy and Fred Wiersema, "How Market Leaders Keep Their Edge," *Fortune,* Feb. 6, 1995, pp. 88–90+; their ideas are fully described in Michael Treacy and Fred Wiersema, *The Discipline of Market Leaders,* Addison-Wesley Inc., Boston, 1995.

35. Mark Gimein, "Starbucks Makes a Net Play," *Fortune,* Mar. 6, 2000, p. 72; Terry Lefton, "Schultz' Caffeinated Crusade," *Brandweek,* July 5, 1999, pp. 20+; Mark Hamstra, "Starbucks' Pasqua Purchase Dovetails with Food-Café Tests," *Nation's Restaurant News,* Jan. 4, 1999, pp. 3, 104; Lee, loc. cit.; Carvell, loc. cit., and Schwartz, loc. cit.

Chapter 21

1. Bruce Orwall, "Disney Plans to Narrow Portal's Focus," *The Wall Street Journal,* Jan. 28, 2000, p. A3; Eric Schmuckler, "Making a Play," *Mediaweek,* Dec. 13, 1999, p. 68; "Go.com, Disney's Internet Portal, and Its Other Internet Assets, Lost More than $1 Billion in 1999," *Broadcasting & Cable,* Dec. 13, 1999, p. 129; Karen Rodriguez, "Walt Disney Strives to Create Web Empire," *Denver Business Journal,* Oct. 22, 1999, p. 29A; Marc Graser, "Mouse House Makes Case for Cyberspace," *Variety,* July 19, 1999, p. 10; Ron Grover, "Disney: Out on a Limb," *Business Week,* July 19, 1999, pp. 40–42; and Geraldine Fabrikant and Saul Hansell, "Disney to Merge Internet Holdings with Infoseek," *The New York Times,* July 13, 1999, p. C1.

2. Charles H. Noble and Michael P. Mokwa, "Implementing Marketing Strategies: Developing and Testing a Managerial Theory," *Journal of Marketing,* October 1999, pp. 57–73.

3. Neal Templin, "Your Room Costs $250 . . . No! $200 . . . No . . . ," *The Wall Street Journal,* May 5, 1999, pp. B1, B16.

4. Ram Charan and Geoffrey Colvin, "Why CEOs Fail," *Fortune,* June 21, 1999, pp. 69–72+.

5. See, for example, Brenda Paik Sunoo, "Redesigning the Company at Donna Karan," *Workforce,* July 1998, pp. 27+.

6. Seven elements of a horizontal organization are described in John A. Byrne, "The Horizontal Corporation," *Business Week,* Dec. 20, 1993, pp. 76–81.

7. Evelyn Theiss, "Research Shows Good Service Is Getting Harder to Find," *St. Louis Post-Dispatch,* June 28, 1999, p. BP22.

8. Avan R. Jassawalla and Hemant C. Sashittal, "Building Collaborative Cross-Functional New Product Teams," *The Academy of Management Executive,* August 1999, p. 50; and Donald Gerwin, "Team Empowerment in New Product Development," *Business Horizons,* July–August 1999, pp. 29+.

9. The Modicon example is from Byrne, op. cit., p. 80.

10. Frank V. Cespedes, "Beyond Teamwork: How the Wise Can Synchronize," *Marketing Management,* Spring 1996, pp. 25–37.

11. For a discussion of two organizational forms—a marketing exchange company and a marketing coalition company—that are designed to cope with complex and dynamic business environments, see Ravi S. Achrol, "Evolution of the Marketing Organization: New Forms for Turbulent Environments," *Journal of Marketing,* October 1991, pp. 77–93.

12. Melissa Campanelli, "A New Focus," *Sales & Marketing Management,* September 1995, pp. 56, 58.

13. Rick Brooks, "FDX Plans Restructuring of Sales Force," *The Wall Street Journal,* Jan. 17, 2000, p. A3.

14. Don E. Schultz, "Structural Straitjackets Stifle Integrated Success," *Marketing News,* Mar. 1, 1999, p. 8.

15. Mike Smith, "Accord Reached on Product Guarantees," *The Financial Times,* Mar. 23, 1999, p. 2.

16. J. Joseph Muller, "Three Key Issues in Consideration of Product Liability," *Mid-Missouri Business Journal,* Feb. 16–29, 1995, p. 22.

17. "Tobacco Takes a Hit," *Time,* July 19, 1999, p. 34, and Marianne Lavelle, "A Hazy Tobacco Verdict," *U.S. News & World Report,* July 19, 1999, p. 29.

18. "Curbs on Product Liability Sought," *Chemical Market Reporter,* Aug. 16, 1999, p. 29. For the description of a simulation model of product liability costs, see Conway Lackman and John Lanasa, "Product Liability Cost as a Marketing Tool," *Industrial Marketing Management,* May 1993, pp. 149–154.

19. "Seen 'n Heard," *Compliance Reporter,* Nov. 8, 1999, p. 8; and Ted Gest, "Product Paranoia," *U.S. News & World Report,* Feb. 24, 1992, pp. 67–69.

20. Jerry Edgerton, "Promises, Promises," *Money,* February 1999, p. 173.

21. Stephen Rushmore, "The Guarantee Payoff," *Lodging Hospitality,* April 1998, p. 12. For research in the context of services that recommends money-back guarantees, see Glenn B. Voss, A. Parasuraman, and Dhruv Grewal, "The Roles of Price, Performance, and Expectations in Determining Satisfaction in Service Exchanges," *Journal of Marketing,* October 1998, pp. 46+.

22. Dirk Van den Poel and Joseph Leunis, "Consumer Acceptance of the Internet as a Channel of Distribution," *Journal of Business Research,* July 1999, pp. 249–256. The Shopping.com guarantee is drawn from Timothy Hanrahan, "Price Isn't Everything," *The Wall Street Journal,* July 12, 1999, p. R20.

23. Jennifer E. Gully, "Image Technical Services, Inc. v. Eastman Kodak Co.," *Berkeley Technology Law Journal,* 1998, pp. 339–353; and Wendy Bounds, "Jury Finds Kodak Monopolized Markets in Services and Parts for Its Machines," *The Wall Street Journal,* Sept. 19, 1995, p. A4.

24. "Business Bulletin," *The Wall Street Journal,* Jan. 20, 2000, p. A1; and Lorrie Grant, "Online Returns a Hassle, Even with a Storefront," *USA Today,* Oct. 28, 1999, p. 3B.

25. John W. Verity, "The Gold Mine of Data in Customer Service," *Business Week,* Mar. 21, 1994, p. 114.

26. Jagdish N. Sheth and Rajendra S. Sisodia, "Feeling the Heat," *Marketing Management,* Fall 1995, p. 22; and Scott McCartney, "PC Makers Cure Customer Ills with Virtual House Calls," *The Wall Street Journal,* Mar. 21, 1995, p. B10.

27. William Flannery, "Too Many Firms Have Workers Who Think the Customer Isn't Always Right. Training Could Help," *St. Louis Post-Dispatch,* Apr. 18, 1999, pp. E1+. The quote is from Stephen W. Brown, "Service Recovery through IT," *Marketing Management,* Fall 1997, p. 25.

28. "Business Bulletin," *The Wall Street Journal,* Feb. 3, 2000, p. A1. For useful recommendations, see Mary C. Gilly and Richard W. Hansen, "Consumer Complaint Handling as a Strategic Marketing Tool," *The Journal of Product and Brand Management,* Summer 1992, pp. 5–16. Also see Roland T. Rust, Bala Subramanian, and Mark Wells, "Making Complaints a Management Tool," *Marketing Management,* Vol. 1, No. 3, 1992, pp. 41–45.

29. For an overview of this technique, see Dennis W. Means, "A Marketing Audit Checklist," *Agency Sales Magazine,* October 1998, pp. 54+.

30. Dale Terry, "How Does Your Bank's Marketing Size Up?" *Bank Marketing,* January 1995, pp. 53–58. For a similar view, see Douglas Brownlie, "The Conduct of Marketing Audits," *Industrial Marketing Management,* January 1996, pp. 11–22.

31. For the original discussion of the marketing audit, see Abe Schuchman, "The Marketing Audit: Its Nature, Purpose, and Problems," in *Analyzing and Improving Marketing Performance: "Marketing Audits" in Theory and Practice,* American Management Association, New York, Management Report No. 32, 1959, p. 14.

32. For more on this concept and its link to strategy, see Gordon A. Wyner, "Customer Profitability," *Marketing Management,* Winter 1999, pp. 8–9.

33. Keith L. Alexander, "Go.com Aims for Net Future with Alliance," *USA Today,* May 24, 2000, p. 28; "Contented Site," *Tele.com,* Feb. 7, 2000, p. 29; "Disney Will Launch Site Aimed at Youth and Extreme Sports," *The Wall Street Journal,* Feb. 3, 2000, p. C20; Laura Rich, "Big-Name Hunting," *The Industry Standard,* Dec. 27, 1999–Jan. 3, 2000, p. 127; and Orwall, loc. cit.

Chapter 22

1. W. W. Grainger website <www.grainger.com>, December 1999; Douglas A. Blackmon, "Selling Motors to Mops, Unglamorous Grainger Is a Web-Sales Star," *The Wall Street Journal,* Dec. 13, 1999, pp. B1+; Bob Violino, "E-Business 100: The Leaders of E-Business," *InformationWeek,* Dec. 13, 1999, pp. 62+; Erick Schonfeld, Marc Gunther, Daniel Roth, and Melanie Warner, "The E-volution of Big Business: 10 Companies That Get It," *Fortune,* Nov. 8, 1999, pp. 115+; Shelly Branch, "The 100 Best Companies to Work for in America," *Fortune,* Jan. 11, 1999, pp. 118+; Thomas A. Stewart, "The Information Wars: What You Don't Know Will Hurt You," *Fortune,* June 12, 1995, pp. 119+.

2. Kevin Maney, "The Net Effect: Evolution or Revolution?" *USA Today,* Aug. 9, 1999, pp. B1+.

3. Much of this discussion is based on Ravi Kalakota, Ralph A. Oliva, and Bob Donath, "Move Over, E-Commerce," *Marketing Management,* Fall 1999, pp. 22–31.

4. Shawn Tully, "How Cisco Mastered the Net," *Fortune,* Aug. 17, 1998, pp. 207–210.

5. Kendra Parker, "Got Questions? All You Have to Do Is Ask," *American Demographics,* November 1999, pp. 36–39.

6. Peter Svensson, "Business Deals Are Pushing Beanie Baby Auctions Aside," *St. Louis Post-Dispatch,* Nov. 24, 1999, p. C7.

7. Paul Davidson, "Manufacturers Must Alter Strategy for Retail Success," *USA Today,* June 4, 1999, p. 1B.

8. Heather Green, "Mona Leaser," *Business Week,* Dec. 20, 1999, p. 46.

9. Leigh Buchanan, "The Best of the Small Business Web," *Inc.,* Nov. 16, 1999, pp. 62+.

10. Richard Vlosky and Renee J. Fontemot, "Learning to Love Extranets," *Marketing Management,* Fall 1999, pp. 33–35.

11. Andrea Ahles, "Internet Is Bracing for an Explosion of Business-to-Business Transactions," *St. Louis Post-Dispatch,* Oct. 8, 1999, p. C19.

12. George Anders, "Buying Frenzy," *The Wall Street Journal,* July 12, 1999, pp. R6+.

13. The structure for this section comes from Gary Hamel and Jeff Sampler, "The E-Corporation," *Fortune,* Dec. 7, 1998, pp. 80–92.

14. Otis Port, "Customers Move into the Driver's Seat," *Business Week,* Oct. 4, 1999, pp. 103–106.

15. Ibid.

16. Adam Cohen, "The Attic of E," *Time,* Dec. 27, 1999, pp. 74–80.

17. Andrew Edgecliffe-Johnson, "Fingerhut Wins Wal-Mart Deal," *Financial Times,* June 22, 1999, p. 26.

18. Christopher Bowe, "U.S. Retailers Take Online Business in Their Stride," *Financial Times,* Dec. 16, 1999, p. 18.

19. Michael Casey, "Internet Changes the Face of Supply and Demand," *The Wall Street Journal,* Oct. 18, 1999, p. A43K.

20. Kara Swisher and Nick Wingfield, "Behind the Wedding of Bricks and Clicks: Need to Woo New Customers," *The Wall Street Journal,* Dec. 17, 1999, pp. B1+.

21. This description is based largely on Kathryn Kranhold, "Researchers Track the Movements of Consumers 'Internet Clicking,'" *The Wall Street Journal,* Oct. 13, 1999, p. B15.

22. Ibid.

23. Susan Gregory Thomas, "Getting to Know You.Com," *U.S. News & World Report,* Nov. 15, 1999, pp. 102–112.

24. Ibid.

25. Stewart Alsop, "The Dawn of E-Service," *Fortune,* Nov. 9, 1998, pp. 243–244.

26. Gregory L. White, "GM Will Connect Drivers to the World Wide Web," *The Wall Street Journal,* Nov. 3, 1999, pp. B1+.

27. Paul Davidson, "Manufacturers Squeeze the Hands That Sell Them," *USA Today,* June 4, 1999, p. 1B.

28. Ibid.

29. "Amway Joins Rush to the Net with an Online Store," *St. Louis Post-Dispatch,* Mar. 3, 1999, p. C7.

30. Maricris G. Briones, "What Technology Wrought: Distribution Channels in Flux," *Marketing News,* Feb. 1, 1999, pp. 1+.

31. Diane Brady, "Insurers Step Gingerly into Cyberspace," *Business Week,* Nov, 22, 1999. pp. 160+.

32. *The Second Annual Ernst & Young Internet Shopping Study,* sponsored by the National Retail Merchants Association, 1999, p. 6.

33. Thomas, loc. cit.

34. Heather Green and Linda Himelstein, "To the Victors Belong the Ads," *Business Week,* Oct. 4, 1999, p. 39.

35. Ivillage website <www.ivillage.com>, December 1999.

36. Dana James, "Linked for Success," *Marketing News,* Jan. 3, 2000, p. 3.

37. Green and Himelstein, loc. cit.

38. Daniel Eisenberg, "The Net Loves Old Media," *Time,* Nov. 1, 1999, pp. 60–61.

39. Ellen Neuborne and Robert D. Hof, "Branding on the Net," *Business Week,* Nov. 9, 1999, pp. 76+.

40. Cohen, loc. cit.

41. Lisa Bransten, "Buying the Buyer," *The Wall Street Journal,* Nov. 22, 1999, p. R42.

42. Matthew Fordahl, "Web Sites Linked by 19 Clicks: Researchers," *South Bend Tribune,* Sept. 9, 1999, p. A7.

43. Rebecca Quick and Ken Bessinger, "Sleaze E-Commerce," *The Wall Street Journal,* May 5, 1999, p. W1.

44. George Anders, "The Clout of the Online Critic," *The Wall Street Journal,* June 28, 1999, p. B1+.

45. Brady, loc. cit.

46. Hamel and Sampler, loc. cit.

47. *Ernst & Young Internet Shopping Study,* loc. cit.

48. Sandeep Dayal, Helene Landesberg, and Michael Zeisser, "How to Build Trust Online," *Marketing Management,* Fall 1999, pp. 64–69.

49. Heather Green, "Privacy Online: The FTC Must Act Now," *Business Week,* Nov. 29, 1999, p. 48.

50. "New Internet Rules on Kids' Privacy," *South Bend Tribune,* Oct. 21, 1999, p. A3.

51. Gordon A. Wyner, "The Future of Customers," *Marketing Management,* Fall 1999, pp. 8–10.

52. Marcia Stepanek, "Protecting E-Privacy: Washington Must Step In," *Business Week,* July 26, 1999, p. EB30.

53. Ian Katz and Elisabeth Malkin, "Battle for the Latin American Net," *Business Week,* Nov. 1, 1999, pp. 194+.

54. Leslie Chang, "China's Web Boom Attracts Crowd of Entrepreneurs," *The Wall Street Journal,* Oct. 27, 1999, pp. A13+.

55. John Barham, Ken Warn, and Andrea Mandel Campbell, "Online Invaders from a Neighbour to the North," *Financial Times,* Nov. 17, 1999, p. 12.

56. Christopher Cooper and Stephanie Gruner, "U.S. Internet Firms Must Hustle to Catch Up in Europe," *The Wall Street Journal,* Nov. 15, 1999, pp. A25+.

57. Brandon Mitchener, "Border Crossings," *The Wall Street Journal,* Nov. 22, 1999, p. R41.

58. Neal R. Boudette, "In Europe, Surfing a Web of Red Tape," *The Wall Street Journal,* Oct. 29, 1999, p. B1+.

59. Katz and Malkin, loc. cit.

60. Lisa Bransten, "The Bottom Line," *The Wall Street Journal,* July 12, 1999, pp. R8+.

61. Several of the points made in this section are from Richard Tomkins, "Reinventing the Dinosaur," *Financial Times,* June 8, 1999, p. 13.

62. Abigail Goldman, "Father of Amazon.Com Says E-Tail Never Will Replace Mall," *The Idaho Statesman,* Dec. 27, 1999, p. 6B.

63. W. W. Grainger website. loc. cit.; Blackmon, loc. cit.; Violino, loc. cit.; Schonfeld et. al., loc. cit.; Branch, loc. cit.

Photo Credits

Chapter 16

452 Courtesy SuperValu.

460 Courtesy W.W. Grainger, Inc.

464 © Kevin Horan.

466 Courtesy Lord Sullivan & Yoder.

477 Allen Tannenbaum/Corbis/Sygma.

Chapter 17

488 Courtesy Pacific Sunwear.

492 Courtesy J.C. Penney Co.

493 OSCAR MAYER, OSCAR MAYER Rhomboid and Design and WIENERMOBILE are trademarks of Kraft Foods, Inc. and are used with permission.

497 Einzig Photography.

500 Courtesy Excite.com.

502 Courtesy Coupon pages.com.

504 Courtesy Hain Food Group.

Chapter 18

514 Courtesy Johnson Controls, Inc.

519 Courtesy L.L. Bean, Inc.

523 Charles Thatcher/Stone.

524 Courtesy In Focus Systems.

531 Tom Wagner/Saba.

Chapter 19

538 Firefly Productions/The Stock Market.

544 Courtesy DaimlerChrysler.

546 Courtesy Saucony, Inc.

552 Courtesy Ford Motor Company.

555 Courtesy Motel 6.

559 Courtesy Catalina Marketing Corporation.

Chapter 20

576 Jonathan Drake/Sygma.

579 Courtesy eCompanystore.com.

584 Courtesy Windjammer Barefoot Cruises Ltd.

589 © 2000, by The McGraw-Hill Companies, Inc.

590 Courtesy Carnival.

Chapter 21

600 Digital Productions, Inc.

603 Courtesy Omni Hotels.

610 Courtesy Hyundai Motor America.

612 Courtesy Liveperson, Inc.

Chapter 22

628 Courtesy W.W. Grainger, Inc.

632 Text and artwork copyright © 2000 by Yahoo! Inc. All rights reserved. Yahoo! and the Yahoo! logo are trademarks of Yahoo! Inc.

636 Courtesy Prairie Frontier.

637 Courtesy CSX Corporation.

639 Courtesy MWW/Savitt.

642 MY DESIGN, BARBIE and related trademarks are owned by and used with permission of Mattel, Inc. © 2000 Mattel, Inc. All Rights Reserved.

646 Reprinted with permission of Land's End, Inc.

Glossary

A

accessory equipment Business goods that have substantial value and are used in an organization's operations.

activity indicator of buying power A market factor that is related to sales and expenditures and serves as an indirect estimate of purchasing power.

administered vertical marketing system An arrangement that coordinates distribution activities through the market and/or economic power of one channel member or the shared power of two channel members.

adoption process The set of successive decisions an individual or organization makes before accepting an innovation.

adoption rate The speed or ease with which a new product is accepted.

advertising All activities involved in presenting to an audience a nonpersonal, sponsor-identified, paid-for message about a product or an organization.

advertising agency An independent company that provides specialized advertising services and may also offer more general marketing assistance.

advertising campaign All the tasks involved in transforming a theme into a coordinated advertising program to accomplish a specific goal for a product or brand.

advertising media The communications vehicles (such as newspapers, radio, and television) that carry advertising as well as other information and entertainment.

agent middleman A firm that never actually takes title to (i.e., owns) products it helps market but does arrange the transfer of title.

agent wholesaling middleman An independent firm that engages primarily in wholesaling by actively negotiating the sale or purchase of products on behalf of other firms but does not take title to the products being distributed.

agribusiness Farms, food-processing firms, and other large-scale farming-related enterprises.

AIDA A sequence of steps in various forms of promotion, notably personal selling and advertising, consisting of attracting *Attention*, holding *Interest*, arousing *Desire*, and generating buyer *Action*.

annual marketing plan A written document that presents the master blueprint for a year's marketing activity for a specified organizational division or major product.

Asia-Pacific Economic Cooperation forum (APEC) A trade pact among 18 Pacific Rim nations that seeks the elimination of major trade barriers.

Association of Southeast Asian Nations (ASEAN) An agreement creating a free-trade zone among Brunei, Indonesia, Malaysia, the Philippines, Singapore, and Thailand.

attitude A learned predisposition to respond to an object or class of objects in a consistently favorable or unfavorable way.

auction company An agent wholesaling middleman that helps assembled buyers and sellers complete their transactions by providing auctioneers who do the selling and physical facilities for displaying the sellers' products.

automatic vending A form of nonstore retailing where the products are sold through a machine with no personal contact between the buyer and seller.

average fixed cost The total fixed cost divided by the number of units produced.

average fixed cost curve A graph of average fixed cost levels showing a decline as output increases because the total of the fixed costs is spread over an increasing number of units.

average revenue The unit price at a given level of unit sales. It is calculated by dividing total revenue by the number of units sold.

average total cost The total cost divided by the number of units produced.

average total cost curve A graph of average total costs, which starts high, then declines to its lowest point, reflecting optimum output with respect to total costs (not variable costs), and then rises because of diminishing returns.

average variable cost The total variable cost divided by the number of units produced.

average variable cost curve A graph of average variable cost levels, which starts high, then declines to its lowest point, reflecting optimum output with respect to variable costs (not total costs), and then rises.

B

baby boomers Americans born during the 10 years following World War II.

balance of payments The accounting record of all of a country's transactions with all the other nations of the world.

balance sheet A financial statement that summarizes the assets, liabilities, and net worth of a company at a given time.

banner ad A boxed-in promotional message often appearing at the top of a Web page.

barter The exchange of goods and/or services for other products.

base price The price of one unit of the product at its point of production or resale. Same as *list price*.

behavioral segmentation Market segmentation based on consumers' product-related behavior, typically the benefits desired from a product and the rate at which the consumer uses the product.

Boston Consulting Group (BCG) matrix A strategic planning model that classifies strategic business units or major products according to market shares and growth rates.

boycott A refusal to buy products from a particular company or country.

brand A name and/or mark intended to identify and differentiate the product of one seller or a group of sellers.

brand equity The value a brand adds to a product.

brand label The application of the brand name alone to a product or package.

brand licensing See *trademark licensing*.

brand manager See *product manager*.

brand mark The part of a brand that appears in the form of a symbol, design, or distinctive color or type of lettering.

brand name The part of a brand that can be vocalized—words, letters, and/or numbers.

breadth The number of product lines offered for sale by a firm.

break-even analysis A method of calculating the level of output at which total revenue equals total costs, assuming a certain selling price.

break-even point The level of output at which total revenue equals total costs, assuming a certain selling price.

bribes Something given in exchange for services or protection, it is common in foreign markets.

broker An agent wholesaling middleman that brings buyers and sellers together and provides market information to either party and that ordinarily neither physically handles products being distributed nor works on a continuing basis with those sellers or buyers.

browser A program that enables its users to access electronic documents included in the World Wide Web on the Internet.

business analysis One stage in the new-product development process, consisting of several steps to expand a surviving idea into a concrete business proposal.

business cycle The three recurring stages in an economy, typically prosperity, recession, and recovery.

business format franchising An agreement, covering an entire method (or format) for operating a business, under which a successful business sells the right to operate the same business in different geographic areas.

business market The total of all business users.

business marketing The marketing of goods and services to business users, as contrasted to ultimate consumers.

business product A product that is intended for purchase and resale or for purchase and use in producing other products or for providing services in an organization.

business services market The total set that deals in data and information such as marketing research firms, ad agencies, public utilities, and financial, insurance, legal, or real estate firms.

business-to-business advertising Advertising that is directed at businesses.

business users Business, industrial, or institutional organizations that buy goods or services to use in their own organizations, to resell, or to make other products.

buy classes Three typical buying situations in the business market—namely new-task buying, modified rebuy, and straight rebuy.

buying center In an organization, all individuals or groups involved in the process of making a purchase decision.

buying motive The reason why a person or an organization buys a specific product or makes purchases from a specific firm.

buying roles The users, influencers, deciders, gatekeepers, and buyers who make up a buying center.

C

cannibalization Situation in which a firm introduces new products to stimulate sales but the profit comes at the expense of other products sold by that firm.

cartel A group of companies that produce similar products and act collectively to restrain competition in manufacturing and marketing.

cash discount A deduction granted to buyers for paying their bills within a specified period.

category-killer store A type of retail institution that has a narrow but very deep assortment, low prices, and few to moderate customer services. It is de-

signed to "destroy" all competition in a specific product category.

change agent In the process of diffusion, a person who seeks to accelerate the spread of a given innovation.

channel assembly Strategy in which a distributor takes over the final assembly role, which allows products to be customized, thus shortening delivery time because manufacturers often delay custom projects so they don't disrupt their production processes.

channel conflict A situation in which one channel member perceives another channel member to be acting in a way that prevents the first member from achieving its distribution objectives.

channel control The actions of a firm to regulate the behavior of other companies in its distribution channel.

channel power The ability of a firm to influence or determine the behavior of another channel member.

client market Individuals and/or organizations that are the recipients of a nonprofit organization's money or services. Same as *recipient market*.

clustering Electronic research technique that tracks the pages visited, the amount of time at a page, and the items purchased by individuals as they navigate a site.

collaborative filtering Electronic research technique that compares a person's selections and the purchases of previous visitors and enables a site to recommend current products that may be of interest to the visitor.

collaborative planning, forecasting, and replenishment (CPFR) Method by which a producer or wholesaler and a customer, ordinarily a retail chain, jointly and interactively develop sales forecasts through a shared website.

cobranding Agreement between two separate companies, or two divisions within the same company, to place both of their respective brands on a particular product or enterprise; also called dual branding.

commercial information environment As contrasted with the social information environment, all communications directed to consumers by organizations and individuals involved in marketing.

Common Market of the South (MERCO-SUR) An agreement between Argentina, Brazil, Paraguay, and Uruguay to allow 90% of trade, among these countries, to occur tariff-free.

communication The verbal or nonverbal transmission of information between someone wanting to express an idea and someone else expected or expecting to get that idea. The four elements are a message, a source of the message,

a communication channel, and a receiver.

company sales branch See *manufacturer's sales branch*.

comparative advertising A form of selective-demand advertising in which an advertiser either directly (by naming a rival brand) or indirectly (through inference) points out the differences among competing brands.

competitive intelligence The process of gathering and analyzing publicly available information about the activities and plans of competitors.

concentration strategy See *single-segment strategy*.

Consolidated Metropolitan Statistical Area (CMSA) A giant urban center consisting of two or more adjacent Primary Metropolitan Statistical Areas.

consumer advertising Advertising that is directed at consumers.

consumer buying-decision process The series of logical stages, which differ for consumers and organizations, that a prospective purchaser goes through when faced with a buying problem.

consumer product A product that is intended for purchase and use by household consumers for nonbusiness purposes.

Consumer Product Safety Act Federal legislation that created the Consumer Product Safety Commission (CPSC), which has authority to establish mandatory safety standards for many consumer products.

containerization A cargo-handling system in which shipments of products are enclosed in large metal or wood receptacles that are then transported unopened from the time they leave the shipper's facilities until they reach their destination.

contract logistics An arrangement under which a firm outsources various physical distribution activities to one or more independent firms.

contract manufacturing An arrangement in which a firm in one country arranges for a firm in another country to produce the product in the foreign country.

contracting A legal relationship that allows a firm to enter a foreign market indirectly, quickly establish a market presence, and experience a limited amount of risk.

contractual vertical market system An arrangement under which independent firms—producers, wholesalers, and retailers—operate under contracts specifying how they will operate in order to improve their distribution efficiency and effectiveness.

contribution-margin approach In marketing cost analysis, an accounting method in which only direct expenses are allocated to each marketing unit being analyzed.

convenience goods A category of tangible consumer products that the consumer has prior knowledge of and purchases with minimum time and effort.

convenience store A type of retail institution that concentrates on convenience-oriented groceries and nonfoods, typically has higher prices than other grocery stores, and offers few customer services.

cookie An inactive data file, placed on the computer's hard drive after the user connects to a particular website, used to record the visitor's activities while connected to the site.

cooperative advertising Advertising promoting products of two or more firms that share its cost.

corporate chain An organization of two or more centrally owned and managed stores that generally handle the same lines of products.

corporate vertical marketing system An arrangement under which a firm at one level of a distribution channel owns the firms at the next level or owns the entire channel.

correlation analysis A statistical refinement of the direct-derivation method, an approach to demand forecasting that takes into account how close the association is between potential sales of the product and the market factor affecting its sales.

cost of goods sold A financial figure showing the value of the merchandise sold during a given period, calculated by adding the value of any merchandise on hand at the beginning of the period to the net cost of what is purchased during the period and then deducting the value of whatever remains at the end of the period.

cost per thousand (CPM) The media cost of gaining exposure to 1,000 persons with an ad.

cost-plus pricing A major method of price determination in which the price of a unit of a product is set at a level equal to the unit's total cost plus a desired profit on the unit.

countertrade An arrangement under which domestically made products are traded for imported goods.

culture A complex of symbols and artifacts created by a society and handed down from generation to generation as determinants and regulators of human behavior.

cumulative discount A quantity discount based on the total volume purchased over a specified period.

customer specialization One method of organizing selling activities in which each

sales person is assigned a specific group of customers, categorized by type of industry or channel of distribution, to which to sell. Same as *market specialization*.

D

database A set of related data that are organized, stored, and updated in a computer.

data mining Method used to identify patterns and meaningful relationships in masses of data that would be unrecognizable to researchers.

data warehouse A collection of data from a variety of internal and external sources, compiled by a firm for use in conducting transactions.

decision support system (DSS) A procedure that allows a manager to interact with data and methods of analysis to gather, analyze, and interpret information.

decline stage The fourth, and final, part of a product life cycle during which the sales of a generic product category drop and most competitors abandon the market.

Delphi method A forecasting technique, applicable to sales forecasting, in which a group of experts individually and anonymously assesses future sales, after which each member has the chance to offer a revised assessment as the group moves toward a consensus.

demand forecasting The process of estimating sales of a product during some future period.

demographic segmentation Subdividing markets into groups based on population factors such as size, age, and growth.

demographics The characteristics of human populations, including such factors as size, distribution, and growth.

department store A large-scale retail institution that has a very broad and deep product assortment, tries not to compete on the basis of price, and offers a wide array of customer services.

depth The relative variety of sizes, colors, and models offered within a product line.

descriptive label The part of a product that gives information about its use, construction, care, performance, and/or other pertinent features.

desk jobber See *drop shipper*.

differential advantage Any feature of an organization or brand perceived by customers to be desirable and different from those of the competition.

differential disadvantage Any feature of an organization or brand perceived by customers to be undesirable and different from those of the competition.

diffusion A process by which an innovation spreads throughout a social system over time.

direct costs Separate expenses that are incurred totally in connection with one market segment or one unit of the sales organization. Same as *separable expenses*.

direct-derivation method An approach to demand forecasting that directly relates the behavior of a market factor to estimated demand.

direct foreign investment A method through which a company can build or acquire production or distribution facilities in a foreign country.

direct distribution A channel consisting only of producer and final customer, with no middlemen providing assistance.

direct investment The actions of a company to build or acquire its own production facilities in a foreign country.

direct marketing A form of nonstore retailing that uses advertising to contact consumers who, in turn, purchase products without visiting a retail store.

direct selling A form of nonstore retailing in which personal contact between a sales person and a consumer occurs away from a retail store. Sometimes called *in-home selling*.

direct tests Measuring or predicting the sales volume attributable to a single ad or an entire advertising campaign.

directory Collection of lists of websites organized by topics and subtopics.

disintermediation The replacement of some traditional intermediaries in a process due to the growth of Internet-based sales.

discount retailing A retailing approach that uses price as a major selling point by combining comparatively low prices and reduced costs of doing business.

discount store A large-scale retail institution that has a broad and shallow product assortment, low prices, and few customer services.

distribution center A facility that has under one roof an efficient, fully integrated system for the flow of products—taking orders, filling them, and preparing them for delivery to customers.

distribution channel The set of people and firms involved in the transfer of title to a product as the product moves from producer to ultimate consumer or business user.

donor market Individuals and/or organizations that contribute money, labor, or materials to a nonprofit organization. Same as *contributor market*.

drop shipper A merchant wholesaler that does not physically handle the product being distributed, but instead sells merchandise for delivery directly from the producer to the customer. Same as *desk jobber*.

dumping The process of selling products in foreign markets at prices below the prices charged for these goods in their home market.

dynamic pricing A form of price adjustment that occurs instantly and frequently in accordance with what the market will bear.

E

early adopters A group of consumers that includes opinion leaders, is respected, has much influence on its peers, and is the second group (following the innovators) to adopt an innovation.

early majority A group of fairly deliberate consumers that adopts an innovation just before the "average" adopter in a social system.

economic environment A set of factors, including the business cycle, inflation, and interest rates, that affect the marketing activities of an organization.

economic order quantity (EOQ) The optimal quantity for reorder when replenishing inventory stocks, as indicated by the volume at which the sum of inventory-carrying costs and order-processing costs are at a minimum.

80–20 principle A situation in which a large proportion of the total orders, customers, territories, or products account for only a small share of the company's sales or profit, and vice versa.

elasticity of demand A price-volume relationship such that a change of one unit on the price scale results in a change of more than one unit on the volume scale.

electronic commerce The buying and selling of goods and services through the use of electronic networks.

electronic data interchange (EDI) Computer-to-computer transmission of orders, invoices, or other business information.

electronic information A form of networking involving the creation of a corporate website to post information about the firm.

electronic networks Individuals or organizations linked via some form of telecommunications.

electronic transactions Purchases made directly from a firm's website.

enterprise resource planning (ERP) systems Strategy in which the various business functions of sales, manufacturing, purchasing, distribution, financial management, and human resources are integrated through the use of computer programs; also called enterprise software.

environmental monitoring The process of gathering information regarding a company's external environment, analyzing it, and forecasting the impact of whatever trends the analysis suggests. Same as *environmental scanning*.

environmental scanning See *environmental monitoring*.

ethics The rules and standards of moral behavior that are generally accepted by a society.

European Union (EU) A political and economic alliance among most of the countries of Western Europe that seeks to liberalize trade among its members.

evaluation The stage of the management process during which an organization determines how well it is achieving the goals set in its strategic planning.

everyday low pricing (EDLP) A pricing strategy that involves consistently low prices and few, if any, temporary price reductions.

exchange The act of voluntarily providing a person or organization something of value in order to acquire something else of value.

exclusive dealing The practice by which a manufacturer prohibits its dealers from carrying products of its competitors.

exclusive distribution A strategy in which a supplier agrees to sell its product only to a single wholesaling middleman and/or retailer in a given market.

exclusive-territory policy The practice by which a producer requires each middleman to sell only to customers located within an assigned territory.

executive judgment A method of sales forecasting that consists of obtaining opinions regarding future sales volume from one or more executives.

expected price The price at which customers consciously or unconsciously value a product—what they think the product is worth.

experiment A method of gathering primary data in which the researcher measures the results of changing one variable in a situation while holding all others constant.

export agent A middleman that operates either in a manufacturer's country or in the destination country and that negotiates the sale of the product in another country and may provide additional services such as arranging for international financing, shipping, and insurance on behalf of the manufacturer.

export merchant A middleman operating in a manufacturer's country that buys goods and exports them.

exporting The activities by which a firm sells its product in another country, either directly to foreign importers or through import-export middlemen.

express warranty A statement in written or spoken words regarding restitution from seller to customer if the seller's product does not perform up to reasonable expectations.

extranet A network that links a large number of firms at different levels of a distribution channel.

F

fabricating materials Business goods that have received some processing and will undergo further processing as they become part of another product.

fabricating parts Business goods that already have been processed to some extent and will be assembled in their present form (with no further change) as part of another product.

fad A product or style that becomes immensely popular nearly overnight and then falls out of favor with consumers almost as quickly.

family A group of two or more people related by blood, marriage, or adoption living together in a household.

family branding A strategy of using the company name for branding purposes.

family life cycle The series of life stages that a family goes through, starting with young single people, progressing through married stages with young and then older children, and ending with older married and single people.

family packaging A strategy of using either highly similar packages for all products or packages with a common and clearly noticeable feature.

fashion A style that is popularly accepted and purchased by successive groups of people over a reasonably long period of time.

fashion-adoption process A series of buying waves by which a style becomes popular in a market; similar to diffusion of an innovation.

fashion cycle Wavelike movements representing the introduction, rise, popular acceptance, and decline of the market's acceptance of a style.

fashion obsolescence See *style obsolescence*.

Federal Trade Commission Act A federal law, passed in 1914, prohibiting unfair competition and establishing the Federal Trade Commission.

first-mover advantage Strategy of entering a market during the introductory stage of a product in order to build a dominant position; also called pioneer advantage.

fixed cost A cost that remains constant regardless of how many items are produced or sold.

flat-rate pricing Arrangement where a purchaser pays a stipulated single price and then can consume as much or as little of the product as desired.

flexible-price strategy A pricing strategy under which a seller charges different prices to similar customers who buy identical quantities of a product. Same as *variable-price strategy*.

FOB (free on board) factory pricing A geographic pricing strategy whereby the seller quotes the selling price at the point of production and the buyer selects the mode of transportation and pays all freight costs. Same as *FOB mill pricing*.

FOB mill pricing See *FOB factory pricing*.

focus group A preliminary data-gathering method involving an interactive interview of 4 to 10 people.

forecast demand The process of estimating sales of a product during some future period. Same as *demand forecasting*.

for-profit services firms Those that sell to consumers or other businesses with profitable operations as a primary goal.

franchising A type of contractual vertical marketing system that involves a continuing relationship in which a franchiser (the parent company) provides the right to use a trademark plus various management assistance in return for payments from a franchisee (the owner of the individual business unit).

freight absorption pricing A geographic pricing strategy whereby the seller pays for (absorbs) some of the freight charges in order to penetrate more distant markets.

freight forwarder A specialized marketing institution that serves firms by consolidating less-than-carload or less-than-truckload shipments into carload or truckload quantities and arranging for door-to-door shipping service.

freight in Freight charges paid by a buyer.

fulfillment The act of packing and shipping orders to customers.

full-cost approach In marketing cost analysis, an accounting method in which all expenses—direct and indirect—are allocated to the marketing units being analyzed.

full-service wholesaler An independent merchant middleman that performs a full range of wholesaling functions (from creating assortments to warehousing).

functional discount See *trade discount*.

functional obsolescence See *technological obsolescence*.

G

General Agreement on Tariffs and Trade (GATT) An organization, formed in 1948 and now comprising over 100 countries, that seeks to develop fair-trade practices among its members.

General Electric (GE) business screen A planning model developed by General Electric that classifies strategic business units or major products based on two factors, market attractiveness and business position.

Generation X Those people in the U.S. who were born between approximately 1966 and 1976. Also called *baby busters*, *twentysomethings*, or *boomerangers*.

Generation Y Those people in the U.S. who were born between either 1976 and 1994, or 1978 and 1982. Also called *echo boomers*, or *millennium generation*.

generic product A product that is packaged in a plain label, is sold with no advertising and without a brand name, and goes by its generic name, such as "tomatoes" or "paper towels."

geographic segmentation Subdividing markets into groups based on their locations.

geographic specialization One method of organizing selling activities, in which each sales person is assigned a specific geographic area—called a territory—in which to sell.

global sales teams A type of personal selling where a team of sales people is responsible for all of its company's sales to an account anywhere in the world.

global strategy A strategy in which essentially the same marketing program is employed around the world.

goal See *objective*.

government market The segment of the business market that includes federal, state, and local units buying for government institutions such as schools, offices, hospitals, and military bases.

grade label The part of a product that identifies the products judged quality (grade) by means of a letter, number, or word.

gray marketing Practice of buying a product in one country, agreeing to distribute it in a second country but diverting it to a third country; also called export diversion.

Green River ordinance Law that restricts door-to-door salespeople by requiring them to register and purchase a license.

gross margin The amount of money that is left after cost of goods sold is subtracted from net sales.

gross margin percentage The ratio of gross margin to net sales.

growth stage The second part of a product life cycle during which the sales and profits of a generic product category rise and competitors enter the market, causing profits to decline near the end of this part of the cycle.

H

heterogeneity A characteristic of a service indicating that each unit is somewhat different from other units of the same service.

hierarchy of effects The stages a buyer goes through in moving toward a purchase, specifically awareness, knowledge, liking, preference, conviction, and purchase.

high-low pricing A pricing strategy that combines frequent price reductions and aggressive promotion to convey an image of very low prices.

horizontal business market A situation where a given product is usable in a wide variety of industries.

horizontal conflict A form of channel conflict occurring among middlemen (either of the same type or different types) at the same level of distribution.

household A single person, a family, or any group of unrelated persons who occupy a housing unit.

hypothesis A tentative supposition that if proven would suggest a possible solution to a problem.

I

iceberg principle A concept related to performance evaluation stating that the summary data (tip of the iceberg) regarding an activity may hide significant variations among segments of this activity.

implementation The stage of the management process during which an organization attempts to carry out its strategic plans.

implied warranty An intended but unstated assurance regarding restitution from seller to customer if the seller's product does not perform up to reasonable expectations.

import-export agent An agent wholesaling middleman that brings together sellers and buyers in different countries. Export agents work in the country in which the product is made; import agents work in the country in which the product will be sold.

import quota A limit on the amount of a particular product that can be brought into a country.

impulse buying A form of low-involvement decision making; purchases made with little or no advance planning.

income statement See *operating statement*.

independent retailer A company with a single retail store that is not affiliated with a contractual vertical marketing system.

indirect costs Expenses that are incurred jointly for more than one marketing unit and therefore cannot be totally charged to one market segment.

indirect distribution A channel consisting of producer, final customer, and at least one level of middleman.

indirect tests Measuring or predicting the effects of advertising by using a factor other than sales volume.

inelastic demand A price-volume relationship such that a change of one unit on the price scale results in a change of less than one unit on the volume scale.

inflation A rise in the prices of goods and services.

informal investigation The stage in a marketing research study at which preliminary, readily available data are gathered from people inside and outside the company—middlemen, competitors, advertising agencies, and consumers.

infrastructure The country's levels and capabilities with respect to transportation, communications, and energy.

in-home selling See *direct selling*.

innovation adopter categories Groups of people differentiated according to when they accept a given innovation.

innovators A group of venturesome consumers that are the first to adopt an innovation.

inseparability A characteristic of a service indicating that it cannot be separated from the creator-seller of the service.

inside selling Situation where the customer comes to the sales person, includes retail stores and telephone order takers.

installations Manufactured products that are an organization's major, expensive, and long-lived equipment and that directly affect the scale of operations in an organization producing goods or services.

institutional advertising Advertising that presents information about the advertiser's business or tries to create a favorable impression—build goodwill—for the organization.

intangibility A characteristic of a service indicating that it has no physical attributes and, as a result, is impossible for customers to taste, feel, see, hear, or smell before they buy it.

integrated marketing communications A strategy in which each of the promotion-mix components is carefully coordinated.

intensity of distribution The number of middlemen used by a producer at the retail and wholesale levels in a particular territory.

intensive distribution A strategy in which a producer sells its product through every available outlet in a market where a consumer might reasonably look for it.

interest rates The percentage amounts either charged to lend money or paid to acquire money.

intermodal transportation The use of two or more modes of transportation to move a shipment of freight.

international market Sales, market potential, or sales potential in foreign (or nondomestic) areas.

international marketing The activities of an organization to market its products in two or more countries.

Internet Global network of networks linking millions of users, originally created to link researchers at many different sites and allow them to exchange information.

Internet selling The offering of goods or services to customers over the Internet.

Internet survey A method of gathering data by posting questionnaires on a firm's website or by e-mailing them to a sample of individuals.

intranet A local electronic network created by linking the personal computers of individuals in a company or department.

introduction stage The first part of a product life cycle during which a generic product category is launched into the market in a full-scale marketing program. Same as *pioneering stage*.

invention In international marketing, the development of an entirely new product for a foreign market.

inverse demand A price-volume relationship such that the higher the price, the greater the unit sales.

ISO 9000 quality standards The International Organization for Standardizations certification to assure that firms conform to specific standards in processes, procedures, operations, controls, and management.

J

joint venture A partnership arrangement in which a foreign operation is owned in part by a domestic company and in part by a foreign company.

just-in-time (JIT) A form of inventory control, purchasing, and production that involves buying parts and supplies in small quantities just in time for use in production and then producing in quantities just in time for sale.

K

kinked demand A condition in which total revenue declines when a product's price is increased or decreased in relation to the prevailing market level.

L

label The part of a product that carries information about the product and the seller.

laggards A group of tradition-bound consumers who are the last to adopt an innovation.

Landham Trademark Act A federal law passed in 1946 that made it illegal for organizations to make false claims about their own products.

late majority A group of skeptical consumers who are slow to adopt an innovation but eventually do so to save money or in response to social pressure from their peers.

leader In leader pricing, an item on which price is cut.

leader pricing A pricing and promotional strategy in which temporary price cuts are made on a few items to attract customers.

learning Changes in behavior resulting from observation and experience.

level of involvement The amount of effort that is expended in satisfying a need.

licensing A business arrangement whereby one firm sells to another firm (for a fee or royalty) the right to use the first company's brand, patents, or manufacturing processes.

life-style Habits that relate to a person's activities, interests, and opinions.

limited-line store A type of retail institution that has a narrow but deep product assortment and customer services that vary from store to store.

line extension One form of product-mix expansion in which a company adds a similar item to an existing product line with the same brand name.

list price See *base price*.

local strategy A strategy used to develop customized marketing programs for each distinct area.

local-content law A regulation specifying the proportion of a finished product's components and labor that must be provided by the importing country.

local operating laws A constraint on how, when, or where retailing can be conducted.

logistics See *physical distribution*.

loss leader In leader pricing, an item on which price is cut to a level that is below the store's cost.

loyalty Faithfulness in a particular brand or retailer so that the consumer purchases that brand or from that retailer without considering alternatives.

M

mail survey A method of gathering data by mailing a questionnaire to potential respondents, and asking them to complete it and return it by mail.

major-accounts organization A variation of customer specialization that usually involves team selling to better service key accounts.

management The process of planning, implementing, and evaluating the efforts of a group of people working toward a common goal.

manufacturers' agent An agent wholesaling middleman that sells part or all of a manufacturer's product mix in an assigned geographic territory. Same as *manufacturers' representative*.

manufacturers' representative See *manufacturers' agent*.

manufacturer's sales branch A manufacturer's sales facility that carries a stock of the product being sold. Same as *company sales branch*.

manufacturer's sales facility An establishment that engages primarily in wholesaling and is owned and operated by a manufacturer but is physically separated from manufacturing plants.

manufacturer's sales office A manufacturer's sales facility that does not carry a stock of the product being sold.

marginal cost The cost of producing and selling one more unit; that is, the cost of the last unit produced or sold.

marginal cost curve A graph of marginal cost levels, which slopes downward until marginal costs start to increase, at which point it rises.

marginal revenue The income derived from the sale of the last unit.

markdown A reduction from the original selling price.

markdown percentage The ratio of the total dollar markdowns to total net sales during a given period.

market People or organizations with wants to satisfy, money to spend, and the willingness to spend the money. Alternatively, any person or group with whom an individual or organization has an existing or potential exchange relationship.

market aggregation strategy A plan of action under which an organization treats its total market as a single segment—that is, as one mass market whose members are considered to be alike with respect to demand for the product—and thus develops a single marketing mix to reach most of the customers in the entire market. Same as *mass-market strategy* and *undifferentiated-market strategy*.

market factor An item or element that (1) exists in a market, (2) may be measured quantitatively, and (3) is related to the demand for a good or service.

market-factor analysis A sales forecasting method that assumes the future demand for a product is related to the behavior of certain market factors and, as a result, involves determining what these factors are and then measuring their relationships to sales activity.

market-orientation stage The third stage in the evolution of marketing management in which companies identify what customers want and tailor all their activities to satisfy those needs as efficiently as possible.

market-penetration pricing A strategy in which the initial price of a product is set low in relation to the target market's range of expected prices.

market potential The total sales volume that all organizations selling a product during a stated time period in a specific market could expect to achieve under ideal conditions.

market-response system A form of inventory control in which a purchase by a final customer activates a process to produce and deliver a replacement item.

market segmentation The process of dividing the total market for a good or service into several smaller groups, such that the members of each group are similar with respect to the factors that influence demand.

market segments Within the same general market, groups of customers with different wants, buying preferences, or product-use behavior.

market share The proportion of total sales of a product during a stated time period in a specific market that is captured by a single firm.

market-share analysis A detailed analysis of the company's share of the market in total as well as by product line and market segment.

market-skimming pricing A strategy in which the initial price of a product is set high in relation to the target market's range of expected prices.

market specialization See *customer specialization*.

market tests One stage in the new-product development process, consisting of acquiring and analyzing actual consumers' reactions to proposed products.

marketer Any person or organization that desires to stimulate and facilitate exchanges.

marketing A total system of business activities designed to plan, price, promote, and distribute want-satisfying products to target markets to achieve organizational objectives.

marketing audit A comprehensive review and evaluation of the marketing function in an organization—its philosophy, environment, goals, strategies, organizational structure, human and financial resources, and performance.

marketing concept A philosophy of doing business that emphasizes customer orientation and coordination of marketing activities in order to achieve the organization's performance objectives.

marketing cost analysis A detailed study of the Operating Expenses section of a company's profit and loss statement.

marketing information system (MkIS) An ongoing, organized procedure to generate, analyze, disseminate, store, and retrieve information for use in making marketing decisions.

marketing intermediary An independent business organization that directly aids in the flow of products between a marketing organization and its markets.

marketing mix A combination of the four elements—product, pricing structure, distribution system, and promotional activities—used to satisfy the needs of an organization's target market(s) and, at the same time, achieve its marketing objectives.

marketing research The development, interpretation, and communication of decision-oriented information to be used in the strategic marketing process.

markon See *markup*.

markup The amount added to the cost of a product to arrive at the price at which the seller would like to make a transaction. Alternatively, the difference between the selling price of an item and its cost. Same as *markon*.

Maslow's need hierarchy A structure of five need levels, arrayed in the order in which people seek to gratify them.

mass customization Developing, producing, and delivering affordable products with enough variety and uniqueness that nearly every potential customer can have exactly what he or she wants.

mass-market strategy See *market aggregation strategy*.

maturity stage The third part of a product life cycle during which the sales of a generic product category continue to increase (but at a decreasing rate), profits decline largely because of price competition, and some firms leave the market.

merchant middleman A firm that actually takes title to (i.e., owns) products it helps to market.

merchant wholesaler An independently owned firm that engages primarily in wholesaling and takes title to products being distributed. Sometimes called a *wholesaler*.

methods of sales-force compensation The three types of compensation plans are salary, straight commission, and a combination plan.

Metropolitan Statistical Area (MSA) An urban area in the U.S. with a center of population of at least 50,000 and a total MSA population of at least 100,000.

middleman A business firm that renders services directly related to the purchase and/or sale of a product as it flows from producer to consumer.

micromarketing The concept of marketing to a small segment of consumers.

middleman's brand A brand owned by a retailer or a wholesaler.

misdirected marketing effort Marketing endeavors that do not produce results commensurate with the resources expended.

mission An organization's statement of what customers it serves, what needs it satisfies, and what types of products it offers.

mix extension One form of product-mix expansion in which a company adds a new product line to its present assortment.

modified rebuy In the business market, a purchasing situation between a new task and a straight rebuy in terms of time and people involved, information needed, and alternatives considered.

motive A need sufficiently stimulated to move an individual to seek satisfaction.

multinational corporation A truly worldwide enterprise, in which the foreign and the domestic operations are integrated and are not separately identified.

multiple-brand strategy A strategy in which a firm has more than one brand of essentially the same product, aimed either at the same target market or at distinct target markets.

multiple correlation analysis A more sophisticated form of correlation analysis that allows the inclusion of more than one market factor in the calculation.

multiple-distribution channels The use by a producer of more than one channel of distribution for reasons such as achieving broad market coverage or avoiding total dependence on a single arrangement.

multiple packaging The practice of placing several units of the same product in one container.

multiple-segment strategy A plan of action that involves selecting two or more different groups of potential customers as the firm's target markets.

N

net cost of delivered purchases A financial figure calculated by taking gross purchases at billed cost, deducting sales returns, sales allowances, and cash discounts for early payment, and adding freight in.

net profit The amount of revenue that remains after a firm pays the cost of merchandise and its operating expenses.

net profit percentage The ratio of net profit to net sales.

net sales The net amount of sales revenue, out of which the company will pay for the products and all its expenses.

networks Individuals or organizations linked together to share data, exchange information and ideas, and perform tasks.

new product A vague term that may refer to (1) really innovative, truly unique products, (2) replacement products that are significantly different from existing ones, or (3) imitative products that are new to a particular firm but are not new to the market.

new-product department An organizational structure for product planning and development that involves a small unit, consisting of five or fewer people, and that reports to the president.

new-product development process A set of six stages that a new product goes through, starting with idea generation and continuing through idea screening, business analysis, prototype development, market tests, and eventually commercialization (full-scale production and marketing).

new-product strategy A statement identifying the role a new product is expected to play in achieving corporate and marketing goals.

new-task buying In the business market, a purchasing situation in which a company for the first time considers buying a given item.

niche marketing A strategy in which goods and services are tailored to meet the needs of small market segments.

niche marketers Sellers that pursue single segments within the total market.

niche markets A small, targeted segment.

nonadopters Those consumers that never adopt an innovation.

nonbusiness market The total set of churches, colleges and universities, museums, hospitals and other health institutions, political parties, labor unions, and charitable organizations.

noncumulative discount A quantity discount based on the size of an individual order of one or more products.

nonprice competition A strategy in which a seller maintains stable prices and attempts to improve its market position by emphasizing other (nonprice) aspects of its marketing program.

nonprofit organizations Those groups that provide services but do not have a profit objective.

nonstore retailing Retailing activities resulting in transactions that occur away from a retail store.

North American Free Trade Agreement (NAFTA) An agreement among the United States, Canada, and Mexico to eliminate tariffs between the countries.

North American Industry Classification System (NAICS) Coding system similar to the SIC, but has 20 rather than 10 industry sectors, to provide a more detailed and contemporary classification scheme.

not-for-profit services organizations (N-F-P) Those groups that have a profit goal because growth and existence depend on generating revenue in excess of costs.

nutrition labeling The part of a product that provides information about the amount of calories, fat, cholesterol, sodium, carbohydrates, and protein contained in the package's contents.

O

objective A desired outcome. Same as *goal*.

observation method A method of gathering primary data by observing the actions of a person without direct interaction.

odd pricing A psychological pricing strategy that consists of setting prices at uneven (or odd) amounts, such as $4.99, rather than at even amounts, such as $5, in the belief that these seemingly lower prices will result in larger sales volume.

off-price retailer A type of retail institution, often found in the areas of apparel and shoes, that has a narrow and deep product assortment, low prices, and few customer services.

oligopoly A market structure dominated by a few firms, each marketing similar products.

one-price strategy A pricing strategy under which a seller charges the same price to all similar customers who buy identical quantities of a product.

one-stop shipping A transportation firm offers multiple modes of transportation of goods to its customers.

online retailing Electronic transactions made over the Internet in which the purchaser is the ultimate consumer.

operating expense ratio Operating expenses divided by net sales.

operating expenses The marketing, administrative, and miscellaneous costs, but not the cost of goods purchased or manufactured, incurred by a firm.

operating statement A financial statement summarizing the firm's income, expenses, and profit or loss over a given period of time. Same as *income statement* and *profit and loss statement*.

operating supplies The "convenience" category of business goods, consisting of tangible products that are characterized by low dollar value per unit and a short life and that aid in an organization's operations without becoming part of the finished product.

organizational strategies Broad plans of action by which an organization intends to achieve its goals and fulfill its mission. These plans are for (1) the total organization in a small, single-product company or (2) each SBU in a large, multiproduct or multibusiness organization.

outside sales The kind of personal selling group in which sales people go to the customers, making contact by mail, telephone, or face-to-face.

P

package-delivery firms Companies that specialize in the delivery of small packages and high-priority mail.

packaging All the activities of designing and producing the container or wrapper for a product.

past sales analysis A method of sales forecasting that applies a flat percentage increase to the volume achieved last year or to the average volume of the past few years.

patronage buying motives The reasons why a consumer chooses to shop at a particular store.

perception The process carried out by an individual to receive, organize, and assign meaning to stimuli detected by the five senses.

perfect competition A market structure in which product differentiation is absent, buyers and sellers are well informed, and the seller has no discernible control over the selling price.

perishability A characteristic of a service indicating that it is highly transitory and cannot be stored.

personal interview A face-to-face method of gathering data in a survey.

personal selling The personal communication of information to persuade somebody to buy something. Alternatively, the direct (face-to-face or over-the-phone) presentation of a product to a prospective customer by a representative of the organization selling it.

personal selling process The logical sequence of prospecting, preapproach, presenting, and postsale services that a sales person takes in dealing with a prospective buyer.

personality An individual's pattern of traits that influences behavioral responses.

physical distribution All the activities involved in the flow of products as they move physically from producer to consumer or industrial user. Same as *logistics*.

physical distribution management The development and operation of processes resulting in the effective and efficient physical flow of products.

physical facilities The building—including its location, design, and layout—that serves as a store for a retail firm.

piggyback service The transporting of loaded truck trailers on railroad flatcars.

pioneering stage See *introduction stage*.

planned obsolescence A strategy that is intended to make an existing product out of date and thus to increase the market for replacement products. There are two forms: technological and style.

planning The process of deciding now what we are going to do later, including when and how we are going to do it.

political and legal forces A set of factors, including monetary and fiscal policies, legislation, and regulations, that affect the marketing activities of an organization.

portal An entrance and guide to the World Wide Web.

position The way a product, brand, or organization is viewed in relation to the competition by current and prospective customers.

positioning A product's image in relation to directly competitive products as well as other products marketed by the same company. Alternatively, a firm's strategies and actions related to favorably distinguishing itself from competitors in the minds of selected groups of consumers. Same as *product positioning*.

postage stamp pricing See *uniform delivered pricing*.

postpurchase cognitive dissonance The anxiety created by the fact that in most purchases the alternative selected has some negative features and the alternatives not selected have some positive features.

postsale service Maintenance and repairs as well as other services that are provided to customers in order to fulfill the terms of a firm's warranty and/or to augment the firm's revenues.

price The amount of money and/or other items with utility needed to acquire a product.

price competition A strategy in which a firm regularly offers products priced as low as possible, usually accompanied by a minimum of services.

price customization Method of establishing prices based on how much different people value a product.

price differential The difference in prices of an identical brand from one area to another.

price discrimination A situation in which different customers pay different prices for the same product.

price elasticity of demand The responsiveness of quantity demanded to price changes.

price lining A pricing strategy whereby a firm selects a limited number of prices at which it will sell related products.

price war A form of price competition that begins when one firm decreases its price in an effort to increase its sales volume and/or market share, the other firms retaliate by reducing prices on competing products, and additional price decreases by the original price cutter and/or its competitors usually follow.

pricing above competition One form of market-based pricing in which price is set above the prevailing market level.

pricing below competition One form of market-based pricing in which price is set below the level of your main competitors.

pricing objective The desired outcome that management seeks to achieve with its pricing structure and strategies.

pricing to meet competition A pricing method in which a firm ascertains

what the market price is and, after allowing for customary markups for middlemen, arrives at its own selling price.

primary data New data gathered specifically for the project at hand.

primary-demand advertising Advertising that is designed to stimulate demand for a generic category of a product.

Primary Metropolitan Statistical Area (PMSA) A Metropolitan Statistical Area in the U.S. that has a population of at least 1 million.

Printer's Ink statutes State legislation intended to punish "untrue, deceptive, or misleading" advertising.

private warehouse A warehouse that is owned and operated by the firm whose products are being stored and handled at the facility.

producer's brand A brand that is owned by a manufacturer or other producer.

product A set of tangible and intangible attributes, which may include packaging, color, price, quality, and brand, plus the seller's services and reputation. A product may be a good, service, place, person, or idea.

product abandonment A decision and subsequent action by a firm to drop a product that has insufficient and/or declining sales and lacks profits.

product advertising Advertising that focuses on a particular product or brand.

product alteration A strategy of improving an existing product.

product and trade name franchising A distribution agreement under which a supplier (the franchiser) authorizes a dealer (the franchisee) to sell a product line, using the parent company's trade name for promotional purposes.

product color The hue(s) given to a particular product, including its packaging.

product counterfeiting The unscrupulous placement of a brand name on a product without the legal right to do so.

product design The arrangement of elements that collectively form a good or service.

product differentiation A strategy in which a firm uses promotion to distinguish its product from competitive brands offered to the same aggregate market.

product liability A legal action alleging that an illness, accident, or death resulted from the named product because it was harmful, faulty, or inadequately labeled.

product life cycle The aggregate demand over an extended period of time for all brands comprising a generic product category.

product line A broad group of products intended for essentially similar uses and having similar physical characteristics.

product manager An organizational structure for product planning and development that makes one person responsible for planning new products as well as managing established products. Same as *brand manager*.

product-market growth matrix A planning model that consists of four alternative growth strategies based on whether an organization will be selling its present products or new products to its present markets or new markets.

product mix The set of all products offered for sale by a company.

product-mix contraction A strategy in which a firm either eliminates an entire line or simplifies the assortment within a line.

product-mix expansion A strategy in which a firm increases the depth within a particular line and/or the number of lines it offers to consumers.

product-orientation stage The first stage in the evolution of marketing management, in which the basic assumption is that making a good product will ensure business success.

product-planning committee An organizational structure for product planning and development that involves a joint effort among executives from major departments and, especially in small firms, the president and/or another top-level executive.

product positioning See *positioning*.

product quality See *quality*.

product specialization One method of organizing selling activities so that each sales person is assigned one or more product lines to sell.

profit and loss statement See *operating statement*.

promotion The element in an organization's marketing mix that serves to inform, persuade, and remind the market of a product and/or the organization selling it in the hope of influencing the recipients' feelings, beliefs, or behavior.

promotional allowance A price reduction granted by a seller as payment for promotional services performed by buyers.

promotional budgeting method The means used to determine the amount of dollars allocated to promotion in general and/or to specific forms of promotion.

promotional mix The combination of personal selling, advertising, sales promotion, public relations, and publicity that is intended to help an organization achieve its marketing objectives.

psychoanalytic theory Freudian theory that argues people have subconscious drives that cannot be satisfied in socially acceptable ways.

psychographic segmentation Subdividing markets into groups based on personality dimensions, life-style characteristics, and values.

psychological obsolescence See *style obsolescence*.

public relations Communications efforts that are designed to favorably influence attitudes toward an organization, its products, and its policies.

public warehouse An independent firm that provides for a fee storage and handling facilities for individuals or companies.

publicity A special form of public relations that involves any communication about an organization, its products, or its policies through the media that is not paid for by the sponsoring organization.

pull strategy Promotional effort directed primarily at end users so they will ask middlemen for the product.

push strategy Promotional efforts directed primarily at middlemen that are the next link forward in the distribution channel for a product.

Q

qualitative evaluation bases In sales-force evaluation, subjective criteria for appraising the performance of sales people.

quality The degree to which a product meets the expectations of the customer. Same as *product quality*.

quantitative evaluation bases In sales-force evaluation, specific, objective criteria for appraising the performance of sales people.

quantity discount A deduction from a seller's list price that is offered to a buyer when a large quantity of the product is purchased.

R

raw materials Business goods that become part of another tangible product prior to being processed in any way.

rebate A discount on a product that a customer obtains by submitting a form or certificate provided by the seller.

recipient market See *client market*.

reference group A group of people who influence a person's attitudes, values, and behavior.

refusal to deal A situation in which a producer that desires to select and perhaps control its channels declines to sell to some middlemen.

regional strategy A strategy used to market a product to different regions by recognizing distinctions in climate, custom, or taste.

relationship marketing An ongoing interaction between a buyer and a seller in which the seller continuously improves its understanding of the buyer's needs, and the buyer becomes increasingly loyal to the seller because its needs are being so well satisfied.

relationship selling An attempt by a sales person or organization to develop a deeper, longer-lasting relationship built on trust with key customers—usually larger accounts.

repositioning Reestablishing a product's attractiveness in the target market.

resale price maintenance A pricing policy whereby a manufacturer seeks to control the prices at which middlemen resell their products.

reseller market One segment of the business market, consisting of wholesaling and retailing middlemen that buy products for resale to other organizations or to consumers.

retail scanners The electronic devices at retail checkouts that read the bar code on each item.

retail trade See *retailing*.

retailer A firm engaged primarily in retailing.

retailer cooperative A type of contractual vertical marketing system that is formed by a group of small retailers who agree to establish and operate a wholesale warehouse.

retailing The sale, and all activities directly related to the sale, of goods and services to ultimate consumers for personal, nonbusiness use. Same as *retail trade*.

return on investment A commonly used measure of managerial performance, calculated by dividing net profit by either total assets or equity.

return on marketing investment A way for firms to measure profit gain from marketing expenditures.

Robinson-Patman Act A federal law passed in 1936 that was intended to curb price discrimination by large retailers and the granting by manufacturers of proportionally unequal promotional allowances to large retailers or wholesalers.

S

sales allowance A situation in which a customer who is dissatisfied with a product keeps it but is given a reduction from the selling price.

sales-force automation (SFA) Strategy of equipping sales people with laptop computers, cellular phones, fax machines, and pagers to give them access to databases, the Internet, and e-mail to help them manage accounts more effectively.

sales-force composite A method of forecasting sales that consists of collecting from all sales people estimates of sales for their territories during the future period of interest.

sales forecast An estimate of probable sales for one company's brand of a product during a stated time period in a specific market and assuming the use of a predetermined marketing plan.

sales-orientation stage The second stage in the evolution of marketing management, in which the emphasis is on using various promotional activities to sell whatever the organization produces.

sales potential The portion of market potential that a specific company could expect to achieve under ideal conditions.

sales promotion Demand-stimulating devices designed to supplement advertising and facilitate personal selling.

sales return A situation in which a customer returns merchandise and receives a refund equal to the full purchase price in cash or credit.

sales team See *selling center*.

sales-volume analysis A detailed study of the Net Sales section of a company's profit and loss statement.

scrambled merchandising The main source of horizontal channel conflict, a strategy under which a middleman diversifies by adding product lines not traditionally carried by its type of business.

seasonal discount A deduction from the list price that is offered to a customer for placing an order during the seller's slack season.

secondary data Available data, already gathered for some other purpose.

selective-demand advertising Advertising that is intended to stimulate demand for individual brands.

selective distribution A strategy in which a producer sells its product through multiple, but not all possible, wholesalers and retailers in a market where a consumer might reasonably look for it.

selective perception The process of screening all the marketing stimuli to which an individual is exposed on a daily basis.

self-concept The way a person sees himself/herself. Same as *self-image*.

self-image See *self-concept*.

selling agent An agent wholesaling middleman that essentially takes the place of a manufacturer's marketing department by marketing the manufacturer's entire output.

selling center A group of people representing a sales department as well as other functional areas in a firm (such as finance, production, and research and development) that work cooperatively to achieve a sale. Sometimes called a *sales team* or *team selling*.

separable expenses See *direct costs*.

service An identifiable, intangible activity that is the main object of a transaction designed to provide want-satisfaction to customers.

service encounter In services marketing, a customer's interaction with any service employee or with any tangible element, such as a service's physical surroundings.

service quality The degree to which an intangible offering meets the expectations of the customer.

shopping center A planned grouping of retail stores that lease space in a structure that is typically owned by a single organization and that can accommodate multiple tenants.

shopping goods A category of tangible consumer products that are purchased after the buyer has spent some time and effort comparing the price, quality, perhaps style, and/or other attributes of alternative products in several stores.

single-price strategy An extreme variation of a one-price strategy in which all items sold by a firm carry a single price.

single-segment strategy A plan of action that involves selecting one homogeneous segment from within a total market to be the firm's target market. Same as *concentration strategy*.

single-source data A data-gathering method in which exposure to television advertising and product purchases can be traced to individual households.

situation analysis The act of gathering and studying information pertaining to one or more specified aspects of an organization. Alternatively, a background investigation that helps in refining a research problem.

situational influences A temporary force, associated with the immediate purchase environment, that affects behavior.

slotting allowance A fee that some retailers charge a manufacturer in order to place its product on store shelves.

small-order problem A situation confronting many firms, in which revenue from an order is less than allocated expenses because several costs, such as billing and direct selling, are essentially the same regardless of order size.

social and cultural forces A set of factors, including life-styles, social values, and beliefs, that affect the marketing activities of an organization.

social class A division of, or ranking within, society based on education, occupation, and type of residential neighborhood.

social information environment As contrasted with the commercial information environment, all communications among family members, friends, and acquaintances about products.

societal marketing concept A revised version of the marketing concept under which a company recognizes that it should be concerned about not only the buyers of its products but also other people directly affected by its operations and with not only tomorrow but also the long term.

specialty goods A category of tangible consumer products for which consumers have a strong brand preference and are willing to expend substantial time and effort in locating and then buying the desired brand.

specialty store A type of retail institution that has a very narrow and deep product assortment (often concentrating on a specialized product line or even part of a specialized product line), that usually strives to maintain manufacturers' suggested prices, and that typically provides at least standard customer services.

stages in the adoption process The six steps a prospective buyer goes through in deciding whether to purchase something new.

Standard Industrial Classification (SIC) system A coding system developed by the federal government that groups firms into similar types of businesses and thus enables a company to identify and analyze small segments of the business market.

standards and certification A requirement that a product contain or exclude certain ingredients or that it be tested and certified as meeting certain restrictive standards.

stimulus-response theory The theory that learning occurs as a person (1) responds to some stimuli and (2) is rewarded with need satisfaction for a correct response or penalized for an incorrect one.

stockturn rate The number of times the average inventory is turned over, or sold, during the period under study.

straight rebuy In the business market, a routine, low-involvement purchase with minimal information needs and no great consideration of alternatives.

strategic alliance A formal, long-term agreement between firms to combine their capabilities and resources to accomplish global objectives.

strategic business unit (SBU) A separate division for a major product or market in a multiproduct or multibusiness organization.

strategic company planning The level of planning that consists of (1) defining the organization's mission, (2) analyzing the situation, (3) setting organizational objectives, and (4) selecting appropriate strategies to achieve these objectives.

strategic marketing planning The level of planning that consists of (1) conducting a situation analysis, (2) developing marketing objectives, (3) determining positioning and differential advantage, (4) selecting target markets and measuring market demand, and (5) designing a strategic marketing mix.

strategic planning The managerial process of matching a firm's resources with its market opportunities over the long run.

strategic window The limited amount of time in which a firm's resources coincide with a particular market opportunity.

strategy A broad plan of action by which an organization intends to reach its objectives.

style A distinctive manner of presentation or construction in any art, product, or endeavor.

style obsolescence A form of planned obsolescence in which superficial characteristics of a product are altered so that the new model is easily differentiated from the previous model and people become dissatisfied with it. Same as *fashion obsolescence* and *psychological obsolescence*.

subculture Groups in a culture that exhibit characteristic behavior patterns sufficient to distinguish them from other groups within the same culture.

suggested list price A pricing policy whereby a manufacturer recommends to retailers a final (retail) price that should provide them with their normal markups.

supercenter A combination of a discount house and a complete grocery store.

supermarket A type of retail institution that has a moderately broad and moderately deep product assortment spanning groceries and some nonfood lines, that offers relatively few customer services, and that ordinarily emphasizes price in either an offensive or defensive way.

supermarket retailing A retailing method that features several related product lines, a high degree of self-service, largely centralized checkout, and competitive prices.

suppliers The people or firms that supply the goods or services that an organization needs to produce what it sells.

supply chain management The combination of distribution channels and physical distribution to make up the total marketing system.

survey A method of gathering primary data by interviewing people in person, by telephone, or by mail.

survey of buyer intentions A form of sales forecasting in which a firm asks a sample of current or potential customers how much of a particular product they would buy at a given price during a specified future period.

SWOT assessment Identifying and evaluating an organization's most significant strengths, weaknesses, opportunities, and threats.

systems approach to physical distribution The unification of individual physical distribution activities.

systems selling Providing a total package of related goods and services to solve a customer's problem (needs).

T

tactic A specific means by which a strategy is implemented.

target market A group of customers (people or organizations) for whom a seller designs a particular marketing mix.

tariff A tax imposed on a product entering a country.

team selling See *selling center*.

technological obsolescence A form of planned obsolescence in which significant technical improvements result in a more effective product. Same as *functional obsolescence*.

technology Applications of science for industrial and commercial purposes.

telemarketing A form of nonstore retailing in which a sales person initiates contact with a shopper and also closes the sale over the telephone.

Telephone Consumer Protection Act Federal law that requires telemarketers to keep a "do-not-call" list of consumers who request that they not receive telephone solicitations, it restricts the indiscriminant use of automatic telephone dialing systems, and it prohibits marketers from sending advertising to a facsimile machine without first obtaining the recipient's permission.

telephone survey A method of gathering data by interviewing people over the telephone.

test marketing A method of demand forecasting in which a firm markets its new product in a limited geographic area, measures the sales, and then—from this sample—projects the company's sales over a larger area. Alternatively, a marketing research technique that uses this same approach to judge consumers' responses to a strategy before committing to a major marketing effort.

total cost The sum of total fixed cost and total variable cost for a specific quantity produced or sold.

total cost concept In physical distribution, the recognition that the best relationship between costs and profit must be established for the entire physical distribution system, rather than for individual activities.

total quality management (TQM) A philosophy as well as specific procedures, policies, and practices that commit an organization to continuous quality improvement in all of its activities.

total variable cost The sum of all variable costs.

trade balance In international business, the difference between the value of a nation's imports and the value of its exports.

trade barriers Created by governments to restrict trade and protect domestic industries, these are the most common legal forces affecting international marketers.

trade discount A reduction from the list price that is offered by a seller to buyers in payment for marketing functions the buyers will perform. Same as *functional discount*.

trademark A brand that has been adopted by a seller and given legal protection.

trademark infringement Act of manufacturing products with names and packaging similar to well-known goods in order to achieve sales.

Trademark Law Revision Act A federal law, passed in 1988, that broadened the Landham Trademark Act to encompass comparisons made in promotional activity.

trademark licensing A business arrangement in which the owner of a trademark grants permission to other firms to use the owner's brand name, logotype, and/or character on the licensee's products in return for a royalty on sales of those products. Same as *brand licensing*.

trading down A product-line strategy wherein a company adds a lower-priced product to a line to reach a market that cannot afford the higher-priced items or that see them as too expensive.

trading up A product-line strategy wherein a company adds a higher-priced product to a line in order to attract a broader market and, through its added prestige, helps the sale of its existing lower-priced products.

trend analysis A statistical method of forecasting sales over the long term by using regression analysis or over the short term by using a seasonal index of sales.

trickle-across theory In fashion adoption, a fashion cycle that moves horizontally and simultaneously within several socioeconomic levels.

trickle-down theory In fashion adoption, a fashion cycle that flows downward through several socioeconomic levels.

trickle-up theory In fashion adoption, a fashion cycle in which a style first becomes popular with lower socioeconomic levels and then flows upward to become popular among higher levels.

truck distributor See *truck jobber*.

truck jobber A merchant wholesaler that carries a selected line of perishable products and delivers them by truck to retail stores. Same as *truck distributor*.

tying contract The practice by which a manufacturer sells a product to a middleman only under the condition that the middleman also buy another (possibly unwanted) product from the manufacturer.

U

ultimate consumers People who buy goods or services for their own personal or household use in order to satisfy strictly nonbusiness wants.

undifferentiated-market strategy See *market aggregation strategy*.

unfair-practices acts State laws intended to regulate some forms of leader pricing that are intended to drive other products or companies out of business. Same as *unfair-sales acts*.

unfair-sales acts See *unfair-practices acts*.

uniform delivered pricing A geographic pricing strategy whereby the same delivered price is quoted to all buyers regardless of their locations. Same as *postage stamp pricing*.

universal design The design of products in such a way that they can be used by all consumers, including disabled individuals, senior citizens, and others needing special considerations.

unsought goods A category of consumer tangible products that consists of new products the consumer is not yet aware of or products the consumer is aware of but does not want right now.

utility The attribute in an item that makes it capable of satisfying human wants.

V

value The ratio of perceived benefits to price and any other incurred costs.

value added The dollar value of a firm's output minus the value of the inputs it purchased from other firms.

value chain The combination of a company, its suppliers, and intermediaries, performing their own activities, to add value to a product.

value pricing A form of price competition in which a firm seeks to improve the ratio of a product's benefits to its price and related costs.

values Intangible principles that are a reflection of people's needs, adjusted for the realities of the world in which they live.

variable cost A cost that changes directly in relation to the number of units produced or sold.

variable-price strategy See *flexible-price strategy*.

venture team An organizational structure for product planning and development that involves a small group, with representatives from engineering, production, finance, and marketing research, that operates like a separate small business, and that typically reports directly to top management.

vertical business market A situation where a given product is usable by virtually all the firms in only one or two industries.

vertical conflict A form of channel conflict occurring among firms at different levels of the same channel, typically producer versus wholesaler or producer versus retailer.

vertical marketing system (VMS) A tightly coordinated distribution channel designed to improve operating efficiency and marketing effectiveness.

viral marketing Strategy of spreading positive information about a company from one person to another, often utilized by smaller firms.

voluntary chain A type of contractual vertical marketing system that is sponsored by a wholesaler who enters into a contract with interested retailers.

W

warehouse club A combined retailing and wholesaling institution that has a very broad but very shallow product assortment, very low prices, few customer services, and is open only to members. Same as *wholesale club*.

warning label The part of a product that tells consumers not to misuse the product and informs them of almost every conceivable danger associated with using it.

warranty An assurance given to buyers that they will be compensated in case the product does not perform up to reasonable expectations.

website A collection of Web files beginning with a home page that is accessible through a unique address.

Wheeler-Lea Act A federal law, passed in 1938, that amended the Federal Trade Commission Act by strengthening the prohibition against unfair competition, especially false or misleading advertising.

wholesale club See *warehouse club*.

wholesale trade See *wholesaling*.

wholesaler See *merchant wholesaler*.

wholesaling The sale, and all activities directly related to the sale, of goods and services to businesses and other organizations for resale, use in producing other goods and services, or the operation of an organization.

wholesaling middleman A firm engaged primarily in wholesaling.

wholly owned subsidiary A business arrangement in foreign markets in which a company owns the foreign operation in order to gain maximum control over its marketing program and production operations.

World Trade Organization (WTO) Created in 1995, as the governing body of global commerce, consisting of 135-member countries and accounting for 90% of world trade.

World Wide Web Collection of hyperlinked multimedia databases stored all over the world and accessible via the Internet.

Z

zone-delivered pricing A geographic pricing strategy whereby a seller divides its market into a limited number of broad geographic zones and then sets a uniform delivered price for each zone.

Name Index

A

A. C. Nielsen, 182
ABB Automation, 418
Abbott, John, 655
ABC, 553, 601
About.com, 645
ACCESS, 667
Ace, 433, 501
Acmepet.com, 425
Acosta, 403
Acrilan, 271
Acuvue, 225, 245, 596
Adidas, 52–54, 56, 70, 78, 105, 245, 333
Adidas-Salomon A.G., 53, 70
Advanced Micro Devices, 539, 543
Advanced Photo System, 225
Advertising Age, 190, 539, 541–542, 549, 670
Advertising Research Foundation, 200
Aetna, 399
Aficio, 135
Agilent Technologies, 267
Agins, Teri, 259, 509
AIBO, 112
Aim, 268
Air Canada, 69
Air France, 345
Air Jordans, 571
Airborne Freight, 476
AirPort, 384
Alaska Airlines, 268, 389
Albertson's, 99, 441, 577, 658
Alcoa, 329
Alfa Romeo, 276
All Products Search Questions, 446
All Sport, 152, 593
AllAdvantage, 503
Allied Van Lines, 268
Allpets, 425
Allstate, 302, 635
Almega Corp., 170
Alonzo, Vincent, 532
Alpha Beta, 155
AltaVista, 643
AM General Corporation, 123
AM/PM Mini Marts, 441
Amana, 254, 459
Amazon, 3, 9, 12, 60, 66, 82–84, 143, 191, 193, 269, 378, 390–391, 411, 425, 445–446, 448, 450, 473, 477, 482, 637, 640, 644–645, 647, 657
America Dairy Farmers and Milk Processors, 105
America Online (AOL), 6, 214, 307, 377, 450, 491, 600–601, 625, 632, 640, 648
America West, 323
American Airlines, 221, 300, 323, 344
American Association of Retired Persons (AARP), 34
American Basketball League, 243

American Booksellers Association, 44, 373
American Can Company, 142
American Cancer Society, 5, 214, 294, 307
American Community Survey (ACS), 190
American Demographics, 190, 193
American Electric Power, 542
American Express, 12, 37, 114, 153, 185, 296
American FactFinder, 189
American Greeting Cards, 499
American Heart Association, 282, 294
American Home Products, 225
American Lung Association, 302, 307
American Marketing Association, 190, 193, 200, 294, 510, 645
American Medical Association (AMA), 294
American Red Cross, 302
American Stores, 428
AmeriSuites hotels, 275
Ameritrade, 267
Amway, 443, 642
Anacin, 215
Anders, George, 46, 85, 392, 411, 483, 659
Anderson Consulting, 658
Anheuser-Busch, 40, 67, 140, 227, 242–243, 265, 414, 546
Ann Taylor, 123, 277, 517
Ansoff, H. Igor, 589, 597
Apollo, 247
Appel, David, 250
Apple Computer, 214, 228, 254, 284, 362–364, 384–385, 506, 551
Aquatred, 365
Archer Daniel Midland Company, 502
Arco, 441
Ariba, 144
Arizona, 263
Arm & Hammer, 264, 275
Armani, 218, 255
Armor All Products, 274
Armstrong, 38
Armstrong, Larry, 483
Aroma, 10
Arrow, 406
Arrow Electronics, 418
Arthur Andersen, 332
Asahi, 268
Asea Brown Boveri, 328
Assmus, Gert, 408
Associated Wholesale Grocers, 417
Association Yellow Book, 662
AT&T, 179, 201, 264, 283, 310, 503, 509, 522, 541, 584, 604, 643
Athlete's Foot, 431, 435
Athletic Store, 377
Atlanta Braves, 298
Atlanta Motor Speedway, 204
Au Bon Pain, 268
AucNet, 343

Audi, 89
Audits & Surveys, 181
Austin Gray, 272
Autobytel, 12, 641
Autolatina, 39
Automobile Strategy Board, 207
Automotive Systems Group (ASG), 515–516, 536
AutoNation USA, 377, 440
Autos.com, 269
Avis, 302
Avon, 76, 306–307, 394–396, 404, 421, 444, 518, 544, 592
AZT, 330

B

B. F. Goodrich, 651
Baby Center, 481
Bailey Controls, 418
Ball, Jeffrey, 19
Baltimore Orioles, 92
Ban, 268
Banana Republic, 258
Band-Aid, 270
Bandai, 39
Bank of America, 312
Bank, David, 46, 343, 392
Bank One, 290–291, 304, 312, 592, 668
Bannon, Lisa, 483
Barbecue Renew, 552
Barbie dolls, 22, 228, 411, 642
Barbour, John, 482
Barer, Coleen, 388
Barnes & Noble, 10, 44, 82–84, 373, 440, 446, 577
Barq's, 653
Barrett, Amy, 655
Barron, Kelly, 485
Barshefsky, Charlene, 421
Barter First Inc., 324
Bass, 67, 440
Bass Hotels & Resorts, 274
Battaglia, Andy, 206
Batteries Plus, 439
Bausch & Lomb, 593
Baxter Healthcare, 125, 418
Baxter International, 523
Bayer, 214, 264
Beanie Babies, 81, 381
Beauty and the Beast, 569
Beauty Center, 395
Beautyrest, 268
Beck, Ernest, 165, 438
Beck, Rachel, 317, 483
Beech Aircraft, 223
Beech-Nut, 504
Beeper Kid, 232
Bell Atlantic, 644
Bell Labs, 179
Bellagio, 368
Ben & Jerry's Ice Cream, 102

Mr. Transmission, 435
MR-Spyder, 156
MSN, 601
MTV, 489, 503, 549, 640
Munk, Nina, 85
Munsingwear, 223, 264
Murphy, Claire, 82
Musicland, 383
MVP.com, 503
MXG Media, 194
MXGonline, 194
MyHome.com, 343
MySimon.com, 446

N

Nabisco, 275, 284, 501–502, 523, 526, 667
Nagai, Jyunichi, 316
NASA, 124
NASCAR, 204, 296, 545
Nasser, Jacques, 207
National Advertising Division (NAD), 510
National Alliance of Breast Cancer Organizations, 307
National Basketball Association, 78, 297
National Car Rental, 297, 406
National Collegiate Athletic Association, 569
National Fluid Milk Processor Promotion Board, 543
National Football League, 553, 601
National Semiconductor, 467–468
National Total-Market Audit, 181
National Trade and Professional Associations of the United States, 662
Nationwide Insurance, 302
Navistar, 129
NBC, 302, 625
NCR Corp., 186
Neighborhood Markets, 432
Neiman Marcus, 427
Nelson, Emily, 438
Neoforma, 126
Neptune, 317
Nescafé 82, 76, 253
Nestea, 33, 653
Nestlé 82, 33, 70, 165, 253, 522, 545
Net2Phone, 267
Net Effect Systems, 613
NetFinity, 401
NetGrocer.com, 657, 659
NetJet, 16, 142–143, 148–150, 175
Netscape, 632
Networking in the Public Interest, 667
Neuborne, Ellen, 36, 269
Neutrogena, 40, 104
New Balance, 151
New Coke, 653
New Pig, 400
New Products Showcase and Learning Center, 224
New York Times, 82–83, 190
Newsweek, 547
Newton, 254
NexTag.com, 446
NextCard, 641
Nike, 8, 25, 36, 40, 53, 78, 104, 151,
223, 264, 333, 405, 485, 570–571, 596, 666
Nikon, 218
99cents Only, 377
Nintendo, 254, 268, 315–317, 473
Nios'93me, 368
Nissan, 38, 70, 276, 331
No-Cal Cola, 254
Nobel Learning Communities, 166
Noise magazine, 492
Noiseonline.com, 492
Nokia, 276, 284
Noodle Kidoole, 439
Nordstrom, 269, 272, 417, 445, 585
Norm Thompson, 519
Northwest Airlines, 323
Northwestern Mutual, 517, 526
Northwestern University, 526
Novak, David, 568
Novartis Consumer Health, 508
Noxema, 152
Nussel, Karen B., 485
Nutella, 558
NutraSweet, 127, 221, 246, 502, 564

O

Ocean Spray, 275, 277, 508
Ody, Penelope, 12
Off, 558
Office Depot, 635
Office Products Dealer, 501
Oil of Olay, 152
Olayk, 277
Old Navy Clothing Co., 247
Oldman, Mark, 662
Oldsmobile, 595
Olean, 135
Olympic Games, 319
Omidyar, Pierre, 22
Omni Hotels Corp., 602–603
OmniCHARM, 602–603
1–800-Flowers.com, 445
One-A-Day vitamins, 162
Onsale, 3, 390–392, 463
Onstar system, 641
Opel Zaifira, 70
Oracle Corp., 207, 469, 649
Oral-B, 382
Orangina, 654
Orderzone, 650–651
Ordonez, Jennifer, 82
O'Reilly, Brian, 485
Oreo, 215, 526
Organization of Petroleum Exporting Countries (OPEC), 74
Oroweat, 595
Ortho Pharmaceuticals, 252
Oscar Mayer, 493–494, 595
Oshkosh Truck Company, 152
Otis Elevator, 509, 610–611
Owens-Corning, 283
Oxydol, 380

P

Pacific Northwest, 15
Pacific Specialty Insurance, 643
Pacific Sunwear (PacSun), 488–490, 522
Pack Mail, 484
Packard Bell, 277
Paine Webber, 93
Palm Inc., 254, 592
Palmolive Optims, 195
Pampered Chef, 443
Pampers, 273
Papa John, 567–568
Paperbacks and More, 350
Pappas, Ben, 317
Paramount Products, 419
Parent, 510
Parker, Kendra, 12
Parker Pens, 76
Parker-Pope, Tara, 99, 102
Pasternak, Volker, 326
Patek Philippe, 345
Patton, Gen. George, 327
Payless ShoeSource, 440
PBS, 193
Peapod, 143, 656, 658–659
Pearle Vision, 309
Pedigree, 247
Pelayo, Cristina, 521
Pentium, 248, 365, 539, 564
Penzoil, 132
People, 547
People Express, 267
Pepsi One, 594, 654
PepsiCo, 36, 68, 74, 95, 152, 195, 223–224, 253–254, 287, 390, 541, 568–569, 589, 593–594, 597, 654–655
Perfect YardSale, 346
Perfecto Gas Grill, 419
Periera, Joseph, 253, 483
Perrier, 165
Personal Computing, 501
Pert Plus, 76, 267, 279
Petco.com, 425, 450
PetJungle, 425
Petopia, 425, 450, 647
Petrogylph Ceramic Lounge, 439
Pets.com, 425, 445, 450, 647
PETsMART, 424–425, 445, 449–450, 592, 647, 664
Petstore.com, 425, 449, 647
Peugeot, 545
Pfizer, 518
Phelps Dodge, 331
Philip Morris, 22, 126, 266, 273, 541, 588
Phillips, 70
Phillips, David, 557
Pierre Cardin, 278
Pillet, Charles, 483
Pillsbury, 6, 59, 102, 223, 235, 246
Pitney-Bowes, 525
Pizza Hut, 10, 74, 268, 567–570, 589
Pizza Outlet, 567
Pizzeria Uno, 405
Planet Hollywood, 581
Planet Ketchup, 159
PlayStation, 315–317
Pledge, 274
Pleion Corp., 455
Pokémon, 253, 278

Visa, 25, 37, 114, 295, 301, 641
Vogue, 263
Voigt, John, 659
Volkswagen, 39, 73, 90, 96, 116, 163, 283, 545
Volvo, 16, 244
Vons, 123

W

W. W. Grainger, 460, 524, 628–630, 635, 641, 648, 650–651, 668
Wal-Mart, 11–12, 37, 59, 70, 91, 156, 265, 273, 291, 332, 344, 365, 377–378, 380, 402, 406, 409, 411, 416, 418, 426, 428, 432, 436–438, 440–442, 445, 471–472, 481–482, 491, 522, 591, 593, 596, 607, 635, 639–640, 656, 668
Walgreen, 264
Walker, Jay, 322–323, 346
Walker, Karen, 389
Walker, Sam, 297, 509
Walkman, 252, 254
Wall Street Journal, 390, 564, 670
Wallpaper to Go, 435
Walton, Sam, 11, 438
Ward's, 447
Warner, Fara, 411, 592
Warner-Lambert, Inc., 472
Warrilow, Clive, 89
Wash and Go, 76
Water Tower Place, 432
Waterford, 276–277, 345
Watkins, Edward, 320
Watney, 67
Waxler, Caroline, 194
WD-40 Co., 242, 267
Web of Culture, 521
Web Digest for Marketers, 190
Web Marketing Today Info Center, 190
Weber, Joseph, 22, 245, 509
WebHouse Club Inc., 346–347
WebOutfitter, 564
WebTV, 317

Webvan, 473, 656–659
Webvan Group Inc., 477
Wechsler, Pat, 169
Wega, 315
Weigand, Robert E., 408
Weimer, De'Ann, 126
Welch, David, 209
Welch, Jack, 37
Wellman, David, 659
Wells Fargo, 312
Wells, Melanie, 194
Wendy's, 166–167, 406, 543
Wesson, 277
Western Auto, 406, 415, 433
Wexler, Mark, 521
Weyerhauser, 132
Wheaties, 246
Whiddom, Robert, 659
Whirlpool, 170, 531, 634
Whiskas, 227
White Castle, 275
White Cloud, 223
White, Gregory I., 209
White, Joseph B., 592
Whitehall-Robins Healthcare, 242
Whittle Communications, 169, 549
Wiese, Carsten, 408
Wight, Michael, 453
Wilder, Clinton, 483
Wildstrom, Stephen H., 317
Williams, Frances, 649
Williams, Stephen, 521
Willman, John, 45
Wilson Sporting Goods, 127
Windex, 279
Windjammer Barefoot Cruises, 584
Windows, 140, 256, 363, 384
Wingfield, Nick, 269, 491
Wingspan, 290–292, 312, 592, 668
Wink Communications, 310
Winn-Dixie, 155, 426
Wireless Dimension, 446
Wiseman, Paul, 496
Wolfe, Richard, 644
Wollenberg, Skip, 509

Women's National Basketball Association, 243
Women's World Cup, 560
The Works, 272
World Wide Web, 144, 551
Wow!, 42
Wrangler, 167–168, 471
Wrigley's, 110, 164–165, 590
Wysocki, Bernard, 343

X

X-Box, 317
Xerox, 270, 471, 522, 604, 614
XYR, 156

Y

Yahoo!, 3, 207–208, 269, 391, 491, 593, 600–601, 625, 632, 640
Yamos, 58
Yang, Catherine, 383
Yeltsin, Boris, 569
YMCA, 302, 310
Yoshida, Reiji, 317
Young & Rubicam, 571
YourSherpa.com, 448
Yugo, 214
Yves Saint Laurent, 258, 266

Z

Zane's Cycles, 447
Zellner, Wendy, 389
Zenith, 119
Zenith Data Systems (ZDS), 124
Zest, 152
Zill, Nicholas, 36
Zima, 224
Ziploc, 276
Znap, 260
Zoots, 304
Zuber, Amy, 570

Subject Index

A

Acceleration principle, 129
Accessory equipment, 221–222
Accounts organization, 607
Activity costs analysis, 618
  by product or market, 619–620
Activity indicator of buying power, 133
Actual self-concept, 111
Administrated vertical marketing system, 406
Adoption process, 230
  adoption rate, 233–234
  characteristics affecting, 233–234
  compatibility and, 233
  complexity and, 233
  fashion-adoption, 257–258
  innovation adopters categories, 231–233
  innovators and, 231–232
  new products, 230–231
  nonadopters, 233
  observability, 234
  relative advantage, 233–234
  stages in, 231
  trialbility and, 234
Adoption rate, 233
Adoption stage, 231
Advertising
  business-to-business, 542
  cable television, 14
  careers in, 665
  celebrity spokespersons, 104
  as commercial information, 101
  comparative advertising, 543
  consumer, 542
  corrective advertising, 508
  cost versus personal selling cost, 541–542
  demand-sustaining advertising, 543
  differential advantage, 543
  direct-action advertising, 543
  expenditures on, 540
  indirect-action advertising, 543
  institutional, 543
  international marketing, 76–77
  marketing research and, 181
  nature and scope of, 540–543
  network television advertising, 13
  as percentage of sales, 540–541
  perception and, 109
  pioneering, 542
  place-based television, 549
  point-of-purchase, 548
  primary-demand, 542
  Printers' Ink statutes, 509
  product, 543
  production costs, 76
  selective-demand advertising, 542–543
  services marketing, 306–307
  standardization, 76
  substantiation of claims, 508
  summary, 563–564

  types of, 542
  virtual, 553
Advertising agencies, 554–555
  inside department, 555
  internal departments, 554
  outside agency, 555
Advertising allowance, 546
Advertising campaign, 543–544
  appeal and, 546
  attention and, 546
  audience coverage, 548
  budget for, 545–546
  cooperative advertising, 546
  creating a message, 546–547
  defined, 543–544
  evaluating, 553–554
  execution and, 546–547
  features of, 540
  influence and, 546
  media cost, 548
  objectives of, 544–545, 548
  requirements of message, 548
  selecting the media; *see* Advertising media
  sponsor, 540
  summary, 563–564
  time and location of buying decision, 548
  verbal/visual message, 540
Advertising media, 21, 547–552
  billboards, 551
  category of, 547
  characteristics of, 548
  cost per thousand (CPT), 548
  delivery via media, 540
  direct mail, 550
  factors influencing choice of, 547–548
  global conditions, 552
  interactive, 551–552
  magazines, 550–551
  newspapers, 548–549
  out-of-home advertising, 551
  outdoor, 551
  payment by sponsor, 540
  prime-time advertising costs, 549
  radio, 550
  specific vehicles, 548
  television, 549
  type of, 547
  yellow pages, 550
African Americans, 35, 92, 95
Age distributions, 34–35, 93
Agent, 304
Agent middlemen, 397
Agent wholesaling middlemen, 457, 461–463
  auction company, 463
  brokers, 462
  import-export agent, 463
  manufacturers' agents, 461–462
  selling agent, 463
Agribusiness, 20, 121–122, 129, 220

Agricultural activity, measures of, 133
AIDA (Attention, Interest, Desire, and Action), 527
Aided recall, 554
Airline Deregulation Act, 43
Airline industry, 108, 149
All funds available budgeting method, 506
Allocating costs, 621
Allowances, 369–372; *See* also Discounts
Alternatives and decision making
  business buying-decision process, 135–136
  evaluation of, 98
  identification of, 98
American Marketing Association, 510
Analytical ratios, 356–359
  gross margin percentage, 356
  markdown percentage, 357–358
  net profit percentage, 357
  operating expense ratio, 357
  return on investment, 358–359
  stockturn rate, 357
Andean Common Market (ANCOM), 65
Annual marketing plan, 581, 586–588
  evaluation procedures, 587
  executive summary, 587
  financial schedules, 587
  objectives, 587
  purposes and responsibilities, 587
  recommended contents, 587–588
  situation analysis, 587
  strategies, 587
  tactics, 587
  timetable, 587
Annual Survey of Manufacturers, 133
Antitrust laws, 44, 74
Apparel industry, 20
Appeal in an ad, 546
Arbitrage, 73
Asia-Pacific Economic Cooperation forum (APEC), 20, 64–65
Asian Americans, 35, 95
Asian tigers, 39
Association promotional strategy, 296
Association of Southeast Asian Nations (ASEAN), 65
Athletic shoe industry, 53
ATM machines, 103, 309
Atmosphere, 113
Attention of an audience, 546
Attitudes, 111–112
Attribute, positioning in relation to, 244
Auction company, 463
Auctions, 3, 145
Audience coverage, 548
Audience perspective, IMC and, 494
Automatic replenishment, 471
Automatic vending, 444–445
Automobile industry, 20, 37, 71, 89, 110, 116, 213–214, 244, 376–377
Automobile Information Disclosure Act, 43